The Oxford Handbook of Autism and Co-Occurring Psychiatric Conditions

OXFORD LIBRARY OF PSYCHOLOGY

The Oxford Handbook of Autism and Co-Occurring Psychiatric Conditions

Edited by

Susan W. White,

Brenna B. Maddox, and

Carla A. Mazefsky

OXFORD
UNIVERSITY PRESS

2020

OXFORD
UNIVERSITY PRESS

Oxford University Press is a department of the University of Oxford.
It furthers the University's objective of excellence in research, scholarship,
and education by publishing worldwide. Oxford is a registered trade mark of
Oxford University Press in the UK and certain other countries.

Published in the United States of America by Oxford University Press
198 Madison Avenue, New York, NY 10016, United States of America.

Library of Congress Control Number: 2020933023

ISBN 9780190910761

SHORT CONTENTS

FOREWORD

Before diving into co-occurring conditions, I'd like to introduce readers to autism and illustrate the relationship between autism and all that accompanies it, whatever the definitions or terms used. As an autistic adult, I have lived this all my life and experienced many of the associations described in this book.

I grew up in the 1960s before autism was recognized in verbal children. My language was clear; I didn't have speech delay or intellectual disability. From a very early age, adults remarked on my technical prowess, but they were equally struck by my absence of social skills. I was forever misreading cues and saying the wrong thing. Those problems worsened as I moved through school. My parents were college professors, but they had no idea how to solve my myriad social problems.

Teachers and counselors had differing views of my trouble. Some said I was lazy. Another put me in language lab, where I repeated phrases thousands of times, till my diction was honed to perfection. The guidance department sent me to groups for emotionally disturbed children, where we talked about failing. A coach thought toughening up was the answer and suggested Outward Bound. If grades were the measure, nothing worked.

Despite so-called gifts in reading and science, I still failed classes. After exhausting the high school's resources, I took up the study of engineering at the University of Massachusetts at age 13, only to drop out when I quit high school a few years later. I could not sit still for classes—today we recognize that as a trait of attention deficit hyperactivity disorder (ADHD)—but I'd taught myself by experimenting in the labs and pestering the grad students when I had questions.

Once out of school I continued my experimentation with electronics. I went through several phases. First, I took things apart to learn how they worked. Then I figured out how to fix them. Next, I taught myself how to build circuits and finally how to invent my own, to suit whatever purpose I had in mind. That's a different path than students follow to learn engineering in school, but it worked for me. I acquired the ability to create useful circuits and that got me work in the music industry.

By age 21, I could manipulate complex wave patterns in my mind. The math they taught in school remained a mystery, but the system I'd devised served me fine. I designed electronic circuits to transform waves, but I could not hold an ordinary conversation. Luckily my technical skills allowed me to earn a living despite significant disability in social settings. No one had a word for that, other than to call me a freak. It wasn't until I turned 40 that I learned I am on the autism spectrum, and for the first time I had a nonjudgmental explanation for why I am the way I am.

I also learned something remarkable. When the neurologists finished their tests, they explained that my abilities were unusual and rare. All the time I worked in engineering, I assumed a real engineer could do everything better than me. After all, I was just a self-taught experimenter. It was the neuroscientists who showed me that the ability to visualize circuits was a rare gift, as was the power to manipulate patterns.

In the 1970s my job included creating sound effects for live music performances. I imagined music as waves, and then I envisioned circuits to reshape the waves to make different sounds. The scientists said I was harnessing synesthesia—which they described as a cross-connecting of the brain—to do something unique. I'd always assumed anyone could do the same.

Prior to my encounters with the neuroscientists, I had seen myself as a second-rate human. My social disability had been obvious from the beginning, as were my failures in school. I had absolutely no idea any of my abilities were exceptional. One result was that I devalued everything I did—hence my assumption that a real engineer could do anything I did better.

Now I see that isn't the case at all. I am not an uneducated loser; I am a self-educated person. At one time, everyone was self-educated like me. In the past few hundred years the education industry has grown to the point where a college degree often seems to matter more than actual job knowledge. If a developmental disability prevents a person from getting that credential, that person has a problem. I am extraordinarily lucky that the work I did was visible to the public, and it spoke for me quite effectively, given that disability kept me from finishing school.

My circuit designs have stood the test of time, and they've entertained millions of people. I may have failed high school, but I am now the Neurodiversity Scholar at William & Mary, one of the top public universities in America. I'm also the neurodiversity advisor for Landmark College, one of the only colleges in America expressly for autistic and neurodivergent students. Autism has disabled me in many ways, but it's also made those achievements possible. In my case, autism is more than just disability.

But getting back to psychiatry.... Prior to my autism diagnosis and subsequent evaluations, I was fully aware of my deficiencies. Every autistic person is painfully aware of what we can't do. Schools are full of critics, and kids are the meanest. It took great clinical insight to identify autism in me—a seemingly successful, articulate adult. The recognition that my life achievements were both unusual and facilitated by autism was life changing—but it took a professional to help me see it.

We are disabled, but many of us are also exceptional. Every one of us knows how we fail and what we can't do, but most of us have no idea of any exceptional skills we may have or what they might be. You (the reader) can help us find them and, in doing so, help us see a positive path forward.

Knowledge of autism proved so transformational for me that I decided to write a book about my experiences. I took up disability advocacy and educated myself on autism and the issues surrounding it. Autism organizations began seeking my opinion on research directions, and I saw a huge gap between what autistic people asked for and what was actually done. For the past decade I have volunteered with government and private foundations to provide an autistic perspective on research. Today, in addition to writing and teaching, I serve on the Interagency Autism Coordinating Committee, the senior autism committee for the U.S. government.

In 2008, American public health agencies began involving more members of affected communities in the guidance of research. Disability advocates have long had a mantra—*nothing about us, without us*. It seemed the government was embracing that. At the same time, private foundations began seeking autistic input into research for or about autism. It's becoming more and more common for researchers to seek input from autistic people when designing studies. Clinicians also can benefit from discussing diagnostic and treatment issues with autistic people.

I've had the honor of providing my autistic perspective to a number of organizations. To do so, I've invested countless hours learning the issues, which are varied and complex. The same autistic concentration that allowed me to learn electronic engineering serves me well in advocacy and policy. It's almost as if I took up a new career. In doing so, I met hundreds and then thousands of people like me—diagnosed with autism and other neurological differences.

The release of my first book[1] brought me to the attention of people I'd worked with over the previous 30 years. In some cases, they wrote me to say they too had gotten autism diagnoses later in life. My first wife (we were by then divorced) was diagnosed at age 50, following the diagnosis of our 18-year-old son. As I learned more about autism and realized how many of my friends had also turned out to be on the spectrum, I saw that it was everywhere.

Part of the emerging neurodiversity vision is that individuals recognize others who were different like them. That is a less formal thing than medical diagnosis, but as I observed, the people who seemed "like me" also happened to have autism diagnoses, in many cases. That wasn't always true, but it was true often enough to make me consider the convergence.

It was a bit startling to discover my first wife (we became friends at age 13) and several of my friends from engineering jobs were autistic. None of us had any idea when we first met, though we described ourselves as geeks or misfits. We shared feelings of loneliness but did not think of ourselves as disabled. We were, instead, rejects or outcasts doing our best to make friends, and make a living.

With our mutual midlife introduction to autism, we realized we must have been drawn to each other unconsciously. Modern studies confirm this, suggesting people with developmental differences are more likely to be friends with neurologically similar individuals. Today some autistics talk about recognizing autism in others as a sixth sense, "autdar" in the way others describe "gaydar."

Autistic people have distinctive patterns of speech, characteristic expressions, and ways of moving that set us apart from nonautistic society. Ironically, none of those traits are part of the present diagnostic definition of autism. That may change tomorrow, given that autism's definition has been in a state of flux all of this century and half of the last.

[1] Robison, *Look me in the eye: My life with autism*, Crown, 2007.

For me, the choice of an arcane word in casual conversation, or the way one moves a hand to the face, tells me more than any observation of behavioral criteria from a guidebook. It's interesting that clinicians sometimes dismiss such lay observations, in the same way a bright child who can't show his work solving a math problem is told the correct answer alone doesn't count. Clinicians who take such positions fail to recognize that lay observations—and not clinical tests—are the way people have recognized members of human groups since time immemorial.

A few years ago, I served on the World Health Organization committee that produced the first International Compendium of Function (ICF) autism core set. The ICD (International Compendium of Disease and Disorder) is the world's standard set of medical definitions. The ICF is the standard catalog for function and ability. The contribution I am most proud of is the committee's recognition that autism and ADHD confer both disability and exceptionality. They are unique in the medical lexicon in that regard.

Autism is a medical diagnosis, but it's also a learning disability, and its various manifestations are often noticed by teachers and counselors. Most diagnoses happen before completion of school, and most autism services are rendered to children. Public health supports for adult autism remain very limited in most places, even though autism is a lifelong condition.

Adults who came of age before the diagnostic revisions of the *Diagnostic and Statistical Manual of Mental Disorders*, fourth edition (DSM-IV) did not generally get autism diagnoses unless they were nonspeaking. For those individuals, autism is often hidden behind depression, anxiety, ADHD, and behavioral problems. One British public health study (Brugha, 2009–2011) found the same prevalence in older adults as children, when current screening tools are used. Most older adults were not aware they were on the autism spectrum, though they often recognized other psychiatric challenges.[2] Attitudes toward autism vary. Some autistic people (or their families) wish fervently for a cure. Others reject talk of cure but wish for help in specific areas and accommodations.

If most autistic adults are undiagnosed, it falls to today's mental health professionals to recognize autism in the context of whatever causes a person to seek help. Identification of autism in adults can be difficult, particularly as there are no screening tools specially validated for older people. Yet the recognition of adult autism is important, even when a patient seeks help for something else, because autism may be a thread tying together other issues, and its presence may impact treatment for symptoms unrelated to the autism.

Whatever its specific impacts, autism has a strong influence over the whole person. Medical texts characterize autism as a communication disability. That's true, but far from the whole story. Lifelong communication impairment leads to anxiety, depression, and many other challenges. Autism is said to be a neurological difference, an alternative wiring of the brain. Other so-called wiring differences are associated with epilepsy, Tourette's, and dyslexia, all of which frequently accompany autism.

[2] Brugha, Epidemiology of autism spectrum disorders in adults in the community in England, *JAMA Psychiatry*, May 2011.

Autism is associated with a wide range of medical and mental health conditions from intestinal distress to sleep dysfunction.

Although the exact mix of co-occurring conditions varies from person to person, every autistic is somehow affected. However, individuals may not realize that conditions present since birth can be treatable. Researchers are just beginning to unravel the ways autism and co-occurring conditions are intertwined. One reason that's important is that co-occurring conditions are often harder to treat in autistic people. Therapies that are highly effective on nonautistics frequently have limited effect on autistic patients. It's not clear why this is the case.

There are few medical treatments for the core symptoms of autism, though promising studies are underway. Prior to recognition of autism by the medical profession, acceptance or accommodation was the only option. Today there are behavioral and occupational therapies that can help, though the essence of the autistic person remains immutable.

One result of the medical focus is a tendency to see autism exclusively as a disability. No one goes to the doctor to discuss their exceptionality. Talk of how autistic people are oblivious to subtle facial expressions can lead us to overlook extraordinary sensitivity to the behavior of a machine. Lacking cognitive flexibility is said to be a disability, except when an adult does one thing all day at work and does it well. Then it's an advantage. Disability when talking to humans isn't so important for someone who works with animals all day.

Obviously, some autistic people have far more serious challenges, and they may have few autistic advantages. For those individuals, mental health professionals may still help with co-occurring conditions, and they may also identify nonpsychiatric conditions that may be amenable to treatment. Psychiatric and general medical problems often go hand in hand.

Genetic studies have identified hundreds of variations associated with autism. Some are inherited, and stable from generation to generation. Others appear in families with no history of autism. Those de novo mutations are associated with more severe impairment, and often intellectual disability. One day we may distinguish many subtypes of autism via biomarker tests. Right now, we have diagnosis by observation, so autisms with very different biological foundations are lumped together.

It's likely that different biological foundations will be associated with specific mixes of co-occurring conditions, which may respond to different treatment strategies. Two examples we recognize today are fragile X and Rett syndrome.

Clinicians should expect to see tremendous variation in the presentation of autism. Some autistic people have social disabilities that are not apparent at first glance; others have obvious language or cognitive impairments, and the need for support is unmistakable. Individuals with cognitive disability are more likely to have significant medical challenges accompanying autism and a diminished ability to describe the problems. With such a diverse population, it's no wonder individual perceptions of autism are so varied.

Community attitudes toward autism have also shifted with time. Autism has probably been part of humanity forever, but it's only recently been recognized as a medical condition. Unusual skills, or strange behaviors, which we might now link to autism, were interpreted in the context of the day.[3] Some autistic people emerged as respected leaders, whereas others were described as lazy, stupid, or defiant. Nonspeaking autistics were called deaf and dumb or idiots.

Today there are a number of films and television shows whose characters exhibit traits of autism. In some cases, they are actually described as autistic. Media tends to present a less disabling side of autism, focusing on the technical prowess of the characters while playing social disability for comedic effect.

In the real world, stories of autistic people in academia and tech companies are legion. We've all heard comments like, "Half the math professors are undiagnosed autistics," and there is no doubt a kernel of truth to some such talk. At the same time, many of us know autistic people with significant intellectual impairment. It's clear that autistic people exist at all points on the intellectual curve. If there is any generalization to be made, it is that autistic intellect has been woefully underestimated. Modern technology is showing us how much nonspeaking autistics have to say, given assistive devices to make communication easier.

Some autistic people have unusual skills. One example is calendar calculating—figuring out what day of the week a certain date fell on, or how many days separate two events. The mechanism by which untrained people acquire those skills is unknown, but it's clear that mastery of the calendar would be life-critical knowledge for a primitive society. Some see calendar skills as an example of a mind shaped by evolution for the benefit of the tribe.

Other students of history look at ancient cave art[4] and draw parallels with modern autistic illustrators. Mastery of figurative art was at one time key to survival also. Today, with our reliance on technology, extraordinary abilities are relegated to the status of parlor tricks. That is evidenced by terminology used to describe people with this ability for most of the 20th century: idiot savant.

Autistics find that phrase offensive but still use the word savant without the idiot prefix. For a person to be credited with a savant skill, it must be outstanding in the context of the individual's overall cognitive ability, and also exceptional with respect to abilities of the general population. Studies have suggested anywhere from 10% to 30% of autistic people have such abilities.[5]

Savant skills per se are not a disability, but when they appear in a person with cognitive limitations, they may magnify other disabilities by comparison. Savant skills may also be disbelieved or interpreted as trickery, with negative results for the savant.

Special skills aside, most autistic people are not visibly disabled. That is one reason many autistics escape notice, particularly those who were not diagnosed in school. Adults may feel they are eccentric or suffer from some of the many conditions

[3] Silberman, Neurotribes, Avery, 2015, see description of Cavendish and others.

[4] Humphrey, Cave art, autism, and the evolution of the human mind, *Cambridge Archaeological Journal*, 1998 and Kellman, Ice age art, autism, and vision: How we see/how we draw, *Studies in Art Education*, 1998.

[5] Howlin, Savant skills in autism: Psychometric approaches and parental reports, *Philosophical Transactions*, May 2009. Also see Treffert, The savant syndrome: An extraordinary condition. A synopsis: past, present, future, *Philosophical Transactions*, May 2009, and his several books on this topic.

that accompany autism, but once out of school they are unlikely to learn about autism itself.

In the past decade employers have begun to recognize that certain autistic people are particularly good at specialized tasks. Software testing was one area where autistics excelled. Other autistic people did well in stockrooms thanks to prodigious memory. These observations led to today's Autism at Work[6] programs, which are led by companies as varied as SAP, Microsoft, HP Enterprise, Ernst and Young, and Home Depot.

Other programs, like Project Search,[7] are putting intellectually impaired autistic people to productive work by creating environments where they are understood and supported. The success of initiatives like those shows that society can change to better accommodate autistic people.

Autism as a definition is fairly new, but the underlying condition is old. The behaviors we now call autism first came to the attention of medical doctors in the 19th century. The field of psychiatry was in its infancy, and the idea of psychiatric conditions being rooted in the mind was still solidifying. Many doctors still attributed psychiatric problems to attacks of nerves. The greatest challenge was dementia praecox, later known as schizophrenia. That was the context in which autistic behavior was first described by Eugen Bleuler in the first part of the 20th century. Leo Kanner posited autism as a distinct disorder in 1943, and its definition has been revised continuously ever since.[8]

This book will discuss the convergence of autism and schizophrenia in a later chapter. In reading that chapter, it's worth remembering the two conditions have been alternately intertwined and separated by psychiatrists since the definitions were created. Meanwhile, geneticists and biologists are finding they share genetic markers and biomarkers, and they may be closely connected indeed.

In 1911, Blueler's schizophrenia was based on abnormal associations, autistic behaviors and thoughts, abnormal affect, and ambivalence. His description was the first to use the word "autism" in the context we know today. Prior to that, the term only existed as a combination of Greek roots that loosely translate to *into oneself.*

Blueler's schizophrenic autism was interpreted as withdrawing into fantasy or delusion. At least that's the interpretation offered by more contemporary psychiatrists, none of which presented themselves as autistic or possessed of first-person knowledge.

As an autistic person, I read Blueler's case studies of autistic withdrawal and see accounts of people like me. When adults looked at me as a child, they said I was lost in my own world—autistic—but I was the farthest one could be from delusional or psychotic. I had an imagination, but I clearly understood what was real and what existed only in my mind. Most of the time.

[6] Eng, Where autistic workers thrive, *Fortune*, June 2018. Also see Differently Abled People – Diversity and Inclusion on SAP.com.

[7] Project Search is an international program that prepares young people with significant disabilities for success in an integrated, competitive employment. Online at projectsearch.us

[8] Evans, How autism became autism, *History of the Human Sciences*, July 2013.

My first-person experience raises the question—how can an observer ever distinguish one from the other? We cannot truly know what's inside another mind. When I was a child, therapists discussed the possibility that I had childhood schizophrenia. Looking back, I imagine they saw my detachment and interpreted it as psychosis, and my imagination as delusion.

That misunderstanding is an excellent example of why it's so important for clinicians and scientists to talk with autistic adults. Researchers have been talking with parents for decades, and they provide their own valuable perspective, but nonautistic parents and researchers are both liable to misread autistic expressions and behaviors. We say autism is a communication disability, but between autistic and typical people, the communication challenges go both ways. Trained professionals misunderstood my thoughts and intentions because autism masked them. But a perceptive autistic adult would see right through that, just as I do now.

The original framers of schizophrenia and autism did not involve affected adults in the process of definition, and I believe that hindered their development of understanding. I hope the researchers of tomorrow learn from that mistake. Bleuler was a student of Greek, and he derived the word "schizophrenia" from roots that meant, loosely translated, a splitting of the soul. In his thinking, a person's psyche could split in two, and also split away from the rest of human society. Today neurodivergent people and psychiatrists see those things differently, but at that time Blueler treated them as one.

At this moment, autism and schizophrenia are fairly distinct. The autism label is given to a person who shows persistent deficits in social communication and social interaction across multiple contexts and restricted, repetitive patterns of behavior, interests, or activities. To gain a diagnosis, every autistic person must have those attributes to such an extent that their functioning is impaired.

The distinction has not always been so clean. Studies of long-term institutionalized adults with schizophrenia find a number of them are actually autistic, when modern diagnostic standards and tools are applied.

For some autistic people, deficits in interpersonal communication are limited to an inability to read body language or facial expressions. That is a serious social disability, but it's a rather different one from lack of response to spoken language or an inability to form sentences and answer questions. All those behaviors fall under the heading of communication disability, and any can be indicative of autism. That is but one example of autism's heterogeneity.

The restricted repetitive interests take a similarly wide range of forms. A child who will only do one thing is disabled in school where he or she is asked to switch tasks every 45 minutes. The same person, as an adult, may be well suited to a work environment where he or she can do a single thing all day long. Fixation in a child can become superior focus and concentration in an adult. With examples like that, some autistic disability is universal; other disability is social or contextual.

Autistic people may concentrate so deeply on a topic of interest that we don't notice or respond to the world around us. I've experienced that when I've been wrapped up in thought or observation and not noticed someone calling out to me. They are upset over being ignored, and I have no idea anything is even happening.

Neither of us is connecting with the other. It's easy for an observer to misinterpret those exchanges, and mental health workers are just as vulnerable to misjudgments as anyone else.

Autism is a neurological difference that shapes us growing up and remains with us all our lives. Ask any autistic adult, and you will hear stories of childhood disability. We know what it's like to be marginalized and bullied, because autism made us act different. Autism isolates us and fills us with frustration when we can't accomplish what others do with ease. The legacy of disability follows us into adulthood and becomes the foundation for conditions discussed in this book. That said, for most of us, autistic disability itself recedes with age, or becomes less visible.

From a treatment perspective, the greatest opportunity to address core symptoms of autism is while the brain is still developing. Childhood is when we learn social skills, and autistic people with communication disabilities benefit from help. Those of us with language impairments often benefit from speech therapy. Some of us gain from occupational therapy. Medication helps also, as with ADHD or anxiety.

One consideration with all these therapies is that autistic people are neurologically different, so we will always exhibit differences when compared to nonautistic peers. Being different is okay, provided it does not lead to bullying or place a child at risk for injury. Some autistic adults believe misunderstanding of autism and misguided interventions have caused children far more harm than autism itself. The goal of therapy should always be to protect subjects and help them to have the best quality of life.

Autistic children are often developmentally delayed. An autistic child who can't read at age 8 might worry his parents, but the same child may be reading at college level 5 years later. It is difficult to know when to intervene and when to wait for nature.

Most autistic people learn adaptive coping skills before adulthood even as they lag behind nonautistic peers with respect to developmental milestones. Psychiatric interventions and therapy may help by teaching basic skills in childhood and helping understand the complexities of adult behavior later on.

School is a big challenge for many autistic people. Communication disability and issues with structure and executive function may prevent us from completing academic requirements. For typical students, school is a very social place, and that can be hard for kids with social disability. Autistic students may reach adulthood with no experience of romance and little experience of friendship.

Every autistic person displays a wide range of other behaviors. Some are "being human," whereas others meet diagnostic criteria for conditions described in this book. Are they truly additional stand-alone diagnoses, or are they and autism all symptomatic of some larger, unnamed thing? That question vexed Bleuler and Kanner as they devised the first descriptions of autism, and it remains a question scientists wrestle with today.

It's also something autistic people live with. Consider those autistic deficits in social communication. The words sound rather sterile. The reality is not. Autistic people often can't read body language or facial expressions. My own life illustrates the impact of that. When I am around strangers, I am in a state of constant anxiety. Why? Because I can't tell what they might do next. Praise or attack seems equally likely.

Some autistic people turn inward and disconnect from other people. For others, childhood communication failures lead to lifelong isolation. Many autistics are targeted by bullies. Some studies suggest autistic people are far more likely to suffer from posttraumatic stress disorder.

A person (even one who is trained as a mental health care provider) who does not live with autism might not understand these common autistic social outcomes. Someone who was good at reading other people might well find autistic social anxiety totally inexplicable. He might know that a third of autistic people qualified for anxiety diagnoses, but without autistic insight, the reason could easily escape him. An autistic person who lived that experience would know every autistic person suffers from anxiety, given the right (wrong) set of circumstances.

Anxiety is one result of autistic social disability, but not the only one. Social failures add up, and the result is depression. Depression goes unresolved, and suicidal ideation often comes next. Studies suggest that most autistic people have thoughts of suicide, and it is nine times more common among autistics. Some of us can break this chain, whether through luck or hard work. Others can't and it proves fatal.

Most people become depressed by social failure and isolation, but others become angry. For some autistic teens the pain is too much, and they become violent. Autistic people may also become violent in response to prolonged mistreatment. They may also react with violence when frustrations overwhelm them. Most autistic people are not dangerous. Those who are present a serious problem.

Self-injury is another problem for autistic individuals. This may take the form of cutting or self-mutilation, scratching till bloody, hair pulling, or headbanging to the point injury is sustained. There are a number of theories to explain self-injurious behaviors, but successful treatments are few.

There are other less acute psychiatric conditions that exist alongside autism, like ADHD. According to the current data, at least a third of autistic people also meet the criteria for an ADHD diagnosis. It's not clear how one would be the result of the other, from a behavioral standpoint. But geneticists find many shared differences between the two conditions, and scientists who map the brain find many of the same areas are affected in both. The evidence that these two diagnoses are first cousins or closer is strong.

Addiction is another mental health issue that converges with autism. Most substance abuse and alcohol counselors don't even consider autism when talking to patients. But the pain of autistic social isolation can be a powerful force pushing some of us toward drugs or alcohol. A desire to be liked can have the same effect for others. When someone says they drink or use drugs to escape the pain, it's worth remembering that autism often magnifies social pain.

Sensory sensitivities are another common problem for autistic people. Some autistics are extremely sensitive to sounds, smells, or light. They may run from a room to escape an overload or cry out in pain, even when other people don't notice anything out of the ordinary. The connection between flashing lights and epilepsy is well known. Autistic people who are not prone to seizures may nonetheless be effectively shut down by sensory overload, and they may not recognize or be able to articulate the cause. This makes awareness and knowledge on the therapist's part that much more important.

Although excessive sensory sensitivity is commonly described as a disability, it must be said that autistic people are often the proverbial canaries in the coal mine. Flickering lights or noises in a classroom may send the autistic student to the therapist, but the truth is, every student in the class would benefit from remediation of the sensory insult.

Furthermore, exceptional sensory sensitivity is not always a disability. It may be a great gift for a musician, and there are many other circumstances where the same may be said. That does not mean a person with great sensitivity will not feel overwhelmed in some circumstances, but rather, this can be an example of disability and exceptionality wrapped into one trait.

Autistic people may also have the opposite problem—sensory insensitivity. They may be oblivious to sounds, smells, or lights that others take note of. This is particularly true when autistic people are in a state of focus or concentration. As with sensitivity, insensitivity can confer benefits in certain situations.

Sensory sensitivity can go hand in hand with synesthesia. Everyone has some sense of synesthesia, as evidenced by its appearance in everyday language. Music shimmers, cymbals are brilliant, and strobe lights flash with the roar of an explosion. People who imagine themselves as totally typical still understand those examples of sensory crossover. Autistic people are likely to experience more intense interconnections. In *Born on a Blue Day*, Daniel Tammet[9] described his perception of numbers as objects with tangible color and feel, and how manipulating them as visual objects helped him solve math problems.

Psychiatrists have traditionally viewed synesthesia as a pathology, but people like Tammet show that synesthesia enhances cognitive powers, at least for some. Personal accounts of autistic people sometimes describe synesthesia as confusing, but it's not generally characterized as a disability by the affected individuals. Consider as another example the symphony conductor. I know one who refers to individual violinists as red, blue, and green. For him, synesthesia helps separate the sounds of similar instruments so he can better conduct the performance.[10]

Autistic people are not often given to delusion, but descriptions of synesthesia may be mistaken for psychosis and delusion.[11] Savant abilities may also be misjudged as imagination or delusion, because the mental feats seem so improbable, especially in an individual with no known training. Highly educated people

[9] Tammet, *Born on a blue day*, Simon & Schuster, 2006.

[10] As another example, in Sweet Man: The Real Duke Ellington, author Don George quotes Duke Ellington on his synesthesia: "I hear a note by one of the fellows in the band and it's one color. I hear the same note played by someone else and it's a different color." Penguin Press, 1981.

[11] Bouvit, When synesthesia and savant abilities are mistaken for hallucinations and delusions: Contribution of a cognitive approach for their differential diagnosis, *Clinical Neuropsychology*, November 2017.

sometimes forget that humans mastered complex cognitive tasks long before universities existed.

This book is exclusively focused on psychiatric conditions that accompany autism, but mental health professionals should be alert to the likelihood of untreated general medical issues in autistic people they see. Autistic people may not recognize symptoms like intestinal pain or tremors as signs of treatable conditions, and a mental health worker may set them on the road to treatment, to their great benefit.

Perhaps one quarter of autistic people suffer from some level of epilepsy. For these individuals, epilepsy may range from unrecognized mild tremors to life-threatening seizures. Some public health researchers believe undiagnosed seizures are one of the leading causes of early death among autistic people.

Gastrointestinal distress is another common companion to autism. Many researchers think there is a link between brain and gut, and there is certainly a relationship between intestinal pain and behavior. At least a third of autistic people have some kind of gastrointestinal issue, and for many it's a serious, lifelong problem.

Autism is part of a complex package of which psychiatric co-occurrences are only a part. If properly evaluated, most autistic people will qualify for a number of other diagnoses.

Autistic people range from intellectually disabled to eccentric genius. That huge spread of affect, and the degree to which autism is intertwined with many other conditions, touches upon an emergent topic that psychiatrists should be aware of: neurodiversity. The word is a conjunction of neurology and diversity. It posits that some degree of neurological diversity is a normal part of humanity. Autism is a term rooted in deficit, whereas neurodiversity is based in strength.[12] One word belongs to the medical community, the other to the people.

Idealists believe all diversity should be honored and respected. Most medical professionals respect diversity but believe there is a point where healthy natural variation shades into pathology.

Lay proponents of neurodiversity believe the term encompasses some autism, ADHD, dyslexia, and other inborn neurological differences. Doctors see autism as the most disabling of those conditions, and scientists describe an imperfect fit between the neurodiversity and autism paradigms.

Autism is the label nosologists in the medical community have given to a certain collection of observed behaviors as defined in the ICD and DSM. Neurodiversity is a less specific label lay philosophers have given to the reality that neurodivergence (neurological diversity) is just as much a part of human diversity as are variations in height, hair color, or body type. Individuals who embrace the neurodiversity paradigm tend to feel they can live with autism, and believe it confers benefit along with disability. Those who reject neurodiversity generally see autism as a disability they would like to cure. When neurodivergent people form those opinions with respect to themselves, both viewpoints are valid.

*

[12] Austin, Neurodiversity as a competitive advantage, *Harvard Business Review*, May 2017.

My different ways of thinking helped me design electronic circuits and create photography. Childhood fixations turned into adult perfectionism, which serves me well in almost everything I do, from writing and science to restoring classic motorcars. But autism has also caused me a lot of pain and suffering. My social disabilities have made it hard to sustain relationships and contributed to chronic depression, anxiety, and loneliness. For many years I wished I could be "like everyone else," yet now I see that being different was the thing that got me to where I am today.

Every day I am reminded that I am lucky to have this balance, and I am part of a minority in that respect. Others see nothing good about autism. They may lay a lifetime of failure at its feet just as I credit autism for my success. Both our experiences are equally real and valid. Those of us with good outcomes can often thank mental health professionals, whether for understanding autism or for helping us with myriad co-occurring conditions from anxiety to posttraumatic stress disorder.

Our autism may simultaneously weave together and conceal a diverse package of psychiatric and general medical conditions, with a sprinkling of social problems on top. Mental health professionals should always be alert for co-occurring conditions in autistic people and expect the unexpected. Some co-occurring conditions escape our notice for years because we never realize they are treatable.

With all of autism's complexity, working with our population is tremendously challenging. As successes are shared, it is also exceptionally rewarding. I hope this guide helps professionals to better serve our community.

John Elder Robison

Springfield, Massachusetts
March 2019

ABOUT THE EDITORS

Dr. Susan W. White is Professor and Doddridge Saxon Chair in Clinical Psychology at the University of Alabama. Her research interests include assessment and intervention for co-occurring and core social problems in autism spectrum disorder. She is Editor of the *ABCT Series on Implementation of Clinical Approaches* and Associate Editor for the *Journal of Clinical Child and Adolescent Psychology* and the *Journal of Autism and Developmental Disorders*. Her research has been funded by the National Institutes of Health and she is coauthor of the Emotion Awareness and Skills Enhancement (EASE) program and developer of the Stepped Transition in Education Program for Students with ASD (STEPS).

Dr. Carla A. Mazefsky is an Associate Professor of Psychiatry and Psychology at the University of Pittsburgh School of Medicine. Supported by federal (e.g., National Institutes of Health, Department of Defense), state, and foundation grants, she focuses on emotion regulation and psychiatric and behavioral problems in autism spectrum disorder, and the development of assessment and treatment approaches. She is coauthor of the Emotion Awareness and Skills Enhancement (EASE) program and developer of the Emotion Dysregulation Inventory. She is an Associate Editor for the *Journal of Autism and Developmental Disorders* and recipient of the Ritvo-Slifka Award for Innovation in Autism Research from the International Society for Autism Research.

Dr. Brenna B. Maddox is a PostDoctoral fellow and clinical psychologist at the Penn Center for Mental Health, located at the University of Pennsylvania. Her research program focuses on the intersection of autism services and implementation science. Her PostDoctoral research, funded by the National Institute of Mental Health and the FAR Fund, aims to improve community mental health services for adults on the autism spectrum. Her clinical interests include the assessment and treatment of co-occurring difficulties within autism, such as anxiety and depression. Dr. Maddox is an Associate Editor for the *Journal of Autism and Developmental Disorders* and *Autism in Adulthood*.

LIST OF CONTRIBUTORS

Laura Gutermuth Anthony, PhD
University of Colorado School of Medicine
Children's Hospital of Colorado
Julia Barnes, PhD BCBA
University of Colorado School of Medicine/Anschutz Medical Campus
Karen Bearss, PhD
University of Washington
Steven J. Berkowitz
Lauren Brookman-Frazee, PhD
University of California
Autism Discovery Institute at Rady Children's Hospital-San Diego
Sarah Cassidy, PhD
University of Nottingham
Colby Chlebowski, PhD
University of California
Child and Adolescent Services Research Center
Chelsea M. Day, MS
Case Western Reserve University
Jeroen Dewinter, PhD
Tilburg University
Tranzo & GGzE
Amy Drahota, PhD
Michigan State University
Katelyn M. Dyason, BPsych(Hons)
Griffith University
Rebecca Elias, PhD
University of California Los Angeles
Andrea N. Evans, BA
Emory University School of Medicine
Mareike Eydt-Beebe
Vanderbilt University Medical Center
Julie McPherson Farmer, LMFT
Vice President of Child
Youth and Family Services
Community Research Foundation
Lara J. Farrell, PhD
Griffith University
Jill C. Fodstad, PhD
Indiana University School of Medicine
Jennifer H. Foss-Feig, PhD
Seaver Autism Center for Research and Treatment
Icahn School of Medicine at Mount Sinai
Robin L. Gabriels, PsyD
University of Colorado School of Medicine/Anschutz Medical Campus
Katherine Gotham, PhD
Vanderbilt University Medical Center
Kirstin Greaves-Lord
Donna L. Griffiths, DClinPsych
Griffith University
Jennifer N. Haddock, PhD BCBA-D
Kennedy Krieger Institute
Johns Hopkins University School of Medicine
Louis P. Hagopian, PhD BCBA-D
Kennedy Krieger Institute
Johns Hopkins University School of Medicine
University of Maryland
Baltimore County
Gloria T. Han, MA
Vanderbilt University
Olive Healy, PhD
Trinity College Dublin
Catherine G. Herrington, PhD
Vanderbilt University Medical Center
Barry Hill
Maya F. Hubert, MD
Icahn School of Medicine at Mount Sinai
Stefanie Zavodny Jackson
Małgorzata Janas-Kozik
Aaron J. Kaat, PhD
Northwestern University
Lauren Kenworthy, PhD
George Washington University Medical School

Connor M. Kerns, PhD
University of British Columbia
Bryan H. King
Yael Koenig, LCSW
County of San Diego Health and Human Services Agency
Behavioral Health Services
Emily S. Kuschner, PhD
University of Pennsylvania and The Children's Hospital of Philadelphia
Virginia Carter Leno, PhD
King's College London
Stacey Lurie, MA
Ferkauf Graduate School of Psychology
Yeshiva University
Seaver Autism Center for Research and Treatment
Icahn School of Medicine at Mount Sinai
Brenna B. Maddox, PhD
University of Pennsylvania
Sharna L. Mathieu, BPsych(Hons)
Griffith University
Carla A. Mazefsky, PhD
University of Pittsburgh
Micah O. Mazurek, PhD
University of Virginia
Julie McPherson
Lennart Pedersen, MSc
Center for Autism
Florencia Pezzimenti, MEd
Vanderbilt University Medical Center
Cara E. Pugliese, PhD
Children's National Health System and George Washington University
Chandler Puhy
Drexel University
Department of Psychology
John Elder Robison
College of William & Mary
Landmark College
Dana L. Rofey, PhD
University of Pittsburgh School of Medicine
Agnieszka Rynkiewicz, MD MAT PhD
University of Rzeszow
Eleonora Sadikova, BA
Children's National Health System
Shivali Sarawgi, PhD
The Warren Alpert Medical School of Brown University and Bradley Hospital
Lawrence Scahill, MSN PhD
Professor of Pediatrics Emory University School of Medicine
Marcus Autism Center
Emily Simonoff, MD FRCPsych
King's College London
Margaret C. Souders, PhD CRNP
University of Pennsylvania
Mark A. Stokes, PhD
Deakin University
John F. Strang, PsyD
Children's National Medical Center and George Washington University
Briana J. Taylor, PhD
Maine Medical Center Research Institute
Marta Tyszkiewicz-Nwafor, MD Ph.D
Psychiatry Poznan University of Medical Sciences Poland
Patricia J. M. van Wijngaarden-Cremers, PhD MD
Dimence and University of Nijmegen
Gregory L. Wallace, PhD
George Washington University
Susan W. White, PhD ABPP
Center for Youth Development and Intervention
University of Alabama
Katherine Nguyen Williams, PhD
University of California at San Diego
Rady Children's Hospital at San Diego.
Benjamin E. Yerys, PhD
Children's Hospital of Philadelphia
University of Pennsylvania

TABLE OF CONTENTS

Part 3 • Related Problems

Part 4 • Current Clinical Practices and Promising Research Approaches

PART 1

Overview

CHAPTER

1

Autism Spectrum Disorder and Co-Occurring Psychiatric Conditions: A Conceptual Framework

Virginia Carter Leno *and* Emily Simonoff

Abstract

There is strong evidence to suggest that individuals with autism spectrum disorder (ASD) are at heightened risk for developing co-occurring psychiatric conditions. However, the reasons behind this increased risk remain unclear. This chapter describes multiple conceptual models of the reasons for comorbidity and appraises the strength for each in relation to currently available evidence. The first section considers the evidence to suggest the reported increase in prevalence can be explained by purely artefactual factors (e.g., issues in sample acquisition or symptom measurement) and concludes this is unlikely as a complete explanation. The second section discusses more theoretical models, and how these could manifest in autistic individuals (e.g., increased prevalence or potency of established risk factors, and the role of ASD-specific risk factors). There is evidence to support multiple mechanisms playing a role in explaining the increased prevalence of psychiatric conditions, and these mechanisms are unlikely to be mutually exclusive. As the current literature is limited, priority areas for future research are suggested, including the need for accurate measurement of predictors and outcomes, more sensitive research designs, and the inclusion of underrepresented groups.

Keywords: autism, comorbidity, mental health problems, epidemiology, risk factors

Introduction

A considerable body of research over the past decade has demonstrated that co-occurring psychiatric conditions are highly prevalent in individuals with autism spectrum disorder (ASD; Gadow, DeVincent, & Drabick, 2008; Gjevik, Eldevik, Fjæran-Granum, & Sponheim, 2011; Leyfer et al., 2006; Lundström et al., 2014; Salazar et al., 2015; Simonoff et al., 2008). Around 70% of young people with ASD meet diagnostic criteria for an additional psychiatric disorder (Gjevik et al., 2011; Leyfer et al., 2006; Simonoff et al., 2008), far higher than in typically developing individuals, where prevalence, using similar instruments and diagnostic algorithms, is estimated at 10% to 13% (Costello, Mustillo, Erkanli, Keeler, & Angold, 2003; H. Green, McGinnity, Ford, & Goodman, 2004). These higher rates of psychiatric difficulties are found across the lifespan—present in early childhood (Salazar et al., 2015; Lecavalier, 2006), adolescence (Simonoff et al., 2013), and adulthood (Hofvander et al., 2009). Given the ubiquity of psychiatric conditions in individuals with ASD, a complete understanding of ASD must take account of these co-occurring difficulties. This chapter will outline the different theoretical models that may be useful when thinking about why the rates of co-occurring psychiatric conditions are elevated in individuals with ASD. Critically appraising different conceptual frameworks is important both theoretically and clinically, as different models suggest different mechanisms that drive interindividual variation in individuals with ASD and consequently suggest different forms of intervention. Where relevant evidence for specific models or arguments was able to be identified, it has been described. However, because of the limited research in this field, the absence of evidence does not negate the existence of a mechanism or theoretical viewpoint. This is a relatively new field of research, and much more work is needed before we fully understand what underpins the increased prevalence of psychiatric conditions in people with ASD.

This chapter will serve as a framework and outline some conceptual issues and questions that arise when attempting to understand the phenomenology and etiology of co-occurring psychiatric conditions in individuals with ASD. The chapter begins by discussing in greater detail why considering conceptual frameworks is important, and then moves onto discussing alternative models that could explain the increased prevalence rates of psychiatric conditions in individuals with ASD. The models outlined in the first section are concerned with potential confounding factors (e.g., methodological issues), whereas those described in the second section are concerned with theoretical causal mechanisms.

Symptoms that are currently not part of the diagnostic criteria for ASD are at times referred to as both "co-occurring" and "comorbid" difficulties/symptoms; for clarity the term "co-occurring psychiatric conditions" will be used throughout to refer to additional mental health symptoms that are not currently part of the diagnostic criteria for ASD.

How Does A Conceptual Framework Help to Understand the Prevalence of Psychiatric Conditions in ASD?

Key findings from the literature relating to theoretical frameworks of comorbidity (Angold, Costello, & Erkanli, 1999; Krueger & Markon, 2006; Neale & Kendler, 1995) can be applied to co-occurring psychiatric conditions in individuals with ASD. The first section will discuss arguments that suggest that the high rate of psychiatric conditions in individuals with ASD is due to a number of potential confounding factors (i.e., is artefactual). The second section will discuss more theoretical and mechanistic models that could explain the heightened prevalence. There is no theoretical requirement as to why these two types of models (confounders, mechanistic) should be mutually exclusive, and in practice it seems highly unlikely that they are.

How these co-occurring conditions are conceptualized has important implications in terms of our understanding of ASD, but also more widely our understanding of psychiatric nosology. The issue of how best to conceptualize co-occurring conditions is not a new idea, and certainly is not specific to ASD. For decades, comorbidity—physical or psychiatric—has been recognized as a common problem in describing and understanding medical conditions. Progress in understanding psychiatric comorbidity has been slower than that for physical disorders, at least in part because difficulties in accurately measuring psychiatric symptoms and risk factors make it harder to investigate underpinning mechanisms. Changes in diagnostic classification systems over time have also altered the issues surrounding comorbidity. The most recent manifestation of this debate has argued that psychiatry should move away from diagnostic categories and focus instead on objectively measured symptoms and their underpinning neurobiological mechanisms (Cuthbert & Insel, 2013; Insel et al., 2010).

Critically appraising patterns of co-occurrence between ASD and psychiatric conditions across the lifespan can lead to generation of testable hypotheses regarding underpinning mechanisms. Given the significant heterogeneity within the behavioral presentation of ASD, a complete understanding of the condition must account for both inter- and intraindividual variation not only in core symptoms but also in other significant aspects of the phenotype (e.g., co-occurring psychiatric conditions). Studying the interface and overlap between ASD and other diagnostic categories can also highlight shared and distinct etiological mechanisms that could have important clinical implications. Finally, evaluating different models regarding the etiology of the overlap between ASD and other psychiatric disorders will tell us more about models of brain and behavioral development more generally, as different models presuppose differences in the relationship between risk factors (be these genetic or environmental) and behavioral manifestations.

In terms of real-life consequences of this nosological debate, the explanatory framework that is used will influence approaches to intervention. Whether co-occurring conditions are part of the phenotype of ASD or are separable entities will determine which type of intervention is most likely to be effective. If these co-occurring conditions are part of (and therefore inseparable from) ASD, what follows is that the same factors are driving both core ASD and co-occurring symptoms. This would suggest that interventions aimed at modifying the core dysfunction in ASD (be this viewed through a neurobiological, cognitive, or psychological lens) would also improve co-occurring difficulties. However, if the latter model is true and these conditions are independent from the core symptoms (and underlying dysfunction) of ASD, it would follow that they would also have independent factors driving their emergence. Thus, treating these conditions separately from interventions for the core symptoms of ASD would be more appropriate, as the factors that cause the additional disorders have little to do with the factors that cause ASD. Of course, the situation does not need to be the same for different clusters of co-occurring symptoms (e.g., attention deficit hyperactivity disorder [ADHD] and anxiety symptoms). Leading from this is the issue of whether existing interventions that have been developed in non-ASD populations should be amended to be tailored to individuals with ASD or whether novel interventions should be sought. This again depends on whether these co-occurring conditions are comparable in individuals with and without a diagnosis of ASD, in terms of presentation and underlying etiology. Therefore, it is crucial to have the most accurate model for understanding co-occurring psychiatric conditions in individuals with ASD, as the choice of intervention largely rests on this understanding. Using an incorrect model could lead to a choice of inappropriate and potentially less effective treatment, thereby limiting the benefits individuals with ASD will gain from an intervention. If the end goal is to improve the lives of individuals with ASD and promote positive outcomes, then the accuracy of these theoretical models, and their corresponding implications, is an important research priority.

For an example of how theoretical models of comorbidity can impact on clinical practice, in older versions of diagnostic manuals, both the *Diagnostic and Statistical Manual of Mental Disorders* (DSM) and the World Health Organization *International Classification of Disease* (ICD), a diagnosis of ADHD could not be given to someone with an existing diagnosis of ASD. This exclusion has been removed in the most recent editions, which now permit a dual diagnosis. A similar exclusionary rule currently exists in the DSM regarding the occurrence of disruptive mood dysregulation disorder (DMDD) in individuals with ASD, despite evidence suggesting that the disorder may be vastly elevated in ASD populations (Copeland et al., 2019) and that emotion regulation problems are a significant issue for individuals with ASD (Mazefsky et al., 2013).

Confounding Factors That Could Explain Increased Prevalence of Psychiatric Conditions in ASD Populations

Bias in Sample Acquisition

It is widely recognized that the type of sample used to estimate prevalence can affect results, regardless of core diagnosis. Specifically considering how this might apply to ASD, different methods of sample ascertainment will lead to different estimations of the prevalence of psychiatric conditions in individuals with ASD, with selected populations often reporting higher rates of co-occurrence. Complete ascertainment from well-defined populations is the most rigorous method of sampling. This is when every individual who is part of the target population (e.g., people with ASD in a given geographical location and within a given age range) is included. The design can be varied to select only a proportion of eligible participants, but the probability of selection should be well defined and accounted for in the statistical analysis using probability weights. Samples drawn through this method are representative of the disorder, but this is reliant upon accurate identification of caseness. This should not always be assumed. Population-based studies that have included individuals with an established ASD diagnosis but also screened individuals who might be at risk of having an undiagnosed ASD (e.g., those who have registered special educational needs) have highlighted differences in prevalence rates based on how caseness is identified (Baird et al., 2006). The prevalence of ASD based on existing diagnoses was 44.1 per 10,000, whereas including all individuals who had been screened and received a diagnosis upon entry to the study yielded an estimated prevalence of 116.1 per 10,000. However, population-based samples that use the complete ascertainment method described previously (i.e., where research methods are used to identify caseness) are few and far between, mostly due to the enormous costs associated with this type of sample design.

Another widely used method is selective sampling. This is when participants either are recruited through clinical services or are volunteers from the community (i.e., not those exclusively in contact with clinical services). Both methods may induce certain biases into the sample and therefore the information researchers seek to obtain. With regard to clinical samples, it is widely recognized that individuals who are in contact with clinical services have a more severe presentation than those who are not (e.g., Berkson's bias; Berkson, 1946) and come from families that feel more burdened by these problems (Angold et al., 1998). Therefore, if studies solely rely on data obtained from individuals with ASD who present to services more broadly, this will likely lead to an overestimation of the prevalence rates of psychopathology in ASD. However, this seems an unlikely explanation as studies that have utilized population-based samples (e.g., Simonoff et al., 2008) and those that have recruited from specialist schools

(Gjevik et al., 2011) find comparable rates of psychopathology in ASD to those found in clinics (Gadow, DeVincent, Pomeroy, & Azizian, 2004, 2005). Furthermore, in their population-based study Simonoff and colleagues (2008) did not find that rates of co-occurring psychiatric disorders differed dependent on whether ASD had already been recognized, as indicated by the presence or absence of a clinical diagnosis of ASD. However, with increasing recognition of co-occurring mental disorders in ASD, this may change in the future when mental health providers are more willing to recognize and treat co-occurring psychiatric disorders in individuals with ASD. Volunteer samples (e.g., individuals recruited through advertisement or word of mouth) are also likely to induce bias. Individuals or families who volunteer to take part may be those with a more complex presentation (this may be more likely in the case of intervention studies, as these may be seen to offer support and thus are taken up by families who feel they need more help), or conversely, it may be primarily those with a less severe presentation (and therefore are more likely to consent to attending a day of assessments or multiple appointments as they may not require as many resources and preparation). It is rare that researchers are able to test exactly how these issues impact on results, but they should be held in mind when drawing conclusions from the literature as a whole, as these may lead to over- or underestimation of prevalence rates or delineation of specific correlates/predictors of psychiatric conditions that are only present in certain subpopulations of individuals with ASD.

Related to the second point about exploring correlates or predictors, if the research being conducted requires participants with ASD, especially young people, to complete cognitive tasks, then other factors may influence participation rates. First, the age of the participants and the severity of certain co-occurring conditions (e.g., ADHD) will most certainly impact on whether participants are able to complete the given assessments. The presence of disorders such as social anxiety and panic disorder may also play a role, for example, if the research requires participants to complete face-to-face assessments or tolerate being in a scanner or wearing an electrode cap. Therefore, one should bear in mind not only who consented to take part in the research but also who was able to successfully complete the research assessments.

Another factor that can bias prevalence estimates and correlates/predictors of psychiatric conditions is the proportion of the sample who have intellectual disability. A significant proportion of people with ASD have some form of intellectual disability (Charman et al., 2011), and this overlap between ASD and intellectual disability could theoretically account for the increased prevalence of psychiatric conditions in ASD populations, as intellectual disability in and of itself is a risk factor for mental health problems (Emerson, 2003). However, this seems unlikely, as although the literature is variable regarding how variation in IQ in individuals with ASD is associated with variation in psychiatric symptoms, there is consistency in that individuals with ASD both with and without intellectual disability have increased rates of psychopathology (Bradley, Summers, Wood, & Bryson, 2004; Kim, Szatmari, Bryson, Streiner, & Wilson, 2000; Salazar et al., 2015; Simonoff et al., 2008). Additionally, comparative studies find that rates of co-occurring psychiatric problems in ASD are higher than in those with intellectual disability (Brereton, Tonge, & Einfeld, 2006; Farmer & Aman, 2011), suggesting that the increased prevalence of psychiatric conditions in individuals with ASD is unlikely to be solely due to the unmeasured impact of intellectual disability in ASD samples. Reviewing the evidence discussed previously, it is unlikely that sampling bias can fully account for the increased rate of psychiatric conditions in individuals with ASD. However, differences in sampling approach will likely contribute to the variability across studies and so should be held in mind when drawing conclusions from the literature as a whole.

Bias in Symptom Measurement

Another potential explanation for the increased prevalence rates of co-occurring psychiatric conditions in ASD is difficulties in measuring symptoms. There are several issues to consider here: first, the suitability of existing instruments to measure symptoms of psychopathology in ASD populations, and second, the more conceptual issue of how and when the symptoms of additional psychiatric conditions and the symptoms of ASD should be differentiated.

Difficulties in measuring psychopathology in individuals with ASD. Currently, there are few specialized instruments designed to assess psychiatric conditions in individuals with ASD (Hanratty et al., 2015; Leyfer et al., 2006). Studies often use measures designed for non-ASD populations, which have not been appraised and validated for use in populations with neurodevelopmental conditions. To give an example of how this could influence prevalence rates, increased rates of callous–unemotional traits are found in young people with ASD (Carter Leno et al., 2015). However, to our knowledge, instruments to measure callous-unemotional traits have not been validated for use in ASD populations. As some behavioral characteristics associated with callous–unemotional traits may be superficially similar to features of ASD (such as difficulties in social reciprocity), instruments designed to measure callous–unemotional traits in typically developing populations may not be sensitive enough to discriminate between superficially overlapping aspects of ASD and callous–unemotional traits, thus leading to an inflation of estimates. Similar points could be made with regard to differentiating between the symptoms of ADHD and ASD, for example, "pure" attentional difficulties versus narrow perceptual focus leading to atypical concentration levels, or fidgeting and difficulties sitting still versus complex mannerisms and stereotyped behavior. Questionnaires developed for non-ASD populations may not elicit the types of fine-grained description required to differentiate between the symptoms of ASD and other psychiatric conditions.

There are also other issues to consider regarding the use of instruments not specifically developed for individuals with ASD. Characteristics such as wording, the type of scale used (e.g., Likert, sliding continuous response option), and age dependency of an instrument should all be held in mind.

The identification of psychiatric symptoms may also be hindered by the limited emotional literacy and communication/language impairments found in people with ASD; these could lead to difficulties both in identifying one's own emotional states and in communicating distressing emotional experiences to others. This point may be especially relevant when considering internalizing disorders such as anxiety and depression, where identification of symptoms relies primarily on both insight into subjective internal experiences and the ability to communicate those experiences (as compared to behavioral disorders such as ADHD, which are typically diagnosed on the basis of observable symptoms). This point should be held in mind when interpreting literature reporting that rates of internalizing disorders are lower in individuals with ASD who are minimally verbal (Hallett et al., 2013; Sukhodolsky et al., 2008). It remains unclear if this reflects the true prevalence or instead difficulties in accurately measuring internalizing symptoms in minimally verbal populations using existing measures. For young children and individuals who are minimally verbal, one must often rely on caregivers or teachers to identify symptoms of internalizing disorders, which could lead to misinterpretation and inaccurate estimation of prevalence. It is possible that lower IQ and communication abilities may prevent the communication of internal states, meaning that parents are less aware of these emotions in general. Alternatively, it may be that a certain level of IQ is required to engage in higher order cognitions such as worrying about past and future events or other people's opinions, as is found in anxiety disorders, or feeling hopeless and helpless, as is found in depression. These considerations regarding identification and measurement of internalizing difficulties are not exclusive to autistic individuals who are minimally verbal. In individuals with ASD who verbally able, difficulties in emotional insight and literacy could be present and similarly impact upon identification of mental health problems, although these difficulties may be overlooked due to seemingly typical levels of cognitive and verbal ability. If unacknowledged, these underlying difficulties could also bias estimations of the prevalence of emotional symptoms in these groups of individuals.

The debate regarding how best to measure symptoms of internalizing disorders in individuals with ASD, especially those who are minimally verbal, is still ongoing. Developing technology that allows accurate but nonobtrusive measurement of physiological characteristics linked to anxiety (e.g., skin conductance, heart rate) may be helpful in this regard. Currently, there is a lack of consensus as to whether and how symptom definitions should be amended to take account of the specific characteristics of individuals with ASD. Bespoke instruments, for example, similar to diagnostic manuals specifically created for people with intellectual disability (Fletcher, Loschen, Stavrakaki, & First, 2007), may offer more sensitive measurement and thus more accurate identification of additional difficulties. However, because they are then autism specific and not used in other populations, it is not possible to make direct comparisons with non-ASD samples. Conversely, although standardized instruments may allow group comparisons, they may be insensitive, as outlined in the examples earlier, and potentially lead to inaccurate estimates of additional psychopathology. Indeed, some have found that using a diagnostic interview modified to account for ASD-specific presentations of psychiatric symptoms led to a substantial reduction in rates of psychiatric conditions (Mazefsky et al., 2012). Carruthers and colleagues report that standardized anxiety questionnaires developed in non-ASD samples perform adequately in ASD samples, especially questionnaires that focus more on the observable symptoms of anxiety (Carruthers, Kent, Hollocks, & Simonoff, 2018), whereas others suggest that another oft-used anxiety measure may measure different constructs in ASD as compared to non-ASD samples (White et al., 2015).

Difficulties in differentiating between symptoms of ASD and symptoms of co-occurring psychiatric conditions. Setting aside difficulties in measuring psychiatric symptoms, a further issue is that there may be real overlap between the symptoms of ASD and other psychiatric conditions. This is not a problem specific to ASD, as many have noted that the absence of clear dividing lines between psychiatric disorders in general means currently there is uncertainty in how one differentiates one disorder from another (Angold & Costello, 2009). One particularly unclear instance is in the case of obsessive-compulsive disorder (OCD). It can be difficult to distinguish between rituals and compulsions indicative of OCD and the repetitive behaviors and interests characteristic of ASD. The issue of how to separate the two clusters of symptoms and when these symptoms are distinct and severe enough to warrant a separate diagnosis of OCD is still under debate (Postorino et al., 2017a). The superficial similarity between the two disorders could potentially contribute to elevated prevalence if certain ASD symptoms are being routinely interpreted as evidence for the presence of OCD. There are other instances where difficulty differentiating symptoms could result in falsely elevated prevalence rates of psychiatric conditions. In some clinical settings a diagnosis of ASD may be made based on social impairments and poor communication, but these may be in fact due to the downstream impact of the symptoms of other disorders (e.g., problems in inhibition characteristic of ADHD impacting on social reciprocity) rather than indicating the presence of ASD. Not all social and communication impairments are due to ASD; misdiagnosis of this sort could lead to individuals with existing underlying disorders being given an additional (inappropriate) diagnosis of ASD, which in turn would inflate the rate of individuals who have co-occurring disorders. It is important to note that this section aims to address a slightly different point to those that have been made previously regarding the impact of nonspecific symptoms on psychiatric comorbidity in general. Some diagnostic criteria effectively include the same symptoms across different disorders (e.g., irritability being a symptom of oppositional defiant disorder [ODD], bipolar, and depression), which could increase the probability of an individual receiving two diagnoses from the same constellation of symptoms (Angold et al., 1999). Here, instead, we are concerned with superficial similarities in symptoms, rather than repetition of symptoms across diagnostic categories, as the core symptoms of ASD are relatively specific. Here, differentiation of ASD-specific types of impairments versus those caused by symptoms of other disorders is key. Taking a full developmental history and accounting for the nature and manifestations of social communicative impairments and restrictive and repetitive behaviors, and how and when any additional symptoms wax and wane, is helpful in these instances.

The counterargument to the argument that superficial similarity is driving the preponderance of co-occurring conditions is that certain disorders that have less superficial symptomatic overlap with ASD, for example, externalizing behaviors (conduct disorder [CD]/ODD) or Tourette syndrome, remain elevated in individuals with ASD. Furthermore, some suggest that prevalence rates may in fact underestimate additional psychiatric conditions in individuals with ASD as the symptoms of these are missed through diagnostic overshadowing, as is well documented in intellectual disability (Jopp & Keys, 2001; Reiss & Szyszko, 1983).

Problematic Nosology

An alternative explanation for the high prevalence of co-occurring psychiatric conditions in ASD populations is that our current diagnostic systems are problematic. This argument differs from the proposal described earlier, which considered that the field may not be measuring co-occurring psychiatric symptoms accurately. In this model, the emphasis is on the conceptualization of ASD, which some see as too narrow (Gillberg, 2010). The consequence of this narrow definition is that all additional symptoms, which do not fit under the category of ASD, by default become "co-occurring" symptoms. Diagnostic practice may also be influenced by external factors. For example, if reimbursement systems for certain interventions require specific diagnoses, practitioners may decide to add additional diagnoses for pragmatic reasons, regardless of the evidence about underpinning etiology and classification.

There are multiple ways to address the debate regarding the nature and range of the ASD phenotype. One approach is to use the twin design, where studies suggest that what is inherited is broader than the core diagnostic criteria, as cotwins of affected individuals are characterized by similar, albeit more subtle, socio-cognitive impairments and restrictive and repetitive patterns of behavior (Bolton et al., 1994; Le Couteur et al., 1996). Unfortunately, these older studies did not measure co-occurring psychiatric symptoms, as the prevalence of these additional difficulties has not been appreciated until recently. It is of note that family studies systematically report higher rates of psychiatric disorders in relatives of individuals with ASD (Bolton, Pickles, Murphy, & Rutter, 1998; Piven & Palmer, 1999; Piven et al, 1991; Smalley, McCracken, & Tanguay, 1995), which are not purely due to the consequence of having a child with ASD, as many report the onset of parental psychiatric difficulties before the birth of the child. Although one could speculate that these additional difficulties occur as a consequence of the broader characteristics of ASD, no association has been found between the psychiatric disorder and the presence of the broader autism phenotype (Piven & Palmer, 1999), suggesting the psychiatric difficulties present in relatives of individuals with ASD are not likely to be either an indirect result of the broad autism phenotype or the direct result of the genes causing the broad autism phenotype.

Another way to differentiate co-occurring psychiatric conditions in individuals with ASD from a core ASD diagnosis is to track symptom variation over time. Although few studies have looked at this, there is some evidence to suggest that the onset of anxiety disorders peaks in key developmental periods (e.g., adolescence) in individuals with ASD in a similar manner to that found in non-ASD populations (for a review see Kerns et al., 2014). Whether variation in psychiatric symptoms over time is meaningfully correlated with variation in ASD symptoms over time, and whether these correlations differ across different psychiatric symptoms, remains relatively unknown. This is likely in part due to the intensive sampling this type of analysis requires, namely larger samples with frequent and in-depth assessments. It is worth noting that cross-sectionally associations between psychiatric symptoms and the number or severity of ASD symptoms do not appear to be supported (Hartley et al., 2008; Maskey et al., 2013; Renno & Wood, 2013; Simonoff et al., 2008).

An alternative, and more commonly used, approach to exploring whether co-occurring psychiatric conditions in individuals with ASD should be considered independent entities is to test whether they are similar in nature to the "classic" presentation of these psychiatric disorders (i.e., in non-ASD populations). Similarities can be assessed at the level of phenotypic presentation (e.g., do the symptoms look the same in ASD vs. non-ASD populations, or do certain symptoms cluster together in the same way in ASD vs. non-ASD populations?) or underlying correlates/predictors (e.g., are certain symptoms associated with the same neurobiological profile in ASD vs. non-ASD populations?). If certain psychiatric disorders are found to be comparable in ASD and non-ASD populations, this would suggest that they should be viewed as valid and independent co-occurring conditions (rather than part of the ASD phenotype). Although some report that ODD is comparable in non-ASD versus ASD samples in terms of the structure of symptom dimensions and the specific pattern of associations between different dimensions and other forms of psychopathology (Mandy, Roughan, & Skuse, 2014), the strong link between ODD and CD found in non-ASD populations does not appear to be present in ASD populations (where rates of CD are low; Simonoff et al., 2008). Others find children with ASD display a different pattern of associations with anxiety symptoms, in that they are more closely correlated with behavior problems, which is not the case in children without ASD (Evans, Canavera, Kleinpeter, Maccubbin, & Taga, 2005). This is in line with reports that although the factor structure of anxiety in youths with versus without ASD may be similar, symptoms relate to each other differently in youths with ASD (White et al., 2015). Others find a more nuanced picture, with some young people with ASD presenting with "typical" (here defined using DSM criteria) anxiety, but others with "atypical" anxiety (defined as anxiety symptoms that did not match DSM definitions but which might reflect anxiety specific to ASD, e.g., interfering, daily worries regarding schedule or environmental changes or other unusual, likely ASD-related concerns), and some individuals presenting with a combination of both typical and atypical anxiety symptoms (Kerns et al., 2014). Moving away from anxiety disorders, using latent class analysis on a large sample of children with ASD and ADHD, van der Meer and colleagues failed to find a class of individuals with ASD without ADHD (but found statistical support for an ADHD + ASD class), suggesting that in some subgroups of individuals, ASD always presents with co-occurring ADHD (van der Meer et al., 2012). A caveat to this finding is that it used a clinical sample and so may have been more likely to include more severe cases and/or more cases with a co-occurring presentation.

Currently, most research on this topic has compared the phenotypic presentation of disorders between individuals with and without ASD. However, just because the surface level manifestation of a disorder in individuals with ASD is somewhat different from those without ASD, this does not automatically mean that it warrants a different label. The causes of psychiatric conditions in ASD could very well be comparable to those in individuals without ASD, and it is merely the *manifestation* of the disorder that is different. The developmental atypicalities that lead to ASD may also affect how psychological disorders present themselves; however, they could still be considered as unique disorders and comparable in etiology to those reported in non-ASD populations (which in turn would suggest similar treatment approaches). To give a more concrete example, in the previously described studies the neurobiological and physiological manifestations of anxiety were not measured, so it may be that the triggers and presentation of anxiety symptoms are different in individuals with ASD, yet the biological mechanisms underpinning said symptoms are comparable to those found in non-ASD populations. If this were the case, it would suggest that anxiety should still be considered as distinct from ASD. Further work focusing on disentangling phenotypic similarity from etiological independence is required to clarify which psychiatric symptoms and conditions should be considered independent from a core ASD diagnosis.

Even if one views the co-occurrence of ASD and other psychiatric conditions as due to artificial division of a single underlying phenomenon into distinct categories, the question still remains as to why symptoms group together in the way they do. Why is it that some individuals with ASD experience few co-occurring psychiatric symptoms, whereas others experience a multitude? Why do some individuals with ASD develop anxiety, whereas others develop ADHD? Furthermore, from a more practical standpoint, this approach offers limited opportunities for intervention. If these co-occurring psychiatric conditions are really just part of ASD, and therefore should not be viewed as distinct disorders, then it follows that intervention attempts to improve any "core impairment" in ASD should improve all other symptoms (as they are all just manifestations of the same underlying phenomenon). Here, it should be noted that pharmacological interventions designed to improve non-ASD-specific difficulties (e.g., ADHD, behavior problems) have relatively little effect on core ASD symptoms (McDougle et al., 2005; Research Units on Pediatric Psychopharmacology Autism Network, 2005), suggesting at least some degree of independence. Finally, given that currently there is no conclusive theory regarding the etiology of ASD and there are a limited number of empirically supported interventions for core symptoms (Pickles et al., 2016), this viewpoint offers few treatment options for individuals with ASD and co-occurring psychiatric conditions.

Theoretical and Mechanistic Explanations for Increased Prevalence of Psychiatric Conditions in ASD Populations

Increased Prevalence of Established Risk Factors

Moving onto more theoretical models to explain the heightened prevalence of psychiatric conditions in ASD, one proposal is that known risk factors for psychopathology happen to be more prevalent in ASD populations. These risk factors could be environmental (e.g., perinatal adversity, adverse life events), biological (e.g., genetic risk factors, a set of neurobiological vulnerabilities), or cognitive (e.g., information processing biases).

Perinatal adversity. An example of an established risk factor for psychiatric and developmental difficulties that is more prevalent in ASD populations (Gardener, Spiegelman, & Buka, 2011) is perinatal adversity (e.g., significant prematurity, obstetric complications). Here it should be noted that although severe obstetric complications that are associated with clear structural brain abnormality, such as extreme prematurity or environmental deprivation, are unlikely to be due to the developing fetus, it is possible that milder obstetric complications may be in part a consequence of an abnormal fetus (and so are a consequence of atypical development prior to birth, rather than the cause of atypical development after birth; R. Goodman, 1988), and there is evidence to suggest this may be the case in ASD (Bolton et al., 1997). Perinatal adversity (across multiple conceptualizations of this term) is a relatively nonspecific risk factor. There is strong evidence for a link between both milder and more severe perinatal adversity and anxiety, ADHD, executive functioning difficulties, intellectual disability, schizophrenia, and behavior problems (Bhutta, Cleves, Casey, Cradock, & Anand, 2002; Linsell et al., 2018; Marlow, Hennessy, Bracewell, & Wolke, 2007; Serati, Barkin, Orsenigo, Altamura, & Buoli, 2017; Taylor & Rogers, 2005). This is perhaps unsurprising, as perinatal adversity is likely to act diffusely on a variety of neural systems (as opposed to having selective mechanisms of action), and therefore may cause a range of difficulties. Extreme early environmental deprivation may also act in a similarly nonspecific manner, as highlighted by the range of suboptimal outcomes in the English Romanian adoptee study (Rutter et al., 2007). It is important to highlight here that just because these complications may be a consequence of the ASD status of the fetus (as opposed to being a risk factor for ASD) as highlighted by Bolton and colleagues, this does not mean the developing fetus is immune from any additional pathogenic effects of perinatal complications. Given the evidence suggesting obstetric complications are associated with meaningful variation in brain development, cognition, and behavior, it is possible that these complications could affect the phenotypic presentation of ASD and increase risk for other difficulties (e.g., ADHD, cognitive impairments).

Other adverse life events. Beyond the perinatal period, research indicates that young people with ASD are more likely to have experienced a variety of adverse life events, including parental divorce, a parent having had serious mental illness, death of a family member or close relative, bullying, and childhood abuse and sexual coercion (H. Green et al., 2004; Hoover & Kaufmann, 2018; Humphrey & Symes, 2010; Little, 2001; Ohlsson Gotby, Lichtenstein, Långström, & Pettersson, 2018; Roberts et al., 2015).

There is strong evidence from typically developing populations to suggest that experiencing these types of adverse life events is causally related to increased likelihood of psychiatric conditions, and there is no evidence or a priori reason to suggest this would not also be true in ASD populations (Cappadocia, Weiss, & Pepler, 2012; Hoover & Kaufmann, 2018; Kendler, Karkowski, & Prescott, 1999; Singham et al., 2017). The explanatory model of increased exposure to environment stressors in ASD populations could be considered similar to the notion of gene–environment correlation, the phenomenon of an individual's genotype and hence his or her behavior influencing the type of environment he or she encounters (Plomin, DeFries, & Loehlin, 1977). Twin studies have demonstrated a genetic influence on characteristics of children's friends and peer groups (Bullock, Deater-Deckard, & Leve, 2006), social support (Agrawal, Jacobson, Prescott, & Kendler, 2002), exposure to trauma (Stein, Jang, Taylor, Vernon, & Livesley, 2002), and life events and stress (Kendler, Gardner, & Prescott, 2003). Genotype–environment correlation has been subclassified by the mechanism of action: passive, evocative, and active (Plomin et al., 1977). Passive genotype–environment correlation is when the environment a child experiences is correlated with his or her parents', and therefore his or her own, genotype. Parents who are highly anxious may increase the risk of anxiety in a young person with ASD by way of risk for anxiety being passed down through the genome, but also by providing an environment that may inadvertently transmit anxiety-evoking beliefs (e.g., viewing the world as a dangerous and unsafe place). In this way the genetic and environmental risks for anxiety are correlated. Evocative genotype–environment correlation is when an individual's genotype evokes certain reactions from other people, thereby influencing the type of environment he or she encounters. This type of genotype–environment correlation may potentially be relevant to understanding the heightened prevalence of bullying (and potentially abuse) in individuals with ASD. Active genotype–environment correlation is when an individual's genotype influences the types of environments he or she seeks out, selects, or creates for him- or herself. Environmental circumstances that are dependent on individual characteristics (e.g., being fired, getting a divorce) are found to be more heritable than those that are usually unaffected by an individual's behavior (e.g., death of a relative, experiencing a natural disaster; Jaffee & Price, 2007). Developmental theories hypothesize that the passive type may be more important in childhood, whereas the latter two types become more important later in life, as individuals gain more autonomy and therefore are able to make more choices regarding the selection and construction of their environment (Scarr & McCartney, 1983). Currently, there is very little literature focused on these processes in ASD populations, despite the fact that understanding the interplay of genetic and environmental factors with regard to risk for psychiatric conditions may be informative in terms of prevention and intervention.

Neurobiological risk factors. Individuals with ASD may also be more likely to inherit genetic risk for other psychiatric disorders due to overlap between genetic influences for certain psychiatric conditions and genetic influences for ASD. Behavioral genetic studies find substantial overlap in genetic influences on ASD and other neurodevelopmental disorders including ADHD and tic disorders (Lichtenstein et al., 2010), and molecular genetic studies have identified the same copy number variants (CNVs) in samples of ADHD, ASD, and/or intellectual disability (Morrow, 2010; Williams et al., 2010; Mefford et al., 2012). Similarly, family history of schizophrenia is a well-replicated risk factor for ASD (Daniels et al., 2008; Larsson et al., 2005; Sullivan et al., 2012), and individuals with ASD are more likely to have a parent with a serious mental illness (Montes & Halterman, 2007; Yirmiya & Shaked, 2005). A puzzle is that an early genome-wide, cross-disorder study did not find evidence for shared genes between ASD and ADHD (Cross-Disorder Group of the Psychiatric Genomics Consortium, 2013). More recent developments in identifying common variants for both disorders, including the establishment of polygenic risk scores, may shed light on this early finding. It should also be noted that common genetic factors are not found for all other co-occurring mental health disorders, and the genetic influences on internalizing symptoms are found to be largely independent from the genetic influences on core ASD symptoms (Hallett, Ronald, & Happé, 2009; Hallett, Ronald, Rijsdijk, & Happé, 2010). It should be noted that these genetic studies do not exclude an environmental pathway (in addition to the genetic one) in terms of mechanism of action (as has been theorized in non-ASD populations; Goodman & Gotlib, 1999).

In addition to increased likelihood of heritable risk, another potential source of risk for psychopathology is the varied profile of neurocognitive impairments associated with ASD. ASD is characterized by dysfunction in multiple neural systems, as individuals with ASD demonstrate atypical functioning across multiple areas of the brain and in multiple frequencies of neural oscillatory activity (Wang et al., 2013; Wass, 2011). If ASD is associated with dysfunction across multiple neural systems, this is likely to impact on several networks of brain functioning and thereby cognition. Indeed, although traditionally ASD was conceptualized as a disorder of social cognition, research has now highlighted that individuals with ASD demonstrate impairments in a wide range of cognitive domains, not all of which are thought to be ASD specific (e.g., executive functioning, memory, verbal ability; Brunsdon et al., 2015). This is in keeping with the concept of "generalist genes," a hypothesis that argues that it is extremely unlikely that the genetic influences on brain structure and function are modular (Kovas & Plomin, 2006). This hypothesis was formed from the observation that it is rare to find a cognitive process that is selectively associated with brain activity in one specific area. What is more common is that certain cognitive abilities entail a network of brain activity, simultaneously recruiting multiple areas, and that patterns of brain activation overlap across different cognitive abilities. The generalist hypothesis proposes that genes act pleiotropically, in that one gene may affect many areas and therefore functions of the brain (e.g., domains of cognition). Candidate mechanisms by which these genes act across several cognitive processes could be through modulation of neural plasticity, dendritic complexity, or speed of nerve conduction. If one considers that ASD is strongly influenced by genetic factors and applies the idea that genes impact on multiple domains/networks of cognitive functioning, this may explain why individuals with ASD are characterized by such a wide range of cognitive impairments. It follows that if some of these impairments in these domains of cognition are thought to be associated with risk for psychopathology in non-ASD populations, then this may be another mechanism by which risk for psychiatric conditions is increased in individuals with ASD (note that this hypothesis is predicated on the acceptance of the proposed genes–cognition–behavior pathway). To give some examples, impairments in cognitive flexibility is one of the most well-documented cognitive characteristics of individuals with ASD (Landry & Al-Taie, 2016; Ozonoff et al., 2004). Individuals with OCD are also characterized by difficulties in cognitive flexibility (Chamberlain, Fineberg, Blackwell, Robbins, & Sahakian, 2006), which are thought to underpin the compulsive behavior associated with the diagnosis. Further research is required to test whether impairment in cognitive flexibility is a shared risk factor for both ASD and OCD, and whether the same neurobiological mechanism underpins these cognitive impairments in ASD and OCD. Similarly, impairments in executive functioning are also found to be associated with ADHD (Lukito et al., 2017) and anxiety symptoms (Hollocks et al., 2014) in youth with ASD.

In terms of practical implications, this model suggests that interventions developed in non-ASD populations may be applicable to individuals with ASD (e.g., cognitive behavioral therapy [CBT], parenting interventions). Although the interventions may need to be somewhat modified in delivery to promote effectiveness in individuals with ASD (e.g., conducting an extra session on identifying emotions, avoiding excessive use of vague or abstract concepts), the core principles should remain the same. Indeed, modified CBT is effective in reducing anxiety (Sukhodolsky, Bloch, Panza, & Reichow, 2013), and parenting interventions (e.g., parental training) are effective in decreasing externalizing behaviors (Postorino et al., 2017b) in children with ASD. The same argument could be made for psychopharmacological interventions; stimulant medication has been found to reduce ADHD symptoms (albeit to a lesser extent than in non-ASD populations; Research Units on Pediatric Psychopharmacology Autism Network, 2005) in individuals with ASD. Research on selective serotonin reuptake inhibitors (SSRIs) for treating anxiety disorders in individuals with ASD is lacking; however, there is some evidence to suggest their efficacy is limited in ASD populations (King et al., 2009).

INCREASED POTENCY OF ESTABLISHED RISK FACTORS OR INCREASED VULNERABILITY IN PEOPLE WITH ASD

An alternative model is that these established risk factors for psychopathology are not more prevalent in individuals with ASD, but instead they have a stronger causal link with psychopathology. Certain characteristics associated with ASD, such as having a more vulnerable brain (due to atypical development) or having a certain profile of cognitive functioning (e.g., difficulties in problem solving and emotional regulation, increased rumination), could increase the negative impact of certain risk factors. This topic is less well investigated and therefore requires much additional research before any strong conclusions can be drawn, and so theoretical instances are provided for illustration.

One example is the consequences of experiencing adverse life events. Some suggest that the profile of cognitive difficulties associated with ASD, for example, impairments in cognitive flexibility and emotion regulation, may impact posttraumatic processing and appraisals of traumatic memories, and therefore increase risk of developing posttraumatic stress disorder (Kerns, Newschaffer, & Berkowitz, 2015). The communication difficulties associated with ASD may also exacerbate the negative impact of adverse life events, as these may make it harder for individuals with ASD to communicate their distress. This in turn could lead to delays in identifying individuals with ASD who may need additional support following stressful or traumatic events and consequent exacerbation of symptoms.

Another example is inconsistent parenting behavior. In non-ASD populations, associations are found between inconsistent parenting and child externalizing problems (Gardner, 1989), and a wealth of literature has demonstrated the efficacy of interventions aimed at improving parenting practices (including consistency) in decreasing behavior problems (Daley et al., 2014; Dretzke et al., 2009; Weber, Kamp-Becker, Christiansen, & Mingebach, 9), suggesting a causal role for ineffective parenting in the development and maintenance of certain types of psychopathology. In ASD, similar associations between variation in parenting practices and levels of child externalizing behaviors are reported (Boonen et al., 2014; Maljaars, Boonen, Lambrechts, Van Leeuwen, & Noens, 2014). However, it may also be possible that the preference for sameness and predictability in individuals with ASD, combined with difficulties with generalization, mean that inconsistent parenting has a more negative impact on child behavior.

Overall, there is limited research that has empirically tested these hypotheses, and so this section is largely speculative; what is required is a comparison of likelihood for the development of mental health difficulties following exposure to comparable risk factors in individuals with and without a diagnosis of ASD. If this hypothesis were supported, the clinical implications would be similar to those outlined in the first section, in that intervention approaches used in non-ASD populations could also be used in individuals with ASD. What differs in this hypothesis is that individuals with ASD may be particularly vulnerable to the consequences of certain negative environments and experiences. More traditional diathesis–stress approaches (grounded in research from non-ASD populations) would also argue that one should aim to not only treat the immediate symptoms but also ameliorate the underlying vulnerability to decrease the likelihood of future psychological disturbance. Many psychoeducation programs for individuals who work with ASD populations (clinicians, teachers, caregivers) already make them aware of this increased vulnerability, but this could be more widely extended. Strategies could encourage parents to be more consistent in their reinforcement and professionals to be especially vigilant for prodromal signs of psychiatric disturbance following adverse life events in individuals with ASD. In terms of clinical interventions, it may follow that a more intense or longer duration might be necessary to achieve the same improvement in individuals with ASD. There is limited research testing these hypotheses, although it has been found that pharmacological treatment for ADHD is less effective in individuals with ASD (Research Units on Pediatric Psychopharmacology Autism Network, 2005). Additionally, combining pharmacological interventions with psychological ones may give opportunities to learn more adaptive responses to negative life events or stressors, thus encouraging psychological resilience, which is unlikely to be afforded by a pharmacological approach alone.

Decreased Prevalence or Effectiveness of Protective Factors in People With ASD

Another similar but slightly different model to consider is that certain protective factors either are less present or do not act in the same way in ASD populations. Protective factors are not simply the opposite of a risk factor but can be thought of as factors that serve to promote positive outcomes in the face of environmental challenge (Rutter, 1985). One of the most well-established protective factors in the non-ASD literature is social support, which is shown to be causally related to both mental and physical health problems, in that greater social support is linked to more positive outcomes (Case et al., 1992; Dalgard, Bjork, & Tambs, 1995; Kessler, Price & Wortman, 1985). With regard to the mechanisms of effect, research has highlighted that it is not simply the availability of social support systems, but the perception that they are seen as adequate that provides a protective buffer (Henderson, 1981). Along with the quality of social ties, dispositional factors have also been implicated in the successful navigation of life challenges. Specifically, some suggest that an ability to act positively in the face of a challenge or stressful situation, which is in part a function of self-esteem and feelings of self-efficacy, can also lessen maladaptive psychological sequalae (Rutter, 1985). These feelings of positive self-esteem and worth are fostered throughout the lifespan through successful social interactions and positive achievements.

In terms of whether established protective factors operate in the same manner in ASD populations, there is limited work in this area. However, the few studies conducted suggest it is the perception and quality of social support that are important in promoting positive outcomes, in a similar manner to what has been reported in non-ASD populations. Perceived social support is found to be a protective factor against loneliness in adolescents with ASD (Lasgaard, Nielsen, Eriksen, & Goossens, 2010), and in adults with ASD, the perception that support is available, rather than the effects of actual received support, correlates with quality of life (Renty & Roeyers, 2006). Longitudinal work has also found that the quality of family relationships predicts changes in psychiatric symptoms over time in adults with ASD, and these effects are present regardless of whether the individual lives in the family home (suggesting it may not simply be the provision of resources driving the association; Woodman, Smith, Greenberg & Mailick, 2015). Although this research suggests social support may function in the same way as is reported in non-ASD populations (i.e., serves to decrease the likelihood of psychiatric disturbance following life stressors or challenges), it may be less likely to be present for people with ASD. The socio-communicative difficulties associated with ASD may mean that individuals with ASD find it harder to establish the types of satisfactory relationships that buffer against the negative effects of stressful life events. Similarly, with regard to individual characteristics, feelings of self-esteem and confidence may be impacted by certain negative events that are more likely to happen to individuals with ASD (e.g., bullying, victimization, social rejection, as discussed in the previous sections). Increased exposure to these negative experiences in adolescence could lead to a less positive and adaptive response when encountering additional life stressors later in adulthood. Research demonstrating a lack of association between co-occurring psychopathology and IQ in individuals with ASD (Gadow, DeVincent, & Schneider, 2008; Gjevik et al., 2011; Mazurek, Kanne, & Wodka, 2013; Simonoff et al., 2008) suggests that individuals with higher IQ from ASD populations may not benefit from the decreased risk for mental health problems that has been reported for individuals with higher IQ in non-ASD populations (e.g., Gale et al., 2008; Koenen et al., 2009). This raises the possibility that certain well-established protective factors (such as higher IQ) may fail to operate, or may operate differently, in ASD populations. Currently, there is a lack of knowledge regarding how other established risk/protective factors such as socioeconomic status and position function in ASD populations. This is a promising area of research for the future as it could lead to new strategies for promoting resilience in individuals with ASD.

ASD-Specific Risk Factors

The third explanatory model is that the profile of neurocognitive impairments associated with ASD, which are thought to underpin the core symptoms of ASD, also increases risk for other psychiatric conditions. These risk factors can be thought of as relatively specific to individuals with ASD as they are not often found in individuals without ASD, for example, impairments in theory of mind and perceptual processing (although the latter are noted in schizophrenia; Uhlhaas & Mishara, 2007) or an increased desire for predictability. This contrasts with the two previous sections, which were concerned with risk factors that occur in individuals without ASD and are not specific to ASD (e.g., perinatal adversity, bullying, impairments in executive functioning). There are two lines of evidence that support the idea that the risk factors for psychopathology in individuals with ASD are not the same as those found in ASD populations.

Established risk factors for psychopathology in non-ASD populations do not modulate risk in the same way in individuals with ASD. Sex is an established moderator of psychopathology in non-ASD populations, with males exhibiting higher rates of externalizing disorders and females exhibiting higher rates of internalizing disorders (Costello et al., 2003; Maughan, Rowe, Messer, Goodman, & Meltzer, 2004). These sex differences are not as consistently reported in ASD populations. Many studies into externalizing behaviors in individuals with ASD have failed to find sex differences in either prevalence or severity (Brereton et al., 2006; Chandler et al., 2016; Farmer & Aman, 2011; Farmer et al., 2014; Hill et al., 2014; Maskey, Warnell, Parr, Le Couteur, & McConachie, 2013). One study found that symptoms of ODD were more severe in male youths with ASD, but only using teacher report of child behavior problems. No sex differences were found when parent report was used (Gadow, DeVincent, & Schneider, 2008). Another study found sex differences in externalizing behaviors in a younger sample using in-depth parental interviews (Salazar et al., 2015). In terms of internalizing disorders, again the literature in ASD is inconsistent. Some find no effect of sex (Lai et al., 2011; Lugnegård, Hallerbäck, & Gillberg, 2011), whereas others do (Lever & Geurts, 2016; Solomon, Miller, Taylor, Hinshaw, & Carter, 2012). It should be noted that most of the studies exploring sex differences used relatively small samples, so replication is necessary before any conclusions are drawn. A further point for future research to consider is whether the moderating role of sex varies across development in ASD populations in the same manner as is reported in non-ASD populations (e.g., sex differences in risk for depression increasing from early to late adolescence; Hankin et al., 1998).

Lower IQ is one of the most consistently reported risk factors for psychiatric disorders, especially behavioral disorders such as ADHD and CD/ODD, in youths without ASD, yet many studies have failed to find an association between IQ and externalizing behavior in ASD populations (Gadow, DeVincent, & Schneider, 2008; Gjevik et al., 2011; Mazurek, Kanne, & Wodka, 2013; Simonoff et al., 2008).

ASD-specific characteristics thought to underpin core ASD symptoms are also associated with psychiatric symptoms. A characteristic that is relatively specific to individuals with ASD is difficulty in theory of mind, or the ability to accurately understand and predict other people's behavior on the basis of their mental states. A breadth of research has demonstrated that individuals with ASD show difficulty on a range of tasks that tap theory-of-mind abilities (Frith, 2012), and these inherent difficulties in theory of mind are thought to underlie the social and communication symptoms of ASD, as theory-of-mind ability has been found to correlate with symptom severity (Lerner, Hutchins, & Prelock, 2011; Shimoni, Weizman, Yoran, & Raviv, 2012). Researchers have now begun to demonstrate that these cognitive impairments might also contribute to risk for psychiatric conditions. Analyses from a nationwide twin study found that the strongest predictor of child conduct problems was ASD symptoms, specifically in social interaction problems (Kerekes et al., 2014). Performance on theory-of-mind tasks has been found to predict challenging behavior in children with ASD (Carter Leno et al., 2018; Pouw, Rieffe, Oosterveld, Huskens, & Stockmann, 2013), and, although theory of mind was not measured specifically, other studies found that individuals with ASD and externalizing behaviors exhibited greater social and communication problems than those without (Kanne & Mazurek, 2011; Mazurek et al., 2013).

In addition to these impairments in social cognition, individuals with ASD experience both hypo- and hypersensitivity to sensory inputs from auditory, tactile, and visual sources (Baranek, David, Poe, Stone, & Watson, 2006; Crane, Goddard, & Pring, 2009), leading to the most recent edition of the DSM including sensory processing hypo- and hypersensitivities in the diagnostic criteria (American Psychological Association, 2013). These sensory processing difficulties are thought to be underpinned by impairments in underlying neurobiological systems that process incoming sensory and perceptual input (Happé & Frith, 2006; Pellicano & Burr, 2012), and are again thought to be relatively specific to ASD (D. Green, Chandler, Charman, Simonoff, & Baird, 2016). Recent studies have demonstrated that atypicalities in the processing of sensory information are also correlated with psychiatric symptoms in individuals with ASD (Ashburner, Ziviani, & Rodger, 2008; Baker, Lane, Angley, & Young, 2008; Tseng, Fu, Cermak, Lu, & Shieh, 2011). A number of studies have also reported an association between sensory hypersensitivity and anxiety symptoms in individuals with ASD (Lane, Reynolds, & Dumenci, 2012; Lidstone et al., 2014), including one longitudinal study of toddlers that found that sensory oversensitivity predicted increases in anxiety over and above child age, ASD symptom severity, cognitive ability, and maternal anxiety, but anxiety did not predict changes in sensory oversensitivity (S. A. Green, Ben-Sasson, Soto, & Carter, 2012). A similar example is the relatively ASD-specific characteristic of a desire for predictability (or an avoidance of uncertainty). Although little work has been done in this area and so this point is largely speculative, research has found that temporally unpredictable stimuli provoke anxiety behaviors in mice and humans (Herry et al., 2007) and intolerance of uncertainty is associated with anxiety symptoms in individuals with ASD (Boulter, Freeston, South, & Rodgers, 2014). Furthermore, pilot work suggests that interventions focused on increasing tolerance of uncertainty may show promise in typically developing individuals with anxiety disorders (Léger et al., 2003; Payne, Bolton, & Perrin, 2011) and in individuals with ASD (Rodgers et al., 2017).

A final example of a (relatively) ASD-specific driver of psychiatric disturbance to consider may be poor emotion regulation (Mazefsky et al., 2013), with research demonstrating that severe mood dysregulation is highly prevalent in young people with ASD (Simonoff et al., 2012). These difficulties with regulation are thought to stem from the impairments in emotional insight and self-awareness (e.g., alexithymia). Difficulties regulating emotions may be especially important for understanding anxiety and noncompliance in ASD; however, it is often hard to disentangle poor emotion regulation from additional psychiatric diagnoses, meaning that the directionality of associations is unclear (Mazefsky et al., 2013).

If the idea that some risk factors for psychiatric conditions in individuals with ASD may be ASD specific were adopted, this would suggest that at least for some psychiatric conditions, interventions originally developed for individuals without ASD may not be suitable, and that novel interventions targeted toward ASD-specific mechanisms are required. For instance, some aspects of explanatory models of behavior problems developed from non-ASD populations may not be appropriate for certain groups of individuals with ASD, for example, that acts of aggression or self-injurious behavior are deliberate or defiant (although it also remains true that some individuals with ASD will engage in these behaviors in a deliberate manner). In some groups of individuals with ASD, the underpinning mechanisms may differ, in that they may be more driven by difficulties in regulating emotions and anxiety (Evans, Canavera, Kleinpeter, Maccubbin, & Taga, 2005). Therefore, although behavioral interventions found to be effective in non-ASD populations (e.g., reinforcement charts, parenting training) may improve behavior in individuals with ASD, using these in isolation may limit effectiveness. What may be required is an additional focus on managing emotions, while also considering the difficulties with emotional literacy prevalent in individuals with ASD.

To conclude this section on theoretical mechanisms, it is likely that some psychiatric conditions in ASD are caused by more general risk factors (e.g., adverse life events), whereas others are caused by more ASD-specific risk factors (e.g., difficulties in theory of mind), and that different types of risk and protective factors may interact, compounding their effects over time. These models should not be seen as mutually exclusive, but rather as different potential explanatory frameworks, each with a corresponding set of predictions that can be empirically tested. See Table 1.1 for a summary of all explanatory models that have been discussed.

An Interactive and Developmental Approach

All the models outlined thus far (aside from those regarding sampling/measurement bias and issues of nosology) have taken a rather static approach to psychopathology. To fully understand the mechanisms by which individuals with ASD develop additional psychiatric conditions, a developmental and interactional approach must be taken (see Figure 1.1). Take, for example, the theoretical models outlined earlier, that the same factors that increase risk that an individual will develop psychiatric conditions in non-ASD populations are also found in individuals with ASD, but they happen to be more prevalent or exert a stronger effect in ASD populations. Examples of perinatal adversity, adverse life events, individual variation in neurocognitive functioning, and genetic influences were discussed. It is very unlikely these factors act in isolation, but instead act in a reciprocal manner over time (as is proposed in non-ASD populations; Sroufe, 2013). However, it should be held in mind that the interactions between parent and child in ASD populations may be somewhat different from those reported in non-ASD populations, and so there may be certain interactions or risk factors that are more ASD specific that should be

Table 1.1. Summary of Models to Explain Heightened Prevalence of Co-Occurring Psychiatric Conditions in Individuals With Autism Spectrum Disorder (ASD)

Explanatory Model	Factors That May Influence Prevalence
The role of confounders	Bias in sample acquisition and symptom measurement lead to inaccurate estimates of co-occurring psychiatric conditions
Problematic nosology	Inaccurate diagnostic systems; specifically, an overly narrow category for the ASD phenotype. External pressures to make multiple diagnoses
Increased prevalence of risk factors	Factors known to cause mental health problems in non-ASD populations occur more frequently in ASD populations
Heightened vulnerability	Individuals with ASD are more likely to develop mental health problems following exposure to known risk factors
Decreased resilience	Individuals with ASD are less likely to have characteristics or experiences associated with resilience
ASD-specific risk factors	The profile of neurocognitive impairments thought to underpin core symptoms also increases risk for co-occurring psychiatric conditions

considered. If we take the example of the interactive relationship between individual and parent characteristics over time, research finds that children with ASD may be more likely to elicit certain parenting styles, for example, less rule setting and less use of discipline (Maljaars et al., 2014; Osborne, McHugh, Saunders, & Reed, 2008), and parents of children with ASD utilize different linguistic strategies when attempting to engage their child in conversations about past events (Goldman & DeNigris, 2015). These differences in parenting and communication may be due to the child's symptoms of ASD (e.g., rigidity, insistence on routine, lack of social reciprocity), and the contribution of each of these domains to variation in parenting would be a useful topic for future research. Certain differences in parenting may in turn increase the risk of psychiatric symptoms in the developing child, which in turn may then impact back on parenting styles. It should be noted here that children with ASD may be more likely to use externalizing behaviors as a form of communication in the first place due to their difficulties with communication. Observational studies have found (in a similar manner to that in non-ASD populations) that when parents are busy with a non-child-centered task (e.g., preparing supper or washing dishes), children with ASD engage in externalizing behaviors, which often elicit parental attention, thus inadvertently positively reinforcing the use of externalizing behaviors (Lucyshyn et al., 2004). Consequently, interactions may occur in which the parent and child both reciprocally reinforce the use of externalizing behaviors and ineffective parenting practices. Longitudinal work supported this theory, demonstrating how externalizing behaviors and maternal criticism exert bidirectional effects over time in young people with ASD (Greenberg, Seltzer, Hong, & Orsmond, 2006). The idea of interactive and bidirectional associations between ineffective parenting and psychiatric symptoms (especially externalizing symptoms) is not a new concept and forms the basis of many effective parenting interventions in non-ASD populations. This section serves to highlight that there is no reason that these concepts cannot be applied to people with ASD, and indeed argue that to gain a full understanding of co-occurring psychiatric conditions in individuals with ASD, a similarly dynamic and interactive approach should be taken.

Taking a developmental approach to psychopathology requires considering how reciprocal effects may occur not only in childhood but also across the lifespan. In a similar manner to non-ASD populations (Coplan & Weeks, 2009), the high rate of internalizing disorders in individuals with ASD may be due to repeated negative social experiences leading to social avoidance, isolation, anxiety, and depression, which in turn decrease the number of successful social interactions an individual will experience. These reciprocal processes, or negative feedback loops, may be more likely to occur in individuals with ASD due to inherent difficulties in understanding complex social situations and preference for predictable events (which social interactions are not). These processes may be especially pertinent in adolescence and adulthood, when rates of internalizing disorders are at their highest in individuals with ASD.

Therefore, one should consider not only the specific characteristics associated with ASD (be these behavioral characteristics such as rigidity and lack of social awareness or neurocognitive impairments such as difficulties in theory of mind and perceptual processing) but also how these characteristics may elicit and interact with environmental factors (e.g.,

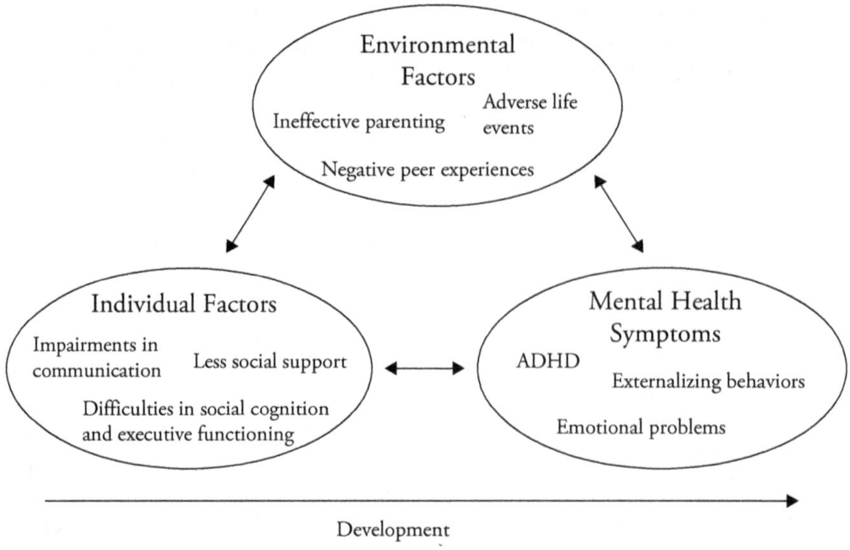

Figure 1.1. Theoretical model of how risk factors and psychiatric conditions may interact over development in individuals with ASD.

variation in parenting practices). A complete model should consider how individual and environmental influences interact together over development to increase risk for different psychiatric conditions. Furthermore, it should be held in mind that different risk and protective factors may exert weaker or stronger influences at different points of the lifespan. Inspecting continuity and change over development in individuals with ASD may offer clues as to specific mechanisms at play.

Research Priorities

There is still much work to be done to fully understand co-occurring psychiatric symptoms in individuals with ASD. This section outlines the key areas where research should focus to have the greatest impact on theoretical understanding and the greatest utility for people with ASD.

Accurate and systematic measurement of co-occurring psychiatric symptoms. As discussed earlier in the chapter, the debate regarding whether to develop new ASD-specific measures or rely on (potentially unsuitable) population-developed and validated measures is ongoing. Careful evaluation of existing measures is required to build an evidence base regarding which of the existing measures are appropriate for use in ASD populations. Consultation with people with ASD and their families and caregivers is an essential part of this process, as they will have important insights regarding what is and is not appropriate that cannot be gleaned from psychometric studies alone. Where measures are found to be inappropriate, developing and validating new measures, which are reliable yet sensitive to change, is required. Currently, there are few existing instruments developed specifically to measure additional psychopathology in individuals with ASD. To ensure these new measures are useful and empirically valid, they should be developed with consultation from individuals with ASD and their caregivers, along with specialist clinicians. Given the high rate of intellectual disability in individuals with ASD, these instruments should also be available across the full range of developmental abilities, whether in a single version or in parallel versions. Furthermore, the psychometric properties of novel instruments should be appropriately assessed (e.g., validity and reliability). Valid and reliable instruments not only are an essential tool for successfully measuring change from intervention but also are required to accurately identify individuals with ASD who may require additional clinical support.

Comprehensive measurement of co-occurring psychiatric conditions and potential driving factors. Given that most individuals with ASD typically have more than one co-occurring psychiatric condition (Simonoff et al., 2008), the full range of psychiatric symptoms should be measured. Furthermore, given the wide range of cognitive impairments (Brunsdon et al., 2015) and strong correlations between functioning in different cognitive domains in individuals with ASD (Carter Leno et al., 2018; Ozonoff et al., 2004), comprehensive measurement of cognitive functioning across a range of domains, along with other relevant risk factors (e.g., ASD severity, IQ, environmental stressors), should also be undertaken. Considering different predictors and outcomes, along with potential confounders, and using multivariate statistical approaches will allow researchers to be more confident about which relevant factors are driving different associations.

Sensitive research designs to critically test causal pathways. Much extant work investigating the potential causes of psychiatric conditions in individuals with ASD has relied on cross-sectional study designs. Although informative, one can only draw limited conclusions from these studies, as any significant associations (e.g., with environmental factors or neurocognitive characteristics) may be due to the downstream impact of having a mental health problem, rather than representing a direct cause. The following study designs allow researchers to more definitively assess the directionality of effects.

Longitudinal designs. As mentioned earlier, cross-sectional studies do not allow researchers to test the directionality of associations. Longitudinal studies allow one to test whether variation in theorized risk factors predict change in mental health symptoms over time, thus illuminating potential causal mechanisms. These types of studies are severely lacking in the field of psychiatric conditions in ASD (although see S. A. Green & Ben-Sasson, 2010; Greenberg et al., 2006; Simonoff et al., 2013, for exceptions). Conducting longitudinal studies would also allow for examination of continuity and change of psychiatric symptoms in individuals with ASD, thus uncovering characteristics that may indicate an individual is at risk of persistent psychiatric difficulties. This type of information will allow a more preventative approach to psychiatric conditions in individuals with ASD.

Experimental studies that modify potential causal mechanisms. These types of studies can be illuminating as well as the more formal trial designs discussed later. These studies typically manipulate an environmental variable and measure the acute response to said variable within an experimental context. This allows one to compare the response between individuals with or without a given psychiatric diagnosis; differences in response can highlight potential causal mechanisms underpinning variation in psychiatric symptoms. These types of studies allow for more rapid testing of hypotheses regarding underpinning mechanisms (especially when compared to longitudinal designs) and typically require fewer resources, and therefore are helpful in informing the selection of predictor, mediator, and outcome variables in wider randomized control trials (RCTs). For example, this type of experimental design has been used to explore the acute physiological impact of stress in individuals with ASD with and without anxiety (Hollocks, Howlin, Papadopoulos, Khondoker, & Simonoff, 2014). Results highlighted how anxiety in individuals with ASD may be associated with a different biological response to stress than is typically found in non-ASD populations. Another example, although not from ASD populations, is work that has investigated the acute cognitive and neurobiological response to pharmacological intervention in youth with ADHD (e.g., An et al., 2013; Rubia et al., 2011). These studies have highlighted how certain pharmacological interventions may "normalize" specific areas of neural and cognitive functioning, therefore implicating them in underpinning the symptoms of ADHD. Looking ahead, the use of developing technology such as wearable devices and mobile phone apps will allow for more objective measurement and larger scale data collection (e.g., more frequent characterization of psychiatric symptoms and greater numbers of participants). This type of experimental design when used in tandem with these new technologies could be especially helpful in understanding the role of variation in neurobiological and cognitive characteristics.

Empirical testing of targeted interventions. The most rigorous test of directionality is to examine whether variation in a theorized risk factor varies as a function of treatment response. Again, these studies are somewhat lacking in psychopathology in ASD (although see Dawson et al., 2012), so to give a clearer illustration of the insights one can gain from these designs, we will again use an example from the ADHD field. Here, pharmacological trials have found limited associations at an individual level between improvement in domains of executive functioning thought to be impaired in ADHD and reduction in ADHD symptoms (Coghill, Hayward, Rhodes, Grimmer, & Matthews, 2013; Coghill et al., 2014), highlighting the pitfalls of assuming causality purely from cross-sectional data. Recent reviews have concluded that the majority of RCTs in ASD are of poor quality (French & Kennedy, 2018), so going forward it is important not only to conduct RCTs but also to conduct them well. The point mentioned earlier regarding the importance of accurate measurement is also of relevance here, as recent work in ASD populations has shown that increased reliability and sensitivity can improve the detection of symptom change (Grzadzinski et al., 2016). Therefore, better powered and more rigorous RCTs, with sensitive and reliable outcome measures, are required to better test the causal relevance of hypothesized risk factors for psychiatric conditions in individuals with ASD. Identification and measurement of potential mediators throughout RCTs are also key to elucidating different underpinning mechanisms, as many interventions may have multiple effects.

Better inclusion of groups of individuals with ASD who have historically been understudied. Most research with individuals with ASD has not included individuals with limited language or intellectual disability. This is likely due to difficulties in recruiting and assessing these individuals, who may be harder to engage, but also has been encouraged as it allows researchers to compare "pure" ASD against typically developing controls without the potentially confounding effects of intellectual disability. A query into the National Database for Autism Research, which includes over 40,000 individuals with ASD, found that only 11% of individuals in the database had a verbal and performance IQ of less than 85, and of this subgroup of individuals, only 1% had some form of neuroimaging data available (Jack & Pelphrey, 2017). Given that a substantial proportion of individuals with ASD have some form of intellectual disability (Charman et al., 2011), studies that do not include individuals with ASD and intellectual disability cannot draw conclusions about ASD as a whole. The lack of data (both behavioral and neuroimaging) for these understudied populations limits testing of any models regarding the etiology of psychiatric conditions in these groups. Researchers should make a concerted effort to include individuals with ASD who have limited language or intellectual disability within future research (although this is not possible in all situations). Protocols should either be designed to suit participants with a wide range of ability or should be amended to be suitable for individuals with limited language or intellectual disability. Assessments that do not rely on verbal outcomes (e.g., physiological recording, neuroimaging, observational coding) may be particularly useful.

Conclusions

It remains relatively unknown why the prevalence of psychiatric conditions is elevated in individuals with ASD, and whether the developmental trajectory and risk factors for mental health difficulties in ASD are the same as those in non-ASD populations. This chapter outlines multiple possible models, some concerning methodological biases, and others concerning theoretical models of causality. The proposed research priorities going forward will help to test these models and better understand the reasons behind the elevated rates of psychopathology in ASD. In addition to improving our theoretical understanding, well-conducted empirical research into co-occurring psychiatric conditions in individuals with ASD will inform clinical practice, specifically which early warning signs and risk factors should be considered when trying to identify individuals with ASD at high risk of developing additional psychiatric conditions, and whether using comparable interventions to those used in non-ASD populations is appropriate. Early and effective detection, combined with evidence-based treatments and support, will promote positive well-being and long-term outcomes in individuals with ASD.

References

Agrawal, A., Jacobson, K., Prescott, C., & Kendler, K. S. (2002). A twin study of sex differences in social support. *Psychological Medicine, 32*, 1155–1164.

American Psychiatric Association. (2013). *Diagnostic and statistical manual of mental disorders* (5th ed.). American Psychiatric Publishing.

An, L., Cao, X.-H., Cao, Q.-J., Sun, L., Yang, L., Zou, Q.-H., . . . Wang, Y.-F. (2013). Methylphenidate normalizes resting-state brain dysfunction in boys with attention deficit hyperactivity disorder. *Neuropsychopharmacology, 38*, 1287.

Angold, A., & Costello, E. J. (2009). Nosology and measurement in child and adolescent psychiatry. *Journal of Child and Adolescent Psychiatry, 50*(1–2), 9–15.

Angold, A., Costello, E. J., & Erkanli, A. (1999). Comorbidity. *Journal of Child Psychology and Psychiatry, 40*(1), 57–87.

Angold, A., Messer, S. C., Stangl, D., Farmer, E., Costello, E. J., & Burns, B. J. (1998). Perceived parental burden and service use for child and adolescent psychiatric disorders. *American Journal of Public Health, 88*(1), 75–80.

Ashburner, J., Ziviani, J., & Rodger, S. (2008). Sensory processing and classroom emotional, behavioral, and educational outcomes in children with autism spectrum disorder. *American Journal of Occupational Therapy, 62*(5), 564–573.

Baird, G., Simonoff, E., Pickles, A., Chandler, S., Loucas, T., Meldrum, D., & Charman, T. (2006). Prevalence of disorders of the autism spectrum in a population cohort of children in South Thames: The Special Needs and Autism Project (SNAP). *Lancet, 368*(9531), 210–215.

Baker, A. E. Z., Lane, A., Angley, M. T., & Young, R. L. (2008). The relationship between sensory processing patterns and behavioural responsiveness in autistic disorder: A pilot study. *Journal of Autism and Developmental Disorders, 38*(5), 867–875.

Baranek, G. T., David, F. J., Poe, M. D., Stone, W. L., & Watson, L. R. (2006). Sensory Experiences Questionnaire: Discriminating sensory features in young children with autism, developmental delays, and typical development. *Journal of Child Psychology and Psychiatry, 47*(6), 591–601.

Berkson, J. (1946). Limitations of the application of fourfold table analysis to hospital data. *Biometrics Bulletin, 2*(3), 47–53.

Bhutta, A. T., Cleves, M. A., Casey, P. H., Cradock, M. M., & Anand, K. S. (2002). Cognitive and behavioral outcomes of school-aged children who were born preterm: A meta-analysis. *JAMA, 288*(6), 728–737.

Bolton, P., Macdonald, H., Pickles, A., Rios, P., Goode, S., Crowson, M.,... Rutter, M. (1994). A case-control family history study of autism. *Journal of Child Psychology and Psychiatry, 35*(5), 877–900.

Bolton, P., Murphy, M., Macdonald, H., Whitlock, B., Pickles, A., & Rutter, M. (1997). Obstetric complications in autism: Consequences or causes of the condition? *Journal of the American Academy of Child & Adolescent Psychiatry, 36*(2), 272–281.

Bolton, P., Pickles, A., Murphy, M., & Rutter, M. (1998). Autism, affective and other psychiatric disorders: Patterns of familial aggregation. *Psychological Medicine, 28*(2), 385–395.

Boonen, H., Maljaars, J., Lambrechts, G., Zink, I., Van Leeuwen, K., & Noens, I. (2014). Behavior problems among school-aged children with autism spectrum disorder: Associations with children's communication difficulties and parenting behaviors. *Research in Autism Spectrum Disorders, 8*(6), 716–725.

Boulter, C., Freeston, M., South, M., & Rodgers, J. (2014). Intolerance of uncertainty as a framework for understanding anxiety in children and adolescents with autism spectrum disorders. *Journal of Autism and Developmental Disorders, 44*(6), 1391–1402.

Bradley, E. A., Summers, J. A., Wood, H. L., & Bryson, S. E. (2004). Comparing rates of psychiatric and behavior disorders in adolescents and young adults with severe intellectual disability with and without autism. *Journal of Autism and Developmental Disorders, 34*(2), 151–161.

Brereton, A. V., Tonge, B. J., & Einfeld, S. L. (2006). Psychopathology in children and adolescents with autism compared to young people with intellectual disability. *Journal of Autism and Developmental Disorders, 36*(7), 863–870.

Brunsdon, V. E. A., Colvert, E., Ames, C., Garnett, T., Gillan, N., Hallett, V.,... Happé, F. (2015). Exploring the cognitive features in children with autism spectrum disorder, their co-twins, and typically developing children within a population-based sample. *Journal of Child Psychology and Psychiatry, 56*(8), 893–902.

Bullock, B. M., Deater-Deckard, K., & Leve, L. D. (2006). Deviant peer affiliation and problem behavior: A test of genetic and environmental influences. *Journal of Abnormal Child Psychology, 34*(1), 27.

Cappadocia, M. C., Weiss, J. A., & Pepler, D. (2012). Bullying experiences among children and youth with autism spectrum disorders. *Journal of Autism and Developmental Disorders, 42*(2), 266–277.

Carruthers, S., Kent, R., Hollocks, M. J., & Simonoff, E. (2018). Brief report: Testing the psychometric properties of the Spence Children's Anxiety Scale (SCAS) and the Screen for Child Anxiety Related Emotional Disorders (SCARED) in autism spectrum disorder. *Journal of Autism and Developmental Disorders*, 1–8.

Carter Leno, V., Charman, T., Pickles, A., Jones, C. R. G., Baird, G., Happé, F., & Simonoff, E. (2015). Callous–unemotional traits in adolescents with autism spectrum disorder. *British Journal of Psychiatry, 207*(5), 392–399.

Carter Leno, V., Vitoratou, S., Kent, R., Charman, T., Chandler, S., Jones, C.,... Simonoff, E. (2018). Exploring the neurocognitive correlates of challenging behaviours in young people with autism spectrum disorder. *Autism.*

Case, R. B., Moss, A. J., Case, N., McDermott, M., & Eberly, S. (1992). Living alone after myocardial infarction. *JAMA, 267*, 515–519.

Chamberlain, S., Fineberg, N., Blackwell, A., Robbins, T., & Sahakian, B. (2006). Motor inhibition and cognitive flexibility in obsessive-compulsive disorder and trichotillomania. *American Journal of Psychiatry, 163*(7), 1282–1284.

Chandler, S., Howlin, P., Simonoff, E., O'Sullivan, T., Tseng, E., Kennedy, J.,... Baird, G. (2016). Emotional and behavioural problems in young children with autism spectrum disorder. *Developmental Medicine & Child Neurology, 58*(2), 202–208.

Charman, T., Pickles, A., Simonoff, E., Chandler, S., Loucas, T., & Baird, G. (2011). IQ in children with autism spectrum disorders: Data from the Special Needs and Autism Project (SNAP). *Psychological Medicine, 41*(3), 619–627.

Coghill, D. R., Hayward, D., Rhodes, S. M., Grimmer, C., & Matthews, K. (2013). A longitudinal examination of neuropsychological and clinical functioning in boys with attention deficit hyperactivity disorder (ADHD): Improvements in executive functioning do not explain clinical improvement. *Psychological Medicine, 44*(5), 1087–1099.

Coghill, D. R., Seth, S., Pedroso, S., Usala, T., Currie, J., & Gagliano, A. (2014). Effects of methylphenidate on cognitive functions in children and adolescents with attention-deficit/hyperactivity disorder: Evidence from a systematic review and a meta-analysis. *Biological Psychiatry, 76*(8), 603–615.

Copeland, W. E., Stringaris, A., Charman, T., Baird, G., Carpenter, K., & Simonoff, E. (2019). Disruptive mood dysregulation disorder in children with autism spectrum disorder. Manuscript submitted for publication.

Coplan, R. J., & Weeks, M. (2009). Shy and soft-spoken: Shyness, pragmatic language, and socio-emotional adjustment in early childhood. *Infant and Child Development, 18*(3), 238–254.

Costello, E. J., Mustillo, S., Erkanli, A., Keeler, G., & Angold, A. (2003). Prevalence and development of psychiatric disorders in childhood and adolescence. *Archives of General Psychiatry, 60*(8), 837–844.

Crane, L., Goddard, L., & Pring, L. (2009). Sensory processing in adults with autism spectrum disorders. *Autism, 13*(3), 215–228.

Cross-Disorder Group of the Psychiatric Genomics Consortium, Lee, S. H., Ripke, S., Neale, B. M., Faraone, S. V., Purcell, S. M.,... International Inflammatory Bowel Disease Genetics Consortium. (2013). Genetic relationship between five psychiatric disorders estimated from genome-wide SNPs. *Nature Genetics, 45*(9), 984–994.

Cuthbert, B., & Insel, T. (2013). Toward the future of psychiatric diagnosis: The seven pillars of RDoC. *BMC Medicine, 11*(1), 126.

Daley, D., van der Oord, S., Ferrin, M., Danckaerts, M., Doepfner, M., Cortese, S., & Sonuga-Barke, E. J. S. (2014). Behavioral interventions in attention-deficit/hyperactivity disorder: A meta-analysis of randomized controlled trials across multiple outcome domains. *Journal of the American Academy of Child & Adolescent Psychiatry, 53*(8), 835–847.e835.

Dalgard, O. S., Bjork, S., & Tambs, K. (1995). Social support, negative life events and mental health. *British Journal of Psychiatry, 166*(1), 29–34.

Daniels, J. L., Forssen, U., Hultman, C. M., Cnattingius, S., Savitz, D. A., Feychting, M., & Sparen, P. (2008). Parental psychiatric disorders associated with autism spectrum disorders in the offspring. *Pediatrics, 121*(5), e1357–e1362.

Dawson, G., Jones, E. J. H., Merkle, K., Venema, K., Lowy, R., Faja, S.,... Webb, S. J. (2012). Early behavioral intervention is associated with normalized brain activity in young children with autism. *Journal of the American Academy of Child & Adolescent Psychiatry, 51*(11), 1150–1159.

Dretzke, J., Davenport, C., Frew, E., Barlow, J., Stewart-Brown, S., Bayliss, S., . . . Hyde, C. (2009). The clinical effectiveness of different parenting programmes for children with conduct problems: A systematic review of randomised controlled trials. *Child and Adolescent Psychiatry and Mental Health, 3*(1), 7.

Emerson, E. (2003). Prevalence of psychiatric disorders in children and adolescents with and without intellectual disabilities. *Journal of Intellectual Disability Research, 47*, 51–58.

Evans, D. W., Canavera, K., Kleinpeter, F. L., Maccubbin, E., & Taga, K. (2005). The fears, phobias and anxieties of children with autism spectrum disorders and down syndrome: Comparisons with developmentally and chronologically age matched children. *Child Psychiatry and Human Development, 36*(1), 3–26.

Farmer, C., & Aman, M. (2011). Aggressive behavior in a sample of children with autism spectrum disorders. *Research in Autism Spectrum Disorders, 5*(1), 317–323.

Farmer, C., Butter, E., Mazurek, M. O., Cowan, C., Lainhart, J., Cook, E. H., . . . Aman, M. (2014). Aggression in children with autism spectrum disorders and a clinic-referred comparison group. *Autism, 19*(3), 281–291.

Fletcher, R., Loschen, E., Stavrakaki, C., & First, M. (2007). *Diagnostic manual - Intellectual disability: S clinical guide for diagnosis of mental disorders in persons with intellectual disability.* USA: National Association for the Dually Diagnosed Press.

French, L., & Kennedy, E. M. M. (2018). Annual research review: Early intervention for infants and young children with, or at-risk of, autism spectrum disorder: A systematic review. *Journal of Child Psychology and Psychiatry, 59*(4), 444–456.

Frith, U. (2012). Why we need cognitive explanations of autism. *Quarterly Journal of Experimental Psychology, 65*(11), 2073–2092.

Gadow, K. D., DeVincent, C. J., & Drabick, D. A. (2008). Oppositional defiant disorder as a clinical phenotype in children with autism spectrum disorder. *Journal of Autism and Developmental Disorders, 38*(7), 1302–1310.

Gadow, K. D., DeVincent, C. J., Pomeroy, J., & Azizian, A. (2004). Psychiatric symptoms in preschool children with PDD and clinic and comparison samples. *Journal of Autism and Developmental Disorders, 34*(4), 379–393.

Gadow, K. D., DeVincent, C. J., Pomeroy, J., & Azizian, A. (2005). Comparison of DSM-IV symptoms in elementary school-age children with PDD versus clinic and community samples. *Autism, 9*(4), 392–415.

Gadow, K. D., DeVincent, C. J., & Schneider, J. (2008). Predictors of psychiatric symptoms in children with an autism spectrum disorder. *Journal of Autism and Developmental Disorders, 38*(9), 1710–1720.

Gale, C. R., Deary, I. J., Boyle, S. H., Barefoot, J., Mortensen, L. H., & Batty, G. D. (2008). Cognitive ability in early adulthood and risk of 5 specific psychiatric disorders in middle age: The Vietnam experience study. *Archives of General Psychiatry, 65*(12), 1410–1418.

Gardener, H., Spiegelman, D., & Buka, S. L. (2011). Perinatal and neonatal risk factors for autism: A comprehensive meta-analysis. *Pediatrics, 128*(2), 344–355.

Gardner, F. E. M. (1989). Inconsistent parenting: Is there evidence for a link with children's conduct problems? *Journal of Abnormal Child Psychology, 17*(2), 223–233.

Gillberg, C. (2010). The ESSENCE in child psychiatry: Early symptomatic syndromes eliciting neurodevelopmental clinical examinations. *Research in Developmental Disabilities, 31*(6), 1543–1551.

Gjevik, E., Eldevik, S., Fjæran-Granum, T., & Sponheim, E. (2011). Kiddie-SADS reveals high rates of DSM-IV disorders in children and adolescents with autism spectrum disorders. *Journal of Autism and Developmental Disorders, 41*(6), 761–769.

Goldman, S., & DeNigris, D. (2015). Parents' strategies to elicit autobiographical memories in autism spectrum disorders, developmental language disorders and typically developing children. *Journal of Autism and Developmental Disorders, 45*(5), 1464–1473.

Goodman, R. (1988). Are complications of pregnancy and birth causes of schizophrenia? *Developmental Medicine and Child Neurology, 30*, 391–406.

Goodman, S. H., & Gotlib, I. H. (1999). Risk for psychopathology in the children of depressed mothers: A developmental model for understanding mechanisms of transmission. *Psychological Review, 106*(3), 458–490.

Green, D., Chandler, S., Charman, T., Simonoff, E., & Baird, G. (2016). Brief report: DSM-5 sensory behaviours in children with and without an autism spectrum disorder. *Journal of Autism and Developmental Disorders, 46*(11), 3597–3606.

Green, H., McGinnity, A., Ford, T., & Goodman, R. (2004). *Mental health of children and young people in Great Britain.* Basingstoke, UK: Palgrave Macmillan.

Green, S. A., & Ben-Sasson, A. (2010). Anxiety disorders and sensory over-responsivity in children with autism spectrum disorders: Is there a causal relationship? *Journal of Autism and Developmental Disorders, 40*(12), 1495–1504.

Green, S. A., Ben-Sasson, A., Soto, T. W., & Carter, A. S. (2012). Anxiety and sensory over-responsivity in toddlers with autism spectrum disorders: Bidirectional effects across time. *Journal of Autism and Developmental Disorders, 42*(6), 1112–1119.

Greenberg, J. S., Seltzer, M. M., Hong, J., & Orsmond, G. I. (2006). Bidirectional effects of expressed emotion and behavior problems and symptoms in adolescents and adults with autism. *American Journal on Mental Retardation, 111*(4), 229–249.

Grzadzinski, R., Carr, T., Colombi, C., McGuire, K., Dufek, S., Pickles, A., & Lord, C. (2016). Measuring changes in social communication behaviors: Preliminary development of the Brief Observation of Social Communication Change (BOSCC). *Journal of Autism and Developmental Disorders, 46*(7), 2464–2479.

Hallett, V., Lecavalier, L., Sukhodolsky, D. G., Cipriano, N., Aman, M. G., McCracken, J. T., . . . Scahill, L. (2013). Exploring the manifestations of anxiety in children with autism spectrum disorders. *Journal of Autism and Developmental Disorders, 43*(10), 2341–2352.

Hallett, V., Ronald, A., & Happé, F. (2009). Investigating the association between autistic-like and internalizing traits in a community-based twin sample. *Journal of the American Academy of Child & Adolescent Psychiatry, 48*(6), 618–627.

Hallett, V., Ronald, A., Rijsdijk, F., & Happé, F. (2010). Association of autistic-like and internalizing traits during childhood: A longitudinal twin study. *American Journal of Psychiatry, 167*(7), 809–817.

Hankin, B. L., Abramson, L. Y., Moffitt, T. E., Silva, P. A., McGee, R., & Angell, K. E. (1998). Development of depression from preadolescence to young adulthood:

Emerging gender differences in a 10-year longitudinal study. *Journal of Abnormal Psychology, 107*(1), 128.
Hanratty, J., Livingstone, N., Robalino, S., Terwee, C. B., Glod, M., Oono, I. P., ... McConachie, H. (2015). Systematic review of the measurement properties of tools used to measure behaviour problems in young children with autism. *PLoS One, 10*(12), e0144649.
Happé, F., & Frith, U. (2006). The weak coherence account: Detail-focused cognitive style in autism spectrum disorders. *Journal of Autism and Developmental Disorders, 36*(1), 5–25.
Hartley, S. L., Sikora, D. M., & McCoy, R. (2008). Prevalence and risk factors of maladaptive behaviour in young children with autistic disorder. *Journal of Intellectual Disability Research, 52*(10), 819–829.
Henderson, S. (1981). Social relationships, adversity and neurosis: An analysis of prospective observations. *British Journal of Psychiatry, 138*(5), 391–398.
Herry, C., Bach, D. R., Esposito, F., Di Salle, F., Perrig, W. J., Scheffler, K., ... Seifritz, E. (2007). Processing of temporal unpredictability in human and animal amygdala. *Journal of Neuroscience, 27*(22), 5958–5966.
Hill, A. P., Zuckerman, K. E., Hagen, A. D., Kriz, D. J., Duvall, S. W., van Santen, J., ... Fombonne, E. (2014). Aggressive behavior problems in children with autism spectrum disorders: Prevalence and correlates in a large clinical sample. *Research in Autism Spectrum Disorders, 8*(9), 1121–1133.
Hofvander, B., Delorme, R., Chaste, P., Nydén, A., Wentz, E., Ståhlberg, O., ... Leboyer, M. (2009). Psychiatric and psychosocial problems in adults with normal-intelligence autism spectrum disorders. *BMC Psychiatry, 9*(1), 35.
Hollocks, M. J., Howlin, P., Papadopoulos, A. S., Khondoker, M., & Simonoff, E. (2014). Differences in HPA-axis and heart rate responsiveness to psychosocial stress in children with autism spectrum disorders with and without co-morbid anxiety. *Psychoneuroendocrinology, 46*, 32–45.
Hoover, D. W., & Kaufman, J. (2018). Adverse childhood experiences in children with autism spectrum disorder. *Current Opinion in Psychiatry, 31*(2), 128–132.
Humphrey, N., & Symes, W. (2010). Perceptions of social support and experience of bullying among pupils with autistic spectrum disorders in mainstream secondary schools. *European Journal of Special Needs Education, 25*(1), 77–91.
Insel, T., Cuthbert, B., Garvey, M., Heinssen, R., Pine, D. S., Quinn, K., ... Wang, P. (2010). Research domain criteria (RDoC): Toward a new classification framework for research on mental disorders. *American Journal of Psychiatry, 167*(7), 748–751.
Jack, A., & Pelphrey, K. (2017). Annual research review: Understudied populations within the autism spectrum—Current trends and future directions in neuroimaging research. *Journal of Child Psychology and Psychiatry, 58*(4), 411–435.
Jaffee, S. R., & Price, T. S. (2007). Gene–environment correlations: A review of the evidence and implications for prevention of mental illness. *Molecular Psychiatry, 12*, 432.
Jopp, D. A., & Keys, C. B. (2001). Diagnostic overshadowing reviewed and reconsidered. *American Journal of Mental Retardation, 106*, 416–433.
Kanne, S. M., & Mazurek, M. O. (2011). Aggression in children and adolescents with ASD: Prevalence and risk factors. *Journal of Autism and Developmental Disorders, 41*(7), 926–937.
Kendler, K. S., Gardner, C. O., & Prescott, C. A. (2003). Personality and the experience of environmental adversity. *Psychological Medicine, 33*(7), 1193–1202.
Kendler, K. S., Karkowski, L., & Prescott, C. (1999). Causal relationship between stressful life events and the onset of major depression. *American Journal of Psychiatry, 156*(6), 837–841.
Kerekes, N., Lundström, S., Chang, Z., Tajnia, A., Jern, P., Lichtenstein, P., ... Anckarsäter, H. (2014). Oppositional defiant- and conduct disorder-like problems: Neurodevelopmental predictors and genetic background in boys and girls, in a nationwide twin study. *PeerJ, 2*, e359.
Kerns, C. M., Kendall, P. C., Berry, L., Souders, M. C., Franklin, M. E., Schultz, R. T., ... Herrington, J. (2014). Traditional and atypical presentations of anxiety in youth with autism spectrum disorder. *Journal of Autism and Developmental Disorders, 44*(11), 2851–2861.
Kerns, C. M., Newschaffer, C. J., & Berkowitz, S. J. (2015). Traumatic childhood events and autism spectrum disorder. *Journal of Autism and Developmental Disorders, 45*(11), 3475–3486.
Kessler, R. C., Price, R. H., & Wortman, C. B. (1985). Social factors in psychopathology: Stress, social support, and coping processes. *Annual Review of Psychology, 36*, 531–72.
Kim, J. A., Szatmari, P., Bryson, S. E., Streiner, D. L., & Wilson, F. J. (2000). The prevalence of anxiety and mood problems among children with autism and Asperger syndrome. *Autism, 4*(2), 117–132.
King, B. H., Hollander, E., Sikich, L., & et al. (2009). Lack of efficacy of citalopram in children with autism spectrum disorders and high levels of repetitive behavior: Citalopram ineffective in children with autism. *Archives of General Psychiatry, 66*(6), 583–590.
Koenen, K. C., Moffitt, T. E., Roberts, A. L., Martin, L. T., Kubzansky, L., Harrington, H., ... Caspi, A. (2009). Childhood IQ and adult mental disorders: A test of the cognitive reserve hypothesis. *American Journal of Psychiatry, 166*(1), 50–57.
Kovas, Y., & Plomin, R. (2006). Generalist genes: Implications for the cognitive sciences. *Trends in Cognitive Sciences, 10*(5), 198–203.
Krueger, R. F., & Markon, K. E. (2006). Reinterpreting comorbidity: A model-based approach to understanding and classifying psychopathology. *Annual Review of Clinical Psychology, 2*(1), 111–133.
Lai, M.-C., Lombardo, M. V., Pasco, G., Ruigrok, A. N. V., Wheelwright, S. J., Sadek, S. A., ... Baron-Cohen, S. (2011). A behavioral comparison of male and female adults with high functioning autism spectrum conditions. *PLoS One, 6*(6), e20835.
Landry, O., & Al-Taie, S. (2016). A meta-analysis of the Wisconsin Card Sort Task in autism. *Journal of Autism and Developmental Disorders, 46*(4), 1220–1235.
Lane, S. J., Reynolds, S., & Dumenci, L. (2012). Sensory over-responsivity and anxiety in typically developing children and children with autism and attention deficit hyperactivity disorder: Cause or coexistence? *American Journal of Occupational Therapy, 66*(5), 595–603.
Larsson, H. J., Eaton, W. W., Madsen, K. M., Vestergaard, M., Olesen, A. V., Agerbo, E., ... Mortensen, P. B. (2005). Risk factors for autism: Perinatal factors, parental psychiatric history, and socioeconomic status. *American Journal of Epidemiology, 161*(10), 916–925.
Lasgaard, M., Nielsen, A., Eriksen, M. E., & Goossens, L. (2010). Loneliness and social support in adolescent boys with autism spectrum disorders. *Journal of Autism and Developmental Disorders, 40*(2), 218–226.

Le Couteur, A., Bailey, A., Goode, S., Pickles, A., Gottesman, I., Robertson, S., & Rutter, M. (1996). A broader phenotype of autism: The clinical spectrum in twins. *Journal of Child Psychology and Psychiatry, 37*(7), 785–801.

Lecavalier, L. (2006). Behavioral and emotional problems in young people with pervasive developmental disorders: Relative prevalence, effects of subject characteristics, and empirical classification. *Journal of Autism and Developmental Disorders, 36*(8), 1101–1114.

Léger, E., Ladouceur, R., Dugas, M. J., & Freeston, M. H. (2003). Cognitive-behavioral treatment of generalized anxiety disorder among adolescents: A case series. *Journal of the American Academy of Child and Adolescent Psychiatry, 42*, 327–330.

Lever, A. G., & Geurts, H. M. (2016). Psychiatric co-occurring symptoms and disorders in young, middle-aged, and older adults with autism spectrum disorder. *Journal of Autism and Developmental Disorders, 46*(6), 1916–1930.

Leyfer, O. T., Folstein, S. E., Bacalman, S., Davis, N. O., Dinh, E., Morgan, J., . . . Lainhart, J. E. (2006). Comorbid psychiatric disorders in children with autism: Interview development and rates of disorders. *Journal of Autism and Developmental Disorders, 36*(7), 849–861.

Lichtenstein, P., Carlstrom, E., Rastam, M., Gillberg, C., & Anckarsater, H. (2010). The genetics of autism spectrum disorders and related neuropsychiatric disorders in childhood. *American Journal of Psychiatry, 167*(11), 1357–1363.

Lidstone, J., Uljarević, M., Sullivan, J., Rodgers, J., McConachie, H., Freeston, M., . . . Leekam, S. (2014). Relations among restricted and repetitive behaviors, anxiety and sensory features in children with autism spectrum disorders. *Research in Autism Spectrum Disorders, 8*(2), 82–92.

Linsell, L., Johnson, S., Wolke, D., Morris, J., Kurinczuk, J. J., & Marlow, N. (2018). Trajectories of behavior, attention, social and emotional problems from childhood to early adulthood following extremely preterm birth: A prospective cohort study. *European Child & Adolescent Psychiatry*, 1–12.

Little, L. (2001). Peer victimization of children with Asperger spectrum disorders. *Journal of the American Academy of Child & Adolescent Psychiatry, 40*(9), 995–996.

Lucyshyn, J. M., Irvin, L. K., Blumberg, E. R., Laverty, R., Horner, R. H., & Sprague, J. R. (2004). Validating the construct of coercion in family routines: Expanding the unit of analysis in behavioral assessment with families of children with developmental disabilities. *Research and Practice for Persons with Severe Disabilities, 29*(2), 104–121.

Lugnegård, T., Hallerbäck, M. U., & Gillberg, C. (2011). Psychiatric comorbidity in young adults with a clinical diagnosis of Asperger syndrome. *Research in Developmental Disabilities, 32*(5), 1910–1917.

Lukito, S., Jones, C. R. G., Pickles, A., Baird, G., Happé, F., Charman, T., & Simonoff, E. (2017). Specificity of executive function and theory of mind performance in relation to attention-deficit/hyperactivity symptoms in autism spectrum disorders. *Molecular Autism, 8*(1), 60.

Lundström, S., Reichenberg, A., Melke, J., Råstam, M., Kerekes, N., Lichtenstein, P., . . . Anckarsäter, H. (2014). Autism spectrum disorders and coexisting disorders in a nationwide Swedish twin study. *Journal of Child Psychology and Psychiatry, 56*(6), 702–710.

Maljaars, J., Boonen, H., Lambrechts, G., Van Leeuwen, K., & Noens, I. (2014). Maternal parenting behavior and child behavior problems in families of children and adolescents with autism spectrum disorder. *Journal of Autism and Developmental Disorders, 44*(3), 501–512.

Mandy, W., Roughan, L., & Skuse, D. (2014). Three dimensions of oppositionality in autism spectrum disorder. *Journal of Abnormal Child Psychology, 42*(2), 291–300.

Marlow, N., Hennessy, E. M., Bracewell, M. A., & Wolke, D. (2007). Motor and executive function at 6 years of age after extremely preterm birth. *Pediatrics, 120*(4), 793.

Maskey, M., Warnell, F., Parr, J. R., Le Couteur, A., & McConachie, H. (2013). Emotional and behavioural problems in children with autism spectrum disorder. *Journal of Autism and Developmental Disorders, 43*(4), 851–859.

Maughan, B., Rowe, R., Messer, J., Goodman, R., & Meltzer, H. (2004). Conduct disorder and oppositional defiant disorder in a national sample: Developmental epidemiology. *Journal of Child Psychology and Psychiatry, 45*(3), 609–621.

Mazefsky, C. A., Herrington, J., Siegel, M., Scarpa, A., Maddox, B. B., Scahill, L., & White, S. W. (2013). The role of emotion regulation in autism spectrum disorder. *Journal of the American Academy of Child & Adolescent Psychiatry, 52*(7), 679–688.

Mazefsky, C. A., Oswald, D. P., Day, T. N., Eack, S. M., Minshew, N. J., & Lainhart, J. E. (2012). ASD, a psychiatric disorder, or both? Psychiatric diagnoses in adolescents with high-functioning ASD. *Journal of Clinical Child & Adolescent Psychology, 41*(4), 516–523.

Mazurek, M. O., Kanne, S. M., & Wodka, E. L. (2013). Physical aggression in children and adolescents with autism spectrum disorders. *Research in Autism Spectrum Disorders, 7*(3), 455–465.

McDougle, C. J., Scahill, L., Aman, M. G., McCracken, J. T., Tierney, E., Davies, M., . . . Ghuman, J. K. (2005). Risperidone for the core symptom domains of autism: Results from the study by the autism network of the research units on pediatric psychopharmacology. *American Journal of Psychiatry, 162*.

Mefford, H. C., Batshaw, M. L., & Hoffman, E. P. (2012). Genomics, intellectual disability, and autism. *New England Journal of Medicine, 366*(8), 733–743.

Montes, G., & Halterman, J. S. (2007). Psychological functioning and coping among mothers of children with autism: A population-based study. *Pediatrics, 119*(5), 1040–1046.

Morrow, E. M. (2010). Genomic copy number variation in disorders of cognitive development. *Journal of the American Academy of Child and Adolescent Psychiatry, 49*(11), 1091–1104.

Neale, M. C., & Kendler, K. S. (1995). Models of comorbidity for multifactorial disorders. *American Journal of Human Genetics, 57*(4), 935–953.

Ohlsson Gotby, V., Lichtenstein, P., Långström, N., & Pettersson, E. (2018). Childhood neurodevelopmental disorders and risk of coercive sexual victimization in childhood and adolescence—A population-based prospective twin study. *Journal of Child Psychology and Psychiatry, 59*, 957–965.

Osborne, L. A., McHugh, L., Saunders, J., & Reed, P. (2008). The effect of parenting behaviors on subsequent child behavior problems in autistic spectrum conditions. *Research in Autism Spectrum Disorders, 2*(2), 249–263.

Ozonoff, S., Cook, I., Coon, H., Dawson, G., Joseph, R. M., Klin, A., . . . Pennington, B. F. (2004). Performance on Cambridge Neuropsychological Test Automated Battery subtests sensitive to frontal lobe function in people with autistic disorder: Evidence from the Collaborative Programs of Excellence in Autism network. *Journal of Autism and Developmental Disorders, 34*(2), 139–150.

Payne, S., Bolton, D., & Perrin, S. (2011). A pilot investigation of cognitive therapy for generalized anxiety disorder in children aged 7–17 years. *Cognitive Therapy and Research, 35*, 171–178.

Pellicano, E., & Burr, D. (2012). When the world becomes "too real": A Bayesian explanation of autistic perception. *Trends in Cognitive Sciences, 16*(10), 504–510.

Pickles, A., Le Couteur, A., Leadbitter, K., Salomone, E., Cole-Fletcher, R., Tobin, H.,... Byford, S. (2016). Parent-mediated social communication therapy for young children with autism (PACT): Long-term follow-up of a randomised controlled trial. *Lancet, 388*(10059), 2501–2509.

Piven, J., Chase, G. A., Landa, R., Wzorek, M., Gayle, J., Cloud, D., & Folstein, S. (1991). Psychiatric disorders in the parents of autistic individuals. *Journal of the American Academy of Child & Adolescent Psychiatry, 30*(3), 471–478.

Piven, J., & Palmer, P. (1999). Psychiatric disorder and the broad autism phenotype: Evidence from a family study of multiple-incidence autism families. *American Journal of Psychiatry, 156*(4), 557–563.

Plomin, R., DeFries, J., & Loehlin, J. (1977). Genotype-environment interaction and correlation in the analysis of human behavior. *Psychological Bulletin, 84*(2), 309–322.

Postorino, V., Kerns, C. M., Vivanti, G., Bradshaw, J., Siracusano, M., & Mazzone, L. (2017a). Anxiety disorders and obsessive-compulsive disorder in individuals with autism spectrum disorder. *Current Psychiatry Reports, 19*(12), 92.

Postorino, V., Sharp, W. G., McCracken, C. E., Bearss, K., Burrell, T. L., Evans, A. N., & Scahill, L. (2017b). A systematic review and meta-analysis of parent training for disruptive behavior in children with autism spectrum disorder. *Clinical Child and Family Psychology Review, 20*(4), 391–402.

Pouw, L. B. C., Rieffe, C., Oosterveld, P., Huskens, B., & Stockmann, L. (2013). Reactive/proactive aggression and affective/cognitive empathy in children with ASD. *Research in Developmental Disabilities, 34*(4), 1256–1266.

Reiss, S., & Szyszko, J. (1983). Diagnostic overshadowing and professional experience with mentally retarded persons. *American Journal of Mental Deficiency, 87*, 396–402.

Renno, P., & Wood, J. J. (2013). Discriminant and convergent validity of the anxiety construct in children with autism spectrum disorders. *Journal of Autism and Developmental Disorders, 43*(9), 2135–2146.

Renty, J. O., & Roeyers, H. (2006). Quality of life in high-functioning adults with autism spectrum disorder: The predictive value of disability and support characteristics. *Autism, 10*(5), 511–524.

Research Units on Pediatric Psychopharmacology Autism Network. (2005). Randomized, controlled, crossover trial of methylphenidate in pervasive developmental disorders with hyperactivity. *Archives of General Psychiatry, 62*(11), 1266–1274.

Roberts, A. L., Koenen, K. C., Lyall, K., Robinson, E. B., & Weisskopf, M. G. (2015). Association of autistic traits in adulthood with childhood abuse, interpersonal victimization, and posttraumatic stress. *Child Abuse & Neglect, 45*, 135–142.

Rodgers, J., Hodgson, A., Shields, K., Wright, C., Honey, E., & Freeston, M. (2017). Towards a treatment for intolerance of uncertainty in young people with autism spectrum disorder: Development of the coping with uncertainty in everyday situations (CUES©) programme. *Journal of Autism and Developmental Disorders, 47*(12), 3959–3966.

Rubia, K., Halari, R., Cubillo, A., Smith, A. B., Mohammad, A.-M., Brammer, M., & Taylor, E. (2011). Methylphenidate normalizes fronto-striatal underactivation during interference inhibition in medication-naïve boys with attention-deficit hyperactivity disorder. *Neuropsychopharmacology, 36*, 1575.

Rutter, M. (1985). Resilience in the face of adversity. Protective factors and resistance to psychiatric disorder. *British Journal of Psychiatry, 147*, 598–611.

Rutter, M., Beckett, C., Castle, J., Colvert, E., Kreppner, J., Mehta, M., Stevens, S., & Sonuga-Barke, E. (2007). Effects of profound early institutional deprivation: An overview of findings from a UK longitudinal study of Romanian adoptees. *European Journal of Developmental Psychology, 4*(3), 332–350.

Salazar, F., Baird, G., Chandler, S., Tseng, E., O'Sullivan, T., Howlin, P.,... Simonoff, E. (2015). Co-occurring emotional and behavioral disorders in preschool and elementary school-aged children with autism spectrum disorder. *Journal of Autism and Developmental Disorders, 45*(8), 2283–2294.

Scarr, S., & McCartney, K. (1983). How people make their own environments: A theory of genotype & environment effects. *Child Development, 54*(2), 424–435.

Serati, M., Barkin, J. L., Orsenigo, G., Altamura, A. C., & Buoli, M. (2017). Research review: The role of obstetric and neonatal complications in childhood attention deficit and hyperactivity disorder—A systematic review. *Journal of Child Psychology and Psychiatry, 58*(12), 1290–1300.

Simonoff, E., Jones, C. R., Baird, G., Pickles, A., Happé, F., & Charman, T. (2013). The persistence and stability of psychiatric problems in adolescents with autism spectrum disorders. *Journal of Child Psychology and Psychiatry, 54*(2), 186–194.

Simonoff, E., Jones, C. R., Pickles, A., Happé, F., Baird, G., & Charman, T. (2012). Severe mood problems in adolescents with autism spectrum disorder. *Journal of Child Psychology and Psychiatry, 53*(11), 1157–1166.

Simonoff, E., Pickles, A., Charman, T., Chandler, S., Loucas, T., & Baird, G. (2008). Psychiatric disorders in children with autism spectrum disorders: Prevalence, comorbidity, and associated factors in a population-derived sample. *Journal of the American Academy of Child & Adolescent Psychiatry, 47*(8), 921–929.

Singham, T., Viding, E., Schoeler, T., & et al. (2017). Concurrent and longitudinal contribution of exposure to bullying in childhood to mental health: The role of vulnerability and resilience. *JAMA Psychiatry, 74*(11), 1112–1119.

Smalley, S. L., McCracken, J., & Tanguay, P. (1995). Autism, affective disorders, and social phobia. *American Journal of Medical Genetics, 60*(1), 19–26.

Solomon, M., Miller, M., Taylor, S. L., Hinshaw, S. P., & Carter, C. S. (2012). Autism symptoms and internalizing psychopathology in girls and boys with autism spectrum disorders. *Journal of Autism and Developmental Disorders, 42*(1), 48–59.

Sroufe, L. A. (2013). Pathways to adaptation and maladaptation: Psychopathology as developmental deviation. In D. V. Cicchetti (Ed.), *The emergence of a discipline* (pp. 27–54). New York, NY: Psychology Press.

Stein, M., Jang, K., Taylor, S., Vernon, P., & Livesley, J. (2002). Genetic and environmental influences on trauma exposure and posttraumatic stress disorder symptoms: A twin study. *American Journal of Psychiatry, 159*(10), 1675–1681.

Sukhodolsky, D. G., Bloch, M. H., Panza, K. E., & Reichow, B. (2013). Cognitive-behavioral therapy for anxiety in children with high-functioning autism: A meta-analysis. *Pediatrics, 132*(5), e1341–e1350.

Sukhodolsky, D. G., Scahill, L., Gadow, K. D., Arnold, L. E., Aman, M. G., McDougle, C. J., . . . Vitiello, B. (2008). Parent-rated anxiety symptoms in children with pervasive developmental disorders: Frequency and association with core autism symptoms and cognitive functioning. *Journal of Abnormal Child Psychology, 36*(1), 117–128.

Sullivan, P. F., Magnusson, C., Reichenberg, A., & et al. (2012). Family history of schizophrenia and bipolar disorder as risk factors for autism. *Archives of General Psychiatry, 69*(11), 1099–1103.

Taylor, E., & Rogers, J. W. (2005). Practitioner review: Early adversity and developmental disorders. *Journal of Child Psychology and Psychiatry, 46*(5), 451–467.

Tseng, M.-H., Fu, C.-P., Cermak, S. A., Lu, L., & Shieh, J.-Y. (2011). Emotional and behavioral problems in preschool children with autism: Relationship with sensory processing dysfunction. *Research in Autism Spectrum Disorders, 5*(4), 1441–1450.

Uhlhaas, P. J., & Mishara, A. L. (2007). Perceptual anomalies in schizophrenia: Integrating phenomenology and cognitive neuroscience. *Schizophrenia Bulletin, 33*(1), 142–156.

van der Meer, J. M., Oerlemans, A. M., van Steijn, D. J., Lappenschaar, M. G., de Sonneville, L. M., Buitelaar, J. K., & Rommelse, N. N. (2012). Are autism spectrum disorder and attention-deficit/hyperactivity disorder different manifestations of one overarching disorder? Cognitive and symptom evidence from a clinical and population-based sample. *Journal of the American Academy of Child & Adolescent Psychiatry, 51*(11), 1160–1172.

Wang, J., Barstein, J., Ethridge, L. E., Mosconi, M. W., Takarae, Y., & Sweeney, J. A. (2013). Resting state EEG abnormalities in autism spectrum disorders. *Journal of Neurodevelopmental Disorders, 5*(1), 24.

Wass, S. (2011). Distortions and disconnections: Disrupted brain connectivity in autism. *Brain and Cognition, 75*(1), 18–28.

Weber, L., Kamp-Becker, I., Christiansen, H., & Mingebach, T. (2019). Treatment of child externalizing behavior problems: A comprehensive review and meta–meta-analysis on effects of parent-based interventions on parental characteristics. *European Child & Adolescent Psychiatry.*

White, S. W., Lerner, M. D., McLeod, B. D., Wood, J. J., Ginsburg, G. S., Kerns, C., . . . Compton, S. (2015). Anxiety in youth with and without autism spectrum disorder: Examination of factorial equivalence. *Behavior Therapy, 46*(1), 40–53.

Williams, N. M., Zaharieva, I., Martin, A., Langley, K., Mantripragada, K., Fossdal, R., . . . Thapar, A. (2010). Rare chromosomal deletions and duplications in attention-deficit hyperactivity disorder: A genome-wide analysis. *Lancet, 376*(9750), 1401–1408.

Woodman, A. C., Smith, L. E., Greenberg, J. S., & Mailick, M. R. (2015). Change in autism symptoms and maladaptive behaviors in adolescence and adulthood: The role of positive family processes. *Journal of Autism and Developmental Disorders, 45*, 111–126.

Yirmiya, N., & Shaked, M. (2005). Psychiatric disorders in parents of children with autism: A meta-analysis. *Journal of Child Psychology and Psychiatry, 46*(1), 69–83.

PART 2

Co-Occurring Conditions

CHAPTER

2 Co-Occurring Mood Problems in Autism Spectrum Disorder

Katherine Gotham, Florencia Pezzimenti, Mareike Eydt-Beebe, Gloria T. Han, *and* Catherine G. Herrington

Abstract

Recent evidence suggests that individuals with autism spectrum disorder (ASD) experience depression at rates approximately four times greater than the general population. Co-occurring mood problems, including depressive and bipolar disorders, are associated with negative outcomes such as lower quality of life, increased adaptive behavior impairments, and greater service use. This chapter discusses what is known about the presentation of unipolar and bipolar depression in people with ASD and describes challenges to establishing sound prevalence estimates of mood disorders in ASD as they relate to methodological design issues and diagnostic assessment practices. It also provides an overview of potential vulnerability factors in the development of depression in this population; these areas of vulnerability include characteristics such as chronological age, cognitive ability, and ASD symptom severity, as well as those individual differences that may represent more direct mechanisms, for example, maladaptive coping styles, attentional biases, social reward profiles, and predisposition to rumination. The current research on interventions specifically designed to treat mood in people with ASD is very limited. However, promising treatments include adapted cognitive behavioral therapy and mindfulness-based approaches. Though most of this chapter focuses on unipolar depression in ASD as the more well-studied mood disorder, the chapter also summarizes the small research base on bipolar disorder in the context of ASD. It ends with a call for improved screening, assessment, and evidence-based treatment options to address this significant public health problem in this special population.

Keywords: depression, mood disorders, bipolar disorder, autism, psychiatric comorbidity

Overview

In this chapter, we discuss the co-occurrence of mood disorders in autism spectrum disorder (ASD) with a specific focus on depression and bipolar disorder. Depressed mood is one of the most common co-occurring conditions in adolescents and adults on the autism spectrum (Lever & Geurts, 2016). Major depressive disorder is also among the most clinically significant dual diagnoses in ASD (Hofvander et al., 2009). When ASD co-occurs with depression, existing difficulties noted in ASD may be exacerbated, such as substantially increased impairments in social motivation and adaptive behavior (Ghaziuddin, Ghaziuddin, & Greden, 2002; Magnuson & Constantino, 2011; Stewart, Barnard, Pearson, Hasan, & O'Brien, 2006). Co-occurring depression has also been linked to increases in some of the most challenging behaviors observed in individuals with ASD, such as aggression and self-injury (Ghaziuddin et al., 2002), as well as highly elevated rates of suicidal ideation compared to the general population (Cassidy et al., 2014). Further, depression is associated with increased medication and service use in people with ASD (in the context of already-scarce resources) and increased burden on families and caregivers (Cadman et al., 2012; Joshi et al., 2013).

The prevalence and impact of mood disorders in the ASD population spurs the need for improved screening, assessment, and treatment tools to address these co-occurring conditions. Accurate detection of mood disorders in ASD is challenging due to symptom overlap (e.g., social withdrawal, irregular sleep patterns, flat affect, and diminished eye contact are features of both ASD and depression). Social communication difficulties characteristic of ASD also impede emotion recognition and expression in ASD, subsequently hindering clinicians from recognizing co-occurring mood disorder symptoms in these individuals. To date, few to no psychometric instruments have been designed and/or validated to assess depressed mood in people with ASD.[1] This is concerning considering growing evidence suggesting that mood-related impairments may manifest differently in individuals with ASD compared to the general population, leading to potential underdiagnosis of mood disorders in ASD when using standard screeners, questionnaires, and structured interviews. Thus, this gap in knowledge warrants a significant and collective effort among researchers, clinicians, and individuals on the spectrum to further our understanding of co-occurring mood disorders in ASD.

In this chapter on unipolar and bipolar mood disorders in ASD, all information about co-occurring depression is presented first, followed by a section summarizing similar considerations in bipolar mood disorder. We explore the presentation of these mood disorders in ASD. We discuss their prevalence rates in ASD, with an eye to explaining the variability in these estimates as it relates to vulnerability factors for mood problems in autism. We include a summary of the current research on etiology, diagnosis, and assessment of depression and bipolar disorder in the ASD population. The limited information available on evidence-based treatment is discussed, and case examples are provided to illustrate effective interventions targeting mood problems in a school-age boy and a young woman, each with co-occurring ASD and depression. Finally, we outline future directions by summarizing the primary challenges in this field and proposing goals and recommendations for continued research and clinical practice.

Unipolar Depression in ASD: Prevalence and Course

Phenomenology

ASD is characterized by two core symptom areas: deficits in social communication, encompassing impairments in social reciprocity and verbal and nonverbal communication, and patterns of restricted or repetitive behaviors and interests (American Psychiatric Association, 2013). Major depressive disorder (MDD) is a mood disorder characterized primarily by feelings of sadness and/or hopelessness and diminished interest or pleasure in almost all activities. Additional symptoms of depression include significant weight change, sleep problems, fatigue, feelings of worthlessness or inappropriate guilt, impaired concentration or indecisiveness, and recurrent thoughts about death or more obvious suicidal ideation. To meet full criteria for MDD, at least five symptoms must be experienced to a significant degree ("nearly every day for most of the day") over a 2-week period (American Psychiatric Association, 2013).

People with ASD can experience some or all of these traditional features of depression (Table 2.1), most notably increased sadness, hopelessness, or tearfulness; changes in appetite and sleeping patterns; increased social withdrawal and lack of motivation; and "cognitive symptoms," such as feelings of guilt, failure, or worthlessness, and negative thoughts about oneself. In fact, although the presentation of depression for individuals on the spectrum was previously thought to be more associated with somatic symptoms (e.g., changes in sleeping

Table 2.1. Symptom Presentation of Depression in Autism Spectrum Disorder (ASD)

Prototypical Depression Symptoms That Commonly Mark Depression in ASD	Depression Symptoms That May Be More Specific to ASD
Loss of pleasure in previously enjoyed activities	Changes in circumscribed interests (CI)
Hopelessness and tearfulness	Loss of pleasure in a CI
Negative beliefs about oneself	*Alternatively:*
Feelings of failure or worthlessness	Significantly increased time/focus on CI
Flat affect	Change to CIs of darker/morbid content
(Increased) Social withdrawal	Increased repetitive behaviors
Appetite changes or increased eating problems	Increased anxiety or insistence on sameness
(Increased) Sleep problems	Greater irritability
Poor concentration abilities	Aggressive behavior (Increased or new onset)
Lack of motivation	Self-injury
Thoughts about death or suicidal ideation	Regressive behavior
	Decline in self-care

From Pezzimenti, Han, Vasa, & Gotham, 2019; reprinted with permission.

[1] At the time of printing, however, at least one is in development; a team led by Dr. Sarah Cassidy of the University of Nottingham is developing a new depression assessment instrument for adults with autism (Icke, 2018).

and eating patterns), cognitive symptoms associated with depressed mood were found to be elevated in young adults with ASD relative to a large similarly aged sample from the general population (Gotham, Unruh, & Lord, 2015).

The prevalence of suicidal ideation, another common symptom in depression, is also significantly higher for individuals with ASD compared to the general population (Segers & Rawana, 2014). A study of 374 adults who had been recently diagnosed with Asperger's syndrome (a discrete ASD diagnosis in the *Diagnostic and Statistical Manual of Mental Disorders*, fourth edition (DSM-IV), characterized by autism features in the absence of language or intellectual impairments; American Psychiatric Association, 2000) in the United Kingdom found that 66% reported suicidal ideation, compared to approximately 17% of the general UK population; those with co-occurring depression were significantly more likely to report suicidal ideation (Cassidy et al., 2014). These findings are consistent with other reports indicating that depression is a leading predictor of suicidal ideation in ASD samples (e.g., Autism and Developmental Disorders Inpatient Research Collaborative et al., 2017; Mayes, Gorman, Hillwig-Garcia, & Syed, 2013). These reports highlight that both suicidality and depressed mood are acute public health concerns for this special population and its stakeholders. Chapter 18 ("Suicidality and Self-Harm in Autism Spectrum Disorder") of this book will elaborate on this topic.

In addition to prototypical depressive symptoms, some behaviors have been suggested to be more autism-specific symptoms of depressed mood (see Table 2.1). For example, loss of pleasure participating in or talking about a special interest may suggest the beginning of a depressive episode in a person with ASD. Further, symptoms of depression among many people with ASD may be best explained as *changes* in existing behaviors, such as increased or decreased intensity of a restricted interest, increased frequency/intensity of repetitive behaviors, or heightened irritability, aggression, or self-injury. Although it is important to be aware of changes from baseline, we also note that behavior changes such as these do not exclusively signal the presence of depression. It is important to consider other possible causes, including ASD-normative responses to life stress (e.g., adjusting to a new teacher or experiencing bullying), an undiagnosed medical issue, or general developmental or pubertal changes.

Importantly, the presence of depressive symptoms may be overlooked in children and adults on the spectrum because they are phenomenologically similar to core features of ASD (e.g., flat affect and social withdrawal). It follows that general depression screening instruments may not be suitable for the ASD population. We will discuss this topic further in the "Diagnosis and Assessment" section.

Estimated Prevalence

Prevalence estimates of MDD in individuals with ASD are notably elevated compared to the general population, though estimates are also highly variable. Significant heterogeneity already exists in autism symptom presentation and level of functioning; this ASD heterogeneity increases when additionally considering co-occurring symptoms. Differences in study methodology (e.g., self-report vs. informant report of diagnostic information; population-based vs. convenience sample estimates) further contribute to the complexity of establishing accurate depression prevalence rates in ASD. Variability in prevalence estimates is discussed in more detail in the "Challenges to Establishing Prevalence Estimates of Depression in ASD" subheading of this section. Overall, the literature indicates that depressive symptoms are common and prevalent in individuals with ASD.

Previously reported lifetime prevalence estimates of co-occurring depression across studies have produced an exceptionally broad range of estimates, rendering them unhelpful (Chandrasekhar & Sikich, 2015; Magnuson & Constantino, 2011). In the single study that employed population-based sampling, only 1.4% of the ASD cohort (n = 112) met criteria for a depression diagnosis, as assessed through parent interview (Simonoff et al., 2008). Although we know of no ideal typically developing (TD) comparison estimate, up to 8.4% of TD peers at the upper age limit of that sample (13 to 14 years old) had diagnoses of either MDD or the milder but long-lasting dysthymia in a large U.S. representative study (Merikangas et al., 2010). However, the age range of the Simonoff et al. ASD sample, at 10 to 14 years old, falls below the ages of significant increase in depressive disorders observed in the general population (Merikangas et al., 2010). The authors further noted that an additional 11% of their sample exhibited significant depressive symptom levels even though they did not meet full diagnostic criteria for MDD (Simonoff et al., 2008). By contrast, several convenience samples of older adolescents and adults have yielded lifetime depression rates in the 50% to 77% range (Hofvander et al., 2009; Joshi et al., 2013; Lugnegård, Hallerbäck, & Gillberg, 2011;

Unruh, Bodfish, & Gotham, 2018), which are remarkably high compared to TD global lifetime prevalence rates of mood disorders of 12% (Kessler et al., 2009). These striking estimates are even more noteworthy considering that the studies used standardized self-report interviews of psychiatric symptoms (e.g., Structured Clinical Interview for DSM-IV or DSM-5; First, Williams, Karg, & Spitzer, 2004), which are considered gold-standard assessment instruments in clinical research.

In a recent meta-analysis, Hudson and colleagues (2018) reviewed 66 articles reporting rates of depression in individuals with ASD. They found that the pooled lifetime prevalence rate of depressive disorders in ASD samples was 14.4% (range = 0.4% to 76.2%), and the pooled current prevalence rate was 12.3% (range = 0.6% to 50.0%). The lifetime prevalence rates of depression were much higher in studies that used structured interviews to assess depression (28.5% compared to reported lifetime prevalence of 6.7% in studies that used other assessment instruments). Studies that collected data using self-report also found higher rates of lifetime depression prevalence (48.6% compared to reported lifetime prevalence of 14.4% in studies where caregivers reported on their child's depressive symptoms). Similarly, higher depression rates were found in ASD samples with average to above-average IQ (52.8% compared to reported lifetime prevalence of 12.2% in studies in which mean IQ was below average) and in studies that only included adults (40.2% compared to reported lifetime prevalence of 7.7% in studies focused on children and adolescents younger than 18 years old; Hudson et al., 2018). It is notable, then, that the current prevalence rate of depression in ASD (12.3%) was still higher than the Centers for Disease Control and Prevention–endorsed current rate of 8.1% in the general adult population (Brody, Pratt, & Hughes, 2018), despite the inclusion of ASD samples weighted toward younger ages (in fact, predominantly child samples) and those assessed during a historical period in which an autism diagnosis tended to overshadow concerns about mood. Ultimately, the extant meta-analysis by Hudson and colleagues (2018) concludes that individuals with ASD are four times more likely to experience depression in their lifetime compared to adults without ASD. This was supported in a recent Scandinavian population–based cohort study not included in the meta-analysis, which sampled over 4,000 young adults with ASD (Rai et al., 2018).

Challenges to Establishing Prevalence Estimates of Depression in ASD

As noted previously, widely ranging depression rates reported in ASD are likely due to variability in methods across studies and to challenges in assessing depressed mood in the context of ASD. First, some studies focus on depression symptoms versus depressive disorders. Many individuals with ASD who present with a high level of depressive symptoms might not meet strict criteria for a formal diagnosis of MDD based on the DSM-5 (e.g., failing to report sufficient severity or duration of symptoms or to endorse one of the two primary and requisite depression symptoms, sad mood or loss of interest). Because of this, studies defining depression based on the DSM-5 diagnosis likely will yield lower prevalence rates than those considering depressive symptoms regardless of diagnostic thresholds. Second, prevalence rates can vary depending on the selection of raters and instruments to assess depression. Studies that used self-report measures generally reported higher depression prevalence rates than studies that used parent or caregiver reports; similarly, studies that used semistructured interviews obtained higher rates than those that used other instruments (Hudson et al., 2018). Challenges regarding assessment and diagnostic methods of depression in ASD will be elaborated later in this chapter under the subheading "Diagnosis and Assessment." Third, depression prevalence rates vary by sample characteristics, as we will discuss next.

Vulnerability Factors for Depressed Mood in ASD

Individual characteristics including chronological and developmental age, gender, cognitive ability, verbal fluency, and ASD symptom severity have been suggested to differentially influence the co-occurrence of depression in persons with ASD. In addition, heightened awareness of social differences, tendency to ruminate, and contextual factors related to stress or trauma exposure make up additional vulnerability processes that increase risk for onset of depression in individuals with ASD. Consistent with perspectives from developmental psychopathology, multiple vulnerability processes likely interact along etiological pathways to depression in ASD (Rutter, 2002).

Though some cross-sectional studies have suggested a lack of association between depression rates and age (see Magnuson & Constantino, 2011, for a review; Strang et al., 2012), many studies assessing independent samples have reported higher prevalence of depression in adolescent and adult samples compared to child ASD samples (Hudson et al., 2018). Independent studies using structured clinical interviews in older adolescents and adults with ASD (combined age ranges of 16 to 60) have noted lifetime depression rates of 70% (Lugnegård et al., 2011), 76% (Gotham et al., 2018), and 77% (Joshi et al., 2013), and current mood disorder rates of 53% (Hofvander et al., 2009), compared to lifetime rates of 7.7% in children with ASD under age 18 (Hudson et al., 2018; see above in the "Estimated Prevalence" subheading). Rates from these more carefully phenotyped studies are consistent with less rigorous estimates of depression in adults with ASD—for example, in 255 adult registrants of the Interactive Autism Network, 75% reported a previous diagnosis of depression (Gotham, Marvin, et al., 2015).

Due to limited prospective longitudinal studies, it is unclear how developmental trajectories of depression in ASD compare to the general population. In general, the risk period for developing depression spikes in adolescence (Kessler et al., 2003), and gender differences intensify between the ages of 15 and 18, with females exhibiting greater risk for depression (Hankin et al., 1998). Available longitudinal data in ASD indicate preliminary support for adolescence as a similar developmental turning point marked by increasing prevalence estimates of depression (Gotham, Brunwasser, & Lord, 2015; see also Greenlee, Mosley, Shui, Veenstra-VanderWeele, & Gotham, 2016). This trajectory is also consistent with social and behavioral observations relevant to ASD. For example, social challenges, expectations, and resulting self-realizations increase with age, and greater social interest that typically starts during adolescence may interact with low social opportunity and negative social feedback to compound onset of depressed mood (Allen & Badcock, 2003).

However, in their longitudinal sample, Gotham and colleagues (2015) reported that boys with ASD tended to have elevated and stable depressive symptoms from childhood through adulthood, whereas girls started in normative symptom level ranges and experienced a steeper increase in depressive symptoms through the adolescent years, a developmental trajectory comparable to that in the general population. It is not clear if males or females with ASD are at greater risk for depression. Unlike typically developing adolescents, some evidence suggests that girls with ASD are no more likely to develop depression than boys with ASD (Brereton, Tonge, & Einfeld, 2006; Hurtig et al., 2009; Mayes, Calhoun, Murray, Ahuja, & Smith, 2011). Such findings open the door to speculation on why males with ASD may be at greater risk for depression than TD males, or conversely, why females with ASD may be at reduced risk compared to TD females: If a shared mechanism between autism and depression topples the typical gender ratio of depression within this predominantly male population, such mechanism(s) likely would illuminate depression science more generally. More research is needed to comment on sex and gender differences, particularly in adults in ASD. Even if risk is equivalent across biological sex and/or traditional gender categories, men and women with ASD may not follow equivalent trajectories in the development of these mood symptoms as noted earlier (Gotham, Brunwasser, et al., 2015). Further, more work is needed to understand how sexual orientation and nonbinary interpretations of gender influence mood in this special population (van Schalkwyk, Klingensmith, & Volkmar, 2015).

Intact intellectual ability is another documented correlate of elevated depressive symptoms for individuals with ASD (De-la-Iglesia & Olivar, 2015). In their meta-analysis, Hudson and colleagues (2018) summarize that individuals on the spectrum with impaired cognitive ability (IQ < 70) had lower rates of current depressive symptoms, compared with individuals with ASD and higher IQ. This finding could be influenced by the relative difficulty of assessing depression in individuals with impaired verbal or cognitive ability. In addition, higher functioning and more socially motivated individuals with ASD may experience greater risk for depression due to greater insight into their social differences, heightened negative self-perception, and diminished self-worth (Capps, Sigman, & Yirmiya, 1995; Ghaziuddin et al., 2002; Gotham, Bishop, Brunwasser, & Lord, 2014; Gotham, Brunwasser, et al., 2015; Mazurek & Kanne, 2010; Sterling, Dawson, Estes, & Greenson, 2008; Vickerstaff, Heriot, Wong, Lopes, & Dossetor, 2007). In either case, it appears that the positive association between IQ and depression is most robust in samples with greater IQ *variability* that include individuals both with and without intellectual disability. For example, a study of 95 children and adolescents ages 6 through 18 years old with IQs of 70 and above did not find any relationship between IQ and depression (Strang et al., 2012). On the other hand, a much more comprehensive study by Mayes and colleagues (2011) included 233 children with ASD and an IQ of 80 and above, as well as 117 children with ASD and an IQ below 80, and observed that the children with greater cognitive abilities were experiencing more depression on average (per parent interview) than the less able group (Mayes et al., 2011). Verbal fluency appears to have a similar effect as IQ on prevalence rates of depression in those with ASD, with individuals with higher verbal scores reporting more depressive symptoms (Sterling et al., 2008); there are fewer studies specifying the role of verbal level explicitly, but it is possible that this could account in part for the negative association between IQ and depression in ASD.

Although less is known about depression in the ASD population with intellectual disability (ASD+ID) because of the greater difficulty making emotional health diagnoses in those with more impaired insight or reduced verbal ability, the risk for depression in ASD+ID samples nevertheless appears to be greater than most non-ASD comparison cohorts with or without ID; in some studies, depression rates in ASD+ID do not lag far behind the elevated rates in ASD comparisons without ID. For example, the Mayes et al. study described previously, assessed more and less cognitively able adolescents with ASD via a comprehensive assessment battery and revealed very high rates of depression for both groups (54% in ASD without ID and 42% in ASD+ID; Mayes et al., 2011). In an online survey, depression diagnoses were reported by 36% of legal representatives of 143 less able adults with ASD (ages 18 to 58; Gotham, Marvin, et al., 2015). Similarly, a longitudinal study spanning late childhood through early adulthood in an ASD sample with mean verbal IQ equal to 56 found that depressive symptoms both began and remained higher in the ASD group than in non-ASD counterparts with developmental delays (Gotham, Brunwasser, et al., 2015). These findings suggest that adults with ASD with or without an ID are at higher risk for developing depression.

A number of studies have reported an association between lower autism severity and higher risk for depression. Vickerstaff et al. (2007) found that children aged 7 to 13 who had less severe autism symptoms demonstrated greater insight into deficits in social competence, leading to negative self-perception that predicted higher levels of depressive symptoms. Consistent with this finding, Mazurek and Kanne (2010) found that individuals with higher ASD severity exhibited fewer symptoms of depression than individuals with less severe ASD symptoms. In both of these studies, however, greater ASD severity was associated with lower IQ, obscuring the role of autism severity. Importantly, a study comparing children with ASD with children with pervasive developmental disorder-not otherwise specified (PDD-NOS), a milder subtype of the autism spectrum per the DSM-IV, found that children with ASD experienced more depressive symptoms even after controlling for IQ (Pearson et al., 2006). This result suggests that autism severity or symptom profiles specific to ASD may uniquely contribute to depression caseness.

The impact of socioeconomic status (SES) on psychopathology in ASD is particularly unclear. In one study, poverty predicted emotional problems at age 16 in people with ASD (Simonoff et al., 2013), whereas in another, SES was not associated with emotional problems (Gray et al., 2012). Similarly, one study found that lower SES predicted less improvement in internalizing symptoms over time (Taylor & Seltzer, 2010), whereas another found that lower SES was associated with overall level of psychopathology but not with changes over time (Midouhas, Yogaratnam, Flouri, & Charman, 2013). Thus, as with prevalence estimates, the relationships between several possible vulnerability factors for psychiatric comorbidity in ASD are difficult to pin down because of design characteristics that impede the comparability of samples and studies. Elevated depression rates across most of the reviewed studies again underscore the need for appropriate screening and treatment options for co-occurring mood problems in the ASD population across age, IQ ranges, level of functioning, sex, and SES.

Unipolar Depression in ASD: Etiology, Diagnosis, and Assessment

Etiology

The vulnerability factors described in the previous section, likely interact with several potential genetic, neurobiological, psychological, and environmental factors to explain the etiology of depression in ASD. Identifying pathways by which mood problems develop in this population is particularly important to specify targets for intervention. These "targets" may be mechanistic (e.g., repetitive self-criticism) or may represent moderator-driven profiles (e.g., focusing certain types of prevention efforts on prepubertal girls) that inform treatment development and selection.

A number of studies have found elevated rates of familial depressive disorders in people with ASD (Magnuson & Constantino, 2011), including more frequent affective disorders in first-degree relatives of children with autism even prior to the additional stress of having a child with special needs (Bolton, Pickles, Murphy, & Rutter, 1998). Twin studies have found that social problems related to depression, anxiety, and autism overlap (Hoekstra, Happé, Baron-Cohen, & Ronald, 2009), with approximately half of the genetic variance related to autism symptom scores conferring susceptibility to other behavioral problems. Similarly, a study of 33,332 psychiatric cases and 27,888 controls found specific genetic variants that precede ASD, schizophrenia, bipolar disorder, and MDD, suggesting transdiagnostic genetic vulnerability (Cross-Disorder Group of the Psychiatric Genomics Consortium, 2013).

There are several atypical biological and neural processes that have been documented in both the general depressed and general ASD populations, for example, anomalous serotonin level and/or function (Muller, Anacker, & Veenstra-VanderWeele, 2016), EEG resting frontal asymmetry (Burnette et al., 2011), neural connectivity disruptions (Just, 2004), anomalous reward circuitry functioning and amygdala activity (Dichter, Damiano, & Allen, 2012), and neural inflammation/microglial dysregulation (Frick, Williams, & Pittenger, 2013). As with most topics in psychiatry and neuroscience, there are likely complicated transactional pathways underlying the link between depression and autism. These pathways may well subsume transactions across genetic, neurobiological, psychological, and environmental domains.

We turn our focus here to a few selected social–psychological–behavioral constructs that are salient to both ASD and depression in the general population. These include rumination, negative self-attributions, maladaptive coping mechanisms more broadly, lack of social connection and loneliness, lower perceived social support in the immediate environment and/or at the societal level, and other stressful environmental factors (e.g., bullying, unemployment, and limited independence). At this point, we also refer readers to a recent review in which additional depression-related psychological mechanisms are located within the Research Domain Criteria (RDoC) matrix, an organizing framework forwarded by the National Institute of Mental Health (White et al., 2018).

Rumination refers to the pattern of thinking repetitively and nonproductively about negative content (Nolen-Hoeksema, Wisco, & Lyubomirsky, 2008). In longitudinal studies within the general population, rumination has been documented as preceding the development of depressive episodes (Nolen-Hoeksema, 2000; Robinson & Alloy, 2003). In the ASD population, rumination is elevated compared to TD controls (Gotham et al., 2018; Crane, Goddard, & Pring, 2013) and is correlated with repetitive behaviors (Gotham et al., 2014; Keenan, Gotham, & Lerner, 2017; Patel, Day, Jones, & Mazefsky, 2017), particularly insistence on sameness. This suggests that individuals on the autism spectrum may be predisposed to getting "stuck" on psychological substrates in addition to interests, rituals, and routines. Further, some studies indicate that adults with ASD have elevated levels of negative self-attributions, such as sense of failure, guilt, and shame, compared to similarly aged TD peers (Gotham, Unruh, et al., 2015). A recent commentary theorizes that people with ASD may be at higher risk for developing internalizing problems as a result of returning to negative self-referential information, coupled with cognitive inflexibility (Burrows, Timpano, & Uddin, 2017). The current empirical literature has not yet determined the incremental contribution of the *self-referential* component of repetitive thinking in the potential rumination-to-depression pathway in ASD, though biases toward negative self-referential thinking in individuals with depression have been documented in the general depression literature (Bargh & Tota, 1988; Nejad, Fossati, & Lemogne, 2013) and likely contribute to the onset and maintenance of depression.

As repetitive thinking is more common in the ASD than TD population, we speculate that it can be conceptualized as a broader cognitive style in many contexts, but also function as a maladaptive coping strategy when it occurs specifically in response to stressors. Maladaptive coping strategies in general may be related to the development of depression and other mood disorders in ASD. A study done by Pouw and colleagues (2013) found that boys with ASD who use adaptive coping strategies, such as working with peers to find solutions, reported less depressive symptoms than those who use maladaptive coping strategies, such as rumination or acting out (Pouw, Rieffe, Stockmann, & Gadow, 2013). Maladaptive coping may be particularly relevant for this population with impaired executive functioning; however, a study by Hollocks et al. (2014) found no significant association between executive functioning and depression in their sample of 90 adolescents with ASD, though they observed a significant negative relation between executive functioning and anxiety.

Next, the literature suggests that lack of social connection and loneliness are associated with depression in people with ASD (Han, Tomarken, & Gotham, 2018; Hedley, Uljarević, Foley, Richdale, & Trollor, 2018; Mazurek, 2014). In the general population, the social connectedness model proposes that lack of social support or engagement leads to loneliness (Cacioppo & Patrick, 2008), which in turn is associated with developing depression. Several groups have theorized that greater desire to fit in socially, in the context of impaired social skills and more negative social interactions, may contribute to depression in people with ASD (Capps et al., 1995; Meyer, Mundy, Van Hecke, & Durocher, 2006; Sterling et al., 2008; Tantam, 2000). In a transdiagnostic adult population, recent evidence suggests that greater self-reported capacity for social reward (construed as social interest or pleasure) was significantly associated with loneliness in the specific context of elevated autism traits (Han et al., 2018). Similarly, a survey study of 185 adolescents and adults with ASD (ages 14 to 80) found that higher reports of loneliness and lower social support satisfaction reports were associated with depression and suicidality (Hedley et al., 2018). In addition to social interest or motivation, social skill deficits may play a key role in the development of depressed mood. For example, people with impaired theory of mind may find it more difficult to understand the mental states of others, or to use this information to understand and predict others' behavior. This might lead them to experience more social isolation or bullying, in turn putting them at greater risk for depression.

Furthermore, there appears to be a relation between social support and/or societal acceptance and the development of depression. Cage, Di Monaco, and Newell (2018) collected data from 111 adults with ASD using an online survey. They found that individuals who experienced a greater degree of acceptance from family, friends, and society had significantly lower depressive symptoms. It is also possible that widespread social stigma influences depression in ASD. In a study of 398 adults with autism who participated in a survey from the Interactive Autism Network ($N = 255$ self-report, $N = 143$ adults legally represented by others), findings revealed that both more and less independent adults with ASD converged in endorsing "societal understanding and acceptance" of ASD as one of their most important priorities for future research (Gotham, Marvin, et al., 2015). Broader social stigma may negatively affect the way some people with ASD view themselves, contributing to cognitive symptoms of depression, such as self-criticism and feelings of worthlessness and failure. In addition, mental illness social stigma has been associated with limitations on resources (e.g., jobs or housing; Wahl, 1999). Based on these findings, societal acceptance and understanding support better outcomes and quality of life in adults with ASD.

Similarly, negative social and environmental circumstances more common among individuals with ASD—such as bullying, unemployment, limited independence, and poor prospects for goal achievement (whether vocational, educational, residential, or romantic; Henninger & Taylor, 2013; Shtayermman, 2007)—likely contribute to depression in people with ASD. Over 50% of young adults with ASD are reportedly not involved with any form of employment or postsecondary education programs for the first 2 years after high school, contributing to this population's tendency to live at home and not engage socially with their peers (Shattuck et al., 2012). Emerging adults on the spectrum who are not gainfully employed or enrolled in a postsecondary program may abruptly transition from a structured, familiar, and relatively busy school day in which their social role is defined (e.g., that of student) and social interaction is built-in to an unstructured, relatively socially isolated and inactive day. One study found that adults with autism who have greater independence and are involved in vocational activities show less internalizing symptomatology, such as withdrawal, inattention, and repetitive habits (Taylor, Smith, & Mailick, 2014). The sudden change in activity, direction, and level of social engagement that people with ASD experience when they transition into adulthood may set the stage for developing depression (Jacobson, Martell, & Dimidjian, 2006). On the other hand, in a study of 36 transition-aged youth with ASD, greater internalizing symptoms before school exit predicted less social participation postexit, rather than the opposite direction of effects (Lounds Taylor, Adams, & Bishop, 2017); this underscores the dynamic interplay between these factors and the overall impact of mood problems in ASD.

Diagnosis and Assessment

Assessment for depressed mood usually includes a semistructured psychiatric interview and standardized questionnaires completed by the individual, parent, and/or teacher, as applicable based on the individual's age and level of functioning. Assessment protocols should be keyed to cover DSM criteria for depressive disorders, with particular attention to assessing behavioral changes, time course, impact on functioning, and suicidal ideation. Medical history and additional medical testing should be considered to rule out causes of mood disturbance related to physical health problems or substance use.

Magnuson and Constantino (2011) developed a clinical approach to guide the diagnosis of depression in people with ASD specifically. Their strategy focuses on identifying predisposing factors that could lead to depression (e.g., family history or negative life events), change in behavior over time (i.e., a behavioral fluctuation from baseline), and consideration of factors that increase the risk of developing depression (e.g., bullying, life dissatisfaction, lack of confidence).

Depression assessment in the general population often relies heavily on self-report, particularly in the lifespan periods in which mood disorders are more common (older school-age through adulthood). Self-report presupposes the ability to recognize internal states and feelings, and the motivation and ability to communicate about them to others. Autism-related difficulties with insight and social communication make it more difficult for some individuals with ASD to recognize or express their emotional state, possibly obfuscating self-report methods (Mazefsky, Kao, & Oswald, 2011).

Inability to recognize or label emotional states in oneself is called *alexithymia* (Bird & Cook, 2013). Several reports suggest that approximately 50% of people with ASD also have alexithymia (Berthoz & Hill, 2005; Hill, Berthoz, & Frith, 2004; Lombardo, Barnes, Wheelwright, & Baron-Cohen, 2007). Impairments in emotional insight likely complicate not only the validity of self-report but also a person's *experience* of depressive symptoms—how or whether they notice, interpret, or tell others about them. Because of difficulties identifying and/or communicating about internal experiences, it is unclear what proportion of the ASD population experiences cognitive or affective symptoms of depression such as negative affect, loss of interest, worthlessness, low self-esteem, and inappropriate guilt.

Beyond problems with emotional insight, other social communication impairments that are central to autism (e.g., low social motivation or less effective communication strategies due to nonverbal communication deficits) further compound difficulties in accurately expressing feeling states to others. For all of these reasons, *observation* of depression symptoms—whether by familiar others or a clinician—can be particularly important to accurate depression diagnosis within the ASD population. However, observing depression symptoms in people with ASD is complicated by the fact that several core symptoms of depression can also be considered behavioral correlates of autism itself. For example, in a typically developing person, flat facial affect and tone of voice are more likely to indicate depressed mood than they are in a person with ASD, for whom these same features might mark nonverbal communication deficits without indicating anything about emotional state. In addition to blunted facial expression and intonation, commonly "overlapping" symptoms include social withdrawal or lack of social motivation, dysregulated eating and sleeping, and poor concentration, all of which can mark ASD, depression, or both.

Across populations, depression assessment often depends on observable *change* from baseline, such as *onset* of social withdrawal or tearfulness. Even if common characteristics of depression may be minimally or not different from "baseline" for many people with ASD, subtle or overt behavioral change may be evident when support teams look for it purposefully—particularly in areas of social and nonsocial pleasure and motivation, self-injury, aggression, irritability, and tearfulness (Turygin, Matson, MacMillan, & Konst, 2013). Behavioral changes that could signal depression in an individual with ASD include reduced pleasure taken in typically preferred topics or activities and, relatedly, increased withdrawal or refusal to engage in previously motivating activities; increased social withdrawal in particular; focus on negative topics, including but not limited to death and dying; decline in self-care; regressive behavior in which the person behaves in a way that is developmentally younger or seems to lose established adaptive behavior skills; exacerbated eating or sleep problems; concentration problems; and weight changes (Charlot et al., 2008; Gotham, Marvin, et al., 2015; Lainhart & Folstein, 1994; Chandrasekhar & Sikich, 2015; see Table 2.1).

With observation that is rooted in awareness of these symptoms and problems, parent or teacher report can be an invaluable tool in assessing depression in people with ASD across the lifespan. However, many studies report large discrepancies between self- and parent-reported depression scores in the ASD population (White & Roberson-Nay, 2009; White, Schry, & Maddox, 2012). Such discrepancies may negatively impact clinicians' confidence in considering a co-occurring diagnosis of depression (despite meta-analytic findings for significantly higher depression rates when self-report measures are used; Hudson et al., 2018). Again, factors like age, intellectual ability, and gender can affect the presentation of depressive symptoms in ASD, and we do not yet have sufficient data to inform an understanding of differential performance of depression self- and other-report measures by participant characteristic profiles. At the moment, at least one depression screener specifically designed for the ASD population is being developed, with efforts led by Dr. Sarah Cassidy and colleagues in the United Kingdom. In the interim, depression measures validated in the general population can still be valuable when interpreted with clinical judgment.

Finally, the screening or assessment process can be difficult for reasons beyond those pertaining to standardized instrumentation or symptom overlap. For example, it may be difficult to motivate a person with depression to seek help or share his or her emotional state and thoughts, given that anhedonia and fatigue are often associated with depressed mood. Even when people with ASD seek assessment for possible depression, a diagnostic "halo effect" can influence clinicians' judgment, such that more apparent and subjectively more severe behaviors associated with ASD often overshadow the detection of or importance placed on internalized states, such as sadness or low self-esteem. Of note, not only can the presence of autism obscure assessment of mood but also the presence of psychiatric disorders, including depression, has been shown to reduce the accuracy of common autism diagnostic instruments in picking up ASD. Havdahl and colleagues (2016) found that non-ASD behavioral and emotional difficulties (e.g., depression) influence the categorical classification on psychometric instruments designed to identify autism. Pine, Guyer, Goldwin, Towbin, and Leibenluft (2008) also found that typically developing youth with mood disorders obtained higher scores on ASD symptom scales compared to healthy youth (replicated in adults in Unruh et al., 2018). Thus, behaviors associated with ASD and depression may mutually impact the utility of diagnostic tools for the other disorder.

Unipolar Depression in ASD: Treatment

Currently, the first line of treatment for depression in individuals with ASD is pharmacological. A study of 129 adults with ASD found that almost 60% took at least one psychotropic medication, with a quarter of the sample taking three or more such medications and 35% on antidepressants in particular (though the number prescribed any of these medications for depression specifically was not reported; Buck et al., 2014). Although psychopharmacology remains a valuable option in treating mood disorders, Kerns, Roux, Connell, and Shattuck (2016) posit that alternative therapy methods could potentially lead to better outcomes and less reliance on continued medication use. Although the research on treatments for depression in ASD is extremely limited, clinical researchers have proposed promising adaptations of cognitive behavioral therapy (CBT), behavioral activation (as a stand-alone treatment modality or an integrated component of CBT), and mindfulness-based therapy for the ASD population.

Reports indicate that CBT is efficacious in treating anxiety in young people with ASD (Storch et al., 2015; White et al., 2013; Wood et al., 2009, 2015) and can be successfully modified to treat depression in adolescents and young adults with ASD (Kerns et al., 2016). A predominant goal of CBT is to help clients identify and change common unhelpful thoughts and behaviors to encourage enduring improvement in mood and overall functioning (Beck & Rush, 1979). In ASD, one study delivered a CBT group intervention to 26 adolescents and adults with ASD and compared outcomes to a waitlist control group (McGillivray & Evert, 2014). Significantly lower depression and perceived stress scores were reported by participants who received the intervention, with benefits maintained at subsequent 3- and 9-month follow-up (McGillivray & Evert, 2014).

As resources for augmented CBT for individuals on the spectrum are scarce, we predominantly draw from a comprehensive overview by Kerns and colleagues (2016) regarding the application of CBT for treatment of depression in ASD. These authors recommend helpful modifications of CBT protocols for the ASD population and emphasize its utility for adolescents and young adults with ASD and average to above-average IQ. The authors note that this age range is a critical period for intervention because individuals are expected to transition into more independent, "adult" social roles with more responsibility while experiencing heightened levels of unpredictability that are part and parcel of real-world settings. A lack of understanding of their diagnosis and variability in self-advocacy skills may also impede individuals' ability to develop more independence as they age. Thus, Kerns and colleagues (2016) emphasize the salient role of psychoeducation to normalize and validate patients' unique experiences while empowering their voice for self-advocacy. In the context of depression, psychoeducation also increases patient awareness of common maladaptive behaviors, such as social withdrawal, isolation, and inactivity, which may aggravate depressive symptoms. The authors also recommend helpful modifications to traditional psychoeducation, such as incorporating age-appropriate hands-on and interactive activities (such as role-play or muscle relaxation exercises), visual guides and worksheets (e.g., fear thermometers), skills practice in real-life situations, and technology (e.g., logging their moods throughout the day on their phones), which make the psychoeducational aspect of CBT more tenable to individuals on the spectrum.

Other considerations for modified CBT include parent involvement, group versus individual programs, and interdisciplinary care (Kerns et al., 2016). Parents may provide initial scaffolding to their adolescent or young adult child, but fading of this structure and cueing should be a part of treatment to support developmentally appropriate movement toward independence. Group CBT programs offer a number of advantages as well, including greater efficiency and cost-effectiveness (one therapist can help multiple clients at once), potentially greater social support, and real-time normalization and practice of social skills. In group therapy, clients are supported and held accountable for their involvement and completion of treatment by their peers rather than their parents, thus providing a more developmentally appropriate experience for adolescents and adults on the autism spectrum. This accountability and social structure may ultimately promote greater maintenance of gains in the long term.

Behavioral activation, a specific component of CBT and potential stand-alone treatment modality, may be particularly effective for treating depression in adolescents and adults on the spectrum. Behavioral activation focuses on building rewarding and goal-directed activities and experiences to improve mood in the context of patients' lives (Jacobson et al., 2006). As previously noted, transitioning from greater to lesser structure in terms of scheduled activities and social opportunities may contribute to the onset of depression in transition-aged individuals with ASD. As such, it may be particularly important to restore structure by equipping individuals with positive, rewarding, and attainable goals and activities as integral parts of patients' daily routines (Kerns et al., 2016).

Mindfulness is another approach that may offer benefits for the treatment of mood disorders in ASD. Mindfulness is broadly defined as paying attention to thoughts, feelings, and experiences in the present moment in an accepting and nonjudgmental manner (Kabat-Zinn, 2003). In contrast to CBT, mindfulness-based interventions do not emphasize the analysis of thoughts, feelings, and behaviors; instead, patients are taught to accept thoughts and feelings as temporary phenomena, which has been shown to reduce maladaptive avoidance behaviors and ruminative thinking associated with negative mood in typically developing depressed adults (Hayes, 2004; Jain et al., 2007). One randomized clinical trial used a modified mindfulness intervention to treat 42 adults with ASD, with significant postintervention decreases observed in depressive and anxiety symptoms (Spek, van Ham, & Nyklíček, 2013). Similarly, a group protocol for mindfulness-based stress reduction (MBSR) that was modified for ASD was found to reduce depressive and anxiety symptoms in adults with ASD (Sizoo & Kuiper, 2017). Even though the published research linking this modality to treatment of depressed mood in ASD is limited, preliminary results suggest that mindfulness is a promising intervention for reducing co-occurring depressive and anxiety symptoms in people with ASD (Cachia, Anderson, & Moore, 2016).

As mechanisms of therapeutic change are likely shared across treatment modalities, we encourage a multimodal approach and multidisciplinary team whenever possible when providing evidence-based treatment to people with ASD. The coordination of services will ensure that all relevant systems (home, vocational, social, and educational environments) are involved in the process (Codding, Feinberg, Dunn, & Pace, 2005). It is always important to take into consideration the patient's level of impairment when trying to determine the most appropriate intervention (e.g., using behavioral treatments for minimally verbal or less cognitively able ASD individuals). Psychotropic medications should be prescribed under the careful oversight of an expert clinician to avoid unnecessary use of multiple medications and unwanted side effects. Of note, some medications commonly prescribed in the ASD population (e.g., atypical antipsychotics) can produce depression-like symptoms such as sadness, despair, and emotional blunting, thereby potentially exacerbating mood problems within ASD. Finally, in tandem with evidence-based treatment strategies, we urge the use of "homegrown" strategies that are either known contributors to well-being (e.g., a balanced diet, regular exercise, meaningful structured activity, better regulated sleep) or creative solutions to build social engagement into the daily routine of persons with ASD (e.g., joining online or local clubs, taking community leisure classes, and creating informal social groups).

We now introduce two case studies of treating depression in individuals with ASD, followed by a summary of shared and unique experiences across the two cases.

Case Example 1: A 10-Year-Old Boy With ASD and MDD

Background. At the start of therapy, "Cody" was a 10-year-old Caucasian male with ASD whose mother sought therapy for her son due to elevated depressive symptoms per his psychiatrist's recommendation. Cody's mother was especially concerned after noticing that Cody experienced a notable decrease in mood and loss of interest in previously pleasurable activities after starting at a new school. Cody met criteria for giftedness and was enrolled in gifted programs. In academic settings, Cody sometimes became argumentative and dismissive of others when he disagreed with teachers and classmates. Thus, Cody had difficulty connecting with peers and forming friendships. Prior to seeking therapy, Cody threatened to harm himself. Cody's mother's goals for her son were for him to learn coping skills for depressed mood and anger management, learn strategies for improving interpersonal skills, and increase cognitive flexibility. Cody's goal for therapy was to "treat depression."

Strengths and barriers. Cody was intellectually gifted and creative. He was receptive to and motivated by learning about coping skills in a way that resonated with his unique interests. Cody also demonstrated a notable level of argumentation and dismissal of the clinician when he disagreed with therapy topics. His rigid thinking style hindered his ability to think flexibly about thoughts and feelings. He also exhibited limited insight into social relationships and had difficulty with perspective taking.

Problem list. *Depressed mood and low frustration tolerance with poor insight into his emotional experience; loneliness, poor interpersonal skills, lack of social awareness.*

At intake, Cody readily articulated a detailed description of his depression experience: "Depression feels like having all your energy sapped and still trying to walk around all week. For me, depression and anger are really similar—it's like the feeling of sitting down at the dinner table and just wanting to push everything off and then smacking your head into the table because you just don't care anymore." Further, he described his diagnostic experience of depression at his psychiatry appointment: "I was so sad when I first came to the doctor and found out I had depression. I was very emotional. Do you know how insulting that is? Being told that I have a mental illness..." At intake, Cody's responses on the Children's Depression Inventory (CDI; Kovacs, 1985) yielded a score of 27, indicating a high level of depressive symptoms.

Every session began with a **10-minute check-in with both Cody and his mother** so that they could share "highs and lows" of the week. The check-in provided an opportunity for the therapist to inform Cody's mother about concepts and skills in therapy that she could reinforce at home. In the first two sessions, Cody was reticent and disengaged for the first 10 to 15 minutes of the session (after check-ins) before participating. In fact, Cody had a fixed belief that it was the "therapist's job to make [him] better" and did not acknowledge his role in the therapeutic process. He also shared that he had done internet searches and watched YouTube videos about depression, which further intensified his dislike of the "label." His research contributed to a very **fixed, rigid, and hopeless perspective about his experience of depression as identity defining** (i.e., "I am a depressed person."). Thus, **emphasis on psychoeducation** was critical to help Cody dispel myths about depression, especially those regarding the immutability of the condition. Cody also became adamant that he did not want to talk about feelings because he "hates feelings" (of note, this contradicted his spontaneous use of a significant emotion vocabulary at intake).

Due to his resistance and apathy, the clinician focused more on **rapport building and establishing reciprocal conversations and interactions** with Cody to acclimate him to a collaborative therapeutic environment. The clinician took note of Cody's unique interests in video games, drawing, and Greek mythology and started each session with a short rapport-building activity that incorporated these interests, such as illustrating his feelings instead of talking about them or doing a mindful breathing exercise with a calm video game tune in the background. This also allowed for a brief **"bidirectional instruction"** activity in which Cody could teach the clinician about an interesting fact, followed by the clinician's introduction of a relevant therapy concept (i.e., psychoeducation). Cody also voiced a preference for a **set structure and written agenda** so that he knew what to expect. Thereafter, the clinician prepared an agenda for each session displayed on a whiteboard and offered Cody the opportunity to modify or add to the agenda at the beginning of each session, which was helpful for acute, time-sensitive issues (e.g., arguments with friends or teachers, recent disappointments).

When the clinician introduced the cognitive behavioral model, Cody demonstrated conceptual understanding of the relationships between thoughts, feelings, and behaviors. He was able to identify cognitive distortions for hypothetical thoughts but was unable to generate evidence that might contradict the accuracy of his *own* thoughts; even when the therapist ultimately suggested parallels between his own thoughts and specific cognitive distortions, he could not or would not engage with the similarities. Because of his strong belief in his negative thoughts, he was resistant to the possibility of changing his emotional experience by changing his thoughts. In response, the clinician focused on **reappraising negative thoughts with behavioral experiments** and using the principles of **behavioral activation** for mood improvement. Cody was receptive to "thinking like a scientist" when hypothesizing about and testing his rigid beliefs in real-world contexts. During periods of anhedonia, he employed a "just do it" mantra to engage in activities for mastery and/or pleasure, which led to mood improvement.

After this initial improvement in mood, Cody shared that he felt very lonely, ugly, and misunderstood in social settings. Cody interpreted **high levels of loneliness** as others' fault for "not understanding him." In session, the clinician observed that he had difficulty with perspective taking and had irrational expectations of others. Specifically, Cody often became argumentative when people used imprecise language or made ambiguous requests. Thus, the clinician incorporated **naturalistic social skills training** in subsequent sessions to improve interpersonal effectiveness. For example, the clinician used an in-the-moment conversational style to practice social skills instead of explicit social skills training to maintain rapport. Cody and the clinician developed a list of "turn-ons" (i.e., prosocial behaviors such as listening to others before interrupting, maintaining an easy manner and vocal tone) and "turn-offs" (i.e., behaviors to minimize, such as talking over others, arguing about minor technicalities, disengaged body language) that he was able to practice during the week. For example, he used an interpersonal effectiveness strategy for anger management that he and the clinician dubbed "gently avoid"; Cody and his mother reported that this significantly decreased arguments with his family. Cody was also encouraged to use diaphragmatic breathing during anger outbursts, which was practiced in session when Cody became frustrated. After six sessions, Cody became more acclimated to the therapy environment. At this point, the clinician also incorporated one of his special interests, drawing, into therapy by assigning an autobiographical drawing activity where Cody was asked to illustrate his self-concept. He illustrated many facets of himself, including his hobbies, unique strengths, and personal experiences. The goals were to help him understand his experience with depression as just one of his many attributes and to increase his ability to think flexibly about his thoughts and feelings in accordance with the cognitive behavioral model. After 10 weekly therapy sessions, Cody's responses on the CDI yielded a score of 12, indicating a mild level of depressive symptoms. Therapy is ongoing, and proximal goals include revisiting the CBT model to focus on reappraisal of thoughts now that Cody is acclimated to the therapeutic process and has experienced significant improvement in mood.

Case Example 2: A 22-Year-Old Woman with ASD and MDD

Background. "Jane" was a 22-year-old Caucasian female who recently graduated from college with an engineering degree. Jane was diagnosed with ASD in middle school by a trained clinician; however, she believed the diagnosis to be invalid. Jane reported that her depressive symptoms worsened during college. Jane's identified stressors during this period included the heavy workload and minimal support from peers and professors. After graduation, Jane applied to many jobs without success. Jane moved back in with her family after having difficulty transitioning to independent living and began therapy at the request of her parents. Her mother's goals for Jane in therapy were to improve mood, develop effective social skills, and increase competence in activities of daily living (e.g., hygiene, time management, job search). Jane's goals for therapy were to improve mood and return to independent living.

Strengths and barriers. Jane was bright and hardworking and demonstrated a logical thinking style that allowed her to think analytically about different situations. She demonstrated an ambivalent attitude toward therapy, which was likely affected by negative impressions of previous therapeutic experiences. She acknowledged a high level of depressive symptoms but had poor insight into her affective experience. Jane also lacked awareness of social cues and expectations, for which she saw no benefit in better understanding. In session, her blunt, straightforward communication style often translated as noncompliant or rude. Misconceptions and dismissal of her ASD diagnosis also hindered her ability to be an effective self-advocate as she navigated social and environmental stressors. Jane had a very tense relationship with her mother and was adamant that she did not want her mother to have any involvement in therapy, which hindered the application and rehearsal of skills learned in session outside of the therapy environment.

Problem list. *Depressed mood with poor insight into her emotional experience; loneliness, poor interpersonal skills, lack of social awareness.*

At the beginning of therapy, Jane reported symptoms of depressed mood most of the day, diminished interest in previously pleasurable activities, significant weight gain, insomnia, fatigue, feelings of worthlessness, and irritability. She sat with her body angled away from the clinician with minimal eye contact for the majority of the session. Through tears, Jane filled out the Beck Depression Inventory, 2nd edition (BDI-II; Beck, Steer, & Brown, 1996) and scored a 9 out of 63, indicating minimal depressive symptoms. However, she rated her overall mood as a 2 out of 10, with 10 being the highest. When the clinician pointed out discrepancies between her BDI-II responses, physical appearance (i.e., tears), and subjective mood rating, she responded that she was experiencing a high level of distress from depression but preferred not to use "subjective" instruments to calibrate her experience. She preferred to focus on physical symptoms that could be tracked, including sleep patterns and weight gain. At the beginning of therapy, Jane's attitude toward the clinician appeared transactional (i.e., "It's your job to help me get better. That's why I'm coming here.") and she did not acknowledge her own role in the therapeutic process. She often responded with one- to two-word answers, leading to stilted, awkward rapport. As a result, the clinician prioritized **rapport building throughout the therapeutic process**. To facilitate this goal, the clinician introduced a **"bidirectional instruction"** activity at the beginning of each session. For example, Jane shared a logic puzzle or taught the clinician about her interests, followed by the clinician's explanation of a therapy skill. Bidirectional instruction dramatically improved rapport; the technique allowed the clinician to teach Jane about the cognitive behavioral model (i.e., the relationship between thoughts, feelings, and behaviors). Jane appeared to understand the connections conceptually but did not agree that thoughts could be reappraised or changed. Though she had an extensive vocabulary, her limited emotion vocabulary hindered her ability to talk about her emotional experience. In contrast, Jane more readily accepted and applied principles of **behavioral activation** into her daily life for mood improvement. She appeared to appreciate using more practical and concrete ways to improve mood. With the clinician, she identified adaptive (e.g., exercise, sleep hygiene, picking up a hobby) and maladaptive (e.g., napping throughout the day, isolating herself) behaviors and used a **mood/activities tracker** to record the relationship between healthy behaviors and mood. Jane demonstrated participation in therapy by creating a personal journal that included data on physical activity, heart rate, sleep cycle, coffee intake, money spending, and her own watercolor artwork (i.e., new hobby). After 4 weeks of using behavioral activation, she reported significant mood improvement, which was congruent with her more pleasant demeanor and engagement in session. She also became amenable to rating mood using a "**mood thermometer**" (i.e., another tracking tool) where she could indicate her relative experience of mood from week to week. This thermometer-like rating scale was used to help her answer other questions with a subjective component ("How did you feel when _____?" or "How willing are you to try _____?") to gauge her willingness to build other skills. In fact, when the clinician encountered moments of impasse in therapy, **motivational interviewing** skills were used to gauge Jane's motivation for change. Specifically, "rolling with the resistance" and encouraging Jane to verbalize her own reasons for or against behavior change facilitated gradual progress toward incremental and adaptive change over time while maintaining rapport.

Jane expressed high levels of loneliness and frustration that she was still living at home. She kept in touch with friends via text but had minimal in-person contact with others. With the clinician, Jane often exhibited poor interpersonal skills that likely hindered her ability to foster friendships outside of therapy. Due to Jane's lack of social insight, the clinician intentionally identified times when Jane's responses, facial expressions, or body language indicated irritability, frustration, or rudeness, though it was likely not her intent. By pointing out moment-to-moment observations of verbal and nonverbal aspects of social communication, Jane became more willing to learn ways to establish social connection. Instead of framing her social functioning as "social difficulties" or a "lack of social skills," it was important to understand her unique and valid social experience and brainstorm practical ways to engage with others on a deeper level. **Role-play and in-session practice** were used to provide a nonthreatening setting to practice social connection. After 16 sessions, Jane reported overall improvement in mood (8 out of 10; she refused to fill out a subjective inventory). After finding a job opportunity in another city, Jane transitioned out of therapy with the clinician but was encouraged to seek and continue therapy with another provider.

Summary Insights for Treating Co-Occurring Depression in People With ASD

These two case reports yield helpful insights into depression treatment for individuals with ASD. Consistent with features of ASD, individuals with co-occurring depression may exhibit a fixed, rigid view of their depression diagnosis. Feelings of hopelessness that are common in depression may be more pronounced in individuals with ASD, who tend to have more difficulty thinking flexibly about their subjective experience. Clients may also identify more readily with the physical symptoms of depression (e.g., fatigue, changes in appetite) rather than their emotional experience. In both cases presented here, the clients expressed a limited understanding of the collaborative nature of the therapeutic environment. There was a strong assumption that attendance and time spent with the clinician would lead to symptom improvement without their own active participation in therapy. This contributed to a unidirectional and awkward rapport. As a result, rapport building was an essential and primary focus throughout the therapy process, which included understanding the unique affinities and proclivities of the patient and actively incorporating these into therapy. One way to achieve this goal was using a bidirectional instruction activity at the beginning of the sessions, which allowed the client to take the lead and teach. Use of a whiteboard, upon which the patient was encouraged to draw, map out, or outline his or her thought content, also facilitated a collaborative and less threatening therapy environment, as the focus of therapy was not always directed *at* the patient. Operating within this "comfort zone" also allowed clients to become more receptive to psychoeducation about the therapeutic process and/or become more willingly engaged in the therapy.

Both clients were highly verbal and intellectually gifted. Thus, they saw the clinician as an expert and prioritized her ability to teach them ways to improve mood; if they felt that the clinician was not effective in this goal, they were likely to lose interest or become dismissive. Though both patients conceptually understood the cognitive behavioral model, they had difficulty applying CBT concepts to their own thoughts, feelings, and behaviors. Both patients were resistant to using cognitive reappraisal and regarded their thoughts as immutable even after psychoeducation and supported practice applying the cognitive model. As a result, implementing behavioral experiments and principles of behavioral activation provided a more practical and direct method for improving mood. Initial mood improvement was considered a prerequisite before revisiting the cognitive model, as the clinician could leverage "buy-in" by suggesting that there is a similar pathway from thoughts to feelings and behaviors as there is from behaviors to thoughts and feelings, which the patient already experienced by applying principles of behavioral activation. After initial mood improvement, both patients also expressed a high level of loneliness and lack of insight into social situations. Thus, moment-to-moment coaching and role-play were used to practice and brainstorm the use of adaptive social skills in real-world situations. Importantly, the ability to do this was dependent on the establishment of trust and strong rapport between the patient and clinician. Throughout therapy, the use of creativity and multiple modalities (e.g., written handouts, visual illustration, experiential role-play, video, music) also complemented the ability for the clinician to convey important therapy concepts.

Bipolar Disorder in ASD

According to the DSM-5 (2013), bipolar disorder (BD) is characterized by at least one manic episode followed by a hypomanic episode (i.e., a less severe manic episode) or by a depressive episode, with individuals with BD alternating between these two states. A manic episode is defined as a period of abnormally elevated and energetic behavior that lasts at least 1 week and persists for most of the day, nearly every day. A manic episode may include inflated ideas of grandiosity or self-esteem, decreased need for sleep, talking more than usual, flight of ideas (e.g., a new business venture), being easily distracted, increasingly goal-directed activities (e.g., retiling the kitchen floor overnight), and increasingly risky behaviors (e.g., gambling or unprotected sexual relations). Hypomania is a distinct period of persistently elevated or irritable mood and increased activity or energy, experienced most of every day for at least 4 days, that must include three or more of the same seven symptom criteria marking a manic episode.

Very little has been published estimating the rate of BD in the ASD population. The prevalence rate of BD in typically developing adults is around 4% according to the National Institute of Mental Health (NIMH, 2017). Reported prevalence rates of BD in ASD samples vary widely: Skokauskas and Frodl (2015) report that documentation of this comorbidity ranges from 0% to 56.9% due to inconsistent methodological approaches, with some studies reporting "artificial" co-occurrence due to study design or the diagnostic criteria used to assess ASD and BD. For example, some studies reported high rates of ASD in their BD patient populations but determined ASD caseness using autism screening instruments that are known to be inflated by non-ASD behavioral issues (Hus, Bishop, Gotham, Huerta, & Lord, 2013). Other studies only collected data on psychiatric diagnoses of BD from parent reports, rather than structured diagnostic interviews (Skokauskas & Frodl, 2015). To our knowledge, no population-based studies on BD within ASD samples exist. Prevalence rates are difficult to establish, as no specific psychometric instruments have been developed to assess BD in children or adults with ASD, and research on this topic often relies on very small and selective clinical samples (e.g., Ghaziuddin, 2010).

Most of the research conducted in dual ASD and BD populations has been in children and adolescents (Bryson, Corrigan, Mcdonald, & Holmes, 2008; Giovinazzo et al., 2013; Leyfer et al., 2006; Mazefsky et al., 2012; Mukaddes & Fateh, 2009; Munesue et al., 2008; Pine et al., 2008; Rosenberg, Kaufmann, Law, & Law, 2011; Wozniak et al., 1995). Some have found that the clinical phenomenology of BD in ASD is similar overall to BD in typically developing youth populations (Wozniak et al., 1995). Other studies report that manic episodes in ASD are less likely to present with elation or euphoria, but rather with more irritable, dysphoric mood, often accompanied by aggressive and violent behavior (Frazier, Doyle, Chiu, & Coyle, 2002). Instead of engaging in risky behavior (e.g., overspending or promiscuous sexual behavior), individuals with ASD may appear restless, socially intrusive (e.g., asking unwelcome or overly personal questions), and verbally aggressive when experiencing a manic or hypomanic episode (Skokauskas & Frodl, 2015). See Table 2.2 for a summary of BD symptoms thought to be more common in ASD samples.

Table 2.2. Symptom Presentation of Bipolar Disorder (BD) in Autism Spectrum Disorder (ASD)

BD symptoms proposed as common in ASD
Irritability
Dysphoric mood
Mood lability or cyclicity
Social intrusiveness[a]
Unusual thoughts or delusions
Restlessness
Sleep problems
Increased stereotypies
Increased distractibility
Self-injury
Aggressive behaviors
Strange language patterns[b] and overtalkativeness
Risk-taking behaviors

[a] Characterized by unwelcome questions, overly personal interactions, invading someone's personal space, etc.
[b] Examples of BD-related strange language patterns might include expansive vocabulary to describe grandiose ideas present in manic states or markedly rapid speech, both of which are different than the stereotyped speech commonly observed in people with ASD.

The effects of age, development, gender, and cognitive ability on BD course and presentation within ASD are not yet known, though findings from one study suggest that manic episodes appear at a younger age in people with ASD and BD than in people with BD alone (Joshi et al., 2013). It is challenging to describe the symptomatology of BD symptoms in ASD as the literature is very limited on this topic. A recent study compared 40 children and adolescents ages 6 to 18 with co-occurring ASD and BD to a sex- and age-matched ASD control group without history of mania (Sapmaz, Baykal, & Akbaş, 2018). The researchers found that a great percentage of the children with co-occurring ASD and BP experienced risk-taking behavior (92.5%), reduced sleep (90%), and overtalkativeness (82.5%; Sapmaz et al., 2018; see Table 2.2).

A crucial difference between the two disorders is that bipolar symptoms are episodic and cyclical, whereas ASD behaviors are chronic and persistent. Frazier and colleagues (2002) put forward the idea of diagnosing BD in a person with ASD in the context of cognitive and language decline with "cyclicity" in behaviors and mood problems. In addition, characteristic features of autism, such as social withdrawal and stereotypies, may be exaggerated during manic episodes (Frazier et al., 2002). As with unipolar depression, care must be taken to tease apart symptom overlap in ASD and BD. For example, strange language patterns that may be commonly observed in youth with ASD (e.g., stereotyped speech) should be differentiated from the grandiose ideas present in manic states (Carlson, 2012). Similarly, "unusual thoughts" or ideas necessary for a BD diagnosis must be differentiated from idiosyncratic thoughts or language often present in ASD (Vannucchi et al., 2014). For example, the idea that one will author a book on a scientific topic that has just recently sparked one's interest might represent an unusual thought consistent with BD, whereas referring to rain as "the sky is crying" might be idiosyncratic language more typical of ASD. It is also possible for bipolar symptoms to overshadow ASD symptoms, especially when the bipolar presentation includes aggressive symptoms or intense, sudden changes in mood. A common misdiagnosis for BD is schizophrenia, due to the overlap in delusional symptoms and erratic behavior during manic episodes (Skeppar et al., 2013).

In addition to clinical correlates between ASD and BD, previous work has also examined familial correlates between the two disorders. DeLong and Nohria (1994) found that 14 out of a sample of 20 individuals with ASD had a family history of major affective disorder, and in their families, 14 (11.4%) of 123 relatives had BD. Per these data, family history of BD may be associated with diagnosis of ASD (Rosen, Mazefsky, Vasa, & Lerner, 2018). Of the biological factors potentially shared across ASD and BD, inflammation and maternal infection during pregnancy appear to be the most commonly studied (Skokauskas & Frodl, 2015), with one study finding that exposure to maternal influenza makes the risk of BD four times greater (Parboosing, Bao, Shen, Schaefer, & Brown, 2013).

Multiple medications have been found to be effective for adults with BD in the general population. There are very few randomized controlled trials on the efficacy of these treatments in ASD. In fact, in a review of the literature, Vannucchi and colleagues (2014) note that most clinical trials exclude individuals with atypical behavior patterns and comorbidity with other mental disorders. Still, the authors note that recommended treatment for adults with ASD includes mood stabilizers, in combination with therapy or other drugs. Antipsychotics were recommended as the last resource and used at the lowest effective dose for the shortest period of time (Vannucchi et al., 2014). Unfortunately, the difficulty in differential diagnosis between bipolar and schizophrenia spectrum disorders has important implications for pharmacological treatment.

To summarize, the co-occurrence of BD and ASD is a nascent field of study, and the findings are scarce and sometimes inconsistent. Given that a co-occurring diagnosis of BD and ASD is a severe state of psychopathology, long-term controlled studies in large samples are needed to explore this comorbidity and its potential treatments (Vannucchi et al., 2014). Even though the prevalence of co-occurring ASD and BD varies depending on study design and assessment instruments used, this comorbidity appears to be higher in people with ASD than in the general population (Skokauskas & Frodl, 2015). Accurate diagnosis of BD in people with ASD is necessary to help determine more effective treatments and reduce hospitalization rates due to incorrect differential diagnosis or ineffective implementation of pharmacological treatment. Additionally, a better understanding of the presentation of this comorbidity would help the individual's support network recognize the need for interventions beyond ASD alone and coordinate care and decisions regarding social and psychological treatments (Vannucchi et al., 2014).

Summary and Future Directions

Based on the current literature, significantly depressed mood is common in ASD and associated with several negative outcomes, many of which extend beyond the individual to the surrounding support system, as well as throughout the lifespan. As noted herein, it may be more difficult to recognize or assess depression in people with ASD because of difficulties with insight and recognition of and/or communication about emotional states. Further, it may be uniquely challenging for others to recognize mood symptoms in those people with ASD who have limited language and intellectual disability, although the literature we have reviewed here indicates that depressed mood does indeed affect these subpopulations within the autism spectrum. The lack of validated psychometric instruments to assess for mood disorders in ASD contributes to the challenge of diagnosing this comorbidity, though we note on page 4 that efforts are being made to address this gap in the clinical and research fields. It is important to focus research initiatives on developing not only new or revised measures but also overall better assessment practices for depression, bipolar disorder, and related mood disorders in individuals with ASD across the ranges of age and verbal ability. These methods could be used in larger population-based studies to determine more accurate prevalence estimates of mood disorders in ASD and to provide more information about their presentation in the ASD population (Chandrasekhar, 2015).

Similarly, we have a grave need to test standard and adapted protocols for treating depressed mood in the ASD population. Some traditional and novel psychotherapy approaches, including CBT, behavioral activation, and mindfulness, show promise for successful adaptation in treating depression in the ASD community. Behaviorally based treatments may be preferable in less cognitively or verbally able ASD individuals, or in those for whom cognitive rigidity makes generalization of the cognitive model particularly difficult. Examining the risk factors and contributing mechanisms associated with depression in individuals with ASD should be a priority in future research to facilitate the identification of specific targets for intervention to increase the effectiveness of treatments for mood problems in ASD.

Overall, research on mood disorders in ASD is growing rapidly, thanks in part to acknowledgment by stakeholders and funding agencies of its importance and urgency. As this field grows, family members, affected individuals, educators, physicians, and other health care team members and supporters must work together to ensure that individuals with ASD and suspected co-occurring mood disorders receive the most appropriate assessment and treatment currently available. We recognize with regret that evidence-based treatment to address mood problems in the ASD population is not available in many areas. We are encouraged, however, that many people are working to change this. Interim proposals for diagnostic assessment plans (Frazier et al., 2002; Magnuson & Constantino, 2011) and adaptations of evidence-based treatments (Kerns et al., 2016; White et al., 2018) that have been efficacious in the general population are a step in the right direction for identifying and helping individuals with ASD and co-occurring mood disorders.

References

Allen, N. B., & Badcock, P. B. T. (2003). The social risk hypothesis of depressed mood: Evolutionary, psychosocial, and neurobiological perspectives. *Psychological Bulletin, 129*(6), 887–913. https://doi.org/10.1037/0033-2909.129.6.887

American Psychiatric Association. (2000). *Diagnostic and statistical manual of mental disorders* (4th ed., text revision, DSM-IV-TR, Vol. 1). Arlington, VA: American Psychiatric Association. https://doi.org/10.1176/appi.books.9780890423349

American Psychiatric Association. (2013). Diagnostic and statistical manual of mental disorders (5th ed.; DSM-5). Arlington, VA: Author. Retrieved from https://search.library.wisc.edu/catalog/9910187853902121

Autism and Developmental Disorders Inpatient Research Collaborative (ADDIRC), Horowitz, L. M., Thurm, A., Farmer, C., Mazefsky, C., Lanzillo, E.,... Siegel, M. (2017). Talking about death or suicide: Prevalence and clinical correlates in youth with autism spectrum disorder in the psychiatric inpatient setting. Journal of Autism and Developmental Disorders, 48(11), 3702–3710.https://doi.org/10.1007/s10803-017-3180-7

Bargh, J. A., & Tota, M. E. (1988). Context-dependent automatic processing in depression: Accessibility of negative constructs with regard to self but not others. *Journal of Personality and Social Psychology, 54*(6), 925–939.

Beck, A. T., & Rush, A. J. (Eds.). (1979). *Cognitive therapy of depression.* New York, NY: Guilford Press.

Beck, A. T., Steer, R., & Brown, G. (1996). *Manual for the Beck Depression Inventory-II.* San Antonio, TX: Psychological Corporation.

Berthoz, S., & Hill, E. L. (2005). The validity of using self-reports to assess emotion regulation abilities in adults with autism spectrum disorder. *European Psychiatry: The Journal of the Association of European Psychiatrists, 20*(3), 291–298. https://doi.org/10.1016/j.eurpsy.2004.06.013

Bird, G., & Cook, R. (2013). Mixed emotions: The contribution of alexithymia to the emotional symptoms of autism. *Translational Psychiatry, 3*(7), e285. https://doi.org/10.1038/tp.2013.61

Bolton, P. F., Pickles, A., Murphy, M., & Rutter, M. (1998). Autism, affective and other psychiatric disorders: Patterns of familial aggregation. *Psychological Medicine, 28*(2), 385–395.

Brereton, A. V., Tonge, B. J., & Einfeld, S. L. (2006). Psychopathology in children and adolescents with autism compared to young people with intellectual disability. *Journal of Autism and Developmental Disorders, 36*(7), 863–870. https://doi.org/10.1007/s10803-006-0125-y

Brody, D. J., Pratt, L. A., & Hughes, J. P. (2018). Prevalence of depression among adults aged 20 and over: United States, 2013–2016. *NCHS Data Brief,* (303), 1–8.

Bryson, S. A., Corrigan, S. K., Mcdonald, T. P., & Holmes, C. (2008). Characteristics of children with autism spectrum disorders who received services through community mental health centers. *Autism, 12*(1), 65–82. https://doi.org/10.1177/1362361307085214

Buck, T. R., Viskochil, J., Farley, M., Coon, H., McMahon, W. M., Morgan, J., & Bilder, D. A. (2014). Psychiatric comorbidity and medication use in adults with autism spectrum disorder. *Journal of Autism and Developmental Disorders, 44*(12), 3063–3071. https://doi.org/10.1007/s10803-014-2170-2

Burnette, C. P., Henderson, H. A., Inge, A. P., Zahka, N. E., Schwartz, C. B., & Mundy, P. C. (2011). Anterior EEG asymmetry and the modifier model of autism. *Journal of Autism and Developmental Disorders, 41*(8), 1113–1124. https://doi.org/10.1007/s10803-010-1138-0

Burrows, C. A., Timpano, K. R., & Uddin, L. Q. (2017). Putative brain networks underlying repetitive negative thinking and comorbid internalizing problems in autism. *Clinical Psychological Science, 5*(3), 522–536. https://doi.org/10.1177/2167702616683506

Cachia, R. L., Anderson, A., & Moore, D. W. (2016). Mindfulness, stress and well-being in parents of children with autism spectrum disorder: A systematic review. *Journal of Child and Family Studies, 25*(1), 1–14. https://doi.org/10.1007/s10826-015-0193-8

Cacioppo, J., & Patrick, B. (2008). *Loneliness: Human nature and the need for social connection.* New York, NY: W. W. Norton & Company.

Cadman, T., Eklund, H., Howley, D., Hayward, H., Clarke, H., Findon, J.,... Glaser, K. (2012). Caregiver burden as people with autism spectrum disorder and attention-deficit/hyperactivity disorder transition into adolescence and adulthood in the United Kingdom. *Journal of the American Academy of Child & Adolescent Psychiatry, 51*(9), 879–888. https://doi.org/10.1016/j.jaac.2012.06.017

Cage, E., Di Monaco, J., & Newell, V. (2018). Experiences of autism acceptance and mental health in autistic adults. *Journal of Autism and Developmental Disorders, 48*(2), 473–484. https://doi.org/10.1007/s10803-017-3342-7

Capps, L., Sigman, M., & Yirmiya, N. (1995). Self-competence and emotional understanding in high-functioning children with autism. *Development and Psychopathology, 7*(1), 137. https://doi.org/10.1017/S0954579400006386

Carlson, G. A. (2012). Differential diagnosis of bipolar disorder in children and adolescents. *World Psychiatry, 11*(3), 146–152. https://doi.org/10.1002/j.2051–5545.2012.tb00115.x

Cassidy, S., Bradley, P., Robinson, J., Allison, C., McHugh, M., & Baron-Cohen, S. (2014). Suicidal ideation and suicide plans or attempts in adults with Asperger's syndrome attending a specialist diagnostic clinic: A clinical cohort study. *Lancet Psychiatry, 1*(2), 142–147. https://doi.org/10.1016/S2215-0366(14)70248–2

Chandrasekhar, T., & Sikich, L. (2015). Challenges in the diagnosis and treatment of depression in autism spectrum disorders across the lifespan. *Dialogues in Clinical Neuroscience, 17*(2), 219–227.

Charlot, L., Deutsch, C. K., Albert, A., Hunt, A., Connor, D. F., & McIlvane, W. J. (2008). Mood and anxiety symptoms in psychiatric inpatients with autism spectrum disorder and depression. *Journal of Mental Health Research in Intellectual Disabilities, 1*(4), 238–253. https://doi.org/10.1080/19315860802313947

Codding, R. S., Feinberg, A. B., Dunn, E. K., & Pace, G. M. (2005). Effects of immediate performance feedback on implementation of behavior support plans. *Journal of Applied Behavior Analysis, 38*(2), 205–219. https://doi.org/10.1901/jaba.2005.98–04

Crane, L., Goddard, L., & Pring, L. (2013). Autobiographical memory in adults with autism spectrum disorder: The role of depressed mood, rumination, working memory and theory of mind. *Autism, 17*(2), 205–219. https://doi.org/10.1177/1362361311418690

Cross-Disorder Group of the Psychiatric Genomics Consortium. (2013). Identification of risk loci with shared effects on five major psychiatric disorders: A genome-wide analysis. *Lancet, 381*(9875), 1371–1379. https://doi.org/10.1016/S0140-6736(12)62129–1

De-la-Iglesia, M., & Olivar, J.-S. (2015). Risk factors for depression in children and adolescents with high functioning autism spectrum disorders. *Scientific World Journal, 2015*, 1–17. https://doi.org/10.1155/2015/127853

DeLong, R., & Nohria, C. (1994). Psychiatric family history and neurological disease in autistic spectrum disorders. *Developmental Medicine and Child Neurology, 36*(5), 441–448.

Dichter, G. S., Damiano, C. A., & Allen, J. A. (2012). Reward circuitry dysfunction in psychiatric and neurodevelopmental disorders and genetic syndromes: Animal models and clinical findings. *Journal of Neurodevelopmental Disorders, 4*(1), 19. https://doi.org/10.1186/1866-1955-4-19

First, M., Williams, J., Karg, R., & Spitzer, R. (2004). *Structured Clinical Interview for DSM-5 Disorders–Research Version (SCID-5-RV)*. American Psychiatric Association, Arlington, VA.

Frazier, J. A., Doyle, R., Chiu, S., & Coyle, J. T. (2002). Treating a child with Asperger's disorder and comorbid bipolar disorder. *American Journal of Psychiatry, 159*(1), 13–21. https://doi.org/10.1176/appi.ajp.159.1.13

Frick, L. R., Williams, K., & Pittenger, C. (2013). Microglial dysregulation in psychiatric disease. *Clinical and Developmental Immunology, 2013*, 1–10. https://doi.org/10.1155/2013/608654

Ghaziuddin, M. (2010). Should the DSM V drop Asperger syndrome? *Journal of Autism and Developmental Disorders, 40*(9), 1146–1148. https://doi.org/10.1007/s10803-010-0969-z

Ghaziuddin, M., Ghaziuddin, N., & Greden, J. (2002). Depression in persons with autism: Implications for research and clinical care. *Journal of Autism and Developmental Disorders, 32*(4), 299–306.

Giovinazzo, S., Marciano, S., Giana, G., Curatolo, P., & Porfirio, M.-C. (2013). Clinical and therapeutic implications of psychiatric comorbidity in high functioning autism/Asperger syndrome: An Italian study. *Open Journal of Psychiatry, 3*(3), 329–334. https://doi.org/10.4236/ojpsych.2013.33034

Gotham, K., Bishop, S. L., Brunwasser, S., & Lord, C. (2014). Rumination and perceived impairment associated with depressive symptoms in a verbal adolescent-adult ASD sample: Depression in ASD. *Autism Research, 7*(3), 381–391. https://doi.org/10.1002/aur.1377

Gotham, K., Brunwasser, S. M., & Lord, C. (2015). Depressive and anxiety symptom trajectories from school age through young adulthood in samples with autism spectrum disorder and developmental delay. *Journal of the American Academy of Child & Adolescent Psychiatry, 54*(5), 369–376.e3. https://doi.org/10.1016/j.jaac.2015.02.005

Gotham, K., Marvin, A. R., Taylor, J. L., Warren, Z., Anderson, C. M., Law, P. A., . . . Lipkin, P. H. (2015). Characterizing the daily life, needs, and priorities of adults with autism spectrum disorder from Interactive Autism Network data. *Autism, 19*(7), 794–804. https://doi.org/10.1177/1362361315583818

Gotham, K., Siegle, G., Han, G., Crist, R., Simon, D., & Bodfish, J. (2018). Pupil response to social-emotional materials is associated with rumination and depressive symptoms in adults with autism spectrum disorder. *PLOS One*, 13(8): e0200340. https://doi.org/10.1371/journal.pone.0200340

Gotham, K., Unruh, K., & Lord, C. (2015). Depression and its measurement in verbal adolescents and adults with autism spectrum disorder. *Autism, 19*(4), 491–504. https://doi.org/10.1177/1362361314536625

Gray, K., Keating, C., Taffe, J., Brereton, A., Einfeld, S., & Tonge, B. (2012). Trajectory of behavior and emotional problems in autism. *American Journal on Intellectual and Developmental Disabilities, 117*(2), 121–133. https://doi.org/10.1352/1944-7588-117-2.121

Greenlee, J. L., Mosley, A. S., Shui, A. M., Veenstra-VanderWeele, J., & Gotham, K. O. (2016). Medical and behavioral correlates of depression history in children and adolescents with autism spectrum disorder. *Pediatrics, 137*(Supplement), S105–S114. https://doi.org/10.1542/peds.2015-2851I

Han, G. T., Tomarken, A. J., & Gotham, K. O. (2018). Social and non-social reward moderate the relation between autism symptoms and loneliness in adults with ASD, depression, and controls. Manuscript submitted for publication.

Hankin, B. L., Abramson, L. Y., Moffitt, T. E., Silva, P. A., McGee, R., & Angell, K. E. (1998). Development of depression from preadolescence to young adulthood: Emerging gender differences in a 10-year longitudinal study. *Journal of Abnormal Psychology, 107*(1), 128–140. https://doi.org/10.1037/0021-843X.107.1.128

Havdahl, K. A., Hus Bal, V., Huerta, M., Pickles, A., Øyen, A.-S., Stoltenberg, C., . . . Bishop, S. L. (2016). Multidimensional influences on autism symptom measures: Implications for use in etiological research. *Journal of the American Academy of Child & Adolescent Psychiatry, 55*(12), 1054–1063.e3. https://doi.org/10.1016/j.jaac.2016.09.490

Hayes, S. C. (2004). Acceptance and commitment therapy, relational frame theory, and the third wave of behavioral and cognitive therapies. *Behavior Therapy, 35*(4), 639–665. https://doi.org/10.1016/S0005-7894(04)80013–3

Hedley, D., Uljarević, M., Foley, K.-R., Richdale, A., & Trollor, J. (2018). Risk and protective factors underlying depression and suicidal ideation in autism spectrum disorder. *Depression and Anxiety, 35*(7), 648–657. https://doi.org/10.1002/da.22759

Henninger, N. A., & Taylor, J. L. (2013). Outcomes in adults with autism spectrum disorders: A historical perspective. *Autism, 17*(1), 103–116. https://doi.org/10.1177/1362361312441266

Hill, E., Berthoz, S., & Frith, U. (2004). Brief report: Cognitive processing of own emotions in individuals with autistic spectrum disorder and in their relatives. *Journal of Autism and Developmental Disorders, 34*(2), 229–235.

Hoekstra, R. A., Happé, F., Baron-Cohen, S., & Ronald, A. (2009). Association between extreme autistic traits and intellectual disability: Insights from a general population twin study. *British Journal of Psychiatry, 195*(6), 531–536. https://doi.org/10.1192/bjp.bp.108.060889

Hofvander, B., Delorme, R., Chaste, P., Nydén, A., Wentz, E., Ståhlberg, O., . . . Leboyer, M. (2009). Psychiatric and psychosocial problems in adults with normal-intelligence autism spectrum disorders. *BMC Psychiatry, 9*(1), 35. https://doi.org/10.1186/1471-244X-9–35

Hollocks, M. J., Jones, C. R. G., Pickles, A., Baird, G., Happé, F., Charman, T., & Simonoff, E. (2014). The association between social cognition and executive functioning and symptoms of anxiety and depression in adolescents with autism spectrum disorders: Neurocognitive ability, anxiety, and depression. *Autism Research, 7*(2), 216–228. https://doi.org/10.1002/aur.1361

Hudson, C. C., Hall, L., & Harkness, K. L. (2018). Prevalence of depressive disorders in individuals with autism spectrum disorder: A meta-analysis. *Journal of Abnormal Child Psychology*, 47, 165–175. https://doi.org/10.1007/s10802-018-0402-1

Hurtig, T., Kuusikko, S., Mattila, M.-L., Haapsamo, H., Ebeling, H., Jussila, K., . . . Moilanen, I. (2009). Multi-informant reports of psychiatric symptoms among high-functioning adolescents with Asperger syndrome or autism. *Autism, 13*(6), 583–598. https://doi.org/10.1177/1362361309335719

Hus, V., Bishop, S., Gotham, K., Huerta, M., & Lord, C. (2013). Factors influencing scores on the social responsiveness scale: Factors influencing the SRS. *Journal of Child Psychology and Psychiatry, 54*(2), 216–224. https://doi.org/10.1111/j.1469–7610.2012.02589.x

Icke, J. (2018, February 16). Better tools needed to diagnose depression in people with autism—The University of Nottingham. Retrieved July 25, 2018, from https://www.nottingham.ac.uk/news/pressreleases/2018/february/better-tools-needed-to-diagnose-depression-in-people-with-autism.aspx

Jacobson, N. S., Martell, C. R., & Dimidjian, S. (2006). Behavioral activation treatment for depression: Returning to contextual roots. *Clinical Psychology: Science and Practice, 8*(3), 255–270. https://doi.org/10.1093/clipsy.8.3.255

Jain, S., Shapiro, S. L., Swanick, S., Roesch, S. C., Mills, P. J., Bell, I., & Schwartz, G. E. R. (2007). A randomized controlled trial of mindfulness meditation versus relaxation training: Effects on distress, positive states of mind, rumination, and distraction. *Annals of Behavioral Medicine: A Publication of the Society of Behavioral Medicine, 33*(1), 11–21. https://doi.org/10.1207/s15324796abm3301_2

Joshi, G., Wozniak, J., Petty, C., Martelon, M. K., Fried, R., Bolfek, A., . . . Biederman, J. (2013). Psychiatric comorbidity and functioning in a clinically referred population of adults with autism spectrum disorders: A comparative study. *Journal of Autism and Developmental Disorders, 43*(6), 1314–1325. https://doi.org/10.1007/s10803-012-1679-5

Just, M. A. (2004). Cortical activation and synchronization during sentence comprehension in high-functioning autism: Evidence of underconnectivity. *Brain, 127*(8), 1811–1821. https://doi.org/10.1093/brain/awh199

Kabat-Zinn, J. (2003). Mindfulness-based interventions in context: Past, present, and future. *Clinical Psychology: Science and Practice, 10*, 144–156. https://doi.org/10.1093/clipsy.bpg016

Keenan, E. G., Gotham, K., & Lerner, M. D. (2017). Hooked on a feeling: Repetitive cognition and internalizing symptomatology in relation to autism spectrum symptomatology. *Autism, 22*(7), 814–824. https://doi.org/10.1177/1362361317709603

Kerns, C. M., Roux, A. M., Connell, J. E., & Shattuck, P. T. (2016). Adapting cognitive behavioral techniques to address anxiety and depression in cognitively able emerging adults on the autism spectrum. *Cognitive and Behavioral Practice, 23*(3), 329–340. https://doi.org/10.1016/j.cbpra.2016.06.002

Kessler, R. C., Aguilar-Gaxiola, S., Alonso, J., Chatterji, S., Lee, S., Ormel, J., . . . Wang, P. S. (2009). The global burden of mental disorders: An update from the WHO World Mental Health (WMH) surveys. *Epidemiologia E Psichiatria Sociale, 18*(1), 23–33.

Kessler, R. C., Berglund, P., Demler, O., Jin, R., Koretz, D., Merikangas, K. R., . . . Wang, P. S. (2003). The epidemiology of major depressive disorder: Results from the National Comorbidity Survey Replication (NCS-R). *JAMA, 289*(23), 3095. https://doi.org/10.1001/jama.289.23.3095

Kovacs, M. (1985). The Children's Depression Inventory (CDI). *Psychopharmacology Bulletin, 21*(4), 995–998.

Lainhart, J. E., & Folstein, S. E. (1994). Affective disorders in people with autism: A review of published cases. *Journal of Autism and Developmental Disorders, 24*(5), 587–601.

Lever, A. G., & Geurts, H. M. (2016). Psychiatric co-occurring symptoms and disorders in young, middle-aged, and older adults with autism spectrum disorder. *Journal of Autism and Developmental Disorders, 46*(6), 1916–1930. https://doi.org/10.1007/s10803-016-2722-8

Leyfer, O. T., Folstein, S. E., Bacalman, S., Davis, N. O., Dinh, E., Morgan, J., . . . Lainhart, J. E. (2006). Comorbid psychiatric disorders in children with autism: Interview development and rates of disorders. *Journal of Autism and Developmental Disorders, 36*(7), 849–861. https://doi.org/10.1007/s10803-006-0123-0

Lombardo, M. V., Barnes, J. L., Wheelwright, S. J., & Baron-Cohen, S. (2007). Self-referential cognition and empathy in autism. *PLoS ONE, 2*(9), e883. https://doi.org/10.1371/journal.pone.0000883

Lounds Taylor, J., Adams, R. E., & Bishop, S. L. (2017). Social participation and its relation to internalizing symptoms among youth with autism spectrum disorder as they transition from high school. *Autism Research: Official Journal of the International Society for Autism Research, 10*(4), 663–672. https://doi.org/10.1002/aur.1709

Lugnegård, T., Hallerbäck, M. U., & Gillberg, C. (2011). Psychiatric comorbidity in young adults with a clinical diagnosis of Asperger syndrome. *Research in Developmental Disabilities, 32*(5), 1910–1917. https://doi.org/10.1016/j.ridd.2011.03.025

Magnuson, K. M., & Constantino, J. N. (2011). Characterization of depression in children with autism spectrum disorders. *Journal of Developmental & Behavioral Pediatrics, 32*(4), 332–340. https://doi.org/10.1097/DBP.0b013e318213f56c

Mayes, S. D., Calhoun, S. L., Murray, M. J., Ahuja, M., & Smith, L. A. (2011). Anxiety, depression, and irritability in children with autism relative to other neuropsychiatric disorders and typical development. *Research in Autism Spectrum Disorders, 5*(1), 474–485. https://doi.org/10.1016/j.rasd.2010.06.012

Mayes, S. D., Gorman, A. A., Hillwig-Garcia, J., & Syed, E. (2013). Suicide ideation and attempts in children with autism. *Research in Autism Spectrum Disorders, 7*(1), 109–119. https://doi.org/10.1016/j.rasd.2012.07.009

Mazefsky, C. A., Kao, J., & Oswald, D. P. (2011). Preliminary evidence suggesting caution in the use of psychiatric self-report measures with adolescents with high-functioning autism spectrum disorders. *Research in Autism Spectrum Disorders, 5*(1), 164–174. https://doi.org/10.1016/j.rasd.2010.03.006

Mazefsky, C. A., Oswald, D. P., Day, T. N., Eack, S. M., Minshew, N. J., & Lainhart, J. E. (2012). ASD, a psychiatric disorder, or both? Psychiatric diagnoses in adolescents with high-functioning ASD. *Journal of Clinical Child and Adolescent Psychology: The Official Journal for the Society of Clinical Child and Adolescent Psychology, American Psychological Association, Division 53, 41*(4), 516–523. https://doi.org/10.1080/15374416.2012.686102

Mazurek, M. O. (2014). Loneliness, friendship, and well-being in adults with autism spectrum disorders. *Autism, 18*(3), 223–232. https://doi.org/10.1177/1362361312474121

Mazurek, M. O., & Kanne, S. M. (2010). Friendship and internalizing symptoms among children and adolescents with ASD. *Journal of Autism and Developmental Disorders, 40*(12), 1512–1520. https://doi.org/10.1007/s10803-010-1014-y

McGillivray, J. A., & Evert, H. T. (2014). Group cognitive behavioural therapy program shows potential in reducing symptoms of depression and stress among young people with ASD. *Journal of Autism and Developmental Disorders, 44*(8), 2041–2051. https://doi.org/10.1007/s10803-014-2087-9

Merikangas, K. R., He, J., Burstein, M., Swanson, S. A., Avenevoli, S., Cui, L., . . . Swendsen, J. (2010). Lifetime prevalence of mental disorders in U.S. adolescents: Results from the National Comorbidity Survey Replication–Adolescent Supplement (NCS-A). *Journal of the American Academy of Child & Adolescent Psychiatry, 49*(10), 980–989. https://doi.org/10.1016/j.jaac.2010.05.017

Meyer, J. A., Mundy, P. C., Van Hecke, A. V., & Durocher, J. S. (2006). Social attribution processes and comorbid psychiatric symptoms in children with Asperger syndrome. *Autism: The International Journal of Research and Practice, 10*(4), 383–402. https://doi.org/10.1177/1362361306064435

Midouhas, E., Yogaratnam, A., Flouri, E., & Charman, T. (2013). Psychopathology trajectories of children with autism spectrum disorder: The role of family poverty and parenting. *Journal of the American Academy of Child & Adolescent Psychiatry, 52*(10), 1057–1065.e1. https://doi.org/10.1016/j.jaac.2013.07.011

Mukaddes, N. M., & Fateh, R. (2009). High rates of psychiatric co-morbidity in individuals with Asperger's disorder. *World Journal of Biological Psychiatry, 11*(2 Pt 2), 486–492. https://doi.org/10.1080/15622970902789130

Muller, C. L., Anacker, A. M. J., & Veenstra-VanderWeele, J. (2016). The serotonin system in autism spectrum disorder: From biomarker to animal models. *Neuroscience, 321*, 24–41. https://doi.org/10.1016/j.neuroscience.2015.11.010

Munesue, T., Ono, Y., Mutoh, K., Shimoda, K., Nakatani, H., & Kikuchi, M. (2008). High prevalence of bipolar disorder comorbidity in adolescents and young adults with high-functioning autism spectrum disorder: A preliminary study of 44 outpatients. *Journal of Affective Disorders, 111*(2–3), 170–175. https://doi.org/10.1016/j.jad.2008.02.015

Nejad, A. B., Fossati, P., & Lemogne, C. (2013). Self-referential processing, rumination, and cortical midline structures in major depression. *Frontiers in Human Neuroscience, 7*, 666. https://doi.org/10.3389/fnhum.2013.00666

NIMH. (2017). Bipolar disorder. Retrieved July 25, 2018, from https://www.nimh.nih.gov/health/statistics/bipolar-disorder.shtml#part_155458

Nolen-Hoeksema, S. (2000). The role of rumination in depressive disorders and mixed anxiety/depressive symptoms. *Journal of Abnormal Psychology, 109*(3), 504–511.

Nolen-Hoeksema, S., Wisco, B. E., & Lyubomirsky, S. (2008). Rethinking rumination. *Perspectives on Psychological Science, 3*(5), 400–424. https://doi.org/10.1111/j.1745-6924.2008.00088.x

Parboosing, R., Bao, Y., Shen, L., Schaefer, C. A., & Brown, A. S. (2013). Gestational influenza and bipolar disorder in adult offspring. *JAMA Psychiatry, 70*(7), 677. https://doi.org/10.1001/jamapsychiatry.2013.896

Patel, S., Day, T. N., Jones, N., & Mazefsky, C. A. (2017). Association between anger rumination and autism symptom severity, depression symptoms, aggression, and general dysregulation in adolescents with autism spectrum disorder. *Autism, 21*(2), 181–189. https://doi.org/10.1177/1362361316633566

Pearson, D. A., Loveland, K. A., Lachar, D., Lane, D. M., Reddoch, S. L., Mansour, R., & Cleveland, L. A. (2006). A comparison of behavioral and emotional functioning in children and adolescents with autistic disorder and PDD-NOS. *Child Neuropsychology, 12*(4–5), 321–333. https://doi.org/10.1080/09297040600646847

Pine, D. S., Guyer, A. E., Goldwin, M., Towbin, K. A., & Leibenluft, E. (2008). Autism Spectrum Disorder Scale scores in pediatric mood and anxiety disorders. *Journal of the American Academy of Child & Adolescent Psychiatry, 47*(6), 652–661. https://doi.org/10.1097/CHI.0b013e31816bffa5

Pouw, L. B. C., Rieffe, C., Stockmann, L., & Gadow, K. D. (2013). The link between emotion regulation, social functioning, and depression in boys with ASD. *Research in Autism Spectrum Disorders, 7*(4), 549–556. https://doi.org/10.1016/j.rasd.2013.01.002

Rai, D., Heuvelman, H., Dalman, C., Culpin, I., Lundberg, M., Carpenter, P., & Magnusson, C. (2018). Association between autism spectrum disorders with or without intellectual disability and depression in young adulthood. *JAMA Network Open, 1*(4), e181465–e181465. https://doi.org/10.1001/jamanetworkopen.2018.1465

Robinson, M. S., & Alloy, L. B. (2003). Negative cognitive styles and stress-reactive rumination interact to predict depression: a prospective study. *Cognitive Therapy and Research, 27*(3), 275–291.

Rosen, T. E., Mazefsky, C. A., Vasa, R. A., & Lerner, M. D. (2018). Co-occurring psychiatric conditions in autism spectrum disorder. *International Review of Psychiatry, 30*(1), 40–61. https://doi.org/10.1080/09540261.2018.1450229

Rosenberg, R. E., Kaufmann, W. E., Law, J. K., & Law, P. A. (2011). Parent report of community psychiatric comorbid diagnoses in autism spectrum disorders. *Autism Research and Treatment, 2011*, 1–10. https://doi.org/10.1155/2011/405849

Rutter, M. (2002). The interplay of nature, nurture, and developmental influences: The challenge ahead for mental health. *Archives of General Psychiatry, 59*(11), 996–1000.

Sapmaz, D., Baykal, S., & Akbaş, S. (2018). The clinical features of comorbid pediatric bipolar disorder in children with autism spectrum disorder. *Journal of Autism and Developmental Disorders, 48*(8), 2800–2808. https://doi.org/10.1007/s10803-018-3541-x

Segers, M., & Rawana, J. (2014). What do we know about suicidality in autism spectrum disorders? A systematic review: Systematic review of suicidality in ASD. *Autism Research, 7*(4), 507–521. https://doi.org/10.1002/aur.1375

Shattuck, P. T., Narendorf, S. C., Cooper, B., Sterzing, P. R., Wagner, M., & Taylor, J. L. (2012). Postsecondary education and employment among youth with an autism spectrum disorder. *Pediatrics, 129*(6), 1042–1049. https://doi.org/10.1542/peds.2011–2864

Shtayermman, O. (2007). Peer victimization in adolescents and young adults diagnosed with Asperger's syndrome: A link to depressive symptomatology, anxiety symptomatology and suicidal ideation. *Issues in Comprehensive Pediatric Nursing, 30*(3), 87–107. https://doi.org/10.1080/01460860701525089

Simonoff, E., Jones, C. R. G., Baird, G., Pickles, A., Happé, F., & Charman, T. (2013). The persistence and stability of psychiatric problems in adolescents with autism spectrum disorders: Stability of psychiatric symptoms in autism spectrum disorders. *Journal of Child Psychology and Psychiatry, 54*(2), 186–194. https://doi.org/10.1111/j.1469–7610.2012.02606.x

Simonoff, E., Pickles, A., Charman, T., Chandler, S., Loucas, T., & Baird, G. (2008). Psychiatric disorders in children with autism spectrum disorders: Prevalence, comorbidity, and associated factors in a population-derived sample. *Journal of the American Academy of Child & Adolescent Psychiatry, 47*(8), 921–929. https://doi.org/10.1097/CHI.0b013e318179964f

Sizoo, B. B., & Kuiper, E. (2017). Cognitive behavioural therapy and mindfulness based stress reduction may be equally effective in reducing anxiety and depression in adults with autism spectrum disorders. *Research in Developmental Disabilities, 64*, 47–55. https://doi.org/10.1016/j.ridd.2017.03.004

Skeppar, P., Thoor, R., Agreen, S., Isakson, A.-C., Skeppar, I., Persson, B., & Fitzgerald, M. (2013). Neuro-developmental disorders with co-morbid affective disorders sometimes produce psychiatric conditions traditionally diagnosed as "schizophrenia." *Clinical Neuropsychiatry, 10*, 123–133.

Skokauskas, N., & Frodl, T. (2015). Overlap between autism spectrum disorder and bipolar affective disorder. *Psychopathology, 48*(4), 209–216. https://doi.org/10.1159/000435787

Spek, A. A., van Ham, N. C., & Nyklíček, I. (2013). Mindfulness-based therapy in adults with an autism spectrum disorder: A randomized controlled trial. *Research in Developmental Disabilities, 34*(1), 246–253. https://doi.org/10.1016/j.ridd.2012.08.009

Sterling, L., Dawson, G., Estes, A., & Greenson, J. (2008). Characteristics associated with presence of depressive symptoms in adults with autism spectrum disorder. *Journal of Autism and Developmental Disorders, 38*(6), 1011–1018. https://doi.org/10.1007/s10803-007-0477-y

Stewart, M. E., Barnard, L., Pearson, J., Hasan, R., & O'Brien, G. (2006). Presentation of depression in autism and Asperger syndrome: A review. *Autism, 10*(1), 103–116. https://doi.org/10.1177/1362361306062013

Storch, E. A., Lewin, A. B., Collier, A. B., Arnold, E., De Nadai, A. S., Dane, B. F., . . . Murphy, T. K. (2015). A randomized controlled trial of cognitive-behavioral therapy versus treatment as usual for adolescents with autism spectrum disorders and comorbid anxiety: CBT for adolescents with ASD and anxiety. *Depression and Anxiety, 32*(3), 174–181. https://doi.org/10.1002/da.22332

Strang, J. F., Kenworthy, L., Daniolos, P., Case, L., Wills, M. C., Martin, A., & Wallace, G. L. (2012). Depression and anxiety symptoms in children and adolescents with autism spectrum disorders without intellectual disability. *Research in Autism Spectrum Disorders, 6*(1), 406–412. https://doi.org/10.1016/j.rasd.2011.06.015

Tantam, D. (2000). Psychological disorder in adolescents and adults with Asperger syndrome. *Autism, 4*(1), 47–62. https://doi.org/10.1177/1362361300004001004

Taylor, J. L., & Seltzer, M. M. (2010). Changes in the autism behavioral phenotype during the transition to adulthood. *Journal of Autism and Developmental Disorders, 40*(12), 1431–1446. https://doi.org/10.1007/s10803-010-1005-z

Taylor, J. L., Smith, L. E., & Mailick, M. R. (2014). Engagement in vocational activities promotes behavioral development for adults with autism spectrum disorders. *Journal of Autism and Developmental Disorders, 44*(6), 1447–1460. https://doi.org/10.1007/s10803-013-2010-9

Turygin, N. C., Matson, J. L., MacMillan, K., & Konst, M. (2013). The relationship between challenging behavior and symptoms of depression in intellectually disabled adults with and without autism spectrum disorders. *Journal of Developmental and Physical Disabilities, 25*(4), 475–484. https://doi.org/10.1007/s10882-012-9321-1

Unruh, K. E., Bodfish, J. W., & Gotham, K. O. (2018). Adults with autism and adults with depression show similar attentional biases to social-affective images. *Journal of Autism and Developmental Disorders*. https://link.springer.com/article/10.1007/s10803-018-3627-5

van Schalkwyk, G. I., Klingensmith, K., & Volkmar, F. R. (2015). Gender identity and autism spectrum disorders. *Yale Journal of Biology and Medicine, 88*(1), 81–83.

Vannucchi, G., Masi, G., Toni, C., Dell'Osso, L., Erfurth, A., & Perugi, G. (2014). Bipolar disorder in adults with Asperger's syndrome: A systematic review. *Journal of Affective Disorders, 168*, 151–160. https://doi.org/10.1016/j.jad.2014.06.042

Vickerstaff, S., Heriot, S., Wong, M., Lopes, A., & Dossetor, D. (2007). Intellectual ability, self-perceived social competence, and depressive symptomatology in children with high-functioning autistic spectrum disorders. *Journal of Autism and Developmental Disorders, 37*(9), 1647–1664. https://doi.org/10.1007/s10803-006-0292-x

Wahl, O. F. (1999). Mental health consumers' experience of stigma. *Schizophrenia Bulletin, 25*(3), 467–478. https://doi.org/10.1093/oxfordjournals.schbul.a033394

White, S. W., Ollendick, T., Albano, A. M., Oswald, D., Johnson, C., Southam-Gerow, M. A., . . . Scahill, L. (2013). Randomized controlled trial: Multimodal anxiety and social skill intervention for adolescents with autism spectrum disorder. *Journal of Autism and Developmental Disorders, 43*(2), 382–394. https://doi.org/10.1007/s10803-012-1577-x

White, S. W., & Roberson-Nay, R. (2009). Anxiety, social deficits, and loneliness in youth with autism spectrum disorders. *Journal of Autism and Developmental Disorders, 39*(7), 1006–1013. https://doi.org/10.1007/s10803-009-0713-8

White, S. W., Schry, A. R., & Maddox, B. B. (2012). Brief report: The assessment of anxiety in high-functioning adolescents with autism spectrum disorder. *Journal of Autism and Developmental Disorders, 42*(6), 1138–1145. https://doi.org/10.1007/s10803-011-1353-3

White, S. W., Simmons, G. L., Gotham, K. O., Conner, C. M., Smith, I. C., Beck, K. B., & Mazefsky, C. A. (2018). Psychosocial treatments targeting anxiety and depression in adolescents and adults on the autism spectrum: Review of the latest research and recommended future directions. *Current Psychiatry Reports, 20,* 82. https://doi.org/10.1007/s11920-018-0949-0

Wood, J. J., Drahota, A., Sze, K., Har, K., Chiu, A., & Langer, D. A. (2009). Cognitive behavioral therapy for anxiety in children with autism spectrum disorders: A randomized, controlled trial. *Journal of Child Psychology and Psychiatry, 50*(3), 224–234. https://doi.org/10.1111/j.1469–7610.2008.01948.x

Wood, J. J., Ehrenreich-May, J., Alessandri, M., Fujii, C., Renno, P., Laugeson, E., . . . Storch, E. A. (2015). Cognitive behavioral therapy for early adolescents with autism spectrum disorders and clinical anxiety: A randomized, controlled trial. *Behavior Therapy, 46*(1), 7–19. https://doi.org/10.1016/j.beth.2014.01.002

Wozniak, J., Biederman, J., Kiely, K., Ablon, J. S., Faraone, S. V., Mundy, E., & Mennin, D. (1995). Mania-like symptoms suggestive of childhood-onset bipolar disorder in clinically referred children. *Journal of the American Academy of Child and Adolescent Psychiatry, 34*(7), 867–876. https://doi.org/10.1097/00004583-199507000-00010

CHAPTER 3

Schizophrenia and Other Psychotic Disorders in Autism Spectrum Disorder

Jennifer H. Foss-Feig, Stacey Lurie, *and* Maya F. Hubert

Abstract

There is substantial data pointing to evidence of heightened rates of psychotic experiences and schizophrenia spectrum disorders in individuals with autism spectrum disorder (ASD). Given overlapping genetics and neurobiology between the two disorders, the prevalence of this comorbidity is not surprising. And yet, psychosis in ASD has received relatively little attention in either the scientific or the clinical literatures. Following an introduction to the shared historical context of schizophrenia and ASD, this chapter reviews the diagnostic criteria for psychosis and the assessment tools available for evaluating symptoms. Difficulties in differentiating true psychotic symptoms from several hallmark ASD features, as well as in diagnosing psychosis in minimally verbal individuals with ASD, are highlighted, and recommendations for making this diagnostic distinction are offered. With regard to treatment, there is a striking absence of literature addressing how to treat psychosis when it presents in individuals with ASD. This chapter highlights best practice treatments for childhood-onset and adult schizophrenia and related disorders and discusses how these treatments might apply or need adaptation when treating an individual with ASD. Finally, this chapter offers recommendations for future research regarding the nature, prevalence, developmental course, assessment, and most effective treatments for schizophrenia and other psychotic disorders when they present in individuals with ASD.

Keywords: autism, psychosis, schizophrenia, diagnosis, treatment

Overview

Autism and schizophrenia share a long history, wherein autism was initially subsumed within the schizophrenia diagnosis (de Lacy & King, 2013). Later diagnostic criteria came to prohibit a schizophrenia diagnosis in those with developmental autism, where onset of social withdrawal and comorbid symptoms occurred early in childhood (American Psychiatric Association, 1980). More recently, however, the exclusion for diagnosing psychosis in autism was removed, and increased attention has been paid to the overlap in both biology and clinical symptoms between the two disorders. Before beginning our description of diagnosing and treating psychotic symptoms in those with autism spectrum disorder (ASD), we take a brief look at the intertwined history of the two disorders. This history provides a backdrop that helps explain the relative paucity of information currently available to guide clinicians working with individuals with ASD where a psychotic disorder must be ruled out or treated.

In 1893, Emil Kraeplin coined the term "dementia praecox," differentiating a condition of "mental weakness occurring at a young age" from manic depression (Aderibigbe, Theodoridis, & Vieweg, 1999; Berrios & Hauser, 1988). Two decades later, Eugen Bleuler would define a more specific syndrome, now called "schizophrenia," characterized by exacerbations and declines. According to Bleuler, the core symptoms of schizophrenia could be categorized into four "A's": flattened affect, impaired association of ideas, ambivalence, and autism (Bleuler, 1911, 1950). By "autism," Bleuler meant "the inclination to divorce oneself from reality" (Bleuler, 1911, p. 14).

By using this term to describe a feature of schizophrenia that would later be expanded to encompass social withdrawal, internal preoccupation, and response to internal stimuli, Bleuler set the stage for later confusion when the same term would be proposed as a diagnostic label associated with a very different set of symptoms alongside the social isolation and internal focus Bleuler observed in his patients.

In a seminal paper published in 1943, Leo Kanner brought the term "autism" into its next context (Kanner, 1943). Describing a series of 11 patients he surmised previously might have been viewed as schizophrenic, Kanner proposed a new syndrome: "early infantile autism." This disorder, according to Kanner, was characterized by autistic aloneness, insistence on sameness, speech disturbances such as language delay and echolalia, large heads, clumsy gait, aversion to sensory input, and excellent rote memory. In the context of early infantile autism, Kanner defined an *extreme autistic aloneness* that, "whenever possible, disregards, ignores, shuts out anything that comes to the child from the outside" (Kanner, 1943, p. 242). Of particular note relative to schizophrenia, the onset of social withdrawal occurred much younger in Kanner's early infantile autism than in schizophrenia: "The outstanding 'pathognomonic' fundamental disorder is the children's *inability to relate themselves* in the ordinary way to people and situations from the beginning of life." (Kanner, 1943, p. 242). Whereas schizophrenia was associated with a decline in patient functioning, in early infantile autism, the aloneness Kanner described was present from the very beginning. The associated symptoms of early infantile autism were also distinct from schizophrenia.

In 1968, the first nod to Kanner's autism appeared in the second edition of the *Diagnostic and Statistical Manual of Mental Disorders* (DSM; American Psychiatric Association, 1975). Although early infantile autism was not given its own diagnostic category, "autism" was mentioned under the label "schizophrenia, childhood type," wherein symptoms appeared before puberty and were "manifested by autistic, atypical and withdrawn behavior." And yet, the idea that there were dissociable subtypes of childhood psychoses remained on the minds of clinicians. In his 1971 *Studies in the Childhood Psychoses*, Israel Kolvin noted three groups of psychoses in childhood that could be distinguished by their age of onset: onset younger than age 3 years, akin to Kanner's infantile autism; onset between 3 and 5 years; and onset after age 5, akin to adult schizophrenia (Kolvin, 1971). However, confusion remained as both the diagnosis that we now know as schizophrenia and that we now call ASD were considered "schizophrenias." Both also had the word "autism" at their core. In 1972, Michael Rutter made a push for differentiating infantile autism, as delineated by Kanner, as a separate diagnostic classification (Rutter, 1972). And yet, around the same time, in a paper focusing on vestibular functioning across schizophrenia and autism, Ornitz reminded the field that symptoms of more traditional schizophrenia can emerge even in autistic children (Ornitz, 1970). Thus, the complicated nature of the relation between the two disorders remained salient.

The publishing of the DSM-III in 1980 (American Psychiatric Association, 1980) represented a significant step forward for recognizing autism as a separate entity with unique diagnostic criteria and treatment needs. Criteria for infantile autism in the DSM-III included onset before 30 months of age, lack of responsiveness to others, deficits in language development and peculiar speech patterns where speech was present, and bizarre responses to the environment including resistance to change and peculiar interests. Although for autism the DSM-III represented progress, for the notion of psychosis co-occurring in those with autism it represented a setback: The final criterion for diagnosing infantile autism was that there be an "absence of delusions, hallucinations, loosening of associations, and incoherence as in schizophrenia." In short, the DSM-III proclaimed that autism could not be diagnosed in those with schizophrenia, and that those with autism ought not display psychotic symptoms. From a diagnostic standpoint, comorbid autism and psychosis was off the table.

And yet, clinically, the presence of psychotic features in those with autism continued to be noted. In 1984, Leonora Petty and colleagues published a paper entitled *Autistic Children Who Become Schizophrenic* (Petty, Ornitz, Michelman, & Zimmerman, 1984). In the paper, they documented three cases of children displaying unambiguous features of autism in early childhood, with hallmark symptoms of schizophrenia emerging later on. Early history for case one includes "that 'he did not point'... he stroked textured surfaces, eg, wood and wall coverings, repetitively... he 'pulled at hands to move the hand to pick up an object'... he did not speak... he was described as having limited eye contact and being quite withdrawn... [and] he lined objects in straight rows and would not touch any item that was slightly sticky..." (Petty et al., 1984, p. 130). In short, he exhibited many of the hallmark social communication and restricted/repetitive behaviors associated with ASD. By adolescence, ASD symptoms were still present, as he "showed fleeting eye contact... and frequent hand flapping." However, traditional psychosis symptoms had also emerged: "Thoughts included delusions of being controlled by life-threatening 'witch craftery... the fearful force.' There were hallucinations of 'hearing voices,' including commands. Much of the patient's language was incomprehensible because of mumbling subvocalizations and loose associations.... [T]he requirements for chronicity were also met" (Petty et al., 1984, p. 130). In this and the other two case examples, Petty and her colleagues presented a compelling case for the notion of comorbid schizophrenia in children with autism, even as the DSM-III precluded clinicians from making concurrent diagnoses.

In 1994, with the publication of the DSM-IV (American Psychiatry Association, 1994), the option to diagnose schizophrenia and related disorders in those with autism was reinstated, making room for accurate classification of patients like those described by Petty. However, to this day, there remain lasting repercussions of the movement to dissociate and dichotomize the two disorders. Indeed, papers published over the next decades have argued the impossibility of their co-occurrence (Crespi & Badcock, 2008). Confusion is likely made more prominent because, at their most basic, several clinical features (e.g., social withdrawal, flat affect, theory-of-mind difficulties, sensory sensitivities) can be associated with either autism, schizophrenia, or both (American Psychiatry Association, 1994; Baron-Cohen, Leslie, & Frith, 1985; Bora, Yucel, & Pantelis, 2009; Couture et al., 2010; Frith & Corcoran, 1996; Pinkham, Hopfinger, Pelphrey, Piven, & Penn, 2008a; Sugranyes, Kyriakopoulos, Corrigall, Taylor, & Frangou, 2011). In this chapter, we review what is currently known about the prevalence and developmental course of psychosis in ASD and provide a guide to the complex diagnostic and treatment considerations relevant when weighing the possibility of comorbid psychosis in individuals with ASD.

Prevalence and Course

Prevalence

Estimates of the rate of psychotic experiences and formal schizophrenia spectrum disorders in ASD vary widely across studies. However, the majority of studies point to higher rates of psychosis in ASD than would be expected in the general population, where approximately 0.75% to 0.87% of individuals develop schizophrenia during their lifetime (Moreno-Küstner, Martín, & Pastor, 2018; Perälä et al., 2007).

Epidemiological studies suggest rates 5% to 35% higher in individuals with an ASD diagnosis than in the general population, with a recent meta-analysis suggesting an odds ratio of 3.55 for the prevalence of psychosis in ASD versus controls (Z. Zheng, Zheng, & Zou, 2018). In two studies using the Danish Psychiatric Central Registry that identified individuals with ASD and tracked psychiatric admissions and diagnoses over the subsequent two to five decades, 6.6% of 118 individuals with infantile autism received schizophrenia spectrum diagnoses, including formal schizophrenia diagnoses in 3.4% (Mouridsen, Rich, Isager, & Nedergaard, 2008). In a parallel study focused on 89 children with "atypical autism" (approximating the DSM-IV diagnosis of pervasive developmental disorder—not otherwise specified), 34.8% went on to receive a later schizophrenia spectrum disorder diagnosis (Mouridsen, Rich, Isager, et al., 2008). Data from a Swedish registry provides corroborating evidence for the increased rate of psychotic disorder diagnoses in those with prior ASD history (Selten, Lundberg, Rai, & Magnusson, 2015). In individuals registered as having ASD before age 16 compared to controls from the same database, the odds ratio for nonaffective psychotic disorder was 5.6 if the individual had no intellectual disability (ID) and 3.5 if there was comorbid ID. Interestingly, if criteria for registering an ASD diagnosis was expanded to age 28, the odds ratio for nonaffective psychotic disorder was 12.3 if the individual had no ID and 6.4 if there was comorbid ID.

Studies conducting chart reviews also tend to report elevated rates of psychotic symptoms and disorders in adults with historical ASD diagnoses. For example, among 60 adults with ASD (defined by Wing and Gould's [1979] criteria using clinical interview, chart review, and informant report) who had normal intelligence but remained quite impaired into adulthood (i.e., were socially isolated, largely unemployed, and largely unable to live independently), 11.7% were diagnosed with a psychotic disorder as per the International Classification of Diseases, ninth revision (ICD-9) criteria and based on clinical interviews, history, and collateral report from treating physicians and family members (Tantam, 1988). In another series of case reports by the same author, 21% of adults with Asperger syndrome, defined by the DSM and using Wing and Gould's "triad of impairment" criteria, had comorbid psychotic symptoms, with 4% receiving schizophrenia diagnoses (Tantam, 1991). In reviewing charts of 163 adolescents and adults with well-documented autism histories, Volkmar and Cohen (1991) identified unequivocal schizophrenia in just one individual. However, 40 others had symptoms that could be interpreted as positive symptoms of schizophrenia (e.g., unusual sensory experiences, bizarre preoccupations, difficulty distinguishing fantasy from reality), but it was noted that possible delusions and hallucinations were ambiguous in these patients.

Increased rates of psychotic experiences and diagnoses have also been identified in studies conducting direct, contemporaneous clinical evaluations of psychotic and ASD symptoms in individuals with prior ASD diagnoses. In 129 adults with ASD consecutively referred to a neuropsychiatric outpatient setting, 7.8% received a diagnosis of schizophrenia or another psychotic disorder, and an additional 7% met criteria for bipolar disorder with psychotic features (Stahlberg, Soderstrom, Rastam, & Gillberg, 2004). In this study, psychosis symptoms were assessed with the Structured Clinical Interview for DSM Diagnoses (SCID; First, Gibbon, Spitzer, & Williams, 1996) as well as semistructured collateral interviews with caregivers where possible. In a second study, among 16 individuals with ASD followed up 11 to 27 years after their initial ASD diagnosis at a specialized clinic for treating children with ASD, 25% exhibited hallucinations, 18.8% paranoid ideation, and 6.3% magical thinking, as indicated during structured interviews in adulthood (Szatmari, Bartolucci, Bremner, Bond, & Rich, 1989). In 14 adult males with ASD assessed for schizophrenia and related symptoms using the SCID, Scale for Assessment of Positive Symptoms (SAPS; Andreasen, 1984), and Scale for Assessment of Negative Symptoms (SANS; Andreasen, 1981), 50% met criteria for schizophrenia, disorganized type on the SCID. On the SAPS, 35.7% showed significant positive symptoms of psychosis, and 42.9% exhibited significant negative symptoms on the SANS (Konstantareas & Hewitt, 2001). Finally, in 71 adults who exceeded diagnostic thresholds for ASD on the Autism Diagnostic Observation Schedule (ADOS; Lord, Rutter, DiLavore, & Risi, 2003) and Autism Diagnostic Interview—Revised (ADI-R; Rutter, Le Couteur, & Lord, 2003) and also received a DSM-IV-TR diagnosis of a psychotic disorder on the Diagnostic Interview for Psychosis (DIP; Castle et al., 2005) or Psychiatric Assessment Schedule for Adults with Developmental Disabilities (Mini PAS-ADD; Moss et al., 1993), more than 80% had delusions, more than 80% had hallucinations, and approximately 35% had thought disorder (Larson et al., 2017). Diagnostically, 52% of these individuals with ASD and comorbid psychosis were categorized as having psychotic disorder—not otherwise specified, whereas approximately 35% had affective psychosis and 13% met full criteria for schizophrenia.

Though the prevalence of psychosis and psychotic experiences does appear to be elevated in ASD, some caution must be taken in interpreting heightened scores on instruments designed to assess psychosis symptoms. Case series highlight how circumscribed interests, atypical language used to describe relatively common experiences, and disorganized behavior in the context of disruptions of routines and lack of schedule can be misinterpreted as psychotic symptoms in those with ASD (Dossetor, 2007; Van Schalkwyk, Peluso, Qayyum, McPartland, & Volkmar, 2015). Additionally, Konstantareas and Hewitt (2001) point out that though more than a third of their participants with ASD met criteria for positive symptoms of psychosis, this finding was mainly due to bizarre behavior, whereas none of their participants with ASD had hallucinations or delusions. Finally, some negative symptoms of psychosis (e.g., reduced emotional expression) are also hallmark features of a primary ASD diagnosis. These findings underscore the importance of careful ascertainment of psychosis symptoms in the context of diagnostic evaluations, as will be discussed in detail in the assessment section later. Nonetheless, best estimates suggest that rates of psychosis in ASD are nontrivial and higher than would be expected in the general population.

Developmental Course

The developmental course of the onset of psychotic experiences and diagnosis of formal psychotic disorders in ASD has not been studied via systematic longitudinal studies. However, in general, registry and chart review studies tend to identify the emergence of psychotic concerns and diagnoses in late adolescence and adulthood (Mouridsen, Rich, & Isager, 2008; Mouridsen, Rich, Isager, et al., 2008; Selten et al., 2015; Szatmari et al., 1989; Tantam, 1988). This pattern is consistent with the more general developmental timing for schizophrenia spectrum disorders, which tend to have onset in early adulthood (Hollis & Rapoport, 2011). In one study of adults with comorbid ASD and psychosis, though age of onset varied (i.e., ranging from age 6 to age 55), for 93.1% onset occurred between age 12 and 45, with only 5.2% of participants experiencing psychotic disorder onset prior to the age of 12 (Larson et al., 2017). In 42% of patients in this study, psychotic disorder diagnosis followed an insidious decline over 6 or more months, consistent with broader patterns associated with schizophrenia where a prodromal period precedes formal diagnosis. Indeed, among help-seeking individuals at clinical high risk for psychosis, those with and without prior ASD diagnoses show similar positive symptoms of psychosis during the prodrome phase and have similar risk of converting to full-blown psychotic illness (Foss-Feig, Velthorst, et al., in press). However, Larson and colleagues (2017) find that, although 53% of individuals with ASD and comorbid psychosis experienced at least one psychotic episode lasting 2 or more years, for many individuals in their study, the illness duration did not meet the duration criteria for schizophrenia (i.e., 6 months of disturbance with 1 month of active symptoms). This final statistic suggests the course of psychotic illness may be more transient and/or acute when it occurs in individuals with ASD, which could translate into DSM-5 diagnoses such as brief psychotic disorder or unspecified schizophrenia spectrum and other psychotic disorder being more common in ASD than the narrower schizophrenia diagnosis.

There are two particular cases where psychosis symptoms can appear earlier in those with ASD than is typical of the usual course of psychosis onset in the general population: childhood-onset schizophrenia (COS) and multiple complex developmental disorder (MCDD). Although neither of these diagnoses can be formally applied according to the DSM or the ICD (World Health Organization, 1992), both have a substantial research base and a strong overlap with ASD.

COS is defined as onset of psychosis before age 13, though typically after age 7 (Rapoport, Chavez, Greenstein, Addington, & Gogtay, 2009). Though very rare (< 0.04% of the population; Driver, Gogtay, & Rapoport, 2013), both positive and negative symptoms of schizophrenia are present in children with COS and prognosis is poor (Hollis & Rapoport, 2011). COS is separate from ASD, falling under the spectrum of psychotic illnesses. However, in a review of 97 individuals with COS, 28.9% had prior ASD diagnoses based on DSM-IV criteria (Rapoport et al., 2009). Moreover, for any given DSM-IV ASD symptom, between 16% and 58% of the COS sample met criteria. One hundred percent of children with COS had one symptom of ASD-related social impairment, and 78% had two or more. Eighty-four percent had one and 53% had two or more symptoms of ASD-related communication impairment. In the restricted and repetitive behavior domain, 74% of children with COS displayed one ASD feature, and 37% had two or more. Overall, 58% of the COS sample had impairment in all three impairment categories associated with an ASD diagnosis in the DSM-IV, and a full 100% had impairment in at least two ASD domains. Thus, although COS remains exceedingly uncommon in the general population and its rates in ASD have never been prospectively measured, it does tend to occur most often in children with pre-existing ASD diagnoses and be associated with subthreshold ASD features. As such, emergence of psychotic symptoms in children with ASD under the age of 13 could indicate the presence of comorbid COS.

MCDD is characterized by social impairment in tandem with inappropriate affect, mood lability, and thought disorder, including bizarre and disorganized thinking and difficulties separating fantasy from reality (Towbin, Dykens, Pearson, & Cohen, 1993). It was initially categorized as falling under the pervasive developmental disorder (PDD) umbrella (Buitelaar & Van der Gaag, 1998; Cohen, Paul, & & Volkmar, 1986); however, core ASD symptoms may be on the milder side in those with MCDD as compared to those with a formal ASD diagnosis (Van der Gaag et al., 1995), and not all children with MCDD will meet full ASD criteria (de Bruin, de Nijs, Verheij, Hartman, & Ferdinand, 2007). Still, 44% of children meeting MCDD criteria do meet criteria for an ASD diagnosis (de Bruin et al., 2007). And by adolescence, 78% meet clinical high risk for psychosis criteria (Sprong et al., 2008). Thus, MCDD may represent a particular case along the ASD spectrum where early social deficits co-occur alongside thought disturbances. In this subset of children, clinicians may observe a distinct developmental course whereby features often associated with both ASD and psychosis present in parallel early in development. This developmental pattern would contrast with the more typical trajectory of comorbidity wherein later-emerging psychotic symptoms become overlaid on a primary ASD diagnosis.

Etiology, Diagnosis, and Assessment

Etiology

The overlap between ASD and schizophrenia spectrum disorders is not surprising given shared biological risk factors. Epidemiological studies reveal that family history of schizophrenia increases the risk of ASD (Daniels et al., 2008; Sullivan et al., 2012), suggesting shared etiological risk factors. Indeed, there is substantial overlap in risk genes for ASD and schizophrenia (Charney, Buxbaum, Sklar, & Nestler, 2018). ASD and psychosis are both common outcomes in individuals with velocardiofacial syndrome, which is caused by 22q11.2 deletion (Vorstman et al., 2006), as well as in Phelan McDermid syndrome, caused by 22q13.3 deletion (Durand et al., 2007; Gauthier et al., 2010). Moreover, several rare copy number variants, including 2p16.3 deletion (H.-G. Kim et al., 2008; Rujescu et al., 2009), 3q29 deletion (Burbach & van der Zwaag, 2009; Levinson et al., 2011; Sagar et al., 2013), 7q35 rearrangement (Arking et al., 2008; Friedman et al., 2008), 15q13.3 deletion (Ben-Shachar et al., 2009; Miller et al., 2009; Stefansson et al., 2008), 16p11.2 deletion and duplication (McCarthy et al., 2009; Weiss et al., 2009), and 17q12 deletion (Moreno-De-Luca et al., 2010) confer increased risk for both ASD and schizophrenia.

Many of the genes that are implicated across both ASD and schizophrenia code for proteins functioning in synaptic development and plasticity (Carroll & Owen, 2009; Liu, Li, Fan, Zhang, & Chen, 2017). Thus, it is not surprising that parallel neuroimaging research in ASD and schizophrenia cohorts reveals overlapping findings that implicate synaptic and network functioning. Across many studies, alterations in neural synchrony (Uhlhaas & Singer, 2006), excitatory/inhibitory neurotransmission balance (Foss-Feig et al., 2017), and resting state functional connectivity (Chen et al., 2017) have been implicated in both disorders. These processes all play a role in the tuning within and communication across local and longer range network systems and suggest that alterations in these functions could play a contributing role in shared features across disorders. At the same time, nuances of these alterations (e.g., which networks are most affected; the degree, direction, and universality of excitatory/inhibitory imbalance) may contribute to the specific phenotype that is ultimately expressed (Mastrovito, Hanson, & Hanson, 2018). In turn, these nuanced differences in network-level brain alterations may help explain how ASD and schizophrenia may overlap to a disproportionate degree yet still have distinct phenotypic aspects among individuals who are not dually diagnosed.

Few studies have directly compared brain functioning between ASD and schizophrenia samples, and only one has examined an ASD sample divided into subsets with and without psychosis comorbidity. In research comparing the two disorders directly, findings suggest that social brain network alterations in the right amygdala, fusiform face area, and left ventrolateral prefrontal cortex during task (Pinkham, Hopfinger, Pelphrey, Piven, & Penn, 2008b) and functional and structural insula abnormalities (Radeloff et al., 2014) may be common across ASD and schizophrenia. Additionally, though cerebellar and temporal lobe gray matter volume was reduced in ASD versus typically developing controls regardless of psychosis status within the ASD group, insular gray matter and cerebellar gray and white matter volume reductions were particularly marked in individuals with ASD with comorbid psychosis in comparison to others with ASD alone (Toal et al., 2009). Thus, these two brain regions may be of particular interest when considering the neural underpinnings of comorbid ASD and psychosis. The research in this area is, however, quite sparse, and more work must be done to clarify specific brain alterations in those diagnosed with both ASD and psychosis.

Diagnosis

In the DSM-5, schizophrenia spectrum and other psychotic disorders encompass schizophrenia, schizophreniform disorder, brief psychotic disorder, schizoaffective disorder, delusional disorder, catatonia, schizotypal personality disorder, and substance-induced psychosis. All are defined by the presence of features in one or more of five symptom domains: hallucinations, delusions, disorganized thinking and speech, grossly disorganized or abnormal motor behavior, and negative symptoms. The number of symptom clusters expressed, duration of symptoms, absence or presence of co-occurring mood symptoms, use of psychosis-inducing medications or drugs of abuse, and presence or absence of an underlying medical condition are used to determine which schizophrenia spectrum disorder is most appropriate for an individual expressing psychotic symptoms. Before describing the assessment tools most commonly used to evaluate psychotic symptoms, we briefly describe each symptom domain and articulate specific considerations that may be important when assessing symptoms in the unique case of evaluating an individual with ASD for possible comorbid psychosis.

According to the DSM-5, hallucinations are perceptual experiences that occur in the absence of external sensory stimulation while an individual is fully awake. Hypnagogic (while falling asleep) and hypnopompic (while waking up) hallucinations, on the other hand, are not indicators of psychosis. Across psychotic disorders, auditory hallucinations, and voice hearing in particular, are most common. However, hallucinations can occur in any sensory modality (e.g., visual, tactile, gustatory). In ASD, hypersensitivity to external sensory stimuli and lack of reflective and introspective capacity to recognize and discuss one's own internal monologue could be confounding symptoms. These features ought to be considered when evaluating whether an individual is truly experiencing hallucinations.

Delusions involve fixed beliefs that are implausible, not shared by others from the same culture or consistent with ordinary experiences, and unable to be changed even in the face of conflicting evidence. Common content for delusions associated with psychosis includes persecutory beliefs (e.g., that one is being or will be harmed, targeted, or harassed by a particular individual or institution), grandiosity (e.g., that one has exceptional abilities or personal relationships with famous individuals), bizarre somatic complaints (e.g., that something has been implanted in the body, that thoughts have been implanted or withdrawn), referential thinking (e.g., that events, signs, or other cues from the environment are directed specifically to the individual), and atypical religious beliefs (e.g., that one can communicate directly with God, is an angel, or has some particular special mission, where the belief is not shared by others of the same culture and faith). However, other content is possible, and the more bizarre, implausible, and immutable a belief is, particularly in light of conflicting evidence, the more likely it is to be a delusion versus simply a strongly held idea. In ASD, delusions must be carefully differentiated from restricted interests, particularly when the content and quality of the interest may be particularly intense, fantastical, and/or bizarre.

Disorganized thinking is observed via how an individual is able to communicate his or her ideas in speech. It can involve loose associations, derailment, tangentiality, and/or incoherence. An individual with disorganized speech has difficulty making a point concisely, may answer questions with unrelated content, or may exhibit "word salad" that is virtually incomprehensible to another person. In essence, disorganized speech is considered an observable proxy for disorganized underlying thought processes. During differential diagnosis, at times it may be difficult to differentiate the stereotyped language, one-sided persistence on topics of interest, and difficulty with reporting of sequential events that can characterize the speech of individuals with ASD from the disorganized thinking and speech of individuals with psychotic disorders.

Abnormal motor behavior can include difficulty performing goal-directed behavior as well as catatonia. The latter symptom is characterized by decreased motor reactivity to the environment and can include a total lack of motor and verbal response and/or holding of rigid, awkward postures. For others, catatonia is accompanied by excessive, purposeless motor activity, stereotyped movements, and echolalia. Of note, catatonia can also be associated with ASD in the absence of psychosis, particularly in adolescence (Billstedt, Gillberg, & Gillberg, 2005; Wing & Shah, 2000).

Negative symptoms of psychosis can bear the most overlap with primary symptoms of ASD. In particular, diminished emotional expression associated with psychosis can include reductions in eye contact and restrictions in range of facial expressions, gestures, and prosody, all of which are also core nonverbal communication features disrupted in ASD. Negative symptoms of psychosis also include avolition (i.e., loss of motivation and ability to self-initiate and engage with activities), anhedonia (i.e., deriving decreased pleasure from activities), alogia (i.e., reduced speech output), and asociality (i.e., lack of interest or opportunities for social interactions). In the context of ASD, it may be important to consider whether negative symptoms appear increased relative to the individual's own previous baseline versus whether they appear similar in nature and severity to difficulties in nonverbal communication and socialization that the person had expressed earlier in his or her development.

Assessment

The most common diagnostic tool to evaluate for psychosis is the Structured Clinical Interview for the DSM-5 (SCID-5; First, Williams, Karg, & Spitzer, 2015, 2016), which is a semistructured interview that includes a schizophrenia spectrum disorder module to probe for psychotic symptoms and, if present, differentiate among the several specific disorders falling under the schizophrenia spectrum umbrella. Several other instruments exist to track the severity of psychotic symptoms more acutely at a given time point. The Positive and Negative Syndrome Scale (PANSS; Kay, Fiszbein, & Opler, 1987), Brief Psychiatric Rating Scale (BPRS; Overall & Gorham, 1962), and combined SAPS (Andreasen, 1984) and SANS (Andreasen, 1981) are all commonly used clinician-administered symptom rating scales. Whereas the PANSS and BPRS contain summary codes for many symptom domains (e.g., hallucinations, delusions), the SAPS and SANS allow for coding of more precise symptom manifestations (e.g., types of delusions, sensory modality of hallucinations). The Structured Interview of Psychosis-Risk Syndromes (SIPS; McGlashan, Walsh, & Woods, 2001) and Comprehensive Assessment of the At-Risk Mental States (CAARMS; Yung et al., 2005) are two tools meant to detect clinical high risk for psychosis in help-seeking individuals showing early psychotic symptoms who may not have yet developed a full-blown psychotic illness but require monitoring and trajectory tracking over time.

To date, there are no targeted instruments designed to assess for psychosis in ASD. However, the Psychiatric Assessment Schedule for Adults with Developmental Disability (PAS-ADD) is a semistructured interview utilized to detect psychopathology, including ASD, psychosis, and other common mental health problems, in individuals with ID (Moss et al., 1993). Alternate versions of the measure have been developed, including the PAS-ADD Checklist (Moss et al., 1998) and the Mini PAS-ADD (Prosser et al., 1998), which are symptom checklists designed to be administered by individuals with and without specific mental health training that aim to ascertain the presence of psychiatric symptoms and provide initial diagnostic clarification. Importantly, items on the Mini PAS-ADD that specifically screen for ASD were designed in conjunction with Rutter and colleagues, creators of the original Autism Diagnostic Interview (Rutter et al., 2003), one of the gold-standard diagnostic assessments for ASD.

Across measures, direct report during the clinical interview with the individual suspected of having psychosis is important for making symptom ratings and determining diagnosis. However, collateral information can also factor in. In particular, clinical observations of behavior during interview and information from caregivers, peers, and supervisors regarding an individual's functioning in the community can both be critical to promote accurate symptom ratings and diagnosis. These components of a comprehensive evaluation are crucial when a patient is guarded, lacks insight into his or her illness, or has communication difficulties. The latter two situations can occur often in ASD. Specifically, difficulty with introspection, concrete thinking and literal interpretation of questions, theory-of-mind deficits, and idiosyncratic language are all common ASD features, even in verbal and cognitively able individuals. These features may make information gathered via direct interview difficult to interpret without context and collateral input when assessing for psychosis in ASD.

When considering the possibility of making a psychosis diagnosis in an individual with pre-existing ASD, there are several important factors to keep in mind. First, according to the DSM, "An individual with autism spectrum disorder or communication disorder must have symptoms that meet full criteria for schizophrenia, with prominent hallucinations or delusions for at least 1 month, in order to be diagnosed with schizophrenia as a comorbid condition" (American Psychiatric Association, 2013, p. 105). Thus, whereas the presence of disorganized thinking plus one or the other of disorganized motor behavior or negative symptoms could be enough for a schizophrenia diagnosis in non-ASD individuals, when the patient being evaluated has ASD, this symptom combination is insufficient. This nuance to the official criteria for diagnosing psychosis in the context of ASD reflects the overlap in core autism and schizophrenia spectrum symptoms and diagnostic criteria. It also helps to ensure the comorbid psychosis diagnosis is only made in ASD when symptoms manifest that clearly are not better explained by the primary ASD diagnosis.

ASD history must be taken into consideration in making a psychosis diagnosis. In Volkmar and Cohen's study of adolescents and adults with historical autism diagnoses, almost 25% had symptoms that could suggest schizophrenia at first glance (Volkmar & Cohen, 1991). These symptoms included bizarre preoccupations and interests, difficulty distinguishing reality from fantasy, and unusual sensory experiences. However, in all but one case, there were no unequivocal delusions and hallucinations. This study highlights that symptoms better explained by the primary ASD diagnosis must not be fit carelessly in support of diagnostic criteria for psychosis. To this point, as previously mentioned, negative symptoms such as decreased emotional expressivity and lack of social interests can be hallmark ASD symptoms. In a study of 14 adult males with ASD assessed with the SCID, SAPS, and SANS, 50% showed significant negative symptoms of schizophrenia and, as a result, met criteria for disorganized-type schizophrenia, despite none showing the delusions or hallucinations that would in most cases be necessary for a psychosis diagnosis (Konstantareas & Hewitt, 2001). Thus, one should not substantiate a psychosis diagnosis in an individual with ASD based in large part on negative symptoms unless there has been a marked change or exacerbation of negative symptoms and the quality of atypicalities in gestures, prosody, facial expressions, and/or social withdrawal has changed substantially relative to the individual's baseline ASD symptoms.

Likewise, unusual framing of interests and use of language could make some thoughts or described behaviors sound atypical, either in their content (where delusions must be ruled out) or in the way they are communicated (where disorganized thoughts must be ruled out). Use of neologisms, cognitive vulnerabilities, and theory-of-mind deficits could all contribute to the impression of bizarreness in the reports of individuals with ASD (Dossetor, 2007). In Konstantareas and Hewitt's 2001 study, five of 14 ASD participants met criteria for displaying bizarre behavior or having formal thought disorder, which relies on ratings of both motor behavior and speech patterns. Whether awkward gait, stereotyped motor movements, and/or idiosyncratic language have been a part of the individual with ASD's historical clinical profile is therefore important to ascertain in considering whether thoughts and behavior are bizarre in a way that may be indicative of a new-onset psychotic disorder. Additionally, in attempting to differentiate delusions from restricted interests, the content, fixedness, and bizarreness of topics of interest—as well as the degree to which they are a close extension of (vs. differ qualitatively from) the individual's prior restricted interests across development—should be considered.

Two case series of individuals with ASD misdiagnosed with comorbid psychotic disorders have been published and offer guidance about how to differentiate questionable symptoms that may be better understood as part of underlying ASD. Van Schalwyck and colleagues (2015) highlight that if symptoms worsen during disrupted routine, resolve with structure, or improve without further medication, it may be safest to consider these symptoms as part of the core ASD phenotype rather than indicators of new-onset psychosis. Other factors that may weight clinical thinking away from a comorbid psychosis diagnosis in ASD include lack of co-occurring developmental or academic deterioration, improvement of symptoms with interventions to address anxiety or reduce family and social stress, symptoms isolated to expression with particular familiar people, and lack of symptom response to traditional antipsychotic treatment (Dossetor, 2007).

On the other hand, it is important for diagnosticians not to allow the ASD diagnosis to overshadow thorough consideration of the possible emergence of psychosis. New-onset symptoms and a decline in functioning are not typical of the standard ASD developmental course through adolescence and adulthood. Per the DSM-5, "Autism spectrum disorder is not a degenerative disorder, and it is typical for learning and compensation to continue throughout life. Symptoms are often most marked in early childhood and early school years, with developmental gains typical in later childhood in at least some areas (e.g., increased interest in social interaction)" (American Psychiatric Association, 2013, p. 56). Thus, when deterioration of functioning occurs, clinicians should be on alert and should subsequently assess for the presence of new-onset symptoms, particularly delusions and hallucinations that would most clearly not be attributable to the underlying ASD. Van Schalwyck and colleagues (2015) highlight that true comorbid psychosis may be best differentiated where there is new onset of sustained hallucinations and disorganized behavior that represent a decline from baseline, are responsive to antipsychotic medications, worsen when medication adherence is poor, and do not improve with structure and other environmental accommodations often effective in ASD. In one study of individuals with gold-standard ASD diagnoses plus comorbid psychosis defined by DSM or ICD criteria, greater than 80% had hallucinations and/or delusions, whereas only a third had thought disorder (Larson et al., 2017). This finding again underscores the importance of hallucinations and delusions as key indicators to support increased confidence in a true comorbid psychosis diagnosis in an individual with ASD.

Finally, MCDD and COS are important diagnostic considerations to keep in mind. First, though MCDD is not a formal diagnosis presently recognized in the DSM, it may be worthwhile for clinicians to keep it in mind when evaluating a child with ASD showing symptoms of thought disorder and mood disturbance. It is very possible that there exists some yet-unnamed disorder (MCDD or otherwise) at the intersection of ASD and psychosis whose particular symptoms and developmental trajectory will become clearer as research in this area improves. Thus, children presenting with MCDD-like symptom profiles may benefit from their clinicians utilizing available literature on this research diagnosis as a reference point and framework for treatment. On the other hand, when children previously diagnosed with ASD begin expressing psychotic symptoms, it may be helpful to re-evaluate their historical ASD symptoms in light of a possible childhood-onset schizophrenia diagnosis. For some, ASD and COS may be comorbid. For others, it may be the case that an earlier ASD diagnosis was more likely a mischaracterization of the precursors and earliest stages of COS in the absence of information about subsequent development and symptom emergence. For these children, reclassification of the ASD diagnosis and shift to a primary COS diagnosis may be most beneficial for subsequent clinical conceptualization and treatment.

Of note, the question of psychosis in minimally verbal individuals with ASD is a particularly challenging one on which there has been little research. Assessment tools for psychosis all require self-report, which is impossible if the individual for whom there are psychosis concerns does not have language. In fact, even in those who have language, reliability of report on psychosis symptoms is reduced when cognitive ability is low (Volkmar & Tsatsanis, 2002). Indeed, little is known about how psychosis presents in individuals with severe intellectual disability and minimal language abilities. Teasing apart possible psychosis symptoms in minimally verbal individuals can be incredibly challenging for caregivers or clinicians attempting to observe and interpret concerning behaviors without the luxury of verbal report from the individual about whom they are concerned. It can be near impossible, for example, to tell whether a new-onset fear or other emotional reaction uncorrelated to external stimuli or an apparent increase in internal preoccupation might be due to hallucinations. Likewise, changes in motor and other behavior, including new stereotypies, catatonic reactions, erratic responding or outbursts, and declines in daily functioning, could—or could not—be possible markers of psychosis. At present, there are no clear guidelines for assessing and diagnosing psychosis in this population; the most common approaches are often either to watch and wait or to attempt treatment with medication and observe for symptom improvement as evidence in support of the diagnosis.

Treatment

Data on optimal treatment for psychosis in ASD is strikingly absent in the scientific literature. Despite the fact that a recent meta-analysis revealed that one in six youth with ASD were treated with an antipsychotic (Park et al., 2016), these medications are generally prescribed in ASD for secondary symptoms, including irritability and aggression (Fung et al., 2016), rather than for psychosis itself. What little evidence exists describing medication of psychotic symptoms in ASD suggests that treatment of psychosis in ASD may be particularly complicated and require multiple medication trials. For example, in a single case study of a young boy with ASD, attention deficit hyperactivity disorder (ADHD), and childhood-onset schizophrenia, stimulant medication, aripiprazole, risperidone, and valproate were ineffective in managing perceptual disturbances; olanzapine helped with psychotic symptoms but left premorbid impulsivity unimproved; and paliperidone was ultimately most effective both for addressing perceptual disturbances and for managing pre-existing symptoms concurrently (Taskiran & Coffey, 2013). Indeed, a study of 10- to 17-year-old children and adolescents with first-episode psychosis highlights that history of ASD diagnosis in particular (but not other neurodevelopmental disorders or ID) is associated with multiple treatment failures using antipsychotic medications, due either to insufficient treatment response or to intolerable side effects (Downs et al., 2017).

Here, in the absence of a well-developed literature on treating psychosis in ASD, we review the literature on treatment of psychotic symptoms in childhood-onset and adult schizophrenia, with the caveat that application of these treatments in ASD may be more complicated and/or have more muted success. We include summaries of pharmacological treatments, as well as individual, family, and system-level supports and newer intervention approaches.

In COS, clozapine has been shown to be the most effective antipsychotic treatment (Kasoff, Ahn, Gochman, Broadnax, & Rapoport, 2016; Krause et al., 2018), though olanzapine, risperidone, lurasidone, aripiprazole, quetiapine, paliperidone, and asenapine were also found to be more effective than placebo (Krause et al., 2018). Clozapine shows the highest effect size over placebo, as well as in direct comparison to other medications (Krause et al., 2018). Kasoff and colleagues (2016) estimated that 72% of COS patients were clozapine responders and noted that long-term compliance was high with this medication. Patients also showed a clear preference for taking clozapine versus other options. In terms of relative effectiveness of clozapine across patients, research suggests that those with a higher *N*-desmethylclozapine-to-clozapine ratio in plasma are most likely to respond successfully to this treatment (Sporn et al., 2007).

First-line treatment of psychosis in broader schizophrenia virtually always includes antipsychotic medications (Lehman, 2004, APA guidelines).

First-generation antipsychotics, which primarily target D2 receptors, can be effective in reducing positive symptoms and improving negative symptoms. However, they have high rates of extrapyramidal side effects (e.g., akathisia and dystonia acutely, tardive dyskinesia and neuroleptic malignant syndrome longer term). Second-generation antipsychotics target both dopamine and serotonin receptors; they tend to be effective for positive symptom reduction and have fewer extrapyramidal side effects, but weight gain is a common side effect for this medication class. Clozapine has historically been the primary medication of choice for treatment-resistant schizophrenia (Kane, Honigfeld, Singer, & Meltzer, 1988); however, risperidone (particularly for positive symptoms) and olanzapine (particularly for negative symptoms) may also be effective in those patients who fail multiple treatment trials (Samara et al., 2016).

Additional medications are often prescribed to treat secondary symptoms associated with psychosis. Benzodiazepines are effective for treating catatonia, when present (Lehman et al., 2004; Sienaert, Dhossche, Vancampfort, De Hert, & Gazdag, 2014), and also can be helpful for agitation and anxiety associated with the psychotic illness (Lehman et al., 2004). Antidepressants and mood stabilizers can be helpful adjunct therapies where mood symptoms are prominent concurrent with a psychotic episode (Lehman, 2004). Finally, benztropine and diphenhydramine are sometimes prescribed to guard against extrapyramidal symptoms (Pringsheim, Doja, Belanger, & Patten, 2011), and, more recently, treating psychiatrists are often adding metformin to treatment with antipsychotics in an attempt to minimize weight gain and prevent metabolic syndromes and prediabetes associated with the primary treatment (de Silva et al., 2016; Siskind, Leung, Russell, Wysoczanski, & Kisely, 2016).

Several other medical-based approaches have also been studied for treatment of primary schizophrenia in adult patients. Though electroconvulsive shock therapy (ECT) has not been shown to be independently effective for treating psychosis, there is some evidence that the combination of ECT and antipsychotic medications may result in superior treatment effects in schizophrenia, particularly for patients experiencing catatonia (Pompili et al., 2013; Zervas, Theleritis, & Soldatos, 2012), as well as in treatment-resistant schizophrenia (Lally et al., 2016; W. Zheng et al., 2016). Additionally, there is some evidence that repetitive transcranial magnetic stimulation (rTMS) may have a moderate effect for improving, in particular, negative symptoms of schizophrenia (Lefaucheur et al., 2014; Shi, Yu, Cheung, Shum, & Chan, 2014).

Once acute positive symptoms are more stable, psychosocial interventions can play an important role in improving functional outcomes. Psychoeducation-based interventions, administered both to patients and to their families, can reduce relapse rates and readmissions, increase knowledge about the disorder, and improve treatment compliance (Xia, Merinder, & Belgamwar, 2011). Importantly, though cognitive behavioral therapy (CBT), when added to antipsychotic medication, was initially thought to be a promising approach for more effectively treating positive symptoms of schizophrenia (Zimmermann, Favrod, Trieu, & Pomini, 2005), more recently reviews suggest that where benefits exist, the effect sizes are modest (Wykes, Steel, Everitt, & Tarrier, 2008). Some reviews have gone further in concluding that the evidence in favor of cognitive behavioral therapy for schizophrenia is limited (Jones & Cormac, 2010; Jones, Hacker, Cormac, Meaden, & Irving, 2012; Lynch, Laws, & McKenna, 2010; Newton-Howes & Wood, 2013), with effect sizes for improving symptoms small at best (Jauhar et al., 2014; Laws, Darlington, Kondel, McKenna, & Jauhar, 2018).

Research instead seems to favor more comprehensive, multidisciplinary treatments, often involving families and typically including community integration components. For example, assertive community treatment, which involves a multidisciplinary, team-based approach to providing integrated services, focusing on both medication management and functional daily living skills within the community, has been shown to be effective in decreasing psychiatric hospital use, improving quality of life, decreasing symptom severity, improving global assessment of functioning (GAF) scores, and increasing community integration (Bond, Drake, Mueser, & Latimer, 2001; T.-W. Kim et al., 2015; Lehman et al., 2004). Family-based interventions may also decrease relapse rates (Pitschel-Walz, Leucht, Bäuml, Kissling, & Engel, 2001). In youth at risk for psychosis but without formal psychotic disorder, a group- and family-based CBT program was effective in decreasing positive symptoms of psychosis, including delusions and suspiciousness/persecution, as well as in reducing active social avoidance and improving social engagement (Landa et al., 2016). This study suggests that, where children and adolescents are expressing subclinical psychotic symptoms and have not yet converted to full-blown psychosis, psychosocial interventions, often in tandem with pharmacological treatment, may be helpful in reducing symptoms and improving function before the clinical picture exacerbates.

For treating secondary symptoms, there is evidence that cognitive remediation—whether administered in a computer-based or paper-and-pencil fashion, can be effective for improving cognitive performance in diagnosed individuals (Hogarty et al., 2004; Hogarty, Greenwald, & Eack, 2006; Morin & Franck, 2017; Wykes, Huddy, Cellard, McGurk, & Czobor, 2011), as well as for improving both cognitive and social outcomes in individuals at ultra-high risk for psychosis (Glenthøj, Hjorthøj, Kristensen, Davidson, & Nordentoft, 2017) and patients with schizophrenia early in their course of illness (Eack et al., 2009). Likewise, social skills training can improve social functioning and specific conversational and problem-solving skills while reducing negative symptoms of schizophrenia (Aleman et al., 2017; Bellack, 2004; Bustillo, Lauriello, Horan, & Keith, 2001; Elis, Caponigro, & Kring, 2013; Morin & Franck, 2017; Mueser & Penn, 2004; Pilling et al., 2002). However, neither of these two treatments effectively address core positive symptoms, making them more useful as adjunct therapies for patients whose cognitive and social deficits may be contributing to poor functional outcomes.

Whether interventions most effective for psychosis in patients with primary schizophrenia diagnoses will be equally effective in individuals whose psychosis is comorbid with a primary ASD diagnosis remains largely unknown. However, until systematic evidence and best practice recommendations for treatment of psychosis in ASD exist, a few rules of thumb may be applied. First, medication trials ought to be closely monitored with an eye toward adjusting dosing and/or attempting an alternative medication relatively rapidly after several weeks without symptom reduction. In terms of adjunct therapies, whereas cognitive behavioral treatments may only be appropriate for those individuals with ASD having adequate cognitive and reflective capacity, social skills interventions may be particularly helpful given the double hit of ASD and psychosis on social functioning. Additionally, the same cognitive enhancement therapy shown to be effective in schizophrenia has also shown positive results in nonpsychotic adults with ASD (Eack et al., 2018), making it a promising intervention for those with comorbid diagnoses. Psychoeducation about psychosis, both for the individual with ASD and for his or her family, will likely also be critical, given the added complexity of psychosis overlaid with the pre-existing ASD diagnosis and all its associated treatment and functional impacts. Finally, applying multidisciplinary, team-based, and community-integrated treatments may be critical for fully addressing the needs of individuals with ASD who develop comorbid psychotic disorders. Involvement of professionals expert in both ASD and inpsychosis will likely facilitate the most appropriate care that takes into account all of the challenges and treatment needs stemming from both the original ASD diagnosis and the newer onset psychosis.

Case Example

The complexity of differential diagnosis and importance of identifying psychosis comorbidity for driving treatment recommendations can be illustrated by the case of "Jake" (name changed to protect confidentiality). Jake presented for evaluation at the age of 11, with a history of language and social difficulties and increasing concern about a possible psychotic process at play. Jake had been receiving accommodations in the school setting as well as individual psychotherapy, but at the time of his evaluation, few treatments targeting either ASD or psychosis were in use.

Jake's early development was quite consistent with an ASD diagnosis. Despite motor milestones on track, language milestones were delayed, with first words between age 2 and 2.5 years, and first sentences between 4 and 5 years of age. Once language emerged, idiosyncratic language including frequent neologisms was noted, understanding of nonliteral language was poor, and conversation skills were lacking, resulting in brief back-and-forth exchanges with little to no social chit-chat or attempts to build dialogue. Beginning in early childhood, Jake had difficulty with eye contact, with sharing interest, and with demonstrating a range of facial affect to communicate. He had unusual preoccupations, such as in water, difficulties with transitions, and insistence on routines and about placement of objects in his environment. All of these difficulties persisted into school-age years, and Jake had significant difficulty with peer interactions. He never had friends and had substantial difficulty with both initiating and sustaining interactions with children his age. On both the Autism Diagnostic Observation Schedule (ADOS) and the Social Communication Questionnaire—Lifetime (SCQ-L), assessing his current symptoms and developmental history, respectively, Jake met criteria for ASD diagnosis.

Psychosis concerns emerged due to observations of parents, educators, and clinicians that Jake was increasingly internally preoccupied. Adults in his life were increasingly observing him to pace, appear distracted, become difficult to communicate with, and gesture and make facial expressions as if interacting with someone not present. Though Jake had seemed to daydream at times from a young age, the frequency (daily), intensity, and atypicality of the "episodes" had become concerning over the last 9 months. At school, episodes of internal preoccupation and distractedness were interfering with classwork and engagement, and, in the community, Jake was liable to walk into traffic or a busy parking lot while internally preoccupied. Abnormal motor behavior, including rocking and pacing not typical of Jake previously, was also noted.

Concern was also raised in the context of behavioral observations made during testing. Jake would gaze off to the corner of the room and smile as if engaging with someone not present. When not engaged by the examiner, he talked to himself and to the corner of the room. Per Jake's own report during his evaluation, both auditory and visual hallucinations were described. He described seeing things others cannot and that aren't there, hearing voices, and feeling as if someone else controlled his thoughts, though he could not describe who or how it might work. He described a set of characters who spoke to him and to whom he spoke, and he described seeing the characters in the room with him, including appearing as a shadow during the evaluation. Thus, based on the convergent evidence from self-report, caregiver descriptions, and clinical observations, Jake met criteria for a schizophrenia diagnosis. Clear hallucinations were present, delusional thinking possible (though poorly articulated), and abnormal motor behaviors noted. Negative symptoms, including decreased range of facial expressions, gestures, and prosody, were readily observable; however, it was unclear that these were any different or worse than the nonverbal communication deficits Jake had exhibited from a young age as child with ASD. Disorganized speech was not clearly present, despite atypical language patterns consistent with ASD.

In terms of differential diagnosis, the timeline of Jake's symptoms, presence of clear positive symptoms (hallucinations), and recent deterioration were all key pieces supporting the psychosis diagnosis. Additionally, his symptoms were present across settings and worsening despite having few home or social stressors, clear and predictable schedules and routines, and anxiety-focused individual therapy sessions. To make the diagnostic distinction, observations of both clinicians and caregivers (parents, educators) were critical. Without these pieces, obtaining a clear picture of Jake's symptoms would have been near impossible due to his weak complex language skills and apparent difficulty with introspection and self-observation and self-report.

Treatment for Jake included a mix of both ASD-related interventions and additional treatments addressing the newer onset psychosis. To address his autism-related needs, Jake was referred for both social skills interventions and speech–language therapy to improve his pragmatic language and conversation skills. Academically, a small classroom setting with visual supports, clear routines and assistance with transitions, and paraprofessional support was recommended. However, additional interventions and support were also critical to fully meet Jake's needs. First and foremost, treatment with antipsychotic medication was advised. Goals for individual therapy shifted toward improving reality testing and increasing coping skills, with additional social skills training in that context pushed to lower priority. Importantly, caregivers were also to be brought into the therapy process more formally, with treatment focused on psychoeducation about psychosis, medication monitoring and compliance, maintaining safety, and creating an environment more tailored to Jake's complex needs.

Summary and Future Directions

This chapter summarizes what is known about psychosis in individuals with ASD. Despite a relative paucity of research on this topic, at the current juncture, several things are evident. Individuals with ASD can and do experience psychotic symptoms and develop full-blown psychotic illnesses. Indeed, there are strong biological reasons that this overlap occurs, as there are many genes and brain-based alterations that contribute both to ASD and to schizophrenia, making individuals with one diagnosis more vulnerable to the second. However, what is less clear at present is how best to assess for and diagnose psychosis in ASD, and whether treatments researched and implemented in individuals with primary psychotic disorders are equally effective in individuals with ASD whose psychosis is secondary. Virtually all of what is known about treatment for psychosis comes from either the adult or childhood-onset schizophrenia literatures. Moreover, available diagnostic tools do not account for symptom overlap between ASD and schizophrenia. They also do not provide adequate guidance or structure for evaluating psychosis symptoms when their presentation can be muddied by primary ASD symptoms or when primary ASD symptoms may be mistakenly interpreted as evidence for psychotic symptoms. At present, what is most apparent is that there is a critical need for more research into the nature of psychotic experiences in ASD, as well as into how best to identify and treat them.

One major research need is the clarification of psychotic experiences as they present in individuals with ASD across the lifespan and, in particular, across the functioning spectrum. Research differentiating delusions of psychosis from restricted interests of ASD, disorganized thinking and speech of psychosis from stereotyped language of ASD, and negative symptoms of psychosis from nonverbal communication and social interaction deficits in ASD will continue to be important. Assessment tools to help clinicians parse these features during differential diagnosis will also be important to develop. Better tools are also needed to help diagnose psychosis in individuals with ASD who are verbal but have difficulty with introspection, are concrete in their thinking, or have theory-of-mind deficits that all make traditional clinical interviews less effective tools for probing symptom expression. Finally, tools for detecting and differentiating psychosis in minimally verbal and intellectually disabled individuals with ASD represent a glaring need. Here, research likely must start with gaining a better understanding of how psychotic symptoms present in this population. Once this information is better understood, new diagnostic tools specifically designed for this population will be needed.

A second important area for future research is the trajectory of psychotic symptoms and illnesses in individuals with ASD. In particular, given the high rates of psychotic symptoms identified in some studies in adults with ASD, it will be important to clarify whether individuals with ASD are at greater risk for experiencing isolated and/or transient psychotic symptoms versus whether they are also at risk for developing long-term, chronic psychotic illnesses comorbid with their primary ASD. Answering this question will be important for understanding the degree to which psychotic symptoms warrant intensive treatment versus ought to be monitored and treated more conservatively. In primary schizophrenia spectrum diagnoses, there is often a prodrome period preceding illness onset that is characterized by functional declines, onset of attenuated positive symptoms, and premorbid cognitive deficits. Whether there is an identifiable prodrome period for individuals with ASD who develop psychosis, whether prodrome symptoms in ASD mirror those seen in the general clinical population at high risk for psychosis, and whether prodrome symptoms are equally predictive of transition to comorbid psychotic disorders in ASD are all questions that remain to be clarified in prospective studies.

An additional important area of inquiry includes continued research into genetic, neurological, phenotypic, and developmental profiles that may predict which individuals with ASD will go on to develop psychosis. For example, given the high rates of premorbid ASD symptoms and diagnoses in children with COS, it may be the case that there are particular features within larger groups of children with ASD that could differentiate those who go on to develop psychotic illnesses from those who do not. Studies exploring, in young individuals with ASD without psychotic disorders, the predictive value of brain-based and behavioral profiles that are more characteristic of schizophrenia or of psychosis prodrome than of traditional ASD findings could also be important. Likewise, longitudinal studies in individuals with ASD at genetic or familial high risk for psychosis (i.e., either because of a genetic finding known to be implicated in schizophrenia or because of a close family member with a psychotic illness) could also be important for identifying predictors of psychosis conversion in individuals with ASD who are at increased psychosis risk.

If research can identify strong predictors of who with ASD is most likely to go on to develop psychosis, progress can be made in several directions. First, this work may allow for opportunities for preventative action or differential intervention approaches in young individuals with ASD, prior to psychosis onset, given concern about future developments. Second, this work may pave the way for developing new, objective biomarkers. Such biomarkers could enable stratification of the ASD population into those at low versus high risk for psychosis, measurement of change in psychosis liability over time, and evaluation of response to treatment. Additionally, the identification of reliable biomarkers of psychosis risk in ASD would be of particular value for assessment of minimally verbal individuals with ASD. Many potential biomarkers (e.g., those collected from blood, those measured using structural neuroimaging or passive functional imaging and electrophysiology) require little or no response or comprehension from the assessed individual. Therefore, identification of such biomarkers would be a major breakthrough for circumventing the current challenges of assessing for psychotic symptoms in minimally verbal ASD populations.

Finally, and perhaps most critically, there is a clear need for additional research into the most effective treatments for psychosis in the context of ASD. At present, virtually all treatment for psychotic illness in ASD is administered based on knowledge gained in individuals without ASD, who almost certainly have quite different neurobiological, developmental, and psychosocial foundations. Research is needed to determine which medications are most effective for treating psychosis when it is comorbid with ASD and to develop clinical best practice guidelines for this scenario. Likewise, research must be conducted to evaluate the effectiveness of psychosocial interventions for schizophrenia when implemented with individuals with ASD. Most likely, these interventions will, at minimum, require modifications to improve their fit for individuals with ASD who often will have additional, compounding social, communication, and functional difficulties affecting their ability to engage with and benefit from intervention. Some interventions effective in primary psychotic disorders may not be advised for individuals with ASD and comorbid psychosis, and new interventions may need to be developed to address the unique challenges of individuals with ASD who also develop psychotic illness. Finally, treatment recommendations for minimally verbal individuals with ASD who may develop psychotic experiences are of critical importance and warrant attention in future research.

In sum, it is clear that schizophrenia, other psychotic disorders, and milder psychotic experiences are all important conditions that will affect a nontrivial proportion of individuals with ASD across the lifespan. Although significant research remains to be conducted to better understand the etiology of this comorbidity and to improve our ability to assess and treat it, increased attention to the overlap between ASD and psychosis in recent years bodes well for improving the mass and quality of empirical literature in this area. Until more is known, however, the onus remains on clinicians evaluating and treating individuals with ASD to be on the lookout for possible symptoms of psychosis. When suspicion of psychosis arises, it is the clinician's responsibility to assess symptoms critically, to seek consultation and referrals when needed to improve differential diagnosis, to treat carefully but also assertively, and to monitor regularly over time to head off declines and increase intervention intensity in cases where symptoms progress or worsen.

References

Aderibigbe, Y. A., Theodoridis, D., & Vieweg, W. V. R. (1999). Dementia praecox to schizophrenia: The first 100 years. *Psychiatry and Clinical Neurosciences, 53*(4), 437–448.

Aleman, A., Lincoln, T. M., Bruggeman, R., Melle, I., Arends, J., Arango, C., & Knegtering, H. (2017). Treatment of negative symptoms: Where do we stand, and where do we go? *Schizophrenia Research, 186*, 55–62. https://doi.org/10.1016/j.schres.2016.05.015

American Psychiatric Association. (1980). *Diagnostic and statistical manual of mental disorders* (DSM-III). Author.

American Psychiatric Association. (2013). *Diagnostic and statistical manual of mental disorders* (DSM-5). American Psychiatric Publishing.

American Psychiatric Association, Nomenclature, C. on, & Statistics. (1975). *Diagnostic and statistical manual of mental disorders* (DSM-II). American Psychiatric Association.

American Psychiatry Association. (1994). *Diagnostic and statistical manual of mental disorders* (DSM-IV). Washington, DC: Author.

Andreasen, N. C. (1981). Scale for the Assessment of Negative Symptoms (SANS).

Andreasen, N. C. (1984). *Scale for the Assessment of Positive Symptoms (SAPS)*. Iowa City, IA: University of Iowa.

Arking, D. E., Cutler, D. J., Brune, C. W., Teslovich, T. M., West, K., Ikeda, M., . . . Chakravarti, A. (2008). A common genetic variant in the neurexin superfamily member CNTNAP2 increases familial risk of autism. *American Journal of Human Genetics, 82*(1), 160–164. https://doi.org/10.1016/j.ajhg.2007.09.015

Baron-Cohen, S., Leslie, A. M., & Frith, U. (1985). Does the autistic child have a "theory of mind"? *Cognition, 21*(1), 37–46.

Bäuml, J., Froböse, T., Kraemer, S., Rentrop, M., & Pitschel-Walz, G. (2006). Psychoeducation: A basic psychotherapeutic intervention for patients with schizophrenia and their families. *Schizophrenia Bulletin, 32*(Suppl 1), S1–S9. https://doi.org/10.1093/schbul/sbl017

Bellack, A. S. (2004). Skills training for people with severe mental illness. *Psychiatric Rehabilitation Journal, 27*(4), 375–391. https://doi.org/10.2975/27.2004.375.391

Ben-Shachar, S., Lanpher, B., German, J. R., Qasaymeh, M., Potocki, L., Nagamani, S. C. S., . . . Sahoo, T. (2009). Microdeletion 15q13.3: A locus with incomplete penetrance for autism, mental retardation, and psychiatric disorders. *Journal of Medical Genetics, 46*(6), 382–388. https://doi.org/10.1136/jmg.2008.064378

Berrios, G. E., & Hauser, R. (1988). The early development of Kraepelin's ideas on classification: A conceptual history. *Psychological Medicine, 18*(4), 813–821. https://doi.org/10.1017/S0033291700009740

Billstedt, E., Gillberg, C., & Gillberg, C. (2005). Autism after adolescence: Population-based 13- to 22-year follow-up study of 120 individuals with autism diagnosed in childhood. *Journal of Autism and Developmental Disorders, 35*(3), 351–360. https://doi.org/10.1007/s10803-005-3302-5

Bleuler, E. (1911). *Dementia Praecox oder Gruppe der Schizophrenien*. Leipzig, Germany: Deuticke.

Bleuler, E. (1950). *Dementia praecox or the group of schizophrenias* (J. Zinkin, Trans.). New York, NY: International Universities Press.

Bond, G. R., Drake, R. E., Mueser, K. T., & Latimer, E. (2001). Assertive community treatment for people with severe mental illness: Critical ingredients and impact on patients. *Disease Management and Health Outcomes, 9*(3), 141–159. https://doi.org/10.2165/00115677-200109030-00003

Bora, E., Yucel, M., & Pantelis, C. (2009). Theory of mind impairment in schizophrenia: Meta-analysis. *Schizophrenia Research, 109*(1–3), 1–9.

Buitelaar, J. K., & Van der Gaag, R. J. (1998). Diagnostic rules for children with PDD-NOS and multiple complex developmental disorder. *Journal of Child Psychology and Psychiatry and Allied Disciplines, 39*(6), 911–919.

Burbach, J. P. H., & van der Zwaag, B. (2009). Contact in the genetics of autism and schizophrenia. *Trends in Neurosciences, 32*(2), 69–72. https://doi.org/10.1016/j.tins.2008.11.002

Bustillo, J. R., Lauriello, J., Horan, W. P., & Keith, S. J. (2001). The psychosocial treatment of schizophrenia: An update. *American Journal of Psychiatry, 158*(2), 163–175. https://doi.org/10.1176/appi.ajp.158.2.163

Carroll, L. S., & Owen, M. J. (2009). Genetic overlap between autism, schizophrenia and bipolar disorder. *Genome Medicine, 1*(10), 102. https://doi.org/10.1186/gm102

Castle, D. J., Jablensky, A., McGrath, J. J., Carr, V., Morgan, V., Waterreus, A., . . . Farmer, A. (2005). The Diagnostic Interview for Psychoses (DIP): Development, reliability and applications. *Psychological Medicine, 36*(1), 69. https://doi.org/10.1017/S0033291705005969

Charney, D. S., Buxbaum, J. D., Sklar, P., & Nestler, E. J. (2018). *Neurobiology of mental illness* (5th ed.). Oxford University Press.

Chen, H., Uddin, L. Q., Duan, X., Zheng, J., Long, Z., Zhang, Y., . . . Chen, H. (2017). Shared atypical default mode and salience network functional connectivity between autism and schizophrenia. *Autism Research, 10*(11), 1776–1786. https://doi.org/10.1002/aur.1834

Chien, W. T., Leung, S. F., Yeung, F. K., & Wong, W. K. (2013). Current approaches to treatments for schizophrenia spectrum disorders, part II: Psychosocial interventions and patient-focused perspectives in psychiatric care. *Neuropsychiatric Disease and Treatment, 9*, 1463–1481. https://doi.org/10.2147/NDT.S49263

Cohen, D. J., Paul, R., & Volkmar, F. R. (1986). Issues in the classification of pervasive and other developmental disorders: Toward DSM-IV. *Journal of the American Academy of Child Psychiatry, 25*(2), 213–220. https://doi.org/10.1016/S0002-7138(09)60228-4

Couture, S. M., Penn, D. L., Losh, M., Adolphs, R., Hurley, R., & Piven, J. (2010). Comparison of social cognitive functioning in schizophrenia and high functioning autism: More convergence than divergence. *Psychological Medicine, 40*(4), 569–579.

Crespi, B., & Badcock, C. (2008). Psychosis and autism as diametrical disorders of the social brain. *Behavioral and Brain Sciences, 31*(3). https://doi.org/10.1017/S0140525X08004214

Daniels, J. L., Forssen, U., Hultman, C. M., Cnattingius, S., Savitz, D. A., Feychting, M., & Sparen, P. (2008). Parental psychiatric disorders associated with autism spectrum disorders in the offspring. *Pediatrics, 121*(5), e1357–e1362. https://doi.org/10.1542/peds.2007–2296

de Bruin, E. I., de Nijs, P. F. A., Verheij, F., Hartman, C. A., & Ferdinand, R. F. (2007). Multiple complex developmental disorder delineated from PDD-NOS. *Journal of Autism and Developmental Disorders, 37*(6), 1181–1191. https://doi.org/10.1007/s10803-006-0261-4

de Lacy, N., & King, B. H. (2013). Revisiting the relationship between autism and schizophrenia: Toward an integrated neurobiology. *Annual Review of Clinical Psychology, 9*(1), 555–587. https://doi.org/10.1146/annurev-clinpsy-050212–185627

de Silva, V. A., Suraweera, C., Ratnatunga, S. S., Dayabandara, M., Wanniarachchi, N., & Hanwella, R. (2016). Metformin in prevention and treatment of antipsychotic induced weight gain: A systematic review and meta-analysis. *BMC Psychiatry, 16*(1). https://doi.org/10.1186/s12888-016-1049-5

Dossetor, D. R. (2007). "All that glitters is not gold": Misdiagnosis of psychosis in pervasive developmental disorders—A case series. *Clinical Child Psychology and Psychiatry, 12*(4), 537–548. https://doi.org/10.1177/1359104507078476

Downs, J. M., Lechler, S., Dean, H., Sears, N., Patel, R., Shetty, H., . . . Pina-Camacho, L. (2017). The association between comorbid autism spectrum disorders and antipsychotic treatment failure in early-onset psychosis: A historical cohort study using electronic health records. *Journal of Clinical Psychiatry, 78*(9), e1233–e1241. https://doi.org/10.4088/JCP.16m11422

Driver, D. I., Gogtay, N., & Rapoport, J. L. (2013). Childhood onset schizophrenia and early onset schizophrenia spectrum disorders. *Child and Adolescent Psychiatric Clinics of North America, 22*(4), 539–555. https://doi.org/10.1016/j.chc.2013.04.001

Durand, C. M., Betancur, C., Boeckers, T. M., Bockmann, J., Chaste, P., Fauchereau, F., . . . Bourgeron, T. (2007). Mutations in the gene encoding the synaptic scaffolding protein SHANK3 are associated with autism spectrum disorders. *Nature Genetics, 39*(1), 25–27. https://doi.org/10.1038/ng1933

Eack, S. M., Hogarty, G. E., Cooley, S. J., DiBarry, A. L., Hogarty, S. S., Greenwald, D. P., . . . Keshavan, M. S. (2009). Cognitive enhancement therapy for early course schizophrenia: Effects of a two-year randomized controlled trial. *Psychiatric Services (Washington, D.C.), 60*(11), 1468–1476. https://doi.org/10.1176/appi.ps.60.11.1468

Eack, S. M., Hogarty, S. S., Greenwald, D. P., Litschge, M. Y., Porton, S. A., Mazefsky, C. A., & Minshew, N. J. (2018). Cognitive enhancement therapy for adult autism spectrum disorder: Results of an 18-month randomized clinical trial. *Autism Research, 11*(3), 519–530. https://doi.org/10.1002/aur.1913

Elis, O., Caponigro, J. M., & Kring, A. M. (2013). Psychosocial treatments for negative symptoms in schizophrenia: Current practices and future directions. *Clinical Psychology Review, 33*(8), 914–928. https://doi.org/10.1016/j.cpr.2013.07.001

First, M. B., Gibbon, M., Spitzer, R. L., & Williams, J. B. (1996). *User's guide for the Structured Clinical Interview for DSM-IV axis I disorders—Research version.* New York, NY: Biometrics Research Department, New York State Psychiatric Institute.

First, M., Williams, J., Karg, R., & Spitzer, R. (2015). *Structured Clinical Interview for DSM-5—Research Version (SCID-5 for DSM-5, Research Version; SCID-5-RV).* Arlington, VA: American Psychiatric Association.

First, M., Williams, J., Karg, R., & Spitzer, R. (2016). *Structured Clinical Interview for DSM-5 Disorders, Clinician Version (SCID-5-CV).* Arlington, VA: American Psychiatric Association.

Foss-Feig, J. H., Adkinson, B. D., Ji, J. L., Yang, G., Srihari, V. H., McPartland, J. C.,... Anticevic, A. (2017). Searching for cross-diagnostic convergence: Neural mechanisms governing excitation and inhibition balance in schizophrenia and autism spectrum disorders. *Biological Psychiatry, 81*(10), 848–861. https://doi.org/10.1016/j.biopsych.2017.03.005

Foss-Feig, J. H., Velthorst, E., Smith, L., Reichenberg, A., Addington, J., Cadenhead, K.S.,... Bearden, C. (2019). Clinical profiles and conversion rates among young individuals with autism spectrum disorder who present to clinical high risk for psychosis services. *Journal of the American Academy of Child & Adolescent Psychiatry, 58*(6), 582-588.

Friedman, J. I., Vrijenhoek, T., Markx, S., Janssen, I. M., Vliet, W. A., van der, Faas, B. H. W.,... Veltman, J. A. (2008). *CNTNAP2* gene dosage variation is associated with schizophrenia and epilepsy. *Molecular Psychiatry, 13*(3), 261–266. https://doi.org/10.1038/sj.mp.4002049

Frith, C. D., & Corcoran, R. (1996). Exploring "theory of mind" in people with schizophrenia. *Psychological Medicine, 26*(3), 521–530.

Fung, L. K., Mahajan, R., Nozzolillo, A., Bernal, P., Krasner, A., Jo, B.,... Hardan, A. Y. (2016). Pharmacologic treatment of severe irritability and problem behaviors in autism: A systematic review and meta-analysis. *Pediatrics, 137*(Suppl 2), S124–135. https://doi.org/10.1542/peds.2015-2851K

Gauthier, J., Champagne, N., Lafrenière, R. G., Xiong, L., Spiegelman, D., Brustein, E.,... the S2D Team. (2010). De novo mutations in the gene encoding the synaptic scaffolding protein *SHANK3* in patients ascertained for schizophrenia. *Proceedings of the National Academy of Sciences, 107*(17), 7863–7868. https://doi.org/10.1073/pnas.0906232107

Glenthøj, L. B., Hjorthøj, C., Kristensen, T. D., Davidson, C. A., & Nordentoft, M. (2017). The effect of cognitive remediation in individuals at ultra-high risk for psychosis: a systematic review. *NPJ Schizophrenia, 3*. https://doi.org/10.1038/s41537-017-0021-9

Hogarty, G. E., Flesher, S., Ulrich, R., Carter, M., Greenwald, D., Pogue-Geile, M.,... Zoretich, R. (2004). Cognitive enhancement therapy for schizophrenia: Effects of a 2-year randomized trial on cognition and behavior. *Archives of General Psychiatry, 61*(9), 866–876. https://doi.org/10.1001/archpsyc.61.9.866

Hogarty, G. E., Greenwald, D. P., & Eack, S. M. (2006). Special Section: A memorial tribute: Durability and mechanism of effects of cognitive enhancement therapy. *Psychiatric Services, 57*(12), 1751–1757. https://doi.org/10.1176/ps.2006.57.12.1751

Hollis, C., & Rapoport, J. (2011). Child and adolescent schizophrenia. In *Schizophrenia* (pp. 24–46). Wiley-Blackwell. https://doi.org/10.1002/9781444327298.ch3

Jauhar, S., McKenna, P. J., Radua, J., Fung, E., Salvador, R., & Laws, K. R. (2014). Cognitive–behavioural therapy for the symptoms of schizophrenia: Systematic review and meta-analysis with examination of potential bias. *British Journal of Psychiatry, 204*(1), 20–29. https://doi.org/10.1192/bjp.bp.112.116285

Jones, C., & Cormac, I. (2010). Cognitive behaviour therapy for schizophrenia, 74.

Jones, C., Hacker, D., Cormac, I., Meaden, A., & Irving, C. B. (2012). Cognitive behavioural therapy versus other psychosocial treatments for schizophrenia. *Cochrane Database of Systematic Reviews, 4*, CD008712. https://doi.org/10.1002/14651858.CD008712.pub2

Kane, J., Honigfeld, G., Singer, J., & Meltzer, H. (1988). Clozapine for the treatment-resistant schizophrenic: A double-blind comparison with chlorpromazine. *Archives of General Psychiatry, 45*(9), 789–796. https://doi.org/10.1001/archpsyc.1988.01800330013001

Kanner, L. (1943). Autistic disturbances of affective contact. *Nervous Child, 2*(3), 217–250.

Kasoff, L. I., Ahn, K., Gochman, P., Broadnax, D. D., & Rapoport, J. L. (2016). Strong treatment response and high maintenance rates of clozapine in childhood-onset schizophrenia. *Journal of Child and Adolescent Psychopharmacology, 26*(5), 428–435. https://doi.org/10.1089/cap.2015.0103

Kay, S. R., Fiszbein, A., & Opler, L. A. (1987). The Positive and Negative Syndrome Scale (PANSS) for schizophrenia. *Schizophrenia Bulletin, 13*(2), 261–276.

Kim, H.-G., Kishikawa, S., Higgins, A. W., Seong, I.-S., Donovan, D. J., Shen, Y.,... Gusella, J. F. (2008). Disruption of neurexin 1 associated with autism spectrum disorder. *American Journal of Human Genetics, 82*(1), 199–207. https://doi.org/10.1016/j.ajhg.2007.09.011

Kim, T.-W., Jeong, J.-H., Kim, Y.-H., Kim, Y., Seo, H.-J., & Hong, S.-C. (2015). Fifteen-month follow up of an assertive community treatment program for chronic patients with mental illness. *BMC Health Services Research, 15*. https://doi.org/10.1186/s12913-015-1058-y

Kolvin, I. (1971). Studies in the childhood psychoses I. Diagnostic criteria and classification. *British Journal of Psychiatry, 118*(545), 381–384.

Konstantareas, M. M., & Hewitt, T. (2001). Autistic disorder and schizophrenia: Diagnostic overlaps. *Journal of Autism and Developmental Disorders, 31*(1), 10.

Krause, M., Zhu, Y., Huhn, M., Schneider-Thoma, J., Bighelli, I., Chaimani, A., & Leucht, S. (2018). Efficacy, acceptability, and tolerability of antipsychotics in children and adolescents with schizophrenia: A network meta-analysis. *European Neuropsychopharmacology, 28*(6), 659–674. https://doi.org/10.1016/j.euroneuro.2018.03.008

Lally, J., Tully, J., Robertson, D., Stubbs, B., Gaughran, F., & MacCabe, J. H. (2016). Augmentation of clozapine with electroconvulsive therapy in treatment resistant schizophrenia: A systematic review and meta-analysis. *Schizophrenia Research, 171*(1–3), 215–224. https://doi.org/10.1016/j.schres.2016.01.024

Landa, Y., Mueser, K. T., Wyka, K. E., Shreck, E., Jespersen, R., Jacobs, M. A.,... Walkup, J. T. (2016). Development of a group and family-based cognitive behavioral therapy program for youth at risk for psychosis. *Early Intervention in Psychiatry, 10*(6), 511–521. https://doi.org/10.1111/eip.12204

Larson, F. V., Wagner, A. P., Jones, P. B., Tantam, D., Lai, M.-C., Baron-Cohen, S., & Holland, A. J. (2017). Psychosis in autism: Comparison of the features of both conditions in a dually affected cohort. *British Journal of Psychiatry, 210*(4), 269–275. https://doi.org/10.1192/bjp.bp.116.187682

Laws, K. R., Darlington, N., Kondel, T. K., McKenna, P. J., & Jauhar, S. (2018). Cognitive behavioural therapy for schizophrenia—Outcomes for functioning, distress and quality of life: A meta-analysis. *BMC Psychology, 6*. https://doi.org/10.1186/s40359-018-0243-2

Lefaucheur, J.-P., André-Obadia, N., Antal, A., Ayache, S. S., Baeken, C., Benninger, D. H.,... Garcia-Larrea, L. (2014). Evidence-based guidelines on the therapeutic use of repetitive transcranial magnetic stimulation (rTMS). *Clinical*

Neurophysiology, 125(11), 2150–2206. https://doi.org/10.1016/j.clinph.2014.05.021

Lehman, A. F., Lieberman, J. A., Dixon, L. B., McGlashan, T. H., Miller, A. L., Perkins, D. O., . . . Regier, D. (2004). Practice guideline for the treatment of patients with schizophrenia, second edition. *American Journal of Psychiatry, 161*(2 Suppl). Retrieved from \

Levinson, D. F., Duan, J., Oh, S., Wang, K., Sanders, A. R., Shi, J., . . . Gejman, P. V. (2011). Copy number variants in schizophrenia: Confirmation of five previous findings and new evidence for 3q29 microdeletions and VIPR2 duplications. *American Journal of Psychiatry, 168*(3), 302–316. https://doi.org/10.1176/appi.ajp.2010.10060876

Liu, X., Li, Z., Fan, C., Zhang, D., & Chen, J. (2017). Genetics implicate common mechanisms in autism and schizophrenia: Synaptic activity and immunity. *Journal of Medical Genetics*,. https://doi.org/10.1136/jmedgenet-2016–104487

Lord, C., Rutter, M., DiLavore, P. C., & Risi, S. (2003). *Autism Diagnostic Observation Schedule: ADOS*. Los Angeles, CA: Western Psychological Services.

Lynch, D., Laws, K. R., & McKenna, P. J. (2010). Cognitive behavioural therapy for major psychiatric disorder: Does it really work? A meta-analytical review of well-controlled trials. *Psychological Medicine, 40*(1), 9–24. https://doi.org/10.1017/S003329170900590X

Mastrovito, D., Hanson, C., & Hanson, S. J. (2018). Differences in atypical resting-state effective connectivity distinguish autism from schizophrenia. *NeuroImage: Clinical, 18*, 367–376. https://doi.org/10.1016/j.nicl.2018.01.014

McCarthy, S., Makarov, V., Kirov, G., Addington, A., McClellan, J., Yoon, S., . . . Sebat, J. (2009). Microduplications of 16p11.2 are associated with schizophrenia. *Nature Genetics, 41*(11), 1223–1227. https://doi.org/10.1038/ng.474

McGlashan, T. H., Walsh, B. C., & Woods, S. W. (2001). *Structured Interview for Psychosis-risk syndromes*. New Haven, CT: Yale School of Medicine.

Miller, D. T., Shen, Y., Weiss, L. A., Korn, J., Anselm, I., Bridgemohan, C., . . . Wu, B.-L. (2009). Microdeletion/duplication at 15q13.2q13.3 among individuals with features of autism and other neuropsychiatric disorders. *Journal of Medical Genetics, 46*(4), 242–248. https://doi.org/10.1136/jmg.2008.059907

Moreno-De-Luca, D., Mulle, J. G., Kaminsky, E. B., Sanders, S. J., Myers, S. M., Adam, M. P., . . . Ledbetter, D. H. (2010). Deletion 17q12 is a recurrent copy number variant that confers high risk of autism and schizophrenia. *American Journal of Human Genetics, 87*(5), 618–630. https://doi.org/10.1016/j.ajhg.2010.10.004

Moreno-Küstner, B., Martín, C., & Pastor, L. (2018). Prevalence of psychotic disorders and its association with methodological issues. A systematic review and meta-analyses. *PLoS ONE, 13*(4). https://doi.org/10.1371/journal.pone.0195687

Morin, L., & Franck, N. (2017). Rehabilitation interventions to promote recovery from schizophrenia: A systematic review. *Frontiers in Psychiatry, 8*. https://doi.org/10.3389/fpsyt.2017.00100

Moss, S., Patel, P., Prosser, H., Goldberg, D., Simpson, N., Rowe, S., & Lucchino, R. (1993). Psychiatric morbidity in older people with moderate and severe learning disability (mental retardation). Part I: Development and reliability of the patient interview (the PAS-ADD). *British Journal of Psychiatry, 163*(4), 471–480. https://doi.org/10.1192/bjp.163.4.471

Moss, S., Prosser, H., Costello, H., Simpson, N., Patel, P., Rowe, S., . . . Hatton, C. (1998). Reliability and validity of the PAS-ADD Checklist for detecting psychiatric disorders in adults with intellectual disability. *Journal of Intellectual Disability Research, 42*(2), 173–183. https://doi.org/10.1046/j.1365–2788.1998.00116.x

Mouridsen, S. E., Rich, B., & Isager, T. (2008). Psychiatric disorders in adults diagnosed as children with atypical autism. A case control study. *Journal of Neural Transmission, 115*(1), 135–138. https://doi.org/10.1007/s00702-007-0798-1

Mouridsen, S. E., Rich, B., Isager, T., & Nedergaard, N. J. (2008). Psychiatric disorders in individuals diagnosed with infantile autism as children: A case control study. *Journal of Psychiatric Practice, 14*(1), 5. https://doi.org/10.1097/01.pra.0000308490.47262.e0

Mueser, K. T., & Penn, D. L. (2004). Meta-analysis examining the effects of social skills training on schizophrenia. *Psychological Medicine, 34*(7), 1365–1367. https://doi.org/10.1017/S0033291704213848

Newton-Howes, G., & Wood, R. (2013). Cognitive behavioural therapy and the psychopathology of schizophrenia: Systematic review and meta-analysis. *Psychology and Psychotherapy: Theory, Research and Practice, 86*(2), 127–138. https://doi.org/10.1111/j.2044–8341.2011.02048.x

Ornitz, E. M. (1970). Vestibular dysfunction in schizophrenia and childhood autism. *Comprehensive Psychiatry, 11*(2), 159–173. https://doi.org/10.1016/0010-440X(70)90157–4

Overall, J. E., & Gorham, D. R. (1962). The Brief Psychiatric Rating Scale. *Psychological Reports, 10*, 799–812.

Park, S. Y., Cervesi, C., Galling, B., Molteni, S., Walyzada, F., Ameis, S. H., . . . Correll, C. U. (2016). Antipsychotic use trends in youth with autism spectrum disorder and/or intellectual disability: A meta-analysis. *Journal of the American Academy of Child & Adolescent Psychiatry, 55*(6), 456–468.e4. https://doi.org/10.1016/j.jaac.2016.03.012

Perälä, J., Suvisaari, J., Saarni, S. I., Kuoppasalmi, K., Isometsä, E., Pirkola, S., . . . Lönnqvist, J. (2007). Lifetime prevalence of psychotic and bipolar I disorders in a general population. *Archives of General Psychiatry, 64*(1), 19–28. https://doi.org/10.1001/archpsyc.64.1.19

Petty, L. K., Ornitz, E. M., Michelman, J. D., & Zimmerman, E. G. (1984). Autistic children who become schizophrenic. *Archives of General Psychiatry, 41*(2), 129–135. https://doi.org/10.1001/archpsyc.1984.01790130023003

Pilling, S., Bebbington, P., Kuipers, E., Garety, P., Geddes, J., Orbach, G., & Morgan, C. (2002). Psychological treatments in schizophrenia: I. Meta-analysis of family intervention and cognitive behaviour therapy. *Psychological Medicine, 32*(5), 763–782. https://doi.org/10.1017/S0033291702005895

Pinkham, A. E., Hopfinger, J. B., Pelphrey, K. A., Piven, J., & Penn, D. L. (2008a). Neural bases for impaired social cognition in schizophrenia and autism spectrum disorders. *Schizophrenia Research, 99*(1–3), 164–175.

Pinkham, A. E., Hopfinger, J. B., Pelphrey, K. A., Piven, J., & Penn, D. L. (2008b). Neural bases for impaired social cognition in schizophrenia and autism spectrum disorders. *Schizophrenia Research, 99*(1–3), 164–175. https://doi.org/10.1016/j.schres.2007.10.024

Pitschel-Walz, G., Leucht, S., Bäuml, J., Kissling, W., & Engel, R. R. (2001). The effect of family interventions on relapse and rehospitalization in schizophrenia—A meta-analysis. *Schizophrenia Bulletin, 27*(1), 73–92. https://doi.org/10.1093/oxfordjournals.schbul.a006861

Pompili, M., Lester, D., Dominici, G., Longo, L., Marconi, G., Forte, A., . . . Girardi, P. (2013). Indications for electroconvulsive treatment in schizophrenia: A systematic review. *Schizophrenia Research, 146*(1), 1–9. https://doi.org/10.1016/j.schres.2013.02.005

Pringsheim, T., Doja, A., Belanger, S., & Patten, S. (2011). Treatment recommendations for extrapyramidal side effects associated with second-generation antipsychotic use in children and youth. *Paediatrics & Child Health, 16*(9), 590–598.

Prosser, H., Moss, S., Costello, H., Simpson, N., Patel, P., & Rowe, S. (1998). Reliability and validity of the Mini PAS-ADD for assessing psychiatric disorders in adults with intellectual disability. *Journal of Intellectual Disability Research, 42*(4), 264–272. https://doi.org/10.1046/j.1365–2788.1998.00146.x

Radeloff, D., Ciaramidaro, A., Siniatchkin, M., Hainz, D., Schlitt, S., Weber, B., . . . Freitag, C. M. (2014). Structural alterations of the social brain: A comparison between schizophrenia and autism. *PLoS ONE, 9*(9), e106539. https://doi.org/10.1371/journal.pone.0106539

Rapoport, J., Chavez, A., Greenstein, D., Addington, A., & Gogtay, N. (2009). Autism spectrum disorders and childhood-onset schizophrenia: Clinical and biological contributions to a relation revisited. *Journal of the American Academy of Child & Adolescent Psychiatry, 48*(1), 10–18. https://doi.org/10.1097/CHI.0b013e31818b1c63

Rujescu, D., Ingason, A., Cichon, S., Pietiläinen, O. P. H., Barnes, M. R., Toulopoulou, T., . . . Collier, D. A. (2009). Disruption of the neurexin 1 gene is associated with schizophrenia. *Human Molecular Genetics, 18*(5), 988–996. https://doi.org/10.1093/hmg/ddn351

Rutter, M. (1972). Childhood schizophrenia reconsidered. *Journal of Autism and Childhood Schizophrenia, 2*(3), 315–337. https://doi.org/10.1007/BF01537622

Rutter, M., Le Couteur, A., & Lord, C. (2003). *Autism Diagnostic Interview-Revised.* Los Angeles, CA: Western Psychological Services.

Sagar, A., Bishop, J. R., Tessman, D. C., Guter, S., Martin, C. L., & Cook, E. H. (2013). Co-occurrence of autism, childhood psychosis, and intellectual disability associated with a de novo 3q29 microdeletion. *American Journal of Medical Genetics, Part A, 161*(4), 845–849. https://doi.org/10.1002/ajmg.a.35754

Samara, M. T., Dold, M., Gianatsi, M., Nikolakopoulou, A., Helfer, B., Salanti, G., & Leucht, S. (2016). Efficacy, acceptability, and tolerability of antipsychotics in treatment-resistant schizophrenia: A network meta-analysis. *JAMA Psychiatry, 73*(3), 199–210. https://doi.org/10.1001/jamapsychiatry.2015.2955

Selten, J.-P., Lundberg, M., Rai, D., & Magnusson, C. (2015). Risks for nonaffective psychotic disorder and bipolar disorder in young people with autism spectrum disorder: A population-based study. *JAMA Psychiatry, 72*(5), 483–489. https://doi.org/10.1001/jamapsychiatry.2014.3059

Shi, C., Yu, X., Cheung, E. F. C., Shum, D. H. K., & Chan, R. C. K. (2014). Revisiting the therapeutic effect of rTMS on negative symptoms in schizophrenia: A meta-analysis. *Psychiatry Research, 215*(3), 505–513. https://doi.org/10.1016/j.psychres.2013.12.019

Sienaert, P., Dhossche, D. M., Vancampfort, D., De Hert, M., & Gazdag, G. (2014). A clinical review of the treatment of catatonia. *Frontiers in Psychiatry, 5*. https://doi.org/10.3389/fpsyt.2014.00181

Siskind, D. J., Leung, J., Russell, A. W., Wysoczanski, D., & Kisely, S. (2016). Metformin for clozapine associated obesity: A systematic review and meta-analysis. *PLoS ONE, 11*(6). https://doi.org/10.1371/journal.pone.0156208

Sporn, A. L., Vermani, A., Greenstein, D. K., Bobb, A. J., Spencer, E. P., Clasen, L. S., . . . Gogtay, N. (2007). Clozapine treatment of childhood-onset schizophrenia: Evaluation of effectiveness, adverse effects, and long-term outcome. *Journal of the American Academy of Child & Adolescent Psychiatry, 46*(10), 1349–1356. https://doi.org/10.1097/chi.0b013e31812eed10

Sprong, M., Becker, H. E., Schothorst, P. F., Swaab, H., Ziermans, T. B., Dingemans, P. M., . . . van Engeland, H. (2008). Pathways to psychosis: A comparison of the pervasive developmental disorder subtype multiple complex developmental disorder and the "at risk mental state." *Schizophrenia Research, 99*(1–3), 38–47. https://doi.org/10.1016/j.schres.2007.10.031

Stahlberg, O., Soderstrom, H., Rastam, M., & Gillberg, C. (2004). Bipolar disorder, schizophrenia, and other psychotic disorders in adults with childhood onset AD/HD and/or autism spectrum disorders. *Journal of Neural Transmission, 111*(7). https://doi.org/10.1007/s00702-004-0115-1

Stefansson, H., Rujescu, D., Cichon, S., Pietiläinen, O. P. H., Ingason, A., Steinberg, S., . . . Stefansson, K. (2008). Large recurrent microdeletions associated with schizophrenia. *Nature, 455*(7210), 232–236. https://doi.org/10.1038/nature07229

Sugranyes, G., Kyriakopoulos, M., Corrigall, R., Taylor, E., & Frangou, S. (2011). Autism spectrum disorders and schizophrenia: Meta-analysis of the neural correlates of social cognition. *PloS ONE, 6*(10), e25322.

Sullivan, P. F., Magnusson, C., Reichenberg, A., Boman, M., Dalman, C., Davidson, M., . . . Lichtenstein, P. (2012). Family history of schizophrenia and bipolar disorder as risk factors for autism. *Archives of General Psychiatry, 69*(11), 1099–1103. https://doi.org/10.1001/archgenpsychiatry.2012.730

Szatmari, P., Bartolucci, G., Bremner, R., Bond, S., & Rich, S. (1989). A follow-up study of high-functioning autistic children. *Journal of Autism and Developmental Disorders, 19*(2), 13.

Tantam, D. (1988). Lifelong eccentricity and social isolation: I. Psychiatric, social, and forensic aspects. *British Journal of Psychiatry, 153*(6), 777–782. https://doi.org/10.1192/bjp.153.6.777

Tantam, D. (1991). Asperger syndrome in adulthood. *Autism and Asperger Syndrome, 147.*

Taskiran, S., & Coffey, B. J. (2013). Unremitting impulsive aggression in a child with childhood onset schizophrenia and pervasive development disorder-not otherwise specified: The role of stimulants, atypical antipsychotics and mood stabilizers. *Journal of Child and Adolescent Psychopharmacology, 23*(5), 363–366. https://doi.org/10.1089/cap.2013.2353

Toal, F., Bloemen, O. J. N., Deeley, Q., Tunstall, N., Daly, E. M., Page, L., . . . Murphy, D. G. M. (2009). Psychosis and autism: Magnetic resonance imaging study of brain anatomy. *British Journal of Psychiatry, 194*(5), 418–425. https://doi.org/10.1192/bjp.bp.107.049007

Towbin, K. E., Dykens, E. M., Pearson, G. S., & Cohen, D. J. (1993). Conceptualizing "borderline syndrome of childhood" and "childhood schizophrenia" as a developmental disorder. *Journal of the American Academy of Child & Adolescent Psychiatry, 32*(4), 775–782. https://doi.org/10.1097/00004583-199307000-00011

Uhlhaas, P. J., & Singer, W. (2006). Neural synchrony in brain disorders: Relevance for cognitive dysfunctions and pathophysiology. *Neuron, 52*(1), 155–168. https://doi.org/10.1016/j.neuron.2006.09.020

Van der Gaag, R. J., Buitelaar, J., Ban, E. V. D., Bezemer, M., Njio, L., & Engeland, H. V. (1995). A controlled multivariate chart review of multiple complex developmental disorder. *Journal of the American Academy of Child & Adolescent Psychiatry, 34*(8), 1096–1106. https://doi.org/10.1097/00004583-199508000-00021

Van Schalkwyk, G. I., Peluso, F., Qayyum, Z., McPartland, J. C., & Volkmar, F. R. (2015). Varieties of misdiagnosis in ASD: An illustrative case series. *Journal of Autism and Developmental Disorders, 45*(4), 911–918. https://doi.org/10.1007/s10803-014-2239-y

Volkmar, F. R., & Cohen, D. J. (1991). Comorbid association of autism and schizophrenia. *American Journal of Psychiatry, 148*(12), 1705–1707.

Volkmar, F. R., & Tsatsanis, K. (2002). Childhood schizophrenia. In M. Lewis (Ed.), *Child and adolescent psychiatry* (pp. 745–754). Philadelphia, PA: Lippincott Williams & Wilkins.

Vorstman, J. A. S., Morcus, M. E. J., Duijff, S. N., Klaassen, P. W. J., Heineman-de Boer, J. A., Beemer, F. A.,... van Engeland, H. (2006). The 22q11.2 deletion in children. *Journal of the American Academy of Child & Adolescent Psychiatry, 45*(9), 1104–1113. https://doi.org/10.1097/01.chi.0000228131.56956.c1

Weiss, L. A., Shen, Y., Korn, J. M., Arking, D. E., Miller, D. T., Fossdal, R.,... Daly, M. J. (2009, June 6). Association between microdeletion and microduplication at 16p11.2 and autism. https://doi.org/10.1056/NEJMoa075974

Wing, L., & Gould, J. (1979). Severe impairments of social interaction and associated abnormalities in children: Epidemiology and classification. *Journal of Autism and Developmental Disorders, 9*(1), 11–29. https://doi.org/10.1007/BF01531288

Wing, L., & Shah, A. (2000). Catatonia in autistic spectrum disorders. *British Journal of Psychiatry: The Journal of Mental Science, 176*, 357–362.

World Health Organization. (1992). *The ICD-10 classification of mental and behavioural disorders: Clinical descriptions and diagnostic guidelines* (Vol. 1). Author.

Wykes, T., Huddy, V., Cellard, C., McGurk, S. R., & Czobor, P. (2011). A meta-analysis of cognitive remediation for schizophrenia: Methodology and effect sizes. *American Journal of Psychiatry, 168*(5), 472–485. https://doi.org/10.1176/appi.ajp.2010.10060855

Wykes, T., Steel, C., Everitt, B., & Tarrier, N. (2008). Cognitive behavior therapy for schizophrenia: Effect sizes, clinical models, and methodological rigor. *Schizophrenia Bulletin, 34*(3), 523–537. https://doi.org/10.1093/schbul/sbm114

Xia, J., Merinder, L. B., & Belgamwar, M. R. (2011). Psychoeducation for schizophrenia. *Cochrane Database of Systematic Reviews*, (6), CD002831. https://doi.org/10.1002/14651858.CD002831.pub2

Yung, A. R., Yung, A. R., Pan Yuen, H., Mcgorry, P. D., Phillips, L. J., Kelly, D.,... Killackey, E. (2005). Mapping the onset of psychosis: The comprehensive assessment of at-risk mental states. *Australian and New Zealand Journal of Psychiatry, 39*(11–12), 964–971.

Zervas, I. M., Theleritis, C., & Soldatos, C. R. (2012). Using ECT in schizophrenia: A review from a clinical perspective. *World Journal of Biological Psychiatry, 13*(2), 96–105. https://doi.org/10.3109/15622975.2011.564653

Zheng, W., Cao, X.-L., Ungvari, G. S., Xiang, Y.-Q., Guo, T., Liu, Z.-R.,... Xiang, Y.-T. (2016). Electroconvulsive therapy added to non-clozapine antipsychotic medication for treatment resistant schizophrenia: Meta-analysis of randomized controlled trials. *PLoS ONE, 11*(6). https://doi.org/10.1371/journal.pone.0156510

Zheng, Z., Zheng, P., & Zou, X. (2018). Association between schizophrenia and autism spectrum disorder: A systematic review and meta-Analysis. *Autism Research*. https://doi.org/10.1002/aur.1977

Zimmermann, G., Favrod, J., Trieu, V. H., & Pomini, V. (2005). The effect of cognitive behavioral treatment on the positive symptoms of schizophrenia spectrum disorders: A meta-analysis. *Schizophrenia Research, 77*(1), 1–9. https://doi.org/10.1016/j.schres.2005.02.018

CHAPTER 4

Autism Spectrum Disorder and Co-Occurring Addiction

Patricia J. M. van Wijngaarden-Cremers

Abstract

For many professionals, patients, and relatives of individuals with autism spectrum disorder (ASD), the co-occurrence with addiction to alcohol or drugs seems unimaginable. How could autism be hidden behind addiction and how could someone diagnosed with autism as a child become addicted in adolescence or adulthood? In this chapter, evidence is presented that this comorbidity is far more frequent in high-functioning adolescents and adults with ASD than is often appreciated. Two different perspectives are considered. First, both conditions are related to the neurotransmitter dopamine. Second, individuals with ASD may become addicted when they try and cope with their social difficulties by taking substances that help them overcome their initial shyness and social anxiety, or they do so to soothe their high levels of arousal and/or hypersensitivity to internal or external stimuli. There are established clinical guidelines for both conditions but none for managing the combination of these two disorders. Thus, the clinician, along with being acutely aware of the possible co-occurrence, should manage individual cases by tailoring an individual approach based on the evidence from both fields. This is illustrated by two clinical cases.

Keywords: autism, dopamine, addiction, behavioral addictions, drugs and alcohol

Overview

Autism is a neurodevelopmental disorder characterized by impairment in the development of reciprocal social interaction and communication and restricted, stereotyped, and repetitive patterns of behavior and interest. There is a huge variety in clinical expressions and individuals can present with very different levels of intellectual functioning ranging from profound learning disability to high levels of intelligence (though mostly characterized by disharmonic profiles). Individuals with autism are vulnerable to comorbidities mainly in the areas of affect (anxiety and depression) and cognition (attention deficit hyperactivity disorder [ADHD]), and many are oversensitive to stimuli of all kinds (Baron Cohen, Ashwin, Ashwin, Tavassoli, & Chakrabarti, 2009). The comorbidity with addiction has only recently been described and discovered as a meaningful challenge in high-functioning individuals with autism. Nearly 5% of the adult population has what is stated as an autistic intelligence (Lai, Lombardo, & Baron-Cohen, 2014) and cope well as engineers, technicians, scientists, or computer technology specialists. Yet 1% of the population in Western societies has an impairing condition that can be classified in *Diagnostic and Statistical Manual of Mental Disorders*, fifth edition (DSM-5) terms as autism spectrum disorder (ASD).

But what is addiction? The word "addiction" is generally defined by the inability to "stop doing or using something that is harmful." The American Society for Addiction Medicine's description of addiction more clearly describes the concept as conceptualized within psychiatry:

> Addiction is a primary, chronic disease of brain reward, motivation, memory and related circuitry. Dysfunction in these circuits leads to characteristic

> biological, psychological, social and spiritual manifestations. This is reflected in an individual pathologically pursuing reward and/or relief by substance use and other behaviors.
>
> Addiction is characterized by inability to consistently abstain, impairment in behavioral control, and craving, diminished recognition of significant problems with one's behaviors and interpersonal relationships, and a dysfunctional emotional response. Like other chronic diseases, addiction often involves cycles of relapse and remission. Without treatment or engagement in recovery activities, addiction is progressive and can result in disability or premature death. (https://www.asam.org/resources/definition-of-addiction 2011)

Addiction is far from uncommon and affects nearly 10% of all adults across various layers of society and cultures. Yet few people who specialize in the field of addiction (psychiatry) seem to be familiar with ASD (van Wijngaarden-Cremers & van der Gaag, 2014) or at least do not feel comfortable working with people with both addiction and impaired social skills as seen in autism. Conversely, specialists in the field of ASD might be unaware of addiction and addictive behavior habits (gaming, gambling, stalking, sex, etc.) in their patients and lack the expertise to address these issues. Therefore, despite a relatively high prevalence of comorbid ASD and addiction in clinical populations (Sizoo et al., 2010; Singh, Hellemans, & Dom, 2012; van Wijngaarden-Cremers, Van den Brink, & van der Gaag, 2014), addictions in individuals with ASD and ASD in addicted individuals are often overlooked. This is detrimental for the patients in question and their direct environment. Moreover, it leads to confusion and frustration in therapeutic teams that feel incapable of addressing these challenging behaviors that do not respond to their routine treatment plans and guidelines.

For many parents of individuals with ASD, it is beyond imagination that their autistic child could also be addicted—despite the fact that they have witnessed the endlessly repetitive stereotyped movements that their young child made to soothe him- or herself when too aroused. They were aware of the extreme focus on preoccupations of all sorts (history, dinosaurs, fans, historical dates, or train timetables) and also of the fact that their child could play video games for hours and days in a row, getting in a nearly trance-like condition. *But addicted? No!* On the other hand, professionals working in the field of addiction and even those in the field of dual diagnosis couldn't have imagined that a substantial proportion of the individuals in their care also in fact had a developmental disorder, such as ADHD or ASD. This mutual lack of awareness about the overlap in their field of expertise has been, and continues to be, detrimental for their patients who do not get the proper treatment (Rengit, McKowen, O'Brien, Howe, & McDougle, 2016), especially when one realizes that addiction in an individual with a developmental disorder in clinical practice needs more than the sum of the treatment and guidance methods for both conditions. Above all it is of the uttermost importance to understand the underlying dynamics and cause(s) of addiction in developmental disorders such as ASD. This is crucial because detoxicating is only a first step. Helping individuals with ASD and addiction develop other strategies to cope with the factors that precipitate their use of substances (e.g., social anxiety, feelings of emptiness and worthlessness) is the essential second step. In this chapter we will summarize the overlap between ASD and addiction from theoretical, developmental, and clinical points of view.

Prevalence and Course

Prevalence of Addiction in ASD

Until recently there were no systematic studies on the co-occurrence of addition and ASD, including the prevalence of this comorbidity in large (community) samples (Rengit et al., 2016). On the other hand, there are a series of clinical surveys that illustrate that the co-occurrence is high and should be a matter of concern. In different clinical samples of individuals with ASD, Hofvander et al. (2009) found an overall prevalence of 19% of adult patients with ASD meeting the criteria for substance use disorders (SUDs) according to the DSM-IV and DSM-5 (e.g., alcohol, soft [e.g., cannabis] and hard [e.g., cocaine, amphetamines, heroin] drugs). These figures were very comparable to the 16% found in a community-based sample of adults with ASD (Lugnegard, Hallerbäck, & Gillberg, 2011). These figures are remarkable, though replication on a larger scale is needed. But if these estimates were accurate, one in six to seven high-functioning individuals with ASD would present with co-occurring addition. And it could be even more because these figures did not include assessment of possible addictions to gaming, gambling, or other behavioral addictions. In our own clinical addiction unit the proportion of individuals with an addiction diagnosis and a concurrent developmental disorder (ADHD and/or ASD) ranged from 30% to 35% in two independent year admission cohorts of 102 individuals (Sizoo et al., 2010; van Wijngaarden-Cremers et al., 2014).

It should be noted that all these figures rise well above the prevalence of addiction (estimated to be around 10%), ADHD (3% to 5%), and ASD (1%) collectively in the general population. In our pilot study of 80 admissions to an adult ASD unit (van Wijngaarden-Cremers, 2016), the comorbidity between ASD and SUD was even higher; 65% of the inpatients met clinical criteria for SUD including gambling, gaming, and behavioral addictions (sex, shopping, stalking, etc.). There were no gender differences in overall prevalence rates, but addiction to medication (32% in women vs. none in men) and eating disorders (24% in women vs. 9% in men) were far more common in women, whereas addiction to drugs (13% in men vs. none in women) was far more common in men.

In conclusion, there are clear indications that a possible comorbidity of substance abuse disorder should be considered among adults with ASD, especially considering that our preliminary estimates only focused on a subset of addictions. In other words, other addictive behaviors such as gaming, Internet use, and sex have not been included in most of these studies.

Etiology, Diagnosis, and Assessment

Etiology

Langen, Durston, Kas, van Engeland, and Staal (2011) demonstrated clearly that three, at first glance, completely different conditions, Parkinson's disease, ADHD, and addiction, share a common causal agent—the neurotransmitter dopamine. The differences between the three conditions can be explained by looking into which cortico-striatal pathway is most affected. In Parkinson's disease, this is the sensorimotor loop, leading mainly to motor impairment but also an enhanced vulnerability for depression and flattening of affect. In ADHD, it is the cognitive loop, leading to problems in the areas of attention, focus, inhibition of behavior, and distraction. Collectively, these neurocognitive deficits lead to problems in the planning and organizing of thoughts and behavior. Finally, in addiction, the limbic pathway is most affected, leading to an insatiable craving for substances or habits that induce dopamine depletion. Despite these differences, in all cases, a lack of dopamine activation is in play (Dichter, Damiano, & Allen, 2012). ASD is characterized by a combination of all characteristics seen in all three conditions; along with fundamental problems with reciprocal social interaction and communication, individuals with ASD have motor oddities such as stereotypies and postural rigidity, attentional problems and cognitive disharmonies, and compulsive and obsessive preoccupations and behaviors.

There are different theories to explain the greater vulnerability of individuals with ASD (Ringer et al., 2016). First, heightened vulnerability to addiction in ASD could be linked to high levels of anxiety and comorbidity with affective disorders (Simonoff et al., 2008). As a consequence, they may be more prone to using addictive substances to overcome their social anxiety or depressed mood. This exposure and the repeated usage of addictive substances can lead to habituation and dose enhancement and finally addiction. Le Merrer, Becker, Befort, and Kieffer (2009) found indications for an elevated threshold for frontal dopamine depletion in individuals with ASD. This could explain their lesser sensitivity to typical (social) rewards, which could contribute to a tendency to become bored easily and be inclined to engage in thrill-seeking behaviors to experience excitement and subsequently pleasure. Conversely, some of the repetitive behaviors and preoccupations are, as we mentioned before, strategies to help cope with hypersensitivity to stimuli and excessive worries and feelings of insecurity (Sizoo et al., 2010). In sum, in ASD a developmental dysregulation of the limbic system is certainly in play (Langen et al., 2011; van Wijngaarden-Cremers et al., 2014). This is illustrated in Figure 4.1, in which both the involvement of the different pathways and their relations to psychopathological categories are pictured.

The common depiction of the socially aloof, naïve person with ASD does not easily coalesce with the behavioral presentation of a patient struggling with addition, especially when antisocial behavior is present (e.g., cunning, lying, self-serving).

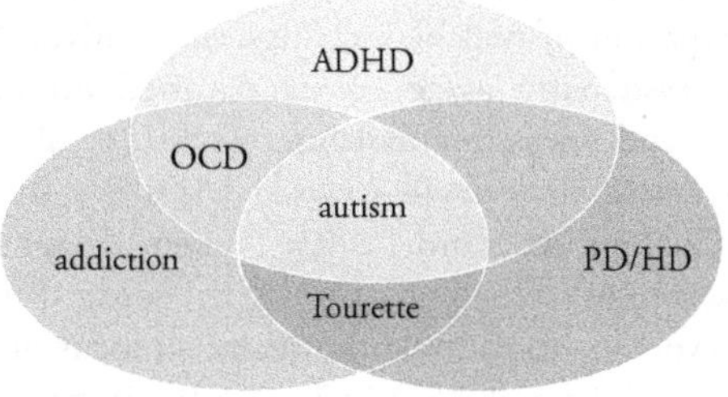

Figure 4.1. The overlap of dopamine-related conditions. ADHD, attention deficit hyperactivity disorder; OCD, obsessive-compulsive disorder; PD/HD.
Langen, M., Durston, S., Kas, M. J., van Engeland, H., & Staal, W. G. (2011). The neurobiology of repetitive behavior: In mice and men. *Neuroscience & Biobehavioral Reviews, 35*, 356–365.

However, there are shared underlying genetic and psychophysiological pathways. There are striking behavioral similarities between both conditions with regard to the extremely detail-oriented perceptions and compulsive tendencies. Perhaps even the developmental pathways leading to an overexposure to addictive substances may be quite similar. In ASD, it could start, for example, with preoccupations (e.g., with spinning objects) and stereotyped movements (rocking, whirling, swinging, sometimes leading to trance-like state). These behaviors may help the child with ASD cope with overarousal and stress. Likewise, addiction often starts with taking substances or engaging in behaviors (gambling) to feel better and regulate stress and tension.

These stimulations of the reward system, by the substance or habit, lead to dopamine depletion, which gives a good feeling and helps one cope with scary situations. So are there common neurobiological characteristics to both conditions? Studies of the developmental course of ASD show that in many high-functioning individuals with ASD, similar to typically developing youth, a strong urge for social relationships emerges at puberty (Lai et al., 2014). But they experience obstacles in their pursuit of social engagement. Difficulty understanding the nuances of social situations and others' perspectives may lead to anxiety. Alcohol and drugs may help them in overcoming their social awkwardness and shyness by making them feel less uncomfortable and more at ease engaging in social contacts. Yet their eagerness and naïve perception of the other makes them easy prey for abusive individuals (e.g., the drug scene). On the other hand, they feel at home in social groups with straightforward rules and comprehensible cues.

Diagnosis and Assessment

ASD is diagnosed using a combination clinical assessment, developmental history, and information from parents (if available), siblings, and relatives along with systematic usage of standardized questionnaires and semistructured interviews (e.g., Autism Diagnostic Interview—Revised [ADI-R], Rutter, Le Couteur, & Lord, 2003; Autism Diagnostic Observation Schedule [ADOS], Lord, Rutter, DiLavore, & Risi, 2001). But these all focus on the core symptoms of ASD including the impairment of reciprocal social interactions and communication and the restricted patterns of behavior and interests. All co-occurring conditions should be teased out by systematically screening all areas of psychopathology including substance abuse and addictive behavior patterns. For these, well-validated questionnaires can be used (National Institute for Health and Care Excellence [NICE] guidelines and American Psychiatric Association [APA] practice parameters), for example, the Mini-International Neuropsychiatric Interview (MINI; Sheehan et al., 1998) or, specific for addiction, the Addiction Severity Index (ASI; McLellan, Luborsky, O'Brien, & Woody 1980).

Treatment

There are no specific guidelines for treatment of co-occurring ASD and SUD. Therefore, one has to turn to guidelines for each of them separately to determine how they could be applied in a pragmatic manner to specifically address the problems encountered when they occur simultaneously in one individual. The state-of-the-art guidelines based on recent evidence widely available in Europe are from NICE on drug misuse (2007, revised in 2011), ASD in children and adolescents (revised in 2011), and ASD in adults (2012, revised in 2016). In the United States, the American Psychiatric Association published a guideline for (general) practitioners (Durand, 2013). Unfortunately, none of these guidelines include the possible comorbidity between ASD and addiction. According to the NICE guideline, ASD should always be the first and utmost focus of attention in the presence of coexisting conditions. This is understandable. As pointed out earlier, individuals with ASD have a very different frame of reference and encounter considerable difficulties in social communication. Some individuals use substances to soothe their anxieties and help them engage more easily in social interactions. Transition to addiction occurs at the point when the primary goal is overclassed by substance/behavior dependence and craving. This happens mostly in high-functioning individuals seeking more independence (Hofvander et al., 2011; Sizoo et al., 2010). But although many individuals with ASD who are functioning at a lower level and are more socially awkward may be protected against substance abuse, in these groups gaming and behavioral addictions are more common and often overlooked (Lau, Smit, Fleming, & Riper, 2017).

So if there is no specific guideline for the combination of ASD and addiction, how should individuals with a combination of ASD and addiction be approached from a therapeutic point of view?

First and of uttermost importance, as pointed out earlier, is to understand the functional dynamics of addiction in ASD in this challenging comorbidity. An essential first step is understanding the specific individual with ASD and addiction within his or her own context. Many individuals with ASD have intense contact with devoted and very involved parents, even in adulthood. Communicating with the individual with ASD and with his parents/social network is very important to understand what has to be done.

From there, a stepwise approach is essential:

> The first step is to offer (adapted) psychoeducation. This should be aimed in a differentiated manner to the patient, his or her parents/guardian, and the professional(s) involved in his or her care.
>
> The next step is to offer psychosocial interventions aimed at the core symptoms of ASD. A comprehensive functional analysis can be completed to identify the strengths and weaknesses of the individual. This may also uncover the sources of stress, and the therapist can then help the individual increase self-awareness of personal triggers. Then it is important to offer alternative strategies to cope with high levels of stress (in a manner other than taking substances or engaging in addictive behaviors).
>
> The individual with ASD will need to be taught and experience a different lifestyle that offers sufficiently salient rewards that will help compensate for the craving for substances, gaming, or other behavioral addictions.
>
> The therapist can work with the client to increase the repertoire of coping strategies. For example, physical activities may help the patient find alternative ways of coping with stress and frustration.
>
> The use of medication to compensate for addictive substances or help soothe withdrawal phenomena should be time limited.

This should be matched with a management strategy for addiction that starts with (a) detoxification combined with specific (b) psychoeducation about how addiction arises, what makes the person vulnerable to addiction, what addiction means, and so forth, and (c) cognitive behavioral therapy, including cue identification and relapse prevention, which will help the patient learn alternative skills to cope with craving, and, finally, coaching for societal reintegration (Volkow & Morales, 2015).

These guiding principles will now be illustrated in two cases. In the first case, the addiction was the primary problem yet was unsuccessfully treated because the ASD was overlooked. In the second case, a young girl diagnosed with ASD gradually became addicted and, in the process, traumatized, mainly because those in her social support system did not suspect that she could ever become addicted.

First case: Example of late diagnosis of ASD in an addicted patient

Susan is a 63-year-old former judge, currently holding an administrative position within the court of appeals, who was admitted to a psychiatric hospital after a severe suicide attempt. She described making this attempt because she "hate[s] living." Besides her job and her animals (12 cats and a dog), there was nothing she liked in her life. That's why, per her admission, she was drinking more than five glasses of alcohol a day and smoking cannabis when she was not at work. She always felt depressed and bad about herself that she drank so much.

Her history tells us that she had a severe car accident when she was 22 years old in which her face became badly mutilated. In the same period, she started drinking more and developed an eating disorder. She had several unsuccessful treatments in addiction clinics, as well as in a clinic for eating disorders. She became more and more depressed, the drinking and eating problems worsened, and she started using marijuana and attempted suicide on several occasions.

During an interview after her last suicide attempt, she got really angry at the person who found her, reproaching him for finding her and calling for help. She does not like people because she sees them as profoundly dishonest. She does not believe anyone would be sad if she died because she would not feel the same if it happened to someone else. She was never convinced that anybody really cared about others and believed that it was only a rule of politeness to say otherwise. As a matter of fact, she did not understand people at all: "Why don't people say what they mean and mean what they say?"

A thorough assessment including interviews with her mother and reading school reports confirmed a diagnosis of Asperger's (captured within ASD by DSM-5) at the age of 63.

It became clear she had difficulties running her life and independently managing her household. She was hoarding useless items, unable to throw things away. In terms of social contacts, it appeared that she was afraid of making a phone call or using email. She never asked for help because she thought that it was her fault she could not do this and she had little hope that she could change. Hence, she started drinking and once drunk had good reason for not doing the things she should do.

Susan was not diagnosed with ASD as a child. She is an example of late diagnosis of ASD in a woman. In retrospect, one can somewhat understand why the diagnosis ASD was not considered before: Susan obviously is intelligent and was gifted in her application of logic, attributes that were very helpful for her to read law and function as a lawyer and finally a judge. Also, the variety of psychiatric symptoms (which were wrongly attributed to the consequences of the car accident) masked the ASD. Her slight eccentricity was broadly accepted and her colleagues would just say "that's just like her." As she aged, she became lonelier—estranging others with her awkward, odd, and sometimes offensive (too blunt) way of interacting socially. Becoming lonely and depressed, she started drinking mainly to help her feel less depressed. As the amounts of alcohol increased, her professional functioning became questionable. Once on sick leave, alone at home, the addiction worsened to the point that she needed professional help. Her general practitioner referred her to an addiction unit where her alcohol dependence and pathological use of cannabis were acknowledged. However, she did not at all fit into the scheme of addiction psychiatry, which is mainly focused on group activities in which patients give each other support and help each other cope with their relapse tendencies.

Susan never completed the full addiction treatment program, as that would necessitate social interest and social skills. Instead, she disrupted the program in a strange manner because she was taking everything literally. Susan really needed one-to-one guidance in which the dynamics of what brought her to drinking—to soothe the affective pain—could be determined. Subsequently, it was a matter of great importance to help her understand that drinking was not helping and merely worsened her condition. The clinical challenge was to explain and make her understand her diagnosis and from there help her understand herself and the world around her as well as learn alternative skills.

Second case: From ASD to substance abuse (drawn from Van Wijngaarden-Cremers and van der Gaag, 2014)

Anna is a 14-year-old adolescent diagnosed with ASD. In elementary school, she was well accepted as a pedantic, verbally eloquent yet clumsy girl with a special interest in all that was related to nature. She collected leaves and feathers and always had a tame rat under her pullover. At school she was left alone and no one ventured to tease or bully her. She did well in elementary school and then went to the gymnasium, the highest secondary school type in the Netherlands with Latin, Greek, and sciences. Her interest shifted from nature to gaming. She would spend hours in a row playing games and chatting with virtual friends. Once in a while, they would organize meetings. There, she met people who drank and smoked pot. She liked it because it helped her overcome her shyness. The group went on to experiment with speed. Her parents were amazed to witness a metamorphosis from socially aloof to suddenly spending time with "friends." One day they got a phone call from the police. Their daughter had been arrested for dealing drugs. She had been used and (sexually) abused by dealers, and used as a drug courier. She confessed in a very naïve manner once in detox. She verbalized thinking that these were her first real friends and she would do anything to be their friend. Once in detox, she reappeared to be the socially isolated and clumsy intelligent young girl.

Reflecting on this case, it appears that Anna is anxious and confused. She experiences flashback memories of "being forced into sex by boys in my junk scene." Often she feels like a complete outsider and a spectator of her own life. She feels filthy and betrayed, because she had started to think that finally she had found some real reliable friends. It felt so much better than having only her pet rat as a companion. In secondary school, her preoccupation was entirely out of tune with her peers, who wanted to date and have fun. She was surprised when a boy showed interest in her rat. He asked her to join him and offered her a joint. When he insisted that they have sex, she complied, not daring to refuse, but feeling awfully miserable. She wanted to be part of the group and gave in. Finally, people seemed interested in her. But as she was abused over and over again, things got out of hand and led to her decompensating.

This case is far more complex than the previous one. It is painfully illustrative for what one often encounters in these individuals with autism that develop an addiction in second place. Alongside the ASD features and emerging addiction problem, Anna's trauma experience played an important role in the dramatic course of her history. This has consequences for the clinical and overall management plan. Psychoeducation should include information about and practice with human relationships, including boundaries between people and how to assert one's position vis-à-vis others, in this case toward boys and men. Relapse prevention should include learning how to discriminate between external and internal cues pointing toward transgression of boundaries and the potential re-enactment of (sexual) abuse and trauma.

Finally, the clinical management plan should deal with working through the traumatization (psychoeducation on posttraumatic stress disorder and working through the various symptoms, including flashbacks, dissociation, and eroticized revenge actions).

The two vignettes show that a proper assessment and functional analysis are important when dealing with coexisting ASD and SUD. It explains why both conditions occur and how they relate to each other. This analysis should also look into other co-occurring problems (e.g., anxiety, depression, posttraumatic stress disorder) as all have to be addressed together in a comprehensive treatment plan that takes a broad perspective and does not just focus on treating the psychopathology. Other considerations such as fostering housing and working/studying are equally important.

Another important lesson is that, in the case of comorbid addiction in ASD, it is important that the ASD be acknowledged to facilitate effective communication with the patient. Without taking the ASD into account, there is no real likelihood that the patient will feel involved and be willing and capable of participating in the addiction treatment. Finally, taking ASD into account may inform why previous interventions did not help and facilitate far more constructive patient engagement.

Summary and Future Directions

Coexisting ASD and addiction are far more common than often assumed. It is of the utmost importance that workers in both fields (autism/addiction) have a solid knowledge of each other's fields of expertise (van Wijngaarden-Cremers & van der Gaag, 2014). Addiction is often missed in individuals with ASD; conversely, addicted individuals with ASD are unlikely to reap the full benefit from standard approaches in the field of addiction treatment (e.g., dynamic group activities). Those approaches really are far more demanding in terms of understanding empathy. Individuals with ASD may benefit more from group interventions that are structured, have an educative aim, and include structured training exercises.

Training professionals to identify and treat SUD in ASD should be implemented in medical education and clinical psychology and be part of postdoctoral training in medical specializations and clinical psychology. But a theoretical background is not sufficient; professionals in the fields of both ASD and addiction should be integrated. The clinical skills needed to most effectively address this co-occurrence should be cultivated through clinical training and supervision. Motivating—confronting and relapse prevention on one hand, thus the usual and evidence based treatment approach in addiction is needed on one hand. On the other hand, individuals with ASD will need individual support, explicit communication, and help in compensating for weak executive functions to benefit from the usual addiction treatment strategies.

We hope this chapter has made a convincing point that continuous diagnostic evaluation is important in detecting underlying problems (such as trauma, anxiety, and depression).

Clinical Guidelines

Guidelines

NICE Guideline on Autism in Adults (2012) ASD in Adults http://guidance.nice.org.uk/CG142

NICE Guideline http://www.nice.org.uk/guidance/cg/published/index.jsp?p=off

CG51	Drug misuse: psychosocial interventions (CG51)	Jul 2007	Mar 2011
CG52	Drug misuse: opioid detoxification (CG52)		

APA Guideline http://www.psych.org/practice/clinical-practice-guidelines

References

Baron-Cohen, S., Ashwin, E., Ashwin, C., Tavassoli, T., & Chakrabarti, B. (2009). Talent in autism: Hyper-systemizing, hyper-attention to detail and sensory hypersensitivity. *Philosophical Transactions of the Royal Society of London B, Biological Sciences, 364*(1522), 1377–1383. doi:10.1098/rstb.2008.0337.

Dichter, G. S., Damiano, C. A., & Allen, J. A. (2012). Reward circuitry dysfunction in psychiatric and neurodevelopmental disorders and genetic syndromes: Animal models and clinical findings. *Journal of Neurodevelopmental Disorders, 4*(1), 19. doi:10.1186/1866-1955-4-19

Gerland, G. (1996). *A real person: Life on the outside.* Karnac Edts.

Hofvander, B., Delorme, R., Chaste, P., Nydén, A., Wentz, E., Ståhlberg, O., . . . Leboyer, M. (2009). Psychiatric and psychosocial problems in adults with normal-intelligence autism spectrum disorders. *BMC Psychiatry, 9*, 35. doi:10.1186/1471-244X-9-35

Lai, M. C., Lombardo, M. V., & Baron-Cohen, S. (2014). Autism. *Lancet, 383*(9920), 896–910.

Langen, M., Durston, S., Kas, M. J., van Engeland, H., & Staal, W. G. (2011). The neurobiology of repetitive behavior: In mice and men. *Neuroscience & Biobehavioral Reviews, 35*, 356–365.

Lau, H. M., Smit, J. H., Fleming, T. M., & Riper, H. (2017). Serious games for mental health: Are they accessible, feasible, and effective? A systematic review and meta-analysis. *Frontiers in Psychiatry, 7*, 209.

Le Merrer, J., Becker, J. A., Befort, K., & Kieffer, B. L. (2009). Reward processing by the opioid system in the brain. *Physiology Review, 89*, 1379–1412.

Lord, C., Rutter, M., DiLavore, P., & Risi, S. (2001). *Autism Diagnostic Observation Schedule (ADOS) manual.* Los Angeles, CA: Western Psychological Services.

Lugnegård, T., Hallerbäck, M. U., & Gillberg, C. (2011). Psychiatric comorbidity in young adults with a clinical diagnosis of Asperger syndrome. *Research in Developmental Disabilities, 32*, 1910–1917.

McLellan, A., Luborsky, L., O'Brien, C., & Woody, G. (1980). An improved diagnostic instrument for substance abuse patients: The addiction severity index. *Journal of Nervous and Mental Diseases, 168*, 26–33.

Rengit, A. C., McKowen, J. W., O'Brien, J., Howe, Y. J., & McDougle, C. J. (2016). Brief report: Autism spectrum disorder and substance use disorder: A review and case study. *Journal of Autism and Developmental Disorders, 46*(7), 2514–2519.

Roozen, H. G., & Van De Wetering, B. J. M. (2007). Neuropsychiatric insights in clinical practice: From relapse prevention toward relapse management. *American Journal on Addictions, 16*(6), 530–531.

Rutter, M., Le Couteur, A., & Lord, C. (2003). *ADI-R: Autism Diagnostic Interview—Revised.* Los Angeles, CA: Western Psychological Services.

Sheehan, D. V., Lecrubier, Y., Sheehan, K. H., Amorim, P., Janavs, J., Weiller, E., . . . Dunbar, G. C. (1998). The Mini-International Neuropsychiatric Interview (M.I.N.I.): The development and validation of a structured diagnostic psychiatric interview for DSM-IV and ICD-10. *Journal of Clinical Psychiatry, 59*(Suppl 20), 22–33; quiz 34–57. PubMed PMID: 9881538.

Simonoff, E., Pickles, A., Charman, T., Chandler, S., Lucas, T., & Baird, G. (2008). Psychiatric disorders in children with autism spectrum disorders: Prevalence, comorbidity and associated factors in population-derived sample. *Journal of the American Academy of Child and Adolescent Psychiatry, 47*(8), 921–929.

Singh, S. K. B., Hellemans, H., & Dom, G. (2012). Autism spectrum disorder and substance use disorder: An unknown comorbidity? *Tijdschrift voor psychiatrie, 54*, 893–897.

Sizoo, B., van den Brink, W., Koeter, M., van Gorissen, E. M., van Wijngaarden-Cremers, P., & van der Gaag, R. J. (2010). Treatment seeking adults with autism or ADHD and co-morbid substance use disorder: Prevalence, risk factors and functional disability. *Drug and Alcohol Dependence, 107*(1), 44–50.

van de Aa, C. (2010). *Do you read me? Value of computer-mediated communication for adults with autism spectrum conditions.* Scriptie, Tilburg University—Dept HAIT (Human Aspects of Information Technology).

van Wijngaarden-Cremers, P. J. (2016). Autism and substance use comorbidity: Screening, identification and treatment. *European Psychiatry, 33*, S21–S22.

van Wijngaarden-Cremers, P. J. M., van den Brink, W., & van der Gaag, R. J. (2014). Addiction and autism: A remarkable comorbidity? *Journal of Alcoholism and Drug Dependence, 2*, 170.

van Wijngaarden-Cremers, P. J. M., & van der Gaag, R. J. (2014). Addiction and autism spectrum disorders. In G. Dom & F. Moggi (Eds.), *Co-occurring addictive and psychiatric disorders* (pp. 193–205). Springer-Verlag—Berlin Heidelberg.

Volkow, N. D., & Morales, M. (2015). The brain on drugs: From reward to addiction. *Cell, 162*(4), 712–725.

CHAPTER

5

Anxiety in Autism Spectrum Disorder

A Case of Blurred Boundaries

Lawrence Scahill *and* Andrea N. Evans

Abstract

Anxiety disorders are relatively common in children and adults in the general population. Available evidence suggests that youth with autism spectrum disorder (ASD) are at elevated risk for anxiety disorders. Moreover, some behavioral manifestations of ASD may overlap and confound the measurement of anxiety in youth and adults with ASD. There is no reason to expect, however, that the emotional and physiological state that defines anxiety would be different in youth or adults with ASD than in youth or adults in the general population. This chapter focuses on common anxiety disorders in children and adolescents, the phenomenology of fear and anxiety, and the challenges of measuring anxiety in youth with ASD. The chapter reviews the traditional fear circuitry and an emerging model that may have a profound impact on our understanding and treatment of anxiety disorders in youth. It summarizes a line of research on improving the measurement of anxiety in youth with ASD. Finally, it provides an update on empirically supported treatments for anxiety in this population.

Keywords: autism spectrum disorder, anxiety, outcome measurement, traditional fear circuitry, emerging model

Overview

Anxiety is a complex emotional and physiological response to perceived threat (LeDoux & Pine, 2016). Anxiety is not, in and of itself, pathological. However, when anxiety interferes with daily living and causes distress, it may rise to the level of anxiety disorder. As a group of conditions, anxiety disorders can be defined as faulty threat detection and a search for safety (Woody & Rachman, 1994). The most common anxiety disorders in pediatric populations include separation anxiety disorder, generalized anxiety disorder, social phobia (also called social anxiety disorder), posttraumatic stress disorder, and specific phobia. These disorders can be chronic and may show diagnostic stability over time. In addition, youth with one anxiety disorder are likely to have at least one other anxiety disorder—suggesting that the boundary lines between diagnoses are not sharp (Merikangas et al., 2010; Walkup et al., 2008).

Generalized anxiety disorder (GAD) is characterized by excessive worry about upcoming events. Youth with GAD worry about competence in activities regarded as important to the child, the family, or both. For example, a young person with GAD may harbor and perhaps express worry about an upcoming school examination, starting a new school, a sports event, or a musical recital. The child or adolescent with GAD often anticipates failure and may seek frequent reassurance that things will work out. If anxiety levels increase, the child may try to avoid the situation altogether. The estimated prevalence of GAD in children and adolescents is 2.2% (Merikangas et al., 2010).

Separation anxiety disorder (SAD) is defined by extreme emotional upset upon impending or actual separation from the child's caregiver. The child may express fear of harm befalling the parent, the child, or both. Many children in the general population may exhibit transient protest at the start of kindergarten or in early elementary school. The protest of a child with SAD persists over time (at least 4 weeks), can be dramatic, and may include school refusal. In many cases, separation anxiety is not confined to school. Children with SAD may become apprehensive and vigilant if the primary caregiver's return home is later than expected. SAD is unique in that it is the only anxiety disorder that, by definition, onsets in childhood. The estimated prevalence of SAD is 7.6% (Merikangas et al., 2010).

Social anxiety disorder (SocAD, also called social phobia) is characterized by excessive worry and apprehension about interaction in the age-appropriate social milieu. Youth with SocAD express intense worry about being accepted by peers and being poorly judged by others. Here again many children and adolescents worry about acceptance, for example, in a new school or when asked to speak in front of the class. The level of anxiety in youth with SocAD causes marked distress and may lead to avoidance of social situations and self-imposed isolation. The estimated prevalence of SocAD is 9.1%, with the highest rate in adolescence (Merikangas et al., 2010).

Posttraumatic stress disorder (PTSD) is emotional disturbance following a traumatic event (exposure to war, disaster, physical abuse, sexual abuse, victim of violent attack, witness of domestic violence or serious accident). The emotional disturbance may include significant avoidance of any reminder of the event, hypervigilance, irritability, sleep problems, distressing memories of the event, and depersonalization. The estimated prevalence of PTSD is 5% (Merikangas et al., 2010).

Specific phobia (SP) is defined by exaggerated fear of a specific object (e.g., dogs, snakes, spiders) or conditions (e.g., thunderstorms). In SP, the exaggerated fear interferes with daily living and persists over time (e.g., at least 6 months). The differentiation between normal and abnormal fears in youth with SP may be difficult because fears of dogs, snakes, spiders, and thunderstorms are common in children and adolescents. In addition, youth with exaggerated anxiety about a particular object may not encounter the feared object day in and day out. In the absence of regular encounter with the feared object, there may be little or no related impairment or distress. For example, in the national survey conducted by Merikangas and colleagues (2010), the variation in the estimated prevalence of SP ranged from 0.6% to 19%—depending on the severity threshold for case definition. That range in the severity threshold can affect the estimated prevalence of SP as well as anxiety disorders in general across the lifespan (WHO World Mental Health Survey Consortium, 2004).

Prevalence and Developmental Course of Anxiety Disorders in ASD

Overall Prevalence of Anxiety Disorders in General Pediatric Population

There is general agreement across studies that these anxiety disorders are slightly more common in girls than boys (Merikangas et al., 2010). The estimated prevalence of anxiety disorders in the general pediatric population ranges from 6.5% to 32%, though several studies fall into a narrower range of 14% to 18% (Beesdo, Knappe, & Pine, 2009; Copeland, Angold, Shanahan, & Costello, 2014; Polanczyk, Salum, Sugaya, Caye, & Rohde , 2005). This narrower range is consistent with a prevalence of 18.1% in adults (Kessler, Chiu, Demler, Merikangas, & Walters, 2005). The differences across prevalence studies in youth are due to differences in sample size, source of the sample, age of the sample, the measures used make the diagnoses, and the severity threshold used to set the diagnosis. For example, the National Comorbidity Study surveyed a nationally representative sample of 10,000 adolescents between 13 and 18 years of age (Merikangas et al., 2010). In that study, 31.9% of youth in the sample met lifetime criteria for at least one anxiety disorder. When the investigators calculated the rate of adolescents with a severe anxiety disorder, the prevalence estimate dropped to 8.3%. As noted earlier, the influence of severity threshold on the prevalence of anxiety disorders is especially evident in specific phobia.

Prevalence of Anxiety in ASD

Compared to the estimated prevalence of anxiety disorders in the general pediatric population, several reports have documented that anxiety disorders are more common in youth with ASD (White, Oswald, Ollendick, & Scahill, 2009; van Steensel, Bogels, & Perrin, 2011; Lecavalier et al., 2019). These reports estimate that 40% of clinically ascertained samples of youth with ASD have at least one anxiety disorder. Based on parent report, youth with ASD also show significantly higher scores on dimensional measures of anxiety than youth in the general population as well as clinically ascertained youth with externalizing disorders (van Steensel & Heeman, 2017). We explored anxiety symptoms in 415 medication-free children with ASD (age 4 to 17 years) using a 20-item, parent-rated, *Diagnostic and Statistical Manual of Mental Disorders*, fourth edition

(DSM-IV)-referenced Child and Adolescent Symptom Inventory (CASI; Gadow & Sprafkin, 2002; Hallett et al., 2013). Anxiety symptoms in this sample ranged from little or no anxiety through mild, moderate, and severe. Scale items that began with "worries" and "complains," however, were rarely endorsed by parents (Hallett et al., 2013). The low rate of these language-dependent items was even more pronounced in nonverbal children and those with IQ below 70. These findings and findings from a study of the parent version of the Spence Children's Anxiety Scale (Glod et al., 2017) suggest that measures of anxiety used in the general pediatric population may not be suitable for youth with ASD.

The observation that two disorders co-occur more often than chance raises questions and debates about the nature of the apparent association. If the association is observed in clinical samples of youth with ASD, there is a distinct possibility of ascertainment bias. Simply stated, children with two disorders may be more likely to come to clinical attention. The term "comorbidity" is often invoked to describe the co-occurrence of two disorders. The term suggests that the anxiety disorder and ASD are independent and that anxiety disorders in ASD are no different than anxiety disorders in the general population. Another take on the co-occurrence of anxiety disorders in youth with ASD is that the presence of ASD increases the risk of developing an anxiety disorder. For example, due to social skill deficits, a middle school–age child with ASD may consistently encounter failure in the social milieu. Over time, social interactions are imbued with anxiety, resulting in social avoidance.

The reported higher than expected co-occurrence of ASD and anxiety disorders may also be due to the potential for symptomatic overlap between ASD and anxiety (Kerns & Kendall, 2012). This proposal can be broken down into several plausible elements. First, in the absence of biological indicators of psychiatric diagnosis, we are constrained to rely on behavioral characteristics to define psychiatric disorders. The same or similar behaviors may be manifestations of both disorders in question. Social avoidance and social isolation could be considered essential elements in ASD, social anxiety disorder, or both. Second, the similarity of behavioral manifestations may result in misattribution of the behavior to one disorder in favor of the other. For example, a parent may report that a child with ASD has a history of protest upon separation from mother. Understandably, the parent may attribute this behavior to separation anxiety. It could be, however, that the child is protesting the deviation from the usual routine—not separation per se. As noted previously, SAD is characterized by fear of harm to the child, the parent, or both. In young children with ASD—especially those with cognitive or language delay—it may be difficult to determine the source of the child's distress. To *manage* the child's presumed separation anxiety, parents may strictly adhere to the routine. In such cases, the parental accommodation may ironically confirm the inference that the child's behavior reflects separation anxiety. Finally, it is possible that insistence on sameness and separation anxiety could each contribute to the child's protest upon separation from the primary caregiver. That two disorders may be intricately blended raises the question that the combined picture may be a distinct diagnostic entity. This has been proposed for the mixed clinical picture of anxiety and depression (Moscati, Flint, & Kendler, 2016). The notion that anxiety disorders and ASD are interwoven has fostered a proposal that anxiety disorders may be fundamentally different in youth with ASD compared to anxiety disorders in the general population (Kerns et al., 2014). This proposal for atypical anxiety in ASD warrants careful consideration of human fear and anxiety.

Etiology: Phenomenology of Fear and Anxiety

Fear and anxiety share some behavioral manifestations and neurobiological features in common (LeDoux, 1998). But there are important differences (LeDoux & Pine, 2016). Fear may be defined as the feelings, physiological responses, and defensive behaviors (escape, avoidance, or both) that occur when source of harm is imminent. By contrast, anxiety is the set of feelings, physiological responses, and defensive behaviors that occur when the source of harm is uncertain. As noted earlier, underlying anxiety disorders is faulty threat detection and often a search for safety (Woody & Rachman, 1994). In SAD, the need for safety may take the form of retreat from social interaction. The protests of a child with separation anxiety may be due to concern about the loss of security and safety with the impending departure of the primary caregiver—who is, the main source of safety. In GAD, the search for safety may be manifested by frequent requests for reassurance about an anxiety-producing upcoming event.

The physical manifestations of fear include increased heart rate and respiration, decreased salivation, increased grooming behavior, fearful expression, freezing, and increased vigilance. Many of these behavioral manifestations can be observed in anxiety. In both fear and anxiety, learning plays an important role. In the classic rodent fear conditioning model, a neutral stimulus (tone or flash of light) is paired with a foot shock. The foot shock induces the fear response (e.g., increased heart rate, freezing, vigilance, decreased salivation, etc.). Over time, the neutral stimulus will provoke the fear response—even in the absence of the foot shock (Davis, 1992). It is also well established that the fear response can be extinguished through repetition of the neutral stimulus without the foot shock (Myers & Davis, 2002).

Learning also plays a role in anxiety (Rachman, 1977). Exposure to an aversive event in a specific situation may result in avoidance of that situation. The child who is ridiculed after speaking up in class may avoid speaking up in the future. Modeling of anxiety by parents or others may provoke anxiety. It has been shown, for example, that anxiety in response to fear-provoking images to young children can be amplified if the child simultaneously sees apprehension in the caretaker (Muris, 2007). Negative reports about an upcoming event may also promote anxiety. For example, predictions from others about the intensive social pressures of junior high school may stoke anxiety in some children.

Implied in each of these three learning paradigms is the supposition that some children are more vulnerable to anxiety than others. Twin studies do indeed show that monozygotic twins are more likely to be mutually affected with anxiety than dizygotic twin pairs. However, heritability in the range of 0.30 to 0.40 strongly suggests that environment also plays a role (Morrison & Ressler, 2014).

Jerome Kagan led a longitudinal study to examine the role of temperament in anxiety. The study began with a sample of 450 Caucasian infants, who were followed forward for 20 years (Kagan et al., 2007). Temperament is an inherited, relatively stable behavioral and personality style. Because temperaments vary and come in many shades, Kagan and colleagues pursued a strategy of studying extremes on what could be called a boldness–caution continuum. The 20% of infants who showed an exaggerated response to mildly provocative stimuli were classified as *high reactives*. The 30% of infants who showed little or no response to the same stimuli were classified as *low reactives*. Cautious infants (high reactives) were presumed to have a low threshold for amygdala excitation, and bold children (low reactives) a high threshold for amygdala excitation. At age 7 years, the high-reactive group expressed more fears and anxieties than the low-reactive group. By 18 years of age, a subgroup of high reactives were described as cautious and prone to anxiety compared to the low reactives. This work highlights the presumed role of the amygdala in the traditional model of fear and anxiety.

Traditional Model of the Fear System

The conventional model of the fear circuit is presumed to be conserved across species (LeDoux, 1998). Activation of the fear circuit begins with a sensory stimulus (sight, sound, or pressure) that is transmitted to the thalamus. The thalamus sends signals to the cortex and the amygdala. The amygdalae are small, almond-shaped, bilateral nuclei in the temporal lobe. In this model, the amygdala serves as the hub of the organism's response (Davis, 1992). Animal studies show that electrical stimulation of the amygdala provokes increased heart rate and respiration, as well as the other behavioral manifestations of fear noted earlier. This extraordinary range of effects is due to the multiple connections of the amygdala to brain regions that control these functions (nucleus accumbens, hypothalamus, parabrachial nucleus, and locus coeruleus, among others). Fear conditioning is blocked in animals with lesions in the amygdala. Humans with amygdala damage do not show the expected physiological responses to threating stimuli and show decreased capacity to recognize fearful facial expressions (Phelps, 2006). This body of evidence has promoted the view that the fear circuit is subcortically driven (Panksepp, Fuchs, & Iacobucci, 2011). Indeed, the role of the amygdala in the fear circuit is supported by neuroimaging studies that show amygdala activation when exposed to threatening images. Amygdala activation is exaggerated in participants with anxiety disorders (Phelps, 2006; LeDoux & Pine, 2016). The role of the cortex in the traditional fear circuit is to evaluate the nature of the threat and initiate defensive actions.

The subcortically driven traditional fear circuit includes two pathways: the so-called low (rapid) pathway and the high (slower) pathway. The rapid pathway travels from the thalamus to the amygdala, which in turn mobilizes the emotional and physiological responses. The slower pathway travels from the thalamus to the cortex to permit reappraisal of the threat by tapping into associations with past events. The rapid and slow pathway model has been applied to anxiety. The cortical reappraisal may modulate amygdala firing in line with the actual threat.

Two-System Framework

LeDoux and Pine (2016) propose an alternative model to the traditional fear circuit. This two-system framework describes integrated, though separate, neural pathways for specific cortical regions and subcortical structures such as the amygdala. In the two-system model, threat detection and feelings of fear or anxiety are cortical in origin. For example, a visual stimulus might register in the visual cortex at a nonconscious level. This information is transmitted to frontal areas (dorsal prefrontal cortices, anterior cingulate, orbital frontal cortices) and parietal areas for interpretation. This sensory information is also transmitted to the amygdala, which then initiates behavioral and physiological responses. Thus, the two-system model stands in contrast to the view that fears and anxiety are exclusively subcortically driven. As noted by LeDoux and Pine (2016), the application of the traditional fear circuit in animal models of drug development for anxiety disorders has been disappointing. For example, a common preclinical strategy in drug development is to place rodents in situations they would predictably avoid such as open, well-lit spaces. A drug that allows test rodents to tolerate an open space could become a candidate as an antianxiety medication. However, drugs that cause this behavioral change in rodents may reduce physiological responses to anxiety—but not affect feelings of anxiety in humans. The two-system model calls for new approaches to drug development as well as the integration of drug treatment and psychotherapy.

Diagnosis and Assessment of Anxiety in Youth with ASD

As noted earlier, cognitive deficits, language delay, and symptom overlap between anxiety and ASD pose challenges to the assessment and quantitative measurement of anxiety in youth with ASD. To improve the measurement of anxiety for youth with ASD, our research group launched a multisite and multistage measure development project (Bearss et al., 2016; Scahill et al., 2019). To carry out these steps, we followed the Food and Drug Administration (FDA) guidance on measure development (Food and Drug Administration, 2009). The FDA monograph emphasizes the importance of involving the patient population in measure development. Patient-reported outcomes (PROs) are also advocated by the British Department of Health and the Patient Reported Outcome Initiative System (Department of Health London, 2008; Food and Drug Administration, 2009; Matza et al., 2013). Given that the ASD patient population includes children with developmental disabilities, we involved primary caregivers as appropriate proxies.

We began with a series of six focus groups involving parents of 45 children (32 boys and 13 girls) with ASD between 3 and 17 years of age. Using an interview guide, we asked parents to describe behavioral manifestations of anxiety in their children. The discussions were transcribed. A recurring issue in the focus group discussions concerned the boundaries of ASD and anxiety. Some parents proposed that child behaviors such as tantrums were driven by anxiety. Further exploration across the six focus groups established a consensus that some tantrums could indeed be driven by anxiety. However, the child's noncompliance, frustration for being denied an object of interest (e.g., an iPad), behavior, or depressed mood could also spark tantrums. The transcripts from the six focus groups were systematically coded to generate a bank of items for possible inclusion in the parent-reported measure for anxiety in youth with ASD. The expert panel reviewed the bank of potential items for validity, clarity, and reading level (Bearss et al., 2016).

The coding of the focus group material and expert panel advice resulted in a pool of 52 items. The items are simple statements such as "Needs a lot of reassurance that things will work out," rated on a 0 to 3 scale (0 [none] = not present; 1 [mild] = present sometimes, not a real problem; 2 [moderate] = often present and a problem; 3 [severe] = very frequent and a major problem).

We also added 20 items from the CASI (Hallett et al., 2013). The 72-item draft survey was placed on a secure website and was completed by parents/primary caretakers of 990 children (ages 5 to 17) with a community diagnosis of ASD.

The survey data set (N = 990) was randomly divided in half to create a test sample and a validation sample (n = 495 per sample). Highly correlated items were assessed and dropped for redundancy. Exploratory factor analyses (EFA) on the test sample (n = 495) reduced the number of items and established the factor structure retained items. The EFA and item response theory (IRT) analysis approaches resulted in a single factor with 25 items. Confirmatory factor analysis in the validation sample (n = 495) and the full sample (N = 990) verified the final 25-item version of the Parent-Rated Anxiety Scale for ASD (PRAS-ASD). The mean score on the PRAS-ASD was 29.04 ± 14.92 (range 0 to 75). Cronbach's alpha and IRT marginal reliability were each above 0.9. The reliability and the standard error curves indicated that the PRAS-ASD is reliable across a wide range of scores (Scahill et al., 2019).

To evaluate the convergent validity and divergent validity of the PRAS-ASD, each site enrolled children and adolescents with ASD (total $N = 116$, ages 5 to 17 years) for a detailed, in-person clinical assessment. The assessment included measures to support the ASD diagnosis, commonly used parent ratings of behavior (e.g., Autism Diagnostic Observation Schedule, Stanford-Binet 5, Vineland II, Screen for Child Anxiety Related Disorders, Repetitive Behavior Survey—Revised, Aberrant Behavior Checklist). Scores on the PRAS-ASD ranged from 1 to 65; mean was 31.5 ± 15.6. In contrast to our prior observation with the 20-item CASI Anxiety scale, the mean scores for participants with IQ of 70 or higher (31.1 ± 15.6) was not different from those with IQ below 70 (30.9 ± 15.9). Pearson correlations of the 25-item PRAS-ASD with parent ratings on disruptive behavior, social disability, and repetitive behavior ranged from 0.33 to 0.66. The PRAS-ASD was most strongly correlated with the Screen for Child Anxiety Related Disorders (SCARED; $r = 0.83$). The SCARED is a parent-rated anxiety measure validated in the general pediatric population (Birmaher et al., 1999). This correlation between the PRAS-ASD and SCARED was significantly higher than any other correlation with parent-rated measure and the PRAS-ASD.

A subsample of 40 participants (32 boys, eight girls; mean age of 11.9 ± 3.4) returned to evaluate the test and retest of the scale at Time 2 (10 to 14 days later) and Time 3 (10 to 14 days after Time 2). The intraclass correlations were 0.88 (from Time 1 to Time 2), 0.93 (from Time 2 to Time 3), and 0.86 (from Time 1 to Time 3). Stable test–retest measurement in the absence of intervention over a relatively brief period is an essential prerequisite for an outcome measure (Kraemer, 1991).

Evidence-Based Treatment for Anxiety in Youth With ASD

In youth with anxiety disorders uncomplicated by ASD, two treatment approaches have supportive evidence for efficacy: medication and cognitive behavioral therapy (CBT; Crowe & McKay, 2017; Strawn, Geracioti, Rajdev, Clemenza, & Levine , 2018). There is also evidence that combined treatment with medication and CBT may be more effective than either modality alone (Walkup et al., 2008).

Cognitive Behavioral Therapy

Crowe and McKay (2017) reviewed the findings of 10 published meta-analyses between 2004 and 2016 that evaluated the efficacy of CBT in youth with anxiety disorders uncomplicated by ASD. The number of studies included in these reviews ranged from seven to 63. Most CBT programs in these meta-analyses included common ingredients such as psychoeducation about the nature of anxiety, self-monitoring of the situations that may trigger anxiety, effective problem solving, reappraisal of negative thought patterns, and in vivo exposure. The mean effect size was 0.42 in the meta-analyses that included trials comparing CBT to an active control. Not surprisingly, the mean effect size was 0.71 in reviews that examined studies without an active control condition (e.g., waitlist).

A meta-analysis of 14 CBT studies in high-functioning youth with ASD and anxiety disorders was completed by Ung, Selles, Small, and Storch (2015). All 14 studies included youth with IQ greater than 70. There were wide ranges in sample sizes (six to 71), age of participants (7 to 17 years), study duration (6 to 32 weeks), and outcome measurement (child report, parent report, or clinician interview). Two of 14 studies were open, and eight randomized trials used a waitlist control. The other four trials had an active control group (e.g., treatment as usual). Several studies were delivered in a group format. Parents were directly involved in 11 of 14 studies. The mean effect size across these studies was 0.71, but the effect sizes varied widely. The extremely wide range of effect sizes is due to differences in design, age, study duration, and choice of outcome measure. This review noted that most studies included familiar CBT techniques. Most studies also included sessions on social skills training. An important limitation of these studies is the exclusion of youth with intellectual disability.

Medication

Strawn and colleagues (2015) conducted a meta-analysis of psychopharmacological treatments for anxiety disorders in the general pediatric population. The review included nine placebo-controlled trials published between 2001 and 2013. Sample sizes ranged from 22 to 320 total participants for active drug and placebo. Selective serotonin reuptake inhibitors (SSRIs) were evaluated in six trials. The other three studies evaluated serotonin/norepinephrine reuptake inhibitors (SNRIs), venlafaxine in two trials, duloxetine in one study. Although there was a range of benefit across these studies, all nine showed superiority to placebo. The mean effect size was 0.62 across all nine trials. Post hoc analysis favored the SSRIs compared to the SNRIs.

Two of these nine trials included a psychotherapeutic study arm (Beidel et al., 2007; Walkup et al., 2008). Beidel and colleagues conducted a three-group study (N = 122): social effectiveness therapy (n = 57), fluoxetine (n = 33), and placebo (n = 32). Social effectiveness therapy includes social skills training and in vivo exposure. In this study, both active treatments were superior to placebo; social effectiveness therapy was superior to fluoxetine on some outcomes. Walkup and colleagues included a fourth study arm of combined treatment with CBT and the SSRI sertraline. This study randomized 488 children (ages 7 to 17) with GAD or SocAD or SAD to sertraline only (n = 133), CBT only (n = 139), combined drug and CBT (n = 140), or placebo (n = 76) for 12 weeks. All three active treatments were superior to placebo. The overall positive response rate was 80.7% for combined therapy, 54.7% for sertraline only, 59.7% for CBT, and 23.7% for placebo. Combined treatment was superior to either CBT or sertraline alone.

Taken together, the results of available meta-analyses and studies by Beidel et al. (2007) and Walkup et al. (2008) suggest that SSRIs are preferred over SNRIs as first-line drug treatments for anxiety in the general population of youth with anxiety disorders. CBT should also be considered a first-line treatment. Combined treatment with CBT and an SSRI appears superior to SSRI or CBT alone.

There are few placebo-controlled trials of SSRIs in youth with ASD and anxiety disorders (Stepanova, Dowling, Phelps, & Findling, 2017). The SSRI citalopram was evaluated in a sample of 149 youth with ASD (ages 5 to 17 years). The target of the treatment was repetitive behavior (King et al., 2009). In that study, citalopram was no better than placebo for reducing repetitive behavior. An important lesson learned from this study is the high risk of SSRI-induced behavioral activation in youth with ASD. Indeed, the only significant difference between citalopram and placebo was the rate of behaviors such as hyperactivity, impulsiveness, decreased concentration, and sleep disturbance. These symptoms of behavioral activation can often be managed by lowering the dose.

Case Example

Bradley is a 14-year-old boy referred for evaluation at the autism center from the guidance counselor at Benson Academy (fictitious name), where he is in the ninth grade. He lives with his parents and older sister in the family's suburban home. The guidance counselor expressed concern about Bradley's increasing isolation and rude comments in the morning community meeting. This is his second year at Benson Academy, which is a small, co-ed, private school for Grades 8 through 12. It has a solid reputation as an inclusive educational environment. He transferred to Benson after 2 years of being bullied at the public middle school. According to the guidance counselor, Bradley frequently complains at morning meeting about student cliques or unfair treatment from teachers.

Brief history. Following an uncomplicated pregnancy, Bradley was delivered at term in vertex position. His mother recalls that Bradley was a passive baby who was difficult to engage. He was breast fed for 2 months. He ate and slept well. By age 13 months, Bradley's mother became concerned about his overall development. He seemed disinterested in others; his motor and language skills were delayed. After multiple consultations with the regular pediatrician, Bradley was referred to a developmental pediatrician, who recommended speech therapy at age 2. He was diagnosed with autism at age 3. He enrolled in a regular kindergarten class at age 5 with special education services in speech and occupational therapy. At the start of his first-grade year, he refused to separate from his mother. He would cry and cling to his mother. With coaxing, he made it into school 1 day out of 5. After 6 weeks of daily struggle, the developmental pediatrician recommended treatment with paroxetine up to 10 mg per day. Bradley's mother also took him to a psychologist to develop and implement a behavioral plan. The combination treatment was successful and gradually he made his way back to school every day. In third grade, teachers raised concern about his inattention. This led to the first of several stimulant trials and a trial with atomoxetine. According to his mother, low-dose extended-release methylphenidate improved inattention without loss of appetite or sleep disturbance.

The middle school years were difficult for Bradley. He had few friends. He was ostracized and he showed increasing social avoidance. In sixth and seventh grade, he became the object of teasing that became intolerable in seventh grade. The transfer to Benson Academy occurred in eighth grade. The first year at Benson was reasonably successful. Although he continued his pattern of social avoidance, he developed a friendship with a fellow male student. Benson Academy fostered social interaction through morning meeting, student clubs, and daily social breaks. During the social breaks students were encouraged to mingle in a naturalistic, though supervised, setting.

Bradley found ways to get out of the social breaks. He told the guidance counselor that he hated going to these events, making comments such as "I won't go up to others and start talking—because I will say something stupid." In the face of continued social anxiety—even though he was not bullied as he had been in public school—he was referred to a child psychiatrist, who gradually increased the dose of paroxetine to 40 mg per day. At the time of the consultation in the autism center, he was on 18 mg of extended-release methylphenidate and paroxetine 40 mg per day.

Medical history. Bradley's medical history is remarkable for frequent bouts of otitis media between age 2 and 3 years. One set of pressure-equalizing tubes was installed about age 3. He has no serious illnesses or injuries. He has not been hospitalized since birth and has not had any major surgeries.

Family history. Bradley's mother reported no history of an anxiety disorder or depression in either parent. No one in the immediate family has a history of a developmental disorder or autism spectrum disorder.

Initial observations. Bradley is a tall, slender Caucasian boy with fair complexion, tousled red hair, and dental braces. Body weight is 130 pounds, height 70 inches, and head circumference 59 centimeters. He came to the evaluation casually dressed in jeans, sneakers, polo shirt, and dark blue Benson Academy hoody. His speech was fluent, slow in tempo, and slightly elevated in volume with nasal tone. His discourse was sparse—but coherent. Bradley was not uncooperative—but seemed mildly annoyed about coming to the center. He occasionally objected to his mother's reports on situations that he avoids due to anxiety with comments such as "That's not true anymore." Table 5.1 shows his scores on the assessment battery.

Formulation. Bradley is a 14-year-old boy of average intellectual ability with a confirmed diagnosis of autism spectrum disorder supported by history, Autism Diagnostic Observation Schedule (ADOS), and Social Communication Questionnaire (SCQ). Although he has a history of language delay, current language appears to be within the average range. However, he has social communication deficits that are amplified by social anxiety disorder. He also meets diagnostic criteria for generalized anxiety disorder. As with the Stanford-Binet, Vineland scores are normed at 100 ± 15. Bradley's Vineland domain scores are far below average and his IQ of 100, suggesting major impairment in adaptive functioning.

Table 5.1. Results of Bradley's Clinical Assessment

Measure	Score	Reference
Autism Diagnostic Observation Schedule (ADOS)	10	Lord et al. (2000)
Social Communication Questionnaire (SCQ—lifetime)	29	Corsello et al. (2007)
Abbreviated Stanford-Binet 5	100	Roid (2003)
Vineland		Sparrow, Cicchetti, and Balla (2006)
Communication	71	
Socialization	48	
Daily Living Skills	54	
Anxiety Diagnostic Inventory Schedule (current)	+ Soc Anxiety, + Generalized Anxiety Disorder	Silverman, Saavedra and Pinna (2001)
Parent-Rated Anxiety Scale-Autism Spectrum Disorder (PRAS-ASD)	48	Scahill et al. (2019)
Pediatric Anxiety Rating Scale-Autism Spectrum Disorder[a]	17	Storch et al. (2012)
Children's Yale-Brown Obsessive-Compulsive Scales-Autism Spectrum Disorder[a]	11	Scahill et al. (2014)
Aberrant Behavior Checklist		Kaat, Lecavalier, and Aman (2014)
Irritability	10	
Social Withdrawal	27	
Stereotypy	10	
Hyperactivity	17	
Inappropriate Speech	8	

[a] Modified versions for ASD.

That anxiety is contributing to his overall disability is supported by the score of 48 on the PRAS-ASD. As noted earlier, results from our online survey with the PRAS-ASD indicated a mean score of 29.04 ± 14.92. A score of 48 is more than a standard deviation above the mean of youth with ASD included in the survey. The Irritability and Hyperactivity subscale scores on the parent-rated Aberrant Behavior Checklist do not suggest problems with disruptive behavior. The score of 27 on the Social Withdrawal subscale is nearly two standard deviation units above available norms for youth with ASD. This score reflects extreme social isolation that is likely influenced by ASD and social anxiety (Cappriola, Maddox, & White, 2017). Despite ongoing treatment with paroxetine, he has prominent anxiety symptoms and social isolation. We recommended that Bradley participate in a social skills group and cognitive behavioral therapy to learn ways to manage anxiety that are more effective than avoidance.

Summary and Future Directions

Measuring anxiety in youth with ASD faces many challenges. Scale items that are dependent on language may not be endorsed by parents—especially in children with language or cognitive delays (Hallett et al., 2013). A detailed review of outcome measures for anxiety in ASD concluded that the absence of an accepted outcome measure of anxiety in ASD is an impediment to intervention research (Lecavalier et al., 2014). Our research group conducted a multisite measure development project. We used qualitative and quantitative methods to build a relevant, valid, reliable, 25-item parent-rated dimensional measure of anxiety for youth with ASD. Future research on the application of CBT in youth with ASD is warranted. Available data suggest that integration of social skills training along with the empirically supported techniques of CBT is recommended. For young children with ASD and those with intellectual disability, CBT techniques in combination with parent training is in order (Cartwright-Hatton et al., 2011). Placebo-controlled trials in youth with ASD and anxiety disorders are overdue. Given the evidence that youth with one anxiety disorder often have another anxiety disorder (Walkup et al., 2008; Merikangas et al., 2010), these studies need not, and probably should not, be disorder specific.

References

American Psychiatric Association. (2013). *Diagnostic and statistical manual of mental disorders* (DSM-5). Washington, DC: American Psychiatric Association.

Bearss, K., Taylor, C. A., Aman, M. G., Whittemore, R., Lecavalier, L., Miller, J.,... Scahill, L. (2016). Using qualitative methods to guide scale development for anxiety in youth with autism spectrum disorder. *Autism, 20*(6), 663–672. doi:10.1177/1362361315601012

Beesdo, K., Knappe, S., & Pine, D. S. (2009). Anxiety and anxiety disorders in children and adolescents: Developmental issues and implications for DSM-V. *Psychiatric Clinics, 32*(3), 483–524.

Beidel, D. C., Turner, S. M., Sallee, F. R., Ammerman, R. T., Crosby, L. A., & Pathak, S. (2007). SET-C versus fluoxetine in the treatment of childhood social phobia. *Journal of the American Academy of Child & Adolescent Psychiatry, 46*(12), 1622–1632.

Birmaher, B., Brent, D. A., Chiappetta, L., Bridge, J., Monga, S., & Baugher, M. (1999). Psychometric properties of the Screen for Child Anxiety Related Emotional Disorders (SCARED): A replication study. *Journal of the American Academy of Child and Adolescent Psychiatry, 38*(10), 1230–1236. doi:10.1097/00004583-199,910,000-00011

Capriola, N. N., Maddox, B. B., & White, S. W. (2017). No offense intended: Fear of negative evaluation in adolescents and adults with autism spectrum disorder. *Journal of Autism and Development Disorders, 47*(12), 3803–3813. doi:10.1007/s10803-016-2827-0, doi:10.1016/j.clinthera.2014.04.006

Cartwright-Hatton, S., McNally, D., Field, A. P., Rust, S., Laskey, B., Dixon, C.,... Woodham, A. (2011). A new parenting-based group intervention for young anxious children: Results of a randomized controlled trial. *Journal of the American Academy of Child and Adolescent Psychiatry, 50*(3), 242–251.e246. doi:10.1016/j.jaac.2010.12.015

Copeland, W. E., Angold, A., Shanahan, L., & Costello, E. J. (2014). Longitudinal patterns of anxiety from childhood to adulthood: The Great Smoky Mountains Study. *Journal of the American Academy of Child and Adolescent Psychiatry, 53*(1), 21–33.

Corsello, C., Hus, V., Pickles, A., Risi, S., Cook, E. H., Jr., Leventhal, B. L., & Lord, C. (2007). Between a ROC and a hard place: Decision making and making decisions about using the SCQ. *Journal of Child Psychology and Psychiatry, 48*(9), 932–940.

Crowe, K., & McKay, D. (2017). Efficacy of cognitive-behavioral therapy for childhood anxiety and depression. *Journal of Anxiety Disorders, 49*, 76–87.

Davis, M. (1992). The role of the amygdala in fear and anxiety. *Annual Review of Neuroscience, 15*, 353–375. doi:10.1146/annurev.ne.15.030192.002033

Department of Health London. (2008). Guidance on the routine collection of patient reported outcome measures (PROMs).

Gadow, K. D., & Sprafkin, J. N. (2002). *Child Symptom Inventory 4: Screening and norms manual.* Checkmate Plus.

Glod, M., Creswell, C., Waite, P., Jamieson, R., McConachie, H., South, M. D., & Rodgers, J. (2017). Comparisons of the factor structure and measurement invariance of the Spence children's anxiety scale—parent version in children with autism spectrum disorder and typically developing anxious children. *Journal of Autism and Developmental Disorders, 47*(12), 3834–3846.

Hallett, V., Lecavalier, L., Sukhodolsky, D. G., Cipriano, N., Aman, M. G., McCracken, J. T.,... Scahill, L. (2013). Exploring the manifestations of anxiety in children with autism spectrum disorders. *Journal of Autism and Developmental Disorders, 43*(10), 2341–2352. doi:10.1007/s10803-013-1775-1

Kaat, A. J., Lecavalier, L., & Aman, M. G. (2014). Validity of the aberrant behavior checklist in children with autism spectrum disorder. *Journal of Autism and Developmental Disorders, 44*(5), 1103–1116. doi:10.1007/s10803-013-1970-0

Kagan, J., Snidman, N., Kahn, V., Towsley, S., Steinberg, L., & Fox, N. A. (2007). The preservation of two infant temperaments into adolescence. *Monographs of the Society for Research in Child Development*, i-95.

Kerns, C. M., & Kendall, P. C. (2012). The presentation and classification of anxiety in autism spectrum disorder. *Clinical Psychology: Science and Practice, 19*(4), 323–347.

Kerns, C. M., Kendall, P. C., Berry, L., Souders, M. C., Franklin, M. E., Schultz, R. T., . . . Herrington, J. (2014). Traditional and atypical presentations of anxiety in youth with autism spectrum disorder. *Journal of Autism and Developmental Disorders, 44*(11), 2851–2861. doi:10.1007/s10803-014-2141-7

Kessler, R. C., Chiu, W. T., Demler, O., Merikangas, K. R., & Walters, E. E. (2005). Prevalence, severity, and comorbidity of 12-month DSM-IV disorders in the National Comorbidity Survey Replication. *Archives of General Psychiatry, 62*(6), 617–627.

King, B. H., Hollander, E., Sikich, L., McCracken, J. T., Scahill, L., Bregman, J. D., . . . Hirtz, D. (2009). Lack of efficacy of citalopram in children with autism spectrum disorders and high levels of repetitive behavior: Citalopram ineffective in children with autism. *Archives of General Psychiatry, 66*(6), 583–590.

Kraemer, H. C. (1991). To increase power in randomized clinical trials without increasing sample size. *Psychopharmacology Bulletin, 27*(3), 217–224.

Lecavalier, L., McCracken, C. E., Aman, M. G., McDougle, C. J., McCracken, J. T., Tierney, E., . . . Swiezy, N. B. (2019). An exploration of concomitant psychiatric disorders in children with autism spectrum disorder. *Comprehensive Psychiatry, 88*, 57–64.

Lecavalier, L., Wood, J. J., Halladay, A. K., Jones, N. E., Aman, M. G., Cook, E. H., . . . Scahill, L. (2014). Measuring anxiety as a treatment endpoint in youth with autism spectrum disorder. *Journal of Autism and Developmental Disorders, 44*(5), 1128–1143. doi:10.1007/s10803-013-1974-9

LeDoux, J. (1998). Fear and the brain: Where have we been, and where are we going? *Biological Psychiatry, 44*(12), 1229–1238.

LeDoux, J. E., & Pine, D. S. (2016). Using neuroscience to help understand fear and anxiety: A two-system framework. *American Journal of Psychiatry, 173*(11), 1083–1093.

Lord, C., Risi, S., Lambrecht, L., Cook, E. H., Jr., Leventhal, B. L., DiLavore, P. C., . . . Rutter, M. (2000). The autism diagnostic observation schedule-generic: A standard measure of social and communication deficits associated with the spectrum of autism. *Journal of Autism and Developmental Disorders, 30*(3), 205–223.

Matza, L. S., Patrick, D. L., Riley, A. W., Alexander, J. J., Rajmil, L., Pleil, A. M., & Bullinger, M. (2013). Pediatric patient-reported outcome instruments for research to support medical product labeling: Report of the ISPOR PRO good research practices for the assessment of children and adolescents task force. *Value in Health, 16*(4), 461–479.

Merikangas, K. R., He, J. P., Burstein, M., Swanson, S. A., Avenevoli, S., Cui, L., . . . Swendsen, J. (2010). Lifetime prevalence of mental disorders in US adolescents: Results from the National Comorbidity Survey Replication–Adolescent Supplement (NCS-A). *Journal of the American Academy of Child and Adolescent Psychiatry, 49*(10), 980–989.

Morrison, F. G., & Ressler, K. J. (2014). From the neurobiology of extinction to improved clinical treatments. *Depression and Anxiety, 31*(4), 279–290. doi:10.1002/da.22214

Moscati, A., Flint, J., & Kendler, K. S. (2016). Classification of anxiety disorders comorbid with major depression: Common or distinct influences on risk? *Depression and Anxiety, 33*(2), 120–127.

Muris, P. (2007). *Normal and abnormal fear and anxiety in children and adolescents*. London: Elsevier.

Myers, K. M., & Davis, M. (2002). Behavioral and neural analysis of extinction. *Neuron, 36*(4), 567–584.

Panksepp, J., Fuchs, T., & Iacobucci, P. (2011). The basic neuroscience of emotional experiences in mammals: The case of subcortical FEAR circuitry and implications for clinical anxiety. *Applied Animal Behaviour Science, 129*(1), 1–17.

Phelps, E. A. (2006). Emotion and cognition: Insights from studies of the human amygdala. *Annual Review of Psychology, 57*, 27–53. doi:10.1146/annurev.psych.56.091103.070234

Polanczyk, G. V., Salum, G. A., Sugaya, L. S., Caye, A., & Rohde, L. A. (2015). Annual research review: A meta-analysis of the worldwide prevalence of mental disorders in children and adolescents. *Journal of Child Psychology and Psychiatry, 56*(3), 345–365.

Rachman, S. (1977). The conditioning theory of fear-acquisition: A critical examination. *Behaviour Research and Therapy, 15*(5), 375–387.

Roid, G. H. (2003). *Stanford-Binet Intelligence Scales* (5th ed.). Rolling Meadows, IL: Riverside.

Scahill, L., Dimitropoulos, A., McDougle, C. J., Aman, M. G., Feurer, I. D., McCracken, J. T., . . . Vitiello, B. (2014). Children's Yale-Brown Obsessive Compulsive Scale in autism spectrum disorder: Component structure of symptom checklist and distribution of severity scales. *Journal of the American Academy of Child and Adolescent Psychiatry, 53*(1), 97–107.

Scahill, L., Lecavalier, L., Schultz, R., Evans, A.N., Maddox, B., . . . Edwards, M. C. (2019). Development of the Parent-Rated Anxiety Scale for youth with autism spectrum disorder. *Journal of the American Academy of Child and Adolescent Psychiatry. E Publication ahead of print.*

Silverman, W. K., Saavedra, L. M., & Pina, A. A. (2001). Test-retest reliability of anxiety symptoms and diagnoses with the Anxiety Disorders Interview Schedule for DSM-IV: Child and parent versions. *Journal of the American Academy of Child Psychiatry, 40*(8), 937–944.

Sparrow, S. S., Cicchetti, D. V., & Balla, D. A. (2005). *Vineland adaptive behavior scales* (2nd ed.). Circle Pines, MN: American Guidance Service.

Stepanova, E., Dowling, S., Phelps, M., & Findling, R. L. (2017). Pharmacotherapy of emotional and behavioral symptoms associated with autism spectrum disorder in children and adolescents. *Dialogues in Clinical Neuroscience, 19*(4), 395.

Storch, E. A., Wood, J. J., Ehrenreich May, J., Lewin, A. B., Jones, A. M., Park, J. M., & Murphy, T. K. (2012). Convergent and divergent validity and reliability of the Pediatric Anxiety Rating Scale. *Journal of Autism and Developmental Disorders, 42*, 2374–2382.

Strawn, J. R., Geracioti, L., Rajdev, N., Clemenza, K., & Levine, A. (2018). Pharmacotherapy for generalized anxiety disorder in adult and pediatric patients: An evidence-based treatment review. *Expert Opinion on Pharmacotherapy, 19*(10), 1057–1070.

Strawn, J. R., Welge, J. A., Wehry, A. M., Keeshin, B., & Rynn, M. A. (2015). Efficacy and tolerability of antidepressants in pediatric anxiety disorders: A systematic review and meta-analysis. *Depression and Anxiety, 32*(3), 149–157.

Ung, D., Selles, R., Small, B. J., & Storch, E. A. (2015). A systematic review and meta-analysis of cognitive-behavioral therapy for anxiety in youth with high-functioning autism spectrum disorders. *Child Psychiatry & Human Development, 46*(4), 533–547.

U.S. Department of Health and Human Services, FDA Center for Drug Evaluation and Research, FDA Center for Biologics Evaluation and Research, & FDA Center for Devices and Radiological Health. (2006). *Health and Quality of Life Outcomes, 4*, 79. https://doi.org/10.1186/1477-7525-4-79

van Steensel, F. J., Bogels, S. M., & Perrin, S. (2011). Anxiety disorders in children and adolescents with autistic spectrum disorders: A meta-analysis. *Clinical Child and Family Psychology Review, 14*(3), 302–317. doi:10.1007/s10567-011-0097-0

van Steensel, F. J. A., & Heeman, E. J. (2017). Anxiety levels in children with autism spectrum disorder: A meta-analysis. *Journal of Child and Family Studies, 26*(7), 1753–1767. doi:10.1007/s10826-017-0687-7

Walkup, J. T., Albano, A. M., Piacentini, J., Birmaher, B., Compton, S. N., Sherrill, J. T.,... Iyengar, S. (2008). Cognitive behavioral therapy, sertraline, or a combination in childhood anxiety. *New England Journal of Medicine, 359*(26), 2753–2766.

White, S. W., Oswald, D., Ollendick, T., & Scahill, L. (2009). Anxiety in children and adolescents with autism spectrum disorders. *Clinical Psychology Review, 29*(3), 216–229. doi:10.1016/j.cpr.2009.01.003

Woody, S., & Rachman, S. (1994). Generalized anxiety disorder (GAD) as an unsuccessful search for safety. *Clinical Psychology Review, 14*(8), 743–753.

World Health Organization Consortium. (2004). Prevalence, severity, and unmet need for treatment of mental disorders in the World Health Organization World Mental Health Surveys. *Journal of the American Medical Association, 291*(21), 2581–2590.

CHAPTER

6 Obsessive-Compulsive and Related Disorders in Autism Spectrum Disorder

Katelyn M. Dyason, Sharna L. Mathieu, Donna L. Griffiths, *and* Lara J. Farrell

Abstract

Obsessive-compulsive and related disorders (OCRDs) are a group of diagnoses that center on compulsive behaviors and/or obsessive thoughts. They include obsessive-compulsive disorder (OCD), body dysmorphic disorder (BDD), hoarding disorder, excoriation disorder, and trichotillomania. Each of the OCRDs are associated with significant psychosocial impairment and family/caregiver burden. Furthermore, these disorders frequently co-occur with autism spectrum disorder (ASD) traits and diagnoses, and differential diagnosis can be difficult. OCD represents the most common of the OCRDs, and also the most well researched to date. Consequently, this chapter focuses on the nature and impact of comorbid OCD and ASD across the lifespan. Unfortunately, preliminary research indicates that individuals with OCD and ASD are significantly more disadvantaged by way of poorer psychosocial functioning, increased family burden/accommodation to symptoms, greater number of other comorbid conditions, and more likely to present with comorbid externalizing disorders. Future research is needed to determine what impact these unique complexities may have on treatment success. Preliminary research suggests that cognitive behavioral therapy (CBT) is of benefit to these individuals with comorbid ASD and OCD; however, modification may be necessary to improve engagement and outcomes (e.g., family inclusion in therapy). This chapter presents a case example of modified CBT for a child with comorbid ASD and OCD, delivered intensively. Future research should focus on the related OCRDs in individuals with ASD, as well as improving current assessment and treatment practices.

Keywords: autism spectrum disorder, ASD, obsessive-compulsive disorder, OCD, comorbidity, obsessive-compulsive related disorders, OCRD

Overview

Obsessive-compulsive and related disorders (OCRDs) are a group of diagnoses that center on compulsive behaviors and/or obsessive thoughts. They include obsessive-compulsive disorder (OCD), body dysmorphic disorder (BDD), hoarding disorder, excoriation disorder, and trichotillomania. The OCRDs have been included as a disorder cluster in the most recent *Diagnostic and Statistical Manual of Mental Disorders* (DSM-5) due to phenomenological overlap and high comorbidity with each other (American Psychiatric Association [APA], 2013). Furthermore, research in this area suggests similar etiological determinants (e.g., Snorrason, Belleau, & Woods, 2012) and underlying difficulties with emotion regulation (e.g., de la Cruz et al., 2013).

OCD, the most common and well-researched disorder of the OCRDs, is an impairing, neuropsychiatric disorder characterized by persistent, distressing, and intrusive thoughts, images, and urges (obsessions) and/or repetitive behaviors or mental acts (compulsions) that an individual feels compelled to perform in an attempt to reduce his or her distressing symptoms (APA, 2013). OCD has been linked to significant and pervasive psychosocial impairment, affecting social, academic/occupational, sleep, and family functioning across the lifespan (Markarian et al., 2010; Piacentini, Bergman,

Keller, & McCracken, 2003; Piacentini, Peris, Bergman, & Chang, 2007) and frequently results in restricted quality of life (Bobes et al., 2001; Huppert, Simpson, Nissenson, Liebowitz, & Foa, 2009; Storch et al., 2007).

In BDD, an individual experiences significant distress related to a perceived physical defect in his or her appearance and consequently engages in time-consuming and repetitive behaviors, such as mirror checking, camouflage or avoidance, and so forth (APA, 2013). Common areas of concern include teeth, eyes/eyebrows, weight, stomach, nose, hair, and skin; however, any body part can become the target of fixation and distress (Phillips et al., 2006; Schneider, Turner, Mond, & Hudson, 2016; Veale et al., 1996). Difficulties associated with this disorder include considerable psychosocial impairment (Phillips et al., 2006), and of particular concern is the significantly higher rates of suicidal ideation/attempts in this population compared to individuals without BDD (Bjornsson et al., 2013; Buhlmann et al., 2010; Phillips et al., 2006). Furthermore, there is a higher tendency to seek physical remedies to the imagined defect (e.g., plastic surgery; Buhlmann et al., 2010) versus psychological support (Marques, Weingarden, & LeBlanc, 2011).

Beyond OCD and BDD, the remaining OCRDs represent less frequently occurring disorders, with relatively limited research attention to date. Hoarding disorder is characterized by extreme distress and difficulty when confronted with the idea, or actuality, of discarding possessions due their perceived need and/or the individual's attachment to said objects (APA, 2013). Trichotillomania is a disorder whereby the individual compulsively pulls out his or her hair and is frequently associated with hair loss/balding, perceived inability to stop the action, and significant distress (APA, 2013). The hair-pulling behaviors can be characterized as either automatic (i.e., habitual) or focused (i.e., intended behavior in response to negative feelings, thoughts, etc.; Arabatzoudis, Rehm, Nedeljkovic, & Moulding, 2017; Flessner et al., 2008; Rehm, Moulding, & Nedeljkovic, 2015; Roberts, O'Connor, & Bélanger, 2013). Although any hair can be targeted, the most common areas include the scalp, eyebrows, and eyelashes (du Toit, van Kradenburg, Niehaus, & Stein, 2001; Franklin et al., 2008; Woods, Flessner, et al., 2006). Of notable concern for individuals with trichotillomania is the presence of life-threatening medical complications resulting from swallowing the pulled hair strands (Bouwer & Stein, 1998; Lynch, Feola, & Guenther, 2003). Excoriation disorder refers to the compulsive picking of one's skin, often resulting in abrasions and scarring, and is similarly described in terms of a perceived inability to stop the behavior despite significant distress (APA, 2013). Each of the remaining OCRDs are associated with considerable impairment, and the social relationships of sufferers are often adversely affected—for example, low self-esteem, shame, and embarrassment resulting in the avoidance of public outings in excoriation disorder (e.g., Tucker, Woods, Flessner, Franklin, & Franklin, 2011) and trichotillomania (e.g., Woods, Flessner, et al., 2006), and the considerable burden experienced by family members of those suffering from hoarding disorder, particularly due to perceived filth and uncleanliness (Drury, Ajmi, de la Cruz, Nordsletten, & Mataix-Cols, 2014).

Autism spectrum disorder (ASD) is not an OCRD yet shares some similar diagnostic features. ASD is a chronic neurodevelopmental disorder marked by restricted and repetitive patterns of behavior or interests, as well as noticeable deficits in communication and social interaction skills. These restricted, repetitive behavioral patterns are noticeable through a broad range of behaviors, such as stereotyped motor mannerisms, repetitive speech, restricted or fixated interests, rigidity in routines and rituals, insistence on sameness, and sensory sensitivities (APA, 2013). Due to the phenotypic similarities between ASD and the OCRDs (e.g., repetitive behaviors, fixated/obsessional features, and rigidity/inflexibility), several challenges face clinicians and researchers alike in determining a differential diagnosis. Additionally, the OCRDs frequently co-occur with ASD, and occur at a higher prevalence in individuals with ASD than in the general population (Croen et al., 2015; Neil, Moum, & Sturmey, 2014; A. J. Russell et al., 2016), so attributing symptoms and behaviors to one disorder only may be misrepresentative of the individual's overall presentation if both disorders are present. The similarities and comorbidities between ASD and the OCRDs raise the question of possible underlying shared mechanisms of risk (Fineberg et al., 2017). At present, it is unknown whether OCD occurs more frequently in individuals with ASD due to shared etiologies, heightened challenges faced by individuals with ASD in their social environment, increased adverse life experiences, or a combination of these or other factors (Postorino et al., 2017); as such, this is an area that requires more research.

Despite phenomenological overlap and significant comorbidities, OCRDs in ASD have received limited research attention regarding the impact these disorders have on an individual's psychosocial functioning, severity of obsessive-compulsive symptoms, and response to treatments. In this chapter we first outline the prevalence, developmental course, and etiology of OCD and the OCRDs across the lifespan in individuals with ASD. We then move on to discuss assessing and diagnosing the OCRDs in individuals with ASD, and observe some difficulties in determining a differential diagnosis. Next, we discuss the current approaches to treatment of the OCRDs and modifications necessary for treatment of OCRDs in individuals with ASD, demonstrated with a clinical case study of comorbid ASD and OCD. Finally, we conclude the chapter with a summary and a discussion of future directions for research. This chapter will focus predominantly on OCD in individuals with ASD, reflecting the relative paucity of research into other OCRDs.

Prevalence and Developmental Course

Comorbid OCD and ASD

Despite affecting approximately 2% to 4% of all children (Geller, 2006; Rapoport, Inoff-Germain, Weissman, & Greenwald, 2000; Zohar, 1999), OCD occurs at a much higher rate in children with ASD, with a mean prevalence rate of 11% across six studies (range = 1.47% to 37.2%; Neil et al., 2014). Similarly, ASD occurs in approximately 1.7% of all children (G. Russell, Rodgers, Ukoumunne, & Ford, 2014), but occurs in 3% to 7% of children with OCD (Chasson et al., 2011). A more recent study reported a much higher prevalence of ASD, with 21% of children (7 to 17 years) seeking treatment for OCD meeting criteria for a diagnosis of ASD (Griffiths, Farrell, Waters, & White 2017b). Even without a diagnosis of ASD, children with OCD also tend to show higher levels of ASD traits than would be expected, often scoring above threshold on screening measures of ASD (Griffiths, Farrell, Waters, & White, 2017a; Stewart et al., 2016).

This pattern of high comorbidity between the two diagnoses is also evident in adults. OCD occurs in approximately 1% of the adult population (Osland, Arnold, & Pringsheim, 2018; Ruscio, Stein, Chiu, & Kessler, 2010), but in 18% to 33% of adults diagnosed with ASD (Buck et al., 2014; A. J. Russell et al., 2016). Roughly comparable to rates in children, ASD occurs in 0.98% of the general adult population (Brugha et al., 2011), but in two samples of clinic-referred adults with OCD, 20% and 28%, respectively, had comorbid ASD (Bejerot, Nylander, & Lindström, 2001; Wikramanayake et al., 2018). Across the lifespan, approximately one quarter (24% in both studies) of clinic-referred adults with ASD experienced OCD at some point in their lives (Buck et al., 2014; Hofvander et al., 2009). Interestingly, even among adults presenting for an ASD assessment in adulthood, OCD was more common among those who ended up receiving a diagnosis of ASD than those who did not meet criteria for diagnosis of ASD (A. J. Russell et al., 2016). When considering only an audit of medical records, the reported prevalence of OCD was lower, with only 8% of individuals with ASD having a recorded diagnosis of OCD (Croen et al., 2015). This highlights the potential for missed diagnosis of OCD when OCD is not the primary presentation to a health service and/or an in-depth assessment of OCD is not conducted. This may in part be due to the difficulties clinicians face in determining whether repetitive behaviors and obsessions are due to ASD or OCD, or perhaps may be related to the often secretive nature of OCD (Geller, 2006; Keyes, Nolte, & Williams, 2017; Robinson, Rose, & Salkovskis, 2017), with many individuals presenting for treatment with other comorbid disorders and only acknowledging OCD symptoms when directly questioned (Rapoport et al., 2000; Nestadt, Bienvenu, Cai, Samuels, & Eaton, 1998). Reported diagnoses and outcome of a comprehensive assessment were compared in one study of adults with ASD, where only 9% of individuals had a reported diagnosis of OCD, but 22% actually met criteria for OCD during their lifetime (Buck et al., 2014).

In a review of the pediatric OCD literature, 11 studies reported the mean age of onset of OCD between 7.5 years and 12.5 years (mean = 10.3 years), with assessment occurring approximately 2.5 years after the age of onset (Geller, 2006). In adulthood, the mean age of onset is 21 years, which suggests a bimodal distribution of disorder origin (Geller, 2006). This being said, childhood-onset OCD often persists across the lifespan, with estimates suggesting 41% of children with OCD experience chronic symptoms into adulthood (Stewart et al., 2004) and have more severe symptoms in adulthood than individuals with an adult onset (do Rosario-Campos et al., 2001). In addition to the difference in age of onset, there may be other differences between childhood- and adult-onset OCD that support a hypothesis of developmental discontinuity (Geller et al., 2001). Although in adulthood OCD affects approximately an equal number of men and women, with a slight female dominance (Torres et al., 2006), pediatric OCD, on the other hand, shows a skew in the distribution toward males, with an average male-to-female ratio of 3:2 (Geller, 2006). Two studies compared children, adolescents, and adults with OCD on a variety of OCD-related variables (Farrell, Barrett, & Piacentini, 2006; Geller et al., 2001). Both studies found consistent differences between the three age groups on: gender distribution; age of onset; obsession/compulsion types, severity and insight; and type of comorbid disorders. As adolescents shared certain features common to adults and children, Farrell and colleagues (2006) suggested OCD may present as specific developmental subtypes at different ages. In individuals with ASD, limited research has examined developmental differences in the expression of OCD symptoms across the lifespan. In individuals with ASD, as in those without ASD, onset of OCD can occur in either childhood (e.g., Neil et al., 2014) or adulthood (Hutton, Goode, Murphy, Le Couteur, & Rutter, 2008). Additionally, in a sample of adults with OCD (Wikramanayake et al., 2018), there were no significant differences in the age of onset or age of first diagnosis of OCD among individuals above and below the clinical cut-off on the Autism-Spectrum Quotient (AQ; Baron-Cohen, Wheelwright, Skinner, Martin, & Clubley, 2001). In line with the general OCD literature, in two samples of adults with ASD there were no significant gender differences in rates of OCD (Hofvander et al., 2009; A. J. Russell et al., 2016). As yet, it does not appear that any study has examined gender differences in OCD rates among youth with ASD, despite or perhaps because of the well-documented male dominance in ASD (APA, 2013).

Aside from the developmental course of OCD being similar in those with and without comorbid ASD, there are other similarities in OCD across the lifespan in individuals both with and without comorbid ASD, including similar self-reported distress, time intensiveness, and interference of OCD symptoms in youth (Lewin, Wood, Gunderon, Murphy, & Storch, 2011) and similar symptom profiles (Cath, Ran, Smit, van Balkom, & Comijs, 2008; Lewin et al., 2011; Mack et al., 2010), although obsessive sameness was found to occur at higher rates in younger (relative to older) children without comorbid ASD, whereas age was not associated with this symptom cluster in patients with comorbid ASD/OCD (Zandt, Prior, & Kyrios, 2007). In relation to differences in OCD between those with and without comorbid ASD, unfortunately, youth with both OCD and ASD tend to be more impaired, their parents report having to engage in more accommodating behaviors, and they tend to have significantly more comorbid conditions, including attention deficit hyperactivity disorder (ADHD; Griffiths et al., 2017b), relative to youth with OCD but without ASD. For adults with OCD, those with comorbid ASD tend to show poorer OCD insight compared to adults with OCD but without comorbid ASD (Wikramanayake et al., 2018).

Other OCRDs in ASD

Across the remaining OCRDs, there is a paucity of information about their occurrence and developmental course in the general population, and even less information about their occurrence and developmental course in individuals with ASD. However, there are published occurrences of each of the OCRDs occurring in individuals with ASD. This illustrates that the OCRDs do indeed co-occur with ASD, but there is currently limited information on how often they co-occur or whether there are differences in profiles between individuals with and without comorbid ASD. Given the high comorbidity between OCD and ASD, and the high comorbidities among the OCRDs, it is likely that the remaining OCRDs also occur more frequently in individuals with ASD; however, this is an area that requires much-needed research attention.

The prevalence of BDD in youth is approximately 2% (Mayville, Katz, Gipson, & Cabral, 1999; Rief, Buhlmann, Wilhelm, Borkenhagen, & Brähler, 2006) and similarly 1.8% in adults (Buhlmann et al., 2010). Exact rates of BDD/ASD co-occurrence are not yet clear. As of 2017, there were only three published case studies of co-occurring BDD and ASD in the literature (that we are aware of): one of an adult with adolescent-onset BDD (Warren, Sanders, & Veenstra-VanderWeele, 2010) and two brief adult case studies published together (Vasudeva & Hollander, 2017). In terms of hoarding disorder there are also varying estimates of prevalence, ranging from 1.5% to 6%, with increasing frequency in older populations (Cath, Nizar, Boomsma, & Mathews, 2017). Although there are no firm estimates of the prevalence of hoarding disorder in individuals with ASD, both children (Ruta, Mugno, D'Arrigo, Vitiello, & Mazzone, 2010) and adults (McDougle, Kresch, Goodman, & Naylor 1995; Pertusa et al., 2012) with OCD and comorbid ASD are more likely to report the presence of hoarding symptoms than those with OCD alone. Despite this, hoarding symptoms have been more strongly linked to attention deficits than ASD traits (Anholt et al., 2010).

Trichotillomania similarly has a prevalence rate of approximately 1% in adolescents (King et al., 1995) and up to 3% in young adults (Grzesiak, Reich, Szepietowski, Hadrys, & Pacan, 2017). There are, however, no reported prevalence statistics of childhood trichotillomania, although it does occur in children (e.g., J. P. Harrison & Franklin, 2012). There is also sparse research into how trichotillomania may develop over the lifespan (Kratochvil & Bloch, 2009). There are several recorded instances of co-occurrence with ASD across the lifespan. For example, Simonoff and colleagues (2008) found 3.9% of children with ASD met criteria for trichotillomania; however, given there are no prevalence estimates of childhood trichotillomania more generally, it is unknown whether this is higher than the general population. Masiran (2018) presented a case study on an adolescent with comorbid ASD and trichotillomania, and in their study of adults with ASD, Hofvander and colleagues (2009) reported one participant ($N = 122$) who met criteria for comorbid trichotillomania. Often co-occurring with trichotillomania (Snorrason et al., 2012), excoriation disorder has a prevalence rate of 1.4% to 5.4% (Hayes, Storch, & Berlanga, 2009; Keuthen, Koran, Aboujaoude, Large, & Serpe, 2010; Kessler, Petukhova, Sampson, Zaslavsky, & Wittchen, 2012). There are no current prevalence estimates for excoriation disorder in ASD (Roi & Bazzano, 2017). In a systematic review of treatment of excoriation in individuals with developmental disabilities, only three case studies (one child, two adolescents) reported on comorbid ASD and excoriation (Lang et al., 2010). Thus, the status of the literature on the prevalence and developmental course of comorbid ASD and the OCRDs is to date extremely limited (beyond research into comorbidity with OCD).

Etiology, Diagnosis, and Assessment

Obsessive-Compulsive Disorder in ASD

Given the high co-occurrence and phenomenological overlap between ASD and OCD, there is likely shared underlying mechanisms, and moreover, some researchers even go so far as to suggest the presence of an ASD subtype within OCD (Bejerot, 2007). An important question for research, therefore, is to determine why people with ASD are more likely to have OCD symptoms and disorder than the wider population, why those with OCD are at greater risk for ASD, and what (if any) are the implications for accurate diagnosis and effective treatment. Given the heterogeneity of both disorders, etiological models for both OCD and ASD are *highly* complex and involve genetic, neurobiological, and psychosocial determinants (Jacob, Landeros-Weisenberger, & Leckman, 2009).

Numerous studies have reported on the genetic overlap of OCD and ASD, including the higher rates of OCD in ASD families (e.g., Bolton, Pickles, Murphy, & Rutter, 1998; Brune et al., 2008; Guo et al., 2017; Hollander, King, Delaney, Smith, & Silverman, 2003; Jacob et al., 2009; Wilcox, Tsuang, Schnurr, & Baida-Fragoso, 2003). These rates are higher again when considering the first-degree relatives of ASD individuals who engage in more repetitive behaviors (vs. those who endorse less; Hollander et al., 2003). Parents of children with ASD are also more likely to report the experience of feeling incomplete and "not just right" sensations (Kloosterman, Summerfedlt, Parker, & Holden, 2013), which are frequently experienced symptoms of OCD (Coles, Frost, Heimberg, & Rheaume, 2003; Coles, Heimberg, Frost, & Steketee, 2005). Furthermore, these "not just right" sensations have also been linked to the sensory sensitivity and sensory avoidance behaviors associated with ASD (Ferrao et al., 2012; Hellriegel, Barber, Wikramanayake, Fineberg, & Mandy, 2017; Taylor, Conelea, McKay, Crowe, & Abramowitz, 2014).

Studies investigating neurocircuitry in ASD and OCD have separately identified common regions of the brain associated with both disorders. For example, in OCD, the cortico-striatal circuit has been implicated in compulsive behaviors, including such regions as the orbitofrontal cortex, anterior cingulate cortex, striatum, and thalamus (Maia, Cooney, & Peterson, 2008; Ting & Feng, 2011; Whiteside, Port, & Abramowitz, 2004). These regions (e.g., anterior cingulate cortex) are also implicated in ASD features such as repetitive behaviors, attention, and emotional awareness (Damasio & Maurer, 1978; Di Martino et al., 2011; Lane et al., 1998; Rapin & Tuchman, 2008; Thakkar et al., 2008). Given the role these frontal brain regions have in executive functioning (Vogt, Finch, & Olson, 1992), it is not surprising that similarities exist between the executive functioning of individuals with ASD and OCD, such as attentional processing biases, impaired social competence and theory of mind, egocentrism—absent-self paradox, and poorer inhibitory control (Anholt et al., 2010; Chasson et al., 2011; Johnson, 2012; Kana, Keller, Minshew, & Just, 2007; Lombardo & Baron-Cohen, 2010; Mosconi et al., 2009).

The most widely accepted psychological model for OCD genesis is the cognitive behavioral model, whereby intrusive thoughts/urges are generally considered "normal" (Rachman & de Silva, 1978; Salkovskis & Harrison, 1984). Instead, an individual's beliefs about the meaning/consequence of these intrusive thoughts and subsequent neutralizing behaviors serve to heighten their salience, distress, and repetitiveness (Salkovskis, 1985). With regard to common OCD-related beliefs, the Obsessive Compulsive Cognitions Working Group (1997) identified six core maladaptive belief biases. These include inflated responsibility, intolerance of uncertainty, perfectionism, exaggerated threat perception, overimportance of thoughts, and the importance of thought control. Therefore, although individuals may have a biological vulnerability to OCD, it is through this biased lens that they become trapped in a reinforcing cycle whereby compulsions are engaged in to neutralize the anxiety/fear/disgust/discomfort or potential threat that arises from one's obsessions. For example, an individual with OCD who fears his or her food may be "off" or poisoned and that consuming said food will make them sick (intrusive thought) may repeatedly check the use-by date and ingredients listed, examine the food for any marks, ask trusted others whether their food is off/poisoned, and/or avoid certain foods that cannot be checked (compulsions) each time he or she eats a meal (triggering situation). Through this process, the individual never learns that he or she can tolerate the doubt and discomfort without a compulsion. Similarly, preliminary research suggests that youth with high-functioning ASD endorse the presence of cognitive beliefs/appraisals associated with anxiety and OCD more so than controls (Sharma, Woolfson, & Hunter, 2013); furthermore, individuals with ASD often engage in repetitive behaviors as an emotion regulation strategy, particularly those associated with sameness (e.g., routines, hoarding, etc.; Lidstone et al., 2014; Rodgers, Glod, Connolly, & McConachie, 2012), such as those used in OCD (Zandt et al., 2007).

Despite overlap in etiological mechanisms associated with OCD and ASD, these presentations remain two distinct diagnoses, and as such, differential diagnosis is important to consider (APA, 2013). In cases where both disorders are present, a thorough assessment will aid in case conceptualization and provide indication as to how best to tailor treatment. First, although there may be social dysfunction in individuals with OCD, it occurs as the result of excessive fears and ritualized behaviors (e.g., avoiding interacting with other people due to a fear of contamination; Markarian et al., 2010). In contrast, the social impairments associated with ASD (e.g., failure to initiate conversation, lack of facial expressions, disinterest in making friends) are the result of a neurodevelopmental disorder and appear much earlier than those reported in OCD cases (APA, 2013) and are often not "driven" by intrusive thoughts or the need to "hide" rituals. Second, the restricted and repetitive behaviors/interests in ASD (e.g., sensory sensitivities, low-level repetitive behaviors such as hand flapping, and high-level repetitive behaviors such as rigid routines and patterns of behaviors; Hollander et al., 2005) are often preferential and not usually experienced with the distress and aversion as those in OCD, and it is upon this distinction that repetitive behaviors are attributed to ASD or OCD (Paula-Perez, 2013; Postorino et al., 2017). Even with this distinction, it is still challenging, particularly when the child is nonverbal or has difficulty articulating thoughts or emotions (Mazefsky & White, 2014; Postorino et al., 2017), or when the behaviors themselves are phenomenologically very similar (Hollander et al., 2005) and when some traditionally OCD-unique experiences (e.g., "not just right") are associated with ASD features such as sensory sensitivity (Hellriegel et al., 2017).

Evidence-based assessment for OCD (Lewin & Piacentini, 2010; Rapp, Bergman, Piacentini, & McGuire, 2016) generally relies upon the clinician-rated Yale-Brown Obsessive-Compulsive Scale (Y-BOCS; Goodman et al., 1989) and its child version (CY-BOCS; Scahill et al., 1997). These checklists allow individuals to endorse the presence or absence of commonly occurring obsessions and compulsions, providing a comprehensive overview of symptoms to the clinician. In addition, frequency of, distress and impairment resulting from, resistance to, and control of obsessions and compulsions are assessed. The Y-BOCS and CY-BOCS have excellent psychometric properties in OCD samples (see Rapp et al., 2016). Furthermore, they have been used extensively in research investigating OCD within ASD and can identify differences between those with ASD and/or OCD (e.g., Cath et al., 2008; McDougle et al., 1995; A. J. Russell, Mataix-Cols, Anson, & Murphy, 2005).

More recently, the CY-BOCS has been modified specifically for use within ASD samples to assess ASD-related repetitive behaviors (Scahill et al., 2014; Scahill et al., 2006). Though sharing many of the original behavior descriptors, the new measure has a distinct factor structure to the original CY-BOCS, including hoarding and rituals, sensory/motor and arranging, insistence on sameness and self-injurious behaviors, stereotypy, and, finally, restricted interests (Scahill et al., 2014). Overall, the new measure demonstrated good psychometric properties; however, the authors note the "resistance" item may not be as applicable to assessing repetitive behaviors among individuals with ASD (Scahill et al., 2014). Given resistance refers to an individual's effort to reduce or stop the behavior/thought, this is consistent with the distinction outlined earlier whereby the repetitive interests and behaviors in ASD are more often a source of enjoyment/comfort versus distress as seen in OCD (Postorino et al., 2017).

In addition to clinician-rated measures, several self-report measures have been recommended in the assessment of OCD generally (see Rapp et al., 2016), for example, the Obsessive-Compulsive Inventory-Revised (OCI-R; Huppert et al., 2007) and its child version (OCI-CV; Foa et al., 2010). The OCI-R has also been used in the assessment of OCD symptoms in adults with ASD alone, ASD with OCD, and OCD alone, and demonstrated good psychometric properties (Cadman et al., 2015). Importantly, the OCI-R was able to differentiate the different groups based on total scores, with the authors concluding that it may be a useful assessment tool in adult ASD samples to reliably identify OCD symptoms (Cadman et al., 2015). Finally, given the tendency for families to report more accommodation behaviors toward OCD symptoms, worse impairment in individuals with ASD and OCD (Griffiths et al., 2017b), and the impact of these behaviors on treatment outcomes (A. J. Russell et al., 2013), family accommodation and impairment should be routinely assessed in OCD/ASD samples. In their review, Postorino and colleagues (2017) acknowledge that more research is needed into assessment measures suitable for OCD within ASD, and multiple methods and multiple informants should be taken into consideration where possible.

Other OCRDs in ASD

In BDD, preliminary research links the striatal abnormalities discussed previously in relation to OCD and ASD, particularly so for detail-oriented attention bias (Feusner et al., 2010; Rauch et al., 2003; Vasudeva & Hollander, 2017), impaired attentional shifting (Jefferies-Sewell, Chamberlain, Fineberg, & Laws, 2017), egocentrism, and poorer emotion recognition (Buhlmann, Etcoff, & Wilhelm, 2006; Vasudeva & Hollander, 2017). BDD (Summers, Matheny, & Cougle, 2017) and hoarding disorder (Finberg et al., 2017) have also been attributed to "not just right" experiences, which are in turn associated with sensory sensitivities such as in ASD (Ferrao et al., 2012; Hellriegel, Barber, Wikramanayake, Fineberg, & Mandy, 2017; Taylor et al., 2014). Similar deficits in executive functioning by way of response inflexibility and inhibitory control in trichotillomania (Bohne et al., 2005) and in excoriation disorder (Odlaug, Hampshire, Chamberlain, & Grant, 2016) have also been observed and parallel those described previously in OCD and ASD. Furthermore, similarities also exist by way of deficits in emotion regulation across each of the OCRDs (de la Cruz et al., 2013; Diefenbach, Tolin, Meunier, & Worhunsky, 2008; Grisham, Martyn, Kerin, Baldwin, & Norberg, 2018; Shusterman, Feld, Baer, & Keuthen, 2009; Snorrason, Smári, & Ólafsson, 2010) and ASD (Mazefsky, Borue, Day, & Minshew, 2014; Mazefsky & White, 2014; Samson, Hardan, Podell, Phillips, & Gross, 2015), as well as the use of repetitive behaviors as regulatory activities in ASD (Joosten, Bundy, & Einfeld, 2008; Rodgers et al., 2012; Spiker, Lin, van Dyke, & Wood, 2012; Sukhodolsky et al., 2008).

Similar challenges arise in differential diagnoses of the other OCRDs within ASD, in particular determining whether the compulsive behaviors in these conditions are not better accounted for by the restricted and repetitive behaviors central to ASD. This issue is further clouded by associations between sensory issues and both stereotypic behaviors and compulsions (Boyd, McBee, Holtzclaw, Baranek, & Bodfish, 2009). Diagnostic assessment tools for the related disorders are a developing area of research, with a tendency to rely on modification to the Y-BOCS or C-YBOCS described previously (McGuire et al., 2012). In the modification of the C-YBOCS for individuals with ASD, the authors note that hair pulling loads on the hoarding/ritualized behavior factor *and* the restricted interest factor, whereas hoarding loads uniquely with ritualized behaviors yet may be *resultant* of restricted interests with certain objects (Scahill et al., 2014). These findings highlight the difficulties that can arise when trying to separate and assess repetitive behaviors. Although the repetitive hair pulling and skin picking associated with the OCRDs are qualitatively similar to repetitive (and sometimes self-injurious) behaviors in ASD, the DSM-5 outlines that those present in ASD have their onset much earlier in life (APA, 2013).

Treatment

Cognitive behavioral therapy (CBT) with exposure and response prevention (ERP) is the predominant evidence-based treatment for OCD, demonstrating superior effects to serotonin reuptake inhibitor (SRI) medication in children (Ivarsson et al., 2015; McGuire et al., 2015; Öst, Riise, Wergeland, Hansen, & Kvale, 2016) and adults (Skapinakis et al., 2016a, 2016b). CBT typically involves psychoeducation as to the reinforcing cycle of OCD, cognitive therapy for obsessive beliefs, ERP, and relapse prevention (March, Franklin, Nelson, & Foa, 2001). It is widely accepted that ERP is the essential component of CBT treatment for OCD (Abramowitz, 2006).

To date, there is preliminary evidence suggesting CBT with ERP may be an effective treatment for individuals with ASD and comorbid OCD, and it has been proposed that the rule-based, rigid style of thinking that is characteristic of ASD may in fact be well suited to interventions within a CBT framework (Farrell, James, Maddox, Griffiths, & White, 2016). For example, youth with OCD and high levels of ASD traits have been shown to respond as well as those without comorbid conditions in group CBT (Farrell, Waters, Milliner, & Ollendick, 2012) and individual CBT (Wolters, de Haan, Hogendoorn, Boer, & Prins, 2016). There is also preliminary evidence to suggest that intensively delivered CBT may be effective (Iniesta-Sepúlveda et al., 2018). On the other hand, studies have concluded that although CBT was shown to have benefit for individuals with OCD and comorbid ASD overall, clients with ASD+OCD responded to treatment significantly less well than matched controls without comorbid ASD (Griffiths et al., 2017b) and were significantly less likely to be in remission at follow-up (Griffiths et al., 2017b; Murray, Jassi, Mataix-Cols, Barrow, & Krebs, 2015). These mixed findings suggest that further investigation is required to elucidate the benefit of CBT protocols in better meeting the needs of these individuals and to improve treatment outcomes. Certain modifications (e.g., family involvement in therapy) may need to be employed (see Kose, Fox, & Storch, 2018).

A series of single-subject case studies have been conducted over the years in youth with comorbid OCD and ASD, describing the effectiveness of certain modifications to standard CBT with ERP aimed at the OCD symptoms. Case studies were conducted with a variety of clients, both male and female individuals, and ages included 7 years (Elliot & Fitzsimons, 2014; Reaven & Hepburn, 2003; Rooney, Alfano, Walsh, & Parr, 2011), 9 years (Nadeau, Arnold, Storch, & Lewin, 2014), 12 years (Lehmkuhl, Storch, Bodfish, & Gekkken, 2008; Ordaz, Lewin, McBride, & Storch, 2018), 14 years (Krebs, Murray, & Jassi, 2016), 16 years (Farrell, James, et al., 2016), and 18 years (Ordaz, Lewin, & Storch, 2018). The modifications described within these studies included parent/family involvement in treatment, limitation of abstract concepts/metaphors, use of visual aids/cues, clear instructions of exposure tasks, integration of restricted interests/idiosyncratic descriptions, use of social stories (Gray, 1994) to increase social understanding and emphasize OCD impact on others, reduction in cognitive restructuring, use of rewards, less reliance on emotional descriptions/subjective units of distress (therapist using other cues, e.g., physiological reactions), problem-solving and emotional regulation skills, home visits, intensive delivery, involvement of other systems (e.g., school), externalization of OCD symptoms, and planning for elopement before treatment begins. In each case study, the individual experienced a substantial reduction in his or her OCD, and treatment gains were maintained at follow-up (up to 12 months; Krebs et al., 2016). In their review of this literature, Kose and colleagues (2018) noted several limitations, including methodological quality, reliance on high-functioning individuals, variability in therapeutic procedures and techniques, and inconsistent use of modifications across studies.

Only one *fully* randomized controlled trial (RCT) examining OCD within ASD has been published to date (several RCTs examining anxiety within ASD more generally have been conducted and in some instances include individuals with OCD; e.g., Storch et al., 2013), as yet precluding the establishment of an evidence base of RCTs. In this lone RCT, A. J. Russell and colleagues (2013) used a predominately adult sample (N = 46, age range 14 to 65 years; 72% adults) to examine the efficacy of a modified CBT protocol for people with comorbid ASD and OCD. Modifications included enhanced education around understanding and rating emotions/anxiety and the use of visual aids, and each session was structured and therapist led. Participants were randomly assigned to either an anxiety management (AM) treatment condition (N = 20) or CBT treatment condition (N = 20). Individuals in both treatment conditions showed significant reductions in OCD symptoms that were maintained over a 12-month follow-up period, with large within-group effect sizes of d = 1.01 for the

CBT condition and $d = 0.6$ for the AM condition. However, there was no difference between the effectiveness of CBT and AM in reducing OCD severity or impairment. Baseline family accommodation to symptoms was the only moderator of treatment outcome, with treatment responders (i.e., > 25% reduction in Y-BOCS score) reporting less family accommodation at baseline. This is an important finding. As described earlier, youth with ASD and OCD report higher levels of family accommodation than neurotypical controls (Griffiths et al., 2017a, 2017b). Given that family accommodation in OCD is associated with coercive and disruptive behaviors (Lebowitz, Storch, MacLeod, & Leckman, 2015), this may be the result of the poor emotion regulation skills seen in ASD, which can lead to meltdowns and aggressive behaviors (Mazefsky & White, 2014). These findings, combined with the overwhelming support for the inclusion of family members in treatment in the case studies reviewed earlier, suggests that these family-based variables are important and warrant further investigation alongside more research into effective treatments more generally.

Other psychological interventions for OCD within ASD remain unevaluated or experimental, and there is limited evidence to suggest the effectiveness of certain pharmacological therapies such as risperidone, fluvoxamine, and fluoxetine (see Neil & Sturney, 2014). In sum, when synthesizing single case studies, case-controlled studies, and RCT evidence, it appears that CBT with ERP may be a useful treatment for OCD within ASD, but that it would benefit from modifications to accommodate for the unique difficulties experienced by individuals with ASD and OCD (Kose et al., 2018; Walters, Loades, & Russell, 2016).

Other OCRDs in ASD

The evidence base for the remaining OCRDs within ASD is even more sparse than that of OCD. Overall, the OCRD/ASD literature is sorely lacking large-scale RCTs, and as a result, no current recommendations can be made as to evidence-based treatment. Although CBT with ERP and SRI treatments are recommended for the treatment of BDD generally, more research is needed (A. Harrison, de la Cruz, Enander, Radua, & Mataix-Cols, 2016), particularly investigating effective treatment of BDD within ASD. Consequently, it is not clear to what extent CBT would be beneficial for comorbid ASD and BDD. However, given shared etiological mechanisms, it has been proposed that deficits in self-referential processing and social engagement may be suitable targets for CBT treatment, and the novel administration of exogenous oxytocin may further assist with social functioning and repetitive behaviors in these uniquely challenged individuals (Vasudeva & Hollander, 2017). There is preliminary evidence suggesting that pharmacological therapies (e.g., fluoxetine) may be useful in treating the repetitive behaviors associated with BDD and comorbid ASD (Hollander et al., 2012).

For hoarding disorder generally, it appears that CBT involving motivation enhancement, ERP, skill development (organization/sorting/disposal), and cognitive restructuring is an effective treatment (although more research is needed; see Tolin, Frost, Steketee, & Muroff, 2015). With regard to hoarding disorder within ASD, there is preliminary evidence in youth samples for anxiety-focused CBT in treating hoarding symptoms, with the authors concluding that improved distress tolerance and general coping skills may be particularly important for these individuals (see Storch, McBride, Timpano, & Murphy, 2016). It is important to note that this CBT protocol included exposure as well as parent/family involvement consistent with modifications made to CBT in treating OCD within ASD discussed earlier.

In treating trichotillomania generally, behavior therapy (including habit reversal) is the recommended psychological intervention, with a meta-analysis of RCTs ($N = 11$) concluding that behavior therapy had large effect sizes for treatment effectiveness, whereas SRI therapy had only moderate effect size (McGuire et al., 2014). Importantly, the behavior therapy RCTs that included components of acceptance and commitment therapy (Woods, Wetterneck, & Flessner, 2006) or dialectical behavior therapy (Keuthen et al., 2012) produced the largest effect sizes, suggesting that the augmentation of emotion regulation and distress tolerance training may be an important treatment component (although the authors note this could also be attributed to the greater time spent in therapy in these studies; McGuire et al., 2014). Similarly, a recent meta-analysis of RCTs and open-trial studies ($N = 12$) of excoriation disorder treatment generally identified CBT, SRI medication, or lamotrigine medication as the most common treatment modalities (Selles, McGuire, Small, & Storch, 2016). However, based on the studies available for analysis, no conclusions could be made regarding the superiority of either treatment modality, suggesting a dire need for more high-quality research in this area (Selles et al., 2016).

With regard to trichotillomania and excoriation disorder within ASD, there is little direct research attention as to which treatments may be most effective, nor whether any suitable modifications to current treatment practices would be best suited to these individuals. Behavioral therapy for repetitive behaviors associated with ASD generally, such as applied behavior analysis techniques, has been shown to be effective (see Boyd, McDonough, & Bodfish, 2012, for review). Although these behaviors are distinct from those diagnosed in excoriation disorder or trichotillomania, the behavioral techniques employed are similar and could be one avenue for future research. Extrapolations can also be made from the emerging body of work in OCD and the other OCRDs suggesting the potential importance of modifications in enhancing treatment gains in CBT. For example, habit reversal therapy was simplified (i.e., only focused on the behavioral components) to successfully treat a 17-year-old female with ASD and chronic skin picking (Cavalari, DuBard Luiselli, & Birtwell, 2013).

A recent interest in the impact of N-acetylcysteine (NAC) in treating OCD and the OCRDs (see Oliver et al., 2015) such as trichotillomania (Grant, Odlaug, & Kim, 2009) and excoriation disorder (Grant et al., 2016) shows promising results in adults. NAC has also been used to treat repetitive and self-injurious behavior (including skin picking) in ASD. Initial single-subject case studies in youth with low-functioning ASD show the effectiveness and tolerability for NAC in reducing restricted interest in hair cutting (parents were cutting the child's hair daily) and aggression (male aged 8 years; Ghanizadeh & Derakhshan, 2012), irritability and aggression (male aged 17 years; Stutzman & Dopheide, 2015), and severe skin picking resulting in substantial lesions (male aged 4 years; Marler, Sanders, & Veenstra-VanderWeele, 2014). Reductions in aggression and stereotypic and repetitive behaviors associated with ASD have been replicated more recently in animal studies (Zhang, Cui, Zhai, Zhang, & Wen, 2017), a case series of youth with ASD (N = 10; Celebi, Koyuncu, & Coskun, 2017), and double-blind RCTs comparing NAC and placebo conditions (N = 36 to 40 youth; Ghanizadeh & Moghimi-Sarani, 2013; Hardan et al., 2012; Nikoo, Radnia, Farokhnia, Mohammadi, & Akhondzadeh, 2015). However, two RCTs failed to find any effect of NAC compared to a placebo in children with ASD, although one acknowledged much lower doses than other previous studies (N = 102; Dean et al., 2017) and the other acknowledged their sample contained higher functioning children (N = 31; Wink et al., 2016). This is potentially problematic as self-injurious behaviors such as skin picking are associated with poorer functioning in ASD (Minshawi et al., 2014).

Overall, more research into treatment is needed for each of the OCRDs within ASD. Given the underlying emotion regulation difficulties of the OCRDs, such as hoarding disorder (de la Cruz et al., 2013; Grisham et al., 2018), trichotillomania (Diefenbach et al., 2008; Shusterman et al., 2009), and excoriation disorder (Snorrason et al., 2010), as well as in ASD (Mazefsky & White, 2014; Samson et al., 2015), understanding the role this may play in the development of successful treatments represents an important avenue for future research (Storch et al., 2016). Furthermore, given the impact of these disorders on family and interpersonal relationships, future research should investigate the impact of family-related variables in treatment and outcomes for ASD and comorbid OCRDs (e.g., hoarding disorder; Drury et al., 2014; Park, Lewin, & Storch, 2014).

A Case Example of Comorbid ASD and OCD: "Jake"

Here, we present a detailed case study of "Jake," a 13-year-old Australian boy with co-occurring ASD and OCD, who presented for treatment of OCD, as an illustration of modified, intensive CBT. Jake's main obsessions related to contamination from people with illnesses (e.g., cancer, diabetes) and disabilities (e.g., amputees, wheelchair users), specifically that if he came into contact with these feared people or objects they had touched, he would contract the illness/disability, would die, or could pass the contamination on to others. These obsessions caused Jake great distress on a daily basis and limited his ability to go to public places where he may encounter feared people, such as shopping centers, the beach, and even walking around his neighborhood. Jake also believed he could become contaminated if he even thought or spoke about illness/disability. To protect himself from contamination, Jake would almost constantly cover his mouth with his T-shirt to avoid breathing in potentially contaminated air, would spit or rinse his mouth with water if he thought he had breathed in contaminated air, and would wash his hands or preferably shower if he believed he been contaminated. If he experienced an intrusive thought while performing any routine action, such as sitting down or writing a sentence, he would have to repeat the action until the thought went away, at which point he would then shower to decontaminate himself. He also sought excessive reassurance from his parents throughout the day and particularly at bedtime that both he and they had not contracted an illness or disability.

Perhaps due to Jake's ASD, his distress tolerance was very low, and he struggled to identify or communicate what had made him distressed. Jake would then become angry, shouting or hitting, and his parents would often be unable to determine the cause of the "meltdown." Jake's parents would punish his behavior during the meltdown, which would only make Jake angrier and further strained family relationships. Jake's anger would reach a point where Jake's parents would accommodate to whatever Jake desired—usually avoidance of a distressing situation or allowing him to complete a compulsion to try and calm him down, which strengthened the cycle of OCD. Jake's parents reported that they felt like they were "walking on eggshells" to avoid anything that might distress Jake. Jake's parents constructed the family's life so that Jake could avoid public places and avoided seeing family or friends to reduce the likelihood that other people might mention illness or disability. At school, Jake was teased by other children who noticed his compulsions even though he tried to hide them. This teasing and Jake's difficulties in communication made him aggressive to other children.

At his initial assessment, based on his mother's report on the Anxiety Disorder Interview Schedule (ADIS-P; Silverman & Albano, 1996), Jake met criteria for OCD with a clinician severity rating of 7 out of a possible 8. On the Kiddie Schedule for Affective Disorders and Schizophrenia—Present and Lifetime version (K-SADS-PL; Kaufman et al., 2016), Jake also met criteria for ASD Level 1. Based on his report on the CY-BOCS, Jake scored in the *severe* range of OCD symptoms.

Overview of Treatment Approach

Jake participated in the intensive OCD Busters program at Griffith University (e.g., Farrell & Oar, 2014; Farrell, Sluis, & Waters, 2016) at the recommendation of his pediatrician after a previous unsuccessful treatment attempt, which did not contain ERP. The OCD Busters program commences with a dedicated psychoeducation session to understand OCD, the self-perpetuating cycle of OCD, and how it is treated through individual CBT with ERP. The cycle of OCD described that situations trigger obsessions (or "sticky thoughts"), which cause distress, anxiety, and/or disgust. To reduce these uncomfortable feelings and/or to prevent feared outcomes from occurring, compulsions are performed, resulting in temporary relief of the uncomfortable feelings, which is translated as prevention of the feared outcome. However, the next time a triggering situation occurs, the cycle is repeated (through the reinforcement experiences of avoidance and neutralizing), and contradictory evidence is never learned (i.e., that even without performing compulsions, anxiety decreases over time and feared outcomes do not come true). However, for Jake it was particularly important throughout the psychoeducation session (and treatment) to provide additional information about emotions and to highlight the impact OCD was having on his and his family's life to increase insight and motivation for ERP.

The rationale for ERP is to break the cycle of OCD, whereby the child is exposed to situations that trigger OCD fears (exposure therapy) and the compulsion is prevented (response prevention) in order to acquire new learning. This is done in a hierarchical fashion, starting with situations that trigger low-level distress and gradually becoming harder. By the time the higher levels are reached, the child should have more distress tolerance and self-efficacy, as he or she has learned that the negative feelings diminish without compulsions and that the feared outcome does not occur (and if it does, that he or she can cope).

Following psychoeducation, the OCD Busters program in this instance consisted of three intensive ERP treatment sessions (3.5 hours each), followed by 4 weeks of home practice of ERP and then a final intensive "booster" session targeting any remaining symptoms. The intensive format is described as a "kickstart" to treating OCD and provides children and their parents with all the tools necessary to keep conducting ERP at home until symptoms have remitted. There were no modifications to session duration for Jake. However, to manage the complexities that occurred in session due to Jake's ASD symptoms, the following additional modifications were made to boost efficacy and engagement.

MODIFICATIONS TO TREATMENT FOR COMORBID ASD

Challenge: Meltdowns, low distress tolerance, and difficulty labeling emotions. To assist with Jake's distress management, both in and out of treatment, two strategies were employed: externalizing OCD and recognizing his distress rising. Throughout treatment, OCD was externalized as a disorder that was separate from Jake in order to decrease frustration aimed at Jake from his family, to cultivate detachment from symptoms for Jake, and to facilitate an alliance between Jake and his family toward OCD, which Jake could learn to fight and resist. It helped strengthen their strained relationship and allowed them to work together toward a common goal. With therapist modeling throughout treatment, Jake's parents also learned how to use the externalization of OCD as a means of communicating empathy with Jake and his distress, rather than becoming angry themselves—for example, "Oh, OCD is making you feel anxious because you had an intrusive thought when I suggested going to the beach. I can tell because you washed your hands." In addition to extra psychoeducation about emotions, over time this helped Jake to identify the link between his obsessions and compulsions and helped him to recognize and label his emotions.

In addition, Jake learned about his "frustration cup," which fills over time with each passing frustration or worry (e.g., see http://www.leakybrakes.ca). When the cup overflows it results in a meltdown, seemingly out of nowhere, particularly as Jake struggles to recognize his internal states. The family were educated that Jake's cup was already half full from managing intrusive thoughts from his OCD and the social confusion and sensory sensitivities resulting from his ASD, leaving little room for additional everyday frustrations or triggering OCD situations before the cup would overflow. The frustration cup analogy was demonstrated concretely to Jake and his parents with water being poured progressively into a cup until it overflowed; each time water was poured in, the therapist or Jake's parents would provide an example of a frustration or worry that might fill Jake's cup. This physical cup was present in all sessions to concretely remind Jake about his own frustration cup. Throughout treatment, Jake was asked to show how full his cup was by pointing to a level on the physical cup, and if it was too full for ERP to be successful (which might result in a meltdown and disengagement from ERP), Jake was encouraged to take a break to do something to empty his cup (such as play a quick game, eat a snack, etc.). When his cup was at a level Jake could manage, ERP would continue. Treatment sessions were conducted in the morning when his cup was the lowest, and he was encouraged to do his home practice during the morning or early afternoon until that task became easy enough to do later in the day when his cup was fuller. Jake's parents reported learning that Jake's meltdowns were due to built-up frustrations and did not appear out of nowhere, and that they could increase compliance and assist with emotion regulation with calming activities and empathic responses.

Challenge: Elopement. During treatment, Jake would often walk away from the ERP task (elopement), which is common with children with ASD (Kiely, Migdal, Vettam, & Adesman, 2016). To mitigate danger, Jake was told that he must stay within the therapist's sight. After a few minutes alone, the therapist would re-engage Jake in the session with empathic talk and would ask him how full his cup was. The therapist would then invite Jake to continue with the ERP task, sometimes after a cup-lowering activity; with the choice to re-engage in his control, he always agreed to continue.

Challenge: Literal thinking. Jake struggled to complete any imaginal exposures because he was unable to temporarily imagine a different situation from reality. For example, a low-level exposure task was playing games with restricted use of his arms/legs, such as hopping races and a popular throwing/catching game where limb use is progressively restricted each time the ball is dropped. When Jake reported no distress at completing these tasks, the therapist queried why. Jake reported that he was not anxious because his arms and legs were still there. When asked to imagine if they were not, he replied, "But my arm is still right here, see?" For the remainder of treatment, Jake's ERP tasks were concrete and in-vivo exposure, which elicited the distress necessary for effective ERP.

Jake's restrictive thinking patterns also meant that he believed his compulsions to be the only logical way to prevent him from contracting an illness or disability. This resulted in poor motivation to engage in treatment. However, after being provided with comprehensive psychoeducation where he learned that OCD is a disorder, and after completing a few exposure "experiments" and realizing that his feared outcome did not occur, Jake realized that his compulsions were not as logical as he first believed, which increased his motivation to complete treatment.

Challenge: Family accommodation. Jake's family engaged in excessive family accommodation to appease Jake's OCD and poor emotion recognition/regulation, such as avoiding going out in public and reducing time spent with family and friends. As such, it was important to discuss family accommodation in the psychoeducation session and identify the ways Jake's family were strengthening the cycle of OCD. Jake and his parents constructed an exposure hierarchy to gradually reduce their accommodation, which was completed in therapy and home practice. Jake's parents were involved throughout each session and learned how to continue to practice ERP at home with Jake to enhance generalization. They also assisted by providing examples of interference that Jake struggled to recognize and by devising ERP tasks. The reduction of family accommodation occurred at a much slower pace than would normally occur with other youth due to Jake's very poor frustration tolerance and his strong desire to be in control of his treatment. Taking this at Jake's pace resulted in greater trust between the therapist and Jake, as well as Jake and his parents.

Outcome of Treatment

Immediately following his first three treatment sessions, Jake's OCD symptoms had decreased slightly, but he remained symptomatic. Jake then completed 4 weeks of home practice and a "booster" treatment session. Jake's OCD significantly improved over this course in time: his score on the ADIS decreased from 7 to 4 (out of 8), just meeting criteria for OCD, and his CY-BOCS total score decreased from 29 to 14, changing from severe to mild OCD. After a further 3 months of practice, Jake no longer met criteria for OCD, and this was maintained at 6-month follow-up. Jake's family reported that they were able to enjoy family outings to public places again—even enjoying chores such as grocery shopping—and no longer feared Jake's meltdowns. Jake reported knowing that even if he did not do what OCD wanted him to do, he was highly unlikely to contract an illness or disease, and even if he did, he knew that he could cope.

Summary and Future Directions

The OCRDs are a cluster of related, yet diverse, disorders that center on compulsive behaviors and/or obsessive thoughts. They include OCD, BDD, hoarding disorder, excoriation disorder, and trichotillomania. The OCRDs are associated with considerable severity and chronicity and result in significant psychosocial impairment and poorer functioning. To date, there has been very limited research examining the correlates and outcomes of individuals who have ASD and co-occurring OCRD diagnoses, despite phenomenological overlap (e.g., repetitive behavior, fixated/obsessional features, and rigidity/inflexibility) and frequently being comorbid. The most well researched of the OCRDs, OCD, occurs significantly more frequently across the whole lifespan in individuals with ASD than in the general population, and likewise, ASD tends to occur more frequently across the lifespan in individuals with OCD. The shared phenomenology but valid comorbidity represents a unique challenge for clinicians and researchers alike in that adequate assessment and differential diagnosis become altogether more important and more difficult. Improved differential diagnostic assessments should be developed to guide diagnosis in individuals with ASD. Additionally, routine screening of the OCRDs is recommended in clinical practice and research with individuals with ASD given the high co-occurrence but underdiagnosis of the OCRDs.

Preliminary findings suggest that in individuals with OCD, having comorbid ASD does not increase symptom distress or time interference (Lewin et al., 2011). However, comorbid OCD/ASD is associated with greater functional impairment, more family accommodation in pediatric samples, higher rates of other comorbid conditions, and poorer insight in adult samples (Griffiths et al., 2017a, 2017b; Wikramanayake et al., 2018). These findings are particularly pertinent given that each of these correlates are associated with poorer response to evidence-based CBT treatment for OCD (Garcia et al., 2010). There is still much research to be conducted to uncover whether there may be an ASD subtype of OCD, how OCD might develop across the lifespan in individuals with comorbid ASD, and whether this is similar or divergent with findings reported in the broader OCD literature.

Research suggests that individual, group, or intensive CBT can be effective for individuals with elevated ASD traits and co-occurring OCD (Farrell et al., 2012; Iniesta-Sepúlveda et al., 2018; Wolters et al., 2016). However, it may be less effective at follow-up for individuals with ASD and OCD compared to those without ASD (Griffiths et al., 2017b; Murray, Jassi, Mataix-Cols, Barrow, & Krebs, 2015). Instead, modifications appear necessary to increase the effectiveness of CBT for individuals with ASD and increase the longevity of gains made in treatment (Krebs et al., 2016). Future research is needed with larger and more rigorous randomized designs to determine the efficacy of modified CBT for individuals with ASD across the lifespan and what modifications are to be recommended (Kose et al., 2018).

Two other commonly underresearched themes emerged throughout this chapter. First, the preponderance of studies examining individuals with ASD without intellectual impairments precludes conclusions from being drawn about potential OCD in individuals with ASD who have accompanying intellectual disability or who are minimally verbal. This may be particularly important given the cognitive capacity necessary to engage in CBT—the recommended treatment for OCD. Second, there is scant research investigating the OCRDs outside of OCD, even in neurotypical individuals. Lack of awareness may make recognition of the other OCRDs potentially more difficult in individuals with ASD, given the possible phenomenological overlap. It also precludes effective treatment guidelines from being developed and implemented for this population. This should be seen as an important and necessary step for future research to provide better clinical care for this vulnerable yet prevalent group of patients.

References

Abramowitz, J. S. (2006). The psychological treatment of obsessive-compulsive disorder. *Canadian Journal of Psychiatry, 51*(7), 407–416. doi:10.1177/070674370605100702

American Psychiatric Association. (2013). *Diagnostic and statistical manual of mental disorders* (5th ed.). Washington, DC: Author.

Anholt, G. E., Cath, D. C., van Oppen, P., Eikelenboom, M., Smit, J. H., van Megen, H., & van Balkom, A. J. (2010). Autism and ADHD symptoms in patients with OCD: Are they associated with specific OC symptom dimensions or OC symptom severity? *Journal of Autism and Developmental Disorders, 40*(5), 580–589. doi:10.1007/s10803-009-0922-1

Arabatzoudis, T., Rehm, I. C., Nedeljkovic, M., & Moulding, R. (2017). Emotion regulation in individuals with and without trichotillomania. *Journal of Obsessive-Compulsive and Related Disorders, 12*, 87–94. doi:10.1016/j.jocrd.2017.01.003

Baron-Cohen, S., Wheelwright, S., Skinner, R., Martin, J., & Clubley, E. (2001). The autism-spectrum quotient (AQ): Evidence from Asperger syndrome/high-functioning autism, males and females, scientists and mathematicians. *Journal of Autism and Developmental Disorders, 31*(1), 5–17. doi:10.1023/A:1005653411471

Bejerot, S. (2007). An autistic dimension: A proposed subtype of obsessive-compulsive disorder. *Autism, 11*(2), 101–110. doi:10.1177/1362361307075699

Bejerot, S., Nylander, L., & Lindström, E. (2001). Autistic traits in obsessive-compulsive disorder. *Nordic Journal of Psychiatry, 55*(3), 169–176. doi:10.1080/08039480152036047

Bjornsson, A. S., Didie, E. R., Grant, J. E., Menard, W., Stalker, E., & Phillips, K. A. (2013). Age at onset and clinical correlates in body dysmorphic disorder. *Comprehensive Psychiatry, 54*(7), 893–903. doi:10.1016/j.comppsych.2013.03.019

Bobes, J., Gonzalez, M. P., Bascaran, M. T., Arango, C., Saiz, P. A., & Bousono, M. (2001). Quality of life and disability in patients with obsessive-compulsive disorder. *European Psychiatry, 16*(4), 239–245. doi:10.1016/S0924-9338(01)00571-5

Bohne, A., Savage, C. R., Deckersbach, T., Keuthen, N. J., Jenike, M. A., Tuschen-Caffier, B., & Wilhelm, S. (2005). Visuospatial abilities, memory, and executive functioning in trichotillomania and obsessive-compulsive disorder. *Journal of Clinical and Experimental Neuropsychology, 27*(4), 385–399. doi:10.1080/13803390490520418

Bolton, P. F., Pickles, A., Murphy, M., & Rutter, M. (1998). Autism, affective and other psychiatric disorders: Patterns of familial aggregation. *Psychological Medicine, 28*(2), 385–395.

Boyd, B. A., McBee, M., Holtzclaw, T., Baranek, G. T., & Bodfish, J. W. (2009). Relationships among repetitive behaviors, sensory features, and executive functions in high functioning autism. *Research in Autism Spectrum Disorders, 3*(4), 959–966. doi:10.1016/j.rasd.2009.05.003

Boyd, B. A., McDonough, S. G., & Bodfish, J. W. (2012). Evidence-based behavioral interventions for repetitive behaviors in autism. *Journal of Autism and Developmental Disorders, 42*(6), 1236–1248. doi:10.1007/s10803-011-1284-z

Brugha, T. S., McManus, S., Bankart, J., Scott, F., Purdon, S., Smith, J., ... Meltzer, H. (2011). Epidemiology of autism spectrum disorders in adults in the community in England. *Archives of General Psychiatry, 68*(5), 459–465. doi:10.1001/archgenpsychiatry.2011.38

Brune, C. W., Kim, S. J., Hanna, G. L., Courchesne, E., Lord, C., Leventhal, B. L., & Cook, E. H. (2008). Family-based association testing of OCD-associated SNPs of SLC1A1 in an autism sample. *Autism Research, 1*(2), 108–113. doi:10.1002/aur.11

Buck, T. R., Viskochil, J., Farley, M., Coon, H., McMahon, W. M., Morgan, J., & Bilder, D. A. (2014). Psychiatric comorbidity and medication use in adults with autism spectrum disorder. *Journal of Autism and Developmental Disorders, 44*, 3063–3071. doi:10.1007/s10803-014-2170-2

Buhlmann, U., Etcoff, N. L., & Wilhelm, S. (2006). Emotion recognition bias for contempt and anger in body dysmorphic disorder. *Journal of Psychiatric Research, 40*(2), 105–111. doi:10.1016/j.jpsychires.2005.03.006

Buhlmann, U., Glaesmer, H., Mewes, R., Fama, J. M., Wilhelm, S., Brähler, E., & Rief, W. (2010). Updates on the prevalence of body dysmorphic disorder: A population-based survey. *Focus, 13*(2), 252–257. doi:10.1176/appi.focus.130217

Cadman, T., Spain, D., Johnston, P., Russell, A., Mataix-Cols, D., Craig, M., ... & Wilson, C. E. (2015). Obsessive-compulsive disorder in adults with high-functioning autism spectrum disorder: What does self-report with the OCI-R tell us? *Autism Research, 8*(5), 477–485. doi:10.1002/aur.1461

Cath, D. C., Nizar, K., Boomsma, D., & Mathews, C. A. (2017). Age-specific prevalence of hoarding and obsessive compulsive disorder: A population-based study. *American Journal of Geriatric Psychiatry, 25*(3), 245–255. doi:10.1016/j.jagp.2016.11.006

Cath, D. C., Ran, N., Smit, J. H., Van Balkom, A. J. L. M., & Comijs, H. C. (2008). Symptom overlap between autism spectrum disorder, generalized social anxiety disorder and obsessive-compulsive disorder in adults: A preliminary case-controlled study. *Psychopathology, 41*(2), 101–110. doi:10.1159/000111555

Cavalari, R. N., DuBard, M., Luiselli, J. K., & Birtwell, K. (2013). Teaching an adolescent with autism and intellectual disability to tolerate routine medical examination: Effects of a behavioral compliance training package. *Clinical Practice in Pediatric Psychology, 1*(2), 121–128. doi:10.1037/cpp0000013

Çelebi, F., Koyuncu, A., & Coşkun, M. (2017). N-acetylcysteine may reduce repetitive behaviors in children with autism: A case series. *Psychiatry and Clinical Psychopharmacology, 27*(2), 185–188. doi:10.1080/24750573.2017.1309817

Chasson, G. S., Timpano, K. R., Greenberg, J. L., Shaw, A., Singer, T., & Wilhelm, S. (2011). Shared social competence impairment: Another link between the obsessive-compulsive and autism spectrums? *Clinical Psychology Review, 31*(4), 653–662. doi:10.1016/j.cpr.2011.02.006

Coles, M. E., Frost, R. O., Heimberg, R. G., & Rhéaume, J. (2003). "Not just right experiences": Perfectionism, obsessive–compulsive features and general psychopathology. *Behaviour Research and Therapy, 41*(6), 681–700. doi:10.1016/S0005-7967(02)00044-X

Coles, M. E., Heimberg, R. G., Frost, R. O., & Steketee, G. (2005). Not just right experiences and obsessive–compulsive features: Experimental and self-monitoring perspectives. *Behaviour Research and Therapy, 43*(2), 153–167. doi:10.1016/j.brat.2004.01.002

Croen, L. A., Zerbo, O., Qian, Y., Massolo, M. L., Rich, S., Sidney, S., & Kripke, C. (2015). The health status of adults on the autism spectrum. *Autism, 19*(7), 814–823. doi:10.1177/1362361315577517

Damasio, A. R., & Maurer, R. G. (1978). A neurological model for childhood autism. *Archives of Neurology, 35*(12), 777–786. doi:10.1001/archneur.1978.00500360001001

de la Cruz, L. F., Landau, D., Iervolino, A. C., Santo, S., Pertusa, A., Singh, S., & Mataix-Cols, D. (2013). Experiential avoidance and emotion regulation difficulties in hoarding disorder. *Journal of Anxiety Disorders, 27*(2), 204–209. doi:10.1016/j.janxdis.2013.01.004

Dean, O. M., Gray, K. M., Villagonzalo, K. A., Dodd, S., Mohebbi, M., Vick, T., . . . Berk, M. (2017). A randomised, double blind, placebo-controlled trial of a fixed dose of N-acetyl cysteine in children with autistic disorder. *Australian & New Zealand Journal of Psychiatry, 51*(3), 241–249. doi:10.1177/0004867416652735

Di Martino, A., Kelly, C., Grzadzinski, R., Zuo, X. N., Mennes, M., Mairena, M. A., . . . Milham, M. P. (2011). Aberrant striatal functional connectivity in children with autism. *Biological Psychiatry, 69*(9), 847–856. doi:10.1016/j.biopsych.2010.10.029

Diefenbach, G. J., Tolin, D. F., Meunier, S., & Worhunsky, P. (2008). Emotion regulation and trichotillomania: A comparison of clinical and nonclinical hair pulling. *Journal of Behavior Therapy and Experimental Psychiatry, 39*(1), 32–41. doi:10.1016/j.jbtep.2006.09.002

do Rosario-Campos, M. C., Leckman, J. F., Mercadante, M. T., Shavitt, R. G., Prado, H. D. S., Sada, P., . . . Miguel, E. C. (2001). Adults with early-onset obsessive-compulsive disorder. *American Journal of Psychiatry, 158*(11), 1899–1903. doi:10.1176/appi.ajp.158.11.1899

Drury, H., Ajmi, S., de la Cruz, L. F., Nordsletten, A. E., & Mataix-Cols, D. (2014). Caregiver burden, family accommodation, health, and well-being in relatives of individuals with hoarding disorder. *Journal of Affective Disorders, 159*, 7–14. doi:10.1016/j.jad.2014.01.023

du Toit, P. L., van Kradenburg, J., Niehaus, D. J. H., & Stein, D. J. (2001). Characteristics and phenomenology of hair-pulling: An exploration of subtypes. *Comprehensive Psychiatry, 42*(3), 247–256. doi:10.1053/comp.2001.23134

Elliott, S. J., & Fitzsimons, L. (2014). Modified CBT for treatment of OCD in a 7-year-old boy with ASD—A case report. *Journal of Child and Adolescent Psychiatric Nursing, 27*(3), 156–159. doi:10.1111/jcap.12,081

Farrell, L., Barrett, P., & Piacentini, J. (2006). Obsessive-compulsive disorder across the developmental trajectory: Clinical correlates in children, adolescents and adults. *Behaviour Change, 23*, 103–120. doi:10.1375/bech.23.2.103

Farrell, L. J., James, S. C., Maddox, B. B., Griffiths, D., & White, S. (2016). Treatment of comorbid obsessive-compulsive disorder in youth with ASD: The case of Max. In E. A. Storch & A. B. Lewin (Eds.), *Clinical handbook of obsessive-compulsive and related disorders: A case-based approach to treating pediatric and adult populations* (pp. 337–355). New York, NY: Springer.

Farrell, L., & Oar, E. (2014). Intensive cognitive behavioural treatment for obsessive compulsive disorder in children and adolescents. *Psychopathology Review, 1*, 182–188. doi:10.5127/pr.034113

Farrell, L. J., Sluis, R., & Waters, A. M. (2016). Intensive treatment of pediatric OCD: The case of Sarah. *Journal of Clinical Psychology: In Session, 72*, 1174–1190. doi:10.1002/jclp.22397

Farrell, L., Waters, A., Milliner, E., & Ollendick, T. (2012). Comorbidity and treatment response in pediatric obsessive-compulsive disorder: A pilot study of group cognitive-behavioral treatment. *Psychiatry Research, 199*(2), 115–123. doi:10.1016/j.psychres.2012.04.035

Ferrao, Y. A., Shavitt, R. G., Prado, H., Fontenelle, L. F., Malavazzi, D. M., de Mathis, M. A., . . . do Rosario, M. C. (2012). Sensory phenomena associated with repetitive behaviors in obsessive-compulsive disorder: An exploratory study of 1001 patients. *Psychiatry Research, 197*(3), 253–258. doi:10.1016/j.psychres.2011.09.017

Feusner, J. D., Moody, T., Hembacher, E., Townsend, J., McKinley, M., Moller, H., & Bookheimer, S. (2010). Abnormalities of visual processing and frontostriatal systems in body dysmorphic disorder. *Archives of General Psychiatry, 67*(2), 197–205. doi:10.1001/archgenpsychiatry.2009.190

Fineberg, N. A., Apergis-Schoute, A. M., Vaghi, M. M., Banca, P., Gillan, C. M., Voon, V., . . . Bullmore, E. T. (2017). Mapping compulsivity in the DSM-5 obsessive compulsive and related disorders: Cognitive domains, neural circuitry, and treatment. *International Journal of Neuropsychopharmacology, 21*(1), 42–58. doi:10.1093/ijnp/pyx088

Flessner, C. A., Conelea, C. A., Woods, D. W., Franklin, M. E., Keuthen, N. J., & Cashin, S. E. (2008). Styles of pulling in trichotillomania: Exploring differences in symptom severity, phenomenology, and functional impact. *Behaviour Research and Therapy, 46*(3), 345–357. doi:10.1016/j.brat.2007.12.009

Foa, E. B., Coles, M., Huppert, J. D., Pasupuleti, R. V., Franklin, M. E., & March, J. (2010). Development and validation of a child version of the obsessive compulsive inventory. *Behavior Therapy, 41*(1), 121–132. doi:10.1016/j.beth.2009.02.001

Franklin, M. E., Flessner, C. A., Woods, D. W., Keuthen, N. J., Piacentini, J. C., Moore, P., . . . Board, T. L. C. S. A. (2008). The child and adolescent trichotillomania impact project: Descriptive psychopathology, comorbidity, functional impairment, and treatment utilization. *Journal of Developmental & Behavioral Pediatrics, 29*(6), 493–500. doi:10.1097/DBP.0b013e31818d4328

Garcia, A. M., Sapyta, J. J., Moore, P. S., Freeman, J. B., Franklin, M. E., March, J. S., & Foa, E. B. (2010). Predictors and moderators of treatment outcome in the Pediatric Obsessive Compulsive Treatment Study (POTS I). *Journal of the American Academy of Child & Adolescent Psychiatry, 49*(10), 1024–1033. doi:10.1016/j.jaac.2010.06.013

Geller, D. A. (2006). Obsessive-compulsive and spectrum disorders in children and adolescents. *Psychiatric Clinics of North America, 29*(2), 353–370. doi:10.1016/j.psc.2006.02.012

Geller, D. A., Biederman, J., Faraone, S., Agranat, A., Cradock, K., Hagermoser, L.,. . . Coffey, B. J. (2001). Developmental aspects of obsessive compulsive disorder: Findings in children, adolescents, and adults. *Journal of Nervous and Mental Disease, 189*(7), 471–477. Retrieved from https://oce-ovid-com.libraryproxy.griffith.edu.au/article/00005053-200,107,000-00009/HTML

Ghanizadeh, A., & Derakhshan, N. (2012). N-acetylcysteine for treatment of autism, a case report. *Journal of Research in Medical Sciences: The Official Journal of Isfahan University Of Medical Sciences, 17*(10), 985–987.

Ghanizadeh, A., & Moghimi-Sarani, E. (2013). A randomized double blind placebo controlled clinical trial of N-acetylcysteine added to risperidone for treating autistic disorders. *BMC Psychiatry, 13*(1), 196. doi:10.1186/1471-244X-13-196

Goodman, W. K., Price, L. H., Rasmussen, S. A., Mazure, C., Fleischmann, R. L., Hill, C. L.,. . . Charney, D. S. (1989). The Yale-Brown Obsessive Compulsive Scale: I. Development, use, and reliability. *Archives of General Psychiatry, 46*(11), 1006–1011. doi:10.1007/978-3-642-18,976-0_11

Grant, J. E., Chamberlain, S. R., Redden, S. A., Leppink, E. W., Odlaug, B. L., & Kim, S. W. (2016). N-Acetylcysteine in the treatment of excoriation disorder: A randomized clinical trial. *JAMA Psychiatry, 73*(5), 490–496. doi:10.1001/jamapsychiatry.2016.0060

Grant, J. E., Odlaug, B. L., & Kim, S. W. (2009). N-acetylcysteine, a glutamate modulator, in the treatment of trichotillomania: A double-blind, placebo-controlled study. *Archives of General Psychiatry, 66*(7), 756–763. doi:10.1001/archgenpsychiatry.2009.60

Gray, C. (1994). *The original social story book.* Arlington, TX: Future Horizons.

Griffiths, D. L., Farrell, L. J., Waters, A. M., & White, S. W. (2017a). ASD traits among youth with obsessive–compulsive disorder. *Child Psychiatry & Human Development, 48*(6), 911–921. doi:10.1007/s10578-017-0714-3

Griffiths, D. L., Farrell, L. J., Waters, A. M., & White, S. W. (2017b). Clinical correlates of obsessive compulsive disorder and comorbid autism spectrum disorder in youth. *Journal of Obsessive-Compulsive and Related Disorders, 14,* 90–98. doi:10.1016/j.jocrd.2017.06.006

Grisham, J. R., Martyn, C., Kerin, F., Baldwin, P. A., & Norberg, M. M. (2018). Interpersonal functioning in hoarding disorder: An examination of attachment styles and emotion regulation in response to interpersonal stress. *Journal of Obsessive-Compulsive and Related Disorders, 16,* 43–49. doi:10.1016/j.jocrd.2017.12.001

Grzesiak, M., Reich, A., Szepietowski, J. C., Hadryś, T., & Pacan, P. (2017). Trichotillomania among young adults: Prevalence and comorbidity. *Acta Dermato-Venereologica, 97*(4), 509–512. doi:10.2340/00015555–2565

Guo, W., Samuels, J. F., Wang, Y., Cao, H., Ritter, M., Nestadt, P. S.,. . . Geller, D. A. (2017). Polygenic risk score and heritability estimates reveals a genetic relationship between ASD and OCD. *European Neuropsychopharmacology, 27*(7), 657–666. doi:10.1016/j.euroneuro.2017.03.011

Hardan, A. Y., Fung, L. K., Libove, R. A., Obukhanych, T. V., Nair, S., Herzenberg, L. A.,. . . Tirouvanziam, R. (2012). A randomized controlled pilot trial of oral N-acetylcysteine in children with autism. *Biological Psychiatry, 71*(11), 956–961. doi:10.1016/j.biopsych.2012.01.014

Harrison, A., de la Cruz, L. F., Enander, J., Radua, J., & Mataix-Cols, D. (2016). Cognitive-behavioral therapy for body dysmorphic disorder: A systematic review and meta-analysis of randomized controlled trials. *Clinical Psychology Review, 48,* 43–51. doi:10.1016/j.cpr.2016.05.007

Harrison, J. P., & Franklin, M. E. (2012). Pediatric trichotillomania. *Current Psychiatry Reports, 14*(3), 188–196. doi:10.1007/s11920-012-0269-8

Hayes, S. L., Storch, E. A., & Berlanga, L. (2009). Skin picking behaviors: An examination of the prevalence and severity in a community sample. *Journal of Anxiety Disorders, 23*(3), 314–319. doi:10.1016/j.janxdis.2009.01.008

Hellriegel, J., Barber, C., Wikramanayake, M., Fineberg, N. A., & Mandy, W. (2017). Is "not just right experience" (NJRE) in obsessive-compulsive disorder part of an autistic phenotype? *CNS Spectrums, 22*(1), 41–50. doi:10.1017/S1092852916000511

Hofvander, B., Delorme, R., Chaste, P., Nydén, A., Wentz, E., Ståhlberg, O.,. . . Råstam, M. (2009). Psychiatric and psychosocial problems in adults with normal-intelligence autism spectrum disorders. *BMC Psychiatry, 9*(1), 35. doi:10.1186/1471-244X-9-35

Hollander, E., Anagnostou, E., Chaplin, W., Esposito, K., Haznedar, M. M., Licalzi, E.,. . . Buchsbaum, M. (2005). Striatal volume on magnetic resonance imaging and repetitive behaviors in autism. *Biological Psychiatry, 58*(3), 226–232. doi:10.1016/j.biopsych.2005.03.040

Hollander, E., King, A., Delaney, K., Smith, C. J., & Silverman, J. M. (2003). Obsessive–compulsive behaviors in parents of multiplex autism families. *Psychiatry Research, 117*(1), 11–16. doi:10.1016/S0165-1781(02)00304-9

Hollander, E., Soorya, L., Chaplin, W., Anagnostou, E., Taylor, B. P., Ferretti, C. J.,. . . Settipani, C. (2012). A double-blind placebo-controlled trial of fluoxetine for repetitive behaviors and global severity in adult autism spectrum disorders. *American Journal of Psychiatry, 169*(3), 292–299. doi:10.1176/appi.ajp.2011.10050764

Huppert, J. D., Simpson, H. B., Nissenson, K. J., Liebowitz, M. R., & Foa, E. B. (2009). Quality of life and functional impairment in obsessive–compulsive disorder: A comparison of patients with and without comorbidity, patients in remission, and healthy controls. *Depression and Anxiety, 26*(1), 39–45. doi:10.1002/da.20506

Huppert, J. D., Walther, M. R., Hajcak, G., Yadin, E., Foa, E. B., Simpson, H. B., & Liebowitz, M. R. (2007). The OCI-R: Validation of the subscales in a clinical sample. *Journal of Anxiety Disorders, 21*(3), 394–406. doi:10.1016/j.janxdis.2006.05.006

Hutton, J., Goode, S., Murphy, M., Le Couteur, A., & Rutter, M. (2008). New onset psychiatric disorders in individuals with autism. *Autism, 12*(4), 373–390. doi:10.1177/1362361308091650

Iniesta-Sepúlveda, M., Nadeau, J. M., Ramos, A., Kay, B., Riemann, B. C. & Storch, E. A. (2018). An initial case series of intensive cognitive-behavioral therapy for obsessive-compulsive disorder in adolescents with autism spectrum disorder. *Child Psychiatry & Human Development, 49*(1), 9–19. doi:10.1007/s10578-017-0724-1

Ivarsson, T., Skarphedinsson, G., Kornør, H., Axelsdottir, B., Biedilæ, S., Heyman, I.,. . . March, J. (2015). The place of and evidence for serotonin reuptake inhibitors (SRIs) for obsessive compulsive disorder (OCD) in children and adolescents: Views based on a systemic review and meta-analysis. *Psychiatry Research, 227*(1), 93–103. doi:10.1016/j.psychres.2015.01.015

Jacob, S., Landeros-Weisenberger, A., & Leckman, J. F. (2009). Autism spectrum and obsessive–compulsive disorders: OC behaviors, phenotypes and genetics. *Autism Research, 2*(6), 293–311. doi:10.1002/aur.108

Jefferies-Sewell, K., Chamberlain, S. R., Fineberg, N. A., & Laws, K. R. (2017). Cognitive dysfunction in body dysmorphic disorder: New implications for nosological systems and neurobiological models. *CNS Spectrums, 22*(1), 51–60. doi:10.1017/S1092852916000468

Johnson, M. H. (2012). Executive function and developmental disorders: The flip side of the coin. *Trends in Cognitive Sciences, 16*(9), 454–457. doi:10.1016/j.tics.2012.07.001

Joosten, A. V., Bundy, A. C., & Einfeld, S. L. (2008). Intrinsic and extrinsic motivation for stereotypic and repetitive behavior. *Journal of Autism and Developmental Disorders, 39*(3), 521–531. doi:10.1007/s10803-008-0654-7

Kana, R. K., Keller, T. A., Minshew, N. J., & Just, M. A. (2007). Inhibitory control in high-functioning autism: Decreased activation and underconnectivity in inhibition networks. *Biological Psychiatry, 62*(3), 198–206. doi:10.1016/j.biopsych.2006.08.004

Kaufman, J., Birmaher, B., Axelson, D., Perepletchikova, F., Brent, D., & Ryan, N. (2016). *The Kiddie SADS—Lifetime version DSM-5 November 2016*. Retrieved from http://pediatricbipolar.pitt.edu/sites/default/files/KSADS_DSM_5_SCREEN_Final.pdf

Kessler, R. C., Petukhova, M., Sampson, N. A., Zaslavsky, A. M., & Wittchen, H. U. (2012). Twelve-month and lifetime prevalence and lifetime morbid risk of anxiety and mood disorders in the United States. *International Journal of Methods in Psychiatric Research, 21*(3), 169–184. doi:10.1002/mpr.1359

Keuthen, N. J., Koran, L. M., Aboujaoude, E., Large, M. D., & Serpe, R. T. (2010). The prevalence of pathologic skin picking in US adults. *Comprehensive Psychiatry, 51*(2), 183–186. doi:10.1016/j.comppsych.2009.04.003

Keuthen, N. J., Rothbaum, B. O., Fama, J., Altenburger, E., Falkenstein, M. J., Sprich, S. E.,... Welch, S. S. (2012). DBT-enhanced cognitive-behavioral treatment for trichotillomania: A randomized controlled trial. *Journal of Behavioral Addictions, 1*(3), 106–114. doi:10.1556/JBA.1.2012.003

Keyes, C., Nolte, L., & Williams, T. I. (2017). The battle of living with obsessive compulsive disorder: A qualitative study of young people's experiences. *Child and Adolescent Mental Health, 23*(3), 177–184. doi:10.1111/camh.12216

Kiely, B., Migdal, T. R., Vettam, S., & Adesman, A. (2016). Prevalence and correlates of elopement in a nationally representative sample of children with developmental disabilities in the United States. *Plos One, 11*(2), e0148337. doi:10.1371/journal.pone.0148337

King, R. A., Scahill, L., Vitulano, L. A., Schwab-Stone, M., Tercyak, K. P., & Riddle, M. A. (1995). Childhood trichotillomania: Clinical phenomenology, comorbidity, and family genetics. *Journal of the American Academy of Child and Adolescent Psychiatry, 34*(11), 1451–1459. doi:10.1097/00004583-199,511,000-00011

Kloosterman, P. H., Summerfeldt, L. J., Parker, J. D., & Holden, J. J. (2013). The obsessive-compulsive trait of incompleteness in parents of children with autism spectrum disorders. *Journal of Obsessive-Compulsive and Related Disorders, 2*(2), 176–182. doi:10.1016/j.jocrd.2012.11.004

Kose, L. K., Fox, L., & Storch, E. A. (2018). Effectiveness of cognitive behavioural therapy for individuals with autism spectrum disorders and comorbid obsessive-compulsive disorder: A review of the research. *Journal of Developmental and Physical Disabilities, 30*(1), 69–87. doi:10.1007/s10882-017-9559-8

Kratochvil, C. J., & Bloch, M. H. (2009). Trichotillomania across the lifespan. *Journal of the American Academy of Child and Adolescent Psychiatry, 48*(9), 879–883. doi:10.1097/CHI.0b013e3181ae09f3

Krebs, G., Murray, K., & Jassi, A. (2016). Modified cognitive behavior therapy for severe, treatment-resistant obsessive-compulsive disorder in an adolescent with autism spectrum disorder. *Journal of Clinical Psychology, 72*(11), 1162–1173. doi:10.1002/jclp.22396

Lane, R. D., Reiman, E. M., Axelrod, B., Yun, L. S., Holmes, A., & Schwartz, G. E. (1998). Neural correlates of levels of emotional awareness: Evidence of an interaction between emotion and attention in the anterior cingulate cortex. *Journal of Cognitive Neuroscience, 10*(4), 525–535. doi:10.1162/089892998562924

Lang, R., Didden, R., Machalicek, W., Rispoli, M., Sigafoos, J., Lancioni, G.,... Kang, S. (2010). Behavioural treatment of chronic skin-picking in individuals with developmental disabilities: A systematic review. *Research in Developmental Disabilities, 31*, 304–315. doi:10.1016/j.ridd.2009.10.017

Lebowitz, E. R., Storch, E. A., MacLeod, J., & Leckman, J. F. (2015). Clinical and family correlates of coercive-disruptive behaviour in children and adolescents with obsessive-compulsive disorder. *Journal of Child & Family Studies, 24*(9), 2589–2597. doi:10.1007/s10826-014-0061-y

Lehmkuhl, H. D., Storch, E. A., Bodfish, J. W., & Geffken, G. R. (2008). Brief report: Exposure and response prevention for obsessive compulsive disorder in a 12-year-old with autism. *Journal of Autism and Developmental Disorders, 38*(5), 977–981. doi:10.1007/s10803-007-0457-2

Lewin, A. B., & Piacentini, J. (2010, April). Evidence-based assessment of child obsessive compulsive disorder: Recommendations for clinical practice and treatment research. *Child & Youth Care Forum, 39*(2), 73–89. doi:10.1007/s10566-009-9092-8

Lewin, A. B., Wood, J. J., Gunderson, S., Murphy, T. K., & Storch, E. A. (2011). Phenomenology of comorbid autism spectrum and obsessive-compulsive disorders among children. *Journal of Developmental and Physical Disabilities, 23*(6), 543–553. doi:10.1007/s10882-011-9247-z

Lidstone, J., Uljarevic, M., Sullivan, J., Rodgers, J., McConachie, H., Freeston, M.,... Leekham, S. (2014). Relations among restricted and repetitive behaviors, anxiety and sensory features in children with autism spectrum disorders. *Research in Autism Spectrum Disorders, 8*(2), 82–92. doi:10.1016/j.rasd.2013.10.001

Lombardo, M. V., & Baron-Cohen, S. (2010), Unraveling the paradox of the autistic self. *WIREs Cognitive Science, 1*, 393–403. doi:10.1002/wcs.45

Lynch, K. A., Feola, P. G., & Guenther, E. (2003). Gastric trichobezoar: An important cause of abdominal pain presenting to the pediatric emergency department. *Pediatric Emergency Care, 19*(5), 343–347. doi:10.1097/01.pec.0000092581.40174.e3

Mack, H., Fullana, M. A., Russell, A. J., Mataix-Cols, D., Nakatani, E., & Heyman, I. (2010). Obsessions and compulsions in children with Asperger's syndrome or high-functioning autism: A case-control study. *Australian & New Zealand Journal of Psychiatry, 44*(12), 1082–1088. doi:10.3109/00048674.2010.515561

Maia, T. V., Cooney, R. E., & Peterson, B. S. (2008). The neural bases of obsessive–compulsive disorder in children and adults. *Development and Psychopathology, 20*(4), 1251–1283. doi:10.1017/S0954579408000606

March, J. S., Franklin, M., Nelson, A., & Foa, E. (2001). Cognitive-behavioral psychotherapy for pediatric obsessive-compulsive disorder. *Journal of Clinical Child Psychology, 30*(1), 8–18. doi:10.1207/S15374424JCCP3001_3

Markarian, Y., Larson, M. J., Aldea, M. A., Baldwin, S. A., Good, D., Berkeljon, A., . . . McKay, D. (2010). Multiple pathways to functional impairment in obsessive–compulsive disorder. *Clinical Psychology Review, 30*(1), 78–88. doi:10.1016/j.cpr.2009.09.005

Marler, S., Sanders, K. B., & Veenstra-VanderWeele, J. (2014). N-acetylcysteine as treatment for self-injurious behavior in a child with autism. *Journal of Child and Adolescent Psychopharmacology, 24*(4), 231–234. doi:10.1089/cap.2013.0137

Marques, L., Weingarden, H. M., LeBlanc, N. J., & Wilhelm, S. (2011). Treatment utilization and barriers to treatment engagement among people with body dysmorphic symptoms. *Journal of Psychosomatic Research, 70*(3), 286–293. doi:10.1016/j.jpsychores.2010.10.002

Masiran, R. (2018). Autism and trichotillomania in an adolescent boy. *BMJ Case Reports, 2018,* 1–4. doi:10.1136/bcr-2018-226,270

Mayville, S., Katz, R. C., Gipson, M. T., & Cabral, K. (1999). Assessing the prevalence of body dysmorphic disorder in an ethnically diverse group of adolescents. *Journal of Child and Family Studies, 8*(3), 357–362. doi:10.1023/A:1022023514730

Mazefsky, C. A., Borue, X., Day, T. N., & Minshew, N. J. (2014). Emotion regulation patterns in adolescents with high-functioning autism spectrum disorder: Comparison to typically developing adolescents and association with psychiatric symptoms. *Autism Research, 7*(3), 344–354. doi:10.1002/aur.1366

Mazefsky, C. A., & White, S. W. (2014). Emotion regulation: Concepts & practice in autism spectrum disorder. *Child and Adolescent Psychiatric Clinics of North America, 23*(1), 15–24. doi:10.1016/j.chc.2013.07.002

McDougle, C. J., Kresch, L. E., Goodman, W. K., & Naylor, S. T. (1995). A case-controlled study of repetitive thoughts and behavior in adults with autistic disorder and obsessive-compulsive disorder. *American Journal of Psychiatry, 152*(5), 772–777. doi:10.1176/ajp.152.5.772

McGuire, J. F., Kugler, B. B., Park, J. M., Horng, B., Lewin, A. B., Murphy, T. K., & Storch, E. A. (2012). Evidence-based assessment of compulsive skin picking, chronic tic disorders and trichotillomania in children. *Child Psychiatry & Human Development, 43*(6), 855–883. doi:10.1007/s10578-012-0300-7

McGuire, J. F., Piacentini, J., Lewin, A. B., Brennan, E. A., Murphy, T. K., & Storch, E. A. (2015). A meta-analysis of cognitive behavior therapy and medication for child obsessive-compulsive disorder: Moderators of treatment efficacy, response and remission. *Depression and Anxiety, 32*(8), 580–593. doi:10.1002/da.22389

McGuire, J. F., Ung, D., Selles, R. R., Rahman, O., Lewin, A. B., Murphy, T. K., & Storch, E. A. (2014). Treating trichotillomania: A meta-analysis of treatment effects and moderators for behavior therapy and serotonin reuptake inhibitors. *Journal of Psychiatric Research, 58,* 76–83. doi:10.1016/j.jpsychires.2014.07.015

Minshawi, N. F., Hurwitz, S., Fodstad, J. C., Biebl, S., Morriss, D. H., & McDougle, C. J. (2014). The association between self-injurious behaviors and autism spectrum disorders. *Psychology Research and Behavior Management, 7,* 125–136. doi:10.2147/PRBM.S44635

Mosconi, M. W., Kay, M., D'cruz, A. M., Seidenfeld, A., Guter, S., Stanford, L. D., & Sweeney, J. A. (2009). Impaired inhibitory control is associated with higher-order repetitive behaviors in autism spectrum disorders. *Psychological Medicine, 39*(9), 1559–1566. doi:10.1017/S0033291708004984

Murray, K., Jassi, A., Mataix-Cols, D., Barrow, F., & Krebs, G. (2015). Outcomes of cognitive behaviour therapy for obsessive–compulsive disorder in young people with and without autism spectrum disorders: A case controlled study. *Psychiatry Research, 228*(1), 8–13. doi:10.1016/j.psychres.2015.03.012

Nadeau, J. M., Arnold, E. B., Storch, E. A., & Lewin, A. B. (2014). Family cognitive-behavioral treatment for a child with autism and comorbid obsessive compulsive disorder. *Clinical Case Studies, 13*(1), 22–36. doi:10.1177/1534650113504488

Neil, N., Moum, L., & Sturmey, P. (2014). Comorbidity among children and youth with autism spectrum disorder. In J. K. Luiselli (Ed.), *Children and youth with autism spectrum disorder (ASD): Recent advances and innovations in assessment, education, and intervention* (pp. 26–41). New York, NY: Oxford University Press.

Neil, N., & Sturmey, P. (2014). Assessment and treatment of obsessions and compulsions in individuals with autism spectrum disorders: A systematic review. *Review Journal of Autism and Developmental Disorders, 1*(1), 62–79. doi:10.1007/s40489-013-0006-1

Nestadt, G., Bienvenu, O. J., Cai, G., Samuels, J., & Eaton, W. W. (1998). Incidence of obsessive-compulsive disorder in adults. *Journal of Nervous and Mental Disease, 186*(7), 401–406.

Nikoo, M., Radnia, H., Farokhnia, M., Mohammadi, M. R., & Akhondzadeh, S. (2015). N-acetylcysteine as an adjunctive therapy to risperidone for treatment of irritability in autism: A randomized, double-blind, placebo-controlled clinical trial of efficacy and safety. *Clinical Neuropharmacology, 38*(1), 11–17.

Obsessive Compulsive Cognitions Working Group. (1997). Cognitive assessment of obsessive-compulsive disorder. *Behaviour Research and Therapy, 35*(7), 667–681. doi:10.1016/S0005-7967(97)00017-X

Odlaug, B. L., Hampshire, A., Chamberlain, S. R., & Grant, J. E. (2016). Abnormal brain activation in excoriation (skin-picking) disorder: Evidence from an executive planning fMRI study. *British Journal of Psychiatry, 208*(2), 168–174. doi:10.1192/bjp.bp.114.155192

Oliver, G., Dean, O., Camfield, D., Blair-West, S., Ng, C., Berk, M., & Sarris, J. (2015). N-acetyl cysteine in the treatment of obsessive compulsive and related disorders: A systematic review. *Clinical Psychopharmacology and Neuroscience, 13*(1), 12–24. doi:10.9758/cpn.2015.13.1.12

Ordaz, D. L., Lewin, A. B., McBride, N. M., & Storch, E. A. (2018). Modular cognitive-behavioral therapy for an early adolescent with autism spectrum disorder and comorbid obsessive compulsive disorder. *Clinical Case Studies, 17*(4), 233–248. doi:10.1177/1534650118782436

Ordaz, D. L., Lewin, A. B., & Storch, E. A. (2018). Modular cognitive-behavioral therapy for a young adult with autism spectrum disorder, comorbid obsessive compulsive disorder, and social anxiety disorder. *Clinical Case Studies, 17*(3), 136–149. doi:10.1177/1534650118770269

Osland, S., Arnold, P. D., & Pringsheim, T. (2018). The prevalence of diagnosed obsessive compulsive disorder and associated comorbidities: A population-based Canadian study. *Psychiatry Research, 268*, 137–142. doi:10.1016/j.psychres.2018.07.018

Öst, L. G., Riise, E. N., Wergeland, G. J., Hansen, B., & Kvale, G. (2016). Cognitive behavioral and pharmacological treatments of OCD in children: A systematic review and meta-analysis. *Journal of Anxiety Disorders, 43*, 58–69. doi:10.1016/j.janxdis.2016.08.003

Park, J. M., Lewin, A. B., & Storch, E. A. (2014). Adult offspring perspectives on parental hoarding behaviors. *Psychiatry Research, 220*(1–2), 328–334. doi:10.1016/j.psychres.2014.07.061

Paula-Perez, I. (2013). Differential diagnosis between obsessive compulsive disorder and restrictive and repetitive behavioural patterns, activities and interests in autism spectrum disorders. *Journal of Psychiatry and Mental Health (English Edition), 6*(4), 178–186. doi:1.1016/j.rpsmen.2012.07.006

Pertusa, A., Bejerot, S., Eriksson, J., Fernández de la Cruz, L., Bonde, S., Russell, A., & Mataix-Cols, D. (2012). Do patients with hoarding disorder have autistic traits? *Depression and Anxiety, 29*(3), 210–218. doi:10.1002/da.20902

Phillips, K. A., Didie, E. R., Menard, W., Pagano, M. E., Fay, C., & Weisberg, R. B. (2006). Clinical features of body dysmorphic disorder in adolescents and adults. *Psychiatry Research, 141*(3), 305–314. doi:10.1016/j.psychres.2005.09.014

Piacentini, J., Bergman, R. L., Keller, M., & McCracken, J. (2003). Functional impairment in children and adolescents with obsessive-compulsive disorder. *Journal of Child and Adolescent Psychopharmacology, 13*(2, Suppl 1), 61–69. doi:10.1089/104454603322126359

Piacentini, J., Peris, T. S., Bergman, R. L., & Chang, S. (2007). Functional impairment in childhood OCD: Development and psychometrics properties of the child obsessive-compulsive impact scale-revised. *Journal of Clinical Child and Adolescent Psychology, 36*(4), 645–653. doi:10.1080/15374410701662790

Postorino, V., Kerns, C. M., Vivanti, G., Bradshaw, J., Siracusano, M., & Mazzone, L. (2017). Anxiety disorders and obsessive-compulsive disorders in individuals with autism spectrum disorder. *Current Psychiatry Reports, 19*(12), 1–8. doi:10.1007/s11920-017-0846-y

Rachman, S., & de Silva, P. (1978). Abnormal and normal obsessions. *Behaviour Research and Therapy, 16*(4), 233–248. doi:10.1016/0005-7967(78)90022-0

Rapin, I., & Tuchman, R. F. (2008). Autism: Definition, neurobiology, screening, diagnosis. *Pediatric Clinics of North America, 55*(5), 1129–1146. doi:10.1016/j.pcl.2008.07.005

Rapoport, J. L., Inoff-Germain, G., Weissman, M. M., & Greenwald, S. (2000). Childhood obsessive–compulsive disorder in the NIMH MECA study. *Journal of Anxiety Disorders, 14*(6), 535–548. doi:10.1016/S0887-6185(00)00048-7

Rapp, A. M., Bergman, R. L., Piacentini, J., & McGuire, J. F. (2016). Evidence-based assessment of obsessive–compulsive disorder. *Journal of Central Nervous System Disease, 8*, 13–29. doi:10.4137/JCNSD.S38359

Rauch, S. L., Phillips, K. A., Segal, E., Makris, N., Shin, L. M., Whalen, P. J., . . . Kennedy, D. N. (2003). A preliminary morphometric magnetic resonance imaging study of regional brain volumes in body dysmorphic disorder. *Psychiatry Research: Neuroimaging, 122*(1), 13–19. doi:10.1016/S0925-4927(02)00117-8

Reaven, J. A., Blakeley-Smith, A., Nichols, S., Dasari, M., Flanigan, E., & Hepburn, S. (2009). Cognitive-behavioral group treatment for anxiety symptoms in children with high-functioning autism spectrum disorders: A pilot study. *Focus on Autism and Other Developmental Disabilities, 24*(1), 27–37. doi:10.1177/1088357608327666

Reaven, J., & Hepburn, S. (2003). Cognitive-behavioral treatment of obsessive-compulsive disorder in a child with Asperger syndrome: A case report. *Autism, 7*(2), 145–164. doi:10.1177/1362361303007002003

Rehm, I. C., Moulding, R., & Nedeljkovic, M. (2015). Psychological treatments for trichotillomania: Update and future directions. *Australian Psychiatry, 23*(4), 365–368. doi:10.1177/1039856215590029

Rief, W., Buhlmann, U., Wilhelm, S., Borkenhagen, A. D. A., & Brähler, E. (2006). The prevalence of body dysmorphic disorder: A population-based survey. *Psychological Medicine, 36*(06), 877–885. doi:10.1017/S0033291706007264

Roberts, S., O'Connor, K., & Bélanger, C. (2013). Emotion regulation and other psychological models for body-focused repetitive behaviors. *Clinical Psychology Review, 33*(6), 745–762. doi:10.1016/j.cpr.2013.05.004

Robinson, K. J., Rose, D., & Salkovskis, P. M. (2017). Seeking help for obsessive compulsive disorder (OCD): A qualitative study of the enablers and barriers conducted by a researcher with personal experience of OCD. *Psychology and Psychotherapy: Theory, Research and Practice, 90*(2), 193–211. doi:10.1111/papt.12090

Rodgers, J., Glod, M., Connolly, B., & McConachie, H. (2012). The relationship between anxiety and repetitive behaviors in autism spectrum disorder. *Journal of Autism and Developmental Disorders, 42*(11) 2404–2409. doi:10.1007/s10803-012-1531-y

Roi, C., & Bazzano, A. (2017). Improvement in excoriation (skin-picking) with use of risperidone in a patient with developmental disability. *Pediatric Reports, 9*(6946), 1–3. doi:10.4081/pr.2017.6946

Rooney, M., Alfano, C. A., Walsh, K. S., & Parr, A. F. (2011). Differential diagnosis and treatment of obsessive-compulsive, inattentive, and sleep symptoms in a 7-year-old with PDD-NOS. *Clinical Case Studies, 10*(2), 133–146. doi:10.1177/1534650111398123

Ruscio, A. M., Stein, D. J., Chiu, W. T., & Kessler, R. C. (2010). The epidemiology of obsessive-compulsive disorder in the National Comorbidity Survey Replication. *Molecular Psychiatry, 15*(1), 53. doi:10.1038/mp.2008.94

Russell, A. J., Jassi, A., Fullana, M. A., Mack, H., Johnston, K., Heyman, I., . . . Mataix-Cols, D. (2013). Cognitive behavior therapy for comorbid obsessive-compulsive disorder in high-functioning autism spectrum disorders: A randomized controlled trial. *Depression and Anxiety, 30*(8), 697–708. doi:10.1002/da.22053

Russell, A. J., Mataix-Cols, D., Anson, M., & Murphy, D. G. (2005). Obsessions and compulsions in Asperger syndrome and high-functioning autism. *British Journal of Psychiatry, 186,* 525–529. doi:10.1192/bjp.186.6.525

Russell, A. J., Murphy, C. M., Wilson, E., Gillan, N., Brown, C., Robertson, D. M.,... Murphy, D. G. M. (2016). The mental health of individuals referred for assessment of autism spectrum disorder in adulthood: A clinic report. *Autism, 20*(5), 623–627. doi:10.1177/1362361315604271

Russell, G., Rodgers, L. R., Ukoumunne, O. C., & Ford, T. (2014). Prevalence of parent-reported ASD and ADHD in the UK: Findings from the millennium cohort study. *Journal of Autism and Developmental Disorders, 44*(1), 31–40. doi:10.1007/s10803-013-1849-0

Ruta, L., Mugno, D., D'Arrigo, V. G., Vitiello, B., & Mazzone, L. (2010). Obsessive–compulsive traits in children and adolescents with Asperger syndrome. *European Child & Adolescent Psychiatry, 19*(1), 17–24. doi:10.1007/s00787-009-0035-6

Salkovskis, P. M. (1985). Obsessional-compulsive problems: A cognitive-behavioural analysis. *Behaviour Research and Therapy, 23*(5), 571–583. doi:10.1016/0005-7967(85)90105-6

Salkovskis, P. M., & Harrison, J. (1984). Abnormal and normal obsessions—A replication. *Behaviour Research and Therapy, 22*(5), 549–552. doi:10.1016/0005-7967(84)90057-3

Samson, A. C., Hardan, A. Y., Podell, R. W., Phillips, J. M., & Gross, J. J. (2015). Emotion regulation in children and adolescents with autism spectrum disorder. *Autism Research, 8*(1), 9–18. doi:10.1002/aur.1387

Scahill, L., Dimitropoulos, A., McDougle, C. J., Aman, M. G., Feurer, I. D., McCracken, J. T.,... Hallett, V. (2014). Children's Yale–Brown Obsessive Compulsive Scale in autism spectrum disorder: Component structure and correlates of symptom checklist. *Journal of the American Academy of Child and Adolescent Psychiatry, 53*(1), 97–107. doi:10.1016/j.jaac.2013.09.018

Scahill, L., McDougle, C. J., Williams, S. K., Dimitropoulos, A., Aman, M. G., McCracken, J. T.,... Ghuman, J. (2006). Children's Yale-Brown Obsessive Compulsive Scale modified for pervasive developmental disorders. *Journal of the American Academy of Child and Adolescent Psychiatry, 45*(9), 1114–1123. doi:10.1097/01.chi.0000220854.79144.e7

Scahill, L., Riddle, M. A., McSwiggin-Hardin, M., Ort, S. I., King, R. A., Goodman, W. K.,... Leckman, J. F. (1997). Children's Yale-Brown Obsessive Compulsive Scale: Reliability and validity. *Journal of the American Academy of Child and Adolescent Psychiatry, 36*(6), 844–852. doi:10.1097/00004583-199,706,000-00023

Schneider, S. C., Turner, C. M., Mond, J., & Hudson, J. L. (2016). Prevalence and correlates of body dysmorphic disorder in a community sample of adolescents. *Australian & New Zealand Journal of Psychiatry, 51*(6), 595–603. doi:10.1177/0004867416665483

Selles, R. R., McGuire, J. F., Small, B. J., & Storch, E. A. (2016). A systematic review and meta-analysis of psychiatric treatments for excoriation (skin-picking) disorder. *General Hospital Psychiatry, 41,* 29–37. doi:10.1016/j.genhosppsych.2016.04.001

Sharma, S., Woolfson, L. M., & Hunter, S. C. (2013). Maladaptive cognitive appraisals in children with high-functioning autism: Associations with fear, anxiety and theory of mind. *Autism, 18*(3), 244–254. doi:10.1177/1362361312472556

Shusterman, A., Feld, L., Baer, L., & Keuthen, N. (2009). Affective regulation in trichotillomania: Evidence from a large-scale internet survey. *Behaviour Research and Therapy, 47*(8), 637–644. doi:10.1016/j.brat.2009.04.004

Silverman, W. K., & Albano, A. M. (1996). *The Anxiety Disorders Interview Schedule for DSM-IV—Child and parent versions.* London, UK: Oxford University Press.

Simonoff, E., Pickles, A., Charman, T., Chandler, S., Loucas, T., & Baird, G. (2008). Psychiatric disorders in children with autism spectrum disorders: Prevalence, comorbidity, and associated factors in a population-derived sample. *Journal of Child and Adolescent Psychiatry, 47*(8), 921–929. doi:10.1097/CHI.0b013e318179964f

Skapinakis, P., Caldwell, D. M., Hollingworth, W., Bryden, P., Fineberg, N. A., Salkovskis, P.,... Lewis, G. (2016a). Pharmacological and psychotherapeutic interventions for management of obsessive-compulsive disorder in adults: A systematic review and network meta-analysis. *Lancet Psychiatry, 3*(8), 730–739. doi:10.1016/S2215-0366(16)30069-4

Skapinakis, P., Caldwell, D., Hollingworth, W., Bryden, P., Fineberg, N., Salkovskis, P.,... Lewis, G. (2016b). A systematic review of the clinical effectiveness and cost-effectiveness of pharmacological and psychological interventions for the management of obsessive-compulsive disorder in children/adolescents and adults. *Health Technology Assessment, 20*(43), 1–392.

Snorrason, Í., Belleau, E. L., & Woods, D. W. (2012). How related are hair pulling disorder (trichotillomania) and skin picking disorder? A review of evidence for comorbidity, similarities and shared etiology. *Clinical Psychology Review, 32*(7), 618–629. doi:10.1016/j.cpr.2012.05.008

Snorrason, Í., Smári, J., & Ólafsson, R.P. (2010). Emotion regulation in pathological skin picking: Findings from a non-treatment seeking sample. *Journal of Behavior Therapy and Experimental Psychiatry, 41*(3), 238–245. doi: 10.1016/j.jbtep.2010.01.009

Spiker, M. A., Lin, C. E., Van Dyke, M., & Wood, J. J. (2012). Restricted interests and anxiety in children with autism. *Autism, 16*(3), 306–320. doi:10.1177/1362361311401763

Stewart, E., Cancilliere, M. K., Freeman, J., Wellen, B., Garcia, A., Sapyta, J., & Franklin, M. (2016). Elevated autism spectrum disorder traits in young children with OCD. *Child Psychiatry & Human Development, 47,* 993–1001. doi:10.1007/s10578-016-0629-4

Storch, E. A., Arnold, E. B., Lewin, A. B., Nadeau, J. M., Jones, A. M., De Nadai, A. S.,... Murphy, T. K. (2013). The effect of cognitive-behavioral therapy versus treatment as usual for anxiety in children with autism spectrum disorders: A randomized, controlled trial. *Journal of the American Academy of Child and Adolescent Psychiatry, 52*(2), 132–142. doi:10.1016/j.jaac.2012.11.007

Storch, E. A., Geffken, G. R., Merlo, L. J., Jacob, M. L., Murphy, T. K., Goodman, W. K.,... Grabill, K. (2007). Family accommodation in pediatric obsessive-compulsive disorder. *Journal of Clinical Child and Adolescent Psychology, 36*(2), 207–216. doi:10.1080/15374410701277929

Storch, E. A., McBride, N., Timpano, K., & Murphy, T. K. (2016). Hoarding in youth with autism spectrum disorders and anxiety: Incidence, clinical correlates, and behavioral treatment response. *Journal of Autism and Developmental Disorders, 46*(5), 1602–1612. doi:10.1007/s10803-015-2687-z

Stutzman, D., & Dopheide, J. (2015). Acetylcysteine for treatment of autism spectrum disorder symptoms. *American Journal of Health-System Pharmacy, 72*(22), 1956–1959. doi:10.2146/ajhp150072

Sukhodolsky, D. G., Scahill, L., Gadow, K. D., Arnold, L. E., Aman, M. G., McDougle, C. J., . . . Vitiello, B. (2008). Parent-rated anxiety symptoms in children with pervasive developmental disorders: Frequency and association with core autism symptoms and cognitive functioning. *Journal of Abnormal Child Psychology, 36*(1), 117–128. doi:10.1007/s10802-007-9165-9

Summers, B. J., Matheny, N. L., & Cougle, J. R. (2017). "Not just right" experiences and incompleteness in body dysmorphic disorder. *Psychiatry Research, 247*, 200–207. doi:10.1016/j.psychres.2016.11.038

Taylor, S., Conelea, C. A., McKay, D., Crowe, K. B., & Abramowitz, J. S. (2014). Sensory intolerance: Latent structure and psychopathologic correlates. *Comprehensive Psychiatry, 55*(5), 1279–1284. doi:10.1016/j.comppsych.2014.03.007

Thakkar, K. N., Polli, F. E., Joseph, R. M., Tuch, D. S., Hadjikhani, N., Barton, J. J., & Manoach, D. S. (2008). Response monitoring, repetitive behaviour and anterior cingulate abnormalities in autism spectrum disorders (ASD). *Brain, 131*(9), 2464–2478. doi:10.1093/brain/awn099

Ting, J. T., & Feng, G. (2011). Neurobiology of obsessive–compulsive disorder: Insights into neural circuitry dysfunction through mouse genetics. *Current Opinion in Neurobiology, 21*(6), 842–848. doi:10.1016/j.conb.2011.04.010

Tolin, D. F., Frost, R. O., Steketee, G., & Muroff, J. (2015). Cognitive behavioral therapy for hoarding disorder: A meta-analysis. *Depression and Anxiety, 32*(3), 158–166. doi:10.1002/da.22327

Torres, A. R., Prince, M. J., Bebbington, P. E., Bhugra, D., Brugha, T. S., Farrell, M., . . . Singleton, N. (2006). Obsessive-compulsive disorder: Prevalence, comorbidity, impact, and help-seeking in the British National Psychiatric Morbidity Survey of 2000. *American Journal of Psychiatry, 163*(11), 1978–1985.

Tucker, B. T., Woods, D. W., Flessner, C. A., Franklin, S. A., & Franklin, M. E. (2011). The Skin Picking Impact Project: Phenomenology, interference, and treatment utilization of pathological skin picking in a population-based sample. *Journal of Anxiety Disorders, 25*(1), 88–95.

Vasudeva, S. B., & Hollander, E. (2017). Body dysmorphic disorder in patients with autism spectrum disorder: A reflection of increased local processing and self-focus. *American Journal of Psychiatry, 174*, 313–316. doi:10.1176/appi.ajp.2016.16050559

Veale, D., Boocock, A., Gournay, K., Dryden, W., Shah, F., Willson, R., & Walburn, J. (1996). Body dysmorphic disorder: A survey of fifty cases. *British Journal of Psychiatry, 169*(2), 196–201.

Vogt, B. A., Finch, D. M., & Olson, C. R. (1992). Functional heterogeneity in cingulate cortex: The anterior executive and posterior evaluative regions. *Cerebral Cortex, 2*(6), 435–443. doi:10.1093/cercor/2.6.435-a

Walters, S., Loades, M., & Russell, A. (2016). A systematic review of effective modifications to cognitive behavioural therapy for young people with autism spectrum disorders. *Review Journal of Autism and Developmental Disorders, 3*(2), 137–153. doi:10.1007/s40489-016-0072-2

Warren, Z. E., Sanders, K. B., & Veenstra-VanderWeele, J. (2010). Identity crisis involving body image in a young man with autism. *American Journal of Psychiatry, 167*, 1299–1303. doi:10.1176/appi.ajp.2010.09091281

Whiteside, S. P., Port, J. D., & Abramowitz, J. S. (2004). A meta–analysis of functional neuroimaging in obsessive–compulsive disorder. *Psychiatry Research: Neuroimaging, 132*(1), 69–79. doi:10.1016/j.pscychresns.2004.07.001

Wikramanayake, W. N. M., Mandy, W., Shahper, S., Kaur, S., Kolli, S., Osman, S., . . . Fineberg, N. A. (2018). Autism spectrum disorders in adult outpatients with obsessive compulsive disorder in the UK. *International Journal of Psychiatry in Clinical Practice, 22*(1), 54–62. doi:10.1080/13651501.2017.1354029

Wilcox, J. A., Tsuang, M. T., Schnurr, T., & Baida-Fragoso, N. (2003). Case-control family study of lesser variant traits in autism. *Neuropsychobiology, 47*(4), 171–177. doi:10.1159/000071210

Wink, L. K., Adams, R., Wang, Z., Klaunig, J. E., Plawecki, M. H., Posey, D. J., . . . Erickson, C. A. (2016). A randomized placebo-controlled pilot study of N-acetylcysteine in youth with autism spectrum disorder. *Molecular Autism, 7*(1), 26. doi:10.1186/s13229-016-0088-6

Wolters, L. H., de Haan, E., Hogendoorn, S. M., Boer, F., & Prins, P. J. M. (2016). Severe pediatric obsessive-compulsive disorder and comorbid autistic symptoms: Effectiveness of cognitive behavioural therapy. *Journal of Obsessive Compulsive and Related Disorders, 10*, 69–77. doi:10.1016/j.jocrd.2016.06.002

Woods, D. W., Flessner, C. A., Franklin, M. E., Keuthen, N. J., Goodwin, R. D., Stein, D. J., & Walther, M. R. (2006). The Trichotillomania Impact Project (TIP): Exploring phenomenology, functional impairment, and treatment utilization. *Journal of Clinical Psychiatry, 67*(12), 1877. Retrieved from https://pdfs.semanticscholar.org/0988/345c03e2cdf2d4833eee04264e39b1c2d55c.pdf

Woods, D. W., Wetterneck, C. T., & Flessner, C. A. (2006). A controlled evaluation of acceptance and commitment therapy plus habit reversal for trichotillomania. *Behaviour Research and Therapy, 44*(5), 639–656. doi:10.1016/j.brat.2005.05.006

Zhang, Y., Cui, W., Zhai, Q., Zhang, T., & Wen, X. (2017). N-acetylcysteine ameliorates repetitive/stereotypic behavior due to its antioxidant properties without activation of the canonical Wnt pathway in a valproic acid-induced rat model of autism. *Molecular Medicine Reports, 16*(2), 2233–2240. doi:10.3892/mmr.2017.6787

Zohar, A. H. (1999). The epidemiology of obsessive-compulsive disorder in children and adolescents. *Child and Adolescent Psychiatric Clinics of North America, 8*(3), 445–460.

CHAPTER

7 Posttraumatic Stress Disorder in Individuals With Autism Spectrum Disorder

Connor M. Kerns, Chandler Puhy, Chelsea M. Day, *and* Steven J. Berkowitz

Abstract

This chapter summarizes current scientific knowledge around the prevalence, etiology, and developmental course of posttraumatic stress disorder (PTSD) in children and adults in the general population, and—based on the limited scientific literature—what is indicated for those with autism spectrum disorder (ASD). Challenges related to differential diagnosis and measurement of PTSD in ASD are considered and illustrated via a case example. The chapter concludes with an overview of evidence-based treatments for PTSD in people without ASD, and their potential applications for those with ASD. Overall, the limited research on PTSD in ASD thus far points to increased rates of adversity and related psychopathology, but few evidence-based approaches to assessment or treatment of PTSD and other trauma-related symptoms in this population. Future investigations should consider not only PTSD in ASD but also a broader range of potential sources and symptoms of trauma in ASD and work quickly to identify empirically supported assessments and treatments.

Keywords: posttraumatic stress disorder, autism spectrum disorder, assessment, treatment, comorbidity

Overview

Posttraumatic stress disorder (PTSD) was first recognized in the *Diagnostic and Statistical Manual* (DSM) in 1980, where it certified an important, but at that time controversial, concept that psychopathology could arise from an event outside the individual. Though the influence of environmental stressors on the development and expression of most forms of psychopathology has since become widely acknowledged, thinking continues to evolve regarding the complex relationship of environmental and biological, external and internal factors (Rutter, Moffitt, & Caspi, 2006). Nonetheless, PTSD remains one of the most salient examples of the influence of external stressors on mental health, and thus it is interesting that it has been so understudied relative to other forms of psychopathology in individuals with autism spectrum disorder (ASD). It is plausible that researchers have shied away from the topic in an effort to distance the field from early, damaging theories of ASD, which erroneously attributed the disorder to maternal rejection and neglect of the child (see Volkmar & McPartland, 2014, for a brief history). Nonetheless, it is clear that individuals with ASD suffer from traumatic events, and further, there is much to suggest that they experience a range of adversities and significant stressors, in part related to their diagnosis, that may influence their emotional development and well-being (Berg, Shiu, Acharya, Stolbach, & Msall, 2016; Kerns, Newschaffer, & Berkowitz, 2015). As such, the comorbidity of PTSD and ASD warrants increased empirical attention.

The present chapter summarizes what is known regarding the prevalence, etiology, and developmental course of PTSD in children and adults in the general population, and—based on the limited scientific literature—what is indicated for those with ASD. Challenges related to differential diagnosis and measurement of PTSD are considered and illustrated via a case example. Finally, an overview of evidence-based treatments for PTSD in the general population and their potential applications for those with ASD is offered.

Prevalence and Developmental Course

Prevalence of Potentially Traumatic Events and PTSD in the General Population

More than 60% of U.S. youth experience a potentially traumatic event (PTE) before adulthood (Copeland, Keeler, Angold, & Costello, 2007; Finkelhor, Ormrod, Turner, & Hamby, 2005), the most common being injuries, physical illnesses, serious accidents, and exposure to violence (e.g., abuse or violent death of a loved one or peer; Copeland et al., 2007). Another significant source of PTEs among youth is maltreatment, which occurs in approximately 12.5% of children in the United States (Wildeman et al., 2014). A recent child maltreatment report published by the U.S. Department of Health and Human Services (USDHHS, 2016) indicated that of over 650,000 substantiated reports, 74.8% children experienced neglect, 18.2% physical abuse, and 8.5% sexual abuse. Though rates for various types of child maltreatment typically decline with age, sexual abuse becomes more common in adolescence (USDHHS, 2016). Further, lifetime prevalence of PTE exposure is greater for adults than children (30.5% vs. 12.5%, respectively; Benjet et al., 2016; Centers for Disease Control and Prevention [CDC], 2016), indicating that although PTEs are most prevalent in childhood, they can continue throughout the lifespan.

A more nuanced investigation reveals that rates of PTE exposure vary by sociodemographic variables, such as sex and race/ethnicity. Females typically experience more PTEs in childhood than males (CDC, 2016; Copeland et al., 2007; Costello, Erkanli, Fairbank, & Angold, 2002); however, beginning in adolescence, males appear to have a higher probability of experiencing PTEs compared to females (Tolin & Foa, 2006). Rates also vary by PTE type, with males typically experiencing higher rates of physical abuse, accidents, and injuries and females experiencing higher rates of sexual abuse and intimate partner violence (Benjet et al., 2016; CDC, 2016; Saunders & Adams, 2014). Individuals of a racial or ethnic minority are more likely to experience certain PTEs, with individuals of African American, Hispanic, American Indian, Alaska Native, and multiple racial descent reporting higher rates of victimization than non-Hispanic Whites (Roberts, Gilman, Breslau, Breslau, & Koenen, 2011; USDHHS, 2013).

Unfortunately, exposure to multiple PTEs, as opposed to a single PTE, in childhood is common and associated with greater physical and psychological detriments in adulthood (CDC, 2016; Felitti et al., 1998). As an example, Finkelhor et al. (2005) found that 22% of a national sample of youth ages 2 to 17 years had experienced four or more different kinds of victimization and that such "poly-victimization" was highly associated with traumatic symptomology. Felitti et al. (1998) also found that adults who had four or more adverse childhood experiences, including but not limited to abuse, had a four- to 12-fold increase in risk for alcoholism, drug abuse, depression, and suicidality compared to those who reported only one.

Despite a high rate of PTE exposure in childhood, results from the National Comorbidity Survey Replication—Adolescent Supplement, a nationally representative sample of over 10,000 adolescents ages 13 to 18 years in the United States, found that only 5% of adolescents met criteria for PTSD in their lifetime (Merikangas et al., 2010). Prevalence rates were greater for girls than boys (8% vs. 2.3%) and increased with age (Merikangas et al., 2010; Kessler et al., 2012). Estimated lifetime prevalence of PTSD in the general population of U.S. adults is between 6% and 9% (Sareen, 2014). These rates vary, with those over 65 years reporting lower rates than younger adults (J. M. Cook & Simiola, 2017). In children, PTSD is shown to occur at the highest rates in those exposed to maltreatment (Gabbay, Oatis, Silva, & Hirsch, 2004). In adults, rates appear highest in adults exposed to abduction, being held captive or tortured, and those who experience rape (Breslau, 2012). In general, high rates of PTSD are also observed for individuals exposed to sexual abuse, regardless of age (Chivers-Wilson, 2006; Herbert, Lavoie, & Blais, 2014; Kelley, Weathers, McDevitt-Murphy, Eakin, & Flood, 2009; Maniglio, 2009; Walsh, Koenen, Aiello, Uddin, & Galea, 2014), as well as more assaultive forms of violence (e.g., sexual assault, combat, mugging, etc.) compared to PTEs such as natural disasters and accidents (Breslau, 2012).

Importantly, the types of events that are considered potentially traumatic have evolved and likely will continue to multiply over time, moving beyond an initially limited set of life-threatening experiences (e.g., war, rape), based on research with adults, to include a broader range of stressors, including the observation of another's trauma and more developmentally sensitive events and experiences, such as chronic childhood maltreatment, peer victimization, and bullying (Idsoe, Dyregrov, & Idsoe, 2012). In addition, much research has focused on the negative impact of adverse childhood experiences (ACEs) on health. Studies of ACEs have explored the influence of financial hardship, systemic racism, parent separation/divorce, mental illness, substance abuse, death, and incarceration as well as maltreatment on child development and health. Though not all ACEs may meet the DSM definition of a qualifying traumatic event for PTSD (i.e., an event that involves direct or indirect exposure to death, threatened death, or actual or threatened serious injury or sexual violence), they have been consistently associated with a succession of negative psychological and physical outcomes as well as premature death (Felitti et al., 1998).

Relatedly, PTSD is just one potential outcome of PTEs (Cloitre et al., 2009; A. Cook et al., 2005; van der Kolk, 2005). A variety of other poor health outcomes have been associated with PTEs in childhood including conduct disorder, hyperactivity, aggression, antisocial behavior, behavioral and emotional dysregulation, anxiety, alcoholism, suicide attempts, depression, and substance abuse (Breslau, Lucia, & Alvarado, 2006; CDC, 2016; Cloitre et al., 2009; Copeland et al., 2007; Koenen, Moffitt, Poulton, Martin, & Caspi, 2007; Storr, Ialongo, Anthony, & Breslau, 2007). Some have argued that children exposed to chronic and varied forms of PTEs, who subsequently develop a broad array of psychiatric symptoms, may be more accurately and parsimoniously recognized as suffering from "complex" or "developmental trauma disorder" (Cloitre et al., 2009; A. Cook et al., 2005; van der Kolk, 2005). These conceptualizations and terms have yet to be adopted by the DSM-5; however, complex PTSD will be included in the 11th revision of the World Health Organization's International Classification of Diseases (ICD-11; Karatzias et al., 2017). Long-term physiological outcomes such as arthritis, back and neck pain, headaches, heart disease, lung and liver disease, high blood pressure, asthma, peptic ulcers, stroke, and early death are associated with ACEs (Atwoli, Stein, Koenen, & McLaughlin, 2015; CDC, 2016; Felitti et al., 1998; L. K. Gilbert et al., 2015). Also of note—several studies have found that children who experience extreme early global privation are more likely to demonstrate autistic-like patterns of behavior (Rutter et al., 1999; Hoksbergen et al., 2005). For the purposes of this chapter, we will focus on PTEs and symptoms of PTSD when apropos, but also acknowledge the broader range of adversities that individuals with ASD experience and which may have an impact on their psychological and physical well-being.

Prevalence of PTEs and PTSD in ASD

Population-based studies and literature reviews suggest youth with ASD, particularly those from financially disadvantaged families, experience more childhood adversity than their typically developing (TD) peers, including increased income insufficiency (ASD 40%; TD 23%), parental divorce (ASD 28%; TD 20%), neighborhood violence (ASD 11%; TD 8%), and household mental health (ASD 18%; TD 7%) and substance use problems (ASD 14%; TD 10%; Berg et al., 2016; Rigles, 2017; Kerns, Newschaffer, Berkowitz, & Lee, 2017). Children with ASD also have higher rates of peer victimization and bullying (Hoover & Kaufman, 2018; Zablotsky, Bradshaw, Anderson, & Law, 2013), as well as more physical injuries, extended separations from their parents, and encounters with law enforcement (Crane, Maras, Hawken, Mulcahy, & Memon, 2016; Croen, Najjar, Ray, Lotspeich, & Bernal, 2006; Solomon & Peltz, 2008). How often these experiences meet the DSM criterion of a qualifying traumatic event for PTSD is unclear. Studies of maltreatment risk are less consistent but thus far suggest that abuse and neglect are equally or more common in youth with ASD relative to the general population (Hall-Lande, Hewitt, Mishra, Piescher, & LaLiberte, 2015; Hoover & Kaufman, 2018; Spencer, 2005). Only two studies have attempted to assess rates of traumatic events in ASD, and definitions of trauma have varied. For example, in a small sample of transition-age youth with ASD, Taylor and Gotham (2016) found that 50% experienced at least one life event (i.e., bullying, death of loved one, separation of parents, abuse) that their parents described as "traumatic." Events were considered traumatic based solely on parent observation of their impact on their child rather than the DSM definition. In a study of 69 children and adolescents attending an autism specialty clinic in Istanbul, Mehtar and Mukkades (2011) found that 26% reported a trauma history (defined as witnessing or being a victim of abuse, violence, or traumatic accidents/disasters) on a semi-structured interview assessing for PTSD.

In addition to adversities indicated for TD populations, individuals with ASD may also experience a wider range of stressors and PTEs not captured by existing trauma screeners due to the unique ways in which they perceive and experience the world, and also the systemic challenges and biases they may face (Kerns et al., 2015; Fuld, 2018; Haruvi-Lamdan, Horesh, & Golan, 2018). ASD may increase vulnerability to certain daily stressors (e.g., changes, sensory experiences, feeling misled by others or socially confused) and conversely also protect against trauma by reducing awareness of some events (Kerns et al., 2015; Taylor & Gotham, 2016). Given the continually evolving understanding of what types of events may result in psychiatric illness, including but not limited to PTSD, more comprehensive investigations of traumatic experiences and traumatic responses in ASD are needed.

Research studies analyzing rates of PTSD among youth with ASD are few and an epidemiological investigation of the prevalence of this comorbidity has yet to be conducted. In the limited studies to date, PTSD rates have ranged from 0% to 17% in youth with ASD (Rumball, 2018). Mehtar and Mukaddes (2011) reported that, of 69 youth ages 6 to 18 years with ASD, 18 reported a trauma history, and 12 (17% overall or 67% of those exposed to a traumatic event) met full DSM-IV criteria for PTSD. Youth were patients in an outpatient autism clinic. Though not selected based on their potential trauma history, patients were informed of the study aims prior to participation. As such, it is plausible that those with trauma histories may have been more inclined to participate. Other studies have reported low PTSD prevalence (0% to 3%; de Bruin, Ferdinand, Meester, de Nijs, & Verheij, 2008; Hofvander et al., 2009; Storch et al., 2013; Ung et al., 2013), even among youth with ASD recruited through inpatient psychiatric settings with a history of sexual, physical, or emotional abuse (2.6% PTSD; Brenner et al., 2017). In her review of studies, Rumball (2018) noted that this range of results may, in part, reflect the varied countries, ages, and clinical presentations of study samples. For example, some studies (Storch et al., 2013; Ung et al., 2013; White et al., 2013) focused on youth with anxiety disorders seeking treatment rather than recruiting a broader range of youth with ASD. Further, studies have thus far relied on measures designed and validated for youth without ASD despite the fact that the sensitivity, specificity, reliability, and validity of these measures for individuals with ASD have yet to be examined. Evaluating the validity of these instruments will be critical given that assessing PTSD in ASD is complicated by communication difficulties, overlapping symptoms, and potentially distinct manifestations of traumatic stress in ASD (Kerns et al., 2015; Mehtar & Mukaddes, 2011). Large-scale, population-based studies conducted with validated and developmentally sensitive instruments are needed to obtain accurate rates of PTSD in ASD.

Notably, numerous deleterious outcomes other than PTSD have been noted for PTE-exposed individuals with ASD. For example, risky sexual behaviors, running away from home, suicide attempts, and an increased likelihood of being sexually abusive were prevalent among sexually abused youth with ASD (Walrath, Manteuffel, Sgro, & Pinto-Martin, 2005). Anxiety, depression, attention, and behavior problems were twice as likely in youth with ASD who reported two or more ACEs in the National Survey of Children's Health (NSCH; Kerns, Newschaffer, Berkowitz, & Lee, 2017). Regressions in communication, daily living, socialization, and motor skills were shown in youth with ASD one year after their exposure to an earthquake (Valenti et al., 2012). Brenner and colleagues (2017) found more intrusive thoughts, distressing memories, loss of interest, irritability, and lethargy in hospitalized children with ASD and a history of maltreatment as compared to ASD alone; however, few children (2.6%) received a diagnosis of PTSD. Mehtar and Mukaddes (2011) also found that youth with ASD and a trauma history (with or without PTSD) displayed increases in stereotypic behavior, aggression, distractibility, sleep disorders, agitation, hyperactivity, self-injury, motor mannerisms, loss of self-care skills, and deterioration of imitation and both verbal and nonverbal communication. These studies suggest a potentially broad range of trauma-related reactions in ASD that may include traditional and ASD-related symptoms and which require further investigation to fully understand the impact of trauma on this population.

Other notable limitations in the extant literature include that very few studies have been conducted with adults (Hofvander et al., 2009; Taylor & Gotham, 2016), populations with intellectual impairments (Haruvi-Lamdan et al., 2018), and females on the spectrum (Rumball, 2018). Reliance on caregiver report alone for rates of PTE exposure in some studies may be a source of bias as well (Adams, Fredstron, Duncan, Holleb, & Bishop, 2014; Becker, Hagenberg, Roessner, Woerner, & Rothenberger, 2004). Thus, future research has many gaps to fill in identifying the rates of PTE exposure and PTSD in individuals with ASD, including a fundamental clarification of the range of events and reactions that may reflect PTEs and trauma-related symptoms in this population.

Developmental Course

Individuals of different ages are more susceptible to certain PTEs (USDHHS, 2013) and to developing PTSD given the sequential and hierarchical nature of neurodevelopment (Lubit, Rovine, Defrancisci, & Eth, 2003; Perry, Pollard, Blaicley, Baker, & Vigilante, 1995; Pynoos et al., 2009). Youth with ASD may be particularly vulnerable to the effects of PTE exposure during sensitive periods, given their already taxed neuropsychological systems (Kerns et al., 2015; Wicks, Hjern, Gunnell, Lewis, & Dalman, 2005). PTE exposure during sensitive periods has, moreover, been shown to differentially affect the presentation of PTSD symptoms in early childhood (e.g., reduced exploration or play, seeking physical or emotional proximity to a parent or caregiver, social withdrawal, re-enacting trauma through play, intrusive memories of trauma that may not appear distressing, extreme temper tantrums; American Psychiatric Association, 2013; Pynoos et al., 2009), middle childhood (e.g., emotional dysregulation, regression to an earlier developmental stage; Dunn, Nichimi, Gomez, Powers, & Bradley, 2018; Yule, Udwin, & Murdoch, 1990), and adolescence (e.g., high-risk or thrill-seeking behaviors such as substance abuse; Pynoos et al., 2009). A revised PTSD algorithm has been introduced in the DSM-5 for children under age 6 years to reflect these developmental differences (APA, 2013). For example, as symptoms of avoidance and negative alterations in mood and cognition can be more difficult to detect in young children, the adjusted diagnostic criteria require fewer of these symptoms to be present for this age group (Scheeringa, Zeanah, & Cohen, 2011). Understanding the developmental age of a child with ASD may thus be critical to accurately identifying PTSD symptoms, as younger developmental age may both increase susceptibility to PTSD and differentially affect symptom presentation.

Etiology, Diagnosis, and Assessment

Etiology

The literature suggests that myriad factors and their interplay determine the development of PTSD. The etiology of PTSD has been extensively covered in the neurotypical population and provides a framework for the conceptualization of PTSD in autism. Following a brief review of the stress response system that is thought to underlie PTSD expression, we will consider how factors at multiple levels are thought to increase vulnerability to traumatic symptoms, and their specific relevance in ASD. Specifically, in accordance with a bioecological framework (Bronfenbrenner, 1977), we consider potential risk factors for PTSD related to the individual (genetic vulnerability, neurobiology, psychiatric comorbidity, and symptomology), the microsystem (close contexts including family and school), the mesosystem (interactions between microsystem participants), and the exosystem (economic, educational, and governmental systems) of the individual.

STRESS RESPONSE SYSTEM

In brief, trauma-related disorders are understood to occur when the stress response system, a constellation of reflexive and initially adaptive survival behaviors, becomes dysregulated and functionally impairing (Sherin & Nemeroff, 2011). The stress response system is regulated by the bidirectional interaction of neurobiological and environmental factors (for a comprehensive review see Sherin & Nemeroff, 2011). Specifically, environmental threats are processed by the amygdala, which projects to the hypothalamic–pituitary–adrenal (HPA) axis, where the "fight, flight, or freeze" response is orchestrated by the release of cortisol and other stress hormones. When threat resolves, feedback processes prevent further release of stress hormones and bring arousal back to baseline. Yet, when these systems become taxed, HPA axis dysregulation can occur, negatively affecting other brain systems, and resulting in functional impairment that may in turn evolve into stress-related disorders, such as PTSD.

INDIVIDUAL-LEVEL RISK FACTORS FOR PTSD

Common associated features of ASD may play a role in PTSD risk. Psychiatric comorbidity, anxiety disorders, and intellectual disability are risk factors for both PTEs and subsequent PTSD (Copeland et al., 2007; Hibbard & Desch, 2007; Koenen, Moffitt, Poulton, Martin, & Caspi, 2007; Reiter, Bryen, & Shachar, 2007). Approximately 80% of youth with ASD present with one or more psychiatric comorbidity (Simonoff et al., 2008), with anxiety disorders being among the most common (40%; van Steensel, Bögels, & Perrin, 2011). Approximately 31% of youth with ASD have co-occurring intellectual disability (ID; Baio et al., 2018). In addition, many youth with ASD demonstrate more diffuse difficulties with emotion regulation that may underlie their psychiatric symptoms and also potentially increase PTSD risk (Bardeen, Kumpula, & Orcutt, 2013; Kerns et al., 2015; Mazefsky et al., 2013). Children with mental health difficulties or delayed development may be more likely to be targeted by others. They may also have fewer emotional, cognitive, and social resources available to cope with a traumatic experience (Mansell, Sobsey, & Moskal, 1998).

Core features of ASD may also confer risk for PTSD. Though often associated with ID, communication deficits may particularly increase the likelihood that a child will be targeted (E. H. Cook, Kieffer, Charak, & Leventhal, 1993; Howlin & Clements, 1995). Struggles to verbally communicate, overall, and specifically about emotional content, may also limit the ability of caregivers and clinicians to recognize trauma-related symptoms and subsequently apply (or seek out) evidence-based interventions for PTSD in ASD (Mevissen, Didden, & de Jongh, 2016; Rosen, Connell, & Kerns, 2016). Further, flattened affect and difficulty expressing emotion in ASD may cause symptoms of PTSD to be underestimated, potentially precluding treatment. These social communication deficits in ASD may limit access to social networks that protect against traumatic exposures and facilitate trauma recovery (Ozer, Best, Lipsey, & Weiss, 2003; Schumm, Briggs-Phillips, & Hobfoll, 2006). Beyond social communication deficits, ASD-related cognitive characteristics such as rigidity and difficulty set-shifting (Hill, 2004) may lead to increased rumination and emotion dysregulation, impeding trauma resolution by preventing use of more adaptive cognitions and behaviors, and ultimately increasing PTSD risk (Kerns et al., 2015; Nolen-Hoekseman & Morrow, 1991; Ehlers, Mayou, & Bryant, 2003; Elwood, Hahn, Olatunji, & Williams, 2009; Johnson, 2009). Further work is needed to examine these theories and directly identify specific risk factors for PTSD among individuals with ASD.

Neurobiological and Physiological Risk Factors

Several neurobiological and physiological similarities between ASD and PTSD have also been noted and may warrant further empirical attention. Genetic markers have been found for PTSD-related reductions in neurogenesis, increases in immune function (e.g., Uddin et al., 2010), HPA axis dysregulation (Binder et al., 2008; Kuan et al., 2017; Logue et al., 2015), and dopamine receptor changes (Wolf et al., 2014). Similar alterations in genes associated with these processes have also been identified in ASD (de Krom et al., 2009; J. Gilbert & Man, 2017; Torres, Westover, & Rosenspire, 2012). Research has also found a heightened cortisol spike in response to certain stressors in both autism (e.g., Corbett, Mendoza, Wegelin, Carmean, & Levine, 2008) and PTSD (e.g., Bremner et al., 2003) compared to controls. Repeated stressors can cause cortisol dysregulation and increasing sensitivity to stress that may lower the threshold for development of PTSD (Nemeroff, 2004). Low baseline cortisol specifically has been identified as a risk factor for (Yehuda, McFarlane, & Shalev, 1998), and a result of, PTSD (Wahbeh & Oken, 2013) and has been observed in autism (Ćurin et al., 2003), though not consistently (Taylor & Corbett, 2014).

Potential neurological differences in ASD might also increase PTSD risk. Studies report increased amygdala volume in ASD before adulthood (Groen, Teluij, Buitelaar, & Tendolkar, 2010; Schumann et al., 2004), which could increase threat detection (De Belis et al., 2000) and subsequent risk for PTSD (Pechtel & Pizzagalli, 2011). Impaired activation of the medial prefrontal cortex (mPFC), which helps inhibit emotional reactivity of the amygdala and contributes to fear extinction (Akirav & Maroun, 2007), has also been reported in ASD and could potentially enhance PTSD risk. Though interesting, if and how these areas of neurobiological overlap in ASD and PTSD contribute to the comorbidity of these disorders requires empirical investigation.

FAMILY AND COMMUNITY-LEVEL RISK FACTORS FOR PTSD

Contextual influences on PTSD risk, such as family and school environments (microsystem), their interaction (mesosystem), and social and cultural factors (macrosystem), may also factor into the etiology of PTSD in ASD. Individuals with developmental disorders are considered vulnerable to maltreatment given their increased reliance on caregivers, and caregivers of dually diagnosed children may face particular demands in trying to seek out, secure, and provide the appropriate medical, emotional, and educational supports for their children (Hibbard & Desch, 2007). Many schools are also not equipped to manage the needs of children with ASD (Sharpe & Baker, 2007), and there is a notable dearth of guidelines regarding evidence-based services for children with ASD and PTSD (Kerns et al., 2019). This is concerning given that assessment and treatment of PTSD are less likely to be pursued in schools with reduced resources or without trauma-informed training (Green et al., 2013). Interactions between the family and service organizations have the ability to positively impact recovery, but largely as a result of the family's ability to advocate for services (Taylor, Hodapp, Burke, Waitz-Kudla, & Rabideau, 2017) and the coordination of care (Sobotka, Francis, & Vander Ploeg Booth, 2016). Coordinating therapeutic and educational services is frequently difficult for families of youth with ASD, particularly those with psychiatric comorbidities

(Ahmedani & Hock, 2011; Vohra, Madhavan, Sambamoorthi, & Peter, 2013).

Lastly, the impact of larger economic, policy, and health care systems (e.g., macrosystem) on individuals with ASD should also be considered as a potential factor in their PTSD risk. Behavioral health and developmental disability systems in the United States are not well coordinated, leaving children with ASD and psychiatric difficulties with limited or poorly integrated treatment (Ervin, Williams, & Merrick, 2014; Siegel & Gabriels, 2014). This issue is compounded by a lack of research on evidence-based treatments for PTSD in ASD and the limited effectiveness of many empirically supported treatments, generally, in community settings (Dingfelder & Mandell, 2011). Further, due to a lack of policy initiatives, individuals on the spectrum often experience a major deficit in supports and services once they graduate from high school, suggesting that transition to adulthood may reflect a particularly vulnerable period (Kerns, Roux, Connell, & Shattuck, 2016; McKenzie, Ouellette-Kuntz, Blinkhorn, & Démoré, 2017; Shattuck, Wagner, Narendorf, Sterzing, & Hensley, 2011). Finally, recognition of PTSD may be impeded by diagnostic overshadowing, or a tendency for health professionals to misattribute new or worsening symptoms to ASD instead of another comorbid disorder, such as PTSD (Sizoo & Lobregt, 2016).

SUMMARY

In conclusion, though studies have yet to examine specific predictors of PTSD in individuals with ASD, the notable areas of psychological and neurobiological overlap between the disorders suggest that such investigations are warranted (see also Kerns et al., 2015; Haruvi-Lamden et al., 2018). In addition, the literature suggests there are multiple environmental factors that may also confer unique risk for those with ASD to have traumatic experiences, be traumatized, and develop PTSD.

Diagnosis and Assessment

Diagnosis of PTSD in individuals with ASD is complicated by communication deficits, which may preclude the reporting of PTEs and symptoms, as well as symptom overlap, the potentially distinct manifestation of traumatic stress in ASD, and a lack of measures designed and validated to contend with these issues.

A diagnosis of PTSD, like many emotional disorders, is highly reliant on self-reported distress and problematic behavior. As such, difficulties with verbal communication in ASD and—even in those with fluent speech—in recognizing and conveying emotions may limit or reduce the accuracy of standard self-report measures. Though parent questionnaires and interviews offer a potentially useful, alternative data source to self-report, they also present challenges. Limited verbal and nonverbal communication of emotions in ASD may also make it difficult for caregivers to discern signs of distress in this population, limiting the accuracy of parent-report measures and interviews. Moreover, observers may struggle to recognize the internal struggles of individuals with ASD, given the notable overlap in ASD and PTSD symptomology (e.g., arousal dysregulation, social withdrawal) and the potential for PTSD symptoms to be misconstrued as an unrelated worsening of ASD symptoms or vice versa (see Kerns et al., 2015; Mehtar & Mukaddes, 2011).

Many symptoms of PTSD reflect core or associated characteristics of ASD, making differential diagnosis of this condition difficult. For example, it may be challenging to determine if behavioral avoidance of certain people or situations reflects a traumatic reaction or rather unrelated anxiety, limited social motivation, or a preference to engage in certain repetitive or restricted behaviors and interests in ASD. Similarly, negative alterations of mood, such as difficulties experiencing positive affect, limited interest in activities, social withdrawal, and low mood, may reflect essential characteristics of ASD or a co-occurring mood disorder that may or may not be related to trauma. Though intrusion symptoms (e.g., unwanted upsetting memories, nightmares, flashbacks, emotional or physical reactivity after traumatic reminders) are likely more specific to a diagnosis of PTSD, they may be particularly difficult to discern unless a clear traumatic event can be identified by the observers or described by the individual. Many traumas, such as abuse and neglect, can be difficult to identify particularly in individuals with communication deficits (Mevissen, Lievegoed, Seubert, & Jongh, 2011). As such, to diagnose PTSD in an individual with ASD, it may be especially important to identify a clear traumatic event or events and to demonstrate changes in behavior and functioning that are consistent with PTSD criteria following that event rather than potentially misattributing behavioral avoidance and alterations in arousal, reactivity, and mood to ASD alone. The DSM PTSD criteria for young children may also provide a helpful framework (Scheeringa et al., 2011; APA, 2013) for youth with ASD. These criteria specifically consider the expression of PTSD in individuals with less developed social–emotional and communication skills and may thus be better suited to assess PTSD in some individuals with ASD.

Finally, as noted earlier, there is growing research to suggest that individuals with ASD may manifest trauma via a broader range of behaviors than is currently included within PTSD criteria and which may resemble a worsening of the ASD phenotype (see Kerns et al., 2015). For example, several studies have noted an increase in self-injurious behavior and stereotypies as well as declines in communication and adaptive functioning (Brenner et al., 2017; Mandell, Walrath, Manteuffel, Sgro, & Pinto-Martin, 2005; Mehtar & Mukaddes, 2011; Valenti et al., 2012) in youth with ASD who experience a traumatic event. As in the general population (Copeland et al., 2007), it is likely that a diagnosis of PTSD captures only a fraction of trauma-related symptoms in individuals with ASD. At the same time, clinicians and researchers must also be cautious not to misattribute natural fluctuations in ASD symptomology to trauma.

Given these challenges, the use of existing, standardized measures to assess PTSD in ASD is likely an important and complicated future direction for research. Standardized measures may provide a useful systematic approach to assessing for PTSD symptoms but are less likely to assess trauma-related symptoms outside of PTSD criteria. Existing measures also do not account for the overlap or provide guidance on the differentiation of PTSD and ASD symptoms. Thus far, research studies have primarily relied on the Kiddie Schedule for Affective Disorders and Schizophrenia—Present and Lifetime Version (Mehtar & Mukkades, 2011; Taylor & Gotham, 2016) and the Anxiety Disorders Interview Schedule—IV—Child/Parent Version (ADIS-IV-C/P; Storch et al., 2013; Ung et al., 2013; White et al., 2013; Wood et al., 2009; 2015) to assess PTSD in ASD. With one exception, evaluations of the reliability and validity of these measures in assessing PTSD in ASD have yet to be conducted. Ung and colleagues (2013) reported excellent interrater agreement on the diagnosis of PTSD using the ADIS-IV-C/P in a sample of youth with ASD seeking treatment for anxiety; however, the base rate of PTSD in the sample was not reported, limiting the conclusions that can be drawn from this finding. Further, though Kerns and colleagues (2017) reported good reliability and validity for an adapted version of the ADIS-IV for ASD (the ADIS/Autism Spectrum Addendum), they did not evaluate the psychometrics of the PTSD module. Similarly, no studies have reported on the validity of PTSD questionnaires for individuals with ASD, though some have been utilized in case reports (see Rumball, 2018, for a review). Valid measurement of PTSD in individuals with ASD thus represents a critical first step to advancing clinical research and practice in this area.

Case Example

In the context of the dearth of standardized measures and approaches, a case example of a child with ASD and a diagnosis of PTSD is offered. As illustrated, particular care is taken by the examiner to (a) discuss Jack's symptoms of PTSD within the context of his development and history of ASD, (b) demonstrate clear changes in Jack's behavior and functioning since the trauma, (c) gather and assess for consistency in reports across observers and environments, and (d) assess for both classic PTSD symptomology using a standardized measure and other signs of stress and significant behavioral and functional deterioration since the trauma.

Jack: A Young Man with ASD Who Experienced a Potentially Traumatic Car Accident

Presenting concern. Jack is a 13-year-old boy who was diagnosed with ASD at age 22 months. He was brought for an evaluation 6 months after he witnessed a hit and run of his mother and 10-year-old sister as they were walking across the street from their house. Jack's sister was killed as she was flung through the air and landed on her head approximately 3 feet from Jack. According to witnesses, her skull was cracked open, and she was unrecognizable. His mother was seriously injured and was hospitalized for 3 months and subsequently required inpatient rehabilitation services. She returned home 1 month ago and still requires a walker and assistance.

Before meeting Jack, all his evaluations and treatment records were requested, along with reports of changes in his behavior seen by school personnel, family, and other important individuals in Jack's life since the car accident. Though it is always useful to obtain records and collateral information, it is especially useful to have records prior to assessing an individual with ASD who has been exposed to a PTE. Understanding Jack's baseline functioning, symptomatology, and, if possible, changes in behavior subsequent to the PTE contributes to a more effective evaluation. However, the impact of this experience on Jack's parents made it exceedingly unlikely that they would have an accurate report of the effects of the PTE on Jack's symptoms and behavior.

Psychological and developmental history. Jack was the first child born to his parents, and his family lived in a suburban area. His father is an engineer and his mother was a school teacher prior to the accident. His deceased sister was reported not to have any emotional or developmental issues and was well liked and a good student. Jack's mother had a difficult pregnancy with him with frequent emesis and was eventually hospitalized due to weight loss. She denied in utero exposure to nicotine, alcohol, illicit substances, psychotropic medications, or opioid medications. Jack was delivered at 41 weeks and was determined to be a healthy baby and discharged after 48 hours.

Reports indicated that Jack had history of broad developmental delays. He did not babble until approximately 10 or 11 months and made little eye contact. He sometimes enjoyed physical contact but at other times refused to be cuddled and would squirm in his parents' arms. He was irritable, cried frequently, and was a poor sleeper. He preferred a bottle to breast-feeding and to this day is a picky eater. Currently, he will only eat noodles with butter, peanut butter and jelly sandwiches, and the occasional hot dog. He will not eat fruit or vegetables and his diet is supplemented with vitamins. He was diagnosed with ASD at 22 months and was referred for early intervention. He was subsequently placed in an applied behavioral analysis (ABA) program with intensive in-home speech therapy, occupational therapy, behavioral therapy, and parent education and support from 22 months to 3 years of age. He was then referred to a specialized center for children with ASD, where he attended school from pre-K through fifth grade. There he received daily speech therapy, twice-a-week occupational therapy, and daily behavioral treatment in a small classroom with an assigned aide. He did not speak his first words until age 26 months, began speaking in phrases around age 4, and spoke in full sentences at age 5.5. Jack's speech improved significantly with early intervention; however, prosody and pragmatic use of language have remained a problem. Jack was transitioned to an inclusion classroom with a one-to-one aide. He generally did well with a lot of support and was removed for reading and math support. There were also reports of echolalia that resolved approximately 3 years ago.

Despite treatment, Jack continued to show little interest in others and made fleeting eye contact unless prompted. In general, Jack engaged in neither functional nor symbolic play. He had been able to engage in play if invited, but only marginally, and did not participate in imaginative play. There were few efforts to engage in activities with others or to share interests and excitement with others. Currently, he does not engage with peers unless part of a structured activity, but he does enjoy watching sporting events and was a "manager" for the football team. Jack has a history of unusual sensitivities (he could not tolerate combing or brushing his hair or tags on clothes) and high pain threshold. He demonstrates unusual sensory interests such as feeling textures repetitively, sweet scents, and prolonged examination of moving objects. He also has a low frustration tolerance and difficulty with transitions. Jack demonstrated stereotypical movements in early childhood, such as hand flapping and rocking; however, they had primarily resolved by adolescence.

Jack was also reported to be hyperactive from early on. Jack had difficulties with change in routine and transitions. Inattention, distractibility, and hyperactivity were evident from preschool on, where he struggled with following instructions in school, often left his seat, and required constant reminders and redirection from teachers. Although Jack was diagnosed with attention deficit hyperactivity disorder (ADHD), combined type, at age 4 years by a psychologist, no pharmacological treatment was recommended at the time. Behavioral interventions in a special education setting significantly improved symptoms of hyperactivity, distractibility, and aggressive behavior, but they continued to be problematic. He was prescribed stimulant medication but became increasingly irritable and labile and had significant appetite suppression, such that the medication was stopped.

Jack's most recent psychological evaluation was conducted 2 years prior to this evaluation by his school district. It supported an ASD classification and revealed a full-scale IQ of 74 with relative strengths in visual spatial skills. Jack also showed poor adaptive skills and delayed socioemotional development.

Per his grandmother's and teacher's reports, Jack never displayed aggressive or self-injurious behavior until the last several months when he began head-banging and putting his hands around his neck in apparent attempts to choke himself. He also recently experienced a re-emergence of several previously resolved symptoms of ASD, including frequent immediate echolalia and body rocking, both of which began approximately 2 months following the accident. In addition to these behaviors, Jack has recently become easily frustrated and oppositional both at home and in the school setting and his academic performance has been declining. In just the past few months, he has refused to complete schoolwork and requires a great deal of support to participate in any school activities including his previously beloved involvement with the football team. He has also been noted to talk to himself more frequently and to laugh for no apparent reason.

Medical history. Jack has a seizure disorder for which he is prescribed levetiracetam (Keppra). He has been seizure free on this medication. Jack has had frequent infections throughout his life and had recurrent otitis media and required myringotomy tube surgery at 2.5 years of age. He has been healthier in the past several years. There is a history of anxiety disorders on both sides of the family and Jack's maternal first cousin was diagnosed with ASD at 18 months.

Social history. The family is upper-middle class and has a good support network in the community. Both paternal grandmother and maternal grandparents live in the area and have been of help to the family since Jack's birth. The maternal grandmother has been very supportive since the accident and she provided the majority of the home observations.

Mental status examination. Jack appeared his age. He was of average height and build and was well groomed and wearing age-appropriate attire. Although he had no dysmorphic features, his eyes were close-set and he had uneven teeth and evidence of a great deal of dental work with multiple crowns and fillings. Jack's speech was generally nasal at times, oddly intonated, and difficult to understand. Sentences were underdeveloped, but he was able to communicate his needs. No abnormal movements or tics were observed, although he appeared to be hyperactive and showed a limited attention span. He made few attempts to initiate or maintain social interaction with others, was inconsistently responsive to social overtures by the examiner, demonstrated poor eye contact, and focused on the paintings on the wall. He responded to yes-or-no but not open-ended questions from the examiner or attempts at conversation that did not involve a direct question. In general, his responses were brief and consisted of one or two words.

Jack described his mood as "fine," though his affect could be best described as labile. Although it was often constricted, he would often smile and laugh in a loud, highly repetitive manner. He was fidgety and unable to sit still, and when the accident was raised he rocked in his chair. He knew the date but was unsure of the why he was meeting the examiner. He was logical and goal directed; there were no delusions, ideas of reference, obsessions, or perceptual disturbances elicited. He denied suicidal or homicidal ideation, intent, or plans. He demonstrated poor insight into his emotional state and reduced judgment. For example, he was unable to provide appropriate responses to situations (e.g., finding a wallet on the street).

During the evaluation, Jack refused to discuss the accident, the death of his sister, or his mother's injuries or absence. Yet, he became emotionally dysregulated when the accident was mentioned in front of him.

PTSD symptoms. Jack denied any changes in behavior or mood since the incident and denied any somatic symptoms such as head or stomach pain or discomfort. The Child PTSD Symptom Scale (CPSS; Foa et al., 2001) was administered to Jack to screen for classic posttraumatic symptomatology. Although the examiner described and elaborated the meaning of each item, Jack denied having any symptoms; however, when the examiner defined the index event, Jack began rocking and laughing inappropriately. He acted similarly when asked about nightmares and intrusive thoughts. In general, Jack was dysregulated throughout the administration of the scale, suggesting elevated distress and avoidance of the scale content.

During the clinical interview with Jack's father, he confirmed changes in Jack's mood, aggression, self-injury, and engagement that had been reported by Jack's grandmother and the school. He confirmed that Jack demonstrated more rocking, more difficulty with transitions, and more oppositionality since the accident. He also agreed that Jack laughed more frequently and at inappropriate times since the accident. He thought that Jack's appetite was worse but did not think he had lost weight. He also reported that Jack had more difficulty sleeping and that he often was up at all hours of the night.

Based on the clear and consistent reports across caregivers and school regarding Jack's behavioral and symptomatic changes since the accident, the examiner gave Jack the diagnosis of PTSD.

Information on Evidence-Based Treatment

PTSD Treatments for Typically Developing Adults

Efficacious psychotherapies for adults with PTSD include cognitive behavioral approaches, including cognitive therapy and prolonged exposure therapy, and eye movement desensitization and reprocessing (EMDR; Watts et al., 2013). Several meta-analyses indicate that mean effect sizes for cognitive behavioral therapy (CBT) range from medium to large in PTSD symptom reduction in adults, with larger effects being reported in studies using waitlist as opposed to active control groups (Gutermann et al., 2016; Frost et al., 2014; Watts et al., 2013), more robust research methods (Gutermann et al., 2016; Newman et al., 2014), and individual as opposed to group treatments (Gutermann et al., 2016; Taylor & Harvey, 2010; Watts et al., 2013) and in women versus men (Watts et al., 2013). In addition, several studies of EMDR have also yielded reductions in PTSD symptoms with large effect sizes (Gutermann et al., 2016; Watts et al., 2013; Seidler & Wagner, 2006); however, some reviews have concluded that research support for CBT is more robust and the contribution of the eye movement component to EMDR has been debated (Lee & Cuijpers, 2013; Seidler & Wagner, 2006).

PTSD Treatments for Typically Developing Children

EMDR and CBT are also among the most widely studied treatments for PTSD in children. In contrast to adult CBT, trauma-focused CBT (TF-CBT) is a family-focused treatment in which parents or caregivers participate equally with their traumatized child or adolescent. In addition, the trauma-specific components of TF-CBT include creating a trauma narrative and using in vivo exposures (Cohen & Mannarino, 2015). In their meta-analysis, Silverman and colleagues (2008) concluded that TF-CBT met the "well-established" criteria for efficacious treatment according to the Task Force on Psychosocial Interventions. In a more recent meta-analysis, Morina, Koerssen, and Pollet (2016) found that TF-CBT produced a large posttreatment effect size in reducing PTSD symptoms when compared to waitlist controls (g = 1.44) and a medium posttreatment effect size in reducing PTSD symptoms (g = 0.56) when compared to active control conditions. Numerous studies have demonstrated the efficacy and effectiveness of TF-CBT in treating youth exposed to a variety of PTEs, including sexual abuse (Cohen, Deblinger, Mannarino, & Steer, 2004; Deblinger, Mannarino, Cohen, & Steer, 2006), natural disasters, domestic violence, and other, acute single-incident PTEs (Scheeringa et al., 2011). Studies suggest that TF-CBT is effective in diverse settings (Jensen et al., 2014; O'Donnell et al., 2014) and populations (National Child Traumatic Stress Network [NCTSN], 2012). TF-CBT has yet to be studied in experimental trials in youth with ASD; however, potential applications for this population are discussed by Grosso (2012).

Several randomized controlled trials have also found that EMDR is associated with reductions in PTSD symptoms with medium effect sizes in children (Ahmad, Larsson, & Sundeline-Wahlsten, 2007; Kemp, Drummond, & McDermott, 2010; Rodenburg, Benjamin, de Roos, Meijer, & Stams, 2009). De Roos and colleagues (2011, 2017) reported comparable effect sizes for EMDR and CBT in reducing symptoms of PTSD, depression, anxiety, and behavior problems in children (EMDR: d = 0.88 to 1.62; CBT: d = 0.62 to 1.40; de Roos et al., 2011, 2017). Like TF-CBT, EMDR has been found to significantly reduce PTSD symptoms in children ages 4 to 18 years (Rodenburg et al., 2009) exposed to a variety of PTEs, including disasters (Brown et al., 2017), automobile accidents (Verardo & Cioccolanti, 2017), and other single-incident traumas (de Roos et al., 2017), demonstrating its applicability to a wide range of youth.

PTSD Treatment in ASD

Research on PTSD interventions in ASD to date have been limited to case studies exploring the feasibility and potential effectiveness of different psychological and pharmacological approaches in ASD. One study (Carrigan & Allez, 2017) described the application of 12-session cognitive therapy for PTSD in a 26-year-old man with ASD and ID who demonstrated significant symptoms of PTSD 3 years following a violent sexual assault. The therapist utilized elements of Ehlers and Clark's cognitive approach (Ehlers, Clark, Hackmann, Mcmanus, & Fennell, 2005) with only minimal adaptations, such as using simpler language and greater explanation of metaphors. Following treatment and at 6-month follow-up, the patient demonstrated significant reductions in intrusion and avoidance symptoms on the Revised Child Impact of Events Scale (CRIES-8; selected due to the young man's young mental age; Yule, 1997), suggesting the potential of this approach for verbal adults on the spectrum.

In addition, several other case studies have described the application of EMDR protocols to reduce PTSD in children and adults with ASD. Ipci, Inci, Ardiç, and Ercan (2017) provided a brief case report of a 6-year-old boy with high-functioning ASD and comorbid obsessive-compulsive disorder, selective mutism, and PTSD following a severe traffic accident. They noted improvement in mood, expressive language, compulsive behaviors, communication, and play following EMDR administered alongside psychotropic medication (aripiprazole); however, few details were provided regarding the length and content of treatment or the measurement of PTSD symptoms. Further, the effects of EMDR were potentially confounded by the use of a psychotropic medication. Another more rigorous case study by Kosatka and Ona (2014) documented a reduction of PTSD symptoms as measured by the PTSD Checklist (Weathers, Litz, Herman, Huska, & Keane, 1993) in a 21-year-old woman with high-functioning ASD and a history of peer victimization, including physical abuse, following eight sessions of EMDR, administered using standard procedures (Shapiro, 2001). This case study illustrates more promising results for EMDR in ASD populations, but the generalizability of these results and effectiveness of EMDR for those with ASD remain unclear. Promisingly, a larger study assessing the efficacy of EMDR in ASD populations is underway (Sizoo & Lobregt, 2016).

Mevissen and colleagues (2011) also published a paper detailing EMDR treatment of four individuals with ASD and/or ID. One 7-year-old girl with ASD and comorbid borderline ID received four sessions of EMDR (adapted into a storytelling method due to cognitive, emotional, and communication levels) that successfully decreased disturbing thoughts, anger, and depressive symptoms and increased positive mood and relaxation. Three other individuals ages 11 to 53 years with mild to moderate levels of ID were treated with two to 13 sessions of EMDR for exposure to a variety of PTEs and showed positive results in decreasing avoidance behavior, anger outbursts, somatic complaints, sleep problems, behavioral problems, panic attacks, and compulsive behaviors, and increasing positive affect, independence, and social relationships. Each of these treatments included numerous recommended adaptations to EMDR, including using caregivers as co-therapists or supports in reinforcing positive behaviors, simplifying language, using visual cues or physical gestures rather than abstract language, and using a directive attitude toward the client. That this treatment was easily adapted to each client's cognitive, emotional, and developmental level shows promise in its applicability to ASD populations. Several other additional case studies have utilized other psychotherapeutic interventions and pharmacological interventions for PTSD in individuals on the spectrum but are difficult to interpret given their limited scientific rigor (E. H. Cook et al., 1993; Harley, Williams, Zamora, & Lakatos, 2014; Ryan, 1994; Trelles Thorne, Khinda, & Coffey, 2015).

Overall, though existing case studies offer potential insights for future research regarding the approaches and adaptations that might be utilized to reduce PTSD symptoms in individuals with ASD, they cannot speak to the efficacy of these approaches. Studies of both psychosocial and pharmacological interventions for PTSD in ASD with rigorous, experimental designs and validated measures are needed to advance clinical research and practice in this area.

Potential Adaptations to CBT for PTSD in ASD: Drawing From the Clinical Literature and Empirically Supported Treatments for Anxiety in ASD

Although no experimental trials have been completed for PTSD interventions in ASD populations, research detailing empirically supported treatments for other anxiety disorders in ASD and other developmentally delayed populations may provide a valuable starting point for tailoring PTSD interventions for individuals with ASD. Particularly, CBT has been successfully adapted to treat anxiety disorders in children with ASD, with two meta-analyses supporting the efficacy of these adapted programs (Sukhodolsky, Bloch, Panza, & Reichow, 2013; Ung, Selles, Small, & Storch, 2015). Studies of CBT for anxiety and depression in adolescents and adults with ASD are less robust, but also promising (Kerns et al., 2016). The adaptations of CBT used in these studies might also be used to improve engagement, comprehension, and efficacy of TF-CBT intervention for those with ASD. In addition, one mixed-methods pilot study of TF-CBT treating PTSD in adults with ID has shown that TF-CBT is feasible, is acceptable, and has the potential to reduce symptoms of complex PTSD in this population (Kroese et al., 2016), underscoring its potential applicability to individuals with ASD and ID. This study also provided suggestions for improving the applicability and effectiveness of the protocol for individuals with a developmental disorder. Further, the National Institute for Health and Care Excellence (NICE, 2013) in the United Kingdom published a paper summarizing different ways professionals can provide support, treatment, and help for individuals with ASD, including several guidelines for adapting CBT for anxiety disorders in ASD. Charlton, Kliethermes, Tallant, Taverne, and Tishelman (2004) also put forth several recommendations for treatment of PTSD in ASD as part of the National Child Traumatic Stress Network Adapted Trauma Treatment Standards Work Group. Finally, Grosso (2012) offered specific recommendations for implementing TF-CBT with children with developmental disabilities. A summary of the adaptations recommended by these papers and utilized in relevant case studies is provided in Table 7.1. Though potentially helpful, these treatment strategies have not yet been evaluated empirically in individuals with ASD and PTSD and will require well-executed clinical trials to establish an evidence base.

In sum, although no empirically supported treatments currently exist for PTSD in ASD populations, work is underway to evaluate adaptations of various empirically supported treatments (i.e., CBT, EMDR) for ASD. Nonetheless, case studies, clinical

Table 7.1. Observed Challenges and Proposed Adaptations When Treating PTSD in ASD Using CBT and EMDR Approaches

Potential Challenges Working With ASD Populations	Proposed Psychotherapeutic Adaptations	Proposed By
General recommendations	Extend treatment via session duration and overall number of sessions	Beebe and Risi (2003)
	Use a more directive approach/attitude	Anderson and Morris (2005; Mevissen et al. (2011)
	Instill structure as well as small, routine, and achievable goals and pleasurable activities in daily life to increase behavioral activation	Kerns et al. (2016)
	For children/adolescents and, as appropriate, young adults, include parents in sessions to promote generalization of skills	Kerns et al. (2016); Moree and Davis (2010); Grosso (2012)
	Use flexible and creative approaches to explain concepts and understand the client's perspective and timeframe for acquiring skills	Kerns et al. (2016)
	Support executive functioning by creating routines, reminders, and checklists	Kerns et al. (2016)
Concrete thinking	Explain metaphors	Carrigan and Allez (2017)
	Use simple and direct language	Moree and Davis (2010)
	Use concrete terms/concepts	Charlton et al. (2004); Kerns et al. (2016)
Higher sensitivity to/ hesitation with in vivo exposures	Focus on and teach concrete skills for managing angry outbursts and rumination	Carrigan and Allez (2017)
	Use very gradual exposure	Grosso (2012)
	Include caregivers in sessions when appropriate to decrease avoidance	National Institute for Health and Care Excellence (2013)
Metacognitive deficiencies (e.g., identifying/labeling emotions and cognitions)	Greater use of both written and visual information; use of storytelling to facilitate EMDR	National Institute for Health and Care Excellence (2013); Moree and Davis (2010); Mevissen et al. (2011)
	Present one concept at a time; speak clearly and concisely; avoid speaking too quickly	Charlton et al. (2004)
	Additional emotion recognition training	National Institute for Health and Care Excellence (2013)
	Provide psychoeducation about the prevalence and interaction of comorbid disorder(s) with ASD for parents and, when appropriate, teens and adults	Kerns et al. (2016)

(continued)

Table 7.1. Continued

Potential Challenges Working With ASD Populations	Proposed Psychotherapeutic Adaptations	Proposed By
Social engagement challenges/response to others/one-sided conversations	As possible and appropriate, schedule conjoint sessions with caregivers throughout treatment	Grosso (2012); Kerns et al. (2016)
	Supplement with interactive, multimodal teaching methods (e.g., drawing and playing materials)	Charlton et al. (2004); Kerns et al. (2016)
	Incorporate a social skills module	Attwood (1999); Moree and Davis (2010)
Difficulties identifying symptoms of trauma separate from other existing problems	Train caregivers to recognize behavioral changes as potential signs of trauma	Charlton et al. (2004)
Externalizing symptoms (e.g., defiance, disobedience, aggression, rule or law breaking, etc.)	Target these symptoms before beginning trauma-specific therapies (e.g., TF-CBT)	Cohen et al. (2004)
	Offer regular breaks	National Institute for Health and Care Excellence (2013)
Restricted interests/ engagement in sessions	Incorporate special interests into treatment to increase engagement; this has been discussed in both CBT and EMDR case studies	Kerns et al. (2016); Moree and Davis (2010); National Institute for Health and Care Excellence (2013); Brand Flu (2012)
Dependence on numerous caregivers/providers	Include additional caregivers in sessions	Grosso (2012); Charlton et al. (2004)
	Coordinate communication between caregivers/providers in different settings (e.g., at home, school, work, etc.)	Kerns et al. (2016)
Sensory differences	Utilize an approach (e.g., self-tapping in EMDR) that matches the individual's comfort level with physical contact and potential sensory sensitivities	Brand Flu (2012)

ASD, autism spectrum disorder; CBT, cognitive behavioral therapy; EMDR, eye movement desensitization and reprocessing; PTSD, posttraumatic stress disorder; TF-CBT, trauma-focused cognitive behavioral therapy.

experience, and empirically supported interventions for reducing anxiety in ASD may provide some potentially useful strategies for practitioners currently supporting youth and adults with ASD and trauma as well as clarify potential future directions for treatment research.

Summary and Future Directions

In a recent multisite study of multidisciplinary ASD providers (N = 673), over 50% reported screening and treating trauma-related symptoms in their patients or students with ASD (Kerns et al., 2019). At the same time, over 75% reported that trauma screening is a needed service for youth with ASD and that a lack of training in trauma-related assessment and treatment were barriers to offering this service. These findings suggest a clear need for evidence-based practice guidelines regarding the assessment and treatment of PTSD as well as other trauma-related symptoms in youth with ASD.

In this chapter we provide an overview of the prevalence, etiology, developmental course, and treatment of PTSD both in the general population and based on the limited literature in individuals with ASD. Where research has yet to be conducted—for example, around the precise risk factors associated with PTSD, the psychometric properties of trauma measures, and the efficacy of trauma-focused psychotherapies in ASD—we have highlighted how findings from research with non-ASD populations may inform and guide future research. Overall, the limited research on PTSD in ASD to date points to increased rates of adversity and related psychopathology in this population, but few evidence-based approaches to assessment or treatment. A growing body of research suggests that peer victimization and other adverse childhood experiences are more common in individuals with versus without ASD and associated with a range of co-occurring psychiatric symptoms and functional impairments. Studies on maltreatment and traumatic events (e.g., adverse events described as traumatic by the individual or caregiver) and PTSD in ASD are few, but also suggest equal or enhanced risk in ASD relative to the general population.

Much of this chapter has focused on and aimed to inform future directions for research on PTSD and ASD. More research is needed on the comorbidity of these conditions and will need to contend with numerous challenges related to the reporting and measurement of PTEs as well as the differential diagnosis and assessment of PTSD and ASD symptoms. Particularly, individuals with ASD may be exposed to more PTEs, in part due to the characteristics of ASD (e.g., communication difficulties, social differences, and naiveté). They may be more likely to experience a distinct array of stressors as traumatic (e.g., stigma, marginalization, chronic social confusion, social isolation, sensory overload; Kerns et al., 2015). They may also manifest symptoms of trauma in a manner distinct from classic PTSD criteria and difficult to disentangle from the core and related symptoms of ASD.

Future research on PTSD and ASD will need to consider how PTEs and trauma-related symptoms in ASD are defined and how they can be validly measured. Taking a broader view of PTEs and trauma-related symptoms in the selection and development of research measures as well as the conceptualization of trauma in ASD going forward may help ensure that the prevalence and impact of trauma exposure is not underestimated in this population. Measures that capture not only classic PTSD symptoms in ASD but also a broader array of trauma-related symptoms will be needed to reach this goal (see also Kerns et al., 2015). Relatedly, whether DSM criteria for PTSD should be adjusted as they have been for young children to better capture those who experience trauma-related psychopathology but do not meet the classic criteria should be considered. Future research will need to contend with the difficulties but also the importance of assessing PTEs and symptoms in individuals with more severe communication impairments. Notably, extant studies have primarily relied on caregiver or observer reports. Multi-informant and multimethod approaches to trauma assessment are recommended and likely to generate more complete and accurate results.

Finally, research is needed to examine the acceptability, feasibility, and effectiveness of trauma-specific treatments for children and adults with ASD. Though studies suggest that cognitive behavioral approaches may be successfully adapted for youth with ASD and intact intellectual abilities, specific adaptations of TF-CBT, other modalities of CBT, and EMDR have yet to be empirically evaluated in ASD. Approaches for working with individuals with ASD and intellectual disability are also needed and may be informed by work assessing and treating PTSD in individuals with intellectual disability (Mevissen et al., 2011, 2016). Finally, very few studies have examined the use of pharmacological interventions for PTSD in ASD. Understanding the impact of stressful and traumatic experiences on individuals with ASD and providing effective treatment is likely a next essential endeavor for this field.

References

Adams, R. E., Fredstrom, B. K., Duncan, A. W., Holleb, L. J., & Bishop, S. L. (2014). Using self- and parent-reports to test the association between peer victimization and internalizing symptoms in verbally fluent adolescents with ASD. *Journal of Autism and Developmental Disorders, 44*(4), 861–872. doi:10.1007/s10803-013-1938-0

Ahmad, A., Larsson, B., & Sundelin-Wahlsten, V. (2007). EMDR treatment for children with PTSD: Results of a randomized controlled trial. *Nordic Journal of Psychiatry, 61*(5), 349–354. doi:10.1080/08039480701643464.

Ahmedani, B. K., & Hock, R. M. (2012). Health care access and treatment for children with co-morbid autism and psychiatric conditions. *Social Psychiatry and Psychiatric Epidemiology, 47*(11), 1807–1814. doi:10.1007/s00127-012-0482-0

Akirav, I., & Maroun, M. (2007). The role of the medial prefrontal cortex–amygdala circuit in stress effects on the extinction of fear. *Neural Plasticity, 2007*, 1–11. doi:10.1155/2007/30873

American Psychiatric Association. (2013). *The diagnostic and statistical manual of mental disorders* (5th ed.). Washington, DC: Author.

Anderson, S., & Morris, J. (2005). Cognitive behaviour therapy for people with Asperger syndrome. *Behavioural and Cognitive Psychotherapy, 34*(3), 293. doi:10.1017/s1352465805002651

Attwood, T. (1999). Modifications to cognitive behaviour therapy to accommodate the cognitive profile of people with Asperger's syndrome. Retrieved from http://www.tonyattwood.com.au/paper2.htm

Atwoli, L., Stein, D. J., Koenen, K. C., & McLaughlin, K. A. (2015). Epidemiology of posttraumatic stress disorder: Prevalence, correlates and consequences. *Current Opinion in Psychiatry, 28*, 307–311. doi:10.1097/YCO.0000000000000167

Baio, J., Wiggins, L., Christensen, D. L., Maenner, M. J., Daniels, J., Warren, Z., . . . Durkin, M. S. (2018). Prevalence of autism spectrum disorder among children aged 8 years—Autism and Developmental Disabilities Monitoring Network, 11 Sites, United States, 2014. *Morbidity and Mortality Weekly Report:*

Surveillance Summaries, 67(6), 1. Retrieved from http://www.jstor.org.ezproxy2.library.drexel.edu/stable/24806108

Bardeen, J. R., Kumpula, M. J., & Orcutt, H. K. (2013). Emotion regulation difficulties as a prospective predictor of posttraumatic stress symptoms following a mass shooting. *Journal of Anxiety Disorders, 27*(2), 188–196. doi:10.1016/j.janxdis.2013.01.003

Becker, A., Hagenberg, N., Roessner, V., Woerner, W., & Rothenberger, A. (2004). Evaluation of the self-reported SDQ in a clinical setting: Do self-reports tell us more than ratings by adult informants? *European Child and Adolescent Psychiatry, 13*(Suppl 2), 17–24. doi:10.1007/s00787-004-2004-4

Beebe, D. W., & Risi, S. (2003). Treatment of adolescents and young adults with high-functioning autism or Asperger syndrome. In M. A. Reinecke, F. M. Dattilio, & A. Freeman (Eds.), *Cognitive therapy with children and adolescents: A casebook for clinical practice* (2nd ed., pp. 369–401. New York, NY: Guilford.

Benjet, C., Bromet, E., Karam, E. G., Kessler, R. C., McLaughlin, K. A., Ruscio, A. M., . . . Koenen, K. C. (2016). The epidemiology of traumatic event exposure worldwide: Results from the World Mental Health Survey Consortium. *Psychological Medicine, 46*(2), 327–343. doi:10.1017/S0033291715001981

Berg, K. L., Acharya, K., Shiu, C. S., & Msall, M. E. (2018). Delayed diagnosis and treatment among children with autism who experience adversity. *Journal of Autism and Developmental Disorders, 48*(1), 45–54. doi:10.1007/s10803-017-3294-y

Berg, K. L., Shiu, C. S., Acharya, K., Stolbach, B. C., & Msall, M. E. (2016). Disparities in adversity among children with autism spectrum disorder: A population-based study. *Developmental Medicine & Child Neurology, 58*(11), 1124–1131. doi:10.1111/dmcn.13161

Binder, E. B., Bradley, R. G., Liu, W., Epstein, M. P., Deveau, T. C., Mercer, K. B., . . . Ressler, K. J. (2008). Association of FKBP5 polymorphisms and childhood abuse with risk of posttraumatic stress disorder symptoms in adults. *JAMA, 299*(11), 1291–1305. doi:10.1001/jama.299.11.1291

Bitsika, V., Sharpley, C. F., Andronicos, N. M., Agnew, L. L., & Mills, R. (2015). Which aspects of sensory features are associated with elevated cortisol concentrations in boys with an autism spectrum disorder? *Journal of Developmental and Physical Disabilities, 27*(5), 661–675. doi:10.1007/s10882-015-9442-4

Bomyea, J., Risbrough, V., & Lang, A. J. (2012). A consideration of select pre-trauma factors as key vulnerabilities in PTSD. *Clinical Psychology Review, 32*(7), 630–641. doi:10.1016/j.cpr.2012.06.008

Brand Flu, R. L. (2012). P-267—Tap, tap, tap—the usefulness of EMDR on kids on the autism spectrum. *European Psychiatry, 27*, 1–1. doi:10.1016/S0924-9338(12)74434–6

Bremner, J. D., Vythilingam, M., Vermetten, E., Adil, J., Khan, S., Nazeer, A., . . . Charney, D. S. (2003). Cortisol response to a cognitive stress challenge in posttraumatic stress disorder (PTSD) related to childhood abuse. *Psychoneuroendocrinology, 28*(6), 733–750. doi:10.1016/S0306-4530(02)00067–7

Brenner, J., Pan, Z., Mazefsky, C., Smith, K. A., Gabriels, R., & the Autism and Developmental Disorders Inpatient Research Collaborative (ADDIRC). (2017). Behavioral symptoms of reported abuse in children and adolescents with autism spectrum disorder in inpatient settings. *Journal of Autism and Developmental Disorders, 48*(11), 3727–3735. doi:10.1007/s10803-017-3183-4.

Breslau, N. (2012). Epidemiology of posttraumatic stress disorder in adults. In J. G. Beck & D. M. Sloan (Eds.), *The Oxford handbook of traumatic stress disorders* (pp. 84–140). New York, NY: Oxford University Press.

Breslau, N., Lucia, V. C., & Alvarado, G. F. (2006). Intelligence and other predisposing factors in exposure to trauma and posttraumatic stress disorder. *Archives of General Psychiatry, 63*(11), 1238. doi:10.1001/archpsyc.63.11.1238

Britton, J. C., Phan, K. L., Taylor, S. F., Fig, L. M., & Liberzon, I. (2005). Corticolimbic blood flow in posttraumatic stress disorder during script-driven imagery. *Biological Psychiatry, 57*, 832–840. doi:10.1016/j.biopsych.2004.12.025

Bronfenbrenner, U. (1977). Toward an experimental ecology of human development. *American Psychologist, 32*(7), 513–531. doi:10.1037/0003-066X.32.7.513

Brown, R. C., Witt, A., Fegert, J. M., Keller, F., Rassenhofer, M., & Plener, P. L. (2017). Psychosocial interventions for children and adolescents after man-made and natural disasters: A meta-analysis and systematic review. *Psychological Medicine, 47*(11), 1893–1905. doi:10.1017/S0033291717000496

Carrigan, N., & Allez, K. (2017). Cognitive behavior therapy for post-traumatic stress disorder in a person with an autism spectrum condition and intellectual disability: A case study. *Journal of Applied Research in Intellectual Disabilities, 30*(2), 326–335. doi:10.1111/jar.12243

Centers for Disease Control and Prevention. (2016). About the CDC-Kaiser ACE Study. Retrieved from https://www.cdc.gov/violenceprevention/acestudy/about.html

Charlton, M., Kliethermes, M., Tallant, B., Taverne, A., & Tishelman, A. (2004). Facts on traumatic stress and children with developmental disabilities. Retrieved from https://www.nctsn.org/resources/facts-traumatic-stress-and-children-developmental-disabilities

Chivers-Wilson, K. A. (2006). Sexual assault and posttraumatic stress disorder: A review of the biological, psychological and sociological factors and treatments. *McGill Journal of Medicine, 9*(2), 111–118. Retrieved from https://www.ncbi.nlm.nih.gov/pmc/articles/PMC2323517/

Cloitre, M., Stolbach, B. C., Herman, J. L., van der Kolk, B., Pynoos, R., Wang, J., & Petkova, E. (2009). A developmental approach to complex PTSD: Childhood and adult cumulative trauma as predictors of symptom complexity. *Journal of Traumatic Stress, 22*(5), 399–408. doi:10.1002/jts.20444

Cohen, J. A., Deblinger, E., Mannarino, A. P., & Steer, R. A. (2004). A multisite, randomized controlled trial for children with sexual-abuse related PTSD symptoms. *Journal of the American Academy of Child & Adolescent Psychiatry, 43*(4), 393–402. doi:0.1097/00004583-200,404,000-00005

Cohen, J. A., & Mannarino, A. P. (2015). Trauma-focused cognitive behavior therapy for traumatized children and families. *Child & Adolescent Psychiatric Clinics, 24*(3), 557–570. doi:10.1016/j.chc.2015.02.005

Cook, A., Spinazzola, J., Ford, J., Lanktree, C., Blaustein, M., Cloitre, M., . . . van der Kolk, B. A. (2005). Complex trauma in children and adolescents. *Psychiatric Annals, 35*(5), 390–398.

Cook, E. H., Kieffer, J. E., Charak, D. A., & Leventhal, B. L. (1993). Autistic disorder and post-traumatic stress disorder. *Journal of the American Academy of Child & Adolescent Psychiatry, 32*(6), 1292–1294. doi:10.1097/00004583-199,311,000-00025

Cook, J. M., & Simiola, V. (2017). Trauma and PTSD in older adults: Prevalence, course, concomitants and clinical considerations. *Current Opinion in Psychology, 14*, 1–4. doi:10.1016/j.copsyc.2016.08.003

Copeland, W. E., Keeler, G., Angold, A., & Costello, E. J. (2007). Traumatic events and posttraumatic stress in childhood. *Archives of General Psychiatry, 64*, 577–584. doi:10.1001/archpsyc.64.5.577

Corbett, B. A., Mendoza, S., Wegelin, J. A., Carmean, V., & Levine, S. (2008). Variable cortisol circadian rhythms in children with autism and anticipatory stress. *Journal of Psychiatry and Neuroscience, 33*, 227. Retrieved from http://link.galegroup.com.ezproxy2.library.drexel.edu/apps/doc/A180862567/AONE?u=drexel_main&sid=AONE&xid=27ccc084

Costello, E. J., Erkanli, A., Fairbank, J. A., & Angold, A. (2002). The prevalence of potentially traumatic events in childhood and adolescence. *Journal of Traumatic Stress, 15*(2), 99–112. doi:10.1023/A:1014851823163

Crane, L., Maras, K. L., Hawken, T., Mulcahy, S., & Memon, A. (2016). Experiences of autism spectrum disorder and policing in England and Wales: Surveying police and the autism community. *Journal of Autism and Developmental Disorders, 46*(6), 2028–2041. doi:10.1007/s10803-016-2729-1

Creamer, M., Burgess, P., & McFarlane, A. C. (2001). Post-traumatic stress disorder: Findings from the Australian National Survey of Mental Health and Well-being. *Psychological Medicine, 31*, 1237–1247. doi:10.1017/S0033291701004287

Croen, L. A., Najjar, D. V., Ray, G. T., Lotspeich, L., & Bernal, P. (2006). A comparison of health care utilization and costs of children with and without autism spectrum disorders in a large group-model health plan. *Pediatrics, 118*, e1203–e1211. doi:10.1542/peds.2006–0127

Ćurin, J. M., Terzić, J., Petković, Z. B., Zekan, L., Terzić, I. M., & Šušnjara, I. M. (2003). Lower cortisol and higher ACTH levels in individuals with autism. *Journal of Autism and Developmental Disorders, 33*(4), 443–448. doi:10.1023/A:1025019030121

Davis, T. E., III, Hess, J. A., Moree, B. N., Fodstad, J. C., Dempsey, T., Jenkins, W. S., & Matson, J. L. (2011). Anxiety symptoms across the lifespan in people diagnosed with autistic disorder. *Research in Autism Spectrum Disorders, 5*(1), 112–118.

De Bellis, M. D., Casey, B. J., Dahl, R. E., Birmaher, B., Williamson, D. E., Thomas, K. M., . . . Ryan, N. D. (2000). A pilot study of amygdala volumes in pediatric generalized anxiety disorder. *Biological Psychiatry, 48*, 51–57. doi:10.1016/j.rasd.2010.02.006

de Bruin, E. I., Ferdinand, R. F., Meester, S., de Nijs, P. F., & Verheij, F. (2007). High rates of psychiatric co-morbidity in PDD-NOS. *Journal of Autism and Developmental Disorders, 37*(5), 877–886. doi:10.1007/s10803-006-0215-x

de Krom, M., Staal, W. G., Ophoff, R. A., Hendriks, J., Buitelaar, J., Franke, B., . . . van Ree, J. M. (2009). A common variant in DRD3 receptor is associated with autism spectrum disorder. *Biological Psychiatry, 65*, 625–630. doi:10.1016/j.biopsych.2008.09.035

de Roos, C., Greenwald, R., den Hollander-Gijsman, M., Noorthoorn, E., van Buuren, S., & de Jongh, A. (2011). A randomised comparison of cognitive behavioural therapy (CBT) and eye movement desensitisation and reprocessing (EMDR) in disaster-exposed children. *European Journal of Psychotraumatology, 2*(1), 5694. doi:10.3402/ejpt.v2i0.5694

de Roos, C., van der Oord, S., Zijlstra, B., Lucassen, S., Perrin, S., Emmelkamp, P., & de Jongh, A. (2017). EMDR and cognitive behavioral writing therapy versus waitlist in pediatric PTSD following single-incident trauma: A multi-center randomized clinical trial. *Journal of Child Psychology and Psychiatry, 58*(11), 1219–1238. doi:10.1111/jcpp.12768

Deblinger, E., Mannarino, A. P., Cohen, J. A., & Steer, R. A. (2006). A follow-up study of a multisite, randomized, controlled trial for children with sexual abuse-related PTSD symptoms. *Journal of the American Academy of Child & Adolescent Psychiatry, 45*(12), 1474–1484. doi:10.1097/01.chi.0000240839.56114.bb

Dingfelder, H. E., & Mandell, D. S. (2011). Bridging the research-to-practice gap in autism intervention: An application of diffusion of innovation theory. *Journal of Autism and Developmental Disorders, 41*(5), 597–609. doi:10.1007/s10803-010-1081-0

Dunn, E. C., Nichimi, K., Gomez, S. H., Powers, A., & Bradley, B. (2018). Developmental timing of trauma exposure and emotion dysregulation in adulthood: Are there sensitive periods when trauma is most harmful? *Journal of Affective Disorders, 227*, 869–877. doi:10.1016/j.jad.2017.10.045

Ehlers, A., Clark, D. M., Hackmann, A., Mcmanus, F., & Fennell, M. (2005). Cognitive therapy for post-traumatic stress disorder: Development and evaluation. *Behaviour Research and Therapy, 43*(4), 413–431. doi:10.1016/j.brat.2004.03.006

Ehlers, A., Mayou, R. A., & Bryant, B. (2003). Cognitive predictors of posttraumatic stress disorder in children: Results of a prospective longitudinal study. *Behaviour Research and Therapy, 4*, 1–10. doi:10.1016/S0005-7967(01)00126–7

Ehring, T., Welboren, R., Morina, N., Wicherts, J. M., Freitag, J., & Emmelkamp, P. M. (2014). Meta-analysis of psychological treatments for posttraumatic stress disorder in adult survivors of childhood abuse. *Clinical Psychology Review, 34*(8), 645–657. doi:10.1016/j.cpr.2014.10.004

Elwood, L. S., Hahn, K. S., Olatunji, B. O., & Williams, N. L. (2009). Cognitive vulnerabilities to the development of PTSD: A review of four vulnerabilities and the proposal of an integrative vulnerability model. *Clinical Psychology Review, 29*(1), 87–100. doi:10.1016/j.cpr.2008.10.002

Ervin, D. A., Williams, A., & Merrick, J. (2014). Primary care: Mental and behavioral health and persons with intellectual and developmental disabilities. *Frontiers in Public Health, 2*, 76. doi:10.3389/fpubh.2014.00076

Felitti, V. J., Anda, R. F., Nordenberg, D., Williamson, D. F., Spitz, A. M., Edwards, V., . . . Marks, J. S. (1998). Relationship of child abuse and household dysfunction to many of the leading causes of death in adults: The Adverse Childhood Experiences (ACE) Study. *American Journal of Preventive Medicine, 14*(4), 245–258. doi:10.1016/S0749-3797(98)00017–8

Finkelhor, D., Ormrod, R., Turner, H., & Hamby, S. L. (2005). The victimization of children and youth: A comprehensive, national survey. *Child Maltreatment, 10*, 5–25. doi:10.1177/10775

Foa, E. B., Asnaani, A., Zang, Y., Capaldi, S., & Yeh, R. (2017). Psychometrics of the Child PTSD Symptom Scale for DSM-5 for trauma-exposed children and adolescents. *Journal of Clinical Child & Adolescent Psychology, 47*(1), 38–46. doi:10.1080/15374416.2017.1350962

Fuchs, E., & Gould, E. (2000). Mini-review: In vivo neurogenesis in the adult brain: Regulation and functional implications.

European Journal of Neuroscience, 12, 2211–2214. https://doi-org.ezproxy2.library.drexel.edu/10.1046/j.1460-9568.2000.00130.x

Fuld, S. (2018). Autism spectrum disorder: The impact of stressful and traumatic life events and implications for clinical practice. *Clinical Social Work Journal, 46*(3), 1–10. doi:10.1007/s10615-018-0649-6

Gabbay, V., Oatis, M. D., Silva, R. R., & Hirsch, G. S. (2004). Epidemiological aspects of PTSD in children and adolescents. In R. R. Silva (Ed.), *Posttraumatic stress disorders in children and adolescents: Handbook* (pp. 1–17). New York, NY: W. W. Norton & Company.

Gilbert, J., & Man, H. (2017). Fundamental elements in autism: From neurogenesis and neurite growth to synaptic plasticity. *Frontiers in Cellular Neuroscience, 11,* 359–384. doi:10.3389/fncel.2017.00359

Gilbert, L. K., Breiding, M. J., Merrick, M. T., Thompson, W. W., Ford, D. C., Dhingra, S. S., & Parks, S. E. (2015). Childhood adversity and adult chronic disease: An update from ten states and the District of Columbia, 2010. *American Journal of preventive Medicine, 48*(3), 345–349. doi:10.1016/j.amepre.2014.09.006

Gotham, K., Brunwasser, S. M., & Lord, C. (2015). Depressive and anxiety symptom trajectories from school age through young adulthood in samples with autism spectrum disorder and developmental delay. *Journal of the American Academy of Child & Adolescent Psychiatry, 54*(5), 369–376. doi:10.1016/j.jaac.2015.02.005

Green, J. G., McLaughlin, K. A., Alegría, M., Costello, E. J., Gruber, M. J., Hoagwood, K.,... Kessler, R. C. (2013). School mental health resources and adolescent mental health service use. *Journal of the American Academy of Child & Adolescent Psychiatry, 52*(5), 501–510. doi:10.1016/j.jaac.2013.03.002

Groden, J., Diller, A., Bausman, M., Velicer, W., Norman, G., & Cautela, J. (2001). The development of a stress survey schedule for persons with autism and other developmental disabilities. *Journal of Autism and Developmental Disorders, 31,* 208–217. doi:10.1023/A:1010755300436.

Groen, W., Teluij, M., Buitelaar, J., & Tendolkar, I. (2010). Amygdala and hippocampus enlargement during adolescence in autism. *Journal of the American Academy of Child & Adolescent Psychiatry, 49*(6), 552–560. doi:10.1016/j.jaac.2009.12.023

Grosso, C. A. (2012). Children with developmental disabilities. In J. A. Cohen, A. P. Mannarino, & E. Deblinger (Eds.), *Trauma-focused CBT for children and adolescents: Treatment applications.* New York, NY: Guilford Press.

Gutermann, J., Schreiber, F., Matulis, S., Schwartzkopff, L., Deppe, J., & Steil, R. (2016). Psychological treatments for symptoms of posttraumatic stress disorder in children, adolescents, and young adults: A meta-analysis. *Clinical Child and Family Psychology Review, 19*(2), 77–93. doi:10.1007/s10567-016-0202-5

Hall-Lande, J., Hewitt, A., Mishra, S., Piescher, K., & LaLiberte, T. (2015). Involvement of children with autism spectrum disorder (ASD) in the child protection system. *Focus on Autism and Other Developmental Disabilities, 30*(4), 237–248. doi:10.1177/1088357614539834

Harley, E. K., Williams, M. E., Zamora, I., & Lakatos, P. P. (2014). Trauma treatment in young children with developmental disabilities: Applications of the child-parent psychotherapy (CPP) model to the cases of "James" and "Juan." *Pragmatic Case Studies in Psychotherapy, 10*(3), 156–195. http://dx.doi.org/10.14713/pcsp.v10i3.1869

Haruvi-Lamdan, N., Horesh, D., & Golan, O. (2018). PTSD and autism spectrum disorder: Co-morbidity, gaps in research, and potential shared mechanisms. *Psychological Trauma: Theory, Research, Practice, and Policy, 10*(3), 290–299. doi:10.1037/tra0000298

Herbert, M., Lavoie, F., & Blais, M. (2014). Post traumatic stress disorder/PTSD in adolescent victims of sexual abuse: Resilience and social support as protection factors. *Ciencia & Saude Coletiva, 19*(3), 685–694. doi:10.1590/1413–81232014193.15972013

Hibbard, R. A., & Desch, L. W. (2007). Maltreatment of children with disabilities. *Pediatrics, 119,* 1018–1025. doi:10.1542/peds.2007–0565

Hill, E. L. (2004). Executive dysfunction in autism. *Trends in Cognitive Sciences, 8,* 26–32. doi:10.1016/j.tics.2003.11.003

Hofvander, B., Delorme, R., Chaste, P., Nydén, A., Wentz, E., Ståhlberg, O.,... Sahlgrenska Academy. (2009). Psychiatric and psychosocial problems in adults with normal-intelligence autism spectrum disorders. *BMC Psychiatry, 9*(1), 35. doi:10.1186/1471-244X-9–35

Hoksbergen, R., Ter Laak, J., Rijk, K., van Dijkum, C., & Stoutjesdijk, F. (2005). Post-institutional autistic syndrome in Romanian adoptees. *Journal of Autism and Developmental Disorders, 35*(5), 615–623. doi:10.1007/s10803-005-0005-x

Hoover, D. W., & Kaufman, J. (2018). Adverse childhood experiences in children with autism spectrum disorder. *Current Opinion in Psychiatry, 31*(2), 128–132. doi:10.1097/YCO.0000000000000390

Howlin, P., & Clements, J. (1995). Is it possible to assess the impact of abuse on children with pervasive developmental disorders? *Journal of Autism and Developmental Disorders, 25,* 337–354. doi:10 0.1007/BF02179372

Idsoe, T., Dyregrov, A., & Idsoe, E. C. (2012). Bullying and PTSD symptoms. *Journal of Abnormal Child Psychology, 40*(6), 901–911. doi:10.1007/s10802-012-9620-0

Ipci, M., Inci, S. B., Ardiç, U. A., & Ercan, E. S. (2017). A case of Asperger syndrome with comorbidity of posttraumatic stress disorder and selective mutism: Significant remission with the combination of aripiprazole and eye movement desensitization and reprocessing. *Journal of Clinical Psychopharmacology, 37*(1), 109–110. doi:10.1097/JCP.0000000000000627

Jensen, T. H., Holt, T., Ormhaug, S. M., Egeland, K., Granly, L., Hoaas, L. C.,... Wentzel-Larson, T. (2014). A randomized effectiveness study comparing trauma-focused cognitive behavioral therapy with therapy as usual for youth. *Journal of Clinical Child & Adolescent Psychology, 43*(3), 356–369, doi:10.1080/15374416.2013.822307

Johnson, D. R. (2009). Emotional attention set-shifting and its relationship to anxiety and emotion regulation. *Emotion, 9*(5), 681–690. doi:10.1037/a0017095

Jones, C. R. G., Pickles, A., Falcaro, M., Marsden, A. J. S., Happé, F., Scott, S. K.,... Charman, T. (2011). A multimodal approach to emotion recognition ability in autism spectrum disorders. *Journal of Child Psychology and Psychiatry, 52*(3), 275–285. doi:10.1111/j.1469–7610.2010.02328.x

Karatzias, T., Cloitre, M., Maercker, A., Kazlauskas, E., Shevlin, M., Hyland, P.,... Brewin, C. R. (2017). PTSD and complex PTSD: ICD-11 updates on concept and measurement in the UK, USA, Germany and Lithuania. *European Journal of Psychotraumatology, 8*(Suppl 7), 1,418,103.

Kelley, L. P., Weathers, F. W., McDevitt-Murphy, M. E., Eakin, D. E., & Flood, A. M. (2009). A comparison of PTSD symptom patterns in three types of civilian trauma. *Journal of Traumatic Stress, 22*(3), 227–235. doi:10.1002/jts.20406

Kemp, M., Drummond, P., & McDermott, B. (2010). A wait-list controlled pilot study of eye movement desensitization and reprocessing (EMDR) for children with post-traumatic stress disorder (PTSD) symptoms from motor vehicle accidents. *Clinical Child Psychology and Psychiatry, 15*(1), 5–25. doi:10.1177/1359104509339086

Kerns, C. M., Berkowitz, S. J., Moskowitz, L. J., Drahota, A., & Lerner, M. D. (2019). Usual Care for Autism Study (UCAS) Consortium, & Newschaffer, C. J. Screening and treatment of trauma-related symptoms in youth with autism spectrum disorder among community providers in the United States. *Autism*, doi: https://doi.org/10.1177/1362361319847908

Kerns, C. M., Newschaffer, C. J., & Berkowitz, S. J. (2015). Traumatic childhood events and autism spectrum disorder. *Journal of Autism and Developmental Disorders, 45*(11), 3475–3486. doi:10.1007/s10803-015-2392-y

Kerns, C. M., Newschaffer, C. J., Berkowitz, S., & Lee, B. K. (2017). Brief report: Examining the association of autism and adverse childhood experiences in the National Survey of Children's Health: The important role of income and co-occurring mental health conditions. *Journal of Autism and Developmental Disorders, 47*(7), 2275–2281. doi:10.1007/s10803-017-3111-7

Kerns, C. M., Renno, P., Kendall, P. C., Wood, J. J., & Storch, E. A. (2017). Anxiety disorders interview schedule–autism addendum: Reliability and validity in children with autism spectrum disorder. *Journal of Clinical Child & Adolescent Psychology, 46*(1), 88–100.

Kerns, C. M., Roux, A. M., Connell, J. E., & Shattuck, P. T. (2016). Adapting cognitive behavioral techniques to address anxiety and depression in cognitively able emerging adults on the autism spectrum. *Cognitive and Behavioral Practice, 23*(3), 329–340. doi:10.1016/j.cbpra.2016.06.002

Kessler, R. C., Avenevoli, S., Costello, E. J., Georgiades, K., Green, J. G., Gruber, M. J., . . . & Sampson, N. A. (2012). Prevalence, persistence, and sociodemographic correlates of DSM-IV disorders in the National Comorbidity Survey Replication Adolescent Supplement. *Archives of General Psychiatry, 69*(4), 372–380. doi:10.1001/archgenpsychiatry.2011.160

Koenen, K. C., Moffitt, T. E., Poulton, R., Martin, J., & Caspi, A. (2007). Early childhood factors associated with the development of post-traumatic stress disorder: Results from a longitudinal birth cohort. *Psychological Medicine, 37*(2), 181–192. doi:10.1017/S0033291706009019

Kosatka, D., & Ona, C. (2014). Eye movement desensitization and reprocessing in a patient with Asperger's disorder: Case report. *Journal of EMDR Practice and Research, 8*(1), 13–18. doi:10.1891/1933–3196.8.1.13

Kroese, B. S., Willott, S., Taylor, F., Smith, P., Graham, R., Rutter, T., . . . Willner, P. (2016). Trauma-focused cognitive-behaviour therapy for people with mild intellectual disabilities: Outcomes of a pilot study. *Advances in Mental Health and Intellectual Disabilities, 10*(5), 299–310. doi:10.1108/AMHID-05-2016-0008

Kuan, P., Waszczuk, M. A., Kotov, R., Clouston, S., Yang, X., Singh, P. K., . . . Luft, B. J. (2017). Gene expression associated with PTSD in world trade center responders: An RNA sequencing study. *Translational Psychiatry, 7*, 1–11. doi:10.1038/s41398-017-0050-1

Lee, C. W., & Cuijpers, P. (2013). A meta-analysis of the contribution of eye movements in processing emotional memories. *Journal of Behavior Therapy and Experimental Psychiatry, 44*(2), 231–239. doi:10.1016/j.jbtep.2012.11.001

Logue, M. W., Smith, A. K., Baldwin, C., Wolf, J., Guffanti, G., Ratanatharathorn, A., . . . Miller, M. W. (2015). An analysis of gene expression in PTSD implicates genes involved in the glucocorticoid receptor pathway and neural responses to stress. *Psychoneuroendocrinology, 57*, 1–13. doi:10.1016/j.psyneuen.2015.03.016

Lopez, C. M., Andrews, A. R., III, Chisolm, A. M., de Arellano, M A., Saunders, B., & Kilpatrick, D. G. (2017). Brief report: Racial/ethnic differences in trauma exposure and mental health disorders in adolescents. *Cultural Diversity and Ethnic Minority Psychology, 23*(3), 382–387. doi:10.1037/cdp0000126

Lubit, R., Rovine, D., Defrancisci, L., & Eth, S. (2003). Impact of trauma on children. *Journal of Psychiatric Practice, 9*(2), 128–138. doi:10.1097/00131746-200,303,000-00004

Mandell, D. S., Walrath, C. M., Manteuffel, B., Sgro, G., & Pinto-Martin, J. A. (2005). The prevalence and correlates of abuse among children with autism served in comprehensive community-based mental health settings. *Child Abuse & Neglect, 29*(12), 1359–1372. doi:10.1016/j.chiabu.2005.06.006

Maniglio, R. (2009). The impact of child sexual abuse on health: A systematic review of reviews. *Clinical Psychology Review, 29*(7), 647–657. doi:10.1016/j.cpr.2009.08.003

Mansell, S., Sobsey, D., & Moskal, R. (1998). Clinical findings among sexually abused children with and without developmental disabilities. *Mental Retardation, 36*(1), 12–22. doi:10.1352/0047–6765(1998)036<0012:CFASAC>2.0.CO;2

Mazefsky, C. A., Herrington, J., Siegel, M., Scarpa, A., Maddox, B. B., Scahill, L., & White, S. W. (2013). The role of emotion regulation in autism spectrum disorder. *Journal of the American Academy of Child & Adolescent Psychiatry, 52*(7), 679–688. doi:10.1016/j.jaac.2013.05.006

McKenzie, K., Ouellette-Kuntz, H., Blinkhorn, A., & Démoré, A. (2017). Out of school and into distress: Families of young adults with intellectual and developmental disabilities in transition. *Journal of Applied Research in Intellectual Disabilities, 30*(4), 774–781. doi:10.1111/jar.12264

Mehtar, M., & Mukaddes, N. M. (2011). Posttraumatic stress disorder in individuals with diagnosis of autistic spectrum disorders. *Research in Autism Spectrum Disorders, 5*(1), 539–546. doi:10.1016/j.rasd.2010.06.020

Merikangas, K. R., He, J. P., Burstein, M., Swanson, S. A., Avenevoli, S., Cui, L., . . . Swendsen, J. (2010). Lifetime prevalence of mental disorders in US adolescents: Results from the National Comorbidity Survey Replication–Adolescent Supplement (NCS-A). *Journal of the American Academy of Child & Adolescent Psychiatry, 49*(10), 980–989. doi:10.1001/archpsyc.64.5.543

Mevissen, L., Didden, R., & de Jongh, A. (2016). Assessment and treatment of PTSD in people with intellectual disabilities. *Comprehensive Guide to Post-Traumatic Stress Disorders*, 281–299. doi:10.1016/j.cpr.2009.12.005

Mevissen, L., Lievegoed, R., Seubert, A., & Jongh, A. D. (2011). Do persons with intellectual disability and limited verbal capacities respond to trauma treatment? *Journal of Intellectual & Developmental Disability, 36*(4), 278–283. doi:10.3109/13668250.2011.621415

Moree, B. N., & Davis, T. E. (2010). Cognitive-behavioral therapy for anxiety in children diagnosed with autism spectrum disorders: Modification trends. *Research in Autism Spectrum Disorders, 4*(3), 346–354. doi:10.1016/j.rasd.2009.10.015

Morina, N., Koerssen, R., & Pollet, T. V. (2016). Interventions for children and adolescents with posttraumatic stress disorder: A meta-analysis of comparative outcome studies. *Clinical Psychology Review, 47*, 41–54. doi:10.1016/j.cpr.2016.05.006

National Child Traumatic Stress Network. (2012). Trauma-focused cognitive behavioral therapy. Retrieved from https://www.nctsn.org/sites/default/files/interventions/tfcbt_fact_sheet.pdf

National Institute for Health and Care Excellence. (2013). Autism: The management and support of children and young people on the autism spectrum. National Clinical Guideline Number 170. Retrieved from https://www.nice.org.uk/guidance/cg170

National Registry of Evidence-Based Programs and Practices. (2016). Trauma-focused cognitive behavioral therapy (TF-CBT). Retrieved from https://nrepp.samhsa.gov/ProgramProfile.aspx?id=96

Nemeroff, C. B. (2004). Neurobiological consequences of childhood trauma. *Journal of Clinical Psychiatry, 65,* 18–28. Retrieved from https://www.ncbi.nlm.nih.gov/pubmed/14728093

Nolen-Hoekseman, S., & Morrow, J. (1991). A prospective study of depression and posttraumatic symptoms after a natural disaster: The 1989 Loma Prieta earthquake. *Journal of Personality and Social Psychology, 61*(1), 115–121. doi:10.1037/0022–3514.61.1.115

O'Donnell, K., Dorsey, S., Gong, W., Ostermann, J., Whetten, R., Cohen, J. A., ... Whetten, K. (2014). Treating maladaptive grief and posttraumatic stress symptoms in orphaned children in Tanzania: Group-based trauma-focused cognitive-behavioral therapy. *Journal of Traumatic Stress, 4*, 664–671. https://doi.org/10.1002/jts.21970

Ozer, E. J., Best, S. R., Lipsey, T. L., & Weiss, D. S. (2003). Predictors of posttraumatic stress disorder and symptoms in adults. *Psychological Bulletin, 129,* 52–73. doi:10.1037/0022–3514.61.1.115

Pechtel, P., & Pizzagalli, D. A. (2011). Effects of early life stress on cognitive and affective function: An integrated review of human literature. *Psychopharmacology, 214,* 55–70. doi:10.1007/s00213-010-2009-2

Perry, B. D., Pollard, R. A., Blaicley, T. L., Baker, W. L., & Vigilante, D. (1995). Childhood trauma, the neurobiology of adaptation, and "use-dependent" development of the brain: How "states" become "traits." *Infant Mental Health Journal, 16*(4), 271–291. doi:10.1002/1097–0355(199524)16:4<271:AID-IMHJ2280160404>3.0.CO;2-B

Pynoos, R. S., Steinberg, A. M., Layne, C. M., Briggs, E. C., Ostrowski, S. A., & Fairbank, J. A. (2009). DSM-V PTSD diagnostic criteria for children and adolescents: A developmental perspective and recommendations. *Journal of Traumatic Stress, 22*(5), 391–398. doi:10.1002/jts.20450

Reiter, S., Bryen, D. N., & Shachar, I. (2007). Adolescents with intellectual disabilities as victims of abuse. *Journal of Intellectual Disabilities, 11,* 371–387. doi:10.1177/1744629507084602

Roberts, A. L., Gilman, S. E., Breslau, J., Breslau, N., & Koenen, K. C. (2011). Race/ethnic differences in exposure to traumatic events, development of post-traumatic stress disorder, and treatment-seeking for post-traumatic stress disorder in the United States. *Psychological Medicine, 41*(1), 71–83. doi:10.1017/S0033291710000401

Rodenburg, R., Benjamin, A., de Roos, C., Meijer, A. M., & Stams, G. J. (2009). Efficacy of EMDR in children: A meta-analysis. *Clinical Psychology Review, 29*(7), 599–606. doi:10.1016/j.cpr.2009.06.008

Rosen, T. E., Connell, J. E., & Kerns, C. M. (2016). A review of behavioral interventions for anxiety-related behaviors in lower-functioning individuals with autism: Behavioral interventions for anxiety in autism. *Behavioral Interventions, 31*(2), 120–143. doi:10.1002/bin.1442

Rumball, F. (2018). A systematic review of the assessment and treatment of posttraumatic stress disorder in individuals with autism spectrum disorders. *Review Journal of Autism and Developmental Disorders,* 1–31. doi:10.1007/s40489-018-0133-9

Rutter, M., Andersen-Wood, L., Beckett, C., Bredenkamp, D., Castle, J., Groothues, C., ... O'Connor, T. G. (1999). Quasi-autistic patterns following severe early global privation. *Journal of Child Psychology and Psychiatry and Allied Disciplines, 40*(4), 537–549. doi:10.1017/S0021963099003935

Rutter, M., Moffitt, T. E., & Caspi, A. (2006). Gene–environment interplay and psychopathology: Multiple varieties but real effects. *Journal of Child Psychology and Psychiatry, 47*(3–4), 226–261. doi:10.1111/j.1469–7610.2005.01557.x

Ryan, R.. (1994). Posttraumatic stress disorder in persons with developmental disabilities. *Community Mental Health Journal, 30*(1), 45–54. doi:10.1007/bf02188874

Samuelson, K. W. (2011). Post-traumatic stress disorder and declarative memory functioning: A review. *Dialogues in Clinical Neuroscience, 13*(3), 346–351. Retrieved from https://www.ncbi.nlm.nih.gov/pmc/articles/PMC3182004/

Sareen, J. (2014). Posttraumatic stress disorder in adults: Impact, comorbidity, risk factors, and treatment. *Canadian Journal of Psychiatry, 59*(9), 460–467. doi:10.1177/070674371405900902

Saunders, B. E., & Adams, Z. W. (2014). Epidemiology of traumatic experiences in childhood. *Child and Adolescent Psychiatric Clinics of North America, 23*(2), 167–184. doi:10.1016/j.chc.2013.12.003

Scheeringa, M. S. (2008). Developmental considerations for diagnosing PTSD and acute stress disorder in preschool and school-age children. *American Journal of Psychiatry, 165*(10), 1237–1239. doi:10.1176/appi.ajp.2008.08070974

Scheeringa, M. S., Weems, C. F., Johen, J. A., Amaya-Jackson, L., & Guthrie, D. (2011). Trauma-focused cognitive-behavioral therapy for posttraumatic stress disorder in three-through six-year-old children: A randomized clinical trial. *Journal of Child Psychology and Psychiatry, 52*(8), 853–60. doi:10.1111/j.1469–7610.2010.02354.x

Schumann, C. M., Hamstra, J., Goodlin-Jones, B. L., Lotspeich, L. J., Kwon, H., Buonocore, M. H., ... Amaral, D. G. (2004). The amygdala is enlarged in children but not adolescents with autism; the hippocampus is enlarged at all ages. *Journal of Neuroscience, 24*(28), 6392–6401. doi:10.1523/JNEUROSCI.1297–04.2004

Schumm, J. A., Briggs-Phillips, M., & Hobfoll, S. E. (2006). Cumulative interpersonal traumas and social support as risk and resiliency factors in predicting PTSD and depression among inner-city women. *Journal of Traumatic Stress, 19*(6), 825–836. doi:10.1002/jts.20159

Seidler, G. H., & Wagner, F. E. (2006). Comparing the efficacy of EMDR and trauma-focused cognitive-behavioral therapy in the treatment of PTSD: A meta-analytic study.

Psychological Medicine, 36(11), 1515–1522. https://doi.org/10.1017/S0033291706007963
Shapiro, F. (2001). *Eye movement desensitization and reprocessing: Basic principles, protocols and procedures* (2nd ed.). New York, NY: Guilford Press.
Sharpe, D. L., & Baker, D. L. (2007). Financial issues associated with having a child with autism. *Journal of Family and Economic Issues, 28*(2), 247–264. doi:10.1007/s10834-007-9059-6
Shattuck, P. T., Wagner, M., Narendorf, S., Sterzing, P., & Hensley, M. (2011). Post–high school service use among young adults with an autism spectrum disorder. *Archives of Pediatrics & Adolescent Medicine, 165*(2), 141–146. doi:10.1001/archpediatrics.2010.279
Sherin, J. E., & Nemeroff, C. B. (2011). Post-traumatic stress disorder: The neurobiological impact of psychological trauma. *Dialogues in Clinical Neuroscience, 13*(3), 263–278. Retrieved from https://www.ncbi.nlm.nih.gov/pmc/articles/PMC3182008/
Siegel, M., & Gabriels, R. L. (2014). Psychiatric hospital treatment of children with autism and serious behavioral disturbance. *Child and Adolescent Psychiatric Clinics, 23*(1), 125–142. doi:10.1016/j.chc.2013.07.004
Silverman, W. K., Ortiz, C. D., Viswesvaran, C., Burns, B. J., Kolko, D. J., Putnam, F. W., & Amaya-Jackson, L. (2008). Evidence-based psychosocial treatments for children and adolescents exposed to traumatic events. *Journal of Clinical Child & Adolescent Psychology, 37*(1), 156–183, doi:10.1080/15374410701818293
Simonoff, E., Pickles, A., Charman, T., Chandler, S., Loucas, T., Baird, G. (2008). Psychiatric disorders in children with autism spectrum disorders: Prevalence, comorbidity, and associated factors in a population-derived sample. *Journal of the American Academy of Child and Adolescent Psychiatry, 47*(4), 921–929. doi:10.1097/CHI.0b013e318179964f
Sizoo, B., & Lobregt, E. (2016). Treating trauma with EMDR in adults with autism spectrum disorders (ASD)—A literature review. *European Psychiatry, 33*(Supplement), S699. doi:10.1016/j.eurpsy.2016.01.2081
Sobotka, S. A., Francis, A., & Vander Ploeg Booth, K. (2016). Associations of family characteristics with perceptions of care among parents of children with autism. *Child: Care, Health and Development, 42*(1), 135–140. doi:10.1111/cch.12290
Solomon, L., & Peltz, L. (2008). Separation, autism, and residential treatment. *Journal of the Canadian Academy of Child and Adolescent Psychiatry, 17*, 26. Retrieved from https://www.ncbi.nlm.nih.gov/pmc/articles/PMC2247444/.
Spencer, N. (2005). Disabling conditions and registration for child abuse and neglect: A population-based study. *Pediatrics, 116*(3), 609–613. doi:10.1542/peds.2004–1882
Storch, E. A., Sulkowski, M. L., Nadeau, J., Lewin, A. B., Arnold, E. B., Mutch, P. J.,... Murphy, T. K. (2013). The phenomenology and clinical correlates of suicidal thoughts and behaviors in youth with autism spectrum disorders. *Journal of Autism and Developmental Disorders, 43*(10), 2450–2459. doi:10.1007/s10803-013-1795-x
Storr, C. L., Ialongo, N. S., Anthony, J. C., & Breslau, N. (2007). Childhood antecedents of exposure to traumatic events and posttraumatic stress disorder. *American Journal of Psychiatry, 164*(1), 119–125. doi:10.1176/appi.ajp.164.1.119
Substance Abuse and Mental Health Services Administration. (2016). Trauma-focused cognitive behavioral therapy (TF-CBT). Retrieved from https://nrepp.samhsa.gov/ProgramProfile.aspx?id=96
Sukhodolsky, D. G., Bloch, M. H., Panza, K. E., & Reichow, B. (2013). Cognitive-behavioral therapy for anxiety in children with high-functioning autism: A meta-analysis. *Pediatrics, 132*(5), e1341-e1350. doi:10.1542/peds.2013–1193
Taylor, J. L., & Corbett, B. A. (2014). A review of rhythm and responsiveness of cortisol in individuals with autism spectrum disorders. *Psychoneuroendocrinology, 49*, 207–228. doi:10.1016/j.psyneuen.2014.07.015
Taylor, J. L., & Gotham, K. O. (2016). Cumulative life events, traumatic experiences, and psychiatric symptomatology in transition-aged youth with autism spectrum disorder. *Journal of Neurodevelopmental Disorders, 8*(28). doi:10.1186/s11689-016-9160-y
Taylor, J. L., Hodapp, R. M., Burke, M. M., Waitz-Kudla, S. N., & Rabideau, C. (2017). Training parents of youth with autism spectrum disorder to advocate for adult disability services: Results from a pilot randomized controlled trial. *Journal of Autism and Developmental Disorders, 47*(3), 846–857. doi:10.1007/s10803-016-2994-z
Tolin, D. F., & Foa, E. B. (2006). Sex differences in trauma and posttraumatic stress disorder: A quantitative review of 25 years of research. *Psychological Bulletin, 132*(6), 959–992. doi:10.1037/0033–2909.132.6.959
Torres, A. R., Westover, J. B., & Rosenspire, A. J. (2012). HLA immune function genes in autism. *Autism Research and Treatment*, 2012, 1–13. http://dx.doi.org/10.1155/2012/959073
Trelles Thorne, M. P., Khinda, N., & Coffey, B. J. (2015). Posttraumatic stress disorder in a child with autism spectrum disorder: Challenges in management. *Journal of Child and Adolescent Psychopharmacology, 25*(6), 514–517. doi:10.1089/cap.2015.29011.mptt
Uddin, M., Aiello, A. E., Wildman, D. E., Koenen, K. C., Pawelec, G., Santos, R. D.,... Galea, S. (2010). Epigenetic and immune function profiles associated with posttraumatic stress disorder. *Proceedings of the National Academy of Sciences, 107*(20), 9470–9475. doi:10.1073/pnas.0910794107
Ung, D., Arnold, E. B., De Nadai, A. S., Lewin, A. B., Phares, V., Murphy, T. K., & Storch, E. A. (2014). Inter-rater reliability of the anxiety disorders interview schedule for DSM-IV in high-functioning youth with autism spectrum disorder. *Journal of Developmental and Physical Disabilities, 26*(1), 53–65. doi:10.1007/s10882-013-9343-3
Ung, D., Selles, R., Small, B. J., & Storch, E. A. (2015). A systematic review and meta-analysis of cognitive-behavioral therapy for anxiety in youth with high-functioning autism spectrum disorders. *Child Psychiatry & Human Development, 46*(4), 533–547. doi:10.1007/s10578-014-0494-y
Ung, D., Wood, J. J., Ehrenreich-May, J., Arnold, E. B., Fuji, C., Renno, P.,... Storch, E. A. (2013). Clinical characteristics of high-functioning youth with autism spectrum disorder and anxiety. *Neuropsychiatry, 3*(2), 147–157. doi:10.2217/npy.13.9
U.S. Department of Health & Human Services. (2016). Child maltreatment 2016. Retrieved from https://www.acf.hhs.gov/cb/resource/child-maltreatment-2016
Valenti, M., Ciprietti, T., Di Egidio, C., Gabrielli, M., Masedu, F., Romassini, A. R., & Sorge, G. (2012). Adaptive response of children and adolescents with autism to the 2009 earthquake in L'Aquila, Italy. *Journal of Autism and Developmental Disorders, 42*, 954–960. doi:10.1007/s10803-011-1323-9
van Denderen, M., de Keijser, J., Stewart, R., & Boelen, P. A. (2018). Treating complicated grief and posttraumatic stress in

homicidally bereaved individuals: A randomized controlled trial. *Clinical Psychology & Psychotherapy, 25*(4), 497–508. doi:10.1002/cpp.2183

van der Kolk, B. A. (2005). Developmental trauma disorder: Toward a rational diagnosis for children with complex trauma histories. *Psychiatric Annals, 35*(5), 401–408. doi:10.3928/00485713-20,050,501-06

van Steensel, F. J. A., Bögels, S. M., & Perrin, S. (2011). Anxiety disorders in children and adolescents with autistic spectrum disorders: A meta-analysis. *Clinical Child and Family Psychology Review, 14*(3), 302–317. doi:10.1007/s10567-011-0097-0

Verardo, A. R., & Cioccolanti, E. (2017). Traumatic experiences and EMDR in childhood and adolescence: A review of the scientific literature on efficacy studies. *Clinical Neuropsychiatry, 14*(5), 313–320. doi:10.1016/j.cpr.2009.04.004

Vohra, R., Madhavan, S., Sambamoorthi, U., & Peter, C. S. (2013). Access to services, quality of care, and family impact for children with autism, other developmental disabilities, and other mental health conditions. *Autism, 18*(7), 815–826. doi:10.1177/1362361313512902

Volkmar, F. R., & McPartland, J. C. (2014). From Kanner to DSM-5: Autism as an evolving diagnostic concept. *Annual Review of Clinical Psychology, 10,* 193–212. doi:10.1146/annurev-clinpsy-032813-153,710

Wahbeh, H., & Oken, B. S. (2013). Salivary cortisol lower in posttraumatic stress disorder: Cortisol in PTSD. *Journal of Traumatic Stress, 26*(2), 241–248. doi:10.1002/jts.21798

Walsh, K., Koenen, K. C., Aiello, A. E., Uddin, M., & Galea, S. (2014). Prevalence of sexual violence and posttraumatic stress disorder in an urban African-American population. *Journal of Immigrant and Minority Health, 16*(6), 1307–1310. doi:10.1007/s10903-013-9840-6

Watts, B. V., Schnurr, P. P., Mayo, L., Young-Yu, Y., Weeks, W. B., & Friedman, M. J. (2013). Meta-analysis of the efficacy of treatments for posttraumatic stress disorder. *Journal of Clinical Psychiatry, 74*(6), e541–e550. doi:10.4088/JCP.12r08225

Weathers, F. W., Litz, B. T., Herman, D. S., Huska, J. A., & Keane, T. M. (1993, October). The PTSD Checklist: Reliability, validity, and diagnostic utility. Paper presented at the annual meeting of the ISTSS, San Antonio, CA. Retrieved from https://www.researchgate.net/publication/313709159_PTSD_Checklist_Reliability_validity_and_diagnostic_utility

White, S. W., Ollendick, T., Albano, A. M., Oswald, D., Johnson, C., Southam-Gerow, M. A., . . . Scahill, L. (2013). Randomized controlled trial: Multimodal anxiety and social skill intervention for adolescents with autism spectrum disorder. *Journal of Autism and Developmental Disorders, 43*(2), 382–394. doi:10.1007/s10803-012-1577-x

Wicks, S., Hjern, A., Gunnell, D., Lewis, G., & Dalman, C. (2005). Social adversity in childhood and the risk of developing psychosis: A national cohort study. *American Journal of Psychiatry, 162,* 1652–1657. doi:10.1176/appi.ajp.162.9.1652

Wildeman, C., Emanuel, N., Leventhal, J. M., Putnam-Hornstein, E., Waldfogel, J., & Lee, H. (2014). The prevalence of confirmed maltreatment among US children, 2004 to 2011. *JAMA Pediatrics, 168*(8), 706–713. doi:10.1001/jamapediatrics.2014.410

Wolf, E. J., Mitchell, K. S., Logue, M. W., Baldwin, C. T., Reardon, A. F., Aiello, A., . . . Miller, M. W. (2014). The dopamine D3Receptor gene and posttraumatic stress disorder: Dopamine D3 receptor gene and PTSD. *Journal of Traumatic Stress, 27*(4), 379–387. doi:10.1002/jts.21937

Wood, J. J., Drahota, A., Sze, K., Har, K., Chiu, A., & Langer, D. A. (2009). Cognitive behavioral therapy for anxiety in children with autism spectrum disorders: A randomized, controlled trial. *Journal of Child Psychology and Psychiatry, 50*(3), 224–234. doi:10.1111/j.1469–7610.2008.01948.x

Wood, J. J., & Gadow, K. D. (2010). Exploring the nature and function of anxiety in youth with autism spectrum disorders. *Clinical Psychology: Science and Practice, 17,* 281–292. doi:10.1111/j.1468–2850.2010.01220.x

Yehuda, R., McFarlane, A. C., & Shalev, A. Y. (1998). Predicting the development of posttraumatic stress disorder from the acute response to a traumatic event. *Biological Psychiatry, 44,* 1305–1313.

Yule, W. (1997). Anxiety, depression and post-traumatic stress disorder in children. In I. Sclare (Ed.), *The NFER Child portfolio* (pp. 43–47). Windsor, UK: NFER-Nelson.

Yule, W., Udwin, O., & Murdoch, K. (1990). The "Jupiter" sinking: Effects on children's fears, depression and anxiety. *Journal of Child Psychology and Psychiatry, 31*(7), 1051–1061. doi:10.1111/j.1469–7610.1990.tb00845.x

Zablotsky, B., Bradshaw, C. P., Anderson, C., & Law, P. A. (2013). The association between bullying and the psychological functioning of children with autism spectrum disorders. *Journal of Developmental and Behavioral Pediatrics, 34,* 1–8. doi:10.1097/DBP.0b013e31827a7c3a

CHAPTER

8

Oppositional Defiant Disorder and Related Disruptive Behaviors in Autism Spectrum Disorder

Karen Bearss *and* Aaron J. Kaat

Abstract

The *Diagnostic and Statistical Manual of Mental Disorders*, fifth edition characterizes oppositional defiant disorder (ODD) as reflecting pervasive patterns of irritable mood, defiant behavior, and/or vindictiveness. Youth with autism spectrum disorder (ASD) exhibit high rates of disruptive behaviors commonly associated with ODD, such as noncompliance, irritability, temper tantrums, and mood dysregulation. This chapter reviews the presentation of ODD in individuals with ASD, including current prevalence estimates, proposed etiology, validated assessment methods, and emerging best practices designed to treat challenging behaviors. Although there is a robust literature describing assessment and treatment procedures for disruptive behaviors in individuals with ASD, conceptualizing these hallmark behaviors within the framework of ODD is relatively novel and not without controversy. Discussion thus includes challenges around the applicability of the diagnostic criteria in this population and future research directions that may provide clarity on this issue.

Keywords: autism spectrum disorder, oppositional defiant disorder, disruptive behavior, applied behavior analysis, parent training

Overview

Up to 50% of children with autism spectrum disorder (ASD) exhibit high rates of disruptive behaviors, such as tantrums, verbal aggression (argumentative behavior), physical aggression, and noncompliance (Hartley, Sikora, & McCoy, 2008; Mazurek, Kanne, & Wodka, 2013). These disruptive behaviors typically occur at higher rates in ASD than among neurotypical children (Bryce & Jahromi, 2013; Mayes, Calhoun, Murray, Ahuja, & Smith, 2011; Mayes et al., 2012). In their own words, parents of children with ASD describe frequent "meltdowns," "outbursts," and other serious behavioral problems in the context of everyday life. When behavioral problems reach levels of clinical significance, children may qualify for the *Diagnostic and Statistical Manual of Mental Disorders*, fifth edition (DSM-5; American Psychiatric Association [APA], 2013) diagnosis of oppositional defiant disorder (ODD; DSM-5 code 313.81). Diagnostic criteria for ODD require at least four symptoms that reflect pervasive patterns (lasting at least 6 months) of irritable mood, argumentative or defiant behavior, and/or vindictiveness.

Although the first symptoms of ODD usually appear during the preschool years, it can be difficult to differentiate between an emotional child and ODD in younger children as misbehavior in early childhood is also normative (Wakschlag, Tolan, & Leventhal, 2010). Thus, clinicians working with individuals with ASD should cautiously consider the developmental level of the child in diagnostic decisions around ODD. The diagnostic criteria acknowledge this, noting a difference in the persistence and frequency of disruptive behavior depending on whether a child is above or below 5 years of age and "other factors" such as the developmental level, gender, and culture of the individual being evaluated; intellectual disability and language disorder are specifically noted as potential differential diagnoses that must be considered (APA, 2013). Appreciating the developmental level of a child with ASD may lead a clinician to recognize that the quality, intensity, and frequency of tantrums are normative for that child's mental age.

It also may be unclear whether a particular clinical characteristic is reflective of ODD versus an associated feature phenotypic of ASD or an entirely separate diagnostic category (Kaat & Lecavalier, 2013; Mazzone, Ruta, & Ruta, 2012). To illustrate, consider two key symptoms of ODD: temper tantrums and noncompliance. Temper dysregulation is diagnostically nonspecific—it can be a precursor for ODD and other disruptive behavior disorders, or it may be a precursor for mood disorders (e.g., disruptive mood dysregulation disorder; APA, 2013; Copeland et al., 2012). Among younger individuals (chronologically or cognitively), it may be typical/normative behavior (Wakschlag et al., 2010; Wakschlag et al., 2012). Noncompliance is also problematic as it can be difficult to determine its developmental appropriateness. Among neurotypical children, noncompliance is expected to increase during the preschool years as the child asserts his or her independence, and then decrease as verbal assertiveness improves (Wakschlag et al., 2010). Noncompliance in this case may demonstrate developmentally appropriate assertiveness. This also may be why functional communication training is well established as effective in reducing noncompliance in ASD, where disruptive behavior is serving communicative purposes (Durand & Merges, 2001). Clinicians need to evaluate the quality and intensity of temper tantrums and the child's communication status prior to endorsing the main diagnostic criteria for ODD.

Applying other diagnostic criteria for ODD in ASD may be equally challenging. For example, the criteria "actively defies or refuses to comply," "deliberately annoys," or is "spiteful or vindictive" require clinicians to demonstrate that the child understands and is intentionally acting in defiance of age-appropriate societal norms (Kaat & Lecavalier, 2013). This requires a higher level of social cognitive knowledge than some children with ASD may achieve. Nonetheless, children with ASD exhibit noncompliance (Lecavalier, 2006), irritability (Mayes et al., 2011), temper loss/mood dysregulation (Simonoff et al., 2012), and other behaviors consistent with an ODD diagnosis. The clinician is given the difficult task of evaluating whether the behaviors are at a high enough frequency and intensity or are so extreme that they cross over from developmentally expected behavior to a psychiatric disorder, not unlike the work done among typically developing preschoolers (Wakschlag et al., 2012).

Prevalence and Course

The prevalence of ODD in the general population ranges from 1% to 11%, with an average prevalence estimate of around 3.3% and rates somewhat higher in males than females (1.4:1) (Canino et al., 2010). Among neurotypical adolescents, the lifetime prevalence rate for ODD has been estimated to be as high as 12.6% overall (Merikangas et al., 2010). Challenges in conceptualizing the nosology of ODD in ASD have hampered epidemiological efforts in estimating prevalence rates within this clinical population. Most research has focused on distinguishing *between* ODD (or disruptive behaviors, more broadly) and ASD, rather than examining their co-occurrence (Kaat & Lecavalier, 2013). Another sizeable number of studies have reported on the frequency of specific behaviors rather than diagnostic categories. For instance, using the Nisonger Child Behavior Rating Form, Lecavalier (2006) reported on the frequency with which parents and teachers endorsed specific items, such as "Defiant" or "Attacks other people," as moderate or severe problems.

Table 8.1 summarizes the limited available data, by age group, on ODD prevalence rates in ASD. To reflect current diagnostic practices, only studies published since 2000 are presented in the table. Additionally, only population-derived epidemiological, convenience community, or diagnostic clinical samples are included. Studies relying on psychiatric clinic referrals were excluded (e.g., Joshi et al., 2010; Witwer & Lecavalier, 2010), because these tend to have considerably higher comorbidity estimates. Studies with overlapping age groups were assigned to a category based on the majority age of the sample.

As reflected in Table 8.1, population-defined prevalence rates within ASD for DSM-defined ODD are broad, ranging from 4% to 37%. High rates of impairment but without a sufficient number of criteria to qualify for ODD (i.e., less than four of eight criteria endorsed) were also observed across studies (ranging from 5% to 43%). As in the general population (Wakschlag et al., 2010), ODD can be diagnosed in preschoolers with ASD (e.g., Gadow, DeVincent, Pomeroy, & Azizian, 2004; Salazar et al., 2015). Although prevalence appears to increase and peak during childhood, decreasing into adolescence, few studies examined age effects within their samples; when age was examined, rates generally did not differ across ages (e.g., Salazar et al., 2015). Kaat and Lecavalier's (2013) published review of ODD prevalence rates in ASD, which included most studies from Table 8.1, reported an estimated weighted average comorbidity rate of 21%, indicating approximately one in five children with ASD met diagnostic criteria for ODD. This would suggest that the rate of ODD in ASD is higher compared to what is observed in the general population of children.

Although there have been some studies to examine the prevalence of ODD comorbid with ASD, there has been a dearth examining its developmental course. In neurotypical samples, the most commonly reported developmental trajectory is from ODD to conduct disorder (Rowe et al., 2010). However, it is rare for an individual to only receive an ODD diagnosis across the lifetime; impulse control disorders, conduct disorder, and mood and anxiety disorders are also common (Nock et al., 2007). Even by adolescence, subdimensions within ODD appear differentially related to mood disorder, conduct disorder, and callous and unemotional traits—a potential precursor for antisocial personality disorder—at age 16 (Whelan et al., 2013). Prior to age 18, 70% of individuals no longer have symptoms of ODD, but the earlier an individual received the initial ODD diagnosis and the more additional comorbid disorders he or she has, the more likely ODD symptoms are to persist into adulthood (Nock et al., 2007).

Much less is known about the developmental course of ODD in ASD. For example, conduct disorder is the most frequently considered subsequent diagnosis in neurotypical samples, but in ASD, most research has emphasized differentiating conduct disorder from ASD rather than investigating their co-occurrence or predictors (c.f. Kaat & Lecavalier, 2013). In one longitudinal study, conduct problems (not equivalent to DSM-defined conduct disorder) were only predicted by neighborhood deprivation and special school placement (Simonoff et al., 2013), which are far fewer predictors than reported in neurotypical samples. Unfortunately, those authors did not specifically evaluate previous ODD diagnosis.

Although more research on longitudinal trajectories of ODD in individuals with ASD is necessary, reasonable hypotheses include (a) maintaining an ODD diagnosis across the lifespan as the developmental self-control skills that help remit ODD in neurotypical samples remain impaired, (b) remission of ODD diagnosis, and (c) conversion of symptoms into a mood problem. Indeed, irritable ODD is most predictive of depressive symptoms, not conduct disorder, in neurotypical samples (Whelan et al., 2013), and preliminary studies applying ODD subgroups to ASD also supports this assertion (Mandy et al., 2014). This does not negate the possibility of a co-occurrence of conduct disorder or antisocial personality disorder (the other common developmental outcomes in neurotypical samples) among individuals with ASD, especially as there is already, albeit limited, evidence for their co-occurrence (c.f. Kaat & Lecavalier, 2013). Instead, the connection between irritability and depressive symptoms supports the more likely developmental trajectory toward mood disorders if diagnostic continuity for ODD does not occur.

Across the lifespan, disruptive behaviors commonly associated with ODD can profoundly impact child and family functioning, including interfering with the child's response to educational intervention, increasing isolation from peers, eroding family quality of life, and increasing caregiver stress due to disruptions in daily activities (Brereton, Tonge, & Einfeld, 2006; Hartley et al., 2008; Hayes & Watson, 2013; Herring et al., 2006; Simonoff et al., 2008; Symon, 2005; Tonge et al., 2006). Compared with parents of neurotypical children, parents of children with ASD report a greater sense of helplessness and are more likely to avoid conflict when facing challenges of parenting (Pisula & Kossakowska, 2010). Disruptive behaviors also pose a barrier to the acquisition and regular performance of daily living skills, resulting in delays in adaptive functioning (Scahill et al., 2012, 2016).

Etiology, Diagnosis, and Assessment

Etiology of ODD in ASD

ODD in neurotypical youth has been connected to a variety of risk factors, including child sex, poor emotion regulation, and inconsistent child-rearing practices, as well as neurobiological markers such as lower heart rate, reduced basal cortisol reactivity, and prefrontal cortex and amygdala abnormalities (APA, 2013). Given the diversity in prevalence rates across studies, it is understandable that studies examining risk factors for ODD in ASD have found inconsistent results. Contrary to neurotypical findings, several studies of children with ASD found no relation between ODD and sex for screened prevalence rates by parent report (Simonoff et al., 2008). Conversely, Salazar and colleagues (2015) found boys were more likely than girls to receive an ODD diagnosis (odds ratio = 3.9) and Gadow and

Table 8.1. Co-Occurrence Rates of Autism Spectrum Disorder and Oppositional Defiant Disorder by Age

First Author and Year	Sample Size	Age Range	Sample Source	% Male	IQ Mean (SD) or % <70	Measure	Comorbidity Rate
Early Childhood (Under 6 Years)							
Gadow 2004[a]	172	3–6	Diagnostic clinic referrals	79	79 (22)	ECI-IV-Parent	13%[a]
Gadow 2004[a]	160	3–6	Diagnostic clinic referrals	79	79 (22)	ECI-IV-Teacher	21%[a]
Hayashida 2010[a]	175	3–6	Partial hospitalization for intensive ASD services	78	72 (27)	ECI-IV-Parent	9%[a] clinical 18%[a] borderline
Hayashida 2010[a]	175	3–6	Partial hospitalization for intensive ASD services	78	72 (27)	CBCL	19%[a] clinical 5%[a] borderline
Salazar 2015	47	4–7.5	UK population-based stratified random sample	56	44%	PAPA	26%
Middle Childhood and Preadolescent (6–13 Years)							
Gadow 2005[a]	284	6–12	Diagnostic clinic referrals	88	92 (22) 14%	CSI-IV-Parent	27%[a]
Gadow 2005[a]	284	6–12	Diagnostic clinic referrals	88	92 (22) 14%	CSI-IV-Teacher	25%[a]
de Bruin 2007	94	6–12	Netherlands-based clinic referrals	88	91 (17)	DISC-IV	37%
Simonoff 2008	112	10–14	UK population-based stratified random sample	88	73 (22)	CAPA	28%
Levy 2010[a]	2,568	8	ADDM Network participants	81	18%	Medical record	4%[a]
Kaat 2013[a]	104	6–12	Diagnostic clinic referrals	86	85 (23) 23%	CASI-4R-Parent	29%[a] full criteria 35%[a] impaired without full criteria
Kaat 2013[a]	88	6–12	Diagnostic clinic referrals	86	85 (23) 23%	CASI-4R-Teacher	21%[a] full criteria 43%[a] impaired without full criteria
Hepburn 2014	42	8–14	Anxiety treatment–seeking youth	81	98 (15)	K-SADS	19% current 19% past
Salazar 2015	54	7.5–9	UK population-based stratified random sample	56	44%	PAPA	30%

Samples That Include Adolescents (At Least Some Participants 13–18 Years)							
Leyfer 2006	109	5–17	Clinic and community samples	94	83 (23) 32%	Modified K-SADS (ACI)	7% full criteria 5% subsyndromal
Kanne 2009[a]	177	3–18	Clinic and community samples	85	NR	CBCL	15%[a]
Kanne 2009[a]	177	3–18	Clinic and community samples	85	NR	CBCL-TRF	9%[a]
Mukaddes 2010	60	6–15	Diagnostic clinic referrals in Turkey	100	0%	K-SADS	32%
Mattila 2010	50	9–16	Clinic and community samples in Finland	76	0%	K-SADS	16% current 16% lifetime
Gjevik 2011	71	6–17	Special school attendees in Norway	82	65 (30) 81%	K-SADS	4%
Mazefsky 2012	35	10–17	Clinic and community samples	80	105 (17) 0%	Modified K-SADS (ACI)	11%

Note: (a) Five studies contributed screening rates by multiple informants (parent- and teacher-completed rating scales), thus creating overlapping samples within a study. (b) One study had a partially overlapping sample, preventing complete independence of screening rates. (c) Six studies (40%; 12% of participants) were from outside the United States, providing representation of autism spectrum disorder comorbidity across the globe.

[a] These are screening rates, not diagnostic rates, as the "diagnostic" measure was either a clinical chart review with unclear diagnostic practices or use of a rating scale.

ASI, Adolescent Symptom Inventory; CAPA, Child and Adolescent Psychiatric Assessment; CASI, Child and Adolescent Symptom Inventory; CBCL, Child Behavior Checklist; CBCL-TRF, Child Behavior Checklist-Teacher Report Form; CSI, Child Symptom Inventory; DISC-IV, Diagnostic Interview Schedule for Children; ECI, Early Childhood Inventory; K-SADS, Schedule for Affective Disorders and Schizophrenia for School-Age Children—Present and Lifetime Version; NR, Not Reported; PAPA, Preschool-Age Psychiatric Assessment.

colleagues (Gadow et al., 2004; Gadow, DeVincent, & Drabick, 2008; Gadow, DeVincent, Pomeroy, & Azizian, 2005) reported males were more likely to be rated as exhibiting ODD behaviors than females when using teacher report. There does seem to be widespread agreement that IQ differences are unrelated to ODD in ASD (Gadow et al., 2004, 2005, 2008; Salazar et al., 2015; Simonoff et al., 2008; Witwer & Lecavalier, 2010). However, there may be other risk factors, including having spoken language (Witwer & Lecavalier, 2010), having more severe ASD (Salazar et al., 2015), having comorbid epilepsy (Simonoff et al., 2008), having ever taken psychotropic medication (though causality is unclear for this risk factor; Gadow, DeVincent, & Schneider, 2008), low parental education (Salazar et al., 2015), or family psychiatric history (Gadow et al., 2008).

Diagnosis and Assessment of ODD in ASD

The assessment of ODD should consider the child, family, and broader systems in which the child operates. Because the core features and associated deficits in ASD, such as language and cognitive delays, make self-reporting on historical events or internal states challenging, clinicians often rely on caregiver report to identify the presence or absence of symptoms in the child. Multimodal (parent, teacher, other caregiver), multimethod (interview, observation, rating scales) assessment will provide the widest range of information that can be used in diagnostic decisions and treatment planning (McMahon & Frick, 2005). Information gathered from multiple informants also is preferred as perspectives between parents as well as between parents and teachers regarding challenging behaviors can be divergent (Stratis & Lecavalier, 2015).

Assessing child history and current parenting practices. Information about the child should include collation of the child's development, including pre-/postnatal complications, medical conditions that may affect the child's development or family functioning, and educational history, including special educational services. For example, compliance with commands is understandably tied to the child's receptive language (RL). An RL threshold of about 12 to 18 months is required for the child to understand simple, one-step commands. Thus, if a child is identified as having notable RL delays, expectations regarding the child's ability to understand and comply with commands will need to be considered.

Family history, including psychiatric conditions in immediate and extended family as well as current medical conditions in family members that may affect caregiving, should be evaluated. Individuals involved in the broader network of caregiving (parents, extended family members, other caregivers) will inform the family support structure and who should be included in treatment planning and implementation. Knowledge of the family structure may also help identify barriers to treatment. For example, while parent training may be a recommended course of treatment and the mother is identified as the primary caregiver, she may be unable to participate in treatment or support her child's therapy due to her work schedule.

Assess the use of current parenting practices, including parental perception of strategies that work versus the strategies that do not work to address challenging behaviors. For example, many parents report they have tried timeout and are convinced that it does not work. In many instances, however, parents misapply timeout (e.g., ending the timeout while the child is still upset, conducting the timeout in front of the television, using the timeout for an escape-maintained behavior). Effective treatment for disruptive behaviors involves implementing new techniques as well as correcting ineffective application of particular strategies.

A focus of the assessment also should be on general parenting perspectives: Is the parent overly harsh (oriented to the authoritarian parenting approach, with an emphasis on punitive discipline strategies) or permissive (appropriate warmth in the parent–child relationship but ineffective limit setting and inadequate follow-through with consequences)? It may also be informative to discuss the parental understanding of what is "driving" the child's behavioral problems. This discussion may delve into parental perceptions on locus of control (LOC), which is the degree to which the parent feels he or she has the ability to influence the child's behavior and development. Parents with an *internal* LOC acknowledge their impact on the child's behavior. During the assessment, these parents may acknowledge their role in the child's behavior (e.g., "I know I don't follow through"). Conversely, a parent with an *external* LOC may attribute the child's behavior to environmental or biological factors, with the implication that the parent has little influence on the child's behavior. Research suggests that an internal LOC is associated with higher maternal esteem, parental satisfaction, and fewer child behavioral problems (Hassal, Rose, & McDonald, 2005; Koeske & Koeske, 1992).

Finally, the presence or absence of behaviors in specific settings or with particular people can inform the appropriate course of treatment. For example, school-based treatment may be the appropriate plan when a parent reports that behavioral problems are only present at school. In some cases, disruptive behaviors are occurring both at school *and* home, but the parent may be underreporting behaviors at home, perhaps a reflection of tolerance of the child's behavior. In such cases, it may be important to "recalibrate" appropriate behavior and parental expectations before initiating treatment. Particularly challenging cases include parents who underreport behavioral problems in the home and may have little motivation to modify their parenting approach. A positive indicator for treatment is when a parent reports behavioral problems in the home that are less prominent at school. This suggests that the child has some ability to regulate behavior at school and may prompt the parent to seek help in managing the child's behavior.

Assessing the topography of target behaviors. Parents raising a child with pervasive defiant behaviors often describe the feeling of "walking on eggshells" and are apprehensive that the child may "go off again." Clarification of more specifically defined target behaviors and their functional properties should occur through an informal or semistructured interview with the family as well as through parent ratings and functional assessment procedures, which include behavioral observation.

Parent interview. Initial discussion should include delineation of the specific behaviors of concern. Parents should be guided to define problems using clear and descriptive behavioral terms: specific behaviors, frequency of occurrence, duration, antecedents, consequences, and impact on the family. These descriptions of behaviors promote a common understanding of the child's target problems and provide useful information on severity.

Discussion can also be guided through the use of standardized, semistructured diagnostic interviews, which provide a framework to review all diagnostic criteria and confirm the presence of symptoms, duration of concern, and functional impairment—the requirements for a DSM-defined diagnosis. Unfortunately, they can be time-consuming and require a fair amount of training. The most frequently used semistructured interview in ASD (c.f. Table 8.1) has been the Schedule for Affective Disorders and Schizophrenia for School-Age Children—Present and Lifetime Version (K-SADS-PL; Kaufman et al., 1997). A modified version of the K-SADS, the Autism Comorbidity Interview (ACI), has also been developed and evaluated in two studies (Leyfer et al., 2006; Mazefsky et al., 2012), but it is not publicly available. The only other diagnostic interview that includes ODD to have undergone psychometric evaluation in an ASD population is the Child Interview of Psychiatric Symptoms—Parent Version (P-CHIPS; Fristad, Teare, Weller, Weller, & Salmon, 1998), which was evaluated by Witwer, Lecavalier, and Norris (2012) in a psychiatric clinic-referred sample.

Parent-report measures. To supplement parent interview, a number of standardized instruments are available to assess the presence of specific disruptive behaviors as well as probe for the presence of DSM-related ODD diagnostic criteria. To follow are brief descriptions of applicable rating scales.

The Aberrant Behavior Checklist, second edition (ABC-2; Aman & Singh, 2017) contains 58 items rated on a 4-point scale from 0 (not a problem) through 3 (the problem is severe). The second edition includes all of the original items, with updated interpretive information and a more comprehensive manual. Items are distributed on five subscales: Irritability (15 items), Social Withdrawal (16 items), Stereotypic Behavior (7 items), Hyperactivity/Noncompliance (16 items), and Inappropriate Speech (4 items). The ABC's original factor structure has been shown to be largely consistent in a large sample of children with ASD (Kaat, Lecavalier, & Aman, 2014). Use of the ABC/ABC-2 has grown significantly over the years, especially among children and adolescents with ASD. While originally validated for individuals age 5 to adulthood, it has more recently been used in preschoolers (Kaat et al., 2014; Karabekiroglu & Aman, 2009). The Irritability subscale, in particular, has been used as the primary outcome measure in a number of large intervention studies targeting irritability in ASD (e.g., Aman et al., 2009; Bearss et al., 2015; Fung et al, 2016; Research Units on Pediatric Psychopharmacology Autism Network, 2002).

The Child Behavior Checklist (CBCL) and Teacher Report Form (TRF; Achenbach & Rescorla, 2001; Achenbach & Ruffle, 2000) are multi-item, multi-informant tools assessing problem behaviors across eight empirically derived syndrome scales and eight syndrome subscales, one of which is Oppositional Defiant Problems. Individual items are rated on a 3-point subjective frequency scale (0 = never; 1 = sometimes; 2 = often). The CBCL has separate versions for young children (ages 1.5 to 5 years) and older children (ages 6 to 18 years) and uses age- and gender-based T-scores, with higher scores indicating more frequent symptoms.

Although several studies have supported the psychometric validity of the CBCL in ASD (e.g., Pandolfi, Magyar, & Dill, 2009, 2012), and it is frequently used in ASD research and clinical settings, it has not been shown to be strongly connected to ODD diagnostic criteria within this population. Note, despite this finding, screening prevalence rates reported in Table 8.1 include use of the CBCL and TRF.

The Children's Scale of Hostility and Aggression: Reactive/Proactive (C-SHARP; Farmer & Aman, 2010) is an informant checklist of several types of aggressive and hostile behavior; it queries five domains of aggression and is best suited to clinical and research applications where aggression is the primary target of assessment or intervention. The C-SHARP was developed from a factor-analytic study of 365 youth aged 3 to 21 years with intellectual and developmental delays and has been shown to have adequate psychometric properties (Farmer & Aman, 2010). The factor validity was subsequently confirmed in a separate clinic-based sample, and the measurement invariance between children with ASD compared to children with other developmental delays was upheld (Farmer et al., 2016). Although reliability and validity for the C-SHARP has been established for assessment, it has not been used as an outcome measure in a treatment study.

The Early Childhood Inventory (ECI; Sprafkin, Volpe, Gadow, Nolan, & Kelly, 2002), Child Symptom Inventory (CSI; Sprafkin, Gadow, Salisbury, Schneider, & Loney, 2010), Adolescent Symptom Inventory (ASI; Nolan, Gadow, & Sprafkin, 2001), and combined Child and Adolescent Symptom Inventory (CASI; Lavigne, Cromley, Sprafkin, & Gadow, 2009) are multi-item, multi-informant (parent-, teacher-, and at some ages self-report) measures that assess a wide range of psychiatric diagnoses, including ODD and ASD. At least one version of the symptom inventories is appropriate from ages 3 to 18 years. Each of them requires respondents to indicate which frequency rating "best describes this youth's overall behavior." Individual items bear one-to-one correspondence with DSM-IV symptoms and are rated on a scale from 0 (never) to 3 (very often). The items in parent and teacher versions are identical; however, a few symptoms/diagnoses that are unlikely to be observed in one setting are omitted from one or the other version (none from the ODD criteria). On the CASI, the last item in each symptom subscale addresses impairment by asking the informant, "How often do the behaviors in [this category] interfere with youth's ability to do schoolwork or get along with others?" There are several scoring procedures, each of which has certain advantages for specific clinical and research applications. The symptom severity score is the sum of all item scores from a specific subscale, which can be converted to a T-score utilizing gender-, age-, and informant-specific norms. The symptom count score is the total number of symptoms in a specific subscale considered to be problematic (i.e., rated often or very often). Youth receive a symptom cutoff score if the informant endorses the prerequisite number of DSM-IV symptoms specified as being necessary for a clinical diagnosis. The ECI, CSI, and CASI have been used in comorbidity screening studies (as in Table 8.1) and in studies examining the phenomenology of comorbidity in neurotypical and in ASD samples. Relevant to this chapter, they have been used to assess the phenotypic overlap of ASD and ODD (Gadow et al., 2008; Guttmann-Steinmetz, Gadow, & DeVincent, 2009) and to confirm the structure of psychiatric diagnoses in ASD (Lecavalier, Gadow, DeVincent, & Edwards, 2009).

The Home Situations Questionnaire—ASD (HSQ; Chowdhury et al., 2016) is a 24-item measure of noncompliance for children ages 3 to 14 with ASD. It is an adaptation of a 16-item scale developed to examine the severity of noncompliant behavior in children with disruptive behavior (Barkley & Edelbrock, 1987). Raters are asked whether a given situation poses a problem for a child. If the answer is yes, severity is evaluated on a scale ranging from 1 (mild severity) to 9 (significant severity). Examples of situations are "when asked to leave the house," "when in public places," or "when parents are on the phone." The total severity score from all items endorsed "yes" is divided by 24 (the number of items) to derive a per-item mean. The HSQ-ASD contains two 12-item factors: Socially Inflexible and Demand Specific. The HSQ-ASD has been used in a number of multisite intervention studies in children with ASD (e.g., Aman et al., 2009; Bearss et al., 2015; Handen et al., 2015).

The Nisonger Child Behavior Rating Form (NCBRF; Aman, Tasse, Rojahn, & Hammer, 1996; Tassé, Aman, Hammer, & Rojahn, 1996) is designed to be used with children and adolescents ages 3 to 16 years. There is a parent and teacher version, with identical content and similar factor structures (Lecavalier, Aman, Hammer, Stoica, & Matthews, 2004). Each version contains two sections, Social Competence and Problem Behaviors. The Social Competence section contains 10 items rated on a 4-point scale and distributed on two subscales: Compliant/Calm and Adaptive/Social. The Problem Behavior section contains 66 items, also rated on a 4-point scale and distributed on six subscales: Conduct Problem, Insecure/Anxious, Hyperactive, Self-Injury/Stereotypic, Self-Isolated/Ritualistic, and Overly Sensitive (parent)/Irritable (teacher). Lecavalier et al. (2004) showed that the original factor structure for the NCBRF held fundamentally true for youth with ASD. Of particular relevance to disruptive behaviors in ASD are the two social competence subscales, as well as the Conduct Problem and Hyperactive subscales. The NCBRF has not been used in large-scale treatment studies of children with ASD but has been used as the primary outcome measure in large trials of children with disruptive behavior without ASD (Aman et al., 2002, 2014).

Functional assessment. Functional assessment involves the use of direct observations of the child in laboratory or naturalistic settings to examine environmental events that precede and follow a target disruptive behavior. Findings from the direct observation are then used to determine the function, or "purpose," of the behavior (Iwata & Worsdell, 2005; Reese, Richman, Belmont, & Morse, 2005), which can in turn inform appropriate intervention strategies (Brosnan & Healy, 2011; Campbell, 2003; Horner, Carr, Strain, Todd, & Reed, 2002).

There are three types of functional assessments: functional analysis, indirect functional assessment, and descriptive functional assessment (Tarbox et al., 2009). Functional analysis (FA) involves observation of the child where environmental events are deliberately manipulated during strictly controlled experimental conditions (Iwata, Dorsey, Slifer, Bauman, & Richman, 1994). FA has been extensively researched and is often recommended as a valid means to identify the function of target behaviors because it allows for a controlled test of factors that lead to disruptive behavior and has been shown to guide the development of successful interventions (Hanley, 2012). However, FA requires specialized training, is time-consuming, and involves setting up experimental conditions that may not be ecologically valid (Conroy, Fox, Crain, Jenkins, & Belcher, 1996; Sturmey, 1995). Although researchers have sought to address all of these limitations (Hanley, 2012; Iwata & Dozier, 2008), FA is not frequently used in practice (Oliver, Pratt, & Normand, 2015).

Providers may instead rely on indirect or descriptive functional assessment (Oliver et al., 2015). Indirect functional assessment involves interviewing parents or teachers to identify antecedents and consequences to a behavior. The provider uses this information to develop hypotheses about the function of the disruptive behavior (Carr & Wilder, 2003; Durand & Crimmins, 1992; Matson & Vollmer, 1995). In comparison, descriptive functional assessment includes direct observation of antecedents and consequences surrounding the child's target behavior in the natural environment to hypothesize the function of the behavioral problem (Carr & Wilder, 2003; Tarbox et al., 2009). Both indirect and descriptive functional assessments have the benefit of being relatively quick to administer and are based on information of the child in the natural environment. Descriptive functional assessment has the additional benefit of focusing on prospective observational data collection instead of requiring informants to recall past events. These forms of functional assessment are limited, however, by the lack of control over extraneous environmental variables, such as attention provided by a sibling or unrestricted access to preferred items. In addition, systematic reviews have identified only a few studies on such assessments, and interventions based on these assessments were less successful than those based on FA (Herzinger & Campbell, 2007). Although FA and descriptive functional assessments are typically conducted by professionals (e.g., board-certified behavior analysts (BCBAs), school personnel; Fettig & Barton, 2013), some research suggests that with instruction from a clinician, parents can be taught to conduct a functional assessment to identify the purpose of behavioral problems that can be used to plan treatment (Frea & Hepburn, 1999; Lindgren et al., 2016; Suess et al., 2016; Wacker et al., 2013).

Treatment

A transdisciplinary "biopsychosocial" or "biobehavioral" approach to the treatment of ODD recognizes that disruptive behavior likely has multiple determinants, including genetic abnormalities, psychiatric and neurological dysfunction, environmental variables such as the availability of reinforcement, and social interactions that may reinforce disruptive behavior (Newcomb & Hagopian, 2018). An integrative biobehavioral approach advocates for the use of behavioral interventions to address problems that stem from social and environmental variables and pharmacological agents to address problems stemming from neuropsychiatric dysfunction (Newcomb & Hagopian, 2018). This combination approach may lead to lower prescribed doses of medication and improved sustainability over time (Hagopian & Caruso-Anderson, 2010).

Treating ODD in ASD: Psychopharmacology

Currently, risperidone and aripiprazole are the only medications approved by the Food and Drug Administration (FDA) for the treatment of irritability and aggression in individuals with ASD (Fung et al., 2016). Specifically, in 2006, the FDA approved risperidone to treat irritability (i.e., aggression, deliberate self-injury, and temper tantrums) based on two 8-week, placebo-controlled trials in 156 patients aged 5 to 16 years (McCracken et al., 2002; Pandina et al., 2007). Subsequently, aripiprazole was approved for irritability, with evidence from two randomized controlled trials supporting its efficacy and safety (Owen et al., 2009; Marcus et al., 2009).

Both medications are now being widely used in patients with ASD (Mandell et al., 2008) but carry a significant risk of metabolic and neurologic adverse events for a subset of patients, including weight gain, sedation, and extrapyramidal symptoms such as tremors, dyskinesia, akathisia, and rigidity (Fung et al., 2016). These concerns mandate consideration of lower risk interventions, even for severe problem behavior, targeting factors such as medical issues or communication challenges that may be potentially contributory to problem behavior (McGuire et al., 2016). Medications are best suited when (a) safety is an issue; (b) the behaviors interfere with functioning to the degree that a change in school or residential placement is at risk; (c) other behavioral/medical treatments have been ineffective; (d) behaviors are judged to be unrelated to psychosocial stressors, communication difficulties, or underlying medial or psychiatric conditions; or (e) lower risk interventions cannot be implemented (Fung et al., 2016; McGuire et al., 2016).

Treating ODD in ASD: Applied Behavior Analysis

Behavioral treatments targeting disruptive behaviors in children with ASD are largely built on a set of basic assumptions: (a) children with ASD primarily engage in unwanted behaviors to gain access to a tangible item of interest, gain access to adult attention, or escape/avoid a nonpreferred situation, and (b) children with ASD are likely to have deficits in functional communication skills. Given the previous two points, children with ASD are at high risk of engaging in disruptive and noncompliant behaviors. They also are likely to have deficits in adaptive behaviors, which can be amplified by noncompliant behavior.

For half a century, applied behavior analysis (ABA) has generated an extensive body of literature detailing a number of procedures that are effective in treating a range of problem behaviors in children with ASD and intellectual disability (Newcomb & Hagopian, 2018), with behavioral interventions relying on functional assessment producing larger effect sizes than those without (Didden et al., 2006). ABA for individuals with ASD can be broadly characterized as "comprehensive" or "problem focused," the latter of which most often targets specific disruptive behaviors such as self-injury, aggression, pica, and elopement. Problem-focused ABA tends to be shorter in duration with more narrowly defined treatment goals, targeting behaviors that appear to be environmental in origin (Matson, 2009). Several meta-analyses have been conducted that support the efficacy of problem-focused ABA treatments in decreasing rates of multiple types of problem behavior for persons with intellectual disabilities, including ASD (Harvey, Boer, Meyer, & Evans, 2009; Heyvaert, Maes, Van Den Noortgate, Kuppens, & Onghena, 2012).

Theoretical foundations of ABA. Operant conditioning is a core component of ABA, which is defined as the systematic application of interventions based on the principles of learning theory to improve socially significant behaviors, reduce maladaptive behavior, and demonstrate that the interventions employed are responsible for the change in behavior (Baer, Wolk, & Risley, 1968). Operant conditioning posits that behavior can be modified through the manipulation of its antecedent, which is the cue for the onset of a learned behavior, or its consequence, which is the event that immediately follows a behavior. By learning more about the events that surround a behavior, one can determine its purpose, or *function*: access to a tangible item (e.g., food or a favorite toy), attention from others (positive reinforcement), escape or avoidance from a demand or an aversive stimuli (negative reinforcement), or sensory and other internal stimulation (automatic reinforcement; Iwata & Worsdell, 2005).

ABA in the context of a behavioral problem begins with the assertion that the child's disruptive behavior is not a random occurrence. This runs counter to what parents often report in clinic: Although they can be eloquent about the actual behavior (i.e., the frequency, duration, intensity), parents often describe meltdowns as unpredictable or coming from "out of nowhere." They are often less able to describe the events and situations that increase the likelihood of the behavior. Faced with behavioral problems that they do not understand, parents may then inadvertently respond in ways that reinforce the child's inappropriate behavior. By understanding the function of the behavior problem, parents learn to change their usual response to teach the child a more appropriate behavior (Horner et al., 2002).

The antecedent–behavior–consequence model breaks down this sequence to identify the environmental circumstances that may provoke the behavior (antecedents) and the responses that maintain it (consequences). This, in turn, facilitates a better understanding of how to manipulate the environment by modifying the antecedents that trigger and consequences that maintain a behavior. Reinforcement and punishment are the core processes through which behaviors are modified. Positive reinforcement (e.g., providing praise for cleaning up toys) and negative reinforcement (e.g., allowing break from schoolwork when the child asks nicely) increase the probability of future behaviors. By contrast, positive punishment (e.g., a reprimand) and negative punishment (e.g., removing a favorite toy for hitting) reduce the future probability of a behavior.

Application of ABA for ODD. A hallmark of ABA in the treatment of disruptive behavior is its individualized approach. Until recently, this stance made large-scale trials generally unsuitable. Instead, decades of single-subject design research, resulting in the publication of many hundreds of studies, have demonstrated the efficacy of ABA in the treatment of behaviors such as noncompliance, aggression, and self-injury for individuals with ASD (Campbell, 2003). Individually, single-subject studies offer proof of concept for effective techniques to reduce maladaptive behavior. Collated, these studies provide the data to support the assertion that ABA is an evidence-based approach in the treatment of disruptive behaviors in individuals with ASD.

The individualized approach of ABA in the treatment of disruptive behavior does not come without challenges. The need for highly trained personnel (typically a BCBA), the lack of manualized approaches, and the scarcity of ABA services outside of specialized centers hinder treatment access (Croen, Grether, Hoogstrate, & Selvin, 2002; Smith et al., 2007). ABA services may also involve work between provider and child specifically within the context of the clinic or school environment, resulting in parents being on the periphery of their child's treatment programming. Compounding the problem is the lack of quality community-based services for youth with ASD and co-occurring disruptive behaviors. Although children with ASD represent 10% to 14% of psychiatrically referred populations (Joshi et al., 2010), only 5% of community mental health therapists consider themselves to have expertise in ASD (Brookman-Frazee, Drahota, & Stadnick, 2012). In addition, parents report frustration about the slow pace of progress in treatment and lack of practical "tools" to manage child behavioral problems (Brookman-Frazee et al., 2012). As a result, the demand for parent support in caring for children with ASD within school and community systems far outpaces the availability of services by skilled providers. This lack of access may result in long delays in securing effective behavioral intervention. Some families may resort to obtaining services in specialty clinics. Other children may go without needed services (Wacker et al., 2013).

Parent training for ODD in ASD. The recognized struggles parents face in raising a child with ASD (Hayes & Watson, 2013; Kogan et al., 2008; Tonge et al., 2006), in combination with challenges accessing treatments in the community, have prompted increased interest in the development of evidence-based, parent-focused interventions for ASD. Parent training (PT) warrants interest as a front-line intervention model because it is traditionally a time-limited approach (typically 10 to 20 sessions) delivered during brief (1- to 1.5-hour) weekly sessions. As such, it may be applicable in a wide range of service settings. PT also emphasizes the role of parents as the change agent. Teaching parents to be the therapist for their child allows for delivery of treatment across settings and contexts (Burrell & Borrego, 2012).

PT involves teaching parents how to implement specific procedures designed to improve parent–child interactions, decrease behavioral problems, and increase prosocial behaviors (Kazdin, 2005; Wierson & Forehand, 1994). For children with ASD, PT also sets the stage for targeting improved adaptive functioning. PT programs targeting disruptive behaviors and based on principles of ABA typically begin with educating parents on the antecedent–behavior–consequence model as a means to better understand the function of their child's disruptive behaviors. The goal is to help parents recognize that their child's behaviors are predictable and how their current responses to behaviors may be inadvertently promoting their reoccurrence. Therapists may then review implementation of antecedent management strategies and consequence-based approaches. Specifically, parents can learn strategies to prevent behaviors from occurring, how to attend to the child's prosocial behaviors while ignoring inappropriate behaviors, and how to decrease the use of punitive and coercive discipline strategies while increasing the use of effective, appropriate, noncoercive child management strategies. These components are the centerpiece of PT for reducing behavioral problems (Kaminski, Valle, Filene, & Boyle, 2008). For children with ASD, PT programs may also include approaches that promote skill acquisition and functional communication as well as maintenance and generalization strategies designed to promote stability in the child's positive behavior change and to ensure application of skills in future situations and settings. Common approaches to promote parent skill acquisition include role playing, in-session guided implementation with the child, and weekly homework and data collection so that parents can practice applying strategies in real life.

Research support for PT. There is a convincing body of evidence built on over 40 years of controlled studies that PT is effective for children with disruptive behavior. Indeed, PT for disruptive behavioral problems is among the most well-established evidence-based treatments in child mental health (Dretzke et al., 2009; Michelson, Davenport, Dretzke, Barlow, & Day, 2013). Within ASD, parent-implemented techniques based on principles of ABA historically demonstrated empirical support through single-subject design studies (Campbell, 2003).

Evidence for the efficacy of PT for disruptive behavior in children with ASD has recently expanded, through a handful of open prospective case series (Bearss, Johnson, Handen, Smith, & Scahill, 2013; Brookman-Frazee et al., 2012; Dabanah & Parish, 2016; Okuno et al., 2011; Roberts & Pickering, 2010; Research Units on Pediatric Psychopharmacology Autism Network , 2007; Wacker et al., 2013) and quasi-experimental trials (Lindgren et al., 2016; Tonge et al., 2014). Additionally, six randomized clinical trials (RCTs) of PT as a stand-alone treatment have been published to date (sample sizes ranged from 26 to 180; Bearss et al., 2015; Ginn, Clionsky, Eyberg, Warner-Metzger, & Abner, 2015; Reitzel et al., 2013; Sofronoff, Leslie, & Brown, 2004; Tellegen & Sanders, 2014; Whittingham, Sofronoff, Sheffield, & Sanders, 2009). Tellegen and Sanders (2014) and Whittingham et al. (2009) conducted RCTs examining the efficacy of the Triple P program. Sofronoff et al. (2004) conducted a three-group study that compared a six-session individual PT program to a 1-day workshop and a waitlist control in youth with Asperger's disorder. Parent–child interaction therapy, which was originally developed for preschoolers with disruptive behaviors without ASD, was examined in 39 children with ASD (Ginn et al., 2015). PT has also been shown to be an effective adjunct treatment to medication: atomoxetine in the treatment of attention deficit hyperactivity disorder and noncompliance (Handen et al., 2015) and risperidone in the treatment of serious behavioral problems (Aman et al., 2009). Most recently, a meta-analysis of eight randomized controlled trials showed that PT is an effective intervention for reducing disruptive behavior in children with ASD (ages 2 to 14 years). The quality and duration of PT varied and effect sizes ranged from small to large, with an overall effect size of 0.58 (Postorino et al., 2017).

The RUBI parent training program. Over the past decade, investigators from the Research Units in Pediatric Psychopharmacology (RUPP) and Research Units in Behavioral Interventions (RUBI) Autism Network developed and tested a PT program for children (ages 3 to 14 years) with ASD accompanied by disruptive behavior problems. To date, the RUBI program is the best studied manualized PT intervention for reducing disruptive behavior and improving adaptive skills in children with ASD (Aman et al., 2009; Bearss et al., 2015; Postorino et al., 2017). The RUBI program consists of 11 core and six supplemental sessions (e.g., toileting, sleep problems, feeding issues) as well as optional booster sessions and home visits. The intervention, which is based on the principles of ABA, involves therapists teaching parents how to modify the child's behavior, setting up the parent as the change agent. The RUBI program targets challenging behaviors such as tantrums, noncompliance, and aggression that occur during daily activities that pose a struggle for parents of children with ASD.

With funding from the National Institute of Mental Health (NIMH), the initial version of the RUBI manual was tested in a multisite feasibility trial with 17 children aged 4 to 13 (RUPP Autism Network, 2007). This was followed by a 6-month, randomized trial comparing risperidone to risperidone plus PT in 124 school-age children with ASD and serious behavioral problems, defined as having an ABC Irritability subscale raw score of 15 or greater. In that study, both treatment arms resulted in substantial reduction of disruptive behavior, but risperidone plus PT was superior to drug only (Aman et al., 2009). The study also showed that risperidone treatment can cause rapid weight gain and detrimental metabolic consequences (Scahill et al., 2016). The manual was then revised for younger children with ASD and disruptive behaviors under the assumption that a downward extension of the manual may prevent the emergence of more severe behaviors in school-age children and avert the need for medication. An open pilot trial of PT as a *stand-alone* treatment in 16 children between the ages of 3 and 7 years supported the feasibility and initial efficacy of the modified PT manual (Bearss et al., 2013).

The RUBI Autism Network then launched an NIMH-funded multisite trial in 180 children (ages 3 to 7 years) with ASD and disruptive behavior. Subjects were randomly assigned to PT or a structured parent education program (PEP) for 6 months. PEP, which was created specifically for this RCT, provided parents with an up-to-date survey of topics related to ASD (e.g., differential diagnosis, genetics, available treatments, and educational placement). It also included strategies for parents to become effective advocates for their child with ASD. However, PEP did not include any information on child behavior management. As with PT, PEP was delivered individually to parents by trained therapists in 13 sessions over 24 weeks. This comparison condition is designed to control for time and attention (i.e., parental contact with the therapist). Outcomes were assessed by parent report and by independent evaluators who were blind to treatment assignment. Children were also followed for up to 24 weeks posttreatment.

In the RUBI trial, independent evaluators, who were masked to treatment assignment, classified 69% of children in PT with a positive response (rated as "much improved" or "very much improved") on the Clinical Global Impressions-Improvement scale (Guy, 1976) compared to 40% in the PEP group (Bearss et al., 2015). A key secondary outcome of interest was change in adaptive skills as measured on the Vineland Adaptive Behavior Scales (Sparrow, Ciccetti, & Balla, 2005). Consistent with the hypothesis that reducing disruptive behavior sets the stage for improvements in adaptive skills, there was a significant improvement in Vineland Daily Living Skills in PT compared to no change in PEP (Scahill et al., 2016). Parents attended 92% of the core therapy sessions and PT attrition was low at 11%. Therapist fidelity to the PT treatment was excellent, averaging 97%. These results provide strong evidence that the RUBI PT program significantly reduces disruptive behavior, parents are engaged in treatment, and therapists can reliably deliver the intervention.

Case Example

Maddie is a 4-year-old Caucasian female who lives with her biological parents and 8-year-old sister. She presents with a confirmed diagnosis of ASD. In terms of communication, Maddie is verbal, using phrase speech to communicate, although her parents note that when frustrated, she is likely to resort to crying, whining, and "baby talk." In terms of adaptive skills, Maddie can undress herself independently, but has more difficulty putting clothes on. She has notable sleep and feeding issues, including coming into her parents' room on a nightly basis and refusing to stay at the table to eat meals. She is not taking any medications aside from vitamins and probiotics. Maddie is in a self-contained special needs preschool classroom. At school, she is receiving speech therapy, 30 minutes per week. Maddie is in private speech therapy 45 minutes per week.

Maddie was referred to the RUBI PT program due to parent-reported concerns of disruptive behaviors involving tantrums and noncompliance as well as difficulties separating from her mother and sleep difficulties. Tantrums, which can take the form of screaming, freezing, yelling, and/or lying down on the ground and kicking her feet, occur two to three times per day and can last up to 20 minutes. Noncompliance, which occurs daily in the context of routines such as dressing, picking up toys, and following mealtime routines, may involve Maddie ignoring her parents' requests or throwing objects while being defiant. In terms of separation issues, Maddie's mother reported that Maddie will rarely let her "out of sight" without having a meltdown or running to her mother and clinging to her leg. Sleep issues include a prolonged history of difficulties with falling and staying asleep as well as coming into her parents' room on a nightly basis.

Assessment battery. Maddie's abbreviated IQ was derived from the Stanford Binet Intelligent Scales, fifth edition (SB-5; Roid, 2003). During testing, she was able to successfully transition to the table and was pleasant throughout the evaluation, completing most testing items that were presented. Maddie received a computed IQ score of 88, which places her in the average range compared to other children her age. Maddie's adaptive skills were derived from the parent-completed Adaptive Behavior Assessment System, third edition (ABAS-III; Harrison & Oakland, 2015). The general adaptive composite score (GAC) summarizes performance across all skill areas, and Maddie obtained a GAC score of 84, which places her current overall adaptive behavior in the low average range. Maddie received a T-score of greater than 90 on the total score of the Social Responsiveness Scale, second edition (SRS-2; Constantino, 2012), indicating she exhibits deficits in reciprocal social behavior that are clinically significant and lead to severe interference with everyday social interactions. Finally, Maddie's parents reported significant disruptive behavior as measured by a raw score of 15 on the ABC Irritability subscale (Aman & Singh, 2017) and a mean severity score of 2.92 on the Home Situations Questionnaire-Autism Spectrum Disorder (HSQ-ASD; Chowdhury et al., 2016). This indicates that Maddie engages in multiple types and topographies of challenging behaviors.

Based on the information provided by Maddie's mother and father regarding her target behaviors and results from standardized testing, it was recommended that Maddie and her family initiate the RUBI PT program.

Treatment course. Maddie's parents began the RUBI program and attended a total of 12 in-person sessions over the course of 15 weeks, followed by a 1-month in-person booster session. Her parents initially collected antecedent–behavior–consequence data to learn more about the function of Maddie's tantrums and noncompliance (Table 8.2). When reviewing this data with the therapist, it was noted that common antecedents to Maddie's target problem behaviors included demands during daily transitions (e.g., getting dressed, getting ready for bed, getting off the iPad) and when being asked to stop engaging in a behavior (e.g., "leave your sister's Kindle alone"). Maddie's parents identified escape/avoidance and "getting what she wants" (tangible) as possible functions of her behavior. We also noted that sometimes it was unclear whether she was engaging in the behavior to "get what she wants" (more time on the iPad) or to "escape" (from having to start her bedtime routine).

Table 8.3 provides a detailed account of treatment activities and generated strategies. Initial prevention strategies focused on aiding Maddie with transitions (e.g., using a timer to provide warnings). The timer was subsequently added as a visual cue to help Maddie know how long she needed to stay at the table for meals, initially focusing on "small doses" (i.e., 5-minute intervals), where she could earn a reinforcer (mini M&Ms) each time she successfully stayed at the table. A visual schedule was introduced at Session 3 to promote understanding of and compliance with the daily routine. This included outlining for Maddie that, in the afternoon, she needed to complete an independent play activity before having a joint playtime with her mother. The schedule was readily accepted by Maddie and even prompted her engagement in tasks that she had previously refused to do (e.g., brushing teeth). Along with targeting staying at the table, reinforcement strategies targeted naturalistic opportunities to tie Maddie's requests for a preferred item to completion of a specific demand (e.g., if Maddie requested her father's phone, her father would prompt her first to pick up a toy, then she could have the phone). Planned ignoring was initially implemented to target negative attention-seeking tantrums, such as when Maddie's mother would set a limit (e.g., no more iPad time) and Maddie would respond with crying and falling on the floor. Timeout was eventually introduced to more directly target attention-seeking tantrums. Compliance training targeted Maddie holding her mother's hand and walking next to her when out in public. This addressed Maddie's tendency to demand to be picked up and carried or fall to the floor when she did not want to leave a place. For the functional communication session, Maddie was taught a more appropriate way to communicate her desire to play with her mother (i.e., saying

Table 8.2. Case Study: Antecedent–Behavior–Consequence Data

Antecedent	Behavior	Consequence	Function
Told "no" she cannot have the phone	Pushing	I said "no thank you" (verbal reprimand)	To get what she wants
Told to put shirt on	Roll away from her mother, fall back on the sofa	Mom took away the iPad	To escape (getting dressed)
Told "it's time for bed"	Shut the door on her parents (she was playing with the iPad)	Mom reopened the door, touched the iPad, and told her to put it away (which she then complied with)	Escape (bedtime) To get what she wants (more iPad time)

Table 8.3. Case Study: Summary of Strategies

Target Behaviors	Prevention	Reinforcement	Consequence	Functional Communication	Skill Training
Tantrums, noncompliance, separation issues, and adaptive skills	Introduce a timer to help with transitions off of preferred activities (e.g., iPad) and to teach waiting. To address dawdling with leaving the bathroom (because she likes to engage in water play), use a timer to set a limit on how long she can brush her teeth, then play with the water. Implement a visual schedule during the morning, afternoon, and evening routine to help with predictability in the routine, showing what "fun" activities follow less preferred demands. On the schedule, require independent play activities in the afternoon prior to being able to have play time with mom. To prevent tantrums around wanting to see the fish at the library, follow the "library" visual schedule, which shows when she will be able to visit the fish (after they have checked out a book).	Reinforce staying at the table for 5 minutes: Use the timer to target sitting at the dinner table for 5 minutes. If she stays in her chair, she can earn a portion of mini M&Ms. If she engages in repetitive requesting of the M&Ms, she loses them for that time period. Create a prize box and set up a reward system so that if she stays in her bed all night, she can pick a prize out of the prize box in the morning.	Ignore the behavior but not the child for repetitive requests; ignore the child and the behavior for tantrums. Use timeout to target "throwing a fit" (whining, crying, screaming, yelling). Use 3 days prior to implementation to point out instances of these behaviors that will get her put in timeout. Create a visual to show what the steps of timeout will look like. Timeout occurs on the stairs. Redirection will be used for escape. One minute of quiet will be required to leave timeout. Practice the four steps of compliance training (get attention, give command, physical prompt, praise) targeting hand holding and walking (vs. being carried). We discussed adding an incentive (reward), offered in advance, if she complies right away with the demand of hand holding and walking.	She is starting to spontaneously vocalize "I want to go home" when out in public. This is an appropriate request that should be rewarded (with immediate, consistent response). If there is a need for her to wait, provide a specific prompt (e.g., we can leave in 3 minutes, then show a visual timer).	Putting on her shirt is the target skill to teach using forward chaining. Prompts will include video modeling and physical prompting.

Table 8.4. Case Study: Parent-Reported Outcomes for the RUBI Parent Training Program

	ABC-I	HSQ-ASD Total Problems	HSQ-ASD Severity	HSQ-ASD Mean Severity
Baseline	15	18	70	2.92
Endpoint	14	16	60	2.5
1-Month follow-up	4	8	16	0.67

ABC-I, Aberrant Behavior Checklist-Irritability subscale; HSQ-ASD, Home Situations Questionnaire-Autism Spectrum Disorder; RUBI, Research Units in Behavioral Interventions.

"Play with me") in place of her current form of communicating this (i.e., whining, clinging to her mother's leg). Maddie's parents also were taught to respond immediately when Maddie appropriately requested to leave an area (stating "I want to go home") instead of waiting for a meltdown to respond. The teaching skills sessions targeted helping Maddie learn how to put on her clothes independently. The supplemental sleep session focused on implementing a reward system for Maddie staying in her room all night. If she stayed in her room, the following morning she could pick out a prize from a prize box as soon as she woke up in the morning.

The RUBI program, overall, emphasized the importance of Maddie's parents implementing all strategies in a manner that promoted consistency and predictability in Maddie's daily routine. Her parents successfully implemented all aspects of these programmatic components. At a 1-month follow up visit, Maddie's parents reported a 77% decrease in noncompliance from baseline on the Home Situations Questionnaire-Autism Spectrum Disorder and a 73% reduction from baseline in her irritability on the ABC Irritability subscale (Table 8.4).

Summary and Future Directions

Over a half a century of literature describing assessment and treatment procedures for disruptive behaviors such as noncompliance, verbal aggression (argumentative behavior), tantrums, and physical aggression in individuals with ASD and related developmental disabilities suggests this field of study is not new. Conceptualizing these hallmark behaviors within the framework of ODD for individuals with ASD, however, is relatively novel. This is reflected in the sparse literature on the prevalence of ODD within this population as well as pharmacological and psychosocial treatment outcome research, which have focused on reductions in related symptomatic behaviors (e.g., irritability, noncompliance) rather than remission or movement out of the diagnostic category of ODD (Aman et al., 2009; Bearss et al., 2015).

Clinically, uncertainty around the applicability of several of the ODD diagnostic criteria in youth with ASD may create reluctance by providers to diagnose ODD and instead lead them to utilize broader terms such as "disruptive," "maladaptive," or "challenging" behaviors when characterizing treatment-seeking youth. Clearly work remains in increasing our understanding of the appropriateness of the current diagnostic criteria of ODD for youth with ASD. For example, although the disruptive behaviors associated with ODD are highly prevalent in children with ASD (Kaat & Lecavalier, 2013), it is not well understood whether these behavioral displays are related to the same impulse control and emotional regulation deficits in the general population or whether they are unique signals of dysregulation within ASD. There are some emerging signals indicating commonalities in the presentation of ODD. The DSM-5 has adopted the tripartite model of ODD ("angry and irritable symptoms [AIS]; "argumentative and defiant behavior [ADB], and "vindictiveness" [V]), with each dimension of oppositionality distinctly associating with other forms of psychopathology (AIS related to mood and anxiety disorders; ADB related to attention deficit hyperactivity disorder; V related to aggressive symptoms of conduct disorder; Stringaris & Goodman, 2009a, 2009b). Although these unique pairings to ODD dimensions were informed by findings from non-ASD populations, Mandy, Roughan, and Skuse (2014) replicated these independent and distinct associations in a sample of 216 high-functioning youth with ASD ages 3 to 16. The burgeoning field of research on emotion regulation in individuals with ASD will hopefully continue to provide clarity on these issues.

Interventions grounded in ABA currently maintain status as the standard of care in ASD for a broad array of targets, including disruptive behaviors. One area making important strides is the development of community-viable, cost-effective, and empirically supported treatments, most notably parent training interventions. As the treatment field expands, there will be a concomitant need for dissemination (spreading the word about the evidence-based intervention) and implementation (deliberate steps to incorporate the treatment into real-world settings) of these novel additions to the field.

References

Achenbach, T. M., & Rescorla, L. A. (2001). *Manual for the ASEBA school-age forms & profiles.* Burlington, VT: Research Centre for Children, Youth and Families, University of Vermont.

Achenbach, T. M., & Ruffle, T. M. (2000). The Child Behavior Checklist and related forms for assessing behavioral/ emotional problems and competencies. *Pediatrics in Review, 21*(8), 265–271.

Aman, M. G., Bukstein, O. G., Gadow, K. D., Arnold, L. E., Molina, B. S. G., McNamara, N. K,... Findling, R. L. (2014). What does risperidone add to parent training and stimulant for severe aggression in child attention deficit/ hyperactivity disorder? *Journal of the American Academy of Child and Adolescent Psychiatry, 53*(1), 47–60.

Aman, M. G., DeSmedt, G., Derivab, A., Lyons, B., Findling, R. L., and the Risperidone Disruptive Behavior Study Group. (2002). Double-blind, placebo-controlled study of risperidone for the treatment of disruptive behaviors in children with sub-average intelligence. *American Journal of Psychiatry, 159*(8), 1337–1346.

Aman, M. G., McDougle, C. J., Scahill, L., Handen, B., Arnold, L. E., Johnson, C.,... Wagner, A. (2009). Medication and parent training in children with pervasive developmental disorders and serious behavior problems: Results from a randomized clinical trial. *Journal of the American Academy of Child and Adolescent Psychiatry, 48*(12), 1143–1154.

Aman, M. G., & Singh, N. N. (2017). *The Aberrant Behavior Checklist* (2nd ed.). Aurora, NY: Slosson.

Aman, M. G., Tasse, M. J., Rojahn, J., & Hammer, D. (1996). The Nisonger CBRF: A child behavior rating form for children with developmental disabilities. *Research in Developmental Disabilities, 17*(1), 41–57.

American Psychiatric Association. (2013). *Diagnostic and statistical manual of mental disorders* (5th ed.). Washington, DC: Author.

Baer, D. M., Wolf, M. M., & Risley, T. R. (1968). Some current dimensions of applied behavior analysis. *Journal of Applied Behavior Analysis, 1*(1), 91–97.

Barkley, R. A., & Edelbrock, C. (1987). Assessing situational variation in children's problem behaviors: The Home and School Situations Questionnaires. In R. Prinz (Ed.), *Advances in behavioral assessment of children and families* (pp. 157–176). Greenwich, CT: JAI Press.

Bearss, K., Johnson, C., Handen, B., Smith, T., & Scahill, L. (2013). A pilot study of parent training in young children with autism spectrum disorders and disruptive behavior. *Journal of Autism and Developmental Disorders, 43*(4), 829–840.

Bearss, K., Johnson, C., Smith, T., Lecavalier, L., Swiezy, N., Aman, M.,... Scahill, L. (2015). Effect of parent training vs parent education on behavior problems in children with autism spectrum disorder: A randomized clinical trial. *Journal of the American Medical Association, 313*, 1524–1533. doi:10.1001/jama.2015.3150

Brereton, A. V., Tonge, B. J., & Einfeld, S. L. (2006). Psychopathology in children and adolescents with autism compared to young people with intellectual disability. *Journal of Autism and Developmental Disorders, 36*(7), 863–870.

Brookman-Frazee, L., Drahota, A., & Stadnick, N. (2012). Training community mental health therapists to deliver a package of evidence-based practice strategies for school-age children with autism spectrum disorders: A pilot study. *Journal of Autism and Developmental Disorders, 42*(8), 1651–1661.

Brosnan, J., & Healy, O. (2011). A review of behavioral interventions for the treatment of aggression in individuals with developmental disabilities. *Research in Developmental Disabilities, 32*(2), 437–446.

Bryce, C. I., & Jahromi, L. B. (2013). Brief report: Compliance and noncompliance to parental control strategies in children with high-functioning autism and their typical peers. *Journal of Autism and Developmental Disorders, 43*, 236–243.

Burrell, T. L., & Borrego, J. J. (2012). Parents' involvement in ASD treatment: What is their role? *Cognitive and Behavioral Practice, 19*(3), 423–432.

Campbell, J. (2003). Efficacy of behavioral interventions for reducing problem behavior in persons with autism: A quantitative synthesis of single-subject research. *Research in Developmental Disabilities, 24*(2), 120–138.

Canino, G., Polanczyk, G., Bauermeister, J.J., Rohde, L.A., & Frick, P.J. (2010). Does the prevalence of CD and ODD vary across cultures? Social Psychiatry and Psychiatric Epidemiology, 145 (7), 695–704.

Carr, J. E., & Wilder, D. A. (2003). *Functional assessment and intervention: A guide to understanding problem behavior* (2nd ed.). Homewood, IL: High Tide Press.

Chowdhury, M., Aman, M. G., Lecavalier, L., Smith, T., Johnson, C., Swiezy, N.,... Scahill, L. (2016). Factor structure and psychometric properties of the Home Situations Questionnaire for autism spectrum disorder: The Home Situations Questionnaire—Autism Spectrum Disorder. *Autism, 20*(5), 528–537.

Conroy, M., Fox, J., Crain, L., Jenkins, A., & Belcher, K. (1996). Evaluating the social and ecological validity of analog assessment procedures for challenging behaviors in young children. *Education and Treatment of Children, 19*(3), 233–256.

Constantino, J. N. (2012). *Social Responsiveness Scale* (2nd ed., *SRS-2*). Torrance, Los Angeles, CA: Western Psychological Services.

Copeland, W.E., Angold, A., Costello, E.J., & Egger, H. (2013). Prevalence, comorbidity, and correlates of DSM-5 proposed disruptive mood dysregulation disorder. *American Journal of Psychiatry, 170*, 173–179.

Croen, L. A., Grether, J. K., Hoogstrate, J., & Selvin, S. (2002). The changing prevalence of autism in California. *Journal of Autism and Developmental Disorders, 32*(3), 207–215.

Dababnah, S., & Parish, S. L. (2016). Feasibility of an empirically based program for parents of preschoolers with autism spectrum disorder. *Autism, 20*(1), 85–95.

de Bruin, E. I., Ferdinand, R. F., Meester, S., de Nijs, P. F. A., & Verheij, F. (2007). High rates of psychiatric co-morbidity in PDD-NOS. *Journal of Autism and Developmental Disorders, 37*, 877–886.

Didden, R., Korzilius, H., van Oorsouw, W., & Sturmey, P. (2006). Behavioral treatment of challenging behaviors in individuals with mild mental retardation: Meta-analysis of single-subject research. *American Journal on Mental Retardation, 111*, 290–298.

Dretzke, J., Davenport, C., Frew, E., Barlow, J., Stewart-Brown, S., Bayliss, S., . . . Hyde, C. (2009). The clinical effectiveness of different parenting programmes for children with conduct problems: A systematic review of randomized control trials. *Child and Adolescent Psychiatry and Mental Health, 3*, 7. doi:10.1186/1753-2000-3-7

Durand, V. M., & Crimmins, D. B. (1992). *The Motivation Assessment Scale (MAS) administration guide*. Topeka, KS: Monaco.

Durand, V. M., & Merges, E. (2001). Functional communication training: A contemporary behavior analytic intervention for problem behaviors. *Focus on Autism and Other Developmental Disorders, 16*, 110–119.

Farmer, C., & Aman, M. (2010). Psychometric properties of the Children's Scale of Hostility and Aggression (C-SHARP). *Research in Developmental Disabilities, 31*(1), 270–280.

Farmer, C. A., Kaat, A. J., Mazurek, M., Lainhart, J., Dewitt, M., Cook, E., ... Aman, M. G. (2016). Confirmation of the factor structure and measurement invariance of the Children's Scale of Hostility and Aggression: Reactive/Proactive (C-SHARP). *Journal of Child and Adolescent Psychopharmacology, 26*(1), 10–18.

Fettig, A., & Barton, E. E. (2013). Parent-implemented interventions for young children with disabilities: A review of fidelity features. *Journal of Early Intervention, 35*(2), 194–219.

Frea, W. D., & Hepburn, S. L. (1999). Teaching parents of children with autism to perform functional assessments to plan interventions for extremely disruptive behaviors. *Journal of Positive Behavior Interventions, 1*(2), 112–116.

Fristad, M. A., Teare, M., Weller, E. B., Weller, R. A., & Salmon, P. (1998). Study III: Development and concurrent validity of the Children's Interview for Psychiatric Syndromes—Parent Version (P-ChIPS). *Journal of Child and Adolescent Psychopharmacology, 8*(4), 221–226.

Fung, L. K., Mahajan, R., Nozzolillo, A., Bernal, P., Krasner, A., Jo, B., . . . Hardan, A. (2016). Pharmacologic treatment of severe irritability and problem behaviors in autism: A systematic review and meta-analysis. *Pediatrics, 137*, 124–135. doi:10.1542/peds.2015-2851K

Gadow, K. D., DeVincent, C. J., & Drabick, D. A. G. (2008). Oppositional defiant disorder as a clinical phenotype in children with autism spectrum disorder. *Journal of Autism and Developmental Disorders, 38*, 1302–1310.

Gadow, K. D., DeVincent, C. J., Pomeroy, J., & Azizian, A. (2004). Psychiatric symptoms in preschool children with PDD and clinic and comparison samples. *Journal of Autism and Developmental Disorders, 34*(4), 379–393.

Gadow, K. D., DeVincent, C. J., Pomeroy, J., & Azizian, A. (2005). Comparison of DSM-IV symptoms in elementary school-age children with PDD versus clinic and community samples. *Autism: The International Journal of Research and Practice, 9*(4), 392–415.

Gadow, K. D., DeVincent, C., & Schneider, J. (2008). Predictors of psychiatric symptoms in children with an autism spectrum disorder. *Journal of Autism and Developmental Disorders, 38*(9), 1710–1720.

Ginn, N. C., Clionsky, L. N., Eyberg, S. M., Warner-Metzger, C., & Abner, J. P. (2015). Child-directed interaction training for young children with autism spectrum disorders: Parent and child outcomes. *Journal of Clinical Child and Adolescent Psychology, 46*(1), 1–9.

Gjevik, E., Eldevik, S., Fjæran-Granum, T., & Sponheim, E. (2011). Kiddie-SADS reveals high rates of DSM-IV disorders in children and adolescents with autism spectrum disorders. *Journal of Autism and Developmental Disorders, 41*, 761–769. doi:10.1007/s10803-010-1095-7

Guttmann-Steinmetz, S., Gadow, K. D., & DeVincent, C. J. (2009). Oppositional defiant and conduct disorder behaviors in boys with autism spectrum disorder with and without attention-deficit hyperactivity disorder versus several comparison samples. *Journal of Autism and Developmental Disorders, 39*, 976–985.

Guy, W. (1976). *ECDEU assessment manual for psychopharmacology: Publication ADM 76–338*. Washington, DC: U.S. Department of Health, Education, and Welfare.

Hagopian, L. P., & Caruso-Anderson, M. E. (2010). Integrating behavioral and pharmacological interventions for severe problem behavior displayed by children with neurogenetic and developmental disorders. In B. K. Shapiro & P. J. Accardo (Eds.), *Neurogenetic syndromes: Behavioral issues and their treatment* (pp. 217–223). Baltimore, MD: Paul H. Brookes Publishing.

Handen, B. L., Aman, M. G., Arnold, L. E., Hyman, S. L., Tumuluru, R. V., Lecavalier, L., . . . Smith, T. (2015). Atomoxetine, parent training, and their combination in children with autism spectrum disorder and attention-deficit/hyperactivity disorder. *Journal of the American Academy of Child & Adolescent Psychiatry, 54*(11), 905–915.

Hanley, G. P. (2012). Functional assessment of problem behavior: Dispelling myths, overcoming implementation obstacles, and developing new lore. *Behavior Analysis in Practice, 5*(1), 54–72.

Harrison, P. L., & Oakland, T. (2015). *Adaptive Behavior Assessment System* (3rd ed.). Torrance, CA: Western Psychological Services.

Hartley, S. L., Sikora, D. M., & McCoy, R. (2008). Prevalence and risk factors of maladaptive behaviour in young children with autistic disorder. *Journal of Intellectual Disability Research, 52*(10), 819–829.

Harvey, S. T., Boer, D., Meyer, L. H., & Evans, I. M. (2009). Updating a meta-analysis of intervention research with challenging behavior: Treatment validity and standards of practice. *Journal of Intellectual and Developmental Disability, 34*, 67–80. doi:10.1080/13668250802690922

Hassall, R., Rose, J., & McDonald, J. (2005). Parenting stress in mothers of children with an intellectual disability: The effects of parental cognitions in relation to child characteristics and family support. *Journal of Intellectual Disability Research, 49*(6), 405–418.

Hayashida, K., Anderson, B., Paparella, T., Freeman, S. F. N., & Forness, S. R. (2010). Comorbid psychiatric diagnoses in preschoolers with autism spectrum disorders. *Behavioral Disorders, 35*(3), 243–254.

Hayes, S. A., & Watson, S. L. (2013). The impact of parenting stress. *Journal of Autism and Developmental Disorders, 43*(3), 629–642.

Hepburn, S. L., Stern, J. A., Blakeley-Smith, A., Kimel, L. K., & Reaven, J. A. (2014). Complex psychiatric comorbidity of treatment-seeking youth with autism spectrum disorder and anxiety symptoms. *Journal of Mental Health Research in Intellectual Disabilities, 7*(4), 359–378.

Herring, S., Gray, K., Taffe, J., Tonge, B., Sweeney, D., & Einfeld, S. (2006). Behaviour and emotional problems in toddlers with pervasive developmental disorders and developmental delay: Associations with parental mental health and family functioning. *Journal of Intellectual Disability Research, 50*, 874–882. doi:10.1111/j.1365–2788.2006.00904.x

Herzinger, C. V., & Campbell, J. M. (2007). Comparing functional assessment methodologies: A quantitative synthesis. *Journal of Autism and Developmental Disorders, 37*, 1430–1445. doi:10.1007/s10803-0219-6

Heyvaert, M., Maes, B., Van Den Noortgate, W., Kuppens, S., & Onghena, P. (2012). A multilevel meta-analysis of single-case and small-n research on interventions for reducing challenging behavior in persons with intellectual disabilities. *Research in Developmental Disabilities, 33*, 766–780. doi:10.1016/j.ridd.2011.10.010

Horner, R., Carr, E., Strain, P., Todd, A., & Reed, H. (2002). Problem behavior interventions for young children. *Journal of Autism and Developmental Disorders, 32*(5), 423–446.

Iwata, B., Dorsey, M., Slifer, K., Bauman, K., & Richman, G. (1994). Toward a functional analysis of self-injury. *Journal of Applied Behavior Analysis, 27*(2), 197–209.

Iwata, B., & Dozier, A. (2008). Clinical application of functional analysis methodology. *Behavior Analysis in Practice, 1*(1), 3–9.

Iwata, B. A., & Worsdell, A. S. (2005). Implications of functional analysis methodology for the design of intervention programs. *Exceptionality, 13*(1), 25–34.

Joshi, G., Petty, C., Wozniak, J., Henin, A., Fried, R., Galdo, M., . . . Biederman, J. (2010) The heavy burden of psychiatric comorbidity in youth with autism spectrum disorders: A large comparative study of a psychiatrically referred population. *Journal of Autism and Developmental Disorders, 40*, 1361. https://doi.org/10.1007/s10803-010-0996-9

Kaat, A. J., Gadow, K. D., & Lecavalier, L. (2013). Psychiatric symptom impairment in children with autism spectrum disorders. *Journal of Abnormal Child Psychology, 41*, 959. https://doi.org/10.1007/s10802-013-9739-7

Kaat, A. J., & Lecavalier, L. (2013). Disruptive behavior disorders in children and adolescents with autism spectrum disorders: A review of the prevalence, presentation, and treatment. *Research in Autism Spectrum Disorders, 7*(12), 1579–1594.

Kaat, A. J., Lecavalier, L., & Aman, M. G. (2014). Validity of the Aberrant Behavior Checklist in children with autism spectrum disorders. *Journal of Autism and Developmental Disorders, 44*(5), 1103–1116.

Kaminski, J. W., Valle, L. A., Filene, J. H., & Boyle, C. L. (2008). A meta-analytic review of components associated with parent training program effectiveness. *Journal of Abnormal Child Psychology, 36*(4), 567–589.

Kanne, S. M., Abbacchi, A. M., & Constantino, J. N. (2009). Multi-informant ratings of psychiatric symptom severity in children with autism spectrum disorders: The importance of environmental context. *Journal of Autism and Developmental Disorders, 39*, 856. https://doi.org/10.1007/s10803-009-0694-7

Karabekiroglu, K., & Aman, M.G. (2009). Validity of the Aberrant Behavior Checklist in a clinical sample of toddlers. *Child Psychiatry and Human Development, 40*, 99-110.

Kaufman, J., Birmaher, B., Brent, D., Rao, U., Flynn, C., Moreci, P., . . . Ryan, N. (1997). Schedule for Affective Disorders and Schizophrenia for School-Age Children—Present and Lifetime Version (KSADS-PL): Initial reliability and validity data. *Journal of the American Academy of Child and Adolescent Psychiatry, 36*, 980–988.

Kazdin, A. E. (2005). *Parent management training: Treatment for oppositional, aggressive, and antisocial behavior in children and adolescents*. New York, NY: Oxford University Press.

Koeske, G. F., & Koeske, R. D. (1992). Parenting locus of control: Measurement, construct validation, and a proposed conceptual model. *Social Work Research Abstracts, 28*, 37–46.

Kogan, M., Strickland, B., Blumberg, S., Singh, G., Perrin, J., & van Dyck, P. (2008). A national profile of the health care experiences and family impact of autism spectrum disorder among children in the United States. *Pediatrics, 122*(6), e1149–e1158.

Lavigne, J. V., Cromley, T., Sprafkin, J., & Gadow, K. D. (2009). The Child and Adolescent Symptom Inventory Progress Monitor: A brief DSM-IV-referenced parent-report scale for children and adolescents. *Journal of Child and Adolescent Psychopharmacology, 19*, 241–252.

Lecavalier, L. (2006). Behavior and emotional problems in young people with pervasive developmental disorders: Relative prevalence, effects of subject characteristics, and empirical classification. *Journal of Autism and Developmental Disorders, 36*(8), 1101–1114.

Lecavalier, L., Aman, M. G., Hammer, D., Stoica, W., & Matthews, G. L. (2004). Factor analysis of Nisonger Child Behavior Rating Form in children with autism spectrum disorders. *Journal of Autism and Developmental Disorders, 34*(6), 709–721.

Lecavalier, L., Gadow, K., DeVincent, C. J., & Edwards, M. C. (2009). Validation of DSM-IV model of psychiatric syndromes in children with autism spectrum disorders. *Journal of Autism and Developmental Disorders, 39*(2), 278–289.

Levy, S. E., Giarelli, E., Lee, L. C., Schieve, L. A., Kirby, R. S., Cunniff, C., . . . Rice, C. E. (2010). Autism spectrum disorder and co-occurring developmental, psychiatric, and medical conditions among children in multiple populations of the United States. *Journal of Developmental and Behavioral Pediatrics, 31*(4), 267–275.

Leyfer, O. T., Folstein, S. E., Bacalmn, S., Davis., N. O., Dinh, E., Morgan, J., . . . Lainhart, J. E. (2006). Comorbid psychiatric disorders in children with autism: Interview development and rates of disorders. *Journal of Autism and Developmental Disorders, 36*(7), 849–861.

Lindgren, S., Wacker, D., Suess, A., Schieltz, K., Pelzel, K., Kopelman, T., . . . Waldron, D. (2016). Telehealth and autism: Treating challenging behavior at lower cost. *Pediatrics. 137*(Suppl 2), S167–S175. doi:10.1542/peds.2015-2851O

Mandell, D. S., Morales, K. H., Marcus, S. C., Stahmer, A. C., Doshi, J., & Polsky, D. E. (2008). Psychotropic medication use among Medicaid-enrolled children with autism spectrum disorders. *Pediatrics, 121*, e441–e448. doi:10.1542/peds.2007–0984

Mandy, W., Roughan, L., & Skuse, D. (2014). Three dimensions of oppositionality in autism spectrum disorder. *Journal of Abnormal Child Psychology, 42*, 291–300.

Marcus, R. N., Owen, R., Kamen, L., Manos, G., McQuade, R. D., Carson, W. H., & Aman, M. G. (2009). A placebo-controlled, fixed-dose study of aripiprazole in children and adolescents with irritability associated with autistic disorder. *Journal of the American Academy of Child and Adolescent Psychiatry, 48*, 1110–1119.

Mattila, M. L., Hurtig, T., Haapsamo, H., Jussila, K., Kuusikko-Gauffin, S., Kielinen, M.,...Moilanen, I. (2010). Comorbid psychiatric disorders associated with Asperger syndrome/high-functioning autism: A community- and clinic-based study. *Journal of Autism and Developmental Disorders, 40*, 1080–1093. doi:10.1007/s10803-010-0958-2

Matson, J. (2009). Aggression and tantrums in children with autism: A review of behavioral treatments and maintaining variables. *Journal of Mental Health Research in Intellectual Disabilities, 2*, 169–187.

Matson, J. L., & Vollmer, T. R. (1995). *The Questions About Behavior Functions (QABF) user's guide.* Baton Rouge, LA: Scientific Publishers.

Mayes, S. D., Calhoun, S. L., Aggarwal, R., Baker, C., Mathapati, S., Anderson, R., & Peterson, C. (2012). Explosive, oppositional and aggressive behavior in children with autism compared to other clinical disorders and typical development. *Research in Autism Spectrum Disorders, 6*(1), 1–10.

Mayes, S. D., Calhoun, S. L., Murray, M. J., Ahuja, M., & Smith, L. A. (2011). Anxiety, depression, and irritability in children with autism relative to other neuropsychiatric disorders and typical development. *Research in Autism Spectrum Disorders, 5*(1), 474–485.

Mazefsky, C. A., Oswald, D. P., Day, T. N., Minshew, N. J., Eack, S. M., & Lainhart, J. E. (2012). ASD, a psychiatric disorder, or both? Psychiatric diagnoses in adolescents with high-functioning ASD. *Journal of Clinical Child and Adolescent Psychology, 41*, 516–523. http://doi.org/10.1080/15374416.2012.686102

Mazurek, M. O., Kanne, S. M., & Wodka, E. L. (2013). Physical aggression in children and adolescents with autism spectrum disorders. *Research in Autism Spectrum Disorders, 7*(3), 455–465.

Mazzone, L., Ruta, L., & Reale, L. (2012). Psychiatric comorbidities in Asperger syndrome and high functioning autism: Diagnostic challenges. *Annals of General Psychiatry*, 11(16), 1-13. https://doi.org/10.1186/1744-859X-11–16

McCracken, J. T., McGough, J., Shah, B., Cronin, P., Hong, D., Aman, M. G.,...Research Units on Pediatric Psychopharmacology Autism Network. (2002). Risperidone in children with autism and serious behavior problems. *New England Journal of Medicine, 347*, 314–321.

McGuire, K., Fung, L. K., Hagopian, L., Vasa, R. A., Mahajan, R., Bernal, P.,...Whitaker, A. H. (2016). Irritability and problem behavior in autism spectrum disorder: A practice pathway for pediatric primary care. *Pediatrics, 137*, 136–148.

McMahon, R. J., & Frick, P. J. (2005). Evidence-based assessment of conduct problems in children and adolescents. *Journal of Clinical Child and Adolescent Psychology, 34*(3), 477–505.

Merikangas, K. R., He, J. P, Burstein, M., Swanson, S. A., Avenevoli, S., Cui, L.,...Swendsen, J. (2010). Lifetime prevalence of mental disorders in US adolescents: Results from the National Comorbidity Study-Adolescent Supplement (NCS-A). *Journal of the American Academy of Child and Adolescent Psychiatry, 49*, 980–989. doi:10.1016/j.jaac.2010.05.017

Michelson, D., Davenport, C., Dretzke, J., Barlow, J., & Day, C. (2013). Do evidence-based interventions work when tested in the "real world"? A systematic review and meta-analysis of parent management training for the treatment of child disruptive behavior. *Clinical Child and Family Psychology Review, 16*, 18–34. doi:10.1007/s10567-013-0128-0

Mukaddes, N. M., Hergüner, S., & Tanidir, C. (2010). Psychiatric disorders in individuals with high functioning autism and Asperger's disorder: Similarities and differences. *World Journal of Biological Psychiatry, 11*, 964–971.

Newcomb, E. T., & Hagopian, L. P. (2018). Treatment of severe problem behavior in children with autism spectrum disorder and intellectual disabilities. *International Review of Psychiatry, 30*, 96–109. doi:10.1080/09540261.2018.1435513

Nock, M.K., Kazdin, A.E., Hiripi, E., & Kessler, R.C. (2007). Lifetime prevalence, correlates, and persistence of oppositional defiant disorder: results from the National Comorbidity Survey Replication. *Journal of Child Psychology and Psychiatry, 48*, 703-713.

Nolan, E. E., Gadow, K. D., & Sprafkin, J. (2001). Teacher reports of DSM-IV ADHD, ODD, and CD symptoms in schoolchildren. *Journal of the American Academy of Child and Adolescent Psychiatry, 40*, 241–249.

Okuno, H., Nagai, T., Sakai, S., Mohri, I., Yamamoto, T., Yoshizaki, A.,...Taniike, M. (2011). Effectiveness of modified parent training for mothers of children with pervasive developmental disorder on parental confidence and children's behavior. *Brain and Development, 33*(2), 152–160.

Oliver, A., Pratt, L., & Normand, M. (2015). A survey of functional behavior assessment methods used by behavior analysts in practice. *Journal of Applied Behavior Analysis, 48*(4), 817–829.

Owen, R., Sikich, L., Marcus, R. N., Corey-Lisle, P., Manos, G., McQuade, R. D.,...Findling, R. L. (2009). Aripiprazole in the treatment of irritability in children and adolescents with autistic disorder. *Pediatrics, 124*, 1533–1540.

Pandina, G. J., Bossie, C. A., Youssef, E., Zhu, Y., & Dunbar, F. (2007). Risperidone improves behavioral symptoms in children with autism in a randomized, double-blind, placebo-controlled trial. *Journal of Autism and Developmental Disorders, 37*, 367–373.

Pandolfi, V., Magyar, C. I., & Dill, C. A. (2009). Confirmatory factor analysis of the Child Behavior Checklist 1.5–5 in a sample of children with autism spectrum disorders. *Journal of Autism and Developmental Disorders, 39*, 986–995. doi.org/10.1007/s10803-009-0716-5

Pandolfi, V., Magyar, C. I., & Dill, C. A. (2012). An initial psychometric evaluation of the CBCL 6–18 in a sample of youth with ASD. *Research in Autism Spectrum Disorders, 6*(1), 96–108.

Pisula, E., & Kossakowska, Z. (2010). Sense of coherence and coping with stress among mothers and fathers of children with autism. *Journal of Autism and Developmental Disorders, 40*(12), 1485–1494.

Postorino, V., Sharp, W. G., McCracken, C. E., Bearss, K., Burrell, T. L., Evans, A. N., & Scahill, L. (2017). A systematic review and meta-analysis of parent training for disruptive behavior in children with autism spectrum disorder. *Clinical Child and Family Psychology Review, 20*, 391–402. doi:10.1007/s10567-017-0237-2

Reese, R. M., Richman, D. M., Belmont, J. M., & Morse, P. (2005). Functional characteristics of disruptive behavior in developmentally disabled children with and without autism. *Journal of Autism and Developmental Disorders, 35*(4), 419–428.

Reitzel, J., Summers, J., Lorv, B., Szatmari, P., Zwaigenbaum, L., Georgiades, S., & Duku, E. (2013). Pilot randomized controlled trial of a functional behavior skills training program for young children with autism spectrum disorder who have significant early learning skill impairments and their families. *Research in Autism Spectrum Disorders, 7*(11), 1418–1432.

Research Units on Pediatric Psychopharmacology (RUPP) Autism Network. (2002). Risperidone in children with autism for serious behavioral problems. *New England Journal of Medicine, 347*(5), 314–321.

Research Units on Pediatric Psychopharmacology (RUPP) Autism Network. (2007). Parent training for children with pervasive developmental disorders: A multi-site feasibility trial. *Behavioral Interventions, 22*(3), 179–199.

Roberts, D., & Pickering, N. (2010). Parent training programme for autism spectrum disorders: An evaluation. *Community Practitioner, 83*(10), 27–30.

Roid, G. H. (2003). *Stanford-Binet Intelligence Scales* (5th ed.). Itasca, IL: Riverside.

Rowe, R., Costello, E.J., Angold. A., Copeland, W.E>, & Maughan, B. (2010). Developmental pathways in oppositional defiant disorder and conduct disorder. Journal of Abnormal Psychology, 119(4), 726–738.

Salazar, F., Baird, G., Chandler, S., Tseng, E., O'Sullivan, T., Howlin, P., . . . Simonoff, E. (2015). Co-occurring psychiatric disorders in preschool and elementary school-aged children with autism spectrum disorder. *Journal of Autism and Developmental Disorders, 45*, 2283. https://doi.org/10.1007/s10803-015-2361-5

Scahill, L., Bearss, K., Lecavalier, L., Smith, T., Swiezy, N., Aman, M., . . . Johnson, C. (2016). Effect of parent training on adaptive behavior in children with autism spectrum disorder and disruptive behavior: Results of a randomized trial. *Journal of the American Academy of Child and Adolescent Psychiatry, 55*(7), 602–609.

Scahill, L., Jeon, S., Boorin, S. G., McDougle, C. J., Aman, M. G., Dziura, J., . . . Vitiello, B. (2016). Weight and metabolic consequences following 6 months exposure to risperidone in young children with autism spectrum disorder and serious behavioral problems. *Journal of the American Academy of Child and Adolescent Psychiatry, 55*(5), 415–423.

Scahill, L., McDougle, C. J., Aman, M. G., Johnson, C., Handen, B., Bearss, K., . . . Vitiello, B. (2012). Effects of risperidone and parent training on adaptive functioning in children with pervasive developmental disorders and serious behavioral problems. *Journal of the American Academy of Child and Adolescent Psychiatry, 51*(2), 136–146.

Simonoff, E.,Jones, C.R.G., Baird, G., Pickles, A., Happé, F., & Charman., T. (2013). The persistence and stability of psychiatric problems in adolescents with autism spectrum disorders. *Journal of Child Psychology and Psychiatry*, 54, 186-194.

Simonoff, E., Jones, C. R., Pickles, A., Happé, F., Baird, G., & Charman, T. (2012). Severe mood problems in adolescents with autism spectrum disorder. *Journal of Child Psychology and Psychiatry, 53*, 1157–1166. doi:10.1111/j.1469–7610.2012.02600.x

Simonoff, E., Pickles, A., Charman, T., Chandler, S., Loucas, T., & Baird, G. (2008). Psychiatric disorders in children with autism spectrum disorders: Prevalence, comorbidity, and associated factors in a population-derived sample. *Journal of the American Academy of Child and Adolescent Psychiatry, 47*(8), 921–929.

Smith, T., Scahill, L., Dawson, G., Guthrie, D., Lord, C., Odom, S., . . . Wagner, A. (2007). Designing research studies on psychosocial interventions in autism. *Journal of Autism and Developmental Disorders, 37*(2), 354–366.

Sofronoff, K., Leslie, A., & Brown, W. (2004). Parent management training and Asperger syndrome: A randomized controlled trial to evaluate a parent based intervention. *Autism, 8*(3), 301–317.

Sparrow, S. S., Ciccetti, D. V., & Balla, D. A. (2005). *Vineland II: Vineland Adaptive Behavior Scales, Second Edition: Survey Forms Manual.* Circle Pines, MN: AGS Publishing.

Sprafkin, J., Gadow, K. D., Salisbury, H., Schneider, J., & Loney, J. (2010). Further evidence of reliability and validity of the Child Symptom Inventory-4: Parent Checklist in clinically referred boys. *Journal of Clinical Child and Adolescent Psychology, 31*, 513–524. doi:10.1207/S15374424JCCP3104_10

Sprafkin, J., Volpe, R. J., Gadow, K. D., Nolan, E. E., & Kelly, K. (2002). A DSM-IV-referenced screening instrument for preschool children: The Early Childhood Inventory-4. *Journal of the American Academy of Child and Adolescent Psychiatry, 41*(5), 604–612.

Stratis, E. A., & Lecavalier, L. (2015). Informant agreement for youth with autism spectrum disorder or intellectual disability: A meta-analysis. *Journal of Autism and Developmental Disorders, 45*(4), 1026–1041.

Stringaris, A., & Goodman, R. (2009a). Three dimensions of oppositionality in youth. *Journal of Child Psychology and Psychiatry, and Allied Disciplines, 50*, 216–223.

Stringaris, A., & Goodman, R. (2009b). Longitudinal outcome of youth oppositionality: Irritable, headstrong, and hurtful behaviors have distinctive predictions. *Journal of the American Academy of Child and Adolescent Psychiatry, 48*, 404–412.

Sturmey, P. (1995). Analog baselines: A critical review of the methodology. *Research in Developmental Disabilities, 16*(4), 269–284.

Suess, A. N., Wacker, D. P., Schwartz, J. E., Lustig, N., & Detrick, J. (2016). Preliminary evidence on the use of telehealth in an outpatient behavior clinic. *Journal of Applied Behavior Analysis, 49*(3), 686–692.

Symon, J. B. (2005). Expanding interventions for children with autism: Parents as trainers. *Journal of Positive Behavior Interventions, 7*(3), 159–173.

Tarbox, J., Wilke, A., Najdowski, E., Findel-Pyles, A., Balasanyan, C., Caveney, R., . . . Tia, D. (2009). Comparing indirect, descriptive, and experimental functional assessments of challenging behavior in children with autism. *Journal of Developmental and Physical Disabilities, 21*(6), 493–514.

Tasse, M. J., Aman, M. G., Hammer, D., & Rojahn, J. (1996). The Nisonger Child Behavior Rating Form: Age and gender effects and norms. *Research in Developmental Disabilities, 17*(1), 59–75.

Tellegen, C. L., & Sanders, M. R. (2014). A randomized controlled trial evaluating a brief parenting program with children with autism spectrum disorders. *Journal of Consulting and Clinical Psychology, 82*(6), 1193–1200.

Tonge, B., Brereton, A., Kiomall, M., Mackinnon, A., King, N., & Rinehart, N. (2006). Effects on parental mental health of an education and skills training program for parents of young children with autism: A randomized controlled trial. *Journal of the American Academy of Child and Adolescent Psychiatry, 45*, 561–569. doi:10.1097/01.chi.0000205701.48324.26

Tonge, B., Brereton, A., Kiomall, M., Mackinnon, A., & Rinehart, N. J. (2014). A randomized group comparison controlled trial of "preschoolers with autism": A parent education and skills training intervention for young children with autistic disorder. *Autism: The International Journal of Research & Practice, 18*(2), 166–177.

Wacker, D. P., Lee, J. F., Padilla Dalmau, Y. C., Kopelman, T. G., Lindgren, S. D., Kuhle, J., . . . Waldron, D. B. (2013). Conducting functional communication training via telehealth to reduce the problem behavior of young children with autism. *Journal of Developmental and Physical Disabilities, 25*(1), 35–48.

Wakschlag, L.S., Choi, S.W., Carter, A.S., Hullsiek, H., Burns, J., McCarthy, K., Leibenluft, E., & Briggs-Gowan, M.J. (2012). Defining the developmental parameters of temper loss in early childhood: Implications for developmental psychopathology. *Journal of Child Psychology and Psychiatry, 53*, 1099-1108.

Wakschlag, L. S., Tolan, P. H., & Leventhal, B. L. (2010). Research review: "Ain't misbehavin": Towards a developmentally-specified nosology for preschool disruptive behavior. *Journal of Child Psychology and Psychiatry, 51*, 3–22.

Whelan, Y.M., Stringaris, A., Maughan, B., & Barker, E.D. (2013). Developmental continuity of oppositional defiant disorder subdimensions at ages 8, 10, and 13 years and their distinct psychiatric outcomes at age 16 years. *Journal of the American Academy of Child and Adolescent Psychiatry, 52*, 961–969.

Whittingham, K., Sofronoff, K., Sheffield, J., & Sanders, M. R. (2009). Stepping Stones Triple P: An RCT of a parenting program with parents of a child diagnosed with an autism spectrum disorder. *Journal of Abnormal Child Psychology, 37*(4), 469–480.

Wierson, M., & Forehand, R. (1994). Parent behavioral training for child noncompliance: Rationale, concepts, and effectiveness. *Current Directions in Psychological Science, 3*(5), 146–150.

Witwer, A. N., & Lecavalier, L. (2010). Validity of comorbid psychiatric disorders in youngsters with autism spectrum disorders. *Journal of Developmental and Physical Disabilities, 22*, 367. https://doi.org/10.1007/s10882-010-9194-0

Witwer, A. N., Lecavalier, L., & Norris, M. (2012). Reliability and validity of the Children's Interview for Psychiatric Syndromes-Parent Version in autism spectrum disorders. *Journal of Autism and Developmental Disorders, 42*, 1949–1958. https://doi.org/10.1007/s10803-012-1442-y

CHAPTER

9

Attention Deficit Hyperactivity Disorder in Autism Spectrum Disorder

A High-Risk Co-Occurring Condition

Benjamin E. Yerys

Abstract

This chapter will review the available evidence on individuals with co-occurring diagnoses of autism spectrum disorder (ASD) and attention deficit hyperactivity disorder (ADHD). This chapter contends that children diagnosed with both disorders (ASD+ADHD) are a subset of the ASD population that is at risk for delayed recognition of their ASD diagnosis, poor treatment response, and poorer functional outcomes compared to those with ASD without ADHD. Specifically, the chapter highlights the best estimates of the prevalence of the comorbidity, the developmental trajectory of people with co-occurring ASD and ADHD, how ADHD symptoms change across development, overlapping genetic and neurobiological risk factors, psychometrics of ADHD diagnostic instruments in an ASD population, neuropsychological and functional impairments associated with co-occurring ASD and ADHD, and the current state of evidence-based treatment for both ASD and ADHD symptoms. Finally, the chapter discusses fruitful avenues of research for improving understanding of this high-risk comorbidity so that *mechanism-to-treatment* pathways for ADHD in children with ASD can be better developed.

Keywords: cognitive neuroscience, neuropsychology, pleiotropy, comorbidity, frontoparietal, executive function, neurodevelopmental disorder

Overview

Attention deficit hyperactivity disorder (ADHD) is a neurodevelopmental disorder characterized by symptoms of inattention and/or hyperactivity/impulsivity (American Psychiatric Association & DSM-5 Task Force, 2013). Examples of inattention symptoms include being easily distracted, being disorganized, having difficulty following instructions, and seeming to not listen when spoken to directly. Examples of hyperactivity/impulsivity symptoms include having difficulty sitting still, fidgeting (or being restless in older teens and adults), interrupting others, and having difficulty waiting their turn. Prior to the release of the *Diagnostic and Statistical Manual of Mental Disorders*, fifth edition (DSM-5; American Psychiatric Association & DSM-5 Task Force, 2013), clinicians were not permitted to make a concurrent diagnosis of autism spectrum disorder (ASD) and ADHD in the same person. This is not the case for other common comorbidities in ASD, including anxiety disorders, other disruptive behavior disorders, mood disorders, or intellectual disability. The thinking behind this early decision, at least as reported in the text-revised fourth edition of the *Diagnostic and Statistical Manual of Mental Disorders* (DSM-IV-TR; American Psychiatric Association, 2000), was that overactivity and inattention problems were a part of the ASD phenotype, and that the behaviors did not warrant a separate ADHD diagnosis. This diagnostic approach was problematic because viewing all behaviors from the lens of ASD left clinicians open to the risk of diagnostic overshadowing—misattributing physical or psychiatric symptoms to a developmental disorder (Miller, 2014). In the case of ASD and ADHD, many children with ASD may have had their ADHD symptoms attributed to their ASD diagnosis and not received potentially efficacious treatment for their ADHD symptoms. Furthermore, diagnostic overshadowing likely had other collateral effects, including delaying research on treatment for ADHD symptoms in ASD as well as basic research on biological and psychological processes contributing to the co-occurrence of the two conditions.

As research was carried out with this exclusionary diagnostic approach for ADHD in children with ASD, a growing body of evidence emerged to demonstrate that those with co-occurring ADHD symptoms were reported to be experiencing a number of other difficulties that were not present in those with ASD alone (Corbett, Constantine, Hendren, Rocke, & Ozonoff, 2009; Matsushima et al., 2008; Sikora, Vora, Coury, & Rosenberg, 2012). Furthermore, psychometric and clinical trial studies also began to evaluate the utility of ADHD diagnostic tools and treatments in ASD, because providers were known to be using them in their clinical work even if they could not make the co-occurring diagnosis. This body of evidence laid the foundation for changing the exclusionary criteria in the DSM-5 (American Psychiatric Association & DSM-5 Task Force, 2013), and it validated a new line of inquiry into the developmental trajectory and profile of individuals with co-occurring ADHD. Epidemiologic research focused on population or community sampling methods, and treatment research into ameliorating ADHD symptoms in individuals with ASD+ADHD or improving ASD symptoms in these people is lagging relative to phenotypic studies; however, the preliminary evidence suggests there is room for improvement in existing treatments. The remainder of this chapter provides an up-to-date summary of what is known about ASD+ADHD from prevalence, the developmental trajectory, genetic and neurobiological etiology, assessment and diagnosis, neuropsychological functioning, functional outcomes, and evidence-based treatment for individuals with ASD+ADHD. Although most of the research to date has focused on children, studies of adults are noted when possible to present a lifespan view. There is also a case example of a child with ASD and ADHD. The chapter ends with a summary and an eye toward future research goals.

Prevalence and Course

Prevalence

Prevalence estimates of ADHD as a co-occurring condition with ASD have varied tremendously across various diagnostic tools and sampling methods. To date, there is only one population-based study that examined neurodevelopmental and psychiatric co-occurring conditions in children with ASD. This study sampled children in the United Kingdom, which likely represents the populations of Western cultures best (Simonoff et al., 2008). From this population cohort of 56,946, a total of 112 children of the 255 identified as having ASD (or high risk) were able to be evaluated for the study. The Child and Adolescent Psychiatric Assessment (Angold & Costello, 1995; Costello, Mustillo, Erkanli, Keeler, & Angold, 2003), a psychiatric interview, was used to assess ADHD. This interview required behavioral descriptions by parents, which was thought to limit the risk of "double counting" a behavior for multiple symptoms. Simonoff and colleagues (2008) reported an ADHD comorbidity rate of 28.2% (95% confidence interval [CI, 13.3 to 43.0]). Other studies using structured or unstructured interviews with convenience sampling approaches (i.e., recruiting through clinics, ASD community events, and local community resources) have reported similar or higher rates. One study implemented a modified version of the Kiddie-Schizoaffective Diagnostic Schedule Present and Lifetime version in a sample of 109 children with ASD (Leyfer et al., 2006). The interview was modified to cue parents to consider the child's ASD symptoms. Approximately 31% of school-age children with ASD met clinical criteria for an ADHD diagnosis in this study, and approximately 25% of children had significant symptoms of ADHD but did not meet full diagnostic criteria. A study from Germany used a psychiatric interview for consecutive cases of school-age children who presented to the clinic with a known ASD diagnosis, and reported that 53% of children met criteria for a co-occurring ADHD diagnosis (Sinzig, Walter, & Doepfner, 2009). Recent studies examining this question in specialty psychiatric clinics and community clinics serving publicly funded patients have reported a co-occurrence rate near 75% in school-aged children (Brookman-Frazee, Stadnick, Chlebowski, Baker-Ericzén, & Ganger, 2018; Joshi et al., 2017).

Few screening tools for ADHD have been used to estimate prevalence in ASD. The ADHD Rating Scale, fourth edition (DuPaul, Power,

Anastopoulos, & Reid, 1998) was recently shown to identify 15% of children with ASD as meeting criteria for ADHD using the "AND" rule of having more than six symptoms of inattention or hyperactivity/impulsivity in two settings (home and school); however, the co-occurrence rate increased to 62% using the "OR" rule of having at least six symptoms of inattention or hyperactivity/impulsivity in at least one setting (Yerys et al., 2017). The "AND" and "OR" rules have been used in the field of ADHD research to capture a range of ADHD symptom presentations—from the most conservative, clear-cut cases of ADHD ("AND" rule) to the least conservative presentations where children may not meet diagnostic criteria in two independent settings ("OR" rule). The Child Behavior Checklist (CBCL) and the companion Teacher Report Form (TRF; Achenbach & Rescorla, 2001) were also recently evaluated in the Simons Simplex Collection, and the CBCL and TRF were observed to have the lowest rates of co-occurring ADHD of any instrument (Hanson et al., 2013). In this study a child receiving a T-score of 70 or higher on the DSM-oriented Attention Deficit/Hyperactivity Problems scale was considered positive for ADHD. Only the CBCL was available on the total sample (n = 1,838), and the CBCL identified 17.6% of children having ADHD. When restricting the sample to children with both the CBCL and TRF (n = 813), the TRF identified 8.34% of the sample as having ADHD. When using the "AND" rule, these two forms identified 2.6% of children with ADHD. A number of factors may contribute to this lower rate, including sample characteristics and the use of the CBCL and TRF as measures of ADHD symptoms. For the sample characteristics, this sample is almost exclusively composed of children with no family history of ASD (i.e., simplex families), which may or may not influence co-occurring disorder rates. In addition, this is the only study to sample children as young as age 4. Regarding the CBCL and TRF, they do not sample all 18 symptoms that comprise an ADHD diagnosis. These are the only two forms reviewed here that do not include all 18 ADHD symptoms. Furthermore, as one might expect, the prevalence of ADHD in ASD is lower when clinicians use multiple sources and the "AND" rule to make a diagnosis of ADHD.

Research in adults with ASD shows comparable rates of co-occurring ADHD as in children with ASD (Anckarsäter et al., 2006; Johnston et al., 2013; Saqr, Braun, Porter, Barnette, & Hanks, 2017). Psychiatrically referred samples have revealed co-occurring ADHD rates between 34% and 52% for adults with ASD. One study following 240 adults referred for a neuropsychological evaluation reported that 34% of adults had co-occurring ASD and ADHD diagnoses, and noted that an additional 7% were considered "in remission" for ADHD (Anckarsäter et al., 2006).

Developmental Trajectory

There is limited research to date regarding the developmental trajectory of co-occurring ADHD in ASD. Based on a thorough literature review, only one longitudinal study of infant siblings at high risk for developing ASD has evaluated these children with an eye toward identification of ADHD as a primary or co-occurring diagnosis (Shephard et al., 2018). In this one study, 104 infants at high risk for developing ASD—defined as having an older sibling with ASD—were evaluated at 7, 14, 24, and 38 months and 7 years of age. Parent-reported measures of activity level and inhibitory control predicted ADHD symptoms, even after controlling for ASD symptoms and anxiety symptoms. This study is one of the first to demonstrate empirically that ADHD and ASD may have unique developmental origins, and that ADHD is not simply a consequence of ASD traits. Another study examined age-related changes in co-occurring ADHD symptoms in children with ASD between the ages of 4 and 7 years over the course of one school year (Llanes, Blacher, Stavropoulos, & Eisenhower, 2018). Parents reported many children with ASD experienced ADHD symptoms at baseline (50%), and ADHD symptoms worsened over the school year for a large portion of children (45%); according to teacher report, fewer children experienced ADHD symptoms (30%), and fewer children had their symptoms worsen (24%). Longitudinal studies that follow individuals with co-occurring ASD and ADHD from childhood into adulthood have shown significant reductions in ADHD symptoms (Gray et al., 2012; Woodman, Mailick, & Greenberg, 2016), which converges with the symptom reduction seen in the ADHD population without ASD (Hechtman et al., 2016; Willcutt et al., 2012). However, Woodman and colleagues (2016) found that 14% of adults with ASD presented with persistent externalizing behaviors—a category that included, but was not exclusive to, inattention and hyperactivity/impulsivity behaviors—across the lifespan. Interestingly, a sample of more than 17,000 people ages 0 to 84 years demonstrated an inverted U-shape trajectory for the relationship between

ASD and ADHD symptoms with a peak correlation during adolescence (defined as ages 12 to 18), suggesting that adolescence may be a critical window for intervening upon both disorders (Hartman, Geurts, Franke, Buitelaar, & Rommelse, 2016). Indeed, a recent follow-up study on the multimodal treatment of ADHD sample revealed that 50% of the sample no longer met criteria for an ADHD diagnosis 16 years after the study (Hechtman et al., 2016). Whether this type of ADHD symptom desistence exists in people with ASD is not yet known. However, understanding the course and possible remission of ADHD in people with ASD is critical, given that recent evidence suggests poorer functional outcomes in adaptive behavior functioning and quality-of-life ratings of children and young adults with ASD+ADHD in comparison to those with ASD alone (Sikora et al., 2012; Yerys et al., 2009; Yerys, Bertollo, Pandey, Guy, & Schultz, 2019).

Etiology, Diagnosis, and Assessment

Genetic Risk Factors

In the last two decades, there have been significant advances in our understanding of the genes contributing to ASD. These discoveries have recast the search from monogenic causal genes being largely responsible for ASD to a pleiotropic approach (many genes carrying small amounts of risk for multiple behaviors involved in ASD and other disorders). This pleiotropic approach encompasses both rare de novo mutations and copy number variants (Abrahams & Geschwind, 2010; Geschwind & Levitt, 2007; Sanders et al., 2015). There is a long history of finding similar linkage disequilibrium in similar locations for both ASD and ADHD populations, such as 16p13 and 17p11 (Lichtenstein, Carlström, Råstam, Gillberg, & Anckarsäter, 2010; Mulligan et al., 2009; Nijmeijer et al., 2010; Ogdie et al., 2003; Rommelse, Franke, Geurts, Hartman, & Buitelaar, 2010; Smalley et al., 2002; Williams et al., 2012); similar candidate genes conferring risk for ADHD symptoms, such as DAT1 and MAOA (Gadow, Roohi, DeVincent, & Hatchwell, 2008; Roohi, DeVincent, Hatchwell, & Gadow, 2009); similar copy number variations, such as CNTN4 (Elia et al., 2012; Gai et al., 2012); and rare mutations placing children at an elevated risk for both disorders, such as fragile X and 22q (Clements et al., 2017; Niklasson, Rasmussen, Oskarsdóttir, & Gillberg, 2005, 2009; Philofsky, Hepburn, Hayes, Hagerman, & Rogers, 2004; Reilly, Senior, & Murtagh, 2015; Schneider et al., 2014; Wheeler et al., 2014).

A recent effort known as the "Brainstorm Consortium" created a collaboration among Genome-Wide Association Studies consortia for 25 brain disorders, which included a sample of 265,218 individuals diagnosed with a psychiatric, neurodevelopmental, or neurological condition (e.g., ASD, ADHD, Alzheimer's) and 784,643 control participants in relation to 17 non-brain-based medical phenotypes (e.g., Crohn's disease) from 1,191,588 individuals. The key finding relevant for this discussion is that ASD and ADHD did not demonstrate significant genetic correlations, and in fact, ASD was highlighted as possibly being more distinct from other psychiatric disorders because of its modest relationships across the board except for schizophrenia (Consortium et al., 2018). At first glance, this type of study appears to throw significant doubt upon the potential genetic overlap of ASD and ADHD; however, large-scale studies of this nature are forced to use lowest common denominators when defining phenotypes, so diagnostic heterogeneity, ascertainment errors, or increased sample sizes may have led to expanded inclusion criteria. Furthermore, the smaller studies that were culled for this Brainstorm Consortium used data from unaffected relatives as controls for ASD cases—dubbed "pseudo-controls." The use of pseudo-controls could be problematic for studying ASD, because under a pleiotropic model issues of assortative mating or preferential ascertainment of multiplex families could diminish the expected difference between cases and the pseudo-controls (Cross-Disorder Group of the Psychiatric Genomics Consortium et al., 2013). In addition, the study only focused on common variants, and important relationships may have been missed by excluding rare variants (e.g., Elia et al., 2012; Gai et al., 2012). Therefore, smaller studies that may have included deeper phenotyping, rare variants, and/or greater controls for ascertainment errors and diagnostic heterogeneity may still hold promise for highlighting the overlapping genetic contributions of ASD and ADHD.

Neurobiological Risk Factors

In terms of neurobiology, the field has learned much about the development and function of the brain in people with ASD and people with ADHD. However, there remains limited evidence on how the brain develops when individuals are diagnosed with both ASD and ADHD. Studies that have looked into brain structure and function individually have highlighted critical overlap in multimodal association areas of the brain that support complex forms of cognition like executive function and social cognition, as well as subcortical structures that play key roles in supporting multimodal association areas of the brain, like the striatum and amygdala. To maintain a narrow focus in line with the comorbidity of ASD and ADHD, this section of the review will cover the few studies explicitly examining the neural correlates of ADHD symptoms in the neurobiology of people with ASD (or mixed diagnostic groups), but it will also cover studies directly comparing individuals with ASD and ADHD to unmask shared neurobiology.

Studies directly targeting the neurobiology of ADHD symptoms in children with ASD are limited to studies of structural and functional connectivity with various forms of magnetic resonance imaging (MRI). This skew toward connectivity studies is likely related to the interest in co-occurring ADHD coinciding with the rise of these modalities as preferred metrics of brain systems and indicators of psychopathology (Gratton et al., 2018; Kana, Uddin, Kenet, Chugani, & Müller, 2014; Vaidya & Gordon, 2013). Structural connectivity relies on diffusion MRI (Basser, Mattiello, & LeBihan, 1994), and this form of imaging is aimed at measuring the structure and architecture of the brain with a particular focus on white matter tracts that connect brain regions, such as the corpus callosum connecting left and right hemispheres (Pierpaoli, Jezzard, Basser, Barnett, & Di Chiro, 1996). Diffusion MRI measures the movement of water in the brain, and it can be used to estimate both macrostructure (estimation of white matter tracts between regions) and microstructure (the quality of the white matter through diffusion metrics like fractional anisotropy) of the brain's white matter. Diffusion MRI has identified structural connectivity differences in children with ASD that are related to their ADHD symptoms, and diffusion MRI has revealed similar structural connectivity differences in ASD-only and ADHD-only samples (Ameis et al., 2016; Aoki et al., 2017; Ray et al., 2014). Similarities across studies show that both ASD and ADHD groups have decreased white matter microstructure (fractional anisotropy and mean diffusivity) in the splenium segment of the corpus callosum (Ameis et al., 2016; Aoki et al., 2017). In particular, the Inattention symptoms scale from the Conners Parent Rating Scales—Revised (Conners, 1997, but see third edition published in 2008) had a negative relationship with mean diffusivity in the splenium in a mixed group of children with ASD, ADHD, and typical development (Aoki et al., 2017). There is also some evidence that the white matter's macro- and microstructure is greater between densely interconnected brain regions that flowed through the corpus callosum in children with ASD compared to matched controls (Ray et al., 2014). In particular, a posterior portion of the corpus callosum, the splenium, was implicated as a key region of interest. These posterior portions of the corpus callosum connect the left and right homologs of the parietal lobes and somatosensory cortex, structures implicated in diverse cognitive processes including attention and cognitive control, episodic memory, and visual spatial processing (Castellanos & Proal, 2012; Cavanna & Trimble, 2006; Cubillo et al., 2010; Fassbender, Krafft, & Schweitzer, 2015; Rubia, Smith, Taylor, & Brammer, 2007; A. B. Smith, Taylor, Brammer, Toone, & Rubia, 2006; Tamm, Menon, & Reiss, 2006). Several of these psychological processes are considered core to ADHD or reflect common components of the ADHD phenotype (Mueller, Hong, Shepard, & Moore, 2017; Willcutt, Doyle, Nigg, Faraone, & Pennington, 2005).

Functional connectivity is the measure of synchronized activity between brain regions (Friston, 1994). In functional MRI, functional connectivity can be measured by correlating the time series of activation between brain regions while the participant is engaged in a task (task-based functional connectivity) or while the participant is directed to rest (rest-state functional connectivity). In one task-based functional connectivity study, adolescents with ASD completed a cognitive control task where they had to suppress a dominant response; for example, if a "red" cue appeared at the start of the trial, the participants had to make a left- or right-hand response that was the opposite of the direction of an arrow in the middle of the screen (Solomon et al., 2009). Functional connectivity between frontal and parietal regions was decreased during these rare-occurring high-cognitive control trials. Furthermore, this decreased functional connectivity between frontal and parietal regions was correlated with greater ADHD symptoms. This observation is convergent with long-standing models of ADHD that posit impairments in frontoparietal brain systems responsible for higher level cognition (Geurts, Verté, Oosterlaan, Roeyers, & Sergeant, 2004; Pennington & Ozonoff, 1996).

A rest-state study of functional connectivity took a transdiagnostic approach to the study of ADHD symptoms across three groups: children with typical development, those with ASD diagnoses, and those with ADHD diagnoses (Di Martino et al., 2013). In this study, a graph theory analytic approach was used by transforming the Pearson correlations into a measure of degree centrality for each voxel of the brain. A voxel is the smallest quantifiable unit from an MRI that takes the form of a cube. Degree centrality is the number of direct connections from each voxel to all other voxels in the brain. In this study the key findings were that degree centrality increased in children with ADHD and ASD+ADHD diagnoses (but not ASD alone), and when collapsing across all children, the degree centrality of the caudate was significantly associated with ADHD symptoms on the Conners Parent/Teacher Rating Scale ADHD index ($R^2 = 0.06$). Furthermore, degree centrality was also decreased in the parietal/precuneus region for those with an ASD diagnosis (regardless of ADHD status) and the ADHD-only group compared to typically developing controls. These findings converge with the structural connectivity findings noted earlier to implicate the fronto-parietal brain systems that have been routinely studied and implicated in ADHD (Casey et al., 1997, 2007; Cubillo et al., 2010; A. B. Smith et al., 2006; Vaidya et al., 2005).

A recent functional MRI study with a sustained attention task examined performance and associated neural correlates in medication-naïve boys with ASD diagnoses, ADHD diagnoses, or typical development (Christakou et al., 2013). In this study, boys were asked to press a button in their dominant hand whenever a visual timer appeared on screen, and its delay was modulated to occur either in short, predictable series of three to five stimuli every 500 ms or after variable delays of 2, 5, or 8 seconds each (20 seconds total). The variable, pseudo-random format of the delay required greater sustained attention. In terms of performance, boys with ADHD diagnoses had greater variability in their response times compared to boys with ASD diagnoses or typical development, suggesting poorer sustained attention skills. However, both clinical groups showed decreased activation, relative to the typical development group, in the parietal cortex (somatosensory cortex, superior parietal), as well as subcortical regions (thalamus, putamen, and hippocampus). The clinical groups also showed increased activation relative to controls in the precuneus cortex. There were also significant differences between the ASD and ADHD groups; specifically, the dorsolateral prefrontal cortex was less activated in the ADHD than the ASD group. However, what is most important to the present review is the shared impairment of atypical activation in parietal and precuneus regions. This study provides another piece of evidence from MRI research regarding the atypical structure and function of the parietal cortex in the shared neurobiology of ASD and ADHD.

Regarding the structure of the brain, there are few studies that have included both an ASD and an ADHD group. One study of 43 children (13 with ASD, 15 with ADHD, 15 controls) examined differences in regional gray matter volumes of the brain using a voxel-based morphometry approach with a structural MRI scan (Brieber et al., 2007). This study reported that both the ASD and ADHD groups demonstrated decreased gray matter in the left inferior parietal gyrus/postcentral gyrus, which is important for sensory processing and attention, and the left hippocampus–amygdala, which is important for processing emotional information and coding information in long-term memory. Interestingly, this study explicitly excluded children in either clinical group exhibiting symptoms of the other disorder. Thus, it is likely that the shared neurobiology here is related to each disorder, and not a result of subclinical features from the other disorder influencing the results. Again, the shared differences in the gray matter of the parietal cortex by both clinical groups implicate this region as playing a role in shared neurobiology and also as a region potentially contributing to ADHD symptoms in children with ASD.

Psychometrics of ADHD Diagnostic Tools

It has been common practice in the research of co-occurring ASD and ADHD—and likely clinical practice—to use ADHD diagnostic tools for screening, diagnosing, and quantifying ADHD symptom severity without addressing the issue of psychometric validity (Corbett et al., 2009; Gomarus, Wijers, Minderaa, & Althaus, 2009; Sinzig, Bruning, Morsch, & Lehmkuhl, 2008; Yerys et al., 2009; Yerys, Kenworthy, Jankowski, Strang, & Wallace, 2013). Thus, some studies have attempted to examine the psychometrics of existing tools for diagnosing ADHD in ASD, and also to develop novel instruments specifically for the ASD population.

To date, there is limited evidence on the psychometric properties of psychiatric interviews for diagnosing ADHD in children with an ASD diagnosis. However, the Autism Comorbidity Interview—Present and Lifetime (ACI-PL) was adapted from the Kiddie Schedule for Affective Disorders and Schizophrenia to evaluate for the presence of psychiatric and neurodevelopmental disorders *in the context of ASD* (Leyfer et al., 2006). That is, the ACI-PL included descriptions of how each disorder may manifest specifically in a child with ASD, and then proceeded with screening questions that have been modified to account for how the specific psychiatric disorder may present in ASD. Using the ACI-PL, clinicians identified that 31% of the 109 school-aged children with confirmed ASD would meet full criteria for a diagnosis of ADHD (i.e., had at least six symptoms in inattention and/or hyperactivity/impulsivity domains). Another 24% of children presented with significant symptoms but did not have six symptoms to meet full criteria; they would likely qualify as other specified ADHD in the DSM-5's nomenclature (American Psychiatric Association & DSM-5 Task Force, 2013). During the course of this study, criterion validity was established by comparing the results of the ACI-PL to whether children received treatment for diagnoses made by the ACI-PL. For ADHD, the sensitivity for an ADHD diagnosis was 100% and specificity was 93%. Although this interview has some merit for diagnosing co-occurring ADHD, it has not been made available to the broader mental health community since its publication in 2006.

There is also limited evidence on the psychometrics of ADHD screening questionnaires in the ASD population. The most commonly used instruments for ADHD include the ADHD Rating Scale (ADHD-RS-IV/V; DuPaul et al., 1998; DuPaul, Power, Anastopoulos, & Reid, 2016), the Behavior Assessment System for Children (BASC-2/3; Reynolds & Kamphaus, 2004, 2015), the CBCL/TRF from the Achenbach System of Empirically Based Assessment (Achenbach & Rescorla, 2001), the Child and Adolescent Symptom Inventory, fourth edition (CASI-4; Gadow & Sprafkin, 2010), and the Conners Parent Rating Form (CPRS-R/3; Conners, 1997, 2008). The ADHD-RS-IV/V, the CPRS-R/3, and the CASI-4 all have ADHD-specific questions that include the 18 symptoms of ADHD from the DSM (fourth and fifth editions) in parent-friendly language, whereas the BASC (second and third editions) and the CBCL are broadband psychiatric screeners that include some items that overlap with DSM language but also contain nonsymptom items (e.g., "acts young for age").

The ADHD-RS-IV has had its psychometric properties evaluated specifically for ADHD symptoms in an ASD population (Yerys et al., 2017). In a large (N = 386) school-aged sample of children with ASD, caregiver ratings on the ADHD-RS-IV showed strong criterion validity with caregiver report on the Behavior Rating Inventory of Executive Function (Gioia, Isquith, Guy, & Kenworthy, 2000), an informant-report executive function measure that includes scales on inhibition (i.e., hyperactivity/impulsivity behaviors) and working memory (i.e., inattention behaviors like forgetfulness and distractibility). Children with ASD also showed a decrease in ADHD symptoms with age on both parent and teacher report; this age-related change was expected as it is also found in the ADHD population (DuPaul et al., 1998). However, the ADHD-RS-IV demonstrated weak factorial validity for both rater types. That is, a confirmatory factor analysis demonstrated a weak fit for both the two-factor (inattention and hyperactivity/impulsivity) and the three-factor models that have been established in the ADHD literature (inattention, hyperactivity, and impulsivity). In particular, three Inattention items (Item 3: difficulty sustaining attention in tasks or play; Item 5: doesn't listen when spoken to directly; Item 15: is easily distracted) cross-loaded onto the inattention and hyperactivity/impulsivity factors for caregiver ratings, whereas for teacher ratings, Item 2 (fidgets or squirms in seat) cross-loaded onto the inattention and hyperactivity/impulsivity factors. My initial arguments were that several of these items may not work well for identifying ADHD as they are originally worded, because of the influence or confounding of social demands/expectations. For example, a child may be rated as not listening when spoken to directly because of social impairments (or social plus attention impairments). At the time, our group suggested that screeners required follow-up interviewing to confirm that symptoms were present after accounting for impairments related to the presence of ASD. However, after publication I became aware of a meta-analysis of factor analyses in ADHD (Willcutt et al., 2012), and several of these same items were identified as weak in the broader ADHD literature. Although postpublication discovery does not invalidate the general conclusions of Yerys and colleagues (2017), it suggests that the weak items may be weak overall and are not specific to the ASD population.

The CASI-4 (Gadow & Sprafkin, 2010) and the preschool version (Early Childhood Inventory, fourth edition) have had their psychometric properties evaluated at a global level in ASD (Lecavalier, Gadow, DeVincent, & Edwards, 2009; Lecavalier, Gadow, Devincent, Houts, & Edwards, 2011). In these two studies, confirmatory factor analyses were carried out to determine if the factor structure, with distinct scales for all psychiatric diagnoses for children (and preschoolers), was valid. The overall model had an acceptable fit with indices ranging from acceptable to good. The most notable exception was that ADHD was not retained as a single factor but was best modeled as separable domains of inattention and hyperactivity/impulsivity (Lecavalier et al., 2011).

The CBCL and the second and third editions of the BASC have not been evaluated for their psychometric validity in children with ASD. Furthermore, psychiatric interviews and screening measures used to evaluate ADHD in adults with ASD have not been well described in the literature.

Current recommendations for diagnosing ADHD in individuals with ASD are largely the same as articulated elsewhere (Yerys et al., 2017), which are for clinicians to exercise caution when interpreting the results of standard ADHD measures. Clinicians will need to carefully consider whether the behaviors being rated are independent of the ASD symptoms. For example, a clinician can consider if a child is easily distracted or fails to sustain play across social and nonsocial situations, as well as the role of sensory factors, insistence on sameness, or circumscribed interest needs interfering with attention-demanding situations.

Neuropsychological Functioning

Executive function and attention are two domains that have been some of the most investigated areas in the study of co-occurring ASD and ADHD (Adamo et al., 2013; Andersen et al., 2015; Andersen, Hovik, Skogli, Egeland, & Oie, 2013; Bühler, Bachmann, Goyert, Heinzel-Gutenbrunner, & Kamp-Becker, 2011; Corbett et al., 2009; Geurts, van den Bergh, & Ruzzano, 2014; Karalunas et al., 2018; Karalunas, Geurts, Konrad, Bender, & Nigg, 2014; Nydén et al., 2010; Sinzig, Bruning, et al., 2008; Sinzig, Morsch, Bruning, Schmidt, & Lehmkuhl, 2008; Wallace et al., 2016; Yerys et al., 2009, 2013). As reviewed elsewhere (Wallace et al., 2016), inhibition is the most commonly assessed executive function process in the context of co-occurring ASD and ADHD. Inhibition, particularly cognitive control tasks requiring the withholding of prepotent responses, is also the most reliable measure for identifying impairments in those with co-occurring ASD and ADHD diagnoses (Adamo et al., 2013; Bühler et al., 2011; Corbett et al., 2009; Sinzig, Bruning, et al., 2008; Yerys et al., 2009, 2013). Other inhibitory processes that require the suppression of distracting information—sometimes referred to as a form of selective attention—are impaired in ASD (Christ, Holt, White, & Green, 2007; Christ, Kester, Bodner, & Miles, 2011) but have not been clearly linked to ADHD symptoms (Corbett et al., 2009). Although a recent study with the largest sample of children with ASD (with and without ADHD) to date reported a response inhibition impairment in children with ASD, it was not linked to ADHD symptoms (Karalunas et al., 2018).

Other executive function processes linked to ADHD symptoms have been found to be impaired in ASD, although less reliably. For example, working memory has been found to be impaired in two of three studies using verbal span tasks (Andersen et al., 2013, 2015; Nydén et al., 2010; Yerys et al., 2009). There is some evidence for differences in a co-occurring ASD and ADHD group from children with ASD or ADHD diagnoses and controls for response time variability (Adamo et al., 2013; Karalunas et al., 2018). Planning and generativity impairments appear to be unrelated to ADHD symptoms in children and adults with ASD (Corbett et al., 2009; Nydén et al., 2010). Studies of flexibility in adults with co-occurring ASD and ADHD diagnoses have revealed mixed findings, with one study demonstrating more impaired performance (high speed–accuracy trade-off) and another showing no differences in an ASD versus an ASD+ADHD group (Johnston et al., 2013; Nydén et al., 2010).

Functional Outcome Measures

When considering functioning in everyday settings, parent-reported measures of executive function, adaptive behavior, and maladaptive behavior are worse in those individuals with co-occurring ASD and ADHD diagnoses compared to those with ASD alone (Ashwood et al., 2015; Lyall, Schweitzer, Schmidt, Hertz-Picciotto, & Solomon, 2017; Rao & Landa, 2014; Sikora et al., 2012; Yerys et al., 2009, 2019). This link between co-occurring ADHD symptoms and adaptive behavior has now been observed in preschoolers through young adults (Lyall et al., 2017; Rao & Landa, 2014; Sikora et al., 2012). In particular, Sikora and colleagues (2012) demonstrated this relationship in all three adaptive behavior domains of communication, daily living skills, and socialization in a large study ($N > 3{,}000$) of children and young adults enrolled in the Autism Treatment Network. This large study also demonstrated that individuals with ASD and ADHD diagnoses were rated as having a lower quality of life by parent report.

Finally, a recent study from our group took a dimensional approach to the study of how ADHD may associate with adaptive behavior functioning in a large sample of 6- to 17-year-olds with ASD (n = 386; Yerys et al., 2019). Rather than splitting our ASD sample into "ASD only" and "ASD+ADHD" groups, we used linear regressions to examine the relationship between ADHD symptoms and adaptive behavior functioning in the home and the school setting. We found that ADHD symptoms predicted significant variance in adaptive behaviors in the school setting, even after controlling for age, cognitive scores, gender, and ASD symptoms (across Communication, Daily Living Skills, and Socialization domains from the Vineland Adaptive Behavior Scales, second edition). We found significant relationships between ADHD symptoms and adaptive behaviors in the home setting too, which replicated prior work that used a categorical approach (Lyall et al., 2017; Rao & Landa, 2014; Sikora et al., 2012; Yerys et al., 2009). Furthermore, our study also demonstrated that these findings were not driven solely by those meeting formal DSM criteria for an ADHD diagnosis; the relationship between ADHD symptoms and adaptive behavior was still significant for the subset of children with ASD who did not have six symptoms in either the Inattention or the Hyperactivity/Impulsivity symptom domains. Although these studies are few in number, some have large sample sizes, and all studies show a consistent relationship between the presence of co-occurring ADHD and worse functioning throughout childhood and into early adulthood.

Treatment

The treatment of ADHD in the general population has been codified into very clear guidelines from the American Academy of Pediatrics (Subcommittee on Attention-Deficit/Hyperactivity Disorder & Steering Committee on Quality Improvement And Management, 2011). For preschoolers, recommendations for primary care pediatricians include prescribing behavioral training (parent or teacher administered) as the first line of treatment, and then methylphenidate can be considered if there is not significant improvement or there is moderate to severe continuing disturbance in the child's behavior. For school-aged children ages 6 to 11 years, recommendations include using U.S. Food and Drug Administration–approved medications for ADHD with particularly strong evidence for stimulant medications and sufficient evidence for nonstimulant medications (atomoxetine, extended-release guanfacine, and extended-release clonidine in this order), as well as academic supports. For adolescents, the recommendations are identical to that of school-aged children with the additional recommendation of obtaining the adolescents' assent and acknowledgment that behavioral interventions have weaker evidence in this age range. The Society of Clinical Child and Adolescent Psychology (American Psychological Association's Division 53; http://effectivechildtherapy.org) provides similar guidelines stating that "medication and/or behavior training for parents and teachers have been shown to be most effective [for treating ADHD]."

Reviews and the Society of Clinical Psychology (American Psychological Association's Division 12) have concluded that a similar medication treatment approach as school-age children and adolescents is appropriate in adults, and that pairing medication treatment with psychosocial treatments for core ADHD and common co-occurring conditions for adults is the most beneficial treatment option (Emilsson et al., 2011; Geffen & Forster, 2018; Kolar et al., 2008).

When evaluating these treatment approaches in children with co-occurring ASD and ADHD diagnoses, the available literature suggests the medication interventions are effective but for a smaller portion of the population. For methylphenidate, a multisite randomized, controlled, crossover trial from the Research Units of Pediatric Psychopharmacology (RUPP) Autism Network found that 49% of children with ASD and ADHD symptoms were classified as responders with an effect size ranging from 0.20 to 0.54, and adverse effects requiring medication discontinuation in 18% of participants (RUPP, 2005). This response rate and side effect rate is notable compared to the more favorable reporting from the Multimodal Treatment of ADHD study, which reported 73.4% of children with ADHD successfully receiving medication management and less than 3% reporting severe side effects (MTA Cooperative Group, 1999). For guanfacine, the same RUPP Autism Network reported that 43.6% of participants with ASD and ADHD diagnoses responded to extended-release guanfacine compared to 13.2% in the placebo group, and both groups had similar severe side effects (13.3% in guanfacine-treated group and 12.5% in placebo; Scahill et al., 2015).

Atomoxetine has been evaluated in a few large-scale randomized clinical trials in school-aged children with co-occurring ASD and ADHD (Arnold et al., 2018; Handen et al., 2015; Harfterkamp et al.,

2012, 2013; T. Smith et al., 2016). Response rates have ranged from 26% (Harfterkamp et al., 2012) to nearly 47% (Handen et al., 2015) across studies with effect sizes ranging from 0.68 to 0.84 (Handen et al., 2015). The response rate is lower than the 60% reported in the ADHD population, but the effect size in the ASD+ADHD population was comparable with what has been found in the ADHD literature (Schwartz & Correll, 2014). One study included a response inhibition task (Go/No-Go task) and a selective attention task (Flanker task) as outcomes and reported that responders improved on response inhibition (fewer false alarms on No-Go trials) but not selective attention (no reliable change on interference control; Van Der Meer et al., 2013). One of these studies examined atomoxetine alone and in conjunction with parent training but reported little additional benefit of parent training (Handen et al., 2015). Another study had a 24-week open-label extension phase and reported that 59% of responders from the original 10-week trial continued to respond, and that 37% of placebo nonresponders responded to atomoxetine at the end of the 24 weeks (T. Smith et al., 2016). Although behavioral parent treatment showed minimal effectiveness on ADHD symptoms in the blinded phase (Handen et al., 2015), it did improve noncompliance for those in the open-label longer term follow-up compared to children without parent training (T. Smith et al., 2016). A third follow-up assessment 1.5 years later showed that children's ADHD symptoms had mildly worsened from the end of the 24-week extension phase but were still significantly better than baseline: 61% of the sample at 24 weeks maintained clinically significant improvement (30% symptom reduction) 1.5 years after the original treatment study versus 67% of the sample having a 30% symptom reduction at the end of the 24-week extension phase (Arnold et al., 2018).

There is some preliminary evidence that children with co-occurring ASD and ADHD diagnoses benefit less from social skills treatment. A small pilot treatment study recruited three groups of children with ASD to complete a social skills treatment: those with ASD and ADHD (n = 25), those with ASD and anxiety (n = 37), and those with ASD alone (n = 21; Antshel et al., 2011). This social skills treatment targeted social communication and social problem-solving skills. The first five sessions focused on emotional awareness of self and others, as well as improving receptive and expressive body language skills so participants could learn how to read others' emotions, "stay on the same page" as others, and "break in" to conversations. The second five sessions focused on friendship, bullying, and teasing with skill building about how to identify social problems, prioritize them, generate feasible alternative strategies, and evaluate outcomes. Children with ASD and co-occurring anxiety or ASD alone showed improvements in the primary outcome variable, the Social Skills Rating System total score, whereas children with ASD and co-occurring ADHD showed no change from baseline to treatment outcome. Although the samples were relatively small, this study was innovative in asking the question of whether comorbidities may influence the outcomes of treatments for impairments related to ASD.

The treatment literature for older adolescents and adults with ASD+ADHD diagnoses is limited to a handful of case reports (Carminati, Deriaz, & Bertschy, 2006; Roy, Dillo, Bessling, Emrich, & Ohlmeier, 2009; van Schalkwyk, Beyer, Martin, & Volkmar, 2016). In two 17-year-olds and a 23-year-old with ASD, intellectual disability, and ADHD, venlafaxine (Effexor) was found to reduce both self-injurious behavior and ADHD symptoms (Carminati et al., 2006). The other two case studies reported on individuals in their mid-20s with ASD without intellectual disability and with ADHD, and both report ADHD symptom reduction with methylphenidate (Roy et al., 2009; van Schalkwyk et al., 2016). Based on a systematic review, there are no clinical trials of behavioral treatments for ADHD in adults with ASD+ADHD diagnoses. Thus, more research is needed to determine how to best treat adults with ASD+ADHD diagnoses.

Case Example

A 9-year-old female, "Tedra," and her biological parents referred themselves to a specialty outpatient psychology or psychiatry clinic because of increasing concerns about her social skills and some unusual behaviors. Tedra received speech and language services starting at age 2 for delayed speech onset. She had a "breakthrough" at age 3 and services were terminated after 6 months of rapid gains. Tedra has an existing diagnosis of ADHD, inattentive presentation from her pediatrician at age 8, but her mother is not sure this diagnosis explains her other problems with social interactions or her unusual behaviors. Her mother was beginning to question if ADHD was an accurate diagnosis for Tedra. Her mother's description of social skill difficulties includes refusing to talk with same-aged peers and adults in social settings (family gatherings, parties) or sometimes responding in odd ways by making sounds ("meep" or "murp") or responding with a cat's meow. In more comfortable settings, Tedra will speak with age-appropriate language but occasionally revert to "baby talk" that is reminiscent of telegraphic speech ("mommy get food"). Tedra is reported to "live within herself" and her preferred activities are reading, using her computer or iPad, and playing with specific brand-name dolls by herself. Tedra does not initiate play with other children and shows difficulties sustaining attention to play when the group switches to an activity that is not her primary interest. Tedra's interest in cats, stuffed animals, coloring, and reading is described as excessive relative to other girls her age, and she has had a strong interest in cats since she was an infant. As noted earlier, Tedra will attempt to act like a cat at inappropriate times in social settings and also at school. Tedra has some notable sensory sensitivities to taste and touch (will eat "deconstructed sandwiches and pizza" and will eat from a small list of foods). Tedra is described as forgetful and has a difficult time with instructions and following through on tasks.

During the evaluation, Tedra and her family completed Module 3 of the Autism Diagnostic Observation Schedule, second edition (ADOS-2; Lord et al., 2012); the Social Communication Questionnaire (SCQ; Rutter, Bailey, & Lord, 2003); the CBCL/TRF (Achenbach & Rescorla, 2001); the Adaptive Behavior Assessment System, third edition (ABAS-3; Harrison & Oakland, 2015); the Behavior Rating Inventory of Executive Function, second edition (BRIEF-2; Gioia, Isquith, Guy, & Kenworthy, 2015); the Wechsler Abbreviated Scales of Intelligence, second edition (WASI-II; Wechsler, 2011); and a clinical interview with components of the Kiddie Schedule for Affective Disorders and Schizophrenia—Present and Lifetime (K-SADS-PL; Kaufman et al., 1997) for diagnosing ADHD. Her IQ estimate from the WASI-II demonstrated a significant split, with a strength in Nonverbal Reasoning (87th percentile) compared to Verbal Reasoning (8th percentile), and her adaptive functioning was rated as moderately delayed (4th percentile overall, and 13th in social). On the BRIEF Tedra's mother rated her Metacognition skills all in the impaired range with a peak impairment in Working Memory, as well as the Shift scale from the Behavioral Regulation Index as impaired. The CBCL revealed clinically elevated scores on Attention problems and ADH Problems scales (both > 97th percentile), and a borderline score on the Withdrawn/Depressed scale (97th percentile). The TRF revealed clinically elevated scores on Social Problems and Thought Problems (> 97th percentile) and a borderline score on the Attention Problems (95th percentile) and Withdrawn/Depressed scale (97th percentile). The SCQ score was well below clinical cut-offs (< 10). The ADOS-2 score fell above the clinical cut-off for an ASD as Tedra demonstrated sufficient difficulties with reciprocal conversation and use of nonverbal communication gestures. She also repeatedly "steered" the conversation to cats, and she struggled to relay stories of nonroutine events. Tedra was able to engage in some turn-taking in conversation and pair it with eye contact, but she never modulated her eye gaze to convey an emotion or direct the examiner's attention. Tedra demonstrated no clear signs of hyperactivity, but she required constant repeating of instructions during the activities, and she was distracted during conversation by both external things in her environment and internal thoughts.

The clinical interview with Tedra and her mother reviewed items on the SCQ that seemed inconsistent with parent report at intake and observations on the ADOS-2, as well as additional questions about attention difficulties. Tedra's mother noted that many social items on the SCQ were not a concern because of supports provided at home and school. For example, Tedra was noted to have a best friend with whom she has regular playdates, and her mother described that Tedra's friend lives on the same street as Tedra's maternal grandmother. Tedra's grandmother regularly invites both girls over and is reported to facilitate the playdates; "otherwise they would end very quickly." During the K-SADS-PL portion of the clinical interview, Tedra and her mother described Tedra's attention as poorly maintained across both social settings (listening to others in a conversation) and nonsocial settings (completing homework). She struggled to complete her homework, and she often forgot to bring it to school or hand it in to the teacher. Tedra's mother described a series of checks she has in place each morning to make sure Tedra gets out of the house with everything she needs for school. Tedra reported having difficulty remembering what her mother and father ask her to get in other rooms, and that sometimes she "spaces out" in conversations and has to figure out what people are talking about. This report by Tedra is consistent with the examiner's experience of having to repeat questions to Tedra during the interview. Tedra also stated that she often refused to talk in social situations because "she doesn't know what to say"; she denied concerns of anticipatory worry before social gatherings, worries of saying something inappropriate, or worries that others may dislike her or view her negatively. Tedra also denied feeling sad or blue, or loss of interest in preferred activities. She has had no significant changes in her eating and sleep habits. Tedra denied suicidal or homicidal ideation.

Tedra was diagnosed with both ASD and ADHD based on this evaluation. Although Tedra's SCQ was below the clinical cut-off, her ADOS-2 score was above clinical cut-off, suggesting the clinician observed significant social reciprocity/communication impairments and some repetitive behaviors, which converged with parent description of both social reciprocity/communication impairments and the presence of multiple repetitive behaviors during the clinical interview. Parent report on questionnaires revealed moderate impairments in adaptive behavior and withdrawn/depressed behaviors related to social isolation. Her teacher reported social problems and thought problems. Taken together, these findings were sufficient to meet criteria for an ASD diagnosis without intellectual disability but with language impairment (based on history and large verbal/nonverbal IQ split). On the K-SADS-PL, Tedra and her mother report at least six pervasive symptoms of inattention (easily distracted, difficulty sustaining attention to tasks or play, often loses things necessary for tasks, disorganized, forgetful, doesn't listen even when spoken to directly) that occur across social and nonsocial settings and cannot be attributed to social difficulties; they did not report any significant hyperactivity or impulsivity symptoms. Both parents and teacher noted some attention problems at home and mild problems at school. Taken together, all of these findings plus clinician observation are sufficient to meet criteria for a diagnosis of ADHD, inattentive presentation (mild).

Although anxiety and depression diagnoses were considered given her refusal to talk in social settings, and parent and teacher report of Withdrawn/Depressed scores, these were not supported by clinical interview (or other CBCL scales) on questions of anxiety or depression.

Summary and Future Directions

This chapter has outlined a number of critical themes in our understanding of ADHD in the context of ASD. Based on the available evidence, ADHD is one of the most common psychiatric comorbidities in ASD alongside anxiety, intellectual disability, and language impairment. Up to 55% of individuals with ASD may experience significant ADHD symptoms and about 30% will meet traditional DSM-based criteria for an ADHD diagnosis. The presence of ADHD symptoms in someone with ASD is associated with worse functional outcomes, including poorer executive and adaptive behavior functioning and quality-of-life ratings. These behavioral differences appear to have similar neural bases as those with ADHD without ASD, including frontoparietal and frontostriatal systems.

This chapter also outlined evaluations of ADHD diagnostic tools in ASD, including recommendations for best practices. ADHD diagnostic interviews and screening forms have largely been applied in the study of ASD without much formal assessment of validity and reliability. The few studies examining psychometrics of these tools suggest that standard measures for screening and diagnosing ADHD may not meet rigid thresholds for psychometric validity, but they are also not grossly invalid. Thus, there is some case to be made for careful interpretation and follow-up interviewing with standard ADHD instruments in a clinical setting for making a diagnosis, and a need to continue refining these measures to improve upon their psychometric properties.

This chapter also addressed the treatment of co-occurring ADHD in ASD. Established treatments that have strong evidence for treating ADHD in those without ASD are also effective in those with ASD+ADHD, albeit a smaller subset than would be expected in the general ADHD population. Effect sizes of methylphenidate and extended-release guanfacine were similar but slightly smaller in the ASD+ADHD population than the ADHD population without ASD. Evaluation of behavioral treatments for ADHD symptoms has been modest in the literature thus far. To date, behavioral parent training has been evaluated and offered little additional benefit over atomoxetine as the medication treatment. However, the use of behavioral parent training was deemed helpful for associated behavioral problems with noncompliance. Another notable development in the treatment literature is how co-occurring ADHD may be predictive of poor treatment response in a social skills intervention.

Future research in co-occurring ASD and ADHD has a number of important issues to address in the coming years. Critical topics in the basic sciences include refining our understanding of shared and unique genetic and neurobiological mechanisms. Although early, small sample studies identified shared genes (e.g., metabotropic glutamate receptors), the very recent large-scale genetic study that combined data from genetic consortiums across the world found weak evidence of shared common variants and a weak correlation between ASD and ADHD. Critical questions to explore include whether the shared genetic risk is coming from rare variants or whether other aspects of the included ASD sample may have biased results.

Neurobiologically, there is some consistency of evidence regarding parietal lobe differences in structure and function, including frontoparietal connectivity, in children with ASD+ADHD diagnoses. However, a portion of this data is culled from studies collapsing across ASD-only and ADHD-only samples where children with co-occurring symptoms were excluded. Thus, it will be important to maintain both a quantitative approach by probing neurobiology in a large ASD sample with a wide range of ADHD symptoms and a quantitative approach in a transdiagnostic sample (those with ASD diagnoses, ADHD diagnoses, and co-occurring ASD+ADHD diagnoses). Furthermore, much of the research has focused squarely on reporting group differences, but it is possible that not all children with co-occurring ASD and ADHD diagnoses may have the same neurobiology underlying their ADHD symptoms. Indeed, although there is strong evidence supporting the frontoparietal-striatal brain system in ADHD (Casey et al., 1997; Rubia et al., 1999; Vaidya et al., 2005; Willcutt et al., 2005), there is also evidence implicating the salience–ventral attention brain system in ADHD (Mueller et al., 2017; Tegelbeckers et al., 2015). Thus, future investigations are needed to determine if children with co-occurring ASD and ADHD diagnoses have one or both systems driving their ADHD symptoms. Increasing specificity of the genetic and neurobiological mechanisms underlying ADHD symptoms is a step toward precision medicine where clinicians can tailor treatments to targeted mechanisms for that individual. The rise of machine-learning approaches in neuroimaging provides some promise to overcoming the obstacles engendered by attempting to translate groupwise differences observed in neuroimaging studies to making inferences about treatment needs at the individual level (Uddin, Dajani, Voorhies, Bednarz, & Kana, 2017).

There is also a critical need to improve diagnostics for identification of ADHD in ASD, so that we may better identify this high-risk comorbidity for early intervention, and to better quantify the developmental trajectory of ADHD in people with ASD. As noted earlier, there is evidence of significant differences in the persistence of ADHD symptoms and the long-term functional outcomes of people with ADHD without ASD (Hechtman et al., 2016), and it appears that this may be true for some adults with ASD+ADHD diagnoses (Gray et al., 2012; Woodman et al., 2016). However, a large number of functional outcomes (medical, social engagement, work) have not been evaluated distinctly for ASD+ADHD versus ASD-only subgroups (Bishop-Fitzpatrick et al., 2016; Howlin, Moss, Savage, & Rutter, 2013; Roux, Shattuck, Rast, Rava, & Anderson, 2015; Taylor & Seltzer, 2011). Furthermore, the field will be limited to engage in such research without validated instruments for screening, diagnosing, and tracking treatment-related change in ADHD symptoms across the lifespan. This is a vital need as waves of children with co-occurring ASD and ADHD diagnoses are now being identified and offered treatments throughout childhood, and it will be imperative to understand if the treatments are effective in improving long-term outcomes as adults.

References

Abrahams, B. S., & Geschwind, D. H. (2010). Connecting genes to brain in the autism spectrum disorders. *Archives of Neurology, 67*(4), 395–399.

Achenbach, T., & Rescorla, L. (2001). *Manual for ASEBA School-Age Forms & Profiles.* Burlington, VT: University of Vermont, Research Center for Children, Youth, & Families.

Adamo, N., Huo, L., Adelsberg, S., Petkova, E., Castellanos, F. X., & Di Martino, A. (2013). Response time intra-subject variability: Commonalities between children with autism spectrum disorders and children with ADHD. *European Child & Adolescent Psychiatry, 23*(2), 69–79.

Ameis, S. H., Lerch, J. P., Taylor, M. J., Lee, W., Viviano, J. D., Pipitone, J., et al. (2016). A diffusion tensor imaging study in children with ADHD, autism spectrum disorder, OCD, and matched controls: Distinct and non-distinct white matter disruption and dimensional brain-behavior relationships. *American Journal of Psychiatry, 173*(12), 1213–1222.

American Psychiatric Association. (2000). *Diagnostic and statistical manual of mental disorders* (4th ed., text revision, DSM-IV-TR). Arlington, VA: American Psychiatric Publishing.

American Psychiatric Association, & DSM-5 Task Force. (2013). *Diagnostic and statistical manual of mental disorders* (5th ed., DSM-5). Arlington, VA: American Psychiatric Association.

Anckarsäter, H., Stahlberg, O., Larson, T., Hakansson, C., Jutblad, S.-B., Niklasson, L., et al. (2006). The impact of ADHD and autism spectrum disorders on temperament, character, and personality development. *American Journal of Psychiatry, 163*(7), 1239–1244.

Andersen, P. N., Hovik, K. T., Skogli, E. W., Egeland, J., & Oie, M. (2013). Symptoms of ADHD in children with high-functioning autism are related to impaired verbal working memory and verbal delayed recall. *PloS One, 8*(5), e64842.

Andersen, P. N., Skogli, E. W., Hovik, K. T., Geurts, H., Egeland, J., & Øie, M. (2015). Working memory arrest in children with high-functioning autism compared to children with attention-deficit/hyperactivity disorder: Results from a 2-year longitudinal study. *Autism, 19*(4), 443–450.

Angold, A., & Costello, E. J. (1995). A test-retest reliability study of child-reported psychiatric symptoms and diagnoses using the Child and Adolescent Psychiatric Assessment (CAPA-C). *Psychological Medicine, 25*(4), 755–762.

Antshel, K. M., Polacek, C., McMahon, M., Dygert, K., Spenceley, L., Dygert, L., et al. (2011). Comorbid ADHD and anxiety affect social skills group intervention treatment efficacy in children with autism spectrum disorders. *Journal of Developmental and Behavioral Pediatrics, 32*(6), 439–446.

Aoki, Y., Yoncheva, Y. N., Chen, B., Nath, T., Sharp, D., Lazar, M., et al. (2017). Association of white matter structure with autism spectrum disorder and attention-deficit/hyperactivity disorder. *JAMA Psychiatry, 74*(11), 1120–1128.

Arnold, L. E., Ober, N., Aman, M. G., Handen, B., Smith, T., Pan, X., et al. (2018). A 1.5-year follow-up of parent training and atomoxetine for attention-deficit/hyperactivity disorder symptoms and noncompliant/disruptive behavior in autism. *Journal of Child and Adolescent Psychopharmacology, 28*(5), 322–330.

Ashwood, K. L., Tye, C., Azadi, B., Cartwright, S., Asherson, P., & Bolton, P. (2015). Brief report: Adaptive functioning in children with ASD, ADHD and ASD + ADHD. *Journal of Autism & Developmental Disorders, 45*(7), 2235–2242.

Basser, P. J., Mattiello, J., & LeBihan, D. (1994). MR diffusion tensor spectroscopy and imaging. *Biophysical Journal, 66*(1), 259–267.

Bishop-Fitzpatrick, L., Hong, J., Smith, L. E., Makuch, R. A., Greenberg, J. S., & Mailick, M. R. (2016). Characterizing objective quality of life and normative outcomes in adults with autism spectrum disorder: An exploratory latent class analysis. *Journal of Autism and Developmental Disorders, 46*(8), 2707–2719.

Brieber, S., Neufang, S., Bruning, N., Kamp-Becker, I., Remschmidt, H., Herpertz-Dahlmann, B., et al. (2007). Structural brain abnormalities in adolescents with autism spectrum disorder and patients with attention deficit/hyperactivity disorder. *Journal of Child Psychology and Psychiatry, 48*(12), 1251–1258.

Brookman-Frazee, L., Stadnick, N., Chlebowski, C., Baker-Ericzén, M., & Ganger, W. (2018). Characterizing psychiatric comorbidity in children with autism spectrum disorder receiving publicly funded mental health services. *Autism, 22*(8), 938–952.

Bühler, E., Bachmann, C., Goyert, H., Heinzel-Gutenbrunner, M., & Kamp-Becker, I. (2011). Differential diagnosis of autism spectrum disorder and attention deficit hyperactivity disorder by means of inhibitory control and "theory of mind." *Journal of Autism and Developmental Disorders, 41*(12), 1718–1726.

Carminati, G. G., Deriaz, N., & Bertschy, G. (2006). Low-dose venlafaxine in three adolescents and young adults with autistic disorder improves self-injurious behavior and attention deficit/hyperactivity disorders (ADHD)-like symptoms. *Progress in Neuro-Psychopharmacology and Biological Psychiatry, 30*(2), 312–315.

Casey, B. J., Castellanos, F. X., Giedd, J. N., Marsh, W. L., Hamburger, S. D., Schubert, A. B., et al. (1997). Implication of right frontostriatal circuitry in response inhibition and attention-deficit/hyperactivity disorder. *Journal of the American Academy of Child and Adolescent Psychiatry, 36*(3), 374–383.

Casey, B. J., Epstein, J. N., Buhle, J., Liston, C., Davidson, M. C., Tonev, S. T., et al. (2007). Frontostriatal connectivity and its role in cognitive control in parent-child dyads with ADHD. *American Journal of Psychiatry, 164*(11), 1729–1736.

Castellanos, F. X., & Proal, E. (2012). Large-scale brain systems in ADHD: Beyond the prefrontal-striatal model. *Trends in Cognitive Sciences, 16*(1), 17–26.

Cavanna, A. E., & Trimble, M. R. (2006). The precuneus: A review of its functional anatomy and behavioural correlates. *Brain, 129*(Pt 3), 564–583.

Christ, S. E., Holt, D. D., White, D. A., & Green, L. (2007). Inhibitory control in children with autism spectrum disorder. *Journal of Autism and Developmental Disorders, 37*(6), 1155–1165.

Christ, S. E., Kester, L. E., Bodner, K. E., & Miles, J. H. (2011). Evidence for selective inhibitory impairment in individuals with autism spectrum disorder. *Neuropsychology, 25*(6), 690–701.

Christakou, A., Murphy, C. M., Chantiluke, K., Cubillo, A. I., Smith, A. B., Giampietro, V., et al. (2013). Disorder-specific functional abnormalities during sustained attention in youth with attention deficit hyperactivity disorder (ADHD) and with autism. *Molecular Psychiatry, 18*(2), 264.

Clements, C. C., Wenger, T. L., Zoltowski, A. R., Bertollo, J. R., Miller, J. S., Marchena, A. B., et al. (2017). Critical region within 22q11.2 linked to higher rate of autism spectrum disorder. *Molecular Autism, 8*, 58.

Conners, C. K. (1997). *Conner's Rating Scales-Revised technical manual.* Toronto, Ontario, Canada: Multi-Health Systems.

Conners, C. K. (2008). *Conners* (3rd ed.). San Antonio, TX: Pearson Assessments.

Consortium, T. B., Anttila, V., Bulik-Sullivan, B., Finucane, H. K., Walters, R. K., Bras, J., et al. (2018). Analysis of shared heritability in common disorders of the brain. *Science, 360*(6395), eaap8757.

Corbett, B. A., Constantine, L. J., Hendren, R., Rocke, D., & Ozonoff, S. (2009). Examining executive functioning in children with autism spectrum disorder, attention deficit hyperactivity disorder and typical development. *Psychiatry Research, 166*(2–3), 210–222.

Costello, E. J., Mustillo, S., Erkanli, A., Keeler, G., & Angold, A. (2003). Prevalence and development of psychiatric disorders in childhood and adolescence. *Archives of General Psychiatry, 60*(8), 837–844.

Cross-Disorder Group of the Psychiatric Genomics Consortium, International Inflammatory Bowel Disease Genetics Consortium (IIBDGC), Lee, S. H., Ripke, S., Neale, B. M., Faraone, S. V., et al. (2013). Genetic relationship between five psychiatric disorders estimated from genome-wide SNPs. *Nature Genetics, 45*(9), 984–994.

Cubillo, A., Halari, R., Ecker, C., Giampietro, V., Taylor, E., & Rubia, K. (2010). Reduced activation and inter-regional functional connectivity of fronto-striatal networks in adults with childhood attention-deficit hyperactivity disorder (ADHD) and persisting symptoms during tasks of motor inhibition and cognitive switching. *Journal of Psychiatric Research, 44*(10), 629–639.

Di Martino, A., Zuo, X.-N., Kelly, C., Grzadzinski, R., Mennes, M., Schvarcz, A., et al. (2013). Shared and distinct intrinsic functional network centrality in autism and attention-deficit/hyperactivity disorder. *Biological Psychiatry, 74*(8), 623–632.

DuPaul, G. J., Power, T. J., Anastopoulos, A. D., & Reid, R. (1998). *ADHD Rating Scale-IV: Checklists, norms, and clinical interpretation*. New York, NY: Guilford Press.

DuPaul, G. J., Power, T. J., Anastopoulos, A. D., & Reid, R. (2016). *ADHD Rating Scale-5 for Children and Adolescents: Checklists, norms, and clinical interpretation*. New York, NY: Guilford Press.

Elia, J., Glessner, J. T., Wang, K., Takahashi, N., Shtir, C. J., Hadley, D., et al. (2012). Genome-wide copy number variation study associates metabotropic glutamate receptor gene networks with attention deficit hyperactivity disorder. *Nature Genetics, 44*(1), 78–84.

Emilsson, B., Gudjonsson, G., Sigurdsson, J. F., Baldursson, G., Einarsson, E., Olafsdottir, H., & Young, S. (2011). Cognitive behaviour therapy in medication-treated adults with ADHD and persistent symptoms: A randomized controlled trial. *BMC Psychiatry, 11*, 116.

Fassbender, C., Krafft, C. E., & Schweitzer, J. B. (2015). Differentiating SCT and inattentive symptoms in ADHD using fMRI measures of cognitive control. *NeuroImage: Clinical, 8*, 390–397.

Friston, K. J. (1994). Functional and effective connectivity in neuroimaging: A synthesis. *Human Brain Mapping, 5*, 56–78.

Gadow, K. D., Roohi, J., DeVincent, C. J., & Hatchwell, E. (2008). Association of ADHD, tics, and anxiety with dopamine transporter (DAT1) genotype in autism spectrum disorder. *Journal of Child Psychology and Psychiatry, 49*(12), 1331–1338.

Gadow, K. D., & Sprafkin, J. (2010). *Child & Adolescent Symptom Inventory* (4th ed. rev.). Stony Brook, NY: Checkmate Plus.

Gai, X., Xie, H. M., Perin, J. C., Takahashi, N., Murphy, K., Wenocur, A. S., et al. (2012). Rare structural variation of synapse and neurotransmission genes in autism. *Molecular Psychiatry, 17*(4), 402–411.

Geffen, J., & Forster, K. (2018). Treatment of adult ADHD: A clinical perspective. *Therapeutic Advances in Psychopharmacology, 8*(1), 25–32.

Geschwind, D. H., & Levitt, P. (2007). Autism spectrum disorders: Developmental disconnection syndromes. *Current Opinion in Neurobiology, 17*(1), 103–111.

Geurts, H. M., van den Bergh, S. F. W. M., & Ruzzano, L. (2014). Prepotent response inhibition and interference control in autism spectrum disorders: Two meta-analyses. *Autism Research, 7*(4), 407–420.

Geurts, H. M., Verté, S., Oosterlaan, J., Roeyers, H., & Sergeant, J. A. (2004). How specific are executive functioning deficits in attention deficit hyperactivity disorder and autism? *Journal of Child Psychology and Psychiatry, 45*(4), 836–854.

Gioia, G. A., Isquith, P. K., Guy, S., & Kenworthy, L. (2000). *BRIEF: Behavior Rating Inventory of Executive Function*. Odessa, FL: Psychological Assessment Resources.

Gioia, G. A., Isquith, P. K., Guy, S., & Kenworthy, L. (2015). *Behavior Rating Inventory of Executive Function* (2nd ed., *BRIEF-2*). Odessa, FL: Psychological Assessment Resources.

Gomarus, H., Wijers, A., Minderaa, R., & Althaus, M. (2009). ERP correlates of selective attention and working memory capacities in children with ADHD and/or PDD-NOS. *Clinical Neurophysiology, 120*(1), 60–72.

Gratton, C., Laumann, T. O., Nielsen, A. N., Greene, D. J., Gordon, E. M., Gilmore, A. W., et al. (2018). Functional brain networks are dominated by stable group and individual factors, not cognitive or daily variation. *Neuron, 98*(2), 439–452.e5.

Gray, K., Keating, C., Taffe, J., Brereton, A., Einfeld, S., & Tonge, B. (2012). Trajectory of behavior and emotional problems in autism. *American Journal on Intellectual and Developmental Disabilities, 117*(2), 121–133.

Handen, B. L., Aman, M. G., Arnold, L. E., Hyman, S. L., Tumuluru, R. V., Lecavalier, L., et al. (2015). Atomoxetine, parent training, and their combination in children with autism spectrum disorder and attention-deficit/hyperactivity disorder. *Journal of the American Academy of Child and Adolescent Psychiatry, 54*(11), 905–915.

Hanson, E., Cerban, B. M., Slater, C. M., Caccamo, L. M., Bacic, J., & Chan, E. (2013). Brief report: Prevalence of attention deficit/hyperactivity disorder among individuals with an autism spectrum disorder. *Journal of Autism and Developmental Disorders, 43*(6), 1459–1464.

Harfterkamp, M., Buitelaar, J. K., Minderaa, R. B., van de Loo-Neus, G., van der Gaag, R.-J., & Hoekstra, P. J. (2013). Long-term treatment with atomoxetine for attention-deficit/hyperactivity disorder symptoms in children and adolescents with autism spectrum disorder: An open-label extension study. *Journal of Child and Adolescent Psychopharmacology, 23*(3), 194–199.

Harfterkamp, M., van de Loo-Neus, G., Minderaa, R. B., van der Gaag, R.-J., Escobar, R., Schacht, A., et al. (2012). A randomized double-blind study of atomoxetine versus placebo for attention-deficit/hyperactivity disorder symptoms in children with autism spectrum disorder. *Journal of the American Academy of Child and Adolescent Psychiatry, 51*(7), 733–741.

Harrison, P. L., & Oakland, T. (2015). *Adaptive Behavior Assessment System Third Edition (ABAS3) manual*. San Antonio, TX: Pearson Assessments.

Hartman, C. A., Geurts, H. M., Franke, B., Buitelaar, J. K., & Rommelse, N. N. J. (2016). Changing ASD-ADHD symptom co-occurrence across the lifespan with adolescence as crucial time window: Illustrating the need to go beyond childhood. *Neuroscience & Biobehavioral Reviews, 71*, 529–541.

Hechtman, L., Swanson, J. M., Sibley, M. H., Stehli, A., Owens, E. B., Mitchell, L. E., et al. (2016). Functional adult outcomes 16 years after childhood diagnosis of attention-deficit/hyperactivity disorder: MTA results. *Journal of the American Academy of Child and Adolescent Psychiatry, 55*(11), 945–954.

Howlin, P., Moss, P., Savage, S., & Rutter, M. (2013). Social outcomes in mid- to later adulthood among individuals diagnosed with autism and average nonverbal IQ as children. *Journal of the American Academy of Child and Adolescent Psychiatry, 52*(6), 572–581.e1.

Johnston, K., Dittner, A., Bramham, J., Murphy, C., Knight, A., & Russell, A. (2013). Attention deficit hyperactivity disorder symptoms in adults with autism spectrum disorders. *Autism Research, 6*(4), 225–236.

Joshi, G., Faraone, S. V., Wozniak, J., Tarko, L., Fried, R., Galdo, M., et al. (2017). Symptom profile of ADHD in youth with high-functioning autism spectrum disorder: A comparative study in psychiatrically referred populations. *Journal of Attention Disorders, 21*(10), 846–855.

Kana, R. K., Uddin, L. Q., Kenet, T., Chugani, D., & Müller, R. A. (2014). Brain connectivity in autism. *Frontiers in Human Neuroscience, 8*, 349.

Karalunas, S. L., Geurts, H. M., Konrad, K., Bender, S., & Nigg, J. T. (2014). Annual research review: Reaction time variability in ADHD and autism spectrum disorders: Measurement and mechanisms of a proposed trans-diagnostic phenotype. *Journal of Child Psychology and Psychiatry, 55*(6), 685–710.

Karalunas, S. L., Hawkey, E., Gustafsson, H., Miller, M., Langhorst, M., Cordova, M., et al. (2018). Overlapping and distinct cognitive impairments in attention-deficit/hyperactivity and autism spectrum disorder without intellectual disability. *Journal of Abnormal Child Psychology, 46*(8), 1705–1716.

Kaufman, J., Birmaher, B., Brent, D., Rao, U., Flynn, C., Moreci, P., et al. (1997). Schedule for Affective Disorders and Schizophrenia for School-Age Children-Present and Lifetime Version (K-SADS-PL): Initial reliability and validity data. *Journal of the American Academy of Child and Adolescent Psychiatry, 36*(7), 980–988.

Kolar, D., Keller, A., Golfinopoulos, M., Cumyn, L., Syer, C., & Hechtman, L. (2008). Treatment of adults with attention-deficit/hyperactivity disorder. *Neuropsychiatric Disease and Treatment, 4*(2), 389–403.

Lecavalier, L., Gadow, K. D., DeVincent, C. J., & Edwards, M. C. (2009). Validation of DSM-IV model of psychiatric syndromes in children with autism spectrum disorders. *Journal of Autism and Developmental Disorders, 39*(2), 278–289.

Lecavalier, L., Gadow, K. D., Devincent, C. J., Houts, C. R., & Edwards, M. C. (2011). Validity of DSM-IV syndromes in preschoolers with autism spectrum disorders. *Autism: The International Journal of Research and Practice, 15*(5), 527–543.

Leyfer, O. T., Folstein, S. E., Bacalman, S., Davis, N. O., Dinh, E., Morgan, J., et al. (2006). Comorbid psychiatric disorders in children with autism: Interview development and rates of disorders. *Journal of Autism and Developmental Disorders, 36*(7), 849–861.

Lichtenstein, P., Carlström, E., Råstam, M., Gillberg, C., & Anckarsäter, H. (2010). The genetics of autism spectrum disorders and related neuropsychiatric disorders in childhood. *American Journal of Psychiatry, 167*(11), 1357–1363.

Llanes, E., Blacher, J., Stavropoulos, K., & Eisenhower, A. (2018). Parent and teacher reports of comorbid anxiety and ADHD symptoms in children with ASD. *Journal of Autism and Developmental Disorders*, 1–12.

Lord, C., Rutter, M., DiLavore, P. C., Risi, S., Gotham, K., & Bishop, S. (2012). *Autism Diagnostic Observation Schedule, second edition (ADOS-2) manual (Part I): Modules 1–4*. Torrance, CA: Western Psychological Services.

Lyall, K., Schweitzer, J. B., Schmidt, R. J., Hertz-Picciotto, I., & Solomon, M. (2017). Inattention and hyperactivity in association with autism spectrum disorders in the CHARGE study. *Research in Autism Spectrum Disorders, 35*, 1–12.

Matsushima, N., Miyawaki, D., Tsuji, H., Takahashi, K., Horino, A., Kawaguchi, T., et al. (2008). Evaluation of attention-deficit/hyperactivity disorder symptoms in male children with high-functioning pervasive developmental disorders. *Osaka City Medical Journal, 54*(1), 1–10.

Miller, J. (2014). DSM-5 and autism spectrum disorders: The changes you haven't heard about yet. *Journal of Clinical Psychiatry, 75*(11), e1326–e1327.

MTA Cooperative Group. (1999). A 14-month randomized clinical trial of treatment strategies for attention-deficit/hyperactivity disorder. *Archives of General Psychiatry, 56*(12), 1073–1086.

Mueller, A., Hong, D. S., Shepard, S., & Moore, T. (2017). Linking ADHD to the neural circuitry of attention. *Trends in Cognitive Sciences, 21*(6), 474–488.

Mulligan, A., Anney, R. J. L., O'Regan, M., Chen, W., Butler, L., Fitzgerald, M., et al. (2009). Autism symptoms in attention-deficit/hyperactivity disorder: A familial trait which correlates with conduct, oppositional defiant, language and motor disorders. *Journal of Autism and Developmental Disorders, 39*(2), 197–209.

Nijmeijer, J. S., Arias-Vásquez, A., Rommelse, N. N. J., Altink, M. E., Anney, R. J. L., Asherson, P., et al. (2010). Identifying loci for the overlap between attention-deficit/hyperactivity disorder and autism spectrum disorder using a genome-wide QTL linkage approach. *Journal of the American Academy of Child and Adolescent Psychiatry, 49*(7), 675–685.

Niklasson, L., Rasmussen, P., Oskarsdóttir, S., & Gillberg, C. (2005). Attention deficits in children with 22q.11 deletion syndrome. *Developmental Medicine and Child Neurology, 47*(12), 803–807.

Niklasson, L., Rasmussen, P., Oskarsdóttir, S., & Gillberg, C. (2009). Autism, ADHD, mental retardation and behavior problems in 100 individuals with 22q11 deletion syndrome. *Research in Developmental Disabilities, 30*(4), 763–773.

Nydén, A., Niklasson, L., Stahlberg, O., Anckarsater, H., Wentz, E., Rastam, M., & Gillberg, C. (2010). Adults with autism spectrum disorders and ADHD neuropsychological aspects. *Research in Developmental Disabilities, 31*(6), 1659–1668.

Ogdie, M. N., Macphie, I. L., Minassian, S. L., Yang, M., Fisher, S. E., Francks, C., et al. (2003). A genomewide scan for attention-deficit/hyperactivity disorder in an extended sample: Suggestive linkage on 17p11. *American Journal of Human Genetics, 72*(5), 1268–1279.

Pennington, B. F., & Ozonoff, S. (1996). Executive functions and developmental psychopathology. *Journal of Child Psychology and Psychiatry, 37*(1), 51–87.

Philofsky, A., Hepburn, S. L., Hayes, A., Hagerman, R., & Rogers, S. J. (2004). Linguistic and cognitive functioning and autism symptoms in young children with fragile X syndrome. *American Journal on Mental Retardation, 109*(3), 208–218.

Pierpaoli, C., Jezzard, P., Basser, P. J., Barnett, A., & Di Chiro, G. (1996). Diffusion tensor MR imaging of the human brain. *Radiology, 201*(3), 637–648.

Rao, P., & Landa, R. J. (2014). Association between severity of behavioral phenotype and comorbid attention deficit hyperactivity disorder symptoms in children with autism spectrum disorders. *Autism, 18*(3), 272–280.

Ray, S., Miller, M., Karalunas, S., Robertson, C., Grayson, D. S., Cary, R. P., et al. (2014). Structural and functional connectivity of the human brain in autism spectrum disorders and attention-deficit/hyperactivity disorder: A rich club-organization study. *Human Brain Mapping, 35*(12), 6032–6048.

Reilly, C., Senior, J., & Murtagh, L. (2015). ASD, ADHD, mental health conditions and psychopharmacology in neurogenetic syndromes: Parent survey. *Journal of Intellectual Disability Research, 59*(4), 307–318.

Research Units of Pediatric Psychopharmacology (RUPP). (2005). Randomized, controlled, crossover trial of methylphenidate

in pervasive developmental disorders with hyperactivity. *Archives of General Psychiatry, 62*(11), 1266–1274.
Reynolds, C., & Kamphaus, R. (2004). *BASC-2: Behavior Assessment System for Children* (2nd ed.). Odessa, FL: Psychological Assessment Resources.
Reynolds, C., & Kamphaus, R. (2015). *BASC-3: Behavior Assessment System for Children* (3rd ed.). Odessa, FL: Psychological Assessment Resources.
Rommelse, N. N. J., Franke, B., Geurts, H. M., Hartman, C. A., & Buitelaar, J. K. (2010). Shared heritability of attention-deficit/hyperactivity disorder and autism spectrum disorder. *European Child & Adolescent Psychiatry, 19*(3), 281–295.
Roohi, J., DeVincent, C. J., Hatchwell, E., & Gadow, K. D. (2009). Association of a monoamine oxidase-a gene promoter polymorphism with ADHD and anxiety in boys with autism spectrum disorder. *Journal of Autism and Developmental Disorders, 39*(1), 67–74.
Roux, A. M., Shattuck, P. T., Rast, J., Rava, J. A., & Anderson, K. A. (2015). *National autism indicators report: Transition into young adulthood.* Philadelphia, PA: Life Course Outcomes Research Program.
Roy, M., Dillo, W., Bessling, S., Emrich, H. M., & Ohlmeier, M. D. (2009). Effective methylphenidate treatment of an adult Aspergers syndrome and a comorbid ADHD: A clinical investigation with fMRI. *Journal of Attention Disorders, 12*(4), 381–385.
Rubia, K., Overmeyer, S., Taylor, E., Brammer, M., Williams, S. C. R., Simmons, A., & Bullmore, E. T. (1999). Hypofrontality in attention deficit hyperactivity disorder during higher-order motor control: A study with functional MRI. *American Journal of Psychiatry, 156*(6), 891–896.
Rubia, K., Smith, A. B., Taylor, E., & Brammer, M. (2007). Linear age-correlated functional development of right inferior fronto-striato-cerebellar networks during response inhibition and anterior cingulate during error-related processes. *Human Brain Mapping, 28*(11), 1163–1177.
Research Units of Pediatric Psychopharmacology (2005). Randomized, controlled, crossover trial of methylphenidate in pervasive developmental disorders with hyperactivity. *Archives of General Psychiatry, 62*(11), 1266–1274.
Rutter, M., Bailey, A., & Lord, C. (2003). *Social Communication Questionnaire (SCQ)*. Los Angeles, CA: Western Psychological Services.
Sanders, S. J., He, X., Willsey, A. J., Ercan-Sencicek, A. G., Samocha, K. E., Cicek, A. E., et al. (2015). Insights into autism spectrum disorder genomic architecture and biology from 71 risk loci. *Neuron, 87*(6), 1215–1233.
Saqr, Y., Braun, E., Porter, K., Barnette, D., & Hanks, C. (2017). Addressing medical needs of adolescents and adults with autism spectrum disorders in a primary care setting. *Autism, 22*(1), 51–61.
Scahill, L., McCracken, J. T., Rockhill, C., Shah, B., Politte, L., Sanders, R., et al. (2015). Extended-release guanfacine for hyperactivity in children with autism spectrum disorder. *American Journal of Psychiatry, 172*(12), 1197–1206.
Schneider, M., Debbané, M., Bassett, A. S., Chow, E. W. C., Fung, W. L. A., van den Bree, M. B. M., et al. (2014). Psychiatric disorders from childhood to adulthood in 22q11.2 deletion syndrome: Results from the international consortium on brain and behavior in 22q11.2 deletion syndrome. *American Journal of Psychiatry, 171*(6), 627–639.
Schwartz, S., & Correll, C. U. (2014). Efficacy and safety of atomoxetine in children and adolescents with attention-deficit/hyperactivity disorder: Results from a comprehensive meta-analysis and metaregression. *Journal of the American Academy of Child and Adolescent Psychiatry, 53*(2), 174–187.
Shephard, E., Bedford, R., Milosavljevic, B., Gliga, T., Jones, E. J. H., Pickles, A., et al. (2018). Early developmental pathways to childhood symptoms of attention-deficit hyperactivity disorder, anxiety and autism spectrum disorder. *Journal of Child Psychology and Psychiatry, 60*(9), 963–974.
Sikora, D. M., Vora, P., Coury, D. L., & Rosenberg, D. (2012). Attention-deficit/hyperactivity disorder symptoms, adaptive functioning, and quality of life in children with autism spectrum disorder. *Pediatrics, 130*(Suppl 2), S91–S97.
Simonoff, E., Pickles, A., Charman, T., Chandler, S., Loucas, T., & Baird, G. (2008). Psychiatric disorders in children with autism spectrum disorders: Prevalence, comorbidity, and associated factors in a population-derived sample. *Journal of the American Academy of Child and Adolescent Psychiatry, 47*(8), 921–929.
Sinzig, J., Bruning, N., Morsch, D., & Lehmkuhl, G. (2008). Attention profiles in autistic children with and without comorbid hyperactivity and attention problems. *Acta Neuropsychiatrica, 20*(4), 207–215.
Sinzig, J., Morsch, D., Bruning, N., Schmidt, M. H., & Lehmkuhl, G. (2008). Inhibition, flexibility, working memory and planning in autism spectrum disorders with and without comorbid ADHD-symptoms. *Child and Adolescent Psychiatry and Mental Health, 2*(1), 4.
Sinzig, J., Walter, D., & Doepfner, M. (2009). Attention deficit/hyperactivity disorder in children and adolescents with autism spectrum disorder: Symptom or syndrome? *Journal of Attention Disorders, 13*(2), 117–126.
Smalley, S. L., Kustanovich, V., Minassian, S. L., Stone, J. L., Ogdie, M. N., McGough, J. J., et al. (2002). Genetic linkage of attention-deficit/hyperactivity disorder on chromosome 16p13, in a region implicated in autism. *American Journal of Human Genetics, 71*(4), 959–963.
Smith, A. B., Taylor, E., Brammer, M., Toone, B., & Rubia, K. (2006). Task-specific hypoactivation in prefrontal and temporoparietal brain regions during motor inhibition and task switching in medication-naive children and adolescents with attention deficit hyperactivity disorder. *American Journal of Psychiatry, 163*(6), 1044–1051.
Smith, T., Aman, M. G., Arnold, L. E., Silverman, L. B., Lecavalier, L., Hollway, J., et al. (2016). Atomoxetine and parent training for children with autism and attention-deficit/hyperactivity disorder: A 24-week extension study. *Journal of the American Academy of Child and Adolescent Psychiatry, 55*(10), 868–876.e2.
Solomon, M., Ozonoff, S., Ursu, S., Ravizza, S., Cummings, N., Ly, S., & Carter, C. S. (2009). The neural substrates of cognitive control deficits in autism spectrum disorders. *Neuropsychologia, 47*(12), 2515–2526.
Subcommittee on Attention-Deficit/Hyperactivity Disorder, & Steering Committee on Quality Improvement and Management. (2011). ADHD: Clinical practice guideline for the diagnosis, evaluation, and treatment of attention-deficit/hyperactivity disorder in children and adolescents. *Pediatrics, 128*(5), 1007–1022.
Tamm, L., Menon, V., & Reiss, A. L. (2006). Parietal attentional system aberrations during target detection in adolescents with attention deficit hyperactivity disorder: Event-related fMRI evidence. *American Journal of Psychiatry, 163*(6), 1033–1043.

Taylor, J. L., & Seltzer, M. M. (2011). Employment and post-secondary educational activities for young adults with autism spectrum disorders during the transition to adulthood. *Journal of Autism and Developmental Disorders, 41*(5), 566–574.

Tegelbeckers, J., Bunzeck, N., Duzel, E., Bonath, B., Flechtner, H.-H., & Krauel, K. (2015). Altered salience processing in attention deficit hyperactivity disorder: Novelty processing in ADHD. *Human Brain Mapping, 36*(6), 2049–2060.

Uddin, L. Q., Dajani, D. R., Voorhies, W., Bednarz, H., & Kana, R. K. (2017). Progress and roadblocks in the search for brain-based biomarkers of autism and attention-deficit/hyperactivity disorder. *Translational Psychiatry, 7*(8), e1218.

Vaidya, C. J., Bunge, S. A., Dudukovic, N. M., Zalecki, C. A., Elliott, G. R., & Gabrieli, J. D. E. (2005). Altered neural substrates of cognitive control in childhood ADHD: Evidence from functional magnetic resonance imaging. *American Journal of Psychiatry, 162*(9), 1605–1613.

Vaidya, C. J., & Gordon, E. M. (2013). Phenotypic variability in resting-state functional connectivity: Current status. *Brain Connectivity, 3*(2), 99–120.

Van Der Meer, J. M. J., Harfterkamp, M., van de Loo-Neus, G., Althaus, M., de Ruiter, S. W., Donders, A. R. T., et al. (2013). A randomized, double-blind comparison of atomoxetine and placebo on response inhibition and interference control in children and adolescents with autism spectrum disorder and comorbid attention-deficit/hyperactivity disorder symptoms. *Journal of Clinical Psychopharmacology, 33*(6), 824–827.

van Schalkwyk, G. I., Beyer, C., Martin, A., & Volkmar, F. R. (2016). College students with autism spectrum disorders: A growing role for adult psychiatrists. *Journal of American College Health, 64*(7), 575–579.

Wallace, G. L., Yerys, B. E., Peng, C., Dlugi, E., Anthony, L. G., & Kenworthy, L. (2016). Assessment and treatment of executive function impairments in autism spectrum disorder: An update. *International Review of Research in Developmental Disabilities, 51*, 85–122.

Wechsler, D. (2011). *Wechsler Abbreviated Scale of Intelligence* (2nd ed., *WASI-II*). San Antonio, TX: Psychological Corporation.

Wheeler, A., Raspa, M., Bann, C., Bishop, E., Hessl, D., Sacco, P., & Bailey, D. B., Jr. (2014). Anxiety, attention problems, hyperactivity, and the Aberrant Behavior Checklist in fragile X syndrome. *American Journal of Medical Genetics, Part A, 164*(1), 141–155.

Willcutt, E. G., Doyle, A. E., Nigg, J. T., Faraone, S. V., & Pennington, B. F. (2005). Validity of the executive function theory of attention-deficit/hyperactivity disorder: A meta-analytic review. *Biological Psychiatry, 57*(11), 1336–1346.

Willcutt, E. G., Nigg, J. T., Pennington, B. F., Solanto, M. V., Rohde, L. A., Tannock, R., et al. (2012). Validity of DSM-IV attention deficit/hyperactivity disorder symptom dimensions and subtypes. *Journal of Abnormal Psychology, 121*(4), 991.

Williams, N. M., Franke, B., Mick, E., Anney, R. J. L., Freitag, C. M., Gill, M., et al. (2012). Genome-wide analysis of copy number variants in attention deficit hyperactivity disorder: The role of rare variants and duplications at 15q13.3. *American Journal of Psychiatry, 169*(2), 195–204.

Woodman, A. C., Mailick, M. R., & Greenberg, J. S. (2016). Trajectories of internalizing and externalizing symptoms among adults with autism spectrum disorders. *Development and Psychopathology, 28*(2), 565–581.

Yerys, B. E., Bertollo, J. R., Pandey, J., Guy, L., & Schultz, R. T. (2019. ADHD symptoms associates with lower adaptive behavior skills in youth with autism. *Journal of the American Academy of Child and Adolescent Psychiatry, 58*(5), 525–533.

Yerys, B. E., Kenworthy, L., Jankowski, K. F., Strang, J., & Wallace, G. L. (2013). Separate components of emotional go/no-go performance relate to autism versus attention symptoms in children with autism. *Neuropsychology, 27*(5), 537–545.

Yerys, B. E., Nissley-Tsiopinis, J., de Marchena, A., Watkins, M. W., Antezana, L., Power, T. J., & Schultz, R. T. (2017). Evaluation of the ADHD rating scale in youth with autism. *Journal of Autism and Developmental Disorders, 47*(1), 90–100.

Yerys, B. E., Wallace, G. L., Sokoloff, J. L., Shook, D. A., James, J. D., & Kenworthy, L. (2009). Attention deficit/hyperactivity disorder symptoms moderate cognition and behavior in children with autism spectrum disorders. *Autism Research, 2*(6), 322–333.

CHAPTER

10 Intellectual Disability in Autism Spectrum Disorder

Jill C. Fodstad, Rebecca Elias, *and* Shivali Sarawgi

Abstract

Intellectual disability (ID) and autism spectrum disorder (ASD) are two neurodevelopmental disorders noted to have a high degree of overlap and co-occurrence. Historically, symptoms of ID were reported to co-occur in approximately 70% or more of those with ASD; however, the rate of co-occurrence is now believed to be around 30%. As the perceptions and diagnostic conceptualization of each condition by itself have changed over time, our knowledge of the overlap and the relationship between ID and ASD has similarly changed. This chapter provides a brief overview of the relationship between ID and ASD and focuses more on the complexities and nuances pertaining to etiology, diagnosis, and assessment of symptoms that may covary or may differentially occur. Finally, the chapter provides a summary of current evidence-based interventions for use in those who have ASD and co-occurring ID, as well as a look toward future directions for investigation.

Keywords: intellectual disability, autism spectrum disorder, differential diagnosis, co-occurring, intervention

Overview

Neurodevelopmental disorders encompass a group of diagnostic conditions originating in childhood and presenting throughout the lifespan (American Psychiatric Association [APA], 2013). Significant overlap exists between conditions characterized by developmental delay, oftentimes without structured guidelines delineating appropriate diagnostic considerations or treatment recommendations. Intellectual disability (ID) and autism spectrum disorder (ASD) are two such neurodevelopmental disorders with significant overlap and co-occurrence. Both conditions are marked by deficits in social abilities, communication, and speech; poor self-referential cognition; and restricted or stereotypic behaviors (Matson & Shoemaker, 2009; Vig & Jedrysek, 1999). Although ID is characterized by core deficits in intellectual and adaptive functioning (APA, 2013), the constellation of social communication and restricted or repetitive behaviors seen in ASD can occur with or without accompanying ID. Thus, the similarities between ASD and ID are complex and make arriving at a differential diagnosis extremely difficult (Pedersen et al., 2017).

Through the years, the incidence of co-occurrence of ASD and ID has changed dramatically: from more than 70% of those with ASD noted to have co-occurring ID (Fombonne, 2009; LaMalfa, Lassi, Bertelli, Salvini, & Placidi, 2004) to more recently only approximately 30% of those with ASD also having ID (Christensen et al., 2018; Zablotsky, Black, & Blumberg, 2017). Many suggest that as diagnostic criteria for both conditions have been clarified and better early-age assessment methods have emerged, rates of diagnostic overshadowing (i.e., attributing symptoms of ASD to ID) have decreased (Matson & Shoemaker, 2009). However, concerns regarding diagnostic substitution (i.e., diagnosing ASD rather than ID) have been raised in instances where obtaining a complete medical and developmental history is unlikely (e.g., adults seeking first diagnosis, foster care; Leonard et al., 2010;

Shattuck, Wagner, Narendorf, Sterzing, & Hensley, 2011). The presence of physical conditions (e.g., limited hearing, vision impairments) or epilepsy or having minimally verbal or nonverbal status may further complicate differential diagnosis (Berg & Plioplys, 2012; Hoevenaars-van den Boom, Antonissen, Knoors, & Vervloed, 2009). Finally, neither ID nor ASD are discrete disorders – they are both heterogeneous conditions with a multitude of symptom profiles (Wing, 1979).

To assist the clinician in arriving at an accurate diagnostic picture and subsequent treatment targets, the following chapter provides an overview on ID and its relationship with ASD. The complexities and nuances pertaining to etiology, diagnosis, and assessment are discussed. Being able to identify the various symptom manifestations that arise in persons with ID, persons with ASD, and persons with both ASD and ID is no easy feat; therefore, we will attempt to provide some clarification on this diagnostic conundrum. Finally, we conclude by focusing on current evidence-based interventions for use in this population, a clinical case example, and future research directions.

Prevalence and Course

ASD is costly not only with respect to observed and perceived individual deficits but also at the financial level. Western countries have examined the economic and financial burden that ASD, with and without co-occurring ID, places on a nation's financial system. Lifetime societal costs of ASD differ with regard to intellectual capacity. A cognitively unimpaired individual with ASD necessitates an individual total support cost across the lifespan of approximately $1.4 million in the United Kingdom and United States (Buescher, Cidav, Knapp, & Mandell, 2014). An individual with ASD and accompanying ID is supported over the lifespan at a total cost of $2.2 million in the United Kingdom and $2.4 million in the United States (Buescher et al., 2014). The largest components contributing to these figures are special education services, productivity lost, and living accommodations (Buescher et al., 2014). These alarming figures suggest that the symptomatology of ASD, especially when it co-occurs with ID, yields hefty financial burdens for caregivers, families, and society as a whole that govern a nation's economy.

Although the financial costs of providing care to those with ASD, with or without ID, are substantial, research indicates that the co-occurrence of both conditions is correlated with higher levels of caregiver burden than either condition separately. Parents of individuals with ASD and co-occurring ID report a higher level of financial difficulty as well as an increased likelihood of leaving the workforce or reducing work hours to care for their child than those parents who had a child with only ASD or ID (Saunders et al., 2015). Furthermore, mothers of children with ASD and ID have also been found to be at risk for higher levels of depression, stress, and feelings of hopelessness regardless of marital status or socioeconomic status when compared to mothers who have a child with either ASD or ID (Olsson & Hwang, 2001) – which is very concerning given that ASD and ID by themselves already vastly increase risk for parental distress (Dunn, Burbine, Bowers, & Tantleff-Dunn, 2001; Hassall, Rose, & McDonald, 2005). Given the vast support costs, establishing accurate prevalence rates is paramount to understanding the impact of these disorders at the individual and societal levels.

Prevalence

Determining the prevalence ASD with co-occurring ID is complicated. Calculating estimates of those affected by these two conditions has changed as the social perception, scholarly literature base, and diagnostic definition of each condition have evolved (Harris, 2006, 2013; King, Toth, Hodapp, & Dykens, 2009). Furthermore, occurrence rates have fluctuated due to inconsistent methods used in defining core symptoms, including variations in study design, terminology definitions, sample size and characteristics, and diagnostic tools (Maulik, Mascarenhas, Mathers, Dua, & Saxena, 2011). With the publication of the fifth edition of the *Diagnostic and Statistical Manual of Mental Disorders* (DSM-5; APA, 2013), researchers and clinicians called for new inquiry into the prevalence of ASD as well as ID given changes in each condition (Lord & Bishop, 2015). That is, concerns were raised regarding continuing to refer to data and/or published articles using an IQ score as the sole criterion for ID status (McKenzie, Milton, Smith, & Ouelette-Kuntz, 2016). Furthermore, researchers also called into question ascertaining prevalence using subtypes – like pervasive developmental disorder—not otherwise specified and Asperger's syndrome – which were no longer considered as distinct and separate conditions (Lord & Bishop, 2015). To address prevalence inconsistencies and to be more in line with the current literature, researchers have begun to conduct meta-analyses or region-specific population studies to better estimate those with ASD, ID, and co-occurring ASD and ID.

For those with either ASD or ID, recent investigations have yielded data indicating that both conditions appear to have somewhat similar prevalence estimates. Internationally, the prevalence of ID across the lifespan is estimated to be 10.37 per 1,000, or 1.04% (Maulik et al., 2011; McKenzie et al., 2016). Looking at rates of ASD in the United States, recent data from the Centers for Disease Control and Prevention (CDC) indicate that in children aged 8 years old the condition occurs in 16.8 in 1,000, or 1.68% (Baio et al., 2018). Estimates from the CDC are in line with other countries that base data on clinical and educational records such as the United Kingdom (1.57% in children ages 5 to 9 years old; Baron-Cohen et al., 2009) and Sweden (1.75% in children ages 6 to 12 years old; Idring et al., 2015). Comparatively, countries that base data on insurance reimbursement records report lower estimates of ASD, such as Germany (0.38% overall prevalence; 0.60% in 6- to 11-year-olds; Bachmann, Gerste, & Hoffmann, 2018), Poland (0.35% in 0 to 16-year-olds; Skonieczna-Żydecka, Gorzkowska, Pierzak Sominka, & Adler, 2017), and France (0.37% in children 7 years-old; van Bakel et al., 2015).

Historically, co-occurrence of ASD and ID was the norm rather than the exception: 70% or more of those diagnosed with ASD were also reported to have ID (Fombonne, 2009; LaMalfa et al., 2004). The belief that autism symptoms (e.g., stereotypies, rigidity in thinking or leisure skills, theory-of-mind deficits, subsumed under the diagnosis of ID often led to diagnostic overshadowing (Harris, 2006; Hartley & Sikora, 2010) and decreased awareness of less severe impairment in those without cognitive delays (Lord & Bishop, 2015). However, as the knowledge of ASD has expanded to include a distinct symptom profile that includes those with and without cognitive impairment, and gold-standard measures (e.g., the Autism Diagnostic Observation Schedule, second edition [ADOS-2]; Lord & Jones, 2012) sensitive to individuals with average or above-average cognitive abilities have been developed, an overall increase in ASD prevalence has occurred (Lord & Bishop, 2015). The CDC's Autism and Developmental Disabilities Monitoring (ADDM) network recently noted that 31.4% of children aged 8 years with an ASD were also diagnosed with ID (Christensen et al., 2018). Their data further indicated that 24.6% of children were noted to have borderline functioning (IQ 71 to 85) and 44.1% had average or above-average intellectual ability (IQ > 85). Although ID and ASD separately are both noted to have a higher male-to-female ratio (Baio et al., 2018; Fombonne, 2009; Maulik et al., 2011), the co-occurrence of these conditions is more likely to occur in females (i.e., in 8-year-olds with ASD, 36.1% of females had co-occurring ID and 29.5% of males had co-occurring ID; Baio et al., 2018), especially at the more severe range of IQ (Maulik et al., 2011; Van Wijngaarden-Cremers et al., 2014). In a recent ADDM report (Christensen et al., 2018), the estimated prevalence of co-occurring ASD and ID was significantly lower for non-Hispanic White children (3.3 per 1,000) compared with non-Hispanic Black children (5.8 per 1,000).

Compared to research in pediatric samples, estimating the prevalence of co-occurring ASD and ID in adult cohorts has been less of a priority. Dunn, Rydzewska, MacIntyre, Rintoul, and Cooper (2018) recently noted that the population prevalence of co-occurrence in adults from Ireland was 0.74 per 1000 (or 0.074%). It is unclear of the generalizability of Dunn and colleagues findings: theirs is the first study to estimate co-occurring ASD and ID using whole country data. Rather researchers tend to look at the prevalence of co-occurrence in adults with ID living in residential or supported settings or in adults with ASD. Outcomes from this research broadly suggest that for adults with ID, a co-occurring diagnosis of ASD is provided in 8–30% of participants (Emerson & Baines, 2010: Hermans & Evenhuis, 2014; Turygin, Matson, & Adams, 2014) with the prevalence higher the more severe the symptoms of ID. Brugha and colleagues (2016) reported ASD in 1.0% of adults with mild/borderline ID and 39.3% in adults with moderate to profound ID. In adults with ASD, Croen and colleagues (2015) found that 19.2% also had a co-occurring diagnosis of ID in their medical record.

Clinical Outcomes

Data suggests that outcomes for those with ASD and/or ID can be improved with access to early and/or focused intervention to improve adaptive skills and overall functioning (Peters-Scheffer, Didden, Korzilius, & Sturmey, 2011); however, clinical outcomes for those with co-occurring ASD and ID are comparatively poor (Howlin, Goode, Hutton, & Rutter, 2004; Marriage, Wolverton, & Marriage, 2009). Although those with ID with or without ASD are more likely to be from a lower socioeconomic status and more disadvantaged background than those with only ASD (Delobel-Ayoub et al., 2015; Maulik et al., 2011), diminished access to resources and supports may not fully account for worse outcomes. It has been noted, for instance, that lower cognitive ability in childhood is generally associated with more severe symptoms of ASD and lower adaptive functioning in adulthood (Magiati, Tay, & Howlin, 2014). Furthermore, lower cognitive and adaptive functioning is correlated with less independence in adulthood (Emerson, 2012), as well as a higher likelihood of other psychopathologies/challenging behaviors, associated health conditions, shorter lifespan, polypharmacy, restrictive treatment practices, and living in residential settings (Bowring et al., 2017; Evenhuis, Henderson, Beange, Lennox, & Chicoine, 2001; Florio & Trollor, 2015; Fusar-Poli et al., 2017; Heslop et al., 2014).

Interestingly, adults with ASD and ID do not differ in their presentation of behavior problems or quality of life when compared to adults with ID only (Totsika, Felce, Kerr, & Hasings, 2010). Differences do emerge, however, in the domain of daily living skills. In adulthood, individuals with ASD and ID tend to perform lower on daily living skills relative to same-aged peers with Down syndrome and similar intellectual profiles. That is, the presence of ASD in individuals with ID appears to hinder improvement in daily living skills throughout adulthood (L. E. Smith, Maenner, & Seltzer, 2012). However, in the domain of productivity and vocational engagement, co-occurring ID in those with ASD appears to serve as a protective factor in adulthood. Young adults diagnosed with ASD and ID are more likely to engage in daytime activities and meaningful employment relative to same-aged peers with ASD who are cognitively able (Taylor & Seltzer, 2011). This outcome is likely related to increased opportunities through government-funded services to receive vocational and recreational training for adults with ID (including those with co-occurring ASD) as opposed to adults with only ASD.

Etiology, Diagnosis, and Assessment

Etiology

Both ASD and ID are believed to be largely heterogeneous conditions (Fombonne, 2009; Luckasson et al., 2002)—often arising from a combination of genetic, medical/biologic, environmental, and psychosocial causes. However, the great deal of overlap and high level of co-occurrence between the two disorders suggest possible genetic similarities. Researchers note that certain genetic syndromes (e.g., fragile X, Rett's syndrome, tuberous sclerosis, Down syndrome, phenylketonuria, CHARGE syndrome, and Angelman's syndrome) associated with more severe ID have a high incidence of ASD (Abrahams & Geschwind, 2008). Conversely, other researchers suggest that ID by itself is more associated with a high number of deletions within an individual's genetic code (Tomac et al., 2017; Veltman & Bruner, 2012), whereas ASD with co-occurring ID is more associated instead with a high number of duplications (C. Richards, Jones, Groves, Moss, & Oliver, 2015; Szatmari et al., 2007). Although research about a shared etiological pathway is still too limited to draw any firm conclusions, it is recognized that individuals with ASD or ID share common struggles, particularly with respect to social and communication skills, which can result in a complex symptom profile making the diagnostic process difficult.

Diagnosis

DIAGNOSTIC CRITERIA

Diagnoses of ASD and ID can co-exist as part of an individual's diagnostic profile. Specifically, a diagnosis of ASD encompasses social communication deficits and restricted and repetitive behaviors (APA, 2013). As part of this symptomatology, in the DSM-5, providers specify if the criteria of ASD are met with or without accompanying intellectual impairment. Specifying the dichotomous level of cognition is independent of a diagnostic co-occurrence of ID. Interestingly, young children most at risk for developing co-occurring diagnoses of ASD and ID can be reliably identified by age 2 (Anderson, Liang, & Lord, 2014), which highlights the importance of ensuring accurate diagnosis and referral to appropriate early intervention services.

Historically, a diagnosis of ID (with or without co-occurring ASD) was solely based on the IQ of the individual, such that any individual with an IQ below 70 met criteria for the disorder (APA, 2000). The DSM-5 presently defines ID as a neurodevelopmental disorder that begins in childhood, is chronic, and includes impairments in areas of cognitive/intellectual functioning and impairments in adaptive functioning (APA, 2013). The DSM-5 does not mandate that an individual receive a specific score on a standardized IQ test to receive a diagnosis of ID; however, IQ in combination with other person-specific factors can be helpful in determining intellectual functioning. In addition to intelligence testing or cognitive testing, measures of adaptive functioning are essential for an accurate diagnosis.

The DSM-5 indicates that severity of impairment is defined based on level of functioning in social, conceptual, and practical domains, not IQ, as a person's ability to function in daily life is what determines the amount of supports required. For diagnostic purposes under the DSM-5, intellectual functioning are still established by way of clinical evaluation and administration of psychometrically sound measures. In addition to scores obtained from assessment and testing, clinical observations and developmental history are necessary for diagnosis.

Assessment

A comprehensive assessment for determining ID as part of the diagnostic profile in an individual with ASD is a multistep process. To provide an accurate picture of the individual's functioning and needs, information should be gathered on his or her developmental history and cognitive ability, as well as on genetic and nongenetic etiologies; pre-, peri-, and postnatal medical history; associated medical conditions (e.g., cerebral palsy, seizure disorder, phenylketonuria); educational history; and mental, emotional, and behavioral conditions that may influence a person's functioning (Harris, 2006; King et al., 2009; S. B. Richards, Brady, & Taylor, 2014; Schalock et al., 2010). Modes of assessment and data collection include a combination of caregiver/individual interview, record review, standardized testing, and clinical observation. A physical examination, genetic evaluation, and metabolic screening or neuroimaging may be included to aid in the determining characteristics that may influence symptom course. This section will briefly touch on biomedical assessment of contributing factors but focus on cognitive and adaptive assessment, which target the main features of ID.

GENETIC

In assessing for ID, identifying possible etiologies may be beneficial but is not necessary or sufficient for the diagnosis. However, when assessing for ID within ASD, identifying etiological variants may provide clarification to factors or conditions that may impact the individual's functioning, quality of life, or increased risk for reduced lifespan, leading many to encourage such inquiry (Beversdorf & Consortium, 2016; Buxbaum et al., 2014). Genetic, metabolic, and neuroimaging assessments may demonstrate the presence of an underlying etiology, leading to further assessment and subsequent diagnosis (Flint, 2001; Szymanski & King, 1999). Genetic testing through microarray analysis is able to identify X-linked chromosomal abnormalities associated with ID and other chromosomal disorders (e.g., Down syndrome, which results from the duplication of chromosome 21). Other biochemical etiologies are detected through biomedical screening, such as the detection of phenylketonuria (PKU) at birth. Brain imaging, such as computed tomography and magnetic resonance imaging, can detect structural etiologies. Errors of metabolism, which may result in ID, may also be detected through biochemical tests. Further etiologies may be detected through electroencephalography, urinary amino acid testing, and blood organic acid and lead level testing. Biomedical assessments, physical examinations, and laboratory tests are indicated in the practice parameters for evaluation of ID by the American Academy of Child and Adolescent Psychiatry (Szymanski & King, 1999).

COGNITIVE TESTING: ASSESSMENT OF INTELLECTUAL FUNCTIONING

Although IQ is no longer the sole qualifier for ID, impairment in intellectual/conceptual functioning must occur for diagnosis. Intelligence testing, which results in an IQ score, is often a first step in assessing for ID with or without co-occurring ASD. There are many standardized intelligence tests that can be utilized to assess IQ in those with ASD such as the Stanford-Binet Intelligence Scale (SB-5; Roid, 2003); the Differential Ability Scales (DAS-II; Elliott, 2007); the Leiter (Leiter-3; Roid, Miller, Pomplun, & Koch, 2013); the Wechsler Intelligence Scale for Children, the Wechsler Adult Intelligence Scale, and the Wechsler Preschool and Primary Scale of Intelligence (WISC-V, WAIS-IV, WPPSI-IV; Wechsler, 2002, 2008, 2014); and the Bayley Scales of Infant Development (Bayley-3; Bayley, 2006); and the Mullen Scales of Early Learning (MSEL; Mullen, 1995).

When assessing for ID in the presence of ASD, there are a few points to consider. First, a long-held belief is that those with ASD have a specific profile of cognitive ability characterized by a higher nonverbal IQ than verbal IQ (Ghazziudin & Mountain-Kimichi, 2004; Ozonoff, South, & Miller, 2000). However, many cognitive profiles occur in those with ASD, especially for those with co-occurring ID (Ankenman, Elgin, Sullivan, Vincent, & Bernier, 2014; Munson et al., 2008). Individuals with severe to profound ID are more likely to have extremely low verbal abilities and low nonverbal abilities; those with mild to moderate ID are more likely to have commensurate verbal and nonverbal cognitive abilities; and others may appear to have ID due to very low verbal abilities but have nonverbal IQ scores on average over 40 points higher (Munson et al., 2008). For the latter, emphasizing adaptive functioning over cognitive abilities is more appropriate for determining support needs. Second, individuals with ASD may perform poorly on standardized tests (Koegel, Koegel, & Smith, 1997). Some may engage in interfering behaviors (e.g., inattentiveness, hyperactivity, noncompliance, echolalia, anxiety, self-injury, or aggression) that hinder testing progress and reduce their ability to respond correctly. Likewise, individuals who are nonverbal or minimally verbal may be judged "untestable" or "low functioning" via conventional IQ assessments on which they may not achieve a basal score due to an overreliance on spoken language or need to demonstrate specific abilities, like finger pointing, which they may lack (Kasari, Brady, Lord, & Tager-Flusberg, 2013).

To ensure individuals with ASD with potential co-occurring ID are able to perform at their best, it is recommended that a "flexible testing" approach be utilized when assessing cognitive abilities. Flexible testing refers to making adaptations to the testing environment or administration procedures to maximize the likelihood of capturing the true abilities of the individual, regardless of functioning level (Courchesne, Girard, Jacques, & Soulières, 2018). Examples of flexible testing procedures include using brief or short-form versions; using a nonverbal test of intelligence; administering items subscale by subscale (e.g., administer the SB-5 Nonverbal Knowledge subscale, then Nonverbal Quantitative Reasoning); taking breaks; allowing parent/caregiver to attend; switching between tests or subscales when attention wavers; counting what the child may spontaneously do for corresponding testing items (e.g., coding spontaneous block stacking for the corresponding MSEL *Fine Motor* item); using a visual countdown to completion; testing in a more comfortable location; using the individual's preferred chair/seating arrangement; allowing alternative response formats for items requiring spoken words; spacing out administration across the day or across a few consecutive days; using motivators (e.g., breaks, tangible item; preferred activity) to reinforce item/subtest completion; and utilizing function-based strategies to address problem behaviors (Courchesne et al., 2018; Minshew, Turner, & Goldstein, 2005; Paynter, 2015). Outcomes from Szarko, Brown, and Watkins (2013) further indicate that examiner familiarity may improve outcomes; therefore, pretest contact between the professional and the individual with ASD is encouraged. Utilizing a flexible testing approach could increase compliance, enhance motivation, improve focus, and reduce the occurrence of interfering behaviors. Courchesne and colleagues (Courchesne, Meilleur, Poulin-Lord, Dawson, & Soulières, 2015; Courchesne et al., 2018) suggest that incorporating or substituting strength-informed tasks, tests, or subtests (e.g., a visual search task, matrices, picture concepts) for conventional standardized intelligence tests appears to help individuals with ASD complete the assessment and provide a better estimate of the true abilities of individuals with ASD who are nonverbal or minimally verbal.

ADAPTIVE TESTING: ASSESSMENT OF ADAPTIVE FUNCTIONING

Discussion continues around the construct of adaptive functioning (Price, Morris, & Costello, 2018; Tassé et al., 2012). However, most agree that adaptive functioning generally refers to an individual's ability to engage in skills independently to meet personal needs and demands of the environment (Price et al., 2018). Schalock and colleagues (2010) specifically define adaptive behavior as conceptual, social, and practical skills used in daily living. Many models of adaptive functioning describe a three-factor structure, though the factors differ slightly based on the measures being used, and may assess communication, social, practical, and/or conceptual skills (Price et al., 2018).

Adaptive functioning assessment begins with a thorough developmental history and clinical observation. Several structured caregiver-report measures of adaptive and social functioning exist that are useful in the assessment and diagnosis of ID in people with ASD. The first standardized assessment for adaptive behavior, the Adaptive Behavior Checklist, was developed by Nihira, Foster, Shellhaas, and Leland (1968) and was revised into the Adaptive Behavior Scale (ABS; Lambert, Nihira, & Leland, 1993). The most commonly used measures of adaptive assessment in people with ASD include the Adaptive Behavior Assessment System (ABAS), which is in its third edition (ABAS-3; Harrison & Oakland, 2015); the Scales of Independent Behavior-Revised (SIB-R; Bruininks, Woodcock, Weatherman, & Hill, 1996); and the Vineland Adaptive Behavior Scales (VABS), mostly recently updated as the VABS-3 (Sparrow, Cicchetti, & Saulnier, 2016). The factors identified and measured by the ABAS-3 and the SIB-R conform to the American Association on

Intellectual and Developmental Disabilities (AAIDD) conceptualization of adaptive behavior and assess social, practical, and conceptual skills (Tassé et al., 2012). The three factors that form the construct of adaptive behavior according to the VABS-3 include communication, daily living (practical), and socialization (social).

The ABAS and VABS are the most psychometrically sound and most widely used measures of adaptive functioning (Price et al., 2018). However, problems regarding the validity of the prior versions of each measure are noted (Floyd et al., 2015). Both measures underwent significant revisions to address validity concerns prior to publishing the newest editions; therefore, it is anticipated that the VABS-3 and ABAS-3 will have improved psychometric properties. The most recent AAIDD manual (Schalock et al., 2010) suggests that impaired adaptive functioning is demonstrated by scores at least two standard deviations below the mean for at least one factor of adaptive behavior or in the overall (composite) score of a standardized adaptive behavior measure.

CO-OCCURRING AND DIFFERENTIAL DIAGNOSIS OF ASD AND ID

The symptom presentations of ASD and ID have noteworthy overlapping features. Specifically, deficits in social competence, communication/language, and stereotypy are often observed among individuals belonging to both diagnostic categories (cf. Matson & Shoemaker, 2009). Few measures exist that clearly differentiate between the two conditions. At this time, the best measures for attempting to parcel out symptoms of ASD versus symptoms of ID (as opposed to just assessing for ID symptoms more broadly) are the Autism Diagnostic Observation Schedule, second edition (ADOS-2; Lord & Jones, 2012) and the Autism Diagnostic Interview-Revised (ADI-R; Le Couteur, Lord, & Rutter, 2003). The ADOS-2 and the ADI-R are highly sensitive to presence of autism symptoms without being influenced by the individual's age, language/speech proficiency, or cognitive ability (Kanne et al., 2011; Shumway et al., 2012).

Individuals who obtain a diagnosis of ASD and/or ID exhibit early variations from the typical developmental trajectory, either via a significant delay or absence of developmentally appropriate traits (Baranek, 1999; Dawson, Meltzoff, Osterling, Rinaldi, & Brown, 1998; Osterling, Dawson, & Munson, 2002; Sigman, Mundy, Sherman, & Ungerer, 1986). Distinguishing differences among infants with ASD, ID, or typical development can be observed by 1 year of age (Bryson et al., 2018; Davidovitch, Stein, Koren, & Friedman, 2018; Wetherby et al., 2004). Infants who are later diagnosed with ASD exhibit deficits in response to name, social orienting, repetitive motor actions, and joint attention behaviors relative to typically developing peers (Dawson et al., 2004; Osterling & Dawson, 1994; Osterling et al., 2002), and also appear to exhibit more externalizing or problematic behavior (e.g., headbanging, tantrums, repetitive motor actions) when compared to other infants with non-ASD delays (Fodstad, Rojahn, & Matson, 2010, 2012). Conversely, infants who are later diagnosed with ID (without co-occurring ASD) show no statistical differences from typically developing infants in orienting to social stimuli and response to name (Osterling et al., 2002). Impairments in joint attention and gestural communication in addition to the presence of repetitive motor actions are apparent across both disorders. However, divergent sociodevelopmental profiles seen in infancy among those who later obtain a diagnosis of ASD or ID are currently insufficient as a primary distinguishing factor to aid in diagnostic clarity, as symptom expression emerges across several domains through early toddlerhood and continues to evolve as the individual ages (Rogers, 2009).

Individuals with ASD show greater quantitative social skill difficulties than individuals with a primary diagnosis of ID (Matson, Dempsey, LoVullo, & Wilkins 2008; Matson & Shoemaker, 2009; Pedersen et al., 2017; Wilkins & Matson, 2009). For those who have co-occurring ASD and ID, social deficits are perceived as more severe than individuals belonging to only one of the diagnostic categories (Matson et al., 2008). Social characteristics that best differentiate ASD from ID include deficits in using nonverbal gestures to modulate social interaction, diminished social–emotional reciprocity, and deficits in initiating and maintaining positive social skills (Hartley & Sikora, 2010; Ingram, Mayes, Troxell, & Calhoun, 2007; Pedersen et al., 2017; Van Bourgondien, Marcus, & Schopler, 1992; Wilkins & Matson, 2009). These deficits remain sensitive differentiating factors among ASD and ID across the lifespan (Wilkins & Matson, 2009).

Although social deficits are consistently reported to be distinguishing factors between ASD and ID, substantial research indicates that communication skills are poor differentiating features (Pedersen et al., 2017; Van Bourgondien et al., 1992). Restricted and repetitive behaviors remain divided in the literature as a present indicator for determining differential diagnosis between ASD and ID (Bishop, Richler, & Lord, 2006; Bodfish, Symons, Parker, & Lewis, 2000; Van Bourgondien et al., 1992; Vig & Jedrysek, 1999). Looking solely at individual DSM-IV-TR criteria, Pedersen and colleagues (2017) determined that restricted and repetitive behaviors specific to adherence to routines, and stereotyped and repetitive behaviors best differentiated those with ASD and co-occurring ID from those with only ID (Pedersen et al., 2017). However, others suggest there is no single topography or collection of repetitive behaviors that best delineates these two groups. Rather, those with ASD and co-occurring ID exhibit more frequent and more severe levels of repetitive behavior—primarily in the areas of compulsive or ritualistic behavior, rigidity, stereotypy, and self-injury—than those with only ID (Bishop et al., 2006; Bodfish et al., 2000; Matson, Dempsey, & Fodstad, 2009).

Lastly, researchers suggest that adaptive function differences exist among those with diagnoses of ASD, ID, and co-occurring presentations. Specifically, individuals with ASD and co-occurring ID demonstrate reduced adaptive skills relative to individuals with only a diagnosis of ASD or ID (Matson, Dempsey, & Fodstad, 2009; Mouga, Almeida, Café, Duque, & Oliveira, 2015). For those with co-occurring ASD, ID, and other psychopathology, adaptive skills are further diminished (Matson, Rivet, Fodstad, Dempsey, & Boisjoli, 2009). Interestingly, this pattern of reduced skills in areas of independence and self-care for those with ASD and co-occurring ID occurs despite there being no difference in motor ability and achievement of motor milestones when compared to peers with only ID of similar cognitive abilities (Bishop, Thurm, Farmer, & Lord, 2016).

Collectively, data suggest that individuals with ASD and co-occurring ID have symptom profiles that can aid in differential diagnosis from those with only ID. Both groups exhibit impairments in areas of social competence, communication, stereotypy, and adaptive skills; however, those with ASD and co-occurring ID appear to exhibit specific and significant difficulties in areas of social communication, social relatedness, and restricted and repetitive patterns of behaviors or interests (APA, 2013). Preliminary research by Pederson and colleagues (2017) indicates that instead of looking within symptom domains, the ideal method to differentiate groups is to look across symptom domains. Specifically, two social criteria (impaired non-verbal social behavior; lack of social reciprocity) and four restricted/repetitive behavior criteria (restricted interests, strict adherence to routines, repetitive/stereotyped behaviors, and preoccupation with parts of objects) best differentiated between diagnostic groups at 92.3% accuracy. Future replication of Pederson and colleagues using DSM-5 criteria will determine the utility of their findings as it relates to differential diagnosis.

Treatment

Although ASD, ID, and co-occurring ID and ASD are permanent, those affected can achieve improvements resulting in a higher quality of life. The overall goal of treatment is to reduce the effects of functional and cognitive impairments to improve the individual's overall functioning level (Harris, 2006). There are three primary categories of treatment for those with ID that would coincide with treatment targets for those with co-occurring ASD: (a) addressing or reducing underlying causes (e.g., immediately beginning a phenylalanine-free diet upon diagnosis of PKU); (b) reducing co-occurring physical, behavioral, or mental health disorders with the aim of improving functioning and life skills; and (c) improving functional impairments through environmental supports, early intervention, educational interventions, psychosocial interventions, facilitation of self-determination and independent living skills, and psychological, behavioral, and pharmacological interventions based on the individual's specific needs (S. B. Richards et al., 2014). In general, most efficacious psychological interventions for psychopathology, including cognitive behavioral therapy (CBT), can be effective for individuals with ASD and mild to moderate ID but will need to be modified (Szymanski, 1980; Willner, 2005).

Given the heterogeneity of those affected, it is critical to provide a plan of care based on the unique profile of abilities, needs, co-occurring conditions, interests, limits, and preferences of the individual. Therefore, a multimodal system where all stakeholders (i.e., the individual [if able], family, case manager, pediatrician, psychologist, behaviorist, various service providers, etc.) are included and communicate among each other is recommended (McAllister, Keehn, Rodgers, & Lock, 2018). It is noteworthy that although there are many interventions used for individuals with ID or ASD, the present chapter will only comment on those that have the most evidence of effectiveness for those with ASD and co-occurring ID.

Behavioral Interventions/Applied Behavior Analysis

Behavioral approaches are the most widely used and most studied modality of treatment for individuals with ID, ASD, and ID with co-occurring ASD. Applied behavior analysis (ABA), a specific behaviorally based technology, is recognized as the most effective treatment strategy for those with ASD (National Autism Center [NAC], 2009; National Institute of Mental Health, 2007). Although the most research to date using ABA has been with those with ASD, the strategies often used in ABA-based interventions are also highly effective for individuals with ID. Several review articles and meta-analyses have been published summarizing the body of literature looking at the effectiveness of ABA for those with ASD, ID, ASD with co-occurring ID, and other related developmental disabilities (Eldevik, Jahr, Eikeseth, Hastings, & Hughes, 2010; Kurtz, Boelter, Jarmolowicz, Chin, & Hagopian, 2011; NAC, 2009; Reichow, 2012). Across all of these studies, which collectively have reviewed thousands of published studies, the support for ABA-based procedures in the assessment and treatment of problem behaviors and in the teaching of socially significant behaviors is strong.

Broadly, ABA refers to the use of basic behavior change principles to promote behaviors that are important, adaptive, and socially acceptable (Miltenberger, 2011). Components or strategies of ABA are used in everyday life to teach, improve, or increase socially desirable behavior and to decrease undesirable behavior. The core principles of behavior analysis and ABA state that by examining and changing elements of an environment, behavior changes correspondingly. Events and variables are examined to identify what is causing a behavior (i.e., the function of the behavior) or, conversely, keeping a behavior from occurring. The behavior (B), its antecedents (A), and its consequences (C) are collectively referred to as a three-term or ABC contingency (Pence, Roscoe, Bourret, & Ahearn, 2009). With respect to intervention, ABA procedures-based strategies for replacement behavior or general behavior skill training, as well as consequence-based strategies (Boutot & Hume, 2012).

ABA-based interventions are generally provided in one of two formats: comprehensive interventions or focused interventions. The goal of comprehensive ABA interventions is to produce changes in specific skills impacting global measures of functioning such as IQ, adaptive skills, and social skills in those with ID and/or ASD (Virués-Ortega, 2010). Research suggests that gains occurring from comprehensive programs are more robust the earlier programming is initiated (Zwaigenbaum et al., 2015). Typically, treatment is provided for an extended period (e.g., 6 months to several years) and can be provided in the home, an intensive educational setting, or a center-based program. Targets for treatment often include increasing attention, language/communication, socialization, and focused academic skills (e.g., reading, math). Specific comprehensive ABA programs described in the literature include Ddiscrete trial training/Lovaas method (Lovaas, 1987), pivotal response training (Koegel, Koegel, Harrower, & Carter, 1999), and treatment and education of autistic and related communication handicapped children (TEACCH; Virués-Ortega, Arnold-Saritepe, Hird, & Phillips, 2017).

Focused ABA interventions are time-limited and focus on specific targeted behaviors that need to be decreased or increased. Behaviors often targeted in focused ABA interventions include problem behaviors (e.g., physical aggression, self-injury, disruptive behavior, pica, noncompliance), social skills, communication, anxiety, specific job skills training, and toileting/life skills. The intervention plan is individualized and specifically addresses the motivating principles of the behavior targeted to be increased or decreased. Strategies often included in individualized ABA plans are differential reinforcement, functional communication training, extinction, token economy, shaping/chaining, response interruption and redirection, and behavioral momentum (see Cooper, Howard, & Heron, 2007, for a more thorough discussion of distinct ABA strategies). Regardless of whether a comprehensive or focused intervention is applied, there are four common features noted across all ABA-approaches: objective measurement of behavior; use of procedures based on scientifically established principles of behavior; control of the environment to allow for objective measurement of outcomes; and generalization of gains across settings.

Psychotherapy

Prevalence of mental health conditions is notable in those with ID and/or ASD, with research indicating that prevalence of depression, mood lability, anxiety, and psychosis is higher than the general population (Platt, Keyes, McLaughlin, & Kaufman, 2019). A growing body of evidence suggests that psychological therapies are feasible and often effective in individuals diagnosed with ID with or without ASD (Prout &

Browning, 2011). Readers should note that there are limited well-controlled data on the use of psychotherapy in only those with ASD and co-occurring ID. Rather, researchers include those with ID and co-occurring ASD in their sample of participants with ID. Therefore, we caution when interpreting outcomes below and urge researchers to develop interventions tailored for those specifically with ASD and co-occurring ID.

Brown, Duff, Karatzias, and Horsburgh (2011) conducted a review of therapies available to people with ID and found that psychodynamic psychotherapy, CBT, counselling, and systemic family therapy can be adapted and often results in positive outcomes. Recent reviews of specific interventions for adults with ID have concluded that there is some evidence to support the use of mindfulness-based interventions (Chapman et al. 2013; Hwang & Kearney 2013), dialectical behavior therapy (J. F. Brown, Brown, & Dibiasio, 2013), and CBT (Nicoll, Beail, & Saxon, 2013; Jennings & Hewitt 2015); however, the present status of data in this area is small. A meta-analysis by Vereenooghe and Langdon (2013) concluded that CBT was an effective treatment for anger and depression in adults with ID with or without co-occurring ASD. The majority of studies looking at psychotherapy in persons with ID have been with adults.

For children with ID, the literature on the application of psychotherapy is scant, but growing research in pediatric samples is relegated to single-case studies or open-label studies of children with mild ID or those with mild ID and co-occurring ASD. The primary therapeutic modality studied in this patient population is CBT, with a recent focus on inclusion of mindfulness-based strategies. Across studies, outcomes indicate that psychotherapy can be adapted for children and adolescents with ID (including those with co-occurring ASD) with preliminary positive outcomes (Kok, Waa, Klip, & Staal, 2016). It is noteworthy that studies including pediatric populations have included parents as therapy participants as well as provided a significant amount of parent training and support (Kok et al., 2016).

Social-Communication Training and Other Supports

Being able to communicate one's needs, wants, and desires is a foundational skill that is a pathway to other complex social behaviors and learning opportunities. For those with ID in the presence of ASD (as well as ID or ASD by itself), deficits in communication can hinder the development of several adaptive behaviors, such as daily living skills and social skills (Park, Yelland, Taffe, & Gray, 2012), and prevent success in many domains, such as educational outcomes, vocational accomplishments, social network, and relationships (Walker & Snell, 2013). Fortunately, there is a wealth of information focused on increasing proficiency in speech, language, and communication ability in those affected. Although multiple communication supports are used, the ultimate goal is to engender independence, self-determination, and increased quality of life.

Functional communication training (FCT). FCT is a differential reinforcement strategy specifically developed to address challenging behaviors (e.g., physical aggression, tantrums, noncompliance, self-injury) often seen in those with ID, ASD, and ASD with co-occurring ID (Carr & Durand, 1985). FCT assumes that challenging behaviors are a means of communicating one's needs when the individual is unable to communicate in more socially acceptable ways, such as through conventional speech (Heath, Ganz, Parker, Burke, & Ninci, 2015). The goal of FCT is to teach a more appropriate alternative behavior that results in the person accessing the same preferred consequence (i.e., attention, escape/avoidance, tangible) as the targeted challenging behavior, lessening the likelihood that the individual has to resort to challenging behavior to get his or her needs met (Hanley, Iwata, & Thompson, 2001). Due to the individualized nature of FCT, the literature is composed of single-case studies. Despite this, researchers utilizing structured and meta-analytic methodologies have found the technique to be a well-established treatment for children with ASD, ID, and ASD with co-occurring ID and a probably efficacious treatment in adults with these conditions (Heath et al., 2015; Kurtz et al., 2011). FCT is effective regardless of the communication modality, which could include speech (Hagopian, Wilson, & Wilder, 2001; Kurtz et al., 2003), signs (Fisher et al., 1993; Wacker et al., 1990), picture cards (Kahng, Hendrickson, & Vu, 2000; Matson, LoVullo, Boisjoli, & Gonzalez, 2008), or a switch device (Wacker et al., 1990). FCT is embedded into treatments with other behavioral techniques including extinction, punishment, noncontingent reinforcement, differential reinforcement, or guided compliance. Kahng et al. (2000) note better outcomes when the communicative response is a specific (e.g., "I want chips") rather than a general request (e.g., "I want a snack").

Augmentative and alternative communication (AAC). AAC refers to an area of evidence-based clinical practice composed of an integrated group of techniques and tools to enhance overall communication for those with specific speech or writing deficits as well as those with limited to no functional language (Beukelman & Mirenda, 2013; Kent-Walsh & Binger, 2018; Sennott, Light, & McNaughton, 2016). AAC interventions include those that are unaided (e.g., manual signs, gestures/facial expressions, vocalizations/verbalizations, finger spelling), requiring the individual to have some degree of motor control, and those that are aided (e.g., picture exchange communication system [PECS] boards, tangible objects, speech-generating devices, voice output devices, a tablet using a specialized communication program), requiring some form of external support. Children and adults with varying levels of verbal ability and cognitive impairment can successfully use both aided and unaided forms of AAC that may be no, low, or high-tech (Sennott et al., 2016). The AAC user must receive specific training to ensure understanding of the chosen modality and be able to use the system meaningfully, flexibility, and interactively across multiple communication partners (Beukelman & Mirenda, 2013; Sennott et al., 2016). Improved outcomes and maintenance of gains occur when caregivers also receive training on the treatment approach and can support the AAC user's needs (Kent-Walsh, Murza, Malani, & Binger, 2015; Shire & Jones, 2015). Furthermore, the use of AAC has been found to improve natural speech when therapy focuses on spoken language development and use of AAC in a multimodal manner (Bird, Gaskell, Babineau, & Macdonald, 2000; Millar, Light, & Schlosser, 2006).

Visual supports and related teaching methods. Learning can be difficult when traditional methods of teaching are utilized for individuals with ID in the presence of ASD (Browder, 2011). Weakness in areas such as processing speed, receptive and expressive language, knowledge, and other cognitive processes noted to occur in this patient population vastly inhibits skill development. Individuals with cognitive impairment often have difficulties with focus, comprehension, sequencing, retention, and ability to retrieve previously mastered material, which are ability areas necessary for learning. When teaching individuals with ASD and co-occurring ID, utilizing visual-based supports, structured teaching strategies, and repetition to build fluency are approaches noted to enhance learning opportunities and skill development (T. E. Smith, Polloway, Patton, & Dowdy, 2014; Spriggs, Mims, Dijk, & Knight, 2017).

Visual supports are an evidence-based practice for teaching a variety of skills to children, adolescents, and adults with ASD and co-occurring ID (Spriggs et al., 2017). Consisting of visual representation of information, visual supports assist in compensating for verbal language and cognitive difficulties. Visual-based strategies employed to enhance independence and learning include graphic organizers, visual activity schedules, pictures/images, concrete items, social stories or scripts, video modeling/prompting, peer modeling, and computer-based supports. Visual activity schedules, one of the most used visual supports, provides the individual with a stimulus prompt to follow a series of activities or tasks independently (Koyama & Wang, 2011). The visual cues associated with the schedule can range in formats depending on the abilities of the individual (e.g., picture, photographs, written words) and can be presented in a variety of ways (e.g., single page; binder, PowerPoint, tablet). Visual activity schedules are successful at promoting success and independence in transitioning between and within activities (Koyama & Wang, 2011), as well as teaching daily living (Mechling, Gast, & Seid, 2010), leisure (Chan, Lambdin, Graham, Fragale, & Davis, 2014), vocational (Carson, Gast, & Ayres, 2008), navigation (Kelley, Test, & Cooke, 2013), and academic (Duttlinger, Ayres, Bevill-Davis, & Douglas, 2013) skills. Across all types of visual supports, the goal is to cue or prime the learner to know what to expect, be better able to understand the desired response, and have to use the least mental processes necessary to be independent and successful.

In addition to visual supports, a variety of teaching methods are recommended for use with those with ID with or without ASD. Strategies used to increase the likelihood of successful learning include errorless learning, shaping successive approximations, reinforcement, priming, prompting, behavioral momentum, environmental modifications, task analysis/chaining, repeated practice, choice/individual interest, incidental teaching, and modeling, just to name a few (NAC, 2009). It is noteworthy that the strategies found to be most effective for teaching those with ID with or without ASD are rooted in ABA, providing further support for behaviorally based principles for this population. When utilized, many of these strategies are combined in an instructional paradigm, as opposed to being used as a single instructional method. For example, Shepley, Smith, Ayres, and Alexander (2017) used peer-based video modeling, task analysis, verbal coaching, and positive feedback to teach four high school students with ASD and co-occurring ID how to film their own videos to use later for self-instruction.

Case Example

Background. Hailey is a 16-year-old female who was admitted to an intensive day hospitalization program due to an escalation in problem behaviors including self-injurious behavior (i.e., hitting head with fist, self-scratching, chin pressing, fingernail biting/pulling), physical aggression (i.e., hitting, kicking, pushing, and biting others), and perseverative comments. Self-injurious behaviors occur daily and are of such severity that she had chewed/pulled off all her fingernails, had significant calluses/scarring on her fingers/arms, and had dislocated her jaw twice in the past 6 months. Hailey has a previous diagnosis of moderate ID. She experienced a significant language delay (first words at 3 years, 10 months); however, she presently speaks in sentences of one to two clauses or phrases. Hailey's parents report that she responds poorly to change/transitions, is hypersensitive to noise, and has a low frustration tolerance; the mother and father recently separated and are living apart.

Assessment. Upon admission, various assessments were conducted to assist with treatment planning. An intake assessment was performed to gather information on medical, developmental, and behavioral history; all available medical and school records were reviewed as well. Hailey's parents rated her adaptive functioning as being in the moderate impairment range via the VABS-3 (Sparrow et al., 2016). Her overall adaptive behavior composite was a standard score of 54. She had a relative strength in the VABS-3 daily living skills (standard score = 60) subdomain compared to social and communication skills (standard scores of 46 and 52, respectively). Based on her performance on the SB-5 (Roid, 2003), Hailey's full-scale IQ was assessed as being in the moderate range of cognitive impairment (standard score = 54), with her nonverbal abilities (standard score = 60) being somewhat more advanced than her verbal abilities (standard score = 50). After a clinical interview, the medical team (i.e., psychologist, psychiatrist, pediatrician, and social worker) noted symptoms of ASD. Hailey's parents and her teacher of record completed the Social Responsiveness Scale, second edition (Constantino & Gruber, 2012), and the Social Skills Improvement Scale (Gresham & Elliot, 2008) to broadly screen for social difficulties as well as specific symptoms of ASD. These measures indicated that Hailey had significant social and communication difficulties and engaged in other restricted behaviors, placing her in the moderate autism risk range. To assess further symptoms of ASD, Module 3 of the ADOS-2 (Lord & Jones, 2012) was administered by a clinical psychologist. On the ADOS-2, Hailey's behavior exceeded the cut-off for autism spectrum (total score = 12), placing her in the moderate severity range. Given all the data collected (some of which is not presented here), Hailey was diagnosed with ASD in addition to her previous diagnosis of moderate ID.

A functional behavior assessment (FBA) was conducted to assess variables maintaining self-injury, physical aggression, and perseverative comments. Many methods were utilized including indirect measures (e.g., the Questions About Behavioral Function; Matson & Vollmer, 1995), a semistructured interview (e.g., O'Neill et al., 1997), and a trial-based functional analysis (Bloom et al., 2011). Hailey's functional analysis included embedded idiosyncratic conditions based on parent/teacher/unit staff input and observations of her behavior. Results of this assessment indicated that Hailey's behaviors were multiply maintained by access to divided attention from a caregiver (i.e., parent is attending to someone else) and escape from/avoidance of verbal arguments, work correction in classroom situations, and noisy/crowded environments.

Treatment. Based on FBA outcomes, an individualized treatment plan was developed. A licensed clinical psychologist (with advanced training in ASD and ID and behavior analysis) supervised the implementation of the intervention. The intervention evaluation occurred across the span of a 4-week partial hospitalization admission – which included all baseline, treatment, and generalization sessions. Prior to the beginning of each treatment phase, and at least once a day, Hailey read (with assistance) a social story providing an overview of the purpose and details of her treatment using language on her developmental level.

Initially treatment was implemented in the milieu under natural conditions with embedded probes of maintaining contingencies. Treatment conditions were conducted by multiple individuals (e.g., licensed psychologist, unit schoolteacher, milieu therapists, parents) to better mimic Hailey's daily life. Each session "probe" lasted 10 minutes; however, if Hailey was having problem behaviors at the end of session time, additional time was added until no target behaviors occurred. Baseline/no-treatment conditions in natural settings involved Hailey receiving attention from the caregiver (if divided) and escape from perceived aversive stimuli contingent upon target behavior (i.e., self-injury, perseverative comments, physical aggression). Treatment initially involved a differential reinforcement (DR) system embedded within a token economy (DR + token economy). Specifically, Hailey earned tokens (a Post-it with a positive statement sticker) if she was able to display behaviors consistent with those listed on her visual "behavior rules" chart. Hailey's "behavior rules" were to keep your hands to yourself, say it once; no hurting yourself or others, and follow directions. Tokens were exchanged at predetermined times for rewards (tangible items, privileges, or approved avoidance of aversive task, demand, or location) identified by a systematic paired-choice reinforcer assessment. Hailey received psychoeducation and focused training in using leisure/distraction skills to manage distress. The training involved using coping skills cards as a visual way to cue adaptive behavior when frustrated. Skills Hailey learned to use when distressed included taking a deep breath, asking for help/a break, taking a walk, reading a book, writing a letter/card, listening to music, drawing a picture, looking out the window, playing with her dog or cat, doing a dance break, and getting a hug from an adult. Each card included a picture of Hailey using the skill to serve as self-model correct use. The skills chosen were embedded into a modified social–emotional competence program (based on CBT) used to increase her emotional awareness and improve problem-solving and emotion regulation skills. During times of stress during naturalistic probes, if Hailey used a coping skill (either independently or after a prompt), she earned an additional token.

During admission, Hailey and her parents participated in family therapy to discuss stressors (parent separation, increase in arguing, different homes) and to develop specific strategies to assist with navigating household changes (e.g., a personalized social story, keeping expectations consistent, limiting arguing in front of Hailey, having a visual calendar to assist with transitions). Parents participated in focused psychoeducation aimed at increasing their understanding of behavioral principles and their application in shaping behaviors in those with neurodevelopmental disabilities. They were trained in Hailey's treatment and were instrumental in ensuring that it could be implemented in home, school, and community settings.

Modifications to Hailey's behavioral plan occurred due to persistence of target behaviors at high and variable levels (Figure 10.1). To increase her ability to understand behavioral expectations, develop self-monitoring skills, and implement problem-solving/distress tolerance strategies, a levels system was added to the intervention. Hailey's three-tiered level system consisted of different privileges/reinforcement provided contingent upon displayed behavior. Hailey began at the "green" level, where she earned/exchanged tokens by meeting behavioral expectations and, when distressed, using problem-solving/coping skills. Contingent upon the frequency or severity of problem behavior, Hailey moved to the "yellow" or "red" level. These levels coincided with altered expectations and reinforcer access—in the "yellow" level tokens were earned (for following directions and using relaxation skills) but not exchanged until promotion to the "green" level; in the "red" level Hailey could not earn or exchange tokens and had to complete a set of basic demands and use at least one relaxation tool before promotion to the "yellow" level. Hailey learned to track her progress with a visual, which also served as a reminder of the rewards/expectations associated with each level. The DR + token economy + levels system was associated with a clinically significant decrease in target behaviors. A stable trend of low rates of target behavior occurred, which persisted even after thinning the reinforcement interval, as well as across home, school, and community generalization probes.

After discharge, Hailey transitioned to an outpatient provider (a licensed clinical psychologist) for continued services. In outpatient therapy, modifications to the behavior plan occurred to assist with ensuring the intervention was able to be implemented across all settings and to maintain treatment gains. For example, the DR interval switched from a fixed time to a variable time to be more akin to natural contingencies and was progressively thinned contingent upon consistently low rates of target behavior and high rates of appropriate and adaptive behavior. Hailey continued to work on increasing her emotional competence, problem solving, social skills, and self-regulation skills, and became involved in a peer-mediated social skills program. Family therapy continued, and her parents

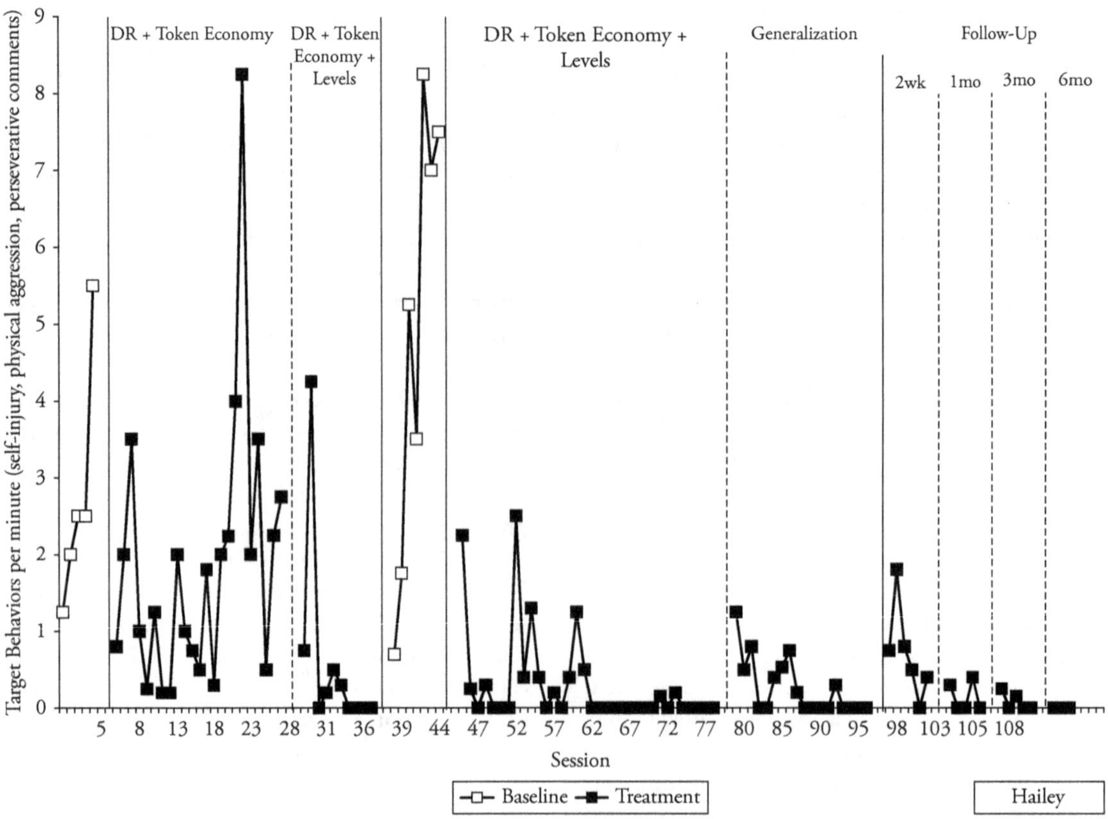

Figure 10.1. Naturalistic setting treatment assessment outcomes. DR + Token Economy = treatment consisting of differential reinforcement and a token economy; DR + Token Economy + Levels = treatment consisting of differential reinforcement, a token economy, and a levels system; wk = week(s); mo = month(s).

sought out individual/marital counseling to address their relationship and personal distress. While data collection postadmission was not consistent, parents reported continued improvement in Hailey's behavior. Her outpatient provider, in coordination with parents and school, conducted follow-up probes at 2 weeks, 1 month, 3 months, and 6 months after admission (see Figure 10.1). Although an initial increase in target behaviors occurred, rates of behaviors were lower than rates observed in baseline conditions.

Summary and Future Directions

The rate of co-occurrence between ASD and ID suggests that attention should be paid to this population in assessment, differential diagnoses, and appropriate and meaningful treatments. Individuals affected by ID, ASD, or ID in the presence of ASD are heterogeneous with varying abilities, needs, and symptom profiles. The history of known etiology and prescribed best practices has been intertwined with sociocultural, religious, and philosophical contexts of the time (Groce & Scheer, 1990; S. B. Richards et al., 2014). As terminology and perceptions of ASD and ID have evolved to be more positive and person centered, a shift toward improving quality of life and self-sufficiency has occurred.

Fortunately, treatments that incorporate behavioral strategies and modifications to suit the unique learning and adaptive profile and individual needs are successful at building skills necessary for long-term positive outcomes. As demonstrated via the case example, treatments for those with ASD and co-occurring ID can incorporate a wide variety of modalities, from purely behavior analytic aimed at skill building through the use of positive reinforcement and structured teaching, to heavily modified CBT to increase socioemotional competence and positive coping strategies, as well as to more traditional psychotherapy that includes handling life stressors (e.g., parents' separation). It is imperative for the clinician to ascertain the most appropriate treatment targets based on the needs and abilities of the patient and other stakeholders (e.g., parents, teachers, service providers) and make adaptations to ensure treatment components match the functioning level and learning style of the patient (Surley & Dagnan, 2019). For Hailey, her treatment program incorporated enhanced visuals, basic language, and hands-on activities suited to her learning style and functioning level. Visual-based strategies (e.g., social stories, coping cards with a self-model, visual rules/level system chart) were utilized to define behavioral expectations and cue appropriate behavior, and positive reinforcement-based strategies were used to increase motivation and shape socially appropriate and adaptive behaviors. Finally, a large focus on training and supporting Hailey's caregivers occurred, as well as ensuring continued outpatient therapy and generalization postdischarge.

When both ASD and ID are present, the individual's prognosis is poorer than if either condition were present on its own (Fusar-Poli et al., 2017). Being able to separate between those who have ASD, ID, or ID with co-occurring ASD can be difficult (Pedersen et al., 2017). Measures exist that can assist with differentiating ASD from ID; however, there are few if any standardized assessments that have a high degree of sensitivity or specificity in differentiating ASD with co-occurring ID from ID only across all severity levels. As described in the case example and throughout the chapter, diagnostic assessments must include many data collection methods (e.g., observation, standardized psychological tests/screeners, medical records review, caregiver report) and may include medical/genetic testing to aid in clarifying symptoms and determining areas that may need to be addressed with appropriate interventions.

More research is needed to clarify the relationship between ASD and ID. Researchers should continue to assist with further delineating and differentiating symptoms when both conditions are present. Unfortunately, attempting to navigate the multitude of etiological pathways for each condition separately may prove to be a roadblock to investigating the unique profile that occurs when both ID and ASD are present. However, research in the area of overlap and co-occurring symptoms must continue. Further research should also attempt to determine how chronological and developmental age impacts symptom expression and the etiological pathways of ID in those with and without ASD. This information could assist with developing assessment measures and tailored interventions for various cohorts. Finally, updating the current research in this area using DSM-5 diagnostic criteria for ID and ASD is imperative—most studies to date use various and outdated perspectives for both conditions.

References

Abrahams, B. S., & Geschwind, D. H. (2008). Advances in autism genetics: On the threshold of a new neurobiology. *Nature Reviews Genetics*, *9*(5), 341.

American Psychiatric Association. (2000). Diagnostic criteria from dsM-iV-tr. American Psychiatric Pub.

American Psychiatric Association. (2013). *Diagnostic and statistical manual of mental disorders* (5th ed.). Washington, DC: Author.

Anderson, D. K., Liang, J. W., & Lord, C. (2014). Predicting young adult outcome among more and less cognitively able individuals with autism spectrum disorders. *Journal of Child Psychology and Psychiatry*, *55*(5), 485–494.

Ankenman, K., Elgin, J., Sullivan, K., Vincent, L., & Bernier, R. (2014). Nonverbal and verbal cognitive discrepancy profiles in autism spectrum disorders: Influence of age and gender. *American Journal on Intellectual and Developmental Disabilities*, *119*(1), 84–99.

Bachmann, C. J., Gerste, B., & Hoffmann, F. (2018). Diagnoses of autism spectrum disorders in Germany: Time trends in administrative prevalence and diagnostic stability. *Autism*, *22*(3), 283–290.

Baio, J., Wiggins, L., Christensen, D. L., Maenner, M. J., Daniels, J., Warren, Z., . . . & Durkin, M. S. (2018). Prevalence of autism spectrum disorder among children aged 8 years—Autism and Developmental Disabilities Monitoring Network, 11 sites, United States, 2014. *Morbidity and Mortality Weekly Report Surveillance Summary*, *67*(SS-6), 1–23. http://dx.doi.org/10.15585/mmwr.ss6706a1

Baranek, G. T. (1999). Autism during infancy: A retrospective video analysis of sensory-motor and social behaviors at 9–12 months of Age. *Journal of Autism and Development Disorders*, *29*(3), 213–224. http://doi.org/0162–3257/99/0600-0213S16.00/0

Baron-Cohen, S., Scott, F. J., Allison, C., Williams, J., Bolton, P., Matthews, F. E., & Brayne, C. (2009). Prevalence of autism-spectrum conditions: UK school-based population study. *British Journal of Psychiatry*, *194*(6), 500–509.

Bayley, N. (2006). *Bayley Scales of Infant and Toddler Development* (3rd ed.). San Antonio, TX: Harcourt Assessment.

Berg, A. T., & Plioplys, S. (2012). Epilepsy and autism: Is there a special relationship? *Epilepsy & Behavior*, *23*(3), 193–198.

Beukelman, D. R., & Mirenda, P. (2013). *Augmentative and alternative communication: Supporting children and adults with complex communication needs*. Baltimore, MD: Paul H. Brookes Publishing.

Beversdorf, D. Q., & Consortium, M. A. S. (2016). Phenotyping, etiological factors, and biomarkers: Toward precision medicine in autism spectrum disorders. *Journal of Developmental and Behavioral Pediatrics*, *37*(8), 659.

Bird, E. K. R., Gaskell, A., Babineau, M. D., & Macdonald, S. (2000). Novel word acquisition in children with Down syndrome: Does modality make a difference? *Journal of Communication Disorders*, *33*(3), 241–266.

Bishop, S., Richler, J., & Lord, C. (2006). Association between restricted and repetitive behaviors and nonverbal IQ in children with autism spectrum disorders. *Child Neuropsychology*, *4*(5), 247–267. http://doi.org/10.1080/09297040600630288

Bishop, S. L., Thurm, A., Farmer, C., & Lord, C. (2016). Autism spectrum disorder, intellectual disability, and delayed walking. *Pediatrics*, *137*(3), e20152959–e20152959. http://doi.org/10.1542/peds.2015–2959

Bloom, S. E., Iwata, B. A., Fritz, J. N., Roscoe, E. M., & Carreau, A. B. (2011). Classroom application of a trial based functional analysis. *Journal of Applied Behavior Analysis, 44,* 19–31. doi:10.1901/jaba.2011.44–19

Bode, M. M., D'Eugenio, D. B., Mettelman, B. B., & Gross, S. J. (2014). Predictive validity of the Bayley, at 2 years for intelligence quotient at 4 years in preterm infants. *Journal of Developmental and Behavioral Pediatrics, 35*(9), 570–575.

Bodfish, J. W., Symons, F. J., Parker, D. E., & Lewis, M. H. (2000). Varieties of repetitive behaviour in autism: Comparison to mental retardation. *Journal of Autism and Developmental Disorders, 30*(3), 237–243. http://doi.org/10.1023/A:1005596502855

Boutot, E. A., & Hume, K. (2012). Beyond time out and table time: Today's applied behavior analysis for students with autism. *Education and Training in Autism and Developmental Disabilities, 47,* 23–38.

Bowring, D. L., Totsika, V., Hastings, R. P., Toogood, S., & McMahon, M. (2017). Prevalence of psychotropic medication use and association with challenging behaviour in adults with an intellectual disability. A total population study. *Journal of Intellectual Disability Research, 61*(6), 604–617.

Browder, D. M. (2011). *Teaching students with moderate and severe disabilities.* New York: Guilford Press.

Brown, J. F., Brown, M. Z., & Dibiasio, P. (2013). Treating individuals with intellectual disabilities and challenging behaviors with adapted dialectical behavior therapy. *Journal of Mental Health Research in Intellectual Disabilities, 6*(4), 280–303.

Brown, M., Duff, H., Karatzias, T., & Horsburgh, D. (2011). A review of the literature relating to psychological interventions and people with intellectual disabilities: Issues for research, policy, education and clinical practice. *Journal of Intellectual Disabilities, 15*(1), 31–45.

Bruininks, R. H., Woodcock, R. W., Weatherman, R. F., & Hill, B. K. (1996). *Scales of Independent Behavior—Revised comprehensive manual.* Itasca, IL: Riverside Publishing.

Brugha, T. S., Spiers, N., Bankart, J., Cooper, S. A., McManus, S., Scott, F. J., . . . & Tyrer, F. (2016). Epidemiology of autism in adults across age groups and ability levels. *The British Journal of Psychiatry, 209*(6), 498–503.

Bryson, S., Garon, N., McMullen, T., Brian, J., Zwaigenbaum, L., Armstrong, V., . . . Szatmari, P. (2018). Impaired disengagement of attention and its relationship to emotional distress in infants at high-risk for autism spectrum disorder. *Journal of Clinical and Experimental Neuropsychology, 40*(5), 487–501.

Buescher, A. V., Cidav, Z., Knapp, M., & Mandell, D. S. (2014). Costs of autism spectrum disorders in the United Kingdom and the United States. *JAMA Pediatrics, 168*(8), 721–728.

Buxbaum, J. D., Bolshakova, N., Brownfeld, J. M., Anney, R. J., Bender, P., Bernier, R., . . . Hallmayer, J. (2014). The autism simplex collection: An international, expertly phenotyped autism sample for genetic and phenotypic analyses. *Molecular Autism, 5*(1), 34.

Carr, E., & Durand, V. (1985). Reducing behavior problems through functional communication training. *Journal of Applied Behavior Analysis, 18*(2), 111–126. http://doi.org/10.1901/jaba.1985.18–111

Carson, K. D., Gast, D. L., & Ayres, K. M. (2008). Effects of a photo activity schedule book on independent task changes by students with intellectual disabilities in community and school job sites. *European Journal of Special Needs Education, 23*(3), 269–279.

Chan, J. M., Lambdin, L., Graham, K., Fragale, C., & Davis, T. (2014). A picture-based activity schedule intervention to teach adults with mild intellectual disability to use an iPad during a leisure activity. *Journal of Behavioral Education, 23*(2), 247–257.

Chapman, M. J., Hare, D. J., Caton, S., Donalds, D., McInnis, E., & Mitchell, D. (2013). The use of mindfulness with people with intellectual disabilities: A systematic review and narrative analysis. *Mindfulness, 4*(2), 179–189.

Christensen, D. L., Braun, K. V. N., Baio, J., Bilder, D., Charles, J., Constantino, J. N., . . . Lee, L. C. (2018). Prevalence and characteristics of autism spectrum disorder among children aged 8 years—Autism and developmental disabilities monitoring network, 11 sites, United States, 2012. *MMWR Surveillance Summaries, 65*(13), 1.

Constantino, J. N., & Gruber, C. P. (2012). *The Social Responsiveness Scale* (2nd ed.). Torrance, CA: Western Psychological Services.

Cooper, J. O., Heron, T. E., & Heward, W. L. (2007). *Applied behavior analysis* (2nd ed.). Upper Saddle River, NJ: Prentice Hall.

Courchesne, V., Girard, D., Jacques, C., & Soulières, I. (2018). Assessing intelligence at autism diagnosis: Mission impossible? Testability and cognitive profile of autistic preschoolers. *Journal of Autism and Developmental Disorders, 49*(3), 1–12.

Courchesne, V., Meilleur, A. A. S., Poulin-Lord, M. P., Dawson, M., & Soulières, I. (2015). Autistic children at risk of being underestimated: School-based pilot study of a strength-informed assessment. *Molecular Autism, 6*(1), 12.

Croen, L. A., Zerbo, O., Qian, Y., Massolo, M. L., Rich, S., Sidney, S., & Kripke, C. (2015). The health status of adults on the autism spectrum. *Autism, 19*(7), 814–823.

Davidovitch, M., Stein, N., Koren, G., & Friedman, B. C. (2018). Deviations from typical developmental trajectories detectable at 9 months of age in low risk children later diagnosed with autism spectrum disorder. *Journal of Autism and Developmental Disorders, 48*(8), 1–16.

Dawson, G., Meltzoff, A. N., Osterling, J., Rinaldi, J., & Brown, E. (1998). Children with autism fail to orient to naturally occurring social stimuli. *Journal of Autism and Developmental Disorders, 28*(6), 479–485. http://doi.org/10.1023/A:1026043926488

Dawson, G., Toth, K., Abbott, R., Osterling, J., Munson, J., Estes, A., & Liaw, J. (2004). Early social attention impairments in autism: Social orienting, joint attention, and attention to distress. *Developmental Psychology, 40*(2), 271–283. http://doi.org/10.1037/0012–1649.40.2.271

Delobel-Ayoub, M., Ehlinger, V., Klapouszczak, D., Maffre, T., Raynaud, J. P., Delpierre, C., & Arnaud, C. (2015). Socioeconomic disparities and prevalence of autism spectrum disorders and intellectual disability. *PloS One, 10*(11), e0141964.

Dunn, M. E., Burbine, T., Bowers, C. A., & Tantleff-Dunn, S. (2001). Moderators of stress in parents of children with autism. *Community Mental Health Journal, 37*(1), 39–52.

Duttlinger, C., Ayres, K. M., Bevill-Davis, A., & Douglas, K. H. (2013). The effects of a picture activity schedule for students with intellectual disability to complete a sequence of tasks following verbal directions. *Focus on Autism and Other Developmental Disabilities, 28*(1), 32–43.

Eldevik, S., Jahr, E., Eikeseth, S., Hastings, R. P., & Hughes, C. J. (2010). Cognitive and adaptive behavior outcomes of behavioral intervention for young children with intellectual disability: Behavior modification. *Behavior Modification, 34*(1), 16–34. http://doi.org/10.1177/0145445510367483

Elliott, C. D. (2007). *Differential Ability Scales* (2nd ed.). New York, NY: Psychological Corporation.

Emerson, E. (2012). Deprivation, ethnicity and the prevalence of intellectual and developmental disabilities. *Journal of Epidemiology and Community Health, 66*(3), 218–224.

Evenhuis, H., Henderson, C. M., Beange, H., Lennox, N., & Chicoine, B. (2001). Healthy ageing–adults with intellectual disabilities: Physical health issues. *Journal of Applied Research in Intellectual Disabilities, 14*(3), 175–194.

Fisher, W., Piazza, C., Cataldo, M., Harrell, R., Jefferson, G., & Conner, R. (1993). Functional communication training with and without extinction and punishment. *Journal of Applied Behavior Analysis, 26*(1), 23–36.

Florio, T., & Trollor, J. (2015). Mortality among a cohort of persons with an intellectual disability in New South Wales, Australia. *Journal of Applied Research in Intellectual Disabilities, 28*(5), 383–393.

Floyd, R. G., Shands, E. I., Alfonso, V. C., Phillips, J. F., Autry, B. K., Mosteller, J. A., . . . Irby, S. (2015). A systematic review and psychometric evaluation of adaptive behavior scales and recommendations for practice. *Journal of Applied School Psychology, 31*(1), 83–113.

Fodstad, J. C., Rojahn, J., & Matson, J. L. (2010). Emergent comorbidity in at risk children with and without autism spectrum disorder—A cross-sectional study. *Journal of Developmental and Physical Disabilities, 22*(4), 381–400.

Fodstad, J. C., Rojahn, J., & Matson, J. L. (2012). The emergence of challenging behaviors in at-risk toddlers with and without autism spectrum disorder: A cross-sectional study. *Journal of Developmental and Physical Disabilities, 24*(3), 217–234.

Fombonne, E. (2009). Epidemiology of pervasive developmental disorders. *Pediatric Research, 65*(6), 591.

Fusar-Poli, L., Brondino, N., Orsi, P., Provenzani, U., De Micheli, A., Ucelli di Nemi, S., . . . Politi, P. (2017). Long-term outcome of a cohort of adults with autism and intellectual disability: A pilot prospective study. *Research in Developmental Disabilities, 60*, 223–231. http://doi.org/10.1016/j.ridd.2016.10.014

Gresham, F. M., & Elliott, S. N. (2008). *Social skills improvement system: Rating scales manual.* NCS Pearson.

Groce, N. E., & Scheer, J. (1990). Introduction to special issue on anthropology and disability. *Social Science and Medicine, 30*, 5–6.

Hagopian, L. P., Wilson, D. M., & Wilder, D. A. (2001). Assessment and treatment of problem behavior maintained by escape from attention and access to tangible items. *Journal of Applied Behavior Analysis, 34*(2), 229–232.

Hanley, G. P., Iwata, B. A., & Thompson, R. H. (2001). Reinforcement schedule thinning following treatment with functional communication training. *Journal of Applied Behavior Analysis, 34*(1), 17–38.

Harris, J. C. (2006). *Intellectual disability: Understanding its development, causes, classification, evaluation, and treatment.* Oxford University Press.

Harris, J. C. (2013). New terminology for mental retardation in DSM-5 and ICD-11. *Current Opinion in Psychiatry, 26*(3), 260–262. http://doi.org/10.1097/YCO.0b013e32835fd6fb

Harrison, P., & Oakland, T. (2015). *Adaptive Behavior Assessment System* (3rd ed.). San Antonio, TX: Pearson.

Hartley, S. L., & Sikora, D. M. (2010). Detecting autism spectrum disorder in children with intellectual disability: Which DSM-IV-TR criteria are most useful? *Focus on Autism and Other Developmental Disabilities, 25*(2), 85–97. http://doi.org/10.1177/1088357609356094

Hassall, R., Rose, J., & McDonald, J. (2005). Parenting stress in mothers of children with an intellectual disability: The effects of parental cognitions in relation to child characteristics and family support. *Journal of Intellectual Disability Research, 49*(6), 405–418.

Heath, A. K., Ganz, J. B., Parker, R., Burke, M., & Ninci, J. (2015). A meta-analytic review of functional communication training across mode of communication, age, and disability. *Review Journal of Autism and Developmental Disorders, 2*(2), 155–166.

Hermans, H., & Evenhuis, H. M. (2014). Multimorbidity in older adults with intellectual disabilities. *Research in Developmental Disabilities, 35*(4), 776–783.

Heslop, P., Blair, P. S., Fleming, P., Hoghton, M., Marriott, A., & Russ, L. (2014). The confidential inquiry into premature deaths of people with intellectual disabilities in the UK: A population-based study. *The Lancet, 383*(9920), 889–895.

Hoevenaars-van den Boom, M. A. A., Antonissen, A. C. F. M., Knoors, H., & Vervloed, M. P. J. (2009). Differentiating characteristics of deafblindness and autism in people with congenital deafblindness and profound intellectual disability. *Journal of Intellectual Disability Research, 53*(6), 548–558.

Howlin, P., Goode, S., Hutton, J., & Rutter, M. (2004). Adult outcome for children with autism. *Journal of Child Psychology and Psychiatry, 45*(2), 212–229.

Hwang, Y. S., & Kearney, P. (2013). A systematic review of mindfulness intervention for individuals with developmental disabilities: Long-term practice and long lasting effects. *Research in Developmental Disabilities, 34*(1), 314–326.

Idring, S., Lundberg, M., Sturm, H., Dalman, C., Gumpert, C., Rai, D., . . . Magnusson, C. (2015). Changes in prevalence of autism spectrum disorders in 2001–2011: Findings from the Stockholm youth cohort. *Journal of Autism and Developmental Disorders, 45*(6), 1766–1773.

Ingram, D. H., Mayes, S. D., Troxell, L. B., & Calhoun, S. L. (2007). Assessing children with autism, mental retardation, and typical development using the Playground Observation Checklist. *Autism, 11*(4), 311–319. http://doi.org/10.1177/1362361307078129

Jennings, C., & Hewitt, O. (2015). The use of cognitive behaviour therapy to treat depression in people with learning disabilities: A systematic review. *Tizard Learning Disability Review, 20*(2), 54–64.

Jones, W., & Klin, A. (2013). Attention to eyes is present but in decline in 2-6-month-old infants later diagnosed with autism. *Nature, 504*(7480), 427–431. http://doi.org/10.1038/nature12715

Kahng, S., Hendrickson, D. J., & Vu, C. P. (2000). Comparison of single and multiple functional communication training responses for the treatment of problem behavior. *Journal of Applied Behavior Analysis, 33*(3), 321–324.

Kanne, S. M., Gerber, A. J., Quirmbach, L. M., Sparrow, S. S., Cicchetti, D. V., & Saulnier, C. A. (2011). The role of adaptive behavior in autism spectrum disorders: Implications for functional outcome. *Journal of Autism and Developmental Disorders, 41*(8), 1007–1018.

Kasari, C., Brady, N., Lord, C., & Tager-Flusberg, H. (2013). Assessing the minimally verbal school-aged child with autism spectrum disorder. *Autism Research, 6*(6), 479–493.

Kaufman, A., & Kaufman, N. (2004). *Kaufman Assessment Battery for Children* (2nd ed.). Circle Pines, MN: American Guidance Service.

Kelley, K. R., Test, D. W., & Cooke, N. L. (2013). Effects of picture prompts delivered by a video iPod on pedestrian navigation. *Exceptional Children, 79*(4), 459–474.

Kent-Walsh, J., & Binger, C. (2018). Methodological advances, opportunities, and challenges in AAC research. *Augmentative and Alternative Communication, 34*(2), 93–103.

Kent-Walsh, J., Murza, K. A., Malani, M. D., & Binger, C. (2015). Effects of communication partner instruction on the communication of individuals using AAC: A meta-analysis. *Augmentative and Alternative Communication, 31*(4), 271–284.

King, B., Toth, K., Hodapp, R., & Dykens, E. (2009). Intellectual disability. In B. Sadock, V. Sadock, & P. Ruiz (Eds.), *Comprehensive textbook of psychiatry* (9th ed., pp. 3444–3474). Philadelphia, PA: Lippincott Williams & Wilkins.

Koegel, L. K., Koegel, R. L., Harrower, J. K., & Carter, C. M. (1999). Pivotal response intervention I: Overview of approach. *Journal of the Association for Persons With Severe Handicaps, 24*(3), 174–185.

Koegel, L. K., Koegel, R. L., & Smith, A. (1997). Variables related to differences in standardized test outcomes for children with autism. *Journal of Autism and Developmental Disorders, 27*(3), 233–243.

Kok, L., van der Waa, A., Klip, H., & Staal, W. (2016). The effectiveness of psychosocial interventions for children with a psychiatric disorder and mild intellectual disability to borderline intellectual functioning: A systematic literature review and meta-analysis. *Clinical Child Psychology and Psychiatry, 21*(1), 156–171.

Koyama, T., & Wang, H. T. (2011). Use of activity schedule to promote independent performance of individuals with autism and other intellectual disabilities: A review. *Research in Developmental Disabilities, 32*(6), 2235–2242.

Kurtz, P. F., Boelter, E. W., Jarmolowicz, D. P., Chin, M. D., & Hagopian, L. P. (2011). An analysis of functional communication training as an empirically supported treatment for problem behavior displayed by individuals with intellectual disabilities. *Research in Developmental Disabilities, 32*(6), 2935–2942. http://doi.org/10.1016/j.ridd.2011.05.009

Kurtz, P. F., Chin, M. D., Huete, J. M., Tarbox, R. S., O'Connor, J. T., Paclawskyj, T. R., & Rush, K. S. (2003). Functional analysis and treatment of self injurious behavior in young children: A summary of 30 cases. *Journal of Applied Behavior Analysis, 36*(2), 205–219.

La Malfa, G., Lassi, S., Bertelli, M., Salvini, R., & Placidi, G. F. (2004). Autism and intellectual disability: A study of prevalence on a sample of the Italian population. *Journal of Intellectual Disability Research, 48*(3), 262–267.

Lambert, N., Nihira, K., & Leland, H. (1993). *Adaptive Behavior Scale—School* (2nd ed.). Austin, TX: PRO-ED.

Le Couteur, A., Lord, C., & Rutter, M. (2003). *The autism diagnostic interview-revised (ADI-R).* Los Angeles, CA: Western Psychological Services, 659–685.

Leonard, H., Dixon, G., Whitehouse, A. J., Bourke, J., Aiberti, K., Nassar, N.,... Glasson, E. J. (2010). Unpacking the complex nature of the autism epidemic. *Research in Autism Spectrum Disorders, 4*(4), 548–554.

Lord, C., & Bishop, S. L. (2015). Recent advances in autism research as reflected in DSM-5 criteria for autism spectrum disorder. *Annual Review of Clinical Psychology, 11,* 53–70.

Lovaas, O. I. (1987). Behavioral treatment and normal educational and intellectual functioning in young autistic children. *Journal of Consulting and Clinical Psychology, 55*(1), 3–9. http://doi.org/10.1037/0022-006X.55.1.3

Luckasson, R., Borthwick-Duffy, S., Buntinx, W. H., Coulter, D. L., Craig, E. M. P., Reeve, A.,... & Tasse, M. J. (2002). Mental retardation: Definition, classification, and systems of supports. American Association on Mental Retardation.

Magiati, I., Tay, X. W., & Howlin, P. (2014). Cognitive, language, social and behavioural outcomes in adults with autism spectrum disorders: A systematic review of longitudinal follow-up studies in adulthood. *Clinical Psychology Review, 34*(1), 73–86.

Marriage, S., Wolverton, A., & Marriage, K. (2009). Autism spectrum disorder grown up: A chart review of adult functioning. *Journal of the Canadian Academy of Child and Adolescent Psychiatry, 18*(4), 322.

Matson, J. L., Dempsey, T., & Fodstad, J. C. (2009). The effect of autism spectrum disorders on adaptive independent living skills in adults with severe intellectual disability. *Research in Developmental Disabilities, 30*(6), 1203–1211.

Matson, J. L., Dempsey, T., LoVullo, S. V., & Wilkins, J. (2008). The effects of intellectual functioning on the range of core symptoms of autism spectrum disorders. *Research in Developmental Disabilities, 29*(4), 341–350. http://doi.org/10.1016/j.ridd.2007.06.006

Matson, J. L., LoVullo, S. V., Boisjoli, J. A., & Gonzalez, M. L. (2008). The behavioral treatment of an 11-year-old girl with autism and aggressive behaviors. *Clinical Case Studies, 7*(4), 313–326.

Matson, J. L., & Rivet, T. T. (2008). Characteristics of challenging behaviours in adults with autistic disorder, PDD-NOS, and intellectual disability. *Journal of Intellectual and Developmental Disability, 33*(4), 323–329.

Matson, J. L., Rivet, T. T., Fodstad, J. C., Dempsey, T., & Boisjoli, J. A. (2009). Examination of adaptive behavior differences in adults with autism spectrum disorders and intellectual disability. *Research in Developmental Disabilities, 30*(6), 1317–1325. http://doi.org/10.1016/j.ridd.2009.05.008

Matson, J. L., & Shoemaker, M. (2009). Intellectual disability and its relationship to autism spectrum disorders. *Research in Developmental Disabilities, 30*(6), 1107–1114. http://doi.org/10.1016/j.ridd.2009.06.003

Matson, J. L., & Vollmer, T. R. (1995). *User's guide: Questions about behavioral function (QABF).* Baton Rouge, LA: Scientific Publishers.

Maulik, P. K., Mascarenhas, M. N., Mathers, C. D., Dua, T., & Saxena, S. (2011). Prevalence of intellectual disability: A meta-analysis of population-based studies. *Research in Developmental Disabilities, 32*(2), 419–436. http://doi.org/10.1016/j.ridd.2010.12.018

McAllister, J. W., Keehn, R. M., Rodgers, R., & Lock, T. M. (2018). Implementation of a shared plan of care: A pilot approach to care coordination with children with neurodevelopmental disabilities. *Journal of Nursing Research and Practice, 2*(2), 1–5.

McKenzie, K., Milton, M., Smith, G., & Ouellette-Kuntz, H. (2016). Systematic review of the prevalence and incidence of intellectual disabilities: Current trends and issues. *Current Developmental Disorders Reports, 3*(2), 104–115. http://doi.org/10.1007/s40474-016-0085-7

Mechling, L. C., Gast, D. L., & Seid, N. H. (2010). Evaluation of a personal digital assistant as a self-prompting device for increasing multi-step task completion by students with moderate intellectual disabilities. *Education and Training in Autism and Developmental Disabilities, 45*(3), 422–439.

Millar, D. C., Light, J. C., & Schlosser, R. W. (2006). The impact of augmentative and alternative communication intervention on the speech production of individuals with developmental disabilities: A research review. *Journal of Speech, Language, and Hearing Research, 49*(2), 248–264.

Miltenberger, R. G. (2011). *Behavior modification: Principles and procedures.* Belmont, CA: Cengage Learning.

Minshew, N. J., Turner, C. A., & Goldstein, G. (2005). The application of short forms of the Wechsler Intelligence scales in adults and children with high functioning autism. *Journal of Autism and Developmental Disorders, 35*(1), 45–52.

Mouga, S., Almeida, J., Café, C., Duque, F., & Oliveira, G. (2015). Adaptive profiles in autism and other neurodevelopmental disorders. *Journal of Autism and Developmental Disorders, 45*(4), 1001–1012.

Mullen, E. M. (1995). *Mullen Scales of Early Learning.* Circle Pines, MN: American Guidance Service.

Munson, J., Dawson, G., Sterling, L., Beauchaine, T., Zhou, A., Koehler, E., . . . Abbott, R. (2008). Evidence for latent classes of IQ in young children with autism spectrum disorder. *American Journal on Mental Retardation, 113*(6), 439–452.

National Autism Center (NAC). (2009). *Findings and conclusions of the National Standards Project: Addressing the need for evidence-based practice guidelines for autism spectrum disorders.* Retrieved from https://www.umass.edu/doegrants/wp-content/uploads/2014/04/NAC-Standards-Report_2009_2011.pdf.

National Institute of Mental Health. (2007). *Autism spectrum disorders.* Bethesda, MD: NIMH.

Nicoll, M., Beail, N., & Saxon, D. (2013). Cognitive behavioural treatment for anger in adults with intellectual disabilities: A systematic review and meta analysis. *Journal of Applied Research in Intellectual Disabilities, 26*(1), 47–62.

Nihira, K., Foster, R., Shellhaas, M., & Leland, H. (1968). *Adaptive Behavior Checklist.* Washington, DC: American Association on Mental Deficiency.

Olsson, M. B., & Hwang, C. P. (2001). Depression in mothers and fathers of children with intellectual disability. *Journal of Intellectual Disability Research, 45*(6), 535–543.

O'Neill, R. E., Horner, R. H., Albin., R. W., Sprague, J. R., Storey, K., & Newton, J. S. (1997). *Functional assessment and program development for problem behavior.* Pacific Grove, CA: Brooks/Cole Publishing.

Osterling, J., & Dawson, G. (1994). Early recognition of children with autism: A study of first birthday home videotapes. *Journal of Autism and Developmental Disorders, 24*, 247–257. http://doi.org/10.1007/BF02172225

Osterling, J., Dawson, G., & Munson, J. (2002). Early recognition of 1-year-old infants with autism spectrum disorder versus mental retardation. *Development and Psychopathology, 14*(2), 239–251. http://doi.org/10.1017/S0954579402002031

Ozonoff, S., South, M., & Miller, J. N. (2000). DSM-IV-defined Asperger syndrome: Cognitive, behavioral and early history differentiation from high-functioning autism. *Autism, 4*(1), 29–46.

Park, C. J., Yelland, G. W., Taffe, J. R., & Gray, K. M. (2012). Brief report: The relationship between language skills, adaptive behavior, and emotional and behavior problems in preschoolers with autism. *Journal of Autism and Developmental Disorders, 42*(12), 2761–2766.

Paynter, J. M. (2015). Assessment of school-aged children with autism spectrum disorder. *Journal of Psychologists and Counsellors in Schools, 25*(1), 104–115.

Pedersen, A. L., Pettygrove, S., Lu, Z., Andrews, J., Meaney, F. J., Kurzius-Spencer, M., . . . Cunniff, C. (2017). DSM criteria that best differentiate intellectual disability from autism spectrum disorder. *Child Psychiatry and Human Development, 48*(4), 537–545. http://doi.org/10.1007/s10578-016-0681-0

Pence, S. T., Roscoe, E. M., Bourret, J. C., & Ahearn, W. H. (2009). Relative contributions of three descriptive methods: Implications for behavioral assessment. *Journal of Applied Behavior Analysis, 42*(2), 425–446.

Peters-Scheffer, N., Didden, R., Korzilius, H., & Sturmey, P. (2011). A meta-analytic study on the effectiveness of comprehensive ABA-based early intervention programs for children with autism spectrum disorders. *Research in Autism Spectrum Disorders, 5*(1), 60–69.

Platt, J. M., Keyes, K. M., McLaughlin, K. A., & Kaufman, A. S. (2019). Intellectual disability and mental disorders in a US population representative sample of adolescents. *Psychological Medicine, 49*(6), 952–961.

Price, J., Morris, Z., & Costello, S. (2018). The application of adaptive behaviour models: A systematic review. *Behavioral Sciences, 8*(1), 11. http://doi.org/10.3390/bs8010011

Prout, H. T., & Browning, B. K. (2011). The effectiveness of psychotherapy with persons with intellectual disabilities. In R. J. Fletcher (Ed.), *Psychotherapy for Individuals with Intellectual Disability* (pp. 265–287). Kingston, NY: NADD Press.

Reichow, B. (2012). Overview of meta-analyses on early intensive behavioral intervention for young children with autism spectrum disorders. *Journal of Autism and Developmental Disorders, 42*(4), 512–520.

Richards, C., Jones, C., Groves, L., Moss, J., & Oliver, C. (2015). Prevalence of autism spectrum disorder phenomenology in genetic disorders: A systematic review and meta-analysis. *Lancet Psychiatry, 2*(10), 909–916.

Richards, S. B., Brady, M. P., & Taylor, R. L. (2014). *Cognitive and intellectual disabilities: Historical perspectives, current practices, and future directions.* New York, NY: Routledge.

Rogers, S. J. (2009). What are infant siblings teaching us about autism in infancy? *Autism Research, 2*(3), 125–137. http://doi.org/10.1002/aur.81

Roid, G. H. (2003). *Stanford Binet Intelligence Scale, Fifth edition. Stanford Binet Intelligence Scale, Fifth edition.* Itasca, IL: Riverside publishing.

Roid, G. H., Miller, L. J., Pomplun, M., & Koch, C. (2013). Leiter international performance scale,(Leiter-3). *Los Angeles: Western Psychological Services.*

Saunders, B. S., Tilford, J. M., Fussell, J. J., Schulz, E. G., Casey, P. H., & Kuo, D. Z. (2015). Financial and employment impact of intellectual disability on families of children with autism. *Families, Systems, & Health, 33*(1), 36.

Schalock, R. L., Borthwick-Duffy, S. A., Bradley, V. J., Buntinx, W. H. E., Coulter, D. L., Craig, E. M.,... Yeager, M. H. (2010). *Intellectual disability: Definition, classification, and systems of supports* (11th ed.). Washington, DC: American Association on Intellectual and Developmental Disabilities.

Sennott, S. C., Light, J. C., & McNaughton, D. (2016). AAC modeling intervention research review. *Research and Practice for Persons with Severe Disabilities, 41*(2), 101–115.

Shattuck, P. T., Wagner, M., Narendorf, S., Sterzing, P., & Hensley, M. (2011). Post–high school service use among young adults with an autism spectrum disorder. *Archives of Pediatrics & Adolescent Medicine, 165*(2), 141–146.

Shepley, S. B., Smith, K. A., Ayres, K. M., & Alexander, J. L. (2017). Use of video modeling to teach adolescents with an intellectual disability to film their own video prompts. *Education and Training in Autism and Developmental Disabilities, 52*(2), 158.

Shire, S. Y., & Jones, N. (2015). Communication partners supporting children with complex communication needs who use AAC: A systematic review. *Communication Disorders Quarterly, 37*(1), 3–15.

Shumway, S., Farmer, C., Thurm, A., Joseph, L., Black, D., & Golden, C. (2012). The ADOS calibrated severity score: Relationship to phenotypic variables and stability over time. *Autism Research, 5*(4), 267–276.

Sigman, M., Mundy, P., Sherman, T., & Ungerer, J. (1986). Social interactions of autistic, mentally retarded and normal children and their caregivers. *Journal of Child Psychology and Psychiatry, and Allied Disciplines, 27*(5), 647–655. http://doi.org/10.1111/j.1469–7610.1986.tb00189.x

Skonieczna Żydecka, K., Gorzkowska, I., Pierzak Sominka, J., & Adler, G. (2017). The prevalence of autism spectrum disorders in West Pomeranian and Pomeranian regions of Poland. *Journal of Applied Research in Intellectual Disabilities, 30*(2), 283–289.

Smith, L. E., Maenner, M. J., & Seltzer, M. M. (2012). Developmental trajectories in adolescents and adults with autism: The case of daily living skills. *Journal of the American Academy of Child & Adolescent Psychiatry, 51*(6), 622–631.

Smith, T. E., Polloway, E. A., Patton, J. R., & Dowdy, C. A. (2014). *Teaching students with special needs in inclusive settings* (Vol. 6). Upper Saddle River, NJ: Pearson.

Sparrow, S., Cicchetti, D., & Saulnier, C. A. (2016). *The Vineland Adaptive Behavior Scales* (3rd ed.). San Antonio, TX: Pearson.

Spriggs, A. D., Mims, P. J., van Dijk, W., & Knight, V. F. (2017). Examination of the evidence base for using visual activity schedules with students with intellectual disability. *Journal of Special Education, 51*(1), 14–26.

Surley, L., & Dagnan, D. (2019). A review of the frequency and nature of adaptations to cognitive behavioural therapy for adults with Intellectual Disabilities. *Journal of Applied Research in Intellectual Disabilities, 32*(2), 219–237.

Szymanski, L. S. (1980). *Emotional disorders of mentally retarded persons: Assessment, treatment, and consultation.* University Park Press.

Szarko, J. E., Brown, A. J., & Watkins, M. W. (2013). Examiner familiarity effects for children with autism spectrum disorders. *Journal of Applied School Psychology, 29*(1), 37–51.

Szatmari, P., Paterson, A. D., Zwaigenbaum, L., Roberts, W., Brian, J., Liu, X. Q.,... Feuk, L. (2007). Mapping autism risk loci using genetic linkage and chromosomal rearrangements. *Nature Genetics, 39*(3), 319.

Szymanski, L., & King, B. H. (1999). Practice parameters for the assessment and treatment of children, adolescents, and adults with mental retardation and comorbid mental disorders. *Journal of the American Academy of Child and Adolescent Psychiatry, 38*(12), 5S–31S. http://doi.org/10.1016/S0890-8567(99)80002–1

Tassé, M. J., Schalock, R. L., Balboni, G., Bersani, H., Borthwick-Duffy, S. A., Spreat, S.,... Zhang, D. (2012). The construct of adaptive behavior: Its conceptualization, measurement, and use in the field of intellectual disability. *American Journal on Intellectual and Developmental Disabilities, 117*(4), 291–303. http://doi.org/10.1352/1944-7558-117.4.291

Taylor, J. L., & Seltzer, M. M. (2011). Employment and post-secondary educational activities for young adults with autism spectrum disorders during the transition to adulthood. *Journal of Autism and Developmental Disorders, 41*(5), 566–574.

Tomac, V., Pušeljić, S., Škrlec, I., Anđelić, M., Kos, M., & Wagner, J. (2017). Etiology and the genetic basis of intellectual disability in the pediatric population. *Southeastern European Medical Journal, 1*(1), 144–153.

Totsika, V., Felce, D., Kerr, M., & Hastings, R. P. (2010). Behavior problems, psychiatric symptoms, and quality of life for older adults with intellectual disability with and without autism. *Journal of Autism and Developmental Disorders, 40*(10), 1171–1180. http://doi.org/10.1007/s10803-010-0975-1

Turygin, N., Matson, J. L., & Adams, H. (2014). Prevalence of co-occurring disorders in a sample of adults with mild and moderate intellectual disabilities who reside in a residential treatment setting. *Research in Developmental Disabilities, 35*(7), 1802–1808.

van Bakel, M. M. E., Delobel-Ayoub, M., Cans, C., Assouline, B., Jouk, P. S., Raynaud, J. P., & Arnaud, C. (2015). Low but increasing prevalence of autism spectrum disorders in a French area from register-based data. *Journal of Autism and Developmental Disorders, 45*(10), 3255–3261.

Van Bourgondien, M. E., Marcus, L. M., & Schopler, E. (1992). Comparison of DSM-III-R and childhood autism rating scale diagnoses of autism. *Journal of Autism and Developmental Disorders, 22*(4), 493–506. http://doi.org/10.1007/BF01046324

Van Wijngaarden-Cremers, P. J., van Eeten, E., Groen, W. B., Van Deurzen, P. A., Oosterling, I. J., & Van der Gaag, R. J. (2014). Gender and age differences in the core triad of impairments in autism spectrum disorders: A systematic review and meta-analysis. *Journal of Autism and Developmental Disorders, 44*(3), 627–635.

Veltman, J. A., & Brunner, H. G. (2012). De novo mutations in human genetic disease. *Nature Reviews Genetics, 13*(8), 565.

Vereenooghe, L., & Langdon, P. E. (2013). Psychological therapies for people with intellectual disabilities: A systematic review and meta-analysis. *Research in Developmental Disabilities, 34*(11), 4085–4102.

Vig, S., & Jedrysek, E. (1999). Autistic features in young children with significant cognitive impairment: Autism or mental retardation? *Journal of Autism and Developmental Disorders, 29*(3), 235–248.

Virués-Ortega, J. (2010). Applied behavior analytic intervention for autism in early childhood: Meta-analysis, meta-regression and dose–response meta-analysis of multiple outcomes. *Clinical Psychology Review, 30*(4), 387–399.

Virués-Ortega, J., Arnold-Saritepe, A., Hird, C., & Phillips, K. (2017). The TEACCH program for people with autism: Elements, outcomes, and comparison with competing models. In J. L. Matson (ED.), *Handbook of treatments for autism spectrum disorder* (pp. 427–436). Cham: Springer.

Vogan, V., Lake, J. K., Weiss, J. A., Robinson, S., Tint, A., & Lunsky, Y. (2014). Factors associated with caregiver burden among parents of individuals with ASD: Differences across intellectual functioning. *Family Relations, 63*(4), 554–567. http://doi.org/10.1111/fare.12081

Wacker, D. P., Steege, M. W., Northup, J., Sasso, G., Berg, W., Reimers, T., . . . Donnlis, A. (1990). A component analysis of functional communication training across three topographies of severe behavior problems. *Journal of Applied Behavior Analysis, 23*(4), 417–429.

Walker, V. L., & Snell, M. E. (2013). Effects of augmentative and alternative communication on challenging behavior: A meta-analysis. *Augmentative and Alternative Communication, 29*(2), 117–131.

Wechsler, D. (2002). *Wechsler Preschool and Primary Scale of Intelligence*. San Antonio, TX: Pearson.

Wechsler, D. (2008). *Wechsler Adult Intelligence Scale* (4th ed., *WAIS–IV*). San Antonio, TX: Pearson.

Wechsler, D. (2014). *The Wechsler Intelligence Scale for Children* (5th ed.). San Antonio, TX: Pearson.

Wetherby, A. M., Woods, J., Allen, L., Cleary, J., Dickinson, H., & Lord, C. (2004). Early indicators of autism spectrum disorders in the second year of life. *Journal of Autism and Developmental Disorders, 34(5)*, 473–493.

Wilkins, J., & Matson, J. L. (2009). A comparison of social skills profiles in intellectually without ASD. *Behavior Modification, 33,* 143–155. http://doi.org/10.1177/0145445508321880

Willner, P. (2005). The effectiveness of psychotherapeutic interventions for people with learning disabilities: A critical overview. *Journal of Intellectual Disability Research, 49*(1), 73–85.

Wing, L., & Gould, J. (1979). Severe impairments of social interaction and associated abnormalities in children: Epidemiology and classification. *Journal of Autism and Developmental Disorders, 9*(1), 11–29. http://doi.org/10.1007/BF01531288

Yu, H., McCoach, D. B., Gottfried, A. W., & Gottfried, A. E. (2018). Stability of intelligence from infancy through adolescence: An autoregressive latent variable model. *Intelligence, 69*, 8–15.

Zablotsky, B., Black, L. I., & Blumberg, S. J. (2017). Estimated prevalence of children with diagnosed developmental disabilities in the United States, 2014–2016. *NCHS Data Brief*, (291), 1–8.

Zahorodny, W., Shenouda, J., Howell, S., Rosato, N. S., Peng, B., & Mehta, U. (2014). Increasing autism prevalence in metropolitan New Jersey. *Autism, 18*(2), 117–126.

Zwaigenbaum, L., Bauman, M. L., Choueiri, R., Kasari, C., Carter, A., Granpeesheh, D., . . . Pierce, K. (2015). Early intervention for children with autism spectrum disorder under 3 years of age: Recommendations for practice and research. *Pediatrics, 136*(Suppl 1), S60–S81.

CHAPTER

11 The Co-Occurrence of Autism and Gender Diversity

John F. Strang, Dana L. Rofey, *and* Eleonora Sadikova

Abstract

Gender diversity refers to gender expressions and/or gender identity experiences that vary from the common experiences of gender. Gender-diverse people may be gender nonconforming, gender nonbinary, gender fluid, gender exploring, transgender, and so forth. Some gender-diverse individuals experience gender dysphoria and/or gender incongruence and may require gender-affirming supports, including gender-affirming medical interventions. The co-occurrence of autism and gender diversity has been highlighted in a series of studies internationally as well as through rich community expressions. Studies in gender-referred individuals reveal high rates of autism traits as well as high rates of existing autism diagnoses. Studies in autistic populations reveal greater gender diversity characteristics. The long-term course of gender diversity in autistic individuals is poorly understood. Clinical guidelines have been developed for adolescents with the co-occurrence, but much work remains: No gender-related measures have been developed and tested for use in neurodiverse populations, no programs exist to support gender-diverse neurodiverse adults, and little is known about co-occurring mental health profiles, risks, or protective factors for people with the co-occurrence. The inclusion of this chapter on co-occurring autism and gender diversity within a book on "co-occurring psychiatric conditions" is problematic, because gender diversity is not a "psychiatric condition," but instead a form of human diversity. The diagnosis of Gender Dysphoria is useful only insomuch as it allows individuals to obtain necessary gender-related supports. The authors' choice to include this chapter in this book reflects a compromise, motivated by the need for educating both autism and gender specialists in this common co-occurrence.

Keywords: autism, gender diversity, gender dysphoria, gender incongruence, transgender

Overview

Gender diversity refers to gender expression or gender identity experiences that vary from common gender experiences. A series of recent studies have reported an overoccurrence of autism spectrum disorder (ASD) and autism spectrum characteristics among gender-diverse individuals. There is also emerging evidence of increased gender diversity characteristics as assessed in autistic individuals. Research evidence for a link between autism and gender diversity is paralleled by diverse community and media references to the co-occurrence (e.g., Autistic Self Advocacy Network, National Center for Transgender Equality, & LGBTQ Task Force, 2016; Kol, 2016).[1]

[1] As noted in the abstract, the authors of this chapter acknowledge that the inclusion of this chapter on co-occurring autism and gender diversity within a book dedicated to autism and "co-occurring psychiatric conditions" is problematic. The authors of this chapter do not consider gender diversity or gender dysphoria a "psychiatric condition," but instead a co-occurring *experience*. Gender Dysphoria is a diagnosis, but we assert that its label as a diagnosis should only exist insomuch as it facilitates medical coverage of supports and treatments necessary for gender affirmation. The decision to include this chapter within a text on co-occurring conditions is a planned compromise driven by the importance of educating both autism and gender diversity

Understanding and interpreting the autism and gender diversity co-occurrence research literature is challenging given the varied methodologies employed across studies, as well as the range of gender diversity–related experiences measured (Van Schalkwyk, Klingensmith, & Volkmar, 2015). One of the primary challenges for both research and clinical endeavors in this field is that most specialists and clinics focus on *either* gender *or* autism (i.e., "silo" expertise). In fact, there are currently relatively few specialists expert in the field of gender care, and even fewer experienced in both areas. This has led to a stratification of both research and clinical supports in this field with many developing out of gender protocols/clinics and some out of autism protocols/clinics. Adding further complexity, gender-related terminology used across studies is inconsistent. Therefore, to appropriately understand and interpret existing research on the co-occurrence, it is necessary to first review the various gender diversity experiences and related gender terminology. The gender-related terminology selected for this chapter reflects the authors' attempts to employ the most current terms used in the research literature while also maintaining a focus on language that is acceptable among gender-diverse communities themselves.

It is important to note that the language used to describe gender diversity–related experiences continues to develop and change rapidly, and some of the terminology used in this chapter may be obsolete in the future as new terms and descriptions are agreed upon. This is also true for language used to describe autistic people and autistic identities; autism-related language continues to be in flux as researchers, diagnosticians, autism advocacy groups, and autistic individuals employ different vocabularies and language constructions to describe the experience of autism (e.g., Autistic Self Advocacy Network, 2011). It is the first author's (J.F.S) personal publishing experience that some of the language used in his publications on the co-occurrence of autism and gender diversity, such as the Initial Clinical Guidelines for adolescents with this co-occurrence (Strang et al., 2016), is already outdated and lacks a sensitivity for both autism neurodiversity and gender diversity elements. In light of the likelihood that language and descriptions of this double-minority group (i.e., autistic gender minority individuals) will develop and become more culturally sensitive over time, the authors of this chapter proactively express regret for any language or descriptions employed that may be experienced as lacking sensitivity to the experiences of autistic, gender-diverse, and autistic gender-diverse individuals.

Gender-Related Concepts and Terminology

"Gender expression" refers to the ways a person expresses gender through behaviors and appearance, whereas "gender identity" describes the gender that a person feels they are (The Gender Unicorn – Trans Student Educational Resources, n.d.). "Gender-diverse" individuals (also referred to as "gender minority" individuals) have gender expressions and/or identities that differ from, or that are outside of the norms for, the gender they were *assumed* at birth. There is some variation in gender expression within the majority binary gender groups; that is, gender-normative males and gender-normative females show a range of behaviors and interests. Gender diversity in this chapter is used to refer to gender identities and gender expressions that vary in *significant* ways from the binary gender majority groups. Gender-diverse individuals represent a heterogeneous group and include people who are transgender, gender nonbinary, gender expansive (e.g., gender nonconforming), agender, gender fluid, and so forth. Gender identity diversity, gender dysphoria, and gender incongruence are gender-related phenomena experienced by *some* gender-diverse individuals, as described next.

Gender Identities

Gender identity diversity is experienced by those whose gender identity differs from their gender assumed at birth. For example, a person who was assumed female at birth and who ultimately knows himself to be male could be described as gender identity diverse. Transgender, gender nonbinary, and agender experiences are examples of gender identity diversity. The term "transgender" often denotes the experience of gender identity diversity in which a person knows him- or herself to be the *other* binary gender than the gender he or she was assumed at birth (i.e., transgender males were assumed female at birth and ultimately know themselves to be male and transgender females were assumed male at birth and ultimately know themselves to be female). Some use the term "transgender"

specialists about this common co-occurrence. Several of the pro forma subheadings employed in this chapter (i.e., "Prevalence and Course," "Etiology, Diagnosis, and Assessment," and "Treatment") were required for the sake of consistency with the other handbook chapters; the authors regret their pathologizing tone.

as an umbrella term to refer to people who know themselves to be any gender different from their gender assumed at birth (including gender nonbinary, agender, etc.). Gender nonbinary individuals know themselves to be a gender other than male or female, and agender individuals experience themselves as having no gender. People who experience their gender as consistent with their gender assumed at birth (i.e., a person who was assumed female at birth experiences herself as female) are referred to as cisgender.

Gender-Related Experiences: Dysphoria, Affirmation, and Incongruence

Gender dysphoria is the distress that a person may experience due to gender-related characteristics, expectations, or indicators, which may be physical or social/interpersonal. There is also a diagnosis known as "Gender Dysphoria,"[2] which consists of some specific experiences of gender-related distress as codified in the *Diagnostic and Statistical Manual of Mental Disorders*, fifth edition (DSM-5; American Psychiatric Association, 2013); the diagnosis of Gender Dysphoria is described in the next paragraph. There is a broad range of possible gender dysphoria experiences, such as the experience of intense discomfort and/or unhappiness related to having male (or female) genitalia, a masculinized (or feminine) voice, a feminine (or masculine) figure, a female (or male) social gender role, and so forth. Gender dysphoria can occur in people regardless of whether they are gender diverse or not. For example, it is not uncommon for prepubertal youth to experience some level of dysphoria regarding gender and aspects of their body and ultimately identify as cisgender (Ristori & Steensma, 2016). On the other hand, not all gender identity–diverse individuals experience gender dysphoria, and gender identity–diverse people who experience gender dysphoria often experience reductions in gender dysphoria after "affirming" gender (also known as "gender transition"). Gender affirmation can include many different actions and experiences such as being referred to by pronouns that match one's gender identity, wearing clothes and styling that is concordant with one's gender identity, and receiving gender-related medical supports such as gender-affirming hormones (previously referred to as "cross-sex" hormones) and gender-affirming surgical procedures (previously referred to as "sex reassignment surgery"). Somewhat similar to the experience of gender dysphoria is the experience of gender incongruence; gender incongruence is the experience of mismatch between gender-related characteristics and one's gender identity. This mismatch can be experienced without distress, and therefore gender incongruence does not always involve dysphoria.

Gender-Related "Diagnoses"

The DSM-5 defines a diagnosis of "Gender Dysphoria." In this chapter the DSM-5 Gender Dysphoria diagnosis will be referred to with the abbreviation "GD," whereas the experience of gender dysphoria will be spelled out in words. The International Classification of Diseases, 11th edition (ICD-11; World Health Organization, 2018) defines a diagnosis of Gender Incongruence and locates this diagnosis in the sexual health section of the ICD (moved from the mental health section in the International Classification of Diseases, 10th edition; World Health Organization, 1993). The diagnosis of "Gender Identity Disorder" (GID) appears in studies published prior to the release of the DSM-5. Critics of the former GID diagnosis, in addition to noting that the name itself is pathologizing, have emphasized its overly inclusive diagnostic criteria for children: Children could meet criteria for GID with just two "symptoms" of gender variance. This overly inclusive diagnosis led to many prepubertal children being diagnosed with GID who ultimately were understood as "gender nonconforming" (e.g., being diverse in terms of their "gender expression" but not gender identity; Newhook et al., 2018; Winters et al., 2018). Critics of both GID and GD diagnoses note that some gender-diverse individuals require gender-related medical supports and experience gender identity diversity but do not experience gender dysphoria and do not meet criteria for DSM gender-related diagnoses. The newer ICD-11 Gender Incongruence diagnosis may solve this problem.

Autism-Related Terminology

In accordance with calls from the autistic self-advocate community, identity-first language rather than person-first language is used frequently in this manuscript. Therefore, the expression "autistic people" is favored over "people with autism spectrum disorder" (Autistic Self Advocacy Network, 2011). However, the latter is also employed in the text at times, particularly to reflect the samples in studies

[2] Gender dysphoria (lowercase) is used to describe the set of experiences of gender dysphoria, whereas Gender Dysphoria (GD; capitalized) refers to a specific diagnostic classification within the DSM-5.

that were identified by meeting criteria for ASD. The term "allistic" is used to refer to people who are not autistic (Hughes, 2015). Allistic people may have other developmental or mental health diversity (e.g., attention deficit hyperactivity disorder, obsessive-compulsive disorder) or not, but the term specifically denotes that a person is not autistic. The term "neurodiversity" is also used from time to time to reflect the increasing understanding of autism as not only a disability but also a source of strength, skills, and identity for many (Baron-Cohen, 2017).

Historical Context of the Autism and Gender Diversity Co-Occurrence

Communications between some of the gender care clinics in the late 1990s and early 2000s included observations that the rates of autism among those seeking gender-related services appeared greater than would be expected by chance (E. Menvielle, personal communication, September 1, 2008). During this earlier period of gender care, a series of case reports were published, including individuals of diverse ages and from various countries, highlighting the co-occurrence of autism and gender diversity (e.g., Gallucci, Hackerman, & Schmidt, 2005; Kraemer, Delsignore, Gundelfinger, Schnyder, & Hepp, 2005; Mukaddes, 2002; Perera, Gadambanathan, & Weerasiri, 2003). One of these case reports highlighted that cognitive behavioral treatment for obsessive-compulsive disorder–related behaviors decreased obsessive-compulsive symptoms in an autistic gender-diverse child, but did not cause any changes in the gender diversity characteristics of the child (Landén & Rasmussen, 1997).

Community Expressions of Co-Occurrence

The co-occurrence of autism and gender diversity is observed across a range of community expressions. For example, the Autistic Women's Network, an advocacy network led by autistic individuals, responded to the diversity of its constituency and adopted the new name, "Autistic Women's & Nonbinary Network" (Falk, 2018). The movie *Transfixed*, a 2016 documentary, follows the gender affirmation process of an autistic transgender woman within the context of her relationship with an autistic cisgender man (Kol, 2016). International media coverage of the death of Kayden Clarke, an autistic transgender man, described his history of having been denied gender affirmation services due to having an autism diagnosis (Wootson, 2017). Community expressions have also included partnership between autistic and gender diversity advocacy organizations: the Autistic Self Advocacy Network, the National LGBTQ Taskforce, and the Transgender Equality Network coauthored a joint statement on the rights of autistic transgender and gender nonconforming individuals (Autistic Self Advocacy Network et al., 2016).

Complexities Interpreting the Co-Occurrence Literature

With no current standardized procedures for characterizing gender diversity in research and a dearth of available gender-related measures, none of which have been tested/validated in neurodiverse/autistic individuals, contextualizing and interpreting the various existing studies of the autism and gender diversity co-occurrence is challenging. The review of gender provided at the beginning of this chapter highlights the complexity and nuance of the range of experiences and identities that make up the umbrella concept of "gender diversity." The various aspects of gender diversity cannot be easily parsed across the existing studies of the co-occurrence with autism. Although a majority of the studies identify an overoccurrence of co-occurring autism and gender diversity, it is not clear which aspects of gender diversity (e.g., gender identity diversity, gender expression diversity, gender dysphoria, etc.) most often co-occur with autism. This is amplified given the diverse health and gender care systems represented in the broadly international studies published thus far on the co-occurrence (e.g., The Netherlands, e.g., de Vries, Noens, Cohen-Kettenis, van Berckelaer-Onnes, & Doreleijers, 2010; van der Miesen, de Vries, Steensma, & Hartman, 2017; United States, e.g., Shumer, Reisner, Edwards-Leeper, & Tishelman, 2016; Strang, Powers, et al., 2018; Canada, e.g., VanderLaan, Postema, et al., 2015; Zucker et al., 2017; Finland, e.g., Kaltiala-Heino, Sumia, Työläjärvi, & Lindberg, 2015; England, e.g., Glidden, Bouman, Jones, & Arcelus, 2016; Nobili et al., 2018; Australia, e.g., George & Stokes, 2017; Strauss et al., 2017; Turkey, e.g., Akgül, Ayaz, Yildirim, & Fis, 2018; Japan, e.g., Tateno, Tateno, & Saito, 2008).

Many of the existing studies of the co-occurrence have focused on youth, and especially adolescents. Review of study findings according to age (e.g., children, adolescents, and adults separately) provides a developmental perspective on the co-occurrence findings. The existing studies can also be organized according to nature of the sample attainment, such as individuals who are gender referred (i.e., referred by themselves, their parents, or a provider for consultation regarding gender-related needs), individuals who have been diagnosed with autism, online samples, and population-based samples. The following sections organize and summarize the existing literature based on these age and sample attainment categories.

Prevalence and Course

Prevalence of Autism in Studies of Children and Adolescents Referred for Gender Care

STUDIES EMPLOYING AUTISM SCREENERS WITH GENDER-REFERRED YOUTH

Several studies of gender-diverse youth have employed standardized parent-reported autism-related screening measures. These studies have consistently reported a disproportionate number of gender-diverse youth obtaining significant score elevations on ASD screeners (in some cases > 20% of youth received scores above clinical cut-offs): in children referred for gender services (VanderLaan, Leef, Wood, Hughes, & Zucker, 2015) and children and adolescents referred for gender services (e.g., Akgül et al., 2018; Shumer et al., 2016; Skagerberg, Di Ceglie, & Carmichael, 2015; van der Miesen et al., 2017). However, concerns have been raised regarding the use of autism screening instruments to assess for autism traits among gender-referred individuals in these studies of youth with the apparent co-occurrence. Turban and van Schalkwyk (2018) note that autism screening questionnaires, such as the Social Responsiveness Scale (SRS; Constantino & Gruber, 2007), may lack specificity for autism and produce score elevations due to a variety of mental health concerns including anxiety and depression, as well as from non-autism-related developmental differences. They suggest that elevations on such screening measures used with gender-referred individuals might result from gender minority stress-related factors and mental health conditions, and therefore suggest that use of these instruments in gender-diverse groups could overestimate the prevalence of co-occurring autistic traits.

STUDIES REPORTING AUTISM DIAGNOSIS/DIAGNOSTICS IN GENDER-REFERRED YOUTH

In response to these concerns, Strang and colleagues proposed a different approach to considering prevalence using extant studies: the identification of studies of gender-diverse individuals that report rates of existing autism diagnoses or report rates of autism as diagnosed as part of study (Strang, Janssen, et al., 2018). Seven studies met these criteria (six with youth/adolescents: de Vries et al., 2010; Holt, Skagerberg, & Dunsford, 2016; Kaltiala-Heino et al., 2015; Nahata, Tishelman, Caltabellotta, & Quinn, 2017; Shumer et al., 2016; Strauss et al., 2017), each reporting rates of autism significantly greater than the most inclusive base rates for autism in the general population (4.1 to 17.5 times ASD population base rates). An additional study of gender-referred youth in a large health management organization found 5% of transgender females had co-occurring ASD (Becerra-Culqui et al., 2018).

STUDIES REPORTING BROADER NEURODIVERSITY CHARACTERISTICS IN GENDER-REFERRED YOUTH

In addition to autism symptoms or diagnostics, some studies have investigated broader neurodiversity characteristics in gender-referred youth, some of which are common in autism as well as other developmental differences. Studies have reported higher rates of obsessional traits by parent report (VanderLaan, Postema, et al., 2015) and teacher report (Zucker et al., 2017) and lower rates of empathizing (Di Ceglie, Skagerberg, Baron-Cohen, & Auyeung, 2014) in gender-referred as compared to cisgender youth. Greater levels of executive function problems across behavioral and metacognitive skills were also identified in gender-diverse young people and suggest a possible overoccurrence of a broader neurodiversity (i.e., beyond autistic traits alone) among gender-referred youth (Akgül et al., 2018).

STUDIES OF GENDER DIVERSITY CHARACTERISTICS IN AUTISTIC INDIVIDUALS

Several studies have examined gender diversity characteristics among autistic people. The earliest of these studies investigated a single item on the Child Behavior Checklist (Achenback & Rescorla, 2001), which reads, "wishes to be the opposite sex"; approximately 5% of parents of autistic youth endorsed this item about their child, which is approximately seven times more often than the item is endorsed among typically developing youth (Janssen, Huang, & Duncan, 2016; Strang et al., 2014). A similar study examined broader neurodiversity categories and suggested a higher prevalence of gender diversity experiences among all mental health–referred youth rather than specifically in autism (May, Pang, & Williams, 2017). Autistic adults assumed female at birth have reported more masculinized gender roles than neurotypical controls (Bejerot & Eriksson, 2014), and autistic adults assumed male or female at birth have reported significantly more gender dysphoria experiences than allistic adults (George & Stokes, 2017). Dewinter, De Graaf, and Begeer (2017) surveyed 675 adults with autism and found that 22% of the participants assigned female at birth and 8% of the participants assigned male at birth reported a different gender identity from the one assigned to them such as "partly male, partly female" or "not male, not female." However, only about 1% of the sample reported being the opposite binary gender (i.e., transgender; Dewinter et al., 2017). Van der Miesen and colleagues examined self-report of the question "wish to be of opposite sex" and found that 11.4% of autistic adults endorsed this item, as compared to 3% to 5% of individuals in the general population (van der Miesen, Hurley, Bal, & de Vries, 2018).

Prevalence of ASD and Autistic Traits in Gender-Diverse Adults

There are fewer studies of autistic traits and autism diagnosis in gender-diverse adults than in youth, and the results of the available adult studies are more equivocal than the studies of youth. Most of the adult studies rely on self-report of autistic traits, especially as reported on the Autism Quotient (AQ; Baron-Cohen, Wheelwright, Skinner, Martin, & Clubley, 2001). Adult self-report studies can be divided between self-reports that were given as part of clinical gender evaluations (i.e., as part of clinical assessments that were conducted to evaluate for potential gender-related medical supports) and self-reports that were collected as part of research studies that had no impact on clinical decision making. This distinction may be important as gender-referred individuals may self-report differently when their medical gender care is linked to clinical assessments (Vermaat et al., 2018).

Of the four studies that assessed autistic traits in gender-referred adults as part of clinical gender evaluations, two studies identified clinically significant ASD traits on the AQ of between 4.85% and 5.5% of gender-referred adults (Heylens et al., 2018; Pasterski, Gilligan, & Curtis, 2014); one study identified elevations on the AQ in 45% of female-identified gender-referred adults, but only on a social engagement–related subscale, which the study authors suggested represented social anxiety and not ASD-related traits (Nobili et al., 2018); and one study found no elevations of autistic traits in Dutch gender-referred adults (Vermaat et al., 2018). The single study to investigate self-reported autistic traits in a nonclinical sample of transgender adults found significant elevations on the AQ in transgender males as compared to a cisgender comparison group (Jones et al., 2012). One study of gender-referred adults included autistic diagnostic assessments as completed through comprehensive clinical record review and found the 6% of gender-referred adults met clear clinical criteria for ASD (Heylens et al., 2018).

The Longitudinal Course of Gender Diversity in Autistic Youth

Little is known about the longitudinal course of gender diversity among autistic people (i.e., how often gender diversity characteristics and experiences in autistic people remain stable, increase, or attenuate over time). Only two studies (de Vries et al., 2010; Strang, Powers, et al., 2018; and the follow-up to de Vries et al., 2010: van der Miesen, Cohen-Kettenis, & de Vries, 2018) and one set of published case reports (Parkinson, 2016) have reported on the stability or change of gender diversity characteristics in autistic individuals followed over time. In total across these studies, the gender trajectories of only 34 autistic postpubertal individuals have been reported.[3] Given this very small number, the broad variation in how long participants were followed across the studies (ranging from 2 to more than 10 years), and varied approaches to assessing gender diversity, no definitive conclusions regarding long-term gender diversity trajectories in autism should be made at this point. However, it is notable that de Vries and colleagues identified that five of nine autistic gender-referred adolescents were ultimately found, through careful gender assessments, appropriate for medical gender-related services (i.e., medical gender affirmation; de Vries et al., 2010). Further, Strang and colleagues identified that 12 of 22 autistic teens followed over 2 years intensified in their gender-diverse expressions over time (Strang, Powers, et al., 2018). There were also individuals in the Strang study and the Parkinson case report who over time showed attenuating gender diversity. Notably, three of 22 autistic youth followed for 2 years who had originally requested gender-related medical supports no longer requested these supports

[3] The longitudinal course of autistic prepubertal gender-diverse children is unknown. De Vries and colleagues reported that most autistic gender-referred prepubertal youth showed an attenuation of gender needs and reduction of gender identity diversity over time (de Vries et al., 2010), but the degree of these children's original gender diversity and gender needs is unclear as they were diagnosed under the overly inclusive Gender Identity Disorder in Childhood diagnosis (see the discussion of the diagnosis of GID in children earlier).

by the 2-year study close (Strang, Powers, et al., 2018). Unfortunately, no appropriate comparison data is available for allistic gender-diverse youth followed over time, so no conclusions can be made about similarities or differences between autistic and allistic gender-diverse youth gender trajectories over time.

Taken as a whole, the limited longitudinal literature suggests diverse gender trajectories among autistic adolescents, without any clear markers identified of which gender-referred autistic teens will ultimately require gender-related medical supports and which will not. As discussed in the study by Strang and colleagues, the gender trajectories of allistic (i.e., nonautistic) gender-referred youth are also poorly understood, so it would be incorrect to assume that examples of gender diversity attenuation are unique to autistic gender-referred youth.

Mental Health Correlates

Little is known about the mental health of autistic gender-diverse individuals; only two studies to date have assessed mental health in people with the co-occurrence. Autistic youth whose parents reported their child had the "wish to be of opposite sex" (WTBOS) had elevated anxiety compared to autistic youth with no report of gender diversity (Strang et al., 2014). However, when comparing autistic youth with parent-reported WTBOS to allistic youth with other neurodevelopmental conditions (e.g., epilepsy) and co-occurring WTBOS, autistic gender-diverse youth showed relatively lower levels of parent-reported anxiety. In their interpretation of these findings, Strang and colleagues wondered if childhood autism spectrum differences could be emotionally protective for some neurodiverse gender-diverse youth given that autistic social differences might to some degree shield gender-diverse youth from awareness of social biases and minority stress commonly experienced by gender minority youth (Strang et al., 2014). However, in an online study of autistic and typically developed adults, autistic adults with co-occurring gender diversity had the greatest levels of emotional difficulties (George & Stokes, 2018). The authors described how each minority status (i.e., autism *and* gender diversity) independently increased emotional/psychiatric burden.

Etiology, Diagnosis, and Assessment

The Nature of the Co-Occurrence

For this chapter we avoid the phrase "etiology of the co-occurrence" as the word "etiology" suggests illness or disorder. We do not consider gender diversity an illness or disorder, and although autism is classified as a disorder, we equally identify the autistic experience as an identity cherished by many and an important form of human neurodiversity (Strang, Janssen, et al., 2018). Several hypotheses have been proposed to explain the apparent overoccurrence of co-occurring autism and gender diversity. For example, it has been suggested that something of the autistic experience (e.g., reduced concern for social expectations and/or conventions) might allow autistic people to more readily express their gender diversity (Strang et al., 2014). Others have noted associations between specific traits of autism and gender diversity (Walsh, Krabbendam, Dewinter, & Begeer, 2018). There have also been suggestions of a possible deeper biological link between autistic traits and gender diversity (Nabbijohn et al., 2018; Shumer, Roberts, Reisner, Lyall, & Austin, 2015). And finally, it has been suggested that some individuals with the apparent co-occurrence may be experiencing a pseudo-autism (i.e., autistic-like presentation) resulting from the experience of minority stress (Turban, 2018). No studies have directly investigated causes for the overoccurrence.

Autism Assessment Challenges in Gender-Diverse Individuals

Evidence suggests autism is often expressed differently in females than in males (Kreiser & White, 2014; Lai, Baron-Cohen, & Buxbaum, 2015). Concerns have been raised regarding the possible underidentification of autism in girls and women (Loomes, Hull, & Mandy, 2017), in part due to autism diagnostic measures developed primarily with males (Halladay et al., 2015; Kirkovski, Enticott, & Fitzgerald, 2013; Lai et al., 2017). No studies thus far have investigated the performance of autism screening or autism diagnostic measures in gender-diverse individuals. Concerns have been raised regarding the possible overidentification of autistic traits among gender-diverse individuals when using screening measures with poor specificity (Turban & van Schalkwyk, 2018). Adding further complexity, multiple clinician reports from gender care programs describe a sizeable group of youth gender referrals with apparent *subclinical* characteristics of autism and who are diagnostically complex in terms of ASD (e.g., L. Edwards-Leeper, personal communication, February 3, 2017; N. Sharon, personal communication, July 7, 2018; L. Willing, personal communication, November 4, 2018). The description of individuals with less overt autistic presentations may be reminiscent of reports of autistic females whose autistic traits may be less clear during childhood and the teen years (Bargiela, Steward, & Mandy, 2016), and may also suggest a broader neurodiversity co-occurrence among a subset of gender-diverse youth (Akgül et al., 2018).

Treatment

Two existing studies provide information regarding autistic gender-diverse individuals' clinical experiences and needs. In a qualitative framework analytic study of the perspectives and experiences of 22 autistic gender-diverse adolescents, several key clinically relevant themes emerged from the youth participants: (a) reported experience of urgent gender needs and gender dysphoria, (b) reported histories of gender diversity–related experiences typically extending back to the prepubertal years, (c) descriptions of a process of gender discernment that unfolds over time (typically many years), and (d) concerns regarding bias and harassment that can impact gender expression and exploration (Strang, Powers, et al., 2018). Additionally, some of the autistic gender-diverse participants in Strang and colleagues' study reported their gender diversity had been questioned due to their autism diagnosis. A small study of three parents of autistic gender-diverse youth (ages 8 to 12) identified several clinical themes from parent interview: (a) parent worries about how transphobia in society might affect their children; (b) parent questions regarding the nature of their child's gender diversity, especially whether it was caused or influenced by autism; and (c) a lack of appropriate resources and supports for families of children with the co-occurrence (Kuvalanka, Mahan, McGuire, & Hoffman, 2017).

Initial clinical guidelines (ICGs) were developed for autistic gender-diverse adolescents by an international team of experts through a multistage blinded Delphi consensus procedure (Strang et al., 2016), with guidelines for both assessment and intervention provided. It is important to note that the recommendations made in these guidelines were specifically developed for adolescents; some care approaches may also be applicable in adults by extension, but this remains untested. The ICG recommendations indicate that a diagnosis of autism should not preclude an adolescent from being considered for gender-affirming medical supports. The importance of assembling a clinical team with expertise in both autism-related care and gender diversity is recommended. The ICG also recommends screening for autism among youth gender referrals and screening for gender diversity and gender-related needs among autistic youth. ICG assessment recommendations emphasize evaluation of urgency and intensity of gender-related needs; "urgency and intensity" of gender needs refers to the level of gender dysphoria and/or incongruence and its clinical impact. Regarding intervention, the ICG notes the importance of "blurring" assessment and intervention practices for many autistic gender-diverse adolescents such that autism-related supports for executive function, communication, self-awareness, and self-advocacy accompany an ongoing gender assessment process. Additionally, the roles of parents and providers in supporting autistic gender-diverse adolescents' process of gender discernment and/or gender affirmation are highlighted; the ICG notes that significantly increased supports may be required for gender-diverse autistic individuals, expanding the support roles of both providers and families. For example, the IGC highlights that supports around sensory concerns, flexibility, or anxiety may be necessary to assist autistic youth who may struggle with medical gender treatments.

Case Example

The following case example is offered to highlight the appropriateness of gender-affirming medical approaches for some autistic youth. Of note, as discussed in a recent longitudinal study of gender-diverse autistic youth (Strang, Powers, et al., 2018), not all autistic gender-diverse youth ultimately want or need medical gender care. In the following case, gender dysphoria characteristics were clearly present over a long period time, and the young person's unwavering commitment to expressing their affirmed gender (as opposed to their gender assumed at birth) convinced the care team of the necessity of gender-affirming medical care.

An autistic 14-year-old had been followed through a pediatric autism program since age 11 and presented to a youth gender clinic requesting gender-affirming hormones. Previously started on medical pubertal suppression at the onset of Tanner Stage 2 of puberty, this young person had shown no apparent pubertal progression; in other words, secondary sex characteristics and physical pubertal progression had been effectively stopped. Further, this person was living full time as their affirmed gender (a gender different from their gender assumed at birth) and had been doing so since age 10. Everyone recognized this young person according to their affirmed gender with appropriate names and pronouns. Clothing and grooming choices were consistent with the affirmed gender, and due to physical characteristics that were not clearly male or female, this young person had no difficulty being immediately perceived as their affirmed gender, simply with the choice of hairstyle and clothing. The communication style of the young person was matter of fact, literal, and, for the most part, terse.

When asked about gender history, the young person struggled to remember much besides when they came out to their parents in late elementary school. When asked about earlier gender diversity experiences through a structured format interview, the young person could only come up with the following: "Don't remember much, except I do remember telling mom I was [affirmed gender] in kindergarten." When asked about the future, the young person noted, "I'm going to be getting a job that pays a couple thousand dollars a month." When asked specifically about gender in the future, the young person explained, "My gender is not going to change. Never! Maybe I'll get [gender-affirming] surgery at 20." When completing written gender assessments, the young person indicated profound gender dysphoria regarding current sexual anatomy and concerns regarding the development of secondary sex characteristics associated with their sex assumed at birth. Further, they endorsed feeling fully like their affirmed gender, with no wavering over the last 4 years. This was confirmed in parent interview, that there was no doubt that this young person's gender identity was different than their gender assumed at birth.

In assessing appropriateness for gender-affirming hormones, the care team carefully reviewed the autism characteristics and their impact on communication and self-advocacy. This young person had a clear history of difficulties advocating and describing inner experiences. In fact, their advocacy around gender needs was remarkable, far outside the norm for this young person in advocating in other areas of their life. Further, and most compelling, the care team noted that there had been a clear and persistent gender dysphoria present from well before pubertal onset, and that this young person had been living full time as their affirmed gender in all settings. Given assessed levels of dysphoria, consistency of presentation over time, and apparent improvements in emotional functioning when pubertal suppression had been commenced previously, the care team recommended this young person for gender-affirming hormones.

Two years later at age 16, this autistic gender-affirmed adolescent continues to live full time according to their affirmed gender. Increased social anxiety has limited their social engagement with peers, which is of growing concern. But decisions regarding gender-affirming medical treatments appear to have relieved much of this young person's gender dysphoria. In fact, this young person's parents note that the gender-related factors are unimportant currently, and that autism-related features are the greatest current challenge.

Ethical Considerations

The vast majority of studies of the co-occurrence have been conducted by researchers without the coauthorship or even engagement of autistic, gender-diverse, or autistic gender-diverse self-advocates. Only two studies thus far have included autistic gender-diverse self-advocates as coresearchers/authors (Strang, Powers, et al., 2018; Strang, Janssen, et al., 2018), and only two studies have directly engaged autistic gender-diverse individuals or their parents to ask about their lived experiences and perspectives (Kuvalanka et al., 2017; Strang, Powers, et al., 2018). Community engagement and research partnerships are increasingly acknowledged as essential in autism-related research to capture person-centered experiences and perspectives that allistic research personnel may easily miss (Nicolaidis et al., 2011). Concerns regarding the lack of self-advocate and key-stakeholder involvement in research investigating the autism and gender diversity co-occurrence have been raised by autistic transgender self-advocates (e.g., Strang, Powers, et al., 2018). Specifically, self-advocates have noted that research on the co-occurrence can directly influence the civil rights of autistic gender-diverse individuals (including access to gender-related medical care) and therefore should richly include the voices and perspectives of individuals who are autistic and gender diverse (i.e., the Autistic Self Advocacy Network's call for "nothing about us without us"; Autistic Self Advocacy Network, 2018).

Decisions regarding medically related gender care for autistic youth are complex. Some expert providers have expressed reluctance to commence potentially irreversible treatments in those autistic youth who present with less clear gender presentations; notably, the ICG expert team was unable to reach consensus around criteria for commencing gender-affirming medical care in autistic youth (Strang et al., 2016). On the other hand, self-advocates have voiced concerns that the risks of "gatekeeping" (i.e., the withholding of requested gender-related medical care) in autistic youth who request gender-related medical treatments put youth at greater risk than the occasional case of an autistic youth regretting moving forward with gender-related medical decisions later in life (Strang, Powers, et al., 2018). Without long-term longitudinal outcome studies, gender-related medical decisions for autistic youth will be best made based on clinical experience and impressions by gender-affirming care providers who have extensive clinical expertise in both autism and the autism and gender diversity co-occurrence. Finally, no studies have investigated potential developmental/cognitive impacts of medical pubertal suppression in autistic youth; we do not know if the suppression of pubertal sex hormones in early puberty might impact a young autistic person's neural/functional development.

Summary and Future Directions

The co-occurrence of gender diversity and autism has been highlighted in a series of studies, with high rates of autism and autism-related traits identified in gender-diverse populations and vice versa. The complex clinical needs of individuals with the co-occurrence have only begun to be identified. Of note, there is some evidence for extra risks for poor mental health outcomes in adulthood (George & Stokes, 2018). A set of initial clinical guidelines have been developed for adolescents with the co-occurrence (Strang et al., 2016), but the needs of autistic gender-diverse adults are unknown. Given risks for reduced access to and usage of appropriate health care in autistic adults (e.g., Anderson & Butt, 2018), adult guidelines will need to consider how such factors might impact autistic adult access to gender care. In spite of much hypothesizing about the nature of the co-occurrence, few studies have directly engaged autistic gender-diverse individuals to understand their experiences and perspectives. Yet, expressions of the co-occurrence are common in the autism and gender diversity communities, and some of the leading transgender activists have been both autistic and gender diverse (Brown, 2014; LGBTQ Oral History Digital Collaboratory & Stonehouse, 2016).

Given possible problems with autism screening and diagnostic measures when used with cisgender male individuals (Lai et al., 2017), future research should evaluate how well existing autism assessment tools work for gender minority individuals, in terms of both acceptability and diagnostic accuracy. Similarly, gender assessments have not been tested and validated in autistic individuals; development of new gender measures should include testing with autistic individuals, such as has been described in the development of a new transgender fertility attitudes questionnaire (Strang, Jarin, et al., 2018). The lack of long-term longitudinal studies makes clinical decision making in this population complex and tentative. Future research designs should follow individuals with the co-occurrence over time, evaluating gender and broader needs as well as autistic traits across developmental periods (e.g., from adolescence into adulthood). And with the extra layers of transphobia and a societal bias to view individuals with developmental disabilities as less capable of self-determination, research on the co-occurrence must take into consideration the civil and human rights–related impact that publications can have on these double-minority individuals.

References

Achenbach, T. M., & Rscorla, L. A. (2001). *Manual for the ASEBA school-age forms & profiles*. Burlington, VT: University of Vermont, Research Center for Children, Youth, & Families.

Akgül, D. G. Y., Ayaz, D. A. B., Yildirim, D. B., & Fis, D. N. P. (2018). Autistic traits and executive functions in children and adolescents with gender dysphoria. *Journal of Sex & Marital Therapy, 0*(ja), 00–00. https://doi.org/10.1080/0092623X.2018.1437489

American Psychiatric Association. (2013). *Diagnostic and statistical manual of mental disorders* (5th ed., DSM-5). Washington, DC: Author.

Anderson, C., & Butt, C. (2018). Young adults on the autism spectrum: The struggle for appropriate services. *Journal of Autism and Developmental Disorders, 48*(11), 3912–3925.

Autistic Self Advocacy Network. (2011). Identity-first language. Retrieved December 16, 2018, from https://autisticadvocacy.org/about-asan/identity-first-language/

Autistic Self Advocacy Network. (2018). Autistic Self Advocacy Network. Retrieved January 17, 2018, from http://autisticadvocacy.org/

Autistic Self Advocacy Network, National Center for Transgender Equality, & LGBTQ Task Force. (2016). *Autistic Self Advocacy Network, National Center for Transgender Equality, and LGBTQ Task Force joint statement on the rights of transgender and gender non-conforming autistic people*. Washington, DC: Author.

Bargiela, S., Steward, R., & Mandy, W. (2016). The experiences of late-diagnosed women with autism spectrum conditions: An investigation of the female autism phenotype. *Journal of Autism and Developmental Disorders, 46*(10), 3281–3294. https://doi.org/10.1007/s10803-016-2872-8

Baron-Cohen, S. (2017). Editorial perspective: Neurodiversity—A revolutionary concept for autism and psychiatry. *Journal of Child Psychology and Psychiatry, 58*(6), 744–747.

Baron-Cohen, S., Wheelwright, S., Skinner, R., Martin, J., & Clubley, E. (2001). The Autism-Spectrum Quotient (AQ): Evidence from Asperger syndrome/high-functioning autism, males and females, scientists and mathematicians. *31*(1), 5–17.

Becerra-Culqui, T. A., Liu, Y., Nash, R., Cromwell, L., Flanders, W. D., Getahun, D., . . . Goodman, M. (2018). Mental health of transgender and gender nonconforming youth compared

with their peers. *Pediatrics, 141*(5). https://doi.org/10.1542/peds.2017-3845
Bejerot, S., & Eriksson, J. M. (2014). Sexuality and gender role in autism spectrum disorder: A case control study. *PloS One, 9*(1), e87961. https://doi.org/10.1371/journal.pone.0087961
Brown, L. (2014, May 14). About. Retrieved December 16, 2018, from https://autistichoya.net/bio/
Constantino, J. N., & Gruber, C. P. (2007). *Social Responsiveness Scale (SRS)*. Los Angeles, CA: Western Psychological Services.
de Vries, A. L. C., Noens, I. L. J., Cohen-Kettenis, P. T., van Berckelaer-Onnes, I. A., & Doreleijers, T. A. (2010). Autism spectrum disorders in gender dysphoric children and adolescents. *Journal of Autism and Developmental Disorders, 40*(8), 930–936. https://doi.org/10.1007/s10803-010-0935-9
Dewinter, J., De Graaf, H., & Begeer, S. (2017). Sexual orientation, gender identity, and romantic relationships in adolescents and adults with autism spectrum disorder. *Journal of Autism and Developmental Disorders, 47*(9), 2927–2934. https://doi.org/10.1007/s10803-017-3199-9
Di Ceglie, D., Skagerberg, E., Baron-Cohen, S., & Auyeung, B. (2014). Empathising and systemising in adolescents with gender dysphoria. *Opticon1826, 16*(6), 1–8.
Falk, C. (2018, April 26). Autistic Women & Nonbinary Network (AWN). Retrieved December 16, 2018, from https://awnnetwork.org/autistic-women-non-binary-network-awn/
Gallucci, G., Hackerman, F., & Schmidt, C. W. (2005). Gender identity disorder in an adult male with Asperger's syndrome. *Sexuality and Disability, 23*(1), 35–40. https://doi.org/10.1007/s11195-004-2078-4
The Gender Unicorn – Trans Student Educational Resources. (n.d.). Retrieved December 16, 2018, from https://www.transstudent.org/gender/
George, R., & Stokes, M. A. (2017). Gender identity and sexual orientation in autism spectrum disorder. *Autism*, 1362361317714587. https://doi.org/10.1177/1362361317714587
George, R., & Stokes, M. A. (2018). A quantitative analysis of mental health among sexual and gender minority groups in ASD. *Journal of Autism and Developmental Disorders, 48*(6), 2052–2063.
Glidden, D., Bouman, W. P., Jones, B. A., & Arcelus, J. (2016). Gender dysphoria and autism spectrum disorder: A systematic review of the literature. *Sexual Medicine Reviews, 4*(1), 3–14.
Halladay, A. K., Bishop, S., Constantino, J. N., Daniels, A. M., Koenig, K., Palmer, K., . . . Szatmari, P. (2015). Sex and gender differences in autism spectrum disorder: Summarizing evidence gaps and identifying emerging areas of priority. *Molecular Autism, 6*, i. https://doi.org/10.1186/s13229-015-0019-y
Heylens, G., Aspeslagh, L., Dierickx, J., Baetens, K., Van Hoorde, B., De Cuypere, G., & Elaut, E. (2018). The co-occurrence of gender dysphoria and autism spectrum disorder in adults: An analysis of cross-sectional and clinical chart data. *Journal of Autism and Developmental Disorders, 48*(6), 2217–2223. https://doi.org/10.1007/s10803-018-3480-6
Holt, V., Skagerberg, E., & Dunsford, M. (2016). Young people with features of gender dysphoria: Demographics and associated difficulties. *Clinical Child Psychology and Psychiatry, 21*(1), 108–118. https://doi.org/10.1177/1359104514558431
Hughes, J. M. F. (2015). *Change conversations around autism: A critical, action implicative discourse analysis of U.S. neurodiversity advocacy online* (Doctoral thesis). Retrieved from Communication Graduate Theses & Dissertations, 52.
Janssen, A., Huang, H., & Duncan, C. (2016). Gender variance among youth with autism spectrum disorders: A retrospective chart review. *Transgender Health, 1*(1), 63–68.
Jones, R. M., Wheelwright, S., Farrell, K., Martin, E., Green, R., Di Ceglie, D., & Baron-Cohen, S. (2012). Brief report: Female-to-male transsexual people and autistic traits. *Journal of Autism and Developmental Disorders, 42*(2), 301–306. https://doi.org/10.1007/s10803-011-1227-8
Kaltiala-Heino, R., Sumia, M., Työläjärvi, M., & Lindberg, N. (2015). Two years of gender identity service for minors: Overrepresentation of natal girls with severe problems in adolescent development. *Child and Adolescent Psychiatry and Mental Health, 9*, 9. https://doi.org/10.1186/s13034-015-0042-y
Kirkovski, M., Enticott, P. G., & Fitzgerald, P. B. (2013). A review of the role of female gender in autism spectrum disorders. *Journal of Autism and Developmental Disorders, 43*(11), 2584–2603. https://doi.org/10.1007/s10803-013-1811-1
Kol, A. (2016). *Transfixed* [Motion Picture]. Toronto, Ontario.
Kraemer, B., Delsignore, A., Gundelfinger, R., Schnyder, U., & Hepp, U. (2005). Comorbidity of Asperger syndrome and gender identity disorder. *European Child & Adolescent Psychiatry, 14*(5), 292–296. https://doi.org/10.1007/s00787-005-0469-4
Kreiser, N. L., & White, S. W. (2014). ASD in females: Are we overstating the gender difference in diagnosis? *Clinical Child and Family Psychology Review, 17*(1), 67–84. https://doi.org/10.1007/s10567-013-0148-9
Kuvalanka, K. A., Mahan, D. J., McGuire, J. K., & Hoffman, T. K. (2017). Perspectives of mothers of transgender and gender-nonconforming children with autism spectrum disorder. *Journal of Homosexuality*, 1–23. https://doi.org/10.1080/00918369.2017.1406221
Lai, M.-C., Baron-Cohen, S., & Buxbaum, J. D. (2015). Understanding autism in the light of sex/gender. *Molecular Autism, 6*, 24. https://doi.org/10.1186/s13229-015-0021-4
Lai, M.-C., Lombardo, M. V., Ruigrok, A. N., Chakrabarti, B., Auyeung, B., Szatmari, P., . . . MRC AIMS Consortium. (2017). Quantifying and exploring camouflaging in men and women with autism. *Autism: The International Journal of Research and Practice, 21*(6), 690–702. https://doi.org/10.1177/1362361316671012
Landén, M., & Rasmussen, P. (1997). Gender identity disorder in a girl with autism—A case report. *European Child & Adolescent Psychiatry, 6*(3), 170–173.
LGBTQ Oral History Digital Collaboratory, & Stonehouse, M. (2016). Martine Stonehouse ORAL HISTORY. Retrieved from http://digitalcollections.clga.ca/exhibits/show/trans-surgery-activism-ontario/item/630
Loomes, R., Hull, L., & Mandy, W. P. L. (2017). What is the male-to-female ratio in autism spectrum disorder? A systematic review and meta-analysis. *Journal of the American Academy of Child and Adolescent Psychiatry, 56*(6), 466–474. https://doi.org/10.1016/j.jaac.2017.03.013
May, T., Pang, K., & Williams, K. J. (2017). Gender variance in children and adolescents with autism spectrum disorder from the National Database for Autism Research. *International Journal of Transgenderism, 18*(1), 7–15. https://doi.org/10.1080/15532739.2016.1241976

Mukaddes, N. M. (2002). Gender identity problems in autistic children. *Child: Care, Health and Development, 28*(6), 529–532.

Nabbijohn, A. N., van der Miesen, A. I. R., Santarossa, A., Peragine, D., de Vries, A. L. C., Popma, A.,...VanderLaan, D. P. (2018). Gender variance and the autism spectrum: An examination of children ages 6–12 years. *Journal of Autism and Developmental Disorders*. https://doi.org/10.1007/s10803-018-3843-z

Nahata, L., Tishelman, A. C., Caltabellotta, N. M., & Quinn, G. P. (2017). Low fertility preservation utilization among transgender youth. *Journal of Adolescent Health: Official Publication of the Society for Adolescent Medicine*. https://doi.org/10.1016/j.jadohealth.2016.12.012

Newhook, J. T., Pyne, J., Winters, K., Feder, S., Holmes, C., Tosh, J.,...Picket, S. (2018). A critical commentary on follow-up studies and "desistance" theories about transgender and gender-nonconforming children. *International Journal of Transgenderism, 19*(2), 212–224.

Nicolaidis, C., Raymaker, D., McDonald, K., Dern, S., Ashkenazy, E., Boisclair, C.,...Baggs, A. (2011). Collaboration strategies in nontraditional community-based participatory research partnerships: Lessons from an academic–community partnership with autistic self-advocates. *Progress in Community Health Partnerships: Research, Education, and Action, 5*(2), 143–150. https://doi.org/10.1353/cpr.2011.0022

Nobili, A., Glazebrook, C., Bouman, W. P., Glidden, D., Baron-Cohen, S., Allison, C.,...Arcelus, J. (2018). Autistic traits in treatment-seeking transgender adults. *Journal of Autism and Developmental Disorders, 48*(12), 3984–3994. https://doi.org/10.1007/s10803-018-3557-2

Parkinson, J. (2016). Re: Gender dysphoria and co-occurring autism spectrum disorders: Review, case examples and treatment considerations, by Jacobs et al. (LGBT Health 2014;1:277–282). *LGBT Health, 3*(2), 175. https://doi.org/10.1089/lgbt.2015.0138

Pasterski, V., Gilligan, L., & Curtis, R. (2014). Traits of autism spectrum disorders in adults with gender dysphoria. *Archives of Sexual Behavior, 43*(2), 387–393. https://doi.org/10.1007/s10508-013-0154-5

Perera, H., Gadambanathan, T., & Weerasiri, S. (2003). Gender identity disorder presenting in a girl with Asperger's disorder and obsessive compulsive disorder. *Ceylon Medical Journal, 48*(2), 57–58.

Ristori, J., & Steensma, T. D. (2016). Gender dysphoria in childhood. *International Review of Psychiatry, 28*(1), 13–20.

Shumer, D. E., Reisner, S. L., Edwards-Leeper, L., & Tishelman, A. (2016). Evaluation of Asperger syndrome in youth presenting to a gender dysphoria clinic. *LGBT Health, 3*(5), 387–390. https://doi.org/10.1089/lgbt.2015.0070

Shumer, D. E., Roberts, A. L., Reisner, S. L., Lyall, K., & Austin, S. B. (2015). Brief report: Autistic traits in mothers and children associated with child's gender nonconformity. *Journal of Autism and Developmental Disorders, 45*(5), 1489–1494. https://doi.org/10.1007/s10803-014-2292-6

Skagerberg, E., Di Ceglie, D., & Carmichael, P. (2015). Brief report: Autistic features in children and adolescents with gender dysphoria. *Journal of Autism and Developmental Disorders, 45*(8), 2628–2632. https://doi.org/10.1007/s10803-015-2413-x

Strang, J. F., Janssen, A., Tishelman, A., Leibowitz, S. F., Kenworthy, L., McGuire, J. K.,...Anthony, L. G. (2018). Revisiting the link: Evidence of the rates of autism in studies of gender diverse individuals. *Journal of the American Academy of Child and Adolescent Psychiatry, 57*(11), 885–887. https://doi.org/10.1016/j.jaac.2018.04.023

Strang, J. F., Jarin, J., Call, D., Clark, B., Wallace, G. L., Anthony, L. G.,...Gomez-Lobo, V. (2018). Transgender Youth Fertility Attitudes Questionnaire: Measure development in nonautistic and autistic transgender youth and their parents. *Journal of Adolescent Health: Official Publication of the Society for Adolescent Medicine, 62*(2), 128–135. https://doi.org/10.1016/j.jadohealth.2017.07.022

Strang, J. F., Kenworthy, L., Dominska, A., Sokoloff, J., Kenealy, L. E., Berl, M.,...Wallace, G. L. (2014). Increased gender variance in autism spectrum disorders and attention deficit hyperactivity disorder. *Archives of Sexual Behavior, 43*(8), 1525–1533. https://doi.org/10.1007/s10508-014-0285-3

Strang, J. F., Meagher, H., Kenworthy, L., de Vries, A. L. C., Menvielle, E., Leibowitz, S.,...Anthony, L. G. (2016). Initial clinical guidelines for co-occurring autism spectrum disorder and gender dysphoria or incongruence in adolescents. *Journal of Clinical Child and Adolescent Psychology*, 1–11. https://doi.org/10.1080/15374416.2016.1228462

Strang, J. F., Powers, M. D., Knauss, M., Sibarium, E., Leibowitz, S. F., Kenworthy, L.,...Anthony, L. G. (2018). "They thought it was an obsession": Trajectories and perspectives of autistic transgender and gender-diverse adolescents. *Journal of Autism and Developmental Disorders, 48*(12), 4039–4055. https://doi.org/10.1007/s10803-018-3723-6

Strauss, P., Cook, A., Winter, S., Watson, V., Wright Toussaint, D., & Lin, A. (2017). *Trans pathways: The mental health experiences and care pathways of trans young people. Summary of results*. Perth, Australia: Telethon Kids Institute.

Tateno, M., Tateno, Y., & Saito, T. (2008). Comorbid childhood gender identity disorder in a boy with Asperger syndrome. *Psychiatry and Clinical Neuroscience, 62*(2), 238.

Turban, J. L. (2018). Potentially reversible social deficits among transgender youth. *Journal of Autism and Developmental Disorders*. https://doi.org/10.1007/s10803-018-3603-0

Turban, J. L., & van Schalkwyk, G. I. (2018). "Gender dysphoria" and autism spectrum disorder: Is the link real? *Journal of the American Academy of Child and Adolescent Psychiatry, 57*(1), 8–9.e2. https://doi.org/10.1016/j.jaac.2017.08.017

van der Miesen, A. I. R., Cohen-Kettenis, P. T., & de Vries, A. L. C. (2018). Is there a link between gender dysphoria and autism spectrum disorder? *Journal of the American Academy of Child and Adolescent Psychiatry, 57*(11), 884–885. https://doi.org/10.1016/j.jaac.2018.04.022

van der Miesen, A. I. R., de Vries, A. L. C., Steensma, T. D., & Hartman, C. A. (2017). Autistic symptoms in children and adolescents with gender dysphoria. *Journal of Autism and Developmental Disorders*. https://doi.org/10.1007/s10803-017-3417-5

van der Miesen, A. I. R., Hurley, H., Bal, A. M., & de Vries, A. L. C. (2018). Prevalence of the wish to be of the opposite gender in adolescents and adults with autism spectrum disorder. *Archives of Sexual Behavior, 47*(8), 2307–2317. https://doi.org/10.1007/s10508-018-1218-3

van Schalkwyk, G. I., Klingensmith, K., & Volkmar, F. R. (2015). Gender identity and autism spectrum disorders. *Yale Journal of Biology and Medicine, 88*(1), 81–83.

VanderLaan, D. P., Leef, J. H., Wood, H., Hughes, S. K., & Zucker, K. J. (2015). Autism spectrum disorder risk factors and autistic traits in gender dysphoric children. *Journal of*

Autism and Developmental Disorders, 45(6), 1742–1750. https://doi.org/10.1007/s10803-014-2331-3
VanderLaan, D. P., Postema, L., Wood, H., Singh, D., Fantus, S., Hyun, J., . . . Zucker, K. J. (2015). Do children with gender dysphoria have intense/obsessional interests? *Journal of Sex Research, 52*(2), 213–219. https://doi.org/10.1080/00224499.2013.860073
Vermaat, L. E. W., van der Miesen, A. I. R., de Vries, A. L. C., Steensma, T. D., Popma, A., Cohen-Kettenis, P. T., & Kreukels, B. P. C. (2018). Self-reported autism spectrum disorder symptoms among adults referred to a gender identity clinic. *LGBT Health, 5*(4), 226–233. https://doi.org/10.1089/lgbt.2017.0178
Walsh, R. J., Krabbendam, L., Dewinter, J., & Begeer, S. (2018). Brief report: Gender identity differences in autistic adults: Associations with perceptual and socio-cognitive profiles. *Journal of Autism and Developmental Disorders, 48*(12), 4070–4078. https://doi.org/10.1007/s10803-018-3702-y
Winters, K., Newhook, J. T., Pyne, J., Feder, S., Jamieson, A., Holmes, C., . . . Tosh, J. (2018). Learning to listen to trans and gender diverse children: A response to Zucker (2018) and Steensma and Cohen-Kettenis (2018). *International Journal of Transgenderism, 19*(2), 246–250.
Wootson, C. R. (2017, February 9). His Asperger's video was inspiring. His death by police was "nonsensical," a lawsuit says. Retrieved December 16, 2018, from https://www.washingtonpost.com/news/post-nation/wp/2017/02/09/his-aspergers-video-was-inspiring-his-death-by-police-was-nonsensical-a-lawsuit-says/
World Health Organization. (1993). *ICD-10, the ICD-10 classification of mental and behavioural disorders: Clinical descriptions and diagnostic guidelines*. Geneva, Switzerland: Author.
World Health Organization. (2018). *International statistical classification of diseases and related health problems* (11th revision). Geneva, Switzerland: Author.
Zucker, K. J., Nabbijohn, A. N., Santarossa, A., Wood, H., Bradley, S. J., Matthews, J., & VanderLaan, D. P. (2017). Intense/obsessional interests in children with gender dysphoria: A cross-validation study using the Teacher's Report Form. *Child and Adolescent Psychiatry and Mental Health, 11*, 51. https://doi.org/10.1186/s13034-017-0189-9

PART 3

Related Problems

CHAPTER

12

Psychosexual Problems, Sexual Deviance, and Promoting Sexual Health in Autistic Adolescents and Adults

Kirstin Greaves-Lord*, Jeroen Dewinter*, Lennart Pedersen, Olive Healy, *and* Mark A. Stokes

Abstract

Although the research base is scarce, clinical practice shows that some autistic individuals demonstrate and experience atypical or deviant sexual behaviors, feelings, and/or thoughts. Moreover, family members and involved professionals are often hesitant to discuss the topic of sexuality, which can cover up or escalate the problems. Therefore, this chapter discusses the relevant background literature, methods to assess psychosexual problems in autistic people, and methods to promote communication about psychosexual health issues and ultimately psychosexual health. Case examples are used to illustrate assessment and intervention. Future directions for research and clinical practice are discussed.

Keywords: psychosexual problems, sexuality, sexual deviance, sexual health, autistic

Overview

Case studies and clinical experience suggest that some autistic individuals (i.e., individuals with a diagnosis of autism spectrum disorder [ASD]; for a discussion on terminology, please see Kenny et al., 2016) display atypical or deviant sexual behaviors, feelings, and/or thoughts. To date, however, research has yet to unequivocally establish an elevated prevalence of atypical or inappropriate sexual development in autistic adolescents and adults when compared to typically developing (TD) or "neurotypical" (NT) peers (for a framework for this terminology, please see Silberman, 2015). Despite a lack of extant research on this topic in ASD, clinical practice indicates that autistic individuals are commonly referred to mental health care with regard to atypical sexual behaviors, feelings, or thoughts. Moreover, professionals often hesitate to discuss sexual well-being with their clients (e.g., Holmes et al., 2014) even though some autistic adolescents and adults have questions and problems relating to sexuality that they would like to discuss. Therefore, the aim of this chapter is to provide an overview of the current state of research and clinical understanding around sexuality in autistic people, and to provide guidelines to promote psychosexual health in autistic people involving different stakeholders such as family members, teachers, other service providers, peers, and loved ones. Before doing so, it is important to discuss and clarify the conceptualizations of "sexuality," "deviance," and "psychosexual problems" versus "sexual dysfunction" and "psychosexual health," as these topics are often highly sensitive and subjective matters. These matters are also impacted by cognitive (dis)ability, which will additionally be discussed. The following section aims to clarify relevant constructs and to promote an open-minded view.

Conceptualizations: Discussion and Clarification of Terminology

At the outset of a chapter addressing psychosexual problems, sexual deviance, and psychosexual health, consideration is in place about what discerns "normality" from "deviance," or "well-being" and "health"

* equally contributed as first authors

from "problems" and "disorders." As sexual behaviors, feelings, and thoughts are subjective matters on continuous dimensions, dichotomous distinctions between normal versus deviant are based on somewhat arbitrary cut-offs and interpretations. Therefore, we will provide the reader with the range of conceptualizations and criteria as a knowledge base that can be used to make informed decisions.

Sexuality is defined by the World Health Organization (WHO, 2006, p. 5) as

> a central aspect of being human throughout life and encompasses sex, gender identities and roles, sexual orientation, eroticism, pleasure, intimacy and reproduction... experienced and expressed in thoughts, fantasies, desires, beliefs, attitudes, values, behaviors, practices, roles and relationships. While sexuality can include all of these dimensions, not all of them are always experienced or expressed. Sexuality is influenced by the interaction of biological, psychological, social, economic, political, cultural, ethical, legal, historical, religious and spiritual factors.

Thus, in this chapter we adopt a broad conceptualization of sexuality, encompassing all these different aspects, and thus—importantly—not merely physical sexual behaviors (e.g., sexual intercourse). Terms such as "*psycho*sexual" (Dekker et al., 2017) or "*socio*sexual" (Hancock, Stokes, & Mesibov, 2017) emphasize the intra- and interpersonal aspects of sexuality. Hancock et al. (2017) highlighted the difference between *sexual behavior*, involving sexual desire, and *sexualized behavior*, which lacks sexual intent but is often sensory based and interpreted by others as sexual (Stokes & Kaur, 2005). Thus, a sexual behavior is used to experience and express one's sexuality—either toward the self or another. Psychosexual problems can emerge in relation to different factors, such as sociocultural, political, or economic factors (e.g., lack of comprehensive information relating to sexuality or health services), factors relating to partner and relationship (e.g., communication problems), psychological factors (e.g., limited pleasure relating to depression), or medical factors (e.g., pain or limited sexual response; Tiefer, Hall, & Tavris, 2002).

Sexual health (WHO, 2006, p. 5) refers to a state of well-being in relation to sexuality, as a combination of the absence of problems, a positive and respectful approach to sexuality and relationships, and the possibility of having pleasurable and safe sexual experiences.

Deviance refers to "the fact or state of diverging from usual or accepted standards, especially in social or sexual behavior" (en.oxforddictionaries.com). In other words, deviance describes an action or behavior that violates social norms, including formally enacted rules (e.g., crimes), as well as informal violations of social norms (e.g., rejecting customs/mores). As such, sexual deviance can be regarded on a continuum, on which sexual behaviors can vary in intensity (i.e., ranging from holding hands, to intercourse, to oral or anal sex) and regarding legal aspects (i.e., ranging from generally accepted, to generally regarded different but legal, to illegal).

In this light, it is important to be aware of the fact that cultural standards (laws, norms, customs, mores) change over time (e.g., descriptions of homosexuality in the different versions of the *Diagnostic and Statistical Manual of Mental Disorders*), differ between cultures, and are gender dependent, often with different standards for men versus women. Cultures are heterogeneous and evolve. For instance, the availability of hormonal contraception for women in the 1960s gave women increased freedom in their own sexuality, resulting in a substantial change in societal mores in many cultures. It is also important to note that although deviance may have a negative connotation, the violation of social norms is in fact not always a negative action; positive deviations exist too. This is when the norm is violated yet the behavior can be classified as positive or acceptable, by part of the society, or by more and more members of a society over time (e.g., tolerance toward same-sex marriages in cultures where this is currently still prohibited).

Finally, it is important to be aware that sexual behaviors and actions should be interpreted while taking into account the individual's level of *intelligence* (e.g., Hellemans, Roeyers, Laplae, Dewaele & Deboutte, 2010) and social emotional development. Individuals in the moderate to severe range of intellectual disability will have an adaptive functioning and understanding of social norms that are at a much lower level than their chronological age. Behavior that could be interpreted as "maladaptive" or nonconforming due to age is perhaps more "normal" (expected level) if conceptualized at the individual's level of cognitive functioning or socioemotional functioning.

Taken together, "sexuality" is a very complex developmental domain with diversity of experience and of expression in people with and without ASD. "Deviance" too is a labyrinthine, perspective-related concept. Given these fluctuating intra- and intercultural perspectives, research on sexuality in ASD has itself changed over time. Therefore, the next section will regard the topic of sexual deviance and development in ASD from a historical perspective.

Historical Perspective on Research Field

Research publications on sexuality in autistic people were very scarce before 1980, after which they slowly began to increase (Figure 12.1). Simultaneously, views on sexuality in autistic people—or more generally people with a developmental disability or a psychiatric condition—changed. Bertilsdotter Rosqvist (2014) described the evolution from an "asexuality discourse to an autistic sexuality," or from a more deficit-oriented discourse to a sexual difference discourse. Next we will further elaborate on how the research and views evolved.

In the 1980s, the majority of literature reported on cases studies of individuals with intellectual disability, focusing on a lack of sexual knowledge or even claims of asexuality in ASD populations (Zigler & Hodapp, 1986). The idea that sexuality and relationships were also of importance to, and a possibility for, autistic people has not long been apparent (Bertilsdotter Rosqvist, 2014; Dekker et al., 2017; Dewinter, Vermeiren, Vanwesenbeeck, & van Nieuwenhuizen, 2013; Kellaher, 2015; Pecora, Mesibov, & Stokes, 2016). Sexual upbringing (by parents/caretakers) and education (by teachers) were regarded as uncomfortable and burdensome rather than an essential part of stimulating healthy development (Torisky & Torisky, 1985). This prevented many autistic people from receiving sufficient sexual education. Moreover, any focus, either clinical or academic, on sexual development in autistic individuals emphasized *preventing* psychosexual *problems* or inappropriate behaviors rather than *promoting* psychosexual *health*.

In the 1990s, larger studies indicated that sexuality in autistic adults was quite common at all levels of intelligence, and that the sexual behavior could be directed to oneself (masturbation) or be person oriented with sexual arousal (Haracopos & Pedersen, 1992; Van Bourgondien, Reichle, & Palmer, 1997). Haracopos and Pedersen (1992) reported that most autistic individuals in their representative sample (16 to 40 years old, with and without intellectual disability) expressed a clear desire for affective, romantic, and/or sexual relationships. Autistic adults without an intellectual disability (mean age = 27 years, SD = 5.6) were reported to have had fewer sexual experiences than adults with mild to moderate

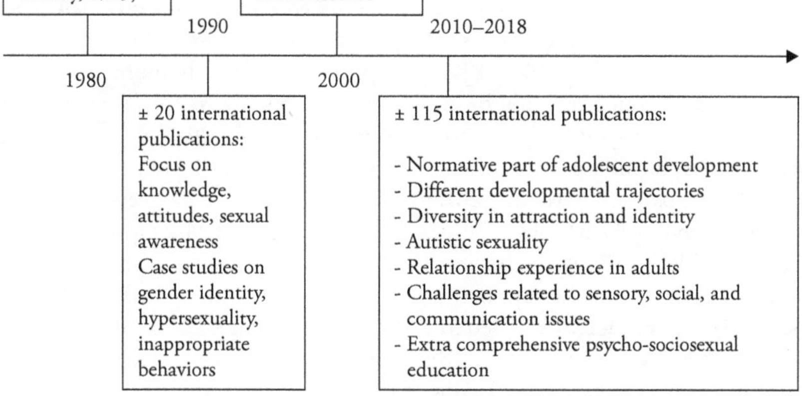

Figure 12.1. Historical overview of research and views on sexuality in autistic people.
Based on systematic literature reviews by Dewinter, J., Vermeiren, R., Vanwesenbeeck, I., & van Nieuwenhuizen, C. (2013). Autism and normative sexual development: A narrative review. *Journal of Clinical Nursing, 22*, 3467–3483. http://doi.org/10.1111/jocn.12397; Pecora, L., Mesibov, G., & Stokes, M. A. (2016). Sexuality in high functioning autism: A systematic review and meta-analysis. *Journal of Autism and Developmental Disorders, 46*(11), 3519–3556. doi: 10.1007/s10803-016-2892-4; and Hancock, G. I. P., Stokes, M. A., & Mesibov, G. B. (2017). Socio-sexual functioning in autism spectrum disorder: A systematic review and meta-analyses of existing literature. *Autism Research, 10*(11), 1823–1833. http://doi.org/10.1002/aur.1831.

degrees of intellectual disability (mean age = 27 years, SD = 6.9), but the interest in sexuality was the same for the two groups (Ousley & Mesibov, 1991).

During the early part of the 21st century, the rise in awareness of ASD in individuals of all levels of functioning, from all ages, was associated with increased awareness that those with ASD often had a normal and healthy interest in sexuality but lacked sexual education and appropriate insight (Hellemans, Colson, Verbraeken, Vermeiren, & Deboutte, 2007; Stokes & Kaur, 2005). Subsequently, consensus grew on the importance of sexuality education and attention to social aspects of dealing with sexuality (Hellemans et al., 2007; Mehzabin & Stokes, 2011; Stokes & Kaur, 2005; Stokes, Newton, & Kaur, 2007).

From 2010 onward, there was more emphasis on sexuality as a normative developmental task for all adolescents, including autistic persons. This went hand in hand with studies on attuned sexuality education for autistic individuals. Research expanded on sexual education programs that were adapted to the specific needs of autistic individuals, involving a very clear and consistent outline and the use of explicit and unambiguous language and illustrations (e.g., Boudesteijn, Van der Vegt, Visser, Tick, & Maras, 2011; Dekker, Van Der Vegt, & Visser, 2015). Autistic adolescents themselves participated more actively in the design and interpretation of sexuality research and reported on their experiences and expectations (Dekker et al., 2015, 2017; Dewinter, Vermeiren, Vanwesenbeeck, Lobbestael, & Van Nieuwenhuizen, 2015; Dewinter, Vermeiren, Vanwesenbeeck, & Van Nieuwenhuizen, 2016; Mehzabin & Stokes, 2011) and their needs relating to psychosexual education (Gougeon, 2013; Hannah & Stagg, 2016; Hatton & Tector, 2010; Travers & Tincani, 2010; Tullis & Zangrillo, 2013; Visser et al., 2015). The skills and attitudes relating to sexuality education in autistic teenagers were explored in representative samples including professionals (Holmes et al., 2014), parents (Ballan, 2012; Holmes & Himle, 2014), and teachers (Kalyva, 2010). Attention to the possible relationship between gender dysphoria and autism, and the support required by these individuals, increased (Bedard, Zhang, & Zucker, 2010; De Vries et al., 2010; Glidden, Bouman, Jones, & Arcelus, 2016; Jacobs, Rachlin, Erickson-Schroth, & Janssen , 2014; Jones et al., 2012; Lehmann & Leavy, 2016; Parkinson, 2014; Pasterski, Gilligan, & Curtis, 2014; Shumer, Reisner, Edwards-Leeper, & Tishelman, 2016; Skagerberg, Di Ceglie, & Carmichael, 2015; Strang et al., 2016; van der Miesen, Hurley & de Vries, 2016; van der Miesen, Hurley, Bal & de Vries, 2018; Van Schalkwyk, Klingensmith, & Volkmar, 2015). In addition, attention to sexual well-being and romantic relationships in autistic adults increased (Byers & Nichols, 2014; Byers, Nichols, & Voyer, 2013; Byers, Nichols, Voyer, & Reilly, 2012; Strunz et al., 2017). Case studies on specific, atypical sexual behaviors and interests and the effects of a variety of interventions in those specific cases continued. Some studies focused on detecting, diagnosing, and treating autistic adolescents and adults in forensic settings and described early guidelines for assessing and treating inappropriate sexual behaviors in autistic adults (Beddows & Brooks, 2016; Bleil Walters et al., 2013, Higgs & Carter, 2015; Sevlever, Roth, & Gillis, 2013). A new paradigm emerged: autistic people developing their own sexual identity and having relationships that suited them, which may be different from those of NT peers (Barnett & Maricka-Tyndale, 2015; Bertilsdotir Rosqvist, 2014).

In the period of 2016 to 2018, a wealth of publications on psychosexual functioning in autistic individuals appeared. A systematic review on potential psychosexual issues experienced by autistic people was published (Pecora et al., 2016), which was supported and extended by the empirical work of Dekker et al. (2017). These studies demonstrated that autistic adolescents as well as their parents indicated more difficulties regarding *psychosexual socialization* (i.e., interpersonal features, such as skills related to friendships, acceptance by peers, and adequately dealing with boundaries) and *psychosexual selfhood* (i.e., intrapersonal features, such as body image, self-perceived social competence, self-esteem, confidence, and psychosexual knowledge). With regard to *sexual/intimate behavior*, only parents reported significantly more problems in autistic adolescents relative to NT peers. A systematic review by Hancock et al. (2017) described a theoretical framework on formal (i.e., in educational setting) and informal (i.e., through peers) psychosexual learning in autistic individuals, emphasizing that these individuals usually lack both formal and informal learning opportunities. This review strengthened the theoretical foundation of ASD-tailored psychosexual education programs, such as "Tackling Teenage Training" (Dekker et al., 2017), which stimulates both formal and informal psychosexual learning experiences in autistic adolescents. The effectiveness of this psychosexual education program was corroborated within a randomized controlled trial (RCT) that was published in the same year (Visser, Greaves-Lord, Tick, Verhulst, Maras & van der Vegt, 2017).

Also in this period, there was a rising awareness of elevated levels of sexual and gender diversity among those on the autism spectrum (Dewinter, De Graaf & Begeer, 2017; Fernandes et al., 2016; George & Stokes, 2016; Van Der Miesen, Hurley, & De Vries, 2016), addressing variation in both sexual orientation (e.g., heteronormativity; George & Stokes, 2018a, Rudolph et al., 2018) and gender roles (George & Stokes, 2016).

Prevalence and Course

As is evident from the overview of research over the last four decades, science-based knowledge on sexuality and autism is still emerging. Our understanding of sexual problems and negative deviance is mostly based on case studies, which only offer a limited basis to make statements about prevalence or course. To follow we offer a limited overview of the available evidence.

Romantic Interest and Sexual Attraction

General societal beliefs are still held that autistic individuals have a reduced romantic/sexual interest and/or attraction relative to NT peers. Yet, comparable numbers of cognitively able autistic adolescent boys and their peers from the general population reported having experience with falling in love and having teenage romantic relationships (Dewinter et al., 2015). The majority of autistic adolescent boys in this study reported experience with masturbation, and about a third had experience with partnered intimate and sexual behaviors, comparable to peers from the general population. The absence of a difference between autistic and NT boys contrasted with earlier findings based on parent and caregiver report (Stokes & Kaur, 2005) and seems explicable by a limited awareness in parents about the sexual activities of their children (Dewinter et al., 2016). When emerging into adulthood, the proportion of autistic young men (aged 16 to 20 years) with partnered experience was lower compared to peers from the general population (Dewinter et al., 2016). Recent studies revealed that about half of cognitively able autistic adults are in a romantic relationship (Byers et al., 2012; Dewinter, De Graaf & Begeer, 2017; Strunz et al., 2017), which is more than earlier findings indicated, yet less than NT peers. Only a third of the single participants regretted this relationship status (Dewinter, De Graaf & Begeer, 2017). In their group of single adults with ASD, Byers et al. (2013) found that those without prior relationship experience were more often younger heterosexual men. Single participants in this study reported positive solitary sexual functioning (i.e., satisfying masturbation). Several explanations for the higher frequency of a single status in autistic individuals have been suggested, such as uncertainty, anxiety, or a lack of skills to initiate a relationship (Byers et al., 2013; Dewinter, Van Parys, Vermeiren & Van Nieuwenhuizen, 2017). Although no differences in attraction patterns were found between ASD and NT adolescent boys (Dewinter et al., 2015), fewer adult autistic men (81.6%) and women (56.6%) reported feeling only heterosexual attraction compared to men (90.4%) and women (87.0%) in the general population (Dewinter, De Graaf & Begeer, 2017; George & Stokes, 2018b; May, Pang & Williams, 2017).

Inappropriate Sexual Behaviors

Systematic research regarding inappropriate sexual behaviors and autism is still limited and most publications are case reports (Dewinter et al., 2013; Hellemans et al., 2007; Stokes & Kaur, 2005). A recent review and meta-analysis of the literature (Hancock et al., 2017) revealed that compared to NT peers, autistic individuals have difficulty adhering to privacy norms (e.g., refraining from demonstrating private behaviors in public), engage in more inappropriate sexual behavior, and have greater concerns regarding their romantic future.

Higher rates of inappropriate sexual behaviors being displayed in public by autistic individuals are referred to in the literature (e.g., Coskun, Karakoc, Kircelli, & Mukaddes, 2009; Hellemans et al., 2007; Holmes & Himle, 2014), including inappropriate touching of genitals in public, touching of others' private body areas, and public masturbation. Some reports suggest that autistic males show much greater interest in sex and hypersexuality, as well as interest in more violent forms of sexuality, than other groups (Fernandes et al., 2016; Schöttle, Briken, Tüscher, & Turner, 2017). In most studies, these behaviors are reported by parents of autistic individuals as compared to NT individuals' parents (Dekker et al., 2017; Ginevra, Nota & Stokes et al., 2016; Stokes & Kaur, 2005), but autistic teens themselves do not report elevated levels of these behaviors (Dekker et al., 2017; Mehzabin & Stokes, 2011). This might be due to a lower self-awareness, a lower awareness of conventions, a lesser ability to apply these conventions, or unjustified hypersensitivity in parents of autistic children. Indeed, lower awareness of privacy norms was reported about autistic individuals as compared to TD groups (Hancock et al., 2017) when using parent report. Yet, when teenagers themselves were asked to judge sexual situations on their appropriateness, no evidence was found that revealed any misconceptions (Visser, Greaves-Lord, Tick, Verhulst, Maras & van der Vegt, 2017b). If differences were found, these revealed stronger adherence to norms when judging situations in the autistic participants. This discrepancy around privacy norms implicates hypersensitivity in parental perceptions, a phenomenon also noted in another study (Stokes, Kornienko, Scheeren, Koot, & Begeer, 2017).

Sexual Problems

To date, studies on sexual problems or dysfunctions are in small, adolescent, predominantly male samples (e.g. Roke et al., 2012) . Studies involving larger samples, more females, and adults are lacking. In the survey by Haracopos and Pedersen (1992), 28% of the autistic participants (16 to 40 years old, with and without intellectual disability) had problems fulfilling their sexual needs due to sexual dysfunctions such as erection problems, orgasm problems, and/or rigidity in sexual activity. In a recent study in the general population, 49% of men and 63% of women ever experienced one or more sexual problems, and 11% of those adult men and 15% of women reported to suffer (severely) from one or more of these sexual problems (de Graaf & Wijsen, 2017). The prevalence of a range of sexual problems over the past 6 months in a small group of adolescent boys with ASD with partnered sexual experience was comparable to rates in general population peers (11% to 50%; Dewinter et al., 2015).

Forensic Issues (Offenses)

Rutten, Vermeiren, and Van Nieuwenhuizen (2017) reviewed the literature on autism and offending in general (i.e., law-breaking behavior, not just pertaining to sex) and found that autism characteristics (e.g., limited social cognition), and not a diagnosis of autism per se, are more prevalent in forensic populations, whereas the rate of offending in autistic groups is lower compared to the general population. In the group of autistic adolescent boys in the studies by Dewinter et al. (2015, 2016) and Dekker et al. (2017), compared to NT peers, similarly low percentages of boys in both groups reported to have forced others to conduct sexual behaviors. In their study in boys accused of sex offenses, 't Hart-Kerkhoffs and colleagues (2009) found higher rates of autism characteristics compared to the general population, yet lower rates compared to peers diagnosed with ASD. In Norway, in a 10-year period of time, 0.35% of all the forensic examinations related to sexual violence reported an ASD diagnosis (Søndenaa et al., 2014). In general, there is not enough evidence available to make any firm statements about the association between autism and sex offenses in particular (Browning & Caulfield, 2011, Baarsma et al., 2016). Bleil and colleagues (2013) found not only high rates of abuse and neglect in adolescents with and without autism who were adjudicated because of sex offenses but also more depressive symptoms in those with a diagnosis of ASD compared to TD peers, especially in the autistic adolescents who reported emotional abuse or neglect. So, although there is no evidence demonstrating higher prevalence of sex offending by autistic adolescents and adults, it is important that the different actors in the criminal justice system are aware of—and sensitive to—the needs of autistic people when these individuals are suspected of sexual offending or inappropriate sexual behaviors.

Sexual Victimization

Findings related to sexual victimization in autistic samples are inconclusive to date. In the group of autistic adolescent boys in the studies by Dewinter et al. (2015, 2016), compared to NT peers, similarly low percentages of boys in both groups reported to have been forced to conduct sexual behaviors that they did not wish to engage in. Additionally, Dekker et al. (2017) found no elevated numbers regarding victimization in their sample of adolescent autistic males. However, other studies found higher rates of sexual victimization and sexual abuse in autistic adolescents and adults compared to their peers (Mandell, Walrath, Manteuffel, Sgro, & Pinto-Martin, 2005; Weiss & Fardella, 2018). The differences in the age of participants in these studies (younger adolescents vs. adults), sex differences (males vs. females), recruitment methods (e.g., screening of files of children who received care), and relatively small sample sizes in several studies might explain the discrepant findings. Based on the existing data, attention to possible sexual victimization of autistic adolescents and adults is warranted.

Etiology, Diagnosis, and Assessment

Psychosexual development is influenced by biological, psychological, and social factors (i.e., can be explained from a bio-psycho-socio-model). In general, research on psychosexual development in autistic adolescents and adults has focused on differences in sexual interest, sexual behaviors, relationship experience, sexuality education, and parental concerns as compared to NT peers. Recently, attention to the lived experience of autistic adolescents and adults has increased (Barnett & Maticka-Tyndale, 2015; Dewinter, Vermeiren, Van Parys & Van Nieuwenhuizen, 2017). Empirical evidence on factors that influence the emergence of atypical or inappropriate sexual behaviors or mechanisms that can explain differences between groups of autistic people and peers from the general population is lacking, although possible explanations have been suggested.

Biological Mechanisms

The general physical maturation and pubertal timing of autistic teenagers are comparable to that of peers from the general population (May, Pang, O'Connel & Williams, 2017). This suggests that there are no large bio-physiological alterations associated with sexuality in people with ASD. Yet, certain mechanisms might influence sexual development. For instance, some genetic syndromes that coincide with autistic features, such as Klinefelter syndrome, have particular issues regarding sexual functioning, including hypersexuality (Fisher et al., 2015; Sinha, Jnanaprakasan, & Andrade, 2012). Co-occurring psychiatric conditions, such as depression or bipolar disorder, are prevelant (e.g. Simonoff et al., 2008), and might also impact on sexual functioning. Also, pharmacological interventions, such as treatment with antidepressants and antipsychotics, can influence sexual functioning (i.e., libido). Finally, some teens and adults reported difficulties recognizing their sexual reactions (Dewinter, Vermeiren, Van Parys & Van Nieuwenhuizen, 2017). Limited interoception (i.e., the ability to recognize internal bodily signs; Dubois, Ameis, Lai, Casanova, & Desarkar, 2016) might play a causative role in this. Schöttle and colleagues (2017) hypothesized that hyposensitivity might relate to masochistic and sadistic interests and behaviors, through a need for stronger stimulation. The authors also suggest a possible influence of a higher sexual drive in autistic men, leading to higher rates of sexuality-related novelty seeking expressed in frequent sexual stimulation and paraphilic interests and behaviors.

Psychological Factors

Autism information processing characteristics/cognitive style features, like limited theory of mind (social cognition), executive functioning, and/or central coherence (e.g., Frith, 2003), might also specifically impact sociosexual functioning in autistic individuals. For example, the tendency to hyperfocus and develop extensive, detailed interests could be directed to dating etiquette and sex techniques; limited mental flexibility and perspective taking/shifting might result in rigid thinking (i.e., difficulty with changing ideas in an interaction with a partner) or relate to stalking (Stokes et al., 2007); and social cognition impairments could result in inappropriate sexual behaviors given a certain social context, such as masturbation in public or too-direct sexual proposals to potential partners. Lower awareness of social norms and lower behavioral control have also been suggested as explanations for higher rates of paraphilic interests and behaviors in autistic individuals (Schöttle et al., 2017). Yet clearly, more research is needed to test these potential explanatory mechanisms.

Social Influences

Socialization probably influences psychosexual development throughout life. People generally learn from others about sexuality in different contexts throughout their lives, starting within our family of origin and continuing through school friends, partners, and other adults we meet at work or during leisure-time activities (Ward & Beech, 2006). This is an informal, mostly unconscious learning process through observation, interpretation, trial-and-error experimentation, and feedback, which has been framed as social learning (e.g., Bandura & Walters, 1963). In their interactions with others, people generally learn socially: They obtain knowledge, attitudes, and ideas about themselves and others and gradually develop a sense of identity as a potential romantic and/or sex partner. Yet this process might unfold differently in autistic people (Bushwick, 2001). Their social limitations often result in a limited social network, thus allowing for only limited opportunities to informally learn about sexuality and relationships from peers (Stokes et al., 2007). In addition, the adult social context (parents, teachers, professionals) can be hesitant to offer early and comprehensive sexuality education or feel less skilled to discuss sexuality and romantic relationships in detail (Ballan, 2012; Holmes et al., 2014; Holmes & Himle, 2014; Nichols & Blakely-Smith, 2009), further limiting the possibilities to more formally gain knowledge, skills, and positive sexual experiences (Fernandes et al., 2016). Hancock et al. (2017) therefore argue that autistic teens have a double disadvantage: They have less access to both *formal* sexuality education and *informal* education through contact with peers. Also, although autistic people do observe their peers' behaviors, remarks, and jokes (Dewinter, Vermeiren, Van Parys & Van Nieuwenhuizen, 2017), they interpret these utilizing their own cognitive style, which can result in misinterpretations and misconceptions. Such flaws and fallacies could result in inappropriate or even deviant behaviors. In addition, the Internet offers information—both accurate and inaccurate—on all kinds of sexual behaviors, yet this is often not accompanied by information that helps with interpreting it (e.g., how to regard and understand explicit pornography). A significant number of autistic adolescents eventually find romantic and sex partners and do learn in practice, although some experience this only at a later age. Negative experiences and victimization might also play a detrimental role in the learning process (Mandell et al., 2005). Finally, the way some treatment facilities and schools are organized (e.g., single sex with little opportunity to meet others, or shared bedrooms) might negatively influence the sexual learning/experimentation experiences of autistic children, teenagers, and adults.

Diagnosis and Assessment

Research on diagnostic procedures pertaining to psychosexual functioning (i.e., ranging from assessing healthy aspects of general sexual development to psychosexual problems or actual deviance) in autistic people is scarce and mostly anecdotal. O'Reilly, Marshall, Carr, and Beckett (2004) suggested interview schedules and item lists when assessing sexual behaviors in adolescents and adults in general, but there are few diagnostic assessment tools related to sexuality specifically developed for—or studied in—autistic people. In this section, we discuss some focal points in assessment and diagnostics based on the existing literature and the clinical experience of the authors, and we suggest some questionnaires and tools that might be helpful.

INTERVIEW ASSESSMENT OF SEXUAL BEHAVIOR AND SEXUAL FUNCTIONING

Understanding sexual behavior requires information acquired through (a) questioning (e.g., interview or questionnaire) the adolescent or adult (depending on the verbal skills of the person), (b) interviewing the parents or caregivers (when appropriate and feasible), and (c) direct observations. However, due to its private nature, discussing sexuality, especially in more detail, is complicated for a lot of parents and professionals. Anxiety or refusal by the adolescent or adult can also make this discussion complicated, as do language and communication issues (e.g., literal interpretations, attributing idiosyncratic meanings to words). Based on the clinical experience of the authors, the following approaches are recommended when discussing sexuality and sexual behavior with autistic people:

- Offer a clear rationale for why you want to discuss sexuality and ensure clarity on how you will deal with the information the person discloses. Talk about the difference between this discussion in the context of mental health care and/or research versus talking about sex with other people in other situations.
- Check your vocabularies: Do you and the autistic person mean the same things using specific words? Especially when it comes to specific interests or very intimate behaviors and experiences, there is a tendency to avoid going into detail or making things concrete, which increases the risk of misunderstandings.
- Adapt to the communication style of your conversation partner: Some people like or need visual support, prefer indirect communication (e-mail, writing), or need a balance between loaded or charged versus easier topics.

When discussing an inappropriate/deviant behavior that did take place, the overall aim of the discussion is to try to understand how someone behaved; what he or she thought, felt, and expected; where he or she learned about this behavior; and how much control someone experienced, to clarify the rationale and intentions behind the behavior.

Although limited diagnostic assessment tools (i.e., interview schedules) of sexual functioning/behavior exist, questionnaires assessing psychosexual development have been developed as part of different research projects. As these questionnaires offer theoretical frameworks to assess sexual functioning and provide possible questions, two examples are discussed next.

QUESTIONNAIRE ASSESSMENT OF SEXUAL BEHAVIOR AND SEXUAL FUNCTIONING

First, the Sexual Behavior Scale (SBS) was developed (Stokes & Kaur, 2005) to assess sexual behavior in autistic children and adolescents aged 10 years and older. The original SBS comprised a parent-report and a self-report version of five scales, namely Social Behavior, Privacy Awareness, Sex Education, Sexual Behavior, and Concerns about the individual's future. As previously described, over time, the awareness increased that beyond these scales, psychosexual functioning should be conceptualized in a broader manner. Therefore, the revised SBS-II (Mehzabin & Stokes, 2011) self-report measure was developed, containing scales that measure Social Contact, Social Insight, Sexualized Behavior, and Concerns. The Sexualized Behavior scale comprises three subscales, namely Self-Directed Public Behavior, Outwardly Directed Behavior, and Invasive Behavior. Within both the SBS-I and the SBS-II, there are 40 items. Reliabilities of most scales with autistic individuals are good (Mehazabin & Stokes, 2011; Stokes & Kaur, 2005). Subsequently, the SBS-III was developed (Hancock, 2017), consisting of both self-report and proxy-report versions of 190 items distributed over 14 scales. These scales are Socializing, Social Insight, Puberty, Sexual Behavior, Romantic Relationships, Attraction, Initial Romantic Interactions, Privacy, Sexual Orientation, Sex Education, Sexual Exchanges, Formulating a Relationship, Concerns, and an optional section containing explicit sexual questions labeled Specific Sexual Behaviors. Psychometric analysis of the SBS-III shows that for both respondents from the general population and autistic respondents, scales are generally reliable, supported by an item analysis using Rasch analysis, though the scales of Puberty, Social Insight, Privacy, and Sexual Exchanges require additional development (Hancock, 2017).

Parallel to the SBS-II and -III, and for the same reason of comprehensiveness, the Teen Transition Inventory (TTI) was developed (Dekker et al., 2017). Based on the gaps noticed in previous research, an initial list of questions, their scoring options, and clustering was constructed by the researchers, that is, covering the topics of Psychosexual Socialization, Psychosexual Selfhood, and Sexual/intimate Behavior. As psychosexuality may be experienced as a rather delicate topic and is probably related to more general aspects of social and physical development, it was decided to structure the TTI in such a way (i.e., build in subheadings) that it starts with less intimate questions on more general adolescent transition issues (such as the experience of the transition to secondary school and building new friendships, physical development, and leisure activities), followed by the more personal questions on psychosexual functioning (i.e., the bulk of the questionnaire, such as building romantic relationships). Psychosexual functioning (i.e., psychosexual socialization, psychosexual selfhood, and sexual/intimate behavior) is covered by a total of 81 items in the parent-report TTI and 123 items in the self-report TTI. Table 12.1 illustrates the scale structure of the TTI divided per domain of psychosexual functioning. The TTI shows sufficient psychometric properties (for details, please see Dekker et al., 2017).

Table 12.1. Domains and Scales of the Teen Transition Inventory

Psychosexual Functioning Domains	Scales
Sexual socialization	Friendship skills
	Social acceptance by peers
	Perceived romantic skills
	Personal openness about intimacy
	Family openness about intimacy
	Adequately dealing with boundaries
Sexual selfhood	Sexual preference
	Body image
	Perceived social competence
	Social desires
	Romantic desires
	Amount of sexual desires
	Self-esteem
	Psychosexual knowledge
Sexual behavior	Amount of sexual behavior
	Types of intimate or sexual behavior and experiences
	Amount of inappropriate sexualized behavior
	Online sexual activity
	Age of onset

From Dekker, L. P., van der Vegt, E. J. M., van der Ende, J., Tick, N., Louwerse, A., Maras, A.,... Greaves-Lord, K. (2017). Psychosexual functioning of cognitively-able adolescents with autism spectrum disorder compared to typically developing peers: The development and testing of the Teen Transition Inventory—A self- and parent report questionnaire on psychosexual functioning. *Journal of Autism and Developmental Disorders, 47*(6), 1716–1738.

ASSESSING SEXUAL SITUATIONS

Besides directly assessing the psychosexual functioning of the autistic person him- or herself, it can be useful to have a tool to assess the level of appropriateness of sexual behaviors, feelings, and thoughts given the social context/situation. Such a tool can have several purposes: for example, professionally judging the behavior of a client by a professional, professionally discussing the behavior of the client with the client and/or his proxies (parents, partner, siblings, etc.), deliberating on how to react to sexual(ized) behaviors, or testing the judgment of sexual situations by the client. The Flag System (Frans, 2018; http://www.flagsystem.org) has been developed for such purposes and can also be applied to situations with autistic adolescents and adults. In this method, six criteria help in the assessment of solo and partnered sexual behaviors and offer guidance to discuss and respond to such behaviors: (a) mutual consent, (b) voluntary engagement, (c) equality, (d) age appropriateness or developmental appropriateness, (e) appropriateness within the context or situation, and (f) self-respect. The Flag System provides a set of 44 drawn illustrations of children and adolescents displaying sexual behaviors in different situations. Depending on whether sexual behaviors, feelings, or thoughts do or do not adhere to one or more of these criteria, they are labeled with a green (acceptable behavior), yellow (debatable behavior), red (unacceptable behavior), or black (offensive behavior with penalty) flag. Green-flag behavior can be respected or confirmed by parents/caregivers/professionals (affirmation). A yellow flag means that there are occasional and slight transgressions regarding one or several criteria, for instance, not age-appropriate sexual contact with a same-aged peer or sexual experimentation between same-aged peers when mutual consent is uncertain or when peer pressure plays a role. Yellow-flag behavior can be limited (but not forbidden) by parents/caregivers and professionals. A red flag means more serious or repeated transgressions of the criteria, such as intimate contact between two adolescents who differ by more than 6 years in age, or sexual behavior with coercion from one party to the other. Red-flag behavior should be forbidden. A black flag is tantamount to sexual abuse or seriously risky sexual behavior, such as rape, forced sex, or exhibitionism. Black-flag behavior is legally forbidden and will be followed up with setting boundaries, punishment, or treatment. To illustrate the usefulness of this system, to follow we discuss two case examples and subsequently judge the sexual behaviors of these cases according to the Flag System criteria (Table 12.2).

CASE EXAMPLES

Case example 1. Tim (aged 34, diagnosed with ASD, IQ above average, living independently) seeks help because he never had a partner. He finds it very difficult to say whether he feels attracted to women, men, or both. His social contacts take place with colleagues at work, and he meets weekly with a small group of friends he has known for years to play board games. His therapist tried to stimulate him to think about his attraction by discussing pictures of all kinds of people and suggested to him to try online dating. During these sessions it becomes clear that Tim experiences sexual arousal and uses pornographic materials to masturbate. He looks for people dressed in leather or rubber with their head covered. He also wears a raincoat to masturbate because that stimulates his arousal.

Table 12.2. Assessing Sexual Situations Using the Flag System

Flag System Criteria	Case Example 1: Tim	Case Example 2: Michael
Mutual consent	v No partner involved	**X** Girl did not consent
Voluntary engagement	v No partner involved and following own feelings	**X** Girl did not volunteer
Equality	v No partner involved	**X** Difference in age, knowledge, and developmental level
Age/developmental appropriateness	v Masturbation is age appropriate, little partnered experience	? Age-appropriate curiosity to opposite-sex body
Appropriateness within the context	v Respects privacy	~ Not in public
Self-respect	v No self-hurting, no negative effects of this behavior	**X** Harmful, because this might lead to police contacts, anger by others, guilt, etc.
Conclusion	Masturbation and interest in leather or rubber are no reason for concern Need for insight in sexuality education, sexual development, and social feelings and skills	- (Unintended) sexual offense Need to explain constructs like mutual agreement, voluntariness, developmentally appropriate experimentation, etc.

v = Flag System criterion is met; **X** = Flag System criterion is not met.
Applied from Frans, E. (2018). *Sensoa Flag System: Reacting to sexually (un)acceptable behaviour of children and young people.* Antwerp-Apeldoorn, Belgium: Garant.

Case example 2 (from Visser, 2017, with permission). Michael (aged 15, average intelligence) was not diagnosed with ASD previously, but his parents always knew that he was different from other children. Michael barely connected with his classmates and never brought friends home to socialize. However, he sometimes played with other children in the neighborhood. One day, he touched the intimate parts of a 9-year-old neighborhood girl and forced her to touch his penis. After this incident, the parents of the girl pressed charges and Michael and his parents were placed in an intensive multisystem therapy program. Because of the incident, Michael and his parents were harassed by people from the small community they lived in. Michael could not go to school anymore. The probation officer was the first to notice how Michael made contact with people in a strange and awkward way.

ASSESSMENT OF AUTISTIC INDIVIDUALS WITH MODERATE TO SEVERE INTELLECTUAL DISABILITY

No assessment tools have been developed exclusively for the group of autistic individuals with moderate to severe intellectual disability. In this group of individuals, self-report will not always be feasible and therefore parent/caregiver reports will be important. Several studies on sexuality in ASD that have included a larger sample of individuals with a lower level of intellectual functioning have used informant-based questionnaires/interviews (Fernandes et al., 2016; Haracopos & Pedersen, 1992; Van Bourgondien et al., 1997). In one study, an investigation of interrater as well as intercode reliability was performed on the questionnaire and showed a concordance of 0.86 and 0.97, respectively (Haracopos & Pedersen, 1992). These kinds of instruments mainly focus on behavior that could be deviant and provide a lesser focus on sexual health. Therefore, they are probably not suitable for planning a broader sexual educational program for the autistic individual, but perhaps useful if problematic behavior is the focus and a behavioral treatment intervention is needed.

Treatment

The goal of treatment should be to support autistic individuals in enjoying relations and/or sexual experiences in their own—neurodiverse—way and at the same time help them to be accepted in contemporary societies and prevent marginalization or illegal acting. In the discussion and evaluation of sexuality with autistic individuals, the complexity of one's own versus others' perspectives/needs (i.e., comparison of own ideas, feelings, and behaviors to societal conventions regarding normality vs. deviance) and the interaction between the individual and the context need to be taken into account.

Studies on the treatment of sexual problems in autistic people are almost absent and mostly consist of case studies. Recently, some authors (Attwood, Hénault, & Dubin, 2014; Higgs & Carter, 2015) discussed how to be responsive to autistic characteristics in the general forensic field. A number of people with autism get involved in the criminal justice system, and in some there is a link between their autism characteristics and their criminal behaviors (Woodbury-Smith & Dein, 2014). The criminal justice system is often not attuned to autistic people and does not offer responsive interventions (Attwood et al., 2014; Higgs & Carter, 2015; Sevlever et al., 2013). Care and treatment of these autistic adults who have sexually offended can be attuned to the needs of autistic people (Higgs & Carter, 2015), yet research on the effects of such attuned interventions is still needed (Woodbury-Smith & Dein, 2014). Given that group-based interventions in forensic settings require participants to carry out introspecting, sharing personal information, and interacting within a group—all activities that an individual with ASD may find challenging—special efforts need to be made to develop interventions that work responsively, safely, appropriately, and effectively. Individual treatment, possibly in combination with a group-based approach, often is advisable in the experience of the authors.

In addition, over the past decade, attention toward sexual education needs increased and attuned programs were developed and evaluated for autistic people. Several publications stressed the importance of proactively (i.e., at the start of sexual maturation) discussing sexuality and relationship issues in a concrete and explicit way that suits the mental age and cognitive style of the autistic adolescent and improving communication skills of parents and professionals (e.g., Dekker et al., 2015; Holmes & Himle, 2014). Also, attention to the relational and/or sexual experiences of autistic adolescents and adults themselves grew, and tolerance and respect toward positive deviation or nonproblematic sexual and relationship diversity have been stressed (e.g., Dewinter, De Graaf & Begeer, 2017). We feel that these are important developments that can add to greater sexual well-being of autistic people and to the prevention of problems.

Based on our clinical experience, offering comprehensive education (as described later) and discussing concrete experiences are often major parts of treatment when autistic adolescents and adults are referred for concerns relating to sexuality and relationships. Often, support to caregivers around these adolescents and adults in dealing with sexual desires and behaviors is important. Apart from this, we mostly apply cognitive behavioral and systemic interventions aimed at specific complaints or problems, taking autistic features and information processing styles into account (see, e.g., Higgs & Carter, 2015). Sometimes, off-label psychopharmacological interventions are used to influence behavioral regulation or sexual responses (Dewinter, van der Miesen & Graham Holmes, 2019, in preparation). Unintended side effects of medication on sexual functioning, such as a diminished sexual response, should also be considered when working with autistic adolescents and adults.

This treatment section starts with information on sexuality education programs. We briefly point out ways to apply the earlier mentioned Flag System in this context. Finally, we discuss sexuality education in autistic people with co-occurring intellectual disability.

Relationship and Sexuality Education

Research has demonstrated the importance of comprehensive sexuality education (CSE) in promoting sexual well-being in NT adolescents (Kendall, 2014). However, CSE is not always comprehensive enough to support autistic children and adolescents to learn about—and deal with—the complexities that come with psychosexual maturation and socialization (Barnett & Maticka-Tyndale, 2015; Dewinter, Van Parys, Vermeiren, & van Nieuwenhuizen, 2017), nor is the educational style always attuned to the detail-focused, literal information processing style of many autistic teenagers. In the evaluation of a standardized CSE program that was specifically tailored to the cognitive style of autistic adolescents (i.e., Tackling Teenage Training; Dekker et al., 2015), some participants asked for additional information on their personal themes like fetishism or gender identity issues (Visser, 2017, George & Stokes, 2017). Although this additional information was provided during this intervention in the light of personalizing the intervention, it was not (yet) a standard part of the curriculum offered to all participants. Based on this input from users, the program was recently updated. Because other studies showed that the more complex themes relating to sexuality development are discussed less by parents and professionals (Holmes et al., 2014; Holmes & Himle, 2014), parent involvement in autism-friendly CSE such as Tackling Teenage Training needs to be optimized.

Several authors explored and discussed how sexuality education should be attuned to the needs of autistic children and adolescents (Ballan & Freyer, 2017; Corona, Fox, Christodulu, & Worlock, 2015; Hannah & Stagg, 2016; Loftin, 2015; Pask, Hughes, & Sutton, 2016). Beddows and Brooks (2015) specifically reviewed the existing research relating to sexuality education for autistic adolescents who demonstrated inappropriate sexual behaviors. Attwood et al. (2014) describe the experiences of the last author relating to his sexuality development and offer advice pertaining to sexuality education for autistic individuals and how to react to inappropriate behaviors.

EVIDENCE-BASED PREVENTIVE INTERVENTION: TACKLING TEENAGE TRAINING

The Tackling Teenage Training (TTT) program (Boudesteijn et al., 2011; Dekker et al., 2015) provides psychoeducation on a variety of psychosexual topics, targeting all domains of psychosexual functioning—that is, sexual behavior, sexual selfhood (i.e., intrapersonal aspects of sexuality), and sexual socialization (i.e., interpersonal aspects of sexuality). The program is specifically tailored to the needs and cognitive style of cognitively able (i.e., average to highly intelligent) adolescents with ASD aged 12 to 18 years old, with a particular focus on obtaining theoretical as well as practical knowledge (e.g., explicit explanation of often implicit rules and practice of conversational skills).

Theoretical Background

Healthy psychosexual functioning requires specific knowledge and skills in all psychosexual domains, for example, regarding personal hygiene, developing and maintaining relationships, recognizing and acknowledging personal boundaries (both of self and others), and intimacy/sexual activity with or without partners ('t Hart-Kerkhoffs et al., 2009; Hénault, 2006; Maniglio, 2012). Research has shown that sex education programs that positively impact sexual behavior in TD individuals incorporate increasing sexual knowledge (Kirby et al., 2007; Rock et al., 2005; Ryan et al., 2007). Psychosexual knowledge may therefore be important with regard to both making informed decisions (e.g., regarding reproduction, intimate behaviors, and understanding boundaries; e.g., Urbano et al., 2013) and promoting healthy psychosexual behavior, such as the use of condoms (e.g., Rock et al., 2005). Theoretical (e.g., definitions of sexual terminology) and practical psychosexual knowledge (e.g., how to appropriately deal with different situations, such as personal hygiene or communication about sexual topics) are important for healthy psychosexual functioning. Limited knowledge of psychosexual topics in autistic adolescents may, in certain cases, escalate into inappropriate behaviors, frustration, or anxiety. This may be a result of limited understanding of private versus public sexual behavior (Nichols & Blakeley-Smith, 2009) or even dangerous situations, for instance, due to the limited ability to identify abusive behavior (Sevlever et al., 2013). Therefore, the TTT program was designed to offer guidance and support with tackling the difficulties that autistic adolescents may encounter regarding psychosexual functioning by increasing their knowledge and skills regarding this topic.

Structure and Content

The TTT program is a manualized individual training program (Boudesteijn et al., 2011), consisting of 18 sessions covering the topics displayed in Table 12.3.

These topics are all discussed and practiced in a structured manner with the adolescent in one-on-one training sessions. The trainer and adolescent have one session a week, during which one topic is discussed, and exercises are practiced, in approximately 45 minutes. The training program can be provided in the school setting, in outpatient or inpatient facilities, or at the home of the adolescent (if certain conditions can be met, such as a private space and no disturbance from family members).

The training starts and ends with an appointment with the adolescent and the parents. After each session, parents are informed through e-mail about the topic of the session (i.e., psychoeducation) and the take-home assignment of the adolescent. In this way the parent is involved in the learning process and is coached to show the right amount of involvement after the program is finished.

Evidence Base

So far, evidence for the effectiveness of the TTT comes from two studies. A first pilot study by Dekker and colleagues (2015) showed that a group of 30 autistic adolescents (77% male; aged 11 to 19 years) had a significant increase in psychosexual knowledge after completing the program. In a subsequent randomized controlled trial among 189 autistic adolescents (78% male; aged 12 to 18 years), significant treatment effects were shown for psychosexual knowledge and adequate insight into boundaries, both posttreatment and after a 6-month follow-up (Visser, Greaves-Lord, Tick, Verhulst, Maras & van der Vegt, 2017). The TTT program was most effective

Table 12.3. Overview of Sessions and Themes in the Tackling Teenage Training Program

Sessions	Themes
Session 1 Talking about puberty	Discussing puberty (i.e., how and with whom)
Session 2 This is me	Appearances
Session 3 A good first impression	First impressions
Session 4 What do you call that?	Appropriately naming body parts
Session 5 Changes during puberty in boys	Male physical changes
Session 6 Changes during puberty in girls	Female physical changes
Session 7 Making love to yourself	Masturbation: conventions and hygiene
Session 8 Friendship	How to become and maintain friends
Session 9 Being in love and stuff...	Falling in love
Session 10 Doubts and confusion during puberty	Sexual orientation
Session 11 Being in love and dating	Falling in love and dating
Session 12 Safe sex	Sexual intercourse, contraception, and sexually transmitted diseases
Session 13 The first time	Sexual intercourse
Session 14 Pregnancy and birth	Pregnancy
Session 15 Where do you draw the line?	Setting and respecting boundaries
Session 16 Yours and other people's boundaries	Setting and respecting boundaries
Session 17 Internet and making contact	Safe Internet use
Session 18 Bad boyfriends (session for girls)	Abusive boyfriends

From: Boudesteijn, F., Van der Vegt, E. J. M., Visser, K., Tick, N. T., & Maras, A. (2011). *Psychoseksuele ontwikkeling bij adolescenten met een autismespectrumstoornis; Ik Puber-training.* Assen, The Netherlands: Van Gorcum BV.

for younger adolescents with ASD (12 to 14 years old), with elevated psychosexual knowledge as well as elevated social functioning in this age group. Currently, research on a group-based version of the intervention is ongoing.

To illustrate how the TTT program is applied, we continue with the previous case example.

Case example 2—continued (from Visser, 2017, with permission). During the intake meeting of the TTT training, Michael came with his mother and told the trainer that—because of what happened—he would never want to have a girlfriend, or anything to do with girls anymore, and he would never want to have sex. To manage expectations, Michael and his mother subsequently received information on the content of the TTT program and agreed on the way that Michael's parents would be kept informed on the progress during the training. Goals of the training were determined: The first aim was to provide Michael with information on the physical changes in puberty for boys and girls and explain body functions, such as sexual arousal. The subsequent aim was to discuss identifying boundaries of others and teach Michael about varying levels of appropriate to inappropriate sexual behaviors.

In the first meeting with Michael, it became clear that he did have a healthy interest in—and normal curiosity toward—sexuality, but that he lacked the information on how he could appropriately handle his changing feelings (e.g., sexual arousal) and his changing body (e.g., getting erections). In the past, he had become curious about the physical differences between boys and girls, which had ultimately led to the incident with the younger neighborhood girl. Even though before the incident Michael did not have severe social problems in school, he did not have close friends with whom he could share personal questions. Michael also never asked his parents questions regarding puberty or sexuality. His parents had assumed that the topic was discussed at school, and that if Michael would have had additional questions, he would address them. As Michael did not take the initiative to talk about his curiosity, his parents also did not start the conversation, because they thought he was not (yet) thinking about sexuality. Given his problems with social cognition (which were only acknowledged after the incident), it was difficult for Michael to think about the consequences of his actions for the younger girl and her feelings. The incident with the girl seemed to be an impulsive act to deal with his curiosity/arousal. After the diagnosis of ASD, parents received psychoeducation regarding ASD and learned that it is often difficult for people with ASD to ask questions/initiate important conversations.

At the start of the training program, Michael still remained reluctant to share personal information and was resistant to complete the assignments. He had decided that he no longer wanted to have anything to do with sexuality/intimate relationships, and therefore he did not find it relevant to learn about sexual themes. To nuance his perspective, the trainer nevertheless started with a few sessions, providing information on psychosexual development, and this period was used to build up a trusting work relationship with Michael. Once Michael realized the trainer was not going to judge him regarding the deviant incident, and that the TTT program provided the opportunity to ask questions regarding a broad range of topics that did after all raise his curiosity (e.g., regarding his changing body and changing feelings), he felt more safe to discuss issues openly and his motivation to follow the TTT program increased. An important part of the intervention for Michael was teaching him to deal with his sexuality in an appropriate (i.e., less extreme in either direction) way. An additional goal of the intervention for Michael and his parents was to stimulate conversations about psychosexual themes among them in the home setting. His parents received guidelines on how to discuss sexuality with Michael, even if he did not (yet) initiate the conversation/ask questions. During the TTT program, Michael started at a new school. This provided the opportunity to focus the training also on starting (casual) conversations with people he did not know before and developing new friendships with peers. The first time Michael went to his new school, his probation officer went with him, and Michael openly told his new class about his ASD and the incident that had happened. This revelation was prepared and evaluated during the TTT training sessions.

In the final evaluation meeting of the TTT program with Michael and his parents, a discussion of how Michael had gained psychosexual knowledge and insight into interpersonal boundaries was conducted, including how he had improved his social skills, such as making eye contact. Parents rated the intervention with an overall grade of 8.5 out of 10, and Michael himself was moderately positive, rating a 6 out of 10 regarding overall satisfaction. Because further improvement of social skills could be beneficial for Michael, he was invited to follow a subsequent social skills training, but Michael declined because of a lack of motivation. The parents were now very much more involved in Michael's life, and they had more conversations about puberty themes at home. They also achieved a rather high control over Michael's behavior, which was not age appropriate but understandable considering their history. His parents therefore were offered additional meetings with a family therapist to gradually guide them toward the age-appropriate separation from their adolescent son. The training ended with the parents expressing pride in how Michael handled his start at the new school and his new social contacts.

Handling Sexual Situations

As discussed earlier, the Flag System (Frans, 2018) offers criteria to evaluate the appropriateness of sexual behaviors in children and adolescents and offers guidelines for caregivers to react to—and deal with—appropriate and inappropriate behaviors in children and adolescents in general. Attention of and reactions by caregivers are probably the most important and powerful ways to influence problematic sexual behaviors. Although originally not developed for these means, the Flag System criteria also offer a framework to evaluate sexual behaviors of adults, and can be used in discussion with adolescents and adults about how they can ensure that they attune their behaviors to a situation in a socially acceptable way. Clinicians can discuss with autistic adolescents and adults in treatment how they can interpret the different criteria (e.g., what is consent, when is someone equal, what are personal and others' desires and boundaries, and how are these communicated) and how to apply these criteria in their daily lives. In this way, the Flag System criteria can also offer guidelines to deal with relationships and sexual situations in a healthy and respectful way.

SEXUAL EDUCATION AND INTERVENTION IN AUTISTIC ADOLESCENTS AND ADULTS WITH INTELLECTUAL DISABILITY

Like the group of autistic individuals in the normal IQ range, the group of autistic individuals with intellectual disability also faces unmet needs of sexuality education programs, information and communication materials (e.g., in simple language and pictures), and provision of multiple sessions to address the content, which is not always accessible at learning institutions (WHO, 2009). Existing sexuality education programs targeted toward individuals with intellectual disability (with or without ASD) seem to lack an autism-friendly approach (i.e., attuning to their cognitive style) and are thus unlikely to be effective (Schaafsma, Stoffelen, Kok, & Curfs, 2013).

Adolescents and adults with intellectual disability often live in group homes or residential settings with staff to provide care and health service to them. Many barriers to sexuality education are identified in such environments, for example, lack of staff member experience dealing with sexuality, concerns about the reactions of other staff members or parents if they would talk about sexuality, or policies on sexuality within organizations that are often inadequate or simply not present (Abbott & Howarth, 2007). When sex education is provided in these kinds of residential settings, it tends to be more reactive (e.g., due to a behavioral problem) than proactive (e.g., to prevent a problem). If there is a sexuality policy for the organization, its implementation is not always guaranteed (e.g., only part of the staff knows the content of it; Schaafsma, Kok, Stoffelen, van Doorn, & Curfs, 2014). Consequence can be misinterpretations of sexual behavior and idiosyncratic responses to similar situations. Differences in response may lead to differences in quality of care (Schaafsma et al., 2014). Methods such as the Flag System (Frans, 2018) can be valuable to strengthen staff collaboration and attention to sexual situations and their reactions to them.

The shortcomings and challenges described have been recognized and discussed in the Danish social and health system. As a result of this discussion, the Danish Social Ministry has published a set of guidelines for sexual health service for adults with disabilities describing the ethical and legal context for this service (Danish Social Ministry, 2012). Besides guidance in how to formulate and implement a sexuality policy within organizations, the guidelines also describe a systematic approach to sexuality counseling and help based on the PLISSIT model. PLISSIT stands for Permission, Limited Information, Specific Suggestions, and Intensive Therapy and is a proposed conceptual scheme for the behavioral treatment of sexual problems (Annon, 1976). According to the PLISSIT model, the counseling and help should start with ensuring that the professionals working with the adult with the sexual problem are prepared to talk about sexuality with the person; the next step could be to provide more general information about the adult body, emotions, intimate relations, and sexual behavior in relation to the problem the adult presents to the professional; a next step is providing specific information about sexual aids and how it is possible to enable a sex life despite a disability. At this level of counseling the adult can also be referred to a medical practitioner or psychologist. At the last level more intensive therapy, direct help, or training in a specific skill (e.g., show the adult how to use a sex device, how to masturbate in a pleasurable, nonpainful way) can be provided. Before a sexual intervention plan is started, according to the guidelines it is mandatory to analyze the specific behavioral problem that gives rise to concerns, make a written report on this analysis, and describe how a plan should progress. The intervention plan should take into consideration the PLISSIT model's stepwise approach, with the social and health professional staff deciding which step in the model will be necessary and sufficient to help the person. Before starting the plan, the staff must get permission from the person him- or herself in written, verbal, or nonverbal format, depending on the person's communicative abilities. If the organization needs assistance implementing the intervention, it can get help from social and health care staff with special education in sexuality (http://www.seksualvejlederuddannelsen.dk) and legal advice from the municipal authorities.

Summary and Future Directions

Limitations Within Research to Date

Before providing a summary, we want to emphasize the fact that the information in this chapter is based on a small (albeit growing) literature base, with several methodological limitations (such as the use of small samples, limited use of multidimensional measures, limited use of a TD control group, nonrepresentative male-to-female gender ratios, use of samples with a narrow age and IQ range, and use of mainly one informant). Although these methodological issues are improving in ongoing research, the reader should keep them in mind when interpreting and applying the findings so far.

Summary

The attention toward sexuality and romantic relationships in autistic people has increased over recent decades. During this time, perspectives on psychosexual development changed from the initial idea that sexuality was less relevant to autistic people to the present idea that psychosexual development is a normative part of development and an important aspect of daily life and well-being in all people, including autistic individuals.

Case reports and a very limited number of empirical studies point out that some autistic adolescents and adults show atypical sexual interests and behaviors. Review of this literature suggests that experiencing the sociosexual aspects of life can be different, and sometimes difficult, for autistic individuals. Some autistic adolescents and adults experience or demonstrate problems relating to sexuality, dating, or dealing with a partner. Others experience other kinds of attraction, stimulation, or relationship types. Many autistic individuals have been deprived of suitable education and support pertaining to sex and relationships, sometimes resulting in inappropriate behaviors. Differing from general norms and values can be stressful for autistic people; however, it is not always harmful or unacceptable. In this chapter, we discussed that atypical sexual interests and behaviors can be deviant from the general cultural norms without being harmful, and that views on what is "normal" change over time and differ across cultures. Therefore, when clinicians encounter issues regarding sexual behaviors, we suggest increased awareness of how to interpret and evaluate specific sexual behaviors in context: Sexuality might initially appear deviant in some cases without being intentionally inappropriate or harmful. Thus, one should be careful in interpretation and response. A thorough knowledge of the cognitive style of autistic people is crucial when assessing sexual behaviors in this population. We recommend the Flag System criteria as a general framework to assess the appropriateness of sexual behaviors in daily life (Frans, 2018).

Little is known about the prevalence and course of atypical sexual interests and "deviant" sexual behaviors in autistic individuals. Case studies and the limited existing research suggest a higher prevalence, compared to NT peers. Although we often view these atypical behaviors as a result of the autistic mind and limited sex education, we have hardly any evidence on underlying etiological mechanisms.

Questionnaires like the SBS and TTI have been developed to study psychosexual functioning in autistic people, and these can support an assessment of psychosexual functioning in autistic adolescents and adults. To our knowledge, no specific diagnostic instruments (i.e., interviews/observation schedules) exist to date.

Guidelines and treatment methods specifically designed to influence sexual behaviors and interests in autistic people are lacking. However, comprehensive and detailed sex education programs such as Tackling Teenage Training exist that promote open and explicit communication. In addition, we formulated some practical guidelines based on our clinical experience. A good understanding of autism characteristics, the experience of individuals, and sexual functioning offers a necessary and sufficient basis to provide attuned support or treatment to autistic individuals presenting with sexuality-related problems.

Taken together, based on the framework of sexual well-being (WHO, 2006), we argue for attention to sexuality and relationships for autistic people at different levels (Frans & De Bruycker, 2012). At the *individual* level, we should prevent sexual or relationship problems, without denying individuals the freedom to explore and experiment. As a *society*, we have to provide the means to offer autistic youngsters the information they need to deal with their sexuality and with relationships in a way that suits them and that is not harmful to themselves or others. This idea includes the notion of diversity and might result in deviance from the general norm. As a society that values well-being and equality for all, regardless of developmental differences, we should provide support to assist autistic individuals to achieve maximal fulfillment and life satisfaction.

Future Directions in Research

Despite the increasing attention to sexuality and romance in autistic children, adolescents, and adults evidenced by the growing number of scientific and popular papers and books, our insight into this developmental domain and part of life is only emerging. In 2018, a special interest group (SIG) at the annual International Society for Autism Research meeting was initiated, titled "Sexuality, Romance and Being Autistic: Learning From the Experience and Needs of Adolescents and Adults." The SIG's aim was to explore directions for future research based on the input of scientists, autistic adults, and other stakeholders (e.g., clinicians, teachers). The focus of this exploration was not solely on deviance and problems—as this is a narrow view—but on understanding diversity and supporting sexual well-being in autistic people. Although preliminary, the following themes emerged (Dewinter, Holmes, & Van der Miesen, 2019)

1. GETTING A BETTER PICTURE

Several questions pertained to gaining a deeper insight into sexual and romantic experiences across the lifespan, across all levels of intellectual functioning, and in different contexts and cultures. Most research has focused on adolescents and emerging adults, so themes related to later adulthood emerged, such as the "success rate" of different kinds of romantic relationships, pregnancy and parenthood, and the associations between sexuality, romance, health, and well-being. A specific topic of interest was the influence of medication on sexual functioning. Also, understanding the experiences and needs of autistic LGBT adolescents and adults, and sexual identity development in general, was found to be important.

2. IMPROVING SUPPORT AND TREATMENT

In all stakeholder groups, the importance of developing and evaluating ways to offer sexuality education, prevention, treatment, and support regarding sexual health/well-being and satisfying relationships was stressed. Participants in these groups referred not only to interventions aimed at autistic individuals but also to ways to involve and support parents, caregivers, and/or partners.

3. INCLUDING AUTISTIC VIEWS AND INFLUENCING SOCIETAL VIEWS

A final theme pertained to how society can be better informed, more tolerant, and more open-minded toward the capabilities of autistic people relating to sexuality and romantic relationships. Acceptance and appreciation of autistic characteristics and strengths in this domain were determined to be important. There was also a wide call for collaborative research with autism advocates, researchers, and other stakeholders to stimulate research that adds to the lives of those whom it is all about.

These findings direct us to gain a better understanding of the whole spectrum of autistic people within different contexts and into complex processes and issues that lie below observable sexual behaviors. Future research should facilitate sexual and relationship well-being in as many autistic people as possible by educating and supporting autistic adolescents and adults as well as by supporting and changing views and attitudes in both the direct context and broader society.

Future Directions in Practice

Despite the need for future research, we already can contribute to the well-being of autistic children, adolescents, and adults relating to sexuality and relationships in daily life. As parents, educators, and professionals, we can address this topic; offer comprehensive education; respond to questions, needs, and desires in an open and respectful way; name positive and negative deviant behaviors; and help in dealing with them in an acceptable way.

In the Netherlands, during the past 4 years, we built an interdisciplinary network to enhance knowledge utilization and dissemination regarding autism (the Academic Workplace Autism [AWA], http://www.academischewerkplaatsautisme.nl/). Within this network, one work group focused on relationships and sexuality in autistic people (http://autisme-samendoen.nl/english). This work group considered the existing, most often used regular education sex education curricula and evaluated the suitability of these for autistic students. The aim of this work group was to provide more knowledge and training to educational staff and parents in order for them to become more comfortable discussing intimate relationship and sexuality topics. One future direction is to further optimize this type of training for educational professionals and evaluate the results.

In line with this, good access to suitable, appropriate educational materials should be improved. This is important given that primarily biased material is currently presented online, which can stimulate the development of ill-conceived and inappropriate ideas and norms (Chia & Gunther, 2006). Many well-developed comprehensive sex education programs are available. Therefore, online access to such programs (i.e., through websites or apps) that are suitable for autistic people should be improved (e.g., video tutorials, online counseling, online web coaching). The guidelines published by the Danish Social Ministry provide an example of how we apply the PLISSIT model in the context of help and support to sexuality-related problems in autistic adolescents and adults while we await evidence on the effectiveness of specific interventions in autistic individuals.

Acknowledgments

We want to thank all our previous coauthors who published with us on this topic, with a special thank you to Dr. Linda Dekker and Dr. Kirsten Visser, given the adapted use of work from their PhD theses.

We also want to thank all organizers and participants of the SIG on sexuality and autism at the International Society for Autism Research 2018 Annual Meeting, with a special thank you to Anna van der Miesen and Dr. Laura Holmes, given their hard work on the preliminary results as presented in the "future directions" section.

References

Abbott, D., & Howarth, J. (2007). Still off-limits? Staff views on supporting gay, lesbian and bisexual people with intellectual disabilities to develop sexual and intimate relationships? *Journal of Applied Research in Intellectual Disabilities, 20*, 116–125.

Annon, J. (1976). *Behavioral treatment of sexual problems. Brief therapy*. Maryland MD: Harper & Row.

Attwood, T., Hénault, I., & Dubin, N. (2014). *The autism spectrum, sexuality and the law: What every parent and professional needs to know*. London, UK: Jessica Kingsley Publishers.

Baarsma, M. E., Boonmann, C., 't Hart-Kerkhoffs,L. A., de Graaf, H., Doreleijers, T. A. H., Vermeiren, R. R. J. M., & Jansen, L. M. C. (2016). Sexuality and autistic-like symptoms in juvenile sex offenders: A follow-up after 8 years. *Journal of Autism and Developmental Disorders, 46*(8), 2679–2691. http://doi.org/10.1007/s10803-016-2805-6

Ballan, M. S. (2012). Parental perspectives of communication about sexuality in families of children with autism spectrum disorders. *Journal of Autism and Developmental Disorders, 42*, 676–684. http://doi.org/10.1007/s10803-011-1293-y

Ballan, M. S., & Freyer, M. B. (2017). Autism spectrum disorder, adolescence, and sexuality education: Suggested interventions for mental health professionals. *Sexuality and Disability, 35*(2), 1–13. http://doi.org/10.1007/s11195-017-9477-9

Bandura, A., & Walters, R.H. (1963). *Social learning and personality development*. New York, NY: Holt Rinehart and Winston.

Barnett, J. P., & Maticka-Tyndale, E. (2015). Qualitative exploration of sexual experiences among adults on the autism spectrum: Implications for sex education. *Perspectives on Sexual and Reproductive Health, 47*(4), 171–179. http://doi.org/10.1363/47e5715

Bedard, C., Zhang, H. L., & Zucker, K. J. (2010). Gender identity and sexual orientation in people with developmental disabilities. *Sexuality and Disability, 28*(3), 165–175. http://doi.org/10.1007/s11195-010-9155-7

Beddows, N., & Brooks, R. (2016). Inappropriate sexual behaviour in adolescents with autism spectrum disorder: What education is recommended and why. *Early Intervention in Psychiatry, 10*(4), 282–289. http://doi.org/10.1111/eip.12265

Bertilsdotter Rosqvist, H. (2014). Becoming an "autistic couple": Narratives of sexuality and couplehood within the Swedish autistic self-advocacy movement. *Sexuality and Disability, 32*(3), 351–363. http://doi.org/10.1007/s11195-013-9336-2

Bleil Walters, J., Hughes, T. L., Sutton, L. R., Marshall, S. N., Crothers, L. M., Lehman, C., . . . Huang, A. (2013). Maltreatment and depression in adolescent sexual offenders with an autism spectrum disorder. *Journal of Child Sexual Abuse, 22*(1), 72–89. http://doi.org/10.1080/10538712.2013.735357

Boudesteijn, F., Van der Vegt, E. J. M., Visser, K., Tick, N. T., & Maras, A. (2011). *Psychoseksuele ontwikkeling bij adolescenten met een autismespectrumstoornis; Ik Puber-training*. Assen, The Netherlands: Van Gorcum BV.

Browning, A., & Caulfield, L. (2011). The prevalence and treatment of people with Asperger's syndrome in the criminal justice system. *Criminology and Criminal Justice, 11*(2), 165–180. http://doi.org/10.1177/1748895811398455

Bushwick, N. L. (2001). Social learning and the etiology of autism. *New Ideas in Psychology, 19*(1), 49–75.

Byers, E. S., Nichols, S., & Voyer, S. D. (2013). Challenging stereotypes: Sexual functioning of single adults with high functioning autism spectrum disorder. *Journal of Autism and Developmental Disorders, 43*, 2617–2627. http://doi.org/10.1007/s10803-013-1813-z

Byers, E. S., Nichols, S., Voyer, S. D., & Reilly, G. (2012). Sexual well-being of a community sample of high-functioning adults on the autism spectrum who have been in a romantic relationship. *Autism, 17*(4), 418–433. http://doi.org/10.1177/1362361311431950

Byers, E. S., & Nichols, S. (2014). Sexual satisfaction of high-functioning adults with autism spectrum disorder. *Sexuality and Disability, 32*(3), 365–382. http://doi.org/10.1007/s11195-014-9351-y

Chia, S. C., & Gunther, A. C. (2006). How Media Contribute to Misperceptions of Social Norms About Sex. Mass Communication & Society, *9*(3), 301–320.

Corona, L. L., Fox, S. A., Christodulu, K. V., & Worlock, J. A. (2015). Providing education on sexuality and relationships to adolescents with autism spectrum disorder and their parents. *Sexuality and Disability, 34*(2), 199–214. http://doi.org/10.1007/s11195-015-9424-6

Coskun, M., Karakoc, S., Kircelli, F., & Mukaddes, N. M. (2009). Effectiveness of mirtazapine in the treatment of inappropriate sexual behaviors in individuals with autistic disorder. *Journal of Child and Adolescent Psychopharmacology, 19*(2), 203–206. http://doi.org/10.1089/cap.2008.020

Danish Social Ministry. (2012). "Seksualitet på dagsordenen En håndbog om professionel støtte til voksne med funktionsnedsættelse." *Socialstyrelsen.*

De Graaf, H., & Wijsen, C. (2017). Seksuele gezondheid in Nederlmand 2017 [Sexual Health in the Netherlands 2017]. Utrecht: Rutgers. Retrieved from https://www.rutgers.nl/sites/rutgersnl/files/PDF-Onderzoek/Seksuele_Gezondheid_in_NL_2017_23012018.pdf

de Vries, A. L. C., Noens, I. L. J., Cohen-Kettenis, P. T., van Berckelaer-Onnes, I. A., & Doreleijers, T. A. (2010). Autism spectrum disorders in gender dysphoric children and adolescents. *Journal of Autism and Developmental Disorders, 40*(8), 930–936. http://doi.org/10.1007/s10803-010-0935-9

Dekker, L. P., van der Vegt, E. J. M., van der Ende, J., Tick, N., Louwerse, A., Maras, A., . . . Greaves-Lord, K. (2017). Psychosexual functioning of cognitively-able adolescents with autism spectrum disorder compared to typically developing peers: The development and testing of the Teen Transition Inventory—A self- and parent report questionnaire on psychosexual functioning. *Journal of Autism and Developmental Disorders, 47*(6), 1716–1738.

Dekker, L. P., Van Der Vegt, E. J. M., & Visser, K. (2015). Improving psychosexual knowledge in adolescents with autism spectrum disorder: Pilot of the Tackling Teenage Training program. *Journal of Autism and Developmental Disorders, 45*(6), 1532–1540. http://doi.org/10.1007/s10803-014-2301-9

Dewinter, J., De Graaf, H., & Begeer, S. (2017). Sexual orientation, gender identity, and romantic relationships in adolescents and adults with autism spectrum disorder. *Journal of Autism And Developmental Disorders, 47*(9), 2927–2934. http://doi.org/10.1007/s10803-017-3199-9

Dewinter, J., Vermeiren, R., Vanwesenbeeck, I., & van Nieuwenhuizen, C. (2013). Autism and normative sexual development: A narrative review. *Journal of Clinical Nursing, 22*, 3467–3483. http://doi.org/10.1111/jocn.12397

Dewinter, J., Vermeiren, R., Vanwesenbeeck, I., Lobbestael, J., & Van Nieuwenhuizen, C. (2015). Sexuality in adolescent boys with autism spectrum disorder: Self-reported behaviours and attitudes. *Journal of Autism and Developmental Disorders, 45*(3), 731–741. http://doi.org/10.1007/s10803-014-2226-3

Dewinter, J., Vermeiren, R., Vanwesenbeeck, I., & Van Nieuwenhuizen, C. (2016). Adolescent boys with autism spectrum disorder growing up: Follow-up of self-reported sexual experience. *European Child & Adolescent Psychiatry, 25*(9), 969–978. http://doi.org/10.1007/s00787-016-0816-7

Dewinter, J., Van Parys, H., Vermeiren, R., & van Nieuwenhuizen, C. (2017). Adolescent boys with an autism spectrum disorder and their experience of sexuality: An interpretative phenomenological analysis. *Autism, 21*(1), 75–82. http://doi.org/10.1177/1362361315627134

Dewinter, J., van der Miesen, A.I.R., & Holmes, L.G. (2019, in preparation). Stakeholder perspectives on priorities for research on autism, sexuality and intimate relationships.

Dubois, D., Ameis, S. H., Lai, M.-C., Casanova, M. F., & Desarkar, P. (2016). Interoception in autism spectrum disorder: A systematic review. *International Journal of Developmental Neuroscience, 52*, 1–16. http://doi.org/10.1016/j.ijdevneu.2016.05.001

Fernandes, L. C., Gillberg, C. I., Cederlund, M., Hagberg, B., Gillberg, C., & Billstedt, E. (2016). Aspects of sexuality in adolescents and adults diagnosed with autism spectrum disorders in childhood. *Journal of Autism and Developmental Disorders, 46*(9), 3155–3165.

Fisher, A. D., Castellini, G., Casale, H., Fanni, E., Bandini, E., Campone, B., . . . Maggi, M. (2015). Hypersexuality, paraphilic behaviors, and gender dysphoria in individuals with Klinefelter's syndrome. *Journal of Sexual Medicine, 12*(12), 2413–2424. http://doi.org/10.1111/jsm.13048

Frans, E., & De Bruycker, A. (2012). Raamwerk seksualiteit en beleid: kwaliteit, preventie en reactie in jouw organisatie [Framework sexuality and policy: Quality, prevention and reacting in your organization]. Antwerpen, Belgium: Sensoa & Child Focus. Retrieved from https://www.seksuelevorming.be/sites/default/files/digitaal_materiaal/2012j047raamwerkseksualiteitenbeleidprintable.pdf

Frans, E. (2018). *Sensoa Flag System: Reacting to sexually (un) acceptable behaviour of children and young people.* Antwerp-Apeldoorn, Belgium: Garant.

Frith, U. (2003). *Autism: Explaining the enigma.* Oxford, UK: Wiley-Blackwell.

George, R., & Stokes, M. A. (2017). Gender identity and sexual orientation in autism spectrum disorder. *Autism 22*(8):970-982. Advance online publication. doi: 10.1177/1362361317714587

George, R., & Stokes, M. (2016). "Gender is not on my agenda!": Gender dysphoria and autism spectrum disorder. In L. Mazzone & B. Vitiello (Eds.), *Psychiatric comorbidities in autism spectrum disorders* (pp. 139–150). London, UK: Springer Publishing. doi:10.1007/978-3-319-29,695-1_10

George, R., & Stokes, M. A. (2018a). Sexual orientation in autism spectrum disorder. *Autism Research, 11*(1), 133–141. doi:10.1002/aur.1892

George, R., & Stokes, M. A. (2018b). A quantitative analysis of mental health among sexual and gender minorities in ASD. *Journal of Autism & Developmental Disorders, 48*(6), 2052–2063. doi:10.1007/s10803-018-3469-1

Ginevra, M. C., Nota, L., & Stokes, M. A. (2016). The differential effects of autism and Down's syndrome on sexual behavior. *Autism Research, 9*(1), 131–140. http://doi.org/10.1002/aur.1504

Glidden, D., Bouman, W. P., Jones, B. A., & Arcelus, J. (2016). Gender dysphoria and autism spectrum disorder: A systematic review of the literature. *Sexual Medicine Reviews, 4*(1), 3–14.

Gougeon, N. A. (2013). *Interest, understanding, and behaviour: Conceptualizations of sexuality education for individuals with an autism spectrum disorder using a socially inclusive lens* (Unpublished doctoral dissertation). University of Ottawa, Ottawa, Canada.

Hancock, G. (2017). *Socio-sexual functioning in autism spectrum disorders* (Unpublished doctoral dissertation). Deakin University, Deakin, Australia.

Hancock, G. I. P., Stokes, M. A., & Mesibov, G. B. (2017). Socio-sexual functioning in autism spectrum disorder: A systematic review and meta-analyses of existing literature. *Autism Research, 10*(11), 1823–1833. http://doi.org/10.1002/aur.1831

Hannah, L. A., & Stagg, S. D. (2016). Experiences of sex education and sexual awareness in young adults with autism spectrum disorder. *Journal of Autism and Developmental Disorders, 46*(12), 3678–3687. http://doi.org/10.1007/s10803-016-2906-2

Haracopos, D., & Pedersen, L. (1992). *Sexuality and autism: The Danish report.* Retrieved from http://www.autismuk.com/?page_id=1293

't Hart-Kerkhoffs, L. A., Jansen, L. M., Doreleijers, T. A., Vermeiren, R., Minderaa, R. B., & Hartman, C. A. (2009). Autism spectrum disorder symptoms in juvenile suspects of sex offenses. *Journal of Clinical Psychiatry, 70*(2), 266–272.

Hatton, S., & Tector, A. (2010). Sexuality and relationship education for young people with autistic spectrum disorder: Curriculum change and staff support. *British Journal of Special Education, 37*(2), 69–76.

Hellemans, H., Colson, K., Verbraeken, C., Vermeiren, R., & Deboutte, D. (2007). Sexual behavior in high-functioning male adolescents and young adults with autism spectrum disorder. *Journal of Autism and Developmental Disorders, 37*(2), 260–269.

Hellemans, H., Roeyers, H., Leplae, W., Dewaele, T., & Deboutte, D. (2010). Sexual behavior in male adolescents and young adults with autism spectrum disorder and borderline/mild mental retardation. *Sexuality and Disability, 28*(2), 93–104. http://doi.org/10.1007/s11195-009-9145-9

Hénault, I. (2006). *Le syndrome d'Asperger et la sexualité. Jessica Kingsley Pub. ISBN 2-7650-0935-X.*

Higgs, T., & Carter, A. J. (2015). Autism spectrum disorder and sexual offending: Responsivity in forensic interventions. *Aggression and Violent Behavior, 22,* 112–119. http://doi.org/10.1016/j.avb.2015.04.003

Holmes, L. G., & Himle, M. B. (2014). Brief report: Parent-child sexuality communication and autism spectrum disorders. *Journal of Autism and Developmental Disorders, 44*(11), 2964–2970. http://doi.org/10.1007/s10803-014-2146-2

Holmes, L. G., Himle, M. B., Sewell, K. K., Carbone, P. S., Strassberg, D. S., & Murphy, N. A. (2014). Addressing sexuality in youth with autism spectrum disorders: Current pediatric practices and barriers. *Journal of Developmental and Behavioral Pediatrics, 35*(3), 172–178. http://doi.org/10.1097/DBP.0000000000000030

Jacobs, L. A., Rachlin, K., Erickson-Schroth, L., & Janssen, A. (2014). Gender dysphoria and co-occurring autism spectrum disorders: Review, case examples, and treatment considerations. *LGBT Health, 1*(4):277–282. http://doi.org/10.1089/lgbt.2013.0045

Jones, R. M., Wheelwright, S., Farrell, K., Martin, E., Green, R., Di Ceglie, D., & Baron-Cohen, S. (2012). Brief report: Female-to-male transsexual people and autistic traits. *Journal of Autism and Developmental Disorders, 42*(2), 301–306. http://doi.org/10.1007/s10803-011-1227-8

Kalyva, E. (2010). Teachers' perspectives of the sexuality of children with autism spectrum disorders. *Research in Autism Spectrum Disorders, 4*(3), 433–437. http://doi.org/10.1016/j.rasd.2009.10.014

Kellaher, D. C. (2015). Sexual behavior and autism spectrum disorders: An update and discussion. *Current Psychiatry Reports, 17*(4). http://doi.org/10.1007/s11920-015-0562-4

Kendall, N. (2014). Sexuality education. In D. L. Tolman & L. M. Diamond (Eds.), *APA handbook of sexuality and psychology* (Vol. 2): *Contextual approaches* (p. 484). Washington, DC: American Psychological Association.

Kenny, L., Hattersley, C., Molins, B., Buckley, C., Povey, C., & Pellicano, E. (2016). Which terms should be used to describe autism? Perspectives from the UK autism community. *Autism, 20*(4), 442–462. http://doi.org/10.1177/1362361315588200.

Kirby DB, Laris BA, Rolleri LA. (2007). Sex and HIV education programs: their impact on sexual behaviors of young people throughout the world. *Journal of Adolescent Health, 40*(3):206–17.

Lehmann, K., & Leavey, G. (2017). Individuals with gender dysphoria and autism: Barriers to good clinical practice. *Journal of Psychiatric and Mental Health Nursing, 24,* 171–177. http://doi.org/10.1111/jpm.12351

Loftin, R. L. (2015). Sex education, sexual health, and autism spectrum disorder. *Pediatrics & Therapeutics, 5*(1), 1–6. http://doi.org/10.4172/2161-0665.1000230

Mandell, D. S., Walrath, C. M., Manteuffel, B., Sgro, G., & Pinto-Martin, J. A. (2005). The prevalence and correlates of abuse among children with autism served in comprehensive community-based mental health settings. *Child Abuse & Neglect, 29*(12), 1359–1372.

Maniglio, R. (2012).The role of parent-child bonding, attachment, and interpersonal problems in the development of deviant sexual fantasies in sexual offenders. *Trauma ViolenceAbuse, 13*(2):83–96. doi:10.1177/1524838012440337.

May, T., Pang, K. C., O'Connell, M. A., & Williams, K. (2017). Typical pubertal timing in an Australian population of girls and boys with autism spectrum disorder. *Journal of Autism and Developmental Disorders, 47*(12), 3983–3993. http://doi.org/10.1007/s10803-017-3281-3

May, T., Pang, K. C., & Williams, K. (2017). Brief report: Sexual attraction and relationships in adolescents with autism. *Journal of Autism and Developmental Disorders, 47*(6), 1910–1916. http://doi.org/10.1007/s10803-017-3092-

Mehzabin, P., & Stokes, M. A. (2011). Self-assessed sexuality in young adults with high functioning autism. *Research in Autism Spectrum Disorders, 5,* 614–621.

Nichols, S., & Blakeley-Smith, A. (2009). "I'm not sure we're ready for this...": Working with families toward facilitating healthy sexuality for individuals with autism spectrum disorders. *Social Work in Mental Health, 8*(1), 72–91. http://doi.org/10.1080/15332980902932383

O'Reilly, G., Marshall, W. L., Carr, A., & Beckett, R. C. (Eds.). (2004). *The handbook of clinical intervention with young people who sexually abuse.* New York, NY: Psychology Press.

Ousley, O. Y., & Mesibov, G. B. (1991). Sexual attitudes and knowledge of high-functioning adolescents and adults with autism. *Journal of Autism and Developmental Disorders, 21*(4), 471–481.

Parkinson, J. (2014). Gender dysphoria in Asperger's syndrome: A caution. *Australasian Psychiatry, 22*(1), 84–85. http://doi.org/10.1177/1039856213497814

Pask, L., Hughes, T. L., & Sutton, L. R. (2016). Sexual knowledge acquisition and retention for individuals with autism.

International Journal of School & Educational Psychology, 3603(March), 1–9. http://doi.org/10.1080/21683603.2016.1130579

Pasterski, V., Gilligan, L., & Curtis, R. (2014). Traits of autism spectrum disorders in adults with gender dysphoria. *Archives of Sexual Behavior, 43*(2), 387–393. http://doi.org/10.1007/s10508-013-0154-5

Pecora, L., Mesibov, G., & Stokes, M. A. (2016). Sexuality in high functioning autism: A systematic review and meta-analysis. *Journal of Autism and Developmental Disorders, 46*(11), 3519–3556. doi:10.1007/s10803-016-2892-4

Rock, E. M., Ireland, M., Resnick, M. D., & McNeely, C. A. (2005). A rose by any other name? Objective knowledge, perceived knowledge, and adolescent male condom use. *Pediatrics, 115*(3), 667–672.

Roke, Y., Buitelaar, J. K., Boot, A. M., Tenback, D., & van Harten, P. N. (2012). Risk of hyperprolactinemia and sexual side effects in males 10–20 years old with autism spectrum disorders or disruptive behavior disorder and treated with risperidone. *Journal of Child and Adolescent Psychopharmacology, 22*(6), 432–439.

Rudolph, C. E. S., Lundin, A., Åhs, J. W., Dalman, C., & Kosidou, K. (2018). Brief report: Sexual orientation in individuals with autistic traits: Population based study of 47,000 adults in Stockholm County. *Journal of Autism and Developmental Disorders, 48*(2), 619–624. http://doi.org/10.1007/s10803-017-3369-9

Rutten, A. X., Vermeiren, R. R. J. M., & Van Nieuwenhuizen, C. (2017). Autism in adult and juvenile delinquents: A literature review. *Child and Adolescent Psychiatry and Mental Health, 11*(1), 45. http://doi.org/10.1186/s13034-017-0181-4

Ryan, S., Franzetta, K., & Manlove, J. (2007). Knowledge, perceptions, and motivations for contraception: influence on teens' contraceptive consistency. *Youth & Society, 39*(2), 182–208.

Schaafsma, D., Stoffelen, J. M. T., Kok, G., & Curfs, L. M. G. (2013). Exploring the development of existing sex education programs for people with intellectual disabilities: An intervention mapping approach. *Journal of Applied Research in Intellectual Disabilities, 26*, 157–166. doi:10.1111/jar.12017

Schaafsma, D., Kok, G., Stoffelen, J. M. T., van Doorn, P., & Curfs, L. M. G. (2014). Identifying the important determinants of teaching sex education to people with intellectual disabilities: Cross-sectional survey among paid care staff. *Journal of Intellectual & Developmental Disability, 39*, 157–166.

Van Schalkwyk, G. I., Klingensmith, K., & Volkmar, F. R. (2015). Gender identity and autism spectrum. *Yale Journal of Biology and Medicine, 88*, 81–83.

Schöttle, D., Briken, P., Tüscher, O., & Turner, D. (2017). Sexuality in autism: Hypersexual and paraphilic behavior in women and men with high-functioning autism spectrum disorder. *Dialogues in Clinical Neuroscience, 19*(4), 381–393.

Sevlever, M., Roth, M. E., & Gillis, J. M. (2013). Sexual abuse and offending in autism spectrum disorders. *Sexuality and Disability, 31*(2), 189–200. http://doi.org/10.1007/s11195-013-9286-8

Shumer, D. E., Reisner, S. L., Edwards-Leeper, L., & Tishelman, A. (2016). Evaluation of Asperger syndrome in youth presenting to a gender dysphoria clinic. *LGBT Health, 3*(5), 387–390. http://doi.org/10.1089/lgbt.2015.0070

Silberman, S. (2015). *Neurotribes: The legacy of autism and the future of neurodiversity* New York, NY: Penguin.

Simonoff, E., Pickles, A., Charman, T., Chandler, S., Loucas, T., & Baird, G. (2008). Psychiatric disorders in children with autism spectrum disorders: Prevalence, comorbidity, and associated factors in a population-derived sample. *Journal of the American Academy of Child and Adolescence Psychiatry, 47*(8), 921–929.

Sinha, P., Jnanaprakasan, P. P., & Andrade, C. (2012). Hyperactive sexual desire in Klinefelter syndrome: Treatment with sertraline. *Psychiatry and Clinical Neurosciences, 66*, 533. http://doi.org/10.1111/j.1440-1819.2012.02375.x

Skagerberg, E., Di Ceglie, D., & Carmichael, P. (2015). Brief report: Autistic features in children and adolescents with gender dysphoria. *Journal of Autism and Developmental Disorders, 45*(8), 2628–2632. http://doi.org/10.1007/s10803-015-2413-x

Søndenaa, E., Helverschou, S. B., Steindal, K., Rasmussen, K., Nilson, B., & Nøttestad, J. A. (2014). Violence and sexual offending behavior in people with autism spectrum disorder who have undergone a psychiatric forensic examination. *Psychological Reports, 115*(1), 32–43. http://doi.org/10.2466/16.15.PR0.115c16z5

Stokes, M., & Kaur, A. (2005). High-functioning autism and sexuality: A parental perspective. *Autism, 9*(3), 266–289. http://doi.org/10.1177/1362361305053258

Stokes, M., Newton, N., & Kaur, A. (2007). Stalking, and social and romantic functioning among of adolescents and adults with autistic spectrum disorder. *Journal of Autism and Developmental Disorders, 37*(10), 1969–1986.

Stokes, M., Kornienko, L., Scheeren, A. M., Koot, H. M., & Begeer, S. (2017). A comparison of children and adolescent's self-report and parental-report of the PEDSQL among those with and without autism spectrum disorder. *Quality of Life Research, 26*(3), 611–624. doi:10.1007/s11136-016-1490-4

Strang, J. F., Meagher, H., Kenworthy, L., de Vries, A. L. C., Menvielle, E., Leibowitz, S., . . . Anthony, L. G. (2018). Initial clinical guidelines for co-occurring autism spectrum disorder and gender dysphoria or incongruence in adolescents. *Journal of Clinical Child & Adolescent Psychology, 47*(1), 105–115. http://doi.org/10.1080/15374416.2016.1228462

Strunz, S., Schermuck, C., Ballerstein, S., Ahlers, C. J., Dziobek, I., & Roepke, S. (2017). Romantic relationships and relationship satisfaction among adults with Asperger syndrome and high-functioning autism. *Journal of Clinical Psychology, 73*(1), 113–125. http://doi.org/10.1002/jclp.22319

Tiefer, L., Hall, M., & Tavris, C. (2002). Beyond dysfunction: A new view of women's sexual problems. *Journal of Sex & Marital Therapy, 28*, 225–232. http://doi.org/10.1080/00926230252851357

Torisky, D., & Torisky, C. (1985). Sex education and sexual awareness building for autistic children and youth: Some viewpoints and considerations. *Journal of Autism and Developmental Disorders, 15*(2), 213–227.

Travers, J., & Tincani, M. (2010). Sexuality education for individuals with autism spectrum disorders: Critical issues and decisionmaking guidelines. *Education and Training in Autism and Developmental Disabilities, 45*(2), 284–293.

Tullis, C. A., & Zangrillo, A. N. (2013). Sexuality education for adolescents and adults with autism spectrum disorders. *Psychology in the Schools, 50*(9), 866–875. http://doi.org/10.1002/pits

Urbano, M. R., Hartmann, K., Deutsch, S. I., Polychronopoulos, G. M. B., & Dorbin, V. (2013). Relationships, Sexuality, and Intimacy in Autism Spectrum Disorders.

Van Bourgondien, M. E., Reichle, N. C., & Palmer, A. (1997). Sexual behavior in adults with autism. *Journal of Autism and Developmental Disorders, 27*(2), 113–125.

van der Miesen, A. I.R, Hurley, H., & de Vries, A. L. (2016). Gender dysphoria and autism spectrum disorder: A narrative review. *International Review of Psychiatry, 28*(1), 70–80.

van Der Miesen, A. I. R., Hurley, H., Bal, A. M., & de Vries, A. L. C. (2018). Prevalence of the wish to be of the opposite gender in adolescents and adults with autism spectrum disorder. *Archives of Sexual Behavior.* Advance online publication. http://doi.org/10.1007/s10508-018-1218-3

Visser, K., Greaves-Lord, K., Tick, N. T., Verhulst, F. C., Maras, A., & van der Vegt, E. J. M. (2015). Study protocol: A randomized controlled trial investigating the effects of a psychosexual training program for adolescents with autism spectrum disorder. *BMC Psychiatry, 15*(1), 207. http://doi.org/10.1186/s12888-015-0586-7

Visser, K., Greaves-Lord, K., Tick, N. T., Verhulst, F. C., Maras, A., & van der Vegt, E. J. M. (2017b). An exploration of the judgement of sexual situations by adolescents with autism spectrum disorders versus typically developing adolescents. *Research in Autism Spectrum Disorders, 36,* 35–43.

Visser, K., Greaves-Lord, K., Tick, N. T., Verhulst, F. C., Maras, A., & van der Vegt, E. J. M. (2017). A randomized controlled trial to examine the effects of the Tackling Teenage psychosexual training program for adolescents with autism spectrum disorder. *Journal of Child Psychology & Psychiatry, 58*(7), 840–850. https://doi.org/10.1111/jcpp.12709

Visser, K. (2017). *Tackling Teenage: A randomized controlled trial to examine a psychosexual training program for adolescent with autism spectrum disorder (ASD)* (Doctoral dissertation). Erasmus University Rotterdam, Rotterdam, The Netherlands.

Ward, T., & Beech, A. (2006). An integrated theory of sexual offending. *Aggression and Violent Behavior, 11,* 44–63. http://doi.org/10.1016/j.avb.2005.05.002

Weiss, J. A., & Fardella, M. A. (2018). Victimization and perpetration experiences of adults with autism. *Frontiers in Psychiatry, 9*(May), 1–10. http://doi.org/10.3389/fpsyt.2018.00203

World Health Organization. (2006). *Defining sexual health: Report of a technical consultation on sexual health 28–31 January 2002, Geneva.* Geneva, Switzerland: World Health Organization.

World Health Organization. (2009). *Promoting sexual and reproductive health for persons with disabilities: WHO/UNFPA guidance note.* Geneva, Switzerland: World Health Organization.

Woodbury-Smith, M., & Dein, K. (2014). Autism spectrum disorder (ASD) and unlawful behaviour: Where do we go from here? *Journal of Autism and Developmental Disorders, 44*(11), 2734–2741. http://doi.org/10.1007/s10803-014-2216-5

Zigler, E., & Hodapp, R. M. (1986). *Understanding mental retardation.* Cambridge, UK: Cambridge University Press.

CHAPTER

13 Eating Issues in Autism Spectrum Disorder

Emily S. Kuschner *and* Gregory L. Wallace

Abstract

Clinicians and researchers have long known that many individuals with autism spectrum disorder (ASD) experience challenges around eating (e.g., "picky eating") that increase risk for negative health sequelae. Nevertheless, as reviewed in this chapter, progress in addressing these challenges has been hampered by disciplinary boundaries, lack of empirical scrutiny of existing interventions, and inconsistency in definition and assessment of eating-related issues. Recent work has begun to overcome these impasses through a greater focus on rigorous evaluation of currently available treatments and the meticulous development of novel and multidisciplinary intervention approaches. Yet, much more work is needed. In addition to the need for consensus on nomenclature and operationalized definitions that directly impact measure development, more work is needed to address the presence and impact of overweight/obesity among people with ASD. Only through cross-disciplinary and collaborative efforts between clinicians and researchers can these obstacles be overcome to improve the health, well-being, and quality of life of people with ASD.

Keywords: autism spectrum disorder, eating, feeding, obesity, treatment

Overview

In Kanner's seminal description (Kanner, 1943), autism spectrum disorder (ASD) was linked with problems related to eating. Although definitions and diagnostic criteria for ASD have changed during the intervening 75 years, problematic behaviors involving eating, such as selective or "picky" eating and overeating, have remained highly prevalent among individuals with ASD. In fact, some data suggest that up to 90% of children with ASD exhibit food selectivity and similar eating-related atypicalities (e.g., Ahearn, Castine, Nault, & Green, 2001; Cornish, 1998; Ledford & Gast, 2006; Sharp et al., 2013; Whiteley, Rodgers, & Shattock, 2000; Williams, Dalrymple, & Neal, 2000).

Nomenclature Challenge

The constructs related to problematic eating in people with ASD are variably defined in the extant literature. For example, food selectivity can be characterized by food intake reported on a dietary recall interview or defined by a set of variables related to food intake, such as food refusal, limited diet variety, or high-frequency intake of a single food (Bandini et al., 2010). In other cases, food selectivity may more broadly capture characteristics that drive food selectivity, such as food neophobia, or the refusal to try new foods (Kuschner et al., 2015; Wallace, Llewellyn, Fildes, & Ronald, 2018). Variable constructs and terminology result from differences by discipline in how problematic eating is conceptualized, differences in the use of state versus trait factors in eating, and differences in whether operationalized definitions are broadband across concepts or more fine-grained. Although the fifth edition of the *Diagnostic and Statistical Manual of Mental Disorders* (DSM-5) delineates several eating-related psychiatric diagnoses, all of which have particular relevance to ASD, most eating challenges in ASD have been conceptualized as co-occurring behaviors rather than comorbid conditions. For the purposes of framing discussion of these concepts in the present chapter, we will describe the most commonly studied eating issues in ASD, whether considered a "free-standing" diagnosis or co-occurring concern.

Picky eating, selective eating, food selectivity. Picky eating is the most commonly reported eating problem for people with ASD, with a multifaceted impact (Cermak, Curtin, & Bandini, 2010; Sharp et al., 2013; Twachtman-Reilly, Amaral, & Zebrowski, 2008). Food selectivity challenges families' daily lives and increases the risk for poor health outcomes, such as nutritional inadequacies (Hyman et al., 2012; Sharp et al., 2013) and obesity (Broder-Fingert, Brazauskas, Lindgren, Iannuzzi, & Van Cleave, 2014). Although diet variety is limited in food selectivity, appetite is usually not (Williams et al., 2000); thus, the often energy-dense, high-sugar, high-fat foods diet of children with ASD (Broder-Fingert et al., 2014; Evans et al., 2012; Schreck & Williams, 2006) increases risk for excess weight gain.

The variability of terms used to describe what is colloquially known as picky eating is in and of itself representative of a conceptual challenge in the field. The broad construct associated with these terms focuses on a child eating a corpus of foods narrower than what would be expected for his or her age, yet the focus of descriptions and research investigations can encompass food repertoire (e.g., the list of foods a child will eat) and associated behavioral challenges (e.g., a child turning his or her head away from a food or spitting out nonpreferred or novel foods at mealtime). It is unclear whether clinicians and researchers make conscious choices about using these terms or if the terms are simply used interchangeably and inconsistently.

When using definitions that enumerate an absolute number of foods in the child's diet, quantification can focus on what is present in food intake (i.e., foods eaten) or what is absent (i.e., food refusal). For example, when examining the number of foods being eaten at least once per month, Zimmer and colleagues (2011) observed that children with ASD (~5 to 11 years old) tried a mean of 33.5 foods per month in contrast to neurotypical controls, who tried a mean of 54.5 foods per month. In a similar sample, Bandini and colleagues (2010) reported a food refusal rate of 41.7% in children with ASD relative to 18.9% in children with neurotypical development.

Many would argue that definitions focused on enumerated food intake or refusal will not account for the idiosyncrasies of food choices and selectivity present for individuals in ASD, and thus these definitions may not fully capture what makes eating different in ASD. In an attempt to test an operationalized definition of food selectivity, Bandini et al. (2010) proposed a definition with three components, including (a) food refusal (number of foods the child will *not* eat from a common list of foods), (b) limited food repertoire (number of unique foods consumed over a discrete period), and (c) high-frequency single-food intake (foods eaten more than four times daily). The authors proposed that this high-frequency single-food intake component might capture the anecdotal reports of unique eating habits in ASD. In a sample of children ages 3 to 11 years, food refusal and limited food repertoire distinguished children with ASD (n = 53) from typically developing (TD) children (n = 58). Although the groups could not be differentiated based on the high-frequency single-food intake variable, the authors highlight that the definition may have been too conservative to mask odd patterns of intake (e.g., macaroni and cheese eaten at three meals of breakfast, lunch, and dinner would not be captured as high-frequency intake, but would be considered unusual). Postorino and colleagues (2015) also saw similarly low rates of high-frequency single-food intake (i.e., four to five times daily) in their sample of 158 children with ASD (ages 3 to 12 years), despite a 92% rate of food refusal.

One of the added challenges of defining food selectivity is establishing what should be considered a reference point for determining "abnormal." Researchers typically examine a group of children with ASD against a control group of neurotypical children with the assumption that the control group is representative of age-matched neurotypical eating; see the descriptions of the Zimmer et al. (2011) and Bandini et al. (2010) studies earlier. An alternative approach used clinically and in research is to examine a child's nutritional profile relative to recommended daily intake. Zimmer and colleagues (2011) showed lower rates of food variety for children with ASD relative to a TD control group (e.g., eating fewer unique foods each month). They then also showed that the children with ASD who were food selective were more likely to have inadequate nutrient intake relative to Estimated Average Requirement/Dietary Reference Intake (EAR/DRI; population-based guidelines for nutritionally sound daily food intake) when compared to both children with ASD without selective eating and children with typical development. In a relatively large sample of

256 children with ASD (2 to 11 years old) from the Autism Speaks Autism Treatment Network (ASD-ATN) sites, Johnson, Turner, Stewart, and Schmidt (2014) demonstrated that severity of nutritional inadequacy could be predicted by the degree of problematic feeding behaviors. All of these analyses, however, occur at the group level. What remains unclear is how, at an individual level, the child with ASD who is selectively eating what might be colloquially known as a "kid diet" (e.g., chicken fingers, pizza, macaroni and cheese) differs from a child with neurotypical development commonly eating a similar makeup of foods. It may be that the neurotypical child still has a smattering of other foods within his or her diet whereas the child with ASD might completely reject particular food groups. This type of criterion has also been used to define food selectivity (e.g., Sharp et al., 2018). Taken together, there is a need for an established definition that can be used at the individual level to define food selectivity, in order to establish standardized norms for what falls in- or outside of a normal distribution.

Food neophobia. Although not an official diagnosis, food neophobia is an eating-related construct defined as difficulty with trying or avoiding *new and unfamiliar* foods. This differs from more global food refusal that could occur with familiar and previously presented foods. Food neophobia occurs frequently in neurotypical development during early childhood; however, when it persists into later childhood and adolescence, concerns arise over dietary and nutritional impacts. For example, food neophobia generally limits variety in dietary intake, with particularly negative consequences upon the consumption of fruits and vegetables that are high in vitamins and minerals (Oliveira et al., 2015). Downstream effects can then occur that might influence broader physical and medical health and development. However, whether there is an association between food neophobia and body mass index (BMI) remains unclear as evidence to date is mixed (Cole, An, Lee, & Donovan, 2017; Webber, Hill, Saxton, Van Jaarsveld, & Wardle, 2009). Although food neophobia may contribute to a narrow food repertoire, children can be food selective for reasons other than an aversion to novelty (e.g., rigidity, sensory issues).

Overweight, obesity. An abundance of data now exists across clinic-referred and epidemiologic samples that individuals with ASD are at significantly increased risk of becoming overweight or obese when compared to the general population as a whole (e.g., Hill, Zuckerman, & Fombonne, 2015; Must et al., 2017) or to individuals with other developmental disabilities (e.g., Phillips et al., 2014). For example, in a population-based study ($n = 9{,}619$), Phillips et al. (2014) found that adolescents (ages 12 to 17 years) with developmental disabilities were 60% more likely to be obese than adolescents without developmental disabilities. More to the point, the ASD subgroup exhibited the highest rates of obesity. Furthermore, a recent meta-analysis found an increased obesity rate among individuals with ASD when compared to controls across numerous large-scale studies (Zheng et al., 2017).

The mechanisms underlying this risk in ASD remain largely unknown or, at best, poorly understood. Obesity risk is increased by usage of certain psychotropic medications often prescribed to address co-occurring conditions with ASD (e.g., depression and anxiety). These medications can affect appetite and metabolic factors. Weight gain is a common side effect of both risperidone and aripiprazole, the only two psychotropic medications approved by the Food and Drug Administration for use with individuals with ASD. Nevertheless, medication is but one contributor to obesity risk. A recent study also highlighted increased obesity risk for children with ASD and disruptive behavior who are unmedicated (Criado et al., 2017). Many studies have focused on lack of physical exercise and sedentary behaviors in ASD (and other developmental disabilities) as culprits. Surprisingly, very little work has examined appetitive factors, although there is some evidence for increased overeating in ASD.

Overeating. Much less well studied than food selectivity in ASD is overeating or eating in the absence of hunger. Overeating is typically defined as eating a large amount of food that is more than nutritionally required. The limited evidence to date suggests that overeating is increased among children with ASD. Two studies by Hess, Matson, and Dixon (2010) and Tureck, Matson, May, Whiting, and Davis (2014) used the Autism Spectrum Disorders-Comorbid for Children scale (ASD-CC; Matson, LoVullo, Rivet, & Boisjoli, 2009) to study co-occurring conditions, including overeating, in children and adolescents with ASD and TD children and adolescents. The Overeating subscale score of the ASD-CC was shown to be significantly elevated among children with ASD as compared to TD children in both studies. However, it is unclear in either of these studies whether participants with ASD were also taking psychotropic medications, which could impact overeating behaviors. An additional study suggests that overeating in people with ASD does not appear to be a behavioral pattern limited to childhood or adolescence. Kobayashi and Murata (1998) examined several behavioral characteristics of 187 young adults (ages 18 to 33 years) with ASD, approximately three quarters of whom also had co-occurring intellectual disability, using a modified version of the Child Behavior Checklist (CBCL; Achenbach & Edelbrock, 1983), which is typically utilized for children and adolescents under 18 years of age. The results showed that 39% of caregivers reported that overeating was either "somewhat or sometimes true" or "very true or often true" of these adults with ASD. However, whether this rate of overeating is atypical as compared to adults without ASD was not determined given that the CBCL norms could not be utilized (this instrument was adapted for use with these young adults but was normed on children) and there was no control group. And just as noted earlier, whether participants were also taking psychotropic medications and how this related to overeating rates was not examined. Finally, overeating has been linked with being overweight/obese in the general population (Hill & Peters, 1998) and other important health indicators, such as elevated blood pressure (Radin et al., 2015), yet these relationships have not been examined in ASD.

Selective overeating. There is increasing recognition that nutritional inadequacies that can result from food selectivity do not solely yield underweight outcomes. Although diet variety may be limited for people with ASD, appetite is often not (Williams et al., 2000). Early animal studies also have supported the observation of a selective overeating construct. In some of his seminal work, Schacter (1971) lesioned the ventromedial hypothalamus to induce obesity in rats. However, an interesting juxtaposition of eating behaviors emerged so that these rats not only were "finicky" (i.e., they would not consume bitter-tasting food) but also, when presented with highly palatable foods, would overeat. This aligns with clinical observation and parental report that children who are highly fussy about eating more nutrient-dense and sometimes less palatable foods (e.g., fruits and vegetables) will still eat age-appropriate (or beyond age-appropriate) amounts of preferred foods, which are most frequently energy-dense, high-sugar, high-fat foods. Thus, those who are selective may actually be more at risk of overweight/obesity than those who have a more varied diet. This anecdotal and clinical observation requires empirical inquiry but highlights the presumed polarity of food selectivity on one hand and overeating on the other, which may be confounded and challenged in people with ASD.

Eating disorders. There is a rapidly increasing focus on co-occurring diagnosis of traditionally defined eating disorders in people with ASD. To date, most research has examined the increased presence of autistic traits in the context of eating disorders, particularly anorexia nervosa (for review, see Westwood & Tchanturia, 2017). However, several studies have examined the co-occurrence of the two conditions, finding that approximately one in four women with anorexia nervosa meet diagnostic criteria for ASD (e.g., Huke, Turk, Saeidi, Kent, & Morgan, 2013; Mandy & Tchanturia, 2015). Much less well studied is the co-occurrence of other eating disorders, such as bulimia nervosa, and ASD.

With the DSM-5 (American Psychiatric Association, 2013), the introduction of avoidant/restrictive food intake disorder (ARFID) has offered a diagnostic, and potentially clinically billable, classification for people previously more colloquially described as picky eaters and food selective. ARFID is characterized by a feeding disturbance that results in failure to meet appropriate nutritional and/or energy needs (American Psychiatric Association, 2013). There is growing empirical support for three ARFID subtypes that align with examples provided in the DSM-5: (a) ARFID with lack of interest in eating, (b) ARFID with restriction based on sensory sensitivity, and (c) ARFID with restriction based on avoidance and fear of aversive consequences of eating (Norris et al., 2017). Although yet to be submitted to empirical inquiry with individuals with ASD, all three subtypes may align with presentations of people with ASD and eating issues. However, given the diagnostic criterion for ARFID, none of these subtypes will capture people with ASD and eating issues who manage to maintain their weight and nutritional adequacy.

Summary of the Nomenclature Challenge

Agreement in the field on eating-related terms and constructs will help align clinicians, researchers, and families. This is a crucial factor when striving to identify mechanisms for treatment change, and what is considered a meaningful treatment outcome (Georgiades & Kasari, 2018). Although some providers might argue that variety of foods eaten is the only true measure of change that will impact health, families in particular can highlight the significantly negative impact of other factors associated with narrow diet variety, including inflexibility, challenging mealtime behaviors, anxiety, or parent–child conflict.

Many parents would argue that improvement in these factors has as much, or in some cases even more, impact on daily life and well-being. Operationalized definitions for these various eating-related constructs, with clear dependent variables for treatment outcome, are necessary. This is particularly applicable when eating or feeding issues like reduced dietary intake or variety are characterized but impact (e.g., behavioral challenges or mealtime disruption) is not also assessed.

Prevalence and Course

In the general population, food selectivity is most prevalent during the preschool years with estimates in the ~15% to 50% range (Carruth, Ziegler, Gordon, & Barr, 2004; Zucker et al., 2015). Within the general population, food selectivity generally declines thereafter, dropping to ~5% to 25% in later childhood (Mascola, Bryson, & Agras, 2010; Micali et al., 2011). Although there are no true epidemiological studies of eating-related issues in ASD, an estimated 70% to 90% of children are food selective (Ledford & Gast, 2006; Whiteley et al., 2000; Williams et al., 2000), which stands in stark contrast to the rates described earlier in the context of typical development. The prevalence of eating issues in adolescents and adults with ASD has not been systematically examined; thus, our knowledge is limited primarily to childhood. In ASD, there appears to be a longer duration of eating issues, extending beyond the preschool years. In a sample of children with ASD aged 2 to 11 years, a subset (approximately 40%) of children originally described as food selective had chronic selectivity issues lasting 2 or more years and 22% remained food selective at age 11 years (Mascola et al., 2010).

In children with ASD, these eating-related issues appear to be developmentally persistent and chronic based on evidence from both cross-sectional studies, which show no association between age and these behaviors in ASD (Bandini et al., 2010; Suarez, Nelson, & Curtis, 2014), and at least two longitudinal studies. Suarez et al. (2014) found not only stable food selectivity issues in ~8-year-old children with ASD over the course of 20 months but also that the relationship between sensory issues and food selectivity is similarly persistent. In another longitudinal study, Bandini and colleagues (2017) examined changes in food selectivity in 18 children with ASD over a ~6.5-year time period (~7 to 13 years of age). Although food refusal diminished somewhat, the repertoire of foods eaten did not significantly expand. Finally, based on our own work and that from other groups, food selectivity clearly persists into the adolescent and adult years in ASD (Karlsson, Råstam, & Wentz, 2013; Kuschner et al., 2015). These studies converge in implicating a much greater preponderance of eating-related issues in ASD than found in the general population and that this selectivity appears to be more developmentally persistent in ASD with selectivity persisting into adulthood.

Evidence thus far suggests that ASD (Huke et al., 2013) and ASD traits (Westwood et al., 2016) are overrepresented in anorexia nervosa, but whether anorexia nervosa and other eating disorders are overrepresented and their developmental course is similar in ASD have not been systematically examined. Future work should seek to assess how prevalent eating disorders (particularly anorexia nervosa and ARFID) are in ASD populations, as well offer characterization of symptom presentation, onset patterns, and diagnostic stability.

Etiology, Diagnosis, and Assessment

Etiology

The etiology of eating issues in people with ASD is complex and likely both individualized and multifactorial. There is also a gap between what is hypothesized or proposed as etiology for eating issues in ASD versus what has been empirically evaluated. Moreover, there are a wealth of constructs and paradigms established in the literature on eating in neurotypically developing children that have not yet been explored for people with ASD (e.g., relative reinforcing value of food for a child with ASD and obesity, family mealtime context). Here we will provide an overview on the theoretical and empirical support for etiological pathways of eating issues in ASD.

ASD-specific features prime issues with eating. The skills needed to navigate eating and mealtime fall squarely in domains that are challenging for children with ASD (reviewed in Twachtman-Reilly et al., 2008). Most prominently, mealtime and food are almost inherently variable. The common fluctuations of eating experiences (e.g., changing menus, utensils, dishes, and eating environment) are in direct contrast to the inflexibility and need for sameness commonly observed in people with ASD (D'Cruz et al., 2013; Yerys et al., 2009). In addition, social demands often accompany eating opportunities. Family meals, lunchroom interactions, and ordering food at a restaurant all tax already compromised social communication skills inherent to the diagnosis. High rates of co-occurring anxiety seen in ASD (Ung, Selles, Small, & Storch, 2015; van Steensel, Bögels, & Perrin, 2011) and difficulty with processing novelty (Maes, Eling, Wezenberg, Vissers, & Kan, 2010) may increase the likelihood that new foods will be avoided and food neophobia will be present. Moreover, difficulties with prototype formation (Klinger & Dawson, 2001) and generalization (Gastgeb, Dundas, Minshew, & Strauss, 2011) in ASD may result in the need for even more repeated exposures to a novel food than would be expected in neurotypical development. In typical development, children often need 12 to 15 exposures to a food to accept the food and integrate it into their food repertoire (Birch & Marlin, 1982; Wardle et al., 2003). In ASD, slight variations in a food (e.g., American cheese in a slice vs. cube) could lead to the food being encoded as a different and novel food, rather than a variation on something familiar. Thus, the typical 12 to 15 exposures may not feel like increasing familiarity with a food, but rather exposure to a new food each time, making eating perhaps even more anxiety provoking. Therefore, it will be even more difficult for someone with ASD to generalize and extract preferred and nonpreferred foods.

Sensory differences. Sensory processing abnormalities have been associated with ASD from the time of its initial conceptualization (e.g., Kanner, 1943); nevertheless, these behaviors did not feature prominently in more recent diagnostic conceptualizations of ASD (e.g., *Diagnostic and Statistical Manual of Mental Disorders*, fourth edition; American Psychiatric Association, 1994) until release of the DSM-5 (American Psychiatric Association, 2013). The DSM-5 has reprioritized these sensory problems and included hyper- and hyporeactivity to sensory input as a core diagnostic feature of ASD in addition to other non–social communication symptoms, like repetitive behaviors and circumscribed interests (American Psychiatric Association, 2013).

Conventional wisdom and anecdotal report by parents suggest that problematic eating behaviors, particularly food selectivity, in children with ASD can be attributed to certain aspects of sensory abnormalities, such as oral texture and taste sensitivities (Kral et al., 2015), and more general sensory processing differences (Nadon, Feldman, Dunn, & Gisel, 2011). Sensory processing abnormalities among people with ASD have been widely researched and documented (for review see Schauder & Bennetto, 2016), with repeated documentation of sensitivities to tastes, textures, and smells (Avery et al., 2018; Chistol, 2018; Hazen, Stornelli, O'Rourke, Koesterer, & McDougle, 2014; Kral et al., 2015; Nadon et al., 2011; Rogers, Hepburn, & Wehner, 2003). For example, Ben-Sasson et al. (2009) conducted a meta-analysis of 14 studies examining the sensory differences between people with ASD and TD control groups and found significant between-group differences. More specifically, people with ASD showed more underresponsivity, more overresponsivity, and more sensation-seeking behaviors than TD control groups. More relevant to eating-related behaviors, research on individual differences in sensory processing in ASD highlights a taste/smell sensory subtype (Lane, Dennis, & Geraghty, 2011; Lane, Molloy, & Bishop, 2014; Lane, Young, Baker, & Angley, 2010), suggesting that sensory differences in taste and smell processing are primary for a subset of children with ASD. Moreover, Lane and colleagues (2010) documented associations between this taste/smell sensitivity and more broadly defined challenging behaviors beyond eating in young children with ASD. This subtyping approach could prove valuable for identifying neurobiological pathways that inform the etiology of eating-related behaviors for a subset of people with ASD.

Prior research has consistently suggested correlations between various aspects of sensory sensitivity and food selectivity behaviors in children with ASD (Ben-Sasson et al., 2009; Cermak et al., 2010; Johnson, Davies, Boles, Gavin, & Bellows, 2015; Lane, Molloy, et al., 2014; Lane, Geraghty, Young, & Rostorfer, 2014; Tanner et al., 2015; Zobel-Lachiusa, Andrianopoulos, Mailloux, & Cermak, 2015). For example, in a study of TD children and children with ASD ages 4 to 6 years, Kral et al. (2015) examined eating behaviors as measured by the Child Feeding Questionnaire (CFQ; Birch et al., 2001) and a modified version of the Food Neophobia Scale (Pliner & Hobden, 1992). Sensory processing was measured by the oral sensory sensitivity subtest of the Sensory Profile Caregiver Questionnaire, including questions such as "Avoids certain tastes or food smells that are typically part of children's diets" and "Shows strong preference for certain tastes" (Dunn, 1999). The results revealed more food avoidance behaviors in children with ASD who had elevated taste and oral texture sensitivities than in children with ASD without these oral sensory sensitivities. Additionally, Nadon et al. (2011) examined the relationship between sensory sensitivities across all modalities (i.e., tactile, smell, taste, visual, and auditory) and eating behaviors (e.g., mealtime behaviors, food preferences, child health) in children with ASD ages 3 to 10 years.

Results showed a significant correlation between sensory processing differences as measured by the total score on the Short Sensory Profile (Dunn, 1999) and the amount of eating problems as measured by the Eating Profile, wherein those with "definite" sensory processing differences demonstrated more eating problems. Specifically, participants who demonstrated tactile sensitivity, taste and smell sensitivity, and visual/auditory sensitivities demonstrated significantly more eating problems than children with ASD with typical sensory processing.

Though progress is being made toward understanding etiological underpinnings of eating behaviors in ASD, this research is in its infancy. The vast majority of studies employ cross-sectional rather than longitudinal designs, thus limiting our ability to make causal inferences. Longitudinal studies will be needed to begin to generate clearer hypotheses about etiology and trajectory.

Neural basis of eating and taste processing. The possible neural underpinnings of eating and taste processing in ASD is only beginning to be explored; however, we have an ever-increasing understanding of the typical neural pathways linked to eating and taste. When consuming food or liquid, taste receptors, primarily on the tongue, transmit information both about taste and mouth somatosensation to the brainstem via cranial nerves. Gustatory perception is then mediated centrally by a complex network involving portions of the brainstem, thalamus, and multiple cortical regions, most crucially, the mid-insula and surrounding operculum. Indeed, the insula and overlying operculum are classified as primary gustatory cortex, based on many nonhuman primate single/multineuron recording and tract-tracing investigations, as well as human functional neuroimaging studies (Baylis, Rolls, & Baylis, 1995; O'Doherty, Rolls, Francis, Bowtell, & McGlone, 2001; Rolls, 2006; Yaxley, Rolls, & Sienkiewicz, 1990). Functional magnetic resonance imaging (fMRI) studies indicate that brain activity within the insula is correlated with the subjective intensity of taste and is likely the critical region involved in taste identification (Grabenhorst, Rolls, & Bilderbeck, 2008). To date and to the best of our knowledge, only two food-related fMRI studies have been completed in a sample of individuals with ASD (Cascio et al., 2012). In the first study of its type, Cascio and colleagues found that when compared to matched controls, an ASD group exhibited greater activity to food pictures in the bilateral mid-insula (Cascio et al., 2012), the same region shown in earlier studies to be primary gustatory cortex (Phillips et al., 2014). Unfortunately, interpreting what this activity in the mid-insula means for models of ASD is complicated by the fact that the often highly idiosyncratic appetitive responses to individual foods were not accounted for in the experimental design. Furthermore, the study did not differentiate between participants with and without food selectivity. More recently, Avery et al. (2018) examined neural response to consumption of small doses of sweet versus neutral tastants in a group of adolescent and young adult males with ASD as compared to a group of age-matched neurotypical males. Although the two groups did not differ in their neural response to the sweet tastant overall, self-reported taste reactivity modulated the hemodynamic response to sweet tastants in the insula/gustatory cortex and food reward centers of the ASD group only. Therefore, much remains unknown and unclear about the neural underpinnings of food-related behaviors in ASD.

Heritability and genetic influences. Very little work has been completed examining the genetic influences on eating and eating-related behaviors in the context of ASD. However, to contextualize etiological influences on eating-related behaviors more broadly, there is an emerging literature examining these influences in the general population that can be examined. One dominant theory, the behavioral susceptibility theory by Jane Wardle and colleagues (Carnell & Wardle, 2008), suggests that appetitive traits, or stable predispositions to foods (food approach behaviors like food enjoyment or food avoidance behaviors like slowness of eating), mediate the genetic risk for obesity. In other words, these various appetitive traits are under genetic control to some extent and act to increase (or decrease) risks for developing obesity. Twin studies (i.e., contrasting concordance rates for traits among monozygotic vs. dizygotic twin pairs and other similar designs) have been the primary vehicle by which the heritability of these appetitive traits have been examined. For example, it has been shown recently that heritability values are modest, albeit influential in trait expression, for emotional overeating (Herle, Fildes, & Llewellyn, 2018; Herle, Fildes, Steinsbekk, Rijsdijk, & Llewellyn, 2017), with shared environmental factors exerting the greatest influence. In contrast, and perhaps most directly relevant to ASD, it has been found that food neophobia (Cooke, Haworth, & Wardle, 2007; Faith, Heo, Keller, & Pietrobelli, 2013; Knaapila et al., 2007) and food fussiness (Smith et al., 2017) are each individually highly heritable traits among children and adults.

Additionally, evidence suggests that these two components of food selectivity share substantial genetic influences (Smith et al., 2017). Complementing these studies are investigations into the heritability of traditional eating disorders. Again, twin and family studies implicate small-moderate heritability values for anorexia nervosa (e.g., Pettersson et al., in press), bulimia nervosa (Bulik et al., 2010), and binge eating disorder (Javaras et al., 2008). Although considerable progress is continuing to be made using quantitative genetic approaches to better understand genetic versus environmental influences on eating habits, traits, and disorders, there have also been studies completed examining potential molecular genetic associations with eating and related phenomena (e.g., taste perception) in the general population and in ASD. For example, the bitter taste receptor gene, TAS2R38, has been identified and shown to be associated with individual differences in perception of bitterness on various psychophysical tasks in the general population (Bufe et al., 2005). Of direct relevance to ASD is a recent study suggesting that children with the haplotype leading to more sensitivity to bitter tastants are more likely to be food selective (Riccio et al., 2018). Taken together, this suggests that food selectivity and related behaviors are largely under genetic control in the general population, yet what potential genetic mechanisms drive this food selectivity in ASD is only beginning to be assessed.

Diagnosis and Assessment

Diagnostic categories. Current diagnostic options in a clinical context include DSM-5 eating disorder diagnoses, including anorexia nervosa, bulimia nervosa, binge eating disorder, and ARFID (American Psychiatric Association, 2013). The shift from the DSM-IV-TR to DSM-5 saw the elimination of more catch-all definitions like other specified feeding and eating disorder and unspecified feeding and eating disorder. The goal was for ARFID to replace the DSM-IV-TR diagnosis of feeding disorder of infancy or early childhood, which was not well understood or used (Attia et al., 2013). However, as noted earlier, some people with ASD and eating issues may still not be captured by one of these diagnostic categories.

In addition, overweight and obesity can be medically diagnosed and coded via International Classification of Diseases, 10th edition (ICD-10). The most commonly utilized metric for determining overweight and obesity, primarily because of its ease in assessment and therefore ubiquity, is body mass index (BMI), which is calculated by dividing a person's weight (in kilograms) by the squared value of his or her height (in meters). For children, percentile scores (accounting for the chronological age and sex of the child) are used to determine cut-offs, with values between the 85th and 95th percentile considered overweight and those at or above the 95th percentile considered obese. For adults, a different scaling is used so that 18.5 to 24.99 is the normal range, 25 to 29.99 is overweight, and 30+ is obese. The obese range is further subdivided into three classes (Class 1 = 30 to 34.99, Class 2 = 35 to 39.99, and Class 3 or severe/extreme obesity = 40+; Centers for Disease Control and Prevention, 2016a, 2016b).

Assessment. Following from issues surrounding nomenclature (discussed earlier), challenges also arise in the assessment of eating-related behaviors and their utility for characterization, diagnosis, and measurement of treatment progress. Two approaches have generally been used: (a) broadband measurement of eating and related behaviors, sometimes with subscales or contributing factors, or (b) tools designed for specific eating-related constructs. Additionally, measures have been developed to assess general population individual differences, and two have been designed to capture eating-related pathology and even autism-specific eating challenges (i.e., Brief Autism Mealtime Behaviors Inventory [BAMBI; Lukens & Linscheid, 2008] and SWedish Eating Assessment for Autism Spectrum Disorders [SWEAA; Karlsson, Råstam, & Wentz, 2013]). Unfortunately, to the best of our knowledge, no commonly used eating disorder screening or diagnostic tools have been validated for use with ASD populations. However, there are many commonly utilized instruments for the assessment of eating disorder symptoms and diagnostic criteria, such as the Eating Disorder Examination (Fairburn & Beglin, 1994), which has been validated for use in both structured interview and questionnaire format for both adolescents and adults. See Table 13.1 for a sampling of measures commonly used in the field. These measures were selected to represent both the gestalt view and specificity of tools currently used in clinical practice and research. Review of the measures presented highlights several key considerations. First, there is significant overlap in content and items across measures, and the user must consider whether an individual item or scale on a broadband measure will meet his or her needs relative to a measure specifically designed for an eating-related construct. Relatedly, the heterogeneity of eating-related issues in ASD increases the possibility of a broadband measure masking individual differences that would be important for measurement of treatment progress and mechanisms of change. In addition, most of these tools are limited by the absence of established norms for providing cut points to indicate clinical concern or diagnosis. Finally, tools have been focused primarily in childhood, though there has been recent effort to develop screening tools for identifying ARFID in adult picky eaters (Zickgraf, Franklin, & Rozin, 2016; Zickgraf & Ellis, 2018). Use of assessment tools with larger sample sizes and a wider age range, including individuals without eating issues, will advance the field tremendously.

Treatment

Despite the high frequency and functional impact of eating problems in children with ASD, few empirically supported (and rigorously evaluated) interventions are available in general and *none* are available for adolescents and adults. In 2017, a systematic review identified only *two* randomized controlled trials available in the literature (Sharp, Volkert, Scahill, McCracken, & McElhanon, 2017); a third trial has just recently been documented evaluating an outpatient parent training program for feeding problems (Johnson et al., 2018). The majority of treatment approaches thus far use behavioral principles, sensory-based strategies, or a combination of the two, and have usually targeted children under the age of 8 years. Although there is a solid evidence base for treating traditional eating disorders in adolescents and adults (see Hilbert, Hoek, & Schmidt, 2017), these treatments have not been examined for use with individuals with ASD and appear to be less effective for ARFID-type presentations, which are likely to be more common in the ASD population (e.g., Forman et al., 2014). More broadly, there are no evidence-based treatments specifically designed or tested for eating issues in adults with ASD.

Treatment of eating issues in ASD is often multidisciplinary but is most frequently implemented by psychologists, speech–language pathologists, or occupational therapists. Consulting dietitians will often guide treatment priorities and target foods. Treatment is most frequently provided in an intensive day-treatment or inpatient context, although there is an increasing presence and effort to establish outpatient treatment options.

Intensive Behavioral Feeding Programs

Chronic feeding problems are regularly treated with behavioral interventions in pediatric clinical feeding programs, with a growing bolus of empirical support for use in the broad population of children with feeding problems (Lukens & Silverman, 2014; Sharp et al., 2017; Sharp, Jaquess, Morton, & Herzinger, 2010). In the context of a time-intensive inpatient or day-treatment environment and a multidisciplinary team (e.g., psychologist, dietician, speech–language pathologist, occupational therapist, social worker, nurse, gastroenterologist), behavioral treatment plans are developed with consideration of the medical risk for the patient as well as other family and system factors. Treatment generally employs systematic desensitization and other behavioral principles to implement therapeutic, structured meals. Intake of novel or nonpreferred foods is shaped to add variety to the diet and often work toward larger quantity of foods. Appetite manipulation and contingency management strategies are often at the forefront of treatment, with integrated plans for managing escape extinction. In many cases, parents are not initially involved in the treatment meals, with the goal of "resetting" the dynamic around eating. As new eating patterns are established, parents are integrated back into treatment meals in preparation for discharge.

Outpatient Treatment Approaches

For children who are medically stable, the time-intensive design of the day-treatment behavioral feeding programs may not be an appropriate fit for treatment. As an alternative, outpatient providers often modify treatment approaches from these intensive behavioral programs for use in an individual therapy model. In recognition of the growing need for outpatient treatment for eating issues in children with ASD, two manualized, outpatient interventions have been specifically designed and empirically evaluated for children with ASD. First, the Autism MEAL Plan (Sharp, Burrell, & Jaquess, 2014) program is a group-based intervention for parents/caregivers of children with ASD and food selectivity (3 to 8 years old; no IQ information included). This program includes eight 1-hour didactic training sessions with parents covering a breadth of behavior modification strategies (6 weeks), as well as more specific support for introducing new foods (2 weeks). Results from a pilot study (n = 19) indicated high social validity of the Autism MEAL Plan, as well as a significant reduction in parent-reported stress following intervention relative to waitlist control. However, the authors reported no significant reduction in challenging behaviors during mealtime and no improvement in diet variety.

Table 13.1. Sampling of Assessment Tools for Eating Issues in People with ASD

	MEASURE DESIGN			CONSTRUCT MEASURED						
Assessment Tool	**ASD Specific?**	**Broadband?**	**Individual Construct?**	Food Intake	Food Selectivity	Food Neophobia	Sensory Processing	Mealtime Challenges	Overeating	Traditional Eating Disorders
BRIEF AUTISM MEALTIME BEHAVIOR INVENTORY Lukens and Linscheid (2008) *18-item parent-report questionnaire designed to measure mealtime behavior problems observed in children with ASD; three factor scores include Limited Variety, Food Refusal, and Autism Features* Internal Consistency α: 0.88 (full scale), 0.87 (Limited Variety), 0.76 (Food Refusal), 0.63 (Autism Features)	Yes	X			X	X	X	X		
CHILDREN'S EATING BEHAVIOR QUESTIONNAIRE Wardle et al. (2001) *35-item parent-report measure with eight subscales (Food Responsiveness, Emotional Overeating, Enjoyment of Food, Desire to Drink, Satiety Responsiveness, Slowness in Eating, Emotional Undereating, and Food Fussiness)* Internal Consistency α: 0.74–0.91	No	X		X	X	X				
EATING IN THE ABSENCE OF HUNGER Tanofsky-Kraff et al. (2008) *14-item parent-report measure assessing children's eating when not hungry and its precipitants* Internal Consistency α: 0.80–0.88	No		X						X	
FOOD NEOPHOBIA SCALE Pliner and Hobden (1992) *10-item self- or parent-report scale assessing avoidance of and reluctance to eat novel foods* Internal Consistency α: 0.78–0.88	No		X			X				
EATING DISORDER EXAMINATION QUESTIONNAIRE Fairburn and Beglin (1994) *Measure of range/severity of eating disorder features* Internal Consistency α: 0.70–0.90	No	X								X

The second parent training program, Parent Training Program for Feeding Problems (Johnson et al., 2018; Johnson, Foldes, DeMand, & Brooks, 2015), extended an efficacious parent training program for children with ASD and challenging behaviors used previously to treat noncompliant behaviors, poor adaptive behavior skills, and sleep problems (Johnson et al., 2007, 2013) to the treatment of feeding problems. In their recently published initial randomized trial (Johnson et al., 2018), 44 children with ASD and feeding problems (2 to 7 years old, approximately half with IQ < 70) were assigned to either parent training for feeding treatment or a waitlist control. Treatment involved 11 sessions (60 to 90 minutes each) individually delivered via parent training. Session content focused first on basic behavior modification principles, nutritional counseling, and strategies for mealtime routines. Grounded in understanding the antecedent–behavior–consequence model for addressing feeding problems, sessions focused on prevention and reinforcement strategies, compliance procedures, and teaching strategies for parents to advance the child's feeding skills as well as how to generalize and maintain skills. Findings from the trial showed high attendance (85%), parent satisfaction (94% would recommend to others), and treatment fidelity (97% therapist integrity, 94% parent adherence). Comparison between groups revealed greater improvement for the treatment group in parent ratings of food selectivity, disruptive mealtime behavior, and parents' perception of their child around mealtimes.

Promising findings from these two outpatient parent training programs suggest that treatment of eating issues for a subset of children with ASD is feasible in an outpatient setting. However, similar to the more intensive behavioral feeding programs, these parent training programs are geared toward an early childhood cohort (i.e., younger than 8 years). The Building Up Food Flexibility and Exposure Treatment (BUFFET; Kuschner et al., 2017) program was developed as the first outpatient intervention to address the unique challenges of school-age youth with ASD and food selectivity. Behavioral feeding principles can be applied for this population to alter what a child eats in an immediate situation but cannot address the distorted or maladaptive thoughts triggering or perpetuating food selectivity. BUFFET was designed to uniquely leverage emerging cognitive skills in later childhood to shift inflexibility and maladaptive thoughts about food while also bolstering autonomy and self-determination in treatment change. BUFFET involves 14 weekly 90-minute multifamily group treatment sessions, with a combination of large group sections (all parents, children, and clinicians together), child-alone and parent-alone sections, and child–parent dyad sections. Treatment targets in BUFFET include reducing anxiety, increasing flexibility, child skill building for managing taste input, and expanding parent skills hypothesized to impact outcomes of food flexibility and diet variety. The first six sessions of the program emphasize psychoeducation and provide training in cognitive strategies for decreasing acute (food-related) anxiety and increasing flexibility. Exposure occurs in a group context as well as individually. Homework assignments provide practice and generalization opportunities. Parents are actively involved throughout all sessions by participating in full group activities, supporting exposure and coping strategy use, and honing specific skills pertinent to parents of youth with food selectivity. An initial open pilot feasibility trial of BUFFET with 11 families (children 8 to 12 years old, verbal IQ ≥80) showed high attendance rates (91%), no attrition, and strong child, parent, and clinician satisfaction ratings (Kuschner et al., 2017). Preliminary data showed an increase in the number of foods children were willing to eat and a reduction in the impact of food selectivity on the family's daily life (Kuschner et al., 2019). Though designed for school-age children, the infusion of elements supporting autonomy and self-determination in BUFFET lay a possible foundation for future adaptation and use with adolescents and adults with ASD.

Treatment for Overweight and Obesity

Established recommendations suggest a staged approach to weight management in neurotypical children and adolescents, starting with preventative management with healthy lifestyle changes (e.g., increasing fruit and vegetable intake, minimizing consumption of sugar-containing beverages, increasing physical activity, decreasing sedentary activity time). If no change is observed, there is a shift to focus on structured weight management, followed by management by a comprehensive multidisciplinary team, and then considerations such as meal replacement, very low-energy diet, medication, and surgery (Spear et al., 2007). Goals transition across the stages from loose guidelines to structured plans. A systems-level approach with integrated messages across environments has also been highlighted as a societal need (Hoelscher, Kirk, Ritchie, Cunningham-Sabo, & Academy Positions Committee, 2013). Treatment efforts are also being targeted toward younger (preschool) ages with the goal of preventing the need for treatment but, when needed, providing evidence-based treatment options (Stark et al., 2017) to change risky health trajectories.

For adults, there is an established treatment algorithm that helps guide primary care physicians through assessing and recommending best practice for patients with weight-related issues (Jensen et al., 2013). Based on calculated body mass index, physicians identify adults at elevated risk for obesity and cardiovascular disease and use the algorithm to recommend an appropriate combination of comprehensive lifestyle changes, dietary strategies for weight loss, and bariatric surgical treatment options. Successful weight loss maintenance is most associated with high levels of physical activity, limited television watching, specific dietary features (e.g., regularly eating breakfast and maintaining a consistent, low-calorie, low-fat diet), low levels of disinhibition, and high levels of self-monitoring (Thomas, Bond, Phelan, Hill, & Wing, 2014; Wing & Hill, 2001).

Although there are some established weight management treatment programs designed for individuals with intellectual and developmental disabilities more broadly (e.g., Beeken et al., 2013; Ptomey, Goetz, Lee, Donnelly, & Sullivan, 2013), very little is available for treatment of overweight or obesity specifically designed for people with ASD. To the best of our knowledge, no exercise programs have been designed specifically for adults with ASD, though there are emerging programs, such as Shape Up-LD (Beeken et al., 2013) designed for individuals with mild to moderate intellectual disabilities that could be adapted for adults on the autism spectrum. In contrast, there are a few emerging programs designed for children with ASD. For example, an exercise intervention administered to children with ASD (6 to 12 years old) showed beneficial effects on metabolic indicators, though nutritional profiles were not evaluated (Toscano, Carvalho, & Ferreira, 2017).

Adaptation and evaluation of existing evidence-based treatment of obesity for people with ASD is a crucial area for research in the coming years and has been highlighted as a key research theme by the Healthy Weight Research Network (Curtin, Must, Phillips, & Bandini, 2017), an interdisciplinary network for children with ASD and developmental disabilities. Although available evidence-based treatment for weight management in neurotypical individuals provides a foundation to expand from, challenges associated with ASD will require unique consideration (e.g., motor skill impairments may limit the range of physical activity opportunities available; executive dysfunction may decrease the likelihood of low levels of disinhibition and high levels of self-monitoring being present). Review of *NIH Reporter* and research grant-giving foundation websites suggests that trials are underway to develop tailored treatments for individuals with ASD to target nutrition and physical activity. We anticipate growth in this area in the coming years.

Interdisciplinary Considerations

Eating issues are often inherently interdisciplinary. Feeding programs in academic medical centers frequently utilize assessment teams with gastrointestinal physicians, psychologists, dieticians, speech therapists, and occupational therapists to provide input and make treatment recommendations. It is also important to maintain this interdisciplinary perspective throughout treatment. Although this is often more readily available for intensive treatment programs that are based in medical centers, it needs to be more thoroughly considered for outpatient treatment options as well. For example, a child may have ongoing issues with constipation due to diet and atypical gastrointestinal function that is managed with a regular dose of a laxative. If through a behavioral treatment the child begins broadening his or her diet and integrating more foods with fiber that promote more regular bowel movement activity, there may be a need to adjust the laxative dose. Similarly, if treatment expands the texture profile of foods the child will tolerate, swallowing could be challenged in a new way and need support from a speech or occupational therapist. Sometimes a multidisciplinary approach may be needed to expand the possibilities of target foods. If a child's fine motor skills are so limited that he or she is making food choices based on avoiding silverware use, occupational therapy will be needed for precursor skills to move beyond finger foods.

Sensory-focused treatment strategies. Sensory-based treatments, such as the sequential oral sensory (SOS) approach (Toomey & Ross, 2011), use systematic desensitization across a hierarchy of textures in a play-based or social context; although commonly used and thought to be effective, they have not undergone rigorous empirical evaluation and are often used separately (or in contrast to) a treatment primarily grounded in a behavioral or cognitive behavioral approach. It may instead be useful to integrate these perspectives more within treatment. There may be sensory-related goals that could be considered precursors to engaging in a behavioral treatment (e.g., systematic desensitization to a particularly reactive texture prior to attempting to eat a food with that texture), or a sensory-focused treatment exercise that could serve as preparation for an eating-focused cognitive behavioral treatment session (e.g., oral–motor "warm-up").

Evidence-Based Treatment Summary

Although the empirical foundation for rigorously evaluated treatment strategies for eating issues in ASD is limited, there is a long history of rather rampantly opposing views in the field regarding the "best" treatment approach for eating issues. Those supporting behavioral strategies have often been diametrically opposed to those behind sensory-based strategies, and vice versa. With the introduction of more outpatient programs for eating issues in ASD, and an emphasis in the field more broadly (and by federal funders) toward a better understanding of mechanisms of treatment in ASD, we propose the need for a more tailored perspective on treatment that considers the medical acuity of the individual's presentation, the desired outcomes, and the family resources available for treatment, all evaluated in a developmental context (see Table 13.2)—and, perhaps most important, a perspective that "one size does not fit all" in treatment planning. For example,

Table 13.2. Considerations for Personalized Treatment of Eating Issues in Autism Spectrum Disorder

Assessment Constructs	Considerations
Where should treatment occur?	Day treatment Inpatient Outpatient Home Multisetting (outpatient + home practice)
What developmental factors need to be considered?	What is the child's chronological age? Developmental age? How can the child communicate about food and eating? Words versus visuals? Does the child have the verbal and abstraction skills to use cognitive strategies in treatment?
Are there any co-occurring conditions to consider?	Medical diagnoses that will impact dietary choices (e.g., celiac disease) Developmental delays or psychiatric conditions that may impact treatment response (e.g., intellectual disability, anxiety)
What is the level of medical acuity?	Child weight and body mass index Risk for need for feeding tube
How will parents be involved in treatment?	Parent training (without the child) Parent training (in parallel to the child receiving treatment) Observing treatment and then reintegrated into an active role after the child makes initial progress Participating collaboratively with child throughout treatment
What are the treatment goals?	Increase diversity of food intake Increase quantity of food intake Improve nutrition value of food intake Decrease conflict and stress related to eating (i.e., reduce daily impact of child's eating on family) Reduce accommodations made to get child to eat (e.g., ability to make one meal for family at dinner time)
Who is choosing the treatment goals?	Parent-driven versus child-driven goals Is the child old enough to identify treatment goals that may be socially motivated?
What will happen at the end of treatment—how do treatment strategies generalize?	A structured approach to eating (structured mealtime, structured food exposure practice) Self-regulatory scripts and strategies that can be applied to any situation with food

the outpatient treatment programs in the literature thus far have been designed specifically for children with ASD; however, interventions developed for general population use (i.e., not ASD specific or geared toward a clinically based feeding program) may offer opportunities for generating novel treatment components for people with ASD. The Tiny Tastes program was designed as a parent-led, home-based intervention to increase intake and liking of vegetables in children ages 3 to 4 years (Remington, Añez, Croker, Wardle, & Cooke, 2011). In a relatively large randomized controlled trial (n = 173), families in the treatment condition presented their children with 12 daily tastes of a vegetable and provided either praise or a sticker for tasting. Relative to a control condition (i.e., no daily tastings), children who completed daily tastings showed a significant increase in their intake and ratings of liking particular vegetables. Although this is perhaps a seemingly simplistic intervention that would not account for the variety of complexities of eating issues for children with ASD, results highlight that there may be strategies validated for use in typical development that could be complementary components to treatments developed for children with ASD. Moreover, it is perhaps a straightforward approach that could be modified via upward extension for adolescents or adults with ASD, a group sorely underserved by currently available treatments. As we think about best practice for outpatient treatment of eating issues for people with ASD, we might think about staged or modular approaches to treatment where something like Tiny Tastes is implemented as a home-based addition to a clinic-based treatment, or as a disseminable and easy-to-administer first-round intervention for a child (or even adolescent/adult) with no medical risks and lower levels of symptoms. It is likely that these multicomponent (and multidiscipline or multitheoretical) treatment programs will be the lynchpin to advancing personalized treatment for eating issues in ASD.

Case Example

Here we offer two case examples to highlight considerations across multiple domains and decision points for determining the most appropriately tailored treatment approach for a child with ASD and eating-related issues.

Case example 1. Leona is a 3-year-old girl with ASD who presents as underweight and with low food intake. Leona has mild language delays but generally shows developmental skills consistent with her chronological age. At mealtime, she eats very small portion sizes that are too small to sustain her weight over time. She does not get upset or have a meltdown when foods are presented, even if they are novel or nonpreferred foods; Leona simply says she is full and doesn't want to eat anymore. Medically based explanations for her small portion sizes are ruled out (e.g., swallowing function is intact, no gastrointestinal disorder). Her parents are at a loss with how to help her eat larger portion sizes. Given her willingness to eat, age-appropriate developmental skills, and positive connection with her parents, an intensive behavioral treatment might be considered the best fit. Her underweight status is concerning and requires a structured approach involving an interdisciplinary team to ensure that she does not lose more weight as the treatment plan is implemented and her dietary choices and strategies are shifted. A treatment plan is developed that starts with a preference assessment to identify foods she currently eats and proximal next steps for treatment goals to expand food options (e.g., chicken nuggets transition to grilled chicken pieces, strawberries transition to raspberries, corn transitions to sweet peas), and a plan is developed for gradually increasing portion size across meals. Reinforcer assessment identifies a Sesame Street toy that is highly preferred and will serve as a reward for bites eaten during treatment sessions. At the start of treatment, Leona responds positively and willingly eats meals and enjoys her Sesame Street toy reward. As treatment progresses and portion size continues to increase, Leona begins to show some avoidance behavior, turning her head away and attempting to leave her seat. With the addition of novel reinforcers and a shift in reinforcement schedule to maximize bites taken prior to reward, these avoidance behaviors decrease. As Leona reaches the end of her treatment, a visual is incorporated to show Leona how many bites must be taken in the session to meet her goal (i.e., target portion size). Her parents receive training on how to provide her meals and use this visual for target bites, and Leona is discharged. By the end of treatment, Leona's parents know how to present foods to support her eating portion sizes that are appropriate for regularly maintained weight gain. Leona has begun to eat these larger meals without difficulty, but her parents are prepared with how to respond by adjusting reinforcement strategies and rewards if she begins to avoid eating full portions at mealtime.

Case example 2 (Figure 13.1). Davis is an 11-year-old boy with ASD who presents with food selectivity. His food repertoire is limited, with nearly no vegetables and only a handful of fruits; thus, his diet is mostly characterized by high-density, high-fat foods. He eats age-appropriate portion sizes and his weight is currently appropriate for his height and waist size, but his parents are concerned that he is at risk for gaining weight and showing nutritional inadequacies given the makeup of his meals and snacks. When his parents suggest he try to eat a new food, he becomes anxious and distressed, and they usually end up in an argument. After years of trying to broaden Davis's diet, his parents gave up and generally feed him only what they know he will eat. Despite making do in daily life, they find the situation very frustrating and believe it negatively impacts their family's quality of life. As Davis has entered middle school in a mainstream education environment (he has cognitive abilities above age expectations in the superior range), he is noticing that his peers eat a wider variety of foods than he does. He has been stuck in a few situations at school events where there were no foods available that he was willing to eat. Davis has also finally made one good friend during sixth grade and knows his rock climbing birthday party is coming up. He is excited about the party, but his friend said that they will have pizza after climbing and Davis is nervous that the pizza won't be the brand he likes to eat; he knows he will be hungry but isn't sure he'll be able to eat the pizza they offer. Both Davis and his parents are beginning to think that they might need to do something about this situation.

With no imminent medical risk, an outpatient treatment context is most likely a good fit for Davis; missing school for a day-treatment program could be challenging for Davis. In adolescence, and with more advanced verbal and cognitive abilities, treatment should focus on giving Davis agency and promoting self-advocacy throughout the process. Davis and his parents enroll in a BUFFET group (Kuschner et al., 2017). Through didactic sessions Davis realizes that when he sees a new food or his parents ask him to try something new his heart starts to race and he begins to think of all the bad things that will happen if he tries to eat the food, which in turn makes him more irritable. Through treatment he begins to develop coping strategies for slowing down his heart rate (e.g., taking deep breaths) and identifies ways to restructure his thoughts about new foods to make the process more manageable (e.g., "Just because kiwi looks funny with black seeds doesn't mean it will taste bad. I like some other fruits and might like the taste of kiwi."). Through exposure opportunities in group snack time Davis also develops a broader food vocabulary and knowledge base. He and his parents begin to see a pattern that he likes foods with a peppery flavor. He learns that he can add pepper to food to change the flavor and add something familiar that he knows he likes. As treatment progresses, he begins to do exposure practice with new foods he and his parents identified as treatment goals. Davis earns "BUFFET Bucks" for completing steps during his exposure practice that he can trade in for extra time with his iPad at home. Treatment goals start with different brands of pizza so he can be flexible for his friend's birthday party. He is nervous about trying the new pizzas, but with his new coping strategies and skills for managing his anxiety and being more flexible, he completes his hierarchy and adds a few brands of pizza into his repertoire. Then he moves onto new foods that will add fruits and vegetables to his repertoire. It takes him a little longer to get through his exposure hierarchies for the vegetables because they make him particularly nervous, but he and his parents test out different ways to prepare them and figure out that vegetables that can be cooked and flavored with pepper are easier for Davis to manage. After 14 weeks of treatment, Davis has become more flexible with pizza brand and added a number of fruits and vegetables into his food repertoire. He and has parents have a better vocabulary for discussing Davis's experiences with food, so rather than immediately arguing and falling into conflict, they are able to use the strategies they've learned in BUFFET to negotiate and make plans for what Davis will eat. Davis no longer panics at the thought of a new food and knows how to build an exposure hierarchy to practice with a new food and use coping strategies to overcome his anxiety and stress.

Case example 2—alternative paths. We can consider how the optimal treatment approach for Davis might vary based on changing a single component of his presentation.

What if Davis were younger? If Davis were 5 years old instead of 11, he would be less capable of engaging in cognitive behavioral strategies and might be a better fit for a more behaviorally oriented outpatient treatment approach that provided exposure practice for systematic desensitization with reinforcement and rewards for trying new foods. A parent training approach could also be a fit, but Davis has more advanced cognitive skills that would allow him to participate in individual therapy sessions.

What if Davis were overweight? With an established medical concern (overweight or obesity), it would be of great importance to integrate evidence-based treatment strategies for obesity (i.e., stricter dietary goals and a plan for physical activity). However, it is crucial to note that although target foods for Davis in this case should have more of a focus on increasing intake of healthy fruits and vegetables and decreasing intake of sweet/salty snacks and sugary beverages, treatment must also help Davis learn how to eat these foods. Though in this case he is overweight and that is a priority concern, he is still selective and does not have the skills needed to eat novel and nonpreferred foods. These foundational skills must be established for Davis to be successful with his nutritionally focused treatment goals.

Summary and Future Directions

There is a rich clinical research history documenting eating-related issues in ASD dating back to seminal descriptions of the disorder. We have made many advances in the interim including the development of effective behavioral interventions for some people with ASD and emerging evidence for the consistently high prevalence and persistence across development of eating-related issues in ASD. Treatment options are expanding, and continued empirical evaluation of efficacy with more advanced treatment designs to examine active agents of treatment and a most optimized treatment (e.g., MOST approach, SMART designs) will further advance the field.

Barriers continue to impede progress in the field, including lack of clarity and consistency in use of concepts, definitions, and nomenclature. This affects not only an accurate census of eating-related challenges and traditional eating disorders (including the newest diagnosis, ARFID) in ASD but also measure development for characterizing individual differences, quantifying severity, and assessing change with treatment. Future research should also seek to move beyond rating scales to utilize experimental paradigms. Building upon a long-standing history in experimental research on eating in the general population, researchers will be able to more precisely pinpoint and understand mechanisms underpinning eating-related atypicalities in ASD, which will in turn inform intervention refinement and development. Similarly, intervention development (as well as measurement development and approach) should look beyond ASD-specific work to utilize and adapt measures (once validated in ASD) previously developed for other populations. Furthermore, our knowledge to date is notably limited to childhood. Eating-related challenges, associated idiosyncrasies less observed in the general population, and potential intervention approaches across the lifespan in ASD need to be evaluated as part of future efforts. Better understanding and treating eating issues may have a crucial downstream impact on the daily life and well-being of adults with ASD, an area of high priority and concern in the field.

Additional work is also needed to clarify whether nutritional intake is truly compromised in ASD. The empirical literature provides mixed evidence and many studies do not directly link eating behaviors with nutritional intake, which is critical to assessing points of entry for intervention and understanding the impact of atypical eating. Relatedly, in spite of the public health importance of potential nutritional inadequacy and an increased risk of obesity in ASD, both basic research into mechanisms and treatments are sorely lacking. More tightly controlled and comprehensive studies of eating-related behavior and their health consequences are needed to optimize well-being and outcomes among people with ASD.

Finally, recognition of self-advocacy and autonomy should be incorporated into personalized treatment approaches and decisions regarding treatment course. Eating issues can result in significant health risk but can also be an extension of the normal distribution of individual differences in eating habits. As measures become more refined and greater consistency is established regarding the clinical significance of eating issues, people with ASD should contribute and maintain a voice regarding treatment decisions.

References

Achenbach, T. M., & Edelbrock, C. (1983). *Manual for the child behavior checklist and revised behavior profile*. Burlington, VT: Department of Psychiatry, University of Vermont.

Ahearn, W. H., Castine, T., Nault, K., & Green, G. (2001). An assessment of food acceptance in children with autism or pervasive developmental disorder-not otherwise specified. *Journal of Autism and Developmental Disorders, 31*(5), 505–511.

American Psychiatric Association. (1994). *Diagnostic and statistical manual of mental disorders* (4th ed.). Arlington, VA: American Psychiatric Publishing.

American Psychiatric Association. (2013). *Diagnostic and statistical manual of mental disorders* (5th ed.). Arlington, VA: American Psychiatric Association.

Attia, E., Becker, A. E., Bryant-Waugh, R., Hoek, H. W., Kreipe, R. E., Marcus, M. D., . . . Wonderlich, S. (2013). Feeding and eating disorders in DSM-5. *American Journal of Psychiatry, 170*(11), 1237–1239. http://doi.org/10.1176/appi.ajp.2013.13030326

Avery, J. A., Ingeholm, J. E., Wohltjen, S., Collins, M., Riddell, C. D., Gotts, S. J., . . . Martin, A. (2018). Neural correlates of taste reactivity in autism spectrum disorder. *NeuroImage: Clinical, 19*, 1–9. http://doi.org/10.1016/j.nicl.2018.04.008

Bandini, L. G., Anderson, S. E., Curtin, C., Cermak, S., Evans, E. W. I., Scampini, R.,... Must, A. (2010). Food selectivity in children with autism spectrum disorders and typically developing children. *Journal of Pediatrics, 157*(2), 259–264. http://doi.org/10.1016/j.jpeds.2010.02.013

Bandini, L. G., Curtin, C., Phillips, S., Anderson, S. E., Maslin, M., & Must, A. (2017). Changes in food selectivity in children with autism spectrum disorder. *Journal of Autism and Developmental Disorders, 47*(2), 439–446. http://doi.org/10.1007/s10803-016-2963-6

Baylis, L. L., Rolls, E. T., & Baylis, G. C. (1995). Afferent connections of the caudolateral orbitofrontal cortex taste area of the primate. *Neuroscience, 64*(3), 801–812. http://doi.org/10.1016/0306-4522(94)00449-F

Beeken, R. J., Spanos, D., Fovargue, S., Hunter, R., Omar, R., Hassiotis, A.,... Croker, H. (2013). Piloting a manualised weight management programme (Shape Up-LD) for overweight and obese persons with mild-moderate learning disabilities: Study protocol for a pilot randomised controlled trial. *Trials, 14*(1), 71. http://doi.org/10.1186/1745-6215-14-71

Ben-Sasson, A., Hen, L., Fluss, R., Cermak, S. A., Engel-Yeger, B., & Gal, E. (2009). A meta-analysis of sensory modulation symptoms in individuals with autism spectrum disorders. *Journal of Autism and Developmental Disorders, 39*(1), 1–11. http://doi.org/10.1007/s10803-008-0593-3

Birch, L. L., Fisher, J. O., Grimm-Thomas, K., Markey, C. N., Sawyer, R., & Johnson, S. L. (2001). Confirmatory factor analysis of the Child Feeding Questionnaire: A measure of parental attitudes, beliefs and practices about child feeding and obesity proneness. *Appetite, 36*(3), 201–210.

Birch, L. L., & Marlin, D. W. (1982). I don't like it; I never tried it: Effects of exposure on two-year-old children's food preferences. *Appetite, 3*(4), 353–360. http://doi.org/10.1016/S0195-6663(82)80053-6

Broder-Fingert, S., Brazauskas, K., Lindgren, K., Iannuzzi, D., & Van Cleave, J. (2014). Prevalence of overweight and obesity in a large clinical sample of children with autism. *Academic Pediatrics, 14*(4), 408–414. http://doi.org/10.1016/j.acap.2014.04.004

Bufe, B., Breslin, P. A. S., Kuhn, C., Reed, D. R., Tharp, C. D., Slack, J. P.,... Meyerhof, W.. (2005). The molecular basis of individual differences in phenylthiocarbamide and propylthiouracil bitterness perception. *Current Biology, 15*(4), 322–327. http://doi.org/10.1016/j.cub.2005.01.047

Bulik, C. M., Thornton, L. M., Root, T. L., Pisetsky, E. M., Lichtenstein, P., & Pedersen, N. L. (2010). Understanding the relation between anorexia nervosa and bulimia nervosa in a Swedish national twin sample. *Biological Psychiatry, 67*(1), 71–77.

Carnell, S., & Wardle, J. (2008). Appetite and adiposity in children: Evidence for a behavioral susceptibility theory of obesity. *American Journal of Clinical Nutrition, 88*(1), 22–29. http://doi.org/10.1093/ajcn/88.1.22

Carruth, B. R., Ziegler, P. J., Gordon, A., & Barr, S. I. (2004). Prevalence of picky eaters among infants and toddlers and their caregivers' decisions about offering a new food. *Journal of the American Dietetic Association, 104*, 57–64. http://doi.org/10.1016/j.jada.2003.10.024

Cascio, C. J., Foss-Feig, J. H., Heacock, J. L., Newsom, C. R., Cowan, R. L., Benningfield, M. M.,...Cao, A. (2012). Response of neural reward regions to food cues in autism spectrum disorders. *Journal of Neurodevelopmental Disorders, 4*(9).

Centers for Disease Control and Prevention. (2016a). Adult overweight and obesity. Retrieved from https://www.cdc.gov/obesity/adult/index.html

Centers for Disease Control and Prevention. (2016b). Childhood overweight and obesity. Retrieved from https://www.cdc.gov/obesity/childhood/index.html

Cermak, S. A., Curtin, C., & Bandini, L. G. (2010). Food selectivity and sensory sensitivity in children with autism spectrum disorders. *Journal of the American Dietetic Association, 110*(2), 238–246. http://doi.org/10.1016/j.jada.2009.10.032

Chistol, L. T. (2018). Sensory sensitivity and food selectivity in children with autism spectrum disorder. *Journal of Autism and Developmental Disorders, 48*(2), 583–591. http://doi.org/10.1007/s10803-017-3340-9

Cole, N. C., An, R., Lee, S.-Y., & Donovan, S. M. (2017). Correlates of picky eating and food neophobia in young children: A systematic review and meta-analysis. *Nutrition Reviews, 75*(7), 516–532. http://doi.org/10.1093/nutrit/nux024

Cooke, L. J., Haworth, C. M., & Wardle, J. (2007). Genetic and environmental influences on children's food neophobia. *American Journal of Clinical Nutrition, 86*(2), 428–433. http://doi.org/10.1093/ajcn/86.2.428

Cornish, E. (1998). A balanced approach towards healthy eating in autism. *Journal of Human Nutrition and Dietetics, 11*(6), 501–509.

Criado, K. K., Sharp, W. G., McCracken, C. E., De Vinck-Baroody, O., Dong, L., Aman, M. G.,... Scahill, L. (2017). Overweight and obese status in children with autism spectrum disorder and disruptive behavior. *Autism, 22*(4), 450–459. http://doi.org/10.1177/1362361316683888

Curtin, C., Must, A., Phillips, S., & Bandini, L. (2017). The healthy weight research network: A research agenda to promote healthy weight among youth with autism spectrum disorder and other developmental disabilities. *Pediatric Obesity, 12*(1), e6–e9. http://doi.org/10.1111/ijpo.12109

D'Cruz, A.-M., Ragozzino, M. E., Mosconi, M. W., Shrestha, S., Cook, E. H., & Sweeney, J. A. (2013). Reduced behavioral flexibility in autism spectrum disorders. *Neuropsychology, 27*(2), 152–160. http://doi.org/10.1037/a0031721

Dunn, W. (1999). *Sensory profile*. San Antonio, TX: Pearson.

Evans, E. W., Must, A., Anderson, S. E., Curtin, C., Scampini, R., Maslin, M., & Bandini, L. (2012). Dietary patterns and body mass index in children with autism and typically developing children. *Research in Autism Spectrum Disorders, 6*(1), 399–405.

Fairburn, C. G., & Beglin, S. J. (1994). Assessment of eating disorder psychopathology: Interview or self-report questionnaire? *International Journal of Eating Disorders, 16*, 363–370.

Faith, M. S., Heo, M., Keller, K. L., & Pietrobelli, A. (2013). Child food neophobia is heritable, associated with less compliant eating, and moderates familial resemblance for BMI. *Obesity (Silver Spring, Md.), 21*(8), 1650–1655. http://doi.org/10.1002/oby.20369

Forman, S. F., McKenzie, N., Hehn, R., Monge, M. C., Kapphahn, C. J., Mammel, K. A., Woods, E. R. (2014). Predictors of outcome at 1 year in adolescents with DSM-5 restrictive eating disorders: Report of the national eating disorders quality improvement collaborative. *J Adolescent Health, 55*(6), 750–756. doi:10.1016/j.jadohealth.2014.06.014

Gastgeb, H. Z., Dundas, E. M., Minshew, N. J., & Strauss, M. S. (2011). Category formation in autism: Can individuals with autism form categories and prototypes of dot patterns? *Journal of Autism and Developmental Disorders, 42*(8), 1694–1704. http://doi.org/10.1007/s10803-011-1411-x

Georgiades, S., & Kasari, C. (2018). Reframing optimal outcomes in autism. *JAMA Pediatrics, 172*(8), 716–712. http://doi.org/10.1001/jamapediatrics.2018.1016

Grabenhorst, F., Rolls, E. T., & Bilderbeck, A. (2008). How cognition modulates affective responses to taste and flavor: Top-down influences on the orbitofrontal and pregenual cingulate cortices. *Cerebral Cortex, 18*(7), 1549–1559. http://doi.org/10.1093/cercor/bhm185

Hazen, E. P., Stornelli, J. L., O'Rourke, J. A., Koesterer, K., & McDougle, C. J. (2014). Sensory symptoms in autism spectrum disorders. *Harvard Review of Psychiatry, 22*(2), 112–124. http://doi.org/10.1097/01.HRP.0000445143.08773.58

Herle, M., Fildes, A., & Llewellyn, C. H. (2018). Emotional eating is learned not inherited in children, regardless of obesity risk. *Pediatric Obesity, 62*, 985. http://doi.org/10.1111/ijpo.12428

Herle, M., Fildes, A., Steinsbekk, S., Rijsdijk, F., & Llewellyn, C. H. (2017). Emotional over- and under-eating in early childhood are learned not inherited. *Scientific Reports, 7*(1), 9092. http://doi.org/10.1038/s41598-017-09519-0

Hess, J. A., Matson, J. L., & Dixon, D. R. (2010). Psychiatric symptom endorsements in children and adolescents diagnosed with autism spectrum disorders: A comparison to typically developing children and adolescents. *Journal of Developmental and Physical Disabilities, 22*(5), 485–496. http://doi.org/10.1007/s10882-009-9185-1

Hilbert, A., Hoek, H. W., & Schmidt, R. (2017). Evidence-based clinical guidelines for eating disorders: International comparison. *Current Opinion in Psychiatry, 30*, 423–437. http://doi.org/10.1097/yco.0000000000000360

Hill, A. P., Zuckerman, K. E., & Fombonne, E. (2015). Obesity and autism. *Pediatrics, 136*(6), 1051–1061. http://doi.org/10.1542/peds.2015-1437

Hill, J. O., & Peters, J. C. (1998). Environmental contributions to the obesity epidemic. *Science, 280*(5368), 1371–1374. http://doi.org/10.1126/science.280.5368.1371

Hoelscher, D. M., Kirk, S., Ritchie, L., Cunningham-Sabo, L., & Academy Positions Committee. (2013). Position of the Academy of Nutrition and Dietetics: Interventions for the prevention and treatment of pediatric overweight and obesity. *Journal of the Academy of Nutrition and Dietetics, 113*(10), 1375–1394. http://doi.org/10.1016/j.jand.2013.08.004

Huke, V., Turk, J., Saeidi, S., Kent, A., & Morgan, J. F. (2013). Autism spectrum disorders in eating disorder populations: A systematic review. *European Eating Disorders Review, 21*(5), 345–351. http://doi.org/10.1002/erv.2244

Hyman, S. L., Stewart, P. A., Schmidt, B., Lemcke, N., Foley, J. T., Peck, R.,... Ng, P.K. (2012). Nutrient intake from food in children with autism. *Pediatrics, 130*(Suppl 2), S145–S153.

Javaras, K. N., Laird, N. M., Reichborn-Kjennerud, T., Bulik, C. M., Pope, H. G., Jr., & Hudson, J. I. (2008). Familiality and heritability of binge eating disorder: Results of a case–control family study and a twin study. *International Journal of Eating Disorders, 41*(2), 174–179.

Jensen, M. D., Ryan, D. H., Apovian, C. M., Ard, J. D., Comuzzie, A. G. Donato, K. A.,... Tomaselli, G.F. (2013). AHA/ACC/TOS guideline for the management of overweight and obesity in adults: A report of the American College of Cardiology/American Heart Association task force on practice guidelines and the Obesity Society. *Journal of the American College of Cardiology, 63*(25), 2985–3025.

Johnson, C. R., Brown, K., Hyman, S. L., Brooks, M. M., Aponte, C., Levato, L.,... Smith, T. (2018). Parent training for feeding problems in children with autism spectrum disorder: Initial randomized trial. *Journal of Pediatric Psychology, 45*, 613–612. http://doi.org/10.1093/jpepsy/jsy063

Johnson, C. R., Foldes, E., DeMand, A., & Brooks, M. M. (2015). Behavioral parent training to address feeding problems in children with autism spectrum disorder: A pilot trial. *Journal of Developmental and Physical Disabilities, 27*(5), 591–607. http://doi.org/10.1007/s10882-015-9437-1

Johnson, C. R., Handen, B. L., Butter, E., Wagner, A., Mulick, J., Sukhodolsky, D. G.,... Smith, T. (2007). Development of a parent training program for children with pervasive developmental disorders. *Behavioral Interventions, 22*, 201–221. http://doi.org/10.1002/bin.237

Johnson, C. R., Turner, K. S., Foldes, E., Brooks, M. M., Kronk, R., & Wiggs, L. (2013). Behavioral parent training to address sleep disturbances in young children with autism spectrum disorder: A pilot trial. *Sleep Medicine, 14*(10), 995–1004. http://doi.org/10.1016/j.sleep.2013.05.013

Johnson, C. R., Turner, K., Stewart, P. A., & Schmidt, B. (2014). Relationships between feeding problems, behavioral characteristics and nutritional quality in children with ASD. *Journal of Autism and Developmental Disorders*, 44, 2175–2184.

Johnson, S. L., Davies, P. L., Boles, R. E., Gavin, W. J., & Bellows, L. L. (2015). Young children's food neophobia characteristics and sensory behaviors are related to their food intake. *Journal of Nutrition, 145*(11), 2610–2616. http://doi.org/10.3945/jn.115.217299

Kanner, L. (1943). Autistic disturbances of affective contact. *Nervous Child, 2*, 217–250.

Karlsson, L., Råstam, M., & Wentz, E. (2013). The SWedish Eating Assessment for Autism spectrum disorders (SWEAA)—Validation of a self-report questionnaire targeting eating disturbances within the autism spectrum. *Research in Developmental Disabilities, 34*, 2224–2233.

Klinger, L. G., & Dawson, G. (2001). Prototype formation in autism. *Development and Psychopathology, 13*(1), 111–124.

Knaapila, A., Tuorila, H., Silventoninen, K., Keskitalo, K., Kallela, M., Wessman, M.,... Perola, M. (2007). Food neophobia shows heritable variation in humans. *Physiology & Behavior, 91*(5), 573–578. http://doi.org/10.1016/j.physbeh.2007.03.019

Kobayashi, R., & Murata, T. (1998). Behavioral characteristics of 187 young adults with autism. *Psychiatry and Clinical Neurosciences, 52*(4), 383–390. http://doi.org/10.1046/j.1440-1819.1998.00415.x

Kral, T. V. E., Souders, M. C., Tompkins, V. H., Remiker, A. M., Eriksen, W. T., & Pinto-Martin, J. A. (2015). Child eating behaviors and caregiver feeding practices in children with autism spectrum disorders. *Public Health Nursing, 32*(5), 488–497. http://doi.org/10.1111/phn.12146

Kuschner, E. S., Eisenberg, I. W., Orionzi, B., Simmons, W. K., Kenworthy, L., Martin, A., & Wallace, G. L. (2015). A preliminary study of self-reported food selectivity in adolescents and young adults with autism spectrum disorder. *Research in Autism Spectrum Disorders, 15–16*, 53–59. http://doi.org/10.1016/j.rasd.2015.04.005

Kuschner, E. S., Maddox, B. B., de Marchena, A., Morton, H. E., Reaven, J., & Anthony, L. G. (2019). The BUFFET Program: Proof-of-concept of a cognitive behavioral treatment for selective eating in youth with autism spectrum disorder. Manuscript in preparation.

Kuschner, E. S., Morton, H. E., Maddox, B. B., Marchena, A., Anthony, L. G., & Reaven, J. (2017). The BUFFET Program: Development of a cognitive behavioral treatment for selective eating in youth with autism spectrum disorder. *Clinical Child and Family Psychology Review, 20*(4), 403–421. http://doi.org/10.1007/s10567-017-0236-3

Lane, A. E., Dennis, S. J., & Geraghty, M. E. (2011). Brief report: Further evidence of sensory subtypes in autism. *Journal of Autism and Developmental Disorders, 41*(6), 826–831. http://doi.org/10.1007/s10803-010-1103-y

Lane, A. E., Geraghty, M. E., Young, G. S., & Rostorfer, J. (2014). Problem eating behaviors in autism spectrum disorder are associated with suboptimal daily nutrient intake and taste/smell sensitivity. *ICAN: Infant, 6*(3), 172–180.

Lane, A. E., Molloy, C. A., & Bishop, S. L. (2014). Classification of children with autism spectrum disorder by sensory subtype: A case for sensory-based phenotypes. *Autism Research, 7*(7), 322–333. http://doi.org/10.1002/aur.1368

Lane, A. E., Young, R. L., Baker, A. E. Z., & Angley, M. T. (2010). Sensory processing subtypes in autism: Association with adaptive behavior. *Journal of Autism and Developmental Disorders, 40*(1), 112–122. http://doi.org/10.1007/s10803-009-0840-2

Ledford, J. R., & Gast, D. L. (2006). Feeding problems in children with autism spectrum disorders: A review. *Focus on Autism and Other Developmental Disabilities, 21*(3), 153–166.

Lukens, C. T., & Linscheid, T. R. (2008). Development and validation of an inventory to assess mealtime behavior problems in children with autism. *Journal of Autism and Developmental Disorders, 38*(2), 342–352. http://doi.org/10.1007/s10803-007-0401-5

Lukens, C. T., & Silverman, A. H. (2014). Systematic review of psychological interventions for pediatric feeding problems. *Journal of Pediatric Psychology, 39*(8), 903–917. http://doi.org/10.1093/jpepsy/jsu040

Maes, J. H. R., Eling, P. A. T. M., Wezenberg, E., Vissers, C. T. W. M., & Kan, C. C. (2010). Attentional set shifting in autism spectrum disorder: Differentiating between the role of perseveration, learned irrelevance, and novelty processing. *Journal of Clinical and Experimental Neuropsychology, 33*(2), 210–217. http://doi.org/10.1080/13803395.2010.501327

Mandy, W., & Tchanturia, K. (2015). Do women with eating disorders who have social and flexibility difficulties really have autism? A case series. *Molecular Autism, 6*(1), 225. http://doi.org/10.1186/2040-2392-6-6

Mascola, A. J., Bryson, S. W., & Agras, W. S. (2010). Picky eating during childhood: A longitudinal study to age 11 years. *Eating Behaviors, 11*(4), 253–257. http://doi.org/10.1016/j.eatbeh.2010.05.006

Matson, J. L., LoVullo, S. V., Rivet, T. T., & Boisjoli, J. A. (2009). Validity of the Autism Spectrum Disorder Comorbid for Children (ASD-CC). *Research in Autism Spectrum Disorders, 3*(2), 345–357.

Micali, N., Simonoff, E., Elberling, H., Rask, C. U., Olsen, E. M., & Skovgaard, A. M. (2011). Eating patterns in a population-based sample of children aged 5 to 7 years: Association with psychopathology and parentally perceived impairment. *Journal of Developmental & Behavioral Pediatrics, 32*(8), 572–580. http://doi.org/10.1097/DBP.0b013e31822bc7b7

Must, A., Eliasziw, M., Phillips, S. M., Curtin, C., Kral, T. V. E., Segal, M.,... Bandini, L.G. (2017). The effect of age on the prevalence of obesity among US youth with autism spectrum disorder. *Childhood Obesity, 13*(1), 25–35. http://doi.org/10.1089/chi.2016.0079

Nadon, G., Feldman, D. E., Dunn, W., & Gisel, E. (2011). Association of sensory processing and eating problems in children with autism spectrum disorders. *Autism Research and Treatment, 2011* (541926) . doi:10.1155/2011/541926

Norris, M. L., Spettigue, W., Hammond, N. G., Katzman, D. K., Zucker, N., Yelle, K.,... Obeid, N.. (2017). Building evidence for the use of descriptive subtypes in youth with avoidant restrictive food intake disorder. *International Journal of Eating Disorders, 51*(2), 170–173. http://doi.org/10.1002/eat.22814

O'Doherty, J., Rolls, E. T., Francis, S., Bowtell, R., & McGlone, F. (2001). Representation of pleasant and aversive taste in the human brain. *Journal of Neurophysiology, 85*(3), 1315–1321. http://doi.org/10.1152/jn.2001.85.3.1315

Oliveira, A., Jones, L., de Lauzon-Guillain, B., Emmett, P., Moreira, P., Charles, M. A., & Lopes, C. (2015). Early problematic eating behaviours are associated with lower fruit and vegetable intake and less dietary variety at 4–5 years of age. A prospective analysis of three European birth cohorts. *British Journal of Nutrition, 114*(5), 763–771. http://doi.org/10.1017/S0007114515002287

Pettersson, E., Lichtenstein, P., Larsson, H., Song, J., Attention Deficit/Hyperactivity Disorder Working Group of the iPSYCH-Broad-PGC Consortium, Autism Spectrum Disorder Working Group of the iPSYCH-Broad-PGC Consortium, et al. (2019). Genetic influences on eight psychiatric disorders based on family data of 4 408 646 full and half-siblings, and genetic data of 333 748 cases and controls. *Psychological Medicine, 49*(7), 1166–1173.

Phillips, K. L., Schieve, L. A., Visser, S., Boulet, S., Sharma, A. J., Kogan, M. D.,... Yeargin-Allsopp, M. (2014). Prevalence and impact of unhealthy weight in a national sample of US adolescents with autism and other learning and behavioral disabilities. *Maternal and Child Health Journal, 18*(8), 1964–1975. http://doi.org/10.1007/s10995-014-1442-y

Pliner, P., & Hobden, K. (1992). Development of a scale to measure the trait of food neophobia in humans. *Appetite, 19*(2), 105–120.

Postorino, V., Sanges, V., Giovagnoli, G., Fatta, L. M., De Pepp, L., Armando, M.,... Mazzone, L. (2015). Clinical differences in children with autism spectrum disorder with and without food selectivity. *Appetite, 92*, 126–132.

Ptomey, L., Goetz, J., Lee, J., Donnelly, J., & Sullivan, D. (2013). Diet quality of overweight and obese adults with intellectual and developmental disabilities as measured by the Healthy Eating Index-2005. *Journal of Developmental and Physical Disabilities, 25*(6), 625-636. http://doi.org/10.1007/s10882-013-9339-z

Radin, R. M., Tanofsky-Kraff, M., Shomaker, L. B., Kelly, N. R., Pickworth, C. K., Shank, L. M., Yanovski, J.A. (2015). Metabolic characteristics of youth with loss of control eating. *Eating Behaviors, 19*, 86–89. http://doi.org/10.1016/j.eatbeh.2015.07.002

Remington, A., Añez, E., Croker, H., Wardle, J., & Cooke, L. (2011). Increasing food acceptance in the home setting: A randomized controlled trial of parent-administered taste exposure with incentives. *American Journal of Clinical Nutrition, 95*(1), 72–77. http://doi.org/10.3945/ajcn.111.024596

Riccio, M. P., Franco, C., Negri, R., Ferrentino, R. I., Maresca, R., D'alterio, E.,... Bravaccio, C.. (2018). Is food refusal in autistic children related to TAS2R38 genotype? *Autism Research, 11*(3), 531–538. http://doi.org/10.1002/aur.1912

Rogers, S. J., Hepburn, S., & Wehner, E. (2003). Parent reports of sensory symptoms in toddlers with autism and those with other developmental disorders. *Journal of Autism and Developmental Disorders, 33*(6), 631–642.

Rolls, E. T. (2006). Brain mechanisms underlying flavour and appetite. *Philosophical Transactions of the Royal Society B: Biological Sciences, 361*(1471), 1123–1136. http://doi.org/10.1098/rstb.2006.1852

Schachter, S. (1971). Some extraordinary facts about obese humans and rats. *American Psychologist*, 26(2), 129–144.

Schauder, K. B., & Bennetto, L. (2016). Toward an interdisciplinary understanding of sensory dysfunction in autism spectrum disorder: An integration of the neural and symptom literatures. *Frontiers in Neuroscience, 10*, 268. http://doi.org/10.3389/fnins.2016.00268

Schreck, K. A., & Williams, K. (2006). Food preferences and factors influencing food selectivity for children with autism spectrum disorders. *Research in Developmental Disabilities, 27*(4), 353–363. http://doi.org/10.1016/j.ridd.2005.03.005

Sharp, W. G., Berry, R. C., McCracken, C., Nuhu, N. N., Marvel, E., Saulnier, C. A., . . . Jazquess, D.L. (2013). Feeding problems and nutrient intake in children with autism spectrum disorders: A meta-analysis and comprehensive review of the literature. *Journal of Autism and Developmental Disorders, 43*(9), 2159–2173. http://doi.org/10.1007/s10803-013-1771-5

Sharp, W. G., Burrell, T. L., & Jaquess, D. L. (2014). The Autism MEAL Plan: A parent-training curriculum to manage eating aversions and low intake among children with autism. *Autism, 18*(6), 712–722. http://doi.org/10.1177/1362361313489190

Sharp, W. G., Jaquess, D. L., Morton, J. F., & Herzinger, C. V. (2010). Pediatric feeding disorders: A quantitative synthesis of treatment outcomes. *Clinical Child and Family Psychology Review, 13*(4), 348–365. http://doi.org/10.1007/s10567-010-0079-7

Sharp, W. G., Postorino, V., McCracken, C. E., Berry, R. C., Criado, K. K., Burrell, T. L., & Scahill, L. (2018). Dietary intake, nutrient status, and growth parameters in children with autism spectrum disorder and severe food selectivity: An electronic medical record review. *Journal of the Academy of Nutrition and Dietetics, 118*(10), 1943–1950. http://doi.org/10.1016/j.jand.2018.05.005

Sharp, W. G., Volkert, V. M., Scahill, L., McCracken, C. E., & McElhanon, B. (2017). A systematic review and meta-analysis of intensive multidisciplinary intervention for pediatric feeding disorders: How standard is the standard of care? *Journal of Pediatrics, 181*, 116–124.e4. http://doi.org/10.1016/j.jpeds.2016.10.002

Smith, A. D., Herle, M., Fildes, A., Cooke, L., Steinsbekk, S., & Llewellyn, C. H. (2017). Food fussiness and food neophobia share a common etiology in early childhood. *Journal of Child Psychology & Psychiatry & Allied Disciplines, 58*(2), 189–196. http://doi.org/10.1111/jcpp.12647

Spear, B. A., Barlow, S. E., Ervin, C., Ludwig, D. S., Saelens, B. E., Schetzina, K. E., & Taveras, E. M. (2007). Recommendations for treatment of child and adolescent overweight and obesity. *Pediatrics, 120*(Suppl 4), S254–S288. http://doi.org/10.1542/peds.2007-2329F

Stark, L. J., Spear Filigno, S., Bolling, C., Ratcliff, M. B., Kichler, J. C., Robson, S. L., . . . Ittenbach,R.F.. (2017). Learning about Activity and Understanding Nutrition for Child Health (LAUNCH): Rationale, design, and implementation of a randomized clinical trial of a family-based pediatric weight management program for preschoolers. *Contemporary Clinical Trials, 52*(C), 10–19. http://doi.org/10.1016/j.cct.2016.10.007

Suarez, M. A., Nelson, N. W., & Curtis, A. B. (2014). Longitudinal follow-up of factors associated with food selectivity in children with autism spectrum disorders. *Autism, 18*(8), 924–932. http://doi.org/10.1177/1362361313499457

Tanner, K., Case-Smith, J., Nahikian-Nelms, M., Ratliff-Schaub, K., Spees, C., & Darragh, A. R. (2015). Behavioral and physiological factors associated with selective eating in children with autism spectrum disorder. *American Journal of Occupational Therapy, 69*(6), 1–8. http://doi.org/10.5014/ajot.2015.019273

Tanofsky-Kraff, M., Ranzenhofer, L. M., Yanovski, S. Z., Schvey, N. A., Faith, M., Gustafson, J., & Yanovski, J. A. (2008). Psychometric properties of a new questionnaire to assess eating in the absence of hunger in children and adolescents. *Appetite, 51*(1), 148–155. http://doi.org/10.1016/j.appet.2008.01.001

Thomas, J. G., Bond, D. S., Phelan, S., Hill, J. O., & Wing, R. R. (2014). Weight-loss maintenance for 10 years in the National Weight Control Registry. *American Journal of Preventive Medicine, 46*(1), 17–23.

Toomey, K. A., & Ross, E. S. (2011). SOS approach to feeding. *Perspectives on Swallowing and Swallowing Disorders (Dysphagia), 20*(3), 82. http://doi.org/10.1044/sasd20.3.82

Toscano, C. V. A., Carvalho, H. M., & Ferreira, J. P. (2017). Exercise effects for children with autism spectrum disorder: Metabolic health, autistic traits, and quality of life. *Perceptual and Motor Skills, 125*(1), 126–146. http://doi.org/10.1177/0031512517743823

Tureck, K., Matson, J. L., May, A., Whiting, S. E., & Davis, T. E. (2014). Comorbid symptoms in children with anxiety disorders compared to children with autism spectrum disorders. *Journal of Developmental and Physical Disabilities, 26*(1), 23–33. http://doi.org/10.1007/s10882-013-9342-4

Twachtman-Reilly, J., Amaral, S. C., & Zebrowski, P. P. (2008). Addressing feeding disorders in children on the autism spectrum in school-based settings: Physiological and behavioral issues. *Language, Speech, and Hearing Services in Schools, 39*(2), 261. http://doi.org/10.1044/0161-1461(2008/025)

Ung, D., Selles, R., Small, B. J., & Storch, E. A. (2015). A systematic review and meta-analysis of cognitive-behavioral therapy for anxiety in youth with high-functioning autism spectrum disorders. *Child Psychiatry and Human Development, 46*(4), 533–547. http://doi.org/10.1007/s10578-014-0494-y

van Steensel, F. J. A., Bögels, S. M., & Perrin, S. (2011). Anxiety disorders in children and adolescents with autistic spectrum disorders: A meta-analysis. *Clinical Child and Family Psychology Review, 14*(3), 302–317. http://doi.org/10.1007/s10567-011-0097-0

Wallace, G. L., Llewellyn, C., Fildes, A., & Ronald, A. (2018). Clinical and subclinical links between autism spectrum disorder and food neophobia. *American Journal of Clinical Nutrition, 108*, 701–707.

Wardle, J., Guthrie, C. A., Sanderson, S., & Rapoport, L. (2001). Development of the children's eating behaviour questionnaire. *Journal of Child Psychology and Psychiatry, 42*(7), 963–970.

Wardle, J., Cooke, L. J., Gibson, E. L., Sapochnik, M., Sheiham, A., & Lawson, M. (2003). Increasing children's acceptance of vegetables: A randomized trial of parent-led exposure. *Appetite, 40*(2), 155–162. http://doi.org/10.1016/S0195-6663(02)00135-6

Webber, L., Hill, C., Saxton, J., Van Jaarsveld, C. H. M., & Wardle, J. (2009). Eating behaviour and weight in children. *International Journal of Obesity, 33*(1), 21–28. http://doi.org/10.1038/ijo.2008.219

Westwood, H., Eisler, I., Mandy, W., Leppanen, J., Treasure, J., & Tchanturia, K. (2016). Using the Autism-Spectrum Quotient to measure autistic traits in anorexia nervosa: A systematic review and meta-analysis. *Journal of Autism and Developmental Disorders, 46*(3), 964–977.

Westwood, H., & Tchanturia, K. (2017). Autism spectrum disorder in anorexia nervosa: An updated literature review. *Current Psychiatry Reports, 19*(7), 1–10. http://doi.org/10.1007/s11920-017-0791-9

Whiteley, P., Rodgers, J., & Shattock, P. (2000). Feeding patterns in autism. *Autism, 4*(2), 207–211.

Williams, P. G., Dalrymple, N., & Neal, J. (2000). Eating habits of children with autism. *Pediatric Nursing, 26*(3), 259.

Wing, R. R., & Hill, J. O. (2001). Successful weight loss maintenance. *Annual Review of Nutrition, 21*, 323–341.

Yaxley, S., Rolls, E. T., & Sienkiewicz, Z. J. (1990). Gustatory responses of single neurons in the insula of the macaque monkey. *Journal of Neurophysiology, 63*(4), 689–700. http://doi.org/10.1152/jn.1990.63.4.689

Yerys, B. E., Wallace, G. L., Harrison, B., Celano, M. J., Giedd, J. N., & Kenworthy, L. E. (2009). Set-shifting in children with autism spectrum disorders: Reversal shifting deficits on the Intradimensional/Extradimensional Shift Test correlate with repetitive behaviors. *Autism, 13*(5), 523–538. http://doi.org/10.1177/1362361309335716

Zheng, Z., Zhang, L., Li, S., Zhao, F., Wang, Y., Huang, L., et al. (2017). Association among obesity, overweight and autism spectrum disorder: A systematic review and meta-analysis. *Scientific Reports, 7*(1), 806. http://doi.org/10.1038/s41598-017-12,003-4

Zickgraf, H. F., Franklin, M. E., & Rozin, P. (2016). Adult picky eaters with symptoms of avoidant/restrictive food intake disorder: Comparable distress and comorbidity but different eating behaviors compared to those with disordered eating symptoms. *Journal of Eating Disorders, 4*, 1–11.

Zickgraf, H. F., & Ellis, J. M. (2018). Initial validation of the Nine Item Avoidant/Restrictive Food Intake disorder screen (NIAS): A measure of three restrictive eating patterns. *Appetite, 123*, 32–42.

Zimmer, M. H., Hart, L. C., Manning-Courtney, P., Murray, D. S., Bing, N. M., & Summer, S. (2011). Food variety as a predictor of nutritional status among children with autism. *Journal of Autism and Developmental Disorders, 42*(4), 549–556. http://doi.org/10.1007/s10803-011-1268-z

Zobel-Lachiusa, J., Andrianopoulos, M. V., Mailloux, Z., & Cermak, S. A. (2015). Sensory differences and mealtime behavior in children with autism. *American Journal of Occupational Therapy: Official Publication of the American Occupational Therapy Association, 69*(5), 6905185050p1–8. http://doi.org/10.5014/ajot.2015.016790

Zucker, N., Copeland, W., Franz, L., Carpenter, K., Keeling, L., Angold, A., & Egger, H. (2015). Psychological and psychosocial impairment in preschoolers with selective eating. *Pediatrics, 136*(3), e582–590. http://doi.org/10.1542/peds.2014-2386

CHAPTER

14

Sleep Problems in Autism Spectrum Disorder

Margaret C. Souders, Briana J. Taylor, *and* Stefanie Zavodny Jackson

Abstract

The aims of this chapter are to present the state of the science of sleep in individuals with autism spectrum disorder (ASD), including hypotheses for the high prevalence of chronic insomnia, possible etiologies of insomnia, and ecological and behavioral interventions for promoting optimal sleep. About two thirds of children with ASD have chronic insomnia, and these sleep problems have been shown to persist. The strongest evidence on promoting sleep in individuals with ASD is for sleep education, ecological changes, behavioral interventions, and exogenous melatonin. In 2012, the Sleep Committee of the Autism Treatment Network developed a practice pathway, based on expert consensus, to capture best practices for screening, identification, and treatment of sleep problems in ASD. An exemplar case is presented to integrate key constructs of the practice pathway.

Keywords: autism, autism spectrum disorder, sleep, insomnia, hyperarousal, practice pathway, behavioral intervention, biological rhythms, melatonin, calming activities

Overview

Sleep is a fundamental necessity for healthy development (Zhao, Zhao, & Veasey, 2017) and optimal daytime functioning in all individuals (Konen, Dirk, & Schmiedek, 2015). At any age, sleep is an essential physiological state that facilitates mental, physical, and emotional health and functioning. During critical periods of neural development, sleep may be particularly important for the maturation of cognitive processes involved in learning and memory as well as emotional and behavioral control (Gomez & Edgin, 2015). Individuals with autism spectrum disorder (ASD) may be particularly vulnerable to sleep disorders (Baker & Richdale, 2015; Baker, Richdale, & Hazi, 2019; Owens, 2008; Richdale, Baker, Short, & Gradisar, 2014). Specifically, a large body of literature has demonstrated that sleep disturbances are associated with increased ASD symptom severity (Schreck, Mulick, & Smith, 2004), deficits in cognitive domains (Maski et al., 2015), challenging daytime behaviors (Johnson et al., 2018), co-occurring psychiatric symptom severity (Nadeau et al., 2015), and even risk for psychiatric hospitalization (Righi et al., 2018). Sleep disturbances also appear to be modifiable in individuals with ASD, and thus may be intervened upon to improve the health and functioning of this vulnerable population (Cuomo et al., 2017). The efficacy of interventions to improve sleep and the origins of sleep disturbance in ASD are still underexamined. For the purposes of improving clinical practice and advancing scientific inquiry, the current chapter evaluates the state of science regarding the prevalence, etiology, developmental trajectory, assessment, and treatment of sleep disturbances in individuals with ASD.

The high prevalence of chronic insomnia in ASD is particularly concerning, given the heightened vulnerability of individuals with ASD to cognitive deficits, emotion dysregulation, and challenging behaviors (Baker & Richdale, 2015; Baker et al., 2019; Hill et al., 2014; Mazefsky et al., 2013; Richdale et al., 2014; Simonoff et al., 2008). Indeed, chronic insomnia in ASD has been associated with greater presentation of mood disorder symptoms, internalizing psychiatric symptoms, externalizing behavior, and attention deficit hyperactivity disorder (ADHD) symptom severity (Allik, Larsson, & Smedje, 2006; Anders, Iosif, Schwichtenberg, Tang, & Goodlin-Jones, 2012; Goldman et al., 2009, 2011; Malow et al., 2006; May, Cornish, Conduit, Rajaratnam, & Rinehart, 2015; Nadeau et al., 2015; Park et al., 2012; Richdale & Baglin, 2015; Richdale et al., 2014). Sleep disturbances have also been associated with increased ASD severity (Adams, Matson, Cervantes, & Goldin, 2014; Mayes & Calhoun, 2009), particularly with respect to social skill deficits (Hoffman et al., 2005; X. L. Yang et al., 2018). Though the studies that compose this literature are cross-sectional, and directionality cannot be determined, it is plausible that sleep disturbances may exacerbate both core and co-occurring psychiatric symptom presentation in ASD. Alternatively, features of the ASD phenotype may make individuals more predisposed to sleep disturbances and may cause them to be more vulnerable to precipitating events/states that trigger episodic sleep disturbance as well as perpetuating factors that prolong the sleep pathology, as discussed later.

Prevalence and Course

The *Diagnostic and Statistical Manual of Mental Disorders*, fifth edition, lists the following sleep–wake disorder categories: insomnia disorder, hypersomnolence disorder, narcolepsy, obstructive sleep apnea hypopnea, central sleep apnea, sleep-related hypoventilation, circadian rhythm sleep–wake disorders, non–rapid eye movement (NREM) sleep arousal disorders, nightmare disorder, rapid eye movement (REM) sleep behavior disorder, restless legs syndrome, and substance/medication-induced sleep disorder (American Psychiatric Association, 2013). It is estimated that 45% to 86% of individuals with ASD experience insomnia as defined by a sleep onset latency of greater than 30 minutes or frequent or prolonged awakenings after sleep onset, and impaired daytime functioning (Baker et al., 2019; Gail Williams, Sears, & Allard, 2004; Goldman et al., 2009; Krakowiak, Goodlin-Jones, Hertz-Picciotto, Croen, & Hansen, 2008; Souders et al., 2009). Thus, this chapter will largely focus on insomnia. The prevalence of insomnia is two to three times more prevalent in individuals with ASD relative to typically developing (TD) individuals (Richdale & Schreck, 2009; Souders et al., 2009). Although the most common sleep disturbances in individuals with ASD are difficulty initiating and maintaining sleep (Gail Williams et al., 2004; Goldman et al., 2009; Krakowiak et al., 2008; Souders et al., 2009), early morning awakenings are also highly common in this population (Hering, Epstein, Elroy, Iancu, & Zelnik, 1999). Prevalence estimates for children are largely based on parent report, due to the pervasiveness of communication deficits and intellectual disability in ASD (Richdale & Schreck, 2009). As such, prevalence estimates may be biased to the extent that parents are aware of their child's sleep status or to the extent that child sleep disturbances disrupt the sleep of parents. However, a meta-analysis by Elrod and Hood (2015) demonstrated that children with ASD indeed exhibit marked disparities via objective measures of sleep: actigraphy, a wristwatch accelerometer that measures movement and can be translated into sleep parameters, and polysomnography, a collective process of monitoring multiple physiological processes during sleep, often including electroencephalographic (EEG) activity, electro-oculogram (EOG), electromyography (EMG) activity, rhythm electrocardiogram (ECG), airflow via nasal pressure thermistor or pneumotachograph, and oxygen saturation via pulse oximetry (American Association of Respiratory Care-Association of Polysomnography Technologists, 1995). Specifically, a meta-analysis of the extant literature reveals that, on average, children with ASD sleep 32.8 minutes less per night, take 10.9 minutes longer to fall asleep, and have 2% less sleep efficiency than their TD peers (Elrod & Hood, 2015). Sleep efficiency is a measure reflecting the percent of time spent asleep after a person first falls asleep (time asleep/[total time in bed—time to fall asleep]). Even though this may not seem like a big difference, small differences in amount of sleep can have a big impact on school performance. A study found that an increase in sleep duration of 34 minutes in high school students was associated with a 4.5% increase in grades (Dunster et al., 2018).

It is unclear if there are particular ASD subgroups at higher risk for insomnia. Although insomnia has been reported across all cognitive levels of ASD (Cortesi, Giannotti, Ivanenko, & Johnson, 2010; Souders et al., 2009), some research suggests that those with ASD and co-occurring intellectual disability have greater sleep problems and/or sleep fewer hours per night (Elrod & Hood, 2015; Taylor, Schreck, & Mulick, 2012). Age-related differences in global sleep disturbance have also been reported in the ASD literature with inconsistent results (Goldman, Richdale, Clemons, & Malow, 2012; Hodge, Hoffman, Sweeney, & Riggs, 2013;

Richdale & Prior, 1995; Sivertsen, Posserud, Gillberg, Lundervold, & Hysing, 2012). Bedtime resistance and sleep anxiety appear to be most common in younger children and decline with age (Goldman et al., 2012; Hodge et al., 2013; Hoffman et al., 2005). Conversely, adolescents with ASD experience greater parent-reported sleep initiation problems and daytime sleepiness (Goldman et al., 2012). Although the evidence is inconsistent (May et al., 2015), sleep disturbances appear to diminish with age from early to late childhood in TD youth, but appear to persist across childhood development in youth with ASD and into adulthood (Hodge, Carollo, Lewin, Hoffman, & Sweeney, 2014; Hohn, de Veld, Mataw, van Someren, & Begeer, 2019). For instance, the meta-analysis by Elrod and Hood (2015) suggests that ASD–TD differences in sleep latency and sleep efficiency increase with age in pediatric samples, suggesting that sleep disturbances persist in a developmentally atypical manner.

Etiology, Diagnosis, and Assessment

Etiology

Sleep is regulated by two primary factors: homeostatic sleep drive and circadian rhythms (Borbely, 1982). Homeostatic sleep drive is a buildup of pressure that starts to accumulate upon waking. The pressure continues to build until the next episode of sleep. Circadian rhythms regulate the timing of sleep and are entrained by the 24-hour light–dark cycle. Homeostatic sleep drive and circadian rhythms interact continuously to facilitate daily rhythms of consolidated sleep sessions. The high prevalence of sleep problems in ASD, from parent reports, actigraphy, and laboratory observations, suggests that individuals with ASD may experience dysfunctions in one or both of the systems that regulate sleep. However, the etiological factors that contribute to the high prevalence of sleep disturbance in ASD are not clear. Numerous psychiatric, behavioral, and neurobiological mechanisms have been proposed, though sleep disturbances in ASD are likely due to multiple factors and are heterogeneous across individuals. The most conventional model of insomnia is outlined by Spielman and colleagues and suggests that insomnia is the consequence of *predisposing* factors that make one vulnerable to sleep disturbance, *precipitating* factors that trigger sleep disturbance episodes, and *perpetuating* factors that prevent an individual from re-establishing normal sleep (i.e., the PPP model of insomnia; Spielman, Caruso, & Glovinsky, 1987; Figure 14.1). Here, we review the factors that are presumed to underlie sleep disturbance in ASD. Due to the

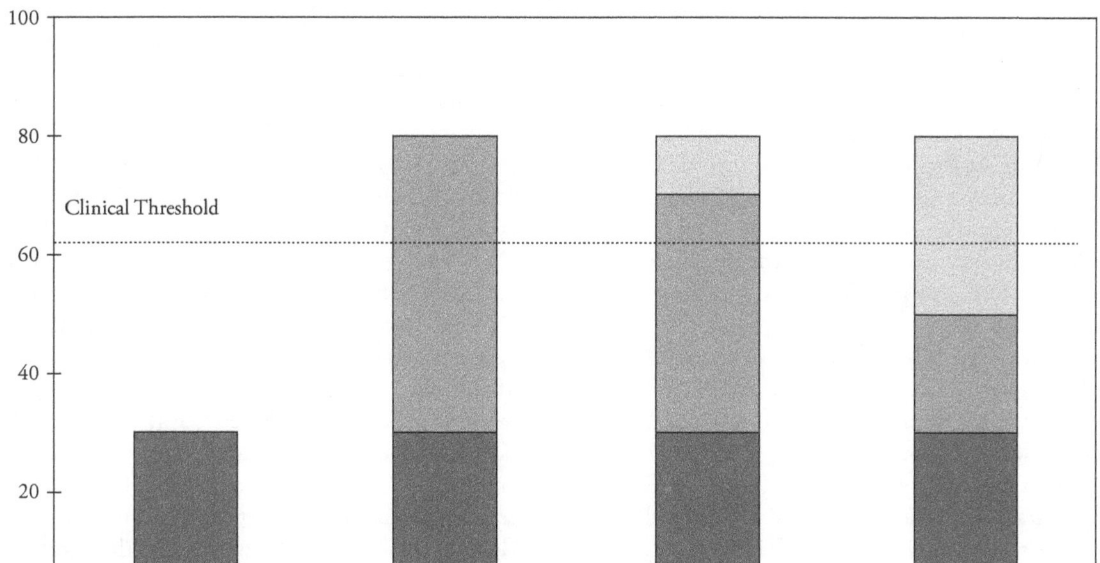

Figure 14.1. The PPP model of insomnia.

Spielman, A. J., Caruso, L. S., & Glovinsky, P. B. (1987). A behavioral perspective on insomnia treatment. *Psychiatric Clinics of North America, 10*(4), 541–553 (adapted with permission from Springer).

cross-sectional and observational nature of most research studies, it is possible that several putative mechanisms leading to sleep disturbances are actually caused by dysregulated sleep and/or circadian factors or by third unmeasured variables. Therefore, when appropriate, the causal roles of sleep and/or circadian factors and additional shared mechanisms are discussed.

PREDISPOSING FACTORS

Predisposing factors reviewed here include the genetics of ASD, abnormal melatonin production and synthesis, neurobiological organization and maturation of the brain, and core neuropsychiatric features of ASD.

Genes

Sleep disturbance in ASD may result from anomalies in circadian-relevant genes. As stated previously, sleep is partially regulated by the circadian system and an endogenous biological clock known as the suprachiasmatic nucleus (SCN; Rusak & Zucker, 1979). The SCN is a small cluster of cells located near the hypothalamus and is largely responsible for synchronizing circadian rhythms in cells located throughout the body (Reppert & Weaver, 2002). Rhythmicity in cells takes the form of molecular transcriptional–translational negative feedback loops that alter clock gene expression. Clock genes PERIOD (PER 1, 2, 3), TIMELESS, NPAS2, and cryptochromes (CRY 1, 2) are activated and suppressed by clock proteins: CLOCK, ARNTL/BMAL1, and NR1D1 (Barnes et al., 2003; Etchegaray, Lee, Wade, & Reppert, 2003; Sasaki, Yoshitane, Du, Okano, & Fukada, 2009; Travnickova-Bendova, Cermakian, Reppert, & Sassone-Corsi, 2002). Circadian clock and clock-relevant genes have been found to be highly polymorphic (i.e., have multiple variants) in those with ASD (Z. Yang et al., 2016) and have even been implicated in the etiology of ASD (Goto et al., 2017; Hu et al., 2009; Wimpory, Nicholas, & Nash, 2002). For instance, clock-controlled genes code for synapse molecules that are implicated in ASD susceptibility (Geoffray, Nicolas, Speranza, & Georgieff, 2016), and several clock genes appear to distinguish severe ASD from mild ASD and control samples (Hu et al., 2009). Clock genes such as hPER1, hPER2, and hPER3 are implicated in social communication (Wimpory et al., 2002) and are known regulators of sleep timing in TD populations. Sleep disturbances in ASD have also been associated with several clock gene mutations (p.F498S in TIMELESS, p.S20R in NR1D1, p.R493C in PER3, p.H542R in CLOCK, p.L473S in ARNTL2, and p.A325V in MTNR1B; Z. Yang et al., 2016).

Melatonin

Sleep disturbance in ASD may be due to circadian-relevant genes involved in the synthesis of the sleep-promoting hormone melatonin. Melatonin is synthesized in the pineal gland and serves as one of the most important synchronizing agents of the circadian system. Melatonin signals back to the SCN via receptors MTNR1A and MTNR1B (Hardeland et al., 2011). In addition, melatonin has been found to promote sleep by inhibiting wake-promoting orexin neurons (Sharma, Sahota, & Thakkar, 2018). Melke and colleagues (2008) have reported that ASD is associated with two polymorphisms in the promotor gene for the last enzyme in the melatonin synthesis pathway: acetylserotonin methyltransferase (ASMT; Melke et al., 2008). The breakdown of melatonin synthesis results in significantly lower levels of ASMT transcripts and melatonin in the blood. In addition, a separate study found significantly reduced ASMT expression and reduced expression of cytochrome P450, another gene involved in melatonin synthesis, among children with ASD and co-occurring sleep onset delay (Veatch, Pendergast, et al., 2015). These findings are consistent with several studies that have found significantly lower levels of melatonin or the major metabolite of melatonin (urinary 6-sulphatoxmelatonin) in the urine, serum, and plasma of those with ASD (Kulman et al., 2000; Melke et al., 2008; Mulder et al., 2010; Nir et al., 1995; Tordjman, Anderson, Pichard, Charbuy, & Touitou, 2005). To date, no systematic investigation has tested the mediating role of endogenous melatonin in the development of sleep disturbance in ASD, though exogenous melatonin has been shown to reduce sleep latency in pediatric ASD samples (Goldman et al., 2014; Malow, Adkins, et al., 2012). Other studies have found no difference in melatonin levels between those with ASD and TD populations (Goldman et al., 2014), and the timing of melatonin secretion does not fully account for the prevalence of sleep disturbance in ASD (Goldman et al., 2017). Taken together, this literature suggests that further work is needed to fully understand the role of melatonin in the high co-occurrence of ASD and sleep disturbance.

Brain Wave Organization and Maturation

The gold-standard method for objectively measuring sleep, polysomnography (PSG), has also revealed differences between ASD and TD populations. One PSG study showed that infants with ASD presented with undifferentiated EEG sleep profiles (Diomedi et al., 1999), which are characteristic of premature infants (Ardura, Andres, Aldana, & Revilla, 1995; Parmelee, Wenner, Akiyama, Schultz, & Stern, 1967). This finding suggested that children with ASD present with immature neural organization patterns. In addition, children with ASD have been shown to present with increased muscle twitching during REM sleep (Elia et al., 2000), higher rates of periodic limb movement syndrome (PLMS; Godbout, Bergeron, Limoges, Stip, & Mottron, 2000), and increased rates of REM sleep behavior disorder (Thirumalai, Shubin, & Robinson, 2002). More recent studies also show various differences in sleep architecture between ASD and TD youth. Differences have included increased Stage 1 sleep, decreased non-REM sleep, decreased slow-wave sleep, decreased REM sleep, fewer Stage 2 sleep spindles, and fewer rapid eye movements during REM sleep (Buckley et al., 2010; Limoges, Mottron, Bolduc, Berthiaume, & Godbout, 2005). These differences suggest maturational differences in neural systems that underlie sleep initiation and/or maintenance.

Core ASD Features

Several studies have found moderate to strong correlations between ASD severity and the severity of sleep problems (Adams et al., 2014; Allik et al., 2006; Mayes & Calhoun, 2009), suggesting that core ASD symptoms may contribute to or may be exacerbated by sleep disturbances. Among the core ASD symptoms, social interaction skill deficits are most strongly associated with disturbed sleep (Taylor, meta-analysis unpublished). In TD populations, sleep has been shown to influence social processes by altering cognitive functioning and stress physiology (Gordon, Mendes, & Prather, 2017). For instance, experimental sleep restriction and habitually short sleep duration have been associated with impaired emotion recognition in others (van der Helm, Gujar, & Walker, 2010), greater neurobiological stress reactivity to emotional stimuli (Yoo, Gujar, Hu, Jolesz, & Walker, 2007), and greater physiological reactivity to social-evaluative threat (Franzen et al., 2011; Prather, Puterman, Epel, & Dhabhar, 2014). Thus, sleep disturbance in people with ASD may exacerbate existing social skill deficits.

Alternatively, social skill deficits may have an influence on sleep via the circadian system, which is informed by environmental "time cues" known in the chronobiology field as zeitgebers (Mistlberger & Skene, 2004). The most powerful time cue is light; however, social motivation to be awake/asleep when others are may also have an impact on circadian timing (Mistlberger & Skene, 2004). In TD, this motivation may manifest as scheduling sleep/wake patterns to be cohesive with those of others or through the automatic detection of social cues that indicate appropriate sleep/wake times. For instance, one study has found that youth with ASD show less susceptibility to contagious yawning than TD controls (Helt, Eigsti, Snyder, & Fein, 2010). Social skill deficits may also prevent a child with ASD from knowing when and where it is unacceptable to sleep during the day, which may increase inappropriate napping (e.g., during school hours) and delay the buildup of homeostatic sleep pressure. Thus, decreased sensitivity to social cues in children with ASD may contribute to less coherence between the sleep/wake patterns of children with ASD and their families (Veatch, Maxwell-Horn, & Malow, 2015).

Another feature of ASD that may delay sleep onset is the tendency to fixate on a particular thought, subject, or restricted interest for longer than is relevant (Maes, Eling, Wezenberg, Vissers, & Kan, 2011). As hypothesized by Kotagal and Broomall (2012), people with ASD have difficulty shifting attention or transitioning. The presence of intrusive thoughts is an established mechanism linking daytime stress and sleep disturbance in TD populations (Berset, Elfering, Luthy, Luthi, & Semmer, 2011; Hall et al., 1997; Zoccola, Dickerson, & Lam, 2009). Thus, daytime stressors may adversely impact sleep in ASD by contributing to intrusive thoughts and rumination (Kotagal & Broomall, 2012).

Another common theory regarding the high prevalence of sleep disturbance in ASD is the pervasiveness of sensory sensitivities in ASD. Many individuals with ASD demonstrate hyperreactivity to sensory stimuli, which may be a consequence of low sensory thresholds (Ausderau et al., 2014; Hohn et al., 2019). This subgroup, as identified by the Sensory Profile (Dunn, 1999) and the Sensory Perception Quotient: Short Version (Tavassoli, Hoekstra, & Baron-Cohen, 2014), has been shown to have greater sleep problems relative to other individuals with ASD, and in turn, hyperreactivity to sensory stimuli has been positively correlated with parent-reported and self-reported sleep problems (Dunn, 1999; Mazurek & Petroski, 2015). Individuals with ASD and hyperreactivity to sensory stimuli may be more agitated by nighttime sounds, light at night, or the tactile sensation of pajamas or bedsheets. These sensitivities may cause difficulty initiating or maintaining sleep. Indeed, Hollway and colleagues (2013) evaluated associations between Sensory Profile subgroups and parent-reported sleep disturbance using 1,347 children from the Autism Treatment Network and found that greater sleep problems were associated with lower auditory filtering capability and lower sensory underresponsivity (Hollway, Aman, & Butter, 2013). Conversely, Tzischinsky and colleagues (2018) found that hypersensitivity to touch using the Caregiver Sensory Profile accounted for the difference in parent-reported sleep problems between 69 children with ASD and 62 age-matched controls. Taken together, these results provide limited but potential support for the role of sensory sensitivities in the high prevalence of sleep disturbances in individuals with ASD.

PRECIPITATING FACTORS

Precipitating factors reviewed here include environmental stressors (e.g., changes in evening routine), psychological stressors (e.g., factors that exacerbate co-occurring psychiatric conditions such as anxiety or ADHD), and physical stressors (e.g., sickness or acute presentations of co-occurring medical conditions such as gastrointestinal dysfunction or epilepsy).

Environmental Stressors

ASD is characterized by an insistence on sameness (IS), which refers to rigid, routinized, and ritualistic behavior that falls under the core ASD feature of restrictive and repetitive behavior. IS and reliance on routine are also common in TD children as sameness and routines can serve an adaptive function. For instance, in early childhood, insistence on a particular routine or order of events may serve as a means to limit unpredictability and thus reduce anxiety surrounding unknown outcomes (Uljarevic, Richdale, Evans, Cai, & Leekam, 2017). The same is likely true of IS in ASD. Given the high co-occurrence of anxiety in ASD, extreme IS may serve to limit contact with unanticipated anxiety-eliciting stimuli. IS can also be adaptive for the development of good sleep hygiene. In fact, the adoption of a consistent nightly bedtime routine is a standard recommendation from behavioral sleep medicine specialists. Bedtime routines can provide cues to the body and brain that it is time to sleep. However, deviations from nightly bedtime routines may have deleterious consequences for sleep, particularly among those with greater IS. To date, only one study has examined the association between IS and sleep problems. Using the Autism Treatment Network, Hundley and colleagues (2016) found no relationship between IS, derived from the Autism Diagnostic Interview-Revised, and parent-reported sleep problems (Hundley, Shui, & Malow, 2016), though the potentially moderating role of adherence to bedtime routine was not examined in this study. In a smaller survey-based study of 167 children with ASD, parent-reported "bedtime rituals" were associated with a 2.4 times greater likelihood for a child having a parasomnia (e.g., wetting the bed at night, moving a lot during sleep; Liu, Hubbard, Fabes, & Adam, 2006). In the latter study, it is unclear if bedtime rituals, or deviations from those rituals, could contribute to the development of a parasomnia or if parents of children with a parasomnia are more likely to establish a bedtime ritual. If parents of children with parasomnias are not more likely to establish a bedtime ritual, it is possible that deviations from the established ritual may act as a trigger for emotion dysregulation and subsequent nighttime problems such as wetting the bed or excessively restless sleep.

PSYCHOLOGICAL STRESSORS

Co-occurring psychiatric disorders are disproportionately common in individuals with ASD and may contribute to the high prevalence of sleep disorders in ASD (Ballester et al., 2019; Matson, Wilkins, & Ancona, 2008). Anxiety is common in the TD population (Zaboski & Storch, 2018) and has been shown to be an independent risk factor for sleep disturbance (Owens, 2008; Peterman et al., 2016; Singh & Zimmerman, 2015). Sleep problems have been shown to be positively correlated with anxiety in individuals with ASD and/or intellectual disability (Hollway et al., 2013; Mazurek & Petroski, 2015; Rzepecka, McKenzie, McClure, & Murphy, 2011), and some research has shown that correlations between anxiety and sleep problems are stronger among ASD youth relative to TD youth (Richdale et al., 2014). Directionality of associations between anxiety and sleep disturbances are unknown, due to the cross-sectional and observational nature of most studies. Rumination on anxiety-producing thoughts may be deleterious for sleep just as poor sleep may impair the regulatory capacity needed to manage daytime anxiety. Only two longitudinal studies have examined temporal precedence across these variables. Both found that sleep disturbances predicted anxiety 1 year later, whereas anxiety did not predict future sleep disturbances (Fletcher et al., 2017; May et al., 2015). Future work is needed to rule out the possibility that bidirectional or feedforward associations exist wherein sleep problems and anxiety exacerbate one another.

ADHD is also common in ASD (Simonoff et al., 2013) and is an independent risk factor for sleep disturbance. The vast majority of studies examining sleep problems in individuals with ASD have excluded for co-occurring ADHD or have not examined ADHD symptoms as a risk factor for sleep problems, despite the high co-occurrence between ASD and ADHD and between ADHD and sleep disturbance (Ramtekkar, 2017). However, two studies have shown that sleep problems are more pronounced in children with ASD who have co-occurring ADHD relative to kids without (Liu et al., 2006; Park et al., 2012). Interestingly, one cross-sectional study showed no differences in parent-reported sleep problems between children with ADHD and those with ADHD and co-occurring ASD (Thomas, Lycett, Papadopoulos, Sciberras, & Rinehart, 2018). However, this study also found that additional co-occurring internalizing symptoms predicted sleep problems in both groups, suggesting that a third factor or confluence of factors may confer the greatest risk. As outlined by Ramtekkar (2017), sleep problems in both neurodevelopmental disorders and their co-occurring presentation may stem from a common pathophysiology. Mechanisms described here such as dysregulated melatonin synthesis and circadian CLOCK genes are also implicated in sleep disturbance for children with ADHD (Baird, Coogan, Siddiqui, Donev, & Thome, 2012; Kohyama, 2016; Van der Heijden, Smits, Van Someren, & Gunning, 2005). Similarly, sleep disordered breathing (SDB) appears to be more prevalent in those with ASD and ADHD relative to TD controls (Youssef, Singh, Huntington, Becker, & Kothare, 2013), and the severity of SDB has been shown to be correlated with attention deficits (Gottlieb et al., 2004). Interestingly, ADHD symptom severity has been shown to improve following treatment for SDB (Chervin et al., 2006). Stimulants to treat hyperactivity and impulsivity have also been known to disrupt sleep (Ramtekkar & Ivanenko, 2015), and current recommendations are to administer medications to treat ADHD symptoms early in the day.

PHYSICAL STRESSORS

Sleep disorders have also been shown to co-occur with medical conditions such as gastrointestinal (GI) disorders (Kang, Wagner, & Ming, 2014; Klukowski, Wasilewska, & Lebensztejn, 2015; Prosperi et al., 2017; X. L. Yang et al., 2018). For instance, in a large correlational study of children with ASD, sleep disorders were associated with constipation (Neumeyer et al., 2018). In a large sample of children with ASD, those with GI dysfunctions were 75% more likely to have a sleep disorder (McCue, Flick, Twyman, & Xian, 2017). In a second study using both the Autism Genetic Resource Exchange and the Simons Simplex Collection, GI problems and sleep problems each conferred a twofold increase in risk for the other (Aldinger, Lane, Veenstra-VanderWeele, & Levitt, 2015). The discomfort associated with GI disorders may impair sleep (Tudor, Walsh, Mulder, & Lerner, 2015), especially among children with no or limited verbal ability who are unable to communicate their discomfort. Though understudied, the same is likely true for chronic pain conditions and medical conditions producing acute pain, such as dental problems. Therefore, medical conditions should always be investigated when sleep disturbances are observed.

Conversely, sleep problems and GI dysfunction may both be due to abnormalities in melatonin production and/or synthesis (Gagnon & Godbout, 2018). For instance, in TD populations, melatonin deficits have been associated with GI problems, and melatonin administration has resulted in significant improvement in GI problems such as constipation relative to placebo administration (Chojnacki, Poplawski, Blasiak, Chojnacki, & Klupinska, 2013). The concentration of melatonin is higher in the GI tract than in the blood or pineal gland (Sotak, Mrnka, & Pacha, 2006), and rodent models suggest that exogenous melatonin modulates intestinal motility (Drago, Macauda, & Salehi, 2002). In addition, melatonin may influence GI functioning by reducing intestinal inflammation (Carrillo-Vico, Guerrero, Lardone, & Reiter, 2005; Swanson et al., 2015), and melatonin levels may alter patients' perceptions of GI symptoms through analgesic properties that reduce pain sensitivity (Song, Leng, Gwee, Moochhala, & Ho, 2005). Lastly, probiotics have been found to improve irritable bowel syndrome symptoms by increasing melatonin production (Wong, Yang, Song, Wong, & Ho, 2015). As previously mentioned, melatonin production and/or synthesis has been shown to be impaired in ASD. Thus, low melatonin levels may act as a shared mechanism contributing to the prevalence of and correlation between sleep and GI disturbances in ASD samples. Other factors may also contribute to the co-occurrence of sleep and GI disturbances. For instance, psychotropic medications such as antipsychotics have been linked with sleep and GI problems in children with ASD (Coury et al., 2012; Lake et al., 2017).

Epilepsy is an additional co-occurring medical condition that is estimated to be present in 4% to 38% of individuals with ASD (Thomas, Hovinga, Rai, & Lee, 2017). Epilepsy is associated with significant impairments in sleep including abnormal sleep architecture (Pereira, Bruni, Ferri, Palmini, & Nunes, 2012) and significant sleep fragmentation (Zanzmera et al., 2012). Epilepsy is also significantly associated with sleep disturbance in children with ASD (Liu et al., 2006). Interestingly, even in the absence of clinical seizures, a large proportion of those with ASD demonstrate epileptiform activity during sleep (Chez et al., 2006). Mouse models have also shown that inflammation in response to bacterial infection during the perinatal period may permanently alter sleep architecture and produce epileptiform activity (Missig et al., 2018). It should also be noted that sleep deprivation, particularly REM sleep, may contribute to seizure susceptibility by affecting neuronal excitability (Civardi & Collini, 2007; Malow, 2004).

PERPETUATING FACTORS

The perpetuation of sleep disturbances is often due to a learned association between sleep and a form of cognitive and/or physiological arousal (Bonnet, 2009; Levenson, Kay, & Buysse, 2015). The theory of cognitive arousal suggests that intrusive thoughts and rumination prevent sleep initiation (Bonnet & Arand, 2010; Feige et al., 2013; Levenson et al., 2015), whereas the theory of somatic/physiological arousal suggests that underlying autonomic activity is dominated by greater activation of the sympathetic nervous system in those with insomnia relative to good sleepers (Healey et al., 1981). Of course, the two forms of arousal are not mutually exclusive and can result in feedback loops that exacerbate one another and further impair sleep. Here we examine the arousal theory of insomnia based on the hypothesis that the cognitive and somatic systems are not mutually exclusive in relation to sleep problems. In addition, we examine the tenets of behavioral sleep medicine that may be employed to break feedback loops that perpetuate sleep disturbances.

Dysregulation of the autonomic nervous system has been identified in people with chronic sleep disturbance, as evidenced by increased heart rate, body temperature, heart rate variability, and norepinephrine (Hall et al., 1997; Healey et al., 1981; Morin, Rodrigue, & Ivers, 2003). The autonomic nervous system (ANS) is composed of three branches: sympathetic, parasympathetic, and enteric. Hyperarousal may be due to overactivity of the sympathetic branch, underactivity of the parasympathetic branch, or dysregulated interaction of the two. Children with ASD may experience increased dysregulation of the ANS relative to the TD population (Lydon et al., 2016). This dysregulation may take the form of "hyper" or "hypo" arousal to external stimuli. Few studies have found evidence for "hyperarousal" in ASD. Ming and colleagues (2005) found that during resting states, children with ASD had lower cardiac vagal tone and cardiac sensitivity to baroreflex with concomitant heightened heart rate, mean arterial pressure, and diastolic blood pressure (Ming, Julu, Brimacombe, Connor, & Daniels, 2005). This group again found evidence for hyperarousal via blunted parasympathetic activation in a separate sample of children with ASD (Ming, Patel, Kang, Chokroverty, & Julu, 2016). A few studies have also found increased electrodermal activation in response to auditory stimuli (Barry & James, 1988; Chang et al., 2012; van Engeland, 1984). However, other studies of autonomic responsivity to auditory sounds have found no differences between ASD and TD (Stevens & Gruzelier, 1984) or blunted reactivity among ASD youth (Palkovitz & Wiesenfeld, 1980). Lower activation of the parasympathetic nervous system (PNS) during the pupillary responses to various social and nonsocial stimuli has also been observed in those with ASD (Daluwatte et al., 2013; Daluwatte, Miles, Sun, & Yao, 2015; Dinalankara, Miles, Nicole Takahashi, & Yao, 2017; Wagner, Luyster, Tager-Flusberg, & Nelson, 2016), whereas other studies of pupillary responses suggest that PNS is blunted in response to emotion-eliciting stimuli (Nuske, Vivanti, & Dissanayake, 2014; Sepeta et al., 2012). Hypoarousal has also been identified in ASD through lower resting EDA levels (Bujnakova et al., 2016; Eilam-Stock et al., 2014) and blunted EDA responses to anxiety-eliciting stimuli (Panju, Brian, Dupuis, Anagnostou, & Kushki, 2015). Parasympathetic dominance has also been identified in ASD samples relative to controls during orthostatic stress (Bricout et al., 2018) and social cognition testing (Kushki, Brian, Dupuis, & Anagnostou, 2014). Finally, decreased sympathetic responses to speech stimuli have also differentiated infants at high and low risk for ASD (Perdue, Edwards, Tager-Flusberg, & Nelson, 2017). Thus, the literature on autonomic arousal in ASD appears to be mixed.

To date, no studies have examined associations between daytime autonomic functioning and nighttime sleep problems. However, one study has examined autonomic functioning during sleep in children with ASD and found evidence for deficits in PNS activation as evidenced by increased heart rate, lower high-frequency heart rate variability, and increased low frequency–to–high frequency ratio during various sleep stages (Harder et al., 2016). Sleep is thought to be protective for autonomic functioning and dominated by the PNS (Tobaldini et al., 2017). However, limited research may suggest that those with ASD do not gain the same benefit from sleep as TD controls. For instance, following one night of normal sleep, adults with ASD demonstrated poorer parasympathetic tone, as evidenced by lower high-frequency heart rate variability, relative to TD adults (Tessier, Pennestri, & Godbout, 2018). Thus, although directionality cannot be confirmed, it is possible that sleep may be less restorative for autonomic functioning in ASD.

The timing of arousal may also be important to consider in the context of sleep disturbance. For instance, presleep arousal is common among people experiencing sleep disturbance (Nicassio, Mendlowitz, Fussell, & Petras, 1985; Palagini, Moretto, Dell'Osso, & Carney, 2017). Presleep arousal is characterized by somatic symptoms (e.g., heart racing, shortness of breath, nausea, perspiration) and/or cognitive symptoms (e.g., worrying about the ability to fall asleep, the inability to shut off intrusive thoughts, enhanced awareness of sounds within the environment). The presleep arousal state is often a maladaptive response to previous sleep problems. Persistent or intermittent sleep problems can cause individuals to focus on their ability/inability to control sleep, which often perpetuates sleep disturbances by increasing arousal (Hantsoo, Khou, White, & Ong, 2013; Morin et al., 2003). Presleep arousal is underexamined in ASD. One small questionnaire-based study showed that adolescents with ASD and average or above-average cognitive abilities report significantly greater presleep arousal than age- and sex-matched TD controls (Richdale et al., 2014). However, one can hypothesize that the prevalence and impact of presleep arousal are dramatic in ASD due to high rates of internalizing symptoms (Malow et al., 2006; Nadeau et al., 2015) and marked difficulties with emotion regulation (Mazefsky et al., 2013).

In addition, maladaptive bedtime practices may evolve around problems with presleep arousal and become perpetuating factors. For instance, caregivers of children with ASD often will initiate multiple ideas to help their child fall asleep and may establish bedtime conditions that inadvertently perpetuate chronic behavioral insomnias (Souders et al., 2009). Sleep onset associations and difficulties with limit setting are the most common types of behavioral insomnia in TD children and in children with ASD (Malow et al., 2014; Meltzer, 2010; Mindell & Meltzer, 2008; Souders et al., 2009). Sleep onset association behavioral insomnia is characterized by the child's dependency on a specific stimulus, whether person, object, or setting, for initiating sleep or returning to sleep. Absence of such a stimulus may produce an arousal, leading to challenging behavior and/or a detriment to sleep. In response, caregivers may increase efforts to make the sleep association stimulus consistently present/available at bedtime. Though it ameliorates momentary reactivity, reliance on a sleep association stimulus will reinforce the association and ultimately perpetuate sleep problems that occur in the absence of the stimulus. Limit-setting behavioral insomnia is characterized by bedtime stalling or refusal behaviors that are a result of difficulties with limit setting by the caregiver. The stalling and refusal behaviors can escalate each night and become quite disruptive. These behaviors may be inadvertently reinforced by postponing bedtime and providing a child with 1:1 attention (Souders et al., 2009). Although soothing a child until he or she falls asleep may diminish arousal, this may inhibit the development of self-soothing techniques. Lack of limit setting may be one reason the prevalence of parent–child cosleeping is significantly higher among children with pervasive developmental disorders (Couturier et al., 2005). Many behavioral sleep medicine professionals recommend that parents gradually diminish their presence at night to avoid dependency and promote the development of self-soothing capabilities in the child.

UNDEREXAMINED FACTORS

Development, specifically the transition from childhood into adolescence, may produce changes in both homeostatic sleep drive and circadian rhythms that may exacerbate sleep problems in youth with ASD. Specifically, during typical adolescent development, homeostatic sleep drive has been shown to accumulate at a slower rate (Jenni, Achermann, & Carskadon, 2005) and the circadian timing of sleep and arousal becomes delayed, resulting in a later propensity for both sleep and waking (Carskadon, Acebo, & Jenni, 2004). As such, adolescents take on an "evening chronotype" characterized by later bed and wake times and difficulty falling asleep when attempting an early bedtime (Roenneberg et al., 2015). This shift toward the evening chronotype is temporary, begins during the preteen years, and persists into the early 20s (Randler, 2011). In addition to behavioral changes, this temporary shift in the processes that regulate sleep has been seen through tightly controlled observations of circadian physiology (Carskadon, Acebo, & Jenni, 2004; Jenni, Achermann, & Carskadon, 2005). Specifically, the timing of melatonin secretion onset has been shown to delay from childhood to adolescence. To date, developmental shifts in homeostatic sleep drive and circadian rhythms have not been examined in youth with ASD across the transition from childhood to adolescence. However, in ASD, parent-reported sleep problems have been shown to shift from bedtime resistance and sleep anxiety in children to sleep initiation problems and daytime sleepiness in adolescents (Goldman et al., 2012). This shift in parental sleep concerns is consistent with TD populations (Carskadon, 1990) and both reduced homeostatic sleep drive and delayed circadian phase (Carskadon, 2011; Crowley et al., 2014; Martin, Gaudreault, Perron, & Laberge, 2016). Developmental changes in sleep and circadian physiology have yet to be examined in ASD and may elucidate critical periods of heightened vulnerability for sleep in this already at-risk population.

Assessment

In ASD, there is great heterogeneity in sleep problem presentation, in that every individual presents a unique case. For this reason, individuals with ASD and their caregivers often will need the support of health care providers in identifying the specific predisposing, precipitating, and perpetuating factors that contribute to insomnia for each individual. Due to the high prevalence of sleep problems in ASD and the high heterogeneity of factors that may contribute to sleep problems, all individuals with ASD should be screened for sleep disturbances at every primary care visit or medical specialty visit. A thorough sleep history should be taken from the caregivers of individuals with ASD and from the individuals themselves, if possible. In addition, providers should utilize a sleep questionnaire, such as the Children's Sleep Habits Questionnaire (CSHQ; Owens, Spirito, & McGuinn, 2000), which has been adapted for use by parents of children with ASD (Katz et al., 2018). For adults with ASD who are able to be their own reporters, the Pittsburgh Sleep Quality Index (PSQI; Buysse, Reynolds, Monk, Berman, & Kupfer, 1989) is recommended. Although not validated for use with an ASD population, the PSQI has been used in adult ASD samples in previous studies (e.g., Baker & Richdale, 2015). Moreover, individuals with ASD should have a thorough review of medical conditions that could be contributing to sleep disturbances. The medical conditions contributing to sleep problems are listed in Table 14.1 (Malow et al., 2012).

More specifically, individuals with ASD should be screened for obstructive sleep apnea (OSA) at every visit. The signs and symptoms of OSA are listed in Table 14.2. Individuals with ASD have an increased prevalence of physical risk factors for OSA such as obesity, hypotonia, and dysmorphic features such as micrognathia (small or receding chin) and palatal defects. Medical conditions should be addressed first prior to moving to other interventions, such as behavioral interventions or sleep medications. Once medical conditions are addressed and an individual continues to have sleep disturbances, then an assessment for sleep disorders should be completed.

Table 14.1. Medical Conditions Contributing to Sleep Problems

Gastrointestinal Disorders
Reflux
Constipation
Pain
Respiratory Disorders
Sleep-disordered breathing
Allergies
Asthma
Neurological Disorders
Epilepsy/seizures
Restless leg syndrome/abnormal movements
Skin and Integumentary Disorders
Dental issues
Eczema/itching
Sensitivity to textures/light/sound
Nutrition
Hunger
Iron deficiency
"Growing pains"

From Malow, B. A., Byers, K., Johnson, K., Weiss, S., Bernal, P., Goldman, S. E., . . . Glaze, D. G. (2012). A practice pathway for the identification, evaluation, and management of insomnia in children and adolescents with autism spectrum disorders. *Pediatrics, 130*(Suppl 2), S106–S124. doi:10.1542/peds.2012-0900I

Table 14.2. Obstructive Sleep Apnea (OSA) Signs/Symptoms and Physical Risk Factors

Signs and Symptoms
Snoring/loud breathing
Snorting/gasping for breath
Periods of apnea (child stops breathing temporarily)
Unrefreshing sleep/daytime sleepiness
Physical Risk Factors
Obesity
Large tonsils and/or adenoids
Hypotonia
Micrognathia (small or receding chin)
Palatal defects

Treatment

Behavioral Therapy for Insomnia

The Autism Treatment Network (ATN; May et al., 2015) recognized that it is critical for clinicians to be well trained in delivering sleep care to this vulnerable population. The ATN Sleep Committee compiled evidence-based ecological and behavioral strategies, resulting in the development of a practice pathway or guideline. The practice pathway published by Malow and colleagues (2012) and the National Initiative for Children's Healthcare Quality offers a clear outline for identifying, evaluating, and managing insomnia in children and adolescents with ASD. A practice pathway has not been developed for adults, but the strategies described in the pathway could be generalizable to the adult population.

The ATN practice pathway was devised from a thorough review of the state of the science and included 20 intervention articles studying individuals with ASD with sample sizes of 10 or greater (Malow, Byers, et al., 2012; Souders et al., 2017). The pathway was based on a consensus of sleep experts that captured best practices for implementing comprehensive sleep care by primary care providers or ASD specialists (Malow, Byers, et al., 2012). The pathway was tested at four pilot sites across the United States. It takes a 10-step approach (Table 14.3) including screening for and treating medical conditions that may be related to poor sleep (Table 14.1) and identifying signs and symptoms of obstructive sleep apnea and its risk factors (Table 14.2). A pilot phase showed that barriers to using the ATN pathway included lack of time during a clinic visit and limited clinician knowledge of and comfort with both assessment and management of insomnia (Malow, Byers, et al., 2012). The following case study illustrates key concepts to increase provider comfort with the assessment and management of insomnia in individuals with ASD.

Table 14.3. Practice Pathway 10-Step Approach

1.	Screen all children with autism spectrum disorder (ASD) for insomnia with sleep questionnaire annually.
2.	Identify any parent or child sleep concerns and discuss.
3.	Screen for medical conditions that may be contributing to insomnia and refer to appropriate subspecialist (see Tables 14.1 and 14.2).
4.	Treat any medical conditions significantly affecting sleep before continuing with the practice pathway.
5.	Determine the willingness and capacity of the family to implement a sleep intervention.
6.	The first-line approach is parent education about environmental modification, positive bedtime routines, and behavioral strategies.
7.	Introduce the Autism Treatment Network Sleep Tool Kit and educational materials with visual schedule.
8.	If the family is unable or unwilling to follow environmental and behavioral strategies, consider consultation to a sleep specialist.
9.	Pharmacological interventions may be considered, starting with melatonin.
10.	Plan for timely follow-up in 2 to 4 weeks for all interventions, as well as annual reassessment for all children with ASD.

From Malow, B. A., Byers, K., Johnson, K., Weiss, S., Bernal, P., Goldman, S. E., . . . Glaze, D. G. (2012). A practice pathway for the identification, evaluation, and management of insomnia in children and adolescents with autism spectrum disorders. *Pediatrics, 130*(Suppl 2), S106–S124. doi:10.1542/peds.2012-0900I

Behavioral interventions are extremely effective in the treatment of insomnia in TD children, and cognitive behavioral therapy for insomnia is effective in the TD adult population (Meltzer, 2010; Mindell & Meltzer, 2008). Behavioral treatments most commonly used to treat insomnia in children with ASD include behavioral modification strategies such as extinction (e.g., withdrawal of reinforcement for inappropriate bedtime behaviors) and positive reinforcement of adaptive sleep behavior. Sleep hygiene instructions (e.g., appropriate sleep schedules and routines) often accompany behavioral modification protocols as described in the ATN sleep toolkit. The evidence base for behavioral interventions for sleep problems in children with ASD has been studied by Malow et al. (2014).

This team developed the ATN Sleep Toolkit, which involves a 1-hour parent education session with emphasis on using an ecological approach with changes to the environment and establishing positive evening routines with a visual schedule (Malow et al., 2014). The ATN Sleep Toolkit was found effective in improving sleep in individuals with ASD. The optimal sleep environment is cool, dark, and unstimulating, and changes to the environment are the easiest and most cost-effective way to improve sleep. The ATN Sleep Toolkit also incorporated the Bedtime Pass, a behavior technique used to encourage a child to self-soothe with calming activities during night wakings. When the child wakes at night, he or she can choose to either trade in the pass for a hug or attention from a parent or keep the pass and claim a reward in the morning. When the child gets out of bed, the parent is taught to redirect the child to bed and take the bedtime pass.

Pharmacotherapy for Insomnia

It must be acknowledged at the outset that no medications are approved by the Food and Drug Administration (FDA) for the purposes of promoting sleep in children and adults with ASD. Melatonin, however, is widely available and has more placebo-controlled trials in the treatment of pediatric insomnia than any sleep-promoting medication licensed by the FDA. Melatonin has also been studied in adults with ASD (Galli-Carminati, Deriaz, & Bertschy, 2009).

MELATONIN

Sixteen treatment studies have shown support for the effectiveness of short-term use of exogenous melatonin, dose range 0.5 mg to 15 mg, with most studies using a 3- to 5-mg dose 30 minutes prior to desired sleep onset, to improve sleep in children with ASD (Andersen, Kaczmarska, McGrew, & Malow, 2008; Cortesi, Giannotti, Sebastiani, Panunzi, & Valente, 2012; De Leersnyder, Zisapel, & Laudon, 2011; Garstang & Wallis, 2006; Giannotti, Cortesi, Cerquiglini, & Bernabei, 2006; Gringras et al., 2012; Gupta & Hutchins, 2005; Ishizaki, Sugama, & Takeuchi, 1999; Jan, Espezel, & Appleton, 1994; Malow, Adkins, et al., 2012; McArthur & Budden, 1998; Paavonen, Nieminen-von Wendt, Vanhala, Aronen, & von Wendt, 2003; Souders et al., 2017; Tordjman et al., 2015; Wasdell et al., 2008; Wirojanan et al., 2009; Wright et al., 2011). However, most of the studies published to date do have some limitations such as small sample sizes, subjective outcome measures (use of diaries rather than actigraphy and polysomnography), lack of screening for medical conditions that can contribute to insomnia, lack of parent and child sleep education, and limited assessment of daytime behavior, family functioning, and predictors of response such as IQ and age.

Five studies with robust data in children with ASD are highlighted to follow. Andersen and colleagues completed the largest retrospective chart review (n = 107) and reported that 85% of children who were treated with melatonin (0.75 to 6 mg) had improvements in sleep (Andersen et al., 2008). Three open-label trials reported decreases in sleep onset latency with exogenous melatonin (Giannotti et al., 2006; Paavonen et al., 2003; Schwichtenberg & Malow, 2015). In addition, in the largest randomized placebo-controlled trial to date, Cortesi and colleaguesstudied 134 children (69 of whom received sustained-release melatonin, 3 mg) and reported reduced sleep onset time and increased sleep duration and efficiency (Cortesi et al., 2012). These improvements were reported for children who received cognitive behavioral therapy and/or melatonin, but not for children in the placebo group. Although the doses of melatonin vary considerably across these studies, the cumulative findings provide evidence that exogenous melatonin is a safe practice when caring for children with ASD, and families have not reported significant adverse events.

Taken together, this body of evidence supports the use of melatonin and extended-release melatonin in children with ASD after environmental and behavioral strategies have been implemented and are insufficient in improving sleep. Some children with ASD, however, do not respond to melatonin, and other families find that melatonin loses its effectiveness over time (Malow, Adkins, et al., 2012; Souders et al., 2009). It is paramount to note that melatonin is not approved by the FDA; it is critical to note that no drug (or supplement) is approved for use in pediatric insomnia. The off-label use of melatonin is common, especially in children with ASD. Based on this review, melatonin is most effective in treating sleep onset difficulties and may be beneficial for other elements of sleep depending on child-specific factors. Additional studies, including large randomized trials, are needed to establish its efficacy and the variables that may influence treatment response.

Case Example

This is the case of a child who participated in a study for children with ASD ages 6 to 10 with insomnia

(Souders et al., 2017). The study involved an intervention designed as a supplement to the ATN Sleep Toolkit. The study also included a home-based weekly intervention delivered by nurses or occupational therapists that included three components: (a) positive evening routines from the ATN Sleep Toolkit; (b) a supplemental bedtime protocol that has children go to bed when they are irresistibly sleepy, equating sleepiness with their bedroom (stimulus control), and (Hall et al.) supplemental calming techniques to decrease arousal level. The environmental changes, bedtime routines, and calming activities were tailored to each child and family, based on the child's arousal/anxiety/ADHD profile and sleep characteristics and the family's identified goals.

Based on the idea that a subgroup of children with ASD are in a hyperaroused state, we developed a module consisting of instructions for calming techniques to supplement the ATN Sleep Tool Kit (Malow et al., 2014) and address the internal factors that threaten sleep and decrease their arousal levels. The calming module includes 12 individualized soothing and relaxing activities that are selected by the children with ASD and their parents: (a) observing your breath exercise, (b) progressive muscle relaxation, (c) yoga poses, (d) massage, (e) activities from the *Moody Cow Meditates* book (e.g., homemade snow globe with sparkles that settle as a visual support to calm their mind), (f) mindfulness exercises, (g) worry box/worry doll, (h) taking a warm bath, (i) gentle rocking or swinging, (j) quietly reading a book, (k) self-soothing: soothing the five senses, and (l) quietly saying prayers. These activities have been found to be successful in calming individuals with arousal/anxiety symptoms (Bagatell, Mirigliani, Patterson, Reyes, & Test, 2010; Dadoly, 2011; Hanh, 2008; Linehan, 1993; MacLean, 2009; Schaaf & Smith Roley, 2006; Seeman, Dubin, & Seeman, 2003; Silva, Schalock, Ayres, Bunse, & Budden, 2009; Silva, Schalock, & Gabrielsen, 2011).

Identifying Information and Presenting Concerns

On joining our study, C.M. was an 8.5-year-old female with a diagnosis of ASD, as well as ADHD, combined type; generalized anxiety disorder; seasonal allergies and asthma; hypotonia and laxity of joints; and intermittent daytime irritability. She frequently became agitated with small changes in routine or if she did not understand the emotional content of an interaction throughout the day as reported by her school teachers and parents. This irritability would escalate into a tantrum one to two times per day. The tantrums consisted of screaming, crying, and flopping to the floor. She was taking 75 mg of sertraline daily for anxiety. She had trialed stimulants for ADHD but had to be discontinued because of increased irritability.

Social history. C.M. was living with her married parents and older sister, aged 9 years, in a comfortable, suburban home outside a major metropolitan area. Both C.M. and her sister share a bedroom. The father completed high school and works as a foreman in a warehouse and the mother is a homemaker and completed her GED.

Birth history and early years. C.M. was an irritable baby who had difficulty feeding and had an immature swallow and persistent tongue thrust behaviors. She received speech–language therapy early for feeding issues and was identified as having speech–language and social delays at age 1.5. She was diagnosed with ASD at 3 years old and her score on the Autism Diagnostic Observation Schedule (ADOS, the gold-standard diagnostic assessment; Lord et al., 1989) was 20, in the range of autism. C.M. received intensive applied behavior analysis and developmental therapies weekly in the preschool years and transitioned to special education in first grade. She had a history of frequent ear infections and received bilateral myringotomy tubes at 15 months with annual follow-ups with an otolaryngologist. She did not have large tonsils or adenoids and did not have symptoms of obstructive sleep apnea.

Current history. At the time of the study, C.M. was in third grade in an autism support classroom with six students. She had weekly speech–language and occupational therapy. Her general cognitive ability was within the normal range. She was followed by a psychiatrist for her ASD; ADHD, combined type; generalized anxiety; and disruptive behaviors. In addition to sertraline, she also took 10 mg of cetirizine daily in the morning for seasonal allergies. C.M. had difficulties falling and staying asleep.

Screen for Sleep Concerns and Associated Psychiatric Disorders

Sleep environment. C.M. slept with her sister on adjacent twin beds. Her bed was covered with stuffed animals and the room was filled with stuffed animals. The bedroom was 70°F during the day and cool (room temperature 65°F) at night, overall dark though with a blue night light, and quiet, with an overhead fan on for white noise.

Sleep questionnaire. C.M.'s mother completed the Children's Sleep Habits Questionnaire (CSHQ;

Owens et al., 2000), a 33-item questionnaire with eight subscales that reflect key sleep domains, help clinicians identify specific sleep problems, and guide behavioral and environmental strategies to improve sleep. Higher scores indicate more sleep problems. A cut-off of 41 for total score has a sensitivity of 0.80 and specificity of 0.72 for a sleep problem that warrants referral to a sleep center (Owens et al., 2000). Table 14.4 shows the expected score for good sleepers with no sleep problems (minimal score of 33; Owens et al., 2000) and C.M.'s CSHQ score of 53. C.M.'s score indicated sleep problems and warranted referral to a sleep expert.

C.M.'s CSHQ revealed high scores for multiple subscales: Sleep Onset Delay, Parasomnias, and Daytime Sleepiness. A closer look at the individual questionnaire items revealed that C.M. took a long time to fall asleep (on average over 1 hour), was a restless sleeper, talked in her sleep, and had daytime sleepiness. These elevated subscales reflected sleep problems, earning sleep diagnoses of behavioral insomnia of childhood and parasomnia: sleep talking.

Anxiety interview and questionnaire. The study psychologist interviewed C.M. and her mother with the Pediatric Anxiety Rating Scale (PARS; Research Units on Pediatric Psychopharmacology Anxiety Study Group, 2002). Her 7-point total severity score was 11, reflecting improved anxiety on sertraline as reported by her mother. Her mother also completed an anxiety questionnaire, the Screen for Child Anxiety Related Disorders (SCARED; Muris et al., 1998). A score above 25 indicates an anxiety disorder, and C.M.'s total score was 17 and improved from 32 from a previous evaluation before medication.

Baseline actigraphy. At baseline, C.M. went to bed on average at 9:30 p.m., took over 60 minutes to fall asleep, and woke just before 7:00 a.m. (Figure 14.2). Over the 7 nights observed with actigraphy, C.M. averaged 590 minutes (9.8 hours) in bed per night, consisting of 440 sleep minutes (7.33 hours).

Intervention. After reviewing her sleep habits and actigraphy data with C.M. and her parents, the study team implemented the intervention (Table 14.5). First, we introduced the visual bedtime schedule from the ATN Sleep Tool Kit, combining the family's current evening routine with three targeted interventions selected by the family from the Calming Module: quietly reading a book, rocking in rocking chair, and saying prayers. C.M. had already been taking a bath in the evening, bringing her total "Calming Activities" during Week 1 to four. These activities were placed on a visual schedule Velcro board.

During Week 2, we implemented significant environmental changes. We made a plan to bring her bedroom into compliance with ideal sleeping standards (cool, dark, and boring). Notable changes included keeping six favorite stuffed animals and putting all the other stuffed animals in plastic bins and away in the closet. We added heavier curtains to block out light at night paired with a red night light in the hallway and her door slightly ajar. It is important to note that the night light is red, because blue light creates an alerting effect on the brain and may prevent melatonin production (Zerbini, Kantermann, & Merrow, 2018). She continued to use a fan at night to serve as white noise and keep the room cool. We placed a rocking chair in the room for reading time and designated the many books in the room as a "before bed only" activity. Additionally, during Week 2 the study team worked with C.M. to practice deep breathing exercises and "Yoga for Insomnia" poses to do at night with her

Table 14.4. Children's Sleep Habits Questionnaire: Minimum Scores and C.M.'s Scores

Subscales	Minimum Score	C.M. Baseline Score	Significance
Bedtime Resistance	6	6	Goes to bed but unable to fall asleep
Sleep Onset Delay	1	3	Prolonged sleep latency
Sleep Duration	3	4	Parental concern about inadequate sleep
Sleep Anxiety	4	6	Afraid to sleep away from home, needs parents
Night Wakings	3	3	None reported
Parasomnias	7	9	Restless, sleep talking
Sleep Disordered Breathing	3	5	Occasional snoring with colds
Daytime Sleepiness	8	17	Takes a long time to be alert in morning, falls asleep watching TV and riding in car, seems tired
Total Score	33	53	Above 41 has been used as a cut-off for sleep problems

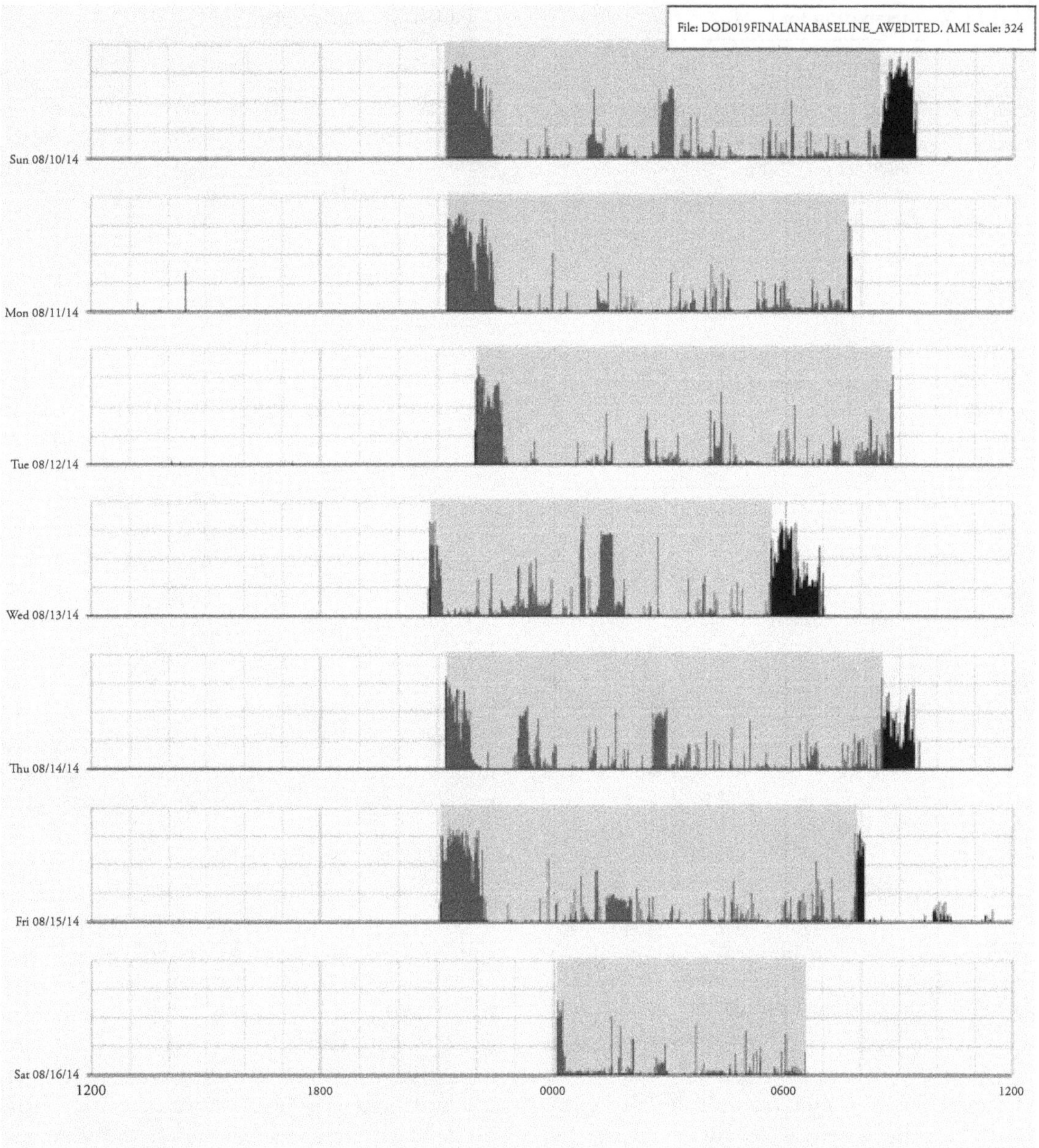

Key

Baseline actigraphy. Seven nights of actigraphy. X-axis is military time with midnight (0000) being in the center of the x-axis. Y-axis is the days of the week starting with Sunday. On average, sleep in minutes for C.M. was 440 minutes per night. Sleep latency was 66 minutes per night and wake in minutes per night was 53 minutes.

Figure 14.2. Baseline actigraphy.

family. C.M. particularly liked doing "yoga legs" paired with the deep breathing exercises and would practice them in bed before going to sleep and again if she woke up in the middle of the night.

Final adjustments to the bedtime routine were made in Week 4, with the addition of a massage at C.M. and the family's request. Each week we monitored the family's use of the interventions and provided feedback on how to implement them consistently. By the fourth week, her family was consistently implementing the visual schedule, with set times every night for calming activities. From Week 4 to Week 8, no significant changes were made to C.M.'s interventions.

Results. By Week 8 (Figure 14.3), C.M. saw improvements, specifically in sleep consolidation and

Table 14.5. Intervention for C.M.

	Interventions
Ecological	Removed 678 stuffed animals from room White noise Night light—red Ceiling fan/open window Six stuffed animals
Positive routines	Shower and teeth brushing Lavender lotion, snuggly PJs Light snack with music
Massage	With lavender lotion
Calming activities	Rocking in chair and reading a book Deep breathing "Yoga legs" in bed Prayer

Table 14.6. Actigraphy

Measure	Baseline	Week 8
Starting Time	21:04:00	21:52:00
Ending time	6:54:00	7:03:00
Duration (min)	590	551
Activity mean (min)	26.71	15.88
Wake minutes	53.5	23.4
Sleep minutes	440.20	488.44
Sleep efficiency	84.21%	91.6%
Sleep latency (min)	66.52	17.83

sleep minutes. She went to bed at 9:52 p.m., took 17.8 minutes to fall asleep, and woke at 7:03 a.m. Over the 5 nights of actigraphy, C.M. averaged 551.2 minutes (9.19 hours) in bed per night, consisting of 488.4 sleep minutes (8.14 hours) and 23.4 wake minutes, reflecting an additional increase of almost 48 minutes per night. Even though the bedtime is later and the amount of time in bed is shorter as a result of the stimulus control bedtime protocol, she had improved her total sleep time and sleep efficiency.

Case Summary

Based on baseline sleep interview, actigraphy, and CSHQ data, C.M. had both early insomnia (prolonged sleep latency) and parasomnias (restlessness and sleep talking). Intervention had a dramatic improvement on her sleep and resolved her early insomnia (Table 14.6). C.M. and her family were able to implement the sleep protocol with fidelity. Parents were able to implement ecological approaches and had the resources to provide an optimal sleep environment. Her parents' perceptions of her sleep habits also improved, based on CSHQ, from a total score of 53 to 44, but they continued to report parasomnias and mild daytime sleepiness. Although by Week 8 C.M.'s sleep had increased from 7 hours per night to 8 hours per night on average, the National Sleep Foundation recommends 9 to 11 hours of sleep per night (National Sleep Foundation, 2016) for a child of C.M.'s age, resulting in inadequate sleep time and residual daytime sleepiness. The plan was for parents to continue the interventions and slowly fade her sleep start time back to 8:45 to 9:00 p.m. in 15-minute increments per the bedtime protocol, in order for her to have a 9- to 10-hour sleep opportunity.

Summary and Future Directions

This chapter provided an overview of the state of the science of sleep in individuals with ASD and hypotheses for the high prevalence of insomnia in this vulnerable population. We presented an ecological approach for promoting optimal sleep using a case presentation. The strongest evidence to date on promoting sleep in ASD is on sleep education, behavioral interventions, and exogenous melatonin. The case presentation highlights the dramatic improvement in sleep achievable with an intensive educational, ecological, and behavioral approach implemented by well-trained providers and highly motivated parents. To be effective, this intervention demands commitment to a nonpharmacological approach by the provider and parent and requires confidence that behavioral change is possible. Moreover, in our experience, ecological changes are quick and cost-effective and parents are very receptive to such environmental changes. The next steps for dissemination of the ATN practice pathway for sleep in children with ASD will need to address local, state, and national barriers to implementation of ecological and behavioral sleep treatment with fidelity. This will require a paradigm shift in the health care arena to mobilize resources to train providers and empower families and communities to implement ecological and behavioral care to improve sleep in individuals with ASD.

Although the clinical importance of insomnia is evident and several promising treatments exist, insomnia remains treatment resistant in a subpopulation of individuals with ASD. Several gaps in knowledge are currently holding back progress in the development of novel interventions to treat insomnia. First, individuals with ASD and co-occurring intellectual disability and/or minimal language abilities are often excluded from research studies that use objective measures of sleep and circadian rhythms. These individuals may present with increased sensory

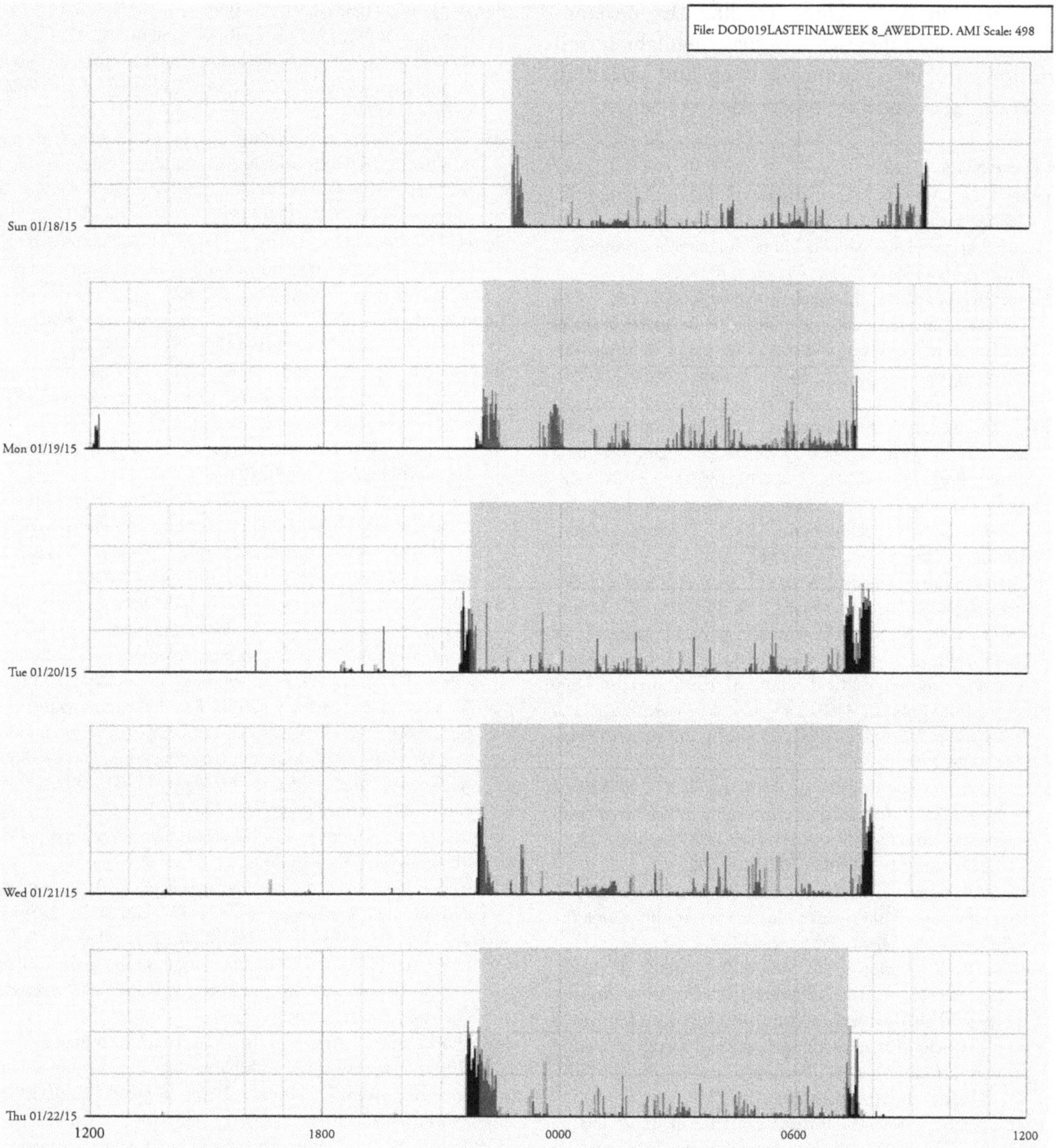

Key

Week 8 postintervention actigraphy. 5 nights of actigraphy. X-axis is military time with midnight (0000) being in the center of the x-axis. Y-axis is the days of the week starting with Sunday. On average, sleep in minutes for C.M. was 488 minimum per night. Sleep latency was 17 minimum and wake in minutes per night was 23 minimum.

Figure 14.3. Follow-up actigraphy at 8 weeks.

sensitivities that make it difficult to tolerate objective sleep and circadian measures (e.g., polysomnography sensors or repeated salivary melatonin sampling). Greater effort to habituate these individuals to gold-standard methods and develop noninvasive sleep and circadian measurement techniques is needed to increase research participation of this subgroup. Including this subgroup in objective rigorous sleep and circadian research may elucidate a richer understanding of sleep disorder phenotypes in ASD and help to individualize sleep treatments to individual subgroups. In addition, the developmental course of sleep and the circadian regulation of sleep have not been tracked objectively from childhood to adulthood in ASD. Understanding the developmental course of these systems may highlight critical windows for intervening on sleep and circadian functioning to optimize prospective outcomes.

References

Adams, H. L., Matson, J. L., Cervantes, P. E., & Goldin, R. L. (2014). The relationship between autism symptom severity and sleep problems: Should bidirectionality be considered? *Research in Autism Spectrum Disorders, 8*(3), 193–199.

Aldinger, K. A., Lane, C. J., Veenstra-VanderWeele, J., & Levitt, P. (2015). Patterns of risk for multiple co-occurring medical conditions replicate across distinct cohorts of children with autism spectrum disorder. *Autism Research, 8*(6), 771–781. doi:10.1002/aur.1492

Allik, H., Larsson, J. O., & Smedje, H. (2006). Insomnia in school-age children with Asperger syndrome or high-functioning autism. *BMC Psychiatry, 6*, 18. doi:10.1186/1471-244X-6-18

American Association of Respiratory Care-Association of Polysomnography Technologists. (1995). Polysomnography. *Respiratory Care, 40*(12), 1336–1343.

American Psychiatric Association. (2013). *Diagnostic and statistical manual of mental disorders* (5th ed.). Washington, DC: Author.

Anders, T., Iosif, A. M., Schwichtenberg, A. J., Tang, K., & Goodlin-Jones, B. (2012). Sleep and daytime functioning: A short-term longitudinal study of three preschool-age comparison groups. *American Journal of Intellectual and Development Disability, 117*(4), 275–290. doi:10.1352/1944-7558-117.4.275

Andersen, I. M., Kaczmarska, J., McGrew, S. G., & Malow, B. A. (2008). Melatonin for insomnia in children with autism spectrum disorders. *Journal of Child Neurology, 23*(5), 482–485. doi:10.1177/0883073807309783

Ardura, J., Andres, J., Aldana, J., & Revilla, M. A. (1995). Development of sleep-wakefulness rhythm in premature babies. *Acta Paediatrica, 84*(5), 484–489.

Ausderau, K. K., Furlong, M., Sideris, J., Bulluck, J., Little, L. M., Watson, L. R.,... Baranek, G. T. (2014). Sensory subtypes in children with autism spectrum disorder: Latent profile transition analysis using a national survey of sensory features. *Journal of Child Psychology and Psychiatry, 55*(8), 935–944. doi:10.1111/jcpp.12219

Bagatell, N., Mirigliani, G., Patterson, C., Reyes, Y., & Test, L. (2010). Effectiveness of therapy ball chairs on classroom participation in children with autism spectrum disorders. *American Journal of Occupational Therapy, 64*(6), 895–903.

Baird, A. L., Coogan, A. N., Siddiqui, A., Donev, R. M., & Thome, J. (2012). Adult attention-deficit hyperactivity disorder is associated with alterations in circadian rhythms at the behavioural, endocrine and molecular levels. *Molecular Psychiatry, 17*(10), 988–995. doi:10.1038/mp.2011.149

Baker, E. K., & Richdale, A. L. (2015). Sleep patterns in adults with a diagnosis of high-functioning autism spectrum disorder. *Sleep, 38*(11), 1765–1774. doi:10.5665/sleep.5160

Baker, E. K., Richdale, A. L., & Hazi, A. (2019). Employment status is related to sleep problems in adults with autism spectrum disorder and no comorbid intellectual impairment. *Autism, 23*(2), 531–536. doi:10.1177/1362361317745857

Ballester, P., Martinez, M. J., Javaloyes, A., Inda, M. D., Fernandez, N., Gazquez, P.,... Peiro, A. M. (2019). Sleep problems in adults with autism spectrum disorder and intellectual disability. *Autism Research, 12*(1), 66–79. doi:10.1002/aur.2000

Barnes, J. W., Tischkau, S. A., Barnes, J. A., Mitchell, J. W., Burgoon, P. W., Hickok, J. R., & Gillette, M. U. (2003). Requirement of mammalian Timeless for circadian rhythmicity. *Science, 302*(5644), 439–442. doi:10.1126/science.1086593

Barry, R. J., & James, A. L. (1988). Coding of stimulus parameters in autistic, retarded, and normal children: Evidence for a two-factor theory of autism. *International Journal of Psychophysiology, 6*(2), 139–149.

Berset, M., Elfering, A., Luthy, S., Luthi, S., & Semmer, N. K. (2011). Work stressors and impaired sleep: Rumination as a mediator. *Stress Health, 27*(2), e71–82.

Bonnet, M. H. (2009). Evidence for the pathophysiology of insomnia. *Sleep, 32*(4), 441–442.

Bonnet, M. H., & Arand, D. L. (2010). Hyperarousal and insomnia: State of the science. *Sleep Medicine Review, 14*(1), 9–15. doi:10.1016/j.smrv.2009.05.002

Borbely, A. A. (1982). A two process model of sleep regulation. *Human Neurobiology, 1*(3), 195–204.

Bricout, V. A., Pace, M., Dumortier, L., Baillieul, F., Favre-Juvin, A., & Guinot, M. (2018). Reduced cardiorespiratory capacity in children with autism spectrum disorders. *Journal of Clinical Medicine, 7*(10). doi:10.3390/jcm7100361

Brown, L. W. (2019). Medications. In J. A. Accardo (Ed.), *Sleep in children with neurodevelopmental disabilities: An evidence-based guide* (pp. 319–329). Springer International Publishing.

Buckley, A. W., Rodriguez, A. J., Jennison, K., Buckley, J., Thurm, A., Sato, S., & Swedo, S. (2010). Rapid eye movement sleep percentage in children with autism compared with children with developmental delay and typical development. *Archives of Pediatric and Adolescent Medicine, 164*(11), 1032–1037. doi:10.1001/archpediatrics.2010.202

Bujnakova, I., Ondrejka, I., Mestanik, M., Visnovcova, Z., Mestanikova, A., Hrtanek, I.,... Tonhajzerova, I. (2016). Autism spectrum disorder is associated with autonomic underarousal. *Physiological Research, 65*(Suppl 5), S673–S682.

Buysse, D. J., Reynolds, C. F., 3rd, Monk, T. H., Berman, S. R., & Kupfer, D. J. (1989). The Pittsburgh Sleep Quality Index: A new instrument for psychiatric practice and research. *Psychiatry Research, 28*(2), 193–213.

Carrillo-Vico, A., Guerrero, J. M., Lardone, P. J., & Reiter, R. J. (2005). A review of the multiple actions of melatonin on the immune system. *Endocrine, 27*(2), 189–200. doi:10.1385/ENDO:27:2:189

Carskadon, M. A. (1990). Patterns of sleep and sleepiness in adolescents. *Pediatrician, 17*(1), 5–12.

Carskadon, M. A. (2011). Sleep in adolescents: The perfect storm. *Pediatric Clinics of North America, 58*(3), 637–647. doi:10.1016/j.pcl.2011.03.003

Carskadon, M. A., Acebo, C., & Jenni, O. G. (2004). Regulation of adolescent sleep: Implications for behavior. *Annals of the New York Academy of Science, 1021*, 276–291. doi:10.1196/annals.1308.032

Chang, M. C., Parham, L. D., Blanche, E. I., Schell, A., Chou, C. P., Dawson, M., & Clark, F. (2012). Autonomic and behavioral responses of children with autism to auditory stimuli. *American Journal of Occupational Therapy, 66*(5), 567–576. doi:10.5014/ajot.2012.004242

Chervin, R. D., Ruzicka, D. L., Giordani, B. J., Weatherly, R. A., Dillon, J. E., Hodges, E. K.,... Guire, K. E. (2006). Sleep-disordered breathing, behavior, and cognition in children before and after adenotonsillectomy. *Pediatrics, 117*(4), e769–e778. doi:10.1542/peds.2005-1837

Chez, M. G., Chang, M., Krasne, V., Coughlan, C., Kominsky, M., & Schwartz, A. (2006). Frequency of epileptiform EEG abnormalities in a sequential screening of autistic patients with no known clinical epilepsy from 1996 to 2005. *Epilepsy and Behavior, 8*(1), 267–271. doi:10.1016/j.yebeh.2005.11.001

Chojnacki, C., Poplawski, T., Blasiak, J., Chojnacki, J., & Klupinska, G. (2013). Does melatonin homeostasis play a role in continuous epigastric pain syndrome? *International Journal of Molecular Science, 14*(6), 12,550–12,562. doi:10.3390/ijms140612550

Civardi, C., & Collini, A. (2007). Sleep deprivation increases cortical excitability in epilepsy: Syndrome-specific effects. *Neurology, 69*(3), 318; author reply 318–319. doi:10.1212/01.wnl.0000275279.98763.14

Cortesi, F., Giannotti, F., Ivanenko, A., & Johnson, K. (2010). Sleep in children with autistic spectrum disorder. *Sleep Medicine, 11*(7), 659–664. doi:10.1016/j.sleep.2010.01.010

Cortesi, F., Giannotti, F., Sebastiani, T., Panunzi, S., & Valente, D. (2012). Controlled-release melatonin, singly and combined with cognitive behavioural therapy, for persistent insomnia in children with autism spectrum disorders: A randomized placebo-controlled trial. *Journal of Sleep Research, 21*(6), 700–709. doi:10.1111/j.1365–2869.2012.01021.x

Coury, D. L., Anagnostou, E., Manning-Courtney, P., Reynolds, A., Cole, L., McCoy, R., . . . Perrin, J. M. (2012). Use of psychotropic medication in children and adolescents with autism spectrum disorders. *Pediatrics, 130*(Suppl 2), S69–S76. doi:10.1542/peds.2012-0900D

Couturier, J. L., Speechley, K. N., Steele, M., Norman, R., Stringer, B., & Nicolson, R. (2005). Parental perception of sleep problems in children of normal intelligence with pervasive developmental disorders: Prevalence, severity, and pattern. *Journal of the American Academy of Child and Adolescent Psychiatry, 44*(8), 815–822. doi:10.1097/01.chi.0000166377.22651.87

Crowley, S. J., Van Reen, E., LeBourgeois, M. K., Acebo, C., Tarokh, L., Seifer, R., . . . Carskadon, M. A. (2014). A longitudinal assessment of sleep timing, circadian phase, and phase angle of entrainment across human adolescence. *PLoS One, 9*(11), e112199. doi:10.1371/journal.pone.0112199

Cuomo, B. M., Vaz, S., Lee, E. A. L., Thompson, C., Rogerson, J. M., & Falkmer, T. (2017). Effectiveness of sleep-based interventions for children with autism spectrum disorder: A meta-synthesis. *Pharmacotherapy, 37*(5), 555–578. doi:10.1002/phar.1920

Dadoly, A. (2011). Two techniques for reducing stress. Retrieved from http://www.health.harvard.edu/blog/two-techniques-for-reducing-stress-201,104,092,235

Daluwatte, C., Miles, J. H., Christ, S. E., Beversdorf, D. Q., Takahashi, T. N., & Yao, G. (2013). Atypical pupillary light reflex and heart rate variability in children with autism spectrum disorder. *Journal of Autism and Developmental Disorders, 43*(8), 1910–1925. doi:10.1007/s10803-012-1741-3

Daluwatte, C., Miles, J. H., Sun, J., & Yao, G. (2015). Association between pupillary light reflex and sensory behaviors in children with autism spectrum disorders. *Research in Developmental Disabilities, 37*, 209–215. doi:10.1016/j.ridd.2014.11.019

De Leersnyder, H., Zisapel, N., & Laudon, M. (2011). Prolonged-release melatonin for children with neurodevelopmental disorders. *Pediatric Neurology, 45*(1), 23–26. doi:10.1016/j.pediatrneurol.2011.02.001

Dinalankara, D. M. R., Miles, J. H., Nicole Takahashi, T., & Yao, G. (2017). Atypical pupillary light reflex in 2-6-year-old children with autism spectrum disorders. *Autism Research, 10*(5), 829–838. doi:10.1002/aur.1745

Diomedi, M., Curatolo, P., Scalise, A., Placidi, F., Caretto, F., & Gigli, G. L. (1999). Sleep abnormalities in mentally retarded autistic subjects: Down's syndrome with mental retardation and normal subjects. *Brain Development, 21*(8), 548–553.

Drago, F., Macauda, S., & Salehi, S. (2002). Small doses of melatonin increase intestinal motility in rats. *Digestive Diseases and Sciences, 47*(9), 1969–1974.

Dunn, W. (1999). *Sensory Profile*. San Antonio, TX: Psychological Corporation.

Dunster, G. P., de la Iglesia, L., Ben-Hamo, M., Nave, C., Fleischer, J. G., Panda, S., & de la Iglesia, H. O. (2018). Sleepmore in Seattle: Later school start times are associated with more sleep and better performance in high school students. *Science Advances, 4*(12), eaau6200. doi:10.1126/sciadv.aau6200

Eilam-Stock, T., Xu, P., Cao, M., Gu, X., Van Dam, N. T., Anagnostou, E., . . . Fan, J. (2014). Abnormal autonomic and associated brain activities during rest in autism spectrum disorder. *Brain, 137*(Pt 1), 153–171. doi:10.1093/brain/awt294

Elia, M., Ferri, R., Musumeci, S. A., Del Gracco, S., Bottitta, M., Scuderi, C., . . . Grubar, J. C. (2000). Sleep in subjects with autistic disorder: A neurophysiological and psychological study. *Brain Development, 22*(2), 88–92.

Elrod, M. G., & Hood, B. S. (2015). Sleep differences among children with autism spectrum disorders and typically developing peers: a meta-analysis. *Journal of Developmental and Behavioral Pediatrics, 36*(3), 166–177. doi:10.1097/DBP.0000000000000140

Etchegaray, J. P., Lee, C., Wade, P. A., & Reppert, S. M. (2003). Rhythmic histone acetylation underlies transcription in the mammalian circadian clock. *Nature, 421*(6919), 177–182. doi:10.1038/nature01314

Feige, B., Baglioni, C., Spiegelhalder, K., Hirscher, V., Nissen, C., & Riemann, D. (2013). The microstructure of sleep in primary insomnia: An overview and extension. *International Journal of Psychophysiology, 89*(2), 171–180. doi:10.1016/j.ijpsycho.2013.04.002

Fletcher, F. E., Foster-Owens, M. D., Conduit, R., Rinehart, N. J., Riby, D. M., & Cornish, K. M. (2017). The developmental trajectory of parent-report and objective sleep profiles in autism spectrum disorder: Associations with anxiety and bedtime routines. Autism, 21(4), 493–503. doi:10.1177/1362361316653365

Food and Drug Administration. (2017). *Autism: Beware of potentially dangerous therapies and products.*

Franzen, P. L., Gianaros, P. J., Marsland, A. L., Hall, M. H., Siegle, G. J., Dahl, R. E., & Buysse, D. J. (2011). Cardiovascular reactivity to acute psychological stress following sleep deprivation. *Psychosomatic Medicine, 73*(8), 679–682. doi:10.1097/PSY.0b013e31822ff440

Gagnon, K., & Godbout, R. (2018). Melatonin and comorbidities in children with autism spectrum disorder. *Current Developmental Disorders Reports, 5*(3), 197–206. doi:10.1007/s40474-018-0147-0

Gail Williams, P., Sears, L. L., & Allard, A. (2004). Sleep problems in children with autism. *Journal of Sleep Research, 13*(3), 265–268. doi:10.1111/j.1365–2869.2004.00405.x

Galli-Carminati, G., Deriaz, N., & Bertschy, G. (2009). Melatonin in treatment of chronic sleep disorders in adults with autism: A retrospective study. *Swiss Medicine Weekly, 139*(19–20), 293–296. doi:smw-12,342

Garstang, J., & Wallis, M. (2006). Randomized controlled trial of melatonin for children with autistic spectrum disorders and sleep problems. *Child: Care, Health, and Development, 32*(5), 585–589. doi:10.1111/j.1365-2214.2006.00616.x

Geoffray, M. M., Nicolas, A., Speranza, M., & Georgieff, N. (2016). Are circadian rhythms new pathways to understand autism spectrum disorder? *Journal of Physiology Paris, 110* (4 Pt B), 434–438. doi:10.1016/j.jphysparis.2017.06.002

Giannotti, F., Cortesi, F., Cerquiglini, A., & Bernabei, P. (2006). An open-label study of controlled-release melatonin in treatment of sleep disorders in children with autism. *Journal of Autism and Developmental Disorders, 36*(6), 741–752. doi:10.1007/s10803-006-0116-z

Godbout, R., Bergeron, C., Limoges, E., Stip, E., & Mottron, L. (2000). A laboratory study of sleep in Asperger's syndrome. *Neuroreport, 11*(1), 127–130.

Goldman, S. E., Adkins, K. W., Calcutt, M. W., Carter, M. D., Goodpaster, R. L., Wang, L., . . . Malow, B. A. (2014). Melatonin in children with autism spectrum disorders: Endogenous and pharmacokinetic profiles in relation to sleep. *Journal of Autism and Developmental Disorders, 44*(10), 2525–2535. doi:10.1007/s10803-014-2123-9

Goldman, S. E., Alder, M. L., Burgess, H. J., Corbett, B. A., Hundley, R., Wofford, D., . . . Malow, B. A. (2017). Characterizing sleep in adolescents and adults with autism spectrum disorders. *Journal of Autism and Developmental Disorders, 47*(6), 1682–1695. doi:10.1007/s10803-017-3089-1

Goldman, S. E., McGrew, S., Johnson, K. P., Richdale, A. L., Clemons, T., & Malow, B. A. (2011). Sleep is associated with problem behaviors in children and adolescents with autism spectrum disorders. *Research in Autism Spectrum Disorders, 5*(3), 1223–1229.

Goldman, S. E., Richdale, A. L., Clemons, T., & Malow, B. A. (2012). Parental sleep concerns in autism spectrum disorders: variations from childhood to adolescence. *Journal of Autism and Developmental Disorders, 42*(4), 531–538. doi:10.1007/s10803-011-1270-5

Goldman, S. E., Surdyka, K., Cuevas, R., Adkins, K., Wang, L., & Malow, B. A. (2009). Defining the sleep phenotype in children with autism. *Developmental Neuropsychology, 34*(5), 560–573. doi:10.1080/87565640903133509

Gomez, R. L., & Edgin, J. O. (2015). Sleep as a window into early neural development: Shifts in sleep-dependent learning effects across early childhood. *Child Development Perspectives, 9*(3), 183–189. doi:10.1111/cdep.12130

Gordon, A. M., Mendes, W. B., & Prather, A. A. (2017). The social side of sleep: Elucidating the links between sleep and social processes. *Current Directions in Psychological Science, 26*(5), 470–475. doi:10.1177/0963721417712269

Goto, M., Mizuno, M., Matsumoto, A., Yang, Z., Jimbo, E. F., Tabata, H., . . . Nagata, K. I. (2017). Role of a circadian-relevant gene NR1D1 in brain development: Possible involvement in the pathophysiology of autism spectrum disorders. *Scientific Reports, 7*, 43,945. doi:10.1038/srep43945

Gottlieb, D. J., Chase, C., Vezina, R. M., Heeren, T. C., Corwin, M. J., Auerbach, S. H., . . . Lesko, S. M. (2004). Sleep-disordered breathing symptoms are associated with poorer cognitive function in 5-year-old children. *Journal of Pediatrics, 145*(4), 458–464. doi:10.1016/j.jpeds.2004.05.039

Gringras, P., Gamble, C., Jones, A. P., Wiggs, L., Williamson, P. R., Sutcliffe, A., . . . Group, M. S. (2012). Melatonin for sleep problems in children with neurodevelopmental disorders: Randomised double masked placebo controlled trial. *BMJ, 345*, e6664. doi:10.1136/bmj.e6664

Gupta, R., & Hutchins, J. (2005). Melatonin: A panacea for desperate parents? (Hype or truth). *Archives of Disease in Childhood, 90*(9), 986–987. doi:10.1136/adc.2005.075218

Hall, M., Buysse, D. J., Dew, M. A., Prigerson, H. G., Kupfer, D. J., & Reynolds, C. F., 3rd. (1997). Intrusive thoughts and avoidance behaviors are associated with sleep disturbances in bereavement-related depression. *Depression and Anxiety, 6*(3), 106–112.

Hanh, T. N. (2008). *Mindful movements: Ten exercises for well-being*. Berkley, CA: Parralax Press.

Hantsoo, L., Khou, C. S., White, C. N., & Ong, J. C. (2013). Gender and cognitive-emotional factors as predictors of pre-sleep arousal and trait hyperarousal in insomnia. *Journal of Psychosomatic Research, 74*(4), 283–289. doi:10.1016/j.jpsychores.2013.01.014

Hardeland, R., Cardinali, D. P., Srinivasan, V., Spence, D. W., Brown, G. M., & Pandi-Perumal, S. R. (2011). Melatonin—A pleiotropic, orchestrating regulator molecule. *Progress in Neurobiology, 93*(3), 350–384. doi:10.1016/j.pneurobio.2010.12.004

Harder, R., Malow, B. A., Goodpaster, R. L., Iqbal, F., Halbower, A., Goldman, S. E., . . . Diedrich, A. (2016). Heart rate variability during sleep in children with autism spectrum disorder. *Clinical Autonomic Research, 26*(6), 423–432. doi:10.1007/s10286-016-0375-5

Healey, E. S., Kales, A., Monroe, L. J., Bixler, E. O., Chamberlin, K., & Soldatos, C. R. (1981). Onset of insomnia: Role of life-stress events. *Psychosomatic Medicine, 43*(5), 439–451.

Helt, M. S., Eigsti, I. M., Snyder, P. J., & Fein, D. A. (2010). Contagious yawning in autistic and typical development. *Child Development, 81*(5), 1620–1631. doi:10.1111/j.1467-8624.2010.01495.x

Hering, E., Epstein, R., Elroy, S., Iancu, D. R., & Zelnik, N. (1999). Sleep patterns in autistic children. *Journal of Autism and Developmental Disorders, 29*(2), 143–147.

Hill, A. P., Zuckerman, K. E., Hagen, A. D., Kriz, D. J., Duvall, S. W., van Santen, J., . . . Fombonne, E. (2014). Aggressive behavior problems in children with autism spectrum disorders: Prevalence and correlates in a large clinical sample. *Research in Autism Spectrum Disorders, 8*(9), 1121–1133. doi:10.1016/j.rasd.2014.05.006

Hodge, D., Carollo, T. M., Lewin, M., Hoffman, C. D., & Sweeney, D. P. (2014). Sleep patterns in children with and without autism spectrum disorders: Developmental comparisons. *Research in Developmental Disabilities, 35*(7), 1631–1638. doi:10.1016/j.ridd.2014.03.037

Hodge, D., Hoffman, C. D., Sweeney, D. P., & Riggs, M. L. (2013). Relationship between children's sleep and mental health in mothers of children with and without autism. *Journal of Autism and Developmental Disorders, 43*(4), 956–963. doi:10.1007/s10803-012-1639-0

Hoffman, C. D., Sweeney, D. P., Gilliam, J. E., Apodaca, D. D., Lopez-Wagner, M. C., & Castillo, M. M. (2005). Sleep problems and symptomology in children with autism. *Focus on Autism and Other Developmental Disabilities, 20*(4), 194–200. http://dx.doi.org/10.1177/10883576050200040101

Hohn, V. D., de Veld, D. M. J., Mataw, K. J. S., van Someren, E. J. W., & Begeer, S. (2019). Insomnia severity in adults with autism spectrum disorder is associated with sensory hyper-reactivity and social skill impairment. *Journal of Autism and Developmental Disorders*. doi:10.1007/s10803-019-03891-8

Hollway, J. A., Aman, M. G., & Butter, E. (2013). Correlates and risk markers for sleep disturbance in participants of the Autism Treatment Network. *Journal of Autism and Developmental Disorders, 43*(12), 2830–2843. doi:10.1007/s10803-013-1830-y

Hu, V. W., Sarachana, T., Kim, K. S., Nguyen, A., Kulkarni, S., Steinberg, M. E., . . . Lee, N. H. (2009). Gene expression profiling differentiates autism case-controls and phenotypic variants of autism spectrum disorders: Evidence for circadian rhythm dysfunction in severe autism. *Autism Research, 2*(2), 78–97. doi:10.1002/aur.73

Hundley, R. J., Shui, A., & Malow, B. A. (2016). Relationship between subtypes of restricted and repetitive behaviors and sleep disturbance in autism spectrum disorder. *Journal of Autism and Developmental Disorders, 46*(11), 3448–3457. doi:10.1007/s10803-016-2884-4

Ishizaki, A., Sugama, M., & Takeuchi, N. (1999). [Usefulness of melatonin for developmental sleep and emotional/behavior disorders—studies of melatonin trial on 50 patients with developmental disorders]. *No To Hattatsu, 31*(5), 428–437.

Jan, J. E., Espezel, H., & Appleton, R. E. (1994). The treatment of sleep disorders with melatonin. *Developmental Medicine and Child Neurology, 36*(2), 97–107.

Jenni, O. G., Achermann, P., & Carskadon, M. A. (2005). Homeostatic sleep regulation in adolescents. *Sleep, 28*(11), 1446–1454.

Johnson, C. R., Smith, T., DeMand, A., Lecavalier, L., Evans, V., Gurka, M., . . . Scahill, L. (2018). Exploring sleep quality of young children with autism spectrum disorder and disruptive behaviors. *Sleep Medicine, 44*, 61–66. doi:10.1016/j.sleep.2018.01.008

Kang, V., Wagner, G. C., & Ming, X. (2014). Gastrointestinal dysfunction in children with autism spectrum disorders. *Autism Research, 7*(4), 501–506. doi:10.1002/aur.1386

Katz, T., Shui, A. M., Johnson, C. R., Richdale, A. L., Reynolds, A. M., Scahill, L., & Malow, B. A. (2018). Modification of the Children's Sleep Habits Questionnaire for children with autism spectrum disorder. *Journal of Autism and Developmental Disabilities, 48*, 2629–2641. doi:10.1007/s10803-018-3520-2.

Klukowski, M., Wasilewska, J., & Lebensztejn, D. (2015). Sleep and gastrointestinal disturbances in autism spectrum disorder in children. *Developmental Period Medicine, 19*(2), 157–161.

Kohyama, J. (2016). Possible neuronal mechanisms of sleep disturbances in patients with autism spectrum disorders and attention-deficit/hyperactivity disorder. *Medical Hypotheses, 97*, 131–133. doi:10.1016/j.mehy.2016.11.001

Konen, T., Dirk, J., & Schmiedek, F. (2015). Cognitive benefits of last night's sleep: daily variations in children's sleep behavior are related to working memory fluctuations. *Journal of Child Psychology and Psychiatry, 56*(2), 171–182. doi:10.1111/jcpp.12296

Kotagal, S., & Broomall, E. (2012). Sleep in children with autism spectrum disorder. *Pediatric Neurology, 47*(4), 242–251. doi:10.1016/j.pediatrneurol.2012.05.007

Krakowiak, P., Goodlin-Jones, B., Hertz-Picciotto, I., Croen, L. A., & Hansen, R. L. (2008). Sleep problems in children with autism spectrum disorders, developmental delays, and typical development: A population-based study. *Journal of Sleep Research, 17*(2), 197–206. doi:10.1111/j.1365-2869.2008.00650.x

Kulman, G., Lissoni, P., Rovelli, F., Roselli, M. G., Brivio, F., & Sequeri, P. (2000). Evidence of pineal endocrine hypofunction in autistic children. *Neuroendocrinology Letters, 21*(1), 31–34.

Kushki, A., Brian, J., Dupuis, A., & Anagnostou, E. (2014). Functional autonomic nervous system profile in children with autism spectrum disorder. *Molecular Autism, 5*, 39. doi:10.1186/2040-2392-5-39

Lake, J. K., Denton, D., Lunsky, Y., Shui, A. M., Veenstra-VanderWeele, J., & Anagnostou, E. (2017). Medical conditions and demographic, service and clinical factors associated with atypical antipsychotic medication use among children with an autism spectrum disorder. *Journal of Autism and Developmental Disorders, 47*(5), 1391–1402. doi:10.1007/s10803-017-3058-8

Levenson, J. C., Kay, D. B., & Buysse, D. J. (2015). The pathophysiology of insomnia. *Chest, 147*(4), 1179–1192. doi:10.1378/chest.14-1617

Limoges, E., Mottron, L., Bolduc, C., Berthiaume, C., & Godbout, R. (2005). Atypical sleep architecture and the autism phenotype. *Brain, 128*(Pt 5), 1049–1061. doi:10.1093/brain/awh425

Linehan, M. M. (1993). *Skills training manual for treating borderline personality disorder*. Guilford Press.

Liu, X., Hubbard, J. A., Fabes, R. A., & Adam, J. B. (2006). Sleep disturbances and correlates of children with autism spectrum disorders. *Child Psychiatry and Human Development, 37*(2), 179–191. doi:10.1007/s10578-006-0028-3

Lord, C., Rutter, M., Goode, S., Heemsbergen, J., Jordan, H., Mawhood, L., & Schopler, E. (1989). Autism diagnostic observation schedule: A standardized observation of communicative and social behavior. *Journal of Autism and Developmental Disorders, 19*(2), 185–212.

Lydon, S., Healy, O., Reed, P., Mulhern, T., Hughes, B. M., & Goodwin, M. S. (2016). A systematic review of physiological reactivity to stimuli in autism. *Developmental Neurorehabilitation, 19*(6), 335–355. doi:10.3109/17518423.2014.971975

MacLean, K. L. (2009). *Moody cow meditates*. Wisdom Publications.

Maes, J. H., Eling, P. A., Wezenberg, E., Vissers, C. T., & Kan, C. C. (2011). Attentional set shifting in autism spectrum disorder: Differentiating between the role of perseveration, learned irrelevance, and novelty processing. *Journal of Clinical and Experimental Neuropsychology, 33*(2), 210–217. doi:10.1080/13803395.2010.501327

Malow, B. A. (2004). Sleep deprivation and epilepsy. *Epilepsy Currents, 4*(5), 193–195. doi:10.1111/j.1535-7597.2004.04509.x

Malow, B. A., Adkins, K. W., McGrew, S. G., Wang, L., Goldman, S. E., Fawkes, D., & Burnette, C. (2012). Melatonin for sleep in children with autism: A controlled trial examining dose, tolerability, and outcomes. *Journal of Autism and Developmental Disorders, 42*(8), 1729–1737; author reply 1738. doi:10.1007/s10803-011-1418-3

Malow, B. A., Adkins, K. W., Reynolds, A., Weiss, S. K., Loh, A., Fawkes, D., . . . Clemons, T. (2014). Parent-based sleep education for children with autism spectrum disorders. *Journal of Autism and Developmental Disorders, 44*, 216–228. doi:10.1007/s10803-013-1866-z

Malow, B. A., Byers, K., Johnson, K., Weiss, S., Bernal, P., Goldman, S. E., . . . Glaze, D. G. (2012). A practice pathway for the identification, evaluation, and management of insomnia in children and adolescents with autism spectrum disorders. *Pediatrics, 130*(Suppl 2), S106–S124. doi:10.1542/peds.2012-0900I

Malow, B. A., Marzec, M. L., McGrew, S. G., Wang, L., Henderson, L. M., & Stone, W. L. (2006). Characterizing sleep in children with autism spectrum disorders: A multidimensional approach. *Sleep, 29*(12), 1563–1571.

Martin, J. S., Gaudreault, M. M., Perron, M., & Laberge, L. (2016). Chronotype, light exposure, sleep, and daytime functioning in high school students attending morning or afternoon school shifts: An actigraphic study. *Journal of Biological Rhythms, 31*(2), 205–217. doi:10.1177/0748730415625510

Maski, K., Holbrook, H., Manoach, D., Hanson, E., Kapur, K., & Stickgold, R. (2015). Sleep dependent memory consolidation in children with autism spectrum disorder. *Sleep, 38*(12), 1955–1963. doi:10.5665/sleep.5248

Matson, J. L., Wilkins, J., & Ancona, M. (2008). Autism in adults with severe intellectual disability: An empirical study of symptom presentation. *Journal of Intellectual and Developmental Disabilities, 33*(1), 36–42. doi:10.1080/13668250701829837

May, T., Cornish, K., Conduit, R., Rajaratnam, S. M., & Rinehart, N. J. (2015). Sleep in high-functioning children with autism: Longitudinal developmental change and associations with behavior problems. *Behavioral Sleep Medicine, 13*(1), 2–18. doi:10.1080/15402002.2013.829064

Mayes, S. D., & Calhoun, S. L. (2009). Variables related to sleep problems in children with autism. *Research in Autism Spectrum Disorders, 3*(4), 931–941.

Mazefsky, C. A., Herrington, J., Siegel, M., Scarpa, A., Maddox, B. B., Scahill, L., & White, S. W. (2013). The role of emotion regulation in autism spectrum disorder. *Journal of the American Academy of Child and Adolescent Psychiatry, 52*(7), 679–688. doi:10.1016/j.jaac.2013.05.006

Mazurek, M. O., & Petroski, G. F. (2015). Sleep problems in children with autism spectrum disorder: Examining the contributions of sensory over-responsivity and anxiety. *Sleep Medicine, 16*(2), 270–279. doi:10.1016/j.sleep.2014.11.006

McArthur, A. J., & Budden, S. S. (1998). Sleep dysfunction in Rett syndrome: A trial of exogenous melatonin treatment. *Developmental Medicine and Child Neurology, 40*(3), 186–192.

McCue, L. M., Flick, L. H., Twyman, K. A., & Xian, H. (2017). Gastrointestinal dysfunctions as a risk factor for sleep disorders in children with idiopathic autism spectrum disorder: A retrospective cohort study. *Autism, 21*(8), 1010–1020. doi:10.1177/1362361316667061

Melke, J., Goubran Botros, H., Chaste, P., Betancur, C., Nygren, G., Anckarsater, H., . . . Bourgeron, T. (2008). Abnormal melatonin synthesis in autism spectrum disorders. *Molecular Psychiatry, 13*(1), 90–98. doi:10.1038/sj.mp.4002016

Meltzer, L. J. (2010). Clinical management of behavioral insomnia of childhood: Treatment of bedtime problems and night wakings in young children. *Behavioral Sleep Medicine, 8*(3), 172–189. doi:10.1080/15402002.2010.487464

Mindell, J. A., & Meltzer, L. J. (2008). Behavioural sleep disorders in children and adolescents. *Annals of the Academy of Medicine Singapore, 37*(8), 722–728.

Ming, X., Julu, P. O., Brimacombe, M., Connor, S., & Daniels, M. L. (2005). Reduced cardiac parasympathetic activity in children with autism. *Brain Development, 27*(7), 509–516. doi:10.1016/j.braindev.2005.01.003

Ming, X., Patel, R., Kang, V., Chokroverty, S., & Julu, P. O. (2016). Respiratory and autonomic dysfunction in children with autism spectrum disorders. *Brain Development, 38*(2), 225–232. doi:10.1016/j.braindev.2015.07.003

Missig, G., Mokler, E. L., Robbins, J. O., Alexander, A. J., McDougle, C. J., & Carlezon, W. A., Jr. (2018). Perinatal immune activation produces persistent sleep alterations and epileptiform activity in male mice. *Neuropsychopharmacology, 43*(3), 482–491. doi:10.1038/npp.2017.243

Mistlberger, R. E., & Skene, D. J. (2004). Social influences on mammalian circadian rhythms: Animal and human studies. *Biological Reviews of the Cambridge Philosophical Society, 79*(3), 533–556.

Morin, C. M., Rodrigue, S., & Ivers, H. (2003). Role of stress, arousal, and coping skills in primary insomnia. *Psychosomatic Medicine, 65*(2), 259–267.

Mulder, E. J., Anderson, G. M., Kemperman, R. F., Oosterloo-Duinkerken, A., Minderaa, R. B., & Kema, I. P. (2010). Urinary excretion of 5-hydroxyindoleacetic acid, serotonin and 6-sulphatoxymelatonin in normoserotonemic and hyperserotonemic autistic individuals. *Neuropsychobiology, 61*(1), 27–32. doi:10.1159/000258640

Muris, P., Merckelbach, H., Mayer, B., van Brakel, A., Thissen, S., Moulaert, V., & Gadet, B. (1998). The Screen for Child Anxiety Related Emotional Disorders (SCARED) and traditional childhood anxiety measures. *Journal of Behavior Therapy and Experimental Psychiatry, 29*(4), 327–339.

Nadeau, J. M., Arnold, E. B., Keene, A. C., Collier, A. B., Lewin, A. B., Murphy, T. K., & Storch, E. A. (2015). Frequency and clinical correlates of sleep-related problems among anxious youth with autism spectrum disorders. *Child Psychiatry and Human Development, 46*(4), 558–566. doi:10.1007/s10578-014-0496-9

Neumeyer, A. M., Anixt, J., Chan, J., Perrin, J. M., Murray, D., Coury, D. L., . . . Parker, R. A. (2018). Identifying associations among co-occurring medical conditions in children with autism spectrum disorders. *Academic Pediatrics.* doi:10.1016/j.acap.2018.06.014

Nicassio, P. M., Mendlowitz, D. R., Fussell, J. J., & Petras, L. (1985). The phenomenology of the pre-sleep state: The development of the pre-sleep arousal scale. *Behavior Research and Therapy, 23*(3), 263–271.

Nir, I., Meir, D., Zilber, N., Knobler, H., Hadjez, J., & Lerner, Y. (1995). Brief report: Circadian melatonin, thyroid-stimulating hormone, prolactin, and cortisol levels in serum of young adults with autism. *Journal of Autism and Developmental Disorders, 25*(6), 641–654.

Nuske, H. J., Vivanti, G., & Dissanayake, C. (2014). Reactivity to fearful expressions of familiar and unfamiliar people in children with autism: an eye-tracking pupillometry study. *Journal of Neurodevelopmental Disorders, 6*(1), 14. doi:10.1186/1866-1955-6-14

Owens, J. A. (2008). Sleep disorders and attention-deficit/hyperactivity disorder. *Current Psychiatry Reports, 10*(5), 439–444.

Owens, J. A., Spirito, A., & McGuinn, M. (2000). The Children's Sleep Habits Questionnaire (CSHQ): Psychometric properties of a survey instrument for school-aged children. *Sleep, 23*(8), 1043–1051.

Paavonen, E. J., Nieminen-von Wendt, T., Vanhala, R., Aronen, E. T., & von Wendt, L. (2003). Effectiveness of melatonin in the treatment of sleep disturbances in children with Asperger disorder. *Journal of Child and Adolescent Psychopharmacology, 13*(1), 83–95. doi:10.1089/104454603321666225

Palagini, L., Moretto, U., Dell'Osso, L., & Carney, C. (2017). Sleep-related cognitive processes, arousal, and emotion dysregulation in insomnia disorder: the role of insomnia-specific rumination. *Sleep Medicine, 30*, 97–104. doi:10.1016/j.sleep.2016.11.004

Palkovitz, R. J., & Wiesenfeld, A. R. (1980). Differential autonomic responses of autistic and normal children. *Journal of Autism and Developmental Disorders, 10*(3), 347–360.
Panju, S., Brian, J., Dupuis, A., Anagnostou, E., & Kushki, A. (2015). Atypical sympathetic arousal in children with autism spectrum disorder and its association with anxiety symptomatology. *Molecular Autism, 6*, 64. doi:10.1186/s13229-015-0057-5
Park, S., Cho, S.-C., Cho, I. H., Kim, B.-N., Shin, M.-S., Chung, U.-S., . . . Yoo, H. J. (2012). Sleep problems and their correlates and comorbid psychopathology of children with autism spectrum disorders. *Research in Autism Spectrum Disorders, 6*, 1068–1072.
Parmelee, A. H., Jr., Wenner, W. H., Akiyama, Y., Schultz, M., & Stern, E. (1967). Sleep states in premature infants. *Developmental Medicine and Child Neurology, 9*(1), 70–77.
Perdue, K. L., Edwards, L. A., Tager-Flusberg, H., & Nelson, C. A. (2017). Differing developmental trajectories in heart rate responses to speech stimuli in infants at high and low risk for autism spectrum disorder. *Journal of Autism and Developmental Disorders, 47*(8), 2434–2442. doi:10.1007/s10803-017-3167-4
Pereira, A. M., Bruni, O., Ferri, R., Palmini, A., & Nunes, M. L. (2012). The impact of epilepsy on sleep architecture during childhood. *Epilepsia, 53*(9), 1519–1525. doi:10.1111/j.1528-1167.2012.03558.x
Peterman, J. S., Carper, M. M., Elkins, R. M., Comer, J. S., Pincus, D. B., & Kendall, P. C. (2016). The effects of cognitive-behavioral therapy for youth anxiety on sleep problems. *Journal of Anxiety Disorders, 37*, 78–88. doi:10.1016/j.janxdis.2015.11.006
Prather, A. A., Puterman, E., Epel, E. S., & Dhabhar, F. S. (2014). Poor sleep quality potentiates stress-induced cytokine reactivity in postmenopausal women with high visceral abdominal adiposity. *Brain, Behavior, and Immunity, 35*, 155–162. doi:10.1016/j.bbi.2013.09.010
Prosperi, M., Santocchi, E., Balboni, G., Narzisi, A., Bozza, M., Fulceri, F., . . . Muratori, F. (2017). Behavioral phenotype of ASD preschoolers with gastrointestinal symptoms or food selectivity. *Journal of Autism and Developmental Disorders, 47*(11), 3574–3588. doi:10.1007/s10803-017-3271-5
Ramtekkar, U. (2017). DSM-5 changes in attention deficit hyperactivity disorder and autism spectrum disorder: Implications for comorbid sleep issues. *Children (Basel), 4*(8). doi:10.3390/children4080062
Ramtekkar, U., & Ivanenko, A. (2015). Sleep in children with psychiatric disorders. *Seminars in Pediatric Neurology, 22*(2), 148–155. doi:10.1016/j.spen.2015.04.004
Randler, C. (2011). Age and gender differences in morningness-eveningness during adolescence. *Journal of Genetic Psychology, 172*(3), 302–308. doi:10.1080/00221325.2010.535225
Reppert, S. M., & Weaver, D. R. (2002). Coordination of circadian timing in mammals. *Nature, 418*(6901), 935–941. doi:10.1038/nature00965
Research Units on Pediatric Psychopharmacology Anxiety Study Group. (2002). The Pediatric Anxiety Rating Scale (PARS): Development and psychometric properties. *Journal of the American Academy of Child and Adolescent Psychiatry, 41*(9), 1061–1069.
Richdale, A. L., & Baglin, C. L. (2015). Self-report and caregiver-report of sleep and psychopathology in children with high-functioning autism spectrum disorder: A pilot study. *Developmental Neurorehabilitation, 18*(4), 272–279. doi:10.3109/17518423.2013.829534
Richdale, A. L., Baker, E., Short, M., & Gradisar, M. (2014). The role of insomnia, pre-sleep arousal and psychopathology symptoms in daytime impairment in adolescents with high-functioning autism spectrum disorder. *Sleep Medicine, 15*(9), 1082–1088. doi:10.1016/j.sleep.2014.05.005
Richdale, A. L., & Prior, M. R. (1995). The sleep/wake rhythm in children with autism. *European Child and Adolescent Psychiatry, 4*(3), 175–186.
Richdale, A. L., & Schreck, K. A. (2009). Sleep problems in autism spectrum disorders: Prevalence, nature, & possible biopsychosocial aetiologies. *Sleep Medicine Review, 13*(6), 403–411. doi:10.1016/j.smrv.2009.02.003
Righi, G., Benevides, J., Mazefsky, C., Siegel, M., Sheinkopf, S. J., Morrow, E. M., . . . Developmental Disabilities Inpatient Research, C. (2018). Predictors of inpatient psychiatric hospitalization for children and adolescents with autism spectrum disorder. *Journal of Autism and Developmental Disorders, 48*(11), 3647–3657. doi:10.1007/s10803-017-3154-9
Roenneberg, T., Keller, L. K., Fischer, D., Matera, J. L., Vetter, C., & Winnebeck, E. C. (2015). Human activity and rest in situ. *Methods in Enzymology, 552*, 257–283. doi:10.1016/bs.mie.2014.11.028
Rusak, B., & Zucker, I. (1979). Neural regulation of circadian rhythms. *Physiological Reviews, 59*(3), 449–526. doi:10.1152/physrev.1979.59.3.449
Rzepecka, H., McKenzie, K., McClure, I., & Murphy, S. (2011). Sleep, anxiety and challenging behaviour in children with intellectual disability and/or autism spectrum disorder. *Research in Developmental Disabilities, 32*(6), 2758–2766. doi:10.1016/j.ridd.2011.05.034
Sasaki, M., Yoshitane, H., Du, N. H., Okano, T., & Fukada, Y. (2009). Preferential inhibition of BMAL2-CLOCK activity by PER2 reemphasizes its negative role and a positive role of BMAL2 in the circadian transcription. *Journal of Biology and Chemistry, 284*(37), 25,149–25,159. doi:10.1074/jbc.M109.040758
Schaaf, R. C., & Smith Roley, S. (2006). *SI: Applying clinical reasoning to practice with diverse population*. San Antonio, TX: Harcourt Assessment.
Schreck, K. A., Mulick, J. A., & Smith, A. F. (2004). Sleep problems as possible predictors of intensified symptoms of autism. *Research in Developmental Disabilities, 25*(1), 57–66.
Schwichtenberg, A. J., & Malow, B. A. (2015). Melatonin treatment in children with developmental disabilities. *Sleep Medicine Clinics, 10*(2), 181–187. doi:10.1016/j.jsmc.2015.02.008
Seeman, T. E., Dubin, L. F., & Seeman, M. (2003). Religiosity/spirituality and health. A critical review of the evidence for biological pathways. *American Psychology, 58*(1), 53–63.
Sepeta, L., Tsuchiya, N., Davies, M. S., Sigman, M., Bookheimer, S. Y., & Dapretto, M. (2012). Abnormal social reward processing in autism as indexed by pupillary responses to happy faces. *Journal of Neurodevelopmental Disorders, 4*(1), 17. doi:10.1186/1866-1955-4-17
Sharma, R., Sahota, P., & Thakkar, M. M. (2018). Melatonin promotes sleep in mice by inhibiting orexin neurons in the perifornical lateral hypothalamus. *Journal of Pineal Research, 65*(2), e12498. doi:10.1111/jpi.12498
Silva, L. M., Schalock, M., Ayres, R., Bunse, C., & Budden, S. (2009). Qigong massage treatment for sensory and self-regulation problems in young children with autism: A randomized controlled trial. *American Journal of Occupational Therapy, 63*(4), 423–432.

Silva, L. M., Schalock, M., & Gabrielsen, K. (2011). Early intervention for autism with a parent-delivered Qigong massage program: A randomized controlled trial. *American Journal of Occupational Therapy, 65*(5), 550–559.

Simonoff, E., Jones, C. R., Baird, G., Pickles, A., Happe, F., & Charman, T. (2013). The persistence and stability of psychiatric problems in adolescents with autism spectrum disorders. *Journal of Child Psychology and Psychiatry, 54*(2), 186–194. doi:10.1111/j.1469-7610.2012.02606.x

Simonoff, E., Pickles, A., Charman, T., Chandler, S., Loucas, T., & Baird, G. (2008). Psychiatric disorders in children with autism spectrum disorders: Prevalence, comorbidity, and associated factors in a population-derived sample. *Journal of American Academy of Child and Adolescent Psychology, 47*, 921–929. doi:10.1097/CHI.0b013e318179964f

Singh, K., & Zimmerman, A. W. (2015). Sleep in autism spectrum disorder and attention deficit hyperactivity disorder. *Seminars in Pediatric Neurology, 22*(2), 113–125. doi:10.1016/j.spen.2015.03.006

Sivertsen, B., Posserud, M. B., Gillberg, C., Lundervold, A. J., & Hysing, M. (2012). Sleep problems in children with autism spectrum problems: A longitudinal population-based study. *Autism, 16*(2), 139–150. doi:10.1177/1362361311404255

Song, G. H., Leng, P. H., Gwee, K. A., Moochhala, S. M., & Ho, K. Y. (2005). Melatonin improves abdominal pain in irritable bowel syndrome patients who have sleep disturbances: A randomised, double blind, placebo controlled study. *Gut, 54*(10), 1402–1407. doi:10.1136/gut.2004.062034

Sotak, M., Mrnka, L., & Pacha, J. (2006). Heterogeneous expression of melatonin receptor MT1 mRNA in the rat intestine under control and fasting conditions. *Journal of Pineal Research, 41*(2), 183–188. doi:10.1111/j.1600-079X.2006.00355.x

Souders, M. C., Mason, T. B., Valladares, O., Bucan, M., Levy, S. E., Mandell, D. S., ... Pinto-Martin, J. (2009). Sleep behaviors and sleep quality in children with autism spectrum disorders. *Sleep, 32*, 1566–1578.

Souders, M. C., Zavodny, S., Eriksen, W., Sinko, R., Connell, J., Kerns, C., ... Pinto-Martin, J. (2017). Sleep in children with autism spectrum disorder. *Current Psychiatry Reports, 19*(34). doi:10.1007/s11920-017-0782-x

Spielman, A. J., Caruso, L. S., & Glovinsky, P. B. (1987). A behavioral perspective on insomnia treatment. *Psychiatric Clinics of North America, 10*(4), 541–553.

Stevens, S., & Gruzelier, J. (1984). Electrodermal activity to auditory stimuli in autistic, retarded, and normal children. *Journal of Autism and Developmental Disorders, 14*(3), 245–260.

Swanson, G. R., Gorenz, A., Shaikh, M., Desai, V., Forsyth, C., Fogg, L., ... Keshavarzian, A. (2015). Decreased melatonin secretion is associated with increased intestinal permeability and marker of endotoxemia in alcoholics. *American Journal of Physiology-Gastrointestinal and Liver Physiology, 308*(12), G1004-1011. doi:10.1152/ajpgi.00002.2015

Tavassoli, T., Hoekstra, R. A., & Baron-Cohen, S. (2014). The Sensory Perception Quotient (SPQ): Development and validation of a new sensory questionnaire for adults with and without autism. *Molecular Autism, 5*, 29. doi:10.1186/2040-2392-5-29

Taylor, M. A., Schreck, K. A., & Mulick, J. A. (2012). Sleep disruption as a correlate to cognitive and adaptive behavior problems in autism spectrum disorders. *Research in Developmental Disabilities, 33*(5), 1408–1417. doi:10.1016/j.ridd.2012.03.013

Tessier, M. P., Pennestri, M. H., & Godbout, R. (2018). Heart rate variability of typically developing and autistic children and adults before, during and after sleep. *International Journal of Psychophysiology, 134*, 15–21. doi:10.1016/j.ijpsycho.2018.10.004

Thirumalai, S. S., Shubin, R. A., & Robinson, R. (2002). Rapid eye movement sleep behavior disorder in children with autism. *Journal of Child Neurology, 17*(3), 173–178. doi:10.1177/088307380201700304

Thomas, S., Hovinga, M. E., Rai, D., & Lee, B. K. (2017). Brief report: Prevalence of co-occurring epilepsy and autism spectrum disorder: The U.S. National Survey of Children's Health 2011–2012. *Journal of Autism and Developmental Disorders, 47*(1), 224–229. doi:10.1007/s10803-016-2938-7

Thomas, S., Lycett, K., Papadopoulos, N., Sciberras, E., & Rinehart, N. (2018). Exploring behavioral sleep problems in children with ADHD and comorbid autism spectrum disorder. *Journal of Attention Disorders, 22*(10), 947–958. doi:10.1177/1087054715613439

Tobaldini, E., Costantino, G., Solbiati, M., Cogliati, C., Kara, T., Nobili, L., & Montano, N. (2017). Sleep, sleep deprivation, autonomic nervous system and cardiovascular diseases. *Neuroscience and Biobehavioral Reviews, 74*(Pt B), 321–329. doi:10.1016/j.neubiorev.2016.07.004

Tordjman, S., Anderson, G. M., Pichard, N., Charbuy, H., & Touitou, Y. (2005). Nocturnal excretion of 6-sulphatoxymelatonin in children and adolescents with autistic disorder. *Biological Psychiatry, 57*(2), 134–138. doi:10.1016/j.biopsych.2004.11.003

Tordjman, S., Davlantis, K. S., Georgieff, N., Geoffray, M. M., Speranza, M., Anderson, G. M., ... Dawson, G. (2015). Autism as a disorder of biological and behavioral rhythms: Toward new therapeutic perspectives. *Frontiers in Pediatrics, 3*, 1. doi:10.3389/fped.2015.00001

Travnickova-Bendova, Z., Cermakian, N., Reppert, S. M., & Sassone-Corsi, P. (2002). Bimodal regulation of mPeriod promoters by CREB-dependent signaling and CLOCK/BMAL1 activity. *Proceedings of the National Academy of Sciences in the USA, 99*(11), 7728–7733. doi:10.1073/pnas.102075599

Tudor, M. E., Walsh, C. E., Mulder, E. C., & Lerner, M. D. (2015). Pain as a predictor of sleep problems in youth with autism spectrum disorders. *Autism, 19*(3), 292–300. doi:10.1177/1362361313518994

Tzischinsky, O., Meiri, G., Manelis, L., Bar-Sinai, A., Flusser, H., Michaelovski, A., ... Dinstein, I. (2018). Sleep disturbances are associated with specific sensory sensitivities in children with autism. *Molecular Autism, 9*, 22. doi:10.1186/s13229-018-0206-8

Uljarevic, M., Richdale, A. L., Evans, D. W., Cai, R. Y., & Leekam, S. R. (2017). Interrelationship between insistence on sameness, effortful control and anxiety in adolescents and young adults with autism spectrum disorder (ASD). *Molecular Autism, 8*, 36. doi:10.1186/s13229-017-0158-4

Van der Heijden, K. B., Smits, M. G., Van Someren, E. J., & Gunning, W. B. (2005). Idiopathic chronic sleep onset insomnia in attention-deficit/hyperactivity disorder: A circadian rhythm sleep disorder. *Chronobiology International, 22*(3), 559–570. doi:10.1081/CBI-200062410

van der Helm, E., Gujar, N., & Walker, M. P. (2010). Sleep deprivation impairs the accurate recognition of human emotions. *Sleep, 33*(3), 335–342.

van Engeland, H. (1984). The electrodermal orienting response to auditive stimuli in autistic children, normal children, mentally retarded children, and child psychiatric patients. *Journal of Autism and Developmental Disorders, 14*(3), 261–279.

Veatch, O. J., Maxwell-Horn, A. C., & Malow, B. A. (2015). Sleep in autism spectrum disorders. *Current Sleep Medicine Reports, 1*(2), 131–140. doi:10.1007/s40675-015-0012-1

Veatch, O. J., Pendergast, J. S., Allen, M. J., Leu, R. M., Johnson, C. H., Elsea, S. H., & Malow, B. A. (2015). Genetic variation in melatonin pathway enzymes in children with autism spectrum disorder and comorbid sleep onset delay. *Journal of Autism and Developmental Disorders, 45*(1), 100–110. doi:10.1007/s10803-014-2197-4

Wagner, J. B., Luyster, R. J., Tager-Flusberg, H., & Nelson, C. A. (2016). Greater pupil size in response to emotional faces as an early marker of social-communicative difficulties in infants at high risk for autism. *Infancy, 21*(5), 560–581. doi:10.1111/infa.12128

Wasdell, M. B., Jan, J. E., Bomben, M. M., Freeman, R. D., Rietveld, W. J., Tai, J., . . . Weiss, M. D. (2008). A randomized, placebo-controlled trial of controlled release melatonin treatment of delayed sleep phase syndrome and impaired sleep maintenance in children with neurodevelopmental disabilities. *Journal of Pineal Research, 44*(1), 57–64. doi:10.1111/j.1600-079X.2007.00528.x

Wimpory, D., Nicholas, B., & Nash, S. (2002). Social timing, clock genes and autism: A new hypothesis. *Journal of Intellectual Disability Research, 46*(Pt 4), 352–358.

Wirojanan, J., Jacquemont, S., Diaz, R., Bacalman, S., Anders, T. F., Hagerman, R. J., & Goodlin-Jones, B. L. (2009). The efficacy of melatonin for sleep problems in children with autism, fragile X syndrome, or autism and fragile X syndrome. *Journal of Clinical Sleep Medicine, 5*(2), 145–150.

Wong, R. K., Yang, C., Song, G. H., Wong, J., & Ho, K. Y. (2015). Melatonin regulation as a possible mechanism for probiotic (VSL#3) in irritable bowel syndrome: A randomized double-blinded placebo study. *Digestive Diseases and Sciences, 60*(1), 186–194. doi:10.1007/s10620-014-3299-8

Wright, B., Sims, D., Smart, S., Alwazeer, A., Alderson-Day, B., Allgar, V., . . . Miles, J. (2011). Melatonin versus placebo in children with autism spectrum conditions and severe sleep problems not amenable to behaviour management strategies: A randomised controlled crossover trial. *Journal of Autism and Developmental Disorders, 41*(2), 175–184. doi:10.1007/s10803-010-1036-5

Yang, X. L., Liang, S., Zou, M. Y., Sun, C. H., Han, P. P., Jiang, X. T., . . . Wu, L. J. (2018). Are gastrointestinal and sleep problems associated with behavioral symptoms of autism spectrum disorder? *Psychiatry Research, 259*, 229–235. doi:10.1016/j.psychres.2017.10.040

Yang, Z., Matsumoto, A., Nakayama, K., Jimbo, E. F., Kojima, K., Nagata, K., . . . Yamagata, T. (2016). Circadian-relevant genes are highly polymorphic in autism spectrum disorder patients. *Brain Development, 38*(1), 91–99. doi:10.1016/j.braindev.2015.04.006

Yoo, S. S., Gujar, N., Hu, P., Jolesz, F. A., & Walker, M. P. (2007). The human emotional brain without sleep—A prefrontal amygdala disconnect. *Current Biology, 17*(20), R877–878. doi:10.1016/j.cub.2007.08.007

Youssef, J., Singh, K., Huntington, N., Becker, R., & Kothare, S. V. (2013). Relationship of serum ferritin levels to sleep fragmentation and periodic limb movements of sleep on polysomnography in autism spectrum disorders. *Pediatric Neurology, 49*(4), 274–278. doi:10.1016/j.pediatrneurol.2013.06.012

Zaboski, B. A., & Storch, E. A. (2018). Comorbid autism spectrum disorder and anxiety disorders: A brief review. *Future Neurology, 13*(1), 31–37. doi:10.2217/fnl-2017–0030

Zanzmera, P., Shukla, G., Gupta, A., Singh, H., Goyal, V., Srivastava, A., & Behari, M. (2012). Markedly disturbed sleep in medically refractory compared to controlled epilepsy—A clinical and polysomnography study. *Seizure, 21*(7), 487–490. doi:10.1016/j.seizure.2012.04.005

Zerbini, G., Kantermann, T., & Merrow, M. (2018). Strategies to decrease social jetlag: Reducing evening blue light advances sleep and melatonin. *European Journal of Neuroscience.* doi:10.1111/ejn.14293

Zhao, Z., Zhao, X., & Veasey, S. C. (2017). Neural consequences of chronic short sleep: Reversible or lasting? *Frontiers in Neurology, 8*, 235. doi:10.3389/fneur.2017.00235

Zoccola, P. M., Dickerson, S. S., & Lam, S. (2009). Rumination predicts longer sleep onset latency after an acute psychosocial stressor. *Psychosomatic Medicine, 71*(7), 771–775. doi:10.1097/PSY.0b013e3181ae58e8

CHAPTER

15 Aggression in Autism Spectrum Disorder

Micah O. Mazurek

Abstract

Aggression is a clinically significant problem for many children, adolescents, and adults with autism spectrum disorder (ASD). The high prevalence and negative outcomes associated with aggression in individuals with ASD make it an especially important treatment target. Emerging research suggests that aggression is associated with both core symptoms and co-occurring conditions among individuals with ASD; however, research on etiology and underlying mechanisms of symptoms remains limited. Although there are few standardized tools developed specifically for assessment of aggression in people with ASD, practitioners are encouraged to use a multi-informant and multimodal assessment approach, with particular focus on identifying the environmental variables that contribute to the occurrence and maintenance of aggression. Treatment strategies with the most empirical evidence include behavioral strategies and medication. Future areas for research include larger scale studies of etiology, underlying mechanisms, and treatment effectiveness across the lifespan.

Keywords: aggression, aggressive behavior, autism spectrum disorder, assessment, treatment

Overview

Aggression can have serious negative consequences for individuals with autism spectrum disorder (ASD) and their families. Although not a diagnostic feature of ASD, aggression commonly co-occurs with ASD across the lifespan. These behaviors can interfere with functioning across environments, can contribute to poor quality of life, and can be dangerous for individuals and their caregivers. For individuals with ASD, aggression can result in increased use of psychotropic medication and polypharmacy (Logan et al., 2015; Tsakanikos, Costello, Holt, Sturmey, & Bouras, 2007), greater likelihood of psychiatric hospitalization (Mandell, 2008), and placement in more restrictive programs and settings (Jacobson & Ackerman, 1993). For families, aggressive and disruptive behaviors are the strongest predictors of parental stress, above and beyond the effects of other child and family characteristics (Estes et al., 2009; Lecavalier, Leone, & Wiltz, 2006; Tomanik, Harris, & Hawkins, 2004). Aggression can also lead to significant stress and burnout among other caregivers, including teachers and therapeutic staff (Freeman, 1994; Hastings & Brown, 2002; Jenkins, Rose, & Lovell, 1997), thereby undermining the effectiveness of the programs and services that are designed to support individuals with ASD. As such, these behaviors are often primary targets of treatment for individuals with ASD.

This chapter will provide a review of current research on the prevalence and development of aggression in individuals with ASD and will review evidence-based methods for assessment and treatment. Before examining these issues, however, it is important to briefly consider terminology and operational definitions of aggression. The term "aggression" is widely used by both scientists and the lay public to refer to specific types of problematic behaviors; however, behavioral scientists have struggled to come to consensus on a consistent definition of the construct. Definitions have ranged from broad to narrow and have varied widely in their emphasis on form, function, and/or outcome of the behavior. For example, an early definition proposed by Dollard, Miller, Doob, Mowrer, and Sears (1939) defined it as "an act whose goal-response is injury to an organism" (p. 11), whereas later well-accepted definitions have added greater specificity (Anderson & Bushman, 2002; Baron & Richardson, 1994; Berkowitz, 1993). For example, Baron and Richardson (1994) described aggression as "any form of behavior directed toward the goal of harming or injuring another living being who is motivated to avoid such treatment" (p. 7), emphasizing both the intent to harm and the perspective of the victim. Some definitions of aggression focus primarily on physical aggression, whereas others have included verbal aggression and other types of disruptive and destructive behavior (e.g., property destruction, defiance). Although a detailed review of historical perspectives on aggression is beyond the scope of the current chapter, these differences in terminology and operational definition are relevant insomuch as they affect the way in which aggression is conceptualized and assessed in ASD research. For the purposes of this chapter, the term "aggression" will be used broadly to describe a range of physically aggressive behaviors, with more specific behavioral descriptions when necessary.

Prevalence and Course

Prevalence of Aggression

Aggression is a clinically significant problem for many children and adults with ASD and has been identified as a treatment priority since the early studies of autism (Rutter, Greenfeld, & Lockyer, 1967). Surprisingly, however, there have been few large-scale studies on the prevalence of aggression in this population. As will be described, prevalence rates have varied widely across existing studies, due in large part to differences in methodology and assessment.

The prevalence of aggression has ranged from 10% to 58% across studies of children and adults with ASD. These studies differ markedly in terms of sample characteristics and how aggression was assessed. Lecavalier (2006) found that 10% to 14% of children and adolescents receiving educational services for autism attacked others, as reported by parents and teachers. In a similar educational sample, Farmer and Aman (2011) found that 23% were reported by parents to shove or push others to a moderate or severe degree. Other aggressive behaviors were also commonly reported, including hitting forcefully (17%), pinching (17%), scratching (13%), biting (10%), lashing out (17%), and charging at others (12%). In a study of both children and adults with ASD, 36% were rated as being "hurtful to others" on the Problem Behavior subscale of the Scales of Independent Behavior—Revised (Woodman, Smith, Greenberg, & Mailick, 2015). Twenty-five percent of a sample of 400 children and adolescents with ASD were rated within the clinically significant range on the Aggressive Behavior Scale T-score of the Child Behavior Checklist (CBCL; Hill et al., 2014), and in a sample of 259 adults with ASD, 14% of men and 5% of women were rated within the clinical range on the Aggressive Behavior Scale of the Adult Behavior Checklist (the adult version of the CBCL; Woodman, Mailick, & Greenberg, 2016). However, it should be noted that the CBCL includes items assessing both physical and verbal aggression, making it difficult to interpret among individuals with minimal language.

In studies using more general definitions, significant aggression has been observed in a majority of children and adolescents with ASD. For example, over half (56%) of 1,380 children and adolescents with ASD participating in the Simons Simplex Collection demonstrated current physical aggression toward caregivers, and almost one third (32%) demonstrated aggression toward noncaregivers (Kanne & Mazurek, 2011). Similar prevalence of physical aggression (53%) was found among 1,584 children and adolescents enrolled in the Autism Treatment Network study (Mazurek, Kanne, & Wodka, 2013). Aggression was also identified as a primary treatment target for over one half (57%) of children with ASD participating in clinical trials conducted by the Research Units on Pediatric Psychopharmacology (RUPP) Autism Network (Carroll et al., 2014). Similar aggression prevalence (58%) has been found among children with ASD and co-occurring intellectual disability (Bronsard, Botbol, & Tordjman, 2010).

Individuals with ASD are generally at greater risk for aggression than those without ASD. For example, children with ASD have been found to show greater aggression than typically developing (TD) children across different methods and measures (Ambler, Eidels, & Gregory, 2015; Chen et al., 2017; Hass, Brown, Brady, & Johnson, 2012; Mayes et al., 2012; Volker et al., 2010). However, the findings have been mixed when comparing children with ASD to those with other clinical diagnoses. For example, Farmer and colleagues (2015) found that children with ASD demonstrated lower levels of aggression than a clinically referred comparison group (comprising children with other developmental and/or behavioral disorders). However, differences between specific diagnostic groups were not examined. In other research, children with ASD have shown higher levels of aggression than those with attention deficit hyperactivity disorder (ADHD) inattentive type, anxiety disorders, and acquired brain injury, but lower levels of aggression than those with ADHD combined type and oppositional defiant disorder (Mayes et al., 2012).

Developmental Course of Aggression

Few studies have examined the developmental course of aggression in individuals with ASD. In the general population, aggressive behavior typically peaks in early childhood and declines with age (Alink et al., 2006). Although evidence in ASD is limited, there is generally evidence of improvement in aggression over time among individuals with ASD. For example, a cross-sectional study of 6- to 17-year-old children and adolescents with ASD found that aggression, as measured by a subset of items from the Aberrant Behavior Checklist, was inversely associated with age (Bitsika et al., 2017). Similarly, cross-sectional data from both the Simons Simplex Collection and the Autism Treatment Network studies demonstrated a higher prevalence of aggression among younger children with ASD (Kanne & Mazurek, 2011; Mazurek et al., 2013). Although not assessing aggression specifically, some studies have also found a general pattern of improvement over time from adolescence through adulthood on more general measures of disruptive behavior (Gray et al., 2012; Taylor & Seltzer, 2010). Woodman and colleagues (2015) examined longitudinal data from 313 individuals with ASD who were between 10 and 49 years of age at enrollment. The prevalence of aggression decreased significantly over the course of 8.5 years, from 36% at baseline to 23% at the final time point. However, it should be noted that aggression remains a clinically significant problem across age groups of individuals with ASD (Hill et al., 2014) and was a continuing problem for nearly half of the adolescents (ages 14 to 17 years) enrolled in the Autism Treatment Network study (Mazurek et al., 2013). Overall, these findings suggest that the rates of aggression among the ASD population do not appear to decline to levels comparable to the general population, even at older ages.

In addition to these general age-related findings, there is also some evidence of distinct developmental trajectories of aggression. Previous studies among the general population have employed sophisticated analytic strategies to characterize the nature and course of aggression across development, from early childhood through adulthood (Broidy et al., 2003; Lahey, Waldman, & McBurnett, 1999). This work has identified a number of individual, family, and community risk and protective factors that characterize different trajectories and outcomes of aggression among children in the general population (Broidy et al., 2003; Lahey et al., 1999; Nagin & Tremblay, 2001; National Institute of Child Health and Human Development [NICHD] Early Child Care Research Network & Arsenio, 2004; Tremblay et al., 2004). Across samples, evidence suggests that aggression declines over time for most children. However, a small percentage of the population demonstrates high levels of aggression that persists across childhood. Consistent predictors of aggression in the general population include low socioeconomic status, lower parental education, less engaged parenting, poorer cognitive and language skills, and male sex (Broidy et al., 2003; Lahey et al., 1999; NICHD Early Child Care Research Network & Arsenio, 2004).

Although similar longitudinal studies have not been conducted among large samples of individuals with ASD, there is some evidence that the course of aggression may differ as a function of individual characteristics. For example, in a longitudinal study of children with ASD followed from 1991 through 2009, Gray and colleagues (2012) found that aggression generally declined over time. However, further examination revealed that aggression actually increased for a subset of individuals, and that those with severe intellectual disability demonstrated a worsening of some behavioral symptoms. Woodman and colleagues (2016) also conducted a longitudinal study of 259 adults with ASD followed over time from 2007 to 2012 and found that 14% of men and 5% of women in the study demonstrated clinically significant levels of aggression across time points. The results also revealed four different trajectories of aggression over time: low and stable symptoms (37%), high initial symptoms with improvement (38%), higher initial symptoms with improvement (21%), and high and stable symptoms (4%).

Correlates and Predictors of Aggression

These emerging findings highlight the importance of understanding potential factors that may relate to the development and maintenance of aggression over time in individuals with ASD. Interestingly, many variables that are predictive of aggression in the general population do not appear to be as strongly associated in individuals with ASD. For example, aggression is much more common among boys than among girls in the general population (Dawson, Meltzoff, Osterling, Rinaldi, & Brown, 1998; NICHD Early Child Care Research Network & Arsenio, 2004), yet prior studies have consistently found that aggression is equally common among boys and girls with ASD (Hill et al., 2014; Kanne & Mazurek, 2011; Mazurek et al., 2013). Similarly, although poor language abilities and cognitive functioning are associated with increased risk for aggression in the general population (Frith, 2001; Lahey et al., 1999; I. M. Smith & Bryson, 1994), these associations have been weaker or absent in prior ASD research (Farmer et al., 2015; Hill et al., 2014; Kanne & Mazurek, 2011; Mazurek et al., 2013; Shic, Bradshaw, Klin, Scassellati, & Chawarska, 2011).

A growing body of research is showing that ASD-specific phenotypic features and common co-occurring medical and behavioral symptoms, rather than demographic characteristics, may play an important role in the occurrence of aggression. Restricted and repetitive behaviors (RRBs) appear to have a particularly strong link with aggression in individuals with ASD. For example, Reese, Richman, Zarcone, and Zarcone (2003) examined the results of functional assessment interviews with caregivers of 100 children with autism and found that disruptive behaviors often served the function of access to perseverative or repetitive behaviors or activities, and that disruptive behaviors were also often demonstrated to escape from sensory stimuli. In a follow-up study, the research team conducted functional behavioral assessment interviews with caregivers of 23 children with ASD and 23 children matched for chronological and developmental age and sex (Reese, Richman, Belmont, & Morse, 2005). The results indicated that for children without ASD and for girls with ASD, the most common functions for disruptive behavior were attention, access to items, or escape from demands. In contrast, for boys with ASD, the most common functions were to escape demands that interfered with repetitive behavior, to gain access to an item used in repetitive behavior, or to avoid sensory stimuli. These findings are consistent with those of a case study of a young adult with ASD who exhibited aggression primarily when stereotyped behaviors were interrupted (Murphy, MacDonald, Hall, & Oliver, 2000). Larger scale studies have also found links between RRBs and aggression in children and adults with ASD (Kanne & Mazurek, 2011; Matson & Rivet, 2008a; Mazurek, Engelhardt, Hilgard, & Sohl, 2016), with particularly strong relationships between aggression, ritualistic behavior, and resistance to change (Kanne & Mazurek, 2011).

Self-injurious behaviors (SIBs) also frequently co-occur with both repetitive behaviors and aggression (Bodfish, Symons, Parker, & Lewis, 2000; Gardner, Campbell, Keisling, & Murphy, 2018; Hadwin, Baron-Cohen, Howlin, & Hill, 1996). Although SIBs and aggression are distinct forms of behavior, they are highly associated (Rojahn, Matson, Lott, Esbensen, & Smalls, 2001) and there is some evidence that SIBs predict the occurrence of later aggression in individuals with intellectual disabilities (Nøttestad & Linaker, 2002). In two large studies of children and adolescents with ASD, SIB was a significant cross-sectional predictor of aggression in both bivariate and multivariate models (Kanne & Mazurek, 2011; Mazurek et al., 2013). Some have hypothesized that these behaviors may share common underlying mechanisms for some individuals, particularly to the extent that they are "automatically" reinforced (Mahan & Matson, 2011; Matson, Gonzalez, & Rivet, 2008; Matson & Rivet, 2008b; Matson, Mahan, Hess, Fodstad, & Neal, 2010).

There is also emerging evidence that anxiety may play a role in aggression for some individuals with ASD. For example, Ambler and colleagues (2015) found that self-reported social anxiety was significantly correlated with teacher-reported physical aggression among teenagers with ASD. Interestingly, similar associations were not found for self-reported physiological anxiety or worry. In a small sample of 20 children with ASD, Pugliese, White, White, and Ollendick (2013) found a curvilinear relationship between fears of social humiliation/rejection and aggressive behavior. The authors suggested that low social fear or inhibition may increase likelihood of aggression, and children with excessive social fears may be more likely to act out aggressively.

Studies have also shown a strong link between sleep disturbance and aggression in individuals with ASD (Goldman et al., 2011; Hill et al., 2014; May, Cornish, Conduit, Rajaratnam, & Rinehart, 2015; Mazurek et al., 2013; Mazurek & Sohl, 2016). In a recent study examining the associations between specific types of sleep and behavioral problems in children with ASD, night awakenings were found to have the strongest relationship with aggression (Mazurek & Sohl, 2016). Although few studies have examined the directionality of these associations, a recent study using nightly sleep observations found that poor sleep significantly predicted challenging daytime behavior in individuals with ASD (Cohen et al., 2018). These findings suggest that sleep disturbance may underlie and/or exacerbate aggressive behavior for some individuals with ASD. It is also possible that there are shared biological or environmental mechanisms that account for these interrelated symptoms, some of which are discussed in the section to follow.

There is also evidence that other common co-occurring medical problems may be associated with aggression in individuals with ASD. For example, clinicians have hypothesized that aggression may be an indicator of gastrointestinal (GI) discomfort in children with ASD (Buie et al., 2010), an important consideration given that individuals with ASD are at high risk for GI problems, such as abdominal pain and constipation (McElhanon, McCracken, Karpen, & Sharp, 2014). However, findings have been somewhat mixed in the few empirical studies that have examined this directly. For example, two separate samples revealed no significant differences in aggression when comparing individuals with ASD with and without GI problems (Maenner et al., 2012; Mazefsky, Schreiber, Olino, & Minshew, 2014). In contrast, in a large sample of 1,584 children and adolescents with ASD, those who demonstrated aggression were more likely to have GI problems (Mazurek, Kanne, & Wodka, 2013) and GI problems were associated with higher scores across subscales of the Aberrant Behavior Checklist in a sample of 499 children with ASD (Chaidez, Hansen, & Hertz-Picciotto, 2014).

Individuals with ASD are also at increased risk for seizures, as compared to the general population (Frye, 2016). Given aggression may occur in some patients with epilepsy (Brodie et al., 2016; Sumer, Atik, Unal, Emre, & Atasoy, 2007), there is reason to predict that the two conditions also co-occur in individuals with ASD. Although there have been few studies to date, existing evidence does support this hypothesis. For example, Mulligan and Trauner (2014) found a higher incidence of aggression in individuals with ASD with epileptiform abnormalities as compared to those without. Similarly, among adults with intellectual disability (ID), those with *combined* ASD and epilepsy had higher rates of aggression and disruptive behavior than those without ASD or epilepsy, those with ASD only, or those with epilepsy only (K. R. Smith & Matson, 2010).

Etiology, Diagnosis, and Assessment

Etiology and Underlying Mechanisms of Aggression

There have been a number of explanatory theories of aggression as it occurs in the general population. Among the most influential have been the frustration–aggression theory (Dollard et al., 1939), social learning theory (Bandura, 1978; Bandura, Ross, & Ross, 1961), and the cognitive–neoassociationist model (Berkowitz, 1989, 1990). The more recent general aggression model (GAM) proposed by Anderson and Bushman (2002) provides a unified theory of aggression that integrates a number of domain-specific theories, including social learning theory (Bandura, 1978; Bandura et al., 1961), script theory (Huesmann, 1998), and cognitive–neoassociationistic models (Berkowitz, 1989, 1990). The GAM predicts that exposure to environmental stimuli jointly interacts with person-level variables to produce heightened levels of aggressive affect, aggressive cognitions, and aggressive arousal (i.e., different internal states), each of which serves as a mechanism by which situational stimuli can increase aggression.

The GAM has received empirical support from numerous experimental laboratory studies (Allen, Anderson, & Bushman, 2018; Anderson & Bushman, 2002; DeWall & Anderson, 2011); however, the model has not been specifically tested among individuals with ASD or other clinical populations at risk for aggression. It is possible that the GAM is not well suited to predict behavioral response among individuals with ASD, particularly because it draws heavily from social–cognitive information processing models. Because individuals with ASD have specific difficulties with social motivation (Chevallier, Kohls, Troiani, Brodkin, & Schultz, 2012), perspective taking (Frith, 2001), and social attention (Dawson et al., 1998; Shic et al., 2011), observational learning may play a less prominent role in the development of aggression and other behaviors. Consistent with this idea, individuals with ASD have difficulty with social imitation (I. M. Smith & Bryson, 1994) and respond less to social provocation than individuals without ASD (Schneider et al., 2015). As such, more specific empirical tests of traditional explanatory models of aggression are needed to determine their applicability within the context of ASD.

Other findings from the larger field of behavioral science have provided evidence for different subtypes of aggression in the general population. The majority of this evidence points to two aggression subtypes with distinct underlying cognitive and physiological mechanisms: proactive and reactive aggression (Buss, 1966; Dodge & Coie, 1987; Dodge, Lochman, Harnish, Bates, & Pettit, 1997; Moyer, 1976; Price & Dodge, 1989). Proactive aggression is characterized by deliberate, unprovoked, goal-directed aggressive behavior and is consistent with the predictions of social learning theory, which proposes that aggressive behavior can be learned through observation and imitation of others, particularly when aggression is rewarded (Bandura, 1978; Bandura et al., 1961). By contrast, reactive aggression is characterized by an impulsive, retaliatory aggressive response to perceived provocation or threat, and is consistent with the predictions of the frustration–aggression theory (Berkowitz, 1962; Dollard et al., 1939).

At the physiological level, proactive aggression is characterized by physiological underarousal both at rest and during stress or provocation (Ortiz & Raine, 2004; Van Goozen, Fairchild, Snoek, & Harold, 2007), whereas reactive aggression is characterized by hyperarousal at rest and heightened physiological reactivity to stress and provocation (Hubbard et al., 2002; Lopez-Duran, Olson, Hajal, Felt, & Vazquez, 2009). At the cognitive processing level, proactive aggression has been associated with later-stage cognitive processing differences, which result in expectations of external rewards for aggression (Crick & Dodge, 1996). In contrast, reactive aggression has been associated with early-stage social information processing biases, specifically hostile causal attributions (Crick & Dodge, 1994). Causal attributions are cognitive processes that allow individuals to reason about why particular events occur, including the intentions of others within particular situations. Individuals with reactive aggression consistently interpret the intentions of others in ambiguous social situations as being hostile or threatening (i.e., hostile attribution biases). Together, these previous findings from the general population suggest that individuals with proactive aggression may engage in aggression to increase physiological arousal (stimulation seeking), and that their aggression is maintained by high expectations for reward and low reactivity. In contrast, individuals with reactive aggression are hypervigilant to threat, both cognitively and physiologically, and may exhibit impulsive aggression as a result of these combined processes.

Recent findings suggest that the proactive/reactive aggression framework may be useful for characterizing and understanding aggression in individuals with ASD. Among a sample of 206 children with ASD and behavioral problems, Carroll and colleagues (2014) found that 31% engaged primarily in reactive aggression, whereas 15% engaged primarily in proactive aggression. Similarly, Farmer and colleagues (2015) found that children and adolescents with ASD were more likely to engage in reactive rather than proactive aggression. Kaartinen and colleagues (2014) also found that boys with ASD were more likely than TD boys to demonstrate reactive aggression in the context of a computerized task. These findings suggest that individuals with ASD may be most likely to engage in reactive aggression and suggest a need for further research to determine if the underlying cognitive and physiological mechanisms of these subtypes of aggression are similar to those in individuals without ASD.

Some preliminary work suggests that empathy and emotion regulation may also play a role in predicting aggression among individuals with ASD. In children without ASD, both reactive and proactive aggression are linked to lower levels of affective empathy (an emotional reaction to another's emotions) and cognitive empathy (the ability to adopt another person's point of view to understand their emotions; Mayberry & Espelage, 2007). Prior research has found that individuals with ASD do not show impairments on affective empathy tasks (Blair, 1999; Dziobek et al., 2008; Jones, Happé, Gilbert, Burnett, & Viding, 2010; Pouw, Rieffe, Oosterveld, Huskens, & Stockmann, 2013) but that they do have greater difficulties with cognitive empathy than individuals without ASD (Dziobek et al., 2008; Jones et al., 2010; Pouw et al., 2013). Puow and colleagues (2013) examined the relationship between these types of empathy and aggression in children with and without ASD. Interestingly, although affective empathy was associated with less reactive aggression in the TD group, for children with ASD, greater affective empathy was associated with greater reactive and proactive aggression, whereas greater cognitive empathy was associated with less reactive aggression. Although preliminary, these findings suggest that children with ASD who experience arousal in the face of others' distress may misinterpret the social situation due to lack of cognitive empathy or theory of mind. This, coupled with difficulties with emotion regulation, may lead to aggressive behavior.

In the general population, the relationship between emotion regulation and aggression has been well studied. There is evidence from both human and animal studies that aggression is associated with brain function in regions responsible for behavioral and emotional control, particularly the amygdala, brainstem, orbitofrontal cortex, and dorsolateral prefrontal cortex (Coccaro, McCloskey, Fitzgerald, & Phan, 2007; Lamm, Granic, Zelazo, & Lewis, 2011; Lozier, Cardinale, VanMeter, & Marsh, 2014; Paus, 2005; Siegel & Victoroff, 2009). There is also evidence of significant interconnectivity between the brain circuits underlying anxiety and aggression (Neumann, Veenema, & Beiderbeck, 2010), pointing to a common emotion regulation pathway that may explain the links between anxiety and aggression in TD children (Bubier & Drabick, 2009). However, very few studies have explored the potential neurobiological underpinning of aggression in individuals with ASD. In an exploratory study, Lundwall and colleagues (2017) recently examined structural magnetic resonance imaging data from 45 boys with ASD and found that smaller brainstem volume was associated with higher aggression. Much more research is needed to examine potential neurocognitive mechanisms of aggression among individuals with ASD to develop more effective and personalized treatment approaches.

Despite the relative lack of attention to cognitive and biological underpinnings of aggression in individuals with ASD, there is a large body of literature focused on understanding aggression from within the context of behavioral principles. From an operant learning perspective, behaviors are maintained by (or are a function of) the consequences that reliably follow them (Skinner, 1953). The application of these principles is integral to the practice of applied behavior analysis (ABA) procedures to understand and modify problem behavior. Within the operant learning paradigm, behavior can be positively reinforced (in which the function is to gain access to a stimulus) or negatively reinforced (in which the function is to remove or avoid a stimulus). In practice, the functions of problem behavior generally fall into one or more categories: access to social attention, access to preferred items or activities, escape from aversive tasks or activities, escape from others, or internal stimulation (automatic or sensory reinforcement; Carr, 1994; Derby et al., 1992; Hanley, Iwata, & McCord, 2003). As will be discussed in more detail in the sections that follow, this framework is central to most evidence-based behavioral interventions. It is also noteworthy that the focus of this framework is largely on the *functions* of behavior, not on the topography of the behavior itself (Carr, 1993; R. G. Smith & Iwata, 1997).

Assessment of Aggression

Accurate assessment of aggression in individuals with ASD is important for treatment planning and progress monitoring. In general, a multimodal, multi-informant approach to assessment is recommended. This should include a comprehensive clinical interview with caregivers and other key informants to determine the nature, severity, and duration of the aggressive behavior and to identify potential contributing factors. Given the high co-occurrence of aggression and medical problems in individuals with ASD, the presence of potential pain, discomfort, and/or insomnia should also be considered as possible contributors to aggressive behavior (McGuire et al., 2016). Standardized rating scales may also be useful to gather information about behavior across settings. Finally, functional behavioral assessment (FBA) methods (described in detail in a later section) may prove most helpful for selecting specific intervention strategies. As will be described next, there are few validated tools that were developed specifically for the ASD population. However, instruments developed for the general population or for those with other developmental disabilities may be useful.

RATING SCALES

Two of the most commonly used broad-band behavior rating scales for children are the Behavior Assessment System for Children (BASC; Kamphaus & Reynolds, 2007) and the CBCL (Achenbach & Rescorla, 2001). Both were developed and normed for use in the general population and demonstrate excellent psychometric properties when used among TD children (Achenbach & Rescorla, 2001; Kamphaus & Reynolds, 2007). Both the BASC and the CBCL provide broad-band Externalizing and Internalizing scores, as well as more specific syndrome or subscale scores for aggressive behavior. Despite the fact that they have been used frequently in studies of children with ASD, few studies have examined their psychometric properties when used in this population. Hass and colleagues (2012) reported Cronbach's alpha for the Aggression subscale of the BASC-2 in an ASD sample and found $\alpha = .88$ for children and $\alpha = .66$ for adolescents. However, other studies have not specifically examined its measurement properties in ASD samples. A handful of studies have examined the psychometric properties of the CBCL in ASD samples, with mixed results. Pandolfi and colleagues (2009, 2012) found support for the factor structure of both age versions of the CBCL in studies of 128 and 122 children with ASD, respectively. However, in a larger sample of children and adolescents with ASD, the CBCL factor structure was supported in younger but not older children with ASD (Medeiros, Mazurek, & Kanne, 2017).

Measures that have been developed specifically for individuals with ASD or other developmental disorders may provide more utility in assessing problem behavior in this population. The Aberrant

Behavior Checklist (ABC; Aman, Singh, Stewart, & Field, 1985) was specifically developed to assess challenging behavior in individuals with developmental disabilities and has been one of the most widely used outcome measures in pharmacological clinical trials for ASD. It contains five empirically derived subscales; however, none assess aggression specifically. The Irritability subscale includes one item assessing physical aggression (i.e., "aggressive to other children or adults"); however, it also includes items assessing mood (e.g., depressed mood, crying), screaming, tantrums, and self-injury.

The Nisonger Child Behavior Rating Form (NCBRF) was developed for children with intellectual disabilities (Aman, Tassé, Rojahn, & Hammer, 1996; Tassé, Aman, Hammer, & Rojahn, 1996) and has demonstrated good psychometric properties among children with ASD (Lecavalier, Aman, Hammer, Stoica, & Mathews, 2004). The NCBRF includes eight subscales (consisting of Social Competence and Problem Behavior domains). The Conduct Problems subscale includes items assessing aggression, anger, and oppositional behavior but does not assess aggression exclusively. The Behavior Problems Inventory (BPI) is another measure developed for assessment of individuals with developmental disabilities (Rojahn et al., 2001) and contains three subscales: Self-Injurious Behavior, Stereotypic Behavior, and Aggression/Destruction. The Aggression/Destruction subscale includes 11 items (nine of which assess physical aggression specifically). Finally, the Developmental Behavior Checklist (Einfeld & Tonge, 1995) was developed for individuals with intellectual disabilities and includes a Disruptive subscale with items assessing aggression, oppositional and defiant behavior, and moodiness. In general, the evidence on the psychometric properties of these tools when used among children and adults with ASD is limited. Of note, these measures were all developed primarily for individuals with intellectual disability, and not specifically for individuals with ASD. As such, it is not clear whether they are appropriate for higher functioning individuals.

The Children's Scale for Hostility and Aggression: Reactive/Proactive (C-SHARP; Farmer & Aman, 2009) is a comprehensive measure of aggression also developed for children with developmental disabilities. The C-SHARP is composed of five empirically derived subscales: Verbal Aggression, Bullying, Covert Aggression, Hostility, and Physical Aggression. Items are rated in terms of their frequency/severity as well as provocation type (reactive/proactive). The C-SHARP has good psychometric properties (Farmer & Aman, 2010) and demonstrated good construct validity and measurement invariance in a large sample of children, adolescents, and young adults with ASD representative of the full range of intellectual functioning (Farmer et al., 2016). The Autism Spectrum Disorder—Problem Behavior—Child Version and Adult Version are two additional scales that were designed specifically for individuals with ASD (Mahan & Matson, 2011; Matson et al., 2008; Matson & Rivet, 2008b). These brief (18- to 20-item) rating scales assess problem behaviors broadly and do not yield a specific aggression subscale, but they do include items targeting physical and verbal aggression.

FUNCTIONAL BEHAVIOR ASSESSMENT

Interventions based on the principles of ABA are generally designed to address the function of the challenging behavior. As such, careful observation and assessment of the behavior and the environmental variables that contribute to and maintain its occurrence are necessary (Carr, 1994; Derby et al., 1992; Hanley, Iwata, & McCord, 2003). This can be done through a systematic process known as FBA. By identifying the variables that contribute to problem behavior, FBA can directly guide the choice of specific behavior intervention strategies. In fact, the effectiveness of behavioral strategies depends in large part on whether they are informed by an understanding of the functions of the behavior. If intervention strategies do not appropriately address behavioral functions, they may inadvertently reinforce the behavior and lead to worsening symptoms (Ingram, Lewis-Palmer, & Sugai, 2005; Newcomer & Lewis, 2004). Furthermore, there is consistent evidence that interventions based on the results of FBA are more effective in reducing problem behaviors than those that did not use FBA (Heyvaert, Saenen, Campbell, Maes, & Onghena, 2014; Horner, Carr, Strain, Todd, & Reed, 2002).

There are many available FBA methods, which vary in terms of both precision and procedural complexity. Decisions about their use generally depend on the severity and complexity of the behavior and the resources available for conducting the assessment. In general, FBA methods can be grouped into three broad categories: informant methods, descriptive observation methods, and experimental functional analysis. Informant methods focus on gathering information from caregivers, teachers, or staff who have observed the target behavior. This information may be collected by interview, rating scale, or other means. The Functional Assessment Interview form

(FAI) is an example of a structured interview format designed to elicit information that can inform the identification of antecedents and consequences of behavior (O'Neill, Horner, Albin, Storey, & Sprague, 1990). The Functional Assessment Checklist: Teachers and Staff (FACTS) is another interview form that was designed specifically for educational settings (March et al., 2000). Informant information about behavioral functions can also be collected using rating scales, such as the Questions About Behavior Function (QABF; Paclawskyj, Matson, Rush, Smalls, & Vollmer, 2000) or the Functional Assessment for Multiple Causality (FACT; Matson et al., 2003), both of which have demonstrated evidence of reliability (Healy, Brett, & Leader, 2013; Matson et al., 2003; Singh et al., 2006). However, others have cautioned that indirect methods alone may not reliably identify functions of behavior (Iwata & Dozier, 2008).

Descriptive FBA methods are often used in conjunction with informant report to further elucidate determinants of problem behavior through systematic direct observation of behavior in natural settings (Crawford, Brockel, Schauss, & Miltenberger, 1992; Kozlowski & Matson, 2012; Lalli, Browder, Mace, & Brown, 1993). Typically, descriptive FBA methods use an antecedent–behavior–consequence format to record each instance of the target behavior along with the specific environmental events that precede it (antecedents) and follow it (consequences). The results of these observations help generate hypotheses about potential functions of the behavior as it occurs in natural environments (Bijou, Peterson, & Ault, 1968; Crawford et al., 1992; Kozlowski & Matson, 2012; Lewis & Sugai, 1996).

In situations in which aggression is infrequent or when indirect or descriptive methods do not yield clear results, assessment of behavior under more controlled conditions may be required. Functional analysis (FA) uses an experimental design to systematically manipulate environmental variables to establish the function of a target behavior (Iwata, Dorsey, Slifer, Bauman, & Richman, 1982; Iwata, Vollmer, & Zarcone, 1990). Although there have been many variations and applications of FA over the past three decades (Beavers, Iwata, & Lerman, 2013; Hanley et al., 2003), they all share a common method of observing behavior under both test and control conditions. In this way, the assessor directly manipulates antecedents and consequences of behavior under highly controlled alternating conditions. The conditions under which high rates of behavior are observed reveal likely behavioral functions (e.g., escape, access to tangibles, etc.; Carr & Durand, 1985; Iwata et al., 1982). FA is generally considered to be the gold-standard method for identifying behavioral functions, and treatments based on FA results have been found to be more effective than those based on other FBA methods (Herzinger & Campbell, 2007). However, conducting an FA with procedural fidelity requires training and expertise in behavior analysis, as well as experience in observing, recording, analyzing, and interpreting behavioral data. Furthermore, the feasibility of implementing rigorous FA procedures may prove difficult in many applied settings, including outpatient clinics and schools. In these situations, less resource-intensive indirect and descriptive FBA procedures may be most helpful as a first step.

Treatment

Behavioral Intervention Approaches

Behavioral interventions have a substantial amount of evidence to support their effectiveness in reducing aggressive behavior in children with ASD (Brosnan & Healy, 2011; Campbell, 2003; Heyvaert et al., 2014; Horner et al., 2002; Matson & Jang, 2014). However, the majority of the evidence to date is based on well-controlled, single-subject designs, and evidence among adults with ASD is limited. By contrast, there have been few large-scale, group-based, or randomized controlled trials to examine the effects of behavioral interventions on aggression in individuals with ASD. For example, in a recent review of 101 studies of behavioral treatments for problem behavior in children with ASD, differential reinforcement, functional communication training, and extinction were the most common interventions for aggression. However, all studies reviewed used single-subject designs (Doehring, Reichow, Palka, Phillips, & Hagopian, 2014), suggesting a need for well-controlled treatment outcome research to continue to extend this evidence base.

In practice, a comprehensive approach to managing aggression is generally required, typically combining elements of preventative strategies, skill instruction, and reinforcement of appropriate behavior. Ultimately, the goal of such interventions should be to prevent the occurrence of aggression while teaching and reinforcing new skills and behaviors that enable the individual to communicate his or her wants and needs. Specific types and components of behavioral intervention strategies are described next.

ANTECEDENT STRATEGIES

Antecedent strategies focus primarily on preventing problem behavior by proactively modifying the environmental variables that trigger its occurrence (Kern, Choutka, & Sokol, 2002; Luiselli, 2008). There are many specific types of antecedent strategies, all with a shared focus on reducing the likelihood of negative behavior and/or prompting desired behavior. Example strategies include offering choices, arranging the environment, providing visual supports, and changing the schedule or routine. As with other behavioral interventions, it is important to select a strategy that directly addresses the function of the behavior. Providing choice-making opportunities has been found to reduce the occurrence of problem behavior in studies of individuals with autism and other developmental disabilities (Dyer, Dunlap, & Winterling, 1990; Romaniuk & Miltenberger, 2001). In a review of 13 single-subject design studies, activity schedules were determined to be effective in reducing disruptive behaviors among children with ASD (Banda & Grimmett, 2008). A similar review of 18 studies also found reductions in challenging behavior after implementation of activity schedules (Lequia, Machalicek, & Rispoli, 2012). Antecedent interventions as a group were found to be effective in a review of school-based interventions for challenging behavior in children with ASD (Machalicek, O'Reilly, Beretvas, Sigafoos, & Lancioni, 2007). As stand-alone interventions, antecedent strategies have the benefit of being relatively low cost and easy to implement. However, there is some evidence that they are relatively less effective than other behavioral strategies in reducing problem behavior in children with ASD (Heyvaert et al., 2014). Thus, these strategies may be most effective when used in conjunction with skill-based or consequence-based approaches, which are described in more detail next.

EXTINCTION

Extinction procedures can be used to reduce the occurrence of challenging behavior by removing the environmental variable that previously reinforced the behavior. If a behavior no longer serves its original function, the likelihood of future occurrence is decreased (Cooper, Heron, & Heward, 2007). As such, extinction is often an important component in behavioral interventions targeting aggression (Lerman & Iwata, 1996). Extinction has been shown to be effective at reducing aggression and other challenging behaviors in previous single-subject studies of individuals with autism and other developmental disabilities (Brosnan & Healy, 2011; Wong et al., 2015). It is important to note that extinction may lead to a temporary increase in the behavior, called an "extinction burst," but this is generally followed by continued reduction or cessation of problem behavior as long as reinforcement continues to be withheld during this period (Cooper et al., 2007). Because of the possibility of this temporary increase in frequency or intensity of behavior, practitioners should carefully consider the use of extinction procedures in individuals with very severe aggression, as an extinction burst may prove dangerous to the individual or others. There is evidence, however, that extinction bursts occur at relatively low frequency in treatment studies using extinction procedures and that they are less likely to occur when extinction is combined with other intervention strategies (Lerman & Iwata, 1995, 1996). Furthermore, other strategies (including reinforcement-based interventions) may be more effective when extinction is included as part of the intervention program (Fisher et al., 1993; Mazaleski, Iwata, Vollmer, Zarcone, & Smith, 1993; Zarcone, Iwata, Mazaleski, & Smith, 1994). As such, extinction is often used as part of a more comprehensive treatment package, generally alongside reinforcement-based strategies.

REINFORCEMENT STRATEGIES

Differential reinforcement procedures are also effective strategies for reducing aggression and other challenging behaviors in individuals with autism (Brosnan & Healy, 2011; Wong et al., 2015). During these procedures, reinforcement is provided when the individual demonstrates a desired behavior. Differential reinforcement of alternative behavior (DRA) is one of the most commonly used applications of the strategy (Vollmer & Iwata, 1992). This procedure includes withholding reinforcing variables after the demonstration of problem behavior (extinction) and presenting reinforcing variables after the individual engages in appropriate behavior (Deitz & Repp, 1983). These procedures are effective for reducing problem behavior and prompting engagement in desired replacement behaviors (Vollmer & Iwata, 1992). Although extinction is generally a critical component to this procedure, there is evidence that DRA can be successful without extinction under some conditions (Athens & Vollmer, 2010; MacNaul & Neely, 2018). This may be an alternative in cases in which extinction is not feasible due to the severity of the behavior or situational circumstances (Athens & Vollmer, 2010). Differential reinforcement of incompatible behavior (DRI) is a variant of this procedure in which reinforcement is provided for an appropriate behavior that is physically incompatible with the challenging behavior (i.e., the two behaviors cannot be performed at the same time; Vollmer & Iwata, 1992). Finally, differential reinforcement of other behavior (DRO) refers to a procedure in which reinforcement is delivered when the individual engages in any appropriate behavior during a specific time period (as long as the challenging behavior is *not* demonstrated; Cooper et al., 2007; Vollmer & Iwata, 1992). A recent systematic review found that DRO procedures appear to be most effective when used in combination with other strategies in reducing challenging behavior in children with ASD (Weston, Hodges, & Davis, 2017).

Functional communication training (FCT) is a specific application of DRA that is also effective for reducing aggressive behavior among individuals with ASD (Horner et al., 2002; Reeve & Carr, 2000; Wong et al., 2015). During FCT procedures, appropriate communication skills are taught and reinforced as desired alternatives to challenging behavior. The goal of FCT is to enable the individual to replace aggression (or other challenging behavior) with more socially acceptable communicative behaviors to access reinforcers (Carr & Durand, 1985). Depending on the abilities of the individual, target communicative behaviors can range from vocal or motor responses to the use of communication systems that include pictures, symbols, or electronic voice output (Brown et al., 2000). In a recent meta-analysis, Chezan, Wolfe, and Drasgow (2018) found good evidence for the effectiveness of FCT in reducing problem behavior in individuals with ASD (large effect size).

PARENT TRAINING AND PARENT-IMPLEMENTED INTERVENTIONS

To increase access to and the generalizability of treatment effects, there has been increasing interest in the development of behavioral interventions that can be delivered by parents or caregivers in natural settings. Parent training interventions for disruptive behavior typically focus on the behavioral principles described earlier (including understanding of antecedents and consequences of behavior); however, they may vary in terms of the specific behavioral strategies emphasized (e.g., antecedent manipulation, reinforcement, FCT, etc.). In a review of the effectiveness of these interventions, Postorino and colleagues (2017) conducted a meta-analysis of the effects of parent training on disruptive behavior in eight randomized controlled trials with children with ASD. The results indicated support for efficacy of these interventions, with medium effect size across studies. However, variability in methods and procedures and the relatively small number of available studies highlighted a need for further research to examine the most effective dose, format, and specific strategies across parent training interventions (Postorino et al., 2017).

Pharmacological Treatment

Several large randomized placebo-controlled clinical trials have demonstrated effectiveness of second-generation antipsychotics (SGAs) in reducing irritability and associated aggressive behavior among children and adults with ASD (Fung et al., 2016; Marcus et al., 2009; McCracken et al., 2002; McDougle et al., 1998; Owen et al., 2009). As a result, both risperidone and aripiprazole have been approved by the U.S. Food and Drug Administration (FDA) for treatment of irritability in children with ASD (Blankenship, Erickson, & McDougle, 2010; Fitzpatrick, Srivorakiat, Wink, Pedapati, & Erickson, 2016). However, it is noteworthy that the Irritability subscale of the ABC was used as the primary treatment outcome measure across most studies (Kent et al., 2013; McCracken et al., 2002; Shea et al., 2004). As noted previously, this subscale does not specifically assess aggression, but captures a wide range of mood and behavioral symptoms (e.g., temper tantrums, depressed mood, screaming, self-injurious behaviors, and one item targeting aggression). In a recent systematic review and meta-analysis, Fung and colleagues (2016) concluded that risperidone and aripiprazole have the strongest evidence of efficacy for treatment of irritability (with large effect sizes across studies); however, both were associated with significant adverse side effects, including sedation, extrapyramidal symptoms, and weight gain. As noted in recent reviews, the evidence to support the use of other medications in treating aggression and irritability in ASD is more limited (Fitzpatrick et al., 2016; Fung et al., 2016). Although some other medications have demonstrated large to moderate effects in single studies, these findings have not been replicated (Fung et al., 2016).

Some studies have also begun to examine the effectiveness of combined pharmacological and behavioral treatment approaches. For example, in a randomized controlled trial of 124 children with ASD, Aman and colleagues (2009) compared the effects of risperidone alone to the effects of a combined risperidone plus behavioral parent training. The results indicated greater reductions in disruptive behavior in the combined treatment group than in the medication-only group (Aman et al., 2009).

Frazier and colleagues (2010) also reported on the effectiveness of combining intensive behavioral intervention (IBI) with different classes of medication in reducing aggression in a sample of 32 children with ASD. Retrospective data indicated that children receiving IBI made more rapid behavioral improvement when also taking antipsychotic medication, whereas medication alone was not associated with significant improvement before IBI was initiated. Aggression decreased notably within the first week of IBI treatment across all groups (including those with and without medication), and the concurrent use of antipsychotic medication was associated with requiring fewer sessions to achieve success. In summary, there is evidence that a combined pharmacological and behavioral treatment approach may be most effective for some children with ASD.

Case Example

Billy was a 4-year-old boy with ASD who was referred for assessment and treatment due to a recent increase in aggressive behaviors. Billy was diagnosed with ASD at 3 years of age and was enrolled in a preschool program in his community at the time of referral. His mother had previously cared for Billy and his 2-year-old brother at home until he started preschool 2 months ago. Although he had participated in playdates and some group-based activities at the public library, this was Billy's first experience in a school setting. Billy's verbal abilities were primarily limited to single words and occasional phrases, most of which were echoed. His parents reported that Billy rarely used words to communicate, although he occasionally made single-word requests, such as "juice," "more," "cookie." He demonstrated understanding of "yes" and "no" and was able to follow simple instructions, such as "close the door" or "sit down." He was also able to point to common objects in a book as they were named. He did not typically make eye contact or initiate social interactions with children or adults, although he was able to respond to others with prompting. Billy's favorite activities were playing in water and playing with Hot Wheels cars. He particularly enjoyed arranging his cars in lines, sorting by color, and watching the wheels spin from different angles. Billy also engaged in frequent repetitive movements, including hand flapping and rocking back and forth.

Due to increasing concerns about his aggressive behavior, Billy's pediatrician, Dr. Gonzales, referred his family to a psychologist with expertise in ASD and behavioral interventions. At the time of referral, Dr. Gonzales consulted with the psychologist, Dr. Wells, to provide information about Billy's medical history and current functioning. Dr. Gonzales reported that Billy had a history of asthma, seasonal allergies, and insomnia, all of which were currently well controlled on medication. During Billy's most recent well-child visit, Dr. Gonzales noted that his sleep problems had responded well to melatonin supplements. No other medical problems were noted and no changes in health status or medications were reported at his most recent visit.

During an initial visit with Dr. Wells, Billy's parents participated in a general clinical interview to provide more detailed information about his history and current functioning. His developmental, medical, educational, and psychosocial history were reviewed. No recent changes or family stressors were identified other than beginning preschool in the fall. Since that time, his parents had noted an increase in aggressive behaviors occurring both at home and at preschool. His parents reported that Billy engaged in tantrums several times per day, which involved screaming, falling down on the floor, and hitting people. Billy's mother had received numerous calls from his preschool due to his disruptive behavior, and she was worried that he would not be able to continue there if his behavior did not improve. His parents were also worried that he may become physically aggressive toward his younger brother in the future.

Dr. Wells also asked Billy's mother and primary teacher to complete a packet of questionnaires to provide information about his behavioral functioning at home and school. The results of the CBCL (parent- and teacher-report forms) indicated consistent clinically significant elevations on the Aggressive Behavior and Withdrawn Syndrome scales as well as the Pervasive Developmental Problems DSM-Oriented Scale (according to both parent and teacher report). No other elevations were noted in other emotional or behavioral domains.

After reviewing the information collected through consultation, interview, and rating scales, Dr. Wells determined that an FBA would be most helpful to guide the selection of behavioral strategies. First, she gathered detailed information about the nature of Billy's behavior through the semistructured Functional Assessment Interview (FAI) conducted with Billy's mother and primary teacher. The results of these interviews indicated that Billy's aggressive behavior at home and at school was characterized by screaming and hitting others (primarily adults) with an open hand. The frequency was multiple episodes per day, and the duration tended to vary significantly from one episode to the next. Billy's mother and teacher both observed that his behavior was most likely to occur when Billy was asked to stop a preferred activity (such as playing with cars) to transition to a different task, or when he was asked to perform a task he did not enjoy (such as brushing his teeth or completing a worksheet). Billy's mother reported that she typically tried to help Billy calm down by allowing him to continue a preferred activity if he started to show signs of distress when asked to begin a nonpreferred task, and she also noted that she had gradually stopped asking Billy to perform certain tasks. His teacher reported that she typically removed unpleasant tasks when Billy screamed or behaved aggressively to minimize classroom disruptions. The FAI indicated a consistent pattern of results across reporters and suggested that Billy's aggressive behavior was occurring most frequently during transitions between activities at his preschool.

Dr. Wells then completed a direct observation in the classroom to further characterize the antecedents, consequences, and nature of Billy's aggressive behavior. After consultation with his teacher, she chose to observe Billy during the classroom period in which his aggression was most likely to occur. She used an antecedent–behavior–consequence recording format to record each instance of the target behavior (operationally defined as hitting another person with an open hand) along with the specific environmental events that preceded (antecedents) and followed (consequences) it. During the 90-minute observation, Billy engaged in 10 episodes of aggressive behavior. Antecedents in all cases included removal of a tangible (preferred item or toy) and/or presentation of a task demand. Consequences included access to a tangible (in two cases) and removal of the task demands (in all cases).

After reviewing all assessment data, Dr. Wells hypothesized that the function of Billy's behavior in most cases was to escape or avoid nonpreferred tasks. Evidence of this was consistent across reporters and settings, and it was clear that Billy's behavior was reinforced in both settings (e.g., parents and teachers allowed him to escape tasks when he engaged in aggressive behaviors). The results of the FBA were used to develop an initial behavior intervention plan. Because Billy was not able to use speech to effectively communicate his needs, an FCT approach was selected to reduce his aggressive behaviors while helping Billy develop more effective means of communication.

As a first step, Dr. Wells worked with his parents and teachers to select an appropriate communication behavior that could be used to replace Billy's aggression. They created a picture communication card indicating "I need a break" and taught Billy to point to or hand the card to his teacher or parent when he wanted a break from a task. At first, Billy required hand-over-hand prompting, and these prompts were gradually faded over time as Billy learned to use the communicative response consistently. In the beginning of the program, each time Billy used the "break" card, he was allowed to escape from the task for 2 minutes (reinforcing the alternative communicative behavior rather than aggressive behavior). Billy's parents and teachers were also instructed not to allow him to escape from the task if he engaged in aggression (removing reinforcement for his aggressive behavior). Over the course of FCT, Billy's aggressive behaviors declined and he began to consistently use the "break" card to communicate his desire to avoid nonpreferred tasks. Over time, the team began to add immediate positive reinforcement for Billy's participation in nonpreferred tasks, gradually increasing the amount of time he was able to tolerate and participate in tasks appropriately. The team also gradually reinforced more complex communication behaviors (moving from the "break" card, to verbalizing the word "break," to using the phrase "break please"). In this way, the intervention team was able to increase Billy's motivation to participate in tasks while also providing him with skills to communicate his needs more effectively.

Summary and Future Directions

In conclusion, aggression is a clinically important issue for many individuals with ASD and their families. These behaviors contribute to negative outcomes for individuals and their families across the lifespan. Although there is some evidence that the frequency and intensity of aggression may decline from childhood to adulthood, these behaviors continue to occur throughout adolescence and adulthood for many individuals. The etiology of aggression among individuals with ASD remains largely unknown, although general theories of aggression may prove useful in understanding its occurrence in this population. Future research focused on subtypes and potential underlying neurobiological mechanisms will be necessary for informing more targeted and personalized treatments. Currently, behavioral principles may provide the most helpful framework for practitioners in understanding the factors that contribute to the occurrence and maintenance of aggression in everyday situations. Because aggression is often a primary treatment target for individuals with ASD, practitioners are encouraged to develop a good working knowledge of evidence-based assessment and treatment strategies.

A comprehensive multimodal assessment including direct observation of behavior is recommended to inform treatment planning. Although there are few psychometrically sound assessment tools that were specifically developed to assess aggression in individuals with ASD, some tools developed for other populations may be useful in characterizing the topography of aggression in this population. More research is needed to examine the psychometric properties of these tools when used among individuals with ASD. Despite the relative lack of standardized assessment tools, much more research has been devoted to developing and refining methods for understanding the functions of challenging behavior and aggression. FBA is strongly recommended to identify the factors that contribute to the occurrence of aggression and to guide behavioral intervention planning. Methods for FBA can range from indirect to direct assessment, depending on the nature of the behavior and available resources. Interventions that are based on the results of FBA are generally more effective, underscoring the importance of selecting an intervention strategy that is directly tied to the purpose of the behavior. Regarding evidence-based treatment strategies, behavioral interventions and certain medications (including second-generation antipsychotics) have the most current evidence of effectiveness.

Although aggression is a clinically significant issue for many individuals with ASD, it has received relatively little attention in large-scale studies. Areas for future research include a greater understanding of the etiology and underlying mechanisms of aggression in ASD, development of psychometrically sound tools for assessment, more consistent operationalization and assessment of aggression across studies, and increased research on both pharmacological and nonpharmacological treatments for aggression in individuals with ASD across the lifespan. Current evidence regarding the effectiveness of behavioral interventions for aggression in individuals with ASD is based almost entirely on single-subject research designs. Future studies using more rigorous designs, such as randomized controlled trials, are needed to continue to inform our understanding of the effectiveness of specific intervention strategies and to determine potential mediators and moderators of treatment effects.

References

Achenbach, T., & Rescorla, L. (2001). *Manual for the Achenbach system of empirically based assessment school-age forms profiles.* Burlington, VT: ASEBA.

Alink, L. R., Mesman, J., Van Zeijl, J., Stolk, M. N., Juffer, F., Koot, H. M.,... Van IJzendoorn, M. H. (2006). The early childhood aggression curve: Development of physical aggression in 10- to 50-month-old children. *Child Development, 77*(4), 954–966.

Allen, J. J., Anderson, C. A., & Bushman, B. J. (2018). The general aggression model. *Current Opinion in Psychology, 19*, 75–80.

Aman, M. G., Singh, N. N., Stewart, A. W., & Field, C. J. (1985). Psychometric characteristics of the Aberrant Behavior Checklist. *American Journal of Mental Deficiency, 89*(5)492.

Aman, M. G., McDougle, C. J., Scahill, L., Handen, B., Arnold, L. E., Johnson, C.,... Research Units on Pediatric Psychopharmacology Autism Network. (2009). Medication and parent training in children with pervasive developmental disorders and serious behavior problems: Results from a randomized clinical trial. *Journal of the American Academy of Child and Adolescent Psychiatry, 48*(12), 1143–1154.

Aman, M. G., Tassé, M. J., Rojahn, J., & Hammer, D. (1996). The Nisonger CBRF: A child behavior rating form for children with developmental disabilities. *Research in Developmental Disabilities, 17*(1), 41–57.

Ambler, P. G., Eidels, A., & Gregory, C. (2015). Anxiety and aggression in adolescents with autism spectrum disorders attending mainstream schools. *Research in Autism Spectrum Disorders, 18*, 97–109.

Anderson, C. A., & Bushman, B. J. (2002). Human aggression. *Annual Review of Psychology, 53*, 27–51.

Athens, E. S., & Vollmer, T. R. (2010). An investigation of differential reinforcement of alternative behavior without extinction. *Journal of Applied Behavior Analysis, 43*(4), 569–589.

Banda, D. R., & Grimmett, E. (2008). Enhancing social and transition behaviors of persons with autism through activity schedules: A review. *Education and Training in Developmental Disabilities, 43*(3)324–333.

Bandura, A. (1978). Social learning theory of aggression. *Journal of Communication, 28*(3), 12–29.

Bandura, A., Ross, D., & Ross, S. A. (1961). Transmission of aggression through imitation of aggressive models. *Journal of Abnormal and Social Psychology, 63*(3), 575.

Baron, R., & Richardson, D. (1994). *Human aggression* (2nd ed.). New York, NY: Plenum.

Beavers, G. A., Iwata, B. A., & Lerman, D. C. (2013). Thirty years of research on the functional analysis of problem behavior. *Journal of Applied Behavior Analysis, 46*(1), 1–21.

Berkowitz, L. (1962). *Aggression: A social psychological analysis.* New York, NY: McGraw-Hill.

Berkowitz, L. (1989). Frustration-aggression hypothesis: Examination and reformulation. *Psychological Bulletin, 106*(1), 59.

Berkowitz, L. (1990). On the formation and regulation of anger and aggression: A cognitive-neoassociationistic analysis. *American Psychologist, 45*(4), 494.

Berkowitz, L. (1993). *Aggression: Its causes, consequences, and control.* Philadelphia, PA: Temple University Press.

Bijou, S. W., Peterson, R. F., & Ault, M. H. (1968). A method to integrate descriptive and experimental field studies at the level of data and empirical concepts. *Journal of Applied Behavior Analysis, 1*(2), 175–191.

Bitsika, V., Sharpley, C. F., Sweeney, J. A., Andronicos, N. M., Agnew, L. L., & Arnold, W. M. (2017). A comparison of age, cognitive, hormonal, symptomatic and mood correlates of aggression towards others in boys with ASD. *Research in Developmental Disabilities, 66*, 44–54.

Blair, R. J. R. (1999). Psychophysiological responsiveness to the distress of others in children with autism. *Personality and Individual Differences, 26*(3), 477–485.

Blankenship, K., Erickson, C. A., & McDougle, C. J. (2010). Pharmacotherapy of autism and related disorders. *Psychiatric Annals, 40*(4), 203–209.

Bodfish, J. W., Symons, F. J., Parker, D. E., & Lewis, M. H. (2000). Varieties of repetitive behavior in autism: Comparisons to mental retardation. *Journal of Autism and Developmental Disorders, 30*(3), 237–243.

Brodie, M. J., Besag, F., Ettinger, A. B., Mula, M., Gobbi, G., Comai, S.,... Steinhoff, B. J. (2016). Epilepsy, antiepileptic drugs, and aggression: An evidence-based review. *Pharmacological Reviews, 68*(3), 563–602.

Broidy, L. M., Nagin, D. S., Tremblay, R. E., Bates, J. E., Brame, B., Dodge, K. A.,... Laird, R. (2003). Developmental trajectories of childhood disruptive behaviors and adolescent delinquency: A six-site, cross-national study. *Developmental Psychology, 39*(2), 222.

Bronsard, G., Botbol, M., & Tordjman, S. (2010). Aggression in low functioning children and adolescents with autistic disorder. *PLoS One, 5*(12), e14358.

Brosnan, J., & Healy, O. (2011). A review of behavioral interventions for the treatment of aggression in individuals with developmental disabilities. *Research in Developmental Disabilities, 32*(2), 437–446.

Brown, K. A., Wacker, D. P., Derby, K. M., Peck, S. M., Richman, D. M., Sasso, G. M.,... Harding, J. W. (2000). Evaluating the effects of functional communication training in the presence and absence of establishing operations. *Journal of Applied Behavior Analysis, 33*(1), 53–71.

Bubier, J. L., & Drabick, D. A. (2009). Co-occurring anxiety and disruptive behavior disorders: The roles of anxious symptoms, reactive aggression, and shared risk processes. *Clinical Psychology Review, 29*(7), 658–669.

Buie, T., Campbell, D. B., Fuchs, G. J., Furuta, G. T., Levy, J., VandeWater, J.,... Winter, H. (2010). Evaluation, diagnosis, and treatment of gastrointestinal disorders in individuals with ASDs: A consensus report. *Pediatrics, 125*(Suppl 1), S1–S18.

Buss, A. H. (1966). Instrumentality of aggression, feedback, and frustration as determinants of physical aggression. *Journal of Personality and Social Psychology, 3*(2), 153.

Campbell, J. M. (2003). Efficacy of behavioral interventions for reducing problem behavior in persons with autism: A quantitative synthesis of single-subject research. *Research in Developmental Disabilities, 24*(2), 120–138.

Carr, E. G. (1993). Behavior analysis is not ultimately about behavior. *Behavior Analyst, 16*(1), 47–49.

Carr, E. G. (1994). Emerging themes in the functional analysis of problem behavior. *Journal of Applied Behavior Analysis, 27*(2), 393–399.

Carr, E. G., & Durand, V. M. (1985). Reducing behavior problems through functional communication training. *Journal of Applied Behavior Analysis, 18*(2), 111–126.

Carroll, D., Hallett, V., McDougle, C. J., Aman, M. G., McCracken, J. T., Tierney, E.,... Scahill, L. (2014). Examination of aggression and self-injury in children with autism spectrum disorders and serious behavioral problems. *Child and Adolescent Psychiatric Clinics of North America, 23*(1), 57–72.

Chaidez, V., Hansen, R. L., & Hertz-Picciotto, I. (2014). Gastrointestinal problems in children with autism, developmental delays or typical development. *Journal of Autism and Developmental Disorders, 44*(5), 1117–1127.

Chen, C., Shen, Y. D., Xun, G. L., Cai, W. X., Shi, L. J., Xiao, L.,... Ou, J. J. (2017). Aggressive behaviors and treatable risk factors of preschool children with autism spectrum disorder. *Autism Research: Official Journal of the International Society for Autism Research, 10*(6), 1155–1162.

Chevallier, C., Kohls, G., Troiani, V., Brodkin, E. S., & Schultz, R. T. (2012). The social motivation theory of autism. *Trends in Cognitive Sciences, 16*(4), 231–239.

Chezan, L. C., Wolfe, K., & Drasgow, E. (2018). A meta-analysis of functional communication training effects on problem behavior and alternative communicative responses. *Focus on Autism and Other Developmental Disabilities, 33*(4), 195–205. http://doi.org/10.1177/1088357617741294.

Coccaro, E. F., McCloskey, M. S., Fitzgerald, D. A., & Phan, K. L. (2007). Amygdala and orbitofrontal reactivity to social threat in individuals with impulsive aggression. *Biological Psychiatry, 62*(2), 168–178.

Cohen, S., Fulcher, B. D., Rajaratnam, S. M., Conduit, R., Sullivan, J. P., St. Hilaire, M. A.,... McConnell, K. (2018). Sleep patterns predictive of daytime challenging behavior in individuals with low-functioning autism. *Autism Research, 11*(2), 391–403.

Cooper, J. O., Heron, T. E., & Heward, W. L. (2007). *Applied behavior analysis* (2nd ed.) Upper Saddle River, NJ: Pearson.

Crawford, J., Brockel, B., Schauss, S., & Miltenberger, R. G. (1992). A comparison of methods for the functional assessment of stereotypic behavior. *Journal of the Association for Persons with Severe Handicaps, 17*(2), 77–86.

Crick, N. R., & Dodge, K. A. (1994). A review and reformulation of social information-processing mechanisms in children's social adjustment. *Psychological Bulletin, 115*(1), 74.

Crick, N. R., & Dodge, K. A. (1996). Social information-processing mechanisms in reactive and proactive aggression. *Child Development, 67*(3), 993–1002.

Dawson, G., Meltzoff, A. N., Osterling, J., Rinaldi, J., & Brown, E. (1998). Children with autism fail to orient to naturally occurring social stimuli. *Journal of Autism and Developmental Disorders, 28*(6), 479–485.

Deitz, D. E., & Repp, A. C. (1983). Reducing behavior through reinforcement. *Exceptional Education Quarterly, 3*(4), 34–46.

Derby, K. M., Wacker, D. P., Sasso, G., Steege, M., Northup, J., Cigrand, K., & Asmus, J. (1992). Brief functional assessment techniques to evaluate aberrant behavior in an outpatient setting: A summary of 79 cases. *Journal of Applied Behavior Analysis, 25*(3), 713–721.

DeWall, C. N., & Anderson, C. A. (2011). The general aggression model. In M. Mikulincer & P. R. Shaver (Eds.), *Understanding and reducing aggression, violence, and their consequences* (pp. 15–33). Washington, DC: American Psychological Association.

Dodge, K. A., & Coie, J. D. (1987). Social-information-processing factors in reactive and proactive aggression in children's peer groups. *Journal of Personality and Social Psychology, 53*(6), 1146.

Dodge, K. A., Lochman, J. E., Harnish, J. D., Bates, J. E., & Pettit, G. S. (1997). Reactive and proactive aggression in school children and psychiatrically impaired chronically assaultive youth. *Journal of Abnormal Psychology, 106*(1), 37.

Doehring, P., Reichow, B., Palka, T., Phillips, C., & Hagopian, L. (2014). Behavioral approaches to managing severe problem behaviors in children with autism spectrum and related developmental disorders: A descriptive analysis. *Child and Adolescent Psychiatric Clinics of North America, 23*(1), 25–40.

Dollard, J., Miller, N. E., Doob, L. W., Mowrer, O. H., & Sears, R. R. (1939). *Frustration and aggression.* New Haven, CT: Yale University Press.

Dyer, K., Dunlap, G., & Winterling, V. (1990). Effects of choice making on the serious problem behaviors of students with severe handicaps. *Journal of Applied Behavior Analysis, 23*(4), 515–524.

Dziobek, I., Rogers, K., Fleck, S., Bahnemann, M., Heekeren, H. R., Wolf, O. T., & Convit, A. (2008). Dissociation of cognitive and emotional empathy in adults with Asperger syndrome using the Multifaceted Empathy Test (MET). *Journal of Autism and Developmental Disorders, 38*(3), 464–473.

Einfeld, S. L., & Tonge, B. J. (1995). The developmental behavior checklist: The development and validation of an instrument to assess behavioral and emotional disturbance in children and adolescents with mental retardation. *Journal of Autism and Developmental Disorders, 25*(2), 81–104.

Estes, A., Munson, J., Dawson, G., Koehler, E., Zhou, X., & Abbott, R. (2009). Parenting stress and psychological functioning among mothers of preschool children with autism and developmental delay. *Autism, 13*(4), 375–387.

Farmer, C. A., & Aman, M. G. (2009). Development of the Children's Scale of Hostility and Aggression: Reactive/Proactive (C-SHARP). *Research in Developmental Disabilities, 30*(6), 1155–1167.

Farmer, C. A., & Aman, M. G. (2010). Psychometric properties of the Children's Scale of Hostility and Aggression: Reactive/Proactive (C-SHARP). *Research in Developmental Disabilities, 31*(1), 270–280.

Farmer, C. A., & Aman, M. G. (2011). Aggressive behavior in a sample of children with autism spectrum disorders. *Research in Autism Spectrum Disorders, 5*(1), 317–323.

Farmer, C. A., Butter, E., Mazurek, M. O., Cowan, C., Lainhart, J., Cook, E. H.,... Aman, M. (2015). Aggression in children with autism spectrum disorders and a clinic-referred comparison group. *Autism, 19*(3), 281–291.

Farmer, C. A., Kaat, A. J., Mazurek, M. O., Lainhart, J. E., Dewitt, M. B., Cook, E. H.,... Aman, M. G. (2016). Confirmation of the factor structure and measurement invariance of the Children's Scale of Hostility and Aggression: Reactive/Proactive in clinic-referred children with and without autism spectrum disorder. *Journal of Child and Adolescent Psychopharmacology, 26*(1), 10–18.

Fisher, W., Piazza, C., Cataldo, M., Harrell, R., Jefferson, G., & Conner, R. (1993). Functional communication training with and without extinction and punishment. *Journal of Applied Behavior Analysis, 26*(1), 23–36.

Fitzpatrick, S. E., Srivorakiat, L., Wink, L. K., Pedapati, E. V., & Erickson, C. A. (2016). Aggression in autism spectrum disorder: Presentation and treatment options. *Neuropsychiatric Disease and Treatment, 12*, 1525–1538.

Frazier, T. W., Youngstrom, E. A., Haycook, T., Sinoff, A., Dimitriou, F., Knapp, J., & Sinclair, L. (2010). Effectiveness of medication combined with intensive behavioral intervention for reducing aggression in youth with autism spectrum disorder. *Journal of Child and Adolescent Psychopharmacology, 20*(3), 167–177.

Freeman, M. (1994). The differential impact on carers dealing with clients with challenging behaviours. *Journal of Community & Applied Social Psychology, 4*(3), 181–187.

Frith, U. (2001). Mind blindness and the brain in autism. *Neuron, 32*(6), 969–979.

Frye, R. E. (2016). Prevalence, significance and clinical characteristics of seizures, epilepsy and subclinical electrical activity in autism. *North American Journal of Medicine and Science, 8*(3), 113–122.

Fung, L. K., Mahajan, R., Nozzolillo, A., Bernal, P., Krasner, A., Jo, B.,... Hardan, A. Y. (2016). Pharmacologic treatment of severe irritability and problem behaviors in autism: A systematic review and meta-analysis. *Pediatrics, 137*(Suppl 2), S124–S135.

Gardner, L. M., Campbell, J. M., Keisling, B., & Murphy, L. (2018). Correlates of DSM-5 autism spectrum disorder levels of support ratings in a clinical sample. *Journal of Autism and Developmental Disorders, 48*(10), 3513–3523.

Goldman, S. E., McGrew, S., Johnson, K. P., Richdale, A. L., Clemons, T., & Malow, B. A. (2011). Sleep is associated with problem behaviors in children and adolescents with autism spectrum disorders. *Research in Autism Spectrum Disorders, 5*(3), 1223–1229.

Gray, K., Keating, C., Taffe, J., Brereton, A., Einfeld, S., & Tonge, B. (2012). Trajectory of behavior and emotional problems in autism. *American Journal on Intellectual and Developmental Disabilities, 117*(2), 121–133.

Hadwin, J., Baron-Cohen, S., Howlin, P., & Hill, K. (1996). Can we teach children with autism to understand emotions, belief, or pretence? *Development and Psychopathology, 8*(2), 345–365.

Hanley, G. P., Iwata, B. A., & McCord, B. E. (2003). Functional analysis of problem behavior: A review. *Journal of Applied Behavior Analysis, 36*(2), 147–185.

Hass, M. R., Brown, R. S., Brady, J., & Johnson, D. B. (2012). Validating the BASC-TRS for use with children and adolescents with an educational diagnosis of autism. *Remedial and Special Education, 33*(3), 173–183.

Hastings, R. P., & Brown, T. (2002). Coping strategies and the impact of challenging behaviors on special educators' burnout. *Mental Retardation, 40*(2), 148–156.

Healy, O., Brett, D., & Leader, G. (2013). A comparison of experimental functional analysis and the Questions About Behavioral Function (QABF) in the assessment of challenging behavior of individuals with autism. *Research in Autism Spectrum Disorders, 7*(1), 66–81.

Herzinger, C. V., & Campbell, J. M. (2007). Comparing functional assessment methodologies: A quantitative synthesis. *Journal of Autism and Developmental Disorders, 37*(8), 1430–1445.

Heyvaert, M., Saenen, L., Campbell, J. M., Maes, B., & Onghena, P. (2014). Efficacy of behavioral interventions for reducing problem behavior in persons with autism: An updated quantitative synthesis of single-subject research. *Research in Developmental Disabilities, 35*(10), 2463–2476.

Hill, A. P., Zuckerman, K. E., Hagen, A. D., Kriz, D. J., Duvall, S. W., Van Santen, J.,... Fombonne, E. (2014). Aggressive behavior problems in children with autism spectrum disorders: Prevalence and correlates in a large clinical sample. *Research in Autism Spectrum Disorders, 8*(9), 1121–1133.

Horner, R. H., Carr, E. G., Strain, P. S., Todd, A. W., & Reed, H. K. (2002). Problem behavior interventions for young children with autism: A research synthesis. *Journal of Autism and Developmental Disorders, 32*(5), 423–446.

Hubbard, J. A., Smithmyer, C. M., Ramsden, S. R., Parker, E. H., Flanagan, K. D., Dearing, K. F., . . . Simons, R. F. (2002). Observational, physiological, and self-report measures of children's anger: Relations to reactive versus proactive aggression. *Child Development, 73*(4), 1101–1118.

Huesmann, L. R. (1998). The role of social information processing and cognitive schema in the acquisition and maintenance of habitual aggressive behavior. In R.G. Green & E. Donnerstein (Eds.), *Human aggression* (pp. 73–109). San Diego, CA: Academic Press.

Ingram, K., Lewis-Palmer, T., & Sugai, G. (2005). Function-based intervention planning: Comparing the effectiveness of FBA function-based and non-function-based intervention plans. *Journal of Positive Behavior Interventions, 7*(4), 224–236.

Iwata, B. A., Dorsey, M. F., Slifer, K. J., Bauman, K. E., & Richman, G. S. (1982). Toward a functional analysis of self-injury. *Analysis and Intervention in Developmental Disabilities, 2*(1), 3–20.

Iwata, B. A., & Dozier, C. L. (2008). Clinical application of functional analysis methodology. *Behavior Analysis in Practice, 1*(1), 3–9.

Iwata, B. A., Vollmer, T. R., & Zarcone, J. R. (1990). The experimental (functional) analysis of behavior disorders: Methodology, applications, and limitations. In A. C. Repp & N. N. Singh (Eds.), *Perspectives on the use of nonaversive and aversive interventions for persons with developmental disabilities* (pp. 301–330). Sycamore, IL: Sycamore Publishing Company.

Jacobson, J. W., & Ackerman, L. J. (1993). Who is treated using restrictive behavioral procedures? A population perspective. *Research in Developmental Disabilities, 14*(1), 51–65.

Jenkins, R., Rose, J., & Lovell, C. (1997). Psychological well-being of staff working with people who have challenging behaviour. *Journal of Intellectual Disability Research, 41*(6), 502–511.

Jones, A. P., Happé, F. G., Gilbert, F., Burnett, S., & Viding, E. (2010). Feeling, caring, knowing: Different types of empathy deficit in boys with psychopathic tendencies and autism spectrum disorder. *Journal of Child Psychology and Psychiatry, 51*(11), 1188–1197.

Kaartinen, M., Puura, K., Helminen, M., Salmelin, R., Pelkonen, E., & Juujärvi, P. (2014). Reactive aggression among children with and without autism spectrum disorder. *Journal of Autism and Developmental Disorders, 44*(10), 2383–2391.

Kamphaus, R., & Reynolds, C. (2007). *BASC-2 behavioral and emotional screening system manual.* Circle Pines, MN: Pearson.

Kanne, S. M., & Mazurek, M. O. (2011). Aggression in children and adolescents with ASD: Prevalence and risk factors. *Journal of Autism and Developmental Disorders, 41*(7), 926–937.

Kent, J. M., Kushner, S., Ning, X., Karcher, K., Ness, S., Aman, M., . . . Hough, D. (2013). Risperidone dosing in children and adolescents with autistic disorder: A double-blind, placebo-controlled study. *Journal of Autism and Developmental Disorders, 43*(8), 1773–1783.

Kern, L., Choutka, C. M., & Sokol, N. G. (2002). Assessment-based antecedent interventions used in natural settings to reduce challenging behavior: An analysis of the literature. *Education and Treatment of Children, 25*(1), 113–130.

Kozlowski, A. M., & Matson, J. L. (2012). Interview and observation methods in functional assessment. In J. Matson (Ed.) *Functional assessment for challenging behaviors* (pp. 105–124). New York, NY: Springer.

Lahey, B. B., Waldman, I. D., & McBurnett, K. (1999). Annotation: The development of antisocial behavior: An integrative causal model. *Journal of Child Psychology and Psychiatry and Allied Disciplines, 40*(5), 669–682.

Lalli, J. S., Browder, D. M., Mace, F. C., & Brown, D. K. (1993). Teacher use of descriptive analysis data to implement interventions to decrease students' problem behaviors. *Journal of Applied Behavior Analysis, 26*(2), 227–238.

Lamm, C., Granic, I., Zelazo, P. D., & Lewis, M. D. (2011). Magnitude and chronometry of neural mechanisms of emotion regulation in subtypes of aggressive children. *Brain and Cognition, 77*(2), 159–169.

Lecavalier, L. (2006). Behavioral and emotional problems in young people with pervasive developmental disorders: Relative prevalence, effects of subject characteristics, and empirical classification. *Journal of Autism and Developmental Disorders, 36*(8), 1101–1114.

Lecavalier, L., Aman, M. G., Hammer, D., Stoica, W., & Mathews, G. L. (2004). Factor analysis of the Nisonger Child Behavior Rating Form in children with autism spectrum disorders. *Journal of Autism and Developmental Disorders, 34*(6), 709–721.

Lecavalier, L., Leone, S., & Wiltz, J. (2006). The impact of behaviour problems on caregiver stress in young people with autism spectrum disorders. *Journal of Intellectual Disability Research, 50*(3), 172–183.

Lequia, J., Machalicek, W., & Rispoli, M. J. (2012). Effects of activity schedules on challenging behavior exhibited in children with autism spectrum disorders: A systematic review. *Research in Autism Spectrum Disorders, 6*(1), 480–492.

Lerman, D. C., & Iwata, B. A. (1995). Prevalence of the extinction burst and its attenuation during treatment. *Journal of Applied Behavior Analysis, 28*(1), 93–94.

Lerman, D. C., & Iwata, B. A. (1996). Developing a technology for the use of operant extinction in clinical settings: An examination of basic and applied research. *Journal of Applied Behavior Analysis, 29*(3), 345–382.

Lewis, T. J., & Sugai, G. (1996). Functional assessment of problem behavior: A pilot investigation on the comparative and interactive effects of teacher and peer social attention on students in general education settings. *School Psychology Quarterly, 11*(1), 1.

Logan, S. L., Carpenter, L., Leslie, R. S., Garrett-Mayer, E., Hunt, K. J., Charles, J., & Nicholas, J. S. (2015). Aberrant behaviors and co-occurring conditions as predictors of psychotropic polypharmacy among children with autism spectrum disorders. *Journal of Child and Adolescent Psychopharmacology, 25*(4), 323–336.

Lopez-Duran, N. L., Olson, S. L., Hajal, N. J., Felt, B. T., & Vazquez, D. M. (2009). Hypothalamic pituitary adrenal axis functioning in reactive and proactive aggression in children. *Journal of Abnormal Child Psychology, 37*(2), 169–182.

Lozier, L. M., Cardinale, E. M., VanMeter, J. W., & Marsh, A. A. (2014). Mediation of the relationship between callous-unemotional traits and proactive aggression by amygdala response to fear among children with conduct problems. *JAMA Psychiatry, 71*(6), 627–636.

Luiselli, J. K. (2008). Antecedent (preventive) intervention. In J. K. Luiselli, D. C. Russo, W. P. Christina, & S. M Wilczynski (Eds.), *Effective practices for children with autism: Educational and behavior support interventions that work* (p. 393). New York, NY: Oxford University Press.

Lundwall, R. A., Stephenson, K. G., Neeley-Tass, E. S., Cox, J. C., South, M., Bigler, E. D., . . . Lainhart, J. E. (2017). Relationship between brain stem volume and aggression in children diagnosed with autism spectrum disorder. *Research in Autism Spectrum Disorders, 34*, 44–51.

Machalicek, W., O'Reilly, M. F., Beretvas, N., Sigafoos, J., & Lancioni, G. E. (2007). A review of interventions to reduce challenging behavior in school settings for students with autism spectrum disorders. *Research in Autism Spectrum Disorders, 1*(3), 229–246.

MacNaul, H. L., & Neely, L. C. (2018). Systematic review of differential reinforcement of alternative behavior without extinction for individuals with autism. *Behavior Modification, 42*(3), 398–421.

Maenner, M., Arneson, C., Levy, S., Kirby, R., Nicholas, J., & Durkin, M. (2012). Brief report: Association between behavioral features and gastrointestinal problems among children with autism spectrum disorder. *Journal of Autism and Developmental Disorders, 42*(7), 1520–1525.

Mahan, S., & Matson, J. L. (2011). Convergent and discriminant validity of the Autism Spectrum Disorder-Problem Behavior for Children (ASD-PBC) against the Behavioral Assessment System for Children (BASC-2). *Research in Autism Spectrum Disorders, 5*(1), 222–229.

Mandell, D. S. (2008). Psychiatric hospitalization among children with autism spectrum disorders. *Journal of Autism and Developmental Disorders, 38*(6), 1059–1065.

March, R. E., Horner, R. H., Lewis-Palmer, T., Brown, D., Crone, D., Todd, A., & Carr, E. (2000). *Functional Assessment Checklist for Teachers and Staff (FACTS)*. Eugene, OR: Educational and Community Supports.

Marcus, R. N., Owen, R., Kamen, L., Manos, G., McQuade, R. D., Carson, W. H., & Aman, M. G. (2009). A placebo-controlled, fixed-dose study of aripiprazole in children and adolescents with irritability associated with autistic disorder. *Journal of the American Academy of Child and Adolescent Psychiatry, 48*(11), 1110–1119.

Matson, J. L., Gonzalez, M. L., & Rivet, T. T. (2008). Reliability of the Autism Spectrum Disorder-Behavior Problems for Children (ASD-BPC). *Research in Autism Spectrum Disorders, 2*(4), 696–706.

Matson, J. L., & Jang, J. (2014). Treating aggression in persons with autism spectrum disorders: A review. *Research in Developmental Disabilities, 35*(12), 3386–3391.

Matson, J. L., Kuhn, D. E., Dixon, D. R., Mayville, S. B., Laud, R. B., Cooper, C. L., . . . Luke, M. A. (2003). The development and factor structure of the Functional Assessment for Multiple Causality (FACT). *Research in Developmental Disabilities, 24*(6), 485–495.

Matson, J. L., Mahan, S., Hess, J. A., Fodstad, J. C., & Neal, D. (2010). Progression of challenging behaviors in children and adolescents with autism spectrum disorders as measured by the Autism Spectrum Disorders-Problem Behaviors for Children (ASD-PBC). *Research in Autism Spectrum Disorders, 4*(3), 400–404.

Matson, J. L., & Rivet, T. T. (2008a). The effects of severity of autism and PDD-NOS symptoms on challenging behaviors in adults with intellectual disabilities. *Journal of Developmental and Physical Disabilities, 20*(1), 41–51.

Matson, J. L., & Rivet, T. T. (2008b). Reliability and factor structure of the Autism Spectrum Disorders-Behavior Problems for Adults (ASD-BPA) with intellectual disabilities and autism. *Journal of Mental Health Research in Intellectual Disabilities, 1*(1), 34–47.

May, T., Cornish, K., Conduit, R., Rajaratnam, S. M., & Rinehart, N. J. (2015). Sleep in high-functioning children with autism: Longitudinal developmental change and associations with behavior problems. *Behavioral Sleep Medicine, 13*(1), 2–18.

Mayberry, M. L., & Espelage, D. L. (2007). Associations among empathy, social competence, & reactive/proactive aggression subtypes. *Journal of Youth and Adolescence, 36*(6), 787.

Mayes, S. D., Calhoun, S. L., Aggarwal, R., Baker, C., Mathapati, S., Anderson, R., & Petersen, C. (2012). Explosive, oppositional, and aggressive behavior in children with autism compared to other clinical disorders and typical children. *Research in Autism Spectrum Disorders, 6*(1), 1–10.

Mazaleski, J. L., Iwata, B. A., Vollmer, T. R., Zarcone, J. R., & Smith, R. G. (1993). Analysis of the reinforcement and extinction components in DRO contingencies with self-injury. *Journal of Applied Behavior Analysis, 26*(2), 143–156.

Mazefsky, C. A., Schreiber, D. R., Olino, T. M., & Minshew, N. J. (2014). The association between emotional and behavioral problems and gastrointestinal symptoms among children with high-functioning autism. *Autism, 18*(5), 493–501.

Mazurek, M. O., Engelhardt, C. R., Hilgard, J., & Sohl, K. (2016). Bedtime electronic media use and sleep in children with autism spectrum disorder. *Journal of Developmental and Behavioral Pediatrics: JDBP, 37*(7), 525–531.

Mazurek, M. O., Kanne, S. M., & Wodka, E. L. (2013). Physical aggression in children and adolescents with autism spectrum disorders. *Research in Autism Spectrum Disorders, 7*(3), 455–465.

Mazurek, M. O., & Sohl, K. (2016). Sleep and behavioral problems in children with autism spectrum disorder. *Journal of Autism and Developmental Disorders, 46*(6), 1906–1915.

McCracken, J. T., McGough, J., Shah, B., Cronin, P., Hong, D., Aman, M. G., . . . Hollway, J. (2002). Risperidone in children with autism and serious behavioral problems. *New England Journal of Medicine, 347*(5), 314–321.

McDougle, C. J., Holmes, J. P., Carlson, D. C., Pelton, G. H., Cohen, D. J., & Price, L. H. (1998). A double-blind, placebo-controlled study of risperidone in adults with autistic disorder and other pervasive developmental disorders. *Archives of General Psychiatry, 55*(7), 633–641.

McElhanon, B. O., McCracken, C., Karpen, S., & Sharp, W. G. (2014). Gastrointestinal symptoms in autism spectrum disorder: A meta-analysis. *Pediatrics, 133*(5), 872–883.

McGuire, K., Fung, L. K., Hagopian, L., Vasa, R. A., Mahajan, R., Bernal, P., . . . Whitaker, A. H. (2016). Irritability and problem behavior in autism spectrum disorder: A practice pathway for pediatric primary care. *Pediatrics, 137*(Suppl 2), S136–S148.

Medeiros, K., Mazurek, M. O., & Kanne, S. (2017). Investigating the factor structure of the child behavior checklist in a large sample of children with autism spectrum disorder. *Research in Autism Spectrum Disorders, 40*, 24–40.

Moyer, K. E. (1976). *The psychobiology of aggression*. New York, NY: Harper & Row.

Mulligan, C. K., & Trauner, D. A. (2014). Incidence and behavioral correlates of epileptiform abnormalities in autism spectrum disorders. *Journal of Autism and Developmental Disorders, 44*(2), 452–458.

Murphy, G., MacDonald, S., Hall, S., & Oliver, C. (2000). Aggression and the termination of "rituals": A new variant of the escape function for challenging behavior? *Research in Developmental Disabilities, 21*(1), 43–59.

Nagin, D. S., & Tremblay, R. E. (2001). Parental and early childhood predictors of persistent physical aggression in boys from kindergarten to high school. *Archives of General Psychiatry, 58*(4), 389–394.

National Institute of Child Health and Human Development (NICHD) Early Child Care Research Network, & Arsenio, W. F. (2004). Trajectories of physical aggression from toddlerhood to middle childhood: Predictors, correlates, and outcomes. *Monographs of the Society for Research in Child Development, 69*(4), i–143.

Neumann, I. D., Veenema, A. H., & Beiderbeck, D. I. (2010). Aggression and anxiety: Social context and neurobiological links. *Frontiers in Behavioral Neuroscience, 4*, 12.

Newcomer, L. L., & Lewis, T. J. (2004). Functional behavioral assessment: An investigation of assessment reliability and effectiveness of function-based interventions. *Journal of Emotional and Behavioral Disorders, 12*(3), 168–181.

Nøttestad, J. A., & Linaker, O. (2002). Predictors for attacks on people after deinstitutionalization. *Journal of Intellectual Disability Research, 46*(6), 493–502.

O'Neill, R. E., Horner, R. H., Albin, R. W., Storey, K., & Sprague, J. R. (1990). *Functional analysis of problem behavior: A practical assessment guide.* Sycamore, IL: Sycamore Publishing.

Ortiz, J., & Raine, A. (2004). Heart rate level and antisocial behavior in children and adolescents: A meta-analysis. *Journal of the American Academy of Child and Adolescent Psychiatry, 43*(2), 154–162.

Owen, R., Sikich, L., Marcus, R. N., Corey-Lisle, P., Manos, G., McQuade, R. D., . . . Findling, R. L. (2009). Aripiprazole in the treatment of irritability in children and adolescents with autistic disorder. *Pediatrics, 124*(6), 1533–1540.

Paclawskyj, T. R., Matson, J. L., Rush, K. S., Smalls, Y., & Vollmer, T. R. (2000). Questions About Behavioral Function (QABF): A behavioral checklist for functional assessment of aberrant behavior. *Research in Developmental Disabilities, 21*(3), 223–229.

Pandolfi, V., Magyar, C. I., & Dill, C. A. (2009). Confirmatory factor analysis of the child behavior checklist 1.5–5 in a sample of children with autism spectrum disorders. *Journal of Autism and Developmental Disorders, 39*(7), 986–995.

Pandolfi, V., Magyar, C. I., & Dill, C. A. (2012). An initial psychometric evaluation of the CBCL 6–18 in a sample of youth with autism spectrum disorders. *Research in Autism Spectrum Disorders, 6*(1), 96–108.

Paus, T. (2005). Mapping brain development and aggression. *Canadian Child and Adolescent Psychiatry Review, 14*(1), 10–15.

Postorino, V., Sharp, W. G., McCracken, C. E., Bearss, K., Burrell, T. L., Evans, A. N., & Scahill, L. (2017). A systematic review and meta-analysis of parent training for disruptive behavior in children with autism spectrum disorder. *Clinical Child and Family Psychology Review, 20*(4), 391–402.

Pouw, L. B., Rieffe, C., Oosterveld, P., Huskens, B., & Stockmann, L. (2013). Reactive/proactive aggression and affective/cognitive empathy in children with ASD. *Research in Developmental Disabilities, 34*(4), 1256–1266.

Price, J. M., & Dodge, K. A. (1989). Reactive and proactive aggression in childhood: Relations to peer status and social context dimensions. *Journal of Abnormal Child Psychology, 17*(4), 455–471.

Pugliese, C. E., White, B. A., White, S. W., & Ollendick, T. H. (2013). Social anxiety predicts aggression in children with ASD: Clinical comparisons with socially anxious and oppositional youth. *Journal of Autism and Developmental Disorders, 43*(5), 1205–1213.

Reese, R. M., Richman, D. M., Belmont, J. M., & Morse, P. (2005). Functional characteristics of disruptive behavior in developmentally disabled children with and without autism. *Journal of Autism and Developmental Disorders, 35*(4), 419–428.

Reese, R. M., Richman, D. M., Zarcone, J., & Zarcone, T. (2003). Individualizing functional assessments for children with autism: The contribution of perseverative behavior and sensory disturbances to disruptive behavior. *Focus on Autism and Other Developmental Disabilities, 18*(2), 89–94.

Reeve, C. E., & Carr, E. G. (2000). Prevention of severe behavior problems in children with developmental disorders. *Journal of Positive Behavior Interventions, 2*(3), 144–160.

Rojahn, J., Matson, J. L., Lott, D., Esbensen, A. J., & Smalls, Y. (2001). The behavior problems inventory: An instrument for the assessment of self-injury, stereotyped behavior, and aggression/destruction in individuals with developmental disabilities. *Journal of Autism and Developmental Disorders, 31*(6), 577–588.

Romaniuk, C., & Miltenberger, R. G. (2001). The influence of preference and choice of activity on problem behavior. *Journal of Positive Behavior Interventions, 3*(3), 152–159.

Rutter, M., Greenfeld, D., & Lockyer, L. (1967). A five to fifteen year follow-up study of infantile psychosis: II. Social and behavioural outcome. *British Journal of Psychiatry, 113*(504), 1183–1199.

Schneider, I., Regenbogen, C., Kohn, N., Zepf, F. D., Bubenzer-Busch, S., Schneider, F., . . . Habel, U. (2015). Reduced responsiveness to social provocation in autism spectrum disorder. *Autism Research, 8*(3), 297–306.

Shea, S., Turgay, A., Carroll, A., Schulz, M., Orlik, H., Smith, I., & Dunbar, F. (2004). Risperidone in the treatment of disruptive behavioral symptoms in children with autistic and other pervasive developmental disorders. *Pediatrics, 114*(5), e634–e641.

Shic, F., Bradshaw, J., Klin, A., Scassellati, B., & Chawarska, K. (2011). Limited activity monitoring in toddlers with autism spectrum disorder. *Brain Research, 1380*, 246–254.

Siegel, A., & Victoroff, J. (2009). Understanding human aggression: New insights from neuroscience. *International Journal of Law and Psychiatry, 32*(4), 209–215.

Singh, N. N., Matson, J. L., Lancioni, G. E., Singh, A. N., Adkins, A. D., McKeegan, G. F., & Brown, S. W. (2006). Questions About Behavioral Function in Mental Illness (QABF-MI): A behavior checklist for functional assessment of maladaptive behavior exhibited by individuals with mental illness. *Behavior Modification, 30*(6), 739–751.

Skinner, B. F. (1953). *Science and human behavior.* New York, NY: Simon and Schuster.

Smith, I. M., & Bryson, S. E. (1994). Imitation and action in autism: A critical review. *Psychological Bulletin, 116*(2), 259.

Smith, R. G., & Iwata, B. A. (1997). Antecedent influences on behavior disorders. *Journal of Applied Behavior Analysis, 30*(2), 343–375.

Smith, K. R., & Matson, J. L. (2010). Behavior problems: Differences among intellectually disabled adults with co-morbid autism spectrum disorders and epilepsy. *Research in Developmental Disabilities, 31*(5), 1062–1069.

Sumer, M., Atik, L., Unal, A., Emre, U., & Atasoy, H. (2007). Frontal lobe epilepsy presented as ictal aggression. *Neurological Sciences, 28*(1), 48–51.

Tassé, M. J., Aman, M. G., Hammer, D., & Rojahn, J. (1996). The Nisonger Child Behavior Rating Form: Age and gender effects and norms. *Research in Developmental Disabilities, 17*(1), 59–75.

Taylor, J. L., & Seltzer, M. M. (2010). Changes in the autism behavioral phenotype during the transition to adulthood. *Journal of Autism and Developmental Disorders, 40*(12), 1431–1446.

Tomanik, S., Harris, G. E., & Hawkins, J. (2004). The relationship between behaviours exhibited by children with autism and maternal stress. *Journal of Intellectual and Developmental Disability, 29*(1), 16–26.

Tremblay, R. E., Nagin, D. S., Seguin, J. R., Zoccolillo, M., Zelazo, P. D., Boivin, M., . . . Japel, C. (2004). Physical aggression during early childhood: Trajectories and predictors. *Pediatrics, 114*(1), e43–e50.

Tsakanikos, E., Costello, H., Holt, G., Sturmey, P., & Bouras, N. (2007). Behaviour management problems as predictors of psychotropic medication and use of psychiatric services in adults with autism. *Journal of Autism and Developmental Disorders, 37*(6), 1080–1085.

Van Goozen, S. H., Fairchild, G., Snoek, H., & Harold, G. T. (2007). The evidence for a neurobiological model of childhood antisocial behavior. *Psychological Bulletin, 133*(1), 149.

Volker, M. A., Lopata, C., Smerbeck, A. M., Knoll, V. A., Thomeer, M. L., Toomey, J. A., & Rodgers, J. D. (2010). BASC-2 PRS profiles for students with high-functioning autism spectrum disorders. *Journal of Autism and Developmental Disorders, 40*(2), 188–199.

Vollmer, T. R., & Iwata, B. A. (1992). Differential reinforcement as treatment for behavior disorders: Procedural and functional variations. *Research in Developmental Disabilities, 13*(4), 393–417.

Weston, R., Hodges, A., & Davis, T. N. (2017). Differential reinforcement of other behaviors to treat challenging behaviors among children with autism: A systematic and quality review. *Behavior Modification, 42*(4), 584–609. http://doi.org/10.1177/0145445517743487.

Wong, C., Odom, S. L., Hume, K. A., Cox, A. W., Fettig, A., Kucharczyk, S., . . . Schultz, T. R. (2015). Evidence-based practices for children, youth, and young adults with autism spectrum disorder: A comprehensive review. *Journal of Autism and Developmental Disorders, 45*(7), 1951–1966.

Woodman, A. C., Mailick, M. R., & Greenberg, J. S. (2016). Trajectories of internalizing and externalizing symptoms among adults with autism spectrum disorders. *Development and Psychopathology, 28*(2), 565–581.

Woodman, A. C., Smith, L. E., Greenberg, J. S., & Mailick, M. R. (2015). Change in autism symptoms and maladaptive behaviors in adolescence and adulthood: The role of positive family processes. *Journal of Autism and Developmental Disorders, 45*(1), 111–126.

Zarcone, J. R., Iwata, B. A., Mazaleski, J. L., & Smith, R. G. (1994). Momentum and extinction effects on self-injurious escape behavior and noncompliance. *Journal of Applied Behavior Analysis, 27*(4), 649–658.

CHAPTER

16

Understanding Executive Function Challenges in Autism Spectrum Disorder

Cara E. Pugliese, Gregory L. Wallace, Laura Gutermuth Anthony, *and* Lauren Kenworthy

Abstract

The construct of executive function (EF) has been referred to as an "umbrella" term for a collection of higher order cognitive processes that guide and manage goal-directed behavior and problem solving. EF impairments are common in autism spectrum disorder (ASD). EF is centrally related to characteristics of ASD and real-world outcomes such as adaptive behavior and quality of life. This chapter describes the profile of EF impairment in ASD and reviews its development across the lifespan and how it affects various aspects of daily functioning (social skills, adaptive behavior, co-occurring psychiatric conditions). The chapter also addresses the challenges assessing of EF and describes promising interventions to promote executive skills in ASD.

Keywords: executive function, autism spectrum disorder, assessment, evidence-based treatment, lifespan

Overview

The construct of executive function (EF) has been referred to as an "umbrella" term for a collection of higher order cognitive processes that guide and manage goal-directed behavior and problem solving. Although there are at least 33 definitions of EF (Sergeant, Geurts, & Oosterlan, 2002), most researchers consider it to be composed of distinct but interrelated self-regulatory abilities, including flexibility, planning, inhibition, working memory, generativity, and organization (Gioia, Isquith, Guy, & Kenworthy, 2000; Miyake et al., 2000; Stuss & Alexander, 2000).

Research into the neural basis of EF has long focused on the prefrontal cortex. ASD was first described as a frontal disorder of executive dysfunction by Damasio and Maurer (1978), based on the inflexibility, insistence on sameness, and presence of perseverative behavior commonly seen in ASD. Since then, over 550 articles have been published on ASD and EF. It remains unclear whether EF is a causal factor of ASD (Ozonoff, Pennington, & Rogers, 1991), but EF has been implicated across several important domains of impairment in ASD, including theory of mind (Pellicano, 2007; Russell, Mauthner, Sharpe, & Tidswell, 1991), social cognition (Ozonoff et al., 1991), social skills (Leung, Vogan, Powell, Anagnostou, & Taylor, 2016), restricted and repetitive behaviors (Kenworthy, Black, Harrison, della Rosa, & Wallace, 2009; Lopez, Lincoln, Ozonoff, & Lai, 2005), adaptive behavior (Pugliese et al., 2015, 2016), and quality of life (de Vries & Geurts, 2015). Table 16.1 presents the most common EF impairments implicated in ASD.

Profile of EF in ASD

Over the last four decades of research, the scientific literature has consistently demonstrated broad executive dysfunction in ASD, with strong evidence that cognitive flexibility and planning skills are robustly impacted, and emerging evidence that inhibition and working memory are also affected in youth with ASD without intellectual disability (ID). However, results of different reviews vary based on moderators such as cognitive ability and task type.

Table 16.1. Domains of Executive Function Most Commonly Implicated in Autism Spectrum Disorder

Flexibility (set shifting)	The ability to intentionally shift to a different thought or action in response to contextual changes (e.g., Rumsey, 1985)
Planning	The ability to sequence actions, monitor progress, re-evaluate the plan, and adjust accordingly to meet a specific goal (e.g., Ozonoff et al., 1991)
Inhibition	The ability to deliberately suppress an automatic behavioral response to reach a goal. Inhibition of a prepotent response refers to suppression of a dominant motor response, whereas interference control reflects the ability to ignore irrelevant information in service of a goal (e.g., Geurts, van den Bergh, & Ruzzano, 2014).
Working memory	The ability to hold information in mind for the purpose of completing a task, encoding information, or generating goals (Bennetto, Pennington, & Rogers, 1996)
Generativity	The ability to generate novel ideas and behaviors (Turner, 1997)
Organization	The ability to integrate information and manage complexity (Kenworthy et al., 2005)

The first review of EF in autism (Pennington & Ozonoff, 1996) indicated that individuals with ASD demonstrate broad deficits in EF compared to typically developing (TD) individuals with a larger effect size (d = 0.98) than in other developmental disorder groups on a variety of neuropsychological tasks across all ages and levels of functioning. The tasks that most successfully discriminated those with and without ASD were the Tower of Hanoi (Hinz, 1989), a test of mental planning, and the Wisconsin Card Sort Task (WCST; Berg, 1948), a widely used neuropsychological test that requires the flexible sorting of cards into piles according to a nonspoken rule the examinee needs to discover based on the examiner's feedback regarding whether the sort was correct or incorrect, which were considered to indicate specific weaknesses in cognitive inflexibility and poor planning, respectively. In these studies, inhibition and working memory remained intact and were not substantially different from controls. A later review by Sergeant, Geurts, and Oosterlaan (2002) also aimed to distinguish differentiating EF features across a variety of neurodevelopmental disorders and found similar results to Pennington and Ozonoff (1996). Sergeant and colleagues (2002) found that the WCST differentiates youth with ASD and average cognitive abilities from TD children and, to a lesser extent, children with ADHD. Youth with ASD tend to make more perseverative errors than those with ADHD, reflecting greater difficulties with cognitive flexibility. Youth with ASD also consistently performed worse than TD youth on Tower tasks, reflecting deficits in planning. Finally, there was also a relative absence of problems with inhibition in autistic youth as compared to those with ADHD and aggressive disorders.

Hill's 2004 review supported prior research indicating core impairment in planning and flexibility but also found difficulties in inhibition of a prepotent response and the ability to generate novel ideas and behaviors. Hill noted that the pattern of strengths and weaknesses may differ across development and the type of test used to assess EF, and called for the use of a wider range of tasks with increasing difficulty to isolate specific EF skills and more thoroughly match control groups to establish clearer performance profiles. Kenworthy, Yerys, Anthony, and Wallace (2008) reviewed studies published after the Hill 2004 review and confirmed and expanded her findings, adding evidence of working memory deficits in cognitively able youth to the previously described flexibility, planning, and inhibition problems in ASD.

More recent meta-analyses and quantitative reviews have sought to examine individual subdomains of EF more thoroughly, particularly in the areas of inhibition and cognitive flexibility, while accounting for moderators that may affect performance, such as level of cognitive ability, age, and type of task. Geurts, van den Bergh, and Ruzzano (2014) undertook a meta-analysis on inhibition in ASD to understand discrepancies in previous research indicating evidence for and against impaired functioning. Their review of 41 studies, which included 1,091 people with ASD (mean age 14.8 years) and 1,306 TD controls (mean age 13.8 years) aged 4 to 83 years, assessed performance on common neuropsychological tasks of prepotent response inhibition (e.g., Go/No-Go and Stop signal tasks) and interference control (e.g., Stroop, Flanker, and Simon). Results indicated an overall performance deficit on inhibition of a prepotent response (suppression of a dominant motor response) and resistance to distractor interference (the ability to ignore irrelevant information to process target stimuli), but a larger effect for the former. Moderator analyses indicated poorer prepotent response inhibition with age and improved interference inhibition with higher IQ.

Leung and Zakanis (2014) questioned whether cognitive flexibility is a hallmark characteristic of all individuals with ASD. In their quantitative review of 72 studies spanning a variety of neuropsychological and questionnaire measures, they found that autistic individuals without ID demonstrated variability in the magnitude of impairment depending on the type of assessment measure used. Self-report and parent report of shifting difficulties on the Behavior Rating Inventory of Executive Function (BRIEF; Gioia et al., 2000) robustly discriminated between autistic and TD individuals. Conversely, none of the neuropsychological tests reached this benchmark. Although individuals with ASD demonstrated impairment on these measures, there was a substantial overlap between individuals with ASD and controls on intact performance, reflecting a lack of ecological validity. To further understand variability in performance, Landry and Al-Taie (2016) conducted a meta-analysis of 31 studies of the WCST spanning 30 years. They confirmed impaired performance on the WSCT in ASD. Results further indicated that older children and adults and individuals with higher performance IQ make fewer perseverative errors (continuing with a previously correct rule despite negative feedback—reflecting less difficulty with cognitive flexibility). Contrary to prior speculation that the social interaction of the task would compound flexibility problems, individuals with ASD had just as much difficulty with flexibility when the task was administered by a computer as when it was administered by a person.

Lai and colleagues (2017) conducted the first meta-analysis to examine the performance on neuropsychological EF tasks in autistic children and adolescents without ID (e.g., IQ > 70, n = 2,986) compared to TD individuals (n = 3,005) while accounting for the impact of co-occurring ADHD. They included 98 studies published since 2015 in the meta-analysis and found that verbal working memory, spatial working memory, flexibility, planning, and generativity were moderately impaired in ASD. After excluding individuals with ASD and co-occurring ADHD or ensuring equivalence of cognitive abilities in both groups, flexibility, generativity, and working memory impairments remained significant, leading the authors to conclude that they represent "core EF deficits" in ASD. In accordance with Leung and Zakanis's (2014) study, there was large variability in effect sizes of cognitive flexibility based on task administered. Generativity was reported to be more impaired in the absence of ADHD and worse when there was a verbal demand. Contrary to the earlier studies, they suggest that planning and inhibition may not be the most prominent deficits in ASD.

Finally, Demetriou and colleagues (2018) conducted the most recent meta-analysis of EF in ASD, using 235 studies up to 2016 encompassing 14,081 participants (ASD = 6,816; neurotypical or sibling controls = 7,265). In an attempt to discern moderators of differential performance, they examined the effects of age, ASD diagnostic tool, and EF assessment tool format (computer vs. traditional administration), among others. There was a moderate effect size of overall executive dysfunction in ASD that was relatively stable across development. Contrary to prior research, individual EF subdomains of concept formation, cognitive flexibility, fluency, planning, response inhibition, and working memory were not differentially impaired and all showed impairments of a moderate effect size. Notably, studies that utilized ratings of EF (self- and parent report) had higher effect sizes, ranging from large to very large, than those using psychometric tests or experimental tasks. Interestingly, a smaller effect size between ASD and neurotypical controls was found when only one of the Autism Diagnostic Observation Schedule (ADOS; Lord et al., 1999) or Autism Diagnostic Interview (ADI; Le Couteur et al., 1989) was used for diagnosis, which the authors attributed to mean that these individuals may have been less severely impacted by ASD.

Overall, recent meta-analyses support the identification of EF as a primary deficit in autism with many domains of EF affected. Over time, more narrowly defined EF deficits in flexibility and planning have been augmented with accumulating evidence of problems across many EF domains, including inhibition, working memory, generativity, and organization, leading some (Demetriou et al., 2018) to argue that EF is globally impaired in autism. This finding is not as inconsistent with the original focus on flexibility and planning as it might appear, because early studies relied heavily on two tests of EF, which, despite being described as measures of flexibility (WCST) and planning (Tower tasks), have been shown to tap multiple EF abilities, or global EF. Evidence from a large factor analytic study of parent-reported EF problems in children with ASD without ID identifies flexibility problems as a key driver of EF deficits in multiple domains (Granader et al., 2014), introducing the possibility that flexibility deficits are uniquely severely impacted and important in the ASD EF profile of global deficits (Craig et al., 2016).

Prevalence and Course

EF is impaired across development from preschool through adulthood in people with ASD without ID (Garon, Smith, & Bryson, 2018; Dijkhuis, Ziermans, Van Rijn, Staal, & Swaab, 2017). Although the majority of research has emphasized deficits in school-age children and adolescents, there is now convincing documentation of the emergence of EF problems in autistic children under 6 years of age and the maintenance of those deficits into adulthood. Although EF is atypical throughout development in autism, it is also plastic. There is consistent evidence that EF abilities improve with time, even though they do not appear to normalize.

Historically, EF problems have not been reliably identified in autistic preschoolers with cognitive delays (Dawson et al., 2002; Griffith, Pennington, & Wehner, 1999; Stahl & Pry, 2002; Yerys, Hepburn, Pennington, & Rogers, 2007), but older preschoolers and those without ID are consistently reported to have EF deficits relative to their TD peers (Dawson, Meltzoff, Osterling, & Rinaldi, 1998; Faja & Dawson, 2013; McEvoy, Rogers, & Pennington, 1993; Pellicano, 2007, 2017; Smithson, 2013). Garon and colleagues (2018) provide a summary of findings regarding preschool EF that shows a clear pattern of deficits in inhibition and attention shifting in children over 54 months of chronological age or over 42 months mental age. For the younger (chronological and mental age) children, findings on EF tasks are mostly within normal limits. Parent-reported EF problems, however, are pervasive throughout the preschool years (Smithson et al., 2013). Garon and colleagues (2018) argue for the importance of developmentally appropriate EF tasks for the younger preschoolers. Using a battery of simple and complex measures of working memory, inhibition, and shifting, they found evidence for global EF impairment across the preschool age and mental ability range. EF deficits were more evident on tasks that were appropriate to the child's developmental level and more substantial for inhibition and shifting than in working memory.

Although still relatively rare, there are an increasing number of longitudinal studies demonstrating that EF improves with age in ASD without ID, but does not reach the levels seen in TD individuals (Luna, Doll, Hegedus, Minshew, & Sweeney, 2007; O'Hearn, Asato, Ordaz, & Luna, 2008). Early investigations of children with ASD and cognitive impairments failed to find age-related gains in EF skills (Griffith et al., 1999; Ozonoff & McEvoy, 1994). More recent longitudinal studies in children with ASD and average cognitive abilities find growth in, but not normalization of, planning, working memory, inhibition, and "hot" EF affective decision-making abilities over time (Kouklari, Tsermentseli, & Monks, 2018; Pellicano, 2010). Rosenthal and colleagues (2013) describe cross-sectional parent-report data that indicate age-related increases in metacognitive (working memory, initiation, organization) problems in adolescents with ASD. This increased concern may reflect the fact that unlike their TD peers, metacognitive abilities in ASD are not improving rapidly enough in late childhood and adolescence to keep pace with increased environmental demands. Despite growth in EF abilities, the gap between environmental expectations and the actual ability of a child with ASD to follow multistep directions, keep school materials organized, and be a "self-starter" may widen over time.

Recent meta-analyses provide evidence of EF deficits across the age span in ASD, a finding that is consistent with the previously cited longitudinal data showing a failure of EF abilities to normalize with age in ASD. Data indicating that some specific subdomains of EF become less discrepant from normative expectations with age is not consistent across studies. Lai et al. (2017) found relatively static deficits across subdomains of EF in children and adolescents with ASD. The exception was flexibility, for which a meta-regression indicated a 0.06 effect size reduction in deficits in ASD for each year of increase in mean age, as compared to TD individuals. Another recent meta-analysis included adults and also found generally static deficits with the exception of working memory (Demetriou et al., 2017). A meta-analysis focused on inhibition found a decrease in prepotent inhibition deficits with age (Geurts et al., 2014).

Studies of EF in ASD during adulthood are growing in number, although they are far fewer than studies of children. As with the broader literature on EF in ASD, most adult studies have excluded individuals diagnosed with ID (in addition to ASD) and have employed performance-based EF tasks as their metrics of interest. Indeed, the first investigations examining EF in ASD were completed with adults (Rumsey, 1985; Rumsey & Hamburger, 1988, 1990). These early studies revealed cognitive flexibility difficulties based on performance on the WCST and the Trail Making Test (Reitan & Wolfson, 1993). Subsequent studies have provided mixed evidence for EF deficits in adults with ASD as compared to TD controls. Some studies demonstrate flexibility, generativity, and spatial working memory deficits in adults with ASD (Ambery, Russell, Perry, Morris, & Murphy, 2006; Geurts & Vissers, 2012; Sachse et al., 2013; Williams, Goldstein, Carpenter, & Minshew, 2005); however, these impairments are not universally documented when utilizing performance-based, laboratory-administered tasks (Geurts & Vissers, 2012; Hill & Bird, 2006; Nakahachi et al., 2006; Sachse et al., 2013; Towgood, Meuwese, Gilbert, Turner, & Burgess, 2009). A smaller set of studies of adults has employed assessment methods meant to better capture real-world functioning, with most studies employing the use of EF-related rating scales. One study utilized other informant ratings from the adult version of the BRIEF (BRIEF-A; Roth, Isquith, & Gioia, 2005) and found deficits in ASD, particularly in flexibility, working memory, and planning/organization (Wallace et al., 2016). These findings parallel not only the pediatric literature using the school-age version of the BRIEF (Granader et al., 2014) but also two recent studies based on self-ratings of EF-related behavioral challenges experienced by adults with ASD (Davids, Groen, Berg, Tucha, & van Balkom, 2016; Dijkhuis, Ziermans, Van Rijn, Staal, & Swaab, 2017).

Akin to the typical emergence and dynamic development of EF skills during childhood and adolescence and into young adulthood, there is a subsequent decline that occurs, albeit more protracted, during middle-later adulthood in the general population. Whether measured using performance-based lab tasks or with ecologically valid assessments, the evidence converges to document age-related declines in EF in the general population, particularly during older adulthood (Crawford, Bryan, Luszcz, Obonsawin, & Stewart, 2000). Studies of the relationship between age and EF in ASD during adulthood have only recently been conducted and thus far have been limited to cross-sectional investigations with mixed findings. For some aspects of EF, such as working memory, there is evidence for a reduced age effect during adulthood in ASD compared to normative expectations (e.g., Lever & Geurts, 2016), whereas for cognitive flexibility, there is indication of greater age-related decline in ASD (e.g., Powell, Klinger, & Klinger, 2017). Yet other studies find no or small differences in the relationship between age and EF performance in ASD compared to normative expectations for these and other EF domains (e.g., Abbott, Happé, & Charlton, 2018). True developmental effects require longitudinal studies to evaluate trajectories of EF change over time during adulthood and to evaluate similarities and discrepancies from neurotypical aging.

The Contribution of EF to Outcome in ASD

ASD persists into adulthood and outcomes are poor compared not only to the TD population but also to individuals with ID and other neurodevelopmental disorders (Howlin, Moss, Savage, & Rutter, 2013; Roux et al., 2013). Many adults with ASD are underemployed, underpaid, and isolated (Shattuck et al., 2012), with 9% in one study remaining consistently employed in full-time competitive positions compared to 90% to 96% of the general U.S. population (Taylor, Henninger, & Mailick, 2015). Even in individuals without ID, who make up two thirds of children with ASD, as few as 9% reach full functional independence as adults (Farley et al., 2009). There is growing evidence that impaired EF is related to factors affecting outcome in ASD in the areas of social cognition and social skills, academic skills, adaptive behavior, co-occurring psychiatric problems, and employment. Understanding and confirming these links is critical to improving outcome via targeting EF through interventions, discussed later in this chapter.

The Impact of EF on Social Cognition and Social Skills

EF abilities drive play skills (Faja et al., 2016), social competence (Pellicano, 2013), and theory of mind (Pellicano, 2007, 2010) in autism. Longitudinal investigations, designed to address causality, indicate that these relationships are consistently found to be unidirectional, as social abilities do not predict later EF abilities. A significant component of social competency for children is developed and expressed in play. Like social interactions themselves, play requires flexible behavior, generation of novel ideas and uses of objects, and inhibition of impulses. EF (inhibition and spatial working memory) in a group of 2- to 4-year-olds with ASD and "basic" expressive or receptive language skills (T-score > 20 on the Mullen Scales of Early Learning; mean group expressive and receptive T-scores = 26) predicted play skills at 5 to 6 years of age and this relationship was unidirectional (Faja et al., 2016).

Griffith et al. (1999) first reported that EF is a precursor to social skills, indicating that flexibility in young children with ASD predicted social communication 1 year later. Pellicano (2013) expanded on this finding, reporting that planning, flexibility, and inhibition predicted later social communication independent of language skills, nonverbal ability, and theory of mind in autistic children. EF, specifically flexibility, is also reported to predict later social skills in adolescents and adults with ASD (Berger, Aerts, Spaendonck, Cools, & Teunisse, 2003; Szatmari, Bartolucci, Bremner, Bond, & Rich, 1989). This relationship has been confirmed using parent report of EF abilities (Pugliese et al., 2015) as well as task-based studies. In addition to these longitudinal investigations, intervention studies show that targeting EF skills in school-age children improves social functioning (Kenworthy, Anthony, Naiman, et al., 2014).

The role of EF abilities as a precursor to social abilities has been most extensively investigated in relationship to social cognition tasks tapping theory of mind (ToM). This relationship was reported over a decade ago by Tager-Flusberg and Joseph (2005), who found performance on measures of working memory predicted ToM abilities 1 year later, independent of initial ToM scores and verbal ability. Pellicano (2010) has extended and confirmed this causal link, showing that planning, flexibility, and inhibition in early childhood predicted ToM abilities 3 years later, even after controlling for the effects of age and cognitive ability. Kouklari and colleagues (2018) confirm Pellicano's unidirectional findings with a "cool" EF measure of working memory and extend them to a "hot" (motivationally salient) delay discounting EF task that uses meaningful rewards and losses for the individual (e.g., would you rather have $10 for sure in 30 days or $2 for sure right now), both of which predict later ToM in children with autism. In an exciting recent publication, these causal linkages have been reframed with an investigation demonstrating that EF abilities, along with general intelligence and anxiety, allow some with autism to compensate for deficits in ToM (Livingston, Colvert, Social Relationships Study Team, Bolton, & Happé, 2018).

The Impact of EF on Academic Skills

Early EF abilities are well-established precursors of academic skills in TD children (e.g., Blair & Raver, 2015), and there have been two recent studies that extend this relationship to autism. One found that preschoolers' inhibitory control and working memory were uniquely related to school readiness (Pellicano, 2017) and the other that performance on a spatial reversal task tapping working memory and flexibility at age 6 predicted math achievement at age 9 beyond the contributions of IQ (St. John, Dawson, & Estes, 2018).

The Impact of EF on Adaptive Behavior

Adaptive behavior is a term used to indicate a person's ability to function independently in his or her environment. Increased emphasis has been placed on understanding real-world adaptive behavior as it relates to functional outcome given that independent living status is more dependent on adaptive behavior than cognitive ability or ASD symptomatology (Farley et al., 2009; Kanne et al., 2011). Adaptive functioning reflects the ability to translate cognitive potential into real-world skills necessary to perform activities of daily living, such as effectively communicating with others, participating in community activities, and developing meaningful relationships (Klin et al., 2007; Sparrow, Balla, & Cicchetti, 1984). For individuals with ASD without ID, the discrepancy between cognitive and adaptive ability spans one to two standard deviations across childhood and adolescence and this discrepancy may increase with age, indicating a failure to acquire adaptive skills at rates corresponding with gains in IQ (Pugliese et al., 2015). To date, the research examining the relationship between EF and adaptive behavior has used samples of youth with ASD without ID. Prior studies have found that IQ, sex, and ASD symptoms generally have small effects on adaptive behavior in cognitively able individuals, whereas ratings of EF in real-world settings may have greater effects on how a child is able to apply cognitive abilities to everyday activities (Gardiner & Iarocci, 2018; Gilotty, Kenworthy, Sirian, Black, & Wagner, 2002; Pugliese et al., 2015, 2016).

McLean, Harrison, Zimak, Joseph, and Morrow (2014) demonstrated that parent-reported EF deficits were related to lower adaptive functioning in a cross-sectional sample of youth with ASD (n = 65) after controlling for age, IQ, and ASD symptom severity. Specifically, metacognitive skills on the BRIEF robustly predicted communication, daily living, and socialization skills on the Vineland Adaptive Behavior Scales (VABS; Sparrow, Cicchetti, & Saulnier, 2016). Negative correlations between the BRIEF and VABS domain scores were also found in a smaller subset (n = 44) of preschoolers.

Investigating the relationship between EF and adaptive behavior in the largest sample of youth with ASD to date spanning early childhood to young adulthood (n = 357), Pugliese and colleagues (2015) replicated the finding that more parent-reported EF problems were associated with worse adaptive behavior on the VABS, above and beyond age and IQ. Specifically, initiation problems robustly predicted lower scores across VABS domains, whereas working memory difficulties were associated with lower communication and daily living skills. Initiation abilities on the BRIEF reflect problems with generativity (e.g., formulating new ideas, complaining about having "nothing to do," having difficulty structuring free time). This finding is in line with results on lab-based tasks indicating impaired generativity in ASD (Hill, 2004; Kenworthy et al., 2008). Working memory problems may particularly impact the ability to carry out multistep activities or follow complex instructions that are crucial to independently navigating daily activities. These results suggest that metacognitive skills are particularly implicated in difficulty acquiring adaptive skills in ASD. Notably, decreased cognitive flexibility also detrimentally affected socialization skills—rigidity, inflexibility, and difficulty with compromising may place strains on social relationships, whereas resisting new situations may prevent access to friendship-making opportunities such as school clubs or sports. Gardiner and Iarocci (2018) provided additional support for the association between metacognitive skills on the BRIEF and adaptive behavior on the activities of daily living, communication, and social skills domains of the Behavior Assessment System for Children, second edition (BASC-2; Kamphaus & Reynolds, 2007) in a smaller, cross-sectional sample of youth with ASD (n = 59). However, the implicated EF subdomains varied from those in the Pugliese et al. (2015) study. Inhibition, shifting, and organization skills predicted activities of daily living, whereas planning and monitoring skills were associated with communication, with monitoring also associated with social skills. Importantly, the studies by Gardiner and Iarocci (2018) and Pugliese and colleagues (2015) were cross-sectional, precluding the nature of causality among EF and adaptive behavior.

In the only longitudinal investigation of EF and adaptive behavior to date in youth with ASD without ID (n = 64), problems with parent-reported total EF skills on the BRIEF contributed to lower adaptive scores above and beyond age, sex, and IQ in the domains of daily living and socialization skills (Pugliese et al., 2016). Impaired self-monitoring skills, or the ability to monitor one's goal-oriented actions and adjust behavior accordingly, were a robust predictor of lower subsequent scores in communication, daily living, and socialization. Inhibition problems uniquely predicted poorer daily living skills, whereas poorer shifting abilities predicted lower socialization scores.

The only study of EF and adaptive behavior in adults to date also found similar trends for the importance of metacognitive skills in adaptive functioning. Interestingly, Wallace, Kenworthy, and colleagues (2016) demonstrated that age and IQ had no predictive value in explaining adaptive behavior on the conceptual, social, and practical skill domains of the Adaptive Behavior Assessment System-II (ABAS-II; Harrison & Oakland, 2003). However, informant-rated metacognition on the BRIEF significantly predicted conceptual and practical skills. When metacognitive skills were isolated, the Planning/Organization subscale was the sole predictor of practical and conceptual skills.

In sum, metacognitive skills appear to be critical to successful execution of adaptive skills in ASD, above and beyond factors that are typically predictive of outcome in neurotypical youth, such as IQ and age. More research is needed to isolate which EF domains specifically predict adaptive skills in ASD, preferably using similar measures of EF and adaptive behavior. There is also a distinct lack of investigation into EF predictors of adaptive outcome in youth with ASD and ID. When consensus is reached, these skills can be targeted through intervention to improve outcome and make the transition to independence and adulthood more successful.

EF Markers of Co-Occurring Psychiatric Problems

A diagnosis of ASD confers greater risk of psychiatric symptoms than in the general population, with approximately 70% to 72% of individuals meeting criteria for at least one psychiatric disorder (Leyfer et al., 2006; Simonoff et al., 2008). Co-occurrence of anxiety and depression is particularly common, with anxiety co-occurring in approximately 40% of youth (van Steensel, Bögels, & Perrin, 2011) and 27% to 50% of adults with ASD (Croen et al., 2015; Hollocks et al., 2018; Lugnegård, Hallerbäck, & Gillberg, 2011) and depression co-occurring in 0.9% to 29% of youth and adolescents (Leyfer et al., 2006; Simonoff et al., 2008; Stewart, Barnard, Pearson, Hasan, & O'Brien., 2006) and 77% of outpatient adults (Joshi et al., 2013; see also Rosen, Mazefsky, Vasa, & Lerner, 2018, for a review).

Poor EF, and in particular, difficulty with flexibility and planning, may be a risk factor for the development of affective psychiatric problems. Similar to what has been found with TD youth, cognitive inflexibility may predispose youth with ASD toward negative processing styles associated with anxiety, such as a failure to flexibly disengage from negative or threatening stimuli (Derryberry & Reed, 2002; Eysenck, Derakshan, Santos, & Calvo, 2007). It is also possible that greater cognitive behavioral rigidity leads to increased anxiety following disruption in routine or violations of expectations (Hollocks et al., 2014).

There is a small literature indicating that the association of EF and psychiatric problems across development is robust to measurement modality. In a large sample of adolescents with ASD (n = 90, FSIQ 50 to 119), Hollocks and colleagues (2014) found that greater anxiety, but not depression, was related to poorer performance on performance-based neuropsychological domains of inhibition, cognitive set shifting, and attentional switching on the Test of Everyday Attention for Children (TEA-Ch; Manly, Robertson, Anderson, & Nimmo-Smith, 1999), WCST, and Trail Making task. Using parent report of EF on the BRIEF in youth aged 6 to 16 without ID, Lawson and colleagues (2014) found that youth with ASD have more problems with inflexibility than those with ADHD, which is predictive of greater anxiety and depression on the Child Behavior Checklist (CBCL; Achenbach, 1991). Greater inflexibility in ASD also predicted more aggression, whereas greater disinhibition predicted greater aggression in the ADHD group.

Thus far, two studies have been conducted in cognitively able adults with ASD that lend support to the idea that impaired EF is also related to anxiety and depression. Zimmerman, Ownsworth, O'Donovan, Roberts, and Gullo (2017) found a significant negative association between anxiety and the Delis-Kaplan Executive Function System (DKEFS; Delis, Kaplan, & Kramer, 2001) Free Sort task in a group of adults with ASD (n = 42), indicating that individuals with better concept formation and cognitive flexibility experienced lower anxiety symptoms. Wallace, Kenworthy, and colleagues (2016) found that greater informant-reported real-world EF problems on the BRIEF-Adult were associated with greater depression and anxiety symptomatology on the Adult Behavior Checklist (Achenbach, 1997). Planning and organization difficulties were predictive of greater depression, whereas shifting problems were predictive of greater anxiety. Taken together, this literature suggests the importance of investigating specific facets of EF as biomarkers for the development of psychiatric problems in ASD.

Etiology, Diagnosis, and Assessment

Genetics of EF in ASD

For the purposes of this chapter, we have split the field of genetics into molecular and behavioral/quantitative genetics. Although there has been very little molecular genetics work investigating, for example, genetic associations with EF in ASD, there is a rich behavioral genetics literature in ASD, some of which includes the examination of EF.

ASD is associated with atypical social communication and the presence of restricted and repetitive patterns of behavior. Increasingly, these two symptom clusters have been conceptualized dimensionally such that social communication behaviors can vary continuously from typical to atypical throughout the general population (e.g., Constantino & Todd, 2003; Ronald, Happé, & Plomin, 2005; Ruzich et al., 2015; Skuse, Mandy, & Scourfield, 2005). Elevated levels of these two symptom clusters that do not reach the threshold of clinical diagnosis are termed the broad autism phenotype (BAP). Unaffected first-degree family members of people with ASD are more likely to display these subclinical characteristics than other members of the general population (Sasson, Lam, Parlier, Daniels, & Piven, 2013; Wheelwright, Auyeung, Allison, & Baron-Cohen, 2010). Based on twin and family studies, the susceptibility for inheritance of ASD is high (for review, see Ronald and Hoekstra, 2011) and likely extends subclinically to include these milder ASD traits (Hurley, Losh, Parlier, Reznick, & Pevin, 2007). Other aspects of the ASD phenotype might also constitute the BAP or cosegregate as part of the BAP. Because EF is such a frequently documented challenge for individuals with ASD across the lifespan, it has also emerged as a candidate endophenotype that could help to bridge biology–disorder links. There is some evidence to suggest that EF performance in unaffected relatives of people with ASD is intermediary between individuals with ASD and TD individuals without autistic family members (Van Eylen et al., 2017), and many studies demonstrate significantly diminished EF, such as cognitive inflexibility and planning difficulties, in parents of children with ASD compared to parents of TD children (e.g., Delorme et al., 2007; Hughes, Leboyer, & Bouvard, 1997; Piven & Palmer, 1997). However, this finding is not universal, with other studies failing to find EF-related deficits in first-degree relatives (e.g., siblings and/or parents) of people with ASD (e.g., Losh et al., 2009; Wong, Maybery, Bishop, Maley, & Hallmayer, 2006). In a complementary approach, instead of focusing on relatives of people with ASD (regardless of whether or not they have the BAP), other studies have examined EF among individuals who have met threshold for the BAP based on either rating scales or interview techniques (e.g., Hurley et al., 2007; Sasson, Lam, Childress, et al., 2013). One study found elevated self-reported EF problems in later life among adults aged 60 years or older with the BAP (Wallace, Budgett, & Charlton, 2016). In a follow-up study utilizing performance-based tasks, again, a separate group of older adults above the BAP cut-off performed more poorly on a range of EF tasks, including those assessing fluency, working memory, and attentional switching, than non-BAP control older adults (Stewart, Charlton, & Wallace, 2018). Taken together, these studies are largely suggestive of the cotransmission of EF deficits alongside the ASD phenotype, even in its subclinical forms.

Neural Substrate of EF in ASD

Much of our knowledge of brain development and brain function in ASD is based on studies employing neuroimaging techniques. With the advent of magnetic resonance imaging (MRI) that enables in vivo examination of brain structure and function, great gains have been made in understanding brain-based differences in ASD. Although early studies focused on brain structure alone, many studies in the last two decades have quantified brain function and/or connectivity as well. EF and its subcomponent processes are underpinned by a complex array of brain regions, with many studies implicating circuits that include the prefrontal and parietal cortices, as well as subcortical regions, particularly the striatum (Goldman-Rakic, 1996; Miller & Cohen, 2001). There is a large literature on structural brain differences in ASD. In one of the largest studies to date, the ENIGMA ASD Working Group recently completed a meta-analysis that compared brain structural metrics from over 1,500 individuals with ASD and over 1,500 TD controls. Their findings suggested that the frontal cortex was larger in ASD and that there were significant interactions between age and brain structure in both frontal and parietal cortices indicative of diverging brain growth trajectories from normative expectations (van Rooij et al., 2018). Some studies suggest atypically enlarged portions of frontal and parietal cortex in ASD early in development (e.g., Hazlett et al., 2011; Raznahan et al., 2012), whereas others reveal that the differences in these regions diminish or disappear later in development (e.g., Wallace et al., 2010, 2013). Paralleling these findings, many studies have implicated atypical structural connectivity in ASD based on quantification of white matter through tractography and other similar methods. Particularly relevant here are studies implicating atypical development of white matter tracts in ASD that include the frontal lobe (e.g., Catani et al., 2016), such as the uncinate fasciculus between the orbitofrontal cortex and limbic and anterior temporal regions (e.g., Jou et al., 2016; Kumar et al., 2010). Turning to brain function, there is a small but emerging set of studies utilizing functional MRI (fMRI) of EF tasks, such as those focused on inhibitory control, working memory, and cognitive flexibility, to examine whether the neural substrates of EF are atypical among individuals with ASD. The key metric in fMRI studies is hemodynamic response or blood flow, which serves as a proxy for brain activity. For task-based fMRI studies, this typically involves comparing hemodynamic response to an experimental (e.g., EF) versus a control (e.g., showing similar visual images without EF demands) task to isolate brain underpinnings of the key cognitive components of the task. For example, fMRI of the most pathognomonic of EF domains, cognitive flexibility, has revealed atypical activation patterns in the dorsolateral prefrontal cortex, anterior cingulate cortex, and parietal cortices among adolescents and young adults with ASD as compared to control participants matched on age and IQ (e.g., Schmitz et al., 2006; Yerys et al., 2015). In addition to task-based fMRI, there is a complementary approach that involves examining brain activity "at rest." For both types of fMRI, "connectivity," or coordination of activity between brain regions, can be assessed by examining the correlation of the hemodynamic function across brain regions. In theory, optimal synchrony between regions leads to more efficient processing of information. Several studies implicate this same network of regions as atypical in ASD. One recent study has demonstrated that the degree to which activity in the frontal and parietal cortices is coordinated in children with ASD was not affected by the introduction of a high-demand EF task (as compared to "rest") and the extent of the connectivity between these regions was positively associated with real-world EF as assessed by parent report on the BRIEF (Lynch et al., 2017). Taken as a whole, these findings suggest that brain regions implicated as critical for EF (e.g., frontal and parietal cortices) demonstrate differences in terms of gray and white matter structural development as well as functional recruitment and coordination in ASD compared to neurotypical controls.

Assessment of EF in ASD

The assessment of EF in autism is complicated by inadequate measurement tools related to the inherent complexity and relative newness of the EF construct; the fact that EF abilities become more differentiated and change dramatically throughout childhood and adolescence (e.g., Mesulam, 2002; Wiebe et al., 2011); the fact that EF is a domain general ability that is expressed through core cognitive skills such as language; and finally, that the expression of EF is sensitive to context variables. These factors have been extensively discussed by the authors in three previous reviews (Kenworthy, Anthony, & Yerys, 2012; Kenworthy et al., 2008; Wallace, Yerys, et al., 2016) and will be briefly addressed here.

EF is a relatively new construct that is still in the process of refinement and operationalization into measurement tools. The debate regarding whether it is a unitary or fractionated construct is slowly resolving in the literature in favor of a view that it is both unified and fractionated into at least three domains (inhibition, working memory, and flexibility; Miyake et al., 2000; Pellicano, 2012), although some suggest fewer domains (Pennington & Ozonoff, 1996; Zelazo, Müller, & Frye, 2003) and others more (Gioia et al., 2015). The trajectory and timing of differentiation from a unified construct in early childhood to a more differentiated set of abilities in adults is still evolving (Wiebe et al., 2008, 2011).

Another measurement problem stems from the fact that EF is a higher order ability that must be expressed through a cognitive modality, such as language or nonverbal problem solving. Variability in a group's capacity to manage the content, or the modality of a task, may obscure information about that group's ability to manage the executive, or process, requirements of the task (Denckla, 2002). As a result, there are few "one size fits all" EF tasks for people with ASD, who have an unusually wide range of language and cognitive abilities (Pellicano, 2012). As Garon and colleagues (2018) point out, this increases the risk of failure to capture EF deficits with laboratory tasks that have inappropriate linguistic or general intellectual demands. This problem has been especially difficult when assessing the very young or people with ASD and ID.

Assessment of EF in ASD is further complicated by the fact that contextual variables can affect EF performance. The highly structured nature of clinical and laboratory settings can produce optimal performance on tasks of EF, whereas real-world environments and demands do not naturally scaffold performance and therefore often elicit EF deficits that might not be apparent in the clinic/lab. Thus, there is a strong tendency in autism and other developmental disabilities for disparate findings depending on whether a well-controlled laboratory task versus an "ecologically valid" task or rating scale was used. Most recently this distinction has been addressed through the application of "hot" EF tasks, which introduce strong affective or motivational components into the laboratory primarily through the promise of real or imagined financial reward (gambling or delay discounting paradigms). These tasks have the potential to provide a stronger link between laboratory and real-world findings (Prencipe et al., 2011; Zelazo, Qu, Müller, & Schneider, 2005) but are not yet fully developed for children, for whom differing amounts of imaginary money may be too abstract to be meaningful (Garon et al., 2018).

In sum, when measuring EF across the lifespan in ASD, we must rely on a relatively new set of assessment tools to capture an uncertain number of EF domains, which mature at different and not yet fully defined rates and require varying degrees of core linguistic and cognitive abilities. It is not surprising, then, that the literature is confusing at times, with premature and even contradictory reification of EF domains and measurement tools (e.g., presentation of performance on a Tower task as indicative of "planning" ability without acknowledgment of the multiple EF domains of inhibition, flexibility, and working memory inherent in this task). The complex aspirations of EF assessment in ASD contrast with the current lack of proven tools that cover all domains of EF across all chronological, linguistic, and cognitive developmental stages and incorporate standardized, yet real-world, motivationally salient demands. Nonetheless, EF drives fundamental outcomes and is plastic throughout childhood and adolescence, making it a strong target for treatment, and thus, its assessment is essential.

Best practices for the assessment of EF in autism currently rely on art, as well as science, and the application of principles that stem from the complexity that is inherent in both EF and autism. These principles include:

1. Complement the use of standard "cool" EF laboratory tasks with measures of EF abilities in real-world and unstructured settings, through use of informant- and self-report measures and other ecologically valid tools (see Kenworthy et al., 2008).

2. For people of school age and older without ID, consider the use of complex EF tasks that require integration of information and tap several discrete processes such as the Tower tasks, the WCST, and the Rey Osterrieth Complex Figure.

3. Given evidence of global EF impairment in ASD, it is important to sample multiple EF subdomains, such as working memory, planning, organization, and generativity.

4. The most consistently reported deficit across development in ASD is flexibility, and thus, administering measures that assess flexibility is recommended. In addition, it is important to observe behavior throughout an in-clinic assessment for signs of inflexibility, such as difficulty transitioning to new tasks, resistance to feedback, or frequent requests for clarification of exactly what will occur during the assessment and when.

5. Account for the heterogeneity of ASD when selecting EF measurement tools. The likely presence of co-occurring psychiatric conditions, particularly ADHD, indicates the utility of the assessment of attention and inhibition. The range of linguistic and cognitive capacities observed within ASD compels careful selection of tools that are appropriate to core capacities.

Treatment

EF is deviant throughout development in autism but plastic and malleable, leading to near-unanimous calls for EF intervention in the preschool years and onward. Though the research described previously has been documenting EF weaknesses in ASD for decades, and those weaknesses have been shown to predict poorer outcomes, there have been very few randomized controlled trials (RCTs) of treatments with EF as a target. Originating with Fisher and Happé's seminal trial in 2005 and Solomon, Goodlin-Jones, and Anders' trial in 2004, there is a small but growing literature on interventions targeting EF in people with ASD, with cognitive behavioral therapy (CBT) for children and cognitive remediation for adults showing the most promise.

Clinic-Based EF Treatment Studies

Several social skills CBT interventions with an EF training component have been evaluated in ASD in uncontrolled single-group studies and reveal improvement on parent-reported EF behaviors (Stichter et al., 2010, 2012) and EF/problem-solving task performance (Bauminger, 2007; Christ et al., 2017; Strichter et al., 2010). Although these studies indicate initial promise for CBT approaches to enhance social awareness and EF in ASD, more rigorous testing of these interventions is needed.

Solomon and colleagues (2004) employed a waitlist control methodology to evaluate the Social Adjustment Enhancement Curriculum, which addressed facial expression recognition, theory of mind, and EF, "with a special emphasis on individual and group problem solving" (p. 652). This 20-week clinic-based group/individual intervention includes more lessons focused on specific EF skills than the interventions described previously. For example, there are lessons on identifying relevant information, prioritizing problems, and generating alternative solutions to problems. The intervention (n = 9) and waitlist control groups (n = 9) were divided into younger (8 to 10 years) and older (10 to 12 years) age groups and the younger intervention group showed significant gains on a problem-solving task following intervention in contrast to the younger waitlist control group, whose mean performance dropped on this measure.

One of the first RCTs of CBT EF interventions in ASD was conducted by Fisher and Happé (2005). It contrasted two brief (five to ten 25-minute sessions) clinic-based trainings with a control group (n = 7), targeting EF (n = 10) and theory of mind (n = 10) skills training, respectively. Both interventions contributed to real-world improvements on behaviors thought to require theory of mind, but neither intervention improved performance on EF tasks. The authors hypothesized that a longer EF intervention that occurred in real-world settings, such as home or school, might be effective.

School-Based EF Treatment Studies

A recent nationwide survey of school professionals reported the use of few evidence-based EF interventions for students with neurodevelopmental disorders and significant EF difficulties (Kenworthy et al., 2018). Evidence-based whole-classroom EF or EF-related interventions, such as the Chicago School Readiness Project (Watts, Gandhi, Ibrahim, Masucci, & Raver, 2018), Promoting Alternative Thinking Strategies (Domitrovich, Cortes, & Greenberg, 2007; Riggs et al., 2006), and Tools of the Mind (Bodrova & Leong, 2007; Diamond, Barnett, Thomas, & Munro, 2007), have been developed for at-risk students, but these have not yet been studied in students with ASD.

Unstuck and On Target (UOT; Cannon et al., 2011, 2018; Kenworthy, Anthony, Alexander, et al., 2014) is a cognitive behavioral treatment that directly addresses EF and self-regulation deficits in elementary school students. It was developed originally for autistic children and subsequently adapted for children with ADHD. UOT is the first evidence-based EF intervention for schools that targets both "hot" and "cool" EF abilities for flexibility, goal setting, and planning through a cognitive behavioral program centered on self-regulatory vocabulary that is consistently modeled and reinforced in school and at home. The vocabulary (e.g., "Big deal/Little deal," "Plan A/Plan B," "Goal-Plan-Do-Check") increases students' ability to regulate their behavioral/emotional responses when frustrated or overwhelmed and to regulate their attention and effort when completing tasks. UOT is designed to foster new EF skills and accommodate EF impairments (Feeney & Ylvisaker, 2008; Ylvisaker & Feeney, 1998). It teaches the what, why, and how of EF skills and uses "supported cognition" (Ylsvisaker & Feeney, 1998): New skills are taught with extensive scaffolding and guided practice with fading supports; parents and school personnel are trained to model use of desired self-regulatory vocabulary; visual cues are provided throughout; and the vocabulary is consistent across home/school settings.

UOT is delivered in a flexible, brief curriculum and, after only 6 hours of interventionist training, is implemented with fidelity by existing school staff (Kenworthy, Anthony, Naiman, et al., 2014). To ensure consistency across settings, UOT is made up of a curriculum of twenty-one 30- to 40-minute lessons (Cannon et al., 2018) that are taught to elementary school students, with reinforcement activities for each lesson to be used in the everyday classroom and home settings, and a parent manual (Kenworthy, Anthony, Alexander, et al., 2014). Furthermore, UOT trains teachers and parents in many best-practice, positive behavior supports, such as maintaining a positive 4:1 praise-to-correction ratio and reframing dysexecutive behavior as things a student "can't" do, as opposed to "won't" do (e.g., the student may be cognitively stuck, as opposed to choosing to be stubborn).

Evidence shows that UOT is effective as delivered in elementary school, including evidence of generalization to the classroom setting, regardless of students' race, ethnicity, or family income. A randomized controlled effectiveness trial in public elementary schools (Kenworthy, Anthony, Naiman, et al., 2014) found that UOT was more effective at improving problem solving, flexibility, goal setting, and planning in students with autism without ID than a published social skills curriculum comparator (Baker, 2003) delivered with an equivalent dose of student, teacher, and parent training. UOT led to improvements in EF and problem solving that not only were clinically meaningful (i.e., medium to large effect sizes) but also were measured through treatment-blinded assessment and included real-world measures in the classroom, such as following directions, making transitions smoothly, and participating in class, as well as treatment-blinded direct assessment of student problem solving, flexibility, and planning. Unexpectedly, UOT also produced improvements in student social skills in the classroom that were equivalent to the social skills comparator.

A second, recently completed comparative effectiveness trial compared UOT to contingency behavior management (CBM) for children with flexibility challenges and autism or ADHD. CBM principles were adapted and manualized into a program called Parents and Teachers Supporting Students (PATSS). Using a cluster randomized controlled design, 24 low-income schools provided UOT (n = 11 schools) or PATSS (n = 13 schools) to 148 third- to fifth-grade students with school-identified EF problems and either ADHD (n = 98) or autism (n = 50). The students were ethnically and racially diverse and 41% spoke a language other than English at home. Interventions were matched for "dose." As in the previous trial, the primary outcome was treatment-blinded classroom observation of six EF behaviors. Overall, the findings indicated significant improvement for ASD students who received UOT, but not consistently for PATSS, and significant improvement for ADHD students regardless of intervention. Implementation and other family/student demographic factors, including family income, which ranged from $8,796 to $400,000, did not relate to classroom outcome. UOT shows promise as an effective, low-cost school-based EF intervention (Kenworthy et al., 2017).

Adult EF Intervention

Baker-Ericzen and colleagues (2018) have been developing the Supported Employment, Comprehensive Cognitive Enhancement, and Social Skills (SUCCESS) intervention for use with adults with ASD and without ID. SUCCESS is a 6-month program embedded in a vocational training setting and delivered in small group settings within the vocational agency combined with staff training to support implementation of strategies. The curriculum content focuses on linking EF, memory, social cognitive, and communication skills to job search or work activities. Specific EF skills that were targeted included sustained attention, use of memory aids, organization, cognitive flexibility, goal-oriented thinking and planning, working memory, and problem solving. Within the social cognition domain, SUCCESS focused on increasing perspective taking, increasing social knowledge and reasoning, decoding social cues, regulating emotion, and building social relationships and networks. Baker-Ericzen and colleagues recently published a small, single-group, uncontrolled pilot study (n = 8) where participants attended twenty-five 1.5-hour sessions across 6 months in a supported employment program focused on teaching technical software testing skills. The pilot data suggest that feasibility, treatment adherence, and acceptability were high and participants increased EF skills, social thinking, and social communication skills, as well as doubled employment rates from pre- to postintervention.

In a larger, well-designed RCT, Eack and colleagues (2018) examined the efficacy of cognitive enhancement therapy (CET) for improving neurocognitive and employment outcomes for adults with autism. Neurocognitive function was measured via a composite index from the MATRICS Consensus Cognitive Battery (Green et al., 2004) and the WCST and captured EF skills including processing speed, attention, working memory, verbal and visual learning, problem solving, social cognition, and cognitive flexibility. Verbal, well-characterized adults with ASD aged 16 to 44 years (n=54) were randomized to an 18-month, single-blind trial of CET or enriched supportive therapy (EST). CET is a comprehensive treatment that was originally designed and proven effective with adults with schizophrenia and was adapted for adults with ASD (Eack et al., 2013). CET is an intensive cognitive remediation approach that integrates 60 hours of computer-based neurocognitive training with 45 group-based training sessions in social cognition. The comparator was an active EST during an individual session focused on supportive therapy (e.g., active listening, correct empathy, psychoeducation) and stress management. Though EST and CET were not matched on number of hours of treatment or on group modality, EST is a better comparator than waitlist control or treatment as usual, as it is an active treatment that could control for the nonspecific treatment effects of CET. CET produced significant differential increases in neurocognitive function relative to EST (d=0.46, p=.013). Both CET and EST were associated with large social cognitive improvements, with CET demonstrating an advantage at 9 (d=0.58, p=.020) but not 18 months (d=0.27, p=.298). Effects on employment indicated that participants in the CET condition were significantly more likely to gain competitive employment than those in EST (odds ratio [OR]=6.21, p=.023), which was mediated by cognitive improvement. CET is an exciting possibility as an effective treatment for core neurocognitive deficits in adult ASD, suggesting that the treatment of EF and social cognitive impairments in this population can contribute to meaningful improvements in adult outcomes and interventions and not only target children and youth with ASD.

Computer-Based EF Training Programs

CHILDREN

Two trials of computer-based interventions to improve EF reveal mixed results. A small, uncontrolled single-group study of a computer game that requires physical activity found gains in parent-reported working memory and metacognitive control (Hilton et al., 2014). On the other hand, a large rigorous RCT of three conditions of Braingame Brian, working memory training with levels of increasing difficulty, flexibility training with levels of increasing difficulty, and an active control condition consisting of EF tasks that did not increase in difficulty (Prins et al., 2013), revealed no significant intervention-specific improvements on a range of working memory, cognitive flexibility, and attention measures. A trend toward improvement in performance on a working memory task that closely resembled the computer-based training activities following the working memory training was reported in a second publication on the same intervention trial (de Vries, Prins, Schmand, & Geuts, 2015).

PARENTS

A recently developed online training for parents of 8- to 12-year-old children with ASD developed by the authors of UOT (e-Unstuck, 3C Institute, in press) was in a trial comparing in-person parent training workshops (n = 51) to an online, individualized parent training program (n = 46). Analysis of variance (ANCOVA) assessing change over time as a result of parent training while controlling for pretraining baseline scores, child IQ, and parent education revealed no group differences in outcomes (all ps > .27). Cohen's d was computed to further explore the main effect of time, in order to capture the impact of the training on parents and children. Significant improvement in parent self-ratings of strain, empowerment, and competence (Cohen's d range = 0.28 to 0.53), as well as parent ratings of their child's EF problems (BRIEF Emotion Regulation Index [ERI] and BRIEF Global Executive

Composite [GEC], Cohen's *ds* = 0.26 and 0.28, respectively), indicated that families in both groups benefited from the training they received (all *ps* < .01). These results are promising, as it makes a parent training program available to parents across the country without needing to find in-person trainings, which are seldom available.

In summary, the increasing number of intervention studies that target specific, well-characterized EF deficits with specific measures of outcome is promising. Another key component of these treatments is the emphasis on ecological validity, which is implicitly recognized in many studies by the use of real-world measures of EF outcomes and is directly invoked in a subset of the studies reviewed here. Kenworthy, Anthony, Naiman, and colleagues (2014) use blinded classroom observations as a tool for measuring transfer of skills to real-world settings, and the adult interventions use employment status as a real-world outcome. Finally, all of the effective approaches demonstrate a blurring of EF and social skills, such that most interventions target some component of both skill sets, and several studies found that purported treatments for EF improved social skills (Fisher & Happé, 2005; Kenworthy, Anthony, Naiman, et al., 2014). This is consistent with evidence that EF abilities may be precursors to theory-of-mind abilities (Flynn, 2007), or in any case are correlated with them (Pellicano, 2007; Perner & Lang, 1999).

Treatment Case Example: Unstuck and On Target

Anthony was referred to the school psychologist by his second-grade teacher because he was consistently disrupting his classmates. Previously diagnosed with autism, he was educated in a mainstream classroom because he was a bright boy with academic skills above grade level. He had poor ability to regulate his emotional and behavioral responses, which frustrated his teacher and peers. Any small change in the classroom routine was stressful for Anthony. He had difficulty accepting feedback from his teacher and was unable to work in groups with peers because he had very specific, rigid ideas about how to do things. He became easily overwhelmed when things did not go as he expected, and had several crying outbursts in class each week that were difficult to recover from. The school psychologist conducted an assessment, including parent and teacher ratings on the second edition of the BRIEF (BRIEF-2; Gioia et al, 2015), which revealed increased EF problems at school and at home in all areas, with peak elevations on the Emotion Regulation Index, reflecting insistence on sameness, inflexible thinking, and emotional outbursts. During a morning classroom observation, the psychologist noted two incidents in which Anthony got stuck on an idea and disrupted the class (he perceived a classmate to have cut in front of him during line-up for lunch, his teacher asked him to make an edit to a writing assignment).

The school psychologist held a team meeting with parents and school staff. She suggested that Anthony participate in a small Unstuck and On Target group and that his parents and school staff work together to reframe their understanding of his challenges and consistently model and reinforce the vocabulary and strategies taught in Unstuck. She helped the team understand Anthony's problems as the result of a specific EF deficit that should be accommodated and could be improved. By reframing a "won't" ("Anthony refuses to listen to me!") into a "can't" ("Anthony has trouble shifting from one thing to another"), the school team and parents were better able to understand the need for accommodations, such as advance warnings of any transitions. Clearly defining and reframing the problem also defused angry power struggles between Anthony and the adults in his life, decreasing the perception of him as a "bad kid."

Anthony participated in weekly Unstuck group sessions, learning first how to identify the size of his feelings on the "Feelings Target," a colored circular target with numbered concentric circles, which was used in his classroom and at home, as well as during group. Anthony quickly learned to identify when he was becoming upset and experimented with coping strategies in group. Visual reminders of his favorite strategies were provided at home and in the classroom. Through a series of fun activities, games, and videos, Anthony also learned a flexibility vocabulary ("flexible," "Plan A/Plan B," and "Big Deal/Little Deal") and how to use it to effectively manage unexpected events, disappointment, and unwanted feedback. Anthony's teachers and parents also used the same language consistently to reinforce skill building. Small visuals in his classroom and at home reminded his teacher and parents to reinforce and model the use of flexibility phrases to regulate behavior and thinking. His parents and teachers provided consistent and specific praise for instances of flexibility, being careful not to criticize him for "getting stuck." If Anthony expressed distress because his teacher asked him to revise a paragraph, for example, she would ask if that was a "big" or "little deal." If he indicated that it was a "big deal," they would work together to collaboratively figure out how to turn it into a "little deal." His teacher found the Unstuck vocabulary and phrases contagious. As she modeled the words, other students in the classroom started using them as well, praising each other and Anthony for flexibility. Following completion of the 21 small group weekly sessions, the school psychologist found that Anthony's disruptive outbursts had dropped from several per week to less than one per month, and, for the first time in his school career, he had a friend to play with at recess. The psychologist readministered the BRIEF-2 and calculated the size of the change in scores from her first assessment, using the Reliable Change Index (RCI) tables provided in the BRIEF-2 manual, which indicted that there had been a significant reduction in Anthony's problems on the Shift and Emotional Control scales.

Summary and Future Directions

Developments in our understanding of EF in ASD have exciting applications for improving and supporting individual outcome. However, there are several gaps in the literature that need to be addressed for this to come to fruition. First, new measurement tools that tap ecological validity and motivational saliency are needed across the age and ability span. Second, individual difference variables including age and cognitive ability also need to be taken into consideration before drawing broad conclusions of a profile of executive dysfunction in autism, and other areas such as gender and symptom severity have not yet thoroughly been studied. Co-occurring conditions, particularly ADHD, are yet to be fully addressed in this literature. In a previous review, we found that inconsistent findings regarding inhibitory control in autism may be the result of failing to account for the presence or absence of ADHD symptoms in study participants (Wallace, Yerys, et al., 2016; see also Yerys et al., 2009). Much of the extant research has been cross-sectional; more longitudinal investigation is needed to confirm cross-sectional findings using batteries that tap multiple domains of EF across the age and ability span. Additionally, more work examining the real-world impact of EF on adult functioning (e.g., quality of life, employment, independent living) is necessary. Importantly, we need renewed efforts to understand EF in individuals with ID, using developmentally appropriate tools, such as those developed by Garon and colleagues (2018).

Finally, in the extant autism literature, we have traditionally examined EF and associated outcomes using a whole-group approach by comparing individuals with ASD to TD individuals, individuals with other psychiatric disorders, or normative data. Given the heterogeneity in ASD symptom presentation and development of co-occurring psychiatric conditions, it is worthwhile to examine within-group differences to elucidate risk and resiliency factors related to distinct EF profiles. There is emerging evidence for variability in EF profiles within the spectrum, and more research is needed to define these profiles to leverage strengths and weaknesses for treatment planning and service supports across the lifespan. This type of approach could use commonplace clinical tools to phenotype youth at risk for outcomes associated with EF impairments, such as psychiatric, academic, or adaptive problems, and potentially ameliorate problems before occurring through targeted EF treatment. Phenotyping can also inform clinicians about which EF supports to utilize during psychiatric treatment for optimal outcomes.

With respect to treatment of EF-related problems, we need to use stronger trial methodology and to expand and refine the characterization of study participants. From a methodological perspective, it will be important to confirm many of the results reported here with better controlled trials that include random assignment to multiple active treatment conditions of equal intensity and treatment-blinded outcome data collection (Dawson & Burner, 2011; Kasari & Lawton, 2010). It is also notable that investigators are studying interventions they themselves have created. For this promising area to fully develop, it will be essential that initial positive findings from RCTs, such as that reported earlier for the Unstuck and On Target intervention and the cognitive enhancement therapy trial, are followed by effectiveness trials run by new investigators that measure the impact of these interventions compared to other promising techniques. There are obvious gaps in the types of people studied in this treatment literature to date, most notably a lack of diversity in participants. All of the research reported here was conducted with participants without ID, indicating a need for new interventions that address EF in those with ASD and ID. Females must also be studied in adequate numbers for treatment response to be evaluated for each sex separately. We also need more treatment studies to explore contributions of cultural factors, family income, insurance benefits, and minority status to treatment outcome. Finally, it is important that EF intervention studies evaluate the full range of co-occurring conditions and abilities in study participants. The presence or absence of depression, impulsivity, anxiety, and social cognitive differences in participants with ASD might interact with EF and therefore impact the chosen intervention and the outcome. It is time to raise the bar in both methodology rigor and inclusiveness.

References

Abbott, P., Happé, F. G., & Charlton, R. A. (2018). Exploratory study of executive function abilities across the adult lifespan in individuals receiving an ASD diagnosis in adulthood. *Journal of Autism and Developmental Disorders*, 1–14.

Achenbach, T. M. (1991). *Integrative guide for the 1991 CBCL/4–18, YSR, and TRF profiles.* Department of Psychiatry, University of Vermont.

Achenbach, T. M. (1997). *Manual for the young adult self-report and young adult behavior checklist.* Department of Psychiatry, University of Vermont.

Ambery, F. Z., Russell, A. J., Perry, K., Morris, R., & Murphy, D. G. (2006). Neuropsychological functioning in adults with Asperger syndrome. *Autism, 10,* 551–564.

Aron, A. R. (2011). From reactive to proactive and selective control: Developing a richer model for stopping inappropriate responses. *Biological Psychiatry, 69*(12), e55–e68.

Baker, J. (2003). *Social skills training for children and adolescents with Asperger syndrome and social-communications problems.* Arlington, TX: Future Horizons.

Baker-Ericzén, M. J., Fitch, M. A., Kinnear, M., Jenkins, M. M., Twamley, E. W., Smith, L., . . . & Leon, J. (2018). Development of the Supported Employment, Comprehensive Cognitive Enhancement, and Social Skills program for adults on the autism spectrum: Results of initial study. *Autism, 22*(1), 6–19.

Barkley, R. A. (2012). *Executive functions: What they are, how they work, and why they evolved.* Guilford Press.

Bauminger, N. (2007). Brief report: Group social-multimodal intervention for HFASD. *Journal of Autism and Developmental Disorders, 37*(8), 1605–1615.

Bennetto, L., Pennington, B. F., & Rogers, S. J. (1996). Intact and impaired memory functions in autism. *Child Development, 67*(4), 1816–1835.

Berg, E. A. (1948). A simple objective technique for measuring flexibility in thinking. *Journal of General Psychology, 39*(1), 15–22.

Berger, H. J., Aerts, F. H., Spaendonck, K. P. V., Cools, A. R., & Teunisse, J. P. (2003). Central coherence and cognitive shifting in relation to social improvement in high-functioning young adults with autism. *Journal of Clinical and Experimental Neuropsychology, 25*(4), 502–511.

Blair, C., & Raver, C. C. (2015). School readiness and self-regulation: A developmental psychobiological approach. *Annual Review of Psychology, 66,* 711–731.

Bodrova, E., & Leong, D. (2007). Tools of the mind: The Vygotskian approach to early childhood education.

Cannon, L., Kenworthy, L., Alexander, K., Anthony, L. G., & Werner, M. (2018). *Unstuck and On Target! Teaching flexibility and goal directed behavior to children with ASD* (2nd ed.). Baltimore, MD: Brookes Publishing.

Cannon, L., Kenworthy, L., Alexander, C., Werner, M. A., & Anthony, L. G. (2011). *Unstuck and On Target. An executive function curriculum to improve flexibility for children with autism spectrum disorders.* Baltimore, MD: Paul H. Brookes.

Catani, M., Dell'Acqua, F., Budisavljevic, S., Howells, H., Thiebaut de Schotten, M., Froudist- Walsh, S., . . . Murphy, D. G. (2016). Frontal networks in adults with autism spectrum disorder. *Brain. 139,* 616–630.

Christ, S. E., Stichter, J. P., O'Connor, K. V., Bodner, K., Moffitt, A. J., & Herzog, M. J. (2017). Social skills intervention participation and associated improvements in executive function performance. *Autism Research and Treatment, 2017.*

Constantino, J. N., & Todd, R. D. (2003). Autistic traits in the general population: A twin study. *Archives of General Psychiatry, 60,* 524–530.

Craig, F., Margari, F., Legrottaglie, A. R., Palumbi, R., De Giambattista, C., & Margari, L. (2016). A review of executive function deficits in autism spectrum disorder and attention-deficit/hyperactivity disorder. *Neuropsychiatric Disease and Treatment, 12,* 1191. doi:10.2147/NDT.S104620

Crawford, J. R., Bryan, J., Luszcz, M. A., Obonsawin, M. C., & Stewart, L. (2000). The executive decline hypothesis of cognitive aging: Do executive deficits qualify as differential deficits and do they mediate age-related memory decline? *Aging, Neuropsychology, and Cognition, 7*(1), 9–31.

Croen, L. A., Zerbo, O., Qian, Y., Massolo, M. L., Rich, S., Sidney, S., & Kripke, C. (2015). The health status of adults on the autism spectrum. *Autism, 19*(7), 814–823.

Damasio, A. R., & Maurer, R. G. (1978). Neurological model for childhood autism. *Archives of Neurology, 35,* 777–786.

Davids, R. C. D., Groen, Y., Berg, I. J., Tucha, O. M., & van Balkom, I. D. C. (2016). Executive functions in older adults with autism spectrum disorder: Objective performance and subjective complaints. *Journal of Autism and Developmental Disorders, 46,* 2859–2873.

Dawson, G., & Burner, K. (2011). Behavioral interventions in children and adolescents with autism spectrum disorder: A review of recent findings. *Current Opinion in Pediatrics, 23*(6), 616–620.

Dawson, G., Meltzoff, A. N., Osterling, J., & Rinaldi, J. (1998). Neuropsychological correlates of early symptoms of autism. *Child Development, 69*(5), 1276–1285.

Dawson, G., Munson, J., Estes, A., Osterling, J., McPartland, J., Toth, K., . . . Abbott, R. (2002). Neurocognitive function and joint attention ability in young children with autism spectrum disorder versus developmental delay. *Child Development, 73*(2), 345–358.

Delis, D. C., Kaplan, E., & Kramer, J. H. (2001). *D-KEFS: Examiners manual.* San Antonio, TX: Psychological Corporation.

Delorme, R., Goussé, V., Roy, I., Trandafir, A., Mathieu, F., Mouren-Siméoni, M. C., Betancur, C., & Leboyer, M. (2007). Shared executive dysfunctions in unaffected relatives of patients with autism and obsessive-compulsive disorder. *European Psychiatry, 22,* 32–38.

Demetriou, E. A., Lampit, A., Quintana, D. S., Naismith, S. L., Song, Y. J. C., Pye, J. E., . . . Guastella, A. J. (2017). Autism spectrum disorders: A meta-analysis of executive function. *Molecular Psychiatry, 23*(5), 1198.

Denckla, M. B. (2002). The behavior rating inventory of executive function: Commentary. *Child Neuropsychology, 8*(4), 304–306.

Derryberry, D., & Reed, M. A. (2002). Anxiety-related attentional biases and their regulation by attentional control. *Journal of Abnormal Psychology, 111*(2), 225.

de Vries, M., & Geurts, H. (2015). Influence of autism traits and executive functioning on quality of life in children with an autism spectrum disorder. *Journal of Autism and Developmental Disorders, 45*(9), 2734–2743.

de Vries, M., Prins, P. J., Schmand, B. A., & Geurts, H. M. (2015). Working memory and cognitive flexibility-training for children with an autism spectrum disorder: A randomized controlled trial. *Journal of Child Psychology and Psychiatry, 56*(5), 566–576.

Diamond, A., Barnett, W. S., Thomas, J., & Munro, S. (2007). Preschool program improves cognitive control. *Science (New York, NY), 318*(5855), 1387.

Domitrovich, C. E., Cortes, R. C., & Greenberg, M. T. (2007). Improving young children's social and emotional competence: A randomized trial of the preschool "PATHS" curriculum. *Journal of Primary Prevention, 28*(2), 67–91.

Dijkhuis, R. R., Ziermans, T. B., Van Rijn, S., Staal, W. G., & Swaab, H. (2017). Self-regulation and quality of life in high-functioning young adults with autism. *Autism, 21*, 896–906.

Eack, S. M., Greenwald, D. P., Hogarty, S. S., Bahorik, A. L., Litschge, M. Y., Mazefsky, C. A., & Minshew, N. J. (2013). Cognitive Enhancement Therapy for adults with autism spectrum disorder: Results of an 18-month feasibility study. *Journal of Autism and Developmental Disorders, 43*, 2866–2877.

Eack, S. M., Hogarty, S. S., Greenwald, D. P., Litschge, M. Y., Porton, S. A., Mazefsky, C. A., & Minshew, N. J. (2018). Cognitive enhancement therapy for adult autism spectrum disorder: Results of an 18-month randomized clinical trial. *Autism Research, 11*(3), 519–530.

Eysenck, M.W., Derakshan, N., Santos, R., & Calvo, M. G. (2007). Anxiety and cognitive performance: Attentional control theory. *Emotion, 7*, 336–353.

Faja, S., & Dawson, G. (2013). Performance on the dimensional change card sort and backward digit span by young children with autism without intellectual disability. *Child Neuropsychology, 20*(6), 692–699.

Faja, S., Dawson, G., Sullivan, K., Meltzoff, A. N., Estes, A., & Bernier, R. (2016). Executive function predicts the development of play skills for verbal preschoolers with autism spectrum disorders. *Autism Research, 9*(12), 1274–1284.

Farley, M. A., McMahon, W. M., Fombonne, E., Jenson, W. R., Miller, J., Gardner, M., . . . Coon, H. (2009). Twenty-year outcome for individuals with autism and average or near-average cognitive abilities. *Autism Research, 2*(2), 109–118.

Feeney, T. J., & Ylvisaker, M. (2008). Context-sensitive cognitive-behavioral supports for young children with TBI: A second replication study. *Journal of Positive Behavior Interventions, 10*, 115–128.

Fisher, N., & Happé, F. (2005). A training study of theory of mind and executive function in children with autistic spectrum disorders. *Journal of Autism and Developmental Disorders, 35*(6), 757.

Flynn, E. (2007). The role of inhibitory control in false belief understanding. *Infant and Child Development, 16*(1), 53e69.

Friedman, N. P., & Miyake, A. (2004). The relations among inhibition and interference control functions: A latent-variable analysis. *Journal of Experimental Psychology: General, 133*(1), 101.

Gardiner, E., & Iarocci, G. (2018). Everyday executive function predicts adaptive and internalizing behavior among children with and without autism spectrum disorder. *Autism Research, 11*(2), 284–295.

Garon, N., Bryson, S. E., & Smith, I. M. (2008). Executive function in preschoolers: A review using an integrative framework. *Psychological Bulletin, 134*(1), 31.

Garon, N., Smith, I. M., & Bryson, S. E. (2018). Early executive dysfunction in ASD: Simple versus complex skills. *Autism Research, 11*(2), 318–330.

Geurts, H. M., & Vissers, M. E. (2012). Elderly with autism: Executive functions and memory. *Journal of Autism and Developmental Disorders, 42*, 665–675.

Geurts, H. M., van den Bergh, S. F., & Ruzzano, L. (2014). Prepotent response inhibition and interference control in autism spectrum disorders: Two meta-analyses. *Autism Research, 7*(4), 407–420.

Gilotty, L., Kenworthy, L., Sirian, L., Black, D. O., & Wagner, A. E. (2002). Adaptive skills and executive function in autism spectrum disorders. *Child Neuropsychology, 8*, 241–248.

Gioia, G., Isquith, P., Guy, S., & Kenworthy, L. (2015). *Behavior Rating Inventory of Executive Function* (2nd ed., *BRIEF-2*). Odessa, FL: Psychological Assessment Resources.

Goldman-Rakic, P. S. (1996). Regional and cellular fractionation of working memory. *Proceedings of the National Academy of Sciences, 93*, 13473–13480.

Granader, Y., Wallace, G. L., Hardy, K. K., Yerys, B. E., Lawson, R. A., Rosenthal, M., . . . Kenworthy, L. (2014). Characterizing the factor structure of parent reported executive function in autism spectrum disorders: The impact of cognitive inflexibility. *Journal of Autism and Developmental Disorders.* doi:10.1007/s10803-014-2169-8.

Green, M. F., Nuechterlein, K. H., Gold, J. M., Barch, D. M., Cohen, J., Essock, S., . . . Marder, S. R. (2004). Approaching a consensus cognitive battery for clinical trials in schizophrenia: The NIMH-MATRICS conference to select cognitive domains and test criteria. *Biological Psychiatry, 56*, 301–307.

Griffith, E. M., Pennington, B. F., Wehner, E. A., & Rogers, S. J. (1999). Executive functions in young children with autism. *Child Development, 70*(4), 817–832.

Harrison, P., & Oakland, T. (2003). *Adaptive Behavior Assessment System (ABAS-II).* San Antonio, TX: Psychological Corporation.

Hazlett, H. C., Poe, M. D., Gerig, G., Styner, M., Chappell, C., Smith, R. G., . . . Piven, J. (2011). Early brain overgrowth in autism associated with an increase in cortical surface area before age 2 years. *Archives of General Psychiatry, 68*, 467–476.

Hill, E. L. (2004). Evaluating the theory of executive dysfunction in autism. *Developmental Review, 24*(2), 189–233.

Hill, E. L., & Bird, C. M. (2006). Executive processes in Asperger syndrome: Patterns of performance in a multiple case series. *Neuropsychologia, 44*, 2822–2835.

Hilton, C. L., Cumpata, K., Klohr, C., Gaetka, S., Artner, A., Johnson, H., & Dobbs, S. (2014). Effects on exergaming on executive function and other motor skills in children with autism spectrum disorder: A pilot study. *American Journal of Occupational Therapy, 68*(1), 57e65.

Hinz, A. M. (1989). The tower of Hanoi. Enseign. *Math, 35*(2), 289–321.

Hollocks, M. J., Jones, C. R., Pickles, A., Baird, G., Happé, F., Charman, T., & Simonoff, E. (2014). The association between social cognition and executive functioning and symptoms of anxiety and depression in adolescents with autism spectrum disorders. *Autism Research, 7*(2), 216–228.

Hollocks, M. J., Lerh, J. W., Magiati, I., Meiser-Stedman, R., & Brugha, T. S. (2018). Anxiety and depression in adults with autism spectrum disorder: A systematic review and meta-analysis. *Psychological Medicine*, 1–14.

Howlin, P., Moss, P., Savage, S., & Rutter, M. (2013). Social outcomes in mid-to later adulthood among individuals diagnosed with autism and average nonverbal IQ as children. *Journal of the American Academy of Child & Adolescent Psychiatry, 52*(6), 572–581.

Hughes, C., Leboyer, M., & Bouvard, M. (1997). Executive function in parents of children with autism. *Psychological Medicine, 27,* 209–220.

Hurley, R. S. E., Losh, M., Parlier, M., Reznick, J. S., & Piven, J. (2007). The broad autism phenotype questionnaire. *Journal of Autism and Developmental Disorders, 37,* 1679–1690.

Joshi, G., Wozniak, J., Petty, C., Martelon, M. K., Fried, R., Bolfek, A.,... Biederman, J. (2013). Psychiatric comorbidity and functioning in a clinically referred population of adults with autism spectrum disorders: A comparative study. *Journal of Autism and Developmental Disorders, 43,* 1314–1325.

Jou, R. J., Reed, H. E., Kaiser, M. D., Voos, A. C., Volkmar, F. R., & Pelphrey, K. A. (2016). White matter abnormalities in autism and unaffected siblings. *Journal of Neuropsychiatry and Clinical Neuroscience, 28,* 49–55.

Kamphaus, R. W., & Reynolds, C. R. (2007). *BASC-2 behavioral and emotional screening system manual.* Circle Pines, MN: Pearson.

Kanne, S. M., Gerber, A. J., Quirmbach, L. M., Sparrow, S. S., Cicchetti, D. V., & Saulnier, C. (2011). The role of adaptive behavior in autism spectrum disorders: Implications for functional outcome. *Journal of Autism and Developmental Disorders, 41*(8), 1007–1018.

Kasari, C., & Lawton, K. (2010). New directions in behavioral treatment of autism spectrum disorders. *Current Opinion in Neurology, 23*(2), 137.

Kenworthy, L., Anthony, L. G., Alexander, K. C., Werner, M. A., Cannon, L. M., & Greenman, L. (2014). *Solving executive function challenges: Simple ways to get kids with autism unstuck and on target.* Paul H. Brookes Publishing Company.

Kenworthy, L., Anthony, L. G., Hardy, K., Safer-Lichtenstein, J., Verbalis, A., Biel, M.,... Anthony, B. (2017, May) *Addressing disparities comparative effectiveness trial of community-based executive function treatments in ASD & ADHD.* Paper presented at the International Meeting for Autism Research, San Francisco.

Kenworthy, L., Anthony, L. G., Naiman, D. Q., Cannon, L., Wills, M. C., Luong-Tran, C.,... & Sokoloff, J. L. (2014). Randomized controlled effectiveness trial of executive function intervention for children on the autism spectrum. *Journal of Child Psychology and Psychiatry, 55*(4), 374–383.

Kenworthy, L., Anthony, L. G., & Yerys, B. E. (2012). Autism spectrum disorders. In S. Hunter & E. Sparrow (Eds.), *Executive function and dysfunction: Identification, assessment, and treatment.* Cambridge Press.

Kenworthy, L., Black, D. O., Harrison, B., Della Rosa, A., & Wallace, G. L. (2009). Are executive control functions related to autism symptoms in high-functioning children? *Child Neuropsychology, 15*(5), 425–440.

Kenworthy, L., Black, D., Wallace, G., Ahluvalia, T., Wagner, A., & Sirian, L. (2005). Disorganization: The forgotten executive dysfunction in autism spectrum disorders. *Developmental Neuropsychology, 28,* 809–827.

Kenworthy, L., Powers, M. D., Verbalis, A., Troxel, M., Anthony L., & Myrick, Y. (2018, May). How do we disseminate?: What school staff and parents need to implement evidence based interventions in public schools. In L. Kenworthy (Chair), *Reaching children where they are: The promise and challenge of school-based intervention for autism.* Symposium conducted at the Annual Meeting of the International Society for Autism Research, Rotterdam, Netherlands.

Kenworthy, L., Yerys, B. E., Anthony, L. G., & Wallace, G. L. (2008). Understanding executive control in autism spectrum disorders in the lab and in the real world. *Neuropsychology Review, 18*(4), 320–338.

Klin, A., Saulnier, C. A., Sparrow, S. S., Cicchetti, D. V., Volkmar, F. R., & Lord, C. (2007). Social and communication abilities and disabilities in higher functioning individuals with autism spectrum disorders: The Vineland and the ADOS. *Journal of Autism and Developmental Disorders, 37(*4), 748–759.

Kouklari, E. C., Tsermentseli, S., & Monks, C. P. (2018). Developmental trends of hot and cool executive function in school-aged children with and without autism spectrum disorder: Links with theory of mind. *Development and Psychopathology,* 1–16.

Kumar, A., Sundaram, S. K., Sivaswamy, L., Behen, M. E., Makki, M. I., Ager, J.,... Chugani, D. C. (2010). Alterations in frontal lobe tracts and corpus callosum in young children with autism spectrum disorder. *Cerebral Cortex, 20,* 2103–2113.

Lai, C. L. E., Lau, Z., Lui, S. S., Lok, E., Tam, V., Chan, Q.,... Cheung, E. F. (2017). Meta- analysis of neuropsychological measures of executive functioning in children and adolescents with high-functioning autism spectrum disorder. *Autism Research, 10*(5), 911–939.

Landry, O., & Al-Taie, S. (2016). A meta-analysis of the Wisconsin Card Sort Task in autism. *Journal of Autism and Developmental Disorders, 46*(4), 1220–1235.

Lawson, R. A., Papadakis, A. A., Higginson, C. I., Barnett, J. E., Wills, M. C., Strang, J. F.,... Kenworthy, L. (2014). Everyday executive function impairments predict comorbid psychopathology in autism spectrum and attention deficit hyperactivity disorders. *Neuropsychology, 29*(3), 445.

Le Couteur, A., Rutter, M., Lord, C., Rios, P., Robertson, S., Holdgrafer, M., & McLennan, J. (1989). Autism diagnostic interview: A standardized investigator-based instrument. *Journal of Autism and Developmental Disorders, 19*(3), 363–387.

Leung, R. C., Vogan, V. M., Powell, T. L., Anagnostou, E., & Taylor, M. J. (2016). The role of executive functions in social impairment in autism spectrum disorder. *Child Neuropsychology, 22*(3), 336–344.

Leung, R. C., & Zakzanis, K. K. (2014). Brief report: Cognitive flexibility in autism spectrum disorders: A quantitative review. *Journal of Autism and Developmental Disorders, 44*(10), 2628–2645.

Lever, A. G., & Geurts, H. M. (2016). Age-related differences in cognition across the adult lifespan in autism spectrum disorder. *Autism Research, 9,* 666–676.

Leyfer, O. T., Folstein, S. E., Bacalman, S., Davis, N. O., Dinh, E., Morgan, J.,... Lainhart, J. E. (2006). Comorbid psychiatric disorders in children with autism: Interview development and rates of disorders. *Journal of Autism and Developmental Disorders, 36,* 849–861.

Livingston, L. A., Colvert, E., Social Relationships Study Team, Bolton, P., & Happé, F. (2018). Good social skills despite poor theory of mind: Exploring compensation in autism spectrum disorder. *Journal of Child Psychology and Psychiatry.*

Lopez, B. R., Lincoln, A. J., Ozonoff, S., & Lai, Z. (2005). Examining the relationship between executive functions and restricted, repetitive symptoms of autistic disorder. *Journal of Autism and Developmental Disorders, 35*(4), 445–460.

Lord, C., Rutter, M., DiLavore, P. C., Risi, S., Gotham, K., & Bishop, S. L. (1999). *ADOS. Autism Diagnostic Observation Schedule. Manual.* Los Angeles, CA: WPS.

Losh, M., Adolphs, R., Poe, M. D., Couture, S., Penn, D., Baranek, G. T., & Piven, J. (2009). Neuropsychological profile of autism and the broad autism phenotype. *Archives of General Psychiatry, 66*, 518–526.

Luna, B., Doll, S. K., Hegedus, S. J., Minshew, N. J., & Sweeney, J. A. (2007). Maturation of executive function in autism. *Biological Psychiatry, 61*(4), 474–481.

Lugnegård, T., Hallerbäck, M. U., & Gillberg, C. (2011). Psychiatric comorbidity in young adults with a clinical diagnosis of Asperger syndrome. *Research in Developmental Disabilities, 32*(5), 1910–1917.

Lynch, C. J., Breeden, A. L., You, X., Ludlum, R., Gaillard, W. D., Kenworthy, L., & Vaidya, C. J. (2017). Executive dysfunction in autism spectrum disorder is associated with a failure to modulate frontoparietal-insular hub architecture. *Biological Psychiatry: Cognitive Neuroscience and Neuroimaging, 2*, 537–545.

Manly, T. I. H. R., Robertson, I. H., Anderson, V., & Nimmo-Smith, I. (1999). *TEA-Ch: The test of everyday attention for children manual.* Bury St. Edmunds, UK: Thames Valley Test Company.

McEvoy, R. E., Rogers, S. J., & Pennington, B. F. (1993). Executive function and social communication deficits in young autistic children. *Journal of Child Psychology and Psychiatry, 34*(4), 563–578.

McLean, R. L., Harrison, A. J., Zimak, E., Joseph, R. M., & Morrow, E. M. (2014). Executive function in probands with autism with average IQ and their unaffected first-degree relatives. *Journal of the American Academy of Child & Adolescent Psychiatry, 53*(9), 1001–1009.

Mesulam, M. (2002). Principles of frontal lobe function. In D. T. Stuss & R. T. Knight (Eds.), *The human frontal lobes: Transcending the default mode through contingent encoding* (pp. 8–30). Oxford, UK: Oxford University Press.

Miller, E. K., & Cohen, J. D. (2001). An integrative theory of prefrontal cortex function. *Annual Review of Neuroscience, 24*, 167–202.

Miyake, A., Friedman N. P., Emerson, M. J., Witzki, A. H., Howerter, A., & Wager, T. D. (2000). The unity and diversity of executive functions and their contributions to complex "frontal lobe" tasks: A latent variable analysis. *Cognitive Psychology, 41*(1), 49–100.

Nakahachi, T., Iwase, M., Takahashi, H., Honaga, E., Sekiyama, R., Ukai, S., . . . Hashimoto, R. (2006). Discrepancy of performance among working memory related tasks in autism spectrum disorders was caused by task characteristics, apart from working memory, which could interfere with task execution. *Psychiatry and Clinical Neurosciences, 60*(3), 312–318.

O'Hearn, K., Asato, M., Ordaz, S., & Luna, B. (2008). Neurodevelopment and executive function in autism. *Development and Psychopathology, 20*(4), 1103–1132.

Ozonoff, S., & McEvoy, R. E. (1994). A longitudinal study of executive function and theory of mind development in autism. *Development and Psychopathology, 6*(3), 415–431.

Ozonoff, S., Pennington, B. F., & Rogers, S. J. (1991). Executive function deficits in high- functioning autistic individuals: Relationship to theory of mind. *Journal of Child Psychology and Psychiatry, 32*(7), 1081–1105.

Pellicano, E. (2007). Links between theory of mind and executive function in young children with autism: Clues to developmental primacy. *Developmental Psychology, 43*(4), 974–990. doi:10.1037/0012-1649.43.4.974

Pellicano, E. (2010). Individual differences in executive function and central coherence predict developmental changes in theory of mind in autism. *Developmental Psychology*, 46(2), 530. doi:10.1037/a0018287

Pellicano, E. (2012). The development of executive function in autism. *Autism Research and Treatment, 2012*, 146132. doi:10.1155/2012/146132

Pellicano, E. (2013). Testing predictive power of cognitive atypicalities in autistic children: Evidence from a 3-year follow-up study. *Autism Research*, 6(4), 258–267.

Pellicano, E., Kenny, L., Brede, J., Klaric, E., Lichwa, H., & McMillin, R. (2017). Executive function predicts school readiness in autistic and typical preschool children. *Cognitive Development, 43*, 1–13.

Pennington, B. F., & Ozonoff, S. (1996). Executive functions and developmental psychopathology. *Journal of Child Psychology and Psychiatry, 37*, 51–87.

Perner, J., & Lang, B. (1999). Development of theory of mind and executive control. *Trends in Cognitive Sciences, 3*(9), 337–344.

Piven, J., & Palmer, P. (1997). Cognitive deficits in parents from multiple- incidence autism families. *Journal of Child Psychology and Psychiatry, 38*, 1011–1021.

Powell, P. S., Klinger, L. G., & Klinger, M. R. (2017). Patterns of age-related cognitive differences in adults with autism spectrum disorder. *Journal of Autism and Developmental Disorders, 47*, 3204–3219.

Prencipe, A., Kesek, A., Cohen, J., Lamm, C., Lewis, M. D., & Zelazo, P. D. (2011). Development of hot and cool executive function during the transition to adolescence. *Journal of Experimental Child Psychology, 108*(3), 621–637. doi:10.1016/j.jecp.2010.09.008

Prins, P. J. M., Brink, E. T., Dovis, S., Ponsioen, A., Geurts, H. M., de Vries, M., & van der Oord, S. (2013). "Braingame Brian": Toward an executive function training program with game elements for children with ADHD and cognitive control problems. *Games for Health Journal, 2*, 44–49.

Pugliese, C. E., Anthony, L., Strang, J. F., Dudley, K., Wallace, G. L., & Kenworthy, L. (2015). Increasing adaptive behavior skill deficits from childhood to adolescence in autism spectrum disorder: Role of executive function. *Journal of Autism and Developmental Disorders, 45*(6), 1579–1587.

Pugliese, C. E., Anthony, L. G., Strang, J. F., Dudley, K., Wallace, G. L., Naiman, D. Q., & Kenworthy, L. (2016). Longitudinal examination of adaptive behavior in autism spectrum disorders: Influence of executive function. *Journal of Autism and Developmental Disorders, 46*(2), 467–477.

Pugliese, C. E., You, X., Powers, M. D., Anthony, L. G., Vaidya, C., & Kenworthy, L. (in prep). *Parsing the heterogeneity of autism through EF profiles to differentiate psychiatric symptoms.* Manuscript in preparation.

Raznahan, A., Lenroot, R., Thurm, A., Gozzi, M., Hanley, A., Spence, S. J., . . . Giedd, J. N. (2012). Mapping cortical anatomy in preschool aged children with autism using surface-based morphometry. *NeuroImage Clinical, 2*, 111–119.

Reitan, R. M., & Wolfson, D. (1993). The Halstead-Reitan neuropsychological test battery: Theory and clinical applications.

Riggs, N. R., Greenberg, M. T., Kusché, C. A., & Pentz, M. A. (2006). The mediational role of neurocognition in the behavioral outcomes of a social-emotional prevention program in elementary school students: Effects of the PATHS curriculum. *Prevention Science, 7*(1), 91–102.

Ronald, A., Happé, F., & Plomin, R. (2005). The genetic relationship between individual differences in social and nonsocial behaviours characteristic of autism. *Developmental Science, 8*, 444–458.

Ronald, A., & Hoekstra, R. A. (2011). Autism spectrum disorders and autistic traits: A decade of new twin studies. *American Journal of Medical Genetics, Part B, Neuropsychiatric Genetics, 156*, 255–274.

Rosen, T. E., Mazefsky, C. A., Vasa, R. A., & Lerner, M. D. (2018). Co-occurring psychiatric conditions in autism spectrum disorder. *International Review of Psychiatry, 30*(1), 40–61.

Rosenthal, M., Wallace, G. L., Lawson, R., Wills, M. C., Dixon, E., Yerys, B. E., & Kenworthy, L. (2013). Impairments in real-world executive function increase from childhood to adolescence in autism spectrum disorders. *Neuropsychology, 27*(1), 13.

Roth, R. M., Isquith, P. K., & Gioia, G. A. (2005). *Behavior Rating Inventory of Executive Function—Adult version (BRIEF-A)*. Lutz, FL: Psychological Assessment Resources.

Roux, A. M., Shattuck, P. T., Cooper, B. P., Anderson, K. A., Wagner, M., & Narendorf, S. C. (2013). Postsecondary employment experiences among young adults with an autism spectrum disorder. *Journal of the American Academy of Child & Adolescent Psychiatry, 52*(9), 931–939.

Rumsey, J. M. (1985). Conceptual problem-solving in highly verbal, nonretarded autistic men. *Journal of Autism and Developmental Disorders, 15*, 23–36.

Rumsey, J. M., & Hamburger, S. D. (1988). Neuropsychological findings in high-functioning men with infantile autism, residual state. *Journal of Clinical and Experimental Neuropsychology, 10*, 201–221.

Rumsey, J. M., & Hamburger, S. D. (1990). Neuropsychological divergence of high-level autism and severe dyslexia. *Journal of Autism and Developmental Disorders, 20*, 155–168.

Russell, J., Mauthner, N., Sharpe, S., & Tidswell, T. (1991). The "windows task" as a measure of strategic deception in preschoolers and autistic subjects. *British Journal of Developmental Psychology, 9*(2), 331–349.

Ruzich, E., Allison, C., Smith, P., Watson, P., Auyeung, B., Ring, H., & Baron-Cohen, S. (2015). Measuring autistic traits in the general population: A systematic review of the autism-spectrum quotient (AQ) in a nonclinical population of 6,900 typical adult males and females. *Molecular Autism, 6*.

Sasson, N. J., Lam, K. S., Parlier, M., Daniels, J. L., & Piven, J. (2013). Autism and the broad autism phenotype: Familial patterns and intergenerational transmission. *Journal of Neurodevelopmental Disorders, 5*.

Sasson, N. J., Lam, K. S. L., Childress, D., Parlier, M., Daniels, J. L., & Piven, J. (2013). The broad autism phenotype questionnaire: Prevalence and diagnostic classification. *Autism Research, 6*, 134–143.

Schmitz, N., Rubia, K., Daly, E., Smith, A., Williams, S., & Murphy, D. G. (2006). Neural correlates of executive function in autistic spectrum disorders. *Biological Psychiatry, 59*, 7–16.

Sergeant, J. A., Geurts, H., & Oosterlaan, J. (2002). How specific is a deficit of executive functioning for attention-deficit/hyperactivity disorder? *Behavioral and Brain Research, 130*, 3–28.

Shattuck, P. T., Narendorf, S. C., Cooper, B., Sterzing, P. R., Wagner, M., & Taylor, J. L. (2012). Postsecondary education and employment among youth with an autism spectrum disorder. *Pediatrics, 129*(6), 1042–1049.

Simonoff, E., Pickles, A., Charman, T., Chandler, S., Loucas, T., & Baird, G. (2008). Psychiatric disorders in children with autism spectrum disorders: Prevalence, comorbidity, and associated factors in a population-derived sample. *Journal of the American Academy of Child and Adolescent Psychiatry, 47*, 921–929.

Skuse, D. H., Mandy, W. P., & Scourfield, J. (2005). Measuring autistic traits: Heritability, reliability and validity of the social and communication disorders checklist. *British Journal of Psychiatry, 187*, 568–572.

Smithson, P. E., Kenworthy, L., Wills, M. C., Jarrett, M., Atmore, K., & Yerys, B. E. (2013). Real world executive control impairments in preschoolers with autism spectrum disorders. *Journal of Autism and Developmental Disorders, 43*, 1967–1975. doi:10.1007/s10803-012-1747-x –

Sparrow, S., Balla, D. A., & Cicchetti, D. (1984). *Vineland Adaptive Behavior Scales (expanded form)*. Circle Pine, MN: American Guidance Service.

Sparrow, S. S., Cicchetti, D. V., & Saulnier, C. A. (2016). *Vineland-3: Vineland Adaptive Behavior Scales*. PsychCorp.

Solomon, M., Goodlin-Jones, B. L., & Anders, T. F. (2004). A social adjustment enhancement intervention for high functioning autism, Asperger's syndrome, and pervasive developmental disorder NOS. *Journal of Autism and Developmental Disorders, 34*(6), 649–668.

Stahl, L., & Pry, R. (2002). Joint attention and set-shifting in young children with autism. *Autism, 6*(4), 383–396.

Stewart, M. E., Barnard, L., Pearson, J., Hasan, R., & O'Brien, G. (2006). Presentation of depression in autism and Asperger syndrome: A review. *Autism, 10*, 103–116.

Stichter, J. P., Herzog, M. J., Visovsky, K., Schmidt, C., Randolph, J., Schultz, T., & Gage, N. (2010). Social competence intervention for youth with Asperger syndrome and high-functioning autism: An initial investigation. *Journal of Autism and Developmental Disorders, 40*(9), 1067–1079.

Stichter, J. P., O'Connor, K. V., Herzog, M. J., Lierheimer, K., & McGhee, S. D. (2012). Social competence intervention for elementary students with Aspergers syndrome and high functioning autism. *Journal of Autism and Developmental Disorders, 42*(3), 354–366.

St. John, T., Dawson, G., & Estes, A. (2018). Brief report: Executive function as a predictor of academic achievement in school-aged children with ASD. *Journal of Autism and Developmental Disorders, 48*(1), 276–283.

Stewart, G. R., Charlton, R. A., & Wallace, G. L. (2018). Aging with elevated autistic traits: Cognitive functioning among older adults with the broad autism phenotype. *Research in Autism Spectrum Disorders, 54*, 27–36.

Stuss, D. T., & Alexander, M. P. (2000). Executive functions and the frontal lobes: A conceptual view. *Psychological Research, 63*(3–4), 289–298.

Szatmari, P., Bartolucci, G., Bremner, R., Bond, S., & Rich, S. (1989). A follow-up study of high-functioning autistic children. *Journal of Autism and Developmental Disorders, 19*(2), 213–225.

Tager-Flusberg, H., & Joseph, R. M. (2005). Theory of mind, language, and executive functions in autism: A longitudinal perspective. In W. Schneider, R. Schumann-Hengsteler, & B. Sodian (Eds.), *Young children's cognitive development: Interrelationships among executive functioning, working memory, verbal ability, and theory of mind* (pp. 239–258). Mahwah, NJ: Erlbaum.

Taylor, J. L., Henninger, N. A., & Mailick, M. R. (2015). Longitudinal patterns of employment and postsecondary education for adults with autism and average-range IQ. *Autism, 19*(7), 785–793.

Towgood, K. J., Meuwese, J. D., Gilbert, S. J., Turner, M. S., & Burgess, P. W. (2009). Advantages of the multiple case series approach to the study of cognitive deficits in autism spectrum disorder. *Neuropsychologia, 47*, 2981–2988.

Turner, M. A. (1997). Towards an executive dysfunction account of repetitive behaviour in autism. In J. Russell (Ed.), *Autism as an executive disorder* (pp. 57–100). Oxford, UK: Oxford University Press.

Van Eylen, L., Boets, B., Cosemans, N., Peeters, H., Steyaert, J., Wagemans, J., & Noens, I. (2017). Executive functioning and local-global visual processing: Candidate endophenotypes for autism spectrum disorder? *Journal of Child Psychology and Psychiatry, 58*, 258–269.

van Rooij, D., Anagnostou, E., Arango, C., Auzias, G., Behrmann, M., Busatto, G. F., . . . Buitelaar, J. K. (2018). Cortical and subcortical brain morphometry differences between patients with autism spectrum disorder and healthy individuals across the lifespan: Results from the ENIGMA ASD working group. *American Journal of Psychiatry, 175*, 359–369. doi:10.1176/appi.ajp.2017.17010100.

van Steensel, F. J., Bögels, S. M., & Perrin, S. (2011). Anxiety disorders in children and adolescents with autistic spectrum disorders: A meta-analysis. *Clinical Child and Family Psychology Review, 14*(3), 302.

Wallace, G. L., Budgett, J., & Charlton, R. (2016). Aging and autism spectrum disorder: Evidence from the broad autism phenotype. *Autism Research, 9*, 1294–1303. doi:10.1002/aur.1620

Wallace, G. L., Dankner, N., Kenworthy, L., Giedd, J. N., & Martin, A. (2010). Age-related temporal and parietal cortical thinning in autism spectrum disorders. *Brain, 133*, 3745–3754.

Wallace, G. L., Kenworthy, L., Pugliese, C. E., Popal, H. S., White, E. I., Brodsky, E., & Martin, A. (2016). Real-world executive functions in adults with autism spectrum disorder: Profiles of impairment and associations with adaptive functioning and co-morbid anxiety and depression. *Journal of Autism and Developmental Disorders, 46*(3), 1071–1083.

Wallace, G. L., Robustelli, B., Dankner, N., Kenworthy, L., Giedd, J. N., & Martin, A. (2013). Increased gyrification but comparable surface area in adolescents with high functioning autism spectrum disorders. *Brain, 136*, 1956–1967.

Wallace, G. L., Yerys, B. E., Peng, C., Dlugi, E., Anthony, L. G., & Kenworthy, L. (2016). Assessment and treatment of executive function impairments in autism spectrum disorder: An update. In R. M. Hodapp & D. J. Fidler (Eds.), *International review of research in developmental disabilities* (pp. 85–122).

Watts, T. W., Gandhi, J., Ibrahim, D. A., Masucci, M. D., & Raver, C. C. (2018). The Chicago School Readiness Project: Examining the long-term impacts of an early childhood intervention. *PloS One, 13*(7), e0200144.

Wheelwright, S., Auyeung, B., Allison, C., & Baron-Cohen, S. (2010). Defining the broader, medium and narrow autism phenotype among parents using the autism spectrum quotient (AQ). *Molecular Autism, 1*.

Wiebe, S. A., Espy, K. A., & Charak, D. (2008). Using confirmatory factor analysis to understand executive control in preschool children: I. Latent structure. *Developmental Psychology, 44*(2), 575.

Wiebe, S. A., Sheffield, T., Nelson, J. M., Clark, C. A., Chevalier, N., & Espy, K. A. (2011). The structure of executive function in 3-year-olds. *Journal of Experimental Child Psychology, 108*(3), 436–452.

Williams, D. L., Goldstein, G., Carpenter, P. A., & Minshew, N. J. (2005). Verbal and spatial working memory in autism. *Journal of Autism and Developmental Disorders, 35*(6), 747.

Wong, D., Maybery, M., Bishop, D. V., Maley, A., & Hallmayer, J. (2006). Profiles of executive function in parents and siblings of individuals with autism spectrum disorders. *Genes, Brain and Behavior, 5*, 561–576.

Yerys, B. E., Antezana, L., Weinblatt, R., Jankowski, K. F., Strang, J., Vaidya, C. J., . . . Kenworthy, L. (2015). Neural correlates of set-shifting in children with autism. *Autism Research, 8*, 386–397.

Yerys, B. E., Hepburn, S. L., Pennington, B. F., & Rogers, S. J. (2007). Executive function in preschoolers with autism: Evidence consistent with a secondary deficit. *Journal of Autism and Developmental Disorders, 37*(6), 1068–1079.

Yerys, B. E., Wallace, G. L., Sokoloff, J. L., Shook, D. A., James, J. D., & Kenworthy, L. (2009). Attention deficit/hyperactivity disorder symptoms moderate cognition and behavior in children with autism spectrum disorders. *Autism Research, 2*(6), 322–333.

Ylvisaker, M., & Feeney, T. (1998). *Collaborative brain injury intervention: Positive everyday routines*. San Diego, CA: Cengage Learning.

Zelazo, P. D., Qu, L., Müller, U., & Schneider, W. (2005). Hot and cool aspects of executive function: Relations in early development. In *Young children's cognitive development: Interrelationships among executive functioning, working memory, verbal ability, and theory of mind* (pp. 71–93). Mahwah, NJ: Lawrence Erlbaum Associates.

Zelazo, P. D., Müller, U., Frye, D., Marcovitch, S., Argitis, G., Boseovski, J., . . . Carlson, S. M. (2003). The development of executive function in early childhood. *Monographs of the Society for Research in Child Development*, i–151.

Zimmerman, D., Ownsworth, T., O'Donovan, A., Roberts, J., & Gullo, M. J. (2017). Associations between executive functions and mental health outcomes for adults with autism spectrum disorder. *Psychiatry Research, 253*, 360–363.

CHAPTER

17

Self-Injurious Behavior in Individuals With Autism Spectrum Disorder

Jennifer N. Haddock *and* Louis P. Hagopian

Abstract

Individuals with autism spectrum disorder (ASD) and other intellectual and developmental disabilities are at increased risk for engaging in one or more types of problem behavior (e.g., aggression, property destruction, self-injury). Self-injurious behavior (SIB)—a broad class of behavior that produces (or could produce) physical injury to an individual's own body—is common among individuals with ASD. SIB poses immediate and long-term risks for the individuals and their caregivers. This chapter summarizes the prevalence and developmental course of SIB in individuals with ASD, as well as research on the etiology, diagnosis, assessment, and evidence-based treatments for SIB. Case examples and suggestions for future research are provided.

Keywords: self-injury, self-injurious behavior, autism, autism spectrum disorder, developmental disability

Overview

Individuals with autism spectrum disorder (ASD) and other intellectual and developmental disabilities (IDD) are at increased risk for engaging in one or more types of problem behavior (e.g., aggression, property destruction, self-injury; Emerson et al., 2001a; Jang, Dixon, Tarbox, & Granpeesheh, 2011; Kurtz, Chin, Huete, & Cataldo, 2012; McClintock, Hall, & Oliver, 2003; McTiernan, Leader, Healy, & Mannion, 2011). Self-injurious behavior (SIB), the focus of the current chapter, refers to behaviors that produce (or could produce) physical injury to an individual's own body (Schroeder, Mulick, & Rojahn, 1980; Tate & Baroff, 1966).[1] Many individuals engage in multiple forms (topographies) of SIB, which include head hitting and headbanging (forceful contact between head and body, objects, or surfaces), self-biting, eye poking or eye gouging, and body-focused repetitive behaviors such as dermatillomania skin picking and trichotillomania, or hair pulling (Kahng, Iwata, & Lewin, 2002; Miltenberger & Spieler, 2016; Oliver, Murphy, & Corbett, 1987; Richards, Davies, & Oliver, 2017). Topographies such as aerophagia (air swallowing), bruxism (teeth grinding), pica (ingesting inedible objects), and rumination (self-induced vomiting) are also considered to be self-injurious (Kahng et al., 2002), though infrequently categorized as SIB in the research literature. The most prevalent topographies of SIB in individuals with ASD are self-biting and self-hitting (Buono, Scannella, & Palmigiano, 2010; Folch et al., 2018; Rice et al., 2015; Richards et al., 2017). In addition to its topography, SIB also varies across other dimensions, including its frequency (rate), intensity (severity), and operant reinforcing function (hereafter referred to as "function").

Decades of behavioral research indicate that the dimension most relevant to understanding and treating SIB is its function. As used here, the term "function" refers to the environmental (social and/

[1] Interestingly, the term "SIB" is applied to IDD populations, whereas the terms "self-mutilation" or "nonsuicidal self-injury (NSSI)" are applied to non-IDD populations (cf. Maddox, Trubanova, & White, 2017; Matson & Turygin, 2012). Research is needed to examine whether selective use of these terms has any clinical or scientific basis.

or biological) variables that are responsible for the continued occurrence, or maintenance, of a given behavior. Through operant learning processes, the events that reliably precede and follow the occurrence of SIB (antecedents and consequences, respectively) come to occasion and reinforce it, making it more likely to occur under similar conditions in the future. The reinforcers that can maintain SIB fall into two broad classes: social reinforcers, which are consequences mediated by other people, and automatic reinforcers, which are biological or physiological consequences directly produced by SIB. Each of these broad classes can be subclassified, or subtyped. Identifying the subclasses of reinforcers that occasion and maintain SIB is critical because treatments informed by the function of an individual's SIB are the most effective in reducing the behavior (Hurl, Wightman, Haynes, & Virues-Ortega, 2016). Functional behavioral assessment (FBA) methods, which will be discussed herein, are used to objectively identify these controlling variables.

SIB can impose direct and immediate risks to the individual, including contusions, concussions, and lacerations. Severe and chronic SIB has been documented to result in body disfigurement and mutilation (e.g., loss of tongue mass, loss of cartilage, erosion of nasal septum), permanent eye damage (e.g., retinal detachment, blindness), infections, hematomas, and brain lesions, and it has been identified as a contributing cause of death (Geddes, Vowles, Nicoll, & Révész, 1999; Hof, Knabe, Bovier, & Bouras, 1991; Hyman, Fisher, Mercugliano, & Cataldo, 1990; D. Kuhn, Hagopian, & Terlonge, 2008; Nissen & Haveman, 1997). In addition to the physical risks, chronic SIB can increase risk of placement into restrictive social, educational, and residential settings (Tausig, 1985), as well as the use of pharmacological and physical restraint (Aman, Lam, & Bourgondien, 2005; Gaskin, McVilly, & McGillivray, 2013; Harris, 1996; McGillivray & McCabe, 2004; Oliver et al., 1987; D. E. Williams & Grossett, 2011).

SIB also can greatly affect the quality of life of caregivers and family members across emotional, social, and financial domains (Emerson, 2003; Hastings, 2002, 2006; Rattaz, Michelon, & Baghdadli, 2015). In addition, parents of children with ASD and/or IDD and problem behavior have been found to be more stressed, psychologically distressed, and in poorer health than those of matched controls (Eisenhower, Baker, & Blacher, 2009; Eisenhower, Blacher, & Baker, 2013; Estes et al., 2009). Over time, decreased quality of life and chronic stress can adversely affect caregivers' health (Miodrag & Hodapp, 2010), which may impair their ability to implement certain treatments for problem behavior (Prinz & Miller, 1996). Treatment infidelity is likely to result in the recurrence of problem behavior (Volkert, Lerman, Call, & Trosclair-Lasserre, 2009), thus creating a self-perpetuating cycle. These problems extend beyond the family unit and are of public health concern in that individuals with ASD and/or IDD require increased health care and specialist services (McDermott, Zhou, & Mann, 2008; Schieve et al., 2012).

Prevalence and Course

Over the last 15 years, the prevalence of SIB in noninstitutionalized infants, children, adolescents, and adults with ASD has been estimated to be between 6% and 74%, but the majority of estimates fall between 30% and 50% (Baghdadli, Pascal, Grisi, & Aussilloux, 2003; Billstedt, Gillberg, & Gillberg, 2005; Buono et al., 2010; Cooper et al., 2009; Dimian et al., 2017; Eaves & Ho, 2008; Folch et al., 2018; Maddox, Trubanova, & White, 2017; Richards, Davies, & Oliver, 2017; Richards, Moss, Nelson, & Oliver, 2016; Richards, Oliver, Nelson, & Moss, 2012; Shattuck et al., 2007; Soke et al., 2016, 2018). Presumably, the discrepancies in prevalence findings are due to differences in study methodologies, the most notable of which include recruitment parameters, sample sizes and characteristics (e.g., age ranges, comorbid diagnoses, diagnostic criteria), definitions of SIB, types of measures and instruments, and the intervals in which SIB was observed or reported to occur (e.g., at the time of sampling, in the 6 months prior, at any point in the individual's lifetime), some of which go unreported.

It is well established that SIB often emerges early and commonly persists across the lifespan of individuals with IDD (e.g., Emerson et al., 2001b; Symons, Sperry, Dropik, & Bodfish, 2005; Taylor, Oliver, & Murphy, 2011). For instance, Taylor et al. (2011) conducted a 20-year follow-up on a population-based study of individuals with IDD in the United Kingdom and found no significant changes in the topographies or severity of SIB in a cohort of 49 individuals, as reported by caregivers. Although individuals with ASD were no doubt subsamples of the population in this and other studies that examined prevalence of SIB in individuals with IDD, less is known about the developmental course (emergence, cessation, and maintenance) of SIB in individuals with ASD specifically.

Infants and toddlers. Neurotypically developing infants frequently engage in repetitive and rhythmic behaviors, including some forms of SIB such as headbanging (e.g., de Lissovoy, 1962; Kravitz & Boehm, 1971; Sallustro & Atwell, 1978; Thelen, 1979). These behaviors often emerge and then diminish in a predictable sequence and are thought to correspond to motor development and maturation of the central nervous system (Wolff, 1967). As neurotypically developing children's motor skills develop and more complex behaviors are acquired, repetitive behaviors are gradually replaced with other, perhaps more adaptive and socially acceptable, topographies of repetitive behaviors (Baghdadli et al., 2003; Kravitz & Boehm, 1971).

However, this does not seem to be the case for infants and toddlers with ASD; in fact, the presence of ASD symptomology has been shown to increase the risk of continued occurrence (maintenance) and increased severity of SIB during early childhood (e.g., Dimian et al., 2017; Fodstad, Rojahn, & Matson, 2012; Soke et al., 2018). For instance, Dimian et al. (2017) found the prevalence of SIB in infants at high familial risk for ASD to be 39% and 32% of the total sample at 12 and 24 months of age, respectively. At 24 months, 20% of these infants met diagnostic criteria for ASD, 74% of whom reportedly engaged in one or more topographies of SIB at either time point, compared to only 47% of those without an ASD diagnosis. Further, at 24 months, the SIB of the ASD subgroup was more likely to have persisted or emerged since the first measure at 12 months—in fact, their risk of SIB at 24 months was nearly twice that of those without ASD symptomology. These results suggest that, in infancy, SIB is more likely to emerge and maintain when ASD symptomology is also present. These results support those of Kurtz et al. (2012), who found that multiple topographies of SIB emerged prior to 12 months of age in infants with ASD; and they converge with those of Fodstad et al. (2012), who found that, although similar topographies of SIB were exhibited across groups of atypically developing infants and toddlers, SIB was more frequent and severe in infants and toddlers with ASD than those without it.

Children and adolescents. Estimates of the prevalence of SIB in children and adolescents with ASD range from 28% to 53% (Baghdadli et al., 2003; Rattaz et al., 2015; Richards et al., 2017; Soke et al., 2016). Recently, Soke et al. (2016) reviewed the educational and health records of 8,065 children with ASD; it was found that approximately 28% of these children engaged in SIB at some point during their education or health care. Curiously, this estimate is nearly half that of Baghdadli et al. (2003) and Fodstad et al. (2012), who both found approximately 50% of caregivers of children with ASD reported SIB at the time of sampling or in their lifetime, respectively.

Little is known about the emergence and course of SIB in children and adolescents with ASD, but a recent longitudinal study suggests it is likely to persist in childhood (Richards et al., 2016). Initially, SIB was reported by 6% of caregivers of children with ASD; after 3 years, 78% of those caregivers reported no change in the frequency, severity, or topography of their children's SIB. Although only a small percentage of the sample engaged in SIB, these data tentatively suggest that SIB in children with ASD may persist in the majority of cases.

Similarly, in one sample of children diagnosed with pervasive developmental disorders, Baghdadli et al. (2008) found that, over the course of a 3-year period, the prevalence of SIB declined from 49% to 33%. Notably, the presence of ASD symptoms and communication deficits was associated with the persistence, worsening, or appearance of SIB at follow-up. Thus, it may be the case that SIB in children with ASD is persistent and chronic, though further research is needed.

Adults. The prevalence of SIB in noninstitutionalized adults with ASD ranges from approximately 8% to 50%, though most estimates fall between 30% and 50% (Billstedt et al., 2005; Bowring, Totsika, Hastings, Toogood, & Griffith , 2017; Cooper et al., 2009; Eaves & Ho, 2008; Folch et al., 2018; Richards et al., 2017). It has been shown that SIB decreases in adults with IDD (Taylor et al., 2011), yet SIB in adults with ASD may be as prevalent as it is in children with ASD (Matson, Mahan, Hess, Fodstad, & Neal, 2010; Richards et al., 2017). For instance, Richards et al. (2017) found that approximately 46% of children and 50% of adults with ASD reportedly engaged in SIB within the past month. Other studies have reported similar prevalence rates of SIB in adults with ASD, despite methodological differences (Billstedt et al., 2005; Eaves & Ho, 2008; Folch et al., 2018). There is even evidence to suggest that some topographies of SIB, such as skin picking and head banging, may increase over time in individuals with ASD (Rice et al., 2016), but more research is needed to clarify the effects of aging on SIB in individuals with ASD.

Etiology, Diagnosis, and Assessment

Etiology

It is important for researchers to make a distinction between the variables responsible for the emergence of SIB (initial occurrence) and those responsible for its maintenance (continued occurrence after the first instance, or chronicity). This distinction is needed because SIB, like other behaviors, is shaped and changes as a function of its interaction with the environment. Research aimed at understanding how SIB emerges requires consideration of developmental factors and numerous biological variables necessitating use of epidemiological, cross-sectional, and longitudinal methods. From a clinical standpoint, identifying the variables responsible for the emergence of SIB could inform prevention and early intervention efforts. Research on the maintenance of SIB, however, is more individual focused and requires analysis of the variables that presently control and maintain it (i.e., its function). Clinically, identifying these variables is the goal of assessment and is essential to successful treatment.

The heterogeneity of SIB—in its form and function—suggests that it has multiple etiologies (Furniss & Biswas, 2012; Richman, 2008). There is a general consensus that SIB has no common pathology among individuals with ASD and that complex environmental–biological interactions contribute to its initial emergence and maintenance over time (e.g., Hagopian & Frank-Crawford, 2017; Langthorne & McGill, 2008; Oliver et al., 2013; Schroeder et al., 2001). However, there is little doubt that ASD symptomology increases the risk of SIB. The presence and severity of ASD core symptomology—particularly communication deficits—has been associated with an increased occurrence of SIB in a number of studies (e.g., Baghdadli et al., 2003; Emerson et al., 2001a; McClintock et al., 2003; Rattaz et al., 2015; Richards et al., 2012, 2016), even when ASD diagnoses were not (Bowring et al., 2017; Lowe et al., 2007). For example, McClintock et al. (2003) found that individuals with ASD diagnoses were approximately 6 times more likely to engage in SIB than individuals with IDD without comorbid ASD, but across groups, the presence of severe or profound IDD and/or receptive and expressive communication deficits significantly increased the risk of SIB as well.

There is a higher prevalence of SIB in individuals with certain genetic syndromes (e.g., Cornelia de Lange, fragile X, Lesch-Nyhan, Prader-Willi, and Smith-Magenis syndromes) than in individuals with other genetic syndromes (e.g., Angelman syndrome) or individuals with IDD of unknown etiology (Oliver et al., 2013; Rice et al., 2016). In fact, SIB is a behavioral phenotype of 12 genetic syndromes, meaning it presents similarly in terms of topographies, age of onset, severity, and chronicity across individuals with that syndrome, which suggests a common, presumably genetic, etiology (for a review, see Huisman et al., 2018). No such patterns have been observed in individuals with ASD (Huisman et al., 2018; cf. Shirley et al., 2016), though the presence of ASD symptomology (not accounted for by degree of IDD) may account for the higher prevalence of SIB in genetic syndromes (Oliver & Richards, 2015). Based on existing evidence regarding genetic and environmental risk markers for SIB, Oliver and Richards (2015) proposed a phenotype–environmental model of the developmental trajectory of SIB in individuals with ASD and genetic syndromes.

Potential risk factors/markers. Other variables that may contribute to the emergence and/or maintenance of SIB in individuals with ASD and/or IDD include, in no particular order, limited social contact (e.g., Hall, Oliver, & Murphy, 2001); stereotypic and ritualistic behaviors (e.g., Duerden et al., 2012); impoverished environments and low vestibular stimulation (Cataldo & Harris, 1982; Devine, 2014); frustrative events (Furniss & Biswas, 2012); comorbid body rocking or yelling (e.g., Barnard-Brak, Rojahn, Richman, Chestnut, & Wei, 2015); level of IDD (e.g., McClintock et al., 2003); sleep disorders and disturbances (e.g., Soke et al., 2017; Symons, Davis, & Thompson, 2000); experience of health problems, physical discomfort, or pain-related events (e.g., Courtemanche, Black, & Reese, 2016; De Winter, Jansen, & Evenhuis, 2011; Folch et al., 2018; Richards et al., 2017); psychiatric medication intake (Folch et al., 2018); behavioral manifestations of anxiety (e.g., Williams, Leader, Mannion, & Chen, 2015); overactivity and impulsive behavior (e.g., Richards et al., 2016, 2017); and factors associated with low socioeconomic status (e.g., Soke et al., 2017).

Additionally, several biological variables are thought to contribute to the emergence and maintenance of SIB and other problem behaviors in individuals with ASD and/or IDD, though the empirical support is quite limited. Reviews of this topic can be found elsewhere (e.g., Schroeder et al., 2001; Summers et al., 2017). Some of these variables include neurological pathophysiologies (Devine, 2014; Duerden et al., 2014; Muehlmann & Lewis, 2012), abnormalities in opiate systems

(Sandman & Kemp, 2011), differences in pain reactivity (Summers et al., 2017), high epidermal nerve fiber density values (Symons et al., 2008), and high cortisol levels (Lydon et al., 2015).

Maintenance of SIB. Finally, regarding the maintenance of SIB, decades of behavioral research indicate that SIB is an operant behavior, meaning (a) it is maintained by its consequences and (b) it is most likely to occur under the conditions in which those consequences are typically produced. The consequences that SIB produces fall into two broad categories: social and automatic, or biological, reinforcers. Both social and automatic reinforcers can be subclassified, or subtyped.

Social reinforcers are those mediated by another person; because these reinforcers are observable and controllable, they are subtyped based on the type of reinforcement it produces, which involves either the addition of preferred stimuli (social-positive reinforcement) or the removal of nonpreferred or aversive stimuli (social-negative reinforcement). In the majority of published cases, SIB was found to be maintained by social-positive reinforcement in the form of attention or access to tangibles (e.g., leisure items, toys, food) or social-negative reinforcement in the form of escape from demands such as academic tasks (Beavers, Iwata, & Lerman, 2013; Iwata, Pace, Dorsey, et al., 1994).

Automatic reinforcement is inferred when SIB persists independent of social reinforcement (evidenced by its maintenance in the absence of social interaction). Automatic reinforcers are presumably biological variables or physiological processes produced by SIB itself; though it is currently not possible to directly observe or identify these processes, they could include peripheral sensory stimulation or some other endogenous process (Cataldo & Harris, 1982; Hagopian & Frank-Crawford, 2017). Conceptually, automatic reinforcers could be subtyped in the same way as social reinforcers, involving automatic-positive (i.e., reinforcing sensory stimulation) and automatic-negative reinforcement (i.e., attenuation of pain; Vaughan & Michael, 1982). Although often discussed, there are no strong empirical demonstrations of automatic-negative reinforcement. There is, however, strong support for subtyping automatic reinforcement based on the extent to which it changes as a function of the level of stimulation in the environment (Haddock, 2017; Hagopian, Rooker, & Yenokyan, 2018), which is quantifiable during assessment and accurately predicts response to first-line behavioral treatment. Identifying the class and subtype of reinforcement for SIB (i.e., its function) through pre-treatment assessment is essential because it directly informs selection of behavioral treatment components such as extinction and differential reinforcement.

Diagnosis and Assessment

There are two classification systems used to diagnose and assess SIB: One is psychiatric diagnosis, which describes the phenomenon, and the other is behavioral, which classifies SIB according to its function (and is used as the basis for treatment selection).

Psychiatric diagnosis. Frequently, individuals with ASD who engage in SIB receive the psychiatric diagnosis of stereotypic movement disorder with self-injury (SMD with SIB), a neurodevelopmental disorder (*Diagnostic and Statistical Manual of Mental Disorders*, fifth edition [DSM-5]; American Psychiatric Association, 2013). A diagnosis of SMD with SIB is based on recurring SIB that began in early childhood, interferes with the individual's daily life, and is not better explained by another condition or disorder. Although this diagnosis is useful in situations in which the presence of SIB must be documented, it has two limitations. First, although the DSM-5 differentiates the repetitive and restrictive behaviors characteristic of ASD from those of SMD *without* SIB, as noted by Symons et al. (2005), the taxon implies that SIB is related to stereotyped movements, yet it remains unclear whether this is indeed the case across all presentations. Second, and more important, the diagnosis is based purely on the presence of SIB—it categorically ignores (and even contradicts) decades of empirical findings demonstrating the most critical dimension of SIB for research and practice is not its presence or its relation to stereotyped movements but its function.

Functional behavior assessment. The function of SIB (i.e., the variables that evoke and maintain it) can be identified through functional behavior assessment (FBA). FBA refers to the process of identifying the antecedent events that occasion and the consequences that reinforce a problem behavior. Several FBA methods exist; these include functional analyses (FAs), indirect assessments, and descriptive assessment.

FAs (e.g., Iwata et al., 1994) are the gold standard in functional behavioral assessment, as they provide direct empirical evidence of cause–effect relations between SIB and the environment. FAs are a rigorous methodology involving systematic implementation of one or more test conditions (in which defined antecedent conditions are arranged and specific consequences are delivered following each instance of SIB). Each test condition simulates situations that are commonly experienced by the individual (such as instructional situation, a condition where an adult is present but busy, or a condition where preferred items are not available or need to be put away). In addition to test conditions where hypotheses about the controlling variables are directly tested, the FBA includes a control condition, which simulates an enriched environment where several reinforcers are freely available. Table 17.1 describes the most commonly included test and control conditions in published FAs of SIB.

The individual is exposed to each test condition and the control condition in a systematic manner. Each condition is replicated (i.e., multiple sessions of each condition are conducted) using a within-subject experimental design (for a thorough description of within-subject experimental designs, see Kazdin, 2011). SIB is operationally defined and each occurrence is recorded via direct behavioral observation. The levels of SIB are compared across conditions in which various contingencies are in place (e.g., test or control). FAs are concluded once each condition has been replicated and patterns of responding are consistent across sessions of the same condition. The results are graphically depicted and examined using established methods (e.g., Iwata, Pace, Dorsey, et al., 1994; Hagopian et al., 1997). Generally speaking, higher and more consistent rates of SIB in any given test condition compared to rates in the control indicate the behavior is sensitive to that reinforcer (i.e., function).

In the majority of cases, FAs identify a single function of problem behavior; rarely are multiple functions identified (Beavers et al., 2013). Data from Beavers et al. (2013)—who summarized data from nearly 1,000 published FAs of problem behavior—indicate that, of 282 published FAs of SIB that produced interpretable results, only 9.2% identified more than one function for SIB. The authors noted that multiple functions were more likely to be found when two or more types of problem behavior (e.g., SIB and aggression) were targeted in the same FA (as opposed to when only one type of problem behavior was targeted). However, the proportion of FAs of SIB that included other types of problem behavior was unclear. Once the function(s) of SIB is identified via FA, the information is used to inform treatments matched to the function. Additionally, because the individual's safety is of utmost concern, safety standards exist, and response blocking and protective equipment are sometimes used during FA sessions (Iwata et al. 1994; Kahng et al., 2015). Although SIB may temporarily increase in frequency during the FA test conditions, this effect is temporary and does not appear to affect the individual's behavior after FA sessions have concluded (Call et al., 2017; Shabani et al., 2013). Given the potential

Table 17.1. Conditions Commonly Included in Functional Analyses of Self-Injurious Behavior (SIB)

Condition	Purpose	Antecedents to SIB	Consequences of SIB	Function[a]
No interaction	Test for automatic reinforcement[b]	Alone or ignored, no leisure or food items available	Biological (no social consequences)	Subtype 1 or 2 automatic reinforcement[c]
Attention	Test for social-positive reinforcement (attention)	Adult/peer attention diverted or removed	Attention delivered	Social-positive reinforcement (attention)
Tangible	Test for social-positive reinforcement	Removal of tangibles (food, leisure items)	Tangibles delivered	Social-positive reinforcement
Demand	Test for social-negative reinforcement	Academic or daily living tasks	Tasks removed	Social-negative reinforcement
Play	Control for social-positive and social-negative reinforcement	Free access to leisure items and attention	No social consequences	Idiosyncratic

[a] The function of SIB is indicated by differentially higher rates of SIB in the relevant test condition than in the control.

[b] Note that there is no true test for automatic reinforcement, as these reinforcers cannot be observed; this condition simply rules out the influence of social variables on SIB.

[c] High rates of SIB in the no-interaction condition would suggest an automatic reinforcement function, regardless of responding in the control. However, differentially higher rates of SIB in this condition relative to the control would suggest Subtype 1 automatic reinforcement; high rates across this and the control condition would suggest Subtype 2 automatic reinforcement.

risks associated with SIB, only those qualified by advanced graduate training and experience should design and conduct or oversee FAs of SIB.

Other FBA methodologies include indirect and descriptive assessments. These methods of information gathering are sometimes implemented prior to conducting an FA, as they allow one to generate hypotheses regarding the function of an individual's SIB, and they can be useful in identifying the types of stimuli to include in FA test and control conditions. Indirect assessments take the form of interviews or questionnaires (e.g., Iwata, DeLeon, & Roscoe, 2013; Matson & Vollmer, 1995); though a relatively quick means of obtaining information, their reliability and validity is limited, as they rely on informant recall and opinions about what events in the environment are causally related to SIB (see Iwata et al., 2013). Descriptive assessments involve naturalistic observation and recording of SIB without any systematic manipulation of the events that precede or follow its occurrence; thus, they yield only correlational data. Given its potential to cause injury, most caregivers react by attempting to stop or distract the individual from continuing to engage in SIB (i.e., provide attention, tangibles, and/or escape from ongoing activities). This occurs even when SIB is maintained by other variables. Thus, descriptive analyses of SIB are likely to yield false-positive results (Thompson & Iwata, 2007). Although frequently used in clinical practice (Oliver, Pratt, & Normand, 2015), descriptive assessments can be time-consuming and, ultimately, do not demonstrate cause–effect relationships between environmental variables and SIB.

Results of indirect and/or descriptive assessments have been shown to correspond with the results of an FA for several individuals (e.g., Alter, Conroy, Mancil, & Haydon, 2008; Smith, Smith, Dracolby, & Pace, 2012); however, mixed findings and noncorrespondence have also been demonstrated (e.g., Iwata et al., 2013; Thompson & Iwata, 2007; Tarbox et al., 2009). Until research empirically identifies the conditions under which indirect and descriptive assessments are likely to produce accurate results, it may be advisable to use more rigorous FBA methods (i.e., FAs) when the behavior of concern poses greater risk or when less rigorous methods have proven insufficient. For example, if SIB is chronic, poses imminent harm, or has proven treatment resistant, an FA should be conducted. On the other hand, if SIB recently emerged and exclusively occurs in certain situations (e.g., during academic tasks), it is possible that the results of an indirect or descriptive assessment could provide enough information to formulate hypotheses to inform an initial intervention.

Treatment

There are several definitions of evidence-based treatments, but they can broadly be defined as treatments with strong empirical support of their efficacy (Sturmey & Didden, 2014). Due to overwhelming evidence of their efficacy, behavioral treatments are supported and recommended by several government, professional, and scientific organizations as best practice in the treatment of problem behavior, including SIB, in individuals with ASD and/or IDD (for a review, see Hagopian, Hardesty, & Gregory, 2015). Behavioral treatments for SIB are based on its function, variations of which will be described in the following section. There is no pharmacological treatment for SIB, yet psychotropic agents are frequently prescribed to individuals with ASD with the intention of ameliorating it (Aman et al., 2005; McGillivray & McCabe, 2004). Thus, pharmacological treatments for SIB will be briefly discussed, with an emphasis on their relevance to and integration with behavioral treatments.

Behavioral Treatments

Behavioral treatments for SIB are based on operant learning principles and, as such, focus on modifying aspects of the events that precede and follow SIB—its antecedents and consequences, respectively. Behavioral treatment is indicated when SIB is not a secondary symptom of a medical condition or neurological disorder (Hagopian & Caruso-Anderson, 2010). Over the last 60 years, behavioral treatments for SIB have consisted mostly of reinforcement-based procedures (Kahng et al., 2002; Minshawi et al., 2014; Morano et al., 2017), which is likely due to the advent of FA methodologies, which identify the reinforcers for SIB. The components of reinforcement-based treatments for SIB can be grouped into three general categories: antecedent manipulations, differential reinforcement, and extinction. Antecedent manipulations and differential reinforcement focus on providing or teaching alternative responses that compete with or replace SIB, respectively. Extinction involves no longer reinforcing SIB, hence the necessity of identifying its function. Procedurally, these components vary according to the function of SIB (Iwata, Pace, Cowdery, et al., 1994). For more information on the variations of these components in the treatment of SIB in ASD, see Minshawi et al. (2014).

Behavioral treatments have been demonstrated effective in reducing SIB and other problem behavior in individuals with ASD and/or IDD in hundreds of studies; these studies have been summarized in a number of reviews and demonstrated to produce robust effects in several reviews and meta-analyses (e.g., Didden, Duker, & Korzilius, 1997; Doehring, Reichow, Palka, Phillips, & Hagopian, 2014; Harvey, Boer, Meyer, & Evans, 2009; Heyvaert, Maes, Van Den Noortgate, Kuppens, & Onghena, 2012; Heyvaert, Saenen, Campbell, Maes, & Onghena, 2014; Horner, Carr, Strain, Todd, & Reed, 2002; Hurl et al., 2016; Kahng et al., 2002; Morano et al., 2017; Weisz, Weiss, Han, Granger, & Morton, 1995; Virués-Ortega, 2010). Additionally, behavioral treatments have been found to be more efficacious than psychotherapy, pharmacological treatments, and other types of interventions alone (e.g., Heyvaert et al., 2012; Morano et al., 2017; Weisz et al., 1995), and those that are based on the function of problem behavior as identified by an FA are more effective than those that are chosen arbitrarily (e.g., Didden et al., 1997; Harvey et al., 2009; Heyvaert et al., 2014; Hurl et al., 2016). Importantly, as is the case with FAs, the design and implementation of behavioral treatments requires a depth of knowledge and expertise only attainable through advanced graduate and professional training in applied behavior analysis.

Hallmarks of behavioral treatments. Although behavioral treatments for SIB are individualized, they share common characteristics (Kahng et al., 2002). All require repeated, direct measures of SIB and other targeted behaviors to evaluate the effects of treatment. All target behaviors are operationally defined and objectively measured. Various methods of data collection exist, but, typically, continuous (second-by-second) observational recording is used to obtain the rate or percentage duration of a given behavior within each treatment session (Mudford, Taylor, & Martin, 2009). A second observer records data on an intermittent basis to ensure the data are reliable and the operational definitions of SIB are valid (House, House, & Campbell, 1981). Data are graphically depicted across sessions and analyzed on an ongoing basis. The effect of treatments and/or their components and parameters on target behavior are evaluated using within-subject experimental designs, in which the individual serves as their own control (Horner et al., 2005; Kazdin, 2011; Kratochwill et al., 2010).

Once desired behavioral changes (e.g., decreases in SIB) are observed and the efficacy of treatment is established (e.g., after replicating the reduction in SIB from baseline to treatment), certain treatment components or their parameters may be modified to promote maintenance and generalization of treatment effects outside of treatment sessions. In practice, this is accomplished through prompt fading, reinforcement schedule thinning, and other procedural and parametric manipulations (see Stokes & Osnes, 2016). Ultimately, the treatment should be implementable by the individual's caregivers with high reliability, or accuracy. Relatedly, behavioral assessment and treatment for SIB and other problem behaviors are often highly successful when caregivers are involved (e.g., Kurtz, Fodstad, Huete, & Hagopian, 2013; Wacker et al., 1998), and there exist several methods of training and monitoring caregivers' implementation of assessment and treatment procedures (e.g., Kuhn, Lerman, & Vorndran, 2003; Vollmer et al., 1994; Wacker et al., 2013).[2]

Treatments for Socially Reinforced SIB

Antecedent manipulations. Antecedents to socially reinforced SIB can be modified in various ways, such as reducing the individual's motivation to engage in SIB or modifying aspects of the stimuli that typically evoke SIB. A common type of antecedent manipulation for socially reinforced SIB involves the use of noncontingent reinforcement (NCR; for a review, see Carr et al., 2000). NCR is an evidence-based treatment for SIB and other problem behaviors in individuals with ASD and/or IDD (Carr, Severtson, & Lepper, 2009; Phillips, Iannaccone, Rooker, & Hagopian, 2017; Richman, Barnard-Brak, Grubb, Bosch, & Abby, 2015). NCR involves "free," or time-based, delivery of the reinforcers that maintain or compete with SIB *prior to* the occurrence of SIB, thus preventing SIB by decreasing the individual's motivation to engage in the behavior. Simply put, during NCR, the individual does not engage in SIB because they already have what SIB would produce (Hagopian, Crockett, Stone, Deleon, & Bowman, 2000). NCR is more effective when functional reinforcers for SIB are used and when it includes an extinction component (Hagopian et al., 2000; Richman et al., 2015).

[2] Notably, these methods of caregiver training are distinct from more general, behaviorally oriented caregiver training methods that are based on behavioral principles but do not teach caregivers to implement specific, individualized procedures (e.g., Aman et al., 2009).

NCR for SIB maintained by social-positive reinforcement (e.g., attention or toys) involves delivery of those reinforcers on a time-based schedule, prior to and independent of SIB. NCR for SIB maintained by social-negative reinforcement (also called noncontingent escape) involves initially not presenting the aversive stimuli, and then gradually increasing their delivery independent of SIB (e.g., Vollmer, Marcus, & Ringdahl, 1995). For instance, NCR for SIB maintained by escape from academic tasks might involve giving the individual a break every few minutes, regardless of whether they completed any tasks.

Sometimes, NCR involves the use of stimuli that have not been demonstrated to be functionally related to SIB but reduce it by evoking a response that competes with SIB (for a review, see Payne & Dozier, 2013). In other words, the individual is given alternative reinforcers that apparently compete with reinforcement for engaging in SIB. For instance, preferred items might be provided when the reinforcement maintaining SIB is not available (toys are made available when attention is not; e.g., Hagopian, Kuhn, Long, & Rush, 2005) or during academic tasks (to treat SIB maintained by social-negative reinforcement; e.g., Slocum & Vollmer, 2015).

There are several other types of antecedent manipulations used in treatments of SIB and other problem behaviors maintained by social-negative reinforcement. These include altering some aspect of the antecedent events, such as task effort, difficulty, or rate of task presentation; the duration of instructional sessions; the use of novel therapists or tasks; interspersing easy and difficult tasks; errorless prompting; and offering a choice of tasks (e.g., Ebanks & Fisher, 2003; Romaniuk et al., 2002; Smith, Iwata, Goh, & Shore, 1995). However, these procedures produced idiosyncratic results and have few replications.

Differential reinforcement. There are several variations of differential reinforcement procedures, and they have collectively been shown to be highly effective in treating socially reinforced problem behavior (for reviews, see Chowdhury & Benson, 2011; Petscher, Rey, & Bailey, 2009). Differential reinforcement treatments for socially reinforced SIB often focus on teaching alternative communication skills using a form of differential reinforcement called functional communication training (FCT; Carr & Durand, 1985). FCT is perhaps the most widely researched and used function-based treatment, and it has strong empirical support (e.g., Heath, Ganz, Parker, Burke, & Ninci, 2015; Kurtz et al., 2011). During FCT, the individual is taught to perform another response (e.g., sign language, picture exchange, vocalization) using prompting and prompt fading. FCT is more effective when it includes an extinction component, meaning the problem behavior does not produce reinforcement (Kurtz et al., 2011). Because the individual is able to produce the same reinforcer as SIB via communication, FCT is highly effective in reducing SIB and other problem behaviors maintained by social reinforcement, and it may be more effective with persons with ASD than ID (Heath et al., 2015).

When FCT is initiated, typically every instance of the communication response produces the reinforcer, and problem behavior is placed on extinction (i.e., it does not produce the reinforcer). Once the communication response occurs reliably without problem behavior, the reinforcer is gradually made less available through the process of schedule thinning. During these periods of reinforcer unavailability, problem behavior often reoccurs (Briggs, Fisher, Greer, & Kimball, 2018; Volkert et al., 2009). The likelihood of SIB recurring during these times can be reduced by providing environmental cues that signal the un/availability of the reinforcer (for a review, see Saini, Miller, & Fisher, 2016) and/or the use of competing stimuli (e.g., Hagopian et al., 2005). See Tiger, Hanley, and Bruzek (2008) for a review of practical issues involved in designing an FCT treatment and discussion of best practice; see Hagopian, Boelter, and Jarmolowicz (2011) for a review of procedures used to teach individuals to wait for reinforcers while maintaining reductions in SIB. Less is known about the maintenance and generalization of FCT effects (see Neely, Garcia, Bankston, & Green, 2018).

Treatments for automatically reinforced SIB. As previously mentioned, the reinforcers for automatically reinforced SIB are assumed to be biological and cannot be observed or controlled, which makes it difficult to develop treatments directly targeting its maintaining variables (Vollmer, 1994). Thus, reinforcement-based treatment for automatically reinforced SIB relies on antecedent manipulations and differential reinforcement because extinction (i.e., ensuring the reinforcer does not follow SIB) is not possible. However, the reinforcement SIB produces can be attenuated via the use of other procedures, such as response blocking (which interrupts the behavior) and protective equipment (which may attenuate the sensory consequences). For a more thorough review of treatments for automatically reinforced SIB, see Rooker, Bonner, Dillon, and Zarcone (2018).

Recent research (e.g., Hagopian et al., 2017) has identified three subtypes of automatically reinforced behavior based on patterns of responding during the FA and the presence of self-restraint (discussed later). Specifically, Subtype 1 automatically reinforced SIB is sensitive to alternative sources of reinforcement, meaning that, when given activities or tasks, the individual will not engage in SIB and will presumably engage in those tasks; thus, Subtype 1 is more likely to respond to reinforcement-based treatments. Subtype 2 automatically reinforced SIB is largely insensitive to other types of stimuli, meaning that relatively few responses compete with SIB, presumably due to the potency of the biological reinforcer; thus, Subtype 2 is likely to require additional procedures such as response blocking, protective equipment, or, in severe cases, temporary restraint.

Subtype 3 automatically reinforced SIB is characterized by co-occurring self-restraint, a debilitating self-limiting behavior characterized by restriction of one's own movement. Examples of self-restraint include wrapping extremities in clothing (e.g., Smith, Lerman, & Iwata, 1996), clutching objects tightly (e.g., Vollmer & Vorndran, 1998), placing objects between body parts (e.g., Rooker & Roscoe, 2005), and sitting on one's hands (e.g., Scheithauer, O'Connor, & Toby, 2015). Some suggest self-restraint may be maintained by automatic-negative reinforcement in the form of escape or avoidance of SIB (Fisher & Iwata, 1996), and there is evidence to support this hypothesis (e.g., Scheithauer et al., 2015). However, it is important to note that, although self-restraint is more likely to co-occur with SIB than not (Richards et al., 2017), the presence of self-restraint does not necessarily indicate SIB is maintained by automatic reinforcement, or even that the two responses are maintained by the same reinforcer (e.g., Derby, Fisher, & Piazza, 1996; Rapp & Miltenberger, 2000; Smith, Iwata, Vollmer, & Pace, 1992; Vollmer & Vorndran, 1998). More research is needed to clarify whether Subtype 3 automatically reinforced SIB is itself composed of subtypes characterized by sensitivity of SIB and self-restraint to alternative sources of reinforcement.

Antecedent manipulations. Antecedent interventions are designed to decrease the probability of the occurrence of automatically reinforced SIB by providing alternative sources of sensory stimulation. The logic is that increasing the level of stimulation in the environment will decrease the motivation to engage in SIB. Initially, antecedent interventions involved alternative stimuli selected using informal methods (Horner, 1980); then stimuli were selected based on having identified them as preferred using a formal preference assessment (Vollmer, Marcus, & LeBlanc, 1994). Contemporary interventions identify stimuli to employ in antecedent interventions based on a competing stimulus assessment (Rooker et al., 2018), a pretreatment assessment that empirically identifies stimuli that reduce SIB when they are made available. Once identified, competing stimuli are delivered using a noncontingent reinforcement schedule. Although highly effective for Subtype 1, this approach has not been demonstrated effective for Subtype 2 or 3 automatically reinforced SIB (Hagopian et al., 2018); for those subtypes, more intensive treatment components (i.e., response blocking, restraint, and protective equipment) are needed to reduce SIB.

Other manipulations. Another empirically supported procedure for decreasing automatically reinforced SIB involves response blocking while simultaneously providing play materials that substitute for, or compete with, the hypothesized stimulation produced by the behavior (e.g., Saini, Greer, et al., 2016). Additionally, more restrictive procedures such as response cost, protective equipment, or restraint may be used temporarily, as a last resort when safety is a concern and less intrusive methods proved ineffective (Vollmer et al., 2011).

Pharmacological Treatments

Although the U.S. Food and Drug Administration (FDA) has approved two medications for the treatment of "irritability" (a loosely defined, heterogeneous construct that lacks definitive parameters; Toohey & DiGiuseppe, 2017) in persons with ASD, there exists no approved pharmacological treatment for the core symptoms of ASD or SIB specifically (Goel, Hong, Findling, & Ji, 2018). However, individuals with ASD and SIB—particularly those with co-occurring psychiatric conditions—are frequently prescribed psychotropic medications with the intention of reducing SIB (Aman et al., 2005; McGillivray & McCabe, 2004). Currently, the FDA has approved two drugs—aripiprazole and risperidone—for treating "irritability" (a construct that includes aggression, SIB, and severe tantrums) in children and adolescents with ASD (FDA, 2006). In general, these two drugs have proved effective in reducing the aggregate symptom domain of irritability, yet their ability to treat SIB specifically is questionable due to lack of precise outcome measures (Oliver & Richards, 2010) and paucity of data regarding the maintenance of reductive effects (cf. Adler et al., 2015).

Other pharmacological agents (e.g., naltrexone) are commonly prescribed to individuals with ID and/or ASD off label (meaning they have not been approved by the FDA for the treatment of SIB or its symptom domain in individuals with ASD), or to treat co-occurring conditions (Aman et al., 2005; West, Brunssen, & Waldrop, 2009). Additionally, polypharmacy, or the prescription of two or more drugs, is also common in individuals with ASD, yet the drug combinations that are often prescribed have not been evaluated (Li, MacNeill, Curiel, & Poling, 2017; cf. Wink et al., 2017). Several reviews of pharmacological treatments for "irritability" and/or SIB in individuals with ASD have been published (e.g., Goel et al., 2018; Stigler & McDougle, 2008; Symons, Thompson, & Rodriguez , 2004), as have diagnostic models and practice parameters for pharmacological treatment of SIB and other problem behaviors (e.g., McGuire et al., 2016).

Integrated Behavioral and Pharmacological Treatments

Regardless of the type or number of psychotropic agents prescribed, when SIB is decreased through pharmacological treatment alone, the mechanisms by which they do so are unknown; it has been suggested that they may be functionally unrelated to SIB for some, and may even be contraindicated for others (Schaal & Hackenberg, 1994; Thompson, 2007). There are findings demonstrating that medications can affect behavioral assessment and treatment outcomes (e.g., Crosland et al., 2003; Symons & Thompson, 1997; Zarcone et al., 2004) in different ways for different individuals. This is why researchers have advocated for integrated behavioral and pharmacological treatment (e.g., Schaal & Hackenberg, 1994), and there exist numerous models for designing interventions based on biological and environmental controlling variables (e.g., Mace & Mauk, 1995; Minshawi, Hurwitz, Morriss, & McDougle, 2015; Pyles, Muniz, Cade, & Silva, 1997; Wachtel & Hagopian, 2006). Although these models are based on empirical findings, there is little evidence of their efficacy.

Case Examples

Individuals in the following case examples were admitted to an inpatient program designed for the assessment and treatment of severe problem behavior. Typically, patients are admitted to this program when they have exhausted all available resources (adequate treatment is unavailable in their area or several treatments have been applied but were unsuccessful) and problem behavior poses a threat to the individual or others. All treatments were based on the results of an FA and were demonstrated effective using within-subject experimental designs. The examples are limited to children. However, because behavioral treatment components are selected based on the function of SIB, treatment components (e.g., competing stimuli, extinction, FCT) would be similar for adults. In all cases, the materials (e.g., leisure stimuli, work tasks) used in the FA and treatment would be individually selected based on their social validity and the individual's preferences.

Social-Positive Reinforcement

Clinical presentation. James was a 12-year-old boy diagnosed with ASD and mild intellectual disability (ID). He was admitted for treatment of aggression, disruption, and severe SIB (self-biting and self-hitting). James could follow simple instructions and used gestures or simple phrases to communicate. At the time of admission, he was not taking medications. After 5 months, he was prescribed Haldol, which was discontinued after 6 weeks; he was subsequently prescribed Depakote and Risperdal, which he took for the remainder of his admission. (This case was reported by Hagopian et al., 2005.)

Assessment. The FA of James's problem behavior included conditions similar to those described in Table 17.1. FA results indicated that James engaged in problem behavior mostly in the tangible condition, in which preferred items were not available until SIB occurred (simulating a situation in which parents attempt to console or appease a child by redirecting him or her to other activities following SIB). In the other conditions of the FA, problem behavior never occurred when he had free access to preferred items and rarely occurred when problem behavior produced removal of academic demands or adult attention, or when by himself (i.e., when no stimuli associated with the delivery of tangible items—other people—were present). In short, FA results indicated his problem behavior was maintained by social-positive reinforcement in the form of access to tangible items. Subsequently, another assessment was conducted to identify alternative activities that James could engage with when he was taught to wait for those items.

Treatment. Treatment baseline was identical to the tangible condition of the FA. Subsequently, FCT with extinction was implemented, meaning he was taught a new response (picture exchange) that produced the same reinforcer that maintained SIB in the FA (preferred items) and SIB no longer produced preferred items. The efficacy of FCT with extinction was evaluated in a reversal design (i.e., baseline and treatment conditions were replicated). Subsequently, James was taught to wait for preferred items after requesting them; this was accomplished using gradually, systematically increasing waiting intervals, and by the use of NCR with competing stimuli (i.e., alternative activities were freely available) during waiting intervals.

Outcomes. During baseline, his rate of problem behavior averaged 1.2 responses per minute. FCT with extinction produced an immediate, 100% reduction in problem behaviors for several sessions. During the last 10 sessions of schedule thinning with NCR, James was able to wait up to 20 minutes for his preferred items without engaging in problem behavior.

Caregiver training. James's mother was subsequently trained to implement the FCT with NCR treatment; this was accomplished using instructions, modeling, and rehearsal, as well as feedback during several in vivo sessions. By the end of training, James's mother implemented all treatment components with 100% accuracy.

Social-Positive and Social-Negative Reinforcement

Clinical presentation. Preston was a 6-year-old boy admitted for treatment of severe self-injury (head hitting and head banging), aggression, disruption, and spitting. Preston was diagnosed with ASD and mild ID. He was prescribed fluoxetine (Prozac) and Claritin. (This case was reported by Hagopian, Wilson, & Wilder, 2001.)

Assessment. The initial FA included attention, demand, and play conditions similar to those described in Table 17.1. Results indicated that Preston's problem behavior occurred almost exclusively in the play condition and rarely in the attention and demand conditions. Although the play condition was intended to be a control, when responding is higher in the control condition than in the test conditions, it suggests an idiosyncratic function (Roscoe, Schlichenmeyer, & Dube, 2015). Due to this unusual pattern of responding, it was hypothesized that Preston's problem behavior was maintained by social-negative reinforcement in the form of escape from adult attention while he engaged with preferred leisure items. Additionally, although his parents reported that they did not deliver tangibles contingent on Preston's problem behavior, direct observations indicated otherwise, and a tangible function was suspected.

These two hypotheses—maintenance by social-positive reinforcement in the form of delivering preferred items and social-negative reinforcement in the form of removal of attention and interaction once preferred items were delivered—were tested in two subsequent FA conditions. (Importantly, inclusion of a test for tangible reinforcement was conducted only once a tangible function was suspected; see Rooker, Iwata, Harper, Fahmie, & Camp, 2011.) During the tangible condition, Preston was deprived of his preferred items and, contingent on problem behavior, his preferred items were delivered for 30 seconds; subsequently, the items were removed and the process was repeated. During the escape-from-attention condition, Preston was given preferred items and every 30 seconds, a therapist interrupted his play to interact with him; contingent on problem behavior, the therapist ceased interaction for 30 seconds, and the process was repeated. Results indicated that Preston's problem behavior was relatively higher in these two conditions than the demand and attention conditions, which suggested Preston's problem behavior was maintained by access to tangibles and escape from attention once those items were delivered.

Treatment. Treatment baseline conditions were identical to the tangible and escape-from-attention FA conditions. Subsequently, FCT treatments (with extinction and NCR components) were implemented across these two conditions in a multiple-baseline design (see Kazdin, 2011). In the tangible treatment condition, Preston was deprived of preferred items and was taught to say "toys please," which produced 30-second access to his preferred items; following this, the items were removed and the process was repeated. In the escape-from-attention condition, Preston had access to preferred items and, when adults interacted with him, he was taught to say "play by myself," which terminated social interaction for 30 seconds. Across both conditions, extinction was in place (i.e., problem behavior no longer produced access to preferred items or terminated adult attention or interaction), as was NCR, in which Preston was given free access to other toys and books on a time-based schedule. Initially, every appropriate communication response produced immediate access to preferred items or escape from attention and interaction.

Outcomes. During treatment baseline sessions, Preston's problem behavior averaged 1.9 and 2.1 responses per minute in the tangible and escape-from-attention conditions, respectively. During FCT with extinction and NCR treatment sessions, Preston's problem behavior averaged 0.1 responses per minute in both conditions. Thus, FCT (with extinction and NCR) produced a 96% reduction in Preston's problem behavior in the access-to-tangibles condition, and a 97% reduction in the escape-from-attention condition.

Once these treatments were demonstrated effective during brief treatment sessions, the procedures were implemented for the entirety of Preston's day, in a simulated school schedule. Prior to implementing treatment, Preston's problem behaviors averaged 20.5 responses per hour; following FCT with extinction and NCR, his problem behaviors reduced to an average of 1.1 responses per hour. Thus, during the simulated school schedule, FCT (with extinction and NCR) produced a 94% reduction in Preston's problem behavior.

Caregiver training. Preston's parents and his school aide were trained to implement the two FCT (with extinction and NCR) procedures using instructions, modeling, and feedback. His parents were trained in 10 sessions, and his aide was trained in seven sessions. By the end of training, Preston's mother and father implemented the treatment components with 100% accuracy, and his school aide implemented it with 98% accuracy.

Automatic Reinforcement

Clinical presentation. Michael was a 5-year-old boy admitted for the assessment and treatment of SIB (hand/fist-to-head hitting, object-to-chest hitting, hand/fist-to-chest hitting), aggression, and tantrums. He was diagnosed with ASD and SMD with SIB, and he communicated vocally. (This case is unpublished, and the treatments for aggression and tantrums have been omitted for the sake of brevity.)

Assessment. An FA was conducted; conditions included those described in Table 17.1. Michael's SIB was high in the absence of social consequences (i.e., the no-interaction condition), which suggested Michael's SIB was maintained by automatic reinforcement. Further, his SIB was not differentially lower in the conditions in the play (control) condition, in which competing stimuli were available, suggesting it was maintained specifically by Subtype 2 automatic reinforcement.

Treatment. Treatment for SIB was initiated following a series of baseline sessions. During the baseline, no social contingencies were placed on SIB. Subsequently, a component analysis of NCR treatment was conducted in a multielement design (see Kazdin, 2011). The first treatment was NCR (free access to three competing stimuli, which were identified to compete with SIB during a pretreatment assessment). During NCR, at the beginning of each session, a therapist placed three competing items within close proximity to Michael. SIB and other problem behaviors were ignored. The second treatment was identical to NCR but involved the additional components of response blocking and representation of competing items: At the beginning of each session, a therapist placed all three competing items within close proximity to Michael. If he did not pick up an item within 5 seconds, the therapist immediately handed him a competing stimulus. If at any time Michael dropped the competing item, the therapist immediately replaced it with another item, in a random order (i.e., representation). Additionally, all SIB attempts/successes were blocked. All other behaviors were ignored.

Outcomes. The mean rate of SIB during treatment baseline was 3.6 responses per minute. Interestingly, the mean rate of SIB during NCR was 6.5 responses per minute, a rate nearly double that of baseline, when no items were present; yet, despite his high rate of SIB during NCR, Michael engaged with the stimuli approximately 66% of session time. When blocking and representation of competing items were added to NCR, his mean rate of SIB decreased to 0.6 per minute, and his engagement averaged 94% of session time. Thus, NCR with blocking and representation of competing items was effective in reducing Michael's SIB by approximately 90%.

Caregiver training. Subsequently, Michael's mother was taught to implement each component of the treatment separately, whereas his father was taught to implement all components at once due to time constraints. Feedback was given on incorrect responses. Michael's mother correctly implemented NCR with representation of competing stimuli an average of 96% of her 19 training sessions, but she was less successful with the blocking component, which she correctly implemented for approximately 83% of SIB occurrences. Michael's father correctly implemented NCR with representation of competing stimuli an average of 99% of his five training sessions, and he was also less successful with the blocking component, which he correctly implemented for approximately 87% of SIB occurrences.

Summary and Future Directions

Summary

SIB commonly occurs in individuals with ASD and presents with considerable heterogeneity across several dimensions (topography, rate, function, severity). Research on the prevalence and developmental course of SIB in persons with ASD shows that it occurs in a substantial proportion of this population, and that it can emerge early in life and maintain for several years, perhaps across the lifespan. The general consensus among researchers is that SIB has no common pathology, but the core deficits and characteristics of ASD (social and communication deficits, propensity to engage in repetitive behaviors) increase the risk of its emergence. After the first instance, biological and social variables will determine the probability of its maintenance, and the longer it maintains in the absence of treatment, the more likely it will be to persist.

Given that SIB is highly heterogeneous, it is unsurprising that there is no universally effective treatment for SIB. Behavioral treatment has a broader base of support and represents a more targeted approach relative to pharmacological treatment. The most effective behavioral treatments for SIB are developed based on empirical demonstrations of its reinforcing function (FAs). Both subtypes of socially reinforced SIB and Subtype 1 automatically reinforced SIB are highly responsive to behavioral treatment; Subtypes 2 and 3 automatically reinforced SIB are less responsive, requiring additional procedures such as response blocking (Hagopian et al., 2017).

Future Directions

Our understanding of the developmental course of SIB in individuals with ASD is limited, as the majority of studies investigating the prevalence, developmental course, and risk factors of SIB in individuals relied on informant recall and lack systematic replication. In future research, these problems could be mitigated by using direct measures of SIB (e.g., Handen et al., 2013), identifying and considering its function, and adopting consistent methodologies.

Future research might also investigate the individual, environmental, and/or genetic characteristics of the ASD subpopulation in which SIB does not occur, as variables that mitigate the emergence of SIB might be identified (Oliver et al., 2017). Identifying protective features could inform research aimed at early intervention and prevention efforts and spawn public health initiatives focused on caregiver training and support.

Given the heterogeneity of both SIB and ASD, by far the most important consideration for all future research on SIB in individuals with ASD and/or IDD is its function and functional subtype. There is, and has been for many years, overwhelming evidence that the most important dimension on which SIB varies (in terms of treatment outcomes) is its function. Indeed, identification of maintenance by social-positive, social-negative, and subtype of automatic reinforcement is imperative for developing effective behavioral treatments. Controlling for the functional subtype of SIB, both experimentally (to identify other functional relations) and statistically (as a predictor variable), would homogenize the sample across the most important dimension of behavior—its function. Initially stratifying research participants based on the empirically demonstrated function of their SIB rather than other individual characteristics (e.g., psychiatric diagnosis, age, gender, race) may elucidate the relevance of individual characteristics and allow for more definitive conclusions to be made with respect to etiology (emergence and maintenance), developmental course, risk factors (both biological and environmental), and the efficacy of pharmacological treatments. Using the latter as an example, certain pharmacological treatments may be more or less effective for different functional subtypes of SIB (e.g., Crosland et al., 2003).

The concept and value of classifying scientific topics of inquiry according to their underlying mechanisms is not novel in the natural sciences (Craver & Darden, 2013). This functional approach underlies the paradigm of precision medicine (Katsnelson, 2013) and applied behavior analysis (Mace, 1994). The myriad reasons a functional approach to SIB has yet to be adopted by the majority of researchers remain speculative. Fortunately, the classification of problems based on a clinical presentation alone is giving way to a more multidimensional approach (Insel et al., 2010).

References

Adler, B. A., Wink, L. K., Early, M., Shaffer, R., Minshawi, N., McDougle, C. J., & Erickson, C. A. (2015). Drug-refractory aggression, self-injurious behavior, and severe tantrums in autism spectrum disorders: A chart review study. *Autism, 19*(1), 102–106. https://doi.org/10.1177/1362361314524641

Alter, P. J., Conroy, M. A., Mancil, G. R., & Haydon, T. (2008). A comparison of functional behavior assessment methodologies with young children: Descriptive methods and functional analysis. *Journal of Behavioral Education, 17*(2), 200–219. https://doi.org/10.1007/s10864-008-9064-3

Aman, M. G., Lam, K. S., & Van Bourgondien, M. E. (2005). Medication patterns in patients with autism: Temporal,

regional, and demographic influences. *Journal of Child & Adolescent Psychopharmacology, 15*(1), 116–126. https://doi.org/10.1089/cap.2005.15.116
Aman, M. G., McDougle, C. J., Scahill, L., Handen, B., Arnold, L. E., Johnson, C., . . . Wagner, A. (2009). Medication and parent training in children with pervasive developmental disorders and serious behavior problems: Results from a randomized clinical trial. *Journal of the American Academy of Child & Adolescent Psychiatry, 48*(12), 1143–1154. https://doi.org/10.1097/CHI.0b013e3181bfd669
American Psychiatric Association. (2013). *Diagnostic and statistical manual of mental disorders* (5th ed.). Arlington, VA: American Psychiatric Publishing.
Baghdadli, A., Pascal, C., Grisi, S., & Aussilloux, C. (2003). Risk factors for self-injurious behaviours among 222 young children with autistic disorders. *Journal of Intellectual Disability Research, 47*(8), 622–627. https://doi.org/10.1046/j.1365–2788.2003.00507.x
Baghdadli, A., Picot, M., Pry, R., Michelon, C., Burzstejn, C., Lazartigues, A., & Aussilloux, C. (2008). What factors are related to a negative outcome of self-injurious behaviour during childhood in pervasive developmental disorders? *Journal of Applied Research in Intellectual Disabilities, 21*(2), 142–149. https://doi.org/10.1111/j.1468–3148.2007.00389.x
Barnard-Brak, L., Rojahn, J., Richman, D. M., Chesnut, S. R., & Wei, T. (2015). Stereotyped behaviors predicting self-injurious behavior in individuals with intellectual disabilities. *Research in Developmental Disabilities, 36*, 419–427. https://doi.org/10.1016/j.ridd.2014.08.017
Beavers, G. A., Iwata, B. A., & Lerman, D. C. (2013). Thirty years of research on the functional analysis of problem behavior. *Journal of Applied Behavior Analysis, 46*(1), 1–21. https://doi.org/10.1002/jaba.30
Billstedt, E., Gillberg, C., & Gillberg, C. (2005). Autism after adolescence: Population-based 13- to 22-year follow-up study of 120 individuals with autism diagnosed in childhood. *Journal of Autism and Developmental Disorders, 35*(3), 351–360. https://doi.org/10.1007/s10803-005-3302-5
Bowring, D. L., Totsika, V., Hastings, R. P., Toogood, S., & Griffith, G. M. (2017). Challenging behaviours in adults with an intellectual disability: A total population study and exploration of risk indices. *British Journal of Clinical Psychology, 56*(1), 16–32. https://doi.org/10.1111/bjc.12118
Briggs, A. M., Fisher, W. W., Greer, B. D., & Kimball, R. T. (2018). Prevalence of resurgence of destructive behavior when thinning reinforcement schedules during functional communication training. *Journal of Applied Behavior Analysis, 51*(3), 620–633. https://doi.org/10.1002/jaba.472
Buono, S., Scannella, F., & Palmigiano, M. B. (2010). Self-injurious behavior: A comparison between Prader-Willi syndrome, Down syndrome and autism. *Life Span and Disability, 2*, 187–201.
Call, N. A., Reavis, A. R., Clark, S. B., Parks, N. A., Cariveau, T., & Muething, C. S. (2017). The effects of conducting a functional analysis on problem behavior in other settings: A descriptive study on potential interaction effects. *Behavior Modification, 41*(5), 609–625. https://doi.org/10.1177/0145445517696052
Carr, E. G., & Durand, V. M. (1985). Reducing behavior problems through functional communication training. *Journal of Applied Behavior Analysis, 18*, 111–126. https://doi.org/10.1901/jaba.1985.18–111
Carr, J. E., Coriaty, S., Wilder, D. A., Gaunt, B. T., Dozier, C. L., Britton, L. N., . . . Reed, C. L. (2000). A review of "noncontingent" reinforcement as treatment for the aberrant behavior of individuals with developmental disabilities. *Research in Developmental Disabilities, 21*(5), 377–391. https://doi.org/10.1016/S0891-4222(00)00050–0
Carr, J. E., Severtson, J. M., & Lepper, T. L. (2009). Noncontingent reinforcement is an empirically supported treatment for problem behavior exhibited by individuals with developmental disabilities. *Research in Developmental Disabilities, 30*(1), 44–57. https://doi.org/10.1016/j.ridd.2008.03.002
Cataldo, M. F., & Harris, J. (1982). The biological basis for self-injury in the mentally retarded. *Analysis and Intervention in Developmental Disabilities, 2*(1), 21–39. https://doi.org/10.1016/0270–4684(82)90004–0
Chowdhury, M., & Benson, B. A. (2011). Use of differential reinforcement to reduce behavior problems in adults with intellectual disabilities: A methodological review. *Research in Developmental Disabilities, 32*(2), 383–394. https://doi.org/10.1016/j.ridd.2010.11.015
Cooper, S. A., Smiley, E., Allan, L. M., Jackson, A., Finlayson, J., Mantry, D., & Morrison, J. (2009). Adults with intellectual disabilities: Prevalence, incidence and remission of self-injurious behaviour, and related factors. *Journal of Intellectual Disability Research, 53*(3), 200–216. https://doi.org/10.1111/j.1365–2788.2008.01127.x
Courtemanche, A. B., Black, W. R., & Reese, R. M. (2016). The relationship between pain, self-injury, and other problem behaviors in young children with autism and other developmental disabilities. *American Journal on Intellectual and Developmental Disabilities, 121*(3), 194–203. https://doi.org/10.1352/1944-7558-121.3.194
Craver, C. F., & Darden, L. (2013). *In search of mechanisms: Discoveries across the life sciences*. The University of Chicago Press, Chicago, IL.
Crosland, K. A., Zarcone, J. R., Lindauer, S. E., Valdovinos, M. G., Zarcone, T. J., Hellings, J. A., & Schroeder, S. R. (2003). Use of functional analysis methodology in the evaluation of medication effects. *Journal of Autism and Developmental Disorders, 33*(3), 271–279. https://doi.org/10.1023/a:1024402500425
de Lissovoy, V. (1962). Head banging in early childhood. *Child Development, 33*(1), 43–56.
De Winter, C. F., Jansen, A. A. C., & Evenhuis, H. M. (2011). Physical conditions and challenging behaviour in people with intellectual disability: A systematic review. *Journal of Intellectual Disability Research, 55*(7), 675–698. https://doi.org/10.1111/j.1365–2788.2011.01390.x
Derby, K. M., Fisher, W. W., & Piazza, C. C. (1996). The effects of contingent and noncontingent attention on self-injury and self-restraint. *Journal of Applied Behavior Analysis, 29*(1), 107–110. https://doi.org/10.1901/jaba.1996.29–107
Devine, D. P. (2014). Self-injurious behaviour in autistic children: A neuro-developmental theory of social and environmental isolation. *Psychopharmacology, 231*(6), 979–997. https://doi.org/10.1007/s00213-013-3279-2
Didden, R., Duker, P. C., & Korzilius, H. (1997). Meta-analytic study on treatment effectiveness for problem behaviors with individuals who have mental retardation. *American Journal on Mental Retardation, 101*(4), 387–399.
Dimian, A. F., Botteron, K. N., Dager, S. R., Elison, J. T., Estes, A. M., Pruett, J. R., . . . Wolff, J. J. (2017). Potential risk

factors for the development of self-injurious behavior among infants at risk for autism spectrum disorder. *Journal of Autism and Developmental Disorders, 47*(5), 1403–1415. https://doi.org/10.1007/s10803-017-3057-9

Doehring, P., Reichow, B., Palka, T., Phillips, C., & Hagopian, L. (2014). Behavioral approaches to managing severe problem behaviors in children with autism spectrum and related developmental disorders: A descriptive analysis. *Child and Adolescent Psychiatric Clinics, 23*(1), 25–40. https://doi.org/10.1016/j.chc.2013.08.001

Duerden, E. G., Card, D., Roberts, S. W., Mak-Fan, K. M., Chakravarty, M. M., Lerch, J. P., & Taylor, M. J. (2014). Self-injurious behaviours are associated with alterations in the somatosensory system in children with autism spectrum disorder. *Brain Structure and Function, 219*(4), 1251–1261. https://doi.org/10.1007/s00429-013-0562-2

Duerden, E. G., Oatley, H. K., Mak-Fan, K. M., McGrath, P. A., Taylor, M. J., Szatmari, P., & Roberts, S. W. (2012). Risk factors associated with self-injurious behaviors in children and adolescents with autism spectrum disorders. *Journal of Autism and Developmental Disorders, 42*(11), 2460–2470. https://doi.org/10.1007/s10803-012-1497-9

Eaves, L. C., & Ho, H. H. (2008). Young adult outcome of autism spectrum disorders. *Journal of Autism and Developmental Disorders, 38*(4), 739–747. https://doi.org/10.1007/s10803-007-0441-x

Ebanks, M. E., & Fisher, W. W. (2003). Altering the timing of academic prompts to treat destructive behavior maintained by escape. *Journal of Applied Behavior Analysis, 36*, 355–359. https://doi.org/10.1901/jaba.2003.36–355

Eisenhower, A., Blacher, J., & Baker, B. L. (2013). Mothers' perceived physical health during early and middle childhood: Relations with child developmental delay and behavior problems. *Research in Developmental Disabilities, 34*(3), 1059–1068. https://doi.org/10.1016/j.ridd.2012.12.002

Eisenhower, A. S., Baker, B. L., & Blacher, J. (2009). Children's delayed development and behavior problems: Impact on mothers' perceived physical health across early childhood. *Social Science & Medicine, 68*(1), 89–99. https://doi.org/10.1016/j.socscimed.2008.09.033

Emerson, E. (2003). Mothers of children and adolescents with intellectual disability: Social and economic situation, mental health status, and the self-assessed social and psychological impact of the child's difficulties. *Journal of Intellectual Disability Research, 47*(4–5), 385–399. https://doi.org/10.1046/j.1365–2788.2003.00498.x

Emerson, E., Kiernan, C., Alborz, A., Reeves, D., Mason, H., Swarbrick, R., . . . Hatton, C. (2001a). Predicting the persistence of severe self-injurious behavior. *Research in Developmental Disabilities, 22*(1), 67–75.

Emerson, E., Kiernan, C., Alborz, A., Reeves, D., Mason, H., Swarbrick, R., . . . Hatton, C. (2001b). The prevalence of challenging behaviors: A total population study. *Research in Developmental Disabilities, 22*(1), 77–93. https://doi.org/10.1016/s0891-4222(00)00062–7

Estes, A., Munson, J., Dawson, G., Koehler, E., Zhou, X.-H., & Abbott, R. (2009). Parenting stress and psychological functioning among mothers of preschool children with autism and developmental delay. *Autism, 13*(4), 375–387. https://doi.org/10.1177/1362361309105658

Fisher, W. W., & Iwata, B. A. (1996). On the function of self-restraint and its relationship to self-injury. *Journal of Applied Behavior Analysis, 29*(1), 93–98. https://doi.org/10.1901/jaba.1996.29–93

Fodstad, J. C., Rojahn, J., & Matson, J. L. (2012). The emergence of challenging behaviors in at-risk toddlers with and without autism spectrum disorder: A cross-sectional study. *Journal of Developmental and Physical Disabilities, 24*(3), 217–234. https://doi.org/10.1007/s10882-011-9266-9

Folch, A., Cortés, M. J., Salvador-Carulla, L., Vicens, P., Irazábal, M., Muñoz, S., . . . Martínez-Leal, R. (2018). Risk factors and topographies for self-injurious behaviour in a sample of adults with intellectual developmental disorders. *Journal of Intellectual Disability Research, 62*(12), 1018–1029. https://doi.org/10.1111/jir.12487

Furniss, F., & Biswas, A. B. (2012). Recent research on aetiology, development and phenomenology of self-injurious behaviour in people with intellectual disabilities: A systematic review and implications for treatment. *Journal of Intellectual Disability Research, 56*(5), 453–475. https://doi.org/10.1111/j.1365–2788.2012.01534.x

Gaskin, C. J., McVilly, K. R., & McGillivray, J. A. (2013). Initiatives to reduce the use of seclusion and restraints on people with developmental disabilities: A systematic review and quantitative synthesis. *Research in Developmental Disabilities, 34*(11), 3946–3961. https://doi.org/10.1016/j.ridd.2013.08.010

Geddes, J., Vowles, G., Nicoll, J., & Révész, T. (1999). Neuronal cytoskeletal changes are an early consequence of repetitive head injury. *Acta neuropathologica, 98*(2), 171–178. https://doi.org/10.1007/s004010051066

Goel, R., Hong, J. S., Findling, R. L., & Ji, N. Y. (2018). An update on pharmacotherapy of autism spectrum disorder in children and adolescents. *International Review of Psychiatry, 30*(1), 78–95. https://doi.org/10.1080/09540261.2018.1458706

Haddock, J. N. (2017). *Predicting treatment effects for problem behavior maintained by automatic reinforcement* (Unpublished doctoral dissertation). University of Florida, Gainesville, FL.

Hagopian, L., & Caruso-Anderson, M. (2010). Integrating behavioral and pharmacological interventions for severe problem behavior displayed by children with neurogenetic and developmental disorders. In B. K. Shapiro & P. J. Accardo (Eds.), *Neurobehavioral disorders: Behavioral issues and their treatment* (pp. 2319–2239). Baltimore, MD: Paul H. Brookes Publishing Co.

Hagopian, L., & Frank-Crawford, M. (2017). Classification of self-injurious behaviour across the continuum of relative environmental–biological influence. *Journal of Intellectual Disability Research, 62*(12), 1108–1113. https://doi.org/10.1111/jir.12430

Hagopian, L. P., Boelter, E. W., & Jarmolowicz, D. P. (2011). Reinforcement schedule thinning following functional communication training: Review and recommendations. *Behavior Analysis in Practice, 4*(1), 4–16. https://doi.org/10.1007/bf03391770

Hagopian, L. P., Crockett, J. L., Stone, M., DeLeon, I. G., & Bowman, L. G. (2000). Effects of noncontingent reinforcement on problem behavior and stimulus engagement: The role of satiation, extinction, and alternative reinforcement. *Journal of Applied Behavior Analysis, 33*(4), 433–449. https://doi.org/10.1901/jaba.2000.33–433

Hagopian, L. P., Fisher, W. W., Thompson, R. H., Owen-DeSchryver, J., Iwata, B. A., & Wacker, D. P. (1997). Toward the development of structured criteria for interpretation of functional analysis data. *Journal of Applied Behavior Analysis, 30*(2), 313–326. https://doi.org/10.1901/jaba.1997.30–313

Hagopian, L. P., Hardesty, S. L., & Gregory, M. (2015). Overview and summary of scientific support for applied behavior analysis. Retrieved from https://www.kennedykrieger.org/sites/default/files/library/documents/patient-care/centers-and-programs/down-syndrome-clinic-and-research-center/aba-scientific-support-9-2015.pdf

Hagopian, L. P., Kuhn, S. A. C., Long, E. S., & Rush, K. S. (2005). Schedule thinning following communication training: Using competing stimuli to enhance tolerance to decrements in reinforcer density. *Journal of Applied Behavior Analysis, 38*(2), 177–193. https://doi.org/10.1901/jaba.2005.43–04

Hagopian, L. P., Rooker, G. W., & Yenokyan, G. (2018). Identifying predictive behavioral markers: A demonstration using automatically reinforced self-injurious behavior. *Journal of Applied Behavior Analysis, 51*(3), 443–465. https://doi.org/10.1002/jaba.477

Hagopian, L. P., Rooker, G. W., Zarcone, J. R., Bonner, A. C., & Arevalo, A. R. (2017). Further analysis of subtypes of automatically reinforced SIB: A replication and quantitative analysis of published datasets. *Journal of Applied Behavior Analysis, 50*(1), 48–66. https://doi.org/10.1002/jaba.368

Hagopian, L. P., Wilson, D. M., & Wilder, D. A. (2001). Assessment and treatment of problem behavior maintained by escape from attention and access to tangible items. *Journal of Applied Behavior Analysis, 34*(2), 229–232. https://doi.org/10.1901/jaba.2001.34-229

Hall, S. S., Oliver, C., & Murphy, G. (2001). Early development of self-injurious behavior: An empirical study. *American Journal on Mental Retardation, 106*(2), 189–199. https://doi.org/10.1352/0895-8017(2001)106<0189:Edosib>2.0.Co;2

Handen, B. L., Johnson, C. R., Butter, E. M., Lecavalier, L., Scahill, L., Aman, M. G.,... Vitiello, B. (2013). Use of a direct observational measure in a trial of risperidone and parent training in children with pervasive developmental disorders. *Journal of Developmental and Physical Disabilities, 25*(3), 355–371. https://doi.org/10.1007/s10882-012-9316-y

Harris, J. (1996). Physical restraint procedures for managing challenging behaviours presented by mentally retarded adults and children. *Research in Developmental Disabilities, 17*(2), 99–134. https://doi.org/10.1016/0891–4222(95)00036–4

Harvey, S., Boer, D., Meyer, L. H., & Evans, I. M. (2009). Updating a meta-analysis of intervention research with challenging behaviour: Treatment validity and standards of practice. *Journal of Intellectual & Developmental Disability, 34*(1), 67–80. https://doi.org/10.1080/13668250802690922

Hastings, R. P. (2002). Parental stress and behaviour problems of children with developmental disability. *Journal of Intellectual & Developmental Disability, 27*(3), 149–160. https://doi.org/10.1080/1366825021000008657

Hastings, R. P. (2006). Longitudinal relationships between sibling behavioral adjustment and behavior problems of children with developmental disabilities. *Journal of Autism and Developmental Disorders, 37*(8), 1485. https://doi.org/10.1007/s10803-006-0230-y

Heath, A. K., Ganz, J. B., Parker, R., Burke, M., & Ninci, J. (2015). A meta-analytic review of functional communication training across mode of communication, age, and disability. *Review Journal of Autism and Developmental Disorders, 2*(2), 155–166. https://doi.org/10.1007/s40489-014-0044-3

Heyvaert, M., Maes, B., Van Den Noortgate, W., Kuppens, S., & Onghena, P. (2012). A multilevel meta-analysis of single-case and small-n research on interventions for reducing challenging behavior in persons with intellectual disabilities. *Research in Developmental Disabilities, 33*(2), 766–780.

Heyvaert, M., Saenen, L., Campbell, J. M., Maes, B., & Onghena, P. (2014). Efficacy of behavioral interventions for reducing problem behavior in persons with autism: An updated quantitative synthesis of single-subject research. *Research in Developmental Disabilities, 35*(10), 2463–2476. https://doi.org/10.1016/j.ridd.2014.06.017

Hof, P., Knabe, R., Bovier, P., & Bouras, C. (1991). Neuropathological observations in a case of autism presenting with self-injury behavior. *Acta neuropathologica, 82*(4), 321–326.

Horner, R. D. (1980). The effects of an environmental "enrichment" program on the behavior of institutionalized profoundly retarded children. *Journal of Applied Behavior Analysis, 13*(3), 473–491. https://doi.org/10.1901/jaba.1980.13–473

Horner, R. H., Carr, E. G., Halle, J., McGee, G., Odom, S., & Wolery, M. (2005). The use of single-subject research to identify evidence-based practice in special education. *Exceptional Children, 71*(2), 165–179. https://doi.org/10.1177/001440290507100203

Horner, R. H., Carr, E. G., Strain, P. S., Todd, A. W., & Reed, H. K. (2002). Problem behavior interventions for young children with autism: A research synthesis. *Journal of Autism and Developmental Disorders, 32*(5), 423–446.

House, A. E., House, B. J., & Campbell, M. B. (1981). Measures of interobserver agreement: Calculation formulas and distribution effects. *Journal of Behavioral Assessment, 3*(1), 37–57. https://doi.org/10.1007/bf01321350

Huisman, S., Mulder, P., Kuijk, J., Kerstholt, M., van Eeghen, A., Leenders, A.,... Hennekam, R. (2018). Self-injurious behavior. *Neuroscience & Biobehavioral Reviews, 84*, 483–491. https://doi.org/10.1016/j.neubiorev.2017.02.027

Hurl, K., Wightman, J., Haynes, S. N., & Virues-Ortega, J. (2016). Does a pre-intervention functional assessment increase intervention effectiveness? A meta-analysis of within-subject interrupted time-series studies. *Clinical Psychology Review, 47*, 71–84. https://doi.org/10.1016/j.cpr.2016.05.003

Hyman, S. L., Fisher, W., Mercugliano, M., & Cataldo, M. F. (1990). Children with self-injurious behavior. *Pediatrics, 85*(3), 437–441.

Insel, T., Cuthbert, B., Garvey, M., Heinssen, R., Pine, D. S., Quinn, K.,... Wang, P. (2010). Research domain criteria (RDoC): Toward a new classification framework for research on mental disorders. *American Journal of Psychiatry, 167*(7), 748–751. https://doi.org/10.1176/appi.ajp.2010.09091379

Iwata, B. A., DeLeon, I. G., & Roscoe, E. M. (2013). Reliability and validity of the Functional Analysis Screening Tool. *Journal of Applied Behavior Analysis, 46*, 271–284. https://doi.org/10.1002/jaba.31

Iwata, B. A., Dorsey, M. F., Slifer, K. J., Bauman, K. E., & Richman, G. S. (1994). Toward a functional analysis of self-injury. *Journal of Applied Behavior Analysis, 27*, 197–209. (Reprinted from *Analysis and Intervention in Developmental Disabilities, 1982*, 1983–1920). https://doi.org/10.1901/jaba.1994.27–197

Iwata, B. A., & Dozier, C. L. (2008). Clinical application of functional analysis methodology. *Behavior Analysis in Practice, 1*(1), 3–9. https://doi.org/10.1007/bf03391714

Iwata, B. A., Pace, G. M., Cowdery, G. E., & Miltenberger, R. G. (1994). What makes extinction work: An analysis of procedural form and function. *Journal of Applied Behavior Analysis, 27,* 131-144. https://doi.org/10.1901/jaba.1994.27–131

Iwata, B. A., Pace, G. M., Dorsey, M. F., Zarcone, J. R., Vollmer, T. R., Smith, R. G.,... Mazaleski, J. L. (1994). The functions of self-injurious behavior: An experimental-epidemiological analysis. *Journal of Applied Behavior Analysis, 27*(2), 215–240. https://doi.org/10.1901/jaba.1994.27–215

Jang, J., Dixon, D. R., Tarbox, J., & Granpeesheh, D. (2011). Symptom severity and challenging behavior in children with ASD. *Research in Autism Spectrum Disorders, 5*(3), 1028–1032. https://doi.org/10.1016/j.rasd.2010.11.008

Kahng, S., Hausman, N. L., Fisher, A. B., Donaldson, J. M., Cox, J. R., Lugo, M., & Wiskow, K. M. (2015). The safety of functional analyses of self-injurious behavior. *Journal of Applied Behavior Analysis, 48,* 107–114. https://doi.org/10.1002/jaba.168

Kahng, S., Iwata, B. A., & Lewin, A. B. (2002). Behavioral treatment of self-injury, 1964 to 2000. *American Journal on Mental Retardation, 107*(3), 212–221. https://doi.org/10.1352/0895–8017(2002)107<0212:btosit>2.0.co;2

Katsnelson, A. (2013). Momentum grows to make personalized medicine more precise. *Nature Medicine, 19,* 249. https://doi.org/10.1038/nm0313-249

Kazdin, A. E. (2011). *Single-case research designs: Methods for clinical and applied settings.* (2nd ed.). New York, NY, US: Oxford University Press.

Kratochwill, T. R., Hitchcock, J., Horner, R., Levin, J. R., Odom, S., Rindskopf, D., & Shadish, W. (2010). *Single-case designs technical documentation.* Retrieved from https://eric.ed.gov/?id=ED510743

Kravitz, H., & Boehm, J. J. (1971). Rhythmic habit patterns in infancy: Their sequence, age of onset, and frequency. *Child Development, 42*(2), 399–413. https://doi.org/10.2307/1127475

Kuhn, D., Hagopian, L., & Terlonge, C. (2008). Treatment of life-threatening self-injurious behavior secondary to hereditary sensory and autonomic neuropathy type II: A controlled case study. *Journal of Child Neurology, 23*(4), 381–388. https://doi.org/10.1177/0883073807309236

Kuhn, S. A., Lerman, D. C., & Vorndran, C. M. (2003). Pyramidal training for families of children with problem behavior. *Journal of Applied Behavior Analysis, 36*(1), 77–88. https://doi.org/10.1901/jaba.2003.36–77

Kurtz, P. F., Boelter, E. W., Jarmolowicz, D. P., Chin, M. D., & Hagopian, L. P. (2011). An analysis of functional communication training as an empirically supported treatment for problem behavior displayed by individuals with intellectual disabilities. *Research in Developmental Disabilities, 32*(6), 2935–2942. https://doi.org/10.1016/j.ridd.2011.05.009

Kurtz, P. F., Chin, M. D., Huete, J. M., & Cataldo, M. F. (2012). Identification of emerging self-injurious behavior in young children: A preliminary study. *Journal of Mental Health Research in Intellectual Disabilities, 5*(3–4), 260–285. https://doi.org/10.1080/19315864.2011.600809

Kurtz, P. F., Fodstad, J. C., Huete, J. M., & Hagopian, L. P. (2013). Caregiver- and staff-conducted functional analysis outcomes: A summary of 52 cases. *Journal of Applied Behavior Analysis, 46*(4), 738–749. https://doi.org/10.1002/jaba.87

Langthorne, P., & McGill, P. (2008). Functional analysis of the early development of self-injurious behavior: Incorporating gene–environment interactions. *American Journal on Mental Retardation, 113*(5), 403–417. https://doi.org/10.1352/2008.113:403–417

Li, A., MacNeill, B., Curiel, H., & Poling, A. (2017). Risperidone in combination with other drugs: Experimental research in individuals with autism spectrum disorder. *Experimental and Clinical Psychopharmacology, 25*(5), 434. https://doi.org/10.1037/pha0000144

Lowe, K., Allen, D., Jones, E., Brophy, S., Moore, K., & James, W. (2007). Challenging behaviours: Prevalence and topographies. *Journal of Intellectual Disability Research, 51*(8), 625–636. https://doi.org/10.1111/j.1365–2788.2006.00948.x

Lydon, S., Healy, O., Roche, M., Henry, R., Mulhern, T., & Hughes, B. M. (2015). Salivary cortisol levels and challenging behavior in children with autism spectrum disorder. *Research in Autism Spectrum Disorders, 10,* 78–92. https://doi.org/10.1016/j.rasd.2014.10.020

Mace, F. C. (1994). The significance and future of functional analysis methodologies. *Journal of Applied Behavior Analysis, 27*(2), 385–392. https://doi.org/10.1901/jaba.1994.27–385

Mace, F. C., & Mauk, J. E. (1995). Bio-behavioral diagnosis and treatment of self-injury. *Developmental Disabilities Research Reviews, 1*(2), 104–110. https://doi.org/10.1002/mrdd.1410010206

Maddox, B. B., Trubanova, A., & White, S. W. (2017). Untended wounds: Non-suicidal self-injury in adults with autism spectrum disorder. *Autism, 21*(4), 412–422. https://doi.org/10.1177/1362361316644731

Matson, J. L., Mahan, S., Hess, J. A., Fodstad, J. C., & Neal, D. (2010). Progression of challenging behaviors in children and adolescents with autism spectrum disorders as measured by the Autism Spectrum Disorders-Problem Behaviors for Children (ASD-PBC). *Research in Autism Spectrum Disorders, 4*(3), 400–404. https://doi.org/10.1016/j.rasd.2009.10.010

Matson, J. L., & Turygin, C. (2012). How do researchers define self-injurious behavior? *Research in Developmental Disabilities, 33*(4), 1021–1026. https://doi.org/10.1016/j.ridd.2012.01.009

Matson, J. L., & Vollmer, T. (1995). *User's guide: Questions About Behavioral Function (QABF).* Baton Rouge, LA: Scientific Publishers.

McClintock, K., Hall, S., & Oliver, C. (2003). Risk markers associated with challenging behaviours in people with intellectual disabilities: A meta-analytic study. *Journal of Intellectual Disability Research, 47*(6), 405–416. https://doi.org/10.1046/j.1365-2788.2003.00517.x

McDermott, S., Zhou, L., & Mann, J. (2008). Injury treatment among children with autism or pervasive developmental disorder. *Journal of Autism and Developmental Disorders, 38*(4), 626–633. https://doi.org/10.1007/s10803-007-0426-9

McGillivray, J. A., & McCabe, M. P. (2004). Pharmacological management of challenging behavior of individuals with intellectual disability. *Research in Developmental Disabilities, 25*(6), 523–537. https://doi.org/10.1016/j.ridd.2004.03.001

McGuire, K., Fung, L. K., Hagopian, L., Vasa, R. A., Mahajan, R., Bernal, P.,... Hardan, A. Y. (2016). Irritability and problem behavior in autism spectrum disorder: A practice pathway for pediatric primary care. *Pediatrics, 137*(Suppl 2), S136–S148. https://doi.org/10.1542/peds.2015-2851I

McTiernan, A., Leader, G., Healy, O., & Mannion, A. (2011). Analysis of risk factors and early predictors of challenging behavior for children with autism spectrum disorder. *Research in Autism Spectrum Disorders, 5*(3), 1215–1222. https://doi.org/https://doi.org/10.1016/j.rasd.2011.01.009

Miltenberger, R. G., & Spieler, C. A. (2016). Body-focused repetitive behaviors. In J. K. Luiselli (Ed.), *Behavioral health promotion and intervention in intellectual and developmental disabilities* (pp. 117–136). Cham: Springer International Publishing.

Minshawi, N. F., Hurwitz, S., Fodstad, J. C., Biebl, S., Morriss, D. H., & McDougle, C. J. (2014). The association between self-injurious behaviors and autism spectrum disorders. *Psychology Research and Behavior Management, 7*, 125. https://doi.org/10.2147/PRBM.S44635

Minshawi, N. F., Hurwitz, S., Morriss, D., & McDougle, C. J. (2015). Multidisciplinary assessment and treatment of self-injurious behavior in autism spectrum disorder and intellectual disability: Integration of psychological and biological theory and approach. *Journal of Autism and Developmental Disorders, 45*(6), 1541–1568. https://doi.org/10.1007/s10803-014-2307-3

Miodrag, N., & Hodapp, R. M. (2010). Chronic stress and health among parents of children with intellectual and developmental disabilities. *Current Opinion in Psychiatry, 23*(5), 407–411. https://doi.org/10.1097/YCO.0b013e32833a8796

Morano, S., Ruiz, S., Hwang, J., Wertalik, J. L., Moeller, J., Karal, M. A., & Mulloy, A. (2017). Meta-analysis of single-case treatment effects on self-injurious behavior for individuals with autism and intellectual disabilities. *Autism & Developmental Language Impairments, 2*, 1–26. https://doi.org/10.1177/2396941516688399

Mudford, O. C., Taylor, S. A., & Martin, N. T. (2009). Continuous recording and interobserver agreement algorithms reported in the Journal of Applied Behavior Analysis (1995–2005). *Journal of Applied Behavior Analysis, 42*(1), 165–169. https://doi.org/10.1901/jaba.2009.42–165

Muehlmann, A. M., & Lewis, M. H. (2012). Abnormal repetitive behaviours: Shared phenomenology and pathophysiology. *Journal of Intellectual Disability Research, 56*(5), 427–440. https://doi.org/10.1111/j.1365–2788.2011.01519.x

Neely, L., Garcia, E., Bankston, B., & Green, A. (2018). Generalization and maintenance of functional communication training for individuals with developmental disabilities: A systematic and quality review. *Research in Developmental Disabilities, 79*, 116–129. https://doi.org/10.1016/j.ridd.2018.02.002

Nissen, J. M. J. F., & Haveman, M. J. (1997). Mortality and avoidable death in people with severe self-injurious behaviour: Results of a Dutch study. *Journal of Intellectual Disability Research, 41*(3), 252–257. https://doi.org.10.1046/j.1365–2788.1997.04545.x

Oliver, A. C., Pratt, L. A., & Normand, M. P. (2015). A survey of functional behavior assessment methods used by behavior analysts in practice *Journal of Applied Behavior Analysis, 48*, 817–829. https://doi.org/10.1002/jaba.256

Oliver, C., Adams, D., Allen, D., Bull, L., Heald, M., Moss, J., . . . Woodcock, K. (2013). Causal models of clinically significant behaviors in Angelman, Cornelia de Lange, Prader–Willi and Smith–Magenis syndromes. *International Review of Research in Developmental Disabilities, 44*, 167–211. https://doi.org/10.1016/b978-0-12-401662-0.00006–3

Oliver, C., Licence, L., & Richards, C. (2017). Self-injurious behaviour in people with intellectual disability and autism spectrum disorder. *Current Opinion in Psychiatry, 30*(2), 97–101. https://doi.org/10.1097/yco.0000000000000313

Oliver, C., Murphy, G. H., & Corbett, J. (1987). Self-injurious behaviour in people with mental handicap: A total population study. *Journal of Intellectual Disability Research, 31*(2), 147–162. https://doi.org/10.1111/j.1365–2788.1987.tb01351.x

Oliver, C., & Richards, C. (2010). Self-injurious behaviour in people with intellectual disability. *Current Opinion in Psychiatry, 23*(5), 412–416. https://doi.org/10.1097/YCO.0b013e32833cfb80

Oliver, C., & Richards, C. (2015). Practitioner review: Self-injurious behaviour in children with developmental delay. *Journal of Child Psychology and Psychiatry, 56*(10), 1042–1054. https://doi.org/10.1111/jcpp.12425

Peters-Scheffer, N., Didden, R., Korzilius, H., & Sturmey, P. (2011). A meta-analytic study on the effectiveness of comprehensive ABA-based early intervention programs for children with autism spectrum disorders. *Research in Autism Spectrum Disorders, 5*(1), 60–69. https://doi.org/10.1016/j.rasd.2010.03.011

Petscher, E. S., Rey, C., & Bailey, J. S. (2009). A review of empirical support for differential reinforcement of alternative behavior. *Research in Developmental Disabilities, 30*(3), 409–425. https://doi.org/10.1016/j.ridd.2008.08.008

Phillips, C. L., Iannaccone, J. A., Rooker, G. W., & Hagopian, L. P. (2017). Noncontingent reinforcement for the treatment of severe problem behavior: An analysis of 27 consecutive applications. *Journal of Applied Behavior Analysis, 50*(2), 357–376. https://doi.org/10.1002/jaba.376

Prinz, R. J., & Miller, G. E. (1996). Parental engagement in interventions for children at risk for conduct disorder. In R. Peters & R. McMahon (Eds.), *Preventing childhood disorders, substance abuse, and delinquency* (pp. 161–183). Thousand Oaks, CA: Sage Publications. https://doi.org/10.4135/9781483327679

Pyles, D. A., Muniz, K., Cade, A., & Silva, R. (1997). A behavioral diagnostic paradigm for integrating behavior-analytic and psychopharmacological interventions for people with a dual diagnosis. *Research in Developmental Disabilities, 18*(3), 185–214. https://doi.org/10.1016/s0891-4222(97)00003-6

Rapp, J. T., & Miltenberger, R. G. (2000). Self-restraint and self-injury: A demonstration of separate functions and response classes. *Behavioral Interventions, 15*(1), 37–51. https://doi.org/10.1002/(SICI)1099-078X(200001/03)15:1<37::AID-BIN40>3.0.CO;2–5

Rattaz, C., Michelon, C., & Baghdadli, A. (2015). Symptom severity as a risk factor for self-injurious behaviours in adolescents with autism spectrum disorders. *Journal of Intellectual Disability Research, 59*(8), 730–741. https://doi.org/10.1111/jir.12177

Rice, L., Gray, K., Howlin, P., Taffe, J., Tonge, B., & Einfeld, S. (2016). The developmental trajectory of self-injurious behaviours in individuals with Prader Willi syndrome, autism spectrum disorder and intellectual disability. *Diseases, 4*(1), 9. https://doi.org/10.3390/diseases4010009

Richards, C., Davies, L., & Oliver, C. (2017). Predictors of self-injurious behavior and self-restraint in autism spectrum disorder: Towards a hypothesis of impaired behavioral

control. *Journal of Autism and Developmental Disorders, 47*(3), 701–713. https://doi.org/:10.1007/s10803-016-3000-5
Richards, C., Moss, J., Nelson, L., & Oliver, C. (2016). Persistence of self-injurious behaviour in autism spectrum disorder over 3 years: A prospective cohort study of risk markers. *Journal of Neurodevelopmental Disorders, 8*(1), 21. https://doi.org/10.1186/s11689-016-9153-x
Richards, C., Oliver, C., Nelson, L., & Moss, J. (2012). Self-injurious behaviour in individuals with autism spectrum disorder and intellectual disability. *Journal of Intellectual Disability Research, 56*(5), 476–489. https://doi.org/10.1111/j.1365–2788.2012.01537.x
Richman, D. M. (2008). Early intervention and prevention of self-injurious behaviour exhibited by young children with developmental disabilities. *Journal of Intellectual Disability Research, 52*(1), 3–17. https://doi.org/10.1111/j.1365–2788.2007.01027.x
Richman, D. M., Barnard-Brak, L., Grubb, L., Bosch, A., & Abby, L. (2015). Meta-analysis of noncontingent reinforcement effects on problem behavior. *Journal of Applied Behavior Analysis, 48*(1), 131–152. https://doi.org/10.1002/jaba.189
Romaniuk, C., Miltenberger, R., Conyers, C., Jenner, N., Jurgens, M., & Ringenberg, C. (2002). The influence of activity choice on problem behaviors maintained by escape versus attention. *Journal of Applied Behavior Analysis, 35*, 349–362. https://doi.org/10.1901/jaba.2002.35–349
Rooker, G. W., Bonner, A. C., Dillon, C. M., & Zarcone, J. R. (2018). Behavioral treatment of automatically reinforced SIB: 1982–2015. *Journal of Applied Behavior Analysis, 51*(4), 974–997. https://doi.org/10.1002/jaba.492
Rooker, G. W., Iwata, B. A., Harper, J. M., Fahmie, T. A., & Camp, E. M. (2011). False-positive tangible outcomes of functional analyses. *Journal of Applied Behavior Analysis, 44*, 737–745. https://doi.org/10.1901/jaba.2011.44–737
Rooker, G. W., & Roscoe, E. M. (2005). Functional analysis of self-injurious behavior and its relation to self-restraint. *Journal of Applied Behavior Analysis, 38*(4), 537–542. https://doi.org/10.1901/jaba.2005.12–05
Roscoe, E. M., Schlichenmeyer, K. J., & Dube, W. V. (2015). Functional analysis of problem behavior: A systematic approach for identifying idiosyncratic variables. *Journal of Applied Behavior Analysis, 48*(2), 289–314. https://doi.org/10.1002/jaba.201
Saini, V., Greer, B. D., Fisher, W. W., Lichtblau, K. R., DeSouza, A. A., & Mitteer, D. R. (2016). Individual and combined effects of noncontingent reinforcement and response blocking on automatically reinforced problem behavior. *Journal of Applied Behavior Analysis, 49*(3), 693–698. https://doi.org/10.1002/jaba.306
Saini, V., Miller, S. A., & Fisher, W. W. (2016). Multiple schedules in practical application: Research trends and implications for future investigation. *Journal of Applied Behavior Analysis, 49*, 421–444. https://doi.org/10.1002/jaba.300
Sallustro, F., & Atwell, C. W. (1978). Body rocking, head banging, and head rolling in normal children. *Journal of Pediatrics, 93*(4), 704–708. https://doi.org/10.1016/s0022-3476(78)80922–6
Sandman, C. A., & Kemp, A. S. (2011). Opioid antagonists may reverse endogenous opiate "dependence" in the treatment of self-injurious behavior. *Pharmaceuticals, 4*(2), 366–381. https://doi.org/10.3390/ph4020366
Schaal, D. W., & Hackenberg, T. (1994). Toward a functional analysis of drug treatment for behavior problems of people with developmental disabilities. *American Journal on Mental Retardation, 99*(2), 123–140.
Scheithauer, M., O'Connor, J., & Toby, L. M. (2015). Assessment of self-restraint using a functional analysis of self-injury. *Journal of Applied Behavior Analysis, 48*(4), 907–911. https://doi.org/10.1002/jaba.230
Schieve, L. A., Gonzalez, V., Boulet, S. L., Visser, S. N., Rice, C. E., Braun, K. V. N., & Boyle, C. A. (2012). Concurrent medical conditions and health care use and needs among children with learning and behavioral developmental disabilities, National Health Interview Survey, 2006–2010. *Research in Developmental Disabilities, 33*(2), 467–476. https://doi.org/10.1016/j.ridd.2011.10.008
Schroeder, S. R., Mulick, J. A., & Rojahn, J. (1980). The definition, taxonomy, epidemiology, and ecology of self-injurious behavior. *Journal of Autism and Developmental Disorders, 10*(4), 417–432. https://doi.org/10.1007/bf02414818
Schroeder, S. R., Oster-Granite, M. L., Berkson, G., Bodfish, J. W., Breese, G. R., Cataldo, M. F., . . . Fisher, W. (2001). Self-injurious behavior: Gene–brain–behavior relationships. *Developmental Disabilities Research Reviews, 7*(1), 3–12. https://doi.org/10.1002/1098–2779(200102)7:1<3::aid-mrdd1002>3.0.co;2-#
Shabani, D. B., Carr, J. E., Pabico, R. S., Sala, A. P., Lam, W. Y., & Oberg, T. L. (2013). The effects of functional analysis test sessions on subsequent rates of problem behavior in the natural environment. *Behavioral Interventions, 28*(1), 40–47.
Shattuck, P. T., Seltzer, M. M., Greenberg, J. S., Orsmond, G. I., Bolt, D., Kring, S., . . . Lord, C. (2007). Change in autism symptoms and maladaptive behaviors in adolescents and adults with an autism spectrum disorder. *Journal of Autism and Developmental Disorders, 37*(9), 1735–1747.
Shirley, M. D., Frelin, L., López, J. S., Jedlicka, A., Dziedzic, A., Frank-Crawford, M. A., . . . Pevsner, J. (2016). Copy number variants associated with 14 cases of self-injurious behavior. *PLoS ONE, 11*(3), e0149646. https://doi.org/10.1371/journal.pone.0149646
Slocum, S. K., & Vollmer, T. R. (2015). A comparison of positive and negative reinforcement for compliance to treat problem behavior maintained by escape. *Journal of Applied Behavior Analysis, 48*, 563–574.
Smith, C. M., Smith, R. G., Dracobly, J. D., & Pace, A. P. (2012). Multiple-respondent anecdotal assessments: An analysis of interrater agreement and correspondence with analogue assessment outcomes. *Journal of Applied Behavior Analysis, 45*, 779–795.
Smith, R. G., Iwata, B. A., Goh, H. L., & Shore, B. A. (1995). Analysis of establishing operations for self-injury maintained by escape. *Journal of Applied Behavior Analysis, 28*(4), 515–535. https://doi.org/10.1901/jaba.1995.28–515
Smith, R. G., Iwata, B. A., Vollmer, T. R., & Pace, G. M. (1992). On the relationship between self-injurious behavior and self-restraint. *Journal of Applied Behavior Analysis, 25*(2), 433–445.
Smith, R. G., Lerman, D. C., & Iwata, B. A. (1996). Self-restraint as positive reinforcement for self-injurious behavior. *Journal of Applied Behavior Analysis, 29*(1), 99–102. https://doi.org/10.1901/jaba.1996.29–99
Soke, G. N., Rosenberg, S. A., Hamman, R. F., Fingerlin, T., Robinson, C., Carpenter, L., . . . Durkin, M. S. (2016). Brief report: Prevalence of self-injurious behaviors among children

with autism spectrum disorder—A population-based study. *Journal of Autism and Developmental Disorders, 46*(11), 3607–3614. https://doi.org/10.1007/s10803-016-2879-1

Soke, G. N., Rosenberg, S. A., Hamman, R. F., Fingerlin, T., Rosenberg, C. R., Carpenter, L., . . . DiGuiseppi, C. (2017). Factors associated with self-injurious behaviors in children with autism spectrum disorder: Findings from two large national samples. *Journal of Autism and Developmental Disorders, 47*(2), 285–296. https://doi.org/10.1007/s10803-016-2951-x

Soke, G. N., Rosenberg, S. A., Rosenberg, C. R., Vasa, R. A., Lee, L. C., & DiGuiseppi, C. (2018). Brief report: Self-injurious behaviors in preschool children with autism spectrum disorder compared to other developmental delays and disorders. *Journal of Autism and Developmental Disorders, 48*(7), 2558–2566. doi:10.1007/s10803-018-3490-4

Stigler, K. A., & McDougle, C. J. (2008). Pharmacotherapy of irritability in pervasive developmental disorders. *Child and Adolescent Psychiatric Clinics of North America, 17*(4), 739–752. https://doi.org/10.1016/j.chc.2008.06.002

Stokes, T. F., & Osnes, P. G. (2016). An operant pursuit of generalization. *Behavior Therapy, 47*(5), 720–732. (Reprinted from *Behavior Therapy, 20*[3], 337–355, 1989). https://doi.org/10.1016/S0005-7894(89)80054-1

Sturmey, P., & Didden, R. (Eds.). (2014). *Evidence-based practice and intellectual disabilities.* London: Wiley Blackwell.

Summers, J., Shahrami, A., Cali, S., D'Mello, C., Kako, M., Palikucin-Reljin, A., . . . Lunsky, Y. (2017). Self-injury in autism spectrum disorder and intellectual disability: Exploring the role of reactivity to pain and sensory input. *Brain Sciences, 7*(11), 140. https://doi.org/10.3390/brainsci7110140

Symons, F. J., Davis, M. L., & Thompson, T. (2000). Self-injurious behavior and sleep disturbance in adults with developmental disabilities. *Research in Developmental Disabilities, 21*(2), 115–123. https://doi.org/10.1016/S0891-4222(00)00028–7

Symons, F. J., Sperry, L. A., Dropik, P. L., & Bodfish, J. W. (2005). The early development of stereotypy and self-injury: A review of research methods. *Journal of Intellectual Disability Research, 49*(2), 144–158. https://doi.org/10.1111/j.1365–2788.2004.00632.x

Symons, F. J., Thompson, A., & Rodriguez, M. C. (2004). Self-injurious behavior and the efficacy of naltrexone treatment: A quantitative synthesis. *Developmental Disabilities Research Reviews, 10*(3), 193–200. https://doi.org/10.1002/mrdd.20031

Symons, F. J., & Thompson, T. (1997). A Review of Self-Injurious Behavior and Pain in Persons with Developmental Disabilities. International Review of Research in Mental Retardation, 69–111. doi:10.1016/s0074-7750(08)60277-3

Symons, F. J., Wendelschafer-Crabb, G., Kennedy, W., Hardrict, R., Dahl, N., & Bodfish, J. W. (2008). Evidence of altered epidermal nerve fiber morphology in adults with self-injurious behavior and neurodevelopmental disorders. *Pain, 134*(1), 232–237. https://doi.org/10.1016/j.pain.2007.07.022

Tarbox, J., Wilke, A. E., Najdowski, A. C., Findel-Pyles, R. S., Balasanyan, S., Caveney, A. C., . . . Tia, B. (2009). Comparing indirect, descriptive, and experimental functional assessments of challenging behavior in children with autism. *Journal of Developmental and Physical Disabilities, 21*(6), 493. https://doi.org/10.1007/s10882-009-9154-8

Tate, B. G., & Baroff, G. S. (1966). Aversive control of self-injurious behavior in a psychotic boy. *Behaviour Research and Therapy, 4*(4), 281-287. https://doi.org/10.1016/0005–7967(66)90084–2

Tausig, M. (1985). Factors in family decision-making about placement for developmentally disabled individuals. *American Journal of Mental Deficiency, 89*(4), 352–361.

Taylor, L., Oliver, C., & Murphy, G. (2011). The chronicity of self-injurious behaviour: A long-term follow-up of a total population study. *Journal of Applied Research in Intellectual Disabilities, 24*(2), 105–117. https://doi.org/10.1111/j.1468–3148.2010.00579.x

Thelen, E. (1979). Rhythmical stereotypies in normal human infants. *Animal Behaviour, 27*, 699–715. https://doi.org/10.1016/0003–3472(79)90006-X

Thompson, R. H., & Iwata, B. A. (2007). A comparison of outcomes from descriptive and functional analyses of problem behavior. *Journal of Applied Behavior Analysis, 40*(2), 333–338. https://doi.org/10.1901/jaba.2007.56–06

Thompson, T. (2007). Relations among functional systems in behavior analysis. *Journal of the Experimental Analysis of Behavior, 87*(3), 423–440. doi:10.1901/jeab.2007.21–06

Thompson, T., Symons, F., Delaney, D., & England, C. (1995). Self-injurious behavior as endogenous neurochemical self-administration. *Mental Retardation and Developmental Disabilities Research Reviews, 1*(2), 137–148. https://doi.org/10.1002/mrdd.1410010210

Tiger, J. H., Hanley, G. P., & Bruzek, J. (2008). Functional communication training: A review and practical guide. *Behavior Analysis in Practice, 1*(1), 16–23. https://doi.org/10.1007/bf03391716

Toohey, M. J., & DiGiuseppe, R. (2017). Defining and measuring irritability: Construct clarification and differentiation. *Clinical Psychology Review, 53*, 93–108. https://doi.org/10.1016/j.cpr.2017.01.009

U.S. Food and Drug Administration. (2006, October). FDA Approves the First Drug to Treat Irritability Associated with Autism, Risperdal. *FDA News.* Retrieved from https://wayback.archive-it.org/7993/20161024051139/http://www.fda.gov/NewsEvents/Newsroom/PressAnnouncements/2006/ucm108759.htm

Vaughan, M. E., & Michael, J. L. (1982). Automatic reinforcement: An important but ignored concept. *Behaviorism, 10*(2), 217–227.

Virués-Ortega, J. (2010). Applied behavior analytic intervention for autism in early childhood: Meta-analysis, meta-regression and dose–response meta-analysis of multiple outcomes. *Clinical Psychology Review, 30*(4), 387–399. https://doi.org/10.1016/j.cpr.2010.01.008

Volkert, V. M., Lerman, D. C., Call, N. A., & Trosclair-Lasserre, N. (2009). An evaluation of resurgence during treatment with functional communication training. *Journal of Applied Behavior Analysis, 42*(1), 145–160. https://doi.org/10.1901/jaba.2009.42–145

Vollmer, T. R. (1994). The concept of automatic reinforcement: Implications for behavioral research in developmental disabilities. *Research in Developmental Disabilities, 15*(3), 187–207. https://doi.org/10.1016/0891–4222(94)90011–6

Vollmer, T. R., Hagopian, L. P., Bailey, J. S., Dorsey, M. F., Hanley, G. P., Lennox, D., . . . Spreat, S. (2011). The association for behavior analysis international position statement on restraint and seclusion. *The Behavior Analyst, 34*(1), 103–110. https://doi.org/10.1007/bf03392238

Vollmer, T. R., Marcus, B. A., & LeBlanc, L. (1994). Treatment of self-injury and hand mouthing following inconclusive functional analyses. *Journal of Applied Behavior Analysis, 27*, 331–344. https://doi.org/10.1901/jaba.1994.27–331

Vollmer, T. R., Marcus, B. A., & Ringdahl, J. E. (1995). Noncontingent escape as treatment for self-injurious behavior maintained by negative reinforcement. *Journal of Applied Behavior Analysis, 28*(1), 15–26. https://doi.org/10.1901/jaba.1995.28–15

Vollmer, T. R., & Vorndran, C. M. (1998). Assessment of self-injurious behavior maintained by access to self-restraint materials. *Journal of Applied Behavior Analysis, 31*(4), 647–650. https://doi.org/10.1901/jaba.1998.31–647

Wachtel, L. E., & Hagopian, L. P. (2006). Psychopharmacology and applied behavioral analysis: Tandem treatment of severe problem behaviors in intellectual disability and a case series. *Israel Journal of Psychiatry and Related Sciences, 43*(4), 265–274. https://search.proquest.com/docview/236952650?accountid=11752

Wacker, D. P., Berg, W. K., Harding, J. W., Derby, K. M., Asmus, J. M., & Healy, A. (1998). Evaluation and long-term treatment of aberrant behavior displayed by young children with disabilities. *Journal of Developmental and Behavioral Pediatrics, 19*(4), 260–266. https://doi.org/10.1097/00004703-199808000-00004

Wacker, D. P., Lee, J. F., Dalmau, Y. C. P., Kopelman, T. G., Lindgren, S. D., Kuhle, J., . . . Waldron, D. B. (2013). Conducting functional analyses of problem behavior via telehealth. *Journal of Applied Behavior Analysis, 46*(1), 31–46. https://doi.org/10.1002/jaba.29

Weisz, J. R., Weiss, B., Han, S. S., Granger, D. A., & Morton, T. (1995). Effects of psychotherapy with children and adolescents revisited: A meta-analysis of treatment outcome studies. *Psychological Bulletin, 117*(3), 450. https://doi.org/10.1037/0033–2909.117.3.450

West, L., Brunssen, S. H., & Waldrop, J. (2009). Review of the evidence for treatment of children with autism with selective serotonin reuptake inhibitors. *Journal for Specialists in Pediatric Nursing, 14*(3), 183–191. https://doi.org/10.1111/j.1744–6155.2009.00196.x

Williams, D. E., & Grossett, D. L. (2011). Reduction of restraint of people with intellectual disabilities: An organizational behavior management (OBM) approach. *Research in Developmental Disabilities, 32*(6), 2336–2339. https://doi.org/10.1016/j.ridd.2011.07.032

Williams, S., Leader, G., Mannion, A., & Chen, J. (2015). An investigation of anxiety in children and adolescents with autism spectrum disorder. *Research in Autism Spectrum Disorders, 10*, 30–40. https://doi.org/10.1016/j.rasd.2014.10.017

Wolff, P. H. (1967). The role of biological rhythms in early psychological development. *Bulletin of the Menninger Clinic, 31*(4), 197.

Zarcone, J. R., Lindauer, S. E., Morse, P. S., Crosland, K. A., Valdovinos, M. G., McKerchar, T. L., . . . Schroeder, S. R. (2004). Effects of risperidone on destructive behavior of persons with developmental disabilities: III. Functional analysis. *American Journal on Mental Retardation, 109*(4), 310–321. https://doi.org/10.1352/0895-8017(2004)109<310:eorodb>2.0.co;2

CHAPTER

18 Suicidality and Self-Harm in Autism Spectrum Conditions

Sarah Cassidy

Abstract

Self-harm and suicidality in autism spectrum conditions (ASCs) have been underresearched. However, there is now convincing evidence that suicide is a leading cause of early death in the autistic community, and the prevalence of self-harm, suicidal thoughts, and suicidal behaviors is significantly elevated in autistic children and adults compared to the general population and psychiatric groups. Less research is currently available exploring the reasons why (etiology), how to assess or measure self-harm and suicidality, or how to treat these difficulties in autistic people. This chapter will summarize existing evidence on this topic and provide recommendations for future research and clinical practice to improve understanding, assessment, and prevention of self-harm and suicidality in ASD.

Keywords: autism spectrum condition, suicidality, self-harm, nonsuicidal self-injury, autistic traits, interpersonal psychological theory of suicide, integrated motivational volitional model of suicide, measurement properties, suicide risk assessment

Overview

Self-harm has traditionally been conceptualized very differently in the context of autism spectrum conditions (ASCs) compared to the general population, which has led to this behavior being overlooked by researchers and clinicians for some time. In people diagnosed with ASC (henceforth autistic people[1]), self-harm has been conceptualized primarily as a challenging and/or restricted repetitive behavior (RRB) characteristic of ASC (Duerden et al., 2012; South, Ozonoff, & McMahon, 2005) and often associated with co-occurring intellectual disability (ID; Minshawi et al., 2014), whereas in the general population, self-harm is conceptualized as a significant risk marker for later suicide attempts (Ribeiro et al., 2016). Hence, it was unknown whether autistic people who displayed self-injurious behaviors (SIBs) as traditionally conceptualized in autism may possibly have been experiencing suicidality or nonsuicidal self-injury (NSSI) as conceptualized in the general population (Cassidy, Bradley, Bowen, Wigham, & Rodgers, 2018a; Hannon & Taylor., 2013). Broadening the conceptualization of SIB in autism to include suicidality and NSSI as defined in the general population is therefore important for improved identification and treatment of a broader range of self-harming behaviors in autistic people.

Research has only started to explore self-harm more broadly in the context of ASC and associations with suicidal thoughts and suicidal behaviors in this group (e.g., Cassidy, Bradley, Shaw, & Baron-Cohen, 2018; Maddox, Trubanova, & White, 2017; Storch et al., 2013; Mayes, Gorman, Hillwig-Garcia, & Syed, 2013), but the topic remains underresearched. In particular, no theoretical framework has yet been proposed to guide future hypothesis-driven research and aid development of new validated assessment tools and treatments to effectively

[1] In this chapter, the preferred language to describe and talk about autism is used, as shown in a recent survey of autistic people's preferences (Kenny et al., 2016), while acknowledging that there are many equally valid individual preferences for describing and talking about autism, which rapidly develop and change over time.

identify and treat self-harm and suicidality in autistic people (Cassidy & Rodgers, 2017).

This chapter therefore aims to summarize the current available evidence regarding the prevalence, etiology, and assessment of self-harm and suicidality in ASC and to consider implications for intervention, prevention, and treatment strategies. Emerging results are considered in the context of relevant theories of self-harm and suicidality originally developed for the general population, to help begin to identify potential common risk markers (shared between the general and autistic population). Subsequently, suggestions are also made regarding risk markers that may be unique to ASC, not yet covered in suicide theory developed for the general population, and thus requiring adapted assessment and treatment approaches for autistic people. From this discussion, recommendations for future research and clinical practice are made to more effectively understand, identify, and prevent self-harm and suicide in the autistic community.

The aim of this chapter is not to be exhaustive or provide definitive conclusions given the preliminary nature of results and early stage of the self-harm and suicidality in the autism research field. Rather, the aim is to provide a more useful way forward for future hypothesis-driven research and evidence-informed assessment and treatment options appropriate for autistic people and tailored to their unique presentations and needs. This is crucial to move the field forward and increase the amount and quality of self-harm and suicidality in ASC research and increase the amount and appropriateness of available assessment, support, and treatment options for this group. This is critical if researchers and clinicians are to prevent the high rates of psychological distress and tragically high rates of death by suicide in this vulnerable group.

Prevalence and Course

Self-harm refers to any form of harm or injury to self, with or without intent to end life (Hawton, Saunders, & O'Connor, 2012). A form of self-harm is NSSI, which refers to any form of socially unsanctioned self-injury without the intent to end life (Nock & Favazza, 2009), whereas suicidality refers to thoughts or behaviors with intent to end life, including death by suicide (Hawton et al., 2012). It is important to note that broader self-harm and NSSI are as equally serious as suicidality and can result in serious injury or death regardless of intent. Hence, many researchers and clinicians argue that it is more useful to aim to understand and prevent self-harm more broadly, rather than just focusing on suicidality (where intent to end life is present; Hawton et al., 1998). In this chapter, various forms of self-harming behavior will be covered, including self-harm (where intent is undefined), NSSI, and suicidality (covering suicidal thoughts, suicidal behaviors, and death by suicide).

SIBs, such as headbanging or biting oneself, are prevalent in autistic people, with approximately 50% having experienced SIBs at some point (Baghdadli, Pascal, Grisi, & Aussilloux, 2003; Bodfish, Symons, Parker, & Lewis, 2000), significantly higher than people with ID or other conditions (Baghdadli et al., 2003; Dominick, Davis, Lainhart, Tager-Flusberg, & Folstein, 2007). However, SIB in ASCs appears to have a different phenomenology compared to the general population, associated with repetitive and challenging behavior (South et al., 2005), particularly in childhood (Minshawi et al., 2014), whereas in the general population, SIB is conceptualized as NSSI, which is usually impulsive and more common in adolescence and adulthood, with the primary form being cutting, and the primary motivation being to cope with emotional pain (Klonsky, 2007). Hence, SIB has been traditionally conceptualized rather differently in ASCs compared to the general population, which has led to autistic people having been routinely excluded from broader self-harm research (Dickstein et al., 2015; Kim et al., 2015). Hence, self-harm in ASCs remains poorly understood and underresearched (Cassidy & Rodgers., 2017). It is unclear, for example, whether autistic people (as in the general population) experience SIB to cope with emotional pain without intent to end life (as in NSSI) or with intent to end life (suicidality; Cassidy et al., 2018a; Hannon & Taylor, 2013).

A growing body of research is starting to explore whether self-harm, NSSI, and suicidality, as traditionally defined and explored in the general population, are also prevalent in autistic people. So far, these studies have tended to focus on autistic people without co-occurring ID, which is a large change from the traditional forms of research outlined earlier exploring SIB in ASC. However, in a recent systematic review of studies exploring suicidality in the autistic and general population, a majority of excluded studies had explored SIB in the context of challenging behavior in autistic people, commonly with ID, rather than suicidality per se (Cassidy et al., 2018a). Far fewer studies had explored suicidality or broader self-harm in autistic people (Cassidy et al., 2018a).

Only three available studies so far have explored NSSI, as traditionally defined in the general population, in autistic people. In a small sample of 42 autistic adults without co-occurring ID, 50% reported lifetime experience of NSSI, higher than previous rates found in the general population (17% to 26%; Maddox et al., 2017). In a larger study of 164 autistic adults, 65% reported NSSI, significantly higher than a matched sample of 169 general population adults (29.8%; Cassidy, Bradley, Shaw, et al., 2018). In 83 autistic children with co-occurring ID, 33% had experienced NSSI based on parental report (Akram, Tariq, & Rafi, 2017). These studies suggest that NSSI is significantly more prevalent in autistic people compared to the general population, in both children and adults. In the one study so far available, the phenomenology of NSSI was broadly similar between autistic and general population young adults, suggesting that the characteristics of NSSI (form, function, and motivations) may not only be prevalent in ASC but also similar to that found in the general (nonautistic) population (Maddox et al., 2017). This challenges previous assumptions about the differing phenomenology of NSSI in autistic individuals compared to the general population, the implication being that NSSI not only has been overlooked in ASC but also clinically may be more likely to be inappropriately attributed to ASC rather than acknowledged and treated in its own right, as in the general population (Maddox et al., 2017). However, to fully explore this possibility, future research must investigate whether autistic people experiencing SIB as traditionally defined in ASC also show characteristics of NSSI and/or suicidality as conceptualized in the general population. This will be particularly important in autistic people with co-occurring ID, where SIB characteristic of ASC is particularly prevalent (Minshawi et al., 2014).

Autistic women appear to be more likely to experience NSSI than autistic men in two studies (Cassidy, Bradley, Shaw, et al., 2018; Maddox et al., 2017), similar to findings in the general population (Klonsky, 2011; Whitlock, Muehlenkamp, & Purington, 2011). The high rates of NSSI in autistic adults (50% to 65%) also appear consistent in the two available online studies using the same online tool, the Non-Suicidal Self-Injury Assessment Tool (NSSI-AT; Whitlock, Exner-Cortens, & Purington, 2014), in nonclinical samples recruited from the general population (Cassidy, Bradley, Shaw, et al., 2018) and college students (Maddox et al., 2017). However, the prevalence in adults appears higher than the rate found in autistic children with co-occurring ID based on parent report (33%; Akram et al., 2017), possibly due to different reporting style (self- vs. proxy report) and type of tool used between these studies. The high rates of NSSI (50% to 65%) in adults cannot be explained by recruitment method or study sample, given these rates are reported from nonclinical general population and college student samples, where we would expect rates to be lower than in clinical samples. Further work is needed to establish whether the prevalence and developmental course of NSSI is different in ASCs compared to the general population.

A relatively larger number of studies have begun to explore suicidality in ASCs, showing consistently increased prevalence in autistic people compared to the general population across both childhood and adulthood (see Hedley & Uljarević, 2018, and Zahid & Upthegrove, 2017, for reviews). First, lifetime prevalence of suicidal ideation in autistic adults ranges between 19.7% (Hedley, Uljarević, Wilmot, Richdale, & Dissanayake, 2017) and 66% (Cassidy et al., 2014). This may reflect the different samples and methods utilized. The highest rate of suicidal ideation was obtained in adults newly diagnosed with Asperger syndrome in adulthood who had struggled without support (66%; Cassidy et al., 2014), whereas the lower bound estimate (19.7%) was obtained from autistic adults involved in a wider study on employment support for autistic people, and may therefore represent a better supported group of autistic people (Hedley et al., 2017). Second, lifetime prevalence of suicide attempts in autistic adults ranges from 1.79% (Croen et al., 2015) to between 35% and 36% (Cassidy et al., 2014; Paquette-Smith, Weiss, & Lunsky, 2014). Again, these large differences in prevalence estimates likely reflect the samples and methods used, with the highest estimates (35% to 36%) typically involving late-diagnosed (Cassidy et al., 2014) or self-selecting samples (Paquette-Smith et al., 2014) using self-report measures, and the lowest estimate (1.79%) involving a larger analysis of medical records (Croen et al., 2015).

Suicidality can be hard to spot in autistic people, and as described earlier, self-harming behavior can be misattributed or overshadowed by an ASC diagnosis. Hence, medical records could underestimate the prevalence of suicide attempts (which could be dismissed as SIB behavior characteristic of ASCs). Equally, it is unclear if self-report measures of suicidality in autistic people may under- or overestimate prevalence in this group, given known differences in cognitive style, such as literal interpretation of language (Happé, 1995), and difficulties in reporting emotional states to others (termed alexithymia; Bird et al., 2010). Issues regarding self-harm and suicidality assessment will be discussed in more detail later in this chapter. Despite the wide range of prevalence estimates, studies consistently indicate increased risk of suicidality in autistic adults (Hedley & Uljaravić, 2018; Zahid & Upthegrove, 2017). However, most studies have used small samples, lack independent confirmation of autism diagnosis, lack appropriate matched comparison groups, and have not used assessment tools with evidence of validity in ASC or other groups (Cassidy et al., 2018a; Hedley & Uljaravić, 2018).

In autistic children and adolescents, a similarly wide range of prevalence estimates are evident as in adults (childhood and adolescence are considered together, as these age groups are commonly grouped in research studies). Between 7% (Mayes et al., 2013) and 41.7% (Mikami et al., 2009) of children and adolescents have attempted suicide, and between 10.9% (Mayes et al., 2013) and 72% (Ghaziuddin, Alessi, & Greden, 1995) show evidence of suicidal ideation. These ranges are similar to those found in adulthood, indicating that perhaps prevalence of suicidality is consistent across ages in ASCs. However, at the time of writing, there are as yet no studies directly exploring or comparing the developmental course of suicidality in ASCs and whether this may differ in comparison to the general population.

To date, only two studies are available exploring the prevalence of death by self-harm (including suicide and self-harm where intent to end life was undetermined) in autistic people. A large population study using national patient register data in Sweden (27,122 autistic and 2.6 million matched controls) showed that a significantly higher proportion of autistic people died by suicide (0.31%) compared to the general population (0.04%), and suicide was a leading cause of early death among autistic people (Hirvikoski et al., 2016). In an ongoing UK study, between 11% and 12% of people who died by suicide had evidence of ASCs, with a majority (9%) not yet diagnosed at the time of their death, despite ample evidence of missed ASC diagnosis from medical records and interviews with informants who knew the person in childhood. This rate of 11% to 12% of ASCs in those who died by suicide is significantly higher than the 1% ASC prevalence in the general alive population, suggesting that ASCs are overrepresented in those who die by suicide (Cassidy et al., 2019).

In summary, a number of research studies suggest significantly increased rates of NSSI and suicidality (including death by self-harm and suicide) in autistic people. However, prevalence estimates are widely variable, due to differences in sampling methods and measures used. High rates of self-harm and suicidality appear to be prevalent across childhood, adolescence, and adulthood, although studies of developmental course are currently lacking. However, it is important to note that suicidal ideation and behavior have been reported in autistic children as young as 6 years old (Mayes et al., 2013), and it will be important for future work to explore whether this may be younger than found in the general population.

Etiology, Diagnosis, and Assessment

Although self-harm and suicidality are more prevalent in autistic people than in the general population, less clear are the reasons why, with little theory or hypothesis-driven research available (Cassidy & Rodgers, 2017). This is problematic, with most research to date having taken a piecemeal approach to understanding suicidality and self-harm in autism. Taking a more systematic, theory-driven approach to future research will likely lead to more tangible progress in the field, particularly in more reliably predicting who is most likely to attempt suicide, and thus providing better clinical opportunities for suicide risk assessment and prevention.

Current suicide theory developed for the general nonautistic population has moved away from merely looking at broad risk markers for suicide, such as depression or unemployment, which in themselves are poor indicators of suicide attempts (O'Connor & Kirtley, 2018; Van Orden et al., 2010). Additionally, not everyone who experiences suicidal ideation will go on to attempt or die by suicide. Hence, it is crucial to be able to understand the different factors underpinning the movement from experiencing suicidal thoughts to attempting suicide. Suicide theories have thus emerged attempting to better model the movement from suicidal ideation to suicide attempts to identify those most at risk of attempting suicide (O'Connor & Kirtley, 2018). Currently, suicide in autism research has not yet joined this important leap, but this is a critical step to increase opportunities to identify and prevent the high rates of suicide in this group.

This section of the chapter therefore aims to first outline current suicide theories developed for the general nonautistic population and subsequently consider how these theories may help us increase our understanding and prediction of suicide in

ASCs. Second, limitations and gaps within these theories will be outlined, and further areas of research identified. Third, the potentially unique aspects of self-harm and suicidality in autism will be discussed in light of our current knowledge regarding autism and emerging research findings.

Applicability of General Population Suicide Theory to ASCs

How can current theories of suicide developed for general nonautistic populations help us understand why autistic people are at increased risk of self-harm and suicidality? Many suicide theories stress the importance of difficulties commonly experienced by autistic people in the formation of suicidal intent, such as rigid thinking (American Psychiatric Association, 2013), reduced social problem-solving ability (Jackson & Dritschel, 2016), perfectionism (Greenaway & Howlin, 2010), and reduced social connections (Orsmond, Shattuck, Cooper, Sterzing, & Anderson, 2013). Hence, ASCs could increase vulnerability to experiencing known risk markers for self-harm and suicidality shared with the general nonautistic population. Additionally, research suggests that autistic traits, that is, behaviors characteristic of ASCs, such as social difficulties, imagination, and attentional switching (APA, 2013), are normally distributed in the general population without an ASC diagnosis (Baron-Cohen, Wheelwright, Skinner, Martin, & Clubley, 2001), termed the "broader autism phenotype" (Piven, Palmer, Jacobi, Childress, & Arndt, 1997). Research is showing not only an association between ASC diagnosis and suicidality (as discussed earlier) but also associations between high autistic traits in the general population and suicidality (Cassidy, Bradley, Shaw, et al., 2018; Pelton & Cassidy, 2017; Takara & Kondo, 2014). Those who attempt suicide (without an ASC diagnosis) also report significantly higher autistic traits than the general population (Richards et al., 2019). Hence, exploring both ASC diagnosis and autistic traits in the general population could be useful to test key components of suicide theory and how these may apply to ASCs. Additionally, it is also important to explore autistic traits in relation to suicide theory, as many people, particularly adults and women, have missed out on the opportunity for ASC diagnosis due to the rapidly changing conceptualization of the autism spectrum over time and availability of diagnostic services (Lai & Baron-Cohen, 2015). People as yet undiagnosed with ASCs are an incredibly important group to include in self-harm and suicidality research, given that many who die by suicide have not yet been diagnosed with ASCs but have high autistic traits indicating likely undiagnosed ASCs (Cassidy et al., 2019).

INTERPERSONAL PSYCHOLOGICAL THEORY OF SUICIDE

Pronounced social difficulties are required for diagnosis of ASCs (APA, 2013). Social difficulties are also a key component of many suicide theories developed for nonautistic populations, and a key example of such a theory is the interpersonal psychological theory of suicide (IPTS; Van Orden et al., 2010). The IPTS argues that two psychological states are required to experience suicidal desire: (a) thwarted belonging (TB), characterized by lack of meaningful social connections ("I am alone"), and (b) perceived burdensomeness (PB), characterized by lack of autonomy and feeling like a hopeless burden on friends and family ("I am a burden"). Humans have an innate desire to be accepted by others and to establish meaningful social connections—a sense of belonging. Traditionally, autism research has been dominated by the unhelpful assumption that autistic people are socially unmotivated (Jaswal & Akhtar, 2018), resulting in factors such as belonging, acceptance, and autonomy in autistic people's mental health being overlooked (Mitchell, Cassidy, & Sheppard, 2019). However, autistic people report belonging and autonomy as key components of their overall well-being (Camm-Crosbie et al., 2019; Milton & Sims, 2016). External indicators of the psychological states of TB and PB are also commonly experienced by autistic people, such as loneliness (Hedley et al., 2017; Hedley, Uljarević, Wilmot, Richdale, & Dissanayake, 2018), social isolation (Orsmond et al., 2013), and unemployment (Riedel et al., 2015). Hence, there appears to be overlap between the constructs of the IPTS and the common experiences of autistic people, who are also at high risk of suicide. Could the IPTS therefore be a promising candidate theory for why autistic people are at high risk of experiencing self-harm and suicide?

The IPTS predicts that presence of ASC diagnosis, or autistic traits characteristic of ASCs in the general population, should be associated with increased risk of experiencing TB and PB, which in turn should increase risk of suicidal desire (Figure 18.1). Emerging findings are consistent with these hypotheses outlined in the theory. For example, in autistic adults, self-reported loneliness predicted suicidal ideation, through depression (Hedley et al., 2018) and lack of social support increased thoughts of suicide and self-harm through depression (Hedley et al., 2017).

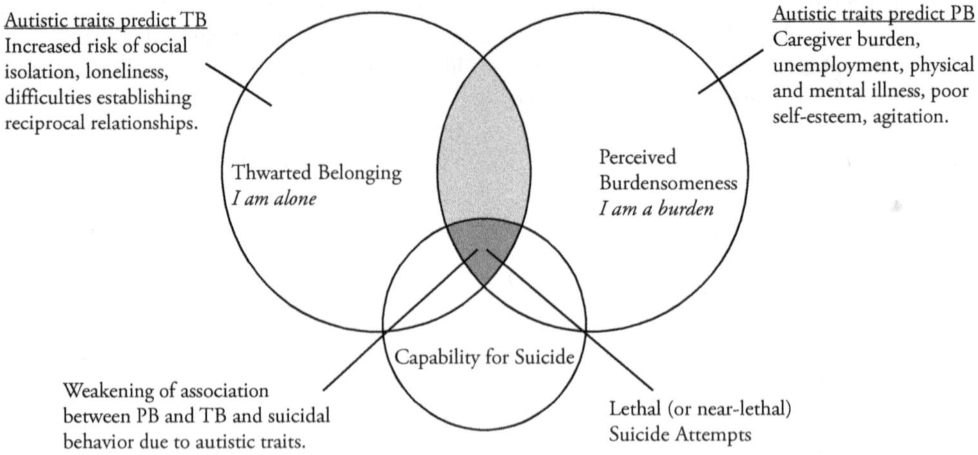

Figure 18.1. The interpersonal psychological theory of suicide and hypothesized interaction with autistic traits. TB, thwarted belongingness, PB, perceived burdensomeness. Adapted from Pelton, M. K., & Cassidy, S. A. (2017). Are autistic traits associated with suicidality? A test of the interpersonal-psychological theory of suicide in a non-clinical young adult sample. *Autism Research, 10*(11), 1891–1904.

Although these studies did not explicitly refer to or test the IPTS, these findings nevertheless show supporting evidence that external indicators of TB (i.e., loneliness) and PB (i.e., lack of support and autonomy) increase suicidal desire through depression in autistic people.

Further support for the relevance of the IPTS to understanding the high rates of suicidal ideation in ASCs comes from Pelton and Cassidy (2017), who directly tested the aforementioned predictions of the IPTS in relation to autistic traits in the general population (Figure 18.1). Specifically, they tested whether autistic traits in the general population increase vulnerability to experiencing TB and PB, and thus suicidal desire. Consistent with predictions, self-reported autistic traits in general population young adults were significantly associated with both TB and PB, and autistic traits predicted suicidality, through each of these constructs (Pelton & Cassidy, 2017). These results thus suggest that ASC diagnosis and autistic traits increase risk of experiencing known risk markers for suicidal desire in the general population and other clinical groups. Together, these findings suggest overlap between risk makers for suicidal desire in both autistic people and the general population as outlined in the IPTS.

However, there are also likely important differences and gaps in the IPTS in the context of suicidal desire in autistic people. For example, contrary to the predictions of the IPTS, the association between depression with TB and PB was attenuated at the highest levels of autistic traits (Pelton & Cassidy, 2017). One likely explanation of this could be that constructs such as depression are not appropriately captured in currently available assessments, given difficulties in reporting emotional distress (alexithymia) in autistic people and those with high autistic traits (Cassidy, Bradley, Bowen, Wigham, & Rodgers, 2018b). It is also possible that existing measures of TB and PB developed for the general population do not as strongly capture these constructs in autistic people and those with high autistic traits as in the general population (Pelton & Cassidy, 2017). For example, to perceive oneself to be a burden on others, one must be able to imagine another's perspective, which is a key area of difficulty for many autistic people (Baron-Cohen, Leslie, & Frith, 1985). If this is the case, then we would expect that the association between PB and suicidality might be attenuated in autistic people compared to the general population (see Figure 18.1). Hence, it will be important for future studies to explore the appropriateness and measurement properties of the tools used to measure the IPTS in the autistic compared to the general population.

An additional important and yet unexplored component of the IPTS in ASCs is capability for suicide. Capability according to the IPTS is characterized by fearlessness of death and increased tolerance to pain, which are required for a person to carry out a lethal or near-lethal suicide attempt (Van Orden et al., 2010). This capability construct, when experienced together with suicidal desire (underpinned by TB and PB), therefore increases the risk of moving from suicidal desire to making a lethal or near-lethal suicide attempt. Given that autistic people are significantly more likely to attempt and die by suicide than the general population, it will be crucial to explore this component of the theory. Capability is thought to be acquired through prolonged experience of painful and provocative events, including (but not limited to) NSSI, adverse events in childhood, drug and alcohol abuse, and traumatic experiences (Van Orden et al., 2010).

Again, ASC diagnosis and/or high autistic traits could increase risk of experiencing known risk markers associated with acquired capability. For example, autistic people are more likely to experience painful and provocative events such as trauma (Kerns, Newschaffer, & Berkowitz, 2015), NSSI (Cassidy, Bradley, Shaw, et al., 2018; Maddox et al., 2017), and drug and alcohol abuse (Butwicka et al., 2017) compared to the general population. Consistent with the theory, NSSI also predicts suicidality in autistic adults, after controlling for a number of demographics and diagnoses (Cassidy, Bradley, Shaw, et al., 2018). Hence, increased vulnerability to experiencing painful and provocative events, such as NSSI, could lead to increased risk of acquired capability, and thus greater risk of attempting suicide in autistic people. However, it will be crucial to test this model in autistic people and those with high autistic traits in the general population. Such research would be extremely valuable in improving understanding and prediction of who will not only experience suicidal desire but also be most likely to go on to make a lethal or near-lethal suicide attempt. As with TB and PB, it will also be important to explore whether the capability construct as defined and measured in the general population applies equally to autistic people. Exploring and developing tools to measure painful and provocative experiences common in autistic people would be especially valuable in helping to better define the acquired capability construct in autistic people and testing whether the predictions of the model accurately distinguish autistic people who experience suicidal desire from those who later go on to attempt suicide.

INTEGRATED MOTIVATIONAL-VOLITIONAL MODEL OF SUICIDAL BEHAVIOR

Another important and influential suicide theory is the integrated motivational–volitional model of suicidal behavior (IMV; O'Connor & Kirtley, 2018; Figure 18.2). The first stage of the IMV model is the premotivational phase, drawn from the diathesis–stress model (Schotte & Clum, 1987), in which individual pre-existing vulnerabilities, when activated by stressors, increase risk of suicidal ideation. These pre-existing vulnerabilities can include

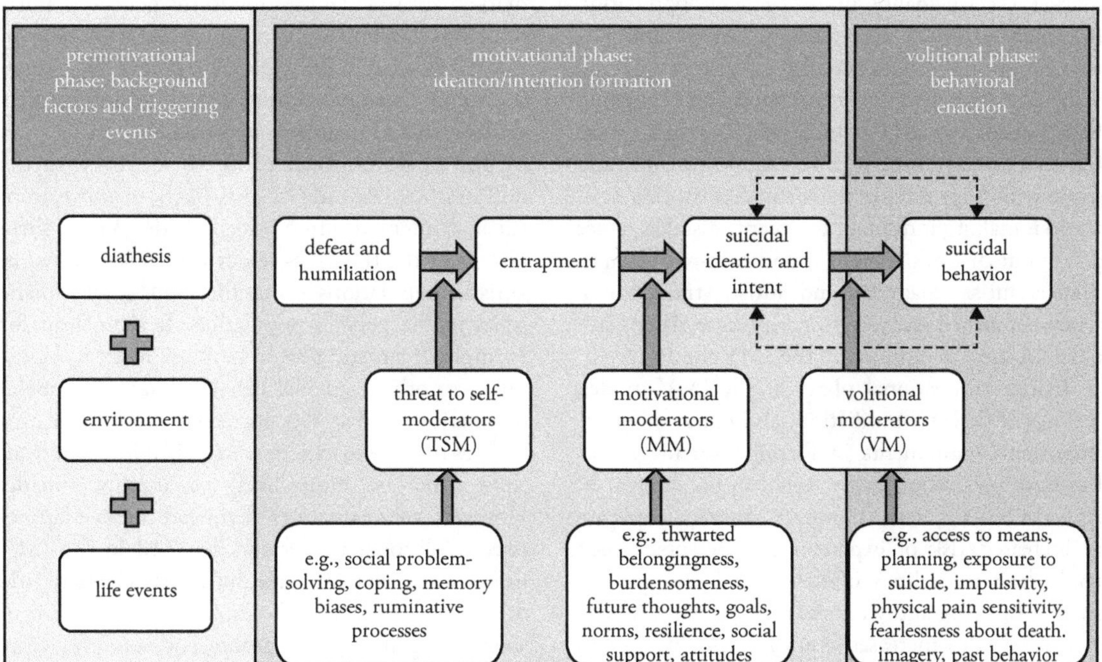

Figure 18.2. The integrated motivational–volitional model of suicidal behaviour.
From O'Connor, R. C., & Kirtley, O. J. (2018). The integrated motivational–volitional model of suicidal behaviour. *Philosophical Transactions of the Royal Society Part B, 373*(1754), 20,170,268.

personality characteristics, such as perfectionism, which, when combined with environmental stressors, can increase risk of suicidal ideation. The next phase of the theory is the motivational phase, drawn from the theory of planned behavior (Ajzen, 1991), which proposes that the strongest predictor of a behavior is an individual's motivation to carry it out. In this phase, feelings of defeat (being brought down) and entrapment (that nothing will ever change, with no prospect of escape or rescue) lead to formation of suicidal intent, where the escape of suicide is seen as the only feasible option. To make a suicide attempt, the final stage of the model (the volitional stage) outlines the capability construct as outlined by the IPTS (Van Orden et al., 2010) described earlier—increased pain tolerance and reduced fear of death. However, the IMV also includes other factors, such as exposure to others' suicidal behavior, which is a social volitional factor.

Again, there are areas of overlap between the experiences and characteristics of autistic people and people with high autistic traits, with the risk markers for suicidality outlined in the IMV model. ASC diagnosis and autistic traits could be considered in the premotivational phase among other personality and characteristics of the individual, which could be activated when exposed to stressors. One example given in the model is perfectionism, a known risk marker for suicidality in the general population (O'Connor, 2007). Interestingly, perfectionism is also commonly experienced by autistic people and associated with depression and anxiety in this group (e.g., Greenaway & Howlin, 2010). The rigid thinking style characteristic of many autistic people and those with high autistic traits could drive this association, making it difficult to accept mistakes or see a way out of one's current mood or circumstance. Hence, autism diagnosis and autistic traits could, when combined with stressors, increase risk of suicidal ideation as outlined in the IMV model.

In the motivational phase of the IMV model, feelings of defeat, humiliation, and entrapment are important components in forming suicide intent but have not been directly tested in the context of ASCs or autistic traits. However, autistic people are at increased risk of experiencing stressors, which could lead to feelings of defeat and entrapment, such as bullying and victimization, which has been associated with increased risk of suicidality in this group (Shtayermman, 2007). Subsequently, a number of key moderators predicted to underpin the movement from defeat and humiliation to entrapment are also commonly experienced by autistic people. These markers include difficulties in social problem solving (Jackson & Dritschel, 2016), memory biases, and ruminative processes (Crane, Goddard, & Pring, 2013). These factors are hypothesized to speed the process of moving from feelings of defeat and humiliation to the psychological state of entrapment, where one cannot find a way out of one's current mood or circumstance. Entrapment as outlined in the IMV model is reminiscent of the "one track" or "black and white" thinking common among many autistic people, and could increase the risk of autistic people experiencing feelings of entrapment and/or amplify this experience. Again, subsequent important moderators outlined in the theory that precipitate the emergence of suicidal intent are commonly experienced by autistic people. These markers include absence of social support (Camm-Crosbie et al., 2019; Cassidy et al., 2018a; Hedley et al., 2017), TB and PB (Pelton & Cassidy, 2017), and difficulties in abstract future thinking (Lind & Bowler, 2010; see Figure 18.2). These factors combine to create a perfect storm of defeat, humiliation, and entrapment, which could, in association with autistic traits such as inflexibility and lack of problem solving and support, amplify these experiences and risk of forming strong suicidal intent. Hence, difficulties characteristic of ASCs and high autistic traits appear to increase vulnerability to experiencing known risk markers for suicidal ideation in the general population, thus potentially explaining the high rates of suicidal ideation in this group. It is crucial for research to explore these predictions directly to inform new evidence-based treatment approaches.

The final volitional phase of the IMV model outlines how an individual is likely to move from suicidal intent to attempting suicide. Again, these aspects of the theory have not yet been explored in autistic populations or in the context of autistic traits in the general population. It is unclear, for example, if autistic people are more likely to be exposed to others suicidal behavior than the general population, and if this increased exposure distinguishes those who experience suicidal ideation from those who are more likely to attempt suicide. However, there are areas of concerning overlap between volitional moderators outlined in the IMV model and behaviors and difficulties characteristic of ASCs, which could also explain unique aspects of suicide attempts in this group. For example, many autistic people are described as impulsive (Mazefsky, 2015), a volitional moderator in the IMV model. However, autistic people also show difficulties in planning and flexible thinking (Sinzig, Morsch,

Bruning, Schmidt, & Lehmkuhl, 2008), which in the general population are volitional moderators in planning a suicide attempt prior to carrying it out. However, in ASCs, this combination may operate counterintuitively in predicting increased risk of attempting suicide. It is possible that this particular combination of difficulties could be more likely to lead to more impulsive suicide attempts absent of a plan in autistic people. This unique presentation of suicidality is consistent with preliminary evidence from surveys and single-case studies showing that autistic adults tend to utilize more impulsive, aggressive, and lethal means of attempting suicide than the general population (Hare, 1997; Kato et al., 2013; Schmid, Truog, & Damian, 2011; Spencer et al., 2011; Takara & Kondo, 2014). This is particularly concerning, as, coupled with the fact that autistic people may be less likely to access appropriate psychiatric support and treatment (Camm-Crosbie et al., 2019; Crane, Adams, Harper, Welch, & Pellicano, 2019; Raja, 2014; Takara & Kondo, 2014), this could mean that autistic people are more likely to die by suicide on their first attempt, without being known to services. Sadly, this clinical picture is emerging from ongoing research exploring the characteristics and circumstances of those who died by suicide who had evidence of ASCs compared to the general population (Cassidy et al., 2019). Another possibility to be aware of is that this presentation of impulsively attempting suicide in the absence of a plan could lead to high suicide risk of autistic people being missed as many suicidality assessments developed for the general population ask about the presence of a suicide plan. This issue is discussed in more detail in the section on assessment later.

UNIQUE RISK AND PROTECTIVE FACTORS IN ASCS

As discussed earlier, there is clearly overlap between known risk markers for self-harm and suicide in the general population, as outlined in current theories of suicide developed for nonautistic populations, consistent with emerging findings from the field of self-harm and suicidality in autism research. However, as also discussed, it is crucial to explore the potentially unique phenomenology, risk, and protective factors for self-harm and suicidality in ASCs compared to the general population to expand and adapt existing suicide theory and improve the applicability and explanatory power of these models to the prediction and prevention of suicide in autistic people.

There is growing evidence of a different phenomenology and risk markers for self-harm and suicidality in autistic people and those with high autistic traits. For example, both ASC diagnosis and autistic traits are independent risk markers for suicidality (Cassidy, Bradley, Shaw, et al., 2018) and suicide attempts (Chen et al., 2017), after controlling for demographic characteristics and co-occurring diagnoses. These findings suggest that ASC diagnosis and autistic traits in the general population explain additional variance in suicidality, not accounted for by other well-known risk markers that are more prevalent in these groups. Hence, high rates of suicidality in autistic people and those with high autistic traits cannot only be explained by increased prevalence of known risk markers such as depression (Cassidy et al., 2014; Hedley et al., 2017, 2018) or social isolation (Hedley et al., 2017; Pelton & Cassidy, 2017). Hence, there are very likely unique risk markers for suicidality in ASCs that are not shared with the general population or other clinical groups, requiring adapted suicide assessment and prevention strategies (Cassidy & Rodgers, 2017).

Studies exploring the characteristics of suicidality in ASCs and those with high autistic traits could provide important clues for possible unique risk markers in this group. For example, the highest rates of suicidal ideation (66%) were reported in adults newly diagnosed with Asperger syndrome (a subgroup on the autism spectrum, without co-occurring language delay or intellectual disability), who had struggled without ASC-specific support or understanding for most of their life given the delay in their diagnosis (Cassidy et al., 2014). Age of diagnosis and adequate access to postdiagnostic support could therefore be particularly important in preventing suicidality in ASC (Cassidy et al., 2014). However, many children and adults not only struggle to obtain their ASC diagnosis (Crane et al., 2018; Jones, Goddard, Hill, Henry, & Crane, 2014) but also struggle to obtain postdiagnostic support to facilitate access to employment, education, and mental health assessment and treatment and to increase social participation (Camm-Crosbie et al., 2019; Crane et al., 2019). Two studies have shown consistent evidence that lack of social support (Hedley et al., 2017) and unmet support needs (Cassidy, Bradley, Shaw, et al., 2018) in autistic adults significantly predict suicidality, even after controlling for a number of demographics and diagnoses (Cassidy, Bradley, Shaw, et al., 2018). Hence, postdiagnostic support appears to be a key and possibly unique protective factor against suicidality in autistic people. Social support is included as a moderator in the IMV model, and thus this model could be expanded to include the support programs useful to autistic people.

A key potential difference in the phenomenology of suicide in the general compared to the autistic population is gender. In the general population the global male-to-female ratio of deaths by suicide is estimated to be 1.7 (World Health Organization, 2018), indicating that males are more likely to die by suicide than females. However, in the one available study exploring death by suicide in the autistic community, autistic females without intellectual disability were at the highest risk of dying by suicide compared to autistic men and general population males and females (odds ratio 13.05; Hirvikoski et al., 2016). Specifically, in this large population study of 27,122 autistic people and 2.6 million matched controls, autistic females (0.32%) were more likely to die by suicide compared to autistic males (0.3%), opposite to the general population, where males (0.05%) were more likely to die by suicide than females (0.03%; Hirvikoski et al., 2016). Given the large sample and effect size, this study suggests potentially a very different role of gender in death by suicide in autistic people compared to the general population.

More large-scale studies are needed to explore whether this different effect of gender in autistic people who die by suicide is present in other countries aside from Sweden, and the reasons why, in order to inform tailored suicide prevention strategies for autistic people. A particularly important starting point, and not explored in this aforementioned pvopulation study by Hirvikoski and colleagues, is differences in methods and motivations for self-harm in autistic men compared to autistic women, which may explain the significantly increased risk of death by suicide in autistic women and how this could best be prevented. For example, in the general population, where men are more likely to die by suicide than women, men tend to experience more suicidal intent and utilize more violent means of self-harm than women (Hawton, 2000). Currently, due to small samples, lack of available relevant data, and lack of validated suicidality assessment tools for autistic people, there is no similarly clear picture of the potentially differing etiology of suicidal behavior between autistic men and women. The few available studies exploring gender differences in suicidality have not found significantly increased risk in autistic women (Cassidy, Bradley, Shaw, et al., 2018; Cassidy et al., 2014), and some systematic reviews have even found that autistic males may be more at risk of experiencing suicidality than females (Hedley & Uljariveć, 2018). More high-quality research is thus needed to explore the role of gender in suicidal ideation, suicidal behaviors, and death by suicide in the autistic community, and whether this differs from the general population.

One possible newly identified risk marker for suicidality in autistic people is "camouflaging," whereby autistic people attempt to camouflage or mask their ASC to try and fit in in social situations (Lai et al., 2011). Research has shown that camouflaging may negatively affect the mental health of autistic people (Livingston, Colvert, Social Relationships Study Team, Bolton, & Happé, 2019; Lai et al., 2017; Hull et al., 2017; Rynkiewicz et al., 2016) and increase risk of suicidality (Cassidy, Bradley, Shaw, et al., 2018), even after controlling for a number of demographics and diagnoses. Camouflaging behavior is also present in people with high autistic traits in the general population and correlated with reduced self-reported well-being (Hull, Mandy, Lai, Baron-Cohen, Allison, Smith, Petrides, 2019). Hence, camouflaging in autistic people and those with high autistic traits in the general population appears to be a potentially important and newly identified risk marker for poor mental health and possibly self-harm and suicidality.

Where might camouflaging fit in with models of suicidality in the general population? Camouflaging could be a potential moderator for increased feelings of TB, as social connections made through being someone you are not may not feel genuine and exacerbate feelings that you do not belong. This is consistent with initial findings suggesting that lack of autism acceptance is a motivator for autistic people camouflaging their ASC, which in turn increases risk of depression (Cage, Di Monaco, & Newell, 2018). Another possibility is that people who are motivated to camouflage may have more insight into their own difficulties—one has to realize one's own difficulties and their negative impact before attempting to camouflage (Cassidy, Bradley, Shaw, et al., 2018). It is therefore also possible that attempts by those with higher insight into their own difficulties to camouflage to fit in but that are unsuccessful, leading to continued experiences of social rejection despite their best efforts, could lead to feelings of defeat and humiliation, a key risk factor for the formation of suicidal intent outlined in the IMV model. Exploring the nature of camouflaging behavior among autistic people and those with high autistic traits in the general population, and how this may be related to key aspects of models of suicidal behavior, such as the IPTS and IMV model, could be an important step toward expanding and adapting these theories to better apply to autistic people and those with high autistic traits.

SUMMARY

In summary, it appears that ASC diagnosis and autistic traits increase vulnerability to experiencing known risk markers for suicidality in the general population and other clinical groups, as outlined in current suicide theories such as the IPTS and IMV model. Research suggests that suicide theories developed outside of ASCs could be useful in understanding why autistic people may be at increased risk of suicide. Exploring suicidality in ASCs using robust and readily available theoretical frameworks such as the IPTS and IMV model could be particularly useful in helping us better predict who will experience suicidal ideation and who will likely go on to attempt suicide. However, it is also important to identify gaps in these models and make adaptations to better accommodate the unique presentation and characteristics of suicidality in ASCs. This is crucial to provide opportunities for clinicians to better identify those at risk and prevent the high rates of suicide in autistic people.

Assessment

One important reason for the wide range of prevalence estimates for self-harm and suicidality summarized in this chapter is the wide range of assessment methods used in previous studies. At the time of writing, only one study of suicidality in adults has used a suicidality assessment tool with evidence of validity (the Suicide Behaviors Questionnaire—Revised [SBQ-R]; Osman et al., 2001), albeit not yet in autistic adults (Cassidy et al., 2018a). No suicidality or self-harm assessment tool has yet been validated in or developed specifically for autistic adults (Cassidy et al., 2018a) or autistic children (Hedley & Uljarević, 2018; Horowitz et al., 2017). This section thus aims to summarize relevant literature and theory relating to more effective assessment of self-harm and suicidality in autistic people. First, challenges for effective assessment in ASCs will be outlined based on what we know about cognition and behavior in this group. Second, potential adaptations to tools will be considered in the context of emerging results regarding the potentially unique presentation of self-harm and suicidality in this group. Third, this discussion will be considered in light of broader debates in use of tools for assessing self-harm and suicidality in the general population and implications for risk assessment in ASCs.

CHALLENGES OF ASSESSMENT IN ASCS

A key challenge in assessment of self-harm and suicidality in ASCs is lack of knowledge regarding the presentation of these difficulties in this group. However, as discussed earlier, there is evidence that autistic people have difficulty accessing mental health and psychiatric services (Camm-Crosbie et al., 2019; Crane et al., 2019; Raja, 2014), could be more at risk of impulsive suicide attempts using more lethal means (Takara & Kondo, 2014), and are more likely to die by suicide than the general population (Cassidy et al, 2019; Hirvikoski et al., 2016). Hence, it is even more crucial for clinicians to take opportunities to ask autistic people presenting in health settings whether they are experiencing suicidal thoughts or behaviors, and not view or misattribute self-harming behaviors as just part of ASCs.

However, how do researchers and clinicians best ask autistic people whether they are considering ending their own life, or if they intend to attempt suicide, and gauge the likelihood of imminent suicide threat? Anecdotally, autistic people can talk about their suicidality in ways that clinicians have difficulty gauging, which can mean that suicidal ideation is more likely to be missed or disregarded. In essence, suicidality can be harder to spot in autistic people. For example, flat affect is a common characteristic of autistic people (APA, 2013), as is literal mindedness and black-and-white thinking (Happé, 1995) and difficulty in articulating their thoughts and feelings to others (Bird et al., 2010). Many autistic people go to great lengths to camouflage or mask their autistic behaviors, in an attempt to fit in and be accepted by others (Cage et al., 2018), and have difficulty understanding the impact of their behavior on others (termed theory of mind; Baron-Cohen, Leslie, & Frith, 1985). All these features can result in a very different presentation of disclosing and talking about suicidal thoughts and behaviors, and future intent, compared to the general population—for example, talking about thoughts of suicide without external indicators of distress due to flat affect or being so used to camouflaging that the extent of one's psychological pain is not recognized by others. Autistic people participating in our research have described how they sometimes do not feel believed by professionals because of the different way they may present to clinicians and services (Camm-Crosbie et al., 2019). This could prevent key opportunities for clinicians to identify and act on significant risks in the clinic, and it is thus very important to be aware of this potentially different presentation and listen to what autistic people are saying.

Another important and related challenge for clinicians is ensuring that the suicide risk of autistic people is not overestimated, which can lead to unneeded hospitalization or medication. For example, in our research, autistic people who have endorsed having previously attempting suicide have included accidents, such as forgetting to space doses of paracetamol, resulting in one extra tablet taken at one time. Emotional regulation difficulties and impulsivity are common in ASCs (Mazefsky, 2015) and anecdotally can result in autistic people expressing suicidal ideation but, on closer inspection, without apparent intent or understanding of death and suicide. It is crucial for future research to explore in depth how autistic people talk about and understand death and suicide to aid clinicians to better balance the risks of missing or overemphasizing risk in their practice.

In ascertaining the best ways of asking autistic people about suicidality, research typically assesses evidence for and against the appropriateness and measurement properties of suicidality assessment tools across a range of contexts. In a recent systematic review (Cassidy et al., 2018a), a validated research tool (the consensus-based Standards for the selection of health measurement instruments (COSMIN); Mokkink et al., 2010) was used to (a) identify which suicidality assessment tools had been most frequently used in the general and autistic populations and (b) assess the quality of the evidence for and against these tools' appropriateness and measurement properties. No studies were found that had used a tool with evidence of validity to explore suicidality in autistic adults, with most using single items from broader mental health assessment tools (e.g., the Patient Health Questionnaire-9 [PHQ-9; [Kroenke & Spitzer, 2002] or Beck Depression Inventory [BDI; Beck, Steer, & Brown, 1996]) or single items created for the purposes of the research project with no evidence for their validity in any population.

There is thus very limited research evidence regarding the best way to assess suicidality in autistic people. It is unknown, for example, how autistic people understand and interpret questions about death, dying, or suicide and whether the high estimates so far revealed are an over- or underestimation of the scale of the problem. However, from previous research we do know about key cognitive differences in ASCs, which could likely affect how questions regarding suicidality could be interpreted. For example, difficulties in effectively identifying and communicating one's feelings (Bird et al., 2010) could impede one's ability to report distress and/or suicidal feelings to others, and thus lead to underendorsement of questions phrased in terms of "How do you feel?" or "Are you feeling suicidal?" Literal interpretation of information is also experienced by many autistic people (Happé, 1995) and could affect responses to questions such as "Have you ever attempted suicide?" As stated earlier, autistic people have reported being uncertain if this included accidentally taking an overdose. Therefore, it is important to probe the context and understanding of questions.

Tools such as the SBQ-R (Osman et al., 2001) ask about communication of suicide threat to others and likelihood of attempting suicide "someday." Such questions are likely to tap into difficulties characteristic of ASCs, which could lead to underendorsement of such items, without necessarily indicating reduced risk (Cassidy et al., 2018a). For example, the social isolation (Orsmond et al., 2013) and communication difficulties (APA, 2013) of autistic people could reduce their opportunities to inform people about their suicidal intent. Autistic people also experience difficulties in abstract future thinking (Lind & Bowler, 2010), and therefore abstract questions about what may happen "someday" or about a suicide plan are likely to be extremely challenging for autistic people to answer.

Current research is starting to explore these hypotheses and how autistic people interpret and respond to suicidality assessment tools, with evidence of validity in nonautistic populations. For example, an online survey comparing responses to the SBQ-R between autistic and general population adults suggested that autistic adults attributed different meaning to items assessing communication of threat of suicide to others and likelihood of attempting suicide someday than general population adults (Cassidy et al., 2019). In-depth interviews with autistic adults explored the nature of these differences in interpretation by asking participants what they were reading and thinking about while answering the questions in the tool (termed "cognitive interviewing"; Willis et al., 2005). Autistic adults reported that they had no one to tell and could not see the relevance of the question about communication of suicide threat to others. However, despite this, having told others about their suicidal intent was statistically more indicative of suicidality overall based on a higher correlation with other items on the tool than the general population. This suggests that although autistic adults experienced difficulty in answering the question on communication of suicide threat to others, it was perhaps more strongly indicative of suicidality. Importantly, this suggests that when autistic people disclose their suicidality to others, it should be taken seriously by professionals and not dismissed, as commonly reported by many autistic people (Camm-Crosbie et al., 2019).

Autistic adults reported that it was impossible to rate likelihood of attempting suicide "someday" as it was simply too abstract and depended on too many variables. Not surprisingly, responses to this question were statistically less indicative of suicidality overall and thus less likely to be clinically useful, at least using the current form and wording of the question (Cassidy et al., 2019). Items probing lifetime and current suicidality did not capture the unique presentation of suicidality in autistic adults. Particular difficulties involved not understanding the concept of a suicide plan and lack of an option covering impulsive suicide attempts without a prior plan when opportunities present themselves at the time.

These results are consistent with our knowledge about cognitive and behavioral differences in ASCs and need to be accounted for in suicidality assessments. For example, although it is important to ask about whether an autistic person has ever told someone about his or her suicidal intent, it will be important to probe the context, such as who has been told and why the autistic person may have not disclosed. Such information will be important for safety planning, which involves communication of imminent suicidal threat to others and help-seeking behavior. Abstract and open-ended questions are likely to be very difficult for autistic people to answer and also not be as informative compared to concrete questions based on past behavior. Although preliminary, autistic people's descriptions of attempting suicide in the absence of a plan when opportunities presented themselves "in the moment" were common and worrying. An important implication for clinical practice is to probe for such instances in the past and the likelihood of such in the future, even if a current plan is not evident.

In discussing the utility of existing suicidality assessment tools in autistic people, it is very important to acknowledge a current debate in the broader field of suicidology regarding the utility of such tools and their place in clinical practice. Specifically, research has suggested that suicidality assessment tools on the whole are poor predictors of later adverse events, such as suicide attempts; may perform worse than clinical judgment without the use of any predefined tool or questions; and are therefore a waste of valuable resources (Quinlivan et al., 2016, 2017). However, our systematic review showed that some tools may be more useful than others in helping clinicians gauge suicide risk in research and/or clinical contexts (Cassidy et al., 2018a). For example, there was moderate evidence in support of the Columbia Suicide Severity Rating Scale (Posner et al., 2011) in successfully predicting future adverse events in clinical practice (Cassidy et al., 2018a). It is therefore very important to highlight that suicide risk assessment tools should form a starting point, as part of a full psychosocial assessment, when assessing suicide risk, as recommended by current clinical guidelines such as those from the National Institute for Health and Care Excellence (NICE, 2011) in the United Kingdom.

Treatment

Treatment of self-harm and suicidality in autistic people is a particularly underresearched area of critical importance but is hampered by lack of high-quality research regarding the etiology in ASCs (Cassidy & Rodgers, 2017). However, a number of key risk markers have been identified for self-harm and suicidality in ASCs, including delay in diagnosis (Cassidy et al., 2014) and lack of access to support (Cassidy, Bradley, Shaw, et al., 2018; Hedley et al., 2017). Providing timely access to diagnosis and postdiagnostic support is thus likely to help prevent suicidality in autistic people, but both remain hard to obtain (Lai & Baron-Cohen, 2015; Crane et al., 2018; Jones et al., 2014).

Given the lack of an available evidence-based treatment for self-harm and suicidality in ASCs, it is important to consider the applicability of existing guidelines and treatments developed for the general nonautistic population to those with ASCs. There are two available psychological therapies for the treatment of suicide attempts in nonautistic groups: cognitive behavioral therapy (CBT; Persons, 1989) for those in the general population who have attempted suicide, and dialectic behavioral therapy (DBT; Robins, Ivanoff, & Linehan, 2001) for people diagnosed with borderline personality disorder with recurrent suicidal ideation and attempts. A number of studies have shown that CBT is effective for treating affective disorders such as anxiety and depression in autistic people (Weston, Hodgekins, & Langdon, 2016). However, no studies have yet explored the potential of DBT in treating autistic people with recurrent suicidal ideation and attempts, despite being successfully adapted for a number of other groups, including those with attention deficit hyperactivity disorder, those with eating disorders, and depressed older people (see Robins & Chapman, 2004, for a review). Exploring how CBT and DBT could be effective in treating autistic people who have attempted suicide or with chronic ongoing suicidal ideation and/or suicidal behavior is extremely important (Cassidy & Rodgers, 2017).

It is also important to consider other current approaches to suicide prevention used in the general population and how these could be more readily implemented and/or adapted for autistic people now. For example, many suicide prevention strategies in the United Kingdom, such as the Campaign Against Living Miserably (CALM), are aimed at men, but as discussed earlier, autistic women might be at higher risk of dying by suicide than autistic men (Hirvikoski et al., 2016). Many strategies also stress the importance of communication and telling someone about suicidality. As discussed in the previous section, communication of suicide threat to others is particularly difficult for autistic people given their communication difficulties and social isolation, but could be particularly informative and therefore needs to be supported (Cassidy et al., 2019). Clinicians and policymakers could therefore consider establishing more accessible means to enable autistic people to more easily communicate their suicidal intent to professionals. For example, technology-based communication has been shown to be particularly effective and desirable by the autistic community (Cassidy et al., 2016) and could potentially be particularly effective for assessment and support for suicidality, as in the general population (Mishara & Kirkoff, 2013). Such tools could be readily adapted for autistic people.

Suicide safety planning also has the potential to be readily adapted for autistic people, given the clear steps involved (e.g., Boudreaux et al., 2017). In the general population, suicide safety planning typically entails a prioritized list of personalized coping strategies and sources of support to prevent and/or alleviate a suicidal crisis. This includes, first, a personalized statement, message, or image to remind the person of his or her reason(s) for living; second, identifying the person's own warning signs of an impending suicidal crisis; third, identifying and employing one's own coping strategies; fourth, utilizing social contacts and social settings to help distract the person from his or her suicidal thoughts; fifth, utilizing family members or friends to help try to resolve the suicidal crisis; sixth, contacting relevant mental health professionals or agencies; and last, making oneself safe by removing access to things that could be used to harm oneself. Safety plans can be written in paper form, or more recently apps have been developed that can incorporate features such as calculating a route to the nearest place of safety (Larsen, Nicholas, & Christensen, 2016).

Suicide safety planning could potentially be extremely valuable to autistic people for a number of reasons. First, as discussed throughout this chapter, autistic people can struggle to identify their own internal emotions (alexithymia). Many autistic people thus report that they do not realize they are approaching a crisis point until it is too late (Camm-Crosbie et al., in 2019; Crane et al., 2019). Hence, many autistic people may struggle to identify their own early signs of approaching suicidal crisis, thus impeding their ability to utilize coping strategies. Suicide safety planning could thus provide autistic people with important tools to help them identify the signs of an approaching suicidal crisis and implement personalized coping strategies to avert that crisis. Suicide safety planning could thus provide scaffolding at a number of stages of severity of suicidal crisis—for example, providing support to the autistic person to identify warning signs of approaching suicidal crisis, developing personalized strategies to avert this, rehearsing instructions for seeking help and support, and restricting access to means of making a suicide attempt.

Case Example

A brief illustrative case example is given, drawn from a range of research studies from our group, to highlight a number of the key themes and issues described in this chapter relating to understanding and assessing autistic people experiencing suicidality. As the example is drawn from a number of different sources, it is not possible to link to any individual, and an anonymous pseudonym is used. The example is then discussed in relation to the underlying research on which it is based and its clinical implications.

"A" was a 26-year-old man who presented to mental health services after attempting to take his own life. "A" had not had any previous mental health problems recorded in his medical records or previous contact with mental health services. "A" had above-average verbal and nonverbal ability assessed with the Weschler Abbreviated Scale of Intelligence. During assessment "A" appeared nervous, and he avoided eye contact during the assessment. His speech had a flat tone, which did not vary in pitch or intonation, and he showed very limited range of facial expressions during the assessment, even when recalling a happy or sad event.

The assessment gathered background information about "A" in the leadup to his suicide attempt. "A" was employed at the time but had experienced a number of job changes in the last few years since leaving college. On exploration, "A" reported that the jobs had been very different than what he had expected from the interviews, tasks that were set were not clear, and he struggled to negotiate and clarify tasks with his employer and colleagues. He also reported becoming very frustrated when others did not carry out tasks in the manner agreed upon or if plans were changed unexpectedly. This led to difficulties at work, and prior to an upcoming performance review in his last job, "A" reported that he had a sudden strong urge to attempt to end his own life, when an opportunity presented itself "in the moment" while walking home from work.

"A" was a high achiever at school, although he struggled making friends and experienced bullying. His parents noted that they saw him wandering around in circles in the playground when he was young, and during his teenage years he did not have many friends with whom he shared an interest outside of an organized group or activity. "A" showed rigid and black-and-white thinking and an "all or nothing" attitude, with "everything planned to the *n*th degree" in his work and personal life from a young age. "A" became frustrated if people and activities did not occur on time or if there was a last-minute change of plans.

"A" thus appeared to present with many symptoms of depression and marked anxiety stemming from a need to control his environment, so a mental health assessment was carried out to confirm this. As part of the mental health assessment, "A" had difficulty describing how he felt, saying that he "didn't know how he felt most of the time." "A" indicated difficulties indicative of depression, including difficulties falling and staying asleep and reduced appetite, scoring above the cut-off for depression on the PHQ-9. However, "A" said that this was his "normal" and that he had always had these difficulties, not just in the past 2 weeks, and was not convinced that he had depression, but was rather struggling in his relationships with others, which were the primary source of his difficulties.

As part of his suicide risk assessment, "A" scored well above the cut-off for suicide risk on the SBQ-R, including being "very likely" to attempt suicide in the future. On exploring this further, "A" said that "anything could happen someday in the future; it is almost impossible to answer," and although he had no plans to take his life, he could not respond "no chance at all."

Summary

This brief case example is an illustration of many themes covered in this chapter. First, many autistic adults are currently undiagnosed, particularly those fitting the profile of Asperger syndrome, a subtype of autism without co-occurring language delay or intellectual disability (Lai & Baron-Cohen, 2015). The most common first concern prior to receiving a diagnosis of ASC in adulthood is a mental health problem (Jones et al., 2014). Autistic people are not only more likely to be diagnosed with a mental health condition at some point than the general population (Lever & Geurts, 2016) but also significantly more likely to disagree with their mental health diagnosis (Au-yeung, Bradley, Robertson, Shaw, Baron-Cohen, Cassidy, 2019. Many autistic people report that the reason for this disagreement is that their ASC-related difficulties, such as social isolation, are their primary concern rather than a mental health condition per se (Au-yeung et al., 2019). Research is also showing that autistic people who attempt or die by suicide are less likely to be in contact with relevant services than nonautistic people (Cassidy et al., 2019; Raja, 2014; Takara & Kondo, 2014). Reasons include autistic people having difficulty recognizing that they have a mental health problem or are approaching crisis, difficulties in asking for or exploring support and treatment options, lack of available services for autistic people with mental health difficulties, and lack of understanding on the part of professionals in autism co-occurring with mental health problems (Camm-Crosbie et al., 2019; Crane et al., 2019). Hence, it can be difficult for clinicians to effectively assess or treat autistic people presenting to mental health settings with suicidal ideation and/or suicidal behavior. It is particularly important, therefore, for clinicians to be aware of the unique presentation of autistic people with mental health difficulties and/or suicidality and to be prepared to explore possible undiagnosed ASCs in those presenting to mental health services for the first time. In our example of "A," his presentation is considered by the clinician to be more indicative of long-standing depression and anxiety than necessarily ASC, which could better fit his presentation and his support needs. This again is a challenge for clinicians, when current mental health assessments such as those for depression fail to disentangle common characteristics of ASCs (such as poor sleep over a lifetime) from depression (Cassidy et al., 2018b; Stewart, Barnard, Pearson, Hasan, & O'Brien, 2006).

Summary and Future Directions

In sum, this chapter has summarized evidence showing that self-harm and suicidality, a neglected topic in ASC research, is highly prevalent in autistic people. Worryingly, autistic people are significantly more likely to die by suicide or self-harming behavior than the general population, and those with evidence of autism (diagnosed or as yet undiagnosed) are significantly overrepresented in those who die by suicide or self-harm. Self-harm and suicidality in ASCs therefore remain a crucial area in much need of further research. However, research exploring the etiology, assessment, and treatment of self-harm and suicidality in ASCs is lacking (Cassidy & Rodgers, 2017). The aim of this chapter was to summarize and make recommendations for future research and clinical practice for a more useful and theoretically guided investigation of suicide in autism, to inform new and more effective assessment and treatment approaches for this vulnerable group. This chapter is very timely, as many research groups internationally are currently addressing many key questions raised herein, which will likely increase understanding and prevention of suicide in ASCs.

This chapter made specific recommendations for future research on suicide in ASCs to focus on. First, research must explore how existing models of suicide developed for the general population, such as the IPTS and IMV model, apply to ASCs. Findings suggest that ASC diagnosis and autistic traits in the general population increase vulnerability to experiencing the key risk markers for self-harm and suicidality outlined in these theories. However, many aspects of these theories have not yet been explored in relation to ASC diagnosis or autistic traits, particularly known risk markers for attempting suicide in the general population, such as capability for suicide. It is also unknown whether and how unique ASC-specific risk markers for self-harm and suicide could expand current suicide theories developed for the general population to increase the applicability and predictive power of these theories for autistic people. For example, camouflaging ASCs has been associated with self-harm and suicidality but not explored in the context of increasing feelings of thwarted belongingness (in the IPTS) or defeat and humiliation (in the IMV model). Exploring the applicability of current theory to understanding suicide in ASCs is an absolutely imperative next step and will likely provide more clinical opportunities to intervene and prevent the high rates of death by suicide in this vulnerable group.

The phenomenology of suicide in autism is also in need of further investigation. For example, possible gender differences in suicidal ideation and suicidal behavior in ASCs are poorly understood, with contradictory findings. One large-scale study suggests that, opposite to the general population, autistic women are more at risk of suicide than autistic men (Hirvikoski et al., 2016), but this picture is not reflected in systematic reviews of suicidal ideation and behavior in ASCs (e.g., Segers & Rawana, 2014). Understanding these gender differences will have important implications for suicide prevention strategies in ASCs. A particularly worrying emerging clinical picture of suicide in ASCs appears to be impulsive and more lethal suicide attempts, which may occur absent of a plan, and thus "fly under the radar" of traditional suicidality assessments developed for the general population. Suicidality assessment tools designed for the general population will therefore need to be adapted to more accurately and usefully identify suicidality in autistic people. Treatment to reduce self-harm and suicidality in ASCs is the most underexplored and crucial area for future research and clinical practice. Many existing suicide prevention and intervention strategies recommended for use in nonautistic populations, such as CBT, DBT, and safety planning, have great potential to be readily adapted for autistic people—CBT approaches have already been successfully adapted to treat depression and anxiety in autistic people.

To reiterate, the aim of this chapter was not to provide a comprehensive review or definitive conclusions, given the preliminary nature of suicide and self-harm in ASC research. This chapter may open discussion, debate, and development of a more useful hypothesis-driven science of self-harm and suicidality in ASCs. This is imperative if we are to better assess, understand, and ultimately prevent the tragically high rates of distress and death by suicide in this vulnerable group and give hope to the many autistic people experiencing self-harm and suicidality, and those supporting them.

References

Ajzen, I. (1991). The theory of planned behavior. *Organizational Behavior and Human Decision Processes, 50*(2), 179–211.

Akram, B., Tariq, A., & Rafi, Z. (2017). Non-suicidal self-injury among children with hearing loss and intellectual disability.

JPMA: Journal of the Pakistan Medical Association, 67(10), 1506–1511.
American Psychiatric Association. (2013). *Diagnostic and statistical manual of mental disorders* (5th ed., DSM-5). American Psychiatric Publishing.
Baghdadli, A., Pascal, C., Grisi, S., & Aussilloux, C. (2003). Risk factors for self-injurious behaviours among 222 young children with autistic disorders. *Journal of Intellectual Disability Research, 47*(8), 622–627.
Baron-Cohen, S., Leslie, A. M., & Frith, U. (1985). Does the autistic child have a "theory of mind"? *Cognition, 21*(1), 37–46.
Baron-Cohen, S., Wheelwright, S., Skinner, R., Martin, J., & Clubley, E. (2001). The autism-spectrum quotient (AQ): Evidence from Asperger syndrome/high-functioning autism, males and females, scientists and mathematicians. *Journal of Autism and Developmental Disorders, 31*(1), 5–17.
Beck, A. T., Steer, R. A., & Brown, G. K. (1996). *Beck Depression Inventory-II* (2nd ed.). San Antonio, TX, The Psychological Corporation.
Bird, G., Silani, G., Brindley, R., White, S., Frith, U., & Singer, T. (2010). Empathic brain responses in insula are modulated by levels of alexithymia but not autism. *Brain, 133*(5), 1515–1525.
Bodfish, J. W., Symons, F. J., Parker, D. E., & Lewis, M. H. (2000). Varieties of repetitive behavior in autism: Comparisons to mental retardation. *Journal of Autism and Developmental Disorders, 30*(3), 237–243.
Boudreaux, E. D., Brown, G. K., Stanley, B., Sadasivam, R. S., Camargo, C. A., Jr., & Miller, I. W. (2017). Computer administered safety planning for individuals at risk for suicide: Development and usability testing. *Journal of Medical Internet Research, 19*(5), e149.
Butwicka, A., Långström, N., Larsson, H., Lundström, S., Serlachius, E., Almqvist, C., . . . Lichtenstein, P. (2017). Increased risk for substance use-related problems in autism spectrum disorders: A population-based cohort study. *Journal of Autism and Developmental Disorders, 47*(1), 80–89.
Cage, E., Di Monaco, J., & Newell, V. (2018). Experiences of autism acceptance and mental health in autistic adults. *Journal of Autism and Developmental Disorders, 48*(2), 473–484.
Camm-Crosbie, L., Bradley, L., Shaw, R., Baron-Cohen, S., & Cassidy, S. (2019). 'People like me don't get support': Autistic adults' experiences of support and treatment for mental health difficulties, self-injury and suicidality. *Autism, 23*(6), 1431–1441.
Cassidy, S. A., Bradley, L., Bowen, E., Wigham, S., & Rodgers, J. (2018a). Measurement properties of tools used to assess suicidality in autistic and general population adults: A systematic review. *Clinical Psychology Review, 62*, 56–70.
Cassidy, S. A., Bradley, L., Bowen, E., Wigham, S., & Rodgers, J. (2018b). Measurement properties of tools used to assess depression in adults with and without autism spectrum conditions: A systematic review. *Autism Research, 11*(5), 738–754.
Cassidy, S. A., Bradley, L., Cogger-Ward, H., Shaw, R., Bowen, E., Glod, M., . . . Rodgers, J. (2019). *Measurement properties of the Suicide Behaviours Questionnaire—Revised in Autistic Adults*. Manuscript submitted for publication.
Cassidy, S. A., Bradley, L., Richards, G., Allison, C., O'Connor, R., Heming, D., . . . Baron-Cohen, S. (2019). *Autism spectrum conditions in people who died by suicide in the UK*. Manuscript submitted for publication.
Cassidy, S., Bradley, P., Robinson, J., Allison, C., McHugh, M., & Baron-Cohen, S. (2014). Suicidal ideation and suicide plans or attempts in adults with Asperger's syndrome attending a specialist diagnostic clinic: A clinical cohort study. *Lancet Psychiatry, 1*(2), 142–147.
Cassidy, S., Bradley, L., Shaw, R., & Baron-Cohen, S. (2018). Risk markers for suicidality in autistic adults. *Molecular Autism, 9*(1), 42.
Cassidy, S., & Rodgers, J. (2017). Understanding and prevention of suicide in autism. *Lancet Psychiatry, 4*(6), e11.
Cassidy, S. A., Stenger, B., Van Dongen, L., Yanagisawa, K., Anderson, R., Wan, V., . . . Cipolla, R. (2016). Expressive visual text-to-speech as an assistive technology for individuals with autism spectrum conditions. *Computer Vision and Image Understanding, 148*, 193–200.
Chen, M. H., Pan, T. L., Lan, W. H., Hsu, J. W., Huang, K. L., Su, T. P., . . . Bai, Y. M. (2017). Risk of suicide attempts among adolescents and young adults with autism spectrum disorder: A nationwide longitudinal follow-up study. *Journal of Clinical Psychiatry, 78*(9), e1174–e1179.
Crane, L., Adams, F., Harper, G., Welch, J., & Pellicano, E. (2019). 'Something needs to change': Mental health experiences of young autistic adults in England. *Autism, 23*(2), 477–493.
Crane, L., Batty, R., Adeyinka, H., Goddard, L., Henry, L. A., & Hill, E. L. (2018). Autism diagnosis in the United Kingdom: Perspectives of autistic adults, parents and professionals. *Journal of autism and developmental disorders, 48*(11), 3761–3772.
Crane, L., Goddard, L., & Pring, L. (2013). Autobiographical memory in adults with autism spectrum disorder: The role of depressed mood, rumination, working memory and theory of mind. *Autism, 17*(2), 205–219.
Croen, L. A., Zerbo, O., Qian, Y., Massolo, M. L., Rich, S., Sidney, S., & Kripke, C. (2015). The health status of adults on the autism spectrum. *Autism, 19*(7), 814–823.
Dickstein, D. P., Puzia, M. E., Cushman, G. K., Weissman, A. B., Wegbreit, E., Kim, K. L., . . . Spirito, A. (2015). Self-injurious implicit attitudes among adolescent suicide attempters versus those engaged in nonsuicidal self-injury. *Journal of Child Psychology and Psychiatry, 56*(10), 1127–1136.
Dominick, K. C., Davis, N. O., Lainhart, J., Tager-Flusberg, H., & Folstein, S. (2007). Atypical behaviors in children with autism and children with a history of language impairment. *Research in Developmental Disabilities, 28*(2), 145–162.
Duerden, E. G., Oatley, H. K., Mak-Fan, K. M., McGrath, P. A., Taylor, M. J., Szatmari, P., & Roberts, S. W. (2012). Risk factors associated with self-injurious behaviors in children and adolescents with autism spectrum disorders. *Journal of Autism and Developmental Disorders, 42*(11), 2460–2470.
Ghaziuddin, M., Alessi, N., & Greden, J. F. (1995). Life events and depression in children with pervasive developmental disorders. *Journal of Autism and Developmental Disorders, 25*(5), 495–502.
Greenaway, R., & Howlin, P. (2010). Dysfunctional attitudes and perfectionism and their relationship to anxious and depressive symptoms in boys with autism spectrum disorders. *Journal of Autism and Developmental Disorders, 40*(10), 1179–1187.
Hannon, G., & Taylor, E. P. (2013). Suicidal behaviour in adolescents and young adults with ASD: Findings from a systematic review. *Clinical Psychology Review, 33*(8), 1197–1204.

Happé, F. G. (1995). Understanding minds and metaphors: Insights from the study of figurative language in autism. *Metaphor and Symbol, 10*(4), 275–295.

Hare, D. J. (1997). The use of cognitive-behavioural therapy with people with Asperger syndrome: A case study. *Autism, 1*, 215–225.

Hawton, K. (2000). Sex and suicide: Gender differences in suicidal behaviour. *British Journal of Psychiatry, 177*(6), 484–485.

Hawton, K., Appleby, L., Platt, S., Foster, T., Cooper, J., Malmberg, A., & Simkin, S. (1998). The psychological autopsy approach to studying suicide: A review of methodological issues. *Journal of Affective Disorders, 50*(2–3), 269–276.

Hawton, K., Saunders, K. E., & O'Connor, R. C. (2012). Self-harm and suicide in adolescents. *The Lancet, 379*(9834), 2373–2382.

Hedley, D., & Uljarević, M. (2018). Systematic review of suicide in autism spectrum disorder: Current trends and implications. *Current Developmental Disorders Reports, 5*(1), 65–76.

Hedley, D., Uljarević, M., Wilmot, M., Richdale, A., & Dissanayake, C. (2017). Brief report: Social support, depression and suicidal ideation in adults with autism spectrum disorder. *Journal of Autism and Developmental Disorders, 47*(11), 3669–3677.

Hedley, D., Uljarević, M., Wilmot, M., Richdale, A., & Dissanayake, C. (2018). Understanding depression and thoughts of self-harm in autism: A potential mechanism involving loneliness. *Research in Autism Spectrum Disorders, 46*, 1–7.

Hirvikoski, T., Mittendorfer-Rutz, E., Boman, M., Larsson, H., Lichtenstein, P., & Bölte, S. (2016). Premature mortality in autism spectrum disorder. *British Journal of Psychiatry, 208*(3), 232–238.

Horowitz, L. M., Thurm, A., Farmer, C., Mazefsky, C., Lanzillo, E., Bridge, J. A., . . . Siegel, M. (2017). Talking about death or suicide: Prevalence and clinical correlates in youth with autism spectrum disorder in the psychiatric inpatient setting. *Journal of Autism and Developmental Disorders, 48*, 3702–3710.

Hull, L., Mandy, W., Lai, M. C., Baron-Cohen, S., Allison, C., Smith, P., & Petrides, K. V. (2019). Development and validation of the camouflaging autistic traits questionnaire (CAT-Q). *Journal of autism and developmental disorders, 49*(3), 819–833.

Hull, L., Petrides, K. V., Allison, C., Smith, P., Baron-Cohen, S., Lai, M. C., & Mandy, W. (2017). "Putting on my best normal": Social camouflaging in adults with autism spectrum conditions. *Journal of Autism and Developmental Disorders, 47*(8), 2519–2534.

Jackson, S. L., & Dritschel, B. (2016). Modeling the impact of social problem-solving deficits on depressive vulnerability in the broader autism phenotype. *Research in Autism Spectrum Disorders, 21*, 128–138.

Jaswal, V. K., & Akhtar, N. (2018). Being vs. appearing socially uninterested: Challenging assumptions about social motivation in autism. *Behavioral and Brain Sciences, 42*, 1–84.

Jones, L., Goddard, L., Hill, E. L., Henry, L. A., & Crane, L. (2014). Experiences of receiving a diagnosis of autism spectrum disorder: A survey of adults in the United Kingdom. *Journal of Autism and Developmental Disorders, 44*(12), 3033–3044.

Kato, K., Mikami, K., Akama, F., Yamada, K., Maehara, M., Kimoto, K., . . . Ichimura, A. (2013). Clinical features of suicide attempts in adults with autism spectrum disorders. *General Hospital Psychiatry, 35*(1), 50–53.

Kenny, L., Hattersley, C., Molins, B., Buckley, C., Povey, C., & Pellicano, E. (2016). Which terms should be used to describe autism? Perspectives from the UK autism community. *Autism, 20*(4), 442–462.

Kerns, C. M., Newschaffer, C. J., & Berkowitz, S. J. (2015). Traumatic childhood events and autism spectrum disorder. *Journal of Autism and Developmental Disorders, 45*(11), 3475–3486.

Kim, K. L., Galvan, T., Puzia, M. E., Cushman, G. K., Seymour, K. E., Vanmali, R., . . . Dickstein, D. P. (2015). Psychiatric and self-injury profiles of adolescent suicide attempters versus adolescents engaged in nonsuicidal self-injury. *Suicide and Life-Threatening Behavior, 45*(1), 37–50.

Klonsky, E. D. (2007). The functions of deliberate self-injury: A review of the evidence. *Clinical Psychology Review, 27*(2), 226–239.

Klonsky, E. D. (2011). Non-suicidal self-injury in United States adults: Prevalence, sociodemographics, topography and functions. *Psychological Medicine, 41*(9), 1981–1986.

Kroenke, K., & Spitzer, R. L. (2002). The PHQ-9: A new depression diagnostic and severity measure. *Psychiatric Annals, 32*(9), 509–515.

Lai, M. C., & Baron-Cohen, S. (2015). Identifying the lost generation of adults with autism spectrum conditions. *Lancet Psychiatry, 2*(11), 1013–1027.

Lai, M. C., Lombardo, M. V., Pasco, G., Ruigrok, A. N., Wheelwright, S. J., Sadek, S. A., . . . MRC AIMS Consortium. (2011). A behavioral comparison of male and female adults with high functioning autism spectrum conditions. *PloS One, 6*(6), e20835.

Lai, M. C., Lombardo, M. V., Ruigrok, A. N., Chakrabarti, B., Auyeung, B., Szatmari, P., . . . MRC AIMS Consortium. (2017). Quantifying and exploring camouflaging in men and women with autism. *Autism, 21*(6), 690–702.

Larsen, M. E., Nicholas, J., & Christensen, H. (2016). A systematic assessment of smartphone tools for suicide prevention. *PloS One, 11*(4), e0152285.

Lever, A. G., & Geurts, H. M. (2016). Psychiatric co-occurring symptoms and disorders in young, middle-aged, and older adults with autism spectrum disorder. *Journal of Autism and Developmental Disorders, 46*(6), 1916–1930.

Lind, S. E., & Bowler, D. M. (2010). Episodic memory and episodic future thinking in adults with autism. *Journal of Abnormal Psychology, 119*(4), 896.

Livingston, L. A., Colvert, E., Social Relationships Study Team, Bolton, P., & Happé, F. (2019). Good social skills despite poor theory of mind: exploring compensation in autism spectrum disorder. *Journal of Child Psychology and Psychiatry, 60*(1), 102–110.

Maddox, B. B., Trubanova, A., & White, S. W. (2017). Untended wounds: Non-suicidal self-injury in adults with autism spectrum disorder. *Autism, 21*(4), 412–422.

Mayes, S. D., Gorman, A. A., Hillwig-Garcia, J., & Syed, E. (2013). Suicide ideation and attempts in children with autism. *Research in Autism Spectrum Disorders, 7*(1), 109–119.

Mazefsky, C. A. (2015). Emotion regulation and emotional distress in autism spectrum disorder: Foundations and considerations for future research. *Journal of Autism and Developmental Disorders, 45*(11), 3405–3408.

Mikami, K., Inomata, S., Hayakawa, N., Ohnishi, Y., Enseki, Y., Ohya, A., . . . Matsumoto, H. (2009). Frequency and clinical features of pervasive developmental disorder in adolescent suicide attempts. *General Hospital Psychiatry, 31*(2), 163–166.

Milton, D., & Sims, T. (2016). How is a sense of well-being and belonging constructed in the accounts of autistic adults? *Disability & Society, 31*(4), 520–534.

Minshawi, N. F., Hurwitz, S., Fodstad, J. C., Biebl, S., Morriss, D. H., & McDougle, C. J. (2014). The association between self-injurious behaviors and autism spectrum disorders. *Psychology Research and Behavior Management, 7*, 125.

Mishara, B., & Kerkhof, A. J. F. M. (Eds.). (2013). *Suicide prevention and new technologies: Evidence based practice*. London: Palgrave Macmillan.

Mitchell, P., Cassidy, S., & Sheppard, E. (2019). The double empathy problem, camouflage, and the value of expertise from experience. *Behavioral and Brain Sciences, 42*, e100.

Mokkink, L. B., Terwee, C. B., Patrick, D. L., Alonso, J., Stratford, P. W., Knol, D. L., . . . De Vet, H. C. (2010). The COSMIN checklist for assessing the methodological quality of studies on measurement properties of health status measurement instruments: An international Delphi study. *Quality of Life Research, 19*(4), 539–549.

National Institute for Health and Care Excellence. (2011). Self-harm in over 8s: Long-term management. Retrieved from https://www.nice.org.uk/guidance/CG133

Nock MK, Favazza A. (2009). Non-suicidal self-injury: Definition and classification. In: Nock MK, editor. Understanding non-suicidal self-injury: Origins, assessment, and treatment. Washington, DC: American Psychological Association, 9–18.

O'Connor, R. C. (2007). The relations between perfectionism and suicidality: A systematic review. *Suicide and Life-Threatening Behavior, 37*(6), 698–714.

O'Connor, R. C., & Kirtley, O. J. (2018). The integrated motivational–volitional model of suicidal behaviour. *Philosophical Transactions of the Royal Society Part B, 373*(1754), 20,170,268.

Orsmond, G. I., Shattuck, P. T., Cooper, B. P., Sterzing, P. R., & Anderson, K. A. (2013). Social participation among young adults with an autism spectrum disorder. *Journal of Autism and Developmental Disorders, 43*(11), 2710–2719.

Osman, A., Bagge, C. L., Gutierrez, P. M., Konick, L. C., Kopper, B. A., & Barrios, F. X. (2001). The Suicidal Behaviors Questionnaire-Revised (SBQ-R): Validation with clinical and nonclinical samples. *Assessment, 8*(4), 443–454.

Paquette-Smith, M., Weiss, J., & Lunsky, Y. (2014). History of suicide attempts in adults with Asperger syndrome. *Crisis, 35*(4), 273–277.

Pelton, M. K., & Cassidy, S. A. (2017). Are autistic traits associated with suicidality? A test of the interpersonal-psychological theory of suicide in a non-clinical young adult sample. *Autism Research, 10*(11), 1891–1904.

Persons, J. B. (1989). *Cognitive therapy in practice: A case formulation approach*. New York, NY: W. W. Norton.

Piven, J., Palmer, P., Jacobi, D., Childress, D., & Arndt, S. (1997). Broader autism phenotype: Evidence from a family history study of multiple-incidence autism families. *American Journal of Psychiatry, 154*(2), 185–190.

Posner, K., Brown, G. K., Stanley, B., Brent, D. A., Yershova, K. V., Oquendo, M. A., . . . Mann, J. J. (2011). The Columbia–Suicide Severity Rating Scale: Initial validity and internal consistency findings from three multisite studies with adolescents and adults. *American Journal of Psychiatry, 168*(12), 1266–1277.

Quinlivan, L., Cooper, J., Davies, L., Hawton, K., Gunnell, D., & Kapur, N. (2016). Which are the most useful scales for predicting repeat self-harm? A systematic review evaluating risk scales using measures of diagnostic accuracy. *BMJ Open, 6*(2), e009297.

Quinlivan, L., Cooper, J., Meehan, D., Longson, D., Potokar, J., Hulme, T., . . . Page, L. (2017). Predictive accuracy of risk scales following self-harm: Multicentre, prospective cohort study. *British Journal of Psychiatry, 210*(6), 429–436.

Raja, M. (2014). Suicide risk in adults with Asperger's syndrome. *Lancet Psychiatry, 1*(2), 99–101.

Ribeiro, J. D., Franklin, J. C., Fox, K. R., Bentley, K. H., Kleiman, E. M., Chang, B. P., & Nock, M. K. (2016). Self-injurious thoughts and behaviors as risk factors for future suicide ideation, attempts, and death: A meta-analysis of longitudinal studies. *Psychological Medicine, 46*(2), 225–236.

Richards, G., Kenny, R., Griffiths, S., Allison, C., Mosse, D., Holt, R., . . . & Baron-Cohen, S. (2019). Autistic traits in adults who have attempted suicide. *Molecular autism, 10*(1w

Riedel, A., Schroeck, C., Ebert, D., Fangmeier, T., Bubl, E., & Tebartz, V. E. (2015). Well educated unemployed—On education, employment and comorbidities in adults with high-functioning autism spectrum disorders in Germany. *Psychiatrische Praxis, 43*, 38–44.

Robins, C. J., & Chapman, A. L. (2004). Dialectical behavior therapy: Current status, recent developments, and future directions. *Journal of Personality Disorders, 18*(1), 73–89.

Robins, C. J., Ivanoff, A. M., & Linehan, M. M. (2001). Dialectical behavior therapy. In W. J. Livesley (Ed.), *Handbook of per- sonality disorders: Theory, research, and treatment* (pp. 117–139). New York: Guilford.

Rynkiewicz, A., Schuller, B., Marchi, E., Piana, S., Camurri, A., Lassalle, A., & Baron-Cohen, S. (2016). An investigation of the "female camouflage effect" in autism using a computerized ADOS-2 and a test of sex/gender differences. *Molecular Autism, 7*(1), 10.

Schmid, A. M., Truog, A. W., & Damian, F. J. (2011). Care of the suicidal pediatric patient in the ED: A case study. *American Journal of Nursing, 111*, 34–43.

Schotte, D. E., & Clum, G. A. (1987). Problem-solving skills in suicidal psychiatric patients. *Journal of Consulting and Clinical Psychology, 55*(1), 49.

Segers, M., & Rawana, J. (2014). What do we know about suicidality in autism spectrum disorders? A systematic review. *Autism Research, 7*(4), 507–521.

Shtayermman, O. (2007). Peer victimization in adolescents and young adults diagnosed with Asperger's syndrome: A link to depressive symptomatology, anxiety symptomatology and suicidal ideation. *Issues in Comprehensive Pediatric Nursing, 30*(3), 87–107.

Sinzig, J., Morsch, D., Bruning, N., Schmidt, M. H., & Lehmkuhl, G. (2008). Inhibition, flexibility, working memory and planning in autism spectrum disorders with and without comorbid ADHD-symptoms. *Child and Adolescent Psychiatry and Mental Health, 2*(1), 4.

South, M., Ozonoff, S., & McMahon, W. M. (2005). Repetitive behavior profiles in Asperger syndrome and high-functioning autism. *Journal of Autism and Developmental Disorders, 35*(2), 145–158.

Spencer, L., Lyketsos, C. G., Samstad, E., Dokey, A., Rostov, D., & Chisolm, M. S. (2011). A suicidal adult in crisis: An unexpected diagnosis of autism spectrum disorder. *American Journal of Psychiatry, 168*(9), 890–892.

Stewart, M. E., Barnard, L., Pearson, J., Hasan, R., & O'Brien, G. (2006). Presentation of depression in autism and Asperger syndrome: A review. *Autism, 10*(1), 103–116.

Storch, E. A., Sulkowski, M. L., Nadeau, J., Lewin, A. B., Arnold, E. B., Mutch, P. J., . . . Murphy, T. K. (2013). The phenomenology and clinical correlates of suicidal thoughts and behaviors in youth with autism spectrum disorders. *Journal of Autism and Developmental Disorders, 43*(10), 2450–2459.

Takara, K., & Kondo, T. (2014). Comorbid atypical autistic traits as a potential risk factor for suicide attempts among adult depressed patients: A case–control study. *Annals of General Psychiatry, 13*(1), 33.

Van Orden, K. A., Witte, T. K., Cukrowicz, K. C., Braithwaite, S. R., Selby, E. A., & Joiner, T. E., Jr. (2010). The interpersonal theory of suicide. *Psychological Review, 117*(2), 575.

Weston, L., Hodgekins, J., & Langdon, P. E. (2016). Effectiveness of cognitive behavioural therapy with people who have autistic spectrum disorders: A systematic review and meta-analysis. *Clinical Psychology Review, 49*, 41–54.

Whitlock, J., Exner-Cortens, D., & Purington, A. (2014). Assessment of nonsuicidal self-injury: Development and initial validation of the Non-Suicidal Self-Injury-Assessment Tool (NSSI-AT). *Psychological Assessment, 26*(3), 935–946.

Whitlock, J., Muehlenkamp, J., & Purington, A. (2011). Nonsuicidal self-injury in a college population: General trends and sex differences. *Journal of American College Health, 59*(8), 691–698.

Willis, G., Lawrence, D., Thompson, F., Kudela, M., Levin, K., & Miller, K. (2005). The use of cognitive interviewing to evaluate translated survey questions: Lessons learned. *Proceedings of the Federal Committee on Statistical Methodology Research Conference*, Arlington, VA.

World Health Organization. (2018). World Health Statistics. Global Health Observatory data. Retrieved from http://apps.who.int/iris/bitstream/handle/10665/272596/9789241565585-eng.pdf?ua=1

Zahid, S., & Upthegrove, R. (2017). Suicidality in autistic spectrum disorders. *Crisis, 38*(4), 237–246.

PART 4

Current Clinical Practices and Promising Research Approaches

CHAPTER

19 Medications to Treat Co-Occurring Psychiatric Conditions in Autism Spectrum Disorder

Bryan H. King, Agnieszka Rynkiewicz, Małgorzata Janas-Kozik, *and* Marta Tyszkiewicz-Nwafor

Abstract

Although there are as yet no drugs specifically indicated for core symptoms of autism spectrum disorder (ASD), medications are frequently used as a component of comprehensive treatment for co-occurring psychiatric conditions in individuals with ASD across the lifespan. As is true for psychopharmacological treatment in general, the selection of particular therapeutic agents is not yet driven by an understanding of the contributions of specific genetic or other abnormalities to the development or expression of psychiatric symptoms. Treatment is thus largely empirical, and the most common therapeutic targets in ASD include hyperactivity and impulsivity, irritability, mood and anxiety symptoms, and insomnia. The literature suggests that individuals with ASD as a group respond less well to common pharmacologic interventions, and they are generally more likely to experience side effects. There is good evidence to support many of the commonly used medication strategies in ASD, particularly the use of stimulants and other drugs typically prescribed for attention deficit hyperactivity disorder, as well as atypical antipsychotics for a cluster of symptoms captured under the umbrella term of irritability. There is growing interest in exploring the role of drugs that act on glutamatergic and GABAergic systems. Overall, the evidence base to inform the practice of psychopharmacology is relatively limited even for situations where a Food and Drug Administration-approved indication exists, and considerable work needs to be done to better inform clinical practice.

Keywords: ADHD, autism spectrum disorder, irritability, depression, psychotropic, randomized controlled trial, sleep

Overview

The foregoing chapters in this volume highlight the multiple and varied conditions that commonly occur in the setting of the diagnosis of autism spectrum disorder (ASD). Although the complexity clearly speaks to the critical need for this handbook, one could also see this extraordinary complexity as an indictment of the psychiatric diagnostic classification system or even of the diagnosis of autism itself. With his effort to define and classify psychiatric illness over a century ago, Mercier (1890) noted that the problem with defining disorders with clear boundaries was that individuals would immediately present with symptoms that straddled those boundaries. "Cases will always occur partaking pretty equally of the nature of two adjoining groups," he wrote, "and other cases will occur which exhibit at one time the features of one group and at another time those of another." The good news about our classification system today in comparison to Mercier's is the general consensus that has been achieved in the field through decades of diagnostic refinement. Autism can be very reliably diagnosed. The bad news is that disorders are still defined by how they look, by the set of symptoms and the progression of symptoms over time. Psychiatric disorders are not yet defined by a knowledge of their underlying pathophysiology, and Mercier's challenge thus persists.

This problem is particularly critical with respect to the use of medication, as what should inform the question of whether a medication is appropriate, or the selection of a particular agent from our overwhelming pharmacopoeia, is the underlying mechanism that is being addressed. If ASD is the downstream or outward expression of a specific physiological abnormality—a deficiency or an overabundance of a particular molecule or protein—the proper treatment will be the one that addresses that particular imbalance.

The challenge for pharmacotherapy of co-occurring conditions or related problems in ASD, then, is that these co-occurring conditions may arise as a consequence of having ASD through shared mechanisms or pathways, or they may arise independently by coincidence. For example, having autism may not protect one from having attention deficit hyperactivity disorder (ADHD). But the more likely case is that some combination of the multiple conditions highlighted in this volume may be the expression of a complex group of symptoms that share the same underlying diathesis in a given individual. Epilepsy, ASD, intellectual disability, anxiety, and cardiac and dermatologic abnormalities may all be expressions of a disruption in the mTOR pathway in tuberous sclerosis complex. As advances in our understanding of the underpinnings of the development and expression of ASD and related conditions reveal new treatment strategies, we may paradoxically identify treatments that are less specific for "ASD" and "co-occurring conditions," but which are also more effective because of their specificity for a particular diathesis. As an example, the optimal medication for sleep disturbance in ASD associated with Phelan-McDermid syndrome may ultimately be revealed to have nothing to do with ASD but everything to do with Phelan-McDermid syndrome.

With these factors in mind, the current state of the field is that medication strategies can be very helpful for co-occurring conditions, but in the risk–benefit considerations for particular drugs, the presence or absence of ASD arguably has as much of an impact on the assessment of risk as it does on the prediction of benefit. The question that must consistently be asked is whether medication for depression or ADHD or anxiety is still indicated if those conditions co-occur with ASD. Is ASD a contraindication for customary pharmacological approaches to addressing specific psychiatric illnesses? That said, the likelihood of being treated with medication in the setting of autism, particularly psychotropic medication, is significantly higher than for the general population, and this increased prescription prevalence is virtually all related to the treatment of co-occurring conditions. There are presently no drugs that have been shown to specifically treat autism or its core features of impairment in social communication, restricted or repetitive behaviors and interests, or sensory sensitivities (e.g., Anagnostou, 2018; Goel, Hong, Findling, & Ji, 2018).

Prevalence of Medication Use in ASD

Several studies from different countries have utilized large insurance or registry databases to examine factors that may predispose to treatment with psychotropic drugs in individuals with ASD (see review by Jobski et al., 2016). House and colleagues (2016) compared 13,100 children who were diagnosed with ASD with 936,731 children in the same database without the diagnosis. Notably, a child or adolescent with the diagnosis of ASD was nine times more likely to receive a psychotropic medication than the general population. The odds ratios by class were 5.80 (stimulants), 9.04 (antidepressants), 9.61 (benzodiazepines), 18.76 (alpha agonists), and 22.51 (antipsychotics). Interestingly, the rate of prescription for oral antibiotics and for antacids was also higher in ASD (1.2 and 3.5 times, respectively). The largest difference in antacid and antibiotic use was in the 0- to 2-year-old age range, presumably before the formal diagnosis of autism had even been made. These data suggest that early on, co-occurring conditions like irritability and sleep disturbance may be driving the selection of medications, and in some cases these symptoms may even herald the diagnosis of ASD.

Although the relative use of psychotropic medications compared to the general population may be dominated by antipsychotics and alpha agonists, studies examining the prevalence by class of drug within the population with ASD typically reveal a different hierarchy. Recently, Rasmussen, Bilenberg, Thomsen Ernst, Abitz Boysen, and Pottegård (2018) examined nationwide registry data to assess the use of psychotropics among children and adolescents with ASD in Denmark. Thirty percent of children and adolescents (6 to 17 years of age) with ASD used at least one of four classes of medication including antipsychotics (5%), antidepressants (5%), ADHD medications (17%), and melatonin (13%). Methylphenidate, sertraline, and risperidone were the specific drugs most often prescribed. Indeed, methylphenidate accounted for 68% of all ADHD medications (stimulants and atomoxetine) in the 6- to 11-year-old cohort and 60% of all ADHD drugs in the 12- to 17-year-olds. Sertraline accounted for 76% of all antidepressants in children and 74% in adolescents, and risperidone accounted for 76% of antipsychotic prescriptions in children and 43% in adolescents. Risperidone and aripiprazole together accounted for 96% of all antipsychotic prescriptions in children and 74% in adolescents. Although overall prescription rates for individuals with ASD appear to be lower in Germany than in the United States (Bachmann, Manthey, Kamp-Becker, Glaeske, & Hoffmann, 2013), analysis of 1,124 subjects from a large insurance database found that methylphenidate accounted for fully 24.4% of all psychotropic prescriptions, followed by risperidone at 13.3% and valproate at 9.1%.

Sex Differences in Psychotropic Medication Use in ASD

For both males and females, although ASD significantly increases the likelihood of receiving one or more psychotropic medications relative to the general population, the prescription rate in females is somewhat lower overall in most studies (Hong et al., 2017; Kamimura-Nishimura et al., 2017). This difference in rates appears to reflect a lower use of stimulants for ADHD (Hong et al., 2017; Madden et al., 2017). Moreover, the elevated prevalence of males with ADHD in the general population also holds for the co-occurrence of ASD and ADHD, but the difference between males and females is less significant (Ramtekkar et al., 2010). Further, the sex difference in ADHD rates in ASD appears to disappear in adulthood (Supekar et al., 2016).

In contrast to stimulant use, for children and adolescents, females may be somewhat more likely to receive antidepressants, anxiolytics, or mood stabilizers than males (Hong et al. 2017; Madden et al., 2017). Co-occurring epilepsy is more common in females with ASD, and this might contribute to higher anticonvulsant use. Two recent studies of large databases, one in the United Kingdom including children and adults (Houghton, Liu, & Bolognani, 2018) and one in Denmark limited to children and adolescents (Rasmussen, 2018), have found significantly higher overall prescription rates in females compared to males with ASD even when controlling for specific comorbidities like ADHD. These findings could support the growing appreciation that ASD is underdiagnosed in females (Begeer et al., 2013; Gould & Ashton-Smith, 2011; Rynkiewicz et al., 2016, 2018; Wilson et al., 2016) and that females may thus have more severe associated symptoms because the diagnostic threshold is higher. Rynkiewicz and colleagues (2016, 2018) highlight that the improvement of current diagnostic assessments may increase identification of autistic females, especially individuals who were not diagnosed early in life and do not have intellectual disability and/or profound communication difficulties (Ormond et al., 2018; Rynkiewicz et al., 2016, 2018). As a result, future studies that specifically examine potential sex differences in drug dose or clinical outcomes may have more representative ASD female subjects and perhaps even yield different outcomes (Rynkiewicz et al., 2018).

Therapeutic Targets for Medication in ASD

ADHD and Related Symptoms of Inattention, Impulsivity, and Hyperactivity

The fact that ADHD medications, specifically stimulants and atomoxetine in most surveys, are the most frequently prescribed of all drugs in ASD underscores how commonly these symptoms are associated with autism. Indeed, hyperactivity is specifically highlighted in some of the earliest descriptions of the disorder. In 1967, Rutter noted that "hand and finger mannerisms, self-injury, and overactivity" were common in autism. When autism officially made its debut in the third edition of the *Diagnostic and Statistical Manual of Mental Disorders* (DSM-III), the reason for the insertion of a "trumping rule" that prevented concurrent diagnoses of autism and ADHD was because hyperactivity was considered so prevalent in pervasive developmental disorders. Thus, though not part of the core diagnostic symptoms because of a lack of specificity, it was expected that ADHD symptoms would be common.

The effectiveness of stimulant medications in ADHD in the general population is well established with nearly 200 controlled trials in children, adolescents, and adults, and the likelihood of being medicated if one has the diagnosis of ADHD is higher than if one has the diagnosis of ASD (Houghton et al., 2018). The literature examining the intersection of ASD and ADHD is much smaller, in part because of the trumping rule in the DSM that made it challenging to study a condition that technically did not exist.

METHYLPHENIDATE

The largest controlled study of methylphenidate for ADHD in ASD was conducted by the Research Units on Pediatric Psychiatry (RUPP) Autism Network (2005a). In this multisite, double-blind, placebo-controlled crossover trial, a total of 72 subjects, 5 to 14 years of age, were enrolled. Interestingly, because of concerns about potential intolerability of methylphenidate in ASD, each of the study subjects was treated for 2 days with escalating doses of methylphenidate prior to randomization. As a result, six subjects were withdrawn, and the remaining 66 subjects were randomized to three different doses of methylphenidate—low, medium, and high—for 1 week each. Subjects received three daily doses of methylphenidate in each of the week-long dose conditions based on weight (low, 0.125 mg/kg/dose; medium, 0.25 mg/kg/dose; and high, 0.5 mg/kg/dose). The primary outcome of the study was the Hyperactivity subscale of the teacher-rated Aberrant Behavior Checklist (ABC).

The ABC was originally developed by Aman and Singh (1985), who sought to develop a scale specifically to assess drug and other treatment effects in individuals with severe intellectual disability residing in institutional settings. The 58 items on the ABC are each rated on a 4-point scale from 0 (not at all a problem) to 3 (the problem is severe). Factor analysis generated five subscales including Irritability (15 items), Hyperactivity (16 items), Lethargy/Social Withdrawal (16 items), Stereotypic Behavior (7 items), and Inappropriate Speech (4 items). The ABC has been shown to be sensitive to change, was subsequently modified to be applicable in community settings, and has since been utilized as an outcome measure in many clinical trials in ASD.

The distribution of best doses among the subjects in the RUPP Autism Network methylphenidate trial was as follows: nine (20%) placebo, 11 (25%) low dose, 14 (32%) medium dose, and 10 (23%) high dose. In terms of adverse effects, seven subjects exited during the crossover phase (one at low, three at medium, and three at high doses) owing to intolerable adverse effects. Thus, 18% of the original 72 subjects were unable to tolerate the drug, with irritability being the primary reason for discontinuation. In addition, parent-rated Lethargy/Social Withdrawal scores during the high dose of methylphenidate were significantly worse than during placebo (p = .004; effect size = 0.37).

Taken together, this trial suggests that the response to methylphenidate for ADHD in ASD differs in important ways from the general population with ADHD alone. First, the overall response rate of 49% is lower than expected. For instance, in the Multimodal Treatment of ADHD (MTA) trial involving 579 children ages 7 to 9 years, 212 (73.4%) of the 289 subjects given medication management and combined treatment were being successfully maintained on methylphenidate by study end at 14 months. Second, the rate of significant side effects is greater in ASD. Nearly one in five children with ASD could not tolerate the highest dose of methylphenidate, whereas only 3% reported severe side effects in the MTA (MTA Cooperative Group, 1999). Finally, the placebo response rate in ASD was significantly higher. This finding has been replicated across a number of different trials.

Although methylphenidate is but one of many options for stimulant medications, other commonly used drugs from this class, including mixed amphetamine salts, the amphetamine prodrug lisdexamphetamine, and long-acting formulations, have not been specifically studied in the setting of ASD.

ALPHA-2 AGONISTS

The alpha agonists clonidine and guanfacine are also frequently used for ADHD symptoms, and guanfacine has a Food and Drug Administration (FDA)–approved indication for this purpose. One controlled trial of guanfacine has been conducted in ASD. In this five-site, 8-week study by Scahill and colleagues (2015), 62 children ages 5 to 14 were randomized to fixed-flexible doses of extended-release guanfacine or placebo. The modal dose of guanfacine was 3 mg daily (range 1 to 4 mg). Compared to placebo, subjects treated with guanfacine showed significantly more improvement on the parent-rated ABC Hyperactivity subscale, the primary outcome of the study. This improvement was also observed in clinician ratings of ADHD as well as ratings of overall change on the Clinical Global Impressions—Improvement scale (CGI-I; Guy, 1976). There were no differences between guanfacine and placebo on tests of working memory or motor planning.

The CGI-I is a 7-point scale that goes from "very much improved," captured with a score of 1, down to a score of 7, which corresponds to "very much worse." A score of 4 represents "no change," and a score of 2 corresponds to "much improved." In several clinical trials in ASD, scores of 1 and 2 are consolidated into "responder" grouping, and all other scores are collapsed into "nonresponders." The "much improved" threshold for defining a response is believed to correspond to change that is clinically meaningful, change that would warrant continued treatment with the medication. In the guanfacine study, the rate of positive response (much improved or very much improved on the CGI-I) was 50% (N = 15/30) for guanfacine compared with 9.4% (N = 3/32) for placebo (p = .0001), corresponding to a number needed to treat of 2.

Side effects were significantly more common in subjects who received guanfacine. The most common of these was drowsiness, which was observed in fully

87% of subjects. Fatigue was also commonly reported (63%). Decreased appetite, dry mouth, irritability, anxiety, and insomnia were also more frequent with guanfacine. In addition, baseline systolic and diastolic blood pressure dropped by about 5 to 10 mmHg by Week 4 of the trial, with recovery close to baseline by Week 8. Resting heart rate dropped by an average of about 10 bpm, was also at its lowest at 4 weeks, and remained low throughout the trial. Overall, treatment for four of 30 guanfacine-treated subjects (13.3%) was discontinued because of adverse events.

One cannot directly compare the results of the extended-release guanfacine 8-week parallel trial to the RUPP Autism Network 4-week fixed-dose methylphenidate crossover trial; however, the effect size and drug tolerability appear somewhat better for guanfacine for reducing ADHD symptoms. Unfortunately, there were no identified predictors of positive response to either drug. Both drugs require careful monitoring in this population.

SEROTONIN NOREPINEPHRINE REUPTAKE INHIBITORS

Atomoxetine, a serotonin norepinephrine reuptake inhibitor (SNRI), has FDA approval for the treatment of ADHD and is widely used for this purpose. A number of controlled trials have been conducted in ASD involving over 200 subjects and it is thus one of the best studied of the ADHD medications in autism.

Harfterkamp and colleagues (2012) enrolled 97 subjects ages 6 to 17 in an 8-week trial who were randomized to double-blind treatment with 1.2 mg/kg/day atomoxetine or placebo. The primary outcome was the ADHD Rating Scale (ADHD-RS) score, and secondary measures included the CGI-I restricted to ADHD, and the Conners Teacher Rating Scale-Revised: Short Form (CTRS-R:S) score. ADHD-RS total and subscale scores improved significantly more in subjects randomized to atomoxetine than the placebo group. The ADHD-RS total change from baseline was 8.2 (standard deviation [SD] = 8.8) for atomoxetine compared to 1.2 (SD = 7.3) for placebo. Total ADHD-RS scores were also lower (atomoxetine: 32.3; placebo: 37.3). However, overall assessment of much or very much improvement on the CGI-I between atomoxetine (20.9% of subjects) and placebo (8.7% of subjects) was not significantly different. Based on a number needed to treat comparison, over twice as many patients would be needed to see a clinically significant response than for methylphenidate or guanfacine.

In the atomoxetine group, 81.3% reported at least one adverse event compared to 65.3% in the placebo group. Nausea, decreased appetite, fatigue, and early morning awakening were all significantly more common in the atomoxetine condition than placebo.

Interestingly, and not unlike the experience with methylphenidate, the overall effect of atomoxetine was smaller in children with combined ADHD and ASD than for children with typical ADHD. Compared to a mean change from baseline in the ADHD-RS of 8.2 points, this change in children with typical ADHD and similar baseline scores has been reported to be in the range of 13 (Michelson et al., 2002) to close to 19 points (Kelsey et al., 2004; Svanborg et al., 2009), although perhaps comparable to the 10.5-point overall change reported in children with combined ADHD and anxiety disorder (Geller et al., 2007). However, following a 20-week open-label extension (Harfterkamp et al., 2013), additional improvement of 7.5 points in the ADHD-RS was observed.

In a follow-up study reporting on secondary outcomes of the 8-week controlled study including ABC subscales, Harfterkamp and colleagues (2014) reported that atomoxetine treatment resulted in significant improvement in the Hyperactivity, Stereotypy, and Inappropriate Speech subscales relative to placebo. These results differ from those reported for guanfacine. Although Scahill and colleagues recruited subjects with higher scores on all of the subscales at baseline, the average improvement in the Hyperactivity subscale relative to placebo was 10.4 points for guanfacine versus only 4.4 points for atomoxetine.

A more recent study by Handen and colleagues (2015) explored the effect of atomoxetine with or without parent behavior training (PT) for ADHD in ASD. In a three-site, 10-week, double-blind trial, 128 children ages 5 to 14 with ASD and symptoms of ADHD were randomized to atomoxetine alone, atomoxetine plus PT, placebo plus PT, or placebo alone. Atomoxetine was adjusted to optimal dose up to a total of 1.8 mg/kg/day over 6 weeks and maintained at that dose for 4 additional weeks. Nine PT sessions were provided. The primary outcome measures were the CGI-I combined with either the parent-rated ADHD symptoms on the Swanson, Nolan, and Pelham (SNAP) scale to assess ADHD or the Home Situations Questionnaire (HSQ; Chowdhury et al., 2010, 2016), a measure used to assess noncompliance.

Atomoxetine, with or without PT, was significantly better than placebo. The response rates were

45.2% for atomoxetine + PT, 46.9% for atomoxetine alone, 29.0% for PT + placebo, and 19.4% for placebo alone. For noncompliance, the response rates were 22.6% for atomoxetine + PT, 43.8% for atomoxetine alone, 38.7% for PT + placebo, and 16.1% for placebo alone.

The overall response rate of 45% to 46% was higher than that in the study by Harfterkamp and colleagues (2014), perhaps reflecting the higher overall dose of atomoxetine used, but response rates were still lower than the 60% responder rate reported for children without ASD (Schwartz et al., 2015).

ATYPICAL ANTIPSYCHOTIC MEDICATIONS

Antipsychotic medications are not FDA approved for the treatment of ADHD. However, the off-label use of this class of drugs for ADHD is widespread. In a national study of Medicaid enrolled children, Matone and colleagues (2012) identified 354,000 youth who were prescribed an antipsychotic. When examining the diagnoses of children and adolescents in this sample, the presence of autism, bipolar disorder, or schizophrenia was associated with proportionally higher use of an antipsychotic prescription. However, a sobering finding was that youth with ADHD accounted for 50% of total antipsychotic use, and fully one in seven users of antipsychotics were youth with ADHD as their only diagnosis. Similar findings were observed by Olfson, King, and Schoenbaum (2015), who found that the most common diagnosis associated with antipsychotic use in the IMS LifeLink LRx longitudinal prescription database, which includes approximately 60% of all retail pharmacies in the United States, was ADHD, in over half of younger children (52.5%) and older children (60.1%) and in a third of adolescents (34.9%).

Within the population of children and adolescents with ASD, Downs and colleagues (2016) explored a large dataset of 3,482 children aged 3 to 17 year with an International Classification of Diseases-10 (ICD-10) diagnosis of ASD who were referred to mental health services between 2008 and 2013. Antipsychotic use was more likely in the setting of comorbid diagnoses including hyperkinetic (odds ratio [OR] = 1.44), psychotic (OR = 5.71), depressive (OR = 2.36), obsessive-compulsive (OR = 2.31), and tic disorders.

Although ADHD symptoms have not been the primary outcome measure in studies evaluating the efficacy of atypical antipsychotic drugs in ASD, improvement in hyperactivity can be significant. For example, in the RUPP Autism Network study of risperidone for symptoms of irritability described in greater detail later in the section on irritability, significant improvement was observed in the ABC Hyperactivity subscale, the same measure used in the guanfacine trial highlighted earlier. Similar improvements in hyperactivity were also observed in trials of aripiprazole.

GLUTAMATERGIC DRUGS

Amantadine is a noncompetitive *N*-methyl-d-aspartate (NMDA) receptor antagonist that modulates glutamatergic activity but that also increases dopaminergic tone; thus, the mechanism by which it might impact ADHD symptoms is both unique and overlapping with established ADHD treatments. King and colleagues (2001) enrolled 39 subjects with ASD and disruptive behaviors captured by the Hyperactivity or Irritability subscales of the ABC. Subjects (5 to 19 years of age) were randomized to amantadine (5 mg/kg/day) or placebo and treated for 4 weeks after a 1-week placebo lead-in. The amantadine-treated group showed statistically significant improvements in absolute changes in clinician-rated ABC-CVs for hyperactivity (amantadine –6.4 vs. placebo –2.1; p = .046) and inappropriate speech (–1.9 vs. 0.4; p = .008), but the changes in the parent-rated scales did not achieve statistical significance. Ratings on the CGI were also higher in the amantadine group with 53% improved versus 25% for placebo, but this relatively small sample was not statistically significant (p = .076). In terms of side effects, amantadine was well tolerated.

Memantine is structurally very similar to amantadine and shares its mechanism of action. Controlled trials have not been performed specifically for irritability or hyperactivity in ASD, but open-label studies have continued to support interest in this class of drug (Mechler et al., 2018). On the contrary, lamotrigine also modulates glutamate release and no significant differences emerged over placebo in a controlled trial in 28 children (27 boys) ages 3 to 11 years with a primary diagnosis of autistic disorder across a number of behavioral outcomes (Belsito et al., 2001).

SUMMARY OF MEDICATIONS COMMONLY USED FOR ADHD IN ASD

Medications used to treat ADHD symptoms are among the most widely prescribed in ASD. The most common of these specific drugs are methylphenidate and other stimulants, atomoxetine, and alpha agonists. Evidence from randomized controlled trials (RCTs) supports the use of each of these agents and, by extension, other representatives from these classes. There is preliminary data to support the continued study of amantadine and memantine in this population. Consistent differences exist between the population with ADHD and autism and the general population with ADHD alone. These differences include a greater sensitivity to side effects in autism, particularly activation, and also a somewhat lower rate of overall response. Direct comparisons of response rates in adults with ASD with or without ADHD have yet to be studied. There are as yet no reliable predictors of susceptibility to specific side effects. In the future, a better understanding of the physiological underpinnings of impulsivity and hyperactivity in autism will certainly inform treatment selection.

Irritability and Related Symptoms of Aggression, Severe Tantrums, and Self-Injury

Like hyperactivity, additional behaviors including aggression, self-injury, and tantrums have long been recognized as commonplace in the setting of ASD. Self-injury was even a core diagnostic feature of childhood onset pervasive developmental disorder in the DSM-III (APA, 1980). Collectively, largely because these behaviors all load onto the ABC Irritability subscale that was used in several pivotal drug trials, "irritability" has come to be used to capture this constellation of symptoms.

Because of the intensity and devastating impact that aggression and self-injury can have for individuals with ASD, as has been highlighted earlier in this volume (see Chapters 15 and 17), the search for effective therapeutics has been intense and has touched on virtually every available class of psychotropic drug. The antipsychotic drugs have been a constant over time, and though in recent years good evidence has emerged to support effectiveness for some members of this class, controversy surrounds their use for a number of reasons.

First, the naming convention for psychotropic medications is nowhere more problematic than for antipsychotic drugs. Initially introduced as "major tranquilizers," the prospect of giving such a drug to a child with autism immediately called into question both the therapeutic rationale and the risk–benefit calculus. Like proposing to treat arthritis with an anticancer drug, connecting an antipsychotic to tantrums in ASD can seem like a disproportionate response and always requires an explanation. But as Sultan, Correll, Zohar, Zalsman, and Veenstra-VanderWeele (2018) have recently highlighted, the mechanism of action of these drugs plays out at specific neurotransmitter receptor or uptake sites and not diagnoses.

Setting aside the mismatch between the name of the drug class and the conditions for which these drugs are used in individuals with ASD, the prescribing patterns of these agents does suggest possible overuse as well as a lack of sophistication, oversight, and respect for well-established side effects, particularly when being prescribed off label (Daviss, Barnett, Neubacher, & Drake, 2016; Matone et al., 2012; Schneider, Taylor, Zalsman, Frangou, & Kyriakopoulos, 2014).

LeVann's (1961) enthusiastic characterization of thioridazine as a drug with "remarkable utility virtually devoid of side-effects" reflected the excitement of having a new therapeutic option for devastating behaviors like self-injury and aggression in institutionalized individuals with developmental disorders, but now underscores the caution that should accompany any medication choice. Thioridazine of course now carries an FDA "black box" warning for risks of cardiac death and has come to be associated with many other short- and long-term side effects.

Haloperidol was the first of the antipsychotic drugs to be formally studied in children with autism. Magda Campbell, who was a pioneer in pediatric psychopharmacology, and her colleagues (1978) randomized 40 children with severe aggression aged 2.6 to 7.2 years to haloperidol (average dose of 1.7 mg/day) or placebo. Haloperidol was associated with significant improvement in symptoms of withdrawal and stereotypy in the children 4.5 years and older, as assessed by the Child Psychiatric Rating Scale (CPRS). Subsequent studies extended these results, including improvement in aggression and angry and labile affect (Malone et al., 2005).

Despite the relatively low doses of haloperidol administered, sedation was very common, occurring in over half of subjects. Additionally, about one third of children developed motor symptoms such as dystonias and dyskinesias. Importantly, using a standard cognitive battery, no adverse effects on cognition were detected. Coupled with the observation that haloperidol treatment seemed to accelerate the acquisition of speech, and harkening back to the earlier study by LeVann, there was little evidence to support the common criticism that the mechanism by which improvements in aggression and other severe behaviors occurred was simply nonspecific sedation (e.g., Gualtieri and Hawk, 1980; Matson & Mahan, 2010). Moreover, there had long been other potentially sedating drugs, the barbiturates, for example, that never really gained any traction in the treatment of these same conditions.

Risperidone was the first medication ever to gain an FDA-approved indication in autism and is indicated "for the treatment of irritability associated with autistic disorder in children and adolescents aged 5–16 years, including symptoms of aggression towards others, deliberate self-injuriousness, temper tantrums, and quickly changing moods" (FDA, 2006). As noted earlier, the definition of "irritability" flows directly from the Irritability subscale of the ABC, highlighted by examples of items from the scale like tantrums and quickly changing moods. The first of the pivotal trials that led to this approval was the RUPP Autism Network risperidone trial briefly highlighted earlier. Investigators at five sites enrolled 101 subjects ages 5 to 17 years who were randomly assigned to either risperidone (0.5 to 3.5 mg/day) or placebo for 8 weeks. The primary outcome was a combination of the scores on the Irritability subscale of the ABC and CGI-I scales.

Risperidone was associated with a 56.9% reduction in the Irritability score, compared with just 14.1% with the placebo ($p < .001$). The overall responder rate, combining a 25% decrease in the Irritability score and a rating of much improved or very much improved on the CGI-I, was 69% for risperidone and 12% in the placebo group ($p < .001$).

Although the trial was just 8 weeks in duration, risperidone was associated with an average weight gain of 2.7 (± 2.9 kg) compared to 0.8 (± 2.2) kg with placebo ($p < .001$). Increased appetite, fatigue, drowsiness, dizziness, and drooling were also significantly more frequent with risperidone. In an open-label extension of this study, two thirds of the children with a positive response to risperidone at 8 weeks maintained that benefit at 6 months.

Shea and colleagues (2004) subsequently replicated these results in an 8-week, randomized, double-blind, placebo-controlled trial in which risperidone or placebo was administered to 79 children ages 5 to 12 years. Children randomized to risperidone (mean dosage: 1.17 mg/day) showed significant improvement on the Irritability subscale of the ABC, and 87% of risperidone-treated subjects met the improvement threshold on the CGI-I compared to 40% of placebo-treated subjects (Shea et al., 2004).

Risperidone has become the most extensively studied medication for irritability symptoms in ASD. Sharma and Shaw (2011) conducted a meta-analysis of these studies and identified five RCTs in which a total of 186 subjects ages 3 to 17 years were randomized to risperidone. Effect sizes ranged from 0.9 to 1.37. A more recent meta-analysis of pharmacological interventions for irritability in ASD by Fung and colleagues (2016) also supported the effectiveness of risperidone.

ARIPIPRAZOLE

The basis for FDA approval for aripiprazole in the treatment of irritability associated with ASD was established with two 8-week, placebo-controlled trials in subjects (6 to 17 years of age). Owen and colleagues (2009) randomized children and adolescents with autistic disorder (n = 98), aged 6 to 17 years, to daily doses of placebo or aripiprazole 2 to 15 mg/day. Scores on the ABC Irritability subscale and on the CGI-I scale were significantly better on aripiprazole compared with placebo. The mean daily dose of aripiprazole at the end of the 8-week treatment was 8.6 mg/day.

Marcus and colleagues (2009) conducted a randomized fixed-dose, 8-week, placebo-controlled trial in 218 children aged 6 to 17 years. Aripiprazole was started at 2 mg/day and increased to 5 mg/day after 1 week. After a second week, it was increased to 10 mg/day for patients in the 10- and 15-mg/day dose arms and increased to 15 mg/day a week later in the 15-mg/day treatment arm. All three doses of aripiprazole significantly improved scores on the ABC Irritability subscale compared with placebo.

Interestingly, a subsequent item analysis of these studies by Aman and colleagues (2010) revealed that self-injurious behavior did not improve significantly in either trial, perhaps owing to the relatively low levels of this behavior exhibited in the enrolled subjects. Thus, although the FDA indication for aripiprazole specifically identifies self-injury as an example of irritability for which the drug is indicated, evidence to support its use for self-injurious behavior is lacking.

Hirsch and Pringsheim (2016) conducted a meta-analysis of these two pivotal trials of aripiprazole in ASD. Their meta-analysis revealed a mean improvement of 6.17 points on the ABC Irritability subscale, 7.93 points on the ABC Hyperactivity subscale, and 2.66 points in the Stereotypy subscale in children treated with aripiprazole relative to children treated with a placebo.

With respect to side effects, children treated with aripiprazole were significantly more likely to gain weight, with a mean increase of 1.13 kg relative to placebo, and had a significantly higher rate of side effects including weight gain, sedation, drooling, and tremor. In Fung and colleagues' comprehensive review (2016), both risperidone and aripiprazole showed elevated rates of extrapyramidal symptoms (EPSs). For risperidone, one in seven treated individuals will experience EPSs, and for aripiprazole, the frequency is one in 20. These frequencies are higher than those reported in RCTs in children with bipolar disorder (Fung et al., 2016), which may indicate more sensitivity to EPSs in ASD. Sedation was also more common for risperidone (50%) than aripiprazole (6%). The absolute excess over placebo in mean weight gain was greater for risperidone (1.6 kg) than for aripiprazole (1.1 kg). The dearth of longer term studies of atypical antipsychotic drugs in individuals with ASD remains a significant gap in the literature.

OTHER ATYPICAL ANTIPSYCHOTIC MEDICATIONS

Although virtually every other available antipsychotic medication has been explored in ASD, none has emerged with convincing efficacy data. In a small placebo-controlled study of olanzapine involving 11 children ages 6 to 14 years, Hollander and colleagues (2006) noted that although more subjects were classified as responders on the CGI-I at the end of the 8-week trial, olanzapine was associated with significantly greater weight gain of 7.5 ± 4.8 lb compared to 1.5 ± 1.5 lb on placebo. Loebel and colleagues (2016) conducted a 6-week randomized, fixed-dose, placebo-controlled study of lurasidone for irritability in youth with ASD, which did not demonstrate benefit relative to placebo at lurasidone doses of 20 and 60 mg daily.

MOOD STABILIZERS

Anticonvulsants

The clinical overlap between some measures of irritability, particularly symptoms like "quickly changing moods," supports the rationale for exploring drugs that seem to act as mood stabilizers, particularly in the setting of bipolar disorder, for the treatment of irritability in ASD. Valproate has been formally evaluated in two RCTs that were included in the meta-analysis by Fung and colleagues (2016). These studies, by Hollander and colleagues (2010) and by Hellings and colleagues (2005), were of comparable size, each randomizing 16 subjects to valproate and assessing the response over 2 or 3 months with the ABC Irritability subscale among other scales. Outcomes were mixed, and changes on the ABC Irritability subscale were quite modest. Side effects associated with valproate are potentially quite significant, however. Valproates are absolutely contraindicated in pregnancy. In women of childbearing age, valproate should be used only if there is no alternative, in combination with an effective birth control method. Some studies have suggested that valproic acid is associated with congenital malformations in 11% and developmental disorders in 30% to 40% of newborns with prenatal exposure. A recent review of the efficacy of valproate and other anticonvulsants for bipolar disorder in childhood by Davico, Canavese, Vittorini, Gandione, and Vitiello (2018) found no evidence for the efficacy of this class of drugs, which, coupled with the side effect profile for valproate, should propel this agent to second- or third-line status among treatments for irritability in ASD.

Lithium

Lithium is one of the oldest pharmacological treatments in psychiatry, and its discovery revolutionized therapy for bipolar disorder. There are no controlled trials of its use specifically for mood dysregulation or irritability in ASD, but clinical experience has certainly accumulated over the years. A relatively recent retrospective review of outcomes in children and adolescents with ASD by Siegel and colleagues (2014) revealed a signal for mania or euphoria/elevated mood, but the side effects require that this agent be used with caution. A growing appreciation for the effects of lithium β-catenin and ERK pathways has generated specific interest in its potential utility for specific genetic conditions associated with ASD like SHANK3 haploinsufficiency and fragile X syndrome. Preliminary clinical experience in both of these conditions supports more extensive trials (see Darville et al., 2016; Egger, Verhoeven, Groenendijk-Reijenga, & Kant, 2017; Hagerman et al., 2014).

OPIATE ANTAGONISTS

Some individuals with self-injurious behavior (SIB) appear to have altered sensitivity to pain as was observed over a century ago (Ireland, 1898). This suggestion, along with data indicating that opioid antagonists can reduce stereotyped movements and self-injury in animal models, has contributed to long-standing interest in this class of drugs. Naltrexone is the opioid antagonist most widely used for SIB based on a literature that is quite mixed and not specifically focused on ASD. Typical doses have ranged from 0.5 to 2.0 mg/kg/day in children up to 200 mg/day in adults. On balance, naltrexone appears to be well tolerated but without compelling evidence for efficacy in ASD. Sedation is the side effect most likely to be observed.

GABAergic and glutamatergic drugs

Benzodiazepines

Abnormalities in the GABAergic system have been identified in many brain regions in ASD as revealed by histochemical, autoradiographic, and biochemical studies (Blatt & Fatemi, 2011). One of the earliest reports of the use of a benzodiazepine in ASD was that of Marrosu, Marrosu, Rachel, and Biggio (1987), who shared their experience with the open-label administration of a single 10-mg intramuscular dose of diazepam to two girls and five boys, all of whom had what were characterized as paradoxical behavioral responses. Specifically, these children became more anxious and dramatically more aggressive after treatment. Kalachnik, Hanzel, Sevenich, and Harder (2003) used a case study to highlight the risks of behavioral worsening associated with clonazepam including agitation, aggression, hyperactivity, irritability, property destruction, and temper tantrums.

Comparing the effectiveness of oral diazepam and midazolam in sedating patients with ASD for dental treatment, Pisalchaiyong, Trairatvorakul, Jirakijja, and Yuktarnonda (2005) used a cross-over design to study 13 subjects aged 5.8 to 14.7 years. Midazolam was found to be significantly more effective than diazepam for sleeping behavior. For movement and crying behaviors, midazolam also proved to be significantly more effective from the start of treatment through the 35- and 40-minute markers. For the remainder of the dental procedure, there was no statistically significant difference in these behaviors between the two drugs, and both diazepam and midazolam were deemed to be effective sedative agents for dental treatment in ASD.

Although epidemiological data indicate that the use of benzodiazepines is at least as likely in individuals with ASD as for the general population (Axmon, Kristensson, Ahlström, & Midlöv, 2017; House et al., 2016; Maddox, Kang-Yi, Brodkin, & Mandell, 2018), the literature is virtually silent with regard to evidence to support ongoing treatment with particular benzodiazepines. Clinicians continue to be generally wary of the risk of paradoxical behavioral responses associated with these drugs in ASD. Such paradoxical responses can present as disinhibition or behavioral activation and essentially result in an increase in frequency or severity of pre-existing problems like aggression or self-injury. Although the anticonvulsant phenobarbital is seldom used any longer because of the introduction of newer and more effective drugs, its mechanism of action is similar to that of the benzodiazepines and it was notorious for increasing hyperactivity, impulsivity, and aggression in some individuals with developmental disorders (Alvarez, 1998).

Arbaclofen

Arbaclofen is the active isomer of baclofen, a GABA-B agonist with downstream effects on glutamatergic function (Henderson et al., 2012; Qin et al., 2015). Arbaclofen has been explored as a treatment for irritability but with inconsistent findings. One open-label study reported significant improvement on irritability ratings (Erickson et al., 2014), but two controlled trials detected no change on irritability ratings relative to placebo (Berry-Kravis et al., 2012; Veenstra-VanderWeele et al., 2016).

N-acetylcysteine

The N-acetyl derivative of L-cysteine, N-acetylcysteine (NAC), is widely used in the treatment of acetaminophen overdose, as a mucolytic in chronic obstructive pulmonary disease, and as a renal protectant in contrast-induced nephropathy (Deepmala et al., 2015). In the brain, NAC impacts regulation of extracellular glutamate levels (Wink et al., 2016). Hardan and colleagues (2012) conducted a 12-week, double-blind, randomized, placebo-controlled study of NAC in 33 children with ASD aged 3.2 to 10.7 years. Subjects randomized to NAC were started at 900 mg daily for 4 weeks, then titrated up to 900 mg three times daily for 4 weeks. Oral NAC was well tolerated with limited side effects. Compared with placebo, NAC resulted in significant improvements on the primary outcome of ABC irritability even though overall scores were relatively low for these subjects at baseline. Though not the primary outcome, neither Wink and colleagues (2016) nor Dean and colleagues (2017) found any difference between active drug and placebo on any measure of irritability in their RCTs of NAC.

Adrenergic drugs

Sagar-Ouriaghli, Lievesley, and Santosh (2018) reviewed evidence for the use of propranolol for behavioral dysregulation symptoms consistent with the construct of irritability. Although a number of studies indicate that propranolol may hold promise, controlled trials are needed to confirm the efficacy of propranolol for emotional dysregulation and irritability in ASD.

Summary

There is good evidence that risperidone and aripiprazole are effective at treating irritability in ASD with moderate to large effect sizes. There is also consensus that their potential benefits should be weighed against the risk of side effects (Howes et al., 2018). Moreover, if an antipsychotic is started, specific treatment targets should be established and progress should be regularly assessed and balanced against side effects.

The British Association of Psychopharmacology (Howes et al., 2018) has also recommended periodic attempts to reduce the daily dosage and discontinue antipsychotic drugs to confirm the need for ongoing exposure. It is also important to keep in mind that obesity, hypertension, diabetes, and epilepsy co-occur in patients with ASD at a higher rate than in the general population. Before commencing treatment with an antipsychotic drug, it is therefore important to assess body weight, height, waist and hip circumference, nutritional state, any diet the patient is following, and the patient's level of physical activity. Additionally, blood pressure and heart rate should be measured and, in some cases, an electrocardiogram should be performed. Fasting blood glucose, glycosylated hemoglobin, lipid profile, and prolactin levels should also be recorded.

There are additional approaches that appear to hold some promise that impact glutamatergic systems directly or indirectly through GABAergic treatment. Although benzodiazepines are commonly used in ASD, there appears to be a risk for making irritability worse in some cases.

Anxiety, Depression, and Compulsive Behavior

SELECTIVE SEROTONIN REUPTAKE INHIBITORS AND BUSPIRONE

As highlighted earlier, selective serotonin reuptake inhibitors (SSRIs) are among the most commonly prescribed medications in ASD (see also Coury et al., 2012). Studies that have been conducted in this population have focused on repetitive behaviors, a core feature of ASD, based on similarities between repetitive behavior in ASDs and obsessive-compulsive disorder and the enduring and ongoing implication of serotonergic abnormalities in autism (Chugani et al., 2016; Montgomery et al., 2018).

A controlled trial with clomipramine, a serotonergic tricyclic antidepressant, found moderate benefit for anger and ritualized behaviors compared with the noradrenergic desipramine hydrochloride. Gordon, State, Nelson, Hamburger, and Rapoport (1993) enrolled 30 patients with ASD aged 6 to 23 years and reported that clomipramine reduced compulsive behavior. Both drugs reduced hyperactivity. But clomipramine was associated with prolongation of the QTc, severe tachycardia, and generalized convulsions. Moreover, a later study comparing clomipramine, haloperidol, and placebo in adults with ASD showed no difference between clomipramine and placebo and a high rate of adverse events. Subsequently, in a study of adults with ASD by McDougle and colleagues (1996), the SSRI fluvoxamine was superior to placebo for repetitive behavior, aggression, and social relatedness. On the other hand, in a placebo-controlled study of fluvoxamine in children, adverse events, including hyperactivity, insomnia, agitation, and aggression, occurred in 14 of 18 children, and only one of the 18 subjects demonstrated improvement (2000).

Although sertraline accounts for roughly 75% of all prescriptions for children and adolescents with ASD in Denmark (Rasmussen et al., 2018), there have been no controlled studies that have investigated the role of SSRIs in treating mood or anxiety disorders in children with ASD. Two larger controlled studies have reported no effect of citalopram and fluoxetine on repetitive behaviors (Hollander et al., 2005; King et al., 2009). Another randomized controlled study of fluoxetine involving 158 patients between the ages of 5 and 17 years was negative and is still yet to be published (EurekAlert, 2009). Importantly, in these trials, there was no suggestion of other potential benefit with respect to irritability, anxiety, or mood symptoms.

Chugani and colleagues (2016) enrolled 166 children ages 2 to 6 years in a study of relatively low doses of the serotonergic anxiolytic buspirone, targeting repetitive behaviors. Although the primary outcome was mixed, a secondary analysis including the outcome of a derived composite measure of anxiety, which included symptoms of anxiety but also measures of mood and affect regulation, suggested evidence for improvement at 2.5 mg of buspirone only. Importantly, the placebo group also showed significant improvement on this measure.

SUMMARY

SSRIs are widely used in ASD, but there are no studies that have focused specifically on the treatment of anxiety or depression as the primary outcome in this population. In light of this limited evidence, the British Association of Psychopharmacology recommends extrapolation from the general population, that is, cautiously following general guidelines for treating anxiety and obsessive-compulsive disorder when present in ASD (Baldwin et al., 2014; Howes et al., 2016). That said, because of the results from studies that have suggested increased sensitivity to side effects of SSRIs in children with ASD (King et al., 2009), it has also been recommend that SSRIs should be used in low doses and titrated up gradually and monitored carefully for side effects (Howes et al., 2016).

Sleep Disturbances and Insomnia

MELATONIN

Melatonin is an effective and well-tolerated treatment for insomnia in children with ASD. Rossignol and Frye (2011) performed a meta-analysis based on five controlled studies that supports the use of melatonin for disorders of sleep in ASD. Outcome measures include sleep latency, sleep duration, and awakenings. Melatonin significantly increases sleep duration with a mean increase of 73 minutes versus baseline and 44 minutes versus placebo. There is also a reduction in sleep onset latency, with a mean decrease of 66 minutes compared with 39 minutes for placebo. There do not appear to be consistent findings with respect to nighttime awakenings in children with ASD (Rossignol & Frye, 2011). Melatonin was not associated with any side effects of significance over periods of exposure up to over 4 years.

Another study by Gringras and colleagues (2010) reported a small increase in total sleep time by a mean of 22 minutes and an improvement in sleep onset with a mean improvement of 38 minutes, though morning wake times were also shifted earlier. Combining melatonin with cognitive behavioral therapy proved better than melatonin or behavioral therapy alone for symptoms of insomnia (Cortesi et al., 2012). Combination treatment for 12 weeks yielded a greater number of responders who reached clinically significant improvement, and there were fewer dropouts (Cortesi, Giannotti, Sebastiani, Panunzi, & Valente, 2012).

Recently, Mehrazad-Saber, Kheirouri, and Noorazar (2018) explored the effects of l-carnosine supplementation on sleep in children with ASD. A total of 43 autistic patients ages 4 to 16 years were randomized to either 500 mg of carnosine or placebo daily for 2 months. Sleep outcomes were captured with the Children's Sleep Habits Questionnaire. Carnosine was associated with significantly reduced sleep duration and improved parasomnias and reduced the total sleep disorders score by 7.59%. There was no benefit on severity of autism core symptoms as assessed by the Gilliam Autism Rating Scale.

Interestingly, there is some evidence to suggest that improvement in sleep may bring additional improvement with respect to other behavioral disturbances in children with ASD. In Malow and colleagues' (2012) open-label study of up to 6 mg of melatonin daily in children ages 3 to 10 years, statistically significant changes in symptoms of attention deficit/hyperactivity, withdrawal, affective problems, stereotyped behaviors, and compulsive behaviors were observed.

Future Directions

Medications are commonly used for co-occurring conditions in children, adolescents, and adults with ASD. Prescribing patterns are remarkably consistent in different countries, with an emphasis on medications targeting ADHD symptoms, irritability, mood and anxiety symptoms, and insomnia. Also consistent in the literature is the finding that individuals with ASD as a group respond less well to common pharmacologic interventions, and they are generally more likely to experience side effects. There is generally good evidence to support many of the commonly used medication strategies in ASD. But overall, even drugs that have gained FDA approval have relatively few studies, particularly to inform long-term treatment. In the future, advances in our understanding of the biological and physiological underpinnings of specific conditions associated with autism should better inform treatment selection.

In the interim, assessment strategies that better parse the heterogeneity of ASD at the point of entry into a clinical trial and that are adequately powered to ensure that responder subgroups will not be lost as wheat in the chaff will be critical. Given the myriad combination therapies in ASD, the ability to leverage large datasets and deploy "big data" strategies, in the service of identifying both therapeutic signals and side effects risks, will also be helpful. The placebo response rate in ASD is vexing from the clinical trials standpoint. It is not uncommon to see placebo response rates above 20% even in trials focused on treating significant behavioral disturbance. Known factors that seem to lower the likelihood of placebo response include higher severity of behaviors at baseline, higher overall symptom burden, and greater caregiver strain (King et al., 2013). But rather than focus on ways to mitigate or prevent placebo responses, the field should seek to understand the active ingredients and exploit those factors for clinical benefit. If children improve with clinical contact that is more frequent in the setting of a clinical trial than treatment as usual, the latter should change. Ultimately, improved understanding of the pathophysiology of ASD and related conditions will likely redefine the diagnostic boundaries around ASD and redefine best practice for pharmacotherapy.

References

Alvarez, N. (1998). Barbiturates in the treatment of epilepsy in people with intellectual disability. *Journal of Applied Research in Intellectual Disabilities*, 42(Suppl 1), 16–23.

Aman, M. G., Kasper, W., Manos, G., Mathew, S., Marcus, R., Owen, R., & Mankoski, R. (2010). Line-item analysis of the Aberrant Behavior Checklist: Results from two studies of aripiprazole in the treatment of irritability associated with autistic disorder. *Journal of Child and Adolescent Psychopharmacology, 20*(5), 415–422.

Aman, M. G., Singh, N. N., Stewart, A. W., & Field, C. J. (1985). The Aberrant Behavior Checklist: A behavior rating scale for the assessment of treatment effects. *American Journal of Mental Deficiency, 89*(5), 485–491.

American Psychiatric Association. (1980). *Diagnostic and statistical manual of mental disorders* (3rd ed., DSM-III). Washington, DC: Author.

Anagnostou, E. (2018). Clinical trials in autism spectrum disorder: Evidence, challenges and future directions. *Current Opinion in Neurology, 31*(2), 119–125.

Anderson, L. T., Campbell, M., Grega, D. M., et al. (1984). Haloperidol in the treatment of infantile autism: Effects on learning and behavioral symptoms. *American Journal of Psychiatry, 141*(10), 1195–1202.

Axmon, A., Kristensson, J., Ahlström, G., & Midlöv, P. (2017). Use of antipsychotics, benzodiazepine derivatives, and dementia medication among older people with intellectual disability and/or autism spectrum disorder and dementia. *Research in Developmental Disabilities, 62*, 50–57.

Bachmann, C. J., Manthey, T., Kamp-Becker, I., Glaeske, G., & Hoffmann, F. (2013). Psychopharmacological treatment in children and adolescents with autism spectrum disorders in Germany. *Research in Developmental Disabilities, 34*(9), 2551–2563.

Berry-Kravis, E. M., Hessl, D., Rathmell, B., Zarevics, P., Cherubini, M., Walton-Bowen, K., et al. (2012). Effects of STX209 (arbaclofen) on neurobehavioral function in children and adults with fragile X syndrome: A randomized, controlled, phase 2 trial. *Science Translational Medicine, 4*, 152ral27.

Biederman, J., Gao, H., Rogers, A. K., & Spencer, T. J. (2006). Comparison of parent and teacher reports of attention-deficit/hyperactivity disorder symptoms from two placebo-controlled studies of atomoxetine in children. *Biological Psychiatry, 60*, 1106–1110.

Blatt, G. J., & Fatemi, S. H. (2011). Alterations in GABAergic biomarkers in the autism brain: Research findings and clinical implications. *Anatomical Record (Hoboken), 294*(10), 1646–1652.

Campbell, M., Anderson, L. T., Meier, M., et al. (1978). A comparison of haloperidol and behavior therapy and their interaction in autistic children. *Journal of the American Academy of Child and Adolescent Psychiatry, 17*, 640–655.

Campbell, M., Armenteros, J., Malone, R. P., et al. (1997). Neuroleptic-related dyskinesias in autistic children: A prospective, longitudinal study. *Journal of the American Academy of Child and Adolescent Psychiatry, 36*(6), 835–843.

Chowdhury, M., Aman, M. G., Lecavalier, L., et al. (2016). Factor structure and psychometric properties of the revised Home Situations Questionnaire for autism spectrum disorder: The Home Situations Questionnaire-Autism Spectrum Disorder. *Autism, 20*(5), 528–537.

Chowdhury, M., Aman, M. G., Scahill, L., et al. (2010). The Home Situations Questionnaire-PDD version: Factor structure and psychometric properties. *Journal of Intellectual Disability Research, 54*, 281–291.

Chugani, D. C., Chugani, H. T., Wiznitzer, M., Parikh, S., Evans, P. A., Hansen, R. L., . . . Autism Center of Excellence Network. (2016). Efficacy of low-dose buspirone for restricted and repetitive behavior in young children with autism spectrum disorder: A randomized trial. *Journal of Pediatrics, 170*, 45–53.

Cortesi, F., Giannotti, F., Sebastiani, T., Panunzi, S., & Valente, D. (2012). Controlled-release melatonin, singly and combined with cognitive behavioural therapy, for persistent insomnia in children with autism spectrum disorders: A randomized placebo-controlled trial. *Journal of Sleep Research, 21*(6), 700–709.

Coury, D. L., Anagnostou, E., Manning-Courtney, P., Reynolds, A., Cole, L., McCoy, R., . . . Perrin, J. M. (2012). Use of psychotropic medication in children and adolescents with autism spectrum disorders. *Pediatrics, 130*(Suppl 2), S69–76.

Darville, H., Poulet, A., Rodet-Amsellem, F., Chatrousse, L., Pernelle, J., Boissart, C., . . . Benchoua, A. (2016). Human pluripotent stem cell-derived cortical neurons for high throughput medication screening in autism: A proof of concept study in SHANK3 haploinsufficiency syndrome. *EBioMedicine, 9*, 293–305.

Davico, C., Canavese, C., Vittorini, R., Gandione, M., & Vitiello, B. (2018). Anticonvulsants for psychiatric disorders in children and adolescents: A systematic review of their efficacy. *Frontiers in Psychiatry, 9*, 270.

Daviss, W. B., Barnett, E., Neubacher, K., & Drake, R. E. (2016). Use of antipsychotic medications for nonpsychotic children: Risks and implications for mental health services. *Psychiatric Services, 67*(3), 339–341.

De Hert, M., Dobbelaere, M., Sheridan, E. M., et al. (2011). Metabolic and endocrine adverse effects of second-generation antipsychotics in children and adolescents: A systematic review of randomized, placebo controlled trials and guidelines for clinical practice. *European Psychiatry, 26*, 144–158.

Dean, O. M., Gray, K. M., Villagonzalo, K. A., Dodd, S., Mohebbi, M., Vick, T., . . . Berk, M. (2017). A randomised, double blind, placebo-controlled trial of a fixed dose of N-acetyl cysteine in children with autistic disorder. *Australian and New Zealand Journal of Psychiatry, 51*(3), 241–249.

Deepmala, Slattery, J., Kumar, N., Delhey, L., Berk, M., Dean, O., et al. (2015). Clinical trials of N-acetylcysteine in psychiatry and neurology: A systematic review. *Neuroscience and Biobehavioral Reviews, 55*, 294–321.

Downs, J., Hotopf, M., Ford, T., Simonoff, E., Jackson, R. G., Shetty, H., . . . Hayes, R. D. (2016). Clinical predictors of antipsychotic use in children and adolescents with autism spectrum disorders: A historical open cohort study using electronic health records. *European Child and Adolescent Psychiatry, 25*(6), 649–658.

Downs, J., Lechler, S., Dean, H., et al. (2017). The association between co-morbid autism spectrum disorders and antipsychotic treatment failure in early-onset psychosis: A historical cohort study using electronic health records. *Journal of Clinical Psychology, 9*, 1233–1241. doi:10.4088/JCP.16m11422

Egger, J. I. M., Verhoeven, W. M. A., Groenendijk-Reijenga, R., & Kant, S. G. (2017). Phelan-McDermid syndrome due to SHANK3 mutation in an intellectually disabled adult male: Successful treatment with lithium. *BMJ Case Reports*.

Erickson, C. A., Veenstra-Vanderweele, J. M., Melmed, R. D., McCracken, J. T., Ginsberg, L. D., Sikich, L., et al. (2014). STX209 (arbaclofen) for autism spectrum disorders: An 8-week open-label study. *Journal of Autism and Developmental Disorders, 44*, 958–964.

EurekAlert. (2019). Autism Speaks reports Neuropharm's SOFIA results. Study of fluoxetine in autism. Retrieved from https://www.eurekalert.org/pub_releases/2009-02/as-asr021809.php

Flygare Wallén, E., Ljunggren, G., Carlsson, A. C., et al. (2018). High prevalence of diabetes mellitus, hypertension and obesity among persons with a recorded diagnosis of intellectual disability or autism spectrum disorder. *Journal of Applied Research in Intellectual Disabilities, 62*, 269–280.

Fung, L. K., Mahajan, R., Nozzolillo, A., Bernal, P., Krasner, A., Jo, B.,... Hardan, A. Y. (2016). Pharmacologic treatment of severe irritability and problem behaviors in autism: A systematic review and meta-analysis. *Pediatrics, 137*(Suppl 2), S124–135.

Geller, D., Donnelly, C., Lopez, F., et al. (2007). Atomoxetine treatment for pediatric patients with attention-deficit/hyperactivity disorder with comorbid anxiety disorder. *Journal of the American Academy of Child and Adolescent Psychiatry, 46*, 1119–1127.

Goel, R., Hong, J. S., Findling, R. L., & Ji, N. Y. (2018). An update on pharmacotherapy of autism spectrum disorder in children and adolescents. *International Review of Psychiatry, 30*(1), 78–95.

Gordon, C. T., State, R. C., Nelson, J. E., Hamburger, S. D., & Rapoport, J. L. (1993). A double-blind comparison of clomipramine, desipramine, and placebo in the treatment of autistic disorder. *Archives of General Psychiatry, 50*(6), 441–447.

Gringras, P., Gamble, C., Jones, A., et al. (2012). Melatonin for sleep problems in children with neurodevelopmental disorders: Randomised double masked placebo controlled trial. *BMJ, 345*, e6664.

Gualtieri, C. T., & Hawk, B. (1980). Tardive dyskinesia and other drug-induced movement disorders among handicapped children and youth. *Applied Research in Mental Retardation, 1*(1–2), 55–69.

Guy, W. (1976). *ECDEU assessment manual for psychopharmacology: Publication ADM 76–338*. Washington, DC: U.S. Department of Health, Education, and Welfare.

Hagerman, R., Lauterborn, J., Au, J., & Berry-Kravis, E. (2012). Fragile X syndrome and targeted treatment trials. *Results and Problems in Cell Differentiation, 54*, 297–335.

Handen, B. L., Aman, M. G., Arnold, L. E., Hyman, S. L., Tumuluru, R. V., Lecavalier, L.,... Smith, T. (2015). Atomoxetine, parent training, and their combination in children with autism spectrum disorder and attention-deficit/hyperactivity disorder. *Journal of the American Academy of Child and Adolescent Psychiatry, 54*(11), 905–915.

Hardan, A. Y., Fung, L. K., Libove, R. A., et al. (2012). A randomized controlled pilot trial of oral N-acetylcysteine in children with autism. *Biological Psychiatry, 71*(11), 956–961.

Harfterkamp, M., Buitelaar, J. K., Minderaa, R. B., van de Loo-Neus, G., van der Gaag, R. J., & Hoekstra, P. J. (2013). Long-term treatment with atomoxetine for attention-deficit/hyperactivity disorder symptoms in children and adolescents with autism spectrum disorder: An open-label extension study. *Journal of Child and Adolescent Psychopharmacology, 23*(3), 194–199.

Harfterkamp, M., Buitelaar, J. K., Minderaa, R. B., van de Loo-Neus, G., van der Gaag, R. J., & Hoekstra, P. J. (2014). Atomoxetine in autism spectrum disorder: No effects on social functioning; some beneficial effects on stereotyped behaviors, inappropriate speech, and fear of change. *Journal of Child and Adolescent Psychopharmacology, 24*(9), 481–485.

Harfterkamp, M., van de Loo-Neus, G., Minderaa, R. B., et al. (2012). A randomized double-blind study of atomoxetine versus placebo for attention-deficit/hyperactivity disorder symptoms in children with autism spectrum disorder. *Journal of the American Academy of Child and Adolescent Psychiatry, 51*, 733–741.

Henderson, C., Wijetunge, L., Kinoshita, M. N., Shumway, M., Hammond, R. S., Postma, F. R., et al. (2012). Reversal of disease-related pathologies in the fragile X mouse model by selective activation of GABA(B) receptors with arbaclofen. *Science Translational Medicine, 4*, 152ra128.

Hirsch, L. E., & Pringsheim, T. (2016). Aripiprazole for autism spectrum disorders (ASD). *Cochrane Database System Reviews*, (6), CD009043.

Hollander, E., Chaplin, W., Soorya, L., et al. (2010). Divalproex sodium vs placebo for the treatment of irritability in children and adolescents with autism spectrum disorders. *Neuropsychopharmacology, 35*, 990–998.

Hollander, E., Phillips, A., Chaplin, W., Zagursky, K., Novotny, S., Wasserman, S., & Iyengar, R. (2005). A placebo controlled crossover trial of liquid fluoxetine on repetitive behaviors in childhood and adolescent autism. *Neuropsychopharmacology, 30*, 582–589.

Hollander, E., Wasserman, S., Swanson, E. N., Chaplin, W., Schapiro, M. L., Zagursky, K., & Novotny, S. (2006). A double-blind placebo-controlled pilot study of olanzapine in childhood/adolescent pervasive developmental disorder. *Journal of Child and Adolescent Psychopharmacology, 16*(5), 541–548.

Houghton, R., Liu, C., & Bolognani, F. (2018). Psychiatric comorbidities and psychotropic medication use in autism: A matched cohort study with ADHD and general population comparator groups in the United Kingdom. *Autism Research*. Advance online publication.

House, S. A., Goodman, D. C., Weinstein, S. J., Chang, C. H., Wasserman, J. R., & Morden, N. E. (2016). Prescription use among children with autism spectrum disorders in northern New England: Intensity and small area variation. *Journal of Pediatrics, 169*, 277–283.

Ireland, W. W. (1898). *Mental affections of children, idiocy, imbecility and insanity*. Oxford, UK: Churchill.

Jobski, K., Höfer, J., Hoffmann, F., & Bachmann, C. (2017). Use of psychotropic drugs in patients with autism spectrum disorders: A systematic review. *Acta Psychiatrica Scandinavica, 135*, 8–28.

Jokiranta, E., Sourander, A., Suominen, A., et al. (2014). Epilepsy among children and adolescents with autism spectrum disorders: A population-based study. *Journal of Autism and Developmental Disorders, 44*, 2547–2557.

Kalachnik, J. E., Hanzel, T. E., Sevenich, R., & Harder, S. R. (2003). Brief report: Clonazepam behavioral side effects with an individual with mental retardation. *Journal of Autism and Developmental Disorders, 33*(3), 349–354.

Kelsey, D. K., Sumner, C. R., Casat, C. D., Coury, D. L., Quintana, H., Saylor, K. E., ... Allen, A. J. (2004). Once-daily atomoxetine treatment for children with attention-deficit/hyperactivity disorder, including an assessment of evening and morning behavior: A double-blind, placebo-controlled trial. *Pediatrics, 114*(1), el–8.

King, B. H., Dukes, K., Donnelly, C. L., Sikich, L., McCracken, J. T., Scahill, L., ... Hirtz, D. (2013). Baseline factors predicting placebo response to treatment in children and adolescents with autism spectrum disorders: A multisite randomized clinical trial. *JAMA Pediatrics, 167*(11), 1045–1052.

King, B. H., Hollander, E., Sikich, L., McCracken, J. T., Scahill, L., Bregman, J. D., ... STAART Psychopharmacology Network. (2009). Lack of efficacy of citalopram in children with autism spectrum disorders and high levels of repetitive behavior: Citalopram ineffective in children with autism. *Archives of General Psychiatry, 66*(6), 583–590.

LeVann, L. J. (1961). Thioridazine (Mellaril): A psycho-sedative virtually free of side-effects. *Alberta Medical Bulletin, 26*, 144–147.

Loebel, A., Brams, M., Goldman, R. S., Silva, R., Hernandez, D., Deng, L., ... Findling, R. L. (2016). Lurasidone for the treatment of irritability associated with autistic disorder. *Journal of Autism and Developmental Disorders, 46*(4), 1153–1163.

Maddox, B. B., Kang-Yi, C. D., Brodkin, E. S., & Mandell, D. S. (2018). Treatment utilization by adults with autism and co-occurring anxiety or depression. *Research in Autism Spectrum Disorders, 51*, 32–37.

Malone, R. P., Gratz, S. S., Delaney, M. A., & Hyman, S. B. (2005). Advances in drug treatments for children and adolescents with autism and other pervasive developmental disorders. *CNS Drugs, 19*(11), 923–934.

Malow, B., Adkins, K. W., McGrew, S. G., Wang, L., Goldman, S. E., Fawkes, D., & Burnette, C. (2012). Melatonin for sleep in children with autism: A controlled trial examining dose, tolerability, and outcomes. *Journal of Autism and Developmental Disorders, 42*, 1729–1737.

Maneeton, N., Maneeton, B., & Putthisri, S. (2018). Risperidone for children and adolescents with autism spectrum disorder: A systematic review. *Neuropsychiatric Disease and Treatment, 14*, 1811–1820.

Marcus, R. N., Owen, R., Kamen, L., Manos, G., McQuade, R. D., ... Aman, M. G. (2009). A placebo-controlled, fixed-dose study of aripiprazole in children and adolescents with irritability associated with autistic disorder. *Journal of the American Academy of Child and Adolescent Psychiatry, 48*(11), 1110–1119.

Marrosu, F., Marrosu, G., Rachel, M. G., & Biggio, G. (1987). Paradoxical reactions elicited by diazepam in children with classic autism. *Functional Neurology, 2*(3), 355–361.

Matone, M., Localio, R., Huang, Y. S., dosReis, S., Feudtner, C., & Rubin, D. (2012). The relationship between mental health diagnosis and treatment with second-generation antipsychotics over time: A national study of U.S. Medicaid-enrolled children. *Health Services Research, 47*(5), 1836–1860.

Matson, J. L., & Mahan, S. (2010). Antipsychotic drug side effects for persons with intellectual disability. *Research in Developmental Disabilities, 31*(6), 1570–1576.

McDougle, C. J., Naylor, S. T., Cohen, D. J., Volkmar, F. R., Heninger, G. R., & Price, L. H. (1996). A double-blind, placebo-controlled study of fluvoxamine in adults with autistic disorder. *Archives of General Psychiatry, 53*(11), 1001–1008.

McDougle, C. J., Scahill, L., Aman, M. G., McCracken, J. T., Tierney, E., Davies, M., ... Vitiello, B. (2005). Risperidone for the core symptom domains of autism: Results from the RUPP Autism Network study. *American Journal of Psychiatry, 162*, 1142–1148.

Mechler, K., Häge, A., Schweinfurth, N., Glennon, J. C., Dijkhuizen, R. M., Murphy, D., ... Tactics Consortium T. (2018). Glutamatergic agents in the treatment of compulsivity and impulsivity in child and adolescent psychiatry: A systematic review of the literature. *Zeitschrift für Kinder- und Jugendpsychiatrie und Psychotherapie, 46*(3), 246–263.

Mehrazad-Saber, Z., Kheirouri, S., & Noorazar, S. G. (2018). Effects of l-carnosine supplementation on sleep disorders and disease severity in autistic children: A randomized, controlled clinical trial. *Basic and Clinical Pharmacology and Toxicology, 123*(1), 72–77.

Michelson, D., Allen, A. J., Busner, J., et al. (2002). Once-daily atomoxetine treatment for children and adolescents with attention deficit hyperactivity disorder: A randomized, placebo-controlled study. *American Journal of Psychiatry, 159*, 1896–1901.

Montgomery, A. K., Shuffrey, L. C., Guter, S. J., Anderson, G. M., Jacob, S., Mosconi, M. W., ... Veenstra-VanderWeele, J. (2018). Maternal serotonin levels are associated with cognitive ability and core symptoms in autism spectrum disorder. *Journal of the American Academy of Child and Adolescent Psychiatry, 57*(11), 867–875.

National Institute for Health Care and Excellence (NICE). (2012). *Autism: Recognition, referral, diagnosis and management of adults on the autism spectrum. Clinical Guideline no. 142.*

Olfson, M., King, M., & Schoenbaum, M. (2015). Treatment of young people with antipsychotic medications in the United States. *JAMA Psychiatry. 72*(9), 867–874.

Ormond, S., Brownlow, C., Garnett, M. S., et al. (2018). Profiling autism symptomatology: An exploration of the Q-ASC parental report scale in capturing sex differences in autism. *Journal of Autism and Developmental Disorders, 48*, 389–403.

Owen, R., Sikich, L., Marcus, R. N., Corey-Lisle, P., Manos, G., McQuade, R. D., ... Findling, R. L. (2009). Aripiprazole in the treatment of irritability in children and adolescents with autistic disorder. *Pediatrics, 124*(6), 1533–1540.

Owley, T., Walton, L., Salt, J., Guter, S. J., Jr., Winnega, M., Leventhal, B. L., & Cook, E. H., Jr. (2005). An open-label trial of escitalopram in pervasive developmental disorders. *Journal of the American Academy of Child and Adolescent Psychiatry, 44*(4), 343–348.

Pisalchaiyong, T., Trairatvorakul, C., Jirakijja, J., & Yuktarnonda, W. (2005). Comparison of the effectiveness of oral diazepam and midazolam for the sedation of autistic patients during dental treatment. *Pediatric Dentistry, 27*(3), 198–206.

Posey, D. J., & McDougle, C. J. (2000). The pharmacotherapy of target symptoms associated with autistic disorder and other pervasive developmental disorders. *Harvard Review of Psychiatry, 8*(2), 45–63.

Qin, M., Huang, T., Kader, M., Krych, L., Xia, Z., Burlin, T., ... Smith, C. B. (2015). R-baclofen reverses a social behavior deficit and elevated protein synthesis in a mouse model of fragile X syndrome. *International Journal of Neuropsychopharmacology, 18*(9).

Rasmussen, L., Bilenberg, N., Thomsen Ernst, M., Abitz Boysen, S., & Pottegård, A. (2018). Use of psychotropic drugs among children and adolescents with autism spectrum disorders in

Denmark: A nationwide drug utilization study. *Journal of Clinical Medicine, 7*(10).

Research Units on Pediatric Psychopharmacology (RUPP) Autism Network. (2002). Risperidone in children with autism and serious behavioral problems. *New England Journal of Medicine, 347*, 314–321.

Research Units on Pediatric Psychopharmacology (RUPP) Autism Network. (2005a). Randomized, controlled, crossover trial of methylphenidate in pervasive developmental disorders with hyperactivity. *Archives of General Psychiatry, 62*(11), 1266–1274.

Research Units on Pediatric Psychopharmacology (RUPP) Autism Network. (2005b). Risperidone treatment of autistic disorder: Longer term benefits and blinded discontinuation after six months. *American Journal of Psychiatry, 162*, 1361–1369.

Riddle, M. A., Bernstein, G. A., Cook, E. H., Leonard, H. L., March, J. S., & Swanson, J. M. (1999). Anxiolytics, adrenergic agents, and naltrexone. *Journal of the American Academy of Child and Adolescent Psychiatry, 38*(5), 546–556.

Rossignol, D. A., & Frye, R. E. (2011). Melatonin in autism spectrum disorders: A systematic review and meta-analysis. *Developmental Medicine and Child Neurology, 53*, 783–792.

Rynkiewicz, A., Lassalle, A., King, B., et al. (2018). Females and autism. In H. Montgomery (Ed.), *Oxford bibliographies in childhood studies*. New York, NY: Oxford University Press. https://www.oxfordbibliographies.com/view/document/obo-9780199791231/obo-9780199791231-0209.xml

Rynkiewicz, A., Schuller, B., Marchi, E., et al. (2016). An investigation of the "female camouflage effect" in autism using a computerized ADOS-2 and a test of sex/gender differences. *Molecular Autism, 7*, 10.

Sagar-Ouriaghli, I., Lievesley, K., & Santosh, P. J. (2018). Propranolol for treating emotional, behavioural, autonomic dysregulation in children and adolescents with autism spectrum disorders. *Journal of Psychopharmacology, 32*(6), 641–653.

Schneider, C., Taylor, D., Zalsman, G., Frangou, S., & Kyriakopoulos, M. (2014). Antipsychotics use in children and adolescents: An on-going challenge in clinical practice. *Journal of Psychopharmacology, 28*(7), 615–623.

Schwartz, S., & Correll, C. (2014). Efficacy and safety of atomoxetine in children and adolescents with attention deficit/hyperactivity disorder: Results from a comprehensive meta-analysis and metaregression. *Journal of the American Academy of Child and Adolescent Psychiatry, 53*, 174–187.

Sharma, A., & Shaw, S. (2012). Efficacy of risperidone in managing maladaptive behaviors for children with autistic spectrum disorder: A meta-analysis. *Journal of Pediatric Health Care, 26*(4), 291–299.

Smith, T., Aman, M. G., Arnold, L. E., Silverman, L. B., Lecavalier, L., Hollway, J., . . . Handen, B. L. (2016). Atomoxetine and parent training for children with autism and attention-deficit/hyperactivity disorder: A 24-week extension study. *Journal of the American Academy of Child and Adolescent Psychiatry, 55*(10), 868–876.

Sultan, R. S., Correll, C. U., Zohar, J., Zalsman, G., & Veenstra-VanderWeele, J. (2018). What's in a name? Moving to neuroscience-based nomenclature in pediatric psychopharmacology. *Journal of the American Academy of Child and Adolescent Psychiatry, 57*(10), 719–721.

Svanborg, P., Thernlund, G., Gustafsson, P. A., Hägglöf, B., Poole, L., & Kadesjö, B. (2009). Efficacy and safety of atomoxetine as add-on to psychoeducation in the treatment of attention deficit/hyperactivity disorder: A randomized, double-blind, placebo-controlled study in stimulant-naïve Swedish children and adolescents. *European Child and Adolescent Psychiatry, 18*, 240–249.

Wink, L. K., Adams, R., Wang, Z., Klaunig, J. E., Plawecki, M. H., Posey, D. J., McDougle, C. J., & Erickson, C. A. (2016). A randomized placebo-controlled pilot study of N-acetylcysteine in youth with autism spectrum disorder. *Molecular Autism, 7*, 26.

CHAPTER

20 A Model for Addressing Crisis Behavior in Youth With Autism Spectrum Disorder Within a Functional and Contextual Framework

Robin L. Gabriels *and* Julia Barnes

Abstract

This chapter provides a model that extends the current resources available for crisis behavior assessment and intervention for youth with autism spectrum disorder (ASD) and co-occurring psychiatric conditions who are in crisis stabilization settings. Visual diagrams and intervention materials incorporated into this chapter illustrate the use of both preventative and responsive behavior management strategies that can be implemented in a time of crisis to stabilize and treat the psychiatric patient with ASD. The chapter begins with a review of a contextual method for evaluating and understanding the function of the presenting crisis behavior by considering the multiple issues that can underlie the crisis presentation. Working from this contextual model, the chapter then provides a blueprint for implementing intervention strategies to address crisis behaviors. This includes a table illustrating key elements to consider when developing a behavior intervention plan for dissemination and generalization.

Keywords: psychiatric, behavioral crisis, autism spectrum disorder, interventions, hospitalization

Overview

Youth with autism spectrum disorder (ASD) and co-occurring psychiatric diagnoses present for treatment in psychiatric hospital settings at much higher rates than youth without ASD (e.g., Croen, Najjar, Ray, Lotspeich, & Bernal, 2006). Compared with the general population, individuals with ASD are also at high risk for having a range of, and sometimes multiple, coexisting psychiatric symptoms and disorders (Joshi et al., 2010; Leyfer et al., 2006; Salazar et al., 2015; Simonoff et al., 2008). Despite the high prevalence of co-occurring psychiatric conditions in youth with ASD, interventions targeting this psychiatric subpopulation have been understudied (Weitlauf et al., 2014). This is a concern because it is common for this population to engage in chronic problem behaviors that require high levels of intensive interventions including psychiatric hospitalization (Doehring, Reichow, Palka, Phillips, & Hagopian, 2014; Joshi et al., 2010; Siegel et al., 2012). Their hospital presentation of dangerous problem behavior and irritability (e.g., physical aggression, severe tantrums, self-injury; Pedersen et al., 2017) combined with the fact that youth with ASD tend to have difficulty self-reporting their internal experiences (Mazefsky, Kao, & Oswald, 2011) presents a complex situation for intensive services providers to disentangle to effectively address the crisis behaviors of youth with ASD.

This chapter extends the resources currently available in the literature by providing a model for addressing the presenting crisis behaviors of youth with ASD in psychiatric settings, particularly on an inpatient or partial hospitalization unit. This model was developed and implemented in a specialized psychiatric hospital unit in the southwestern region of the United States (Gabriels et al., 2012). A review of the literature reveals practice statements and training packages offering general evaluation and treatment guidance to ASD service providers

(Volkmar et al., 2014) as well as to psychiatric hospital service providers (McGuire et al., 2015; Kuriakose et al., 2018). There are also a multitude of well-documented and empirically supported preventative/antecedent interventions (see Smith, 2011, for a review) as well as responsive behavior management strategies for treating problem behaviors (see Fisher & Bouxsein, 2011; Lerman & Toole, 2011; and Vollmer & Athens, 2011, for reviews). However, this chapter will address *why* and *how* these strategies can be utilized in a time of crisis to stabilize and treat the psychiatric patient with ASD. First, this chapter will provide a contextual method for evaluating and understanding the function of the presenting crisis behavior by considering the multiple underlying issues (e.g., ASD features, psychiatric, family, developmental, life events). These issues have been metaphorically described as "driving" the "tip of the iceberg" (Cox & Schopler, 1993; Schopler, 1994) crisis presentation. Working from this contextual model, this chapter will then provide a blueprint for implementing intervention strategies (e.g., replacement behavior and skill training, graduated exposure and self-regulation/monitoring) to address crisis behavior presentations of psychiatric patients with ASD. This will include consideration of a dissemination and generalization plan for successful transition from the crisis stabilization environment back to the natural community environment.

Psychiatric Prevalence and Crisis Behavior Presentation in ASD

Psychiatrically related health care utilization in children and adolescents with ASD is a common occurrence. A large cross-sectional study of pediatric patients in an integrated managed care consortium located in Northern California (Croen et al., 2006) compared patients diagnosed with ASD to those without ASD and revealed that the ASD population had significantly more outpatient psychiatric clinic visits and inpatient psychiatric hospitalizations. For the subset that also had psychiatric diagnoses, the ASD population had significantly more psychotherapeutic medication prescriptions (Croen et al., 2006). A 1994-to-1999 comparison study of Medicaid expenditures in a large Pennsylvania county survey of Medicaid-eligible pediatric patients with and without ASD revealed that this ASD population had nine times more total expenditures and that inpatient psychiatric hospitalization accounted for many of these expenses (Mandell, Cao, Ittenbach, & Pinto-Martin, 2006). Additionally, the ASD patients in this sample had considerably more psychiatric diagnoses (i.e., attention deficit, oppositional defiant, conduct, and mood disorders Mandell et al., 2006). In a different study, Mandell (2008) examined factors that increase risk for psychiatric hospitalization in a sample of youth with ASD, which included those in single-parent families, diagnosed with ASD at a later age, who engage in self-injurious behaviors (SIBs) or aggression, diagnosed with depression or obsessive-compulsive behaviors, or who take psychiatric medications. Examination of the pattern of hospitalization usage between 1999 and 2009 in a pediatric sample of those diagnosed with ASD revealed that the ASD group had a steady rise in hospitalizations, particularly for psychiatric symptoms, with the largest increase in the 10- to 14- and 15- to 18-year-old age groups (Nayfack et al., 2014). A more recent (2009–2010) health care usage study of a large sample including youth with and without ASD (ages 3 to 17 years) from several health care systems indicated more health care usage, including hospitalizations, in the ASD group, and this appeared to be related to the higher rates of psychiatric conditions in this group (Cummings et al., 2016). Given such findings, there appears to be a high need for psychiatric hospital services in ASD youth.

Specialized psychiatric units for individuals with developmental disabilities (DDs) including ASD are becoming more available in the United States (Siegel et al., 2012) and in other parts of the world such as Paris, France (Guinchat et al., 2015). A 2012 survey of nine of these specialized units in the United States indicated long lengths of hospital stay (42.3 days; range 12 to 135 days) and a patient demographic makeup of individuals ages 4 to 21 years with a high percentage of patients diagnosed as having ASD (range 62% to 87%; Siegel et al., 2012). A retrospective study of psychiatrically hospitalized youth with DDs admitted to a general psychiatric unit compared to those admitted to a newly developed DD specialty unit revealed improved outcomes of readmission rate reductions (33.3% general unit vs. 11.5% DD unit) and reductions in average length of stay (45 days general unit vs. 26 days DD unit; Gabriels et al., 2012). A prospective outcome study of another DD specialty unit revealed significant reductions in patients' irritability behaviors (e.g., aggression, tantrums, and SIBs) from admission to discharge, with patients maintaining more lasting reductions in symptoms of irritability outcomes 2 months post discharge if their caregivers practiced implementing a behavior plan during the hospitalization (Siegel et al., 2014). A multisite prospective study of ASD youth admitted to six DD specialty psychiatric units demonstrated significant declines of patients' irritability behaviors from hospital admission to discharge (Pedersen et al., 2017). The preliminary evidence for positive effects of DD specialized units suggests that these types of units may be optimally equipped to meet the particular psychiatric crisis care needs of youth with ASD.

The unique demographic profile of psychiatrically hospitalized youth with ASD has begun to be illuminated by a multisite investigation of DD specialized units in the United States, the Autism Inpatient Collection (AIC; Siegel et al., 2015). In March 2014, the AIC began recruiting youth (ages 4 to 20 years) diagnosed with ASD and admitted to six DD specialized psychiatric units. Preliminary results of the initial 147 enrolled participants revealed that 42.6% also had an intellectual disability, 52.4% either had no language or were minimally verbal, 71.9% had low adaptive functioning levels, and 85.4% exceeded clinical thresholds for irritability behaviors (Siegel et al., 2015). In addition to the developmentally impaired nature of this ASD psychiatric population, several follow-up studies from this growing multisite study sample bring to light additional considerations for their crisis management. In an AIC cohort of 346 participants, there was an association found in ASD participants having poorer adaptive/coping skills (i.e., less flexibility) and more severe problem behaviors (i.e., SIBs, stereotypy, externalizing behaviors, and irritability), even when accounting for age and nonverbal intelligence (Williams, Siegel, & Mazefsky, 2017). In that same AIC cohort (n = 346), those ASD patients' who were verbally fluent displayed more irritability and externalizing behaviors compared to the minimally verbal cohort (Williams et al., 2017). In a study of 302 participants from the AIC cohort, 74% of caregivers said participants engaged in SIBs prior to their hospital admission, but only 25% of those continued to exhibit SIBs on a daily basis during their hospital course (Handen et al., 2018). Participants who had more impaired social and communication skills and low nonverbal intelligence quotients (i.e., below 72) were more likely to continue engaging in SIBs in the hospital setting, and the two most common types of participants' SIBs described by caregivers in this sample were hitting self with own body part or with an object (Handen et al., 2018). In a verbally fluent cohort (n = 107; mean age = 13.86; standard deviation [SD] = 2.26) of the AIC sample, 22% of these participants, including those with nonverbal intelligence quotients in the mild intellectual disability range, talked about death or suicide and this talk lasted over several days per caregiver report (Horowitz et al., 2017). Finally, caregivers reported that 72% of participants in the AIC cohort (n = 350) experienced some type of abuse , (physical, emotional, or sexual) and more caregiver-reported trauma-related symptoms (e.g., thought intrusion, interest loss, distressing memories, irritability, and inactivity) in this abuse subgroup compared to the no abuse subgroup (Brenner, Pan, Mazefsky, Smith, & Gabriels, 2017). These findings reflect that regardless of verbal or cognitive abilities, there are a wide range of issues that warrant consideration to accurately assess the etiologies underlying the presenting psychiatric crisis behaviors of youth with ASD.

Rationale for Using a Functional and Contextual Model to Address Crisis Behaviors in Youth With ASD

At the heart of our proposed functional and contextual framework for addressing crisis behavior in ASD youth is consideration of both the environmental conditions and individual variables that may affect and maintain the presenting behavior of concern. Myriad variables both within the individual (e.g., physiological states, psychological states, communicative and cognitive functioning) and external to the individual (e.g., caregiving relationships, virtual environments, presence of trauma cues) can impact the conceptualization of crisis behavior presentation.

The process of developing a well-integrated conceptualization of crisis behavior involves several phases of information gathering and refined understanding. Often an initial step in this process is to broadly understand "function of behavior" or "behavioral function," which may be particularly due to the influential and growing body of evidence supporting the use of applied behavior analytic methods for assessing and treating individuals with ASD (National Autism Center, 2015). This is especially evident in U.S. public school systems, in which special education teams are required to complete functional behavioral assessments (FBAs) to inform the development of behavior intervention plans that target problem behaviors impeding a student's access to his or her educational curriculum (for additional information on the Individuals With Disabilities Education Act [IDEA] 2004 and special education laws regarding FBAs in schools see Wright & Wright, 2006, as well as http://www.wrightslaw.com). Many crisis situations also require initial understanding of behavioral function, which is refined by gaining a thorough understanding of contextual variables. This section demonstrates this process by reviewing various aspects of completing an FBA within a crisis assessment context.

In general, the function of a behavior is the *purpose* or *role* the behavior serves for the individual in achieving a certain end goal within his or her environment. Generally speaking, this refers to the individual's drive to access or to escape from something (see Cipani & Schock, 2011, pp. 81–132, for details on a function-based diagnostic classification system). In other words, when caregivers, educators, or therapists ask, "*Why* does he or she do X?", they are typically referring to *function*. When referencing the problematic behaviors observed in ASD youth presenting with a psychiatric behavior crisis, this "why" question can take several forms. For example, "Why do they melt down/shut down/run away/become inconsolable/fight/engage in self-harm behavior/talk about death/talk about harming themselves/threaten to harm others, etc.?" or "Why can't they manage frustrations/cope with anxiety/get along with others, etc.?" Depending on the setting or primary theoretical orientation of the evaluator, answers can range from citing specific psychiatric conditions (e.g., "Because she has an anxiety disorder and schoolwork makes her anxious") to descriptions of behavior–environment interactions (e.g., "She is avoiding an aversive task demand"). However, without important context, none of these explanations are necessarily accurate or comprehensive enough to capture the complexity of the circumstances leading to a psychiatric crisis evaluation. Thus, a critical first step is to gather relevant information and develop initial hypotheses to answer this prominent "why" question. Hypotheses generated from this first step help focus and accurately target the subsequent assessment and intervention process. Consider this brief example for the purposes of illustration:

A youth with ASD presents to an emergency department for a crisis evaluation after having engaged in several acts of physical aggression at school targeting his teacher and other classroom staff. Upon initial interview, it becomes clear that the typical setting in which aggressive behaviors occur is at school, usually in the midmorning, and that the behavior has been occurring at an increasing rate for the past 6 weeks. The typical proximal antecedent is a teacher directive to complete some type of reading task in a group setting and the typical consequence for this youth's aggressive behaviors is that school personnel either sends the youth to a quiet, "demand-free" setting in the school for the duration of the reading group or sends the youth home for the rest of the day.

Considering the patterns described in the previous example, perhaps socially mediated negative reinforcement ("escape") is the most appropriate hypothesis regarding behavioral function. However, more information is necessary to develop a comprehensive behavioral hypothesis for assessment and treatment. For example, the patterns described should also lead to an important sequence of follow-up questions, such as some of the following:

- How long has this youth displayed this behavior at school in response to presentation of reading work or to more general academic demands?
- Is reading instruction aversive to the child and, if so, does the child have prerequisite skills to promote engagement and understanding of the reading tasks?
- Is there something about the setting (e.g., people, sensory factors, seating arrangements) that is difficult for the child to tolerate? For example, can the individual access materials needed for participation in the group and can he hear and see adequately?
- Is there something about the time of day and/or physiological/medical considerations (e.g., medication effects, sleep patterns, or hunger) that make attending to a classroom demand more difficult?
- What are the characteristics of the alternative environments that the child accesses when consequences are employed for aggressive behaviors that may make them more appealing than the classroom environment (e.g., is the principal's office or home a quieter or more calming place to be)?
- Have there been any changes in the youth's caregiver environment (separation, divorce, military deployment, etc.) that coincide with the onset or increase in rate of the aggression?

This series of questions illuminates the importance of not only considering and addressing behavioral crises from a functional perspective (e.g., change, reduce, or eliminate this escape behavior in the presence of task demands through escape extinction protocols) but also fully understanding the context so that a holistic set of interventions is developed to improve the functioning and even the quality of life for the individual.

Schopler (1994) advocated for understanding underlying skill deficits and other characteristics of individuals with ASD when evaluating their presenting crisis behavior presentation or "tip of the iceberg" behavior. This analogy has remained popular among practitioners treating this population. A good example of this is The Ziggurat Model by Aspy and Grossman (2007). This approach is also consistent with the increasingly influential field of contextual psychology, defined as

> the study of organisms (both human and nonhuman) interacting in and with a historical and current situational context. It is an approach based on contextualism, a philosophy in which any event is interpreted as an ongoing act inseparable from its current and historical context and in which a radically functional approach to truth and meaning is adopted.

The sections that follow aim to offer guidelines for using a comprehensive approach to managing crisis behaviors of youth with ASD, an approach that is routed in a holistic understanding of how crises develop and are maintained within each individual's unique context.

Functional and Contextual Methods for Stabilization, Assessment, Engagement, and Generalization

The following section provides a general organization for addressing crisis behaviors. Although these are organized in a stepwise fashion, it is important to note that the stabilization and assessment phases occur in tandem and throughout the engagement phase to identify treatment approach modifications that match the dynamic crisis behavior presentations of youth with ASD. Figure 20.1 presents a holistic visual framework for understanding this functional and contextual model and highlights the pivotal role of prospectively and thoroughly examining the contexts of the individual's crisis behavior presentation to formulate a well-informed behavior intervention plan. The absence of taking such a holistic, comprehensive view of a youth's problem behavior can result when there is a nonintegrated group of care providers for youth with ASD (i.e., school teams, applied behavioral analysis [ABA] teams, speech therapists, occupational therapists, family therapists, mental health providers, and various medical providers). Without deliberate efforts to coordinate care, each discipline may operate with a narrow focus, strengthening one particular set of skills or reducing one area of problematic/deficient functioning through various concurrent types and schedules of reinforcement, punishment, and/or extinction procedures. However, attempts to change behavior, in any direction, without a clear understanding of the interplay of all of the contextual variables (e.g., sensory aversions and self-regulation needs; medical/physical aspects of an individual's internal state; individual's communication, cognitive, and social skill level; and the influence of family/community/virtual environments) can lead to selection and use of inappropriate, futile, and/or sometimes countertherapeutic methods. Thus, although many practitioners may consider the work they do to be informed by contextual variables, this is often not the case clinically, or if it is, contexts (e.g., potential pain, possible seizures, psychiatric disturbance, disrupted or abusive relationships at home or school) are considered *only after* a period of treatment failure, lack of progress, or negative reactions to inappropriate intervention methods. The goal of presenting this model is to encourage practitioners who treat youth with ASD presenting with co-occurring psychiatric concerns to consider the complex set of influential contextual variables when understanding performance deficits and other problematic behavior, *even when doing so requires extra time and effort to consider perspectives and information from other disciplines.* Multidisciplinary team assessment, conceptualization, and intervention are essential elements to quality care for this uniquely complex population of youth, as well as for crisis prevention. It is recommended that the effectiveness of such a multidisciplinary team relies on the establishment of respect and understanding among providers to delineate roles and responsibilities to address the issues underlying the crisis behavior presentation (Mohr & Davis, 2004; Thurecht & Davis, 2001).

Phase I: Stabilization

Creating an environment that allows ASD youth presenting with a behavioral crisis to achieve physical safety and regulation, basic psychological comfort, and a sense of familiarity is a critical consideration for all environments that interface with this population. Stabilization is necessary to help manage the extraneous and potentially dysregulating variables inherent in unfamiliar settings (e.g., an emergency department, crisis center, or inpatient hospital unit) for youth with ASD. In essence, creating a stabilizing environment in which youth can be evaluated reduces the "noise" in the already complex body of data to be collected through the subsequent phases of assessment and treatment.

Environmental structure, particularly within psychiatric hospital settings, is an essential primary

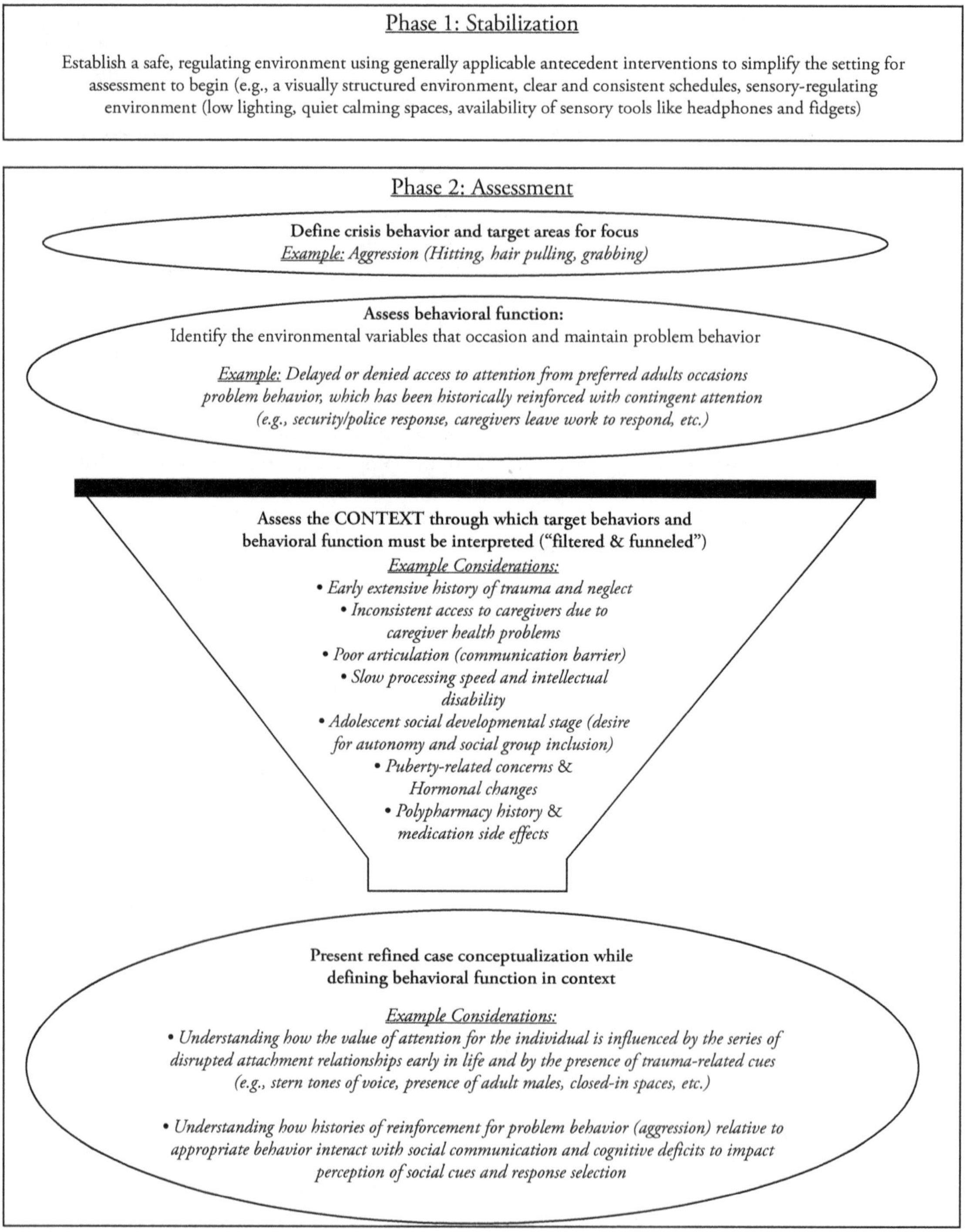

Figure 20.1. A functional and contextual framework for addressing crisis behavior.

consideration for stabilizing/regulating the ASD patient both at the start and throughout his or her treatment. Such environmental structure provides both verbal and minimally verbal ASD youth with a concrete means to understand and functionally communicate within an unfamiliar environment. This is important because a psychiatric hospital unit can bombard patients with novel faces, demands, and sensory stimuli that can further agitate ASD youth, given their diagnostic and developmental needs (e.g., Siegel & Gabriels, 2014; Thunberg, Buchholz, & Nilsson, 2016). Changes in youth's

Phase 3: Engagement

Determine appropriate goals for treatment

Examples:

- *Decrease aggression*
- *Increase safe, communicative requests for attention (including need for help, support, etc.)*
- *Increase prosocial/relationship-building behavior*

Select appropriate PROACTIVE behavior management interventions:

Examples:

- *Visual cues provided to:*
  - *define availability of attention (green card) vs no attention (red card)*
  - *track the length of no-attention periods (e.g., timer)*
  - *prompt use of "more time" request routine to ease transitions away from preferred activities*
  - *increase predictability of schedules and access to preferred activities (e.g., daily "I am working for" schedule)*
- *Frequent positive praise delivered for appropriate social behaviors (differential reinforcement of alternative behavior [DRA])*
- *Preventative schedules of attention from preferred individuals*
- *Structure all activities with specific tasks (e.g., chores, play routines) and clear roles (e.g., staff helper); particularly less-structured independent leisure times*

- *Problem behavior is not reinforced with access to attention from most preferred adult staff; differential attention provided for demonstrating self-regulation and functional communication of needs*
- *Visual cues/supports provided early on in escalation cycle to give clear reminders on self-regulation strategies/routines and to reduce need for social prompting/attention immediately following problem behavior.*
- *Debriefing with visual roadmap following self-regulation routine and calm behavior allows for review of all aggressive incidents using visual roadmap to reflect consequences of behavior*
- *Careful development of crisis intervention plan that reduces risk of exposure to trauma cues (e.g., no physical restraint from males, no closed-door seclusions, etc.)*

Evaluate efficacy of interventions and refine core treatment package

Phase 4: Generalization

- **Caregiver Training** (Examples: Practice differential attention routines and crisis intervention plan)
- **Address environmental factors to reduce likelihood of crisis recurrence.** Examples:
  - Increasing availability of trained caregivers to provide preventative schedules of attention
  - Increasing salience of needed visual cues and making them consistent across the individual's natural environments
  - Increasing availability of independent leisure activities and supporting fluency with independent routines

Figure 20.1 Continued

level of cognitive orientation can also result from psychotropic medications used to provide initial relief from dangerous behaviors, making environmental structure critical to reduce confusion and further disorientation. Structure in relation to ASD interventions "generally describes the organization of time, space, and sequences of events within the environment in order to make learning activities clearer and easier to perform" (Mesibov & Shea, 2010, p. 572). There is empirical support for using environmental structure (e.g., visual cues, physical organization, routines) to decrease disruptive behaviors and increase activity engagement in youth with ASD in a variety of treatment settings (e.g., Davit, Hundley, Bacic, & Hanson, 2011; Kuriakose et al., 2018; O'Reilly, Sigafoos, Lancioni, Edrisinha, & Andrews, 2005; Odom et al., 2003; Rogers, 1999; Scattone, Wilczynski, Edwards, & Rabian, 2002).

The architectural design literature also discusses the importance of manipulating the physical/sensory environment to support the learning process for individuals with ASD (Forcier, 1999; Mostafa, 2008, 2014). There is preliminary clinical evidence for what has been termed sensory design theory such that its implementation improves attention and decreases self-stimulation behaviors in individuals with ASD who are more severely impaired or are beginning treatment (Mostafa, 2008). Sensory design theory involves providing areas for noise reduction, organizing spaces with visual cues (e.g., physical barriers and picture cues) and structure (e.g., designated locations) to coincide with the daily flow of routines, designating a neutral sensory "escape" space within the treatment environment (e.g., quiet area in and outside of the classroom areas), allocating distinct transition areas (e.g., area to check a main routine schedule), and attending to environmental safety (e.g., covering sharp edges; Mostafa, 2014).

The TEACCH (Treatment and Education of Autistic and Related Communication-Handicapped Children) approach is a long-standing (over 30 years) comprehensive example of a visually based program of methods for structuring intervention environments to best match the unique learning style needs and interests of individuals with ASD (Mesibov & Shea, 2010. The aims of this approach include the following: (a) improve an individual's understanding of expectations, (b) increase an individual's interest and engagement in learning new skills and adaptive alternative behaviors, and (c) increase self-supporting behaviors (Mesibov, Browder, & Kirkland, 2002; Mesibov & Shea, 2010). The TEACCH approach is part of a larger body of ASD behavioral intervention methods previously described in detail that have been termed "positive behavior supports" to prevent problem behaviors (Mesibov et al., 2002). Approaches such as TEACCH have particular relevance for youth diagnosed with ASD who present to a psychiatric hospital in a state of crisis because they are in need of expeditious stabilization methods that can effectively engage them in the assessment and treatment process.

The structured environmental routine aspects implemented on specialized inpatient and partial-hospitalization psychiatric units have multiple purposes for youth with ASD, including the following: (a) to expose the youth to familiar daily life routines; (b) to provide opportunities for behavioral exposures, challenges, and mastery; and (c) to facilitate the process of structured observation and assessment (Gabriels et al., 2012; Siegel & Gabriels, 2014). The following examples briefly describe structured unit milieu routines for consideration:

- **Daily living activity routines** provide visual cues for (a) facilitating youths' understanding of how to engage in a sequence of self-care or chore routine steps (e.g., sequenced picture cards), (b) helping youth order a well-balanced meal (e.g., color-coded food cards to match and complete a corresponding color-coded laminated paper meal "plate"), or (c) engaging youth in steps necessary to complete medical procedures, including physical exams, blood draws, or X-rays (e.g., Gabriels, Shah, Young, Gralla, & Goldson, 2018), which are critical to evaluate physiological factors that may be contributing to the crisis behavior presentation.
- **Individualized intervention routines and locations** provide visual cues to promote successful completion of a specific task demand, follow a daily schedule of activities, or learn a new skill. For example:
  - A "First Work, Then Play" schedule with two picture cues can provide a clear and focused rule that can efficiently motivate an agitated youth to complete a demand.
  - An extended (e.g., four -to five- step picture/ icon or written) schedule can motivate a youth throughout the day by clearly outlining the alternating (less preferred and preferred) timeline of daily activities.
  - A "More Time" visual routine card that contains two removable green "more time" cards can be used by the youth to request more time with a preferred activity (e.g., 1 minute per card). When all the green cards have been used (i.e., detached from the routine card), the remaining red card stating "all done" prompts the youth to transition. This particular routine has been clinically useful for youth with slower cognitive processing abilities who need a concrete routine to help ready themselves for a transition.
  - A "Diabetes Blood Sugar Chart" delineates high and low blood sugar numbers in red colored zones above and below the "target" green zone containing the acceptable blood sugar level corresponding with numbers. The routine involves a youth with diabetes placing a sticker on the zone that corresponds to the blood test results and then an adult can review possible symptoms for the corresponding blood sugar level zone with the youth. This routine can help youth with poor food selection or other problematic eating habits better understand adult-imposed restrictions on

their intake, which can often be "triggers" for problem behavior in the ASD population.

- **Leisure period/"choice time" routines** (e.g., toy play area, computers, art and game materials) can motivate patients throughout the day by making leisure choice times contingent on first completing an adult-directed demand/ activity and then allowing the youth to engage in a highly preferred interest activity. Choice boards containing various adult-controlled options through different periods in the day can also help youth make varied leisure choice activities throughout the day, which promotes flexibility (e.g., tolerating when a toy/ activity is not available, occupied by someone else).
- **Self-regulation routines** target youths' (a) understanding of emotions, triggers, warning signs, and use of coping skills (e.g., Gabriels & Gaffey, 2012; Kuypers, 2011) and (b) ability to manage social situations (e.g., Thompson & Johnston, 2013). Such routines can include designating quiet area locations that contain self-regulation materials (e.g., fidgets and headphones) and involve specific routines for their use, such as a quiet area request routine (e.g., "I need a break" card) and a check-out routine (e.g., "How to show I am calm"/"How I can get calm" picture sequence).
- **Social and leisure group routines** provide the following:
  - Targeted instructions for self-regulation and coping skills (e.g., via creative arts, occupational, and speech therapies).
  - Visual group schedule cues (e.g., pictures or containers with materials) to clarify social guidelines and what/how much is to be completed in the group
  - Group leader assistant roles and responsibilities illustrated by visual instruction cues (e.g., laminated group helper instructions) for the group leader assistant to check off after each step is complete
  - Visual cues for monitoring group or individual behavior reinforcement contingencies (e.g., token boards for tracking engagement in target behaviors (e.g., "safe body") and progress toward earning an individual or group reward)
  - Group routines that include a beginning (introduction), middle (themed activity), and end (wrap-up routine)
- **Transition areas and schedule routines** include visually defined transition areas for patients to line up before moving on to the next activity and to reference a "master" schedule that lays out the progression of activities for the day. Individualized transportable daily schedules matched to the learning abilities and needs of each patient (e.g., object, picture, word schedules, or combination) are necessary to help patients make successful transitions and follow a sequence of steps without excessive need for adult prompting (Hume, 2009; Mesibov et al., 2002).

Phase II: Assessment

Careful assessment and case conceptualization are paramount to working with ASD youth and families who are in the midst of dealing with behavioral crises. This is a critical step to create order in the midst of seeming chaos for fatigued caregivers of youth with ASD, who have often spent days to weeks or even months trying to manage the oftentimes dangerous behavior of a youth with ASD prior to presenting for a crisis evaluation. The crisis assessment process may be their first opportunity to pause and critically evaluate what has been going on for them and for their child. An essential part of assessment, case conceptualization and eventually successful intervention of the presenting crisis behavior in youth with ASD routinely requires a multidisciplinary treatment team. For youth in crisis settings, particularly hospitals, involvement from psychologists, psychiatrists, social workers, behavior analysts, occupational therapists, speech–language pathologists, mental health aides, nurses, and a multitude of specialists (e.g., teams from neurology, gastroenterology, and dentistry) are often warranted given the complexity of ASD youth with co-occurring psychiatric and medical concerns.

INDIRECT ASSESSMENTS

Following the process of stabilization, often first achieved partially through the process of transitioning from an emergency/crisis setting to a specialized setting, the next step to manage a youth in a behavioral crisis is often to conduct indirect assessments that can inform an initial case conceptualization. Indirect assessment methods include caregiver surveys, rating scales, and interviews, as well as a review of previous assessments and treatment reports. For a further review of such methods, refer to Kelley, LaRue, Roane, and Gadaire (2011). These methods inform identification of specific target behaviors of concern, as well important details about where, when, and how often concerns are present.

Caregiver surveys should include gathering information about the adaptive strengths and needs of the youth with ASD. A study of caregivers' recommendations for specialized hospital care of their child or adult (ages 2 to 49 years) with ASD highlighted three areas for care providers to consider: (a) communication (e.g., specialized communication tools and techniques), (b) social engagement (e.g., hands-on/concrete-oriented interaction, self-regulation, and instruction materials), and (c) sensory (e.g., auditory, tactile, and oral sensory preferences; Kopecky, Broder-Fingert, Iannuzzi, and Connors, 2013). Several comprehensive surveys are available for use including the Parent/Guardian Survey (Kopecky et al., 2013), which surveys communication and social skills along with sensory issues, and the Child and Caregiver Information Form (Gabriels, 2007), which surveys medical, psychiatric, daily living, and academic issues, as well as previous intervention information. Along with these individually based surveys, normed rating scales of crisis symptom presentation can also be helpful. Measures such as the Aberrant Behavior Checklist – Community (ABC-C; Aman, Singh, Stewart, & Field, 1985), the Sensory Profile-2 (Dunn, 2014), and the Repetitive Behaviors Scales—Revised (Bodfish, Symons, & Lewis, 1999) can provide a norm-referenced picture of the severity of behavioral symptoms that may be pertinent to conceptualization of the crisis for which a youth with ASD is presenting.

Semistructured and structured interviews are also useful tools in surveying a multitude of factors related to problem behavior in youth, both with and without ASD. Because these tools focus on specific characteristics of behavior and environments, they are not syndrome or diagnosis specific. The Functional Assessment Interview (FAI; O'Neill, Horner, Albin, Sprague, Storey, & Newton, J.S., 1997) is one such tool that provides a guided approach to assessing the potential functions for maladaptive behavior. Although the level of detail gleaned from the FAI is certainly informative, the length of the interview may not always be feasible in the context of acute crisis stabilization and treatment. In contrast, the Iceberg Assessment Interview (IAI; Stark, Barnes, Young, & Gabriels, 2015) provides a relatively quick, well-rounded assessment within crisis settings using a one-page, visually organized guide to gather information about complex crisis behaviors (see Stark et al., 2015, for the IAI visual) and was developed within a specialty hospitalization unit (Gabriels et al., 2012). The format for structuring an IAI caregiver interview takes a functional and contextual framework for understanding presenting crisis behavior in youth with ASD. The top section of the IAI guides a broad assessment of the three-term antecedent–behavior–consequence contingencies that relate to the "tip of the iceberg" presenting problem behavior and provides a visual depiction for the caregiver of the possible functional patterns of a youth's presenting crisis behavior. The lower section of the IAI aids in gathering critical contextual information for developing an initial case conceptualization, including information about sensory preferences and self-regulation skills/behavior, developmental skills (cognitive, communication, social, adaptive daily living, and academic), medical and psychiatric history, and influential environments (i.e., virtual, home/caregiving environments). Although the IAI is a caregiver interview tool, the IAI can be used with verbally and cognitively able youth with ASD to facilitate self-report of preferences and concerns. For example, they can report their "triggers" (antecedents to their problem behavior), their experiences of psychiatric conditions like anxiety and depressive symptoms, sensory likes and dislikes, school and home concerns, internal states (e.g., hunger, pain, sleep quality), and experiences within any virtual environments/activities (e.g., amount of time spent engaging with electronics, favorite games/websites and content, online gaming communities or social media forums). The IAI can also be used in conjunction with other caregiver-report tools designed to quickly assess possible functional relations of problem behavior, such as the Functional Assessment Screening Tool (FAST; Iwata, Deleon, & Roscoe, 2013), Questions About Behavior Function (QABF; Matson & Vollmer, 1995), and Motivation Assessment Scale (MAS; Durand & Crimmins, 1988). The discussion that follows highlights several key issues to consider when using the IAI or other indirect assessment methods to determine relevant contextual issues underlying the crisis behavior. Considerations for assessing the additional contextual sections of the IAI not mentioned here are discussed in Stark et al. (2015).

Medical Issues Underlying Crisis Behavior Presentations

A crisis behavior presentation can represent an indirect communication of physical pain or discomfort by the youth with ASD. This is a critical initial consideration for youth with limited communication abilities; however, this is also a necessary consideration for more verbally able youth (van der Outten & Vlaskamp, 2011; Benini et al., 2004; Breau & Burkitt, 2009). For example, medical etiologies (e.g., seizures, dental problems, ear and bladder infections, gastrointestinal issues, constipation, and pain from self-induced or other injuries) were implicated as contributing to acute crisis behavior presentations (e.g., aggression and SIB) in 28% of a psychiatric hospital sample (n = 58) of adolescents with ASD (Guinchat et al., 2015). Of note, two thirds of this sample had minimal to no functional communication skills (Guinchat et al., 2015). SIBs may not only be the manifestation of an attempt to manage pain but also signal a medically related etiology as well as target the location of the pain (Breau & Burkitt, 2009; Siegel & Gabriels, 2014. Psychotropic medication polypharmacy is an important consideration when evaluating the possible underlying exacerbations of crisis behaviors in individuals with ASD and coexisting psychiatric diagnoses (e.g., Esbensen, Greenberg, Seltzer, & Aman, 2009; Logan et al., 2015). Side effects like constipation are sometimes linked to psychotropic medications, which may also help explain an increase in behavior problems such as SIBs and aggression in the ASD population (Christensen et al., 2009).

Use of Electronics/Video Games Underlying Crisis Behavior Presentations

Another potential factor associated with presenting crisis behavior in youth with ASD is their use of electronic media. Youth with ASD spend excessive amounts of their choice time with electronics when compared to non-ASD youth with DDs (Mazurek et al., 2012; Orsmond & Kuo, 2011; Shane & Albert, 2008) and typically developing youth (Paulus et al., 2019). Video gaming is a significant preoccupation for youth with ASD compared to their typically developing siblings (Mazurek & Wenstrup, 2012). A caregiver-report study of the video gaming patterns in a large sample (n = 169) of male youth ages 8 to 18 years revealed that a majority of this sample spent 2.4 hours per day engaged in video gaming and the most common gaming categories were action, platform, and shooter as defined by the Entertainment Software Rating Board website (http://www.esrb.org/index-js.jsp; Mazurek & Engelhardt, 2013). Addictive video gaming behaviors that included role-playing games significantly predicted engagement in oppositional behaviors (Mazurek & Engelhardt, 2013). A follow-up analysis of these data revealed that oppositional behaviors were even more likely when youth had access to electronics in their room and caregivers set no boundaries for the use of electronics (Engelhardt & Mazurek, 2014).

Finally, screening for the presence of suicidal ideation and related self-harm behavior is a critically important component of crisis assessment. Although there are no existing screening tools developed for or validated with the ASD population, screening for known demographic and psychological risk factors can be achieved by gathering information from multiple informants (e.g., youth and caregivers) and, when possible, using standardized screening measures administered by providers with expertise in ASD. Recent research has revealed that risk factors for suicidal ideation and attempts in the ASD population include being male, 10 years of age or older, and Black or Hispanic and having lower socioeconomic status (SES; Mayes, Gorman, Hillwig-Garcia, & Syed, 2013). Additionally, psychological symptoms associated with greater risk of suicidal ideation and attempts in this population include symptoms of depression, behavior problems, and a history of being teased by peers (Mayes et al., 2013). Of note, however, these results reflect caregiver ratings of youth behavior rather than youth self-reports of suicidal ideation. Screening tools that may be appropriate for directly surveying youth with ASD about their experiences related to thoughts of suicide include the Ask Suicide-Screening Questions (ASQ; Horowitz et al. 2012) and the Columbia-Suicide Severity Rating Scale (C-SSRS; Posner et al., 2011). Youth who are positively screened for suicide risk during a crisis assessment process should then undergo a more in-depth and ongoing safety assessment and safety planning as part of their transition of care through various phases of the crisis stabilization (e.g., from an emergency room assessment to inpatient or partial hospitalization, or from hospitalization to an outpatient level of care).

DIRECT ASSESSMENTS

Direct assessments can include naturalistic, semistructured, contrived, and experimental observations. Utilization of these methods is often dependent on a variety factors including patient safety, feasibility of contriving pertinent situations, availability of caregivers, and appropriately trained professionals to conduct experimental procedures. Often a first critical step in the crisis stabilization and assessment process is to assess preferences and potential reinforcers for youth with ASD. Guided by indirect survey information gleaned from caregivers or the youth him- or herself, a variety of assessment methodologies exist to assess relative preferences for various stimuli (food, toys, activities, etc.) that can be incorporated as potential reinforcers within the context of other direct assessments and treatment. Such methodologies include free operant observation and trial-based (single-, paired-, and multiple-stimulus presentation) methods (Cooper, Heron, & Heward, 2007, pp. 274–283). To directly assess the youth's crisis behavior, narrative recording (a form of collecting information about the antecedents, behaviors, and consequences) can be a relatively simple way to gather information about the youth's behavior in a variety of contexts. Assessment contexts can include structured demand contexts (e.g., groups or individual work periods) and unstructured leisure periods (e.g., meals, and caregiver/family interactions). For example, narrative recording could take place during a semistructured family meeting, like an interactive art activity (Gabriels & Gaffey, 2012), to assist in focused assessment of family interaction styles and dynamic roles as the family completes a given task. Narrative recording may be augmented by streamlined antecedent–behavior–consequence checklists, which may be a simpler and more structured method for helping direct care staff collect observations. Readers are directed to Thompson and Borrero (2011) and Cipani and Schock (2011, pp. 33–79) for additional information about direct assessment methods.

In certain contexts and under appropriate conditions, experimental analysis of problem behavior may also be appropriate to consider in assessing the crisis behavior of youth with ASD. Structural and functional analyses of problem behavior may be feasible to conduct, particularly in the context of a well-controlled and highly structured specialized setting for youth with ASD. These assessment methods involve analysis of problem behavior within tightly controlled, contrived situations and allow for assessment of the antecedent-behavior(s) or behavior-consequence relations of presenting crisis behavior. These methodologies and considerations for their use are discussed in Wacker, Berg, Harding, and Cooper-Brown (2011). Ethical and appropriate use of these methods involves supervision by a board-certified behavior analyst (BCBA) and a careful consideration of safety practices, particularly when addressing the often intense and dangerous behaviors displayed by ASD youth in crisis.

Phase III: Engagement

Goal setting is the primary objective of this phase. However, this can be a complicated process that requires a strategic approach to narrow the focus of caregivers' broad treatment goals noted by statements such as "Fix my child" or "Teach my child to have a happy life," which are goals influenced by feeling overwhelmed. An additional complication is having an effective strategy to communicate with ASD youth the "big picture" of their crisis behaviors and resulting outcomes to motivate them to identify and work on treatment goals.

It can be helpful to provide caregivers with a frame of reference to narrow down their goals for their child. Clinical observations of ASD youth presenting in a state of crisis to the psychiatric hospital setting (e.g., Gabriels et al., 2012) have resulted in a frame of reference for treatment targets that tend to cluster under the following categories:

1. **Poor self-regulation skills** indicated by the youth exhibiting dangerous behaviors to self and others
2. **Poor attending skills** indicated by the youth being unable to attend to adult-directed activities such as sitting or waiting for extended periods of time (e.g., for groups, car rides, schools, restaurants, and stores) without becoming aggressive
3. **Poor self-care/independent living skills** indicated by youth's refusal to engage in self-care routines (e.g., hygiene, feeding, dressing, planning, organization, time management) without becoming aggressive toward the caregiver
4. **Poor social interaction skills** indicated by the youth being unable to engage in social routines (e.g., turn-taking and sharing in a school group environment) in a safe manner

Goal setting with ASD youth requires a concrete visual approach that captures their interest, attention, and understanding, such as using a visual roadmap (Figure 20.2). This visual roadmap provides a "bird's-eye view" of the challenging situations that may emotionally trigger a youth with ASD to make unsafe behavior choices. The visual roadmap provides ASD youth with a visually organized way to consider both the undesired consequences of their actions and safer response/coping strategies to use to gain access to more desired outcomes. For example, using the visual roadmap can help youth with ASD see specific connections between their triggers/upsetting situations (e.g., a caregiver leaving, being told "no," having something taken away), their problematic/unsafe behavior (e.g., "hurting teacher"), and their experience of undesired outcomes (e.g., having to stay in the hospital setting or being away from home/caregivers). The visual roadmap outlines the alternative behavior targets/treatment goals that can lead to desired/motivating outcomes. The visual roadmap provides information in a manner that addresses the social cognition deficits (e.g., tendency

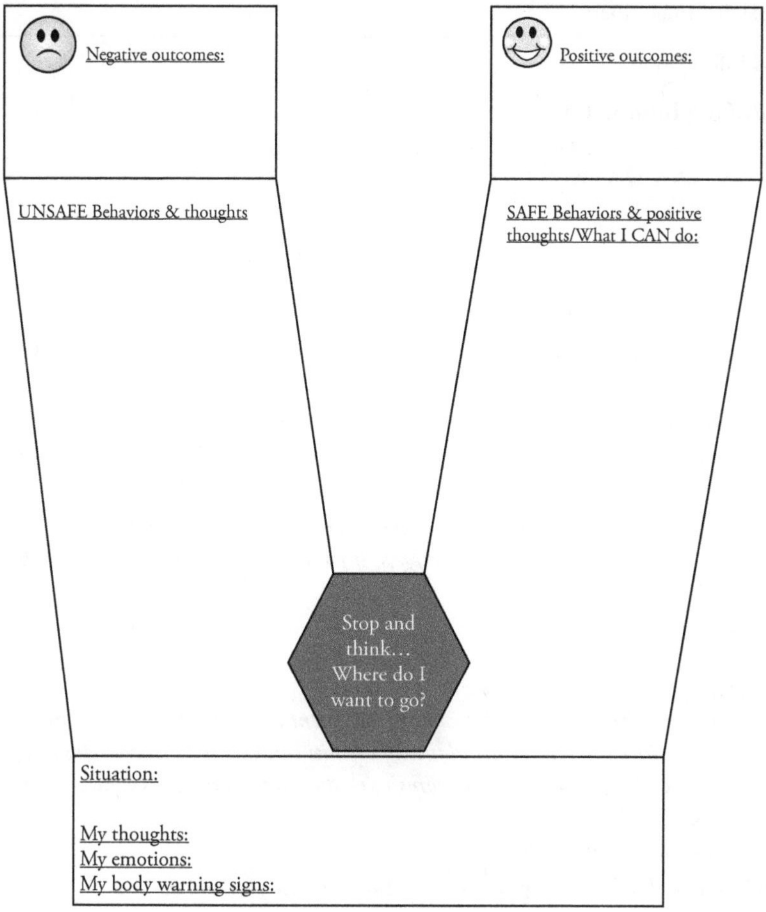

Figure 20.2. Visual problem-solving roadmap.

to inaccurately evaluate others' intentions) common in individuals with ASD (Baron-Cohen, Tager-Flusberg, & Cohen, 2000), skill deficits that can cause them to make incorrect assumptions about why others responded to them in a certain manner rather than recognizing their role/responsibility in the outcome they experienced. For example, the roadmap can include words and/or drawings/pictures in all sections to accommodate for varying communicative abilities. The roadmap visual has demonstrated clinical utility for youth with ASD and co-occurring psychiatric conditions and a variety of cognitive (i.e., mild to moderate intellectual disability) and ability levels (readers and nonreaders). Finally, the roadmap visual can be used throughout treatment to help youth with ASD to (a) reflect on the consequences of their unsafe behaviors in the moment and (b) generate safe alternative response strategies to be trialed immediately with staff support. For example, the roadmap can highlight/positively reinforce safe coping behaviors when debriefing a challenging situation (e.g., "In the past you have chosen this unsafe path of behavior for coping with that situation, but today you chose this other path and the outcome was better for you—do you see that?").

Treatment

The unique context of each patient's crisis behavior presentation requires careful development of a coordinated package of individualized proactive and responsive treatment strategies. Individualized strategies are documented in a set of detailed instructions in a behavior intervention plan to enhance consistency of treatment delivery across caregivers. Table 20.1 provides an outline of sections to consider when constructing an individualized intervention or treatment plan. Case conceptualization and determination of factors that are core to driving the function of problem behaviors are critical areas of focus for developing the plan. For example, if communication barriers are a core impairment for the youth, then focusing on developing communication systems in collaboration with a speech–language

Table 20.1. Sample Treatment Plan

Part I: Background Information

A. **Patient Identifying Information**
   i. Age
   ii. DSM-V Psychiatric Diagnoses
   iii. Medical Diagnosis
   iv. Psychosocial Factors

B. **Patient Strengths**
   i. Support from family/other caregivers
   ii. Communicative abilities and other skill areas of relative strength
   iii. Access to helping agencies

C. **Patient Preferences:** *As reported by caregivers and as observed through initial clinical observations*

D. **Preference Assessment Results:** *Results of free operant, paired-stimulus, or multiple stimulus preference assessments (list examples of high, moderate, and low preference items/activities)*

E. **Presenting Problem Behavior: Summarize presenting concerns, including:**
   - *Aggression (specify common topographies and targets, if possible [particular people, animals, classes of people])*
   - *Self-injury (specify common topographies)*
   - *Property destruction*
   - *Elopement*
   - *Increased functional impairment includes:*
     - *depressive symptoms like anhedonia/decreased engagement in activities of daily living*
     - *anxiety symptoms like maladaptive avoidance of certain contexts (like school refusal) and/or excessive withdrawal from certain contexts (bathrooms with automatic toilets, exposure to particular stimuli [people, animals, environments])*
     - *Suicidal ideation and/or attempts*

F. **Precursor Behaviors** (*list signs or signals that typically precede problem behavior)*

G. **Typical Antecedents to Problem Behavior**
   - *Common examples:*
     - *Change in routine/schedule/timing of anticipated event*
     - *Presentation of expectations/task demands*
     - *Transitions (in settings, caregivers, etc.)*

H. **Historical Consequences to Problem Behavior**
   - *Common examples:*
     - *Gets to leave aversive situation (spends time away from classroom/school; sent to room/"timeout")*
     - *Becomes target of verbal reprimands/other forms of negative attention*
     - *Gets consoled/reassured*
     - *Is physically restrained*
     - *Security/law enforcement responds to situation*

I. **Hypothesized Functions of Presenting Problem Behavior:** *Summarize information from functional behavioral assessment and state hypotheses regarding function of presenting crisis behaviors (e.g., social positive reinforcement ["tangible" and/or "attention" function] social negative reinforcement ["avoidance" or "escape" function], or automatic reinforcement [positive/"self-stimulation" or negative/attenuation of pain or discomfort])*

J. **Contextual Information Related to Presenting Problem Behavior ("Iceberg" Table):** *Summarize information from initial caregiver interviews and review historical document in a table with the following sections (as suggested in the "Iceberg Assessment Interview"; Stark et al. 2015)*
   i. Sensory and Self-Regulation Considerations
   ii. Medical and Psychiatric Considerations

iii. Communication Skill Considerations
iv. Social Skill Considerations
v. Motor Skills and Other Activities of Daily Living Skill Considerations
vi. Cognitive and Academic Skill Considerations
vii. Caregiver, Community, and Virtual Environment Considerations

Part II: Intervention Plan

A. **Outline Youth and Caregiver Treatment Goals**
   Common examples include those related to:
   i. Decreasing dangerous behaviour
   ii. Increasing use of self-regulation and functional replacement behavior

B. **Recommended Structure and Routines**
   i. Schedule type (e.g., object, picture, picture–word, word)
   ii. Visual emotion rating scale type (e.g., 2-point or 4-point)
   iii. Familiar self-care and other daily activity routines: Describe any special requests or information about familiar routines requested by caregivers and/or the patient, as well as recommendations to supporting safe, functional engagement in:
      - *Hygiene (toileting, bathing, teeth or hair brushing)*
      - *Nighttime routines and morning routines*
      - *Family visits and/or phone calls (for inpatient hospitalizations)*

C. **Recommendations from Outside Consultations**
   i. Includes plans and results from consultations with medical (gastroenterology, neurology, etc.) and therapeutic providers (speech–language pathology, occupational therapy, physical therapy)

D. **Target Behaviors for Data Collection and Tracking Treatment Progress:** *Specify*:
   i. Presenting behaviors of concern—include one to two primary targets for decrease in the context crisis stabilization and treatment (e.g., "aggression," "self-injury," "elopement"). For each provide clear operational definition (observable, measurable), as well as one **example** of a behavior that should be counted and at least one **non example** (i.e., a behavior that should *not* be counted)
   ii. Replacement/alternative behavior—include one to two skills to target for increase as a functional "replacement" for the presenting crisis behavior (e.g., "functional communication" of need for breaks) and/or to promote more adaptive coping responses (e.g., " self-regulation/coping skill use")

E. **Milieu Interventions and General Treatment Considerations:** *May include*:
   i. Recommended classroom arrangements (spacing, structure for specific group activities, etc.)
   ii. Protocols for group and/or individual contingencies to implement during milieu/group programming (e.g., individual differential reinforcement systems for promoting safe, cooperative group behavior)
   iii. Recommendations for supporting transitions and low-structure periods throughout the day (playground/gym times, meal times, etc.)

F. **Independent Treatment Work**
   i. Specify individual treatment protocols to be conducted during individual treatment sessions (e.g., functional communication training, self-regulation training, cognitive behavioral therapy skills training).

G. **Crisis Prevention, Injury Prevention, and Precautions**
   i. Specify crisis de-escalation strategies to use at early signs of escalation (e.g., gently prompt the individual to leave the situation, use distraction, or help the individual state the problem and develop potential solutions to try).
   ii. Outline personal protective equipment (head coverings, skin coverings, padding, etc.) to be used to reduce injury to staff, caregivers, and youth.

(*continued*)

Table 20.1. Continued

iii.	Describe any additional environmental safety precautions: Note any past tendency to use accessible items (e.g., clothing, writing implements, etc.) to engage in self- or other-directed harm. Also include notes regarding risk for pica behavior, etc.
iv.	Crisis intervention plan: Specify criteria for using more intensive restraint and/or seclusion interventions (e.g., when individual presents an acute danger to self or others and when the risks of not intervening outweigh the risks of intervening), as well as clear discontinuation criteria for these highly restrictive interventions (e.g., as soon as the individual no longer presents an acute danger to self or others)

pathologist should be a priority for focused care. Continuously adjusting this plan is necessary to match the youth's response to treatment and progress made. Depending on the length of time available for treatment in a crisis stabilization setting, the feasibility and appropriateness of interventions can vary. Areas of focus for consideration include the following.

- **Safety planning** is a critical component of crisis intervention for youth identified as being at risk for suicide, particularly those who initially presented in crisis with suicidal ideations and/or associated behavior. Safety planning includes discussion of early warning signs of a suicidal crisis along with mitigation of a youth's access to means with which to engage in dangerous behaviors. Means safety should include creating a clear plan with caregivers to remove and/or secure (i.e., lock up) firearms, sharps, medications, and other materials that could be used for harm in the youth's environment (McManama O'Brien, Aguinaldo, Almeida, & White, 2016). Use of a visually clear safety plan can draw on the strengths of the ASD population. For example, a plan should identify concrete steps for youth to remain safe even when they experience strong emotions, as well as a list of resources for the youth to access for support (e.g., family, friends, and therapists) with instructions and information (e.g., phone numbers) for contacting these resources. Safety plan templates based on the safety planning intervention (Stanley & Brown, 2012) are available through the Suicide Prevention Resource Center website (http://www.sprc.org), along with a quick guide to safety planning for clinicians. Rosenbaum Asarnow, Berk, Hughes, and Anderson (2015) also provide a helpful visual for the various considerations and phases involved in safety planning with youth and their caregivers, which they implement via the SAFETY Program. Although designed as a 12-week intervention program, this model contains steps that can be initiated in an acute crisis stabilization context. For youth also presenting with homicidal ideation as a crisis behavior, similar safety planning steps are appropriate in addition to consideration of additional steps like "duty to warn" targets of homicidal threats.
- **Medical interventions** may involve adjustment of psychiatric medications along with coordination of care with specialty medical providers. The American Academy of Child and Adolescent Psychiatry (2016) recently developed practice parameters for medical providers of youth with ASD as well as a medication guide for parents. More recently, DeFilippis and Wagner (2016) developed a summary of the evidence base for use of different psychotropic medications in youth with ASD.
- **Teaching and practice of self-regulation skills** in coordination with an occupational therapist. may include breathing, guided imagery, progressive muscle relaxation, sensory regulation routines and other mindfulness techniques (e.g., meditation and breathing techniques) that have some preliminary beneficial evidence base for individuals with ASD (de Bruin et al., 2015).
- **Addressing communication deficits/barriers** that can contribute to problem behavior, ideally in coordination with a speech–language pathologist, can include implementation of communication skill-building protocols. Assessment of additional communication modalities (e.g. augmentative and alternative communication systems) may also be warranted.
- **Teaching functionally matched and safe alternative behaviors** can be implemented for meeting the individual needs (e.g., for attention, help, a break, etc.) that may have been previously met through the occurrence of problem behavior. Use of interventions based in Applied Behavior

Analysis (ABA) are particularly applicable for this part of stabilization. A common example is functional communication training (FCT; initially described by Carr & Durand, 1985; see also Tiger, Hanley, & Bruzek, 2008, for a helpful review of FCT), which trains individuals to use communicative responses (vocal or nonvocal).

- **Targeted use of modified cognitive behavioral therapy (CBT) interventions** to address acute symptoms of anxiety and depression may also be warranted. For example, graduated exposure therapy for addressing avoidance and escape behavior that directly relates to critical levels of functional impairment (e.g., school refusal or significantly impaired self-care routines) may be particularly pertinent to improving a youth's crisis behavior. (For a review of CBT protocols developed for the ASD population, readers are referred to Ung, Selles, Small, & Storch, 2015). Walters, Loades, and Russell (2016) summarized several considerations for modifying CBT interventions for youth with ASD. Attwood and Scarpa (2013) also provide suggestions for CBT modifications for high-functioning youth. Particularly important to the application of CBT interventions within a crisis management setting are:
    - Use of hands-on (e.g., role-play and drawings) and visual representation strategies to enhance training of emotion recognition and regulation skills, as well as emphasis on linking the specific moods, thoughts, and body dysregulation warning signals that precipitated psychiatric crises with the behavior that resulted in hospitalization.
    - Involvement of caregivers along with their youth in identifying caregiving reactions that tend to exacerbate crisis situations (e.g., being "rushed" by caregivers to make cognitive and behavioral shifts or to "talk" when youth are in states of arousal that make these skills more difficult to access without positive behavior supports and adequate wait times). Alternative supportive interventions that caregivers can use should also be identified and practiced (e.g., familiar scripts and routines to cue use of cognitive and behavioral de-escalation tools, and tools for written/other nonvocal communication)
    - Development of clear, concrete, and visual tools to prompt youth and caregivers to understand and disrupt the maladaptive thought–feeling–behavior "spirals" that lead to crisis situations.
- **Family therapy interventions** such as role-playing appropriate interactions, can address maladaptive youth–caregiver and/or youth–sibling interactions that are contributing to the ASD youth's crisis presentation. Family therapy can include making modifications to household rules, contingencies, and reinforcement schedules thought to be contributing to problem behavior occurrence prior to hospitalization. A common example of this involves working with ASD youth and their caregivers to adjust and clearly define when and how often the youth has access to preferred activities (e.g., video games or other screen-time activities).
- **Pivotal response training (PRT;** Koegel & Koegel, 2018) interventions can target skill areas that are considered pivotal behaviors leading to learning skills such as self-management and self-regulation. PRT strategies have particular relevance when teaching self-regulation skills for youth with ASD in crisis intervention settings because motivational procedures (e.g., offering choices, positively reinforcing approximations of target behaviors, and using natural reinforcements) can be employed to motivate the youth's engagement in targeted safe behaviors. For example, a self-monitoring routine that incorporates a positive reinforcement component might include working with the youth with ASD to first generate a checklist of target behaviors to display in a group setting and then, after the group, the youth checks off behaviors he or she exhibited. Reinforcement would then be delivered by staff based on established contingencies and criteria. Through this process, the youth with ASD gains experience with taking an active role to reflect on and reinforce target behaviors.
- **Developing an effective crisis intervention plan** (see Table 20.1) to prevent or minimize the severity of dangerous escalation cycles is critical to reducing risk of crisis recurrence. A crisis plan should define prevention strategies that include specific visual and verbal problem-solving protocols aimed at interrupting the behavior escalation (e.g., asking the youth, "How can I help?" and/or providing immediate and concrete reminders of alternative behavior like saying, "Come walk with me"). Additionally, the plan should carefully outline criteria and guidelines for implementing acute safety interventions like physical, mechanical, and medical restraints or seclusions. Both criteria for using these highly restrictive interventions (e.g., when an individual presents as an acute danger to

self or others and when the risks of not intervening outweigh the risks of intervening) and criteria for discontinuing their use as soon as there is no longer an acute safety concern should be clearly defined in the plan. When considering use of physical or mechanical restraint and/or seclusions, it is critical to consider if the youth has any history of trauma or neglect and then include guidelines for providers to minimize risk of exposure to trauma cues. For example, in some cases the gender of the staff involved in managing the crisis, the specific restraint position (e.g., seated vs. laying down), and the lighting and the visibility of an exit are all critical considerations. A program such as Safety-Care Behavioral Safety Training (Quality Behavioral Solutions) is particularly applicable to training staff to manage youth with ASD in psychiatric environments given this program's emphasis on effective procedures based in ABA and positive behavior interventions and supports (PBISs).

Phase IV: Generalization

Teaching caregivers from multiple community environments (e.g., home and school) to implement individualized behavior and medical management plans is a core aspect of the functional and contextual model. Investment in a plan to disseminate and generalize the youth's individualized behavior intervention plan to a variety of caregivers in the natural environment (e.g., home, school, law enforcement, emergency medical personnel) can increase the likelihood of treatment progress maintenance (e.g., problem behavior reduction) and the youth's behavioral consistency across settings. Teaching opportunities for caregivers (e.g., parents, teachers, and therapists) while the youth is still in the hospital care system can include the following:

- Hospital milieu-based teaching for caregivers to both observe and take an active role in the process of implementing interventions with the youth that are outlined in the youth's individualized behavior intervention plan.
- Community-based skills practice for the youth and caregiver. For example, the youth returns to the community caregiving environment at the end of each hospital care day (e.g., partial hospital setting) with a motivational contingency plan in place for the youth to engage in a preferred activity when he or she returns to the hospital day program if he or she has maintained safe behaviors in the community. Otherwise, if the youth was unsafe in the community, the first activity of the hospital day is to review, using a visual roadmap, the dangerous behavior / incident.
- Caregiver education and training groups that provide a review and practice of proactive and responsive behavior intervention strategies within the functional contextual framework model.

Summary and Future Directions

Although this chapter focuses on youth with ASD, there is a steadily growing population of adults with ASD, and problem behaviors that can lead to crisis intervention. The key elements of the crisis behavior assessment and stabilization outlined in this chapter can also provide guidance for providers working with an adult ASD population. Specifically, these key elements include:

- Stabilizing the environment to match the learning style needs of individuals with ASD presenting with a behavioral crisis to quickly help individuals achieve a level of physical safety and regulation, basic psychological comfort, and a sense of familiarity necessary to engage the individual with ASD in subsequent phases of assessment and treatment
- Having a consideration of the environmental and individual variables that can impact the crisis behavior presentation of the individual with ASD and making every effort to thoroughly assess these variables to gain an accurate conceptualization of the individual and the function(s) of his or her crisis behavior
- Engaging the individual with ASD in goal setting using concrete visual approaches adapted to his or her strengths and needs to capture his or her interest, attention, and understanding such as using a visual roadmap
- Developing a package of individualized proactive and responsive treatment strategies in collaboration with multidisciplinary providers based on case conceptualization and determination of factors that are core to driving the function of problem behaviors
- Providing detailed instructions in a behavior intervention plan to enhance consistency of treatment delivery across caregiving environments

Finally, there is a need for future work to focus on adult crisis management and employing crisis prevention strategies.

References

Aman, M. G., Singh, N. N., Stewart, A. W., & Field, C. J. (1985). The aberrant behavior checklist: A behavior rating scale for the assessment of treatment effects. *American Journal of Mental Deficiency, 89*, 485–491.

American Academy of Child and Adolescent Psychiatry. (2016). *Autism spectrum disorder: Parents' medication guide. Retrieved from*: https://www.aacap.org/App_Themes/AACAP/Docs/resource_centers/autism/Autism_Spectrum_Disorder_Parents_Medication_Guide.pdf

Attwood, T., & Scarpa, A. (2013). Modifications of cognitive-behavioral therapy for children and adolescents with high-functioning ASD and their common difficulties. In A. Scarpa, S.White, & T.Attwood (Eds.) *CBT for Children and Adolescents with High-Functioning Autism SpectrumDdisorders* (pp. 27–44). New York, NY: The Guilford Press.

Baron-Cohen, S., Tager-Flusberg, H., & Cohen, D. J. (Eds.). (2000). *Understanding other minds: Perspectives from developmental cognitive neuroscience* (2nd ed.). Oxford University Press.

Benini, F., Trapanotto, M., Gobber, D., Agosto, C., Carli, G., Drigo, P., . . . Zacchello, F. (2004). Evaluating pain induced by venipuncture in pediatric patients with developmental delay. *Clinical Journal of Pain, 20*(3), 156–163.

Bodfish, J. W., Symons, F. J., & Lewis, M. H. (1999). *The Repetitive Behavior Scale*. Western Carolina Center Research Reports.

Breau, L. M., & Burkitt, C. (2009). Assessing pain in children with intellectual disabilities. *Pain Research and Management, 14*(2), 116–120.

Brenner, J., Pan, Z., Mazefsky, C., Smith, K., & Gabriels, R. (2017). The expression of trauma in children and adolescents with autism spectrum disorder. *Journal of Autism and Developmental Disorders*.

Carr, E. G., & Durand, V. M. (1985). Reducing behavior problems through functional communication training. *Journal of Applied Behavior Analysis, 18*(2), 111–126.

Contextual Psychology. (n.d.). Retrieved from https://contextualscience.org/contextual_psychology

Cooper, J. O., Heron, T. E., & Heward, W. L. (2007). *Applied behavior analysis* (2nd ed.). Upper Saddle River, NJ: Pearson.

Cox, R. D., & Schopler, E. (1993). Aggression and self-injurious behaviors in persons with autism: The TEACCH approach. *Acta Paedopsychiatrica: International Journal of Child & Adolescent Psychiatry*.

Croen, L. A., Najjar, D. V., Ray, G. T., Lotspeich, L., & Bernal, P. (2006). A comparison of health care utilization and costs of children with and without autism spectrum disorders in a large group-model health plan. *Pediatrics, 118*(4), e1203–e1211.

Christensen, T. J., Ringdahl, J. E., Bosch, J. J., Falcomata, T. S., Luke, J. R., & Andelman, M. S. (2009). Constipation associated with self-injurious and aggressive behavior exhibited by a child diagnosed with autism. *Education and Treatment of children, 32*, 89–103.

Cipani, E., & Schock, K. M. (2011). *Functional behavioral assessment, diagnosis, and treatment: A complete system for education and mental health settings* (2nd ed.). New York, NY: Springer Publishing.

Cummings, J. R., Lynch, F. L., Rust, K. C., Coleman, K. J., Madden, J. M., Owen-Smith, A. A., . . . Croen, L. A. (2016). Health services utilization among children with and without autism spectrum disorders. *Journal of Autism and Development Disorders, 46*(3), 910–920.

Davit, C. J., Hundley, R. J., Bacic, J. D., & Hanson, E. M. (2011). A pilot study to improve venipuncture compliance in children and adolescents with autism spectrum disorders. *Journal of Developmental and Behavioral Pediatrics, 32*(7), 521–525.

DeFilippis, M., & Wagner, K. D. (2016). Treatment of autism spectrum disorder in children and adolescents. *Psychopharmacology Bulletin, 46*(2), 18–41.

Doehring, P., Reichow, B., Palka, T., Phillips, C., & Hagopian, L. (2014). Behavioral approaches to managing severe problem behaviors in children with autism spectrum and related developmental disorders: A descriptive analysis. *Child and Adolescent Psychiatric Clinics, 23*(1), 25–40.

Dunn, W. (2014). *Sensory Profile 2 manual: Strengths based approach to assessment and planning*. Bloomington, MN: Pearson.

Durand, V. M., & Crimmins, D. B. (1988). Identifying the variables maintaining self-injurious behavior. *Journal of Autism and Developmental Disorders, 18*(1), 99–117.

Engelhardt, C. R., & Mazurek, M. O. (2014). Video game access, parental rules, and problem behavior: A study of boys with autism spectrum disorder. *Autism, 18*(5), 529–537.

Esbensen, A. J., Greenberg, J. S., Seltzer, M. M., & Aman, M. G. (2009). A longitudinal investigation of psychotropic and non-psychotropic medication use among adolescents and adults with autism spectrum disorders. *Journal of Autism and Developmental Disorders, 39*(9), 1339–1349.

Fisher, W. W., & Bouxsein, K. (2011). Developing function-based reinforcement procedures for problem behavior. In W. Fisher, C. Piazza, and H. Roane (Eds.), *Handbook of applied behavior analysis* (pp. 335–347). New York, NY: The Guilford Press.

Forcier, A. (1999). A place like no other: Students with autism design a space to learn best. *Massachusetts Psychologist, 7*(8).

Gabriels, R. L., Agnew, J. A., Beresford, C., Morrow, M. A., Mesibov, G., & Wamboldt, M. (2012). Improving psychiatric hospital care for pediatric patients with autism spectrum disorders and intellectual disabilities. *Autism Research and Treatment, 2012*.

Gabriels, R. L., & Gaffey, L. J. (2012). Art therapy with children on the autism spectrum. In C. A. Malchiodi (Ed.), *Handbook of art therapy* (pp. 205–221). New York, NY: Guilford Press.

Gabriels, R. L., & Hill, D. E. (Eds.). (2010). *Growing up with autism: Working with school-age children and adolescents*. Guilford Press.

Gabriels, R. L., Shah, J. S., Young, N. D., Gralla, J., & Goldson, E. J. (2018). Picture-schedule reinforcement intervention for children with autism. *Journal of Mental Health Research in Intellectual Disabilities, 11*(2), 173–174.

Guinchat, V., Cravero, C., Diaz, L., Perisse, D., Xavier, J., Amiet, C., . . . Consoli, A. (2015). Acute behavioral crises in psychiatric inpatients with autism spectrum disorder (ASD): Recognition of concomitant medical or non-ASD psychiatric conditions predicts enhanced improvement. *Research in Developmental Disabilities, 38*, 242–255.

Handen, B. L., Mazefsky, C. A., Gabriels, R. L., Pedersen, K. A., Wallace, M., & Siegel, M. (2018). Risk factors for self-injurious behavior in an inpatient psychiatric sample of children with autism spectrum disorder: A naturalistic observation study. *Journal of Autism and Developmental Disorders*, 1–11.

Horowitz, L. M., Bridge, J. A., Teach, S. J., Ballard, E., Klima, J., Rosenstein, D. L., . . . Pao, M. (2012). Ask suicide-screening questions (ASQ): A brief instrument for the pediatric emergency department. *Archives of Pediatrics & Adolescent Medicine, 166*(12), 1170–1176. doi:10.1001/archpediatrics.2012.1276

Horowitz, L. M., Thurm, A., Farmer, C., Mazefsky, C., Lanzillo, E., & Bridge, J. A. (2017). Talking about death or suicide: Prevalence and clinical correlates in youth with autism spectrum disorder in the psychiatric inpatient setting. *Journal of Autism and Developmental Disorders*, 1–9.

Hume, K. (2009). *Steps for implementation: Visual schedules.* Chapel Hill, NC: National Professional Development Center on Autism Spectrum Disorders, Frank Porter Graham Child Development Institute, University of North Carolina.

Iwata, B. A., DeLeon, I. G., & Roscoe, E. M. (2013). Reliability and validity of the functional analysis screening tool. *Journal of Applied Behavior Analysis, 46*, 271–284.

Joshi, G., Petty, C., Wozniak, J., Henin, A., Fried, R., Galdo, M., . . . Biederman, J. (2010). The heavy burden of psychiatric comorbidity in youth with autism spectrum disorders: A large comparative study of a psychiatrically referred population. *Journal of Autism and Developmental Disorders, 40*(11), 1361–1370.

Kelley, M. E., LaRue, R. H., Roane, H. S., & Gadaire, D. M. (2011). Indirect behavioral assessments. In W. Fisher, C. Piazza, and H. Roane (Eds.), *Handbook of applied behavior analysis* (pp. 182–190). New York, NY: The Guilford Press.

Koegel, R. L., & Koegel, L. K. (2018). *Pivotal response treatments for autism* (2nd ed.). Baltimore, MD: Brookes Publishing.

Kopecky, K., Broder-Fingert, S., Iannuzzi, D., & Connors, S. (2013). The needs of hospitalized patients with autism spectrum disorders: a parent survey. *Clinical Pediatrics, 52*(7), 652–660.

Kuriakose, S., Filton, B., Marr, M., Okparaeke, E., Cervantes, P., Siegel, M., . . . Havens, J. (2018). Does an autism spectrum disorder care pathway improve care for children and adolescents with ASD in inpatient psychiatric units? *Journal of Autism and Developmental Disorders*, 1–8.

Kuypers, L. (2011). *The zones of regulation*. San Jose, CA: Think Social Publishing.

Lerman, D. C., & Toole, L. M. (2011). Developing function-based punishment procedures for problem behavior. In W. Fisher, C. Piazza, and H. Roane (Eds.), *Handbook of applied behavior analysis* (pp. 348–381). New York, NY: The Guilford Press.

Leyfer, O. T., Folstein, S. E., Bacalman, S., Davis, N. O., Dinh, E., Morgan, J., . . . Lainhart, J. E. (2006). Comorbid psychiatric disorders in children with autism: Interview development and rates of disorders. *Journal of Autism and Developmental Disorders, 36*(7), 849–861.

Logan, S. L., Carpenter, L. Leslie, R. S., Garrett-Mayer, E., Hunt, K. J., Charles, J., & Nicholas, J. S. (2015). Aberrant behaviors and co-occurring conditions as predictors of psychotropic polypharmacy among children with autism spectrum disorders. *Journal of Child and Adolescent Psychopharmacology, 25*(4), 323–336.

Mandell, D. S. (2008). Psychiatric hospitalization among children with autism spectrum disorders. *Journal of Autism and Developmental Disorders, 38*(6), 1059–1065.

Mandell, D. S., Cao, J., Ittenbach, R., & Pinto-Martin, J. (2006). Medicaid expenditures for children with autistic spectrum disorders: 1994 to 1999. *Journal of Autism and Developmental Disorders, 36*(4), 475–485.

Matson, J. L., & Vollmer, T. R. (1995). *User's guide: Questions About Behavioral Function (QABF)*. Baton Rouge, LA: Scientific Publishers.

Mayes, S. D., Gorman, A. A., Hillwig-Garcia, J., & Syed, E. (2013). Suicide ideation and attempts in children with autism. *Research in Autism Spectrum Disorders, 7*(1), 109–119. https://doi.org/10.1016/j.rasd.2012.07.009

Mazefsky, C., Kao, J., & Oswald, D. (2011). Preliminary evidence suggesting caution in the use of psychiatric self-report measures with adolescents with high-functioning autism spectrum disorders. *Research in Autism Spectrum Disorders, 5*(1), 164–174.

Mazurek, M. O., & Engelhardt, C. R. (2013). Video game use and problem behaviors in boys with autism spectrum disorders. *Research in Autism Spectrum Disorders, 7*(2), 316–324.

McGuire, K., Erickson, C., Gabriels, R. L., Kaplan, D., Mazefsky, C., McGonigle, J., . . . Siegel, M. (2015). Psychiatric hospitalization of children with autism or intellectual disability: Consensus statements on best practices. *Journal of the American Academy of Child and Adolescent Psychiatry, 54*(12), 969–971.

McManama O'Brien, K. H., Aguinaldo, L. D., Almeida, J., & White, E. (2016). The role of parents in safety planning interventions with suicidal adolescents. *International Journal of Emergency Mental Health and Human Resilience, 18*(1), 727–729.

Mesibov, G., Browder, D. M., & Kirkland, C. (2002). Using individualized schedules as a component of positive behavioral support for students with developmental disabilities. *Journal of Positive Behavior Interventions, 4*(2), 73–79.

Mesibov, G., & Shea, V. (2010). The TEACCH program in the era of evidence-based practice. *Journal of Autism and Developmental Disorders, 40*(5), 570–579.

Mohr, C., & Davis, R. (2004). The assessment and treatment of behavioural problems. *Australian Family Physician, 33*(8), 609.

Mostafa, M. (2008). An architecture for autism: Concepts of design intervention for the autistic user. *International Journal of Architectural Research: ArchNet-IJAR, 2*(1), 189–211.

Mostafa, M. (2014). Architecture for autism: Autism ASPECTSS™ in school design. *International Journal of Architectural Research: ArchNet-IJAR, 8*(1), 143–158.

National Autism Center. (2015). Findings and conclusions: National standards project, phase 2.

Nayfack, A. M., Huffman, L. C., Feldman, H. M., Chan, J., Saynina, O., & Wise, P. H. (2014). Hospitalizations of children with autism increased from 1999 to 2009. *Journal of Autism and Developmental Disorders, 44*(5), 1087–1094.

Odom, S. L., Brown, W. H., Frey, T., Karasu, N., Lee Smith-Canter, L., & Strain, P. S. (2003). Evidence-based practices for young children with autism: Contributions for single-subject design research. *Focus on Autism and Other Developmental Disabilities, 18*(3), 166–175.

O'Neill, R. E., Horner, R. H., Albin, R. W., Sprague, J. R., Storey, K., & Newton, J. S. (1997). Functional Assessment and Program Development for Problem Behavior. Pacific Grove, CA: Brooks/Cole Publishing.

O'Reilly, M., Sigafoos, J., Lancioni, G., Edrisinha, C., & Andrews, A. (2005). An examination of the effects of a classroom activity schedule on levels of self-injury and engagement for a child with severe autism. *Journal of Autism and Developmental Disorders, 35*(3), 305–311.

Pedersen, K. A., Santangelo, S. L., Gabriels, R. L., Righi, G., Erard, M., & Siegel, M. (2017). Behavioral outcomes of specialized psychiatric hospitalization in the Autism Inpatient

Collection (AIC): A multisite comparison. *Journal of Autism and Developmental Disorders*, 1–10.

Posner, K., Brown, G. K., Stanley, B., Brent, D.A., Yershova, K.V., Oquendo, M.A., Currier, G.W., Melvin, G.A., Greenhill, L., Shen, S. and Mann, J.J. (2011). The Columbia-Suicide Severity Rating Scale: Initial validity and internal consistency findings from three multisite studies with adolescents and adults. *American Journal of Psychiatry, 168*, 1266–1277.

Rogers, S. J. (1999). Intervention for young children with autism: From research to practice. *Infants & Young Children, 12*(2), 1–16.

Rosenbaum Asarnow, J., Berk, M., Hughes, J. L., & Anderson, N. L. (2015). The SAFETY program: A treatment-development trial of a cognitive-behavioral family treatment for adolescent suicide attempters. *Journal of Clinical Child and Adolescent Psychology, 44*(1), 194–203. doi:10.1080/15374416.2014.940624.

Salazar, F., Baird, G., Chandler, S., Tseng, E., O'Sullivan, T., Howlin, P., . . . Simonoff, E. (2015). Co-occurring psychiatric disorders in preschool and elementary school-aged children with autism spectrum disorder. *Journal of Autism and Developmental Disorders, 45*(8), 2283–2294.

Scattone, D., Wilczynski, S. M., Edwards, R. P., & Rabian, B. (2002). Decreasing disruptive behaviors of children with autism using social stories. *Journal of Autism and Developmental Disorders, 32*(6), 535–543.

Schopler, E. (1994). Behavioral priorities for autism and related developmental disorders. In *Behavioral issues in autism* (pp. 55–77). Boston, MA: Springer.

Siegel, M., Doyle, K., Chemelski, B., Payne, D., Ellsworth, B., Harmon, J., . . . Lubetsky, M. (2012). Specialized inpatient psychiatry units for children with autism and developmental disorders: A United States survey. *Journal of Autism and Developmental Disorders, 42*(9), 1863–1869.

Siegel, M., & Gabriels, R. L. (2014). Psychiatric hospital treatment of children with autism and serious behavioral disturbance. *Child and Adolescent Psychiatric Clinics of North America, 23*(1), 125–142.

Siegel, M., Milligan, B., Chemelski, B., Payne, D., Ellsworth, B., Harmon, J., . . . Smith, K. A. (2014). Specialized inpatient psychiatry for serious behavioral disturbance in autism and intellectual disability. *Journal of Autism and Developmental Disorders, 44*(12), 3026–3032.

Siegel, M., Smith, K. A., Mazefsky, C., Gabriels, R. L., Erickson, C., Kaplan, D., . . . Santangelo, S. L. (2015). The autism inpatient collection: Methods and preliminary sample description. *Molecular Autism, 6*(1), 61.

Simonoff, E., Pickles, A., Chairman, T., Chandler, S., Loucas, T., & Baird, G. (2008). Psychiatric disorders in children with autism spectrum disorders: Prevalence, comorbidity and associated factors in a population-derived sample. *Journal of the American Academy of Child and Adolescent Psychiatry, 47*(8), 921–929.

Smith, R. G. (2011). Developing antecedent interventions for problem behavior. In W. Fisher, C. Piazza, and H. Roane (Eds.), *Handbook of applied behavior analysis* (pp. 297–316). New York, NY: The Guilford Press.

Stanley, B., & Brown, G. K. (2012). Safety planning intervention: A brief intervention to mitigate suicide risk. *Cognitive and Behavioral Practice, 19*, 256–264.

Stark, K. H., Barnes, J. C., Young, N. D., & Gabriels, R. L. (2015). Brief report: Understanding crisis behaviors in hospitalized psychiatric patients with autism spectrum disorder—Iceberg assessment interview. *Journal of Autism and Developmental Disorders, 45*(11), 3468–3474.

Thompson, R. H., & Borrero, J. C. (2011). Direct observation. In W. Fisher, C. Piazza, and H. Roane (Eds.), *Handbook of applied behavior analysis* (pp. 191–205). New York, NY: The Guilford Press.

Thompson, R. M., & Johnston, S. (2013). Use of social stories to improve self-regulation in children with autism spectrum disorders. *Physical & Occupational Therapy in Pediatrics, 33*(3), 271–284.

Thunberg, G., Buchholz, M., & Nilsson, S. (2016). Strategies that assist children with communicative disability during hospital stay: Parents' perceptions and ideas. *Journal of Child Health Care, 20*(2), 224–233.

Thurecht, R., & Davis, R. (2001). Care planning and case conferencing: Building effective multidisciplinary teams. *Australian Family Physician, 30*(1), 78.

Tiger, J. H., Hanley, G. P., & Bruzek, J. (2008). Functional communication training: A review and practical guide. *Behavior Analysis in Practice, 1*(1), 16–23.

Ung, D., Selles, R., Small, B. J., & Storch, E. A. (2015). A systematic review and meta-analysis of cognitive-behavioral therapy for anxiety in youth with high-functioning autism spectrum disorders. *Child Psychiatry & Human Development, 46*(4), 533–547.

van der Putten, A., & Vlaskamp, C. (2011). Pain assessment in people with profound intellectual and multiple disabilities: A pilot study into the use of the Pain Behaviour Checklist in everyday practice. *Research in Developmental Disabilities, 32*(5), 1677–1684.

Volkmar, F., Siegel, M., Woodbury-Smith, M., King, B., McCracken, J., State, M., & of Child, A. A. (2014). Practice parameter for the assessment and treatment of children and adolescents with autism spectrum disorder. *Journal of the American Academy of Child & Adolescent Psychiatry, 53*(2), 237–257.

Vollmer, T. R., & Athens, E. (2011). Developing function-based extinction procedures for problem behavior. In W. Fisher, C. Piazza, and H. Roane (Eds.), *Handbook of applied behavior analysis* (pp. 317–334). New York, NY: The Guilford Press.

Wacker, D., Berg, W., Harding, J., & Cooper-Brown, L.J. (2011). Functional and Structural Approaches to Behavioral Assessment of Problem Behavior. In W. Fisher, C. Piazza, and H. Roane (Eds.), *Handbook of applied behavior analysis (p. 165–181)*. New York, NY: The Guilford Press.

Walters, S., Loades, M., & Russell, A. (2016). A systematic review of effective modifications to cognitive behavioural therapy for young people with autism spectrum disorders. Review. *Journal of Autism and Developmental Disorders, 3*(2), 137–153. doi:10.1007/s40489-016-0072-2.

Weitlauf, A. S., McPheeters, M. L., Peters, B., Sathe, N., Travis, R., Aiello, R., . . . Warren, Z. (2014). *Therapies for children with autism spectrum disorder: Behavioral interventions update.* Rockville, MD.

Williams, D. L., Siegel, M., & Mazefsky, C. A. (2017). Problem behaviors in autism spectrum disorder: Association with verbal ability and adapting/coping skills. *Journal of Autism and Developmental Disorders*, 1–10.

Wright, P. W., & Wright, P. D. (2006). *Wrightslaw: Special education law*. Hartfield, VA: Harbor House Law Press.

CHAPTER

21

Designing Autism Spectrum Disorder Interventions for Community Implementation

Addressing Children's Challenging Behaviors in Publicly Funded Mental Health Services

Lauren Brookman-Frazee, Amy Drahota, Colby Chlebowski, Yael Koenig, Katherine Nguyen Williams, Barry Hill, *and* Julie McPherson

Abstract

There are well-documented gaps between evidence-based interventions (EBIs) developed and tested in controlled research settings and those delivered in routine, community-based care. The field of implementation science has developed in response to identified gaps to study methods to promote the uptake and sustainment of EBIs in community care. Community mental health (MH) services play an important role in caring for individuals with autism spectrum disorder (ASD) across the lifespan who have co-occurring psychiatric conditions. This chapter summarizes over a decade of community-engaged research aimed to (a) characterize MH services for children with ASD, including the training needs of therapists and clinical needs of children with ASD receiving care; (b) develop the AIM HI (An Individualized Mental Health Intervention for ASD) intervention, a package of well-established, evidence-based behavioral strategies designed to reduce challenging behaviors in children served in MH service settings; (c) test the impact of training therapists to deliver AIM HI on child outcomes; (d) identify potential influences on implementation; and (e) test the impact of different implementation strategies to enhance therapist delivery of AIM HI. The chapter includes directions for future research including applying the AIM HI development model to older individuals with ASD and other community service systems and integrating implementation science approaches earlier in the pipeline of research-to-practice translation.

Keywords: implementation science, mental health services, autism, effectiveness research, evidence-based interventions, community services

Services and Implementation Research

There are well-documented gaps between evidence-based interventions (EBIs) developed and tested in controlled research settings and those delivered in routine, community-based health and behavioral health care. It takes approximately 17 years to translate only 14% of original research findings to community delivery, substantially reducing the public health impact of clinical innovations (Balas, 1998; Balas & Boren, 2000). Mental health services research characterizing patterns of routine care has facilitated the identification of research–practice gaps and quality improvement targets at the system/policy, organizational, and individual provider levels (e.g., Garland, Bickman, & Chorpita, 2010; Garland, Brookman-Frazee, et al., 2010; Garland, Hough, et al., 2001; Garland, Lau, et al., 2005). The field of implementation science has developed in response to identified gaps between research and routine care. Implementation science refers to the scientific study of methods to promote the systematic uptake of research findings and EBI into routine care with the goal of improving the quality and effectiveness of health services and care (Eccles & Mittman, 2006). A critical component of implementation science is the distinction between clinical interventions (i.e., EBIs) and implementation strategies (e.g., provider training models, organizational supports or fiscal incentives for new interventions). Implementation strategies are methods used to promote the adaptation, implementation, or sustainment of an EBI of a clinical program or practice that may target different levels (systems, organizations, providers, consumers; Leeman, Birken, Powell, Rohweder, & Shea, 2017; Proctor, Powell, & McMillen, 2013). Furthermore, conceptual models of implementation research differentiate implementation outcomes (e.g., feasibility, uptake, provider fidelity, costs) and client outcomes (symptoms, functioning; Proctor et al., 2013). Implementation science is a rapidly increasing research priority across areas of health and behavioral health to ensure that clinical innovations developed in research setting reach the populations they are intended to impact.

Role of Publicly Funded Mental Health Services for Individuals With ASD

Almost all individuals with ASD experience medical, social–emotional, or behavioral conditions along with their ASD symptoms (Soke, Maenner, Christensen, Kurzius-Spencer, & Schieve, 2018). Given the number and varied intervention needs of individuals with ASD, multiple community service systems are involved in caring for this population (e.g., developmental disability/intellectual disability services; special education; medical; mental health; vocational rehabilitation; juvenile/criminal justice; Brookman-Frazee, Baker- Ericzén, et al., 2009), each intended to target different symptoms. Individuals with ASD are at particularly high risk for experiencing co-occurring psychiatric symptoms (Gray et al., 2012; Lever & Geurts, 2016; Salazar et al., 2015; Wood & Gadow, 2010). Approximately 70% to 80% of children (de Bruin et al., 2007; Gjevik, Eldevik, Fjæran-Granum, & Sponheim, 2011; Leyfer et al., 2006; Simonoff et al., 2008) and adults (Buck et al., 2014; Lever & Geurts, 2016) meet criteria for at least one co-occurring psychiatric disorder. Therefore, the mental health (MH) system is an important community delivery system for individuals with ASD.

Medicaid has long been the single largest payer of MH care in the United States (Mark et al., 2005) and its reach is expected to grow in many states through Medicaid expansion through the Affordable Care Act (Garfield & Zur, 2017). Medicaid MH services are often more comprehensive than private insurance, particularly for children, due to Medicaid's Early, Periodic Screening, Diagnosis, and Treatment (EPSDT) benefit. Over the past decade, there has been growing recognition of the role of publicly funded MH for children with ASD (Brookman-Frazee et al., 2009; Mandell, Walrath, Manteuffel, Sgro, & Pinto-Martin, 2005) and more recently for autistic adults (Maddox & Gaus, 2018; Maddox, Crabbe, et al., 2019). Furthermore, MH providers have requested training and assistance in addressing the complex clinical needs of this population (Brookman-Frazee, Drahota, Stadnick, & Palinkas, 2012; Maddox & Gaus, 2018), and there are urgent calls to build capacity of MH services to care for this population across the lifespan (Lake, Perry, & Lunsky, 2014).

Most of the research on MH services for individuals with ASD conducted to date has focused on services for children. For children with and without ASD, publicly funded MH services for school-age children are often provided in outpatient and school-based programs. A large proportion of children served in these programs are from racial/ethnic minority backgrounds. For example, in 2015–2016, over 74% of children who received psychotherapy and related services provided in California under Medi-Cal (California's Medicaid) were from racial/ethnic minority backgrounds (California Department of Health Care Services, 2018a). Furthermore, children present with clinically complex needs with high rates of multiple psychiatric conditions (Garland, Hough, et al., 2011). Children with ASD represent 10% to 14% of children in the psychiatrically referred population (Joshi et al., 2014), and outpatient MH therapists indicate that children with ASD or suspected ASD represent, on average, 21% of their psychotherapy caseloads (Brookman-Frazee, Drahota, Stadnick, et al., 2012). These data highlight the important role of MH services in caring for school-age children with ASD to address their co-occurring MH symptoms.

Application of Mental Health Services Research and Implementation Science to Research on Mental Health Services for ASD

In response to the growing recognition of the importance of MH services in caring for children with ASD, as well as the urgent need identified by the community MH agency leaders, therapists, and caregivers, to build capacity of MH services for children with ASD, our group initiated a community-engaged line of research aimed to characterize MH services for ASD and develop scalable strategies to effectively serve children with ASD. There are a number of different implementation frameworks to guide implementation science (Tabak, Khoong, Chambers, & Brownson, 2013) that may provide useful guidance for considering a comprehensive set of factors that are likely to contribute to implementing and sustaining EBI in routine care settings (Aarons, Hurlburt, & Horwitz, 2011). We apply one such

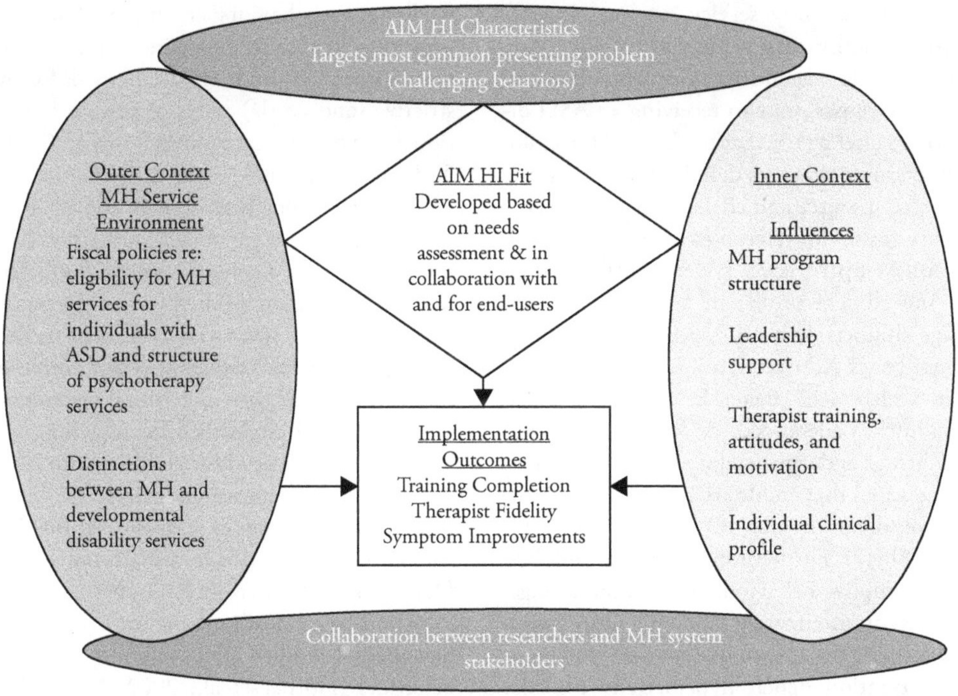

Figure 21.1. Applying the exploration, preparation, implementation, sustainment (EPIS) conceptual model of implementation to An Individualized Mental Health Intervention for ASD (AIM HI) development. ASD, autism spectrum disorder; MH, mental health.

implementation framework, the exploration, preparation, implementation, and sustainment (EPIS) model (Aarons, Hurlburt, & Horwitz, 2011), to frame the development of an MH intervention for children with ASD (AIM HI: *A*n *I*ndividualized *M*ental *H*ealth *I*ntervention for ASD; Brookman-Frazee & Drahota, 2010; Brookman-Frazee, Drahota, & Chlebowski, 2016; Figure 21.1). EPIS highlights factors from multiple levels that potentially influence implementation, including *intervention characteristics, outer context* (e.g., service system) factors, *inner context* (e.g., leader, provider and client characteristics) factors, and *intervention–context fit.* Within this research, there are calls for intervention developers to design interventions based on considerations of the end-user and usual care context to facilitate successful uptake and sustained delivery of EBI across public service systems (Drahota, Chlebowski, Stadnick, Baker-Ericzén, & Brookman-Frazee, 2017).

In the following sections, we summarize over a decade of community-engaged services and implementation research aimed to (a) characterize MH services for children with ASD, including the training needs of therapists and clinical needs of children with ASD receiving care; (b) develop the AIM HI intervention, designed specifically for delivery in MH services; (c) test the impact of training therapists to deliver AIM HI on child outcomes; (d) identify potential determinants of implementation; and (e) test the impact of different implementation strategies to enhance therapist delivery of AIM HI.

Characterizing Mental Health Services for ASD: Challenges and Needs in the Inner and Outer Contexts

Clinical profile of individuals with ASD in MH services: Challenging behaviors as the primary intervention target (inner context). In a mixed qualitative and quantitative study assessing the clinical needs of children with ASD served in outpatient MH programs, parents (Brookman-Frazee, Baker-Ericzén, Stadnick, & Taylor, 2012) and therapists (Brookman-Frazee, Drahota, Stadnick et al., 2012) described a common and complex clinical profile of children with ASD presenting to outpatient MH services. Specifically, most children were considered to have "high functioning" ASD based on their diagnoses and cognitive functioning. Specifically, the children primarily receiving *Diagnostic and Statistical Manual of Mental Disorders*, fourth edition [DSM-IV] diagnoses of pervasive developmental disorder-not otherwise specified [PDD-NOS] and Asperger's disorder and few with intellectual disability. Additionally, very few received developmental disability–focused interventions through the California Regional Center (California's developmental disability service system). Parents described a lengthy diagnostic process involving multiple professionals and receipt of multiple and conflicting diagnoses prior to receiving an ASD diagnosis, often after age 5, that finally "fit" the child. Both parents and therapists described schools as the primary referral source and challenging behaviors as the primary reason for referral to MH services.

Our follow-up research systematically characterizing the clinical profile of a large sample of school-age children with ASD receiving outpatient and school-based MH services (Brookman-Frazee, Stadnick, Chlebowski, Baker Ericzén, & Ganger, 2017; Stadnick, Chlebowski, & Brookman-Frazee, 2017) confirmed and expanded upon earlier findings. Results indicated that children's cognitive functioning was typically in the non-ID range (mean standard score = 88.47). Furthermore, children exhibited ASD and disruptive behaviors in the clinical range. Additionally, approximately 92% of children with ASD met criteria for at least one non-ASD diagnosis (78% attention deficit hyperactivity disorder [ADHD], 58% oppositional defiant disorder, 56% anxiety, 30% mood disorder), with an average of 2.80 non-ASD disorders (range was one to nine diagnoses) based on an adapted version of the Mini-International Neuropsychiatric Interview, parent version (MINI-KID-P; Sheehan et al., 1998; Brookman-Frazee et al., 2017).

Regardless of other clinical factors, the primary presenting problem of school-age children with ASD was challenging behavior (Brookman-Frazee, Drahota, & Stadnick, 2012), with 80% of children in MH services meeting criteria for at least one disorder associated with challenging behaviors (e.g., ADHD, oppositional defiant disorder; Brookman-Frazee et al., 2017). Challenging behaviors are broader than specific symptoms of externalizing diagnoses and can also include the outward demonstration of core ASD symptoms and internalizing (anxiety and mood) psychiatric symptoms. For example, behavioral rigidity (core ASD symptom) can be displayed as hostility and tantrum behaviors when an individual with ASD is asked to adapt within a certain context. Additionally, anxiety can trigger what appears as a challenging behavior but is actually an anxiety-driven response (Wood & Gadow, 2010); for example, a child may engage in tantrum behaviors in response to an anxiety-producing situation like attending a social event. Additionally, children with ASD and depression symptoms may exhibit negative affect through aggression (Kim, Szatmari, Bryson, Streiner, & Wilson, 2000). Such challenging behaviors are often children's most impairing symptoms, hindering academic and social development, and put children at risk for more restrictive (and costly) levels of care in both educational and psychiatric settings (Horner, Carr, Strain, Todd, & Reed, 2002; Matson, Wilkins, & Macken, 2009). Challenging behaviors are also a major source of stress and burden to families and teachers (Hastings, 2003; Lecavalier, Leone, & Wiltz, 2006). Thus, it is not surprising that children with ASD are often referred for MH services to target challenging behaviors.

Gaps between evidence-based interventions and routine MH care. Behavioral interventions are considered well established for targeting outcomes in many areas of need for children with ASD (e.g., academic, communication, social, MH, behavioral) based on independent reviews by the National Autism Center (2015) and National Professional Development Center on ASD (Wong et al., 2015). Function-based positive behavior support strategies have been found to effectively reduce challenging behaviors (Horner et al., 2002; National Autism Center, 2015; Wong et al., 2015). However, despite the resource-intensive investments in the development of efficacious behavioral interventions, these EBIs are often neither consistently nor effectively used in routine MH services for children with ASD (Brookman-Frazee, Taylor, & Garland, 2010). Specifically, although therapists have been observed to deliver some behavioral intervention strategies (e.g., positive reinforcement), they are not typically used intensively. Active teaching strategies needed for skill building (e.g., modeling, behavioral rehearsal, between-session practice) are used less frequently and at low intensity. Furthermore, therapists and parents express concerns about the appropriateness and effectiveness of MH services for children with ASD, and therapists are frustrated by their lack of "tools" to serve this complex population. A number of other challenges contribute to these identified gaps and are described in the following sections.

Structural and fiscal policy challenges (outer context). Outpatient and school-based MH programs are typically expected to serve a broad population of children with psychiatric conditions designated as qualifying for MH services. Although there is substantial variation between states on the specific organization of MH services, fiscal policies aimed to differentiate responsibilities between specialty MH services and developmental disability services have created "silos" between programs serving MH disorders and those serving individuals with developmental disabilities. For example, in California, an

International Classification of Diseases-10 (ICD-10) primary diagnosis of autistic disorder (but not other pervasive developmental disorders) is excluded from eligibility for Medicaid-reimbursed MH services (California Department of Health Care Services, 2018b). It is not known how this policy will change with the transition to the ICD-11, which, like the DSM-5, collapses autistic disorder and other pervasive developmental disorders into one disorder referred to as "autism." Unfortunately, this policy, combined with the perception held by some that psychotherapy is not appropriate for children with ASD, has led to stress and confusion for families as they are faced with navigating multiple service systems (Brookman-Frazee, Baker-Ericzén, et al., 2012) and may unintentionally limit access to children with ASD who meet criteria for other qualifying MH diagnoses (e.g., ADHD, anxiety, oppositional defiant disorder). This is not unique to children and has been identified as similarly impacting MH service access for adults with ASD (Maddox & Gaus, 2018). Furthermore, our data indicate that many children with ASD in MH services do not qualify for developmental disability services (e.g., through California Regional Centers) due to their higher cognitive functioning, resulting in the MH system becoming their default system of care from childhood and likely into adulthood. Taken together, there are a number of outer context factors that influence MH services for individuals with ASD.

Need for therapist training in ASD (inner context). In response to requests from agency leaders and therapists for assistance in building capacity of programs to more effectively serve the growing number of children with ASD in MH programs, we conducted a systematic needs assessment that included identifying the training needs of MH therapists related to ASD. Specifically, we conducted a mixed qualitative and quantitative study examining the perspectives of MH therapists providing services to children with ASD (Brookman-Frazee, Drahota, Stadnick, et al., 2012). Therapists reported delivering psychotherapy to many children with ASD and perceived providing services for this population to be particularly challenging due to their limited training and the children's complex clinical presentations. Specifically, therapists indicated that they have very limited ASD-specific training in graduate school education yet are faced with serving many children with ASD in their routine practice. Therapists described a slow rate of change in the children with ASD and reported that the typical psychotherapeutic strategies used with children without ASD are ineffective with this population. Yet, therapists were highly motivated for comprehensive and structured training on ASD characteristics and evidence-based intervention strategies. Specifically, therapists reported a need for information about ASD symptoms and characteristics and training in ASD EBIs, treatment planning, coordinating care, and strategies for working with parents. Similarly, parents of children with ASD receiving MH services indicated that perceived limited ASD training by therapists influenced the effectiveness of MH care for their children. These themes are consistent with research indicating that parents view limited therapist training in ASD as a barrier to effective services (Kalb, Stuart, Mandell, Olfson, & Vasa, 2017). Similarly, lack of therapist training has been identified as a barrier to access to MH services for adolescents and adults with ASD (Lake et al., 2014; Narendorf, Shattuck, & Sterzing, 2011).

Development of the AIM HI Intervention Protocol and Therapist Training Model

Based on results from the needs assessment described earlier, there was not an existing intervention or training protocol available at the time that adequately fit the clinical needs of children, therapist training needs, and service delivery context (e.g., weekly psychotherapy/counseling session lasting approximately 50 minutes). Thus, in collaboration with MH service system stakeholders (agency leaders, therapists, caregivers), we developed a package of existing, evidence-based strategies designed to fit in the context of routine psychotherapy services. Specifically, based on findings related to the clinical needs of children with ASD receiving MH services and the training needs of therapists, our group developed the AIM HI clinical intervention and therapist training protocol specifically for delivery in MH services. AIM HI is a package of parent-mediated and child-focused strategies designed to reduce challenging behaviors in children with ASD aged 5 to 13 years. It can be used with this population regardless of developmental functioning or type of co-occurring psychiatric symptoms. It includes well-established behavioral intervention strategies, including identifying patterns in the child's challenging behaviors and actively teaching positive alternative skills for children (e.g., emotion regulation, compliance) and complementary strategies for parents to help prevent the occurrence of challenging behaviors and promote the child's use of alternative skills (e.g., prompting, environmental modifications, making transitions predictable, using rewards; Table 21.1). Based on the

Table 21.1. Summary of AIM HI Protocol

Phase	AIM HI Protocol Steps	Within-Session Elements
Treatment planning	Integrate assessment information Complete *Behavior Tracking* with parents Develop *Behavior Plan* Develop *Active Teaching Plan*	**Structuring sessions for skill building and engagement** • Schedules, visual/written materials **Engaging parents and children** • Collaboration/active involvement (parents) • Motivational strategies (children) • Preparing to teach new skills
Active teaching	Teach parent strategies Teach alternative skill(s) to child Promote generalization of alternative skill(s) Teach additional alternative skills to child (as indicated)	**Active teaching with parents and children** • Modeling, practice with feedback, reinforcement, between-session practice
Evaluating progress	Review *Treatment Progress* Develop *Plan for Next Steps*	

AIM HI, An Individualized Mental Health Intervention for ASD.

From Brookman-Frazee, L., Drahota, A., & Chlebowski, C. (2016). *An individualized mental health intervention for children with autism spectrum disorder (AIM HI*; Vol. 2): *Therapist manual.* San Diego, CA: University of California, San Diego.

specific needs of MH therapists who provide weekly psychotherapy/counseling, it also includes "within session elements" used to adapt psychotherapy structure for this population to facilitate engagement and skill building (e.g., maximizing predictability through schedules and warnings, use of visual supports, incorporating the child's special interests into session activities).

The AIM HI therapist training process occurs over a 6-month training/consultation period while the therapist delivers AIM HI with a child on his or her current caseload. The training model includes active, direct, and explicit instructional methods and contains the following components: (a) an introductory training workshop involving didactic lecture, video examples, and planning for AIM HI delivery with a target client; (b) 11 consultation meetings (nine group, two individual) approximately 1 hour in length with an AIM HI trainer over a 6-month period, with didactic instruction and case-specific feedback; (c) performance feedback from trainers based on review of the therapist's session recordings with participating families; and (d) access to a therapist manual and printed and electronic forms.

AIM HI Pilot Study

Following the initial AIM HI development, we conducted a pilot study[1] to examine the feasibility, acceptability, and preliminary outcomes of training 13 therapists practicing in three community MH clinics from one organization in San Diego County (Brookman-Frazee, Drahota, & Stadnick, 2012; Drahota, Stadnick, & Brookman-Frazee, 2014; Stadnick, Drahota, & Brookman-Frazee, 2013). None of the clinics specialized in treatment of children with ASD or in EBIs for other disorders before or during the study period. Participating therapists included staff and trainee therapists at one of the three participating clinics who had an eligible client on his or her current caseload and indicated that they would be employed at the clinic for at least the next 9 months. Therapists came from different MH disciplines including marriage and family therapy (39%), psychology (39%), and social work (23%). Therapists reported an average of 13.61 clients on their caseload, with children with ASD representing an average of 24%. Therapists participated in both initial training and ongoing consultation with low attrition, indicating that participation in the training protocol was feasible for practicing MH therapists. Furthermore, therapists reported that AIM HI was useful, acceptable, and effective (Brookman-Frazee, Drahota, et al., 2012). Specifically, therapists reported that the training and intervention delivery were effective in improving their clinical skills (e.g., competence addressing challenging behaviors, engaging parents) and child and family outcomes (Drahota et al., 2014). Participating therapists were observed to provide the AIM HI intervention with a high degree of fidelity, and children demonstrated statistically and clinically significant decreases in overall parent-reported child problem behaviors (Brookman-Frazee, Drahota, & Stadnick, 2012). Lastly, parents

[1] Funded by National Institute of Mental Health (NIMH) Grant K23MH077584.

reported that they were highly involved in the treatment for their children, perceived a strong therapeutic alliance with their children's therapists, and found that the treatment was improved once their children's therapist began delivering AIM HI (Stadnick et al., 2013).

Effectiveness Trial: Primary Child Outcomes

Building on the promising findings from the pilot study that supported the feasibility of training MH therapists and positive changes in child behaviors, we conducted a randomized controlled community effectiveness trial[2] in 29 publicly funded outpatient and school-based MH programs in San Diego and Los Angeles Counties, with the goal to systematically test the impact of training MH providers on changes in child behaviors over 18 months and identify potential moderators and mediators of trajectories of child behaviors. Programs were randomized to receive immediate AIM HI training or usual care/delayed AIM HI training (waitlist control). Therapist and child dyads were recruited and enrolled from participating programs. A total of 202 children (mean age = 9.13 years; 84% male; 60% Latino) participated (see Figure 21.2 for a description of the multilevel sample). Results indicated that children whose therapists received AIM HI training and ongoing consultation showed greater reductions in the frequency (Eyberg Child Behavior Inventory [ECBI] Intensity scale) and severity (ECBI Problem scale) of parent-reported challenging behaviors over 18 months compared to children whose therapists delivered usual care. Observer-rated therapist fidelity to AIM HI strategies within sessions mediated intervention effects such that children whose therapists received AIM HI training received significantly higher session structure and continuity across sessions (relative to the usual care group, which in turn was associated with lower EBCI scores at 6 months (Brookman-Frazee, Roesch, et al., 2019).

Overall, these key findings provide further evidence for an intervention designed to fit the needs and structure of community services when delivered by therapists who do not specialize in ASD. The significant reductions in the frequency and severity of challenging behaviors as measured by the ECBI suggests that AIM HI was effective in reducing the problem behavior symptoms it was designed to improve. This was the first large-scale community effectiveness trial of an ASD psychosocial intervention tested within the context of publicly funded MH services. Additionally, this study included a large and diverse sample of therapists and children who are representative of the MH workforce (e.g., master's-level licensed and trainees) and clients (primarily ethnic minority and low socioeconomic status with a large proportion of caregivers with limited English proficiency) and supports the effectiveness of AIM HI with diverse populations across

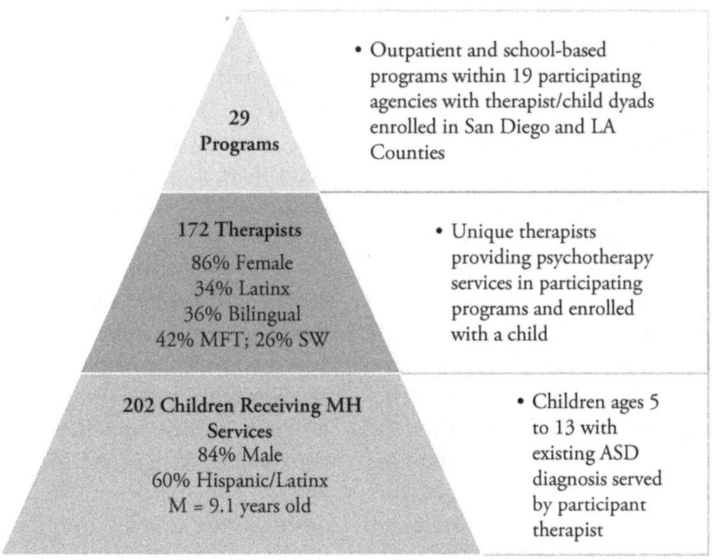

Figure 21.2. An Individualized Mental Health Intervention for ASD (AIM HI) effectiveness trial participants. ASD, autism spectrum disorder; MFT, marriage and family therapist, MH, mental health; SW, social worker.

[2] Funded by NIMH Grant R01MH094317.

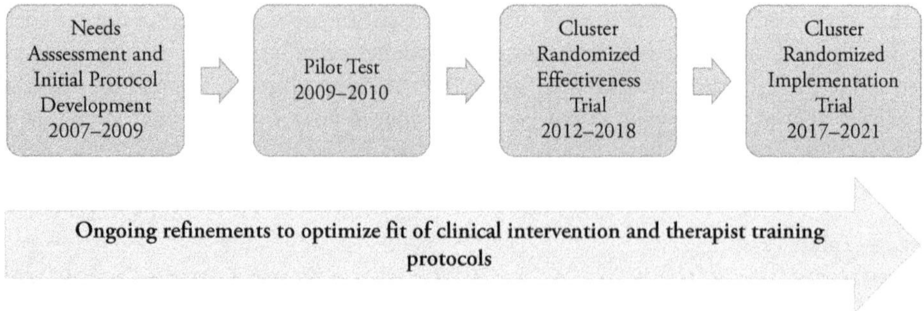

Figure 21.3. Timeline of An Individualized Mental Health Intervention for ASD (AIM HI) research.

settings. The finding related to therapist fidelity as a mediator of outcome highlights the importance of developing and testing implementation strategies aimed to facilitate high therapist fidelity in delivering evidence-based interventions.

Effectiveness Trial: Implementation Processes and Outcomes

A secondary aim of the effectiveness trial was to characterize the implementation process and outcomes (changes to therapist practice, successfully learning AIM HI intervention) and identify inner context factors (organizational and therapist characteristics) influencing these outcomes.

Impact of AIM HI training on therapist practice. One of the key implementation outcomes in this study was therapist delivery of evidence-based intervention strategies included in AIM HI. Observer ratings of therapist adherence to and effectiveness of child-directed and parent-directed strategies were significantly higher in therapists receiving AIM HI training compared to therapists delivering usual care (Brookman-Frazee, Roesch, et al., under review; Table 21.2). These findings are particularly important, as higher scores on AIM HI fidelity effectiveness scores (continuity across sessions, session structure) were associated with improved child behaviors 6 months after the baseline assessment.

AIM HI training outcomes and inner context factors associated with training success. Approximately 74% of the therapists enrolled in the AIM HI training condition of the effectiveness trial completed the requirements for certification in AIM HI (i.e., adhering to AIM HI protocol steps with an actual client during the 6-month training period, reaching the session fidelity criterion on a trainer-rated session recording with a client, and attending 80% of the required consultation/feedback meetings). Although a high proportion of therapists met the certification criteria, there was significant variability in delivery of AIM HI between therapists and across sessions, and the average observer-rated fidelity ratings for therapists trained in AIM HI were in the moderate range (see Table 21.2).

To understand the variability in therapist training outcomes, we compared perspectives of the AIM HI intervention and training process for a subset of therapists in the AIM HI condition of the effectiveness trial based on training certification status (i.e., certified in the AIM HI intervention vs. noncertified; Dyson, Chlebowski, Wright, & Brookman-Frazee, 2017). Overall, both certified and noncertified therapists perceived the AIM HI intervention as useful and effective with their clients, described the increased use of structure and improved clinical skills, and reported intended sustained use of at least parts of the AIM HI protocol. Both certified and noncertified therapists identified program and supervisor support as a facilitator to implementation. This finding is consistent with previous research identifying program and leader support as an important influence on EBI implementation (Aarons & Palinkas, 2007; Brunette et al., 2008; Massatti, Sweeney, Panzano, & Roth, 2008; Nadeem & Ringle, 2016; Palinkas et al., 2013).

Although certified and noncertified therapists experienced similar implementation challenges (i.e., time required for training and intervention delivery and the challenge of delivering a structured intervention within existing program structure), they differed in their approaches to addressing these perceived challenges and how insurmountable they perceived the barriers to be, and these perceptions distinguished certified from noncertified providers. Findings suggest that therapist perceptions and motivation may have a large influence on successful implementation and indicate the need to develop organizational leadership and provider interventions designed to address attitudinal and organizational

Table 21.2. Comparing Observed Therapist Delivery of EBI Strategies for Therapists in AIM HI and Usual Care Groups

Observed Therapist Fidelity (Averaged Across 6 Months)[a]	Usual Care (n = 42 therapists)	AIM HI (n = 130 therapists)
Adherence		
Child-directed strategies	2.78 (.743)	3.55 (.785)
Caregiver-directed strategies	1.84 (.772)	3.22 (.735)
Therapist effectiveness (competence)		
Session structure	2.80 (1.00)	4.55 (0.78)
Continuity across sessions	2.47 (1.10)	4.52 (0.80)
Pursuit of child skill	3.09 (1.53)	3.77 (1.13)
Pursuit of caregiver skill	1.27 (1.30)	3.41 (1.11)

AIM HI, An Individualized Mental Health Intervention for ASD; EBI, evidence-based intervention.

[a] Fidelity ratings were scored by coders naïve to the experimental group on a 7-point Likert scale reflecting the extent to which the strategy was used in a specific session. Scores of 0 indicate that the strategy was not observed. Scores of 1–2, 3–4, and 5–6 reflect low, moderate, and high extensiveness, respectively.

barriers to facilitate the successful training and implementation of evidence-based interventions.

Therapist adaptations to AIM HI. To further understand the fit of AIM HI with therapist practice in community and school settings, we also collected mixed qualitative and quantitative data from a subset of therapists participating in one of the training cohorts of the effectiveness trial. We characterized the types of adaptation therapists reported using when delivering AIM HI to their clients and the reported reasons therapists made these adaptations. Results indicate that the majority of therapists made adaptations that augmented or enhanced the AIM HI protocol, including simplifying intervention language, slowing the pace of intervention delivery, integrating other treatment methods, and involving others, such as other caregivers or professionals, in treatment. These adaptations were made with the goal of enhancing the intervention to fit with their own therapeutic style and to address clients' and caregivers' needs, functioning, and comprehension (Dyson, Chlebowski, & Brookman-Frazee, 2019). The identified adaptations were highly consistent with the AIM HI protocol to individualize intervention for children and their families, suggesting that AIM HI can be successfully and flexibly applied in routine care.

Implementation Trial

The next step in this line of translational research is to move from a primary focus on testing effectiveness to testing strategies to implement AIM HI. The primary goal of an implementation trial is to test a method or methods designed to enhance adoption and uptake of an EBI (Curran, Bauer, Mittman, Pyne, & Stetler, 2012). Findings from the AIM HI effectiveness trial[3] indicated that, even when interventions are systematically developed for the end-users with strong community partnership and best practices in training and consultation, there is variability in training completion and fidelity. These findings are highly consistent with findings from a similarly designed and concurrently conducted effectiveness trial testing the impact of training teachers to deliver a behavioral intervention (CPRT: Classroom Pivotal Response Teaching) for children with ASD in classrooms (Brookman-Frazee & Stahmer, 2018). Because provider fidelity of EBIs is related to child outcomes (Brookman-Frazee, Roesch, et al., 2019; Mandell et al., 2013; Strain & Bovey, 2011), testing methods to improve this key implementation outcome is critical to ensuring positive child-level outcomes when EBIs are implemented in routine care. Findings from both the AIM HI and CPRT effectiveness trials indicate that implementation leadership and climate and provider attitudes toward EBIs are promising inner context targets of implementation interventions (Brookman-Frazee & Stahmer, 2018).

Building directly on the AIM HI and CPRT effectiveness trials, the AIM HI and CPRT research groups are currently conducting two coordinated studies testing the effectiveness of the Translating Evidence-based Interventions (EBI) for ASD: Multilevel Implementation Strategy (TEAMS) model. TEAMS targets implementation leadership and climate, as well as provider motivation to improve key implementation outcomes: provider training completion, intervention fidelity, and subsequent

[3] Funded by NIMH Collaborative R01 Grants R01MH111950 (AIM HI) and R01MH111981 (CPRT)

child outcomes. The TEAMS Leadership Institute applies implementation leadership/climate strategies. TEAMS Individualized Provider Strategies (TIPS) for training applies motivational interviewing strategies to facilitate provider and organizational behavior change. Through a randomized trial, we are testing the effectiveness of TEAMS across settings and participants throughout California. Study 1 is testing the TEAMS model with AIM HI in publicly funded MH services. Study 2 is testing TEAMS with CPRT in education settings. Thirty-seven MH programs and 37 school districts are being randomized to one of four groups (Standard Provider Training Only, Standard Provider Training + Leader Training, Enhanced Provider Training, Enhanced Provider Training + Leader Training) to test the effectiveness of combining standard, EBI-specific training with the two TEAMS modules individually and together on implementation outcomes. The TEAMS project has the potential to increase the quality of care for ASD in routine care services by improving the effectiveness of EBI implementation.

Summary and Future Directions

In this chapter, we describe a decade of research aimed to build the capacity of MH services to address the commonly co-occurring MH conditions in children with ASD (Figure 21.3). We apply an emerging model of intervention development and testing that uses methods to facilitate implementation by end-users in targeted community service systems (Brookman-Frazee & Stahmer, 2018; Wood, McLeod, Klebanoff, & Brookman-Frazee, 2015; Drahota et al., 2017). First, we developed an intervention protocol based on quantitative and qualitative data collected from the targeted service context, including data on observed gaps between EBI and routine MH services and caregiver and therapist perspectives on the clinical needs of children with ASD served in MH programs and the training needs of MH therapists. Second, this research has been conducted through collaboration with researchers and relevant community stakeholders to facilitate the relevance of the research questions and fit of models developed to routine care. Lastly, we developed and tested the effectiveness of clinical intervention and therapist training protocols. In addition to the data supporting the effectiveness of the AIM HI intervention, this research is considered to be highly relevant and impactful in building the capacity of MH services for children with ASD.

As indicated in the introduction to this chapter, individuals with ASD experience high rates of co-occurring psychiatric symptoms and disorders across the lifespan. The research presented in this chapter represents significant advancements in conducting community-engaged, translational research in children's MH services. Because very similar themes regarding barriers to accessing effective MH services have been identified for adolescents and adults, the AIM HI development process has the potential to serve as a guide for building capacity across the lifespan. Additionally, individuals with ASD are served in other public service systems that may experience similar challenges to MH services in caring for this population. As such, ASD services and implementation research could be extended to reach a more comprehensive array of relevant services. Lastly, the focus of this work has been to improve MH services once individuals are already linked to and engaged with these services. As systems build capacity to work with individuals with ASD, ensuring access to these services is essential. Policies related to the financing and organization of public services for ASD are critical to facilitating access to and quality of services for individuals with ASD across the lifespan.

References

Aarons, G. A., Hurlburt, M., & Horwitz, S. M. (2011). Advancing a conceptual model of evidence-based practice implementation in public service sectors. *Administration and Policy in Mental Health and Mental Health Services Research, 38*, 4–23. doi:10.1007/s10488-010-0327-7

Aarons, G. A., & Palinkas, L. A. (2007). Implementation of evidence-based practice in child welfare: Service provider perspectives. *Administration and Policy in Mental Health and Mental Health Services Research, 34*, 411–419. doi:10.1007/s10488-007-0121-3

Balas, E. A. (1998). From appropriate care to evidence-based medicine. *Pediatric Annals, 27*, 581–584. doi:10.3928/0090-4481-19,980,901-11

Balas, E. A., & Boren, S. A. (2000). Managing clinical knowledge for health care improvement. *Yearbook of Medical Informatics, 9*(01), 65–70.

Brookman-Frazee, L., Baker-Ericzén, M., Stadnick, N., & Taylor, R. (2012). Parent perspectives on community mental health services for children with autism spectrum disorders. *Journal of Child and Family Studies, 21*, 533–544. doi:10.1007/s10826-011-9506-8

Brookman-Frazee, L., Baker-Ericzén, M., Stahmer, A., Mandell, D., Haine, R. A., & Hough, R. L. (2009). Involvement of youths with autism spectrum disorders or intellectual disabilities in multiple public service systems. *Journal of Mental Health Research in Intellectual Disabilities, 2*, 201–219. doi:10.1080/19315860902741542

Brookman-Frazee, L., & Drahota, A. (2010). *An individualized mental health intervention for children with autism spectrum disorders (AIM HI): A model to address challenging behaviors in children with ASD—A therapist manual.* San Diego, CA: University of California, San Diego.

Brookman-Frazee, L., Drahota, A., & Chlebowski, C. (2016). *An individualized mental health intervention for children with autism spectrum disorder (AIM HI;* Vol. 2): *Therapist manual.* San Diego, CA: University of California, San Diego.

Brookman-Frazee, L., Drahota, A., & Stadnick, N. (2012). Training community mental health therapists to deliver a package of evidence-based practice strategies for school-age children with autism spectrum disorders: A pilot study. *Journal of Autism and Developmental Disorders, 42,* 1651–1661. doi:10.1007/s10803-011-1406-7

Brookman-Frazee, L., Drahota, A., Stadnick, N., & Palinkas, L. A. (2012). Therapist perspectives on community mental health services for children with autism spectrum disorders. *Administration and Policy in Mental Health and Mental Health Services Research, 39,* 365–373. doi:10.1007/s10488-011-0355-y

Brookman-Frazee, L., Stadnick, N., Chlebowski, C., Baker-Ericzén, M., & Ganger, W. (2017). Characterizing psychiatric comorbidity in children with autism spectrum disorder receiving publicly-funded mental health services. *Autism: International Journal of Research and Practice, 22 (8),* 1–15. doi:10.1177/1362361317712650

Brookman-Frazee, L., Roesch, S., Chlebowski, C., Baker-Ericzén, M., & Ganger, W. (2019). Effectiveness of training therapists to deliver An Individualized Mental Health Intervention for Children with ASD in publicly funded mental health services: A cluster randomized clinical trial. *JAMA Psychiatry, 76*(6), 574–583. doi:10.1001/jamapsychiatry.2019.0011

Brookman-Frazee., L., & Stahmer, A. C. (2018). Effectiveness of a multi-level implementation strategy for ASD interventions: Study protocol for two linked cluster randomized trials. *Implementation Science, 13*(1), 66. doi:10.1186/s13012-018-0757-2

Brookman-Frazee, L., Taylor, R., & Garland, A. F. (2010). Characterizing community-based mental health services for children with autism spectrum disorders. *Journal of Autism and Developmental Disorders, 40,* 1188–1201. doi:10.1007/s10803-010-0976-0

Brunette, M. F., Asher, D., Whitley, R., Lutz, W. J., Wieder, B. L., Jones, A. M., & McHugo, G. J. (2008). Implementation of integrated dual disorders treatment: A qualitative analysis of facilitators and barriers. *Psychiatric Services, 59,* 989–995. doi:10.1176/ps.2008.59.9.989

Buck, T., Viskochil, J., Farley, M., Coon, H., McMahon, W., Morgan, J., & Bilder, D. (2014). Psychiatric comorbidity and medication use in adults with autism spectrum disorder. *Journal of Autism and Developmental Disorders, 44,* 3063–3071. doi:10.1007/s10803-014-2170-2

California Department of Health Care Services. (2018a). *Medi-Cal specialty mental health services policy change supplement.* Retrieved from https://www.dhcs.ca.gov/services/MH/Documents/SMHS-Supplement-May2018-Est-2018-5-14-ADA.pdf

California Department of Health Care Services. (2018b). Medical necessity criteria. Title 9, California Code of Regulations, Chapter 11, Medi-Cal Specialty Mental Health Services, section 1830.210. Retrieved from https://www.dhcs.ca.gov/formsandpubs/MHArchiveLtrs/MH-Ltr01-01_enclosure1.pdf

Curran, G. M., Bauer, M., Mittman, B., Pyne, J. M., & Stetler, C. (2012). Effectiveness-implementation hybrid designs: Combining elements of clinical effectiveness and implementation research to enhance public health impact. *Medical Care, 50,* 217–226. doi:10.1097/mlr.0b013e3182408812

de Bruin, E. I., Ferdinand, R. F., Meester, S., de Nijs, P. F. A., & Verheij, F. (2007). High rates of psychiatric co-morbidity in PDD-NOS. *Journal of Autism and Developmental Disorders, 37*(5), 877–886. doi:10.1007/s10803-006-0215-x

Drahota, A., Chlebowski, C., Stadnick, N., Baker-Ericzén, M. J., & Brookman-Frazee, L. (2017). The dissemination and implementation of behavioral treatments for anxiety in ASD. In C. M. Kerns, P. Renno, E. A. Storch, P. C. Kendall, & J. J. Wood (Eds.), *Anxiety in children and adolescents with autism spectrum disorder: Evidence-based assessment and treatment* (pp. 231–249). Atlanta, GA: Elsevier.

Drahota, A., Stadnick, N., & Brookman-Frazee, L. (2014). Therapist perspectives on training in a package of evidence-based practice strategies for children with autism spectrum disorders served in community mental health clinics. *Administration and Policy in Mental Health and Mental Health Services Research, 41,* 114–125. doi:10.1007/s10488-012-0441-9

Dyson, M. W., Chlebowski, C., & Brookman-Frazee, L. (2019). Therapists' adaptations to an intervention to reduce challenging behaviors in children with autism spectrum disorder in publicly funded mental health services. *Journal of Autism and Developmental Disorders, 49*(3), 924-934. doi.org/10.1007/s10803-018-3795-3

Dyson, M. W., Chlebowski, C., Wright, B., & Brookman-Frazee, L. (2017). How do certified and uncertified therapists differ in their perceptions of a mental health intervention for ASD? *Evidence-Based Practice in Child and Adolescent Mental Health, 2*(3–4), 179–194. doi:10.1080/23794925.2017.1389319

Eccles, M., & Mittman, B. (2006). Welcome to implementation science. *Implementation Science, 1*(1), 1. doi:10.1186/1748-5908-1-1

Garfield, R., & Zur, J. (2017, March). *Medicaid restructuring under the American Health Care Act and implications for behavioral health care in the US.* Washington, DC: Kaiser Family Foundation. Retrieved from https://www.kff.org/medicaid/issue-brief/medicaid-restructuring-under-the-american-health-care-act-and-implications-for-behavioral-health-care-in-the-us/view/footnotes/#footnote-212, 771–6.

Garland, A. F., Bickman, L., & Chorpita, B. (2010). Change what? Identifying quality improvement targets by investigating usual mental health care. *Administration and Policy in Mental Health and Mental Health Services Research, 37.* 15–26. doi:10.1007/s10488-010-0279-y

Garland, A. F., Brookman-Frazee, L., Hurlburt, M. S., Accurso, E. C., Zoffness, R. J., Haine Schlagel, R., & Ganger, W. (2010). Mental health care for children with disruptive behavior problems: A view inside therapists' offices. *Psychiatric Services, 61,* 788–795. doi:10.1176/appi.ps.61.8.788

Garland, A. F., Hough, R. L., McCabe, K. M., Yeh, M. A. Y., Wood, P. A., & Aarons, G. A. (2001). Prevalence of psychiatric disorders in youths across five sectors of care. *Journal of the American Academy of Child & Adolescent Psychiatry, 40,* 409–418. doi:10.1097/00004583-200,104,000-00009

Garland, A. F., Lau, A. S., Yeh, M., McCabe, K. M., Hough, R. L., & Landsverk, J. A. (2005). Racial and ethnic differences in utilization of mental health services among high-risk youths. *American Journal of Psychiatry, 162,* 1336–1343. doi:10.1176/appi.ajp.162.7.1336

Gjevik, E., Eldevik, S., Fjæran-Granum, T., & Sponheim, E. (2011). Kiddie-SADS reveals high rates of DSM-IV disorders in children and adolescents with autism spectrum disorders. *Journal of Autism and Developmental Disorders, 41,* 761–769. doi:10.1007/s10803-010-1095-7

Gray, K., Keating, C., Taffe, J., Brereton, A., Einfeld, S., & Tonge, B. (2012). Trajectory of behavior and emotional problems in autism. *American Association on Intellectual and Developmental Disabilities, 117,* 121–133. doi:10.1352/1944-7588-117-2.121

Hastings, R. P. (2003). Child behaviour problems and partner mental health as correlates of stress in mothers and fathers of children with autism. *Journal of Intellectual Disability Research, 47*(4–5), 231–237. doi:10.1046/j.1365–2788.2003.00485.x

Horner, R. H., Carr, E. G., Strain, P. S., Todd, A. W., & Reed, H. K. (2002). Problem behavior interventions for young children with autism: A research synthesis. *Journal of Autism and Developmental Disorders, 32,* 423–446. doi:10.1023/A:1020593922901

Joshi, G., Faraone, S. V., Wozniak, J., Petty, C., Fried, R., Galdo, M., . . . Biederman, J. (2014). Examining the clinical correlates of autism spectrum disorder in youth by ascertainment source. *Journal of Autism and Developmental Disorders, 44,* 2117–2126. doi:10.1007/s10803-014-2063-4

Kalb, L. G., Stuart, E. A., Mandell, D. S., Olfson, M., & Vasa, R. A. (2017). Management of mental health crises among youths with and without ASD: A national survey of child psychiatrists. *Psychiatric Services, 68,* 1039–1045. doi:10.1176/appi.ps.201600332

Kim, J. A., Szatmari, P., Bryson, S. E., Streiner, D. L., & Wilson, F. J. (2000). The prevalence of anxiety and mood problems among children with autism and Asperger syndrome. *Autism, 4,* 117–132. doi:10.1177/1362361300004002002

Lake, J. K., Perry, A., & Lunsky, Y. (2014). Mental health services for individuals with high functioning autism spectrum disorder. *Autism Research and Treatment, 2014,* 502420. doi:10.1155/2014/502420

Lecavalier, L., Leone, S., & Wiltz, J. (2006). The impact of behaviour problems on caregiver stress in young people with autism spectrum disorders. *Journal of Intellectual Disabilities Research, 50,* 172–183. doi:10.1111/j.1365–2788.2005.00732.x

Leeman, J., Birken, S. A., Powell, B. J., Rohweder, C., & Shea, C. M. (2017). Beyond "implementation strategies": Classifying the full range of strategies used in implementation science and practice. *Implementation Science, 12*(1), 125. doi:10.1186/s13012-017-0657-x

Lever, A. G., & Geurts, H. M. (2016). Psychiatric co-occurring symptoms and disorders in young, middle-aged, and older adults with autism spectrum disorder. *Journal of Autism and Developmental Disorders, 46,* 1916–1930. doi:10.1007/s10803-016-2722-8

Leyfer, O. T., Folstein, S. E., Bacalman, S., Davis, N. O., Dinh, E., Morgan, J., . . . Lainhart, J. E. (2006). Comorbid psychiatric disorders in children with autism: Interview development and rates of disorders. *Journal of Autism and Developmental Disorders, 36,* 849–861. doi:10.1007/s10803-006-0123-0

Maddox, B. B., Crabbe, S. R., Fishman, J. M., Beidas, R. S., Brookman-Frazee, L., Miller, J. S., . . . & Mandell, D. S. (2019). Factors Influencing the Use of Cognitive–Behavioral Therapy with Autistic Adults: A Survey of Community Mental Health Clinicians. *Journal of autism and developmental disorders,* 1–8.

Maddox, B. B., & Gaus, V. L. (2018). Community mental health services for adults: Good news and bad news. *Autism in Adulthood, 1*(1). doi:10.1089/aut.2018.0006

Mandell, D. S., Stahmer, A. C., Shin, S., Xie, M., Reisinger, E., & Marcus, S. C. (2013). The role of treatment fidelity on outcomes during a randomized field trial of an autism intervention. *Autism, 17,* 281–295. doi:10.1177/1362361312473666

Mandell, D. S., Walrath, C. M., Manteuffel, B., Sgro, G., & Pinto-Martin, J. (2005). Characteristics of children with autistic spectrum disorders served in comprehensive community-based mental health settings. *Journal of Autism and Developmental Disorders, 35,* 313–321. doi:10.1007/s10803-005-3296-z

Mark, T. L., Coffey, R. M., Vandivort-Warren, R., Harwood, H. J., King, E. C., & MHSA Spending Estimates Team. (2005). U.S. spending for mental health and substance abuse treatment, 1991–2001. *Health Affairs,* Supplement Web Exclusives W5-133 - W5-142

Massatti, R. R., Sweeney, H. A., Panzano, P. C., & Roth, D. (2008). The de-adoption of innovative mental health practices (IMHP): Why organizations choose not to sustain an IMHP. *Administration and Policy in Mental Health and Mental Health Services Research, 35,* 50–65. doi:10.1007/s10488-007-0141-z

Matson, J., Wilkins, J., & Macken, J. (2009). The relationship of challenging behaviors to severity and symptoms of autism spectrum disorders. *Journal of Mental Health Research in Intellectual Disabilities, 2,* 1931–5864. doi:10.1080/19315860802611415

Nadeem, E., & Ringle, V. A. (2016). De-adoption of an evidence-based trauma intervention in schools: A retrospective report from an urban school district. *School Mental Health, 8,* 132–143. doi:10.1007/s12310-016-9179-y

Narendorf, S. C., Shattuck, P. T., & Sterzing, P. R. (2011). Mental health service use among adolescents with an autism spectrum disorder. *Psychiatric Services, 62,* 975–978. doi:10.1176/appi.ps.62.8.975

National Autism Center. (2015). National Standards Project, Phase 2. Retrieved from http://www.nationalautismcenter.org/national-standards-project/phase-2/

Palinkas, L. A., Weisz, J. R., Chorpita, B. F., Levine, B., Garland, A. F., Hoagwood, K. E., & Landsverk, J. (2013). Continued use of evidence-based treatments after a randomized controlled effectiveness trial: A qualitative study. *Psychiatric Services, 64,* 1110–1118. doi:10.1176/appi.ps.004682012

Proctor, E. K., Powell, B. J., & McMillen, J. C. (2013). Implementation strategies: Recommendations for specifying and reporting. *Implementation Science, 8*(1), 1–11. doi:10.1186/1748-5908-8-1

Salazar, F., Baird, G., Chandler, S., Tseng, E., O'Sullivan, T., Howlin, P., . . . Simonoff, E. (2015). Co-occurring psychiatric disorders in preschool and elementary school-aged children with autism spectrum disorder. *Journal of Autism and Developmental Disorders, 45,* 2283–2294. doi:10.1007/s10803-015-2361-5

Sheehan, D.V., Lecrubier, Y., Sheehan, K.H., Amorim, P., Janavs, J., Weiller, E., Hergueta, T., Baker, R. and Dunbar, G.C., (1998). The Mini-International Neuropsychiatric Interview (M.I.N.I.): The development and validation of a structured diagnostic psychiatric interview for DSM-IV and ICD-10. *Journal of Clinical Psychiatry, 59*(Suppl 20), 22–33, quiz 34–57.

Simonoff, E., Pickles, A., Charman, T., Chandler, S., Loucas, T., & Baird, G. (2008). Psychiatric disorders in children with autism spectrum disorders: Prevalence, comorbidity, and associated factors in a population-derived sample. *Journal of the American Academy of Child & Adolescent Psychiatry, 47,* 921–929. doi:10.1097/chi.0b013e318179964f

Soke, G. N., Maenner, M. J., Christensen, D., Kurzius-Spencer, M., & Schieve, L. A. (2018). Prevalence of co-occurring medical and behavioral conditions/symptoms among 4- and

8-year-old children with autism spectrum disorder in selected areas of the United States in 2010. *Journal of Autism and Developmental Disorders, 48*, 2663–2676. doi:10.1007/s10803-018-3521-1

Stadnick, N., Chlebowski, C., & Brookman-Frazee, L. (2017). Caregiver-teacher concordance of challenging behaviors in children with autism spectrum disorder served in community mental health settings. *Journal of Autism and Developmental Disorders, 47*, 1780–1790. doi:10.1007/s10803-017-3101-9

Stadnick, N., Drahota, A., & Brookman-Frazee, L. (2013). Parent perspectives of an evidence-based intervention for children with autism served in community mental health clinics. *Journal of Child and Family Studies, 22*, 414–422. doi:10.1007/s10826-012-9594-0

Strain, P. S., & Bovey, E. H., II. (2011). Randomized, controlled trial of the LEAP model of early intervention for young children with autism spectrum disorders. *Topics in Early Childhood Special Education, 31*, 133–154. doi:10.1177/0271121411408740

Tabak, R. G., Khoong, E. C., Chambers, D., & Brownson, R. C. (2013). Models in dissemination and implementation research: Useful tools in public health services and systems research. *Frontiers in Public Health Services and Systems Research, 2*(1), 8. doi:10.13023/fphssr.0201.08

Wong, C., Odom, S. L., Hume, K. A., Cox, A. W., Fettig, A., Kucharczyk, S., . . . Schultz, T. R. (2015). Evidence-based practices for children, youth, and young adults with autism spectrum disorder: A comprehensive review. *Journal of Autism and Developmental Disorders, 45*, 1951–1966. doi:10.1007/s10803-014-2351-z

Wood, J. J., & Gadow, K. D. (2010). Exploring the nature and function of anxiety in youth with autism spectrum disorders. *Clinical Psychology-Science and Practice, 17*, 281–292. doi:10.1111/j.1468–2850.2010.01220.x

Wood, J. J., McLeod, B. D., Klebanoff, S., & Brookman-Frazee, L. (2015). Toward the implementation of evidence-based interventions for youth with autism spectrum disorders in schools and community agencies. *Behavior Therapy, 46*, 83–95. doi:10.1016/j.beth.2014.07.003

CHAPTER

22 Synthesis

Current State of the Science and Future Directions

Brenna B. Maddox, Carla A. Mazefsky, *and* Susan W. White

Abstract

Recent research and clinical attention devoted to co-occurring psychiatric conditions within autism spectrum disorder (ASD) has led to significant advances in the understanding of and ability to assess and treat co-occurring problems effectively. This chapter summarizes those advances while also highlighting the substantial gaps that remain in the understanding of co-occurring problems in people with ASD. The chapter provides recommendations for future research directions in the areas of etiology, developmental course, assessment, and treatment. It also offers suggestions for improving the representativeness of research participants and strengthening community–academic partnerships in this important field of study.

Keywords: autism spectrum disorder, co-occurring psychiatric conditions, etiology, mechanisms, lifespan, assessment, treatment

Introduction

The goal of this handbook is to provide a comprehensive resource on co-occurring psychiatric conditions and behavioral concerns in autistic people across the lifespan. This book covers 10 psychiatric conditions or groups of psychiatric conditions from the *Diagnostic and Statistical Manual of Mental Disorders*, fifth edition (DSM-5; American Psychiatric Association [APA], 2013) and seven related topics, such as aggression and sleep problems. We chose to include these seven topics, although not co-occurring diagnoses, because they have a significant impact on many autistic individuals' lives and may require psychiatric treatment. However, it is also important to note that some of the experiences described here (e.g., sexuality, gender diversity) may not be associated with problems and can be viewed as contributing to an autistic person's well-being in general.

For each psychiatric condition and related topic, the expert contributors herein provide information about prevalence and developmental course, review current theories on etiology, and describe the evidence-based assessment and treatment approaches available. In addition, the final chapters highlight important considerations for the psychopharmacological treatment of co-occurring psychiatric conditions in autism spectrum disorder (ASD), the management of crisis behavior in autistic individuals, and the intersection of implementation science and autism services. Recent research and clinical attention devoted to co-occurring psychiatric conditions within ASD has led to significant advances in our understanding and ability to assess and treat co-occurring problems effectively. However, as detailed in this chapter, there remain several substantial gaps in our understanding of co-occurring problems in people with ASD.

Current State of the Science

Co-occurring psychiatric conditions received relatively little attention in ASD research until recent years (Mazurek, 2016). Historically, the DSM precluded certain psychiatric diagnoses (e.g., attention deficit hyperactivity disorder [ADHD], separation anxiety disorder) in people with pervasive developmental or autism spectrum disorders (APA, 1980, 1987, 1994, 2000), based on the belief that symptoms of these disorders presented so frequently in autistic individuals that they were characteristic of ASD and did not warrant additional diagnoses. The current edition of the DSM (DSM-5; APA, 2013) removed these exclusionary criteria and specifically discusses the high rates of co-occurring psychiatric conditions in ASD (pp. 58–59).

As discussed by Leno and Simonoff in Chapter 1, we now know that autistic people of all ages are at a higher risk for experiencing co-occurring psychiatric conditions relative to people without ASD. In fact, autistic individuals often meet diagnostic criteria for multiple co-occurring psychiatric conditions (Leyfer et al., 2006; Simonoff et al., 2008). There is solid evidence of increased risk for certain conditions, such as unipolar depression (Chapter 2), psychosis (Chapter 3), anxiety disorders (Chapter 5), obsessive-compulsive disorder (OCD; Chapter 6), and ADHD (Chapter 9), although prevalence estimates have varied widely across different diagnostic tools and sampling methods. For other conditions, no established prevalence estimates in ASD exist (e.g., bipolar disorder, Chapter 2; substance-related disorders, Chapter 4), or findings on whether there is an increased rate in ASD are mixed (e.g., posttraumatic stress disorder; Chapter 7). In addition, the reasons behind heightened risk of co-occurring psychiatric conditions remain largely unknown; multiple mechanisms likely play a role, as summarized by Leno and Simonoff in Chapter 1. Regardless of the etiology, we know that co-occurring psychiatric conditions can have serious negative consequences and lead to poorer functional outcomes for autistic individuals across the lifespan (e.g., Farley et al., 2009; Sikora, Vora, Coury, & Rosenberg, 2012; Spain, Sin, Linder, McMahon, & Happé, 2018). Co-occurring psychiatric conditions and behavioral concerns often prompt treatment referral for autistic individuals and are associated with adverse effects for the entire family (e.g., Joshi et al., 2010; Lecavalier, Leone, & Wiltz, 2006). Thus, it is not surprising that the topics of co-occurring psychiatric conditions and mental health services are a high research priority for stakeholders in the autistic community (Frazier et al., 2018; Pellicano, Dinsmore, & Charman, 2014).

As discussed throughout this volume, most assessment measures of psychiatric conditions and related problems were not designed specifically for (or even validated for use with) autistic individuals, although some exceptions exist (e.g., Parent-Rated Anxiety Scale for ASD, Scahill et al., 2019; Emotion Dysregulation Inventory, Mazefsky et al., 2018; Brief Autism Mealtime Behaviors Inventory, Lukens & Linscheid, 2008). The accurate detection and diagnosis of co-occurring psychiatric conditions can be challenging due to overlapping symptoms with ASD and certain characteristics of the autistic individual (e.g., cognitive or language limitations, alexithymia). In the context of ASD, psychiatric conditions present with many prototypical symptoms; however, there may also be some signs that are ASD specific, such as increased frequency or intensity of repetitive behaviors (e.g., Rodgers, Glod, Connolly, & McConachie, 2012; Chapter 2, Table 2.1).

The preceding chapters offer many practical tips for distinguishing between ASD characteristics and symptoms of a co-occurring psychiatric condition. In general, a multimodal (e.g., self-report, parent report, teacher report), multimethod (e.g., interview, rating scales, direct observation) assessment is recommended, with a focus on any observable changes from the individual's established baseline, or typical behaviors before concerns first arose. For concerns such as self-injurious behavior and aggression, a functional behavioral assessment is useful to identify the environmental variables that contribute to the occurrence and maintenance of a problem behavior (Chapters 15 and 17).

There are few evidence-based treatments for co-occurring psychiatric conditions in ASD, based on the American Psychological Association Division 12 and Division 53 criteria (Chambless & Hollon, 1998; Society of Clinical Child and Adolescent Psychology, 2019), although preliminary studies show promise. The most researched psychosocial interventions to date include cognitive behavioral therapy (CBT) modified for ASD and co-occurring anxiety (Chapter 5), depression (Chapter 2), and OCD (Chapter 6); CBT for executive function impairments in children (Chapter 16); behavioral interventions (e.g., applied behavior analysis) for disruptive behaviors (Chapters 8 and 15), self-injurious behaviors (Chapter 17), and intellectual disability (Chapter 10); and parent training for disruptive behaviors (Chapters 8 and 15). This handbook includes practical tools for clinicians treating co-occurring psychiatric conditions in autistic individuals. Examples include a summary of modifications to traditional CBT approaches (Chapter 7, Table 7.1), considerations for personalized treatment of eating issues (Chapter 13, Table 13.2), and a sample treatment plan for addressing crisis behaviors (Chapter 20, Table 20.1). In addition, several chapters highlight the importance of multidisciplinary treatment teams and communication between different treatment providers to produce meaningful change.

Although only risperidone and aripiprazole have been approved by the U.S. Food and Drug Administration (FDA) for use in autistic youth, autistic individuals of all ages are commonly prescribed a host of medications for co-occurring conditions, particularly for ADHD, irritability, depression, anxiety, and insomnia (Chapter 19). Unfortunately, autistic individuals tend to respond less well to pharmacologic interventions in general relative to people without ASD, both in terms of symptom improvement and adverse side effects. In Chapter 19 of this volume, King and colleagues describe a number of important qualifications about the use of psychotropic medications in ASD. Overall, pharmacologic interventions for autistic people are understudied compared to the number of studies with non-ASD groups, particularly with regard to long-term use.

Future Directions

There is much work yet to be done in the field of ASD and co-occurring psychiatric conditions. In this section, we summarize some key themes that emerged from the preceding chapters about future research directions. It is fair to say that we have much yet to learn regarding every disorder and behavioral concern covered in this handbook. As highlighted in the preceding chapters, we have particularly limited information about certain psychiatric conditions in ASD, such as bipolar disorder (Chapter 2), body dysmorphic disorder (Chapter 6), hoarding disorder (Chapter 6), and trichotillomania (Chapter 6). Similarly, there is a notable absence of treatment studies for certain conditions or concerns that we know are more common in autistic people, such as psychosis (Chapter 3) and suicidality (Chapter 18).

Improving Understanding About the Etiology and Course of Co-Occurring Psychiatric Conditions in ASD

Future research should focus on examining the risk factors and contributing mechanisms associated with psychiatric conditions in autistic individuals. Longitudinal studies are needed to examine pathways from risk to emergence of different disorders. Given the challenges inherent in differential diagnosis and the frequency with which autistic individuals present with symptoms of multiple psychiatric disorders, there is also value in efforts to identify transdiagnostic mechanisms. This is consistent with the National Institute of Mental Health's Research Domain Criteria (RDoC) initiative, which was developed to encourage a greater focus on processes that may be disrupted across disorders (Insel et al., 2010).

This handbook focuses on autistic people of all ages. However, as most chapters highlight, the vast majority of research on co-occurring psychiatric conditions in autistic people has been conducted with children and adolescents. This is concerning, given emerging research that many autistic adults have mental health concerns and evidence that co-occurring conditions are often chronic and pervasive (Buck et al., 2014; Croen et al., 2015; Maddox & White, 2015). Future studies would benefit from a lifespan approach to better understand the developmental course of co-occurring psychiatric conditions in ASD.

Improving the Assessment and Treatment of Co-Occurring Psychiatric Conditions in ASD

To improve our abilities to detect co-occurring psychiatric conditions in autistic people, we need assessment measures that are validated and reliable for use with this population. In addition, new measures or modifications to existing measures should be developed with careful consideration of sensitivity to change and participant burden. Future research on assessment tools could use data repositories to conduct sensitivity analyses with large sample sizes.

Across all psychiatric conditions, most of the treatment research is composed of pilot studies with small sample sizes. We need replication studies of promising interventions across multiple sites, along with longer term follow-up assessments. These follow-up assessments are especially relevant for psychotropic medication studies, because autistic individuals can be on medications for long periods of time and few studies have examined the effects of long-term use (Chapter 19).

In addition, most of the treatment studies in this field have been conducted in tightly controlled, academic or medical research settings. It is not known how well these treatments work in the community. As discussed by Brookman-Frazee and colleagues in Chapter 21, community mental health services can play an important role in treating co-occurring psychiatric conditions in autistic children, adolescents, and adults. Future work could pull from the implementation science literature to focus on sustainable evidence-based mental health practices in routine, community-based care.

Future treatment studies could focus on transdiagnostic processes, as opposed to disorder-specific targets. Although psychopharmacology in ASD (e.g., risperidone for irritability) and behavioral treatments (e.g., focusing on the function of the behavior) have already embraced this idea, there has been recent increasing attention to the promise of transdiagnostic psychiatric treatments for psychosocial concerns more broadly in ASD (e.g., Weiss, 2014). One empirical example of the promise of this approach is the Emotional Awareness and Skills Enhancement (EASE) program. EASE was developed with stakeholder input to target improved emotion regulation in verbal autistic adolescents and adults, with observed benefits across the domains of emotion dysregulation, depression, anxiety, and problem behavior (Conner et al., 2018).

Increasing the Representativeness of Psychiatric Research in ASD

Most work on co-occurring psychiatric conditions and related behaviors has focused on individuals with average or even above-average cognitive abilities. Very little is known about how psychiatric conditions present in autistic individuals with intellectual disability (Helverschou & Martinsen, 2011) or with minimal language abilities (Lerner et al., 2018). Relatedly, a critical unanswered question is how to accurately diagnose, effectively treat, or monitor symptomatic change in people who do not have the verbal abilities to self-report symptoms or engage in standard psychosocial interventions.

Another largely underrepresented group in this research is racial and ethnic minorities. Significant racial and ethnic disparities exist in the recognition or diagnosis of ASD (e.g., Magaña, Lopez, Aguinaga, & Morton, 2013; Mandell et al., 2009), but it is less clear whether these disparities persist for recognition of co-occurring psychiatric conditions in ASD. Research suggests that non-White autistic children have significantly lower use of psychiatry/psychology subspecialty care (Broder-Fingert, Shui, Pulcini, Kurowski, & Perrin, 2013), which is consistent with findings from non-White children and adults without ASD (Marrast, Himmelstein, & Woolhandler, 2016), but more studies are needed to understand how to improve mental health services for minority groups. Future research on co-occurring psychiatric conditions in ASD should focus on the recruitment and retention of racial and ethnic minorities to close this gap (e.g., Zamora, Williams, Higareda, Wheeler, & Levitt, 2016).

Strengthening Community–Academic Partnerships

We agree with concerns raised in the preceding chapters about the lack of self-advocate and key-stakeholder involvement in research on psychiatric conditions in ASD. Future research would be greatly strengthened by including key stakeholders in all stages (Nicolaidis et al., 2011). For example, partnering with stakeholders in designing interventions and provider training activities increases the probability that these interventions will be implemented successfully in the community (Wood, McLeod, Klebanoff, & Brookman-Frazee, 2015).

We also believe that being mindful of language is important as we move the field forward. Many of the included chapters in this volume begin with a section on nomenclature, citing current confusion due to a wide variety of terms used in research and clinical practice. Another issue to consider is the distinction between strengths-based versus deficits-based language (Kapp, Gillespie-Lynch, Sherman, & Hutman, 2013). To follow a strengths-based approach, we chose to use the term "co-occurring" instead of "comorbid" for this volume's title, because "comorbid" implies that the index condition (ASD in this case) is a disease or morbidity. Our goal in this handbook is to be accurate, clear, and consistent in our terminology. However, it is also true that terminology changes over time, including what is preferred by autistic stakeholders (see Chapter 11 for an excellent discussion of this point).

Rubenstein and Bishop-Fitzpatrick (2019) recently introduced a temporally focused terminology to describe mental and physical health conditions that present with ASD. They argue that focusing on *when* conditions develop is important for better understanding the etiology, prevention, and treatment of these conditions. We agree that using more specific language to talk about mental health conditions experienced by autistic people will help to move the field in a meaningful direction.

Conclusions

The preceding chapters provide a compilation of the state of the science on co-occurring psychiatric conditions in ASD. Such a volume would not have been conceivable even just 10 years ago. Owing to the determination and care of family members and other stakeholders, as well as the work of countless scientists and clinicians in this field, there is now scientific recognition that many such problems (e.g., aggression, irritability, anxiety) can be effectively treated or managed to promote better quality of life. It is our hope that this handbook will provide a launchpad for future scientific and clinical work that will result in better understanding of co-occurring psychiatric conditions and improved quality of life for autistic individuals of all ages.

References

American Psychiatric Association. (1980). *Diagnostic and statistical manual of mental disorders* (3rd ed.). Washington, DC: Author.

American Psychiatric Association. (1987). *Diagnostic and statistical manual of mental disorders* (3rd ed. rev.). Washington, DC: Author.

American Psychiatric Association. (1994). *Diagnostic and statistical manual of mental disorders* (4th ed.). Washington, DC: Author.

American Psychiatric Association. (2000). *Diagnostic and statistical manual of mental disorders* (4th ed. rev.). Washington, DC: Author.

American Psychiatric Association. (2013). *Diagnostic and statistical manual of mental disorders* (5th ed.). Washington, DC: Author.

Broder-Fingert, S., Shui, A., Pulcini, C. D., Kurowski, D., & Perrin, J. M. (2013). Racial and ethnic differences in subspecialty service use by children with autism. *Pediatrics, 132,* 94–100. doi:10.1542/peds.2012-3886

Buck, T. R., Viskochil, J., Farley, M., Coon, H., McMahon, W. M., Morgan, J., & Bilder, D. A. (2014). Psychiatric comorbidity and medication use in adults with autism spectrum disorder. *Journal of Autism and Developmental Disorders, 44,* 3063–3071. doi:10.1007/s10803-014-2170-2

Chambless, D. L., & Hollon, S. D. (1998). Defining empirically supported therapies. *Journal of Consulting and Clinical Psychology, 66,* 7–18. doi:10.1037/0022-006X.66.1.7

Conner, C. M., White, S. W., Beck, K. B., Golt, J., Smith, I. C., & Mazefsky, C. A. (2019). Improving emotion regulation ability in autism: The Emotional Awareness and Skills Enhancement (EASE) program. *Autism, 23,* 1273–1287. doi:10.1177/1362361318810709

Croen, L. A., Zerbo, O., Qian, Y., Massolo, M. L., Rich, S., Sidney, S., & Kripke, C. (2015). The health status of adults on the autism spectrum. *Autism, 19,* 814–823. doi:10.1177/1362361315577517

Farley, M. A., McMahon, W. M., Fombonne, E., Jenson, W. R., Miller, J., Gardner, M., . . . Coon, H. (2009). Twenty-year outcome for individuals with autism and average or near-average cognitive abilities. *Autism Research, 2,* 109–118. doi:10.1002/aur.69

Frazier, T. W., Dawson, G., Murray, D., Shih, A., Sachs, J. S., & Geiger, A. (2018). Brief report: A survey of autism research priorities across a diverse community of stakeholders. *Journal of Autism and Developmental Disorders, 48,* 3965–3971. doi:10.1007/s10803-018-3642-6.

Helverschou, S. B., & Martinsen, H. (2011). Anxiety in people diagnosed with autism and intellectual disability: Recognition and phenomenology. *Research in Autism Spectrum Disorders, 5,* 377–387. doi:10.1016/j.rasd.2010.05.003

Insel, T., Cuthbert, B., Garvey, M., Heinssen, R., Pine, D. S., Quinn, K., . . . Wang, P. (2010). Research domain criteria (RDoC): Toward a new classification framework for research on mental disorders. *American Journal of Psychiatry, 167,* 748–751. doi:10.1176/appi.ajp.2010.09091379

Joshi, G., Petty, C., Wozniak, J., Henin, A., Fried, R., Galdo, M., . . . Biederman J. (2010). The heavy burden of psychiatric comorbidity in youth with autism spectrum disorders: A large comparative study of a psychiatrically referred population. *Journal of Autism and Developmental Disorders, 40,* 1361–1370. doi:10.1007/s10803010-0996-9 9

Kapp, S. K., Gillespie-Lynch, K., Sherman, L. E., & Hutman, T. (2013). Deficit, difference, or both? Autism and neurodiversity. *Developmental Psychology, 49,* 59–71. doi:10.1037/a0028353

Lecavalier, L., Leone, S., & Wiltz, J. (2006). The impact of behaviour problems on caregiver stress in young people with autism spectrum disorders. *Journal of Intellectual Disability Research, 50,* 172–183. doi:10.1111/j.1365-2788.2005.00732.x

Lerner, M. D., Mazefsky, C. A., Weber, R. J., Transue, E., Siegel, M., Gadow, K. D., & the Autism and Developmental Disorders Inpatient Research Collaborative (ADDIRC). (2018). Verbal ability and psychiatric symptoms in clinically referred inpatient and outpatient youth with ASD. *Journal of Autism and Developmental Disorders, 48,* 3689–3701. doi:10.1007/s10803-017-3344-5

Leyfer, O. T., Folstein, S. E., Bacalman, S., Davis, N. O., Dinh, E., Morgan, J., . . . Lainhart, J. E. (2006). Comorbid psychiatric disorders in children with autism: Interview development and rates of disorders. *Journal of Autism and Developmental Disorders, 36,* 849–861. doi:10.1007/s10803-006-0123-0

Lukens, C. T., & Linscheid, T. R. (2008). Development and validation of an inventory to assess mealtime behavior problems in children with autism. *Journal of Autism and Developmental Disorders, 38,* 342–352. doi:10.1007/s10803-007-0401-5

Maddox, B. B., & White, S. W. (2015). Comorbid social anxiety disorder in adults with autism spectrum disorder. *Journal of Autism and Developmental Disorders, 45,* 3949–3960. doi:10.1007/s10803-015-2531-5

Magaña, S., Lopez, K., Aguinaga, A., & Morton, H. (2013). Access to diagnosis and treatment services among Latino children with autism spectrum disorders. *Journal of Intellectual and Developmental Disability, 51,* 141–153. doi:10.1352/1934-9556-51.3.141.

Mandell, D. S., Wiggins, L. D., Carpenter, L. A., Daniels, J., DiGuiseppi, C., Durkin, M. S., . . . Kirby, R. S. (2009). Racial/ethnic disparities in the identification of children with autism spectrum disorders. *American Journal of Public Health, 99,* 493–498. doi:10.2105/AJPH.2007.131243

Marrast, L., Himmelstein, D. U., & Woolhandler, S. (2016). Racial and ethnic disparities in mental health care for children and young adults: A national study. *International Journal of Health Services, 46,* 810–824. doi:10.1177/0020731416662736

Mazefsky, C. A., Day, T. N., Siegel, M., White, S. W., Yu, L., Pilkonis, P. A., & the Autism and Developmental Disorders Inpatient Research Collaborative (ADDIRC). (2018). Development of the Emotion Dysregulation Inventory: A PROMIS®ing method for creating sensitive and unbiased questionnaires for autism spectrum disorder. *Journal of Autism and Developmental Disorders, 48,* 3736–3746. doi:10.1007/s10803-016-2907-1

Mazurek, M. O. (2016). The history of comorbidity in autism spectrum disorders (ASD). In J. L. Matson (Ed.), *Comorbid conditions among children with autism spectrum disorders* (pp. 3–25). Switzerland: Springer International Publishing. doi:10.1007/978-3-319-19,183-6

Nicolaidis, C., Raymaker, D., McDonald, K., Dern, S., Ashkenazy, E., Boisclair, C., . . . Baggs, A. (2011). Collaboration strategies in nontraditional community-based participatory research partnerships: Lessons from an academic–community partnership with autistic self-advocates. *Progress in Community Health Partnerships: Research, Education, and Action, 5*, 143–150. doi:10.1353/cpr.2011.0022

Pellicano, E., Dinsmore, A., & Charman, T. (2014). What should autism research focus upon? Community views and priorities from the United Kingdom. *Autism, 18*, 756–770. doi:10.1177/1362361314529627

Rodgers, J., Glod, M., Connolly, B., & McConachie, H. (2012). The relationship between anxiety and repetitive behaviours in autism spectrum disorder. *Journal of Autism and Developmental Disorders, 42*, 2404–2409. doi:10.1007/s10803-012-1531-y

Rubenstein, E., & Bishop-Fitzpatrick, L. (2019). A matter of time: The necessity of temporal language in research on health conditions that present with autism spectrum disorder. *Autism Research, 12*, 20–25. doi:10.1002/aur.2010

Scahill, L., Lecavalier, L., Schultz, R. T., Evans, A. N., Maddox, B. B., Pritchett, J., . . . Edwards, M. C. (2019). Development of the parent-rated anxiety scale for youth with autism spectrum disorder. *Journal of the American Academy of Child and Adolescent Psychiatry*. Advance online publication. doi:10.1016/j.jaac.2018.10.016

Sikora, D. M., Vora, P., Coury, D. L., & Rosenberg, D. (2012). Attention-deficit/hyperactivity disorder symptoms, adaptive functioning, and quality of life in children with autism spectrum disorder. *Pediatrics, 130*(Suppl 2), S91–97. doi:10.1542/peds.2012-0900G

Simonoff, E., Pickles, A., Charman, T., Chandler, S., Loucas, T., & Baird, G. (2008). Psychiatric disorders in children with autism spectrum disorders: Prevalence, comorbidity, and associated factors in a population-derived sample. *Journal of the American Academy of Child & Adolescent Psychiatry, 47*, 921–929. doi:10.1097/CHI.0b013e318179964f

Society of Clinical Child and Adolescent Psychology. (2019). Effective child therapy: Evidence-based mental health treatment for children and adolescents. Retrieved from http://www.effectivechildtherapy.org

Spain, D., Sin, J., Linder, K. B., McMahon, J., & Happé, F. (2018). Social anxiety in autism spectrum disorder: A systematic review. *Research in Autism Spectrum Disorders, 52*, 51–68. doi:10.1016/j.rasd.2018.04.007

Weiss, J. A. (2014). Transdiagnostic case conceptualization of emotional problems in youth with ASD: An emotion regulation approach. *Clinical Psychology: Science and Practice, 21*, 331–350. doi:10.1111/cpsp.12084

Wood, J. J., McLeod, B. D., Klebanoff, S., & Brookman-Frazee, L. (2015). Toward the implementation of evidence-based interventions for youth with autism spectrum disorders in schools and community agencies. *Behavior Therapy, 46*, 83–95. doi:10.1016/j.beth.2014.07.003

Zamora, I., Williams, M. E., Higareda, M., Wheeler, B. Y., & Levitt, P. (2016). Brief report: Recruitment and retention of minority children for autism research. *Journal of Autism and Developmental Disorders, 46*, 698–703. doi:10.1007/s10803-015-2603-6

INDEX

Note: Figures and tables are indicated by an italic "*f*" and "*t*" respectively, following the page numbers.

D

E

F

Q

R

V

W

Y

www.ingramcontent.com/pod-product-compliance
Lightning Source LLC
Chambersburg PA
CBHW082022080825
30824CB00005B/222
* 9 7 8 0 1 9 0 9 1 0 7 6 1 *